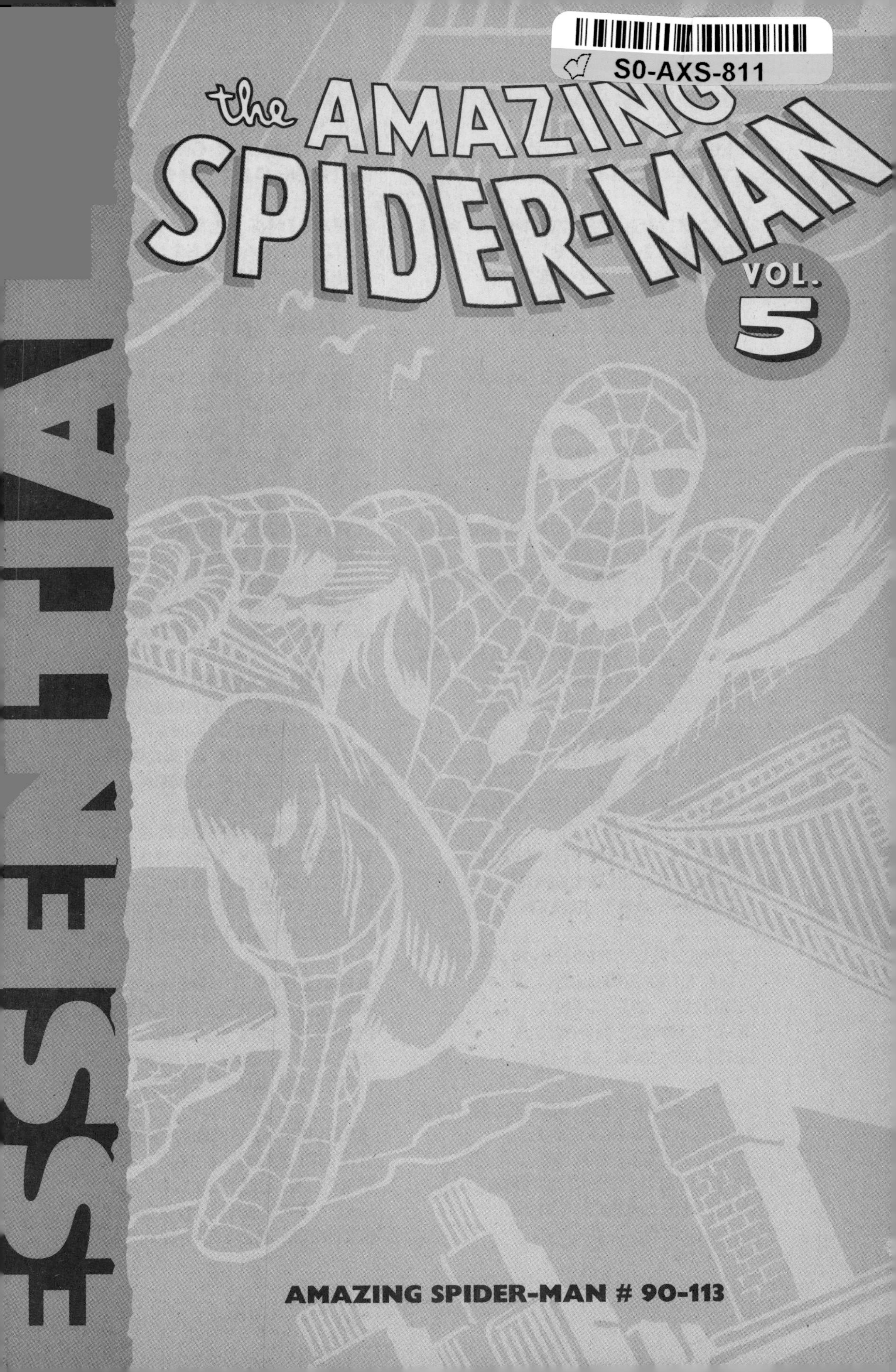
ESSENTIAL
the AMAZING SPIDER-MAN
VOL. 5
AMAZING SPIDER-MAN # 90-113

AMAZING SPIDER-MAN #90
WRITER: **STAN LEE**
PENCILER: **GIL KANE**
INKER: **JOHN ROMITA**
LETTERER: **SAM ROSEN**

AMAZING SPIDER-MAN #91
WRITER: **STAN LEE**
PENCILER: **GIL KANE**
INKER: **JOHN ROMITA**
LETTERER: **SAM ROSEN**

AMAZING SPIDER-MAN #92
WRITER: **STAN LEE**
PENCILER: **GIL KANE**
INKER: **JOHN ROMITA**
LETTERER: **ART SIMEK**

AMAZING SPIDER-MAN #93
WRITER: **STAN LEE**
ILLUSTRATOR: **JOHN ROMITA**
LETTERER: **ART SIMEK**

AMAZING SPIDER-MAN #94
WRITER: **STAN LEE**
PENCILER: **JOHN ROMITA**
INKER: **SAL BUSCEMA**
LETTERER: **ART SIMEK**

AMAZING SPIDER-MAN #95
WRITER: **STAN LEE**
PENCILER: **JOHN ROMITA**
INKER: **SAL BUSCEMA**
LETTERER: **ART SIMEK**

AMAZING SPIDER-MAN #96
WRITER: **STAN LEE**
PENCILER: **GIL KANE**
INKER: **JOHN ROMITA**
LETTERER: **ART SIMEK**

AMAZING SPIDER-MAN #97
WRITER: **STAN LEE**
PENCILER: **GIL KANE**
INKER: **FRANK GIACOIA**
LETTERER: **SAM ROSEN**

AMAZING SPIDER-MAN #98
WRITER: **STAN LEE**
PENCILER: **GIL KANE**
INKER: **FRANK GIACOIA**
LETTERER: **ART SIMEK**

AMAZING SPIDER-MAN #99
WRITER: **STAN LEE**
PENCILER: **GIL KANE**
INKER: **FRANK GIACOIA**
LETTERER: **ART SIMEK**

AMAZING SPIDER-MAN #100
WRITER: **STAN LEE**
PENCILER: **GIL KANE**
INKER: **FRANK GIACOIA**
LETTERER: **ART SIMEK**

AMAZING SPIDER-MAN #101
WRITER: **ROY THOMAS**
PENCILER: **GIL KANE**
INKER: **FRANK GIACOIA**
LETTERER: **ART SIMEK**

AMAZING SPIDER-MAN #102
WRITER: **ROY THOMAS**
PENCILER: **GIL KANE**
INKER: **FRANK GIACOIA**
LETTERER: **ART SIMEK**

AMAZING SPIDER-MAN #103
WRITER: **ROY THOMAS**
PENCILER: **GIL KANE**
INKER: **FRANK GIACOIA**
LETTERER: **ART SIMEK**

AMAZING SPIDER-MAN #104
WRITER: **ROY THOMAS**
PENCILER: **GIL KANE**
INKER: **FRANK GIACOIA**
LETTERER: **ART SIMEK**

AMAZING SPIDER-MAN #105
WRITER: **STAN LEE**
PENCILER: **GIL KANE**
INKER: **FRANK GIACOIA**
LETTERER: **ART SIMEK**

AMAZING SPIDER-MAN #106
WRITER: **STAN LEE**
PENCILER: **JOHN ROMITA**
INKER: **FRANK GIACOIA**
LETTERER: **SAM ROSEN**

AMAZING SPIDER-MAN #107
WRITER: **STAN LEE**
PENCILER: **JOHN ROMITA**
INKER: **FRANK GIACOIA**
LETTERER: **ART SIMEK**

AMAZING SPIDER-MAN #108
WRITER: **STAN LEE**
ILLUSTRATOR: **JOHN ROMITA**
LETTERER: **ART SIMEK**

AMAZING SPIDER-MAN #109
WRITER: **STAN LEE**
ILLUSTRATOR: **JOHN ROMITA**
LETTERER: **ART SIMEK**

AMAZING SPIDER-MAN #110
WRITER: **STAN LEE**
ILLUSTRATOR: **JOHN ROMITA**
LETTERER: **JOHN COSTANZA**

AMAZING SPIDER-MAN #111
WRITER: **GERRY CONWAY**
ILLUSTRATOR: **JOHN ROMITA**
LETTERER: **JOHN COSTANZA**

AMAZING SPIDER-MAN #112
WRITER: **GERRY CONWAY**
ILLUSTRATOR: **JOHN ROMITA**
LETTERER: **ART SIMEK**

AMAZING SPIDER-MAN #113
WRITER: **GERRY CONWAY**
PENCILER: **JOHN ROMITA**
INKERS: **TONY MORTELLARO
& JIM STARLIN**
LETTERER: **ART SIMEK**

REPRINT CREDITS

MARVEL ESSENTIAL DESIGN:
**JOHN "JG" ROSHELL OF
COMICRAFT**
COVER ART:
JOHN ROMITA
COVER COLORS:
MORRY HOLLOWELL
COLLECTION EDITOR:
MARK D. BEAZLEY
ASSISTANT EDITOR:
MICHAEL SHORT
ASSOCIATE EDITOR:
JENNIFER GRÜNWALD
SENIOR EDITOR, SPECIAL PROJECTS:
JEFF YOUNGQUIST

PRODUCTION:
JERRON QUALITY COLOR
VICE PRESIDENT OF SALES:
DAVID GABRIEL
VICE PRESIDENT OF CREATIVE:
TOM MARVELLI
EDITOR IN CHIEF:
JOE QUESADA
PUBLISHER:
DAN BUCKLEY

**SPECIAL THANKS TO
RALPH MACCHIO, TOM
BREVOORT, & POND SCUM**

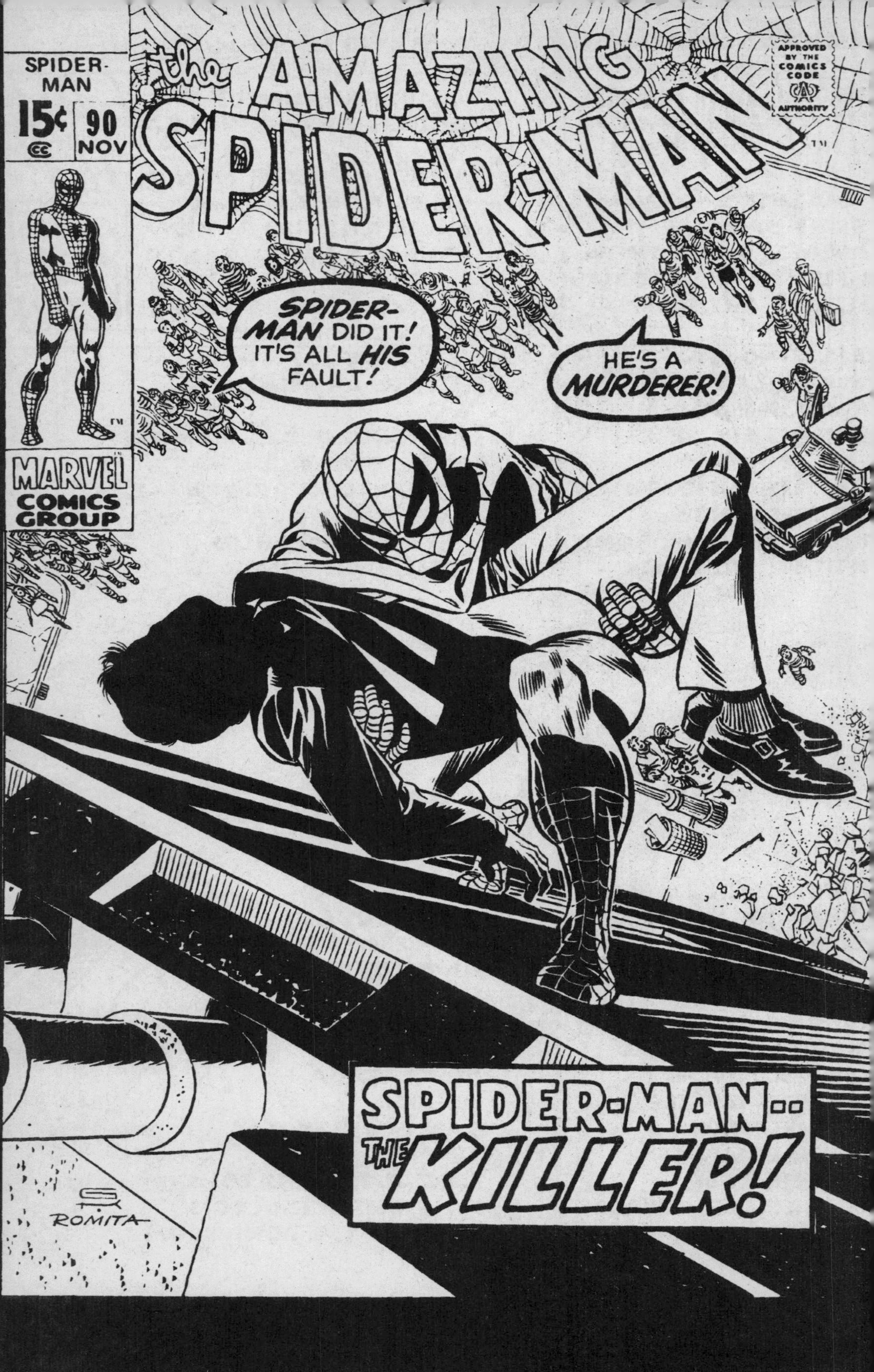

SPIDER-MAN
15¢
90
NOV
the AMAZING SPIDER-MAN
APPROVED BY THE COMICS CODE AUTHORITY
MARVEL COMICS GROUP
SPIDER-MAN DID IT! IT'S ALL HIS FAULT!
HE'S A MURDERER!
SPIDER-MAN.. THE KILLER!
ROMITA

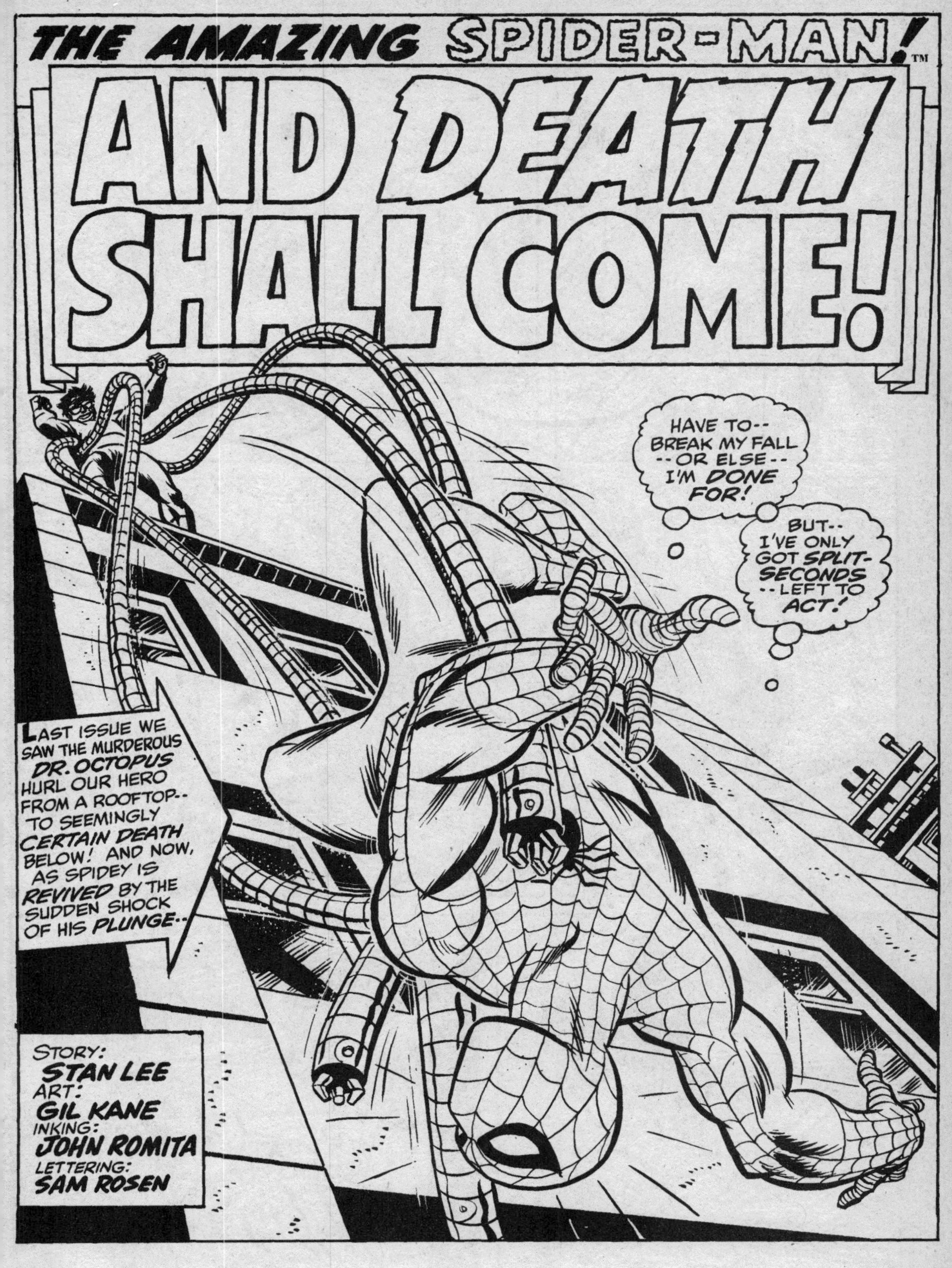
THE AMAZING SPIDER-MAN!™
AND DEATH SHALL COME!
HAVE TO-- BREAK MY FALL --OR ELSE-- I'M DONE FOR!
BUT-- I'VE ONLY GOT SPLIT-SECONDS --LEFT TO ACT!
LAST ISSUE WE SAW THE MURDEROUS DR. OCTOPUS HURL OUR HERO FROM A ROOFTOP-- TO SEEMINGLY CERTAIN DEATH BELOW! AND NOW, AS SPIDEY IS REVIVED BY THE SUDDEN SHOCK OF HIS PLUNGE--
STORY: STAN LEE
ART: GIL KANE
INKING: JOHN ROMITA
LETTERING: SAM ROSEN

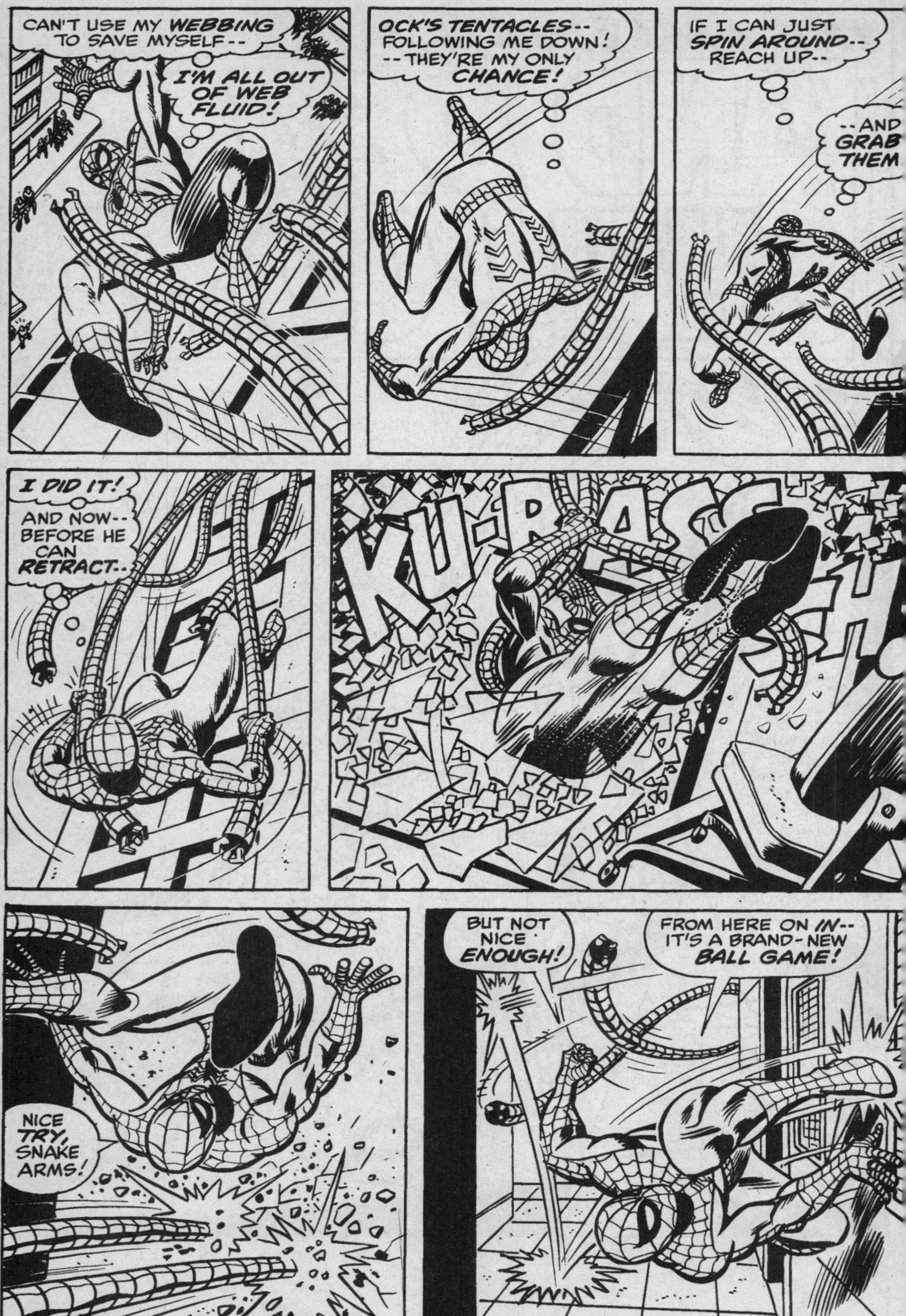
CAN'T USE MY WEBBING TO SAVE MYSELF--
I'M ALL OUT OF WEB FLUID!
OCK'S TENTACLES-- FOLLOWING ME DOWN! --THEY'RE MY ONLY CHANCE!
IF I CAN JUST SPIN AROUND-- REACH UP--
--AND GRAB THEM
I DID IT!
AND NOW-- BEFORE HE CAN RETRACT--
KU-RASSH!
NICE TRY, SNAKE ARMS!
BUT NOT NICE ENOUGH!
FROM HERE ON IN-- IT'S A BRAND-NEW BALL GAME!

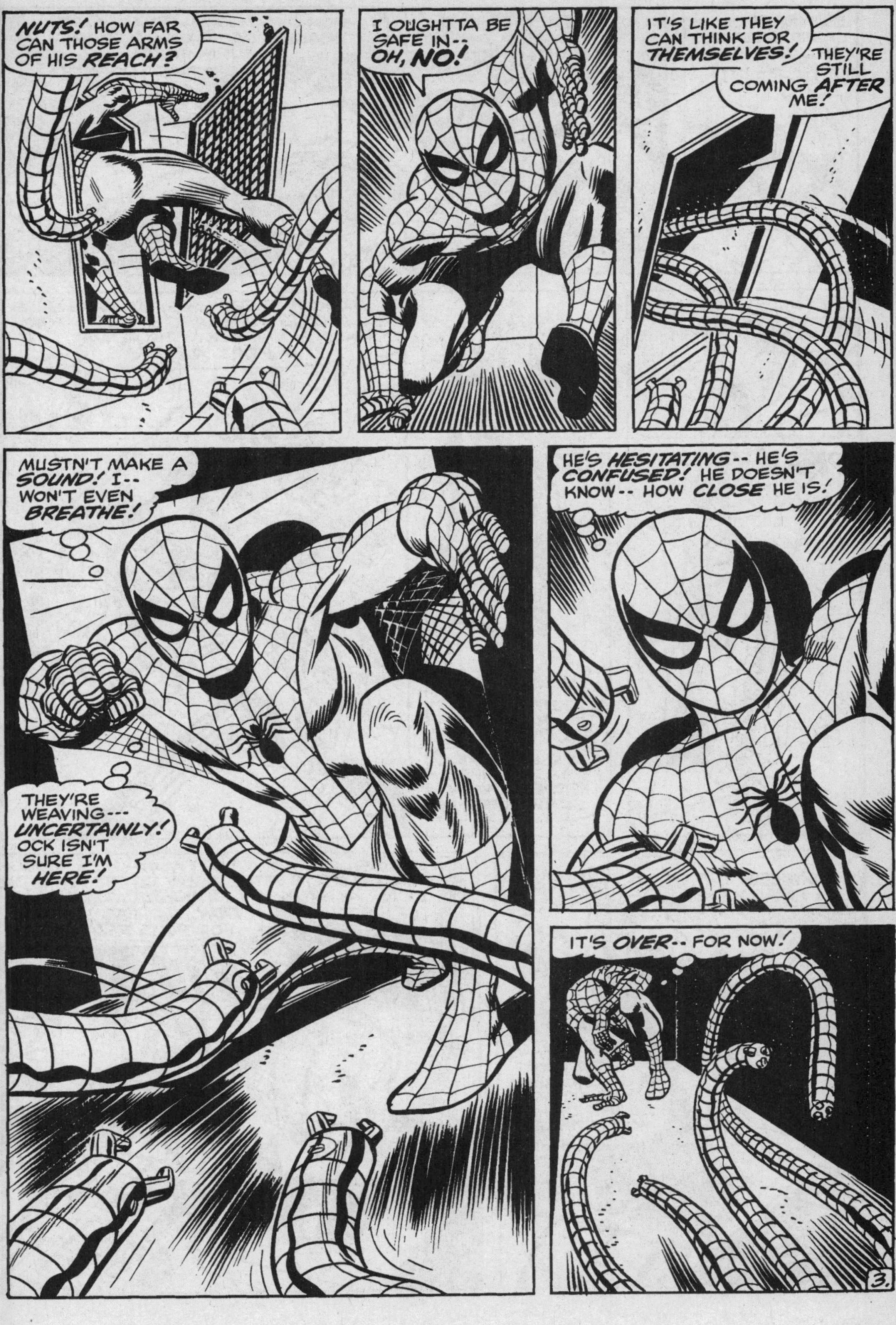
NUTS! HOW FAR CAN THOSE ARMS OF HIS REACH?
I OUGHTTA BE SAFE IN-- OH, NO!
IT'S LIKE THEY CAN THINK FOR THEMSELVES!
THEY'RE STILL COMING AFTER ME!
MUSTN'T MAKE A SOUND! I-- WON'T EVEN BREATHE!
THEY'RE WEAVING--- UNCERTAINLY! OCK ISN'T SURE I'M HERE!
HE'S HESITATING-- HE'S CONFUSED! HE DOESN'T KNOW-- HOW CLOSE HE IS!
IT'S OVER-- FOR NOW!
3.

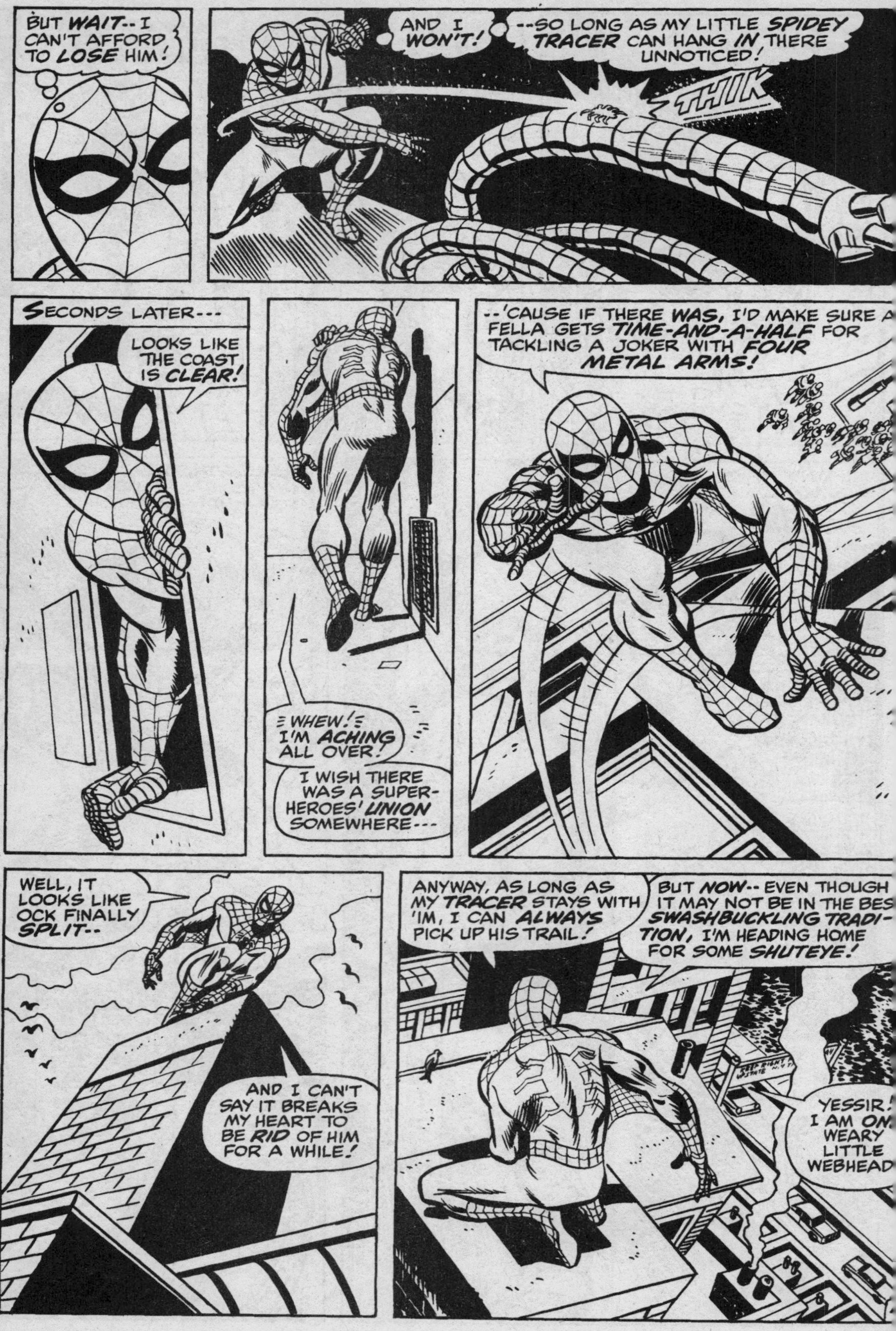
BUT WAIT-- I CAN'T AFFORD TO LOSE HIM!
AND I WON'T!
--SO LONG AS MY LITTLE SPIDEY TRACER CAN HANG IN THERE UNNOTICED!
THIK
SECONDS LATER---
LOOKS LIKE THE COAST IS CLEAR!
WHEW! I'M ACHING ALL OVER!
I WISH THERE WAS A SUPER-HEROES' UNION SOMEWHERE---
--'CAUSE IF THERE WAS, I'D MAKE SURE A FELLA GETS TIME-AND-A-HALF FOR TACKLING A JOKER WITH FOUR METAL ARMS!
WELL, IT LOOKS LIKE OCK FINALLY SPLIT--
AND I CAN'T SAY IT BREAKS MY HEART TO BE RID OF HIM FOR A WHILE!
ANYWAY, AS LONG AS MY TRACER STAYS WITH 'IM, I CAN ALWAYS PICK UP HIS TRAIL!
BUT NOW-- EVEN THOUGH IT MAY NOT BE IN THE BES SWASHBUCKLING TRADI-TION, I'M HEADING HOME FOR SOME SHUTEYE!
YESSIR! I AM ON WEARY LITTLE WEBHEAD

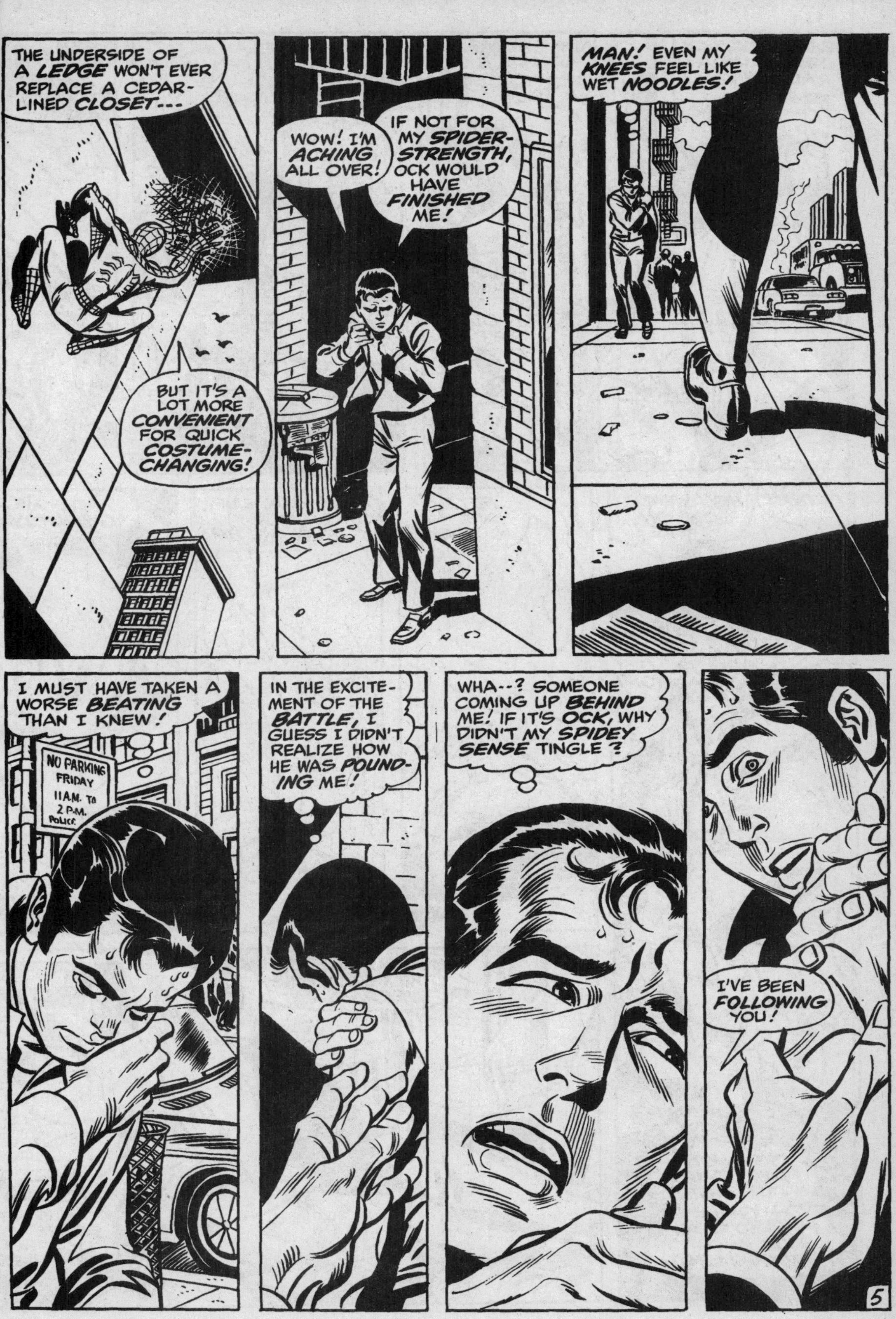
THE UNDERSIDE OF A LEDGE WON'T EVER REPLACE A CEDAR-LINED CLOSET---
BUT IT'S A LOT MORE CONVENIENT FOR QUICK COSTUME-CHANGING!
WOW! I'M ACHING ALL OVER!
IF NOT FOR MY SPIDER-STRENGTH, OCK WOULD HAVE FINISHED ME!
MAN! EVEN MY KNEES FEEL LIKE WET NOODLES!
I MUST HAVE TAKEN A WORSE BEATING THAN I KNEW!
NO PARKING FRIDAY 11 A.M. TO 2 P.M. POLICE
IN THE EXCITEMENT OF THE BATTLE, I GUESS I DIDN'T REALIZE HOW HE WAS POUNDING ME!
WHA--? SOMEONE COMING UP BEHIND ME! IF IT'S OCK, WHY DIDN'T MY SPIDEY SENSE TINGLE?
I'VE BEEN FOLLOWING YOU!
5

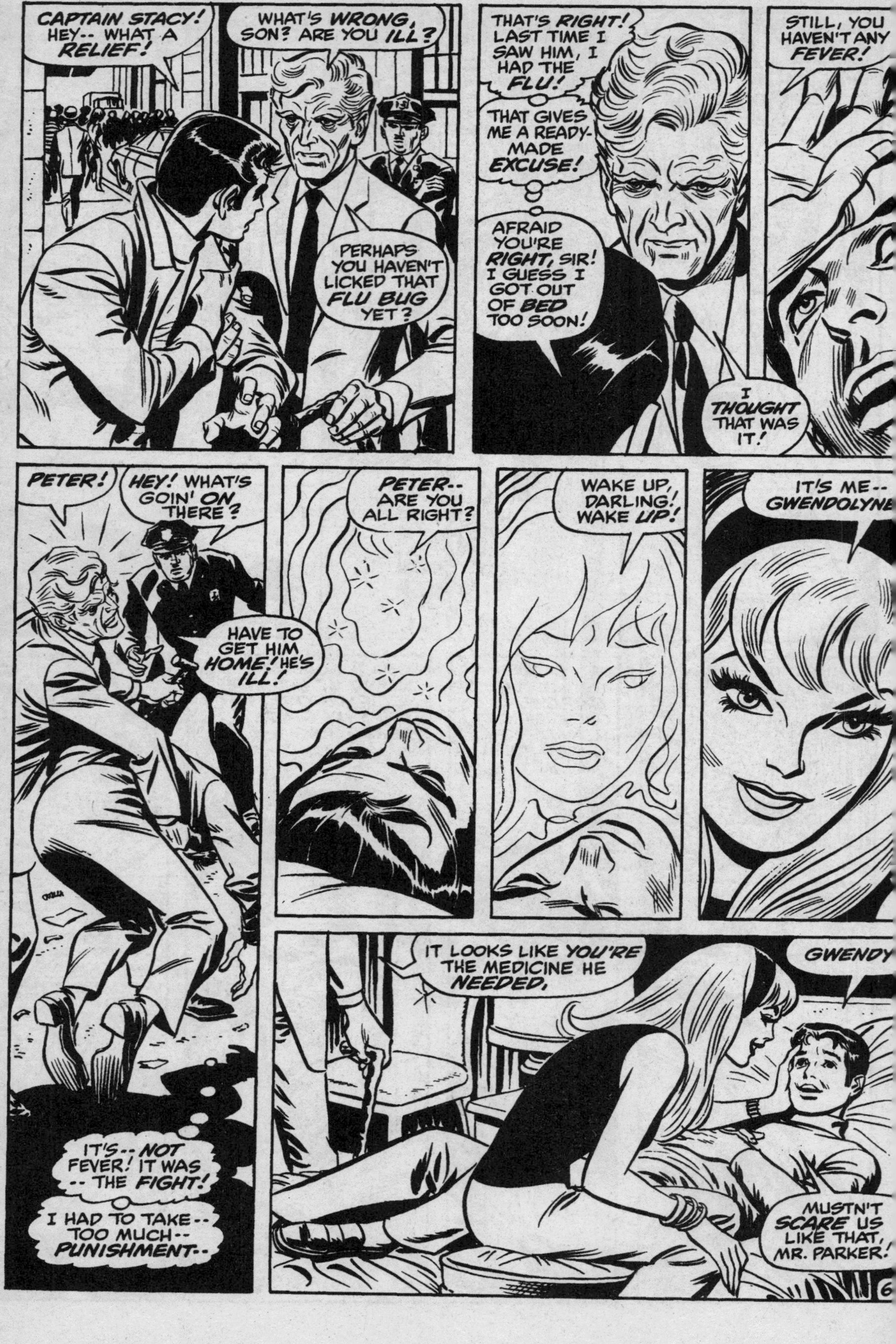

CAPTAIN STACY! HEY-- WHAT A RELIEF!
WHAT'S WRONG, SON? ARE YOU ILL?
PERHAPS YOU HAVEN'T LICKED THAT FLU BUG YET?
THAT'S RIGHT! LAST TIME I SAW HIM, I HAD THE FLU!
THAT GIVES ME A READY-MADE EXCUSE!
AFRAID YOU'RE RIGHT, SIR! I GUESS I GOT OUT OF BED TOO SOON!
STILL, YOU HAVEN'T ANY FEVER!
I THOUGHT THAT WAS IT!
PETER!
HEY! WHAT'S GOIN' ON THERE?
HAVE TO GET HIM HOME! HE'S ILL!
IT'S-- NOT FEVER! IT WAS -- THE FIGHT!
I HAD TO TAKE-- TOO MUCH-- PUNISHMENT--
PETER-- ARE YOU ALL RIGHT?
WAKE UP, DARLING! WAKE UP!
IT'S ME-- GWENDOLYNE
IT LOOKS LIKE YOU'RE THE MEDICINE HE NEEDED,
GWENDY
MUSTN'T SCARE US LIKE THAT, MR. PARKER!

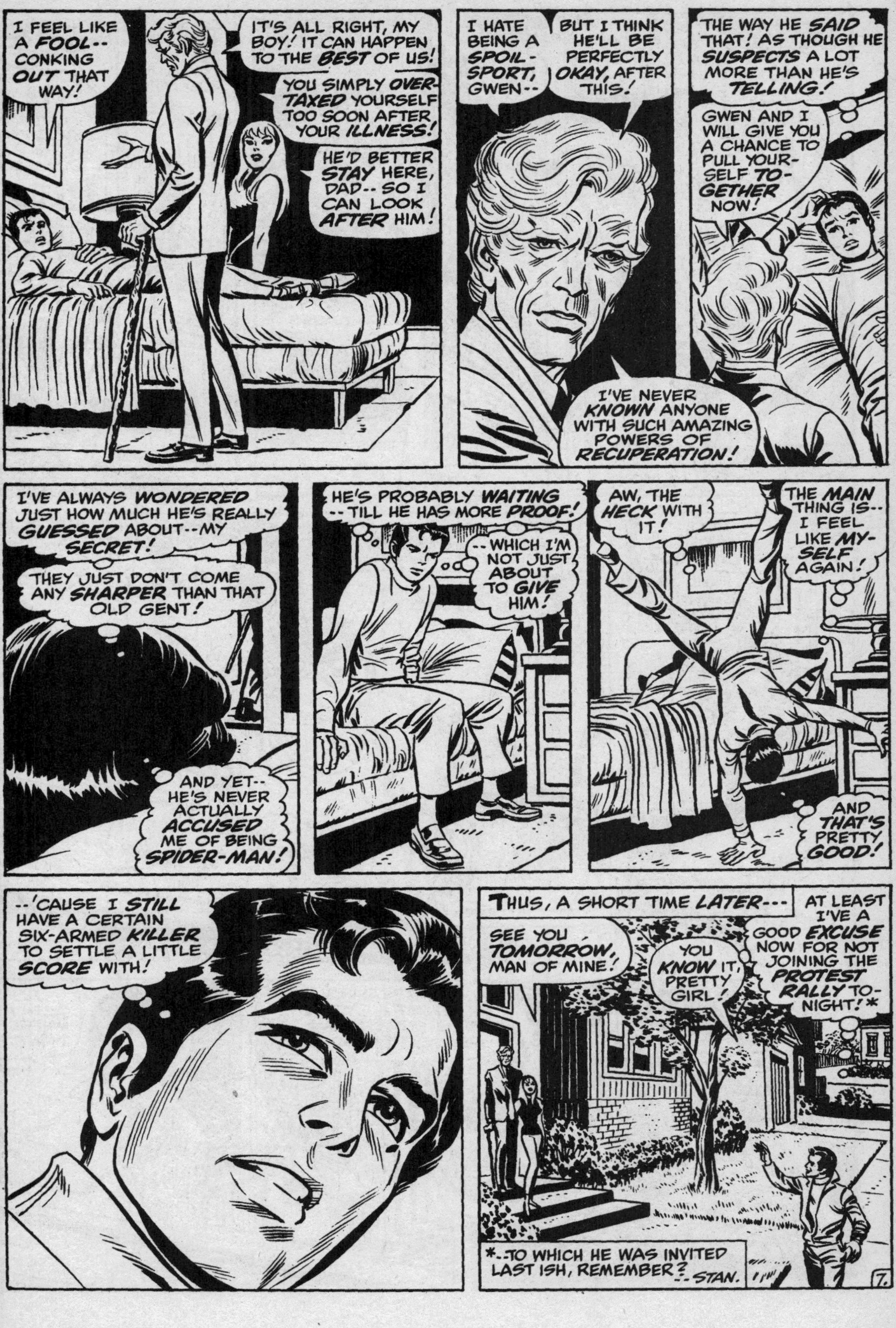
I FEEL LIKE A FOOL-- CONKING OUT THAT WAY!
IT'S ALL RIGHT, MY BOY! IT CAN HAPPEN TO THE BEST OF US!
YOU SIMPLY OVER-TAXED YOURSELF TOO SOON AFTER YOUR ILLNESS!
HE'D BETTER STAY HERE, DAD-- SO I CAN LOOK AFTER HIM!
I HATE BEING A SPOIL-SPORT, GWEN--
BUT I THINK HE'LL BE PERFECTLY OKAY, AFTER THIS!
I'VE NEVER KNOWN ANYONE WITH SUCH AMAZING POWERS OF RECUPERATION!
THE WAY HE SAID THAT! AS THOUGH HE SUSPECTS A LOT MORE THAN HE'S TELLING!
GWEN AND I WILL GIVE YOU A CHANCE TO PULL YOURSELF TOGETHER NOW!
I'VE ALWAYS WONDERED JUST HOW MUCH HE'S REALLY GUESSED ABOUT--MY SECRET!
THEY JUST DON'T COME ANY SHARPER THAN THAT OLD GENT!
AND YET-- HE'S NEVER ACTUALLY ACCUSED ME OF BEING SPIDER-MAN!
HE'S PROBABLY WAITING -- TILL HE HAS MORE PROOF!
-- WHICH I'M NOT JUST ABOUT TO GIVE HIM!
AW, THE HECK WITH IT!
THE MAIN THING IS-- I FEEL LIKE MYSELF AGAIN!
AND THAT'S PRETTY GOOD!
--'CAUSE I STILL HAVE A CERTAIN SIX-ARMED KILLER TO SETTLE A LITTLE SCORE WITH!
THUS, A SHORT TIME LATER---
SEE YOU TOMORROW, MAN OF MINE!
YOU KNOW IT, PRETTY GIRL!
AT LEAST I'VE A GOOD EXCUSE NOW FOR NOT JOINING THE PROTEST RALLY TONIGHT!*
*--TO WHICH HE WAS INVITED LAST ISH, REMEMBER? --STAN.
7.

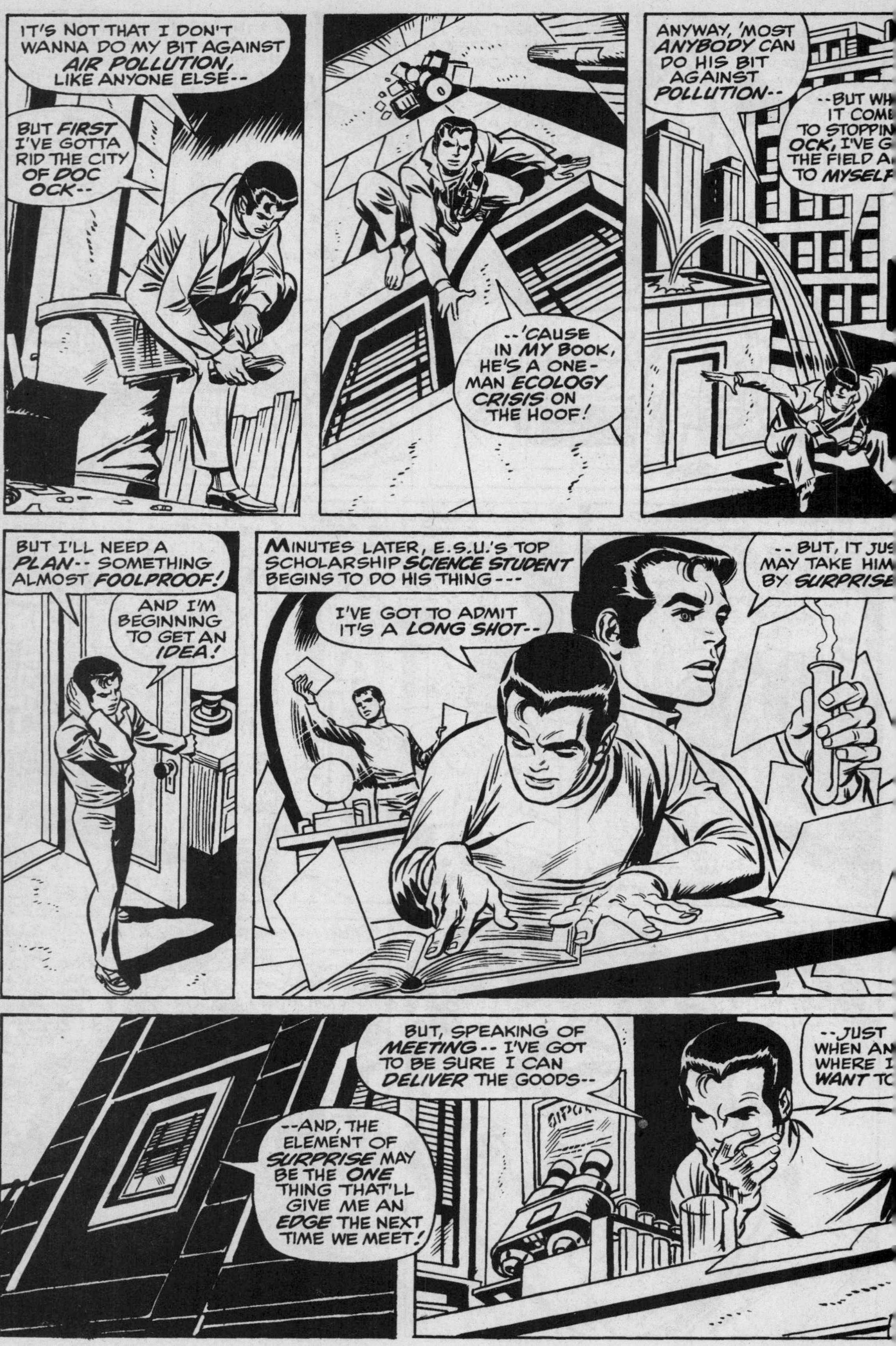
IT'S NOT THAT I DON'T WANNA DO MY BIT AGAINST AIR POLLUTION, LIKE ANYONE ELSE--
BUT FIRST I'VE GOTTA RID THE CITY OF DOC OCK--
--'CAUSE IN MY BOOK, HE'S A ONE-MAN ECOLOGY CRISIS ON THE HOOF!
ANYWAY, 'MOST ANYBODY CAN DO HIS BIT AGAINST POLLUTION--
--BUT WH IT COMB TO STOPPIN OCK, I'VE G THE FIELD A TO MYSELF
BUT I'LL NEED A PLAN-- SOMETHING ALMOST FOOLPROOF!
AND I'M BEGINNING TO GET AN IDEA!
MINUTES LATER, E.S.U.'S TOP SCHOLARSHIP SCIENCE STUDENT BEGINS TO DO HIS THING---
I'VE GOT TO ADMIT IT'S A LONG SHOT--
--BUT, IT JUS MAY TAKE HIM BY SURPRISE
--AND, THE ELEMENT OF SURPRISE MAY BE THE ONE THING THAT'LL GIVE ME AN EDGE THE NEXT TIME WE MEET!
BUT, SPEAKING OF MEETING-- I'VE GOT TO BE SURE I CAN DELIVER THE GOODS--
--JUST WHEN AN WHERE I WANT TO

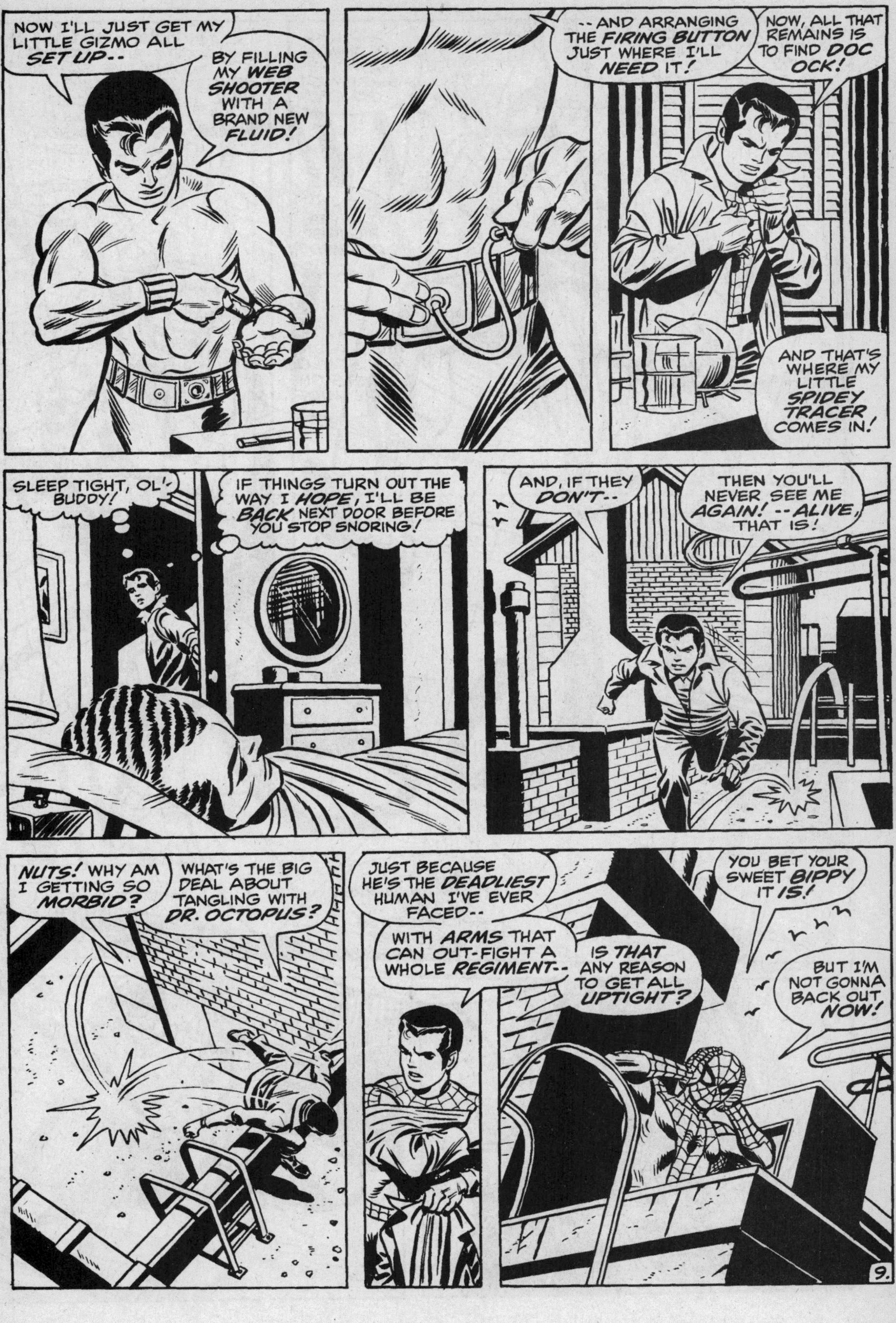
NOW I'LL JUST GET MY LITTLE GIZMO ALL SET UP--
BY FILLING MY WEB SHOOTER WITH A BRAND NEW FLUID!
--AND ARRANGING THE FIRING BUTTON JUST WHERE I'LL NEED IT!
NOW, ALL THAT REMAINS IS TO FIND DOC OCK!
AND THAT'S WHERE MY LITTLE SPIDEY TRACER COMES IN!
SLEEP TIGHT, OL' BUDDY!
IF THINGS TURN OUT THE WAY I HOPE, I'LL BE BACK NEXT DOOR BEFORE YOU STOP SNORING!
AND, IF THEY DON'T--
THEN YOU'LL NEVER SEE ME AGAIN! --ALIVE, THAT IS!
NUTS! WHY AM I GETTING SO MORBID?
WHAT'S THE BIG DEAL ABOUT TANGLING WITH DR. OCTOPUS?
JUST BECAUSE HE'S THE DEADLIEST HUMAN I'VE EVER FACED--
WITH ARMS THAT CAN OUT-FIGHT A WHOLE REGIMENT--
IS THAT ANY REASON TO GET ALL UPTIGHT?
YOU BET YOUR SWEET BIPPY IT IS!
BUT I'M NOT GONNA BACK OUT NOW!
9.

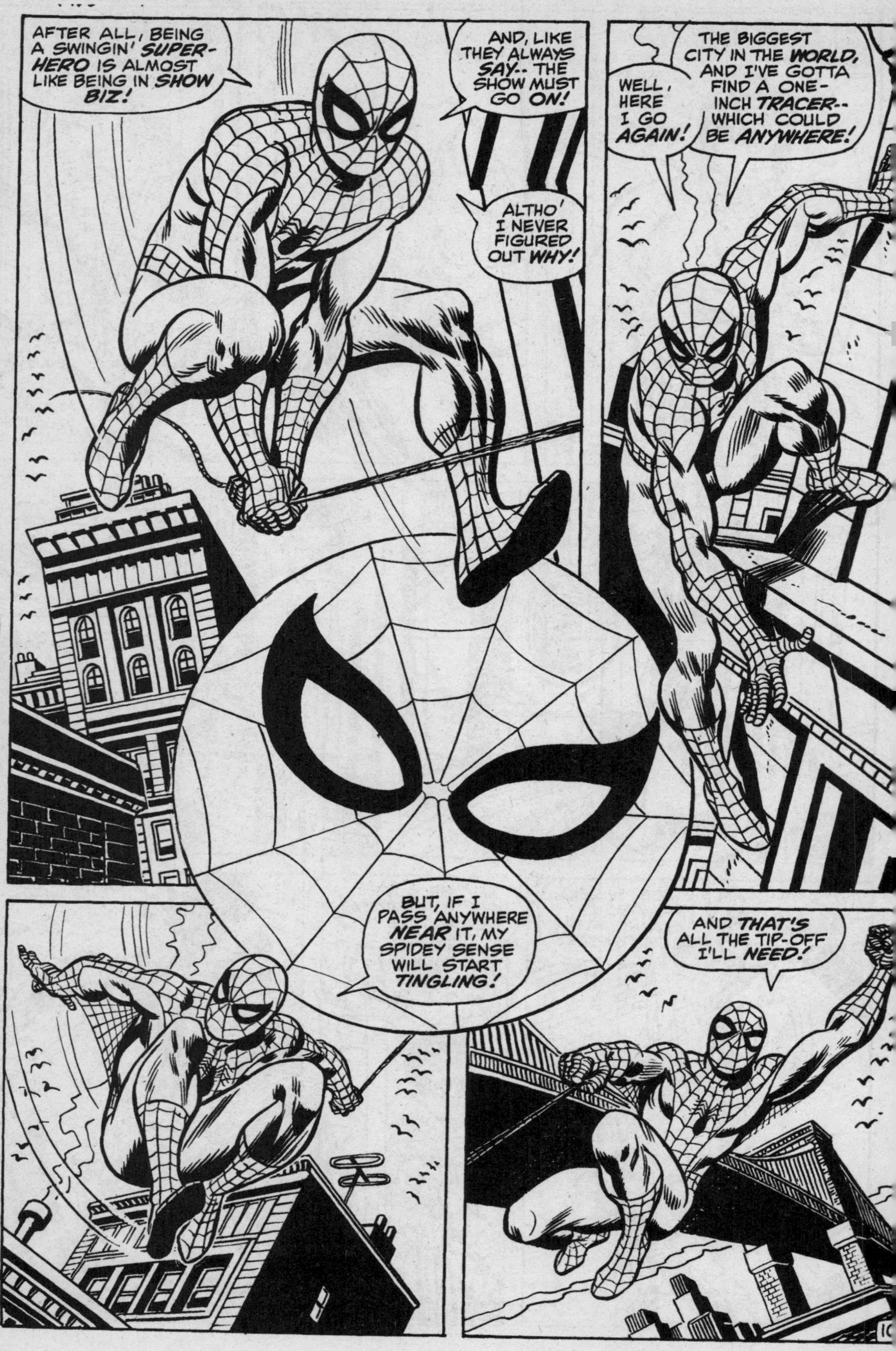
AFTER ALL, BEING A SWINGIN' SUPER-HERO IS ALMOST LIKE BEING IN SHOW BIZ!
AND, LIKE THEY ALWAYS SAY-- THE SHOW MUST GO ON!
ALTHO' I NEVER FIGURED OUT WHY!
WELL, HERE I GO AGAIN!
THE BIGGEST CITY IN THE WORLD, AND I'VE GOTTA FIND A ONE-INCH TRACER-- WHICH COULD BE ANYWHERE!
BUT, IF I PASS ANYWHERE NEAR IT, MY SPIDEY SENSE WILL START TINGLING!
AND THAT'S ALL THE TIP-OFF I'LL NEED!
10

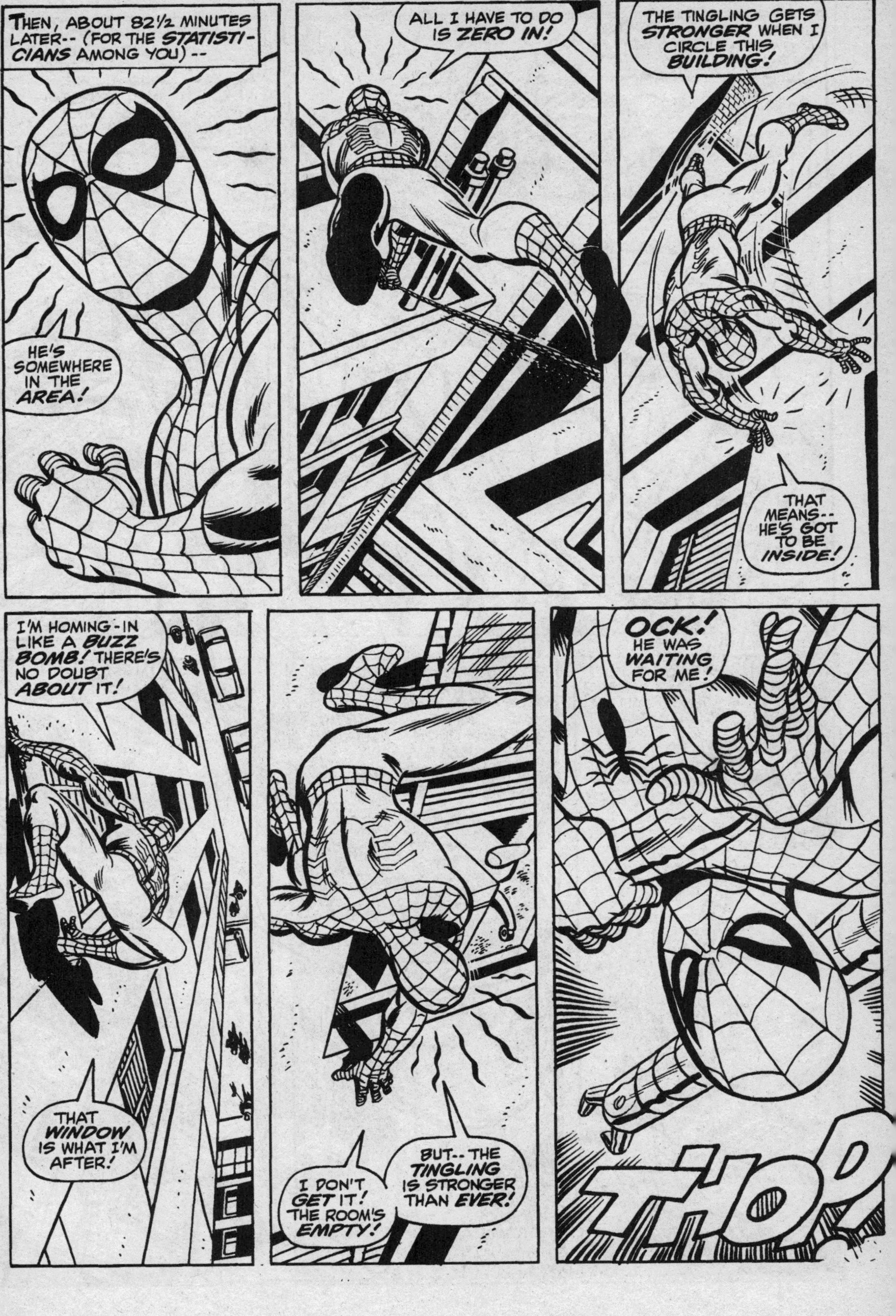
THEN, ABOUT 82 1/2 MINUTES LATER-- (FOR THE STATISTICIANS AMONG YOU) --
HE'S SOMEWHERE IN THE AREA!
ALL I HAVE TO DO IS ZERO IN!
THE TINGLING GETS STRONGER WHEN I CIRCLE THIS BUILDING!
THAT MEANS-- HE'S GOT TO BE INSIDE!
I'M HOMING-IN LIKE A BUZZ BOMB! THERE'S NO DOUBT ABOUT IT!
THAT WINDOW IS WHAT I'M AFTER!
I DON'T GET IT! THE ROOM'S EMPTY!
BUT-- THE TINGLING IS STRONGER THAN EVER!
OCK! HE WAS WAITING FOR ME!
THOP!

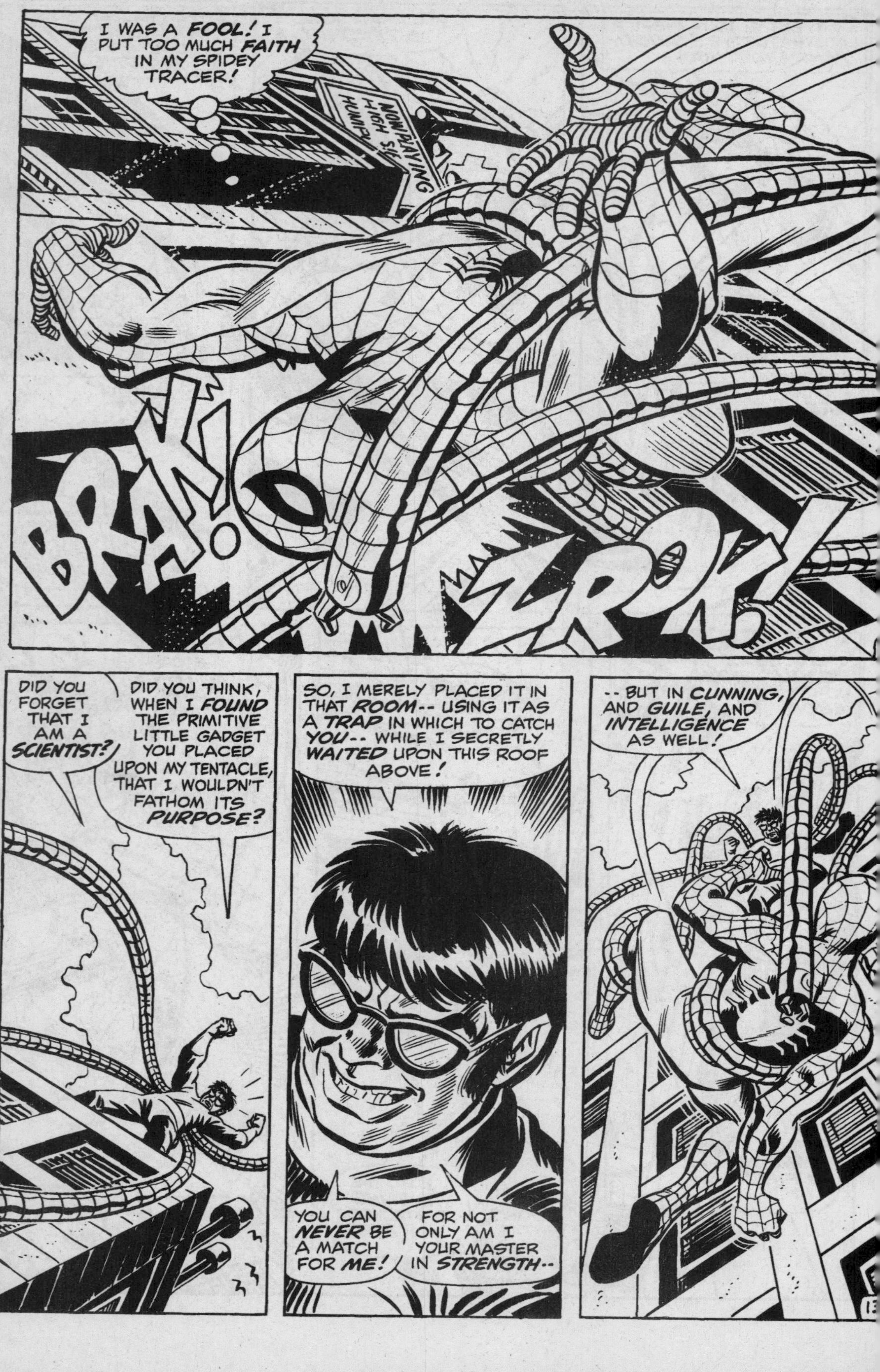
I WAS A FOOL! I PUT TOO MUCH FAITH IN MY SPIDEY TRACER!
BRAK!
ZROK!
DID YOU FORGET THAT I AM A SCIENTIST?
DID YOU THINK, WHEN I FOUND THE PRIMITIVE LITTLE GADGET YOU PLACED UPON MY TENTACLE, THAT I WOULDN'T FATHOM ITS PURPOSE?
SO, I MERELY PLACED IT IN THAT ROOM-- USING IT AS A TRAP IN WHICH TO CATCH YOU-- WHILE I SECRETLY WAITED UPON THIS ROOF ABOVE!
YOU CAN NEVER BE A MATCH FOR ME!
FOR NOT ONLY AM I YOUR MASTER IN STRENGTH--
--BUT IN CUNNING, AND GUILE, AND INTELLIGENCE AS WELL!

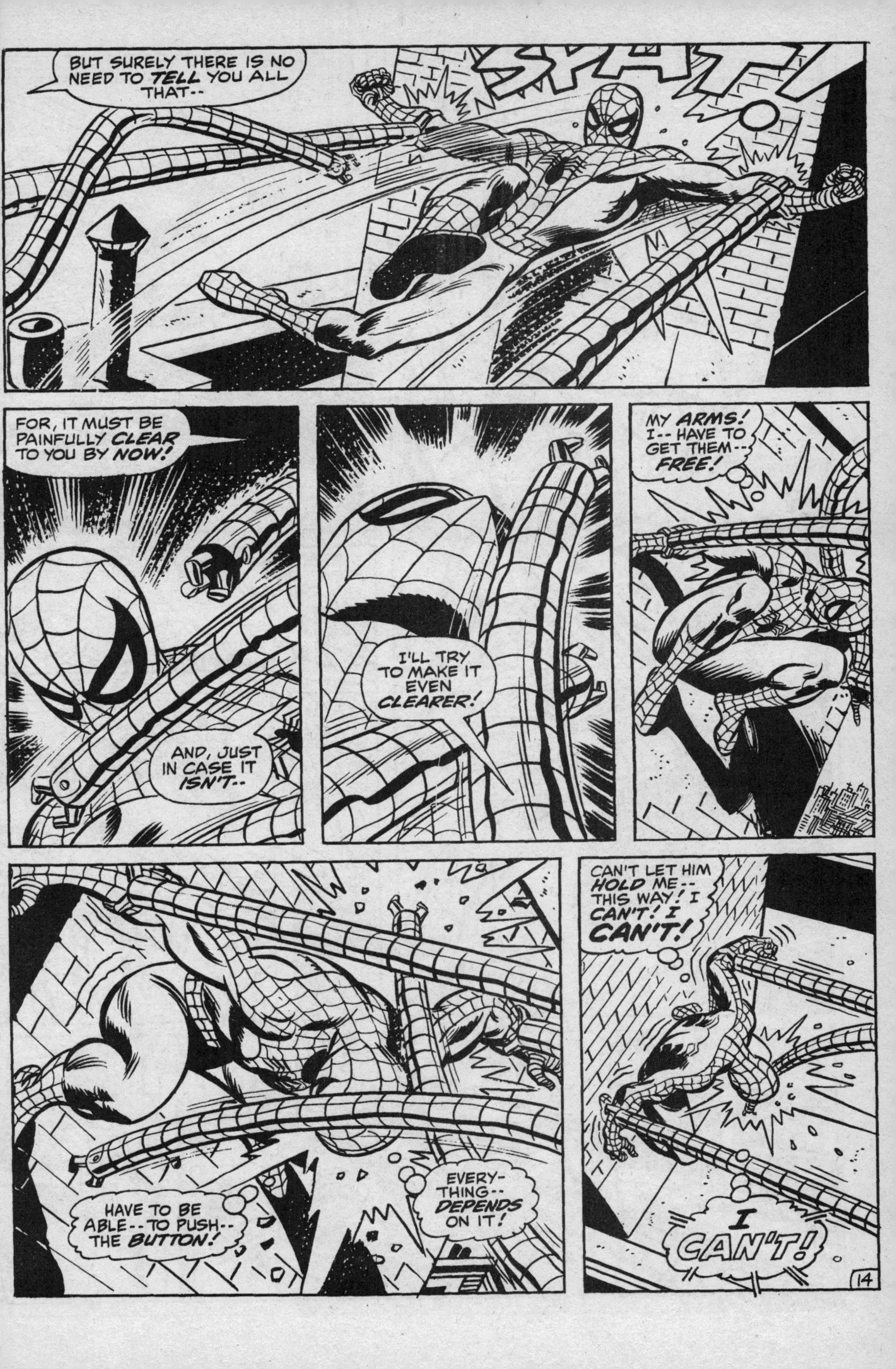
BUT SURELY THERE IS NO NEED TO TELL YOU ALL THAT--
SPAT!
FOR, IT MUST BE PAINFULLY CLEAR TO YOU BY NOW!
AND, JUST IN CASE IT ISN'T..
I'LL TRY TO MAKE IT EVEN CLEARER!
MY ARMS! I-- HAVE TO GET THEM-- FREE!
HAVE TO BE ABLE-- TO PUSH-- THE BUTTON!
EVERY-THING-- DEPENDS ON IT!
CAN'T LET HIM HOLD ME-- THIS WAY! I CAN'T! I CAN'T!
I CAN'T!
14

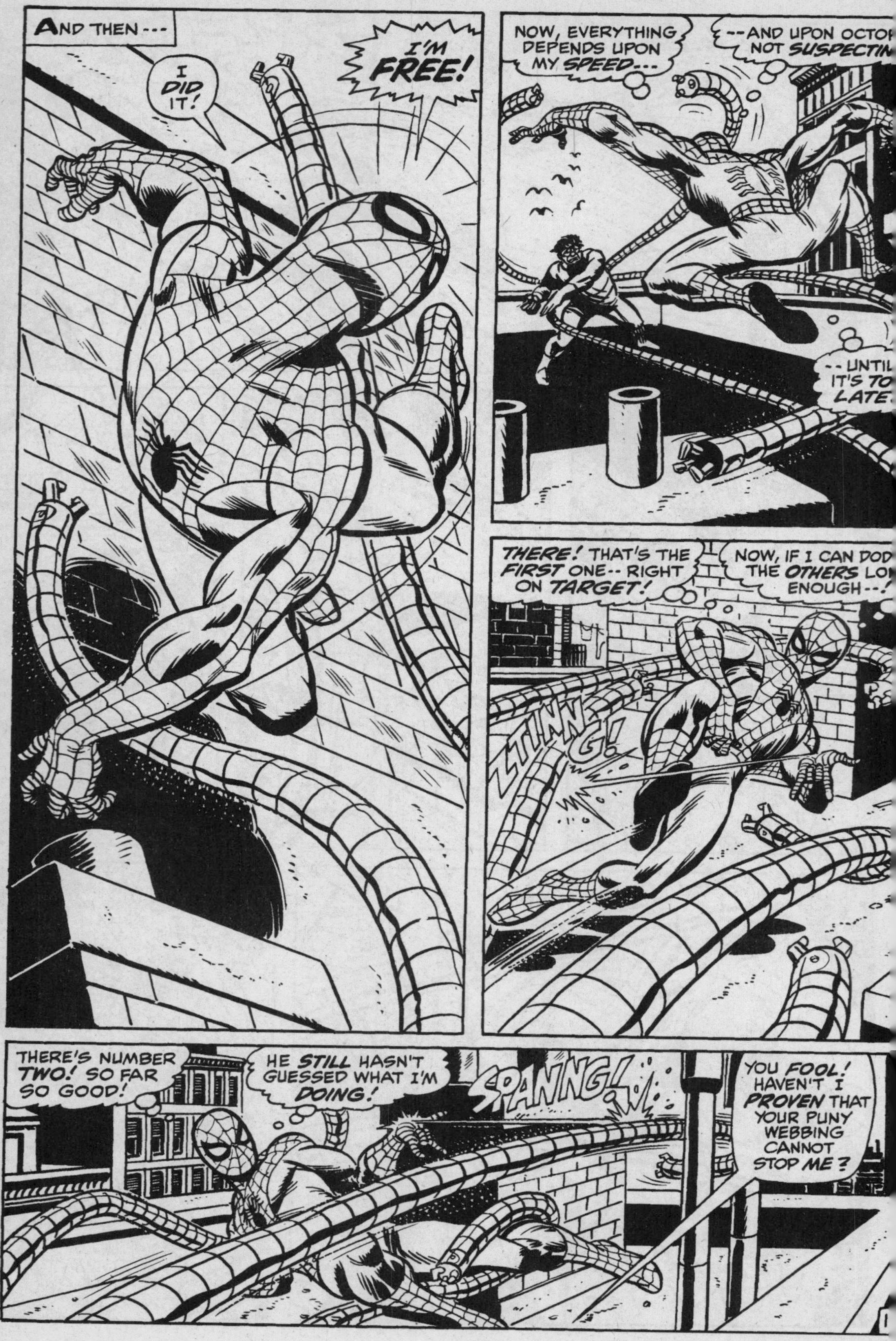
AND THEN ---
I DID IT!
I'M FREE!
NOW, EVERYTHING DEPENDS UPON MY SPEED...
--AND UPON OCTOP NOT SUSPECTIN
--UNTIL IT'S TO LATE
THERE! THAT'S THE FIRST ONE-- RIGHT ON TARGET!
NOW, IF I CAN DOD THE OTHERS LO ENOUGH--!
ZTINNG!
THERE'S NUMBER TWO! SO FAR SO GOOD!
HE STILL HASN'T GUESSED WHAT I'M DOING!
SPANNG!
YOU FOOL! HAVEN'T I PROVEN THAT YOUR PUNY WEBBING CANNOT STOP ME?

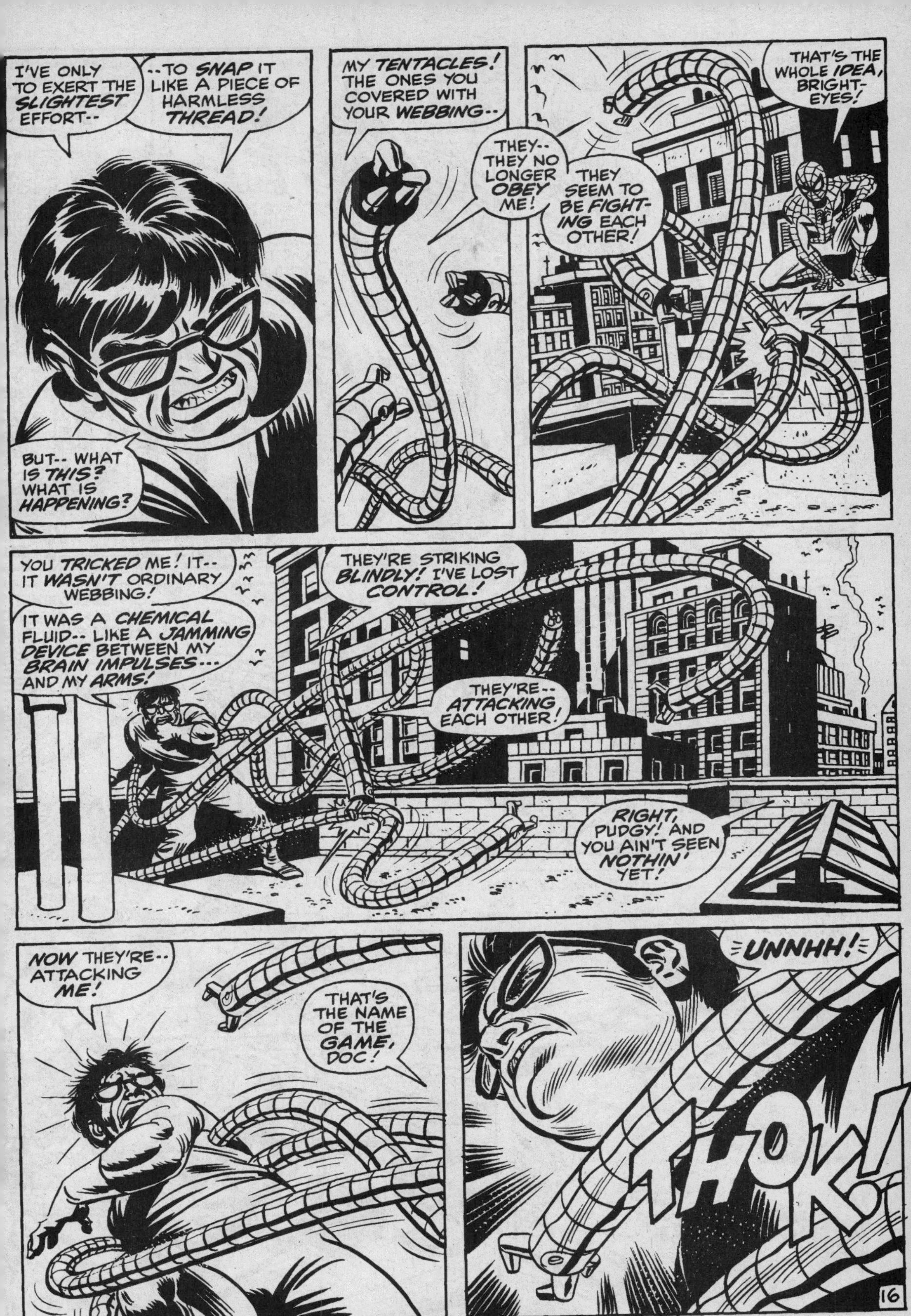
I'VE ONLY TO EXERT THE SLIGHTEST EFFORT--
--TO SNAP IT LIKE A PIECE OF HARMLESS THREAD!
BUT-- WHAT IS THIS? WHAT IS HAPPENING?
MY TENTACLES! THE ONES YOU COVERED WITH YOUR WEBBING--
THEY-- THEY NO LONGER OBEY ME!
THEY SEEM TO BE FIGHTING EACH OTHER!
THAT'S THE WHOLE IDEA, BRIGHT-EYES!
YOU TRICKED ME! IT-- IT WASN'T ORDINARY WEBBING!
IT WAS A CHEMICAL FLUID-- LIKE A JAMMING DEVICE BETWEEN MY BRAIN IMPULSES... AND MY ARMS!
THEY'RE STRIKING BLINDLY! I'VE LOST CONTROL!
THEY'RE-- ATTACKING EACH OTHER!
RIGHT, PUDGY! AND YOU AIN'T SEEN NOTHIN' YET!
NOW THEY'RE-- ATTACKING ME!
THAT'S THE NAME OF THE GAME, DOC!
UNNHH!
THOK!

IT WON'T *WORK!* I'LL BEAT YOU *YET!*

MY *OTHER* ARMS WILL SAVE ME!

IT'S *DOCTOR OCTOPUS*--- FIGHTING *SPIDER-MAN* UP THERE!

THE *BEST* THING THAT COULD HAPPEN FOR THIS TOWN WOULD BE IF THEY *BOTH* FINISH EACH OTHER OFF!

I REACHED HER JUST IN *TIME!*

THEY'RE STILL *BATTLING*--- UP ON THAT *ROO*

BUT T CROW BELO DOES REAL THE DANG

THE MUS CLE THE ARE

I'D BETTER *GET* HIM-- BEFORE HE'S KILLED BY HIS OWN *ARMS!*

SPROK!

OH *BROTHER*: THERE'S JUST N *STOPPING* THE NOW!

HELP ME! HELP ME! I-- I CAN'T *HANDLE* THEM!

DON'T WORRY, MAN! THE *COPS* ARE ON THE WAY RIGHT *NOW!*

--THEY'LL HELP YOU TO A NICE COZY LITTLE *CELL* IN-- *HEY!*

THE CHIMNEY! YOU'VE *TOPPLED* IT!

THEY'VE GONE AMOK! I-- I'M *DONE* FOR!

K

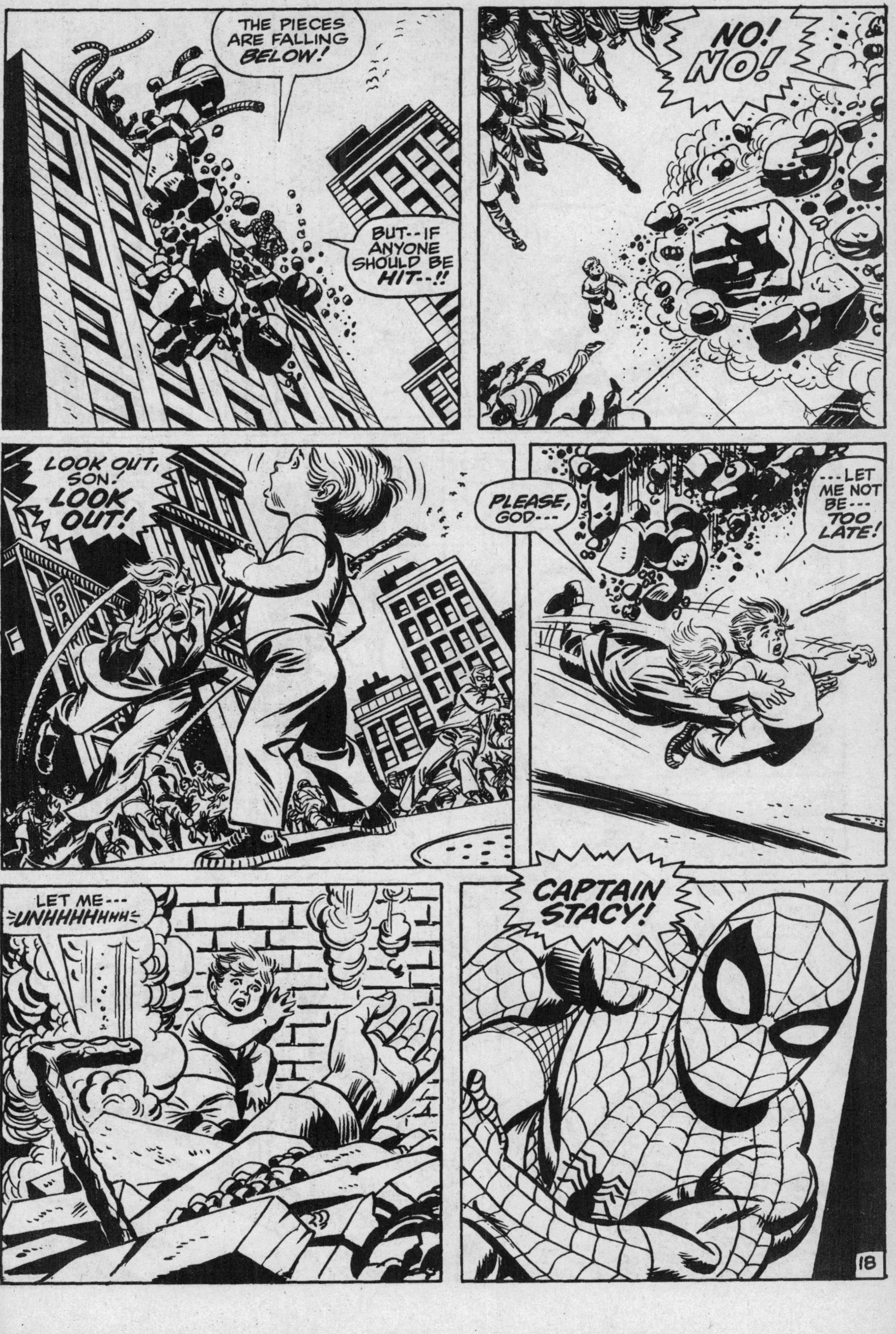
THE PIECES ARE FALLING BELOW!
BUT--IF ANYONE SHOULD BE HIT--!!
NO! NO!
LOOK OUT, SON! LOOK OUT!
PLEASE, GOD---
---LET ME NOT BE--- TOO LATE!
LET ME--- UNHHHHHHH
CAPTAIN STACY!
18

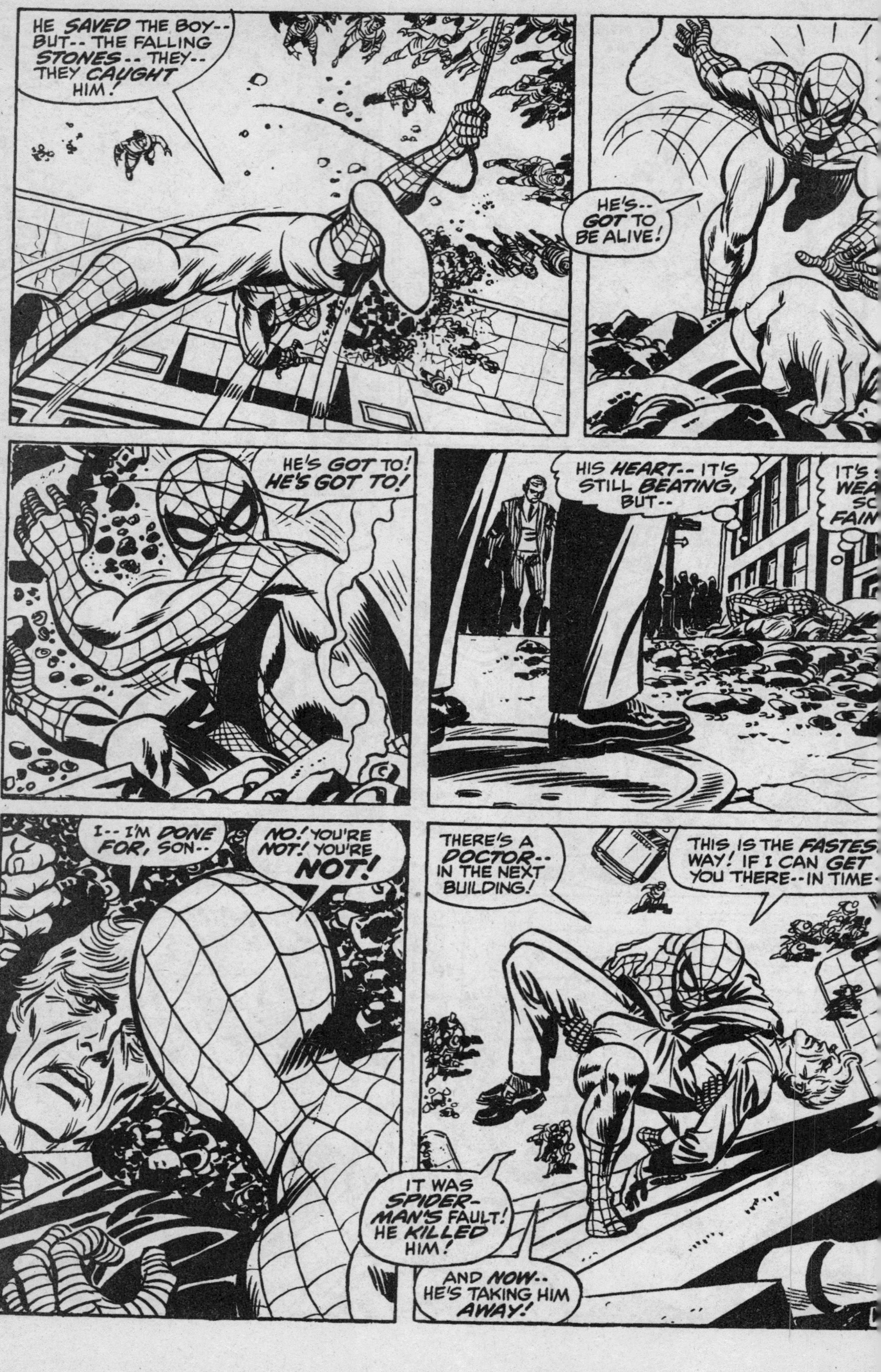
HE SAVED THE BOY-- BUT-- THE FALLING STONES-- THEY-- THEY CAUGHT HIM!
HE'S-- GOT TO BE ALIVE!
HE'S GOT TO! HE'S GOT TO!
HIS HEART-- IT'S STILL BEATING, BUT--
IT'S WEA SO FAIN
I-- I'M DONE FOR, SON--
NO! YOU'RE NOT! YOU'RE NOT!
THERE'S A DOCTOR-- IN THE NEXT BUILDING!
THIS IS THE FASTES WAY! IF I CAN GET YOU THERE--IN TIME-
IT WAS SPIDER-MAN'S FAULT! HE KILLED HIM!
AND NOW-- HE'S TAKING HIM AWAY!

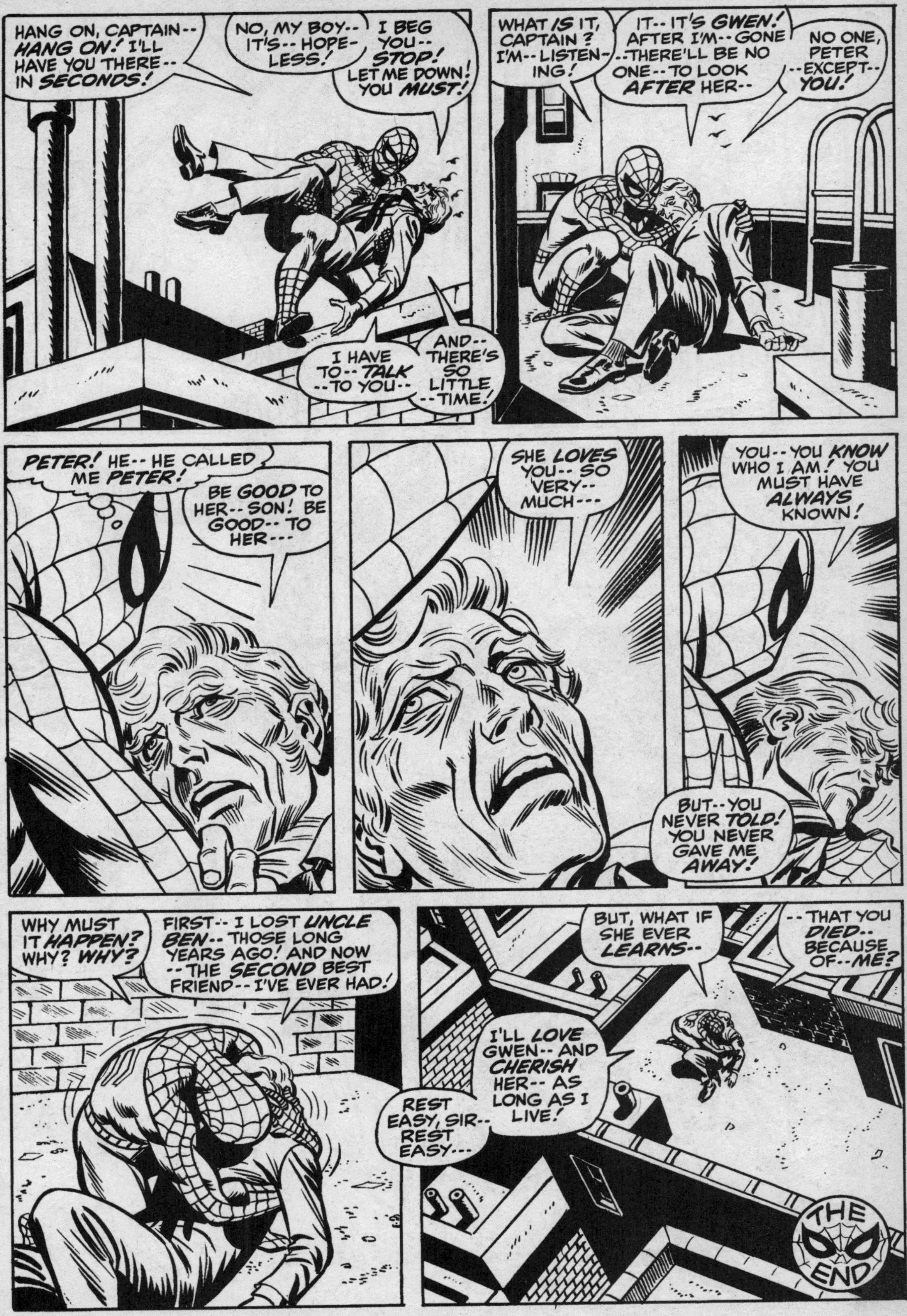
HANG ON, CAPTAIN-- HANG ON! I'LL HAVE YOU THERE-- IN SECONDS!
NO, MY BOY-- IT'S-- HOPE-LESS!
I BEG YOU-- STOP! LET ME DOWN! YOU MUST!
I HAVE TO--TALK --TO YOU--
AND-- THERE'S SO LITTLE --TIME!
WHAT IS IT, CAPTAIN? I'M--LISTEN-ING!
IT-- IT'S GWEN! AFTER I'M--GONE --THERE'LL BE NO ONE-- TO LOOK AFTER HER--
NO ONE, PETER --EXCEPT-- YOU!
PETER! HE-- HE CALLED ME PETER!
BE GOOD TO HER--SON! BE GOOD-- TO HER---
SHE LOVES YOU-- SO VERY-- MUCH---
YOU--YOU KNOW WHO I AM! YOU MUST HAVE ALWAYS KNOWN!
BUT--YOU NEVER TOLD! YOU NEVER GAVE ME AWAY!
WHY MUST IT HAPPEN? WHY? WHY?
FIRST-- I LOST UNCLE BEN-- THOSE LONG YEARS AGO! AND NOW --THE SECOND BEST FRIEND-- I'VE EVER HAD!
BUT, WHAT IF SHE EVER LEARNS--
--THAT YOU DIED-- BECAUSE OF--ME?
I'LL LOVE GWEN-- AND CHERISH HER-- AS LONG AS I LIVE!
REST EASY, SIR-- REST EASY---
THE END

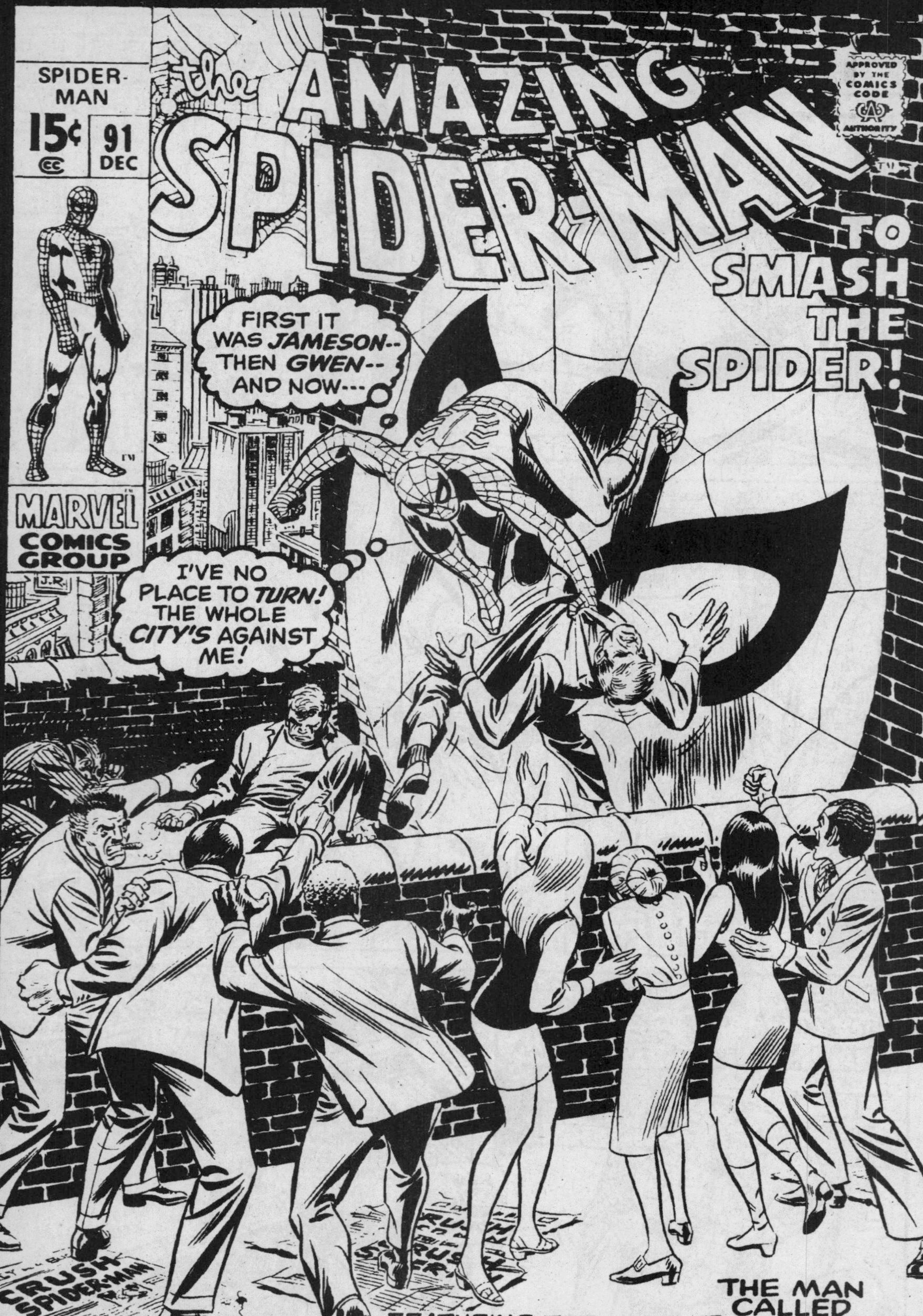
SPIDER-MAN
15¢
91
DEC
MARVEL
COMICS
GROUP
the AMAZING SPIDER-MAN
TO SMASH THE SPIDER!
FIRST IT WAS JAMESON-- THEN GWEN-- AND NOW---
I'VE NO PLACE TO TURN! THE WHOLE CITY'S AGAINST ME!
CRUSH SPIDER-MAN
-FEATURING THE MURDEROUS MENACE OF--
THE MAN CALLED BULLIT!

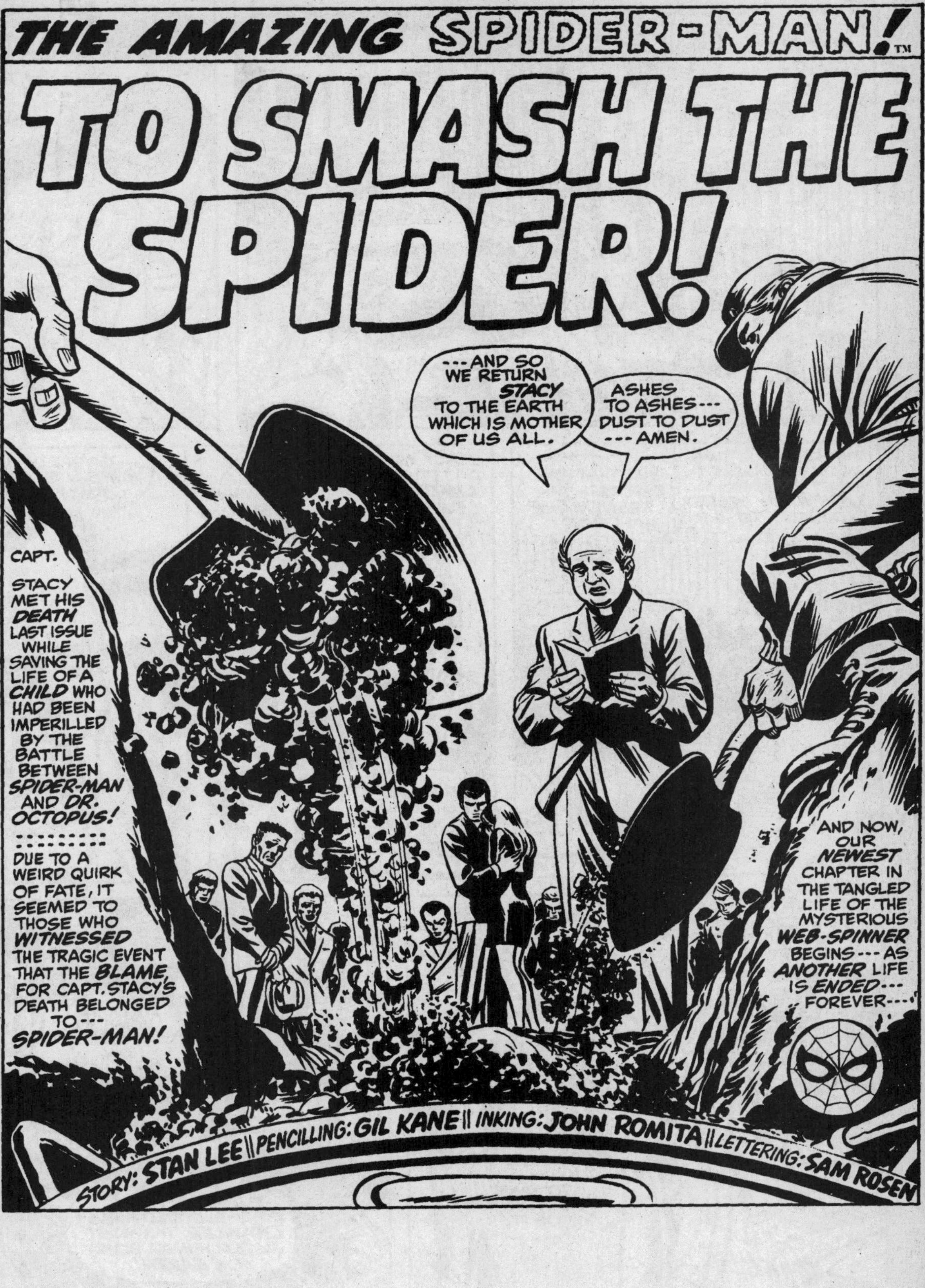
THE AMAZING SPIDER-MAN!™
TO SMASH THE SPIDER!
---AND SO WE RETURN STACY TO THE EARTH WHICH IS MOTHER OF US ALL.
ASHES TO ASHES--- DUST TO DUST ---AMEN.
CAPT. STACY MET HIS DEATH LAST ISSUE WHILE SAVING THE LIFE OF A CHILD WHO HAD BEEN IMPERILLED BY THE BATTLE BETWEEN SPIDER-MAN AND DR. OCTOPUS!
DUE TO A WEIRD QUIRK OF FATE, IT SEEMED TO THOSE WHO WITNESSED THE TRAGIC EVENT THAT THE BLAME FOR CAPT. STACY'S DEATH BELONGED TO--- SPIDER-MAN!
AND NOW, OUR NEWEST CHAPTER IN THE TANGLED LIFE OF THE MYSTERIOUS WEB-SPINNER BEGINS---AS ANOTHER LIFE IS ENDED--- ..FOREVER----!
STORY: STAN LEE || PENCILLING: GIL KANE || INKING: JOHN ROMITA || LETTERING: SAM ROSEN

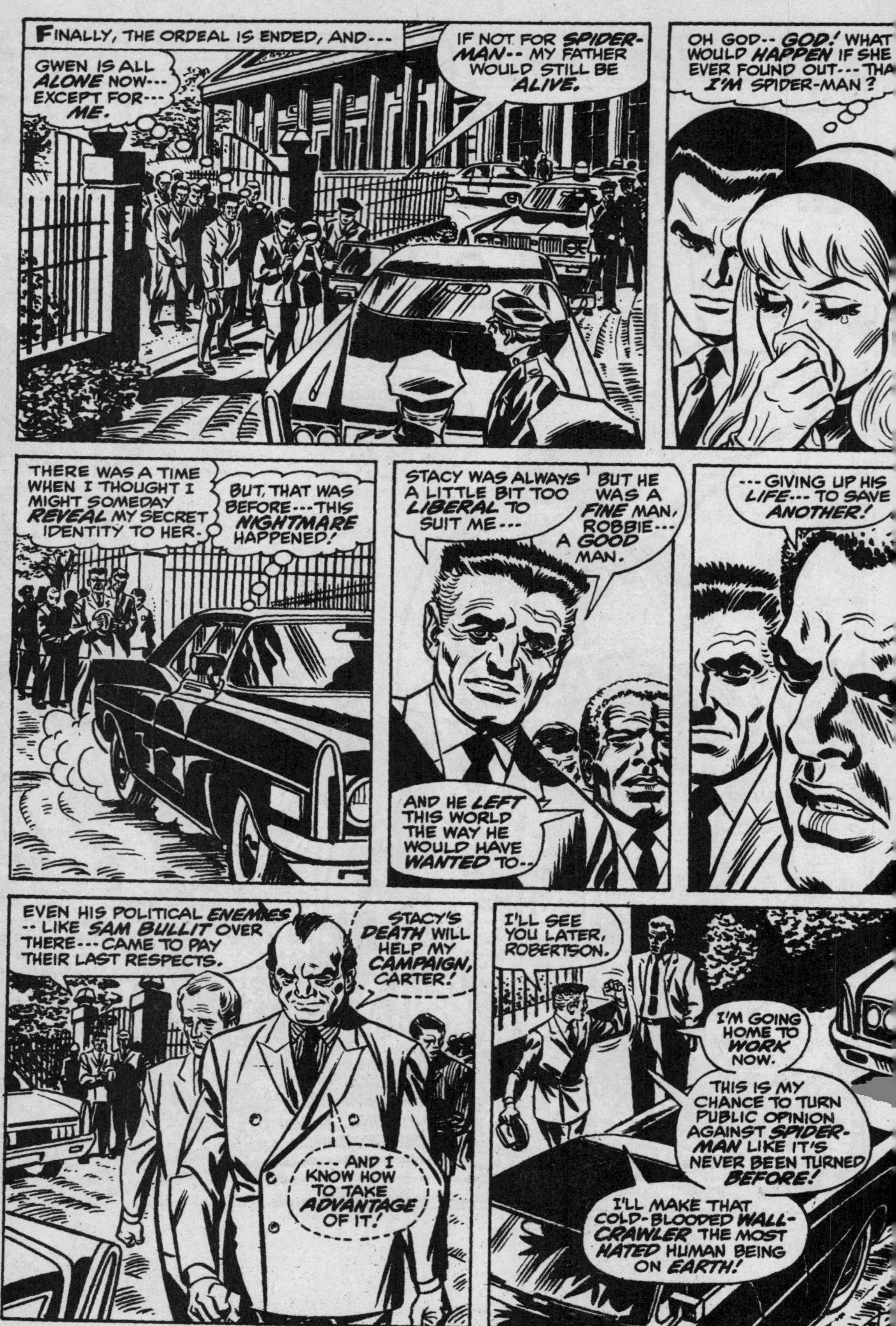
FINALLY, THE ORDEAL IS ENDED, AND---
GWEN IS ALL ALONE NOW--- EXCEPT FOR--- ME.
IF NOT FOR SPIDER-MAN-- MY FATHER WOULD STILL BE ALIVE.
OH GOD-- GOD! WHAT WOULD HAPPEN IF SHE EVER FOUND OUT--- THA I'M SPIDER-MAN?
THERE WAS A TIME WHEN I THOUGHT I MIGHT SOMEDAY REVEAL MY SECRET IDENTITY TO HER.
BUT, THAT WAS BEFORE---THIS NIGHTMARE HAPPENED!
STACY WAS ALWAYS A LITTLE BIT TOO LIBERAL TO SUIT ME---
BUT HE WAS A FINE MAN, ROBBIE--- A GOOD MAN.
AND HE LEFT THIS WORLD THE WAY HE WOULD HAVE WANTED TO--
---GIVING UP HIS LIFE--- TO SAVE ANOTHER!
EVEN HIS POLITICAL ENEMIES -- LIKE SAM BULLIT OVER THERE--- CAME TO PAY THEIR LAST RESPECTS.
STACY'S DEATH WILL HELP MY CAMPAIGN, CARTER!
--- AND I KNOW HOW TO TAKE ADVANTAGE OF IT!
I'LL SEE YOU LATER, ROBERTSON.
I'M GOING HOME TO WORK NOW.
THIS IS MY CHANCE TO TURN PUBLIC OPINION AGAINST SPIDER-MAN LIKE IT'S NEVER BEEN TURNED BEFORE!
I'LL MAKE THAT COLD-BLOODED WALL-CRAWLER THE MOST HATED HUMAN BEING ON EARTH!

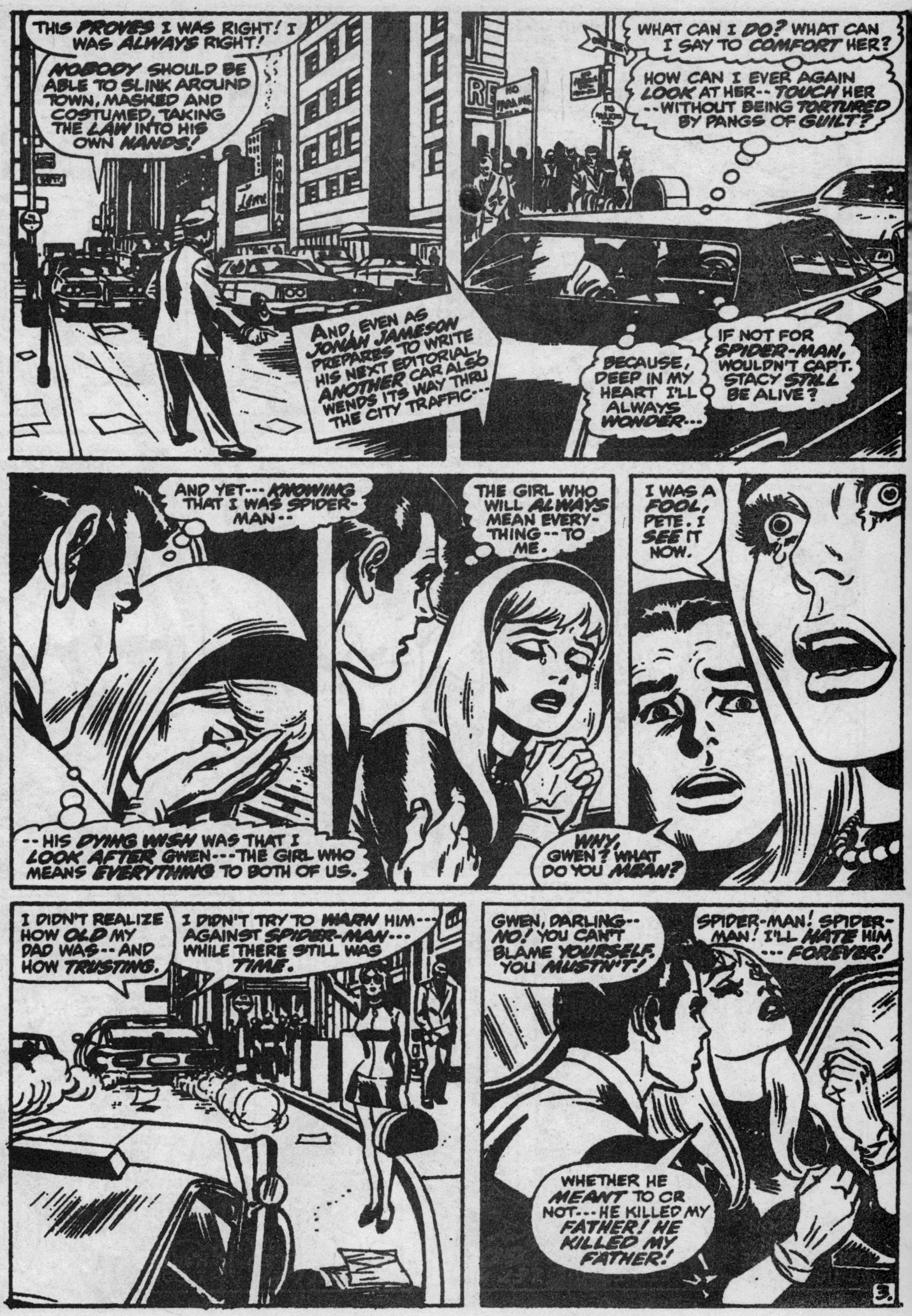
THIS PROVES I WAS RIGHT! I WAS ALWAYS RIGHT!
NOBODY SHOULD BE ABLE TO SLINK AROUND TOWN, MASKED AND COSTUMED, TAKING THE LAW INTO HIS OWN HANDS!
AND, EVEN AS JONAH JAMESON PREPARES TO WRITE HIS NEXT EDITORIAL, ANOTHER CAR ALSO WENDS ITS WAY THRU THE CITY TRAFFIC---
WHAT CAN I DO? WHAT CAN I SAY TO COMFORT HER?
HOW CAN I EVER AGAIN LOOK AT HER-- TOUCH HER --WITHOUT BEING TORTURED BY PANGS OF GUILT?
BECAUSE, DEEP IN MY HEART I'LL ALWAYS WONDER...
IF NOT FOR SPIDER-MAN, WOULDN'T CAPT. STACY STILL BE ALIVE?
AND YET--- KNOWING THAT I WAS SPIDER-MAN--
--HIS DYING WISH WAS THAT I LOOK AFTER GWEN---THE GIRL WHO MEANS EVERYTHING TO BOTH OF US.
THE GIRL WHO WILL ALWAYS MEAN EVERYTHING--- TO ME.
I WAS A FOOL, PETE. I SEE IT NOW.
WHY, GWEN? WHAT DO YOU MEAN?
I DIDN'T REALIZE HOW OLD MY DAD WAS--AND HOW TRUSTING.
I DIDN'T TRY TO WARN HIM--- AGAINST SPIDER-MAN--- WHILE THERE STILL WAS TIME.
GWEN, DARLING-- NO! YOU CAN'T BLAME YOURSELF. YOU MUSTN'T!
SPIDER-MAN! SPIDER-MAN! I'LL HATE HIM ---FOREVER!
WHETHER HE MEANT TO OR NOT---HE KILLED MY FATHER! HE KILLED MY FATHER!
3.

BUT, GWEN, YOU DON'T UNDER-STAND. HE--HE--

IT'S NO USE. WHAT CAN I SAY? THERE JUST AREN'T ANY WORDS.

PETER, I--I'M NOT GOING TO WASTE TIME CRYING. I'M GOING TO WORK--

--TO DO WHAT I CAN TO RID THE CITY OF MENACES LIKE-- SPIDER-MAN!

HOW, GWEN? WHAT DO YOU MEAN?

IN THE COMING ELECTION-- ONE OF THE CANDIDATES, SAM BULLIT, IS RUNNING ON A LAW AND ORDER TICKET!

HE USED TO BE A COP-- JUST LIKE DAD. THEY KNEW EACH OTHER IN THE PAST.

I'M GOIN TO VOLUNT TO HELP I CAMPING

AND SO, THE VERY NEXT DAY--

PERHAPS IT TAKES A HARD MAN LIKE SAM BULLIT TO BRING SOMEONE LIKE SPIDER-MAN TO JUSTICE!

AND IF IT DOES, I'M ALL FOR HIM.

MAY I HELP YO YOUNG LADY?

WHAT AN OFFICE! I DIDN'T REALIZE HE WAS SO SUCCESSFUL!

I'D LIKE TO SEE MR. BULLIT, PLEASE.

I'M CAPTAIN STACY'S DAUGHTER, GWENDOLYN.

WHAT CAN THIS BE?

RRRINNG

STACY'S DAUGHTER TO SEE THE BIG MAN?

SURE, SEND HER RIGHT IN!

4

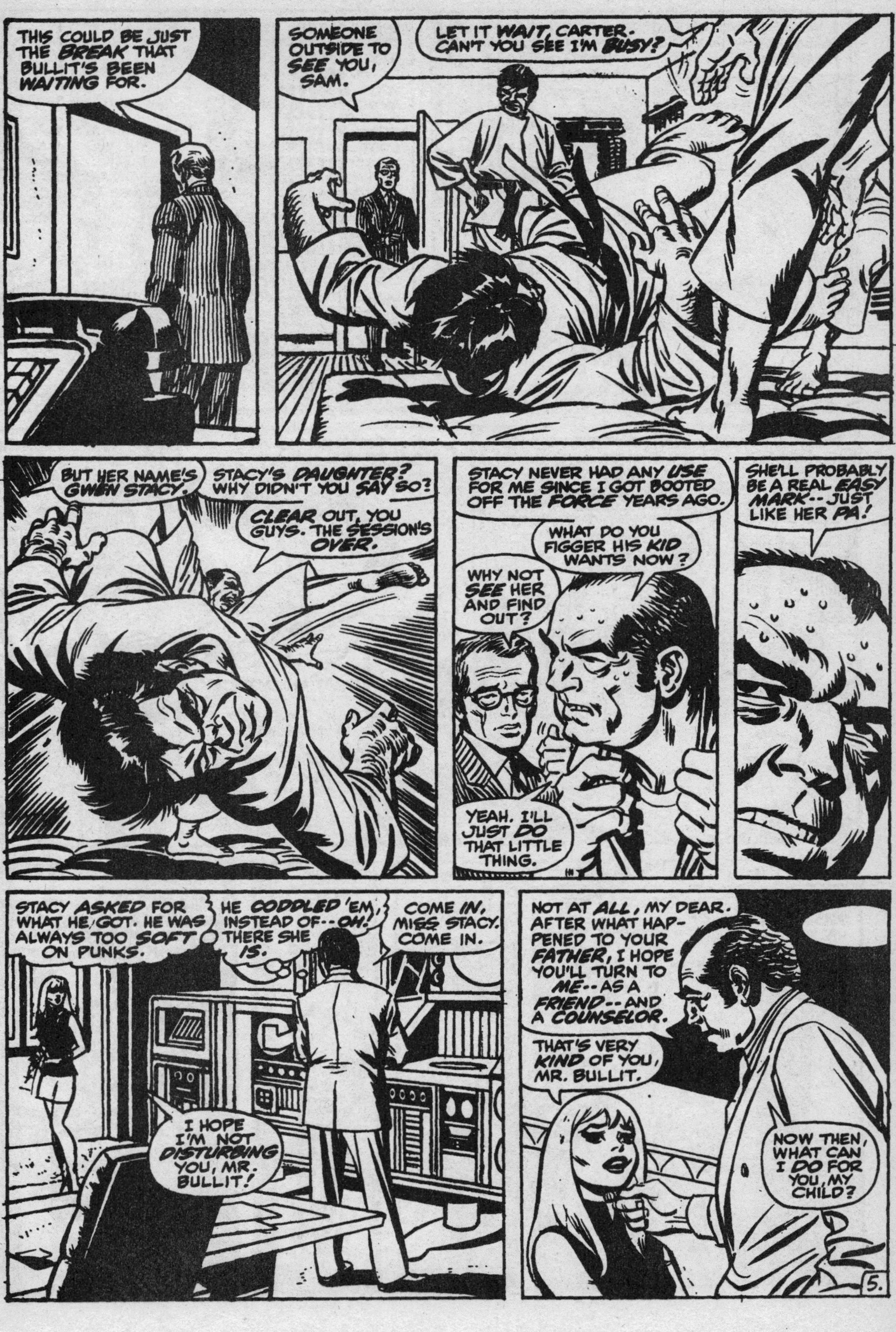
THIS COULD BE JUST THE BREAK THAT BULLIT'S BEEN WAITING FOR.
SOMEONE OUTSIDE TO SEE YOU, SAM.
LET IT WAIT, CARTER. CAN'T YOU SEE I'M BUSY?
BUT HER NAME'S GWEN STACY.
STACY'S DAUGHTER? WHY DIDN'T YOU SAY SO?
CLEAR OUT, YOU GUYS. THE SESSION'S OVER.
STACY NEVER HAD ANY USE FOR ME SINCE I GOT BOOTED OFF THE FORCE YEARS AGO.
WHAT DO YOU FIGGER HIS KID WANTS NOW?
WHY NOT SEE HER AND FIND OUT?
YEAH. I'LL JUST DO THAT LITTLE THING.
SHE'LL PROBABLY BE A REAL EASY MARK-- JUST LIKE HER PA!
STACY ASKED FOR WHAT HE GOT. HE WAS ALWAYS TOO SOFT ON PUNKS.
HE CODDLED 'EM, INSTEAD OF-- OH! THERE SHE IS.
COME IN, MISS STACY. COME IN.
I HOPE I'M NOT DISTURBING YOU, MR. BULLIT!
NOT AT ALL, MY DEAR. AFTER WHAT HAPPENED TO YOUR FATHER, I HOPE YOU'LL TURN TO ME-- AS A FRIEND-- AND A COUNSELOR.
THAT'S VERY KIND OF YOU, MR. BULLIT.
NOW THEN, WHAT CAN I DO FOR YOU, MY CHILD?
5.

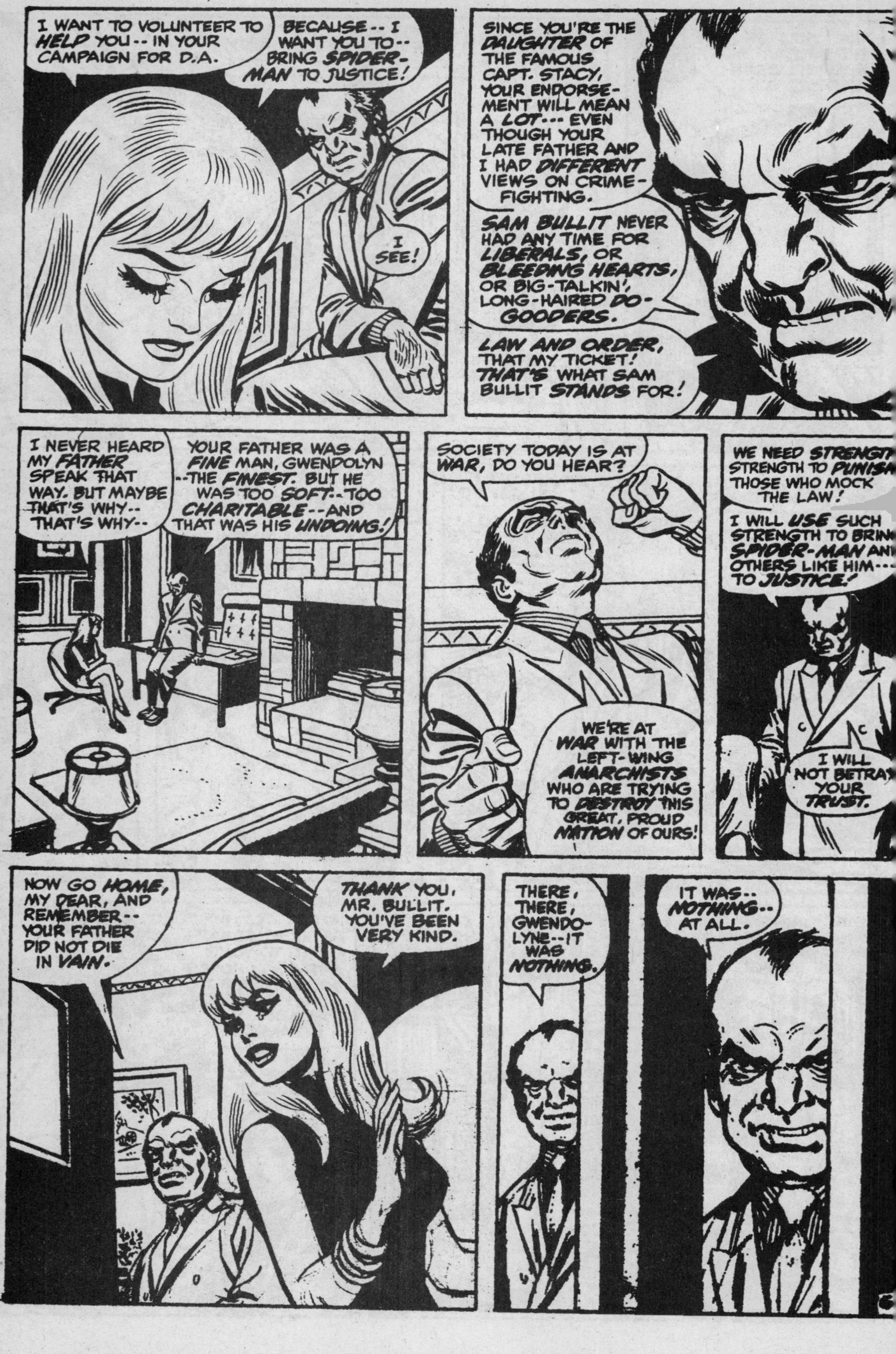
I WANT TO VOLUNTEER TO HELP YOU -- IN YOUR CAMPAIGN FOR D.A.
BECAUSE -- I WANT YOU TO -- BRING SPIDER-MAN TO JUSTICE!
I SEE!
SINCE YOU'RE THE DAUGHTER OF THE FAMOUS CAPT. STACY, YOUR ENDORSEMENT WILL MEAN A LOT--- EVEN THOUGH YOUR LATE FATHER AND I HAD DIFFERENT VIEWS ON CRIME-FIGHTING.
SAM BULLIT NEVER HAD ANY TIME FOR LIBERALS, OR BLEEDING HEARTS, OR BIG-TALKIN', LONG-HAIRED DO-GOODERS.
LAW AND ORDER, THAT MY TICKET! THAT'S WHAT SAM BULLIT STANDS FOR!
I NEVER HEARD MY FATHER SPEAK THAT WAY. BUT MAYBE THAT'S WHY-- THAT'S WHY--
YOUR FATHER WAS A FINE MAN, GWENDOLYN --THE FINEST. BUT HE WAS TOO SOFT--TOO CHARITABLE--AND THAT WAS HIS UNDOING!
SOCIETY TODAY IS AT WAR, DO YOU HEAR?
WE'RE AT WAR WITH THE LEFT-WING ANARCHISTS WHO ARE TRYING TO DESTROY THIS GREAT, PROUD NATION OF OURS!
WE NEED STRENGTH STRENGTH TO PUNISH THOSE WHO MOCK THE LAW!
I WILL USE SUCH STRENGTH TO BRING SPIDER-MAN AND OTHERS LIKE HIM---- TO JUSTICE!
I WILL NOT BETRAY YOUR TRUST.
NOW GO HOME, MY DEAR, AND REMEMBER-- YOUR FATHER DID NOT DIE IN VAIN.
THANK YOU, MR. BULLIT. YOU'VE BEEN VERY KIND.
THERE, THERE, GWENDOLYNE--IT WAS NOTHING.
IT WAS.. NOTHING.. AT ALL.

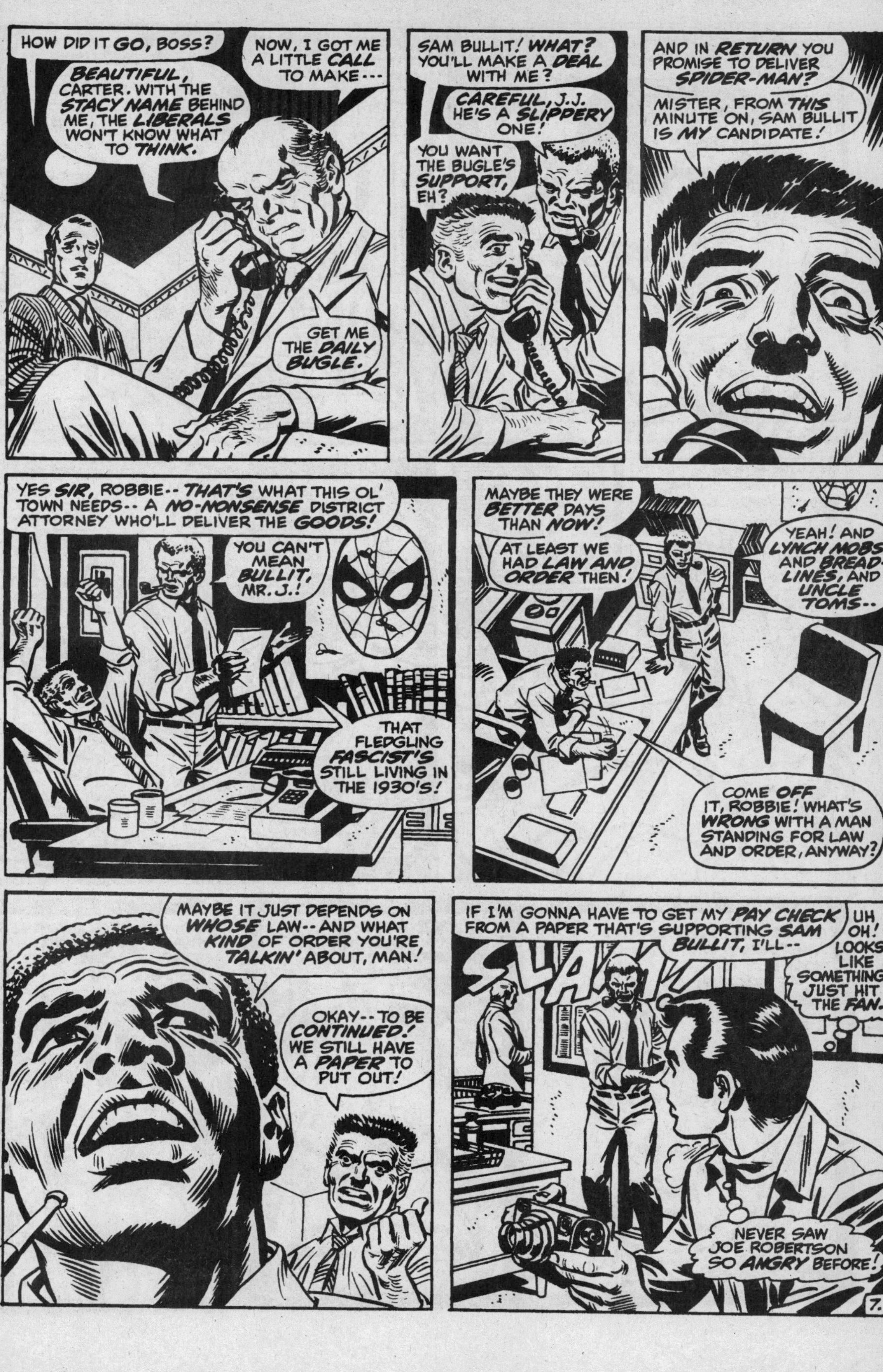
HOW DID IT GO, BOSS?
BEAUTIFUL, CARTER. WITH THE STACY NAME BEHIND ME, THE LIBERALS WON'T KNOW WHAT TO THINK.
NOW, I GOT ME A LITTLE CALL TO MAKE---
GET ME THE DAILY BUGLE.
SAM BULLIT! WHAT? YOU'LL MAKE A DEAL WITH ME?
CAREFUL, J.J. HE'S A SLIPPERY ONE!
YOU WANT THE BUGLE'S SUPPORT, EH?
AND IN RETURN YOU PROMISE TO DELIVER SPIDER-MAN?
MISTER, FROM THIS MINUTE ON, SAM BULLIT IS MY CANDIDATE!
YES SIR, ROBBIE-- THAT'S WHAT THIS OL' TOWN NEEDS-- A NO-NONSENSE DISTRICT ATTORNEY WHO'LL DELIVER THE GOODS!
YOU CAN'T MEAN BULLIT, MR. J.!
THAT FLEDGLING FASCIST'S STILL LIVING IN THE 1930'S!
MAYBE THEY WERE BETTER DAYS THAN NOW!
AT LEAST WE HAD LAW AND ORDER THEN!
YEAH! AND LYNCH MOBS, AND BREAD-LINES, AND UNCLE TOMS--
COME OFF IT, ROBBIE! WHAT'S WRONG WITH A MAN STANDING FOR LAW AND ORDER, ANYWAY?
MAYBE IT JUST DEPENDS ON WHOSE LAW-- AND WHAT KIND OF ORDER YOU'RE TALKIN' ABOUT, MAN!
OKAY-- TO BE CONTINUED! WE STILL HAVE A PAPER TO PUT OUT!
IF I'M GONNA HAVE TO GET MY PAY CHECK FROM A PAPER THAT'S SUPPORTING SAM BULLIT, I'LL--
SLAM!
UH OH! LOOKS LIKE SOMETHING JUST HIT THE FAN.
NEVER SAW JOE ROBERTSON SO ANGRY BEFORE!

AND IF *ROBBIE'S* THAT MAD-- I CAN JUST IMAGINE *JAMESON'S* MOOD!

I'D BETTER *SPLIT!* I'LL ASK HIM ABOUT SOME PHOTO ASSIGNMENTS SOME *OTHER* TIME!

LATER--

ONE THING'S FOR SURE--- I CAN'T HANG AROUND *HERE!*

I'VE GOTTA DO *SOMETHING* TO TAKE MY MIND OFF *GWEN---*

--AND THE WAY SHE FEELS ABOUT *SPIDER-MAN!*

I'VE GOT KEEP *BUSY* TAKING *PICTURES* WALL-CRAWLING-- *ANYTHING.*

MAYBE THERE'S SOMETHING ON THE *BOOB TUBE* THAT'LL---

HEY! WHAT'S *THIS?*

IS IT *TRUE* THAT YOU'VE PROMISED TO APPREHEND *SPIDER-MAN* IF ELECTED, MR. *BULLIT?*

YOU CAN *BET* ON IT, MISTER! I PLEDGED TO MAKE THE STREETS OF THIS CITY *SAFE* FOR DECENT FOLK!

AND THAT MEANS PUTTING AN *END* TO THAT WEB-SPINNING *KILLER!*

WE'VE ALL SEEN WHAT *HAPPENS* WHEN WE CODDLE PUBLIC *MENACES!*

SPIDER-MAN IS RESPONSIBLE FOR THE *DEATH* OF CAPT. GEORGE STACY!

AND UNTIL HE'S *CRUSHED* -- SWIFTLY-- WITHOUT *MERCY--* *NONE* OF US ARE SAFE!

GREAT! THAT'S ALL I NEED-- SOME GUY WORKING UP A LYNCH MOB AGAINST ME!

CLIC--

THE VERY NEXT DAY, AS THOUGH TO LEND *EMPHASIS* TO SPIDEY'S WORDS---

DAILY GLOBE
SPIDER-MAN MUST BE CRUSHED!
SAYS SAM BULLIT

I'LL MAKE OUR CITY'S STREETS SAFE AGAIN!

I SWEAR THAT SPIDER-MAN'S DAYS ARE NUMBERED!

CRUSH SPIDER-MAN!

CRUSH SPIDER-MAN!

CRUSH SPIDER-MAN!

CRUSH SPIDER-MAN!

CRUSH SPIDER-MAN!

CRUSH SPIDER-MAN!

9.

THEN, AS *DARKNESS* SHROUDS THE FEARFUL CITY---

IT'S LIKE A *GHOST TOWN* DOWN THERE, THANKS TO *BULLITT* AND *JAMESON!*

THEY'VE MADE PEOPLE TOO *SCARED* TO LEAVE THEIR *APARTMENTS!*

AND *I'M* THE ONE THEY'RE *SCARED* OF!

OVERNIGHT, TWO UN-THINKING RABBLE-ROUSERS HAVE CREATED A CITY OF *FEAR!*

BUT-- WHAT IF THEY'RE *NOT* UNTHINKING?

WHAT IF--- THEY'RE *RIGHT?*

MAYBE I *DO* BRING TRAGEDY--TO EVERYONE WHO CROSSES MY PATH!

LOOK WHAT I'VE JUST DONE--TO THE GIRL I LOVE!

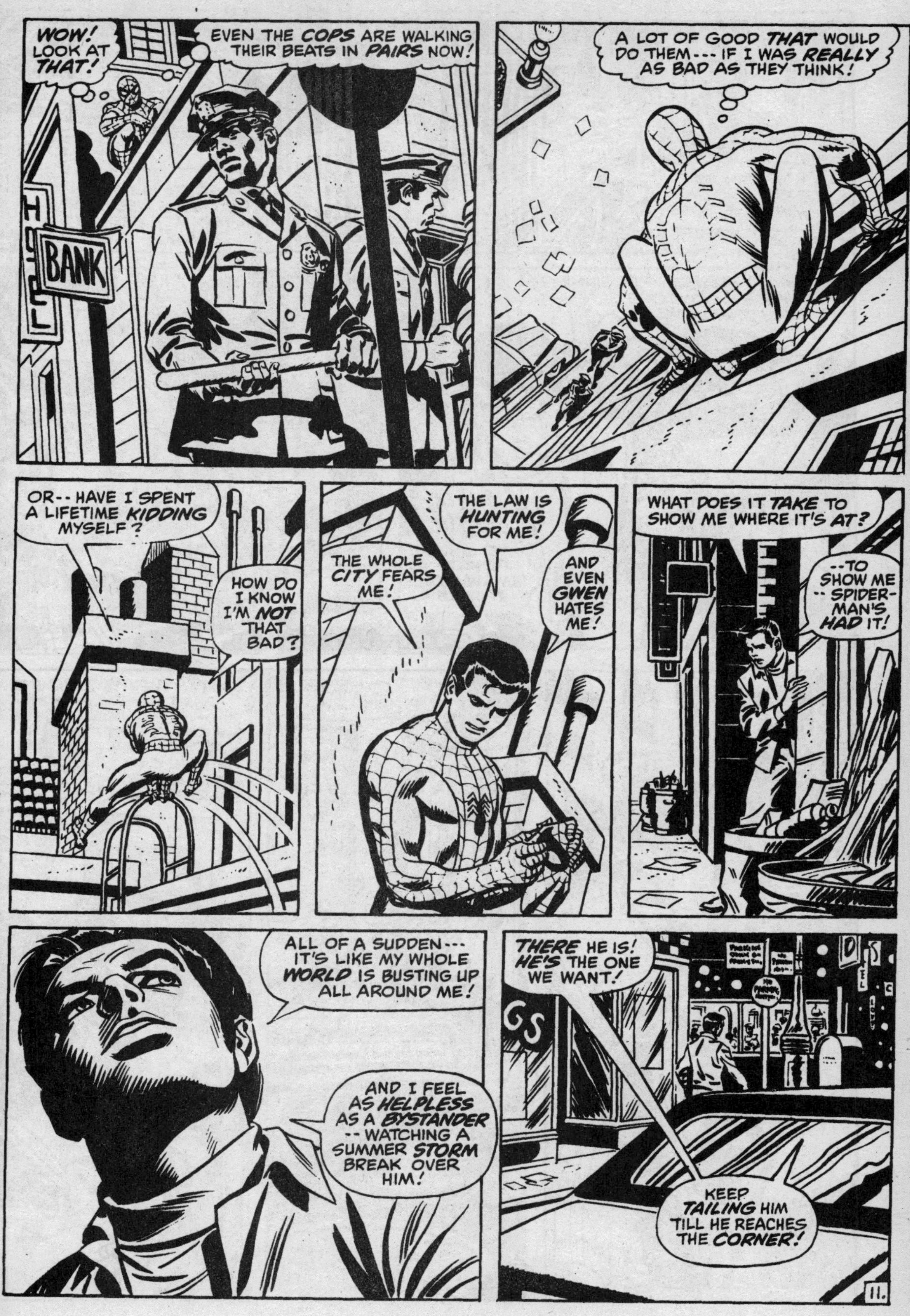
WOW! LOOK AT THAT!
EVEN THE COPS ARE WALKING THEIR BEATS IN PAIRS NOW!
BANK
A LOT OF GOOD THAT WOULD DO THEM--- IF I WAS REALLY AS BAD AS THEY THINK!
OR-- HAVE I SPENT A LIFETIME KIDDING MYSELF?
HOW DO I KNOW I'M NOT THAT BAD?
THE LAW IS HUNTING FOR ME!
THE WHOLE CITY FEARS ME!
AND EVEN GWEN HATES ME!
WHAT DOES IT TAKE TO SHOW ME WHERE IT'S AT?
--TO SHOW ME --SPIDER-MAN'S HAD IT!
ALL OF A SUDDEN--- IT'S LIKE MY WHOLE WORLD IS BUSTING UP ALL AROUND ME!
AND I FEEL AS HELPLESS AS A BYSTANDER --WATCHING A SUMMER STORM BREAK OVER HIM!
THERE HE IS! HE'S THE ONE WE WANT!
KEEP TAILING HIM TILL HE REACHES THE CORNER!
11.

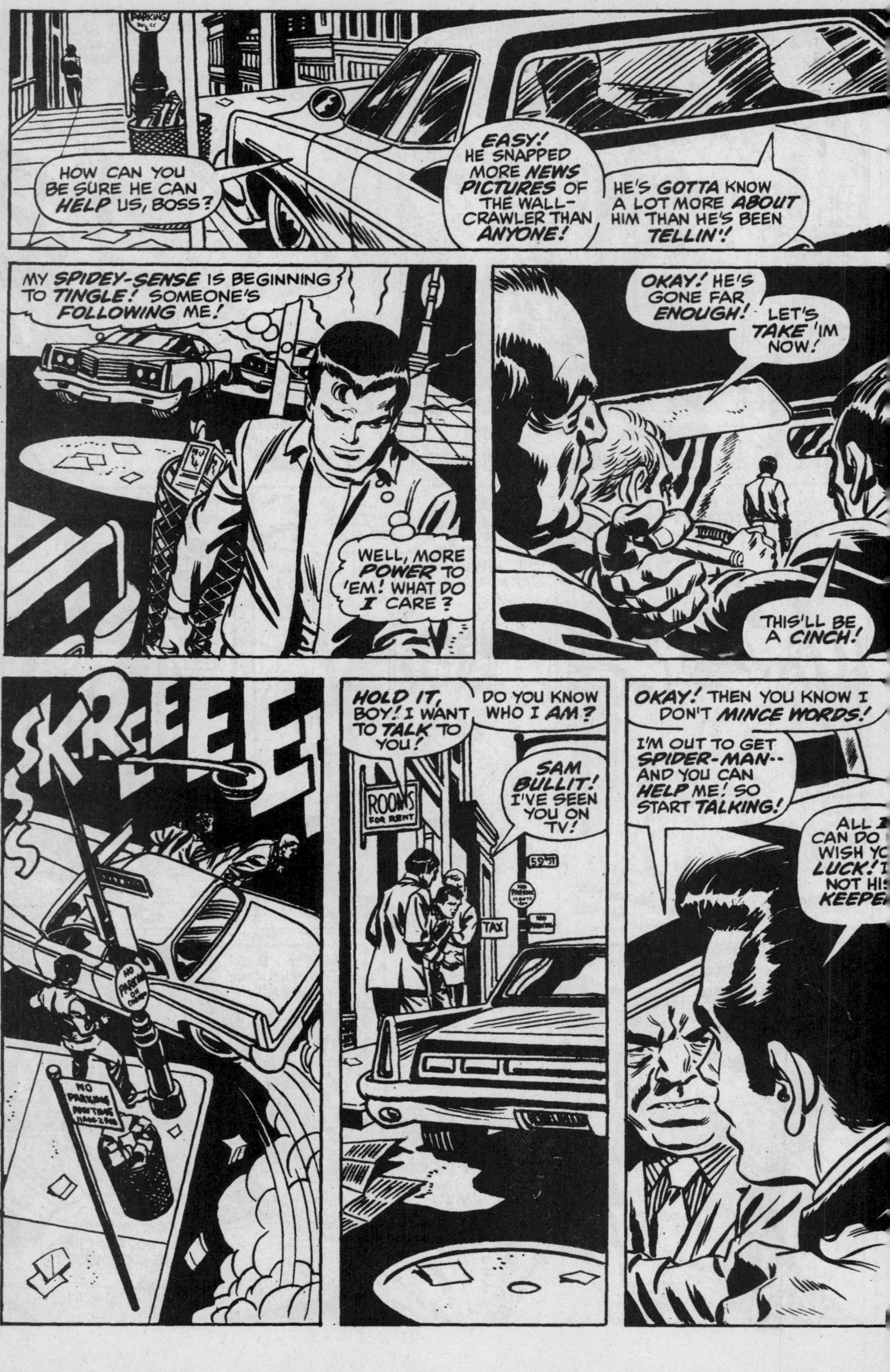
PARKING
HOW CAN YOU BE SURE HE CAN HELP US, BOSS?
EASY! HE SNAPPED MORE NEWS PICTURES OF THE WALL-CRAWLER THAN ANYONE!
HE'S GOTTA KNOW A LOT MORE ABOUT HIM THAN HE'S BEEN TELLIN'!
MY SPIDEY-SENSE IS BEGINNING TO TINGLE! SOMEONE'S FOLLOWING ME!
WELL, MORE POWER TO 'EM! WHAT DO I CARE?
OKAY! HE'S GONE FAR ENOUGH!
LET'S TAKE 'IM NOW!
THIS'LL BE A CINCH!
SKREEEE
NO PARKING ANYTIME
HOLD IT, BOY! I WANT TO TALK TO YOU!
DO YOU KNOW WHO I AM?
SAM BULLIT! I'VE SEEN YOU ON TV!
ROOMS FOR RENT
59th ST
TAX
OKAY! THEN YOU KNOW I DON'T MINCE WORDS!
I'M OUT TO GET SPIDER-MAN-- AND YOU CAN HELP ME! SO START TALKING!
ALL I CAN DO WISH YO LUCK! I NOT HIS KEEPE

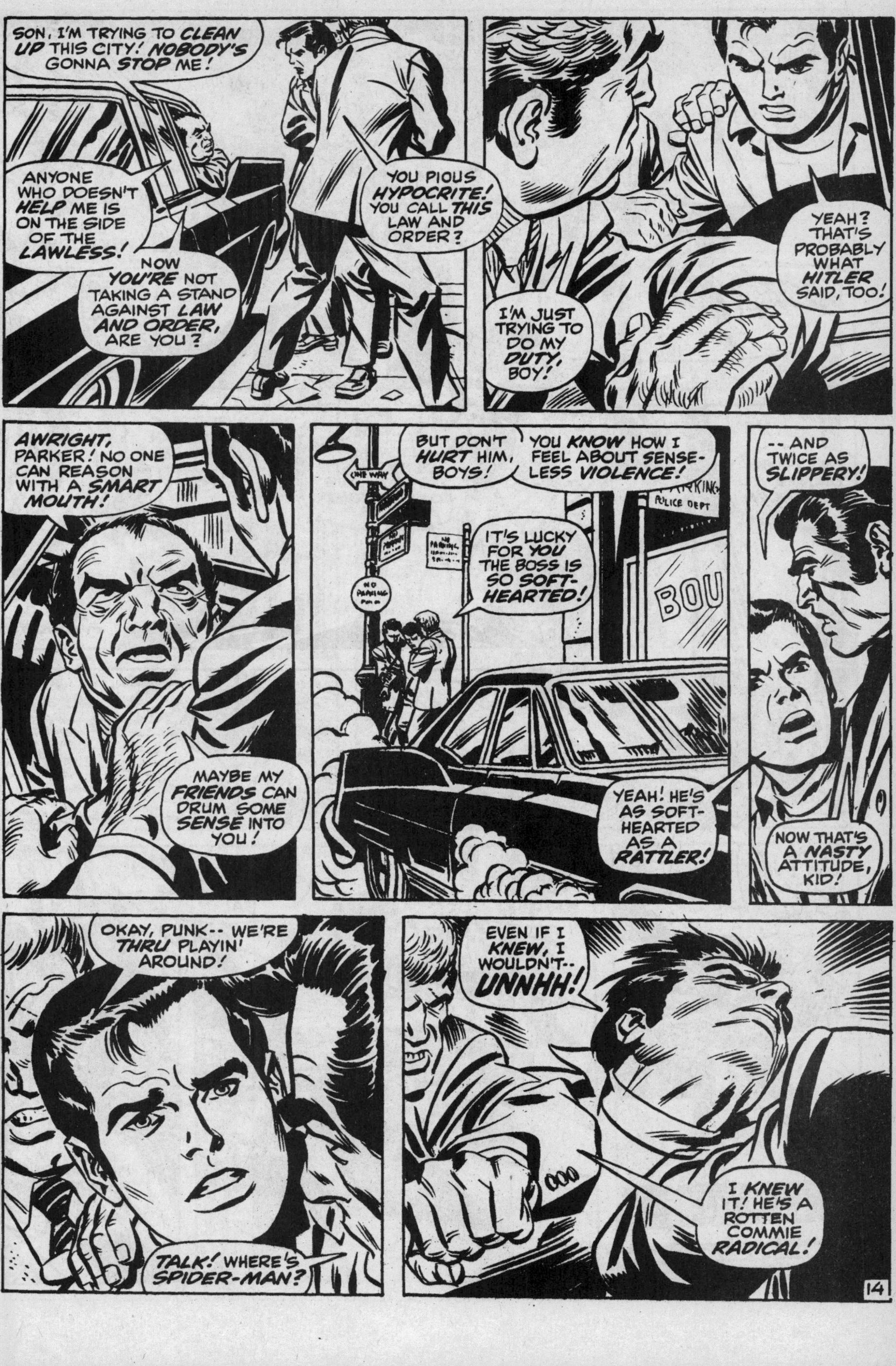
SON, I'M TRYING TO CLEAN UP THIS CITY! NOBODY'S GONNA STOP ME!
ANYONE WHO DOESN'T HELP ME IS ON THE SIDE OF THE LAWLESS!
NOW YOU'RE NOT TAKING A STAND AGAINST LAW AND ORDER, ARE YOU?
YOU PIOUS HYPOCRITE! YOU CALL THIS LAW AND ORDER?
YEAH? THAT'S PROBABLY WHAT HITLER SAID, TOO!
I'M JUST TRYING TO DO MY DUTY, BOY!
AWRIGHT, PARKER! NO ONE CAN REASON WITH A SMART MOUTH!
MAYBE MY FRIENDS CAN DRUM SOME SENSE INTO YOU!
BUT DON'T HURT HIM, BOYS!
YOU KNOW HOW I FEEL ABOUT SENSE-LESS VIOLENCE!
ONE WAY
POLICE DEPT
NO PARKING
IT'S LUCKY FOR YOU THE BOSS IS SO SOFT-HEARTED!
BOU
YEAH! HE'S AS SOFT-HEARTED AS A RATTLER!
-- AND TWICE AS SLIPPERY!
NOW THAT'S A NASTY ATTITUDE, KID!
OKAY, PUNK-- WE'RE THRU PLAYIN' AROUND!
TALK! WHERE'S SPIDER-MAN?
EVEN IF I KNEW, I WOULDN'T.. UNNHH!
I KNEW IT! HE'S A ROTTEN COMMIE RADICAL!

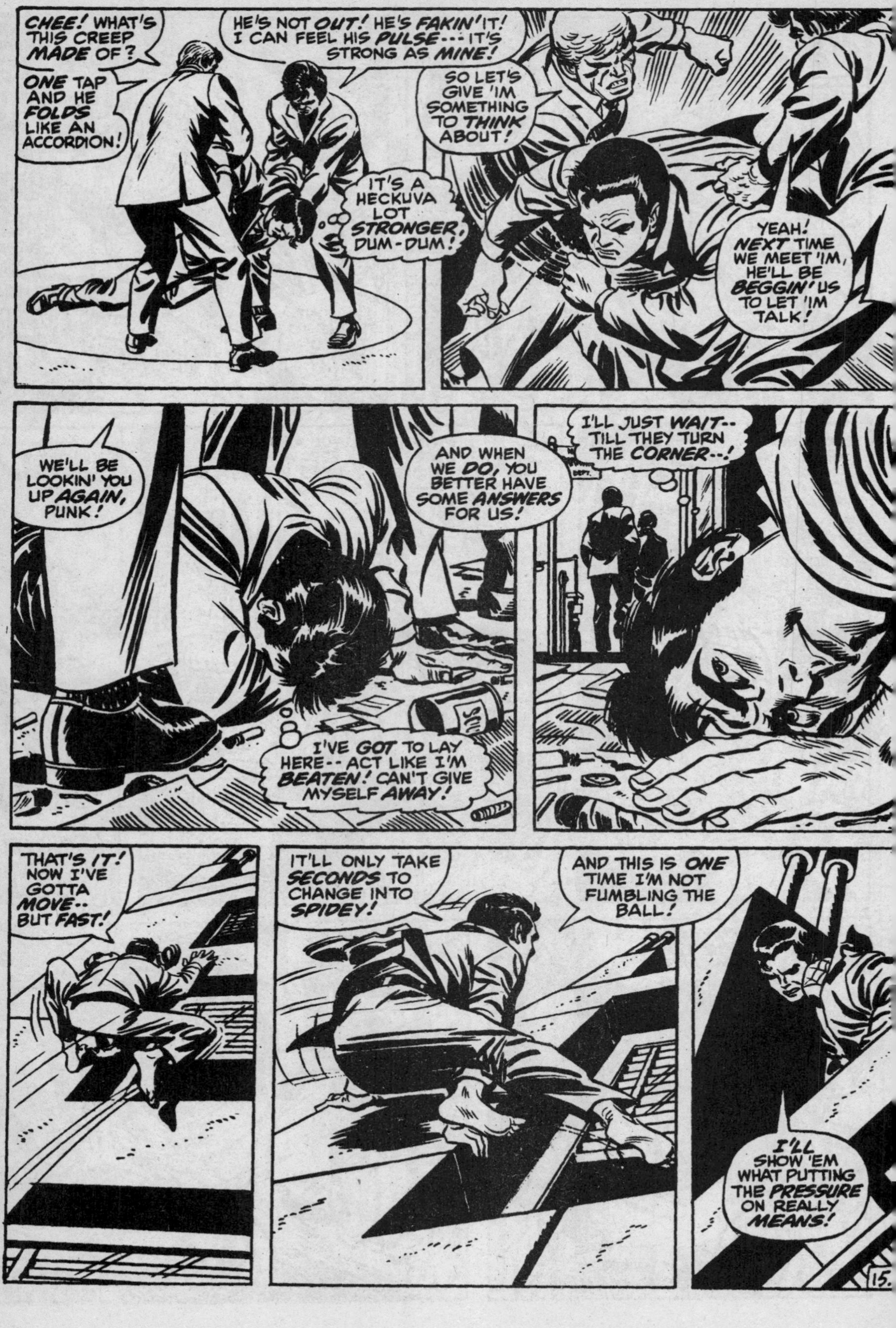
CHEE! WHAT'S THIS CREEP MADE OF?
ONE TAP AND HE FOLDS LIKE AN ACCORDION!
HE'S NOT OUT! HE'S FAKIN' IT! I CAN FEEL HIS PULSE--- IT'S STRONG AS MINE!
IT'S A HECKUVA LOT STRONGER, DUM-DUM!
SO LET'S GIVE 'IM SOMETHING TO THINK ABOUT!
YEAH! NEXT TIME WE MEET 'IM, HE'LL BE BEGGIN' US TO LET 'IM TALK!
WE'LL BE LOOKIN' YOU UP AGAIN, PUNK!
AND WHEN WE DO, YOU BETTER HAVE SOME ANSWERS FOR US!
I'VE GOT TO LAY HERE-- ACT LIKE I'M BEATEN! CAN'T GIVE MYSELF AWAY!
I'LL JUST WAIT-- TILL THEY TURN THE CORNER--!
THAT'S IT! NOW I'VE GOTTA MOVE-- BUT FAST!
IT'LL ONLY TAKE SECONDS TO CHANGE INTO SPIDEY!
AND THIS IS ONE TIME I'M NOT FUMBLING THE BALL!
I'LL SHOW 'EM WHAT PUTTING THE PRESSURE ON REALLY MEANS!
15.

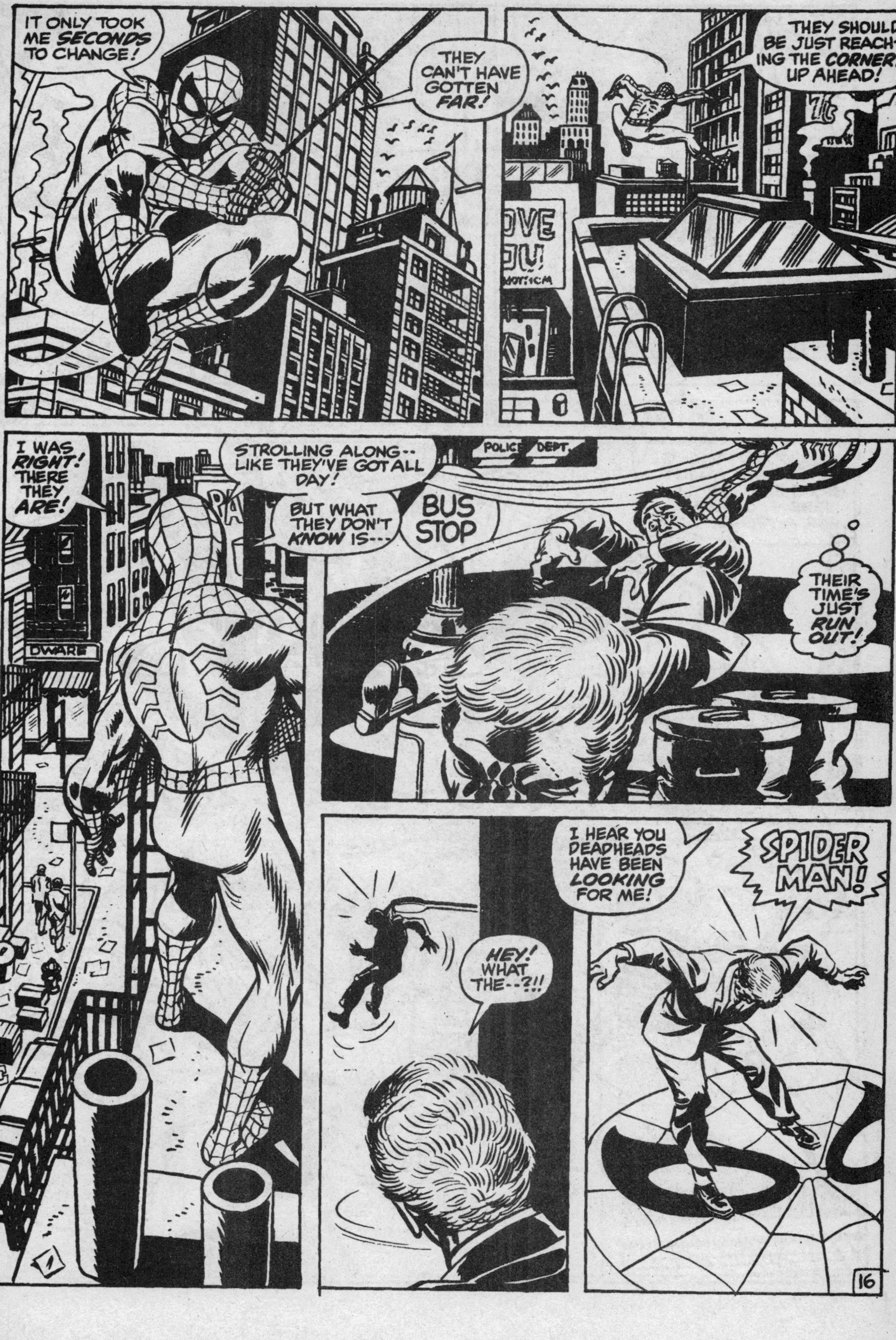
IT ONLY TOOK ME SECONDS TO CHANGE!
THEY CAN'T HAVE GOTTEN FAR!
THEY SHOULD BE JUST REACHING THE CORNER, UP AHEAD!
I WAS RIGHT! THERE THEY ARE!
STROLLING ALONG-- LIKE THEY'VE GOT ALL DAY!
BUT WHAT THEY DON'T KNOW IS---
POLICE DEPT.
BUS STOP
THEIR TIME'S JUST RUN OUT!
HEY! WHAT THE--?!!
I HEAR YOU DEADHEADS HAVE BEEN LOOKING FOR ME!
SPIDER MAN!
16

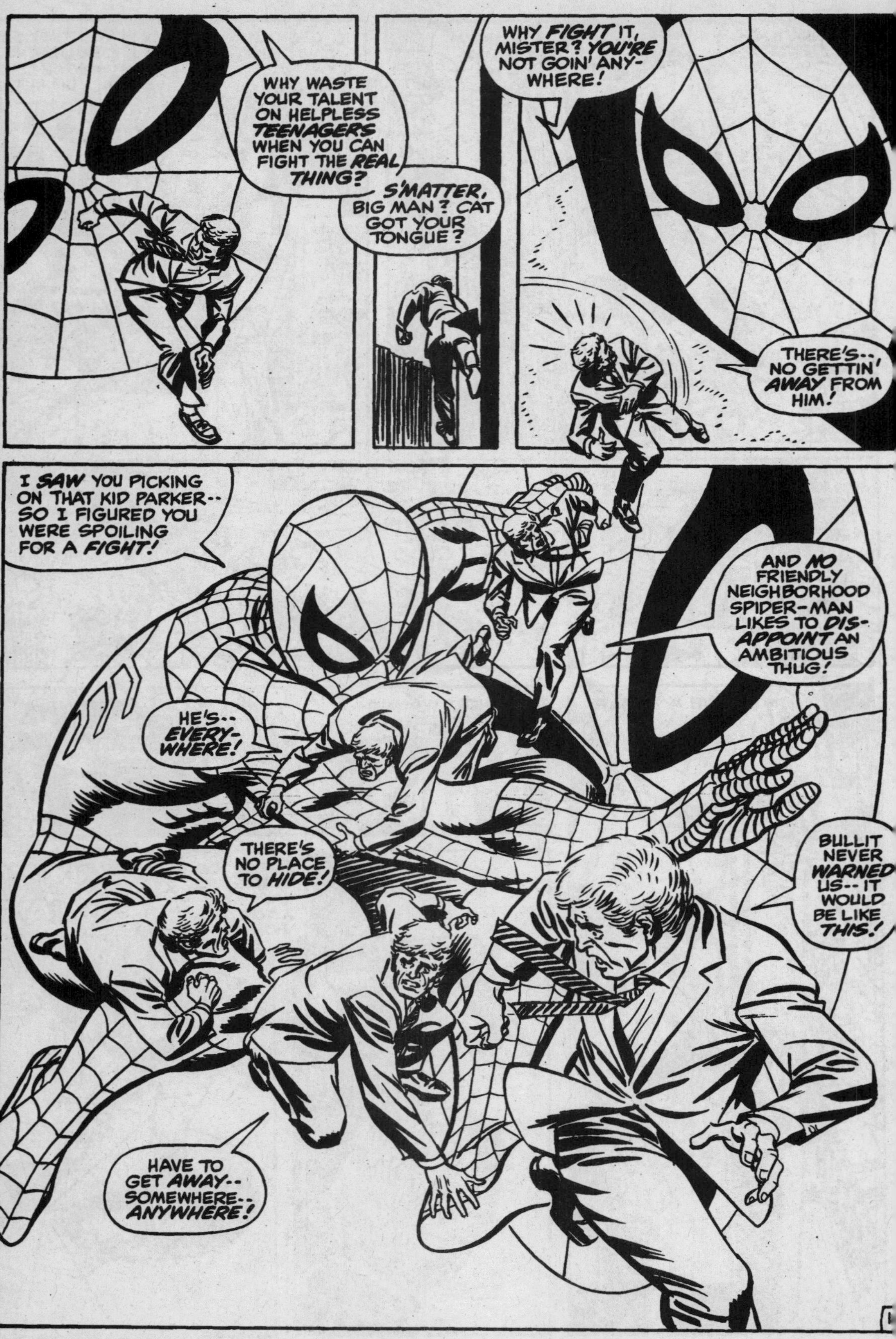
WHY WASTE YOUR TALENT ON HELPLESS TEENAGERS WHEN YOU CAN FIGHT THE REAL THING?
S'MATTER, BIG MAN? CAT GOT YOUR TONGUE?
WHY FIGHT IT, MISTER? YOU'RE NOT GOIN' ANYWHERE!
THERE'S-- NO GETTIN' AWAY FROM HIM!
I SAW YOU PICKING ON THAT KID PARKER-- SO I FIGURED YOU WERE SPOILING FOR A FIGHT!
AND NO FRIENDLY NEIGHBORHOOD SPIDER-MAN LIKES TO DISAPPOINT AN AMBITIOUS THUG!
HE'S-- EVERYWHERE!
THERE'S NO PLACE TO HIDE!
BULLIT NEVER WARNED US-- IT WOULD BE LIKE THIS!
HAVE TO GET AWAY-- SOMEWHERE-- ANYWHERE!

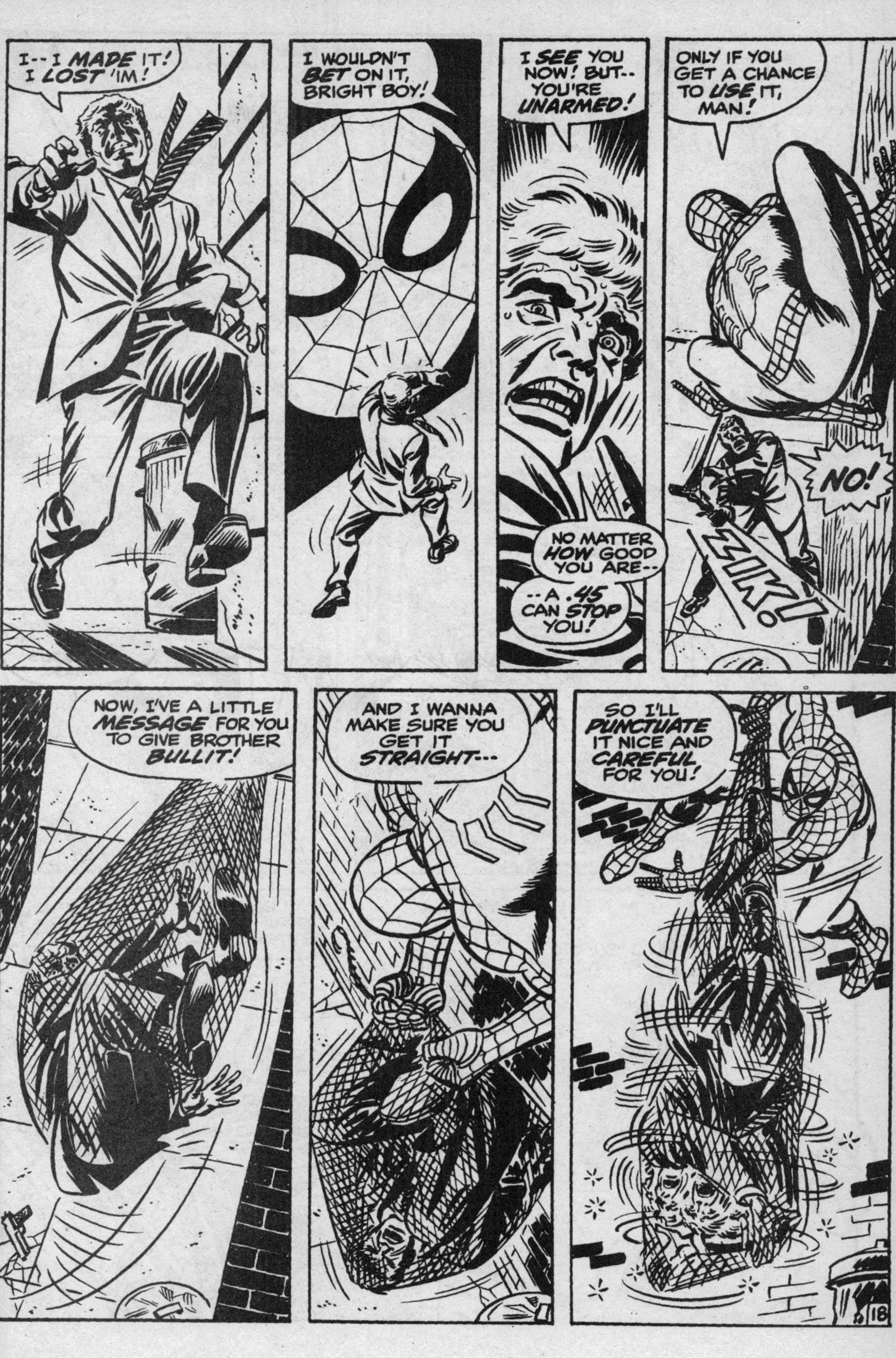

I-- I MADE IT! I LOST 'IM!
I WOULDN'T BET ON IT, BRIGHT BOY!
I SEE YOU NOW! BUT-- YOU'RE UNARMED!
NO MATTER HOW GOOD YOU ARE--
--A .45 CAN STOP YOU!
ONLY IF YOU GET A CHANCE TO USE IT, MAN!
NO!
ZIK!
NOW, I'VE A LITTLE MESSAGE FOR YOU TO GIVE BROTHER BULLIT!
AND I WANNA MAKE SURE YOU GET IT STRAIGHT---
SO I'LL PUNCTUATE IT NICE AND CAREFUL FOR YOU!
18

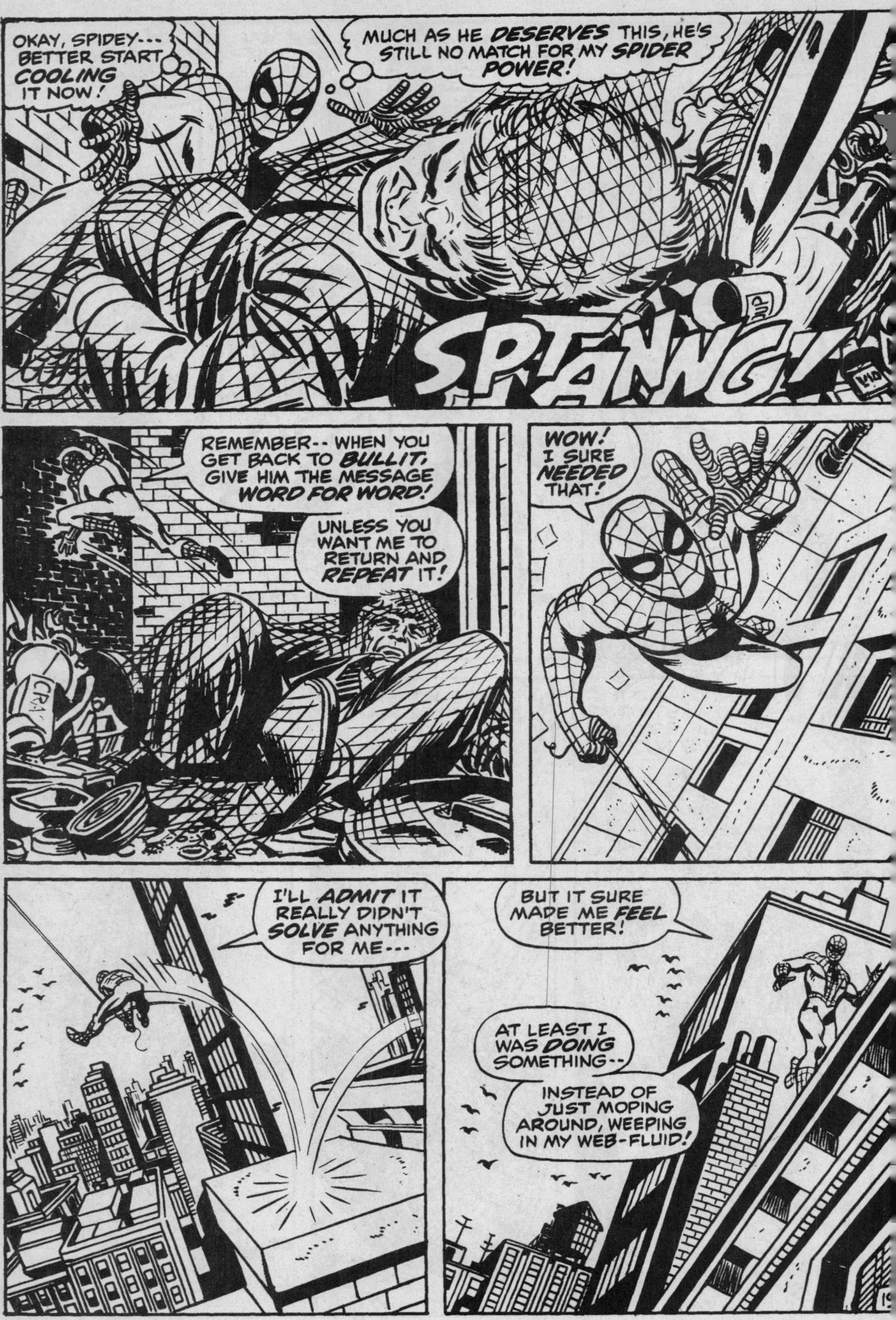
OKAY, SPIDEY--- BETTER START COOLING IT NOW!
MUCH AS HE DESERVES THIS, HE'S STILL NO MATCH FOR MY SPIDER POWER!
SPANNG!
REMEMBER-- WHEN YOU GET BACK TO BULLIT, GIVE HIM THE MESSAGE WORD FOR WORD!
UNLESS YOU WANT ME TO RETURN AND REPEAT IT!
WOW! I SURE NEEDED THAT!
I'LL ADMIT IT REALLY DIDN'T SOLVE ANYTHING FOR ME---
BUT IT SURE MADE ME FEEL BETTER!
AT LEAST I WAS DOING SOMETHING--
INSTEAD OF JUST MOPING AROUND, WEEPING IN MY WEB-FLUID!
19

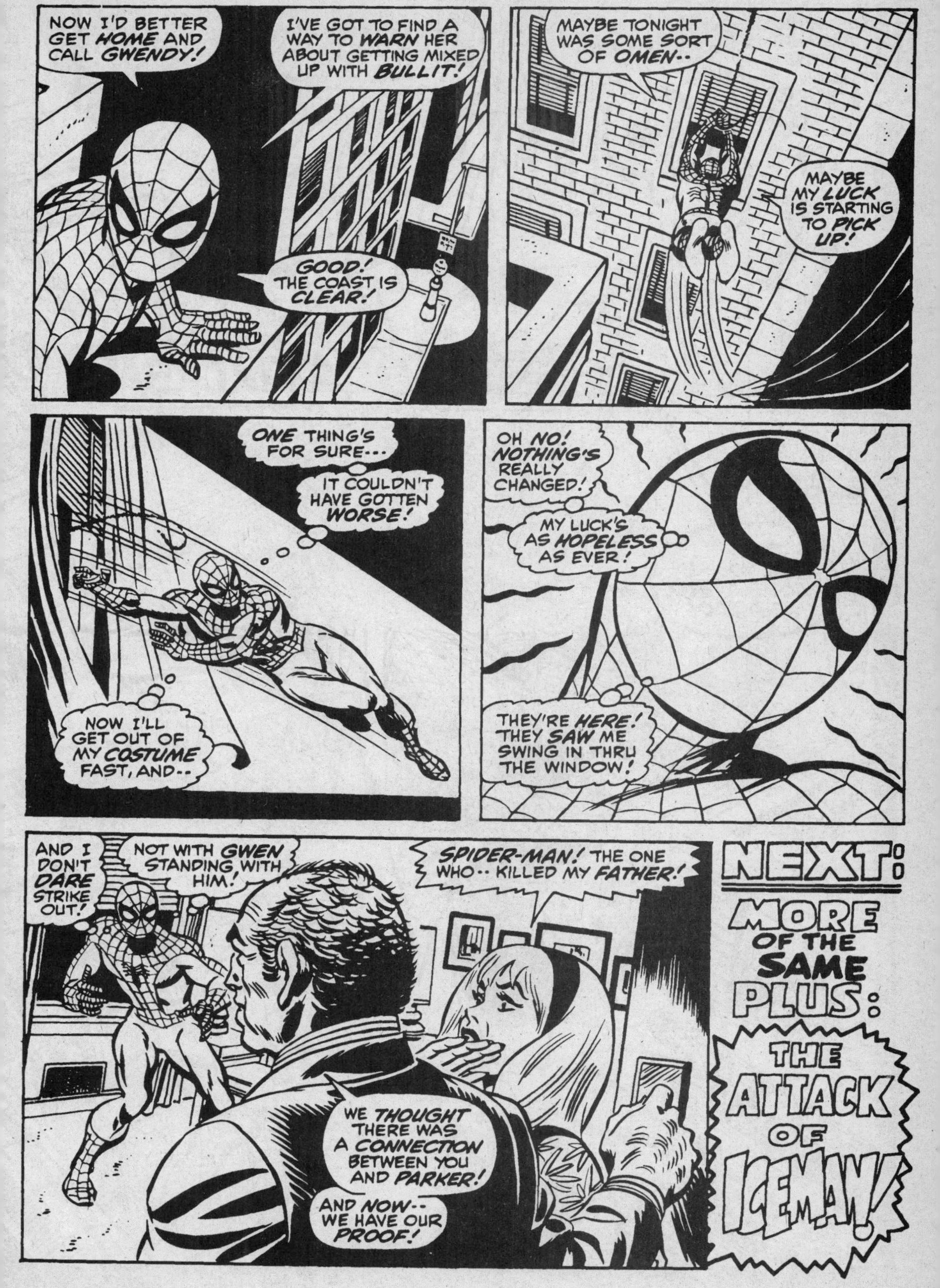
NOW I'D BETTER GET HOME AND CALL GWENDY!
I'VE GOT TO FIND A WAY TO WARN HER ABOUT GETTING MIXED UP WITH BULLIT!
GOOD! THE COAST IS CLEAR!
MAYBE TONIGHT WAS SOME SORT OF OMEN--
MAYBE MY LUCK IS STARTING TO PICK UP!
ONE THING'S FOR SURE...
IT COULDN'T HAVE GOTTEN WORSE!
NOW I'LL GET OUT OF MY COSTUME FAST, AND--
OH NO! NOTHING'S REALLY CHANGED!
MY LUCK'S AS HOPELESS AS EVER!
THEY'RE HERE! THEY SAW ME SWING IN THRU THE WINDOW!
AND I DON'T DARE STRIKE OUT!
NOT WITH GWEN STANDING WITH HIM!
SPIDER-MAN! THE ONE WHO-- KILLED MY FATHER!
WE THOUGHT THERE WAS A CONNECTION BETWEEN YOU AND PARKER!
AND NOW-- WE HAVE OUR PROOF!
NEXT:
MORE OF THE SAME PLUS:
THE ATTACK OF ICEMAN!

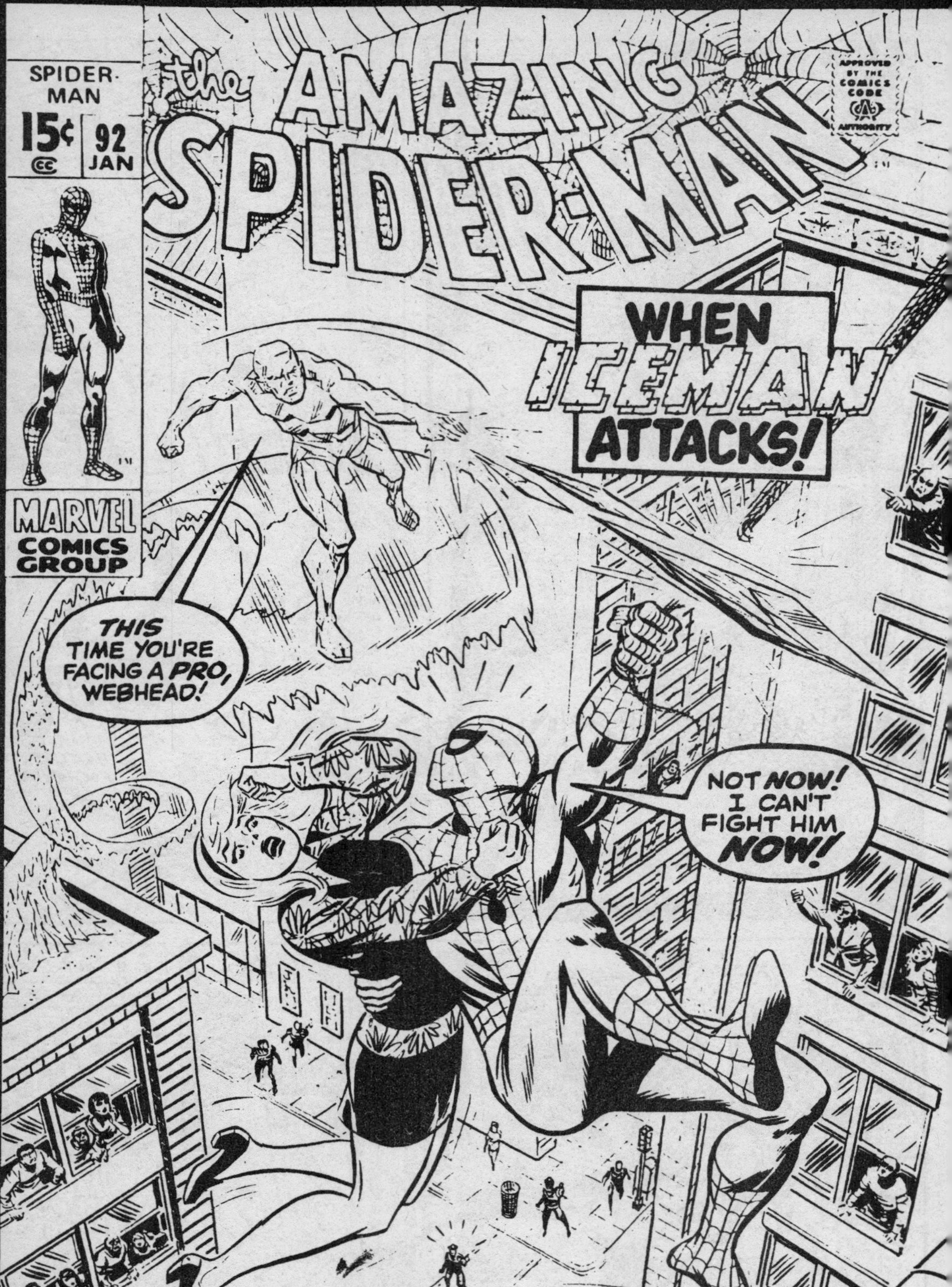
SPIDER-MAN
15¢
92
JAN
MARVEL COMICS GROUP
APPROVED BY THE COMICS CODE AUTHORITY
the AMAZING SPIDER-MAN
WHEN ICEMAN ATTACKS!
THIS TIME YOU'RE FACING A PRO, WEBHEAD!
NOT NOW! I CAN'T FIGHT HIM NOW!

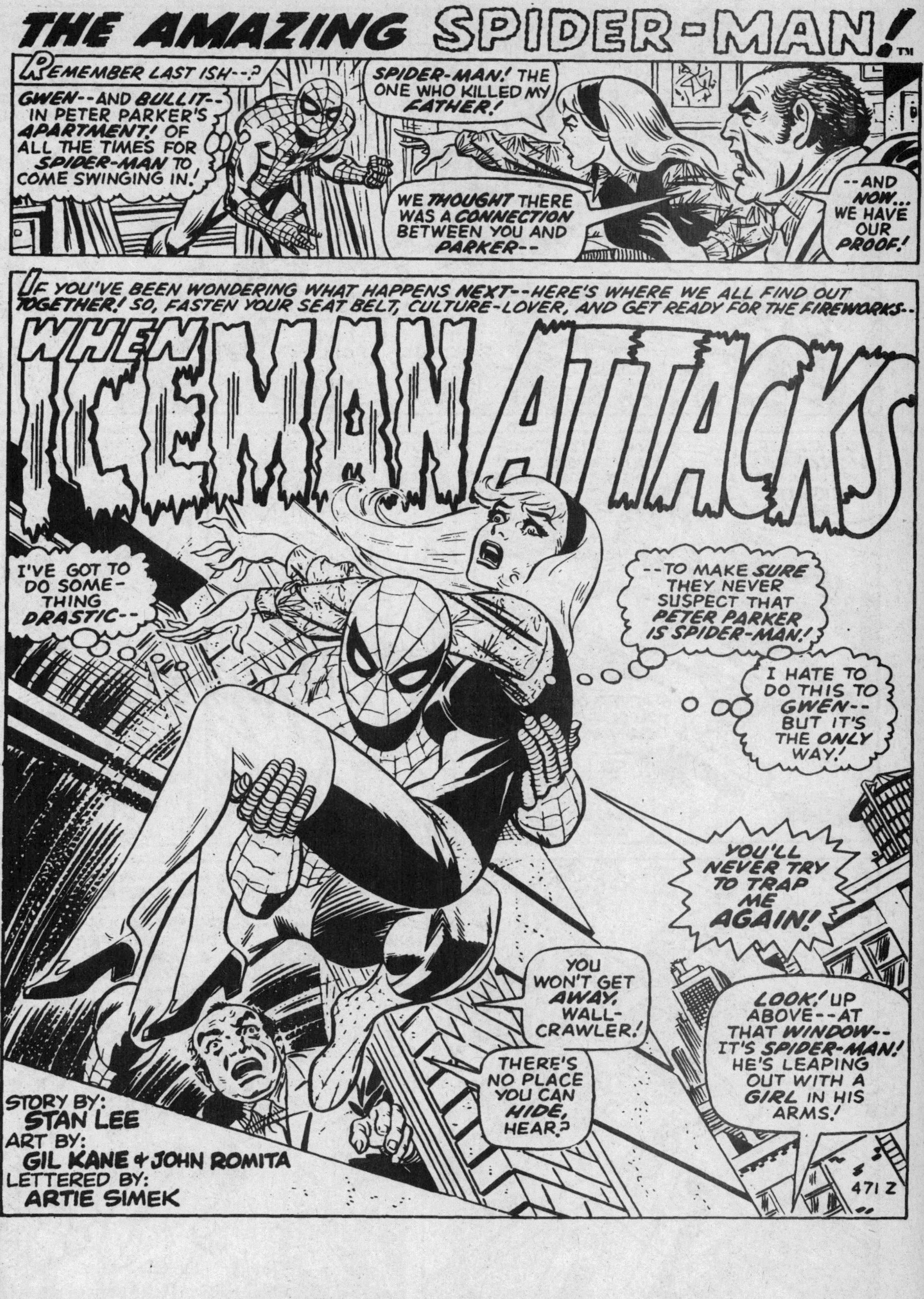
THE AMAZING SPIDER-MAN!™
REMEMBER LAST ISH--?
GWEN--AND BULLIT--IN PETER PARKER'S APARTMENT! OF ALL THE TIMES FOR SPIDER-MAN TO COME SWINGING IN!
SPIDER-MAN! THE ONE WHO KILLED MY FATHER!
WE THOUGHT THERE WAS A CONNECTION BETWEEN YOU AND PARKER--
--AND NOW... WE HAVE OUR PROOF!
IF YOU'VE BEEN WONDERING WHAT HAPPENS NEXT--HERE'S WHERE WE ALL FIND OUT TOGETHER! SO, FASTEN YOUR SEAT BELT, CULTURE-LOVER, AND GET READY FOR THE FIREWORKS--
WHEN ICEMAN ATTACKS
I'VE GOT TO DO SOME-THING DRASTIC--
--TO MAKE SURE THEY NEVER SUSPECT THAT PETER PARKER IS SPIDER-MAN!
I HATE TO DO THIS TO GWEN--BUT IT'S THE ONLY WAY!
YOU'LL NEVER TRY TO TRAP ME AGAIN!
YOU WON'T GET AWAY, WALL-CRAWLER!
THERE'S NO PLACE YOU CAN HIDE, HEAR?
LOOK! UP ABOVE--AT THAT WINDOW--IT'S SPIDER-MAN! HE'S LEAPING OUT WITH A GIRL IN HIS ARMS!
STORY BY: STAN LEE
ART BY: GIL KANE & JOHN ROMITA
LETTERED BY: ARTIE SIMEK
471 Z

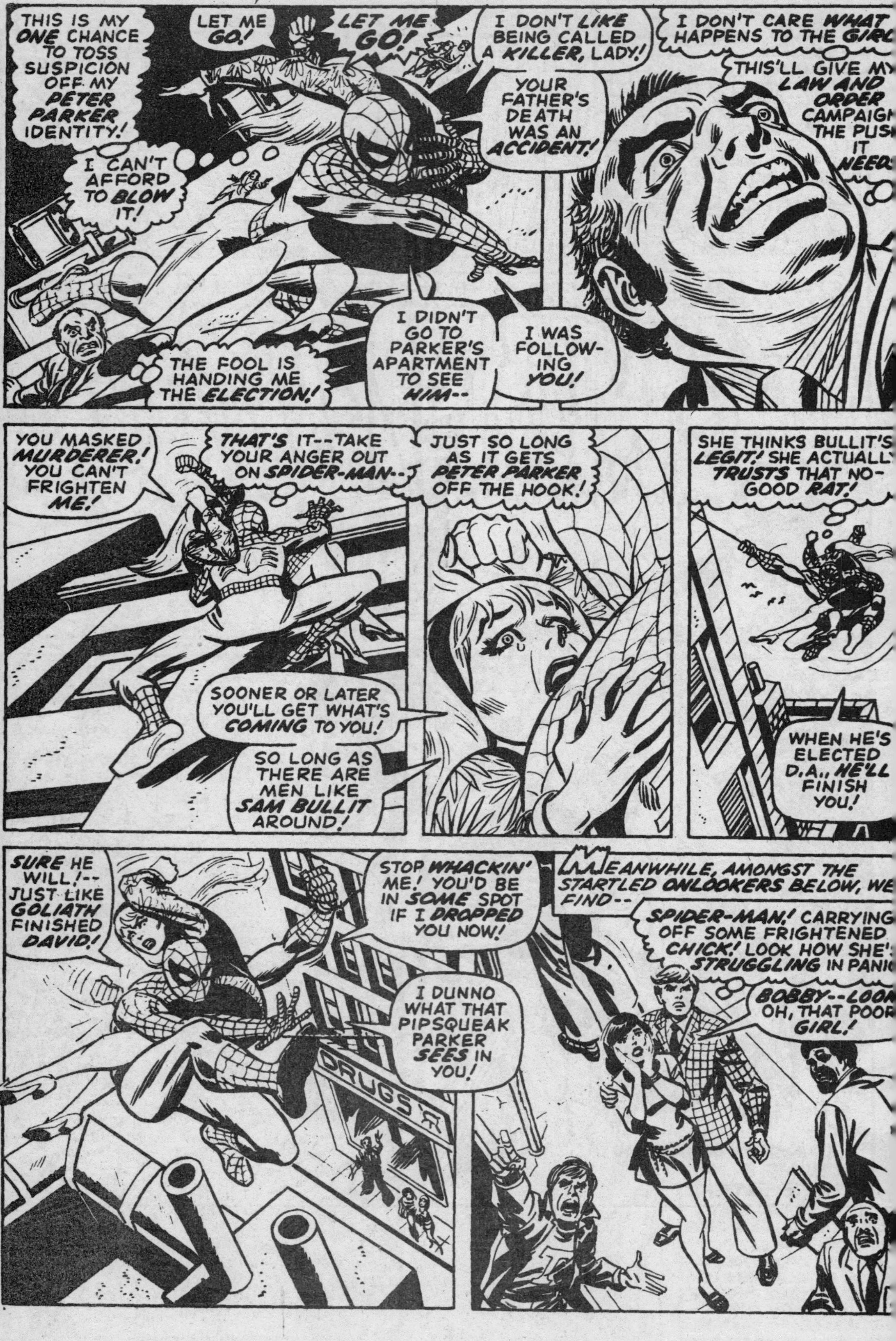
THIS IS MY ONE CHANCE TO TOSS SUSPICION OFF MY PETER PARKER IDENTITY!
I CAN'T AFFORD TO BLOW IT!
LET ME GO!
LET ME GO!
I DON'T LIKE BEING CALLED A KILLER, LADY!
YOUR FATHER'S DEATH WAS AN ACCIDENT!
I DON'T CARE WHAT HAPPENS TO THE GIRL
THIS'LL GIVE MY LAW AND ORDER CAMPAIGN THE PUSH IT NEEDS
THE FOOL IS HANDING ME THE ELECTION!
I DIDN'T GO TO PARKER'S APARTMENT TO SEE HIM--
I WAS FOLLOWING YOU!
YOU MASKED MURDERER! YOU CAN'T FRIGHTEN ME!
THAT'S IT--TAKE YOUR ANGER OUT ON SPIDER-MAN--
JUST SO LONG AS IT GETS PETER PARKER OFF THE HOOK!
SOONER OR LATER YOU'LL GET WHAT'S COMING TO YOU!
SO LONG AS THERE ARE MEN LIKE SAM BULLIT AROUND!
SHE THINKS BULLIT'S LEGIT! SHE ACTUALLY TRUSTS THAT NO-GOOD RAT!
WHEN HE'S ELECTED D.A., HE'LL FINISH YOU!
SURE HE WILL!--JUST LIKE GOLIATH FINISHED DAVID!
STOP WHACKIN' ME! YOU'D BE IN SOME SPOT IF I DROPPED YOU NOW!
I DUNNO WHAT THAT PIPSQUEAK PARKER SEES IN YOU!
DRUGS
MEANWHILE, AMONGST THE STARTLED ONLOOKERS BELOW, WE FIND--
SPIDER-MAN! CARRYING OFF SOME FRIGHTENED CHICK! LOOK HOW SHE'S STRUGGLING IN PANIC
BOBBY--LOOK OH, THAT POOR GIRL!

Panel 1: WHY DOESN'T SOMEBODY *DO* SOMETHING? // AGAINST *SPIDER-MAN*? BITE YOUR *TONGUE*, BABY! // SHE'S *RIGHT*! BUT I HAVE TO GET *RID* OF HER FIRST!

Panel 2: IT'S GETTING *LATE*, HONEY! I'LL CALL A *CAB* FOR YOU! // *LATE*? BUT--! // A GUY NEEDS HIS BEAUTY SLEEP! // *TAXI!*

Panel 3: I HATED TO *DO* THAT! // --SPECIALLY AFTER IT TOOK ME *WEEKS* TO FINALLY GET A *DATE* WITH HER! // BUT THIS IS *MORE* IMPORTANT!

Panel 4: I'VE BEEN OUT OF ACTION WITH THE *X-MEN* LONG ENOUGH, ANYWAY!* // BUT *THIS* TIME, I'LL HAVETA GO IT *ALONE*! // IT'LL ONLY TAKE *SECONDS* TO START FREEZING UP!

*X-MEN: A SECRET GROUP OF *MUTANTS*, EACH WITH A STRANGE, SUPERHUMAN POWER --AS IF YOU DIDN'T KNOW! --STAN.

Panel 5: OKAY, WEB-HEAD! YOU'RE A *BIG MAN* WITH A HELPLESS *FEMALE*-- // BUT LET'S SEE HOW YOU DO AGAINST-- *ICEMAN!!!*

Panel 6: A QUICK-FREEZE *ICE BRIDGE* WILL BE THE FASTEST WAY TO *REACH* HIM! // AND THEN-- IT'LL BE EVERY MAN FOR *HIMSELF*!

3

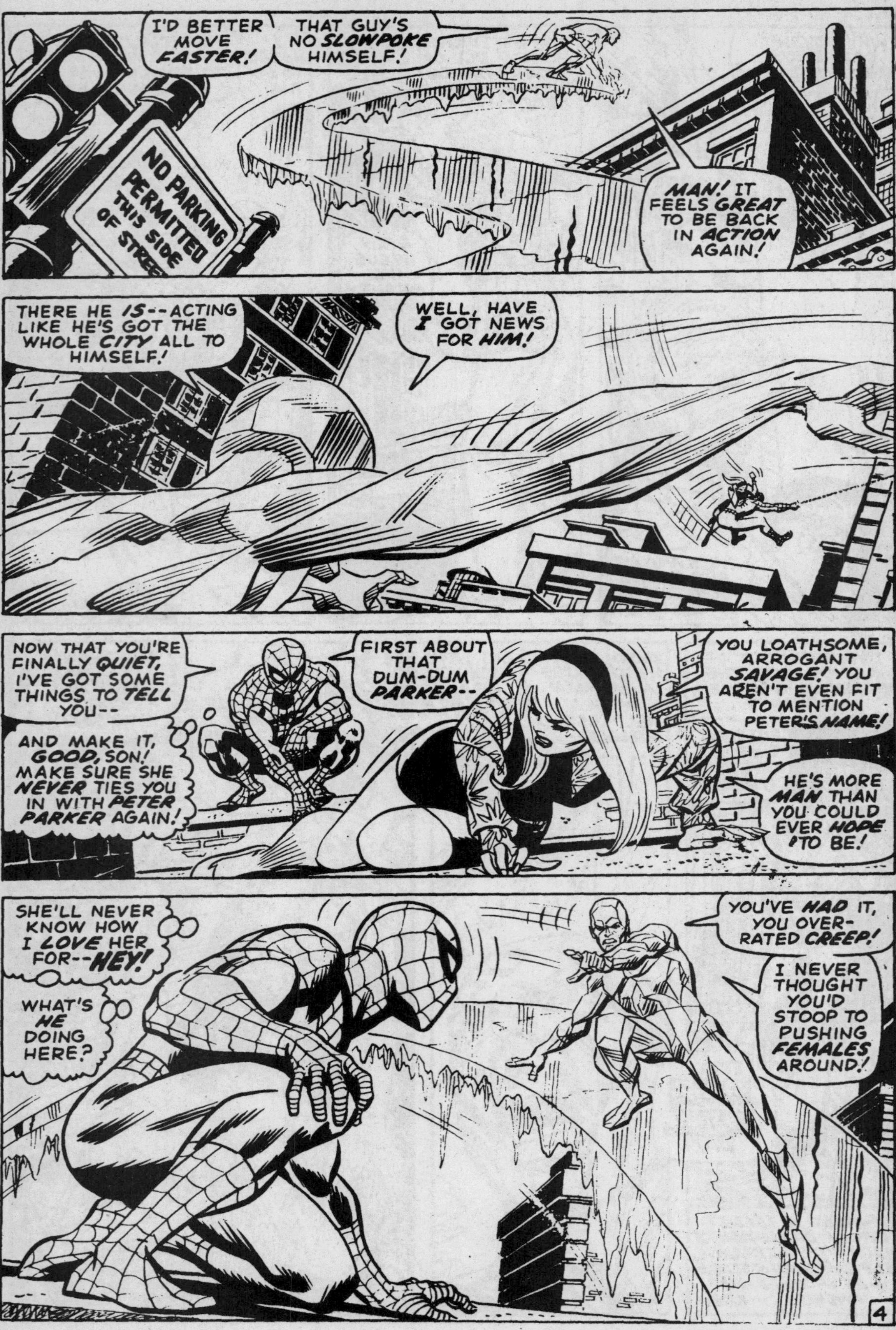
I'D BETTER MOVE FASTER!
THAT GUY'S NO SLOWPOKE HIMSELF!
NO PARKING PERMITTED THIS SIDE OF STREE
MAN! IT FEELS GREAT TO BE BACK IN ACTION AGAIN!
THERE HE IS--ACTING LIKE HE'S GOT THE WHOLE CITY ALL TO HIMSELF!
WELL, HAVE I GOT NEWS FOR HIM!
NOW THAT YOU'RE FINALLY QUIET, I'VE GOT SOME THINGS TO TELL YOU--
AND MAKE IT, GOOD, SON! MAKE SURE SHE NEVER TIES YOU IN WITH PETER PARKER AGAIN!
FIRST ABOUT THAT DUM-DUM PARKER--
YOU LOATHSOME, ARROGANT SAVAGE! YOU AREN'T EVEN FIT TO MENTION PETER'S NAME!
HE'S MORE MAN THAN YOU COULD EVER HOPE TO BE!
SHE'LL NEVER KNOW HOW I LOVE HER FOR--HEY!
WHAT'S HE DOING HERE?
YOU'VE HAD IT, YOU OVER-RATED CREEP!
I NEVER THOUGHT YOU'D STOOP TO PUSHING FEMALES AROUND!
4

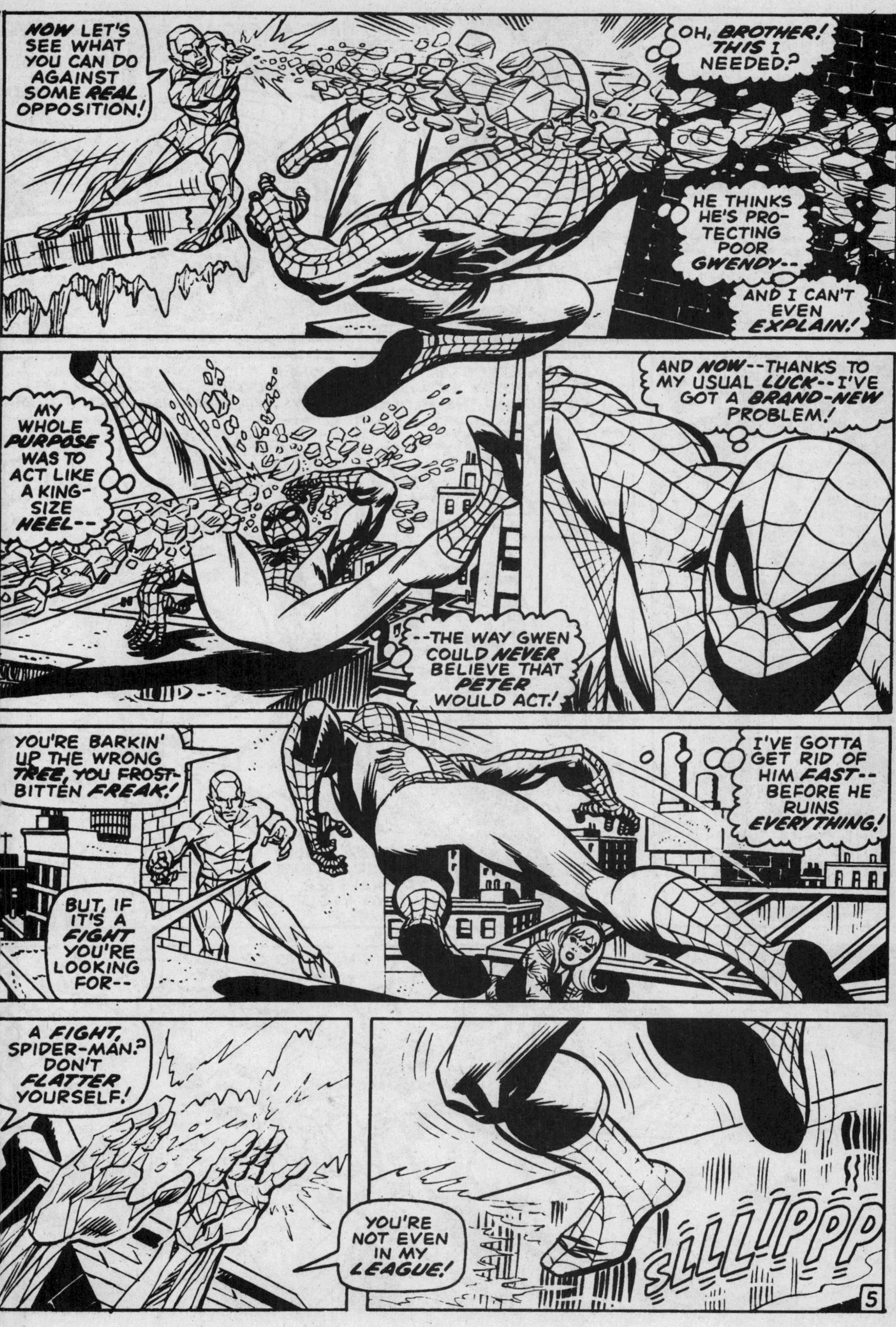
NOW LET'S SEE WHAT YOU CAN DO AGAINST SOME REAL OPPOSITION!
OH, BROTHER! THIS I NEEDED?
HE THINKS HE'S PROTECTING POOR GWENDY--
AND I CAN'T EVEN EXPLAIN!
MY WHOLE PURPOSE WAS TO ACT LIKE A KING-SIZE HEEL--
--THE WAY GWEN COULD NEVER BELIEVE THAT PETER WOULD ACT!
AND NOW--THANKS TO MY USUAL LUCK--I'VE GOT A BRAND-NEW PROBLEM!
YOU'RE BARKIN' UP THE WRONG TREE, YOU FROST-BITTEN FREAK!
BUT, IF IT'S A FIGHT YOU'RE LOOKING FOR--
I'VE GOTTA GET RID OF HIM FAST--BEFORE HE RUINS EVERYTHING!
A FIGHT, SPIDER-MAN? DON'T FLATTER YOURSELF!
YOU'RE NOT EVEN IN MY LEAGUE!
SLLLIPPP
5

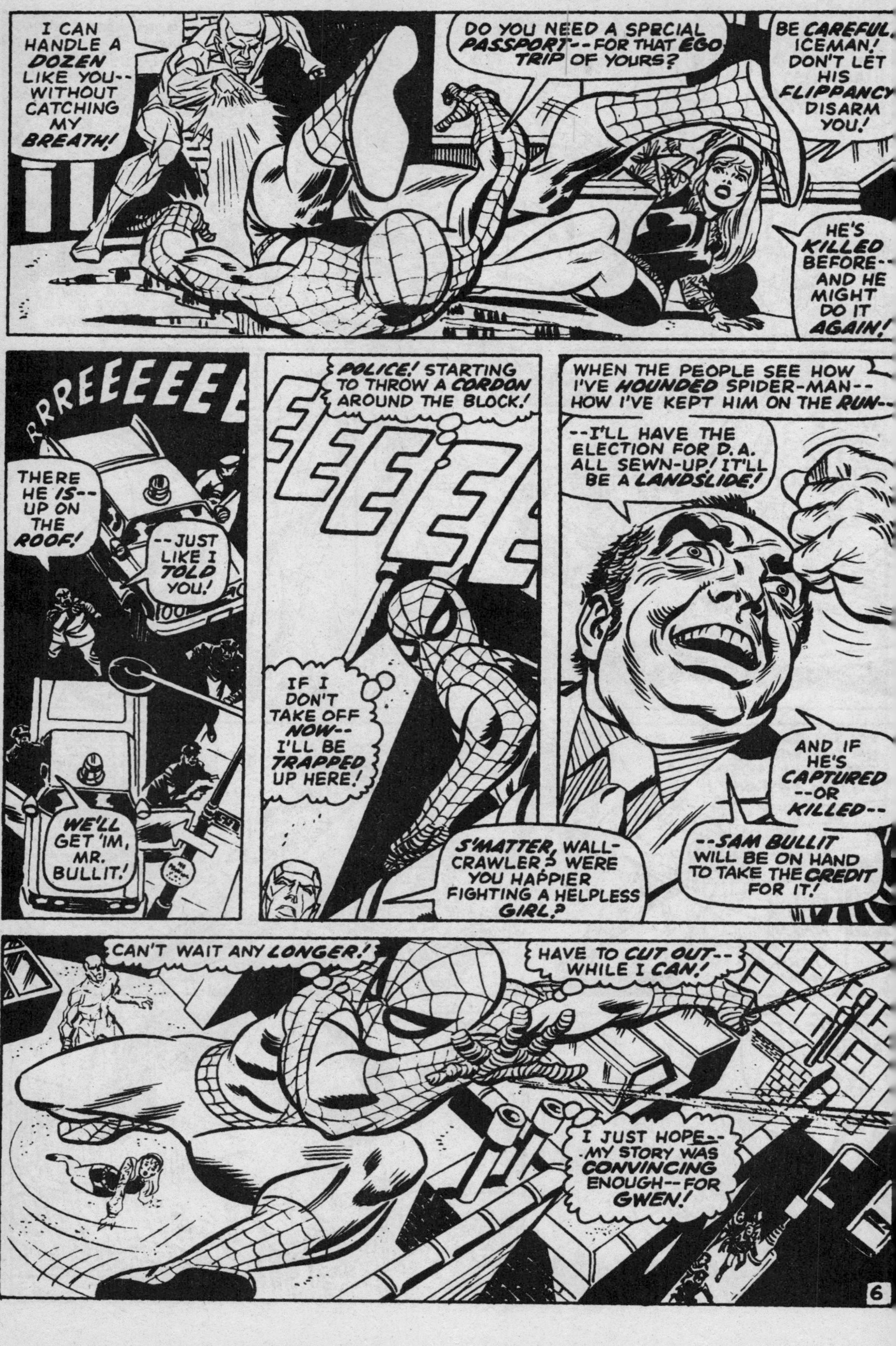
I CAN HANDLE A DOZEN LIKE YOU-- WITHOUT CATCHING MY BREATH!
DO YOU NEED A SPECIAL PASSPORT--FOR THAT EGO-TRIP OF YOURS?
BE CAREFUL, ICEMAN! DON'T LET HIS FLIPPANCY DISARM YOU!
HE'S KILLED BEFORE--AND HE MIGHT DO IT AGAIN!
RRREEEEEEE
THERE HE IS--UP ON THE ROOF!
--JUST LIKE I TOLD YOU!
WE'LL GET 'IM, MR. BULLIT!
POLICE! STARTING TO THROW A CORDON AROUND THE BLOCK!
IF I DON'T TAKE OFF NOW--I'LL BE TRAPPED UP HERE!
S'MATTER, WALL-CRAWLER? WERE YOU HAPPIER FIGHTING A HELPLESS GIRL?
WHEN THE PEOPLE SEE HOW I'VE HOUNDED SPIDER-MAN--HOW I'VE KEPT HIM ON THE RUN--
--I'LL HAVE THE ELECTION FOR D.A. ALL SEWN-UP! IT'LL BE A LANDSLIDE!
AND IF HE'S CAPTURED --OR KILLED--
--SAM BULLIT WILL BE ON HAND TO TAKE THE CREDIT FOR IT!
CAN'T WAIT ANY LONGER!
HAVE TO CUT OUT--WHILE I CAN!
I JUST HOPE--MY STORY WAS CONVINCING ENOUGH--FOR GWEN!
6

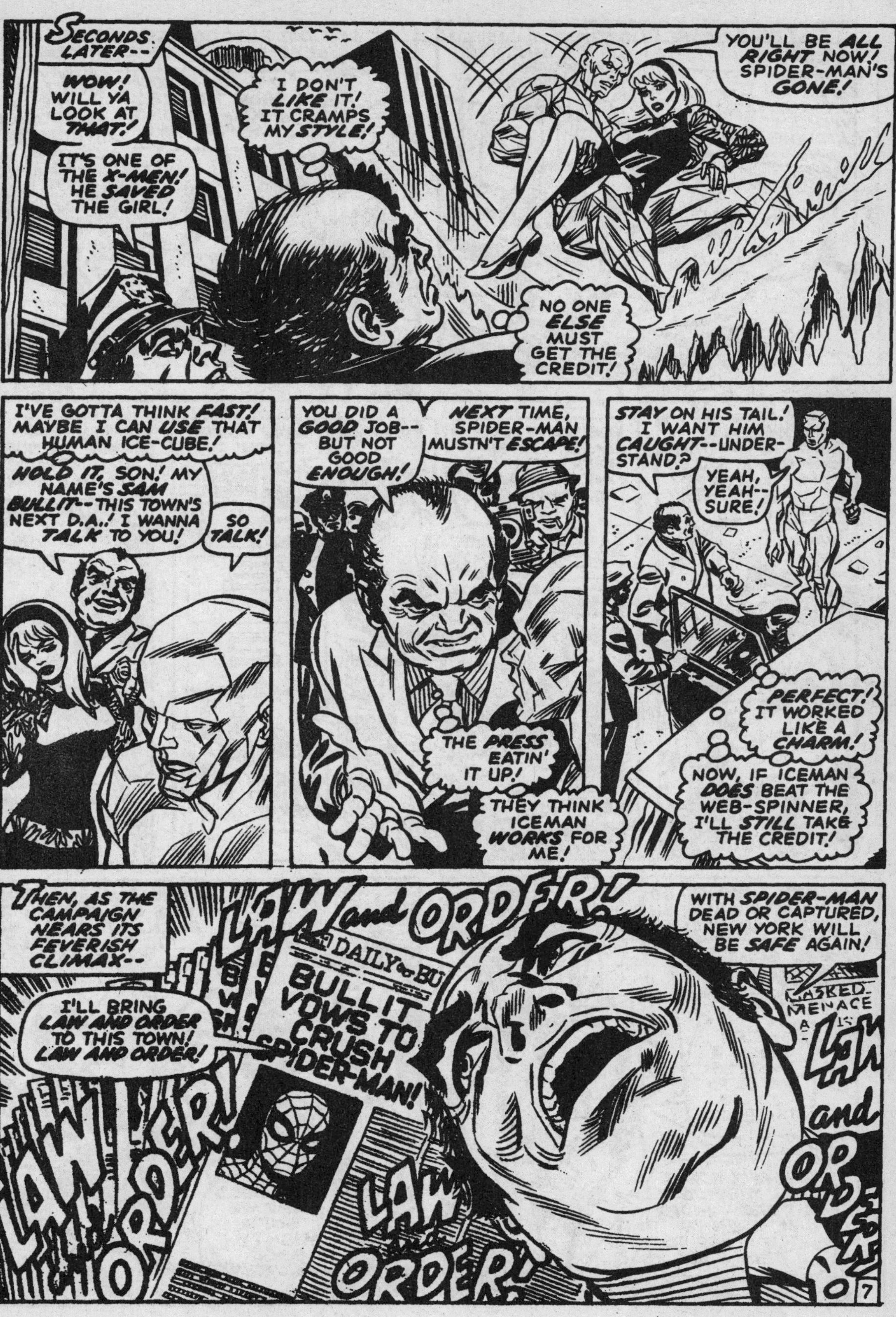
SECONDS LATER--
WOW! WILL YA LOOK AT THAT!
IT'S ONE OF THE X-MEN! HE SAVED THE GIRL!
I DON'T LIKE IT! IT CRAMPS MY STYLE!
YOU'LL BE ALL RIGHT NOW! SPIDER-MAN'S GONE!
NO ONE ELSE MUST GET THE CREDIT!
I'VE GOTTA THINK FAST! MAYBE I CAN USE THAT HUMAN ICE-CUBE!
HOLD IT, SON! MY NAME'S SAM BULLIT-- THIS TOWN'S NEXT D.A.! I WANNA TALK TO YOU!
SO TALK!
YOU DID A GOOD JOB-- BUT NOT GOOD ENOUGH!
NEXT TIME, SPIDER-MAN MUSTN'T ESCAPE!
THE PRESS EATIN' IT UP!
THEY THINK ICEMAN WORKS FOR ME!
STAY ON HIS TAIL! I WANT HIM CAUGHT-- UNDERSTAND?
YEAH, YEAH-- SURE!
PERFECT! IT WORKED LIKE A CHARM!
NOW, IF ICEMAN DOES BEAT THE WEB-SPINNER, I'LL STILL TAKE THE CREDIT!
THEN, AS THE CAMPAIGN NEARS ITS FEVERISH CLIMAX--
LAW and ORDER!
DAILY BU
BULLIT VOWS TO CRUSH SPIDER-MAN!
WITH SPIDER-MAN DEAD OR CAPTURED, NEW YORK WILL BE SAFE AGAIN!
MASKED MENACE
I'LL BRING LAW AND ORDER TO THIS TOWN! LAW AND ORDER!
LAW and ORDER!
LAW ORDER!
LAW and OR
7

TELEPHONE, BULLIT!

ANSWER IT, CARTER! IF IT'S ANOTHER INTERVIEW, SAY I'M TOO BUSY!

I GOT THE ELECTION SEWED UP! DON'T NEED TO BOTHER ANYMORE!

IT'S JAMESON-- FROM THE DAILY BUGLE! SOUNDS IMPORTANT!

I BETTER SEE WHAT THE OLD GOAT WANTS!

WHAT? YOU'RE THINKING OF WITH-DRAWING YOUR PAPER'S SUPPORT OF ME?!!

YOU'RE OUTTA YOUR MIND!

YOU WANT YOUR READERS TO THINK YOU'RE AGAINST LAW AND ORDER? YOU CAN'T BACK OUT NOW!

I CAN'T, HUH? I WOULDN'T BET ON IT, BULLIT!

NOW YOU'RE TALKIN', J.J.!

AND KNOCK OFF THE THREATS, MISTER!

--WE'VE BEEN THREATENED BY EXPERTS!

YEAH, YEAH-- KNOW THE BUGLE SUPPORTED YOU UP TILL NOW--

--BUT THAT WAS BEFORE I LEARNED SOME THINGS!

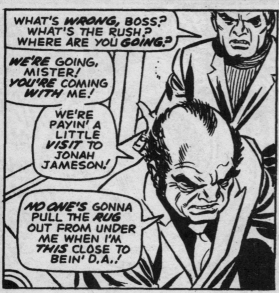

WHAT'S WRONG, BOSS? WHAT'S THE RUSH? WHERE ARE YOU GOING?

WE'RE GOING, MISTER! YOU'RE COMING WITH ME!

WE'RE PAYIN' A LITTLE VISIT TO JONAH JAMESON!

NO ONE'S GONNA PULL THE RUG OUT FROM UNDER ME WHEN I'M THIS CLOSE TO BEIN' D.A.!

AND IF JAMESON THINKS HE'S BIG ENOUGH TO BUCK ME--WE'LL HAVE TO DO A LITTLE CONVINCING!

YEAH, BOSS --AND WE GOT A MIGHTY GOOD ARGUMENT!

THA

MINUTES LATER--

WHAT'S THAT? *BULLIT* OUTSIDE, WITH ONE OF HIS *BODYGUARDS*?

BODYGUARD, MY *LOOT*, J.J! IT'S ONE OF THE *HOODS* ON HIS PAYROLL!

JUST SENT *BULLIT* IN! I DON'T NEED A *CONVENTION*!

NOW YOU'RE WISIN' UP, MAN! BUT *WATCH* YOURSELF!

ALL *RIGHT*, NEWSMAN! IF YOU *KNOW* SOMETHING, SPILL IT!

THAT'S JUST WHAT I *INTEND* TO DO--

--RIGHT ON THE *FRONT PAGE*!

WHEN YOUR *STRONGARM BOYS* TRIED TO PUT THE MUSCLE ON *PARKER* THE OTHER DAY*, THEY FORGOT HE WORKS FOR THE *BUGLE*!

THE KID *TOLD* US WHAT HAPPENED --AND IT *SMELLS*, MISTER!

SO *THAT'S* WHAT YOU GOT IN YOUR CRAW, HUH?

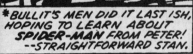

* *BULLIT'S MEN DID IT LAST ISH, HOPING TO LEARN ABOUT SPIDER-MAN FROM PETER! --STRAIGHTFORWARD STAN.*

THERE'S LOTS *MORE*, BULLIT! PARKER'S STORY JUST SERVED TO OPEN JAMESON'S *EYES*--

BUT *I'VE* KEPT A *DOSSIER* ON YOU--

I HAVEN'T BEEN *CITY EDITOR* ALL THESE YEARS FOR *NOTHING*!

I *KNOW* WHERE YOUR SUPPORT COMES FROM! I *KNOW* ABOUT THE LUNATIC *HATE GROUPS* WHO ARE BACKING YOU!

I *KNOW* WHAT YOU *REALLY* MEAN BY-- *LAW AND ORDER*!

I *KNOW* WHAT YOU THINK OF *MINORITY GROUPS*--AND THE *PLANS* YOU'VE GOT FOR THEM!

ANYONE EVER TELL YA YOU KNOW *TOO MUCH*, BLACK MAN?

SHUDDUP! ROBBIE IS GONNA *HANG* YOU, BULLIT!

MY PAPER'S *ACTING* ON THE EVIDENCE HE'S GATHERED! WE'RE *RENOUNCING* OUR SUPPORT OF YOU!

WE'RE SWITCHING TO *NELSON*!

YOU'VE *HAD* IT, BIGOT!

9

AND DON'T THINK WE'RE *BLUFFING*, MAN! I'VE GOT IT ALL *DOWN* HERE--NAMES, DATES AND PLACES!

TELL 'IM HE CAN *SHOVE* IT, JAMESON! EVIDENCE DON'T MEAN *NOTHING* UNLESS YA CAN *USE* IT!

AND *SAMBO* AINT *NEVER* GONNA USE IT!

I THINK HE JUST QUIT OUR *FAN CLUB*, JONAH!

GET *OUT*, BULLIT! YOU'RE TURNING MY *STOMACH*!

NOW AIN' THAT SHAM

I'M GLAD YOU LISTENED TO *PARKER*, JJ! I *HOPED* IT WOULD OPEN YOUR EYES!

NUTS! I HAD BULLIT PEGGED ALL THE *TIME!*

BUT YOU BETTER *WATCH* YOURSELF, ROBBIE!

HE CAN BE *DANGEROUS!*

LATER, IN THE HALL OUTSIDE--

IT'S LUCKY I STAYED AROUND!

THOSE ARE THE SAME TWO HOODS WHO HASSLED ME *BEFORE!*

AND *NOW*-- THEY'RE HEADING FOR *ROBBIE'S* OFFICE!

I *THOUGHT* SOMETHING LIKE THIS MIGHT HAPPEN!

I *THOUGHT* SO! HE'S *LEAVING* WITH THEM!

AND I'M BETTING THAT IT ISN'T 'CAUSE HE LIKES THEIR *COMPANY!*

YOU DON'T REALLY EXPECT TO GET *AWAY* WITH THIS?

JUST KEEP *WALKIN'*, SMART GUY!

I WAS *RIGHT!*

IT'S LIKE WATCHING AN OLD *HUMPHREY BOGART* MOVIE!

ONLY THIS IS FOR *REAL!*

ONE THING ABOUT BULLIT--HE SURE DOESN'T WASTE ANY *TIME!*

AND THE SAME BETTER GO FOR *SPIDER-MAN!*

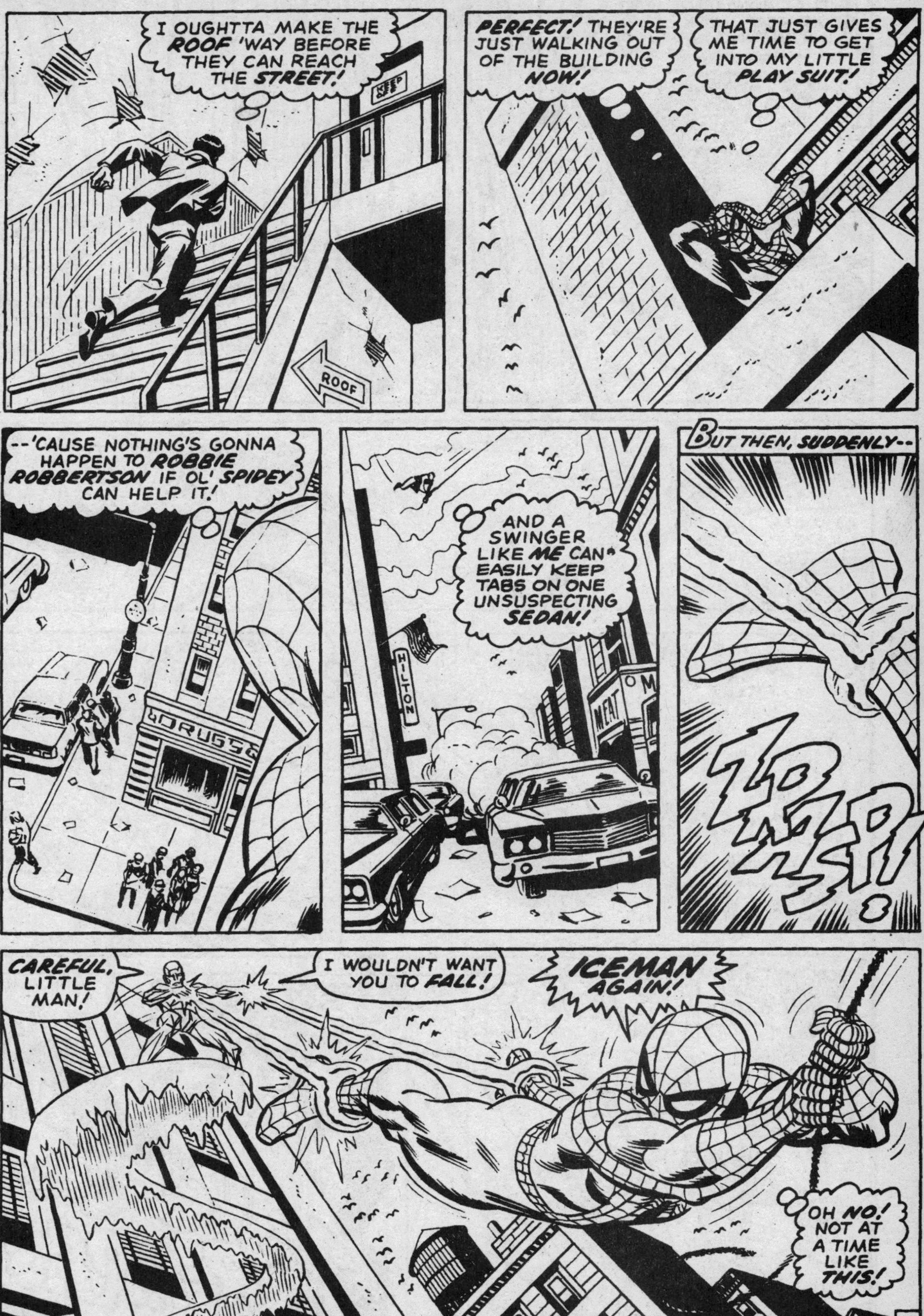

I OUGHTTA MAKE THE ROOF 'WAY BEFORE THEY CAN REACH THE STREET!
ROOF
PERFECT! THEY'RE JUST WALKING OUT OF THE BUILDING NOW!
THAT JUST GIVES ME TIME TO GET INTO MY LITTLE PLAY SUIT!
--'CAUSE NOTHING'S GONNA HAPPEN TO ROBBIE ROBBERTSON IF OL' SPIDEY CAN HELP IT!
DRUGS
AND A SWINGER LIKE ME CAN EASILY KEEP TABS ON ONE UNSUSPECTING SEDAN!
HILTON
MEAT
BUT THEN, SUDDENLY--
ZWASP!
CAREFUL, LITTLE MAN!
I WOULDN'T WANT YOU TO FALL!
ICEMAN AGAIN!
OH NO! NOT AT A TIME LIKE THIS!
11

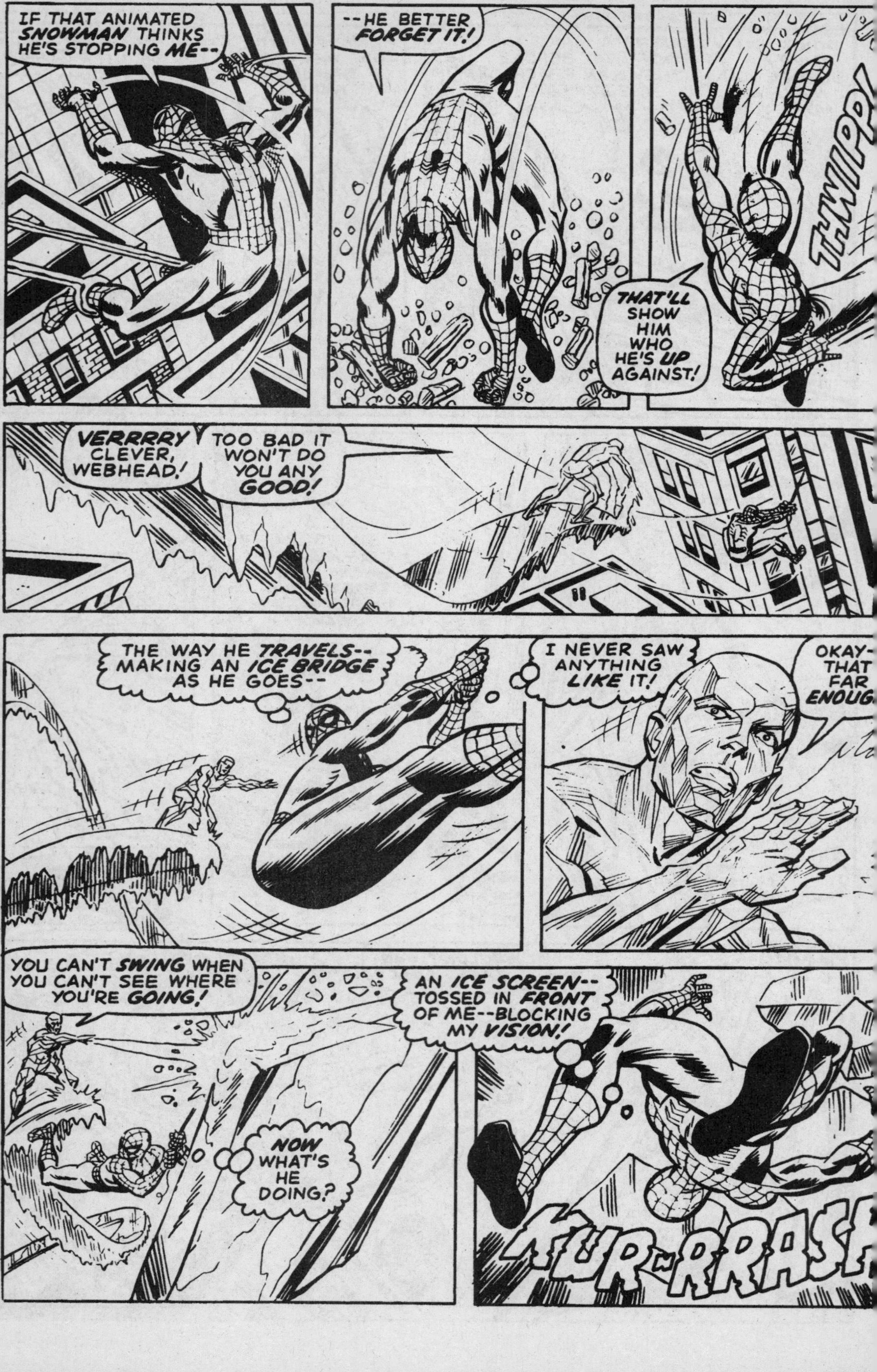
IF THAT ANIMATED SNOWMAN THINKS HE'S STOPPING ME--
--HE BETTER FORGET IT!
THAT'LL SHOW HIM WHO HE'S UP AGAINST!
THWIPP!
VERRRRY CLEVER, WEBHEAD!
TOO BAD IT WON'T DO YOU ANY GOOD!
THE WAY HE TRAVELS--MAKING AN ICE BRIDGE AS HE GOES--
I NEVER SAW ANYTHING LIKE IT!
OKAY-THAT FAR ENOUGH
YOU CAN'T SWING WHEN YOU CAN'T SEE WHERE YOU'RE GOING!
NOW WHAT'S HE DOING?
AN ICE SCREEN--TOSSED IN FRONT OF ME--BLOCKING MY VISION!
KUR-RRASH

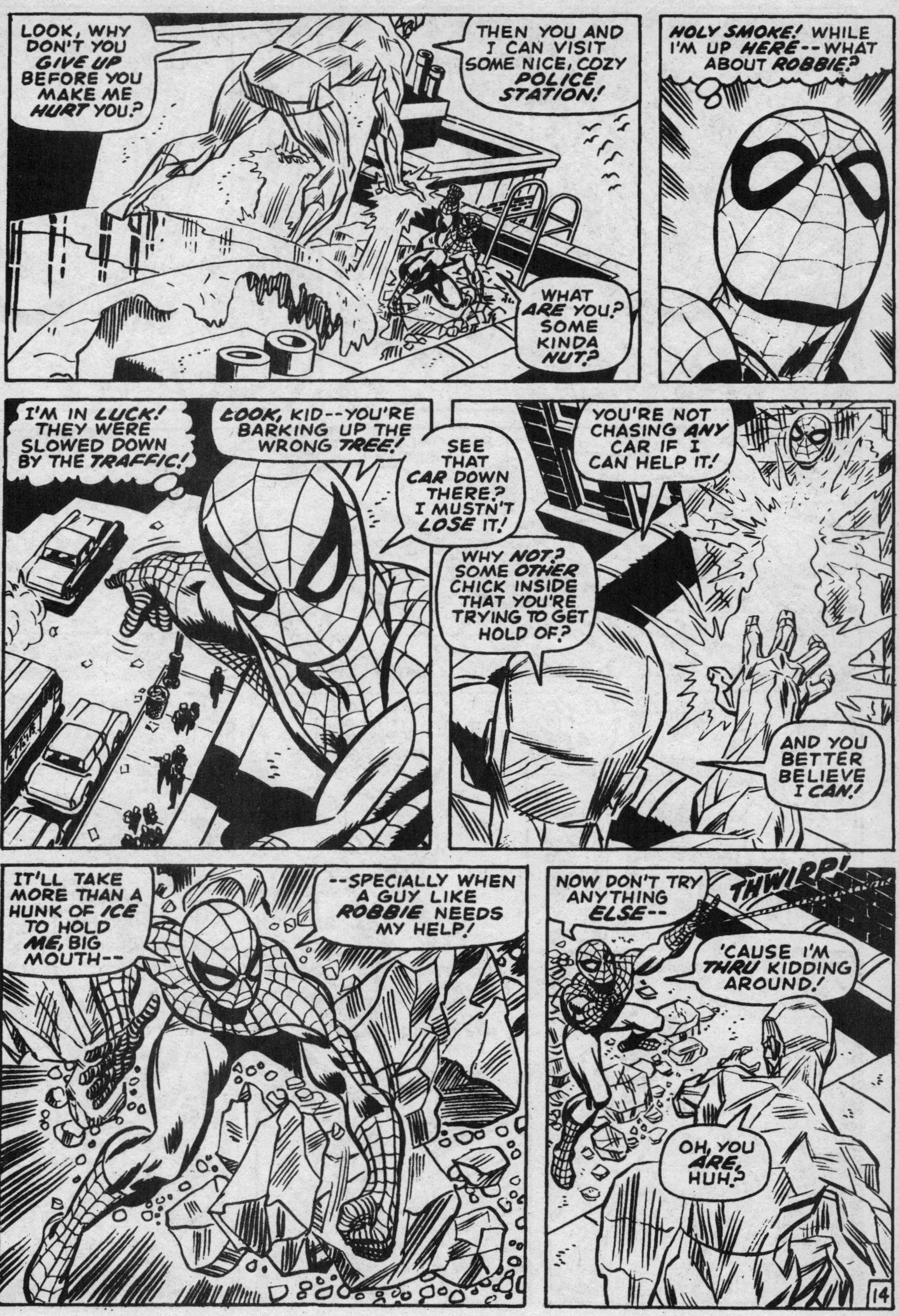
LOOK, WHY DON'T YOU GIVE UP BEFORE YOU MAKE ME HURT YOU?
THEN YOU AND I CAN VISIT SOME NICE, COZY POLICE STATION!
WHAT ARE YOU? SOME KINDA NUT?
HOLY SMOKE! WHILE I'M UP HERE--WHAT ABOUT ROBBIE?
I'M IN LUCK! THEY WERE SLOWED DOWN BY THE TRAFFIC!
LOOK, KID--YOU'RE BARKING UP THE WRONG TREE!
SEE THAT CAR DOWN THERE? I MUSTN'T LOSE IT!
WHY NOT? SOME OTHER CHICK INSIDE THAT YOU'RE TRYING TO GET HOLD OF?
YOU'RE NOT CHASING ANY CAR IF I CAN HELP IT!
AND YOU BETTER BELIEVE I CAN!
IT'LL TAKE MORE THAN A HUNK OF ICE TO HOLD ME, BIG MOUTH--
--SPECIALLY WHEN A GUY LIKE ROBBIE NEEDS MY HELP!
NOW DON'T TRY ANYTHING ELSE--
THWIPP!
'CAUSE I'M THRU KIDDING AROUND!
OH, YOU ARE, HUH?
14

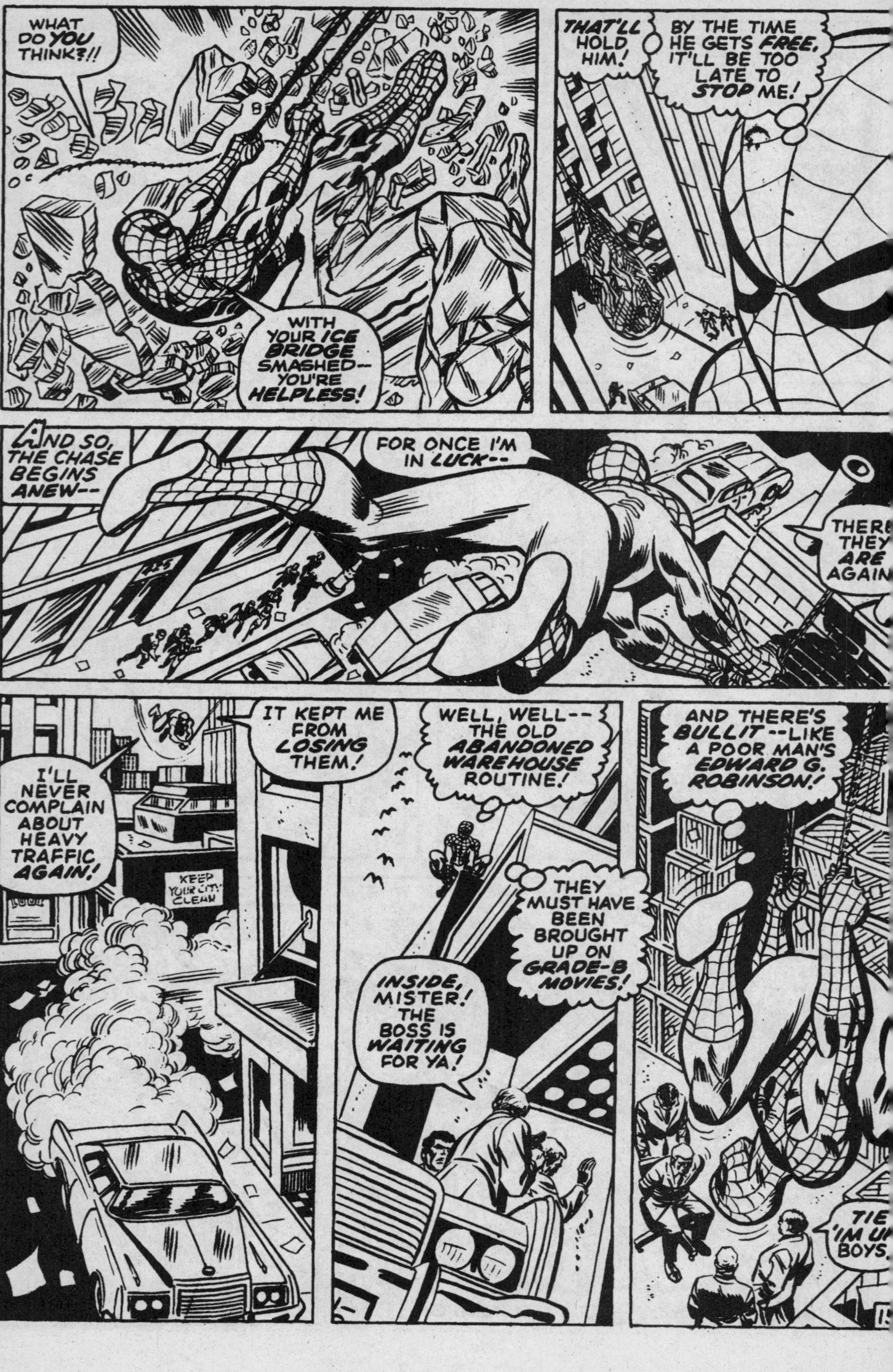
WHAT DO YOU THINK?!!
WITH YOUR ICE BRIDGE SMASHED-- YOU'RE HELPLESS!
THAT'LL HOLD HIM!
BY THE TIME HE GETS FREE, IT'LL BE TOO LATE TO STOP ME!
AND SO, THE CHASE BEGINS ANEW--
FOR ONCE I'M IN LUCK--
THERE THEY ARE AGAIN
I'LL NEVER COMPLAIN ABOUT HEAVY TRAFFIC AGAIN!
IT KEPT ME FROM LOSING THEM!
KEEP YOUR CITY CLEAN
WELL, WELL-- THE OLD ABANDONED WAREHOUSE ROUTINE!
THEY MUST HAVE BEEN BROUGHT UP ON GRADE-B MOVIES!
INSIDE, MISTER! THE BOSS IS WAITING FOR YA!
AND THERE'S BULLIT --LIKE A POOR MAN'S EDWARD G. ROBINSON!
TIE 'IM U BOYS
15

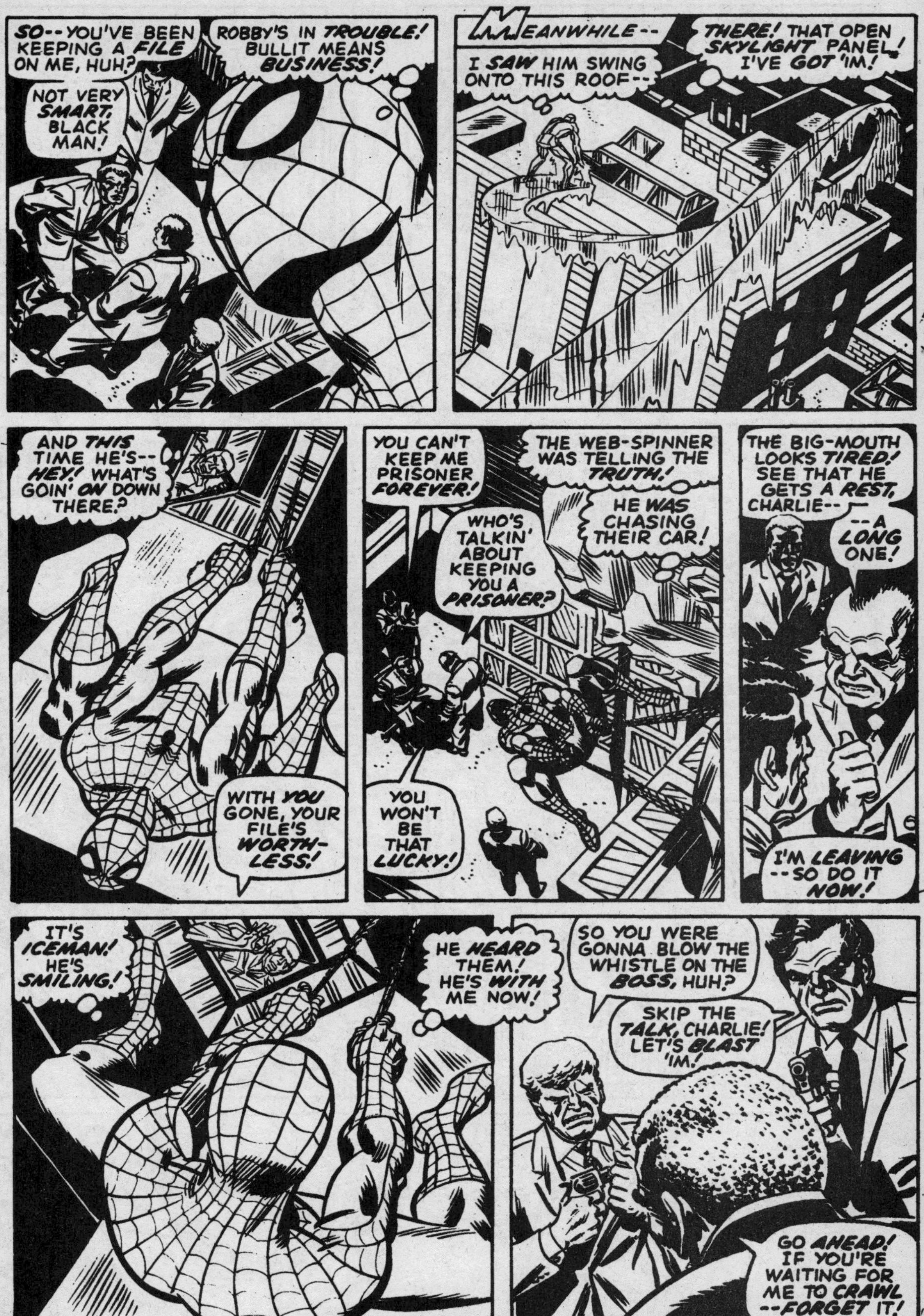
SO--YOU'VE BEEN KEEPING A FILE ON ME, HUH?
ROBBY'S IN TROUBLE! BULLIT MEANS BUSINESS!
NOT VERY SMART, BLACK MAN!
MEANWHILE--
I SAW HIM SWING ONTO THIS ROOF--
THERE! THAT OPEN SKYLIGHT PANEL! I'VE GOT 'IM!
AND THIS TIME HE'S--HEY! WHAT'S GOIN' ON DOWN THERE?
WITH YOU GONE, YOUR FILE'S WORTH-LESS!
YOU CAN'T KEEP ME PRISONER FOREVER!
WHO'S TALKIN' ABOUT KEEPING YOU A PRISONER?
YOU WON'T BE THAT LUCKY!
THE WEB-SPINNER WAS TELLING THE TRUTH!
HE WAS CHASING THEIR CAR!
THE BIG-MOUTH LOOKS TIRED! SEE THAT HE GETS A REST, CHARLIE--
--A LONG ONE!
I'M LEAVING --SO DO IT NOW!
IT'S ICEMAN! HE'S SMILING!
HE HEARD THEM! HE'S WITH ME NOW!
SO YOU WERE GONNA BLOW THE WHISTLE ON THE BOSS, HUH?
SKIP THE TALK, CHARLIE! LET'S BLAST 'IM!
GO AHEAD! IF YOU'RE WAITING FOR ME TO CRAWL --FORGET IT!

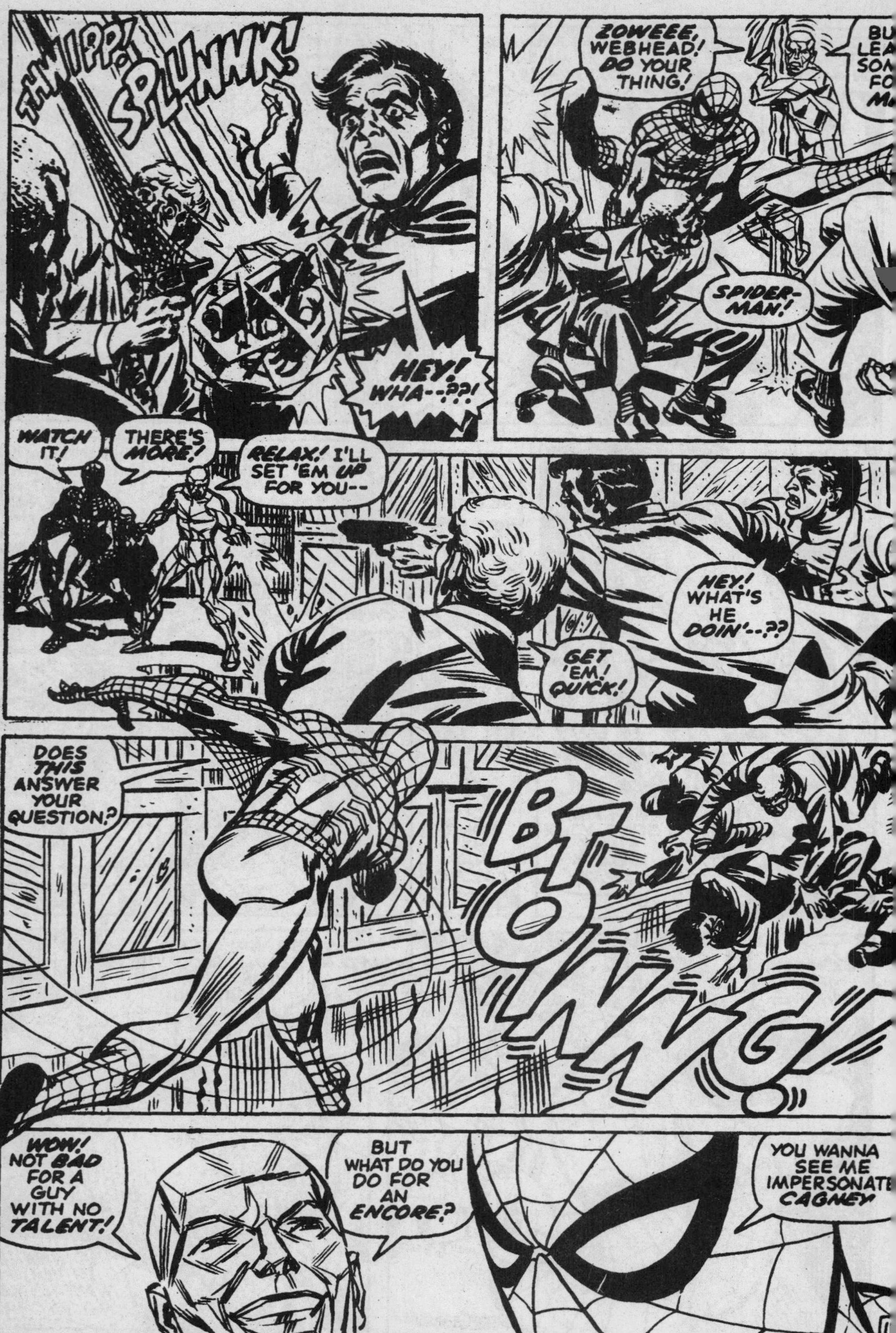
THHIPP! SPLUNNK!
HEY! WHA--??!
ZOWEEE, WEBHEAD! DO YOUR THING!
SPIDER-MAN!
WATCH IT!
THERE'S MORE!
RELAX! I'LL SET 'EM UP FOR YOU--
HEY! WHAT'S HE DOIN'--??
GET 'EM! QUICK!
DOES THIS ANSWER YOUR QUESTION?
BTOONNNG!
WOW! NOT BAD FOR A GUY WITH NO TALENT!
BUT WHAT DO YOU DO FOR AN ENCORE?
YOU WANNA SEE ME IMPERSONATE CAGNEY

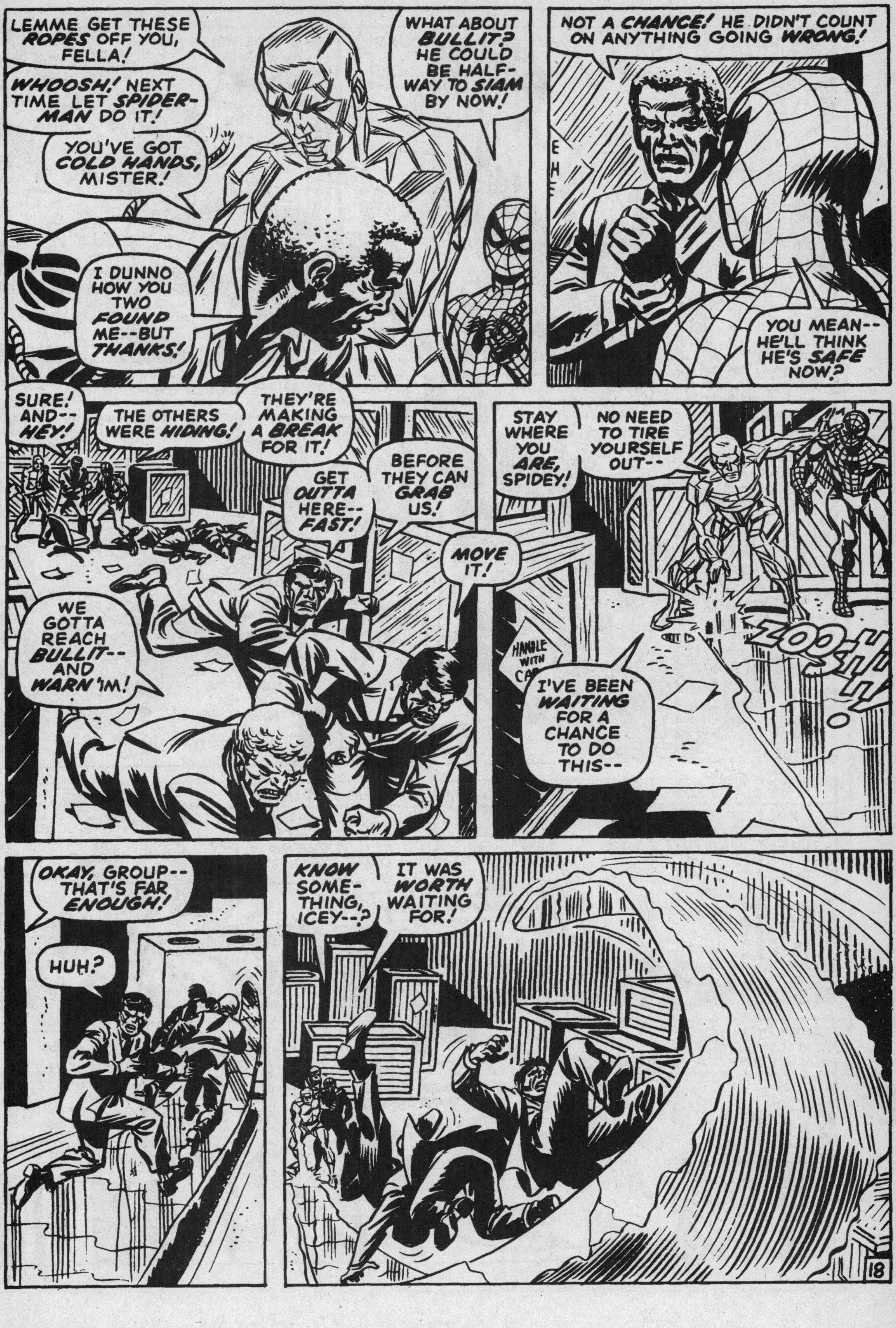
LEMME GET THESE ROPES OFF YOU, FELLA!
WHOOSH! NEXT TIME LET SPIDER-MAN DO IT!
YOU'VE GOT COLD HANDS, MISTER!
I DUNNO HOW YOU TWO FOUND ME--BUT THANKS!
WHAT ABOUT BULLIT? HE COULD BE HALF-WAY TO SIAM BY NOW!
NOT A CHANCE! HE DIDN'T COUNT ON ANYTHING GOING WRONG!
YOU MEAN--HE'LL THINK HE'S SAFE NOW?
SURE! AND--HEY!
THE OTHERS WERE HIDING!
THEY'RE MAKING A BREAK FOR IT!
GET OUTTA HERE--FAST!
BEFORE THEY CAN GRAB US!
MOVE IT!
WE GOTTA REACH BULLIT--AND WARN 'IM!
STAY WHERE YOU ARE, SPIDEY!
NO NEED TO TIRE YOURSELF OUT--
I'VE BEEN WAITING FOR A CHANCE TO DO THIS--
ZOO-
OKAY, GROUP--THAT'S FAR ENOUGH!
HUH?
KNOW SOME-THING, ICEY--?
IT WAS WORTH WAITING FOR!
18

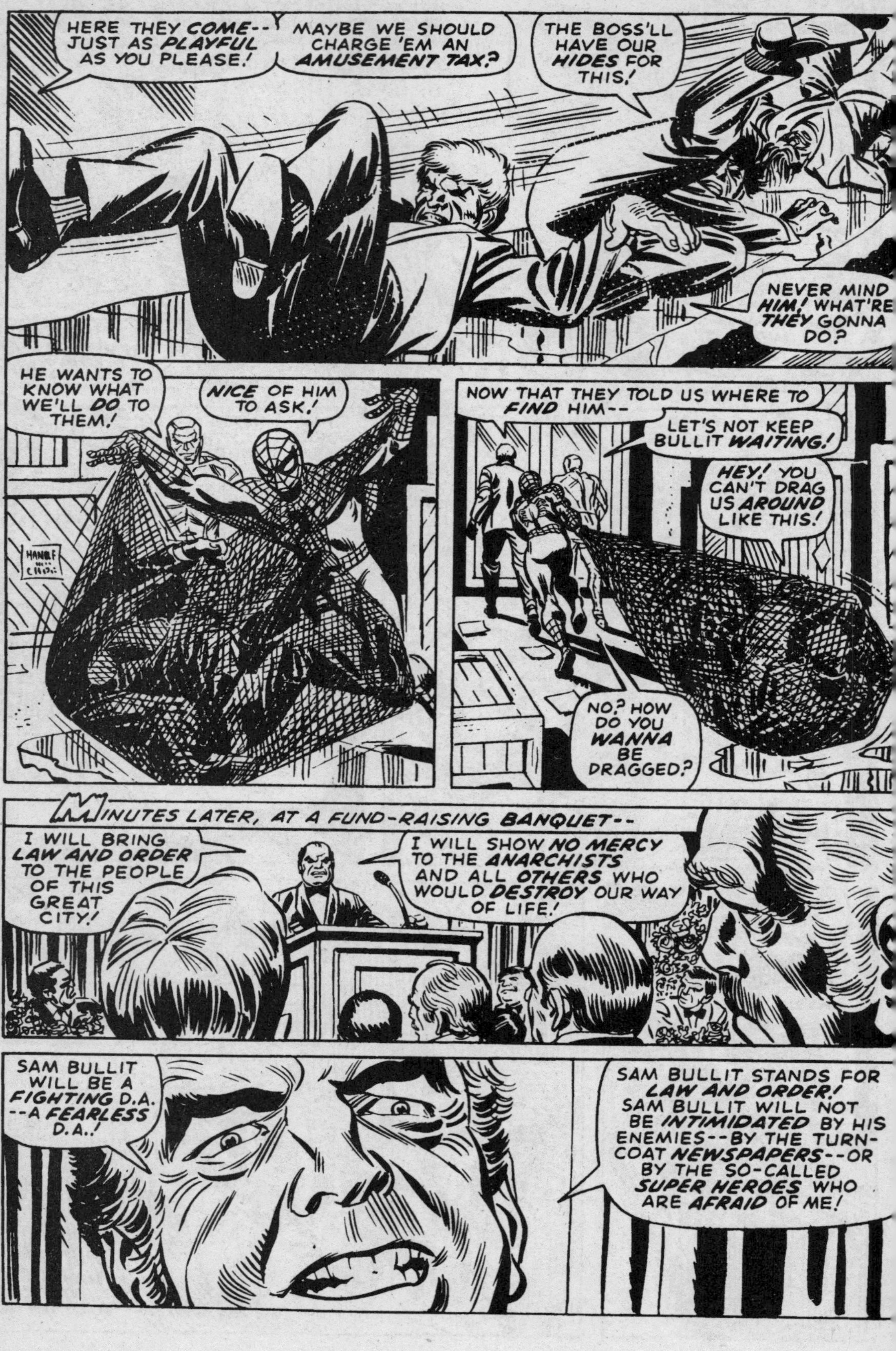
HERE THEY COME-- JUST AS PLAYFUL AS YOU PLEASE!
MAYBE WE SHOULD CHARGE 'EM AN AMUSEMENT TAX?
THE BOSS'LL HAVE OUR HIDES FOR THIS!
NEVER MIND HIM! WHAT'RE THEY GONNA DO?
HE WANTS TO KNOW WHAT WE'LL DO TO THEM!
NICE OF HIM TO ASK!
NOW THAT THEY TOLD US WHERE TO FIND HIM--
LET'S NOT KEEP BULLIT WAITING!
HEY! YOU CAN'T DRAG US AROUND LIKE THIS!
NO? HOW DO YOU WANNA BE DRAGGED?
MINUTES LATER, AT A FUND-RAISING BANQUET--
I WILL BRING LAW AND ORDER TO THE PEOPLE OF THIS GREAT CITY!
I WILL SHOW NO MERCY TO THE ANARCHISTS AND ALL OTHERS WHO WOULD DESTROY OUR WAY OF LIFE!
SAM BULLIT WILL BE A FIGHTING D.A. --A FEARLESS D.A.!
SAM BULLIT STANDS FOR LAW AND ORDER! SAM BULLIT WILL NOT BE INTIMIDATED BY HIS ENEMIES--BY THE TURN-COAT NEWSPAPERS--OR BY THE SO-CALLED SUPER HEROES WHO ARE AFRAID OF ME!

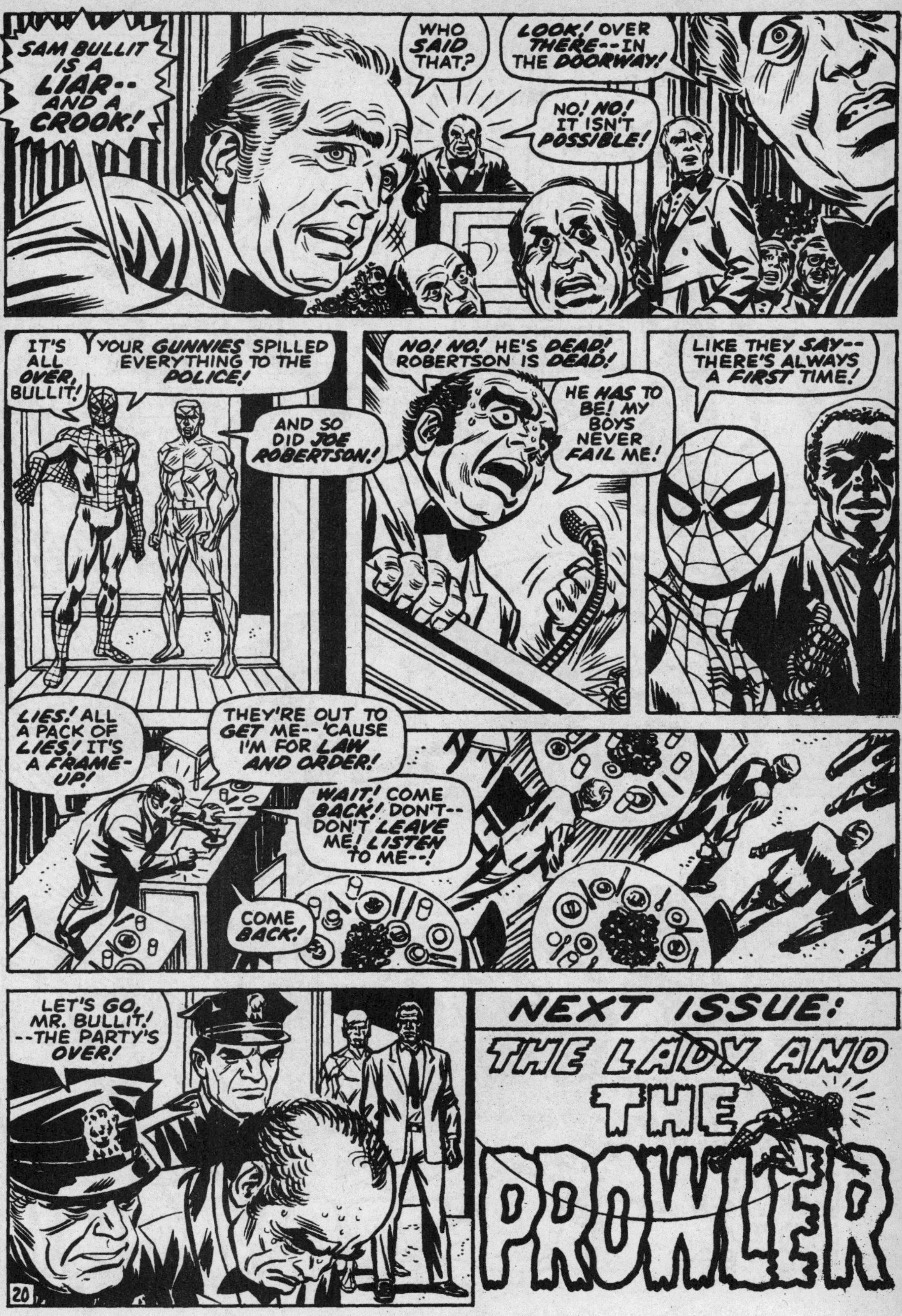

SAM BULLIT IS A LIAR-- AND A CROOK!
WHO SAID THAT?
LOOK! OVER THERE--IN THE DOORWAY!
NO! NO! IT ISN'T POSSIBLE!
IT'S ALL OVER, BULLIT!
YOUR GUNNIES SPILLED EVERYTHING TO THE POLICE!
AND SO DID JOE ROBERTSON!
NO! NO! HE'S DEAD! ROBERTSON IS DEAD!
HE HAS TO BE! MY BOYS NEVER FAIL ME!
LIKE THEY SAY-- THERE'S ALWAYS A FIRST TIME!
LIES! ALL A PACK OF LIES! IT'S A FRAME-UP!
THEY'RE OUT TO GET ME-- 'CAUSE I'M FOR LAW AND ORDER!
WAIT! COME BACK! DON'T-- DON'T LEAVE ME! LISTEN TO ME--!
COME BACK!
LET'S GO, MR. BULLIT! --THE PARTY'S OVER!
NEXT ISSUE:
THE LADY AND THE PROWLER

SPIDER-MAN
15¢ 93 FEB
the AMAZING SPIDER-MAN
APPROVED BY THE COMICS CODE AUTHORITY
MARVEL COMICS GROUP
WHATEVER HAPPENS TO YOU NOW, WEB-SLINGER-- YOU DESERVE IT!
HE'S BACK! MORE DANGEROUS THAN EVER!
IT'S ACTION ALL THE WAY WHEN SPIDEY TACKLES--
THE PROWLER!

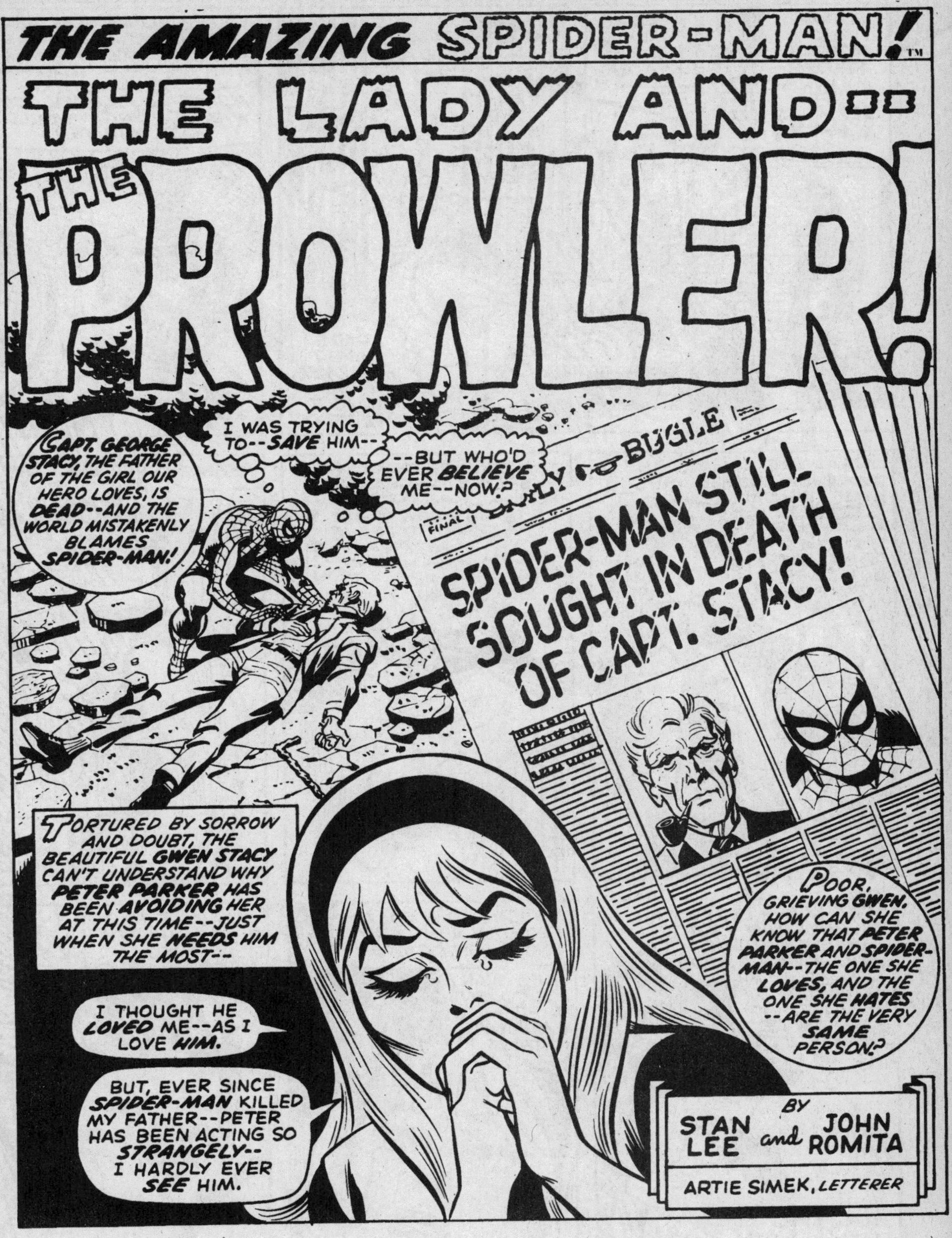
THE AMAZING SPIDER-MAN!™
THE LADY AND--
THE PROWLER!
CAPT. GEORGE STACY, THE FATHER OF THE GIRL OUR HERO LOVES, IS DEAD--AND THE WORLD MISTAKENLY BLAMES SPIDER-MAN!
I WAS TRYING TO--SAVE HIM--
--BUT WHO'D EVER BELIEVE ME--NOW?
BUGLE
FINAL
SPIDER-MAN STILL SOUGHT IN DEATH OF CAPT. STACY!
TORTURED BY SORROW AND DOUBT, THE BEAUTIFUL GWEN STACY CAN'T UNDERSTAND WHY PETER PARKER HAS BEEN AVOIDING HER AT THIS TIME--JUST WHEN SHE NEEDS HIM THE MOST--
POOR, GRIEVING GWEN. HOW CAN SHE KNOW THAT PETER PARKER AND SPIDER-MAN--THE ONE SHE LOVES, AND THE ONE SHE HATES--ARE THE VERY SAME PERSON?
I THOUGHT HE LOVED ME--AS I LOVE HIM.
BUT, EVER SINCE SPIDER-MAN KILLED MY FATHER--PETER HAS BEEN ACTING SO STRANGELY--I HARDLY EVER SEE HIM.
BY STAN LEE and JOHN ROMITA
ARTIE SIMEK, LETTERER

WITHOUT *DAD*-- WITHOUT *PETER*-- MY WHOLE LIFE SEEMS SO *EMPTY*-- SO--

THE *PHONE!* PLEASE-- *PLEASE* LET IT BE *PETER.*

RRRRRINNNGG!

GWENDOLYN, THIS IS YOUR *UNCLE ARTHUR* --IN LONDON.

I JUST LEARNED THE TERRIBLE *NEWS*-- ABOUT POOR *GEORGE.*

DAD'S OLDER *BROTHER.* I HAD ALMOST *FORGOTTEN.*

YOU'RE *ALONE* NOW, DEA[R.] YOUR *AUNT* AND I WAN[T] YOU TO COME AND *STA[Y]* WITH US.

YOU'LL HAVE A *HOME*--A *FAMILY.* IT['S] WHAT *GEORGE* WOULD [HAVE] HAVE WANTED.

THEY WERE ALWAYS THE *DEAREST* COUPLE. BUT, WHAT ABOUT *PETER?*

IT'S SO *KIND* OF YOU BOTH. BUT I NEED TIME TO *THINK.*

OF *COURSE,* CHILD. CALL WHEN YOU *CAN.*

IT WOULD BE *WONDERFUL* --SEEING THEM AGAIN--

BUT HOW CAN I *GO*--AND LEAVE *PETER?*

UNLESS--HE NO LONGER *CARES.*

BZZZ

PETER!

HER *EYES* ARE RED. SHE'S BE[EN] *CRYING.* I--[I FEEL] LIKE SUCH A *HE[EL]* AND YET--

HI, *GWENDY.* SO[RRY] I COULDN'T CO[ME] BY *SOONER*[.]

IS--AN[Y]- THIN[G] *WRON[G],* *PETER*[?]

NOTHING--'CEPT I'M *SPIDER-MAN*--THE ONE YOU THINK *KILLED* YOUR DAD!

NO, HONEY. I--JUST HAD SOME *LOOSE ENDS*--TO TIE UP.

I JUST HAD A *CALL*-- FROM MY AUNT AND UNCLE--IN *LONDON.*

THEY WANT ME TO *GO* THERE--TO *LIVE* WITH THEM.

DO YOU-- *WANT* TO?

I *HAVE* TO, PETER. THERE'S NOTHING TO *KEEP* ME HERE.

I CAN['T] LET HE[R] *LEAVE* ME--I *CAN'T*[.] I HAVE [TO] *PROPOS[E]* NOW...

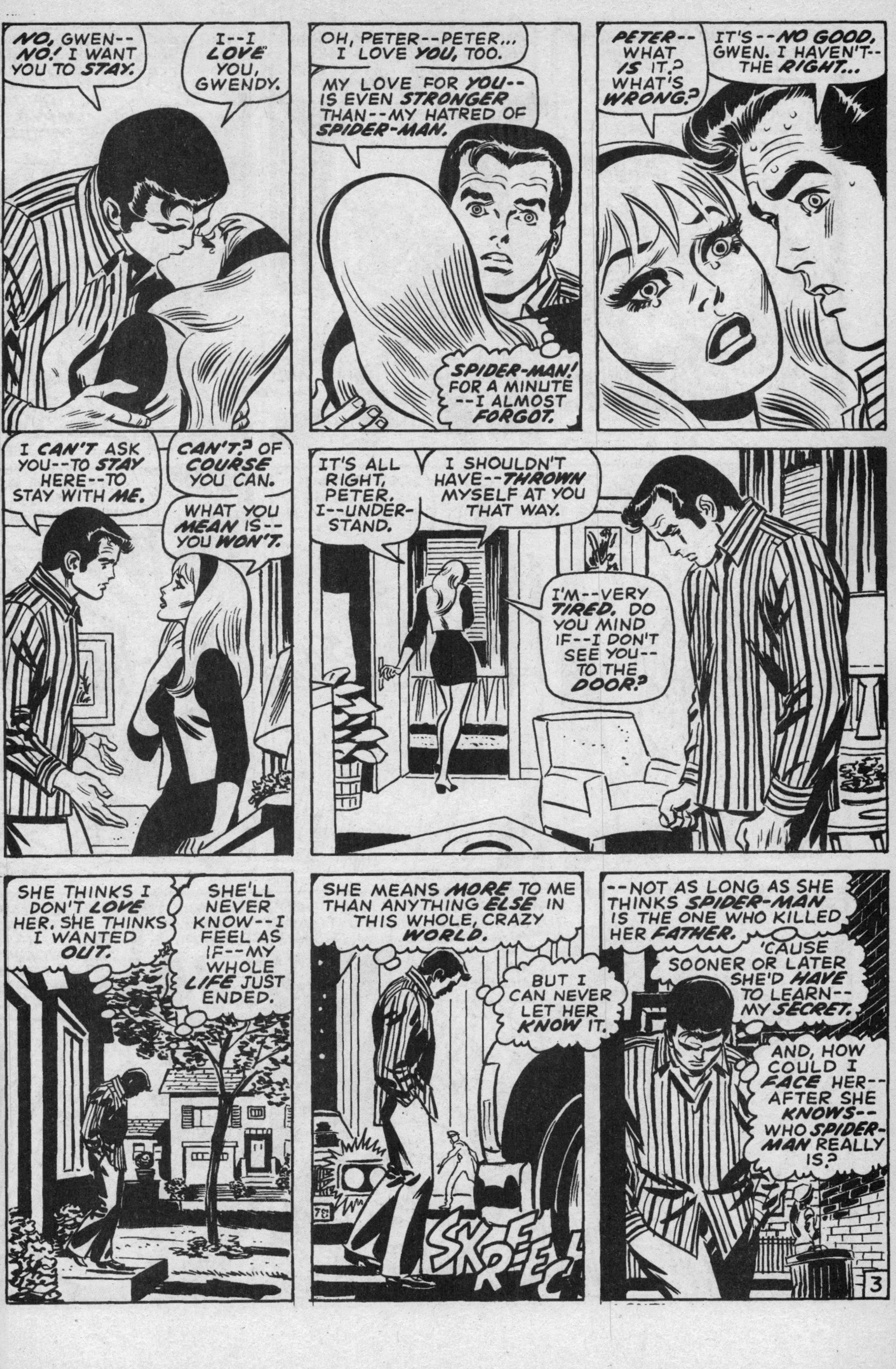
NO, GWEN-- NO! I WANT YOU TO STAY.
I--I LOVE YOU, GWENDY.
OH, PETER--PETER... I LOVE YOU, TOO.
MY LOVE FOR YOU-- IS EVEN STRONGER THAN--MY HATRED OF SPIDER-MAN.
SPIDER-MAN! FOR A MINUTE --I ALMOST FORGOT.
PETER-- WHAT IS IT? WHAT'S WRONG?
IT'S--NO GOOD, GWEN. I HAVEN'T-- THE RIGHT...
I CAN'T ASK YOU--TO STAY HERE--TO STAY WITH ME.
CAN'T? OF COURSE YOU CAN.
WHAT YOU MEAN IS-- YOU WON'T.
IT'S ALL RIGHT, PETER. I--UNDER-STAND.
I SHOULDN'T HAVE--THROWN MYSELF AT YOU THAT WAY.
I'M--VERY TIRED. DO YOU MIND IF--I DON'T SEE YOU-- TO THE DOOR?
SHE THINKS I DON'T LOVE HER. SHE THINKS I WANTED OUT.
SHE'LL NEVER KNOW--I FEEL AS IF--MY WHOLE LIFE JUST ENDED.
SHE MEANS MORE TO ME THAN ANYTHING ELSE IN THIS WHOLE, CRAZY WORLD.
BUT I CAN NEVER LET HER KNOW IT.
SKREEEECH
--NOT AS LONG AS SHE THINKS SPIDER-MAN IS THE ONE WHO KILLED HER FATHER.
'CAUSE SOONER OR LATER SHE'D HAVE TO LEARN-- MY SECRET.
AND, HOW COULD I FACE HER-- AFTER SHE KNOWS-- WHO SPIDER-MAN REALLY IS?
3

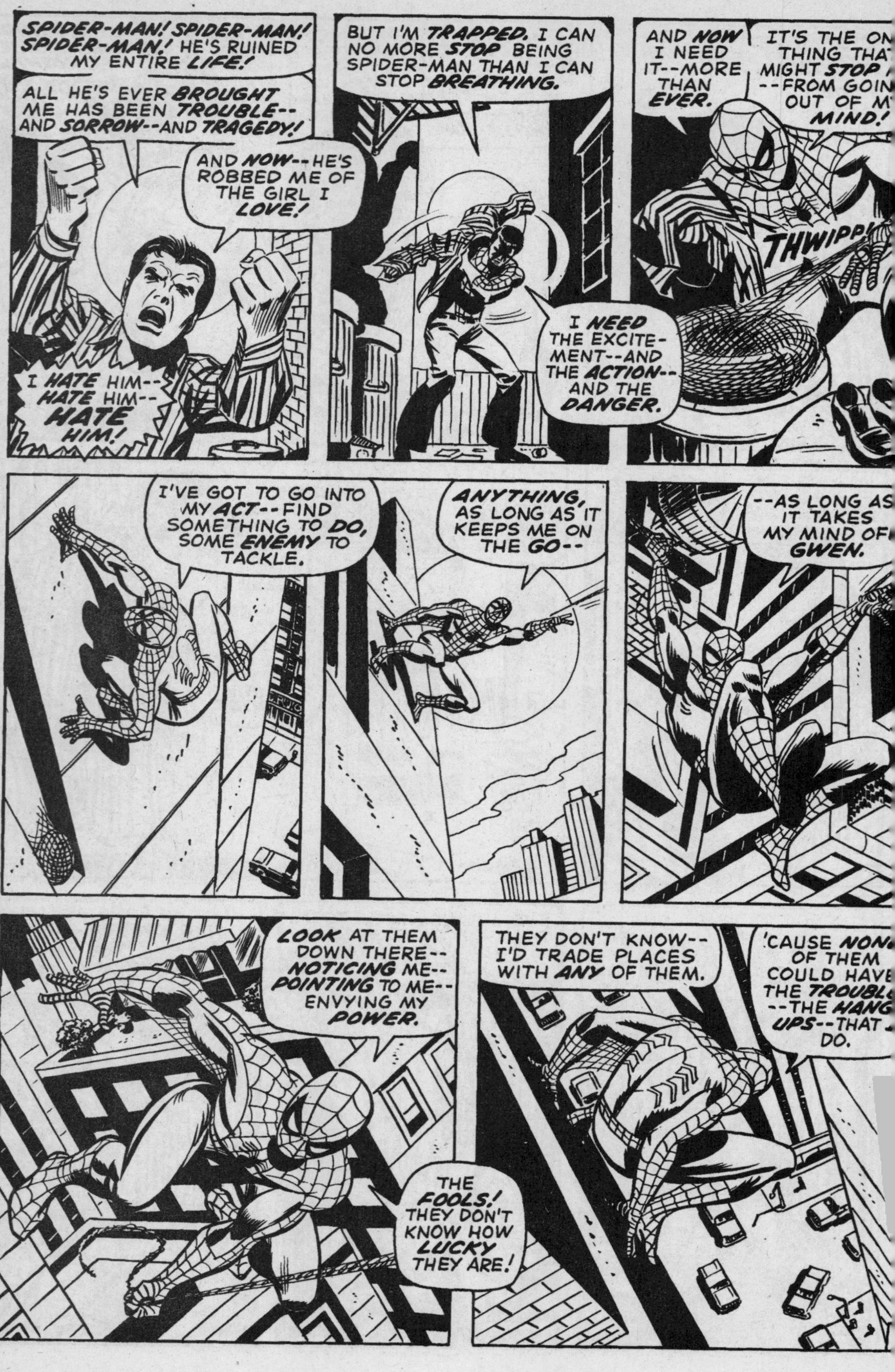

SPIDER-MAN! SPIDER-MAN! SPIDER-MAN! HE'S RUINED MY ENTIRE LIFE!
ALL HE'S EVER BROUGHT ME HAS BEEN TROUBLE--AND SORROW--AND TRAGEDY!
AND NOW--HE'S ROBBED ME OF THE GIRL I LOVE!
I HATE HIM--HATE HIM--HATE HIM!
BUT I'M TRAPPED. I CAN NO MORE STOP BEING SPIDER-MAN THAN I CAN STOP BREATHING.
I NEED THE EXCITEMENT--AND THE ACTION--AND THE DANGER.
AND NOW I NEED IT--MORE THAN EVER.
THWIPP!
I'VE GOT TO GO INTO MY ACT--FIND SOMETHING TO DO, SOME ENEMY TO TACKLE.
ANYTHING, AS LONG AS IT KEEPS ME ON THE GO--
--AS LONG AS IT TAKES
GWEN.
LOOK AT THEM DOWN THERE--NOTICING ME--POINTING TO ME--ENVYING MY POWER.
THE FOOLS! THEY DON'T KNOW HOW LUCKY THEY ARE!
THEY DON'T KNOW--I'D TRADE PLACES WITH ANY OF THEM.
'CAUSE
OF THEM COULD HAVE
--THE
UPS--THAT
DO.

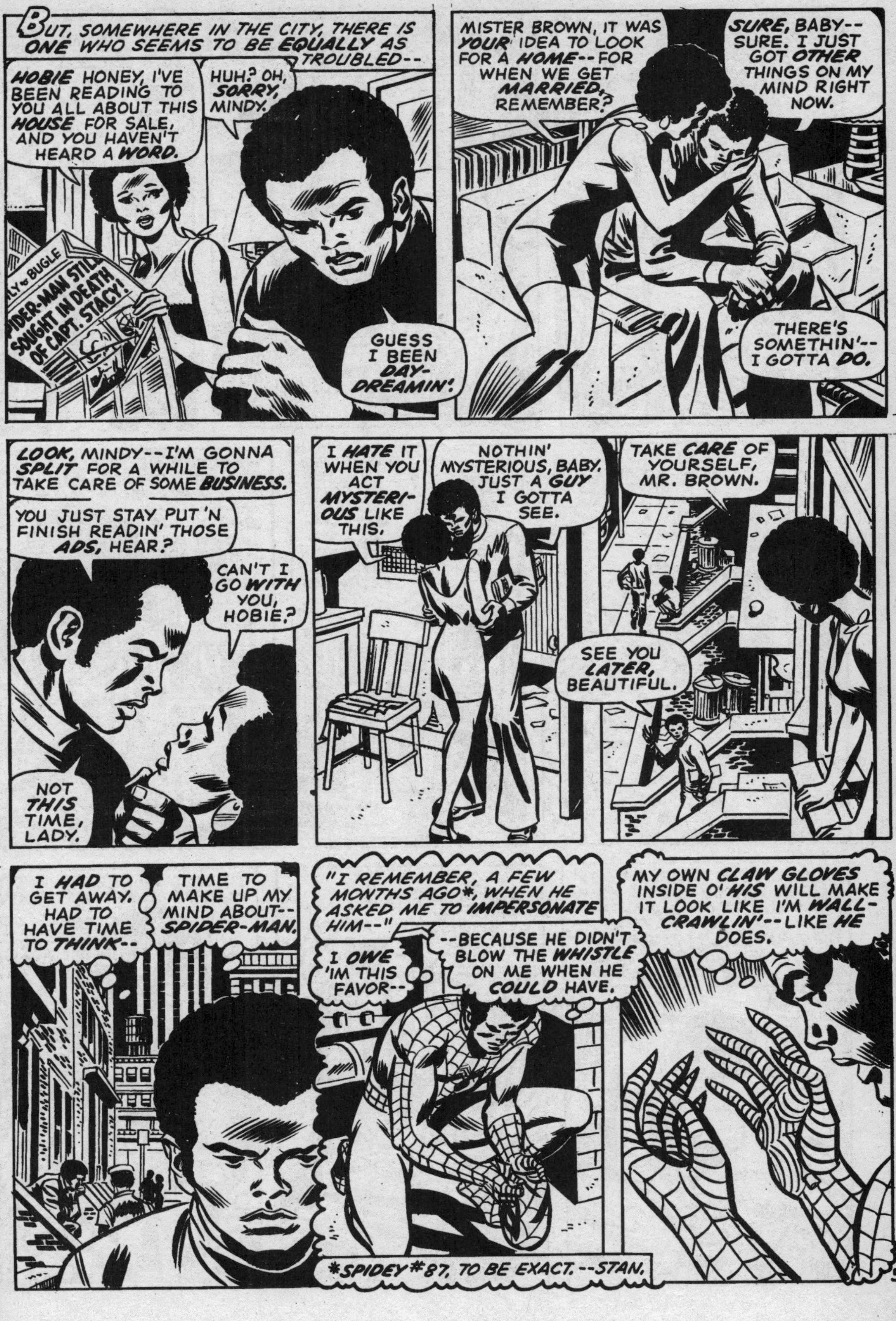

BUT, SOMEWHERE IN THE CITY, THERE IS ONE WHO SEEMS TO BE EQUALLY AS TROUBLED--
HOBIE HONEY, I'VE BEEN READING TO YOU ALL ABOUT THIS HOUSE FOR SALE, AND YOU HAVEN'T HEARD A WORD.
HUH? OH, SORRY, MINDY.
SPIDER-MAN STILL SOUGHT IN DEATH OF CAPT. STACY!
GUESS I BEEN DAY-DREAMIN'.
MISTER BROWN, IT WAS YOUR IDEA TO LOOK FOR A HOME--FOR WHEN WE GET MARRIED, REMEMBER?
SURE, BABY--SURE. I JUST GOT OTHER THINGS ON MY MIND RIGHT NOW.
THERE'S SOMETHIN'--I GOTTA DO.
LOOK, MINDY--I'M GONNA SPLIT FOR A WHILE TO TAKE CARE OF SOME BUSINESS.
YOU JUST STAY PUT 'N FINISH READIN' THOSE ADS, HEAR?
CAN'T I GO WITH YOU, HOBIE?
NOT THIS TIME, LADY.
I HATE IT WHEN YOU ACT MYSTERIOUS LIKE THIS.
NOTHIN' MYSTERIOUS, BABY. JUST A GUY I GOTTA SEE.
TAKE CARE OF YOURSELF, MR. BROWN.
SEE YOU LATER, BEAUTIFUL.
I HAD TO GET AWAY. HAD TO HAVE TIME TO THINK--
TIME TO MAKE UP MY MIND ABOUT--SPIDER-MAN.
"I REMEMBER, A FEW MONTHS AGO*, WHEN HE ASKED ME TO IMPERSONATE HIM--"
I OWE 'IM THIS FAVOR--
--BECAUSE HE DIDN'T BLOW THE WHISTLE ON ME WHEN HE COULD HAVE.
MY OWN CLAW GLOVES INSIDE O' HIS WILL MAKE IT LOOK LIKE I'M WALL-CRAWLIN'--LIKE HE DOES.
*SPIDEY #87, TO BE EXACT. --STAN.

I DUNNO WHY HE WANTS ME TO DO THIS... BUT WHAT THE HECK.

IT'S SPIDER-MAN!

SO FAR SO GOOD.

"I REMEMBER SEEIN' CAPTAIN STACY THERE WITH HIS DAUGHTER 'N A COUPLE OF OTHER KIDS--"

"AND THEN I TOOK OFF--LIKE SPIDER MAN TOLD ME TO D--"

I FORGOT ABOUT THE WHOLE THING--TILL I READ ABOUT STACY'S DEATH.

NOW, I'VE GOTTA KNOW-- DID THE WALL-CRAWLER REALLY KILL 'IM?

DAILY oo BU

SPIDER-MAN SOUGHT IN DEA OF CAPT. STACY!

AND--THE ONE THING THAT'S BEEN HAUNTING ME--

DID SPIDER-MAN MAKE ME SOME SORT OF ACCOMPLICE--WITHOUT MY EVEN KNOWING IT?

WHOEVER HE REALLY IS, I THOUGHT SPIDER-MAN WAS FRIEND OF MINE.

BUT--IF HE USED ME-- IF HE MADE A GOAT OUTTA ME--

I CAN'T TAKE IT LYIN' DOWN.

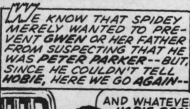

WE KNOW THAT SPIDEY MERELY WANTED TO PREVENT GWEN OR HER FATHER FROM SUSPECTING THAT HE WAS PETER PARKER--BUT, SINCE HE COULDN'T TELL HOBIE, HERE WE GO AGAIN--

AND WHATEVER HOBIE BROWN CAN'T TAKE--

--THE PROWLER CAN'T TAKE EITHER!

I HOPED I'D NEVER HAVE TO USE THIS GET-UP AGAIN--

BUT I CAN'T FIGHT IT ANY LONGER

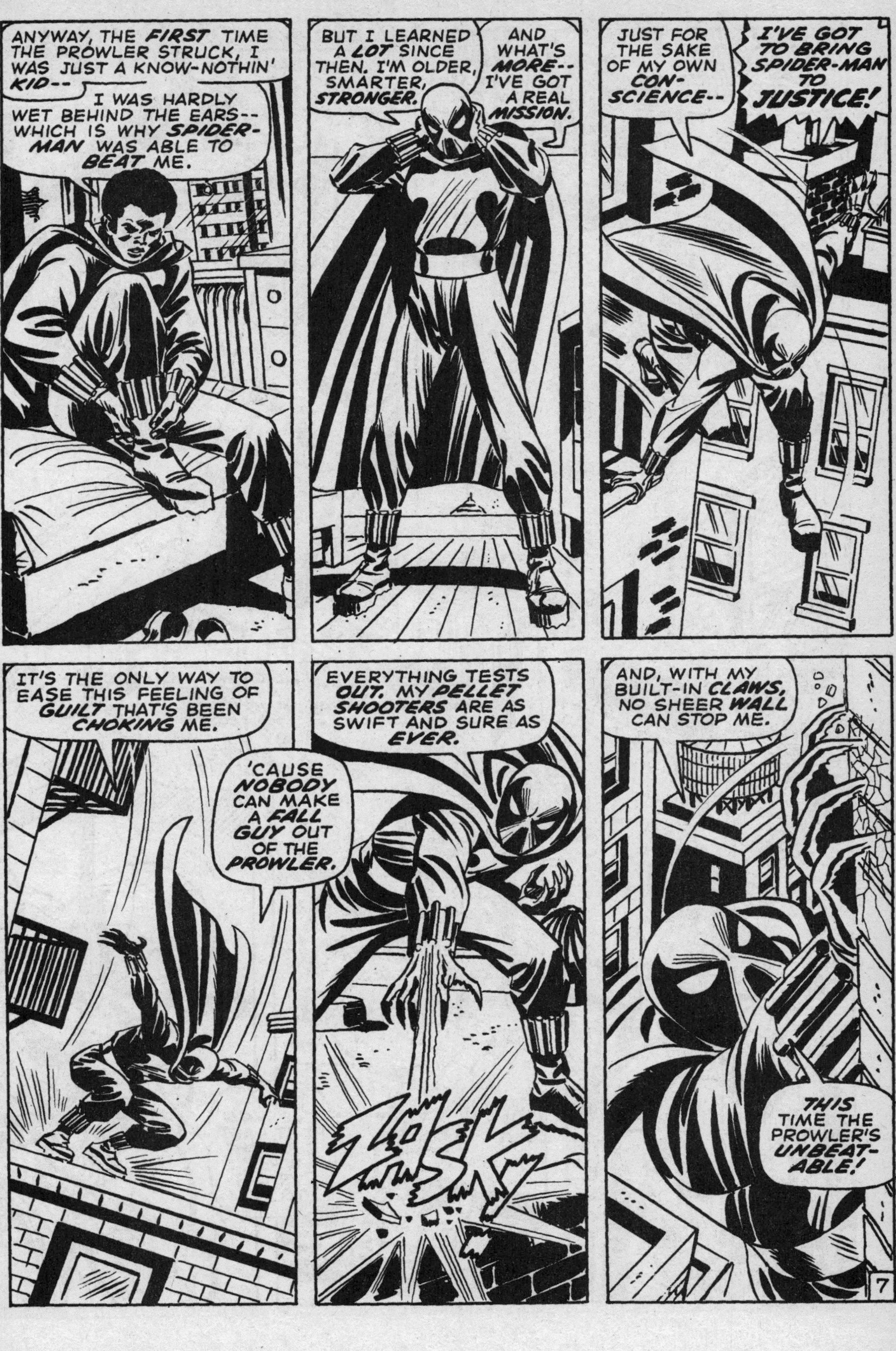
ANYWAY, THE FIRST TIME THE PROWLER STRUCK, I WAS JUST A KNOW-NOTHIN' KID--
I WAS HARDLY WET BEHIND THE EARS-- WHICH IS WHY SPIDER-MAN WAS ABLE TO BEAT ME.
BUT I LEARNED A LOT SINCE THEN. I'M OLDER, SMARTER, STRONGER.
AND WHAT'S MORE-- I'VE GOT A REAL MISSION.
JUST FOR THE SAKE OF MY OWN CON-SCIENCE--
I'VE GOT TO BRING SPIDER-MAN TO JUSTICE!
IT'S THE ONLY WAY TO EASE THIS FEELING OF GUILT THAT'S BEEN CHOKING ME.
'CAUSE NOBODY CAN MAKE A FALL GUY OUT OF THE PROWLER.
EVERYTHING TESTS OUT. MY PELLET SHOOTERS ARE AS SWIFT AND SURE AS EVER.
ZOSK
AND, WITH MY BUILT-IN CLAWS, NO SHEER WALL CAN STOP ME.
THIS TIME THE PROWLER'S UNBEAT-ABLE!
7

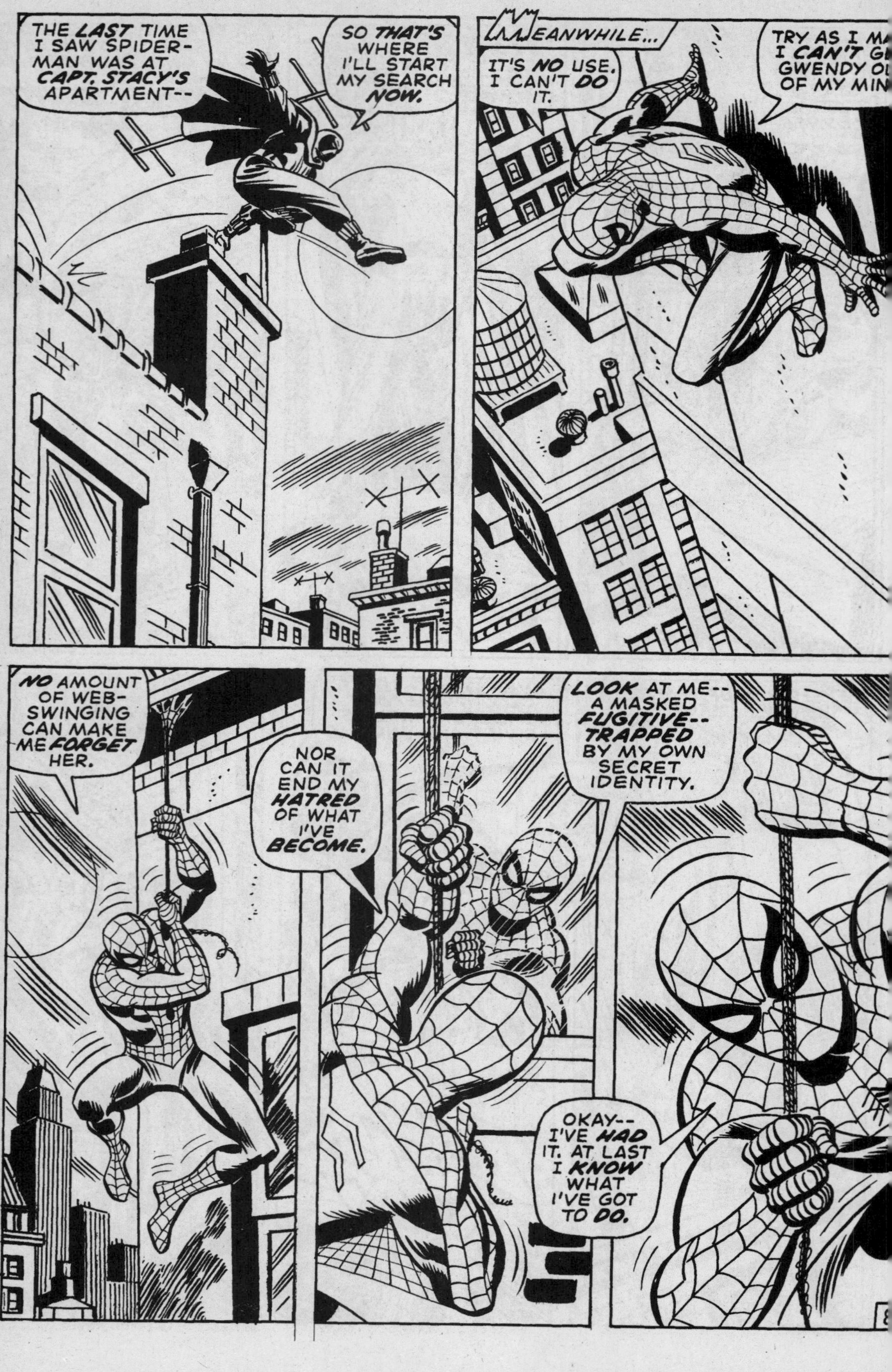
THE LAST TIME I SAW SPIDER-MAN WAS AT CAPT. STACY'S APARTMENT--
SO THAT'S WHERE I'LL START MY SEARCH NOW.
MEANWHILE...
IT'S NO USE. I CAN'T DO IT.
TRY AS I MA
I CAN'T G
GWENDY O
OF MY MIN
NO AMOUNT OF WEB-SWINGING CAN MAKE ME FORGET HER.
NOR CAN IT END MY HATRED OF WHAT I'VE BECOME.
LOOK AT ME-- A MASKED FUGITIVE-- TRAPPED BY MY OWN SECRET IDENTITY.
OKAY-- I'VE HAD IT. AT LAST I KNOW WHAT I'VE GOT TO DO.

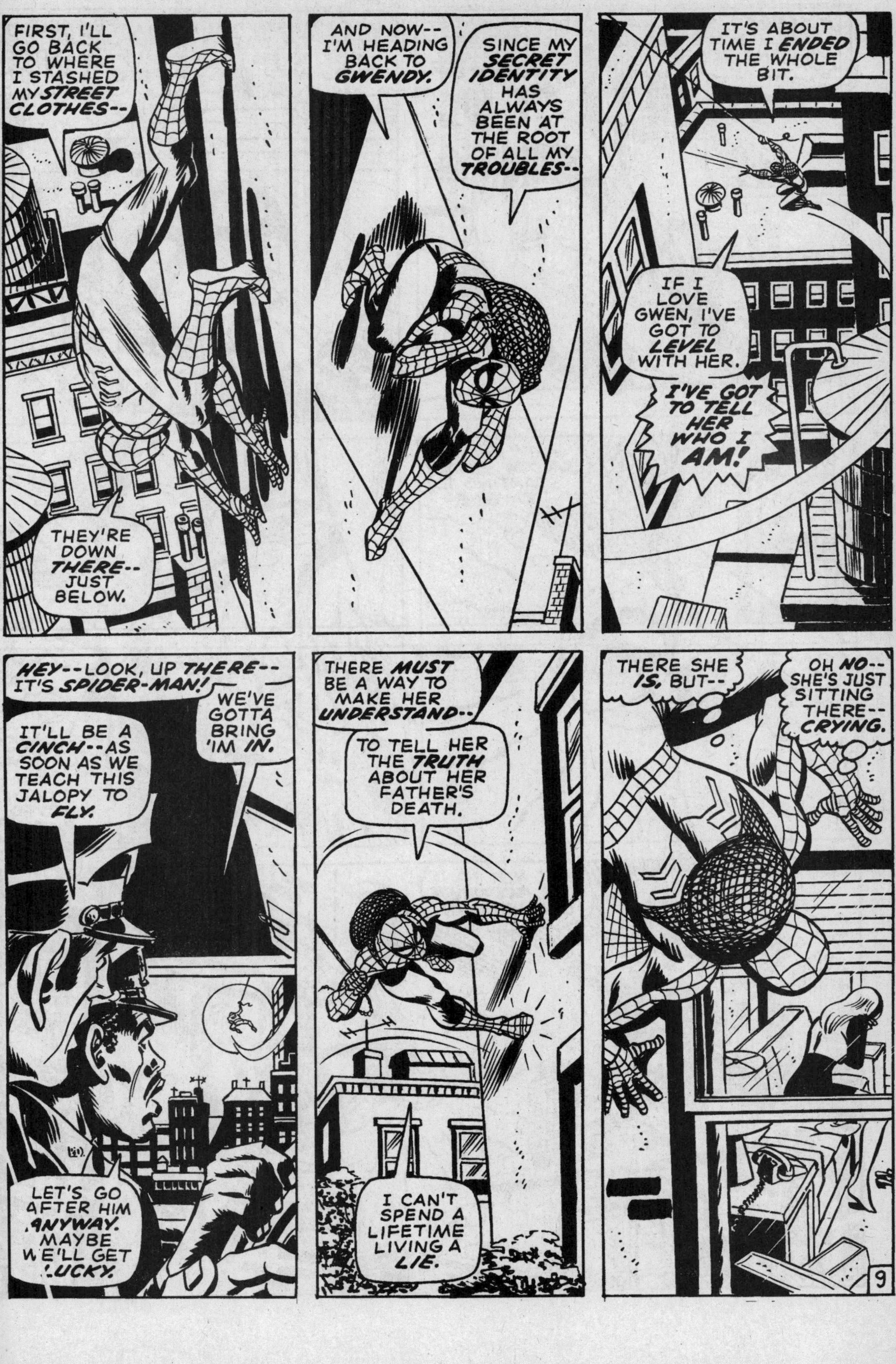
FIRST, I'LL GO BACK TO WHERE I STASHED MY STREET CLOTHES--
THEY'RE DOWN THERE-- JUST BELOW.
AND NOW-- I'M HEADING BACK TO GWENDY.
SINCE MY SECRET IDENTITY HAS ALWAYS BEEN AT THE ROOT OF ALL MY TROUBLES--
IT'S ABOUT TIME I ENDED THE WHOLE BIT.
IF I LOVE GWEN, I'VE GOT TO LEVEL WITH HER.
I'VE GOT TO TELL HER WHO I AM!
HEY--LOOK, UP THERE-- IT'S SPIDER-MAN!
WE'VE GOTTA BRING 'IM IN.
IT'LL BE A CINCH--AS SOON AS WE TEACH THIS JALOPY TO FLY.
LET'S GO AFTER HIM ANYWAY. MAYBE WE'LL GET LUCKY.
THERE MUST BE A WAY TO MAKE HER UNDERSTAND--
TO TELL HER THE TRUTH ABOUT HER FATHER'S DEATH.
I CAN'T SPEND A LIFETIME LIVING A LIE.
THERE SHE IS, BUT--
OH NO-- SHE'S JUST SITTING THERE-- CRYING.
9

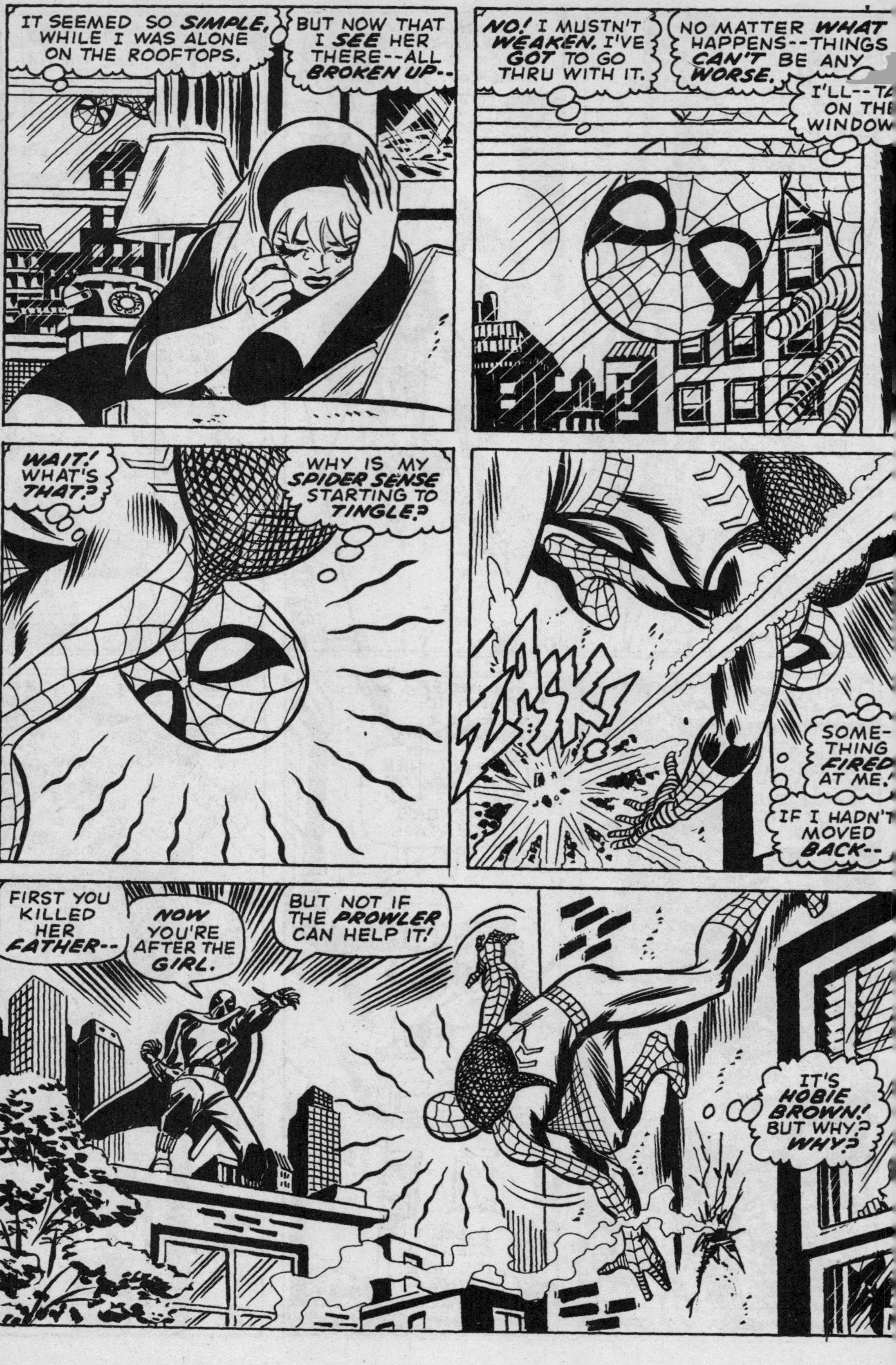

IT SEEMED SO SIMPLE, WHILE I WAS ALONE ON THE ROOFTOPS.
BUT NOW THAT I SEE HER THERE--ALL BROKEN UP--
NO! I MUSTN'T WEAKEN. I'VE GOT TO GO THRU WITH IT.
NO MATTER WHAT HAPPENS--THINGS CAN'T BE ANY WORSE.
WAIT! WHAT'S THAT?
WHY IS MY SPIDER SENSE STARTING TO TINGLE?
ZAK!
SOME-THING FIRED AT ME.
IF I HADN'T MOVED BACK--
FIRST YOU KILLED HER FATHER--
NOW YOU'RE AFTER THE GIRL.
BUT NOT IF THE PROWLER CAN HELP IT!
IT'S HOBIE BROWN! BUT WHY? WHY?

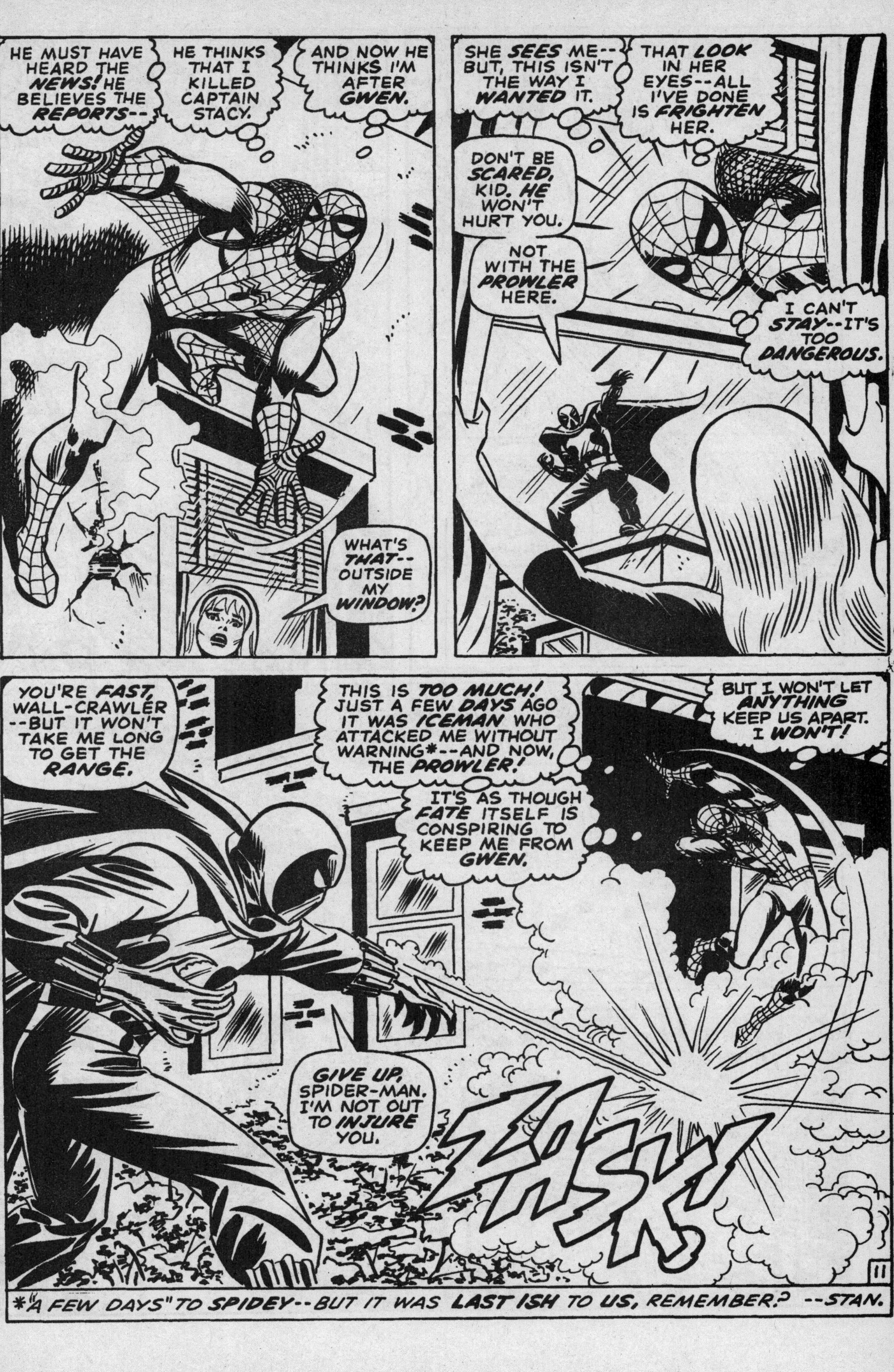
HE MUST HAVE HEARD THE NEWS! HE BELIEVES THE REPORTS--
HE THINKS THAT I KILLED CAPTAIN STACY.
AND NOW HE THINKS I'M AFTER GWEN.
WHAT'S THAT--OUTSIDE MY WINDOW?
SHE SEES ME--BUT, THIS ISN'T THE WAY I WANTED IT.
THAT LOOK IN HER EYES--ALL I'VE DONE IS FRIGHTEN HER.
DON'T BE SCARED, KID. HE WON'T HURT YOU.
NOT WITH THE PROWLER HERE.
I CAN'T STAY--IT'S TOO DANGEROUS.
YOU'RE FAST, WALL-CRAWLER--BUT IT WON'T TAKE ME LONG TO GET THE RANGE.
THIS IS TOO MUCH! JUST A FEW DAYS AGO IT WAS ICEMAN WHO ATTACKED ME WITHOUT WARNING*--AND NOW, THE PROWLER!
IT'S AS THOUGH FATE ITSELF IS CONSPIRING TO KEEP ME FROM GWEN.
BUT I WON'T LET ANYTHING KEEP US APART. I WON'T!
GIVE UP, SPIDER-MAN. I'M NOT OUT TO INJURE YOU.
ZASK!
11
*"A FEW DAYS" TO SPIDEY--BUT IT WAS LAST ISH TO US, REMEMBER? --STAN.

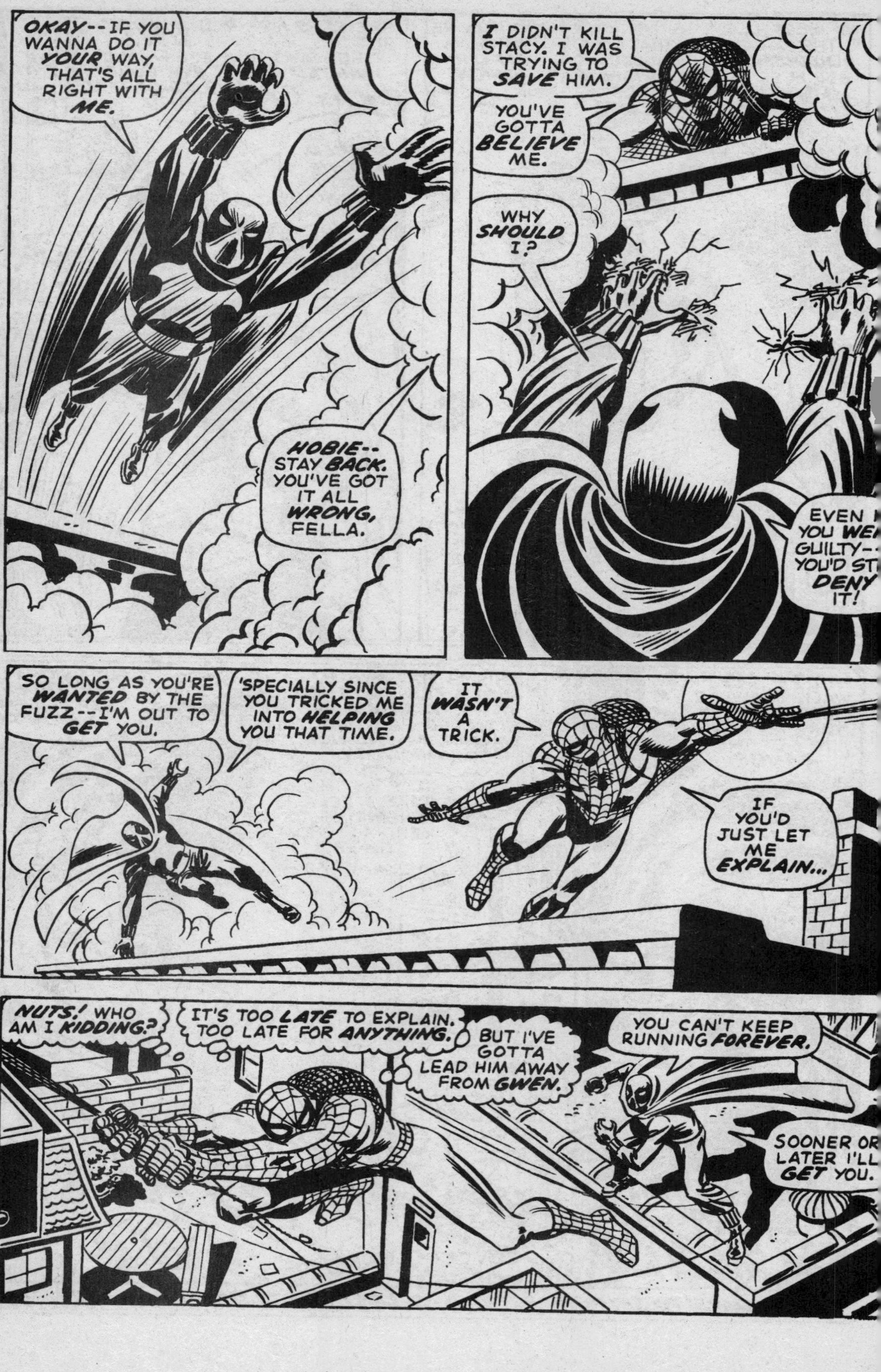
OKAY--IF YOU WANNA DO IT YOUR WAY, THAT'S ALL RIGHT WITH ME.
HOBIE--STAY BACK. YOU'VE GOT IT ALL WRONG, FELLA.
I DIDN'T KILL STACY. I WAS TRYING TO SAVE HIM.
YOU'VE GOTTA BELIEVE ME.
WHY SHOULD I?
EVEN I
YOU WE
GUILTY--
YOU'D ST
DENY
IT!
SO LONG AS YOU'RE WANTED BY THE FUZZ--I'M OUT TO GET YOU.
'SPECIALLY SINCE YOU TRICKED ME INTO HELPING YOU THAT TIME.
IT WASN'T A TRICK.
IF YOU'D JUST LET ME EXPLAIN...
NUTS! WHO AM I KIDDING?
IT'S TOO LATE TO EXPLAIN. TOO LATE FOR ANYTHING.
BUT I'VE GOTTA LEAD HIM AWAY FROM GWEN.
YOU CAN'T KEEP RUNNING FOREVER.
SOONER OR LATER I'LL GET YOU.

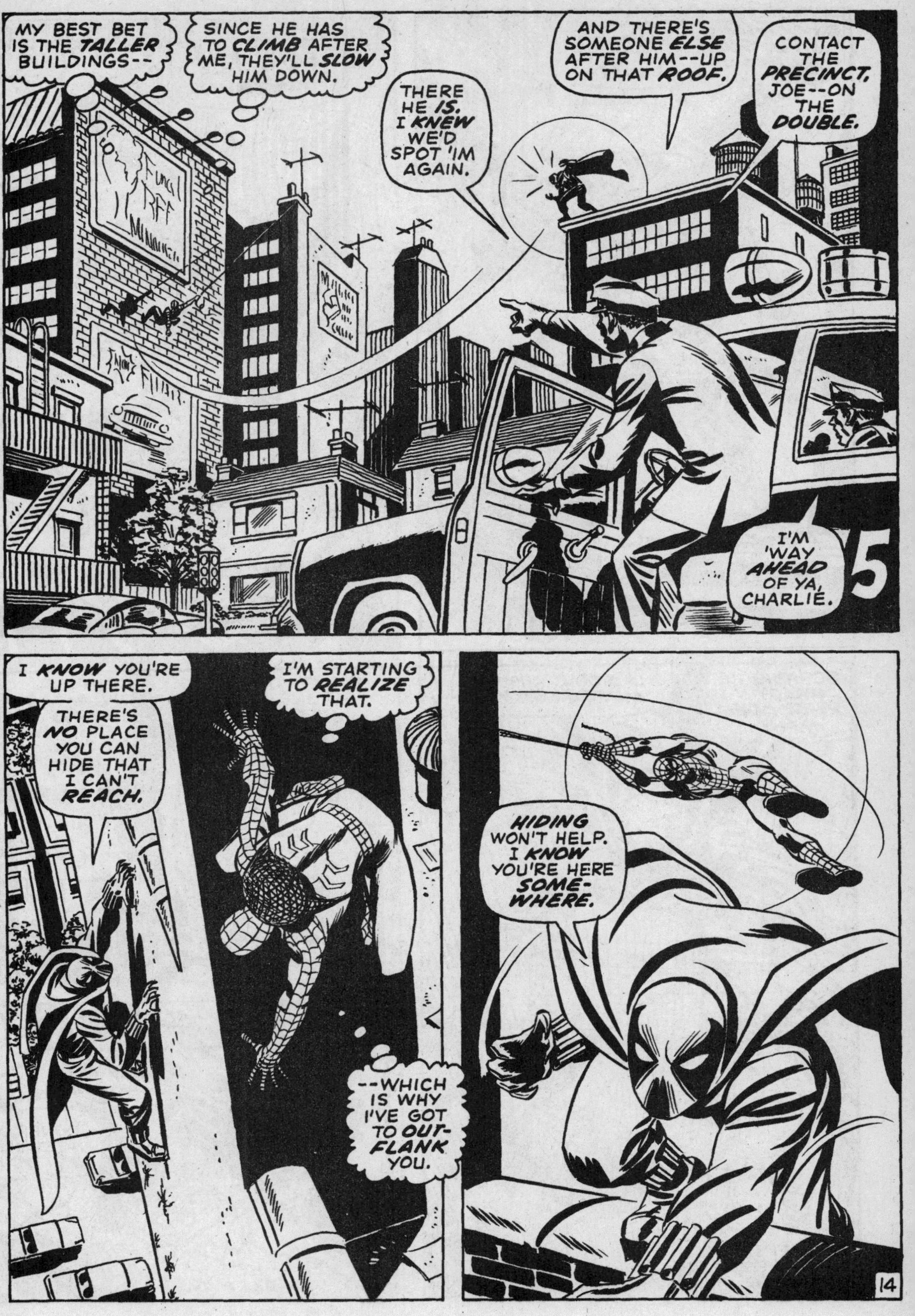
MY BEST BET IS THE TALLER BUILDINGS--
SINCE HE HAS TO CLIMB AFTER ME, THEY'LL SLOW HIM DOWN.
THERE HE IS. I KNEW WE'D SPOT 'IM AGAIN.
AND THERE'S SOMEONE ELSE AFTER HIM--UP ON THAT ROOF.
CONTACT THE PRECINCT, JOE--ON THE DOUBLE.
I'M 'WAY AHEAD OF YA, CHARLIE.
I KNOW YOU'RE UP THERE.
THERE'S NO PLACE YOU CAN HIDE THAT I CAN'T REACH.
I'M STARTING TO REALIZE THAT.
--WHICH IS WHY I'VE GOT TO OUT-FLANK YOU.
HIDING WON'T HELP. I KNOW YOU'RE HERE SOME-WHERE.

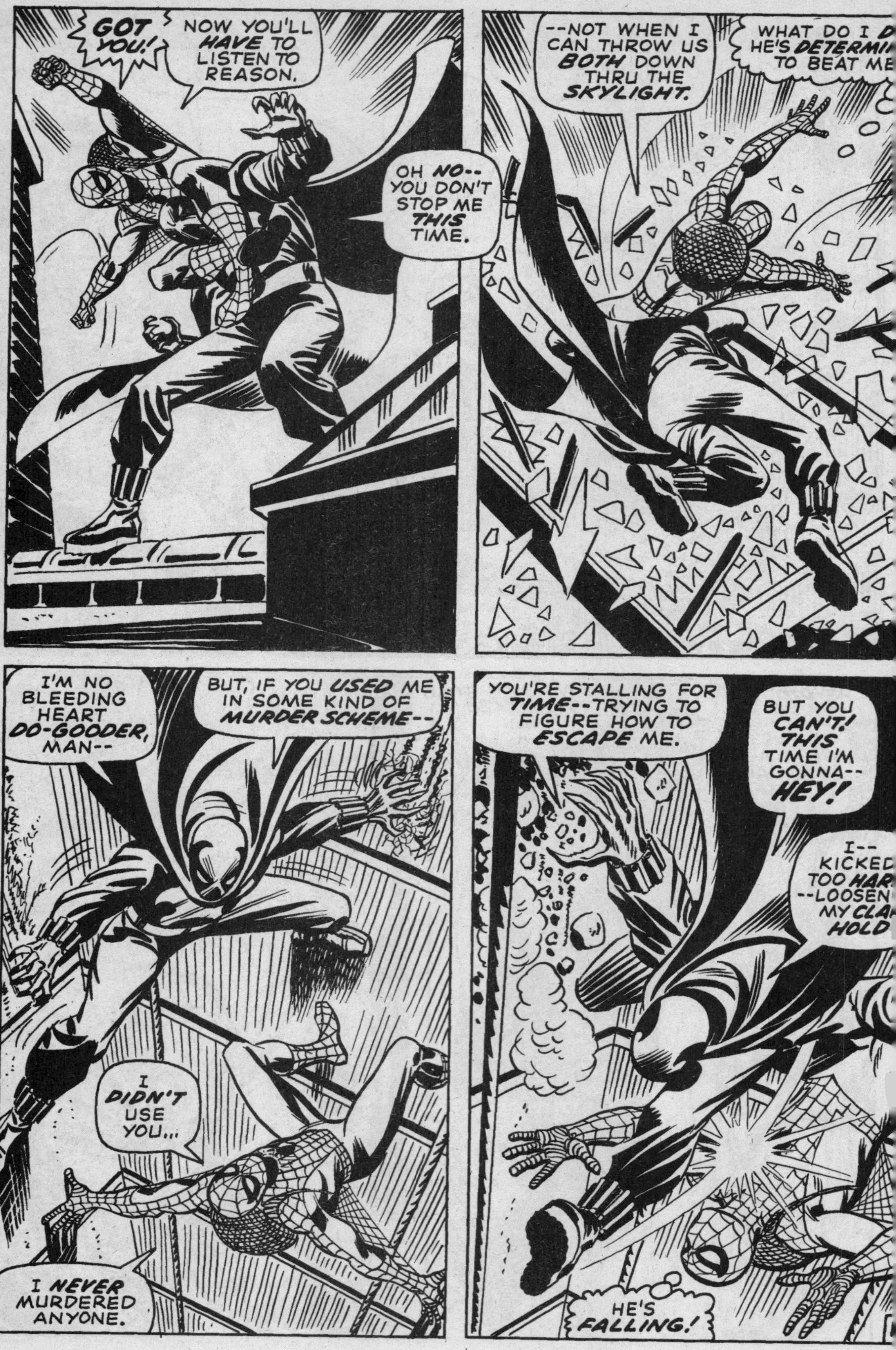

GOT YOU!
NOW YOU'LL HAVE TO LISTEN TO REASON.
OH NO-- YOU DON'T STOP ME THIS TIME.
--NOT WHEN I CAN THROW US BOTH DOWN THRU THE SKYLIGHT.
I'M NO BLEEDING HEART DO-GOODER, MAN--
BUT, IF YOU USED ME IN SOME KIND OF MURDER SCHEME--
I DIDN'T USE YOU...
I NEVER MURDERED ANYONE.
YOU'RE STALLING FOR TIME--TRYING TO FIGURE HOW TO ESCAPE ME.
BUT YOU CAN'T! THIS TIME I'M GONNA-- HEY!
HE'S FALLING!

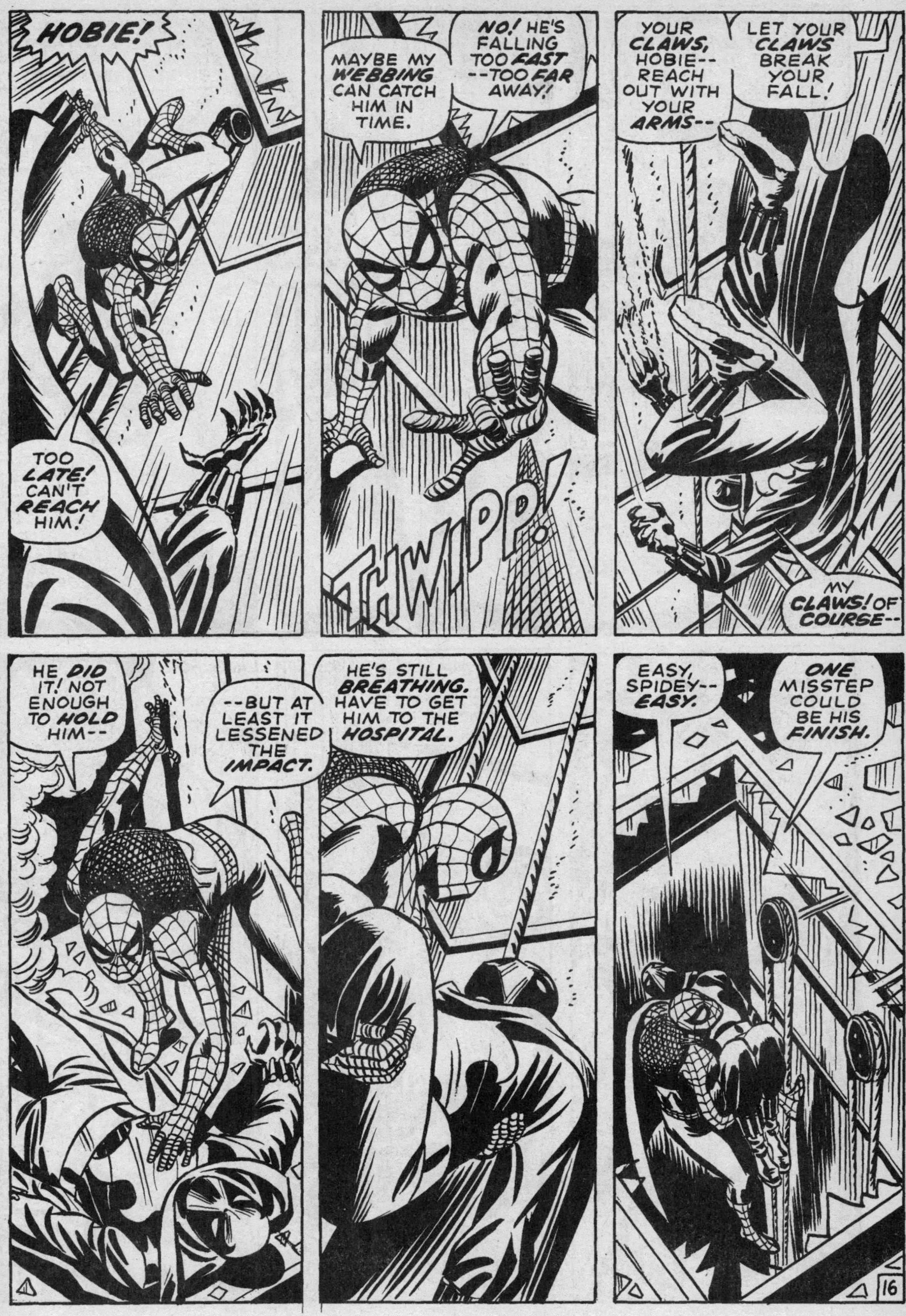
HOBIE!
TOO LATE! CAN'T REACH HIM!
MAYBE MY WEBBING CAN CATCH HIM IN TIME.
NO! HE'S FALLING TOO FAST --TOO FAR AWAY!
THWIPP!
YOUR CLAWS, HOBIE-- REACH OUT WITH YOUR ARMS--
LET YOUR CLAWS BREAK YOUR FALL!
MY CLAWS! OF COURSE--
HE DID IT! NOT ENOUGH TO HOLD HIM--
--BUT AT LEAST IT LESSENED THE IMPACT.
HE'S STILL BREATHING. HAVE TO GET HIM TO THE HOSPITAL.
EASY, SPIDEY-- EASY.
ONE MISSTEP COULD BE HIS FINISH.
16

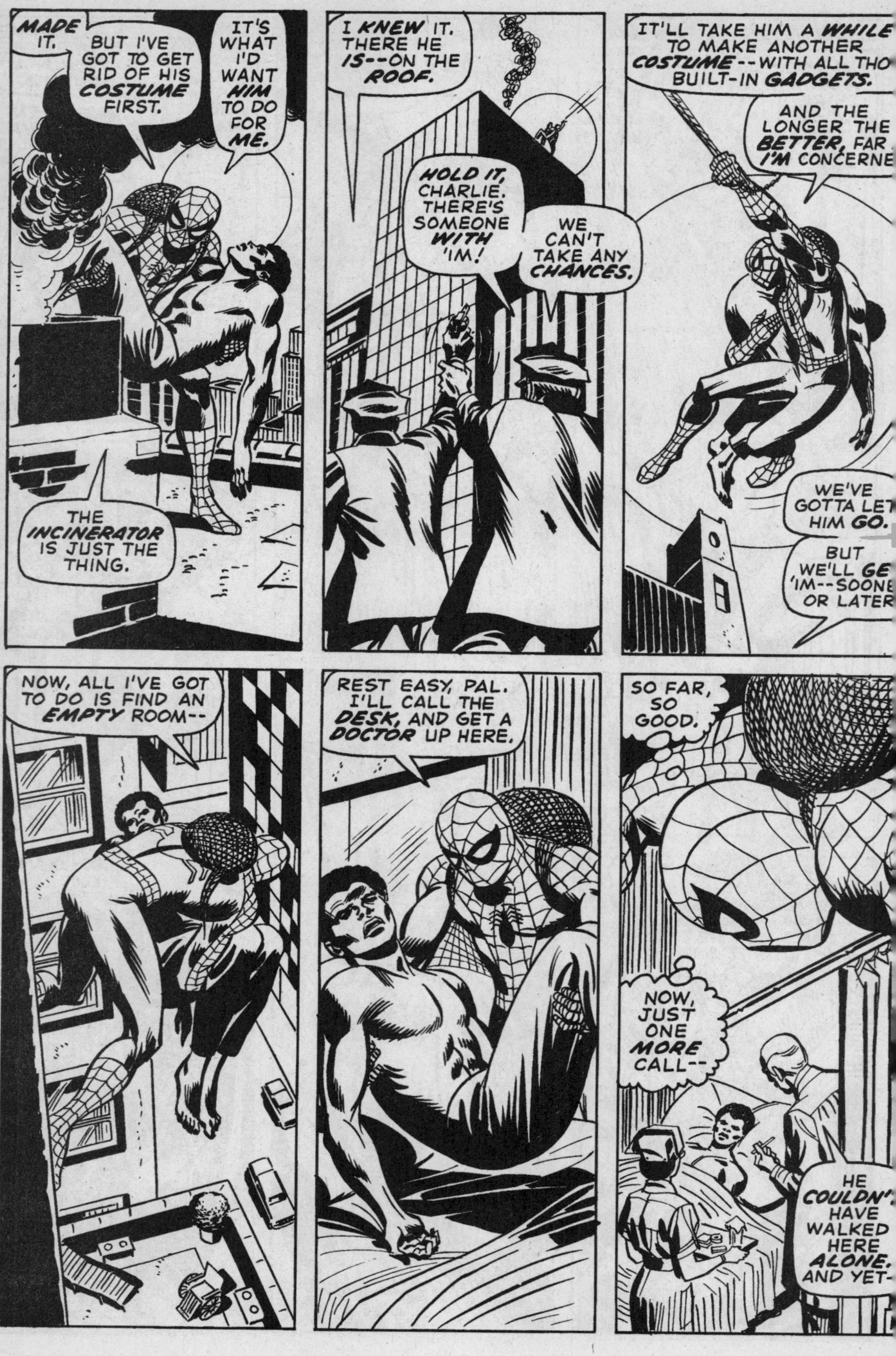
MADE IT.
BUT I'VE GOT TO GET RID OF HIS COSTUME FIRST.
IT'S WHAT I'D WANT HIM TO DO FOR ME.
THE INCINERATOR IS JUST THE THING.
I KNEW IT. THERE HE IS--ON THE ROOF.
HOLD IT, CHARLIE. THERE'S SOMEONE WITH 'IM!
WE CAN'T TAKE ANY CHANCES.
IT'LL TAKE HIM A WHILE TO MAKE ANOTHER COSTUME--WITH ALL THO BUILT-IN GADGETS.
AND THE LONGER THE BETTER, FAR I'M CONCERNE
WE'VE GOTTA LET HIM GO.
BUT WE'LL GE 'IM--SOONE OR LATER
NOW, ALL I'VE GOT TO DO IS FIND AN EMPTY ROOM--
REST EASY, PAL. I'LL CALL THE DESK, AND GET A DOCTOR UP HERE.
SO FAR, SO GOOD.
NOW, JUST ONE MORE CALL--
HE COULDN' HAVE WALKED HERE ALONE. AND YET-

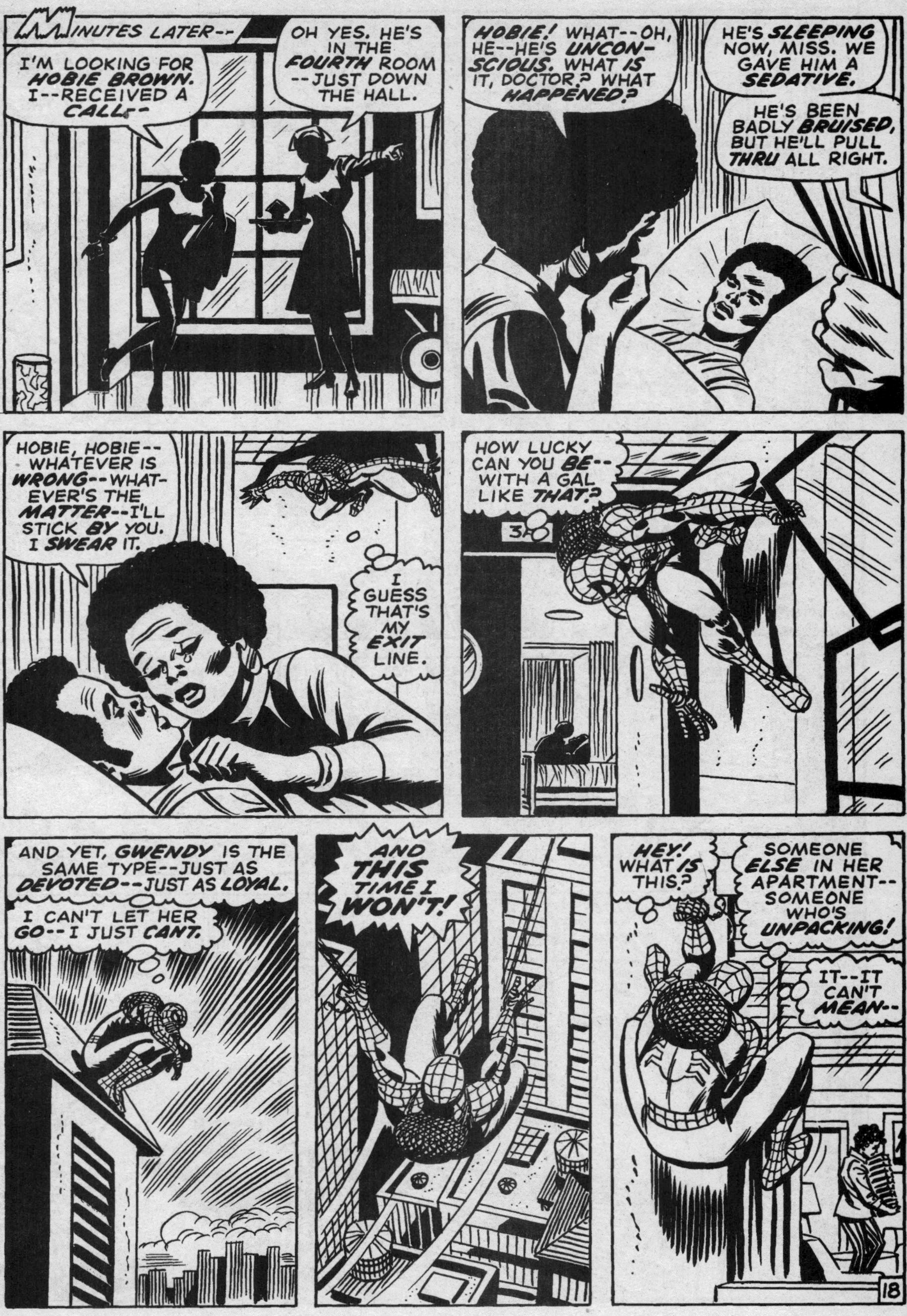
MINUTES LATER--
I'M LOOKING FOR HOBIE BROWN. I--RECEIVED A CALL--
OH YES. HE'S IN THE FOURTH ROOM --JUST DOWN THE HALL.
HOBIE! WHAT--OH, HE--HE'S UNCONSCIOUS. WHAT IS IT, DOCTOR? WHAT HAPPENED?
HE'S SLEEPING NOW, MISS. WE GAVE HIM A SEDATIVE.
HE'S BEEN BADLY BRUISED, BUT HE'LL PULL THRU ALL RIGHT.
HOBIE, HOBIE-- WHATEVER IS WRONG--WHATEVER'S THE MATTER--I'LL STICK BY YOU. I SWEAR IT.
I GUESS THAT'S MY EXIT LINE.
HOW LUCKY CAN YOU BE-- WITH A GAL LIKE THAT?
AND YET, GWENDY IS THE SAME TYPE--JUST AS DEVOTED--JUST AS LOYAL.
I CAN'T LET HER GO--I JUST CANT.
AND THIS TIME I WON'T!
HEY! WHAT IS THIS?
SOMEONE ELSE IN HER APARTMENT-- SOMEONE WHO'S UNPACKING!
IT--IT CAN'T MEAN--
18

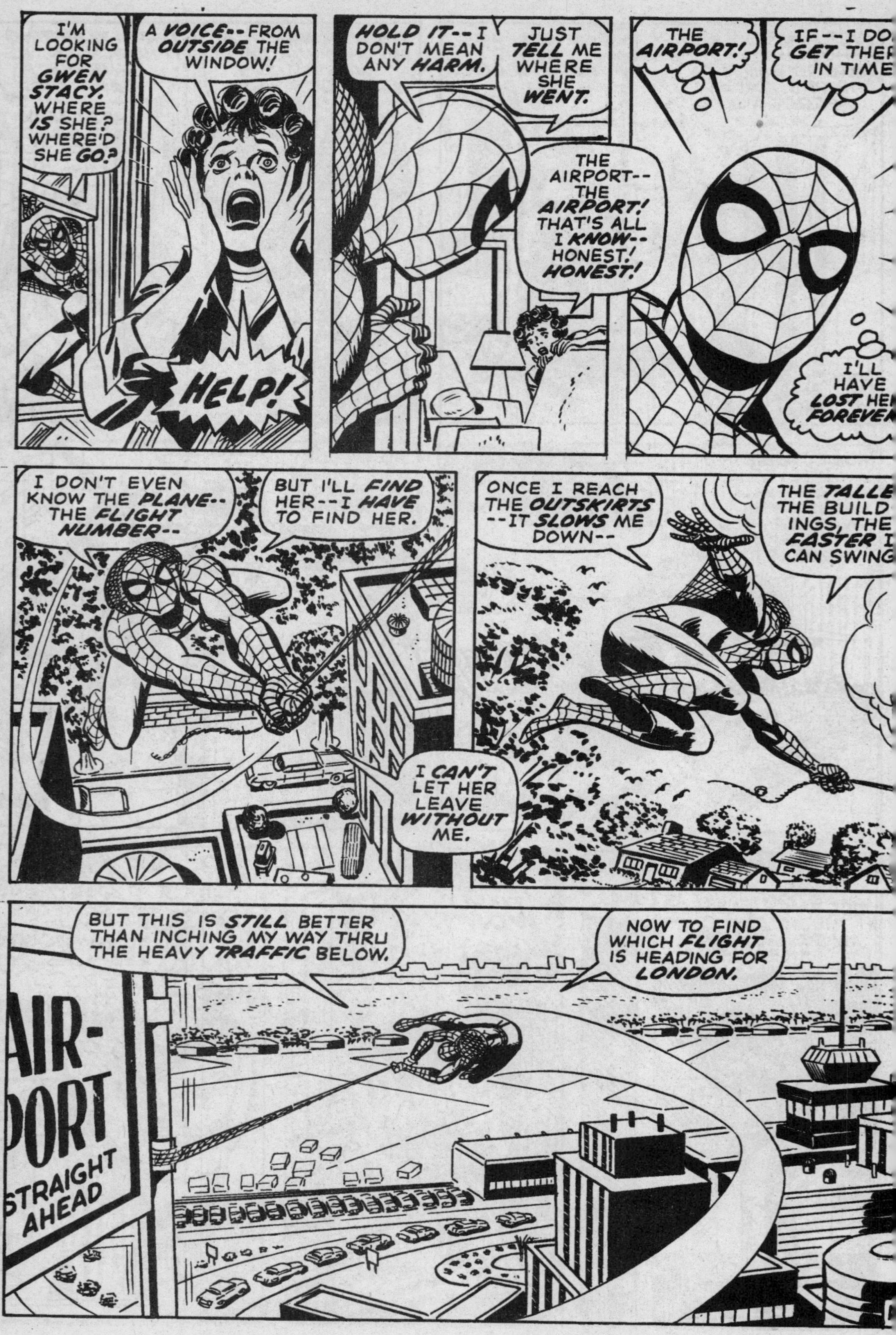
I'M LOOKING FOR GWEN STACY. WHERE IS SHE? WHERE'D SHE GO?
A VOICE--FROM OUTSIDE THE WINDOW!
HELP!
HOLD IT--I DON'T MEAN ANY HARM.
JUST TELL ME WHERE SHE WENT.
THE AIRPORT--THE AIRPORT! THAT'S ALL I KNOW--HONEST! HONEST!
THE AIRPORT!
IF--I DO GET THER IN TIME
I'LL HAVE LOST HE FOREVER
I DON'T EVEN KNOW THE PLANE--THE FLIGHT NUMBER--
BUT I'LL FIND HER--I HAVE TO FIND HER.
I CAN'T LET HER LEAVE WITHOUT ME.
ONCE I REACH THE OUTSKIRTS --IT SLOWS ME DOWN--
THE TALLE THE BUILD INGS, THE FASTER I CAN SWING
BUT THIS IS STILL BETTER THAN INCHING MY WAY THRU THE HEAVY TRAFFIC BELOW.
NOW TO FIND WHICH FLIGHT IS HEADING FOR LONDON.
AIR-PORT STRAIGHT AHEAD

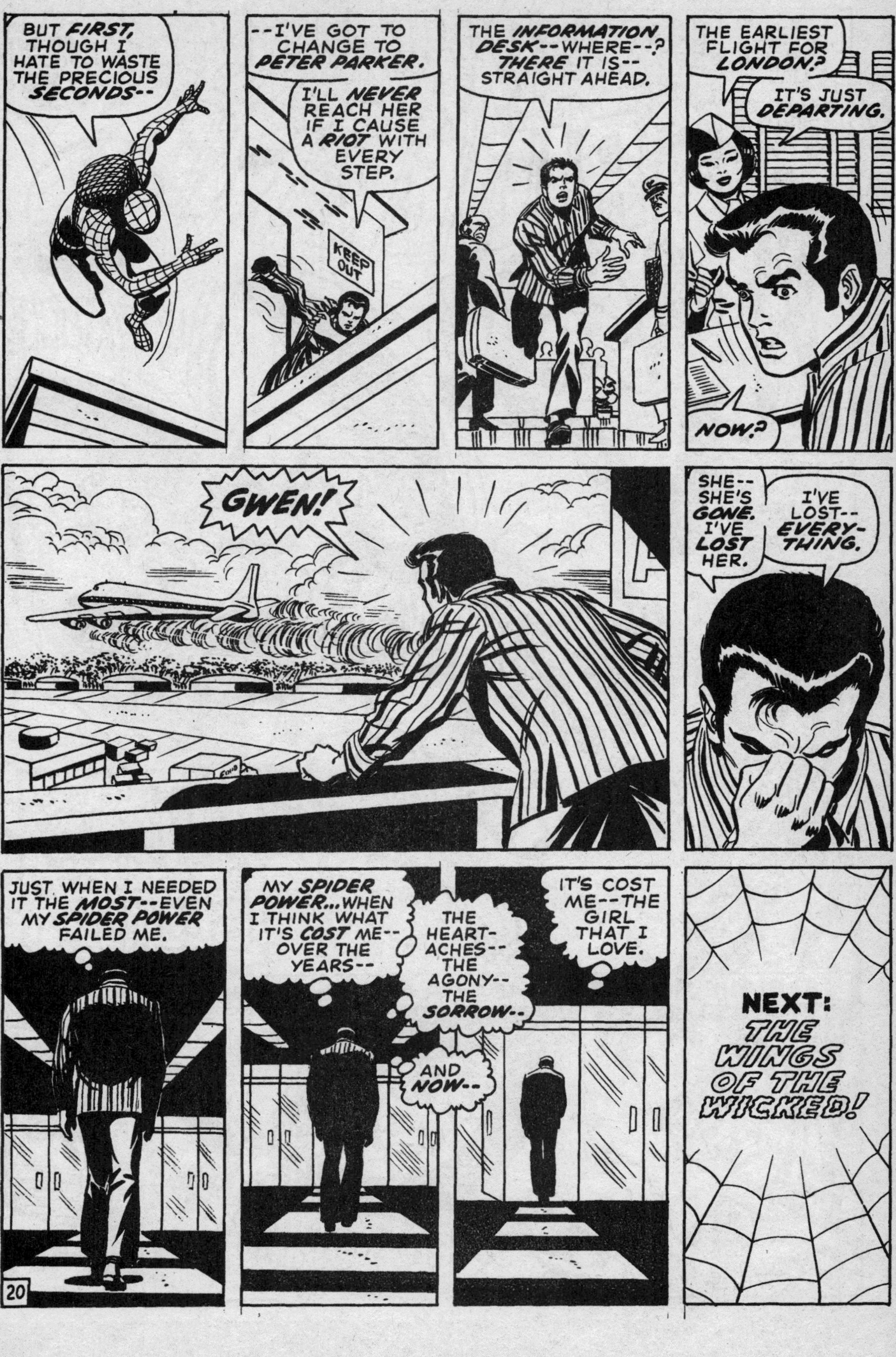
BUT FIRST, THOUGH I HATE TO WASTE THE PRECIOUS SECONDS--
--I'VE GOT TO CHANGE TO PETER PARKER.
I'LL NEVER REACH HER IF I CAUSE A RIOT WITH EVERY STEP.
KEEP OUT
THE INFORMATION DESK--WHERE--? THERE IT IS--STRAIGHT AHEAD.
THE EARLIEST FLIGHT FOR LONDON?
IT'S JUST DEPARTING.
NOW?
GWEN!
SHE--SHE'S GONE. I'VE LOST HER.
I'VE LOST--EVERYTHING.
JUST WHEN I NEEDED IT THE MOST--EVEN MY SPIDER POWER FAILED ME.
MY SPIDER POWER...WHEN I THINK WHAT IT'S COST ME--OVER THE YEARS--
THE HEART-ACHES--THE AGONY--THE SORROW--
AND NOW--
IT'S COST ME--THE GIRL THAT I LOVE.
NEXT: THE WINGS OF THE WICKED!
20

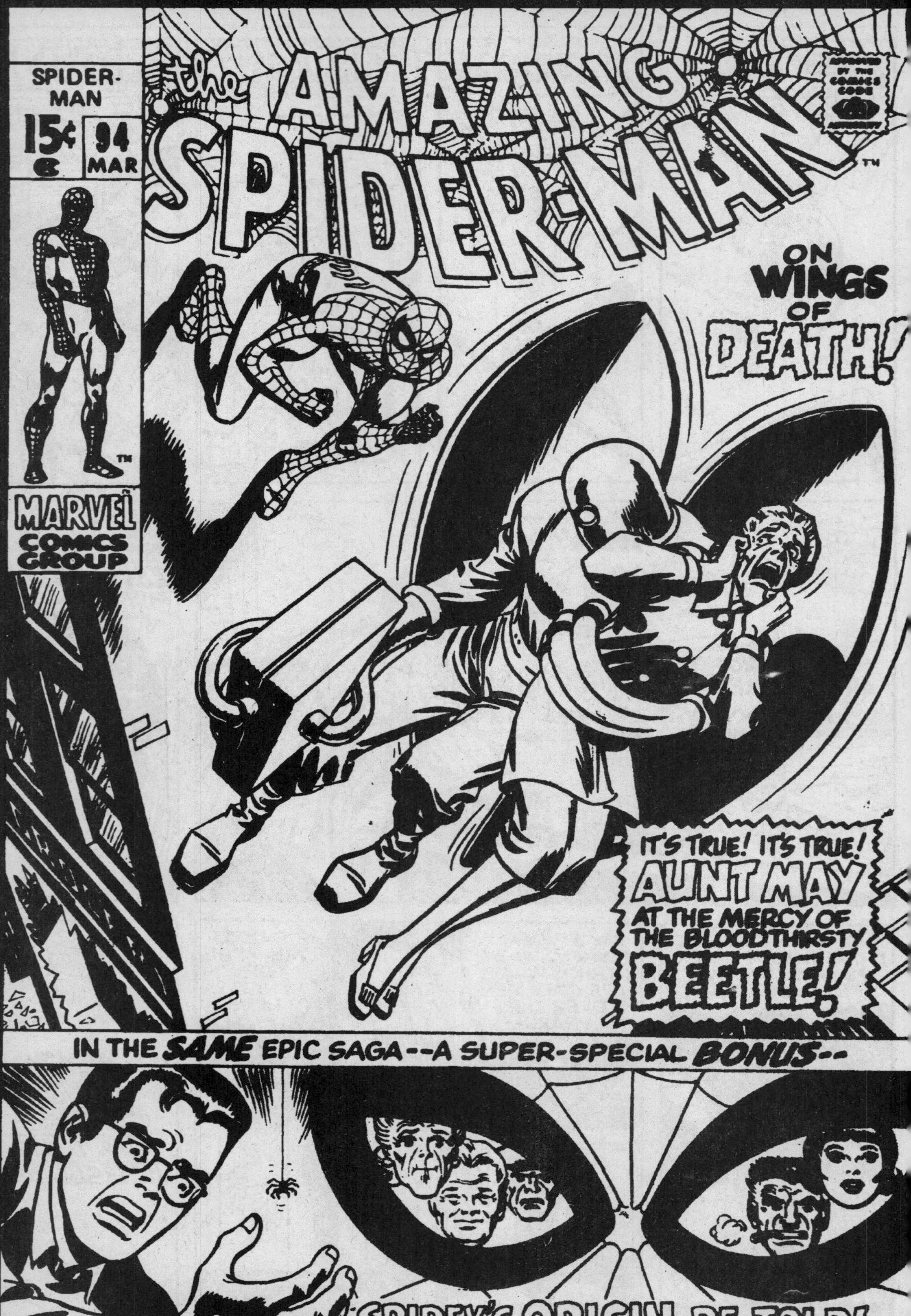

SPIDER-MAN
15¢
94
MAR
THE AMAZING SPIDER-MAN
MARVEL COMICS GROUP
ON WINGS OF DEATH!
IT'S TRUE! IT'S TRUE! AUNT MAY AT THE MERCY OF THE BLOODTHIRSTY BEETLE!
IN THE SAME EPIC SAGA--A SUPER-SPECIAL BONUS--
SPIDEY'S ORIGIN RE-TOLD!

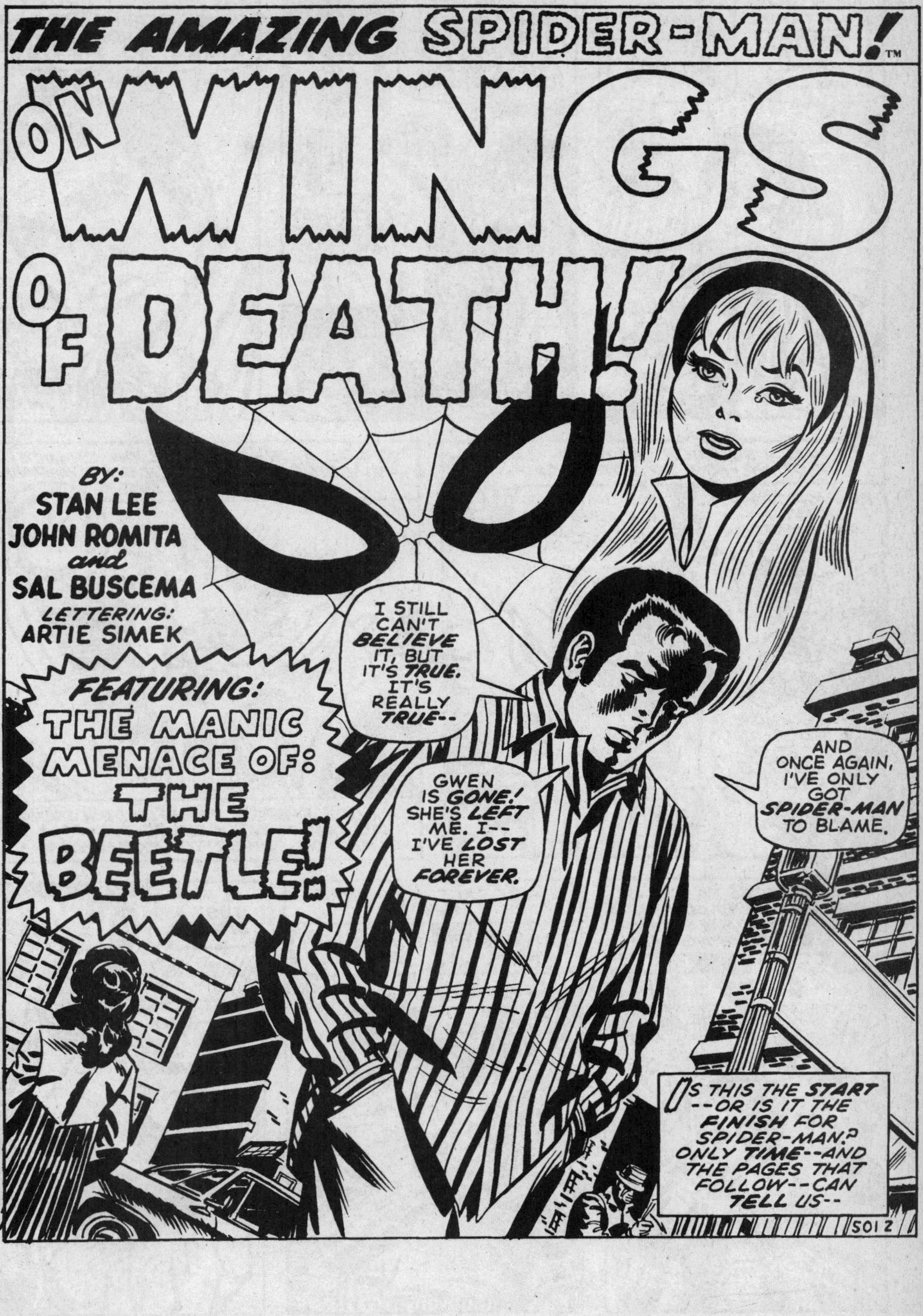

THE AMAZING SPIDER-MAN!™
ON WINGS OF DEATH!
BY: STAN LEE JOHN ROMITA and SAL BUSCEMA LETTERING: ARTIE SIMEK
FEATURING: THE MANIC MENACE OF: THE BEETLE!
I STILL CAN'T BELIEVE IT, BUT IT'S TRUE. IT'S REALLY TRUE--
GWEN IS GONE! SHE'S LEFT ME. I-- I'VE LOST HER FOREVER.
AND ONCE AGAIN, I'VE ONLY GOT SPIDER-MAN TO BLAME.
IS THIS THE START --OR IS IT THE FINISH FOR SPIDER-MAN? ONLY TIME--AND THE PAGES THAT FOLLOW--CAN TELL US--

EVERYTHING *BAD* THAT'S EVER HAPPENED TO ME--ALL OF MY *LIFE*--

WAS BECAUSE OF MY *SECRET IDENTITY*...

--BECAUSE OF-- *SPIDER-MAN.*

BUT, I WASN'T *BORN* WITH SPIDER POWERS--I WASN'T *BORN* WEARING AN ICKY *COSTUME*...

I DON'T *HAVE* TO STAY THIS WAY.

NOTHING'S *STOPPING* ME FROM GIVING IT ALL *UP.*

SOMETIMES--I ALMOST *HATE* TO THINK BACK--TO REMEMBER HOW IT *WAS*--WHEN IT ALL *STARTED*--

I NEVER DREAMED WHAT I WAS GETTING INTO..

"IT WAS A SCIENCE LECTURE--LIKE ANY OTHER--OR, SO I *THOUGHT*--"

RADIOACTIVITY... WHAT A *FASCINATING* SUBJECT.

NOW, IF YOU'LL ALL GIVE ME YOUR CLOSE ATTENTION--

WE KNOW SO *MUCH*, YET SO *LITTLE* ABOUT IT.

"IT WAS A ONE IN A *BILLION* CHANCE-- AN ACCIDENT THAT *COULDN'T* HAPPEN-- AND YET--IT *DID*."

"A LONE *SPIDER*, SILENTLY DESCENDING, WAS UNWITTINGLY SUBJECTED TO A *BLAST* OF POWERFUL *RADIATION*--"

"AND, MINUTES LATER, AS IT KEPT SLOWLY *LOWERING* ITSELF ON A THIN STRAND OF *WEBBING*--"

"I FELT SOMETHING *BITE* ME--"

OWW! WHAT THE--?

SOMETHING *BIT* ME.

THWAK

IT WAS JUST A *SPIDER.*

BUT--WHY DO I FEEL SO-- *STRANGE?*

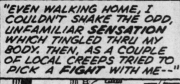

"EVEN WALKING HOME, I COULDN'T SHAKE THE ODD, UNFAMILIAR *SENSATION* WHICH TINGLED THRU MY BODY. THEN, AS A COUPLE OF LOCAL CREEPS TRIED TO PICK A *FIGHT* WITH ME--"

HERE'S SOMETHIN' *FOR YA,* PUNY PARKER.

I--HARDLY *FELT* IT.

CAN'T BECOME A *PUNCHING BAG.* I'VE GOT TO FIGHT *BACK*-- SOMEHOW.

BT5K!

HEY--

TAKE *OFF,* MAN. NOBODY CAN PUNCH LIKE *THAT!*

I--SNAPPED A *LAMP-POST*--WITH MY BARE *FIST!*

BUT HOW? *HOW?*

WHAT'S *HAPPENING* TO ME?

"I WAS SO *SHAKEN* BY WHAT HAPPENED, THAT I DIDN'T HEAR AN APPROACHING *CAR* AS I STEPPED OFF THE CURB --UNTIL--"

HE CAN'T *STOP* IN TIME!

HAVE TO *JUMP* FOR SAFETY!

I *MADE* IT.

BUT--HOW DID I JUMP SO *HIGH?*

AND HOW CAN I *CLING* TO THE SHEER WALL LIKE THIS?

I'M CLIMBING *UP*--EASY AS A *SPIDER!*

"*SPIDER!* THAT GAVE ME THE CLUE. I RACED BACK TO MY ROOM--"

IF THE SPIDER THAT *BIT* ME WAS *RADIO-ACTIVE*--

--IT AFFECTED MY *BLOOD.* I'VE GAINED HIS *POWERS!*

AND, THAT MEANS--

"IN THE DAYS THAT FOLLOWED, I DESIGNED MY *WEB-SHOOTER*--"

ALL I DO IS HIT THE *BUTTON.*

IT *WORKS.* I CAN SNARE *ANY-THING.*

AND MY *SPIDER POWER* GIVES ME SUPERHUMAN *AIM* AND *CONTROL.*

"I CAN'T REMEMBER *WHAT* MADE ME DO IT--BUT, BEFORE LONG, I HAD DE-SIGNED MYSELF A *COSTUME.*"

THERE MUST BE *SOME* WAY TO MAKE *SOME MONEY* OUT OF THIS.

FLAK!

3

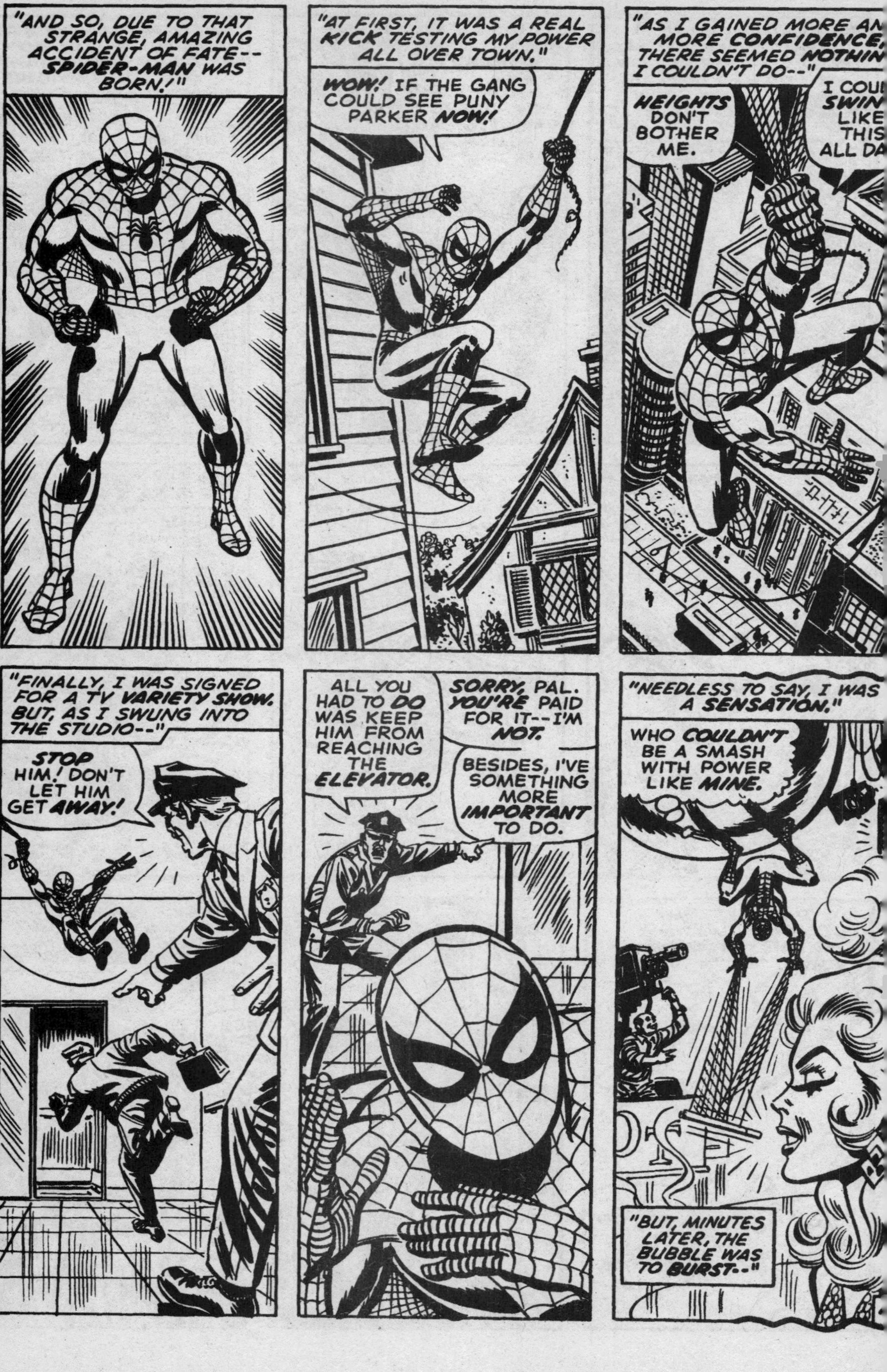
"AND SO, DUE TO THAT STRANGE, AMAZING ACCIDENT OF FATE-- SPIDER-MAN WAS BORN!"
"AT FIRST, IT WAS A REAL KICK TESTING MY POWER ALL OVER TOWN."
WOW! IF THE GANG COULD SEE PUNY PARKER NOW!
"AS I GAINED MORE AN MORE CONFIDENCE, THERE SEEMED NOTHIN I COULDN'T DO--"
HEIGHTS DON'T BOTHER ME.
I COUL SWIN LIKE THIS ALL DA
"FINALLY, I WAS SIGNED FOR A TV VARIETY SHOW. BUT, AS I SWUNG INTO THE STUDIO--"
STOP HIM! DON'T LET HIM GET AWAY!
ALL YOU HAD TO DO WAS KEEP HIM FROM REACHING THE ELEVATOR.
SORRY, PAL. YOU'RE PAID FOR IT--I'M NOT.
BESIDES, I'VE SOMETHING MORE IMPORTANT TO DO.
"NEEDLESS TO SAY, I WAS A SENSATION."
WHO COULDN'T BE A SMASH WITH POWER LIKE MINE.
"BUT, MINUTES LATER, THE BUBBLE WAS TO BURST--"

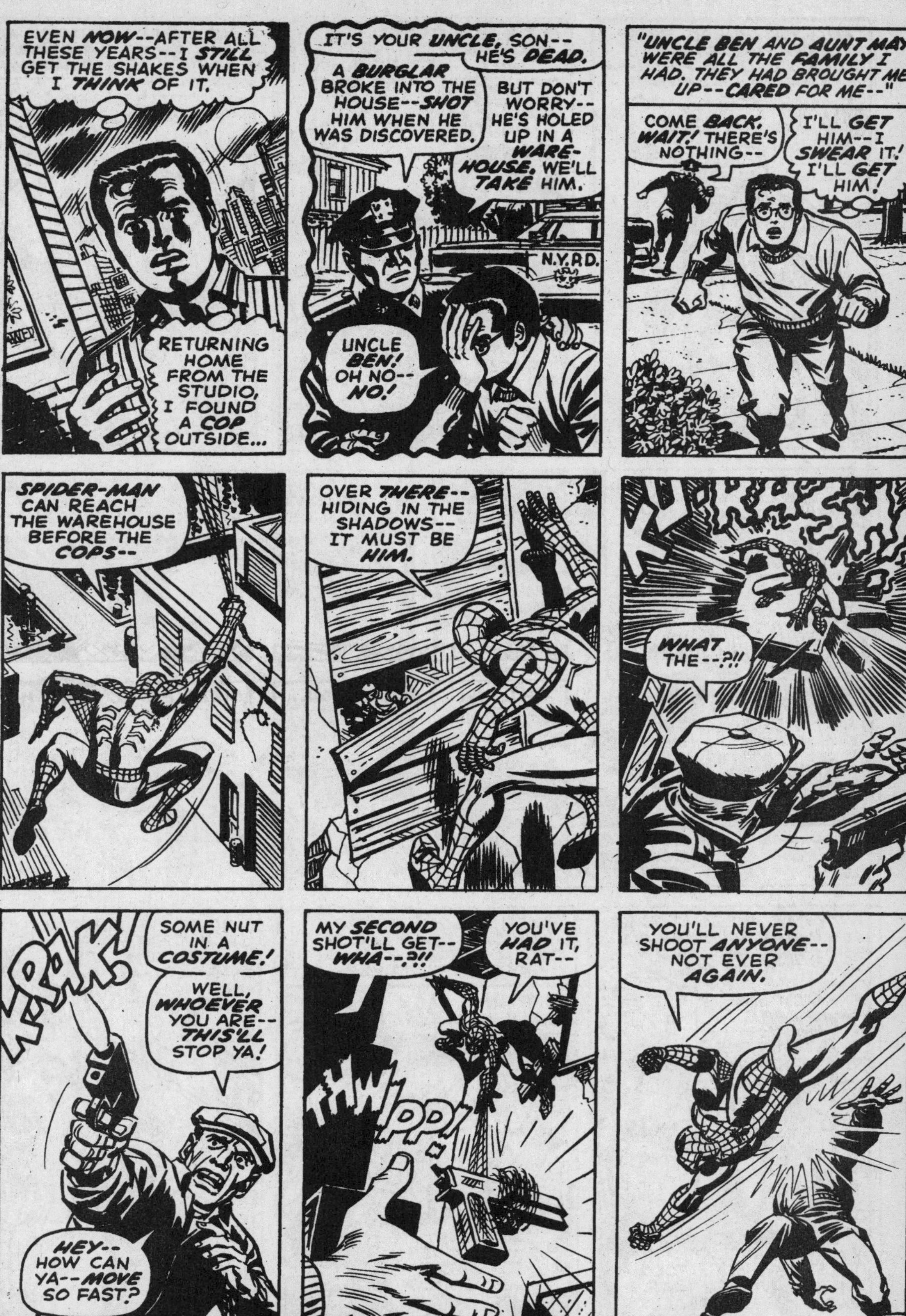
EVEN NOW--AFTER ALL THESE YEARS--I STILL GET THE SHAKES WHEN I THINK OF IT.
RETURNING HOME FROM THE STUDIO, I FOUND A COP OUTSIDE...
IT'S YOUR UNCLE, SON-- HE'S DEAD.
A BURGLAR BROKE INTO THE HOUSE--SHOT HIM WHEN HE WAS DISCOVERED.
BUT DON'T WORRY-- HE'S HOLED UP IN A WARE-HOUSE. WE'LL TAKE HIM.
N.Y.P.D.
UNCLE BEN! OH NO-- NO!
"UNCLE BEN AND AUNT MAY WERE ALL THE FAMILY I HAD. THEY HAD BROUGHT ME UP--CARED FOR ME--"
COME BACK. WAIT! THERE'S NOTHING--
I'LL GET HIM--I SWEAR IT! I'LL GET HIM!
SPIDER-MAN CAN REACH THE WAREHOUSE BEFORE THE COPS--
OVER THERE-- HIDING IN THE SHADOWS-- IT MUST BE HIM.
WHAT THE--?!!
K-RAK!
SOME NUT IN A COSTUME!
WELL, WHOEVER YOU ARE-- THIS'LL STOP YA!
HEY-- HOW CAN YA--MOVE SO FAST?
MY SECOND SHOT'LL GET-- WHA--?!!
YOU'VE HAD IT, RAT--
THWIPP!
YOU'LL NEVER SHOOT ANYONE-- NOT EVER AGAIN.
5

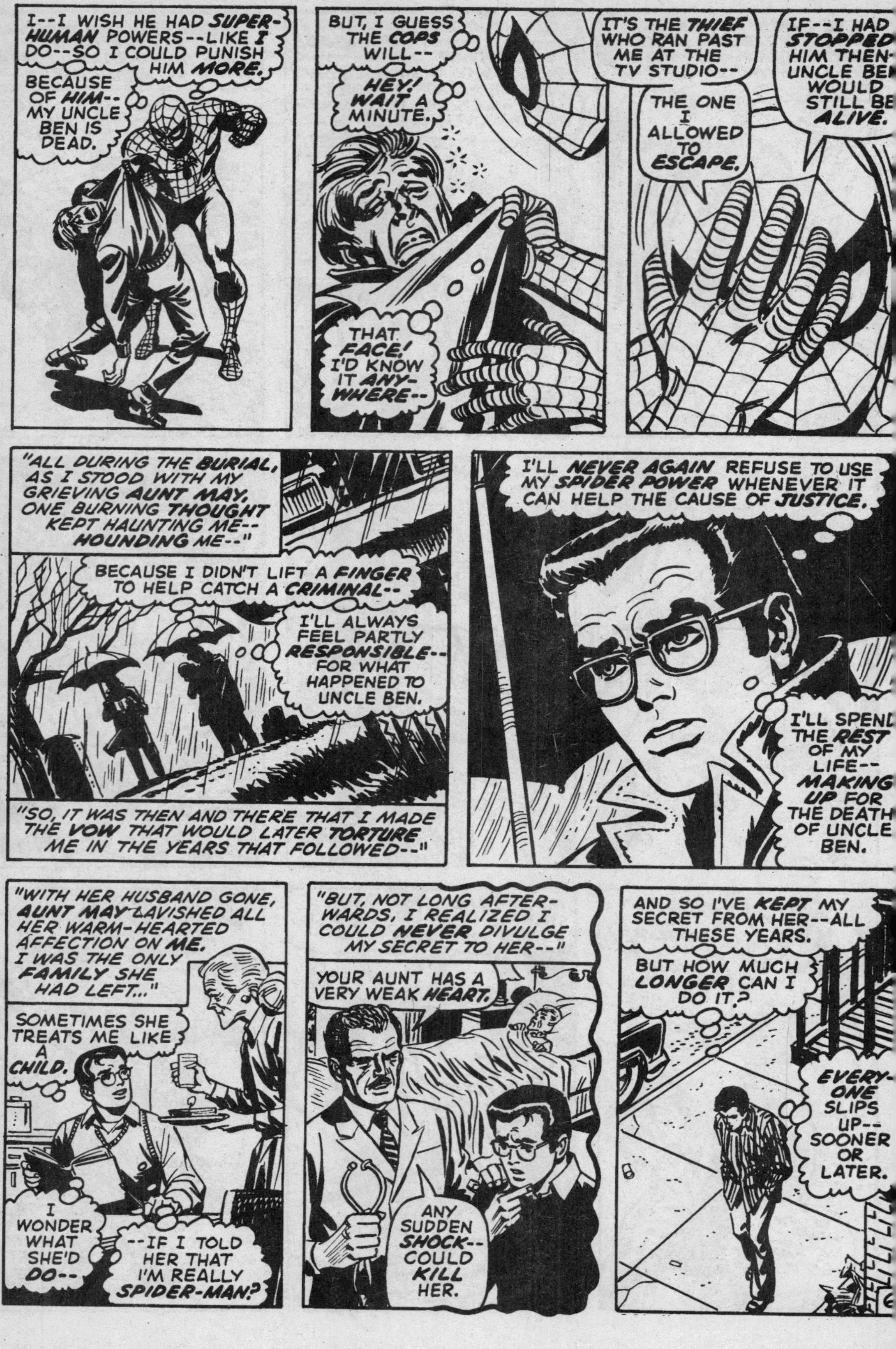
I--I WISH HE HAD SUPER-HUMAN POWERS--LIKE I DO--SO I COULD PUNISH HIM MORE.
BECAUSE OF HIM-- MY UNCLE BEN IS DEAD.
BUT, I GUESS THE COPS WILL--
HEY! WAIT A MINUTE.
THAT FACE! I'D KNOW IT ANY-WHERE--
IT'S THE THIEF WHO RAN PAST ME AT THE TV STUDIO--
THE ONE I ALLOWED TO ESCAPE.
IF--I HAD STOPPED HIM THEN-UNCLE BEN WOULD STILL BE ALIVE.
"ALL DURING THE BURIAL, AS I STOOD WITH MY GRIEVING AUNT MAY, ONE BURNING THOUGHT KEPT HAUNTING ME--HOUNDING ME--"
BECAUSE I DIDN'T LIFT A FINGER TO HELP CATCH A CRIMINAL--
I'LL ALWAYS FEEL PARTLY RESPONSIBLE-- FOR WHAT HAPPENED TO UNCLE BEN.
"SO, IT WAS THEN AND THERE THAT I MADE THE VOW THAT WOULD LATER TORTURE ME IN THE YEARS THAT FOLLOWED--"
I'LL NEVER AGAIN REFUSE TO USE MY SPIDER POWER WHENEVER IT CAN HELP THE CAUSE OF JUSTICE.
I'LL SPEND THE REST OF MY LIFE-- MAKING UP FOR THE DEATH OF UNCLE BEN.
"WITH HER HUSBAND GONE, AUNT MAY LAVISHED ALL HER WARM-HEARTED AFFECTION ON ME. I WAS THE ONLY FAMILY SHE HAD LEFT..."
SOMETIMES SHE TREATS ME LIKE A CHILD.
I WONDER WHAT SHE'D DO--
--IF I TOLD HER THAT I'M REALLY SPIDER-MAN?
"BUT, NOT LONG AFTER-WARDS, I REALIZED I COULD NEVER DIVULGE MY SECRET TO HER--"
YOUR AUNT HAS A VERY WEAK HEART.
ANY SUDDEN SHOCK-- COULD KILL HER.
AND SO I'VE KEPT MY SECRET FROM HER--ALL THESE YEARS.
BUT HOW MUCH LONGER CAN I DO IT?
EVERY-ONE SLIPS UP-- SOONER OR LATER.
6

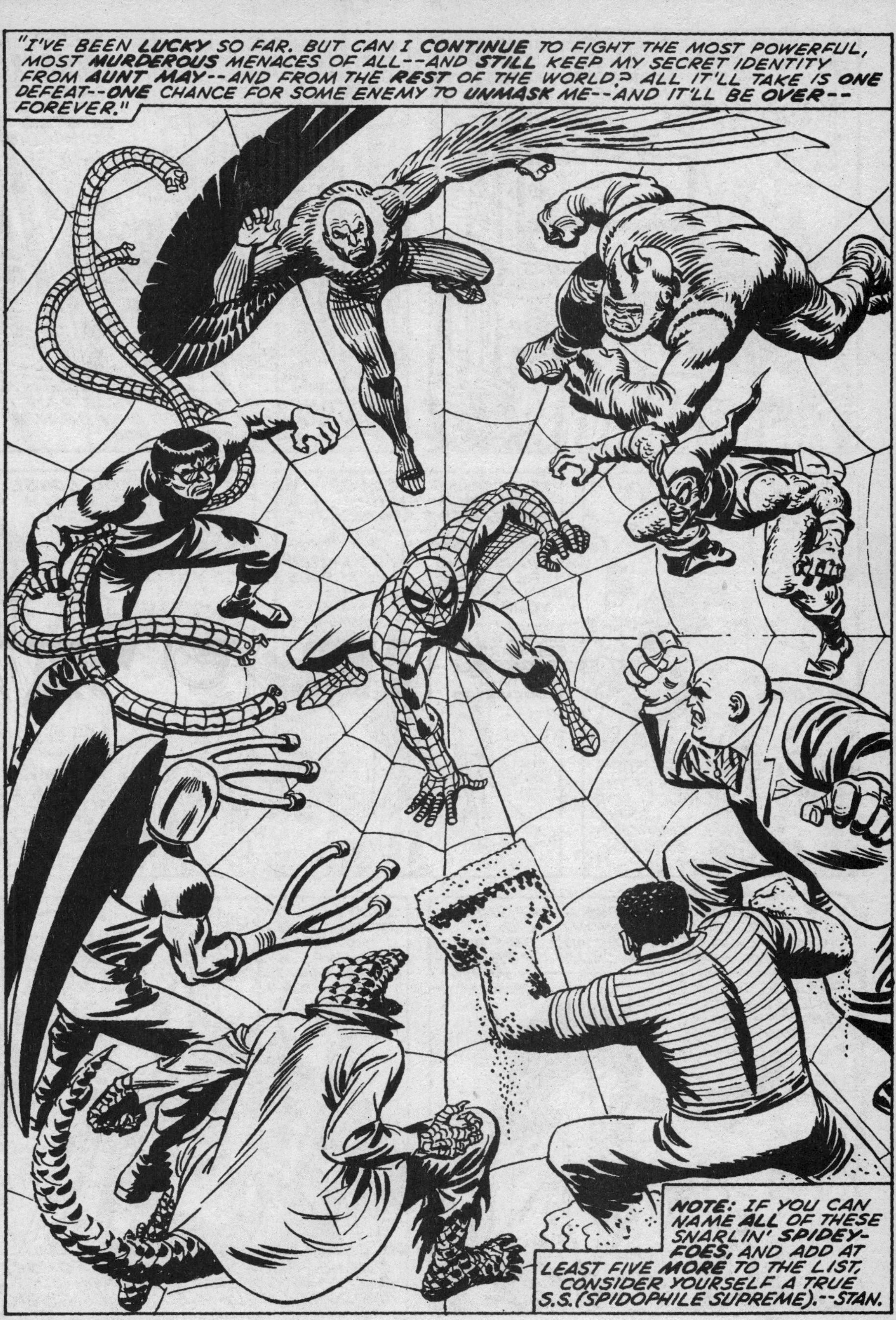

"I'VE BEEN LUCKY SO FAR. BUT CAN I CONTINUE TO FIGHT THE MOST POWERFUL, MOST MURDEROUS MENACES OF ALL--AND STILL KEEP MY SECRET IDENTITY FROM AUNT MAY--AND FROM THE REST OF THE WORLD? ALL IT'LL TAKE IS ONE DEFEAT--ONE CHANCE FOR SOME ENEMY TO UNMASK ME--AND IT'LL BE OVER--FOREVER."
NOTE: IF YOU CAN NAME ALL OF THESE SNARLIN' SPIDEY-FOES, AND ADD AT LEAST FIVE MORE TO THE LIST, CONSIDER YOURSELF A TRUE S.S. (SPIDOPHILE SUPREME).--STAN.

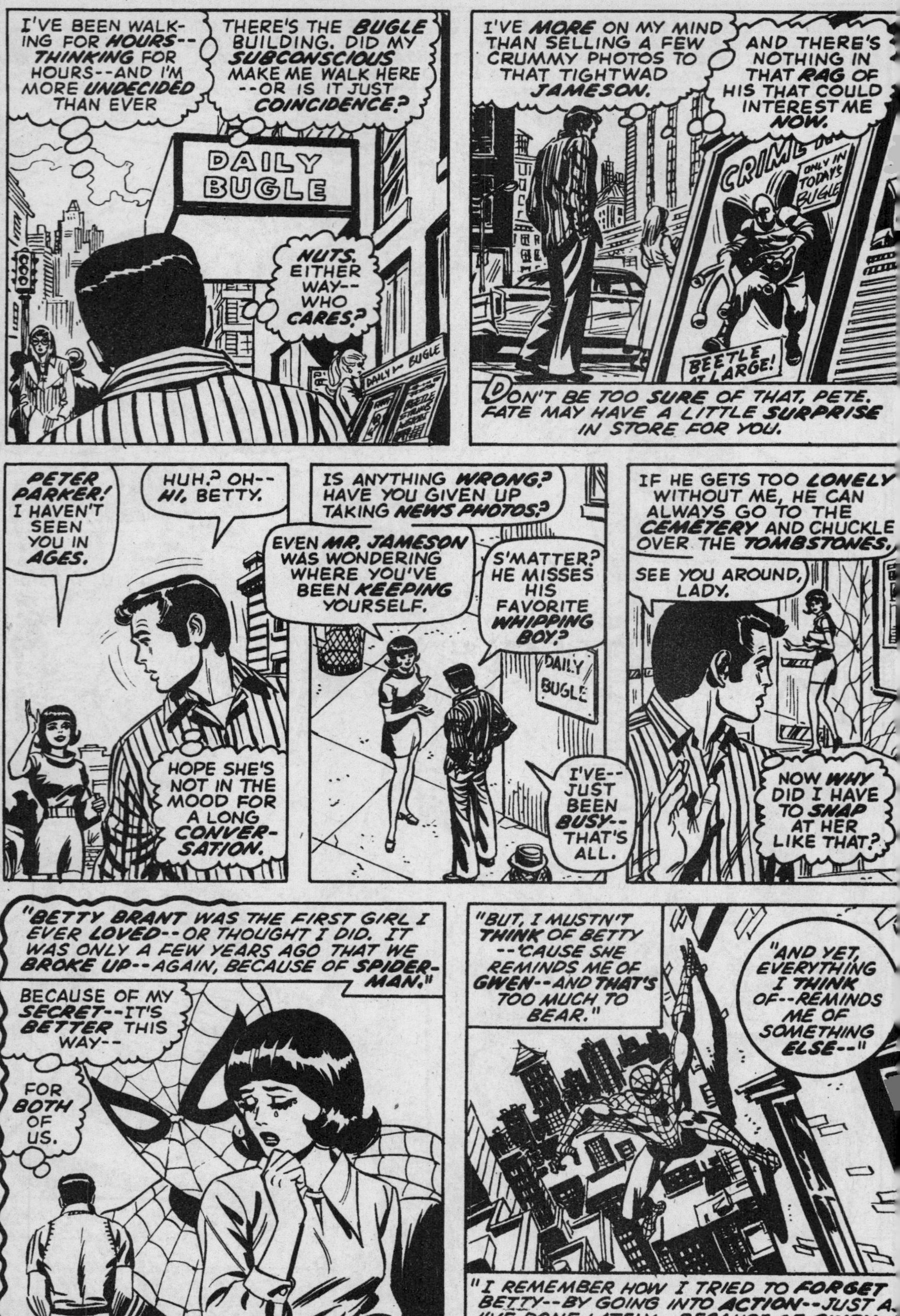
I'VE BEEN WALKING FOR HOURS--THINKING FOR HOURS--AND I'M MORE UNDECIDED THAN EVER
THERE'S THE BUGLE BUILDING. DID MY SUBCONSCIOUS MAKE ME WALK HERE--OR IS IT JUST COINCIDENCE?
DAILY BUGLE
NUTS. EITHER WAY--WHO CARES?
I'VE MORE ON MY MIND THAN SELLING A FEW CRUMMY PHOTOS TO THAT TIGHTWAD JAMESON.
AND THERE'S NOTHING IN THAT RAG OF HIS THAT COULD INTEREST ME NOW.
ONLY IN TODAY'S BUGLE
BEETLE AT LARGE!
DON'T BE TOO SURE OF THAT, PETE. FATE MAY HAVE A LITTLE SURPRISE IN STORE FOR YOU.
PETER PARKER! I HAVEN'T SEEN YOU IN AGES.
HUH? OH--HI, BETTY.
HOPE SHE'S NOT IN THE MOOD FOR A LONG CONVERSATION.
IS ANYTHING WRONG? HAVE YOU GIVEN UP TAKING NEWS PHOTOS?
EVEN MR. JAMESON WAS WONDERING WHERE YOU'VE BEEN KEEPING YOURSELF.
S'MATTER? HE MISSES HIS FAVORITE WHIPPING BOY?
DAILY BUGLE
I'VE--JUST BEEN BUSY--THAT'S ALL.
IF HE GETS TOO LONELY WITHOUT ME, HE CAN ALWAYS GO TO THE CEMETERY AND CHUCKLE OVER THE TOMBSTONES.
SEE YOU AROUND, LADY.
NOW WHY DID I HAVE TO SNAP AT HER LIKE THAT?
"BETTY BRANT WAS THE FIRST GIRL I EVER LOVED--OR THOUGHT I DID. IT WAS ONLY A FEW YEARS AGO THAT WE BROKE UP--AGAIN, BECAUSE OF SPIDER-MAN."
BECAUSE OF MY SECRET--IT'S BETTER THIS WAY--
FOR BOTH OF US.
"BUT, I MUSTN'T THINK OF BETTY--'CAUSE SHE REMINDS ME OF GWEN--AND THAT'S TOO MUCH TO BEAR."
"AND YET, EVERYTHING I THINK OF--REMINDS ME OF SOMETHING ELSE--"
"I REMEMBER HOW I TRIED TO FORGET BETTY--BY GOING INTO ACTION--JUST A I'VE DONE LATELY--BECAUSE OF GWEN..."

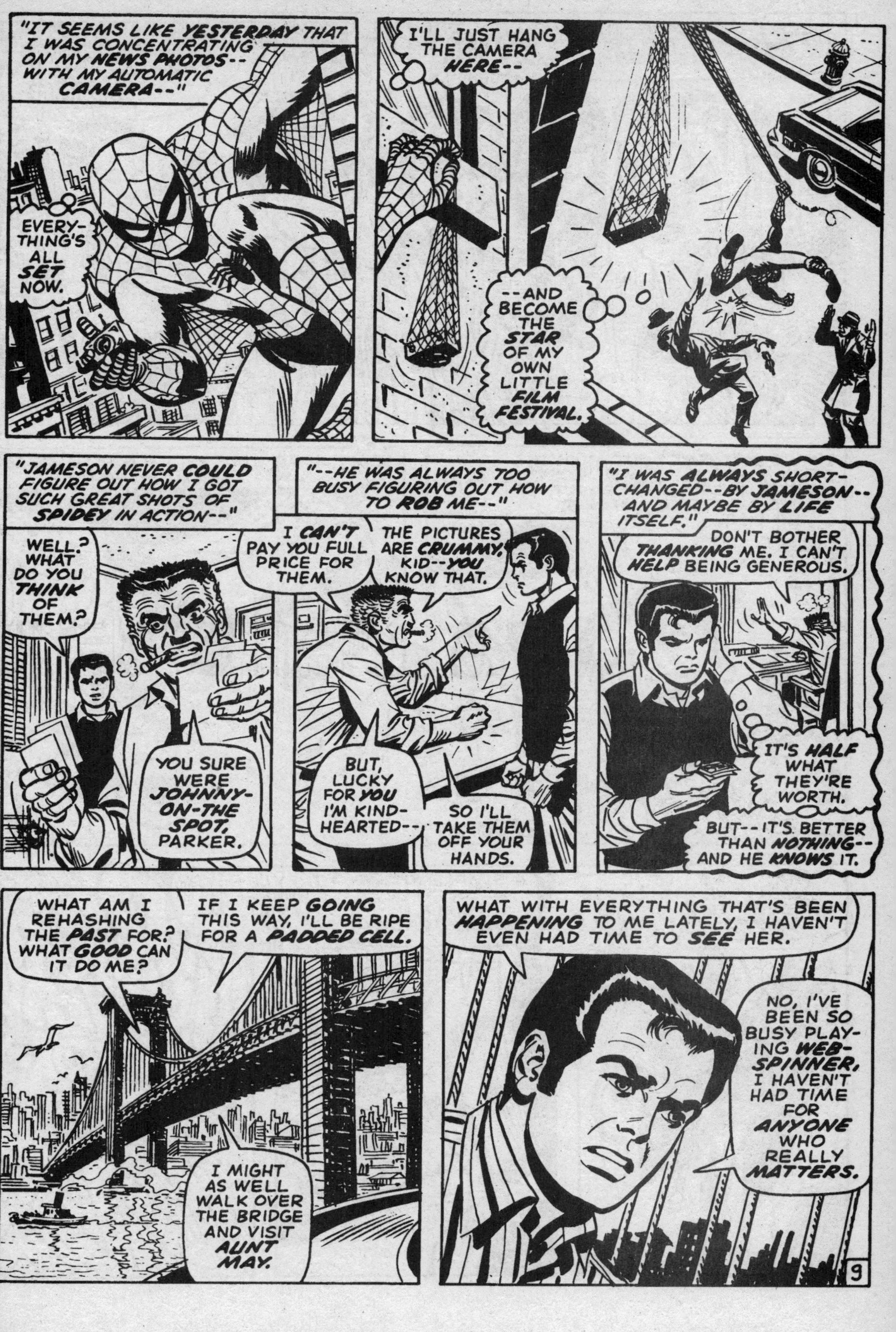
"IT SEEMS LIKE YESTERDAY THAT I WAS CONCENTRATING ON MY NEWS PHOTOS--WITH MY AUTOMATIC CAMERA--"
EVERYTHING'S ALL SET NOW.
I'LL JUST HANG THE CAMERA HERE--
--AND BECOME THE STAR OF MY OWN LITTLE FILM FESTIVAL.
"JAMESON NEVER COULD FIGURE OUT HOW I GOT SUCH GREAT SHOTS OF SPIDEY IN ACTION--"
WELL? WHAT DO YOU THINK OF THEM?
YOU SURE WERE JOHNNY-ON-THE-SPOT, PARKER.
"--HE WAS ALWAYS TOO BUSY FIGURING OUT HOW TO ROB ME--"
I CAN'T PAY YOU FULL PRICE FOR THEM.
THE PICTURES ARE CRUMMY, KID--YOU KNOW THAT.
BUT, LUCKY FOR YOU I'M KIND-HEARTED--
SO I'LL TAKE THEM OFF YOUR HANDS.
"I WAS ALWAYS SHORT-CHANGED--BY JAMESON--AND MAYBE BY LIFE ITSELF."
DON'T BOTHER THANKING ME. I CAN'T HELP BEING GENEROUS.
IT'S HALF WHAT THEY'RE WORTH.
BUT--IT'S BETTER THAN NOTHING--AND HE KNOWS IT.
WHAT AM I REHASHING THE PAST FOR? WHAT GOOD CAN IT DO ME?
IF I KEEP GOING THIS WAY, I'LL BE RIPE FOR A PADDED CELL.
I MIGHT AS WELL WALK OVER THE BRIDGE AND VISIT AUNT MAY.
WHAT WITH EVERYTHING THAT'S BEEN HAPPENING TO ME LATELY, I HAVEN'T EVEN HAD TIME TO SEE HER.
NO, I'VE BEEN SO BUSY PLAYING WEB-SPINNER, I HAVEN'T HAD TIME FOR ANYONE WHO REALLY MATTERS.
9

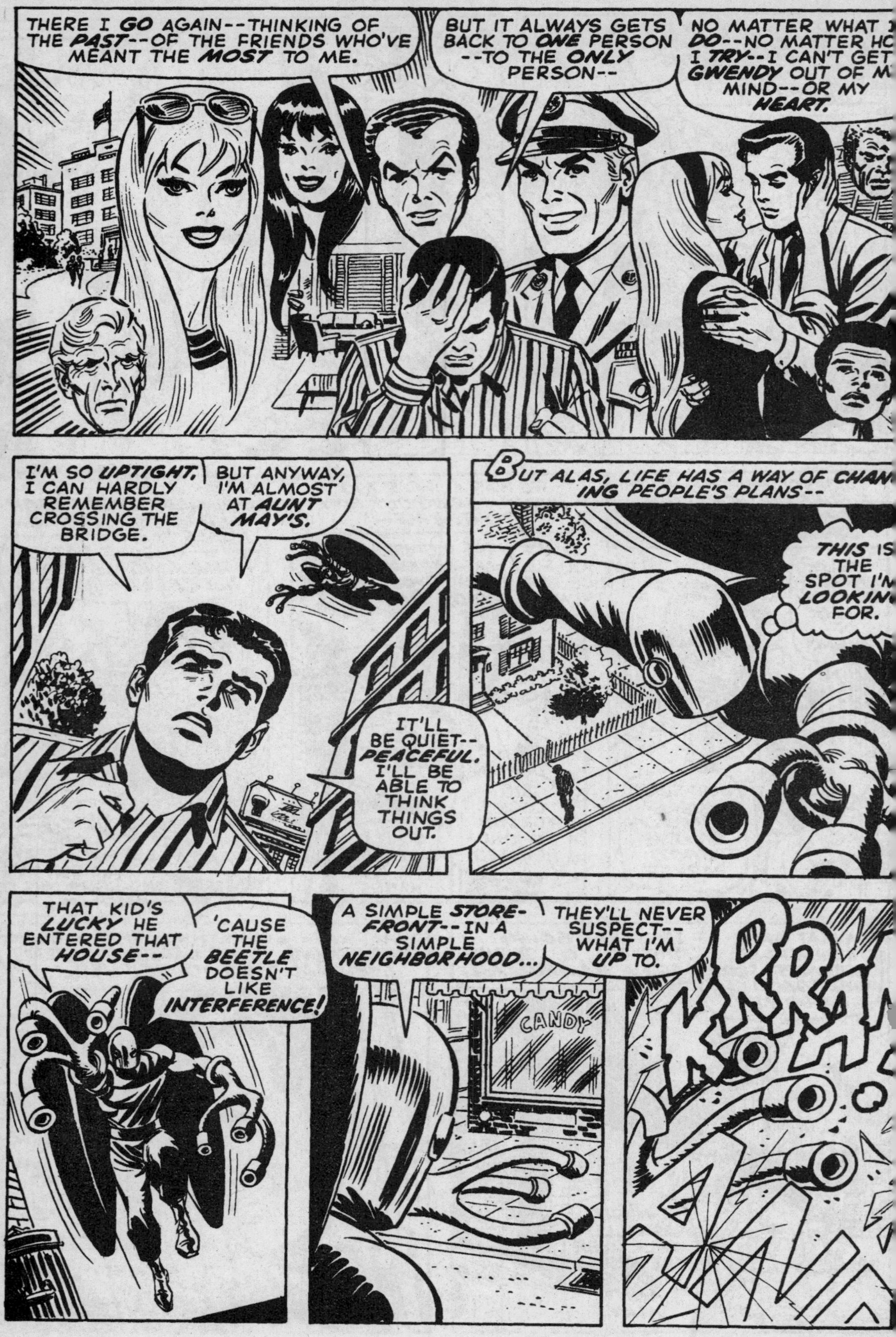
THERE I GO AGAIN--THINKING OF THE PAST--OF THE FRIENDS WHO'VE MEANT THE MOST TO ME.
BUT IT ALWAYS GETS BACK TO ONE PERSON --TO THE ONLY PERSON--
NO MATTER WHAT I DO--NO MATTER HOW I TRY--I CAN'T GET GWENDY OUT OF MY MIND--OR MY HEART.
I'M SO UPTIGHT, I CAN HARDLY REMEMBER CROSSING THE BRIDGE.
BUT ANYWAY, I'M ALMOST AT AUNT MAY'S.
IT'LL BE QUIET--PEACEFUL. I'LL BE ABLE TO THINK THINGS OUT.
BUT ALAS, LIFE HAS A WAY OF CHANGING PEOPLE'S PLANS--
THIS IS THE SPOT I'M LOOKING FOR.
THAT KID'S LUCKY HE ENTERED THAT HOUSE--
'CAUSE THE BEETLE DOESN'T LIKE INTERFERENCE!
A SIMPLE STORE-FRONT--IN A SIMPLE NEIGHBORHOOD...
THEY'LL NEVER SUSPECT--WHAT I'M UP TO.
CANDY
KRRA

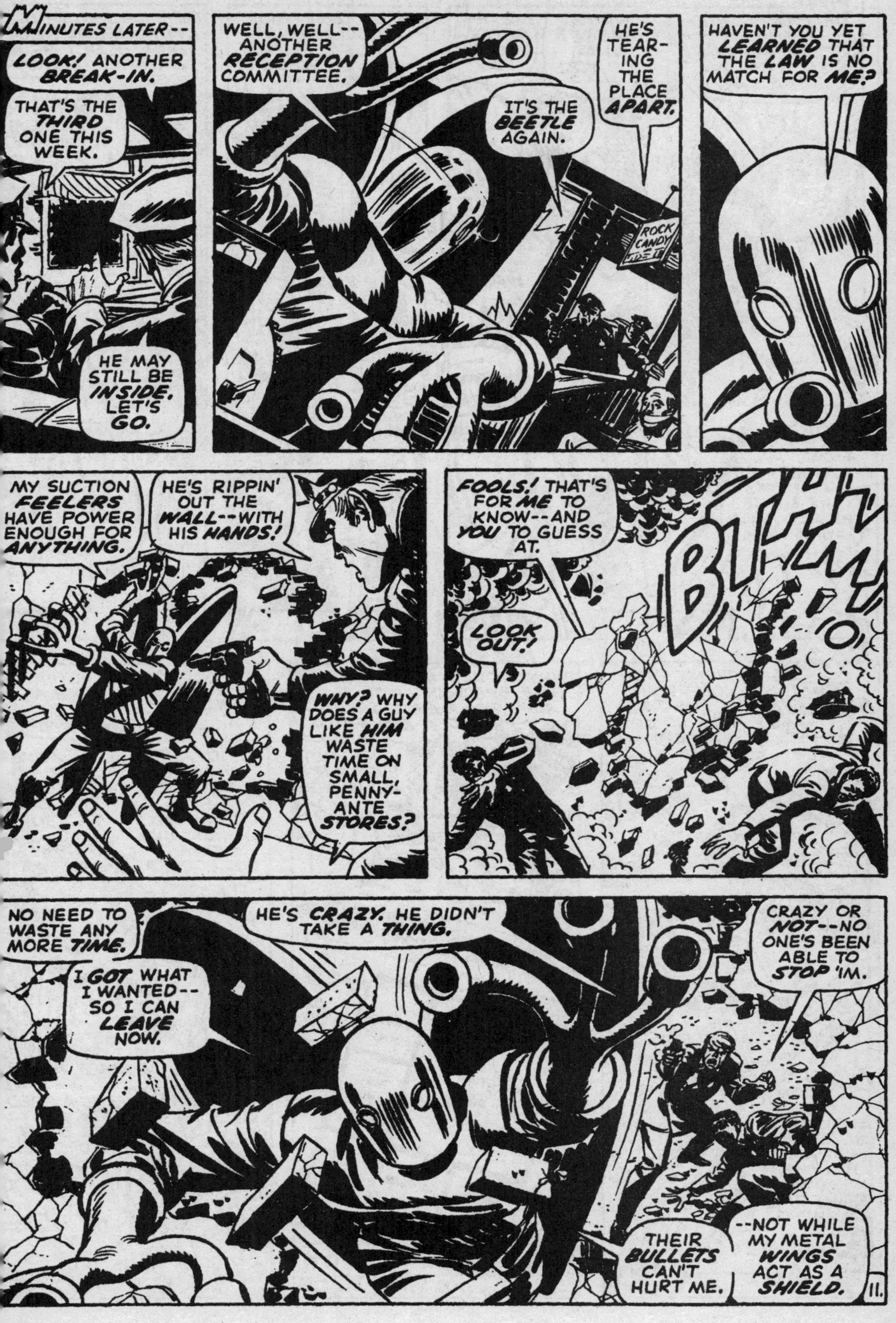
MINUTES LATER--
LOOK! ANOTHER BREAK-IN.
THAT'S THE THIRD ONE THIS WEEK.
HE MAY STILL BE INSIDE. LET'S GO.
WELL, WELL-- ANOTHER RECEPTION COMMITTEE.
HE'S TEARING THE PLACE APART.
IT'S THE BEETLE AGAIN.
ROCK CANDY
HAVEN'T YOU YET LEARNED THAT THE LAW IS NO MATCH FOR ME?
MY SUCTION FEELERS HAVE POWER ENOUGH FOR ANYTHING.
HE'S RIPPIN' OUT THE WALL--WITH HIS HANDS!
WHY? WHY DOES A GUY LIKE HIM WASTE TIME ON SMALL, PENNY-ANTE STORES?
FOOLS! THAT'S FOR ME TO KNOW--AND YOU TO GUESS AT.
LOOK OUT!
BTHOOM
NO NEED TO WASTE ANY MORE TIME.
I GOT WHAT I WANTED-- SO I CAN LEAVE NOW.
HE'S CRAZY. HE DIDN'T TAKE A THING.
CRAZY OR NOT--NO ONE'S BEEN ABLE TO STOP 'IM.
THEIR BULLETS CAN'T HURT ME.
--NOT WHILE MY METAL WINGS ACT AS A SHIELD.

MEANWHILE--

I HEAR *VOICES*, SO I KNOW SHE'S *IN*.

IT SOUNDS LIKE *MRS. WATSON*. SHE MUST BE *VISITING* AUNT MAY.

WHO'S *THERE?* WHAT DO YOU W--?

OH-- PETER-- IT'S *YOU!*

SHE SOUNDS *FRIGHTENED.* WHAT CAN BE *WRONG?*

PETER, DEAR--YOU SHOULD HAVE *CALLED*, TO TELL US YOU WERE *COMING.*

WHY, AUNT MAY? WHY DO YOU *SEEM* SO *NERVOUS?*

YOU JUST GAVE US A *START*, DEAR-- THAT'S ALL.

OH, TELL HIM THE *TRUTH*, MAY.

IT'S THAT HORRIBLE *COSTUMED MENACE* WHO'S BEEN TERRORIZING THE NEIGHBORHOOD.

IT'S ALL *HERE*-- IN THE *PAPER.*

WHO CAN IT *BE?* I HAVEN'T EVEN *LOOKED* AT A PAPER IN DAYS.

MAY I *SEE* IT, MRS. WATSON?

THE *BEETLE!*

I DIDN'T EVEN KNOW HE WAS OUT OF *JAIL*. HE'S NO ONE TO KID *AROUND* WITH.

DAILY BUGLE
BEETLE STRIKES
SNIPERS MENACED

MAP OF

YOU SHOULDN'T HAVE *TOLD* HIM, ANNA. YOU *KNOW* HOW *SENSITIVE* PETER IS. NOW HE'S ALL *UPSET.*

WHY WOULD *HE* WASTE TIME BREAKING INTO A *LAUNDRY*-- A *BIKE SHOP*-- AND A *BAKERY*--

--AND NOT EVEN *TAKE* ANYTHING?

...ICE PHOTOGRAPHED AT RECENT HOLD... ...P BELOW SHOWS LOCATION OF BREAK-INS

BEETLE ATTACKS NUMBERED IN ORDER

1ST NATIONAL BANK		
	LAUNDRY	①
SMITH IMPORTING CO. BUILDING	BIKE SHOP	②
	BAKERY	③
DRESS SHOP	GROCERY	CANDY STORE

...ICE BAFFLED BY... ...TERN

YOU LOOK *TIRED*, PETER. WHY DON'T YOU TAKE A *NAP*--WHILE I FIX YOU A NICE *CHICKEN STEW?*

AND DON'T WORRY ABOUT THE *BEETLE*, DEAR. HE ONLY ATTACKS *STORES*-- NOT HOUSES.

SHE'LL *NEVER* STOP THINKING OF ME A... A FRAIL, TIMID MILKSOP.

BUT, MAYBE IT'S JUST AS *WELL.*

THAT'S A GOOD *IDEA*, AUNT MAY. I *AM* KIND OF TIRED.

THE BEETLE'S THE *LEAST* OF MY *WORRIES* NOW.

BUGLE! ...STRIKES!

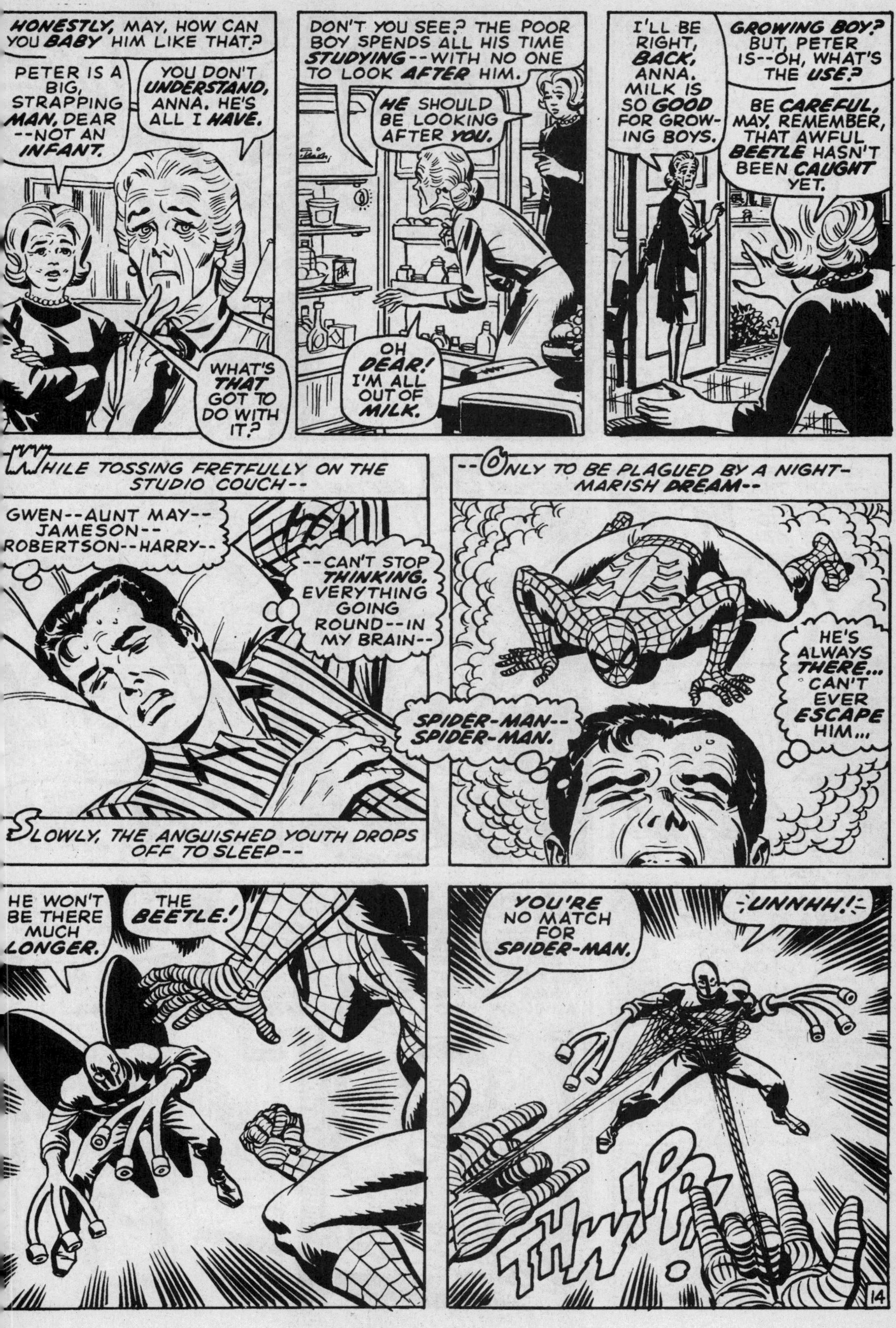
HONESTLY, MAY, HOW CAN YOU BABY HIM LIKE THAT?
PETER IS A BIG, STRAPPING MAN, DEAR --NOT AN INFANT.
YOU DON'T UNDERSTAND, ANNA. HE'S ALL I HAVE.
WHAT'S THAT GOT TO DO WITH IT?
DON'T YOU SEE? THE POOR BOY SPENDS ALL HIS TIME STUDYING--WITH NO ONE TO LOOK AFTER HIM.
HE SHOULD BE LOOKING AFTER YOU.
OH DEAR! I'M ALL OUT OF MILK.
I'LL BE RIGHT, BACK, ANNA. MILK IS SO GOOD FOR GROWING BOYS.
GROWING BOY? BUT, PETER IS--OH, WHAT'S THE USE?
BE CAREFUL, MAY. REMEMBER, THAT AWFUL BEETLE HASN'T BEEN CAUGHT YET.
WHILE TOSSING FRETFULLY ON THE STUDIO COUCH--
GWEN--AUNT MAY--JAMESON--ROBERTSON--HARRY--
--CAN'T STOP THINKING. EVERYTHING GOING ROUND--IN MY BRAIN--
SLOWLY, THE ANGUISHED YOUTH DROPS OFF TO SLEEP--
--ONLY TO BE PLAGUED BY A NIGHT-MARISH DREAM--
SPIDER-MAN--SPIDER-MAN.
HE'S ALWAYS THERE... CAN'T EVER ESCAPE HIM...
HE WON'T BE THERE MUCH LONGER.
THE BEETLE!
YOU'RE NO MATCH FOR SPIDER-MAN.
UNNHH!
THWIPP!
14

MY *WEBBING*-- TURNING INTO *CHAINS!*

I--I'M *TRAPPED!*

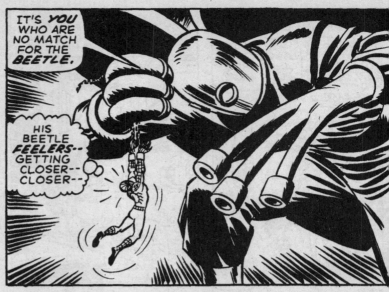

IT'S *YOU* WHO ARE NO *MATCH* FOR THE *BEETLE.*

HIS BEETLE *FEELERS*-- GETTING CLOSER-- CLOSER--

YOU NEVER THOUGHT THAT *I* WOULD BE THE ONE TO *FINISH* YOU.

I--THE *BEETLE.*

THE *BEETLE!*

THE *BEETLE!*

THE *BEETLE!*

PETER-- WAKE *UP.*

THE *BEETLE*-- THE *BEETLE!*

YES--THAT'S WHAT I'VE BEEN TRYING TO *TELL* YOU--

YOUR *AUNT MAY*-- WAS *CAPTURED* BY THE *BEETLE!*

WHAT?

LISTEN-- IT'S ON THE TV *NEWS* RIGHT *NOW*--

--DEFYING THE POLICE IN A LOCAL GROCERY STORE, THE METAL-WINGED *BEETLE* IS STILL HOLDING HIS *HOSTAGE,* INDENTIFIED AS *MRS. MAY PARKER,* A WIDOW WHO LIVES AT--

MY DREAM WAS AN *OMEN:*--A *WARNING.* AUNT MAY WITH HER WEAK *HEART*--

PETER... *WAIT.* COME *BACK.* WHAT ON EARTH CAN *YOU* DO?

I CAN BE *THERE.* AND I *WILL.*

15

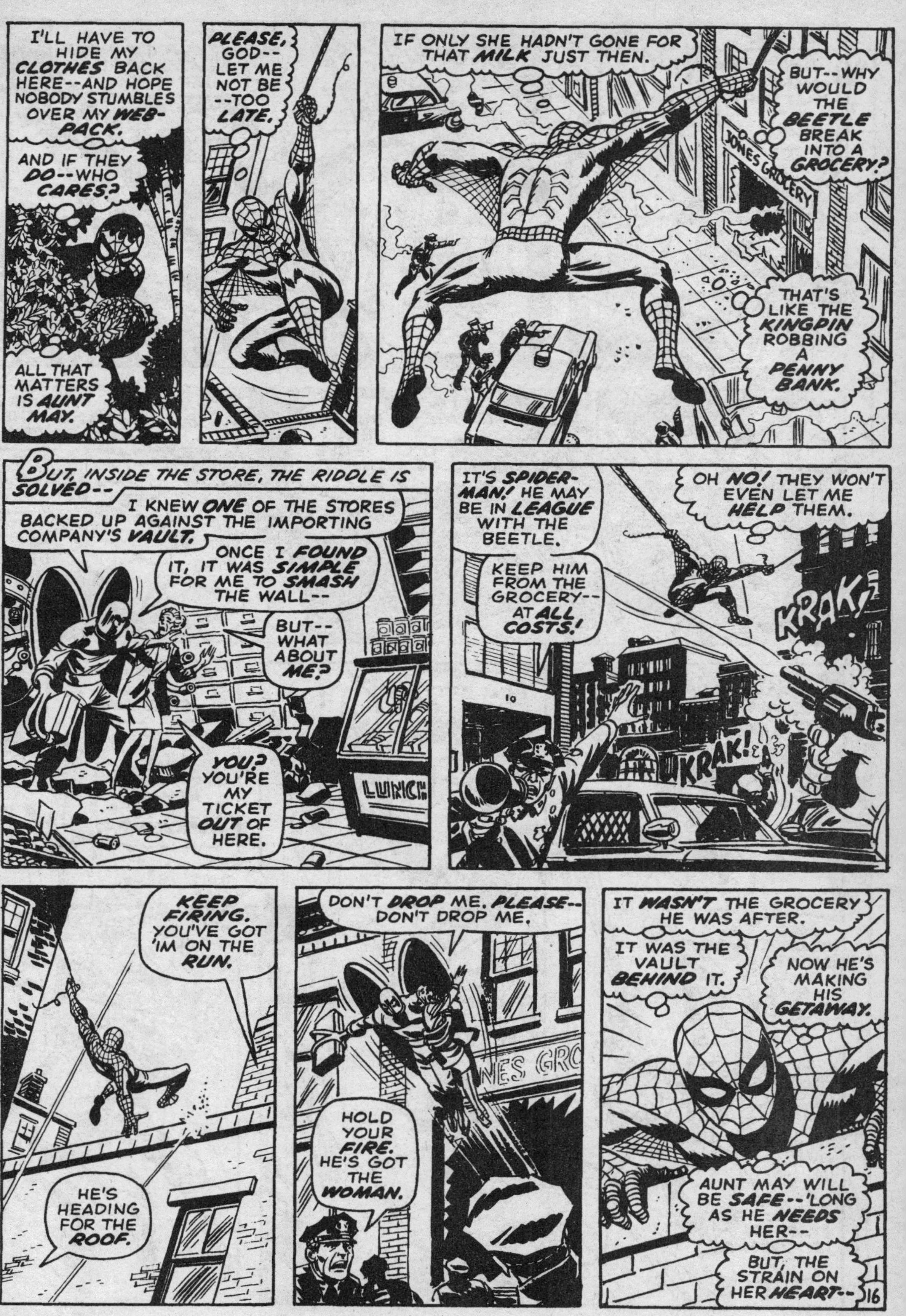
I'LL HAVE TO HIDE MY CLOTHES BACK HERE--AND HOPE NOBODY STUMBLES OVER MY WEB-PACK.
AND IF THEY DO--WHO CARES?
ALL THAT MATTERS IS AUNT MAY.
PLEASE, GOD--LET ME NOT BE--TOO LATE.
IF ONLY SHE HADN'T GONE FOR THAT MILK JUST THEN.
BUT--WHY WOULD THE BEETLE BREAK INTO A GROCERY?
JONES GROCERY
THAT'S LIKE THE KINGPIN ROBBING A PENNY BANK.
BUT, INSIDE THE STORE, THE RIDDLE IS SOLVED--
I KNEW ONE OF THE STORES BACKED UP AGAINST THE IMPORTING COMPANY'S VAULT.
ONCE I FOUND IT, IT WAS SIMPLE FOR ME TO SMASH THE WALL--
BUT--WHAT ABOUT ME?
YOU? YOU'RE MY TICKET OUT OF HERE.
LUNCH
IT'S SPIDER-MAN! HE MAY BE IN LEAGUE WITH THE BEETLE.
KEEP HIM FROM THE GROCERY--AT ALL COSTS!
OH NO! THEY WON'T EVEN LET ME HELP THEM.
KRAK!
KRAK!
KEEP FIRING. YOU'VE GOT 'IM ON THE RUN.
HE'S HEADING FOR THE ROOF.
DON'T DROP ME. PLEASE--DON'T DROP ME.
NES GRO
HOLD YOUR FIRE. HE'S GOT THE WOMAN.
IT WASN'T THE GROCERY HE WAS AFTER.
IT WAS THE VAULT BEHIND IT.
NOW HE'S MAKING HIS GETAWAY.
AUNT MAY WILL BE SAFE--'LONG AS HE NEEDS HER--
BUT, THE STRAIN ON HER HEART--
16

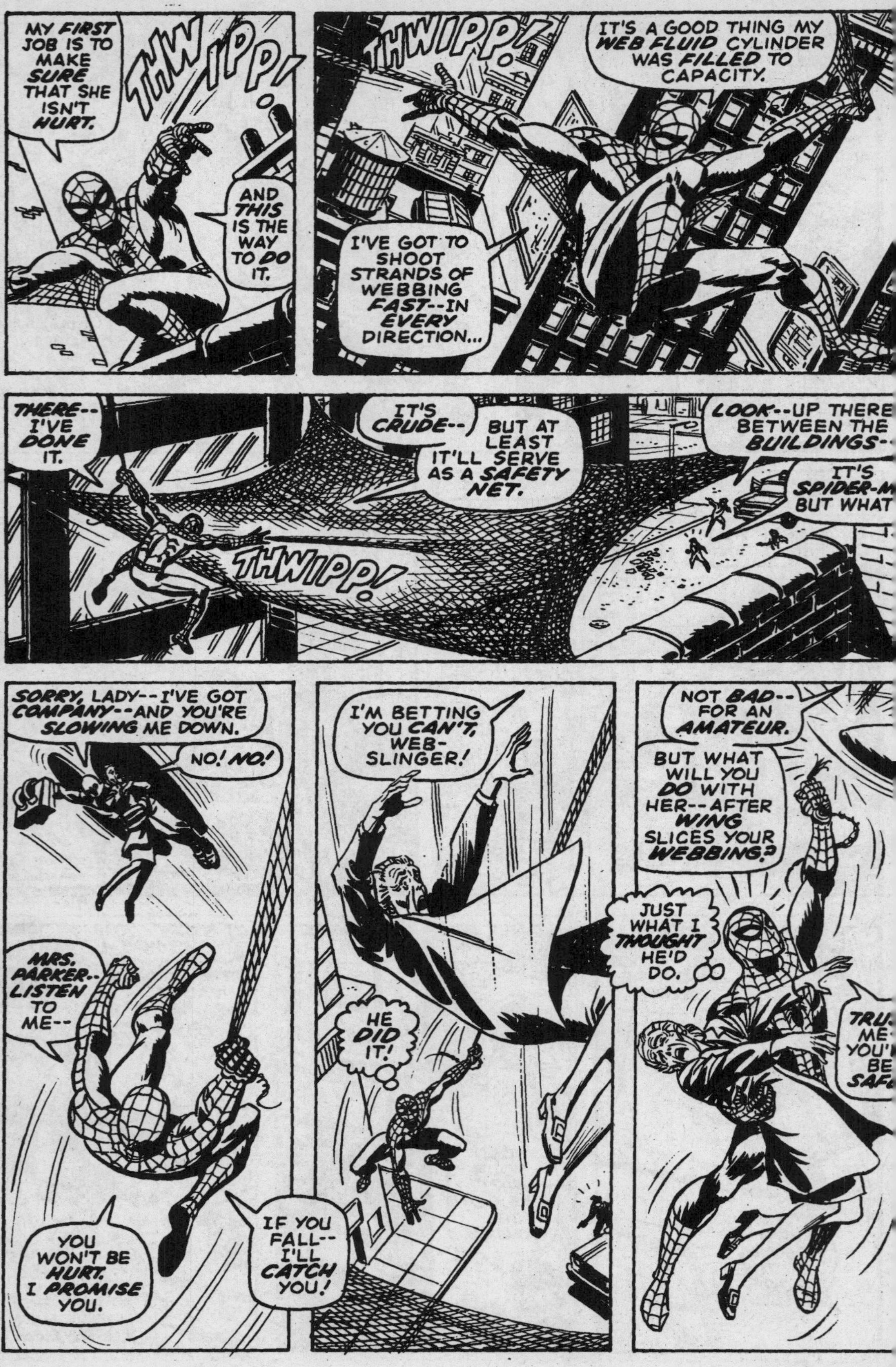

MY FIRST JOB IS TO MAKE SURE THAT SHE ISN'T HURT.
THWIPP!
AND THIS IS THE WAY TO DO IT.
THWIPP!
IT'S A GOOD THING MY WEB FLUID CYLINDER WAS FILLED TO CAPACITY.
I'VE GOT TO SHOOT STRANDS OF WEBBING FAST--IN EVERY DIRECTION...
THERE--I'VE DONE IT.
IT'S CRUDE--
BUT AT LEAST IT'LL SERVE AS A SAFETY NET.
THWIPP!
LOOK--UP THERE BETWEEN THE BUILDINGS--
SORRY, LADY--I'VE GOT COMPANY--AND YOU'RE SLOWING ME DOWN.
NO! NO!
MRS. PARKER--LISTEN TO ME--
YOU WON'T BE HURT. I PROMISE YOU.
I'M BETTING YOU CAN'T, WEB-SLINGER!
IF YOU FALL--I'LL CATCH YOU!
HE DID IT!
NOT BAD--FOR AN AMATEUR.
BUT WHAT WILL YOU DO WITH HER--AFTER WING SLICES YOUR WEBBING?
JUST WHAT I THOUGHT HE'D DO.

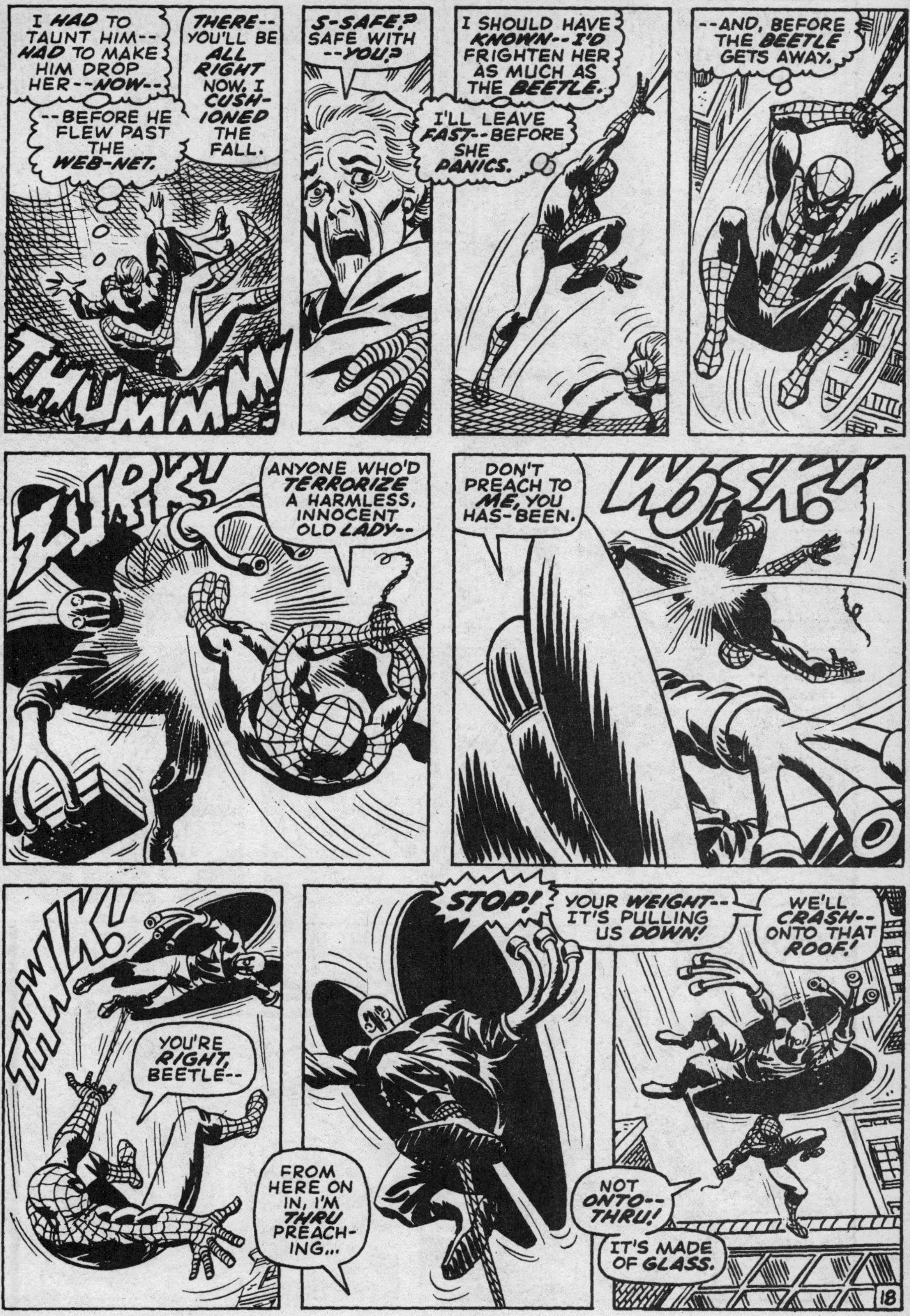

I HAD TO TAUNT HIM-- HAD TO MAKE HIM DROP HER--NOW--
--BEFORE HE FLEW PAST THE WEB-NET.
THERE-- YOU'LL BE ALL RIGHT NOW. I CUSHIONED THE FALL.
THUMMM!
S-SAFE? SAFE WITH --YOU?
I SHOULD HAVE KNOWN--I'D FRIGHTEN HER AS MUCH AS THE BEETLE.
I'LL LEAVE FAST--BEFORE SHE PANICS.
--AND, BEFORE THE BEETLE GETS AWAY.
ZURK!
ANYONE WHO'D TERRORIZE A HARMLESS, INNOCENT OLD LADY--
DON'T PREACH TO ME, YOU HAS-BEEN.
WOSK!
THWK!
YOU'RE RIGHT, BEETLE--
FROM HERE ON IN, I'M THRU PREACHING...
STOP!
YOUR WEIGHT-- IT'S PULLING US DOWN!
WE'LL CRASH-- ONTO THAT ROOF!
NOT ONTO-- THRU!
IT'S MADE OF GLASS.

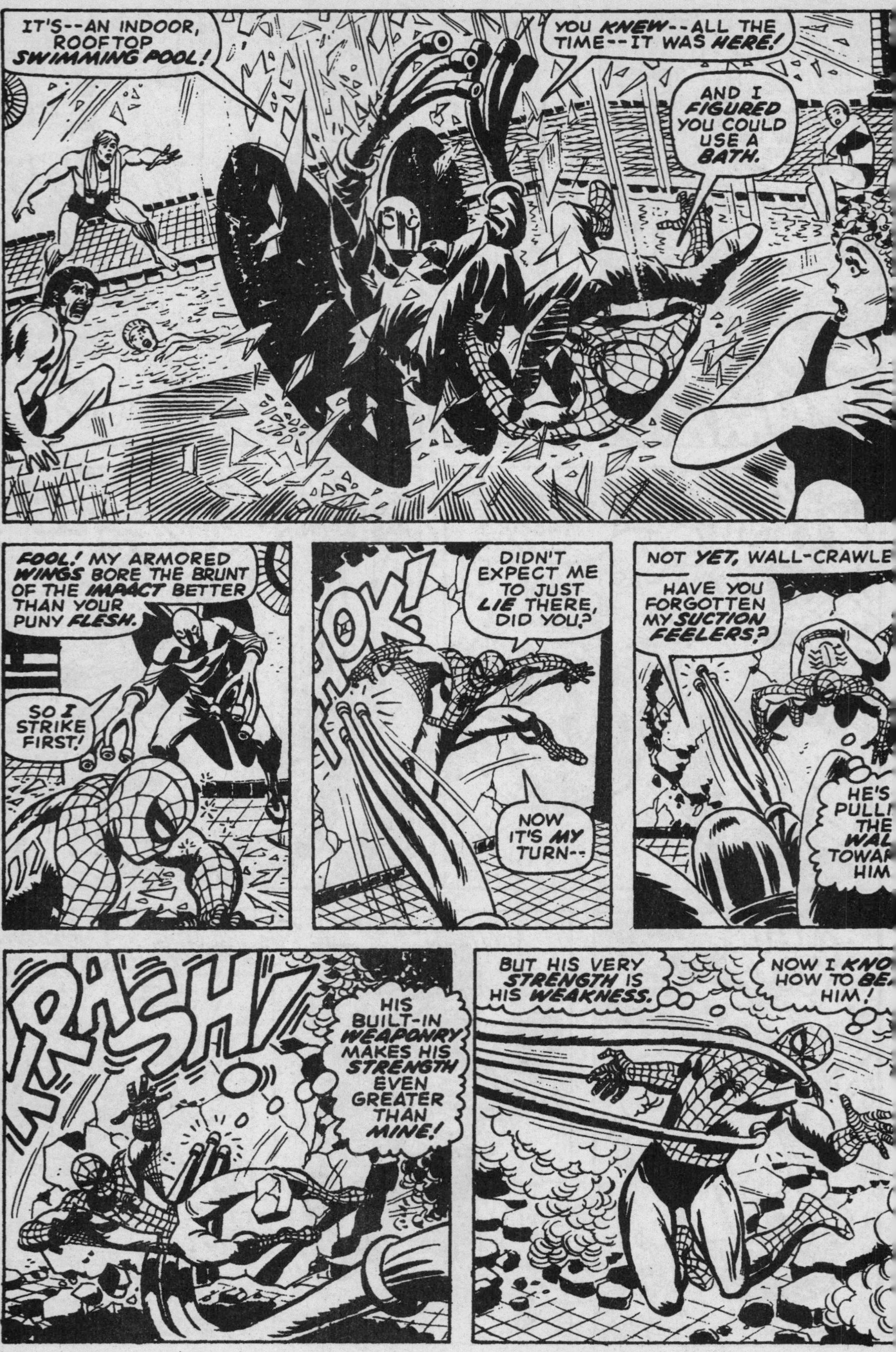
IT'S--AN INDOOR, ROOFTOP SWIMMING POOL!
YOU KNEW--ALL THE TIME--IT WAS HERE!
AND I FIGURED YOU COULD USE A BATH.
FOOL! MY ARMORED WINGS BORE THE BRUNT OF THE IMPACT BETTER THAN YOUR PUNY FLESH.
SO I STRIKE FIRST!
POK!
DIDN'T EXPECT ME TO JUST LIE THERE, DID YOU?
NOW IT'S MY TURN--
NOT YET, WALL-CRAWLE
HAVE YOU FORGOTTEN MY SUCTION FEELERS?
HE'S PULLI THE WAL TOWAR HIM
HIS BUILT-IN WEAPONRY MAKES HIS STRENGTH EVEN GREATER THAN MINE!
BUT HIS VERY STRENGTH IS HIS WEAKNESS.
NOW I KNO HOW TO BE HIM!

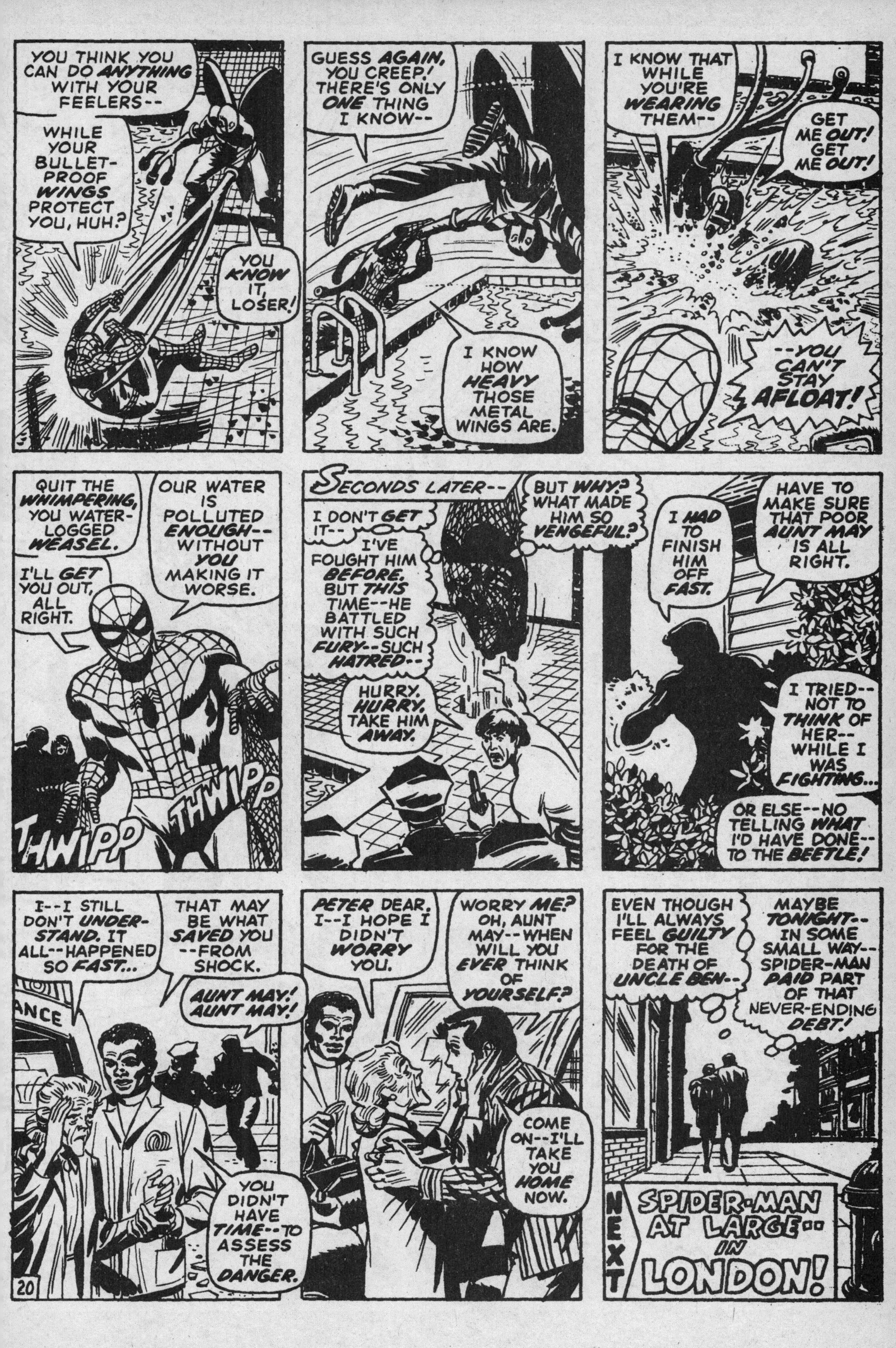
YOU THINK YOU CAN DO ANYTHING WITH YOUR FEELERS--
WHILE YOUR BULLET-PROOF WINGS PROTECT YOU, HUH?
YOU KNOW IT, LOSER!
GUESS AGAIN, YOU CREEP! THERE'S ONLY ONE THING I KNOW--
I KNOW HOW HEAVY THOSE METAL WINGS ARE.
I KNOW THAT WHILE YOU'RE WEARING THEM--
GET ME OUT! GET ME OUT!
--YOU CAN'T STAY AFLOAT!
QUIT THE WHIMPERING, YOU WATER-LOGGED WEASEL.
I'LL GET YOU OUT, ALL RIGHT.
OUR WATER IS POLLUTED ENOUGH--WITHOUT YOU MAKING IT WORSE.
THWIPP
THWIPP
SECONDS LATER--
I DON'T GET IT--
I'VE FOUGHT HIM BEFORE. BUT THIS TIME--HE BATTLED WITH SUCH FURY--SUCH HATRED--
BUT WHY? WHAT MADE HIM SO VENGEFUL?
HURRY. HURRY. TAKE HIM AWAY.
I HAD TO FINISH HIM OFF FAST.
HAVE TO MAKE SURE THAT POOR AUNT MAY IS ALL RIGHT.
I TRIED--NOT TO THINK OF HER--WHILE I WAS FIGHTING...
OR ELSE--NO TELLING WHAT I'D HAVE DONE--TO THE BEETLE!
I--I STILL DON'T UNDER-STAND. IT ALL--HAPPENED SO FAST...
THAT MAY BE WHAT SAVED YOU --FROM SHOCK.
AUNT MAY! AUNT MAY!
ANCE
YOU DIDN'T HAVE TIME--TO ASSESS THE DANGER.
20
PETER DEAR. I--I HOPE I DIDN'T WORRY YOU.
WORRY ME? OH, AUNT MAY--WHEN WILL YOU EVER THINK OF YOURSELF?
COME ON--I'LL TAKE YOU HOME NOW.
EVEN THOUGH I'LL ALWAYS FEEL GUILTY FOR THE DEATH OF UNCLE BEN--
MAYBE TONIGHT--IN SOME SMALL WAY--SPIDER-MAN PAID PART OF THAT NEVER-ENDING DEBT!
NEXT
SPIDER-MAN AT LARGE-- IN LONDON!

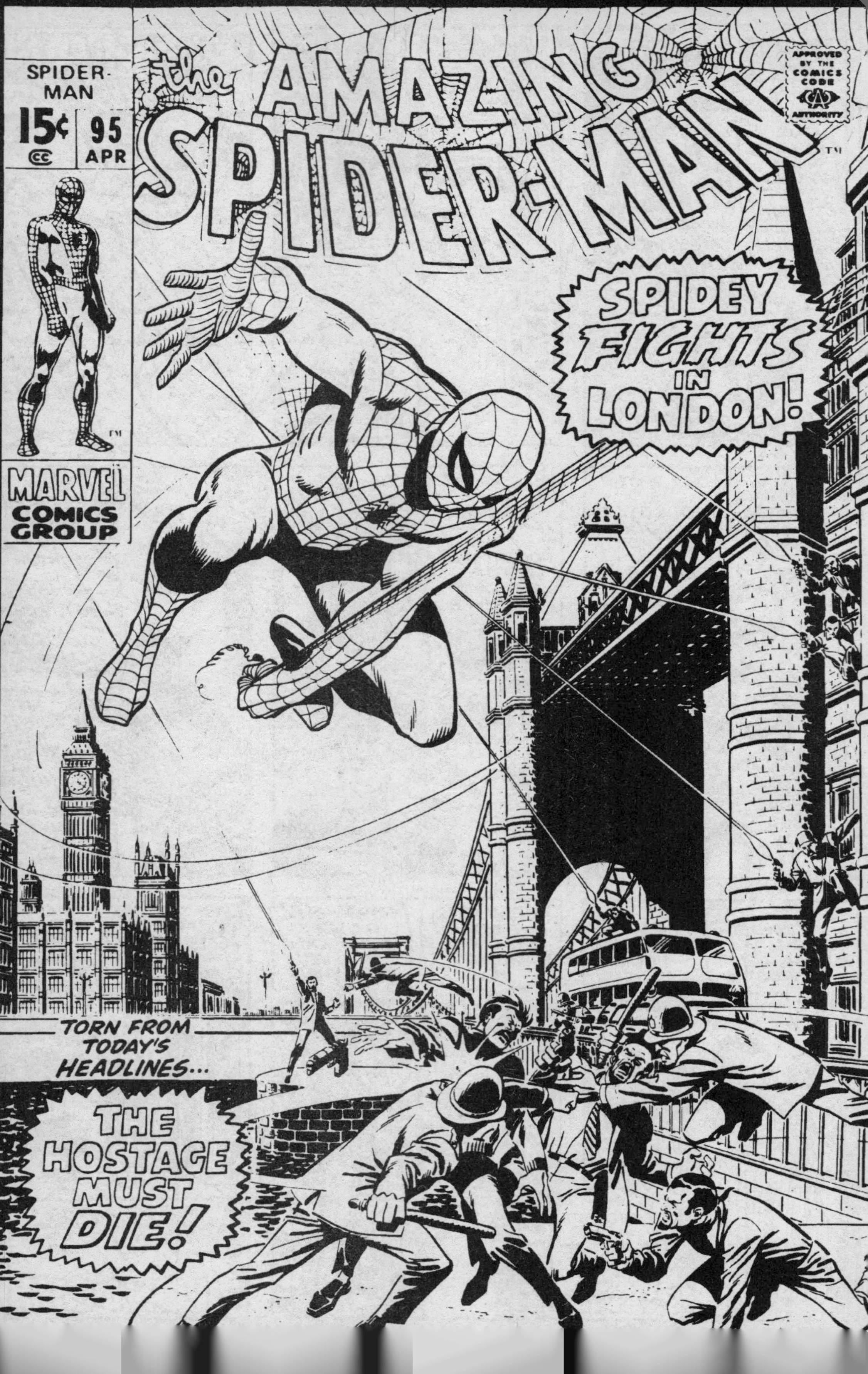

SPIDER-MAN
15¢
CC
95
APR
the AMAZING SPIDER-MAN
TM
APPROVED BY THE COMICS CODE AUTHORITY
MARVEL COMICS GROUP
SPIDEY FIGHTS IN LONDON!
TORN FROM TODAY'S HEADLINES...
THE HOSTAGE MUST DIE!

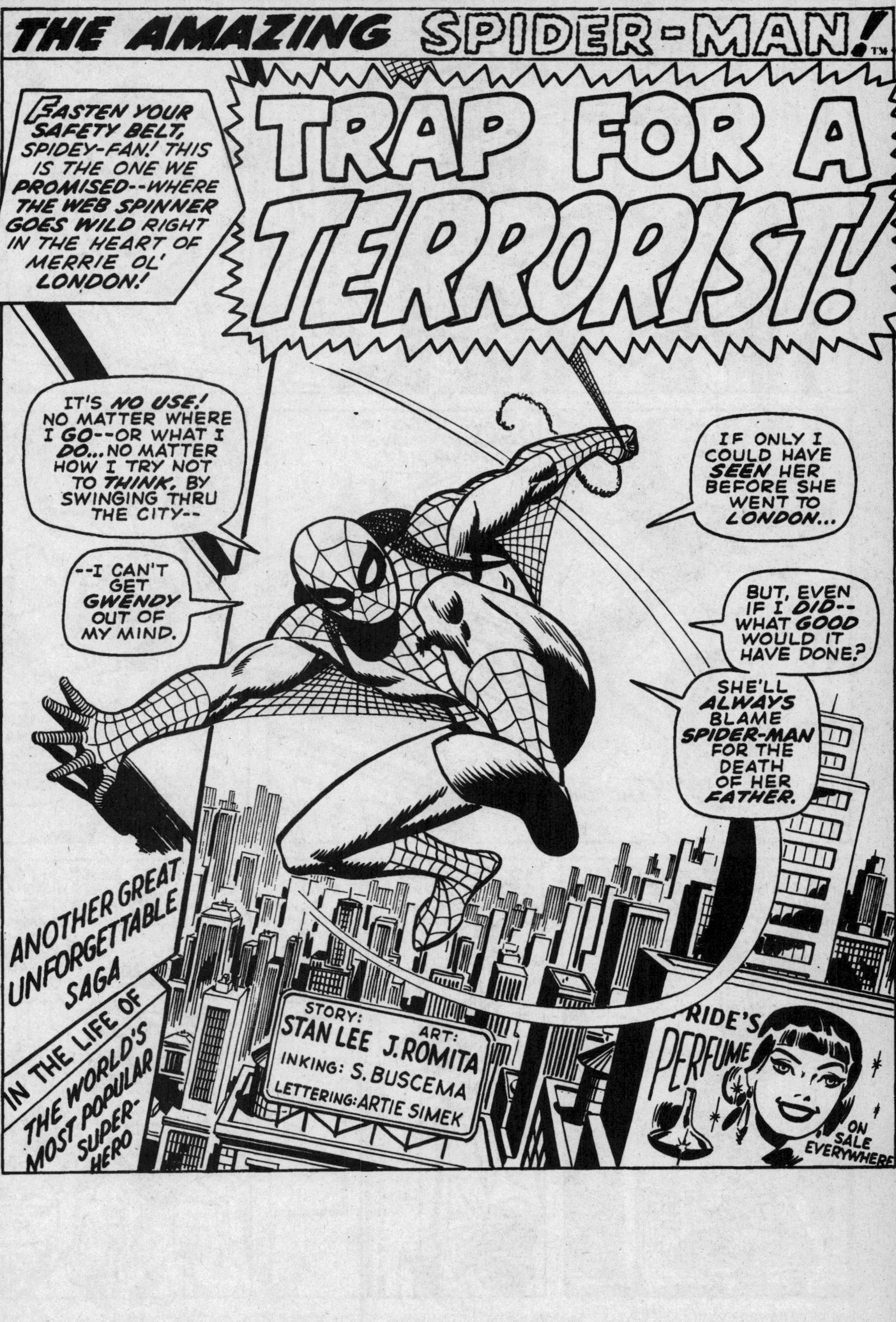
THE AMAZING SPIDER-MAN!™
FASTEN YOUR SAFETY BELT, SPIDEY-FAN! THIS IS THE ONE WE PROMISED--WHERE THE WEB SPINNER GOES WILD RIGHT IN THE HEART OF MERRIE OL' LONDON!
TRAP FOR A TERRORIST!
IT'S NO USE! NO MATTER WHERE I GO--OR WHAT I DO... NO MATTER HOW I TRY NOT TO THINK, BY SWINGING THRU THE CITY--
--I CAN'T GET GWENDY OUT OF MY MIND.
IF ONLY I COULD HAVE SEEN HER BEFORE SHE WENT TO LONDON...
BUT, EVEN IF I DID--WHAT GOOD WOULD IT HAVE DONE?
SHE'LL ALWAYS BLAME SPIDER-MAN FOR THE DEATH OF HER FATHER.
ANOTHER GREAT UNFORGETTABLE SAGA
IN THE LIFE OF
THE WORLD'S MOST POPULAR SUPER-HERO
STORY: STAN LEE ART: J. ROMITA
INKING: S. BUSCEMA
LETTERING: ARTIE SIMEK
RIDE'S PERFUME
ON SALE EVERYWHERE

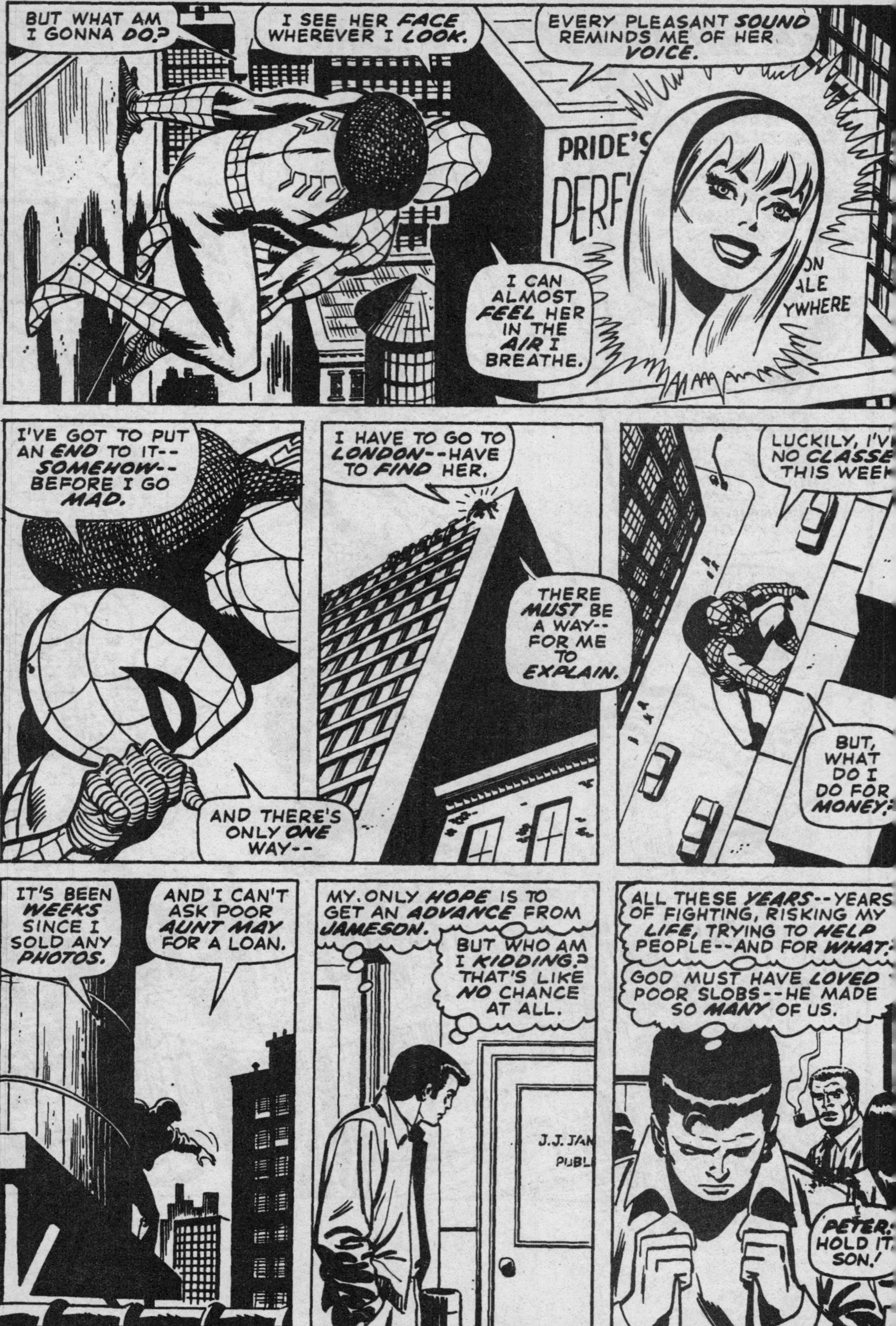

BUT WHAT AM I GONNA DO?
I SEE HER FACE WHEREVER I LOOK.
EVERY PLEASANT SOUND REMINDS ME OF HER VOICE.
PRIDE'S
PERF
ON
ALE
YWHERE
I CAN ALMOST FEEL HER IN THE AIR I BREATHE.
I'VE GOT TO PUT AN END TO IT-- SOMEHOW-- BEFORE I GO MAD.
AND THERE'S ONLY ONE WAY--
I HAVE TO GO TO LONDON--HAVE TO FIND HER.
THERE MUST BE A WAY-- FOR ME TO EXPLAIN.
LUCKILY, I'V NO CLASSE THIS WEEK
BUT, WHAT DO I DO FOR MONEY?
IT'S BEEN WEEKS SINCE I SOLD ANY PHOTOS.
AND I CAN'T ASK POOR AUNT MAY FOR A LOAN.
MY ONLY HOPE IS TO GET AN ADVANCE FROM JAMESON.
BUT WHO AM I KIDDING? THAT'S LIKE NO CHANCE AT ALL.
J.J. JAN
PUBL
ALL THESE YEARS--YEARS OF FIGHTING, RISKING MY LIFE, TRYING TO HELP PEOPLE--AND FOR WHAT?
GOD MUST HAVE LOVED POOR SLOBS--HE MADE SO MANY OF US.
PETER! HOLD IT, SON!

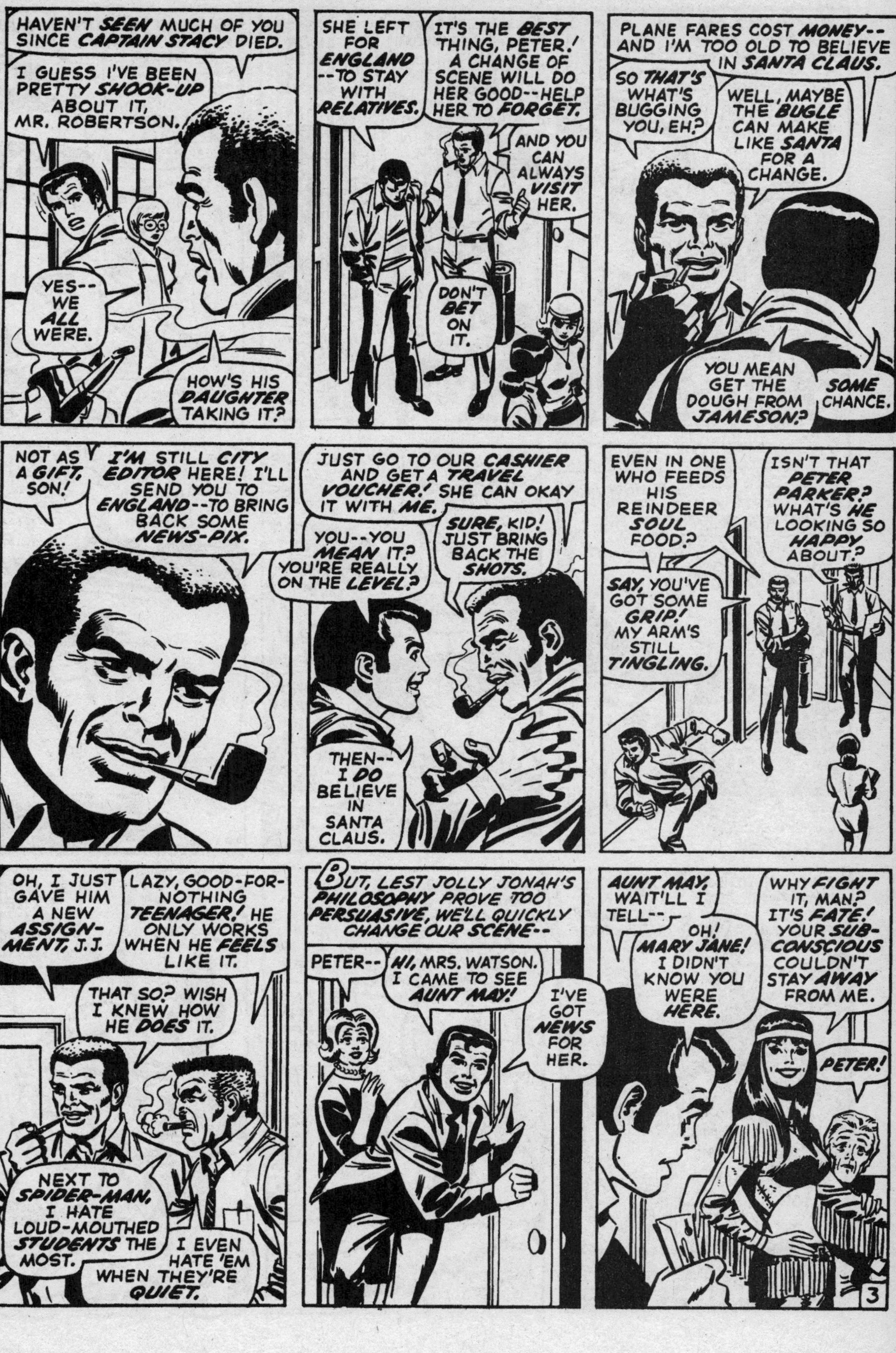

HAVEN'T SEEN MUCH OF YOU SINCE CAPTAIN STACY DIED.
I GUESS I'VE BEEN PRETTY SHOOK-UP ABOUT IT, MR. ROBERTSON.
YES-- WE ALL WERE.
HOW'S HIS DAUGHTER TAKING IT?
SHE LEFT FOR ENGLAND --TO STAY WITH RELATIVES.
IT'S THE BEST THING, PETER.! A CHANGE OF SCENE WILL DO HER GOOD--HELP HER TO FORGET.
AND YOU CAN ALWAYS VISIT HER.
DON'T BET ON IT.
PLANE FARES COST MONEY-- AND I'M TOO OLD TO BELIEVE IN SANTA CLAUS.
SO THAT'S WHAT'S BUGGING YOU, EH?
WELL, MAYBE THE BUGLE CAN MAKE LIKE SANTA FOR A CHANGE.
YOU MEAN GET THE DOUGH FROM JAMESON?
SOME CHANCE.
NOT AS A GIFT, SON!
I'M STILL CITY EDITOR HERE! I'LL SEND YOU TO ENGLAND--TO BRING BACK SOME NEWS-PIX.
JUST GO TO OUR CASHIER AND GET A TRAVEL VOUCHER! SHE CAN OKAY IT WITH ME.
YOU--YOU MEAN IT? YOU'RE REALLY ON THE LEVEL?
SURE, KID! JUST BRING BACK THE SHOTS.
THEN-- I DO BELIEVE IN SANTA CLAUS.
EVEN IN ONE WHO FEEDS HIS REINDEER SOUL FOOD?
SAY, YOU'VE GOT SOME GRIP! MY ARM'S STILL TINGLING.
ISN'T THAT PETER PARKER? WHAT'S HE LOOKING SO HAPPY ABOUT?
OH, I JUST GAVE HIM A NEW ASSIGNMENT, J.J.
LAZY, GOOD-FOR-NOTHING TEENAGER! HE ONLY WORKS WHEN HE FEELS LIKE IT.
THAT SO? WISH I KNEW HOW HE DOES IT.
NEXT TO SPIDER-MAN, I HATE LOUD-MOUTHED STUDENTS THE MOST.
I EVEN HATE 'EM WHEN THEY'RE QUIET.
BUT, LEST JOLLY JONAH'S PHILOSOPHY PROVE TOO PERSUASIVE, WE'LL QUICKLY CHANGE OUR SCENE--
PETER--
HI, MRS. WATSON. I CAME TO SEE AUNT MAY!
I'VE GOT NEWS FOR HER.
AUNT MAY, WAIT'LL I TELL--
OH! MARY JANE! I DIDN'T KNOW YOU WERE HERE.
WHY FIGHT IT, MAN? IT'S FATE! YOUR SUB-CONSCIOUS COULDN'T STAY AWAY FROM ME.
PETER!

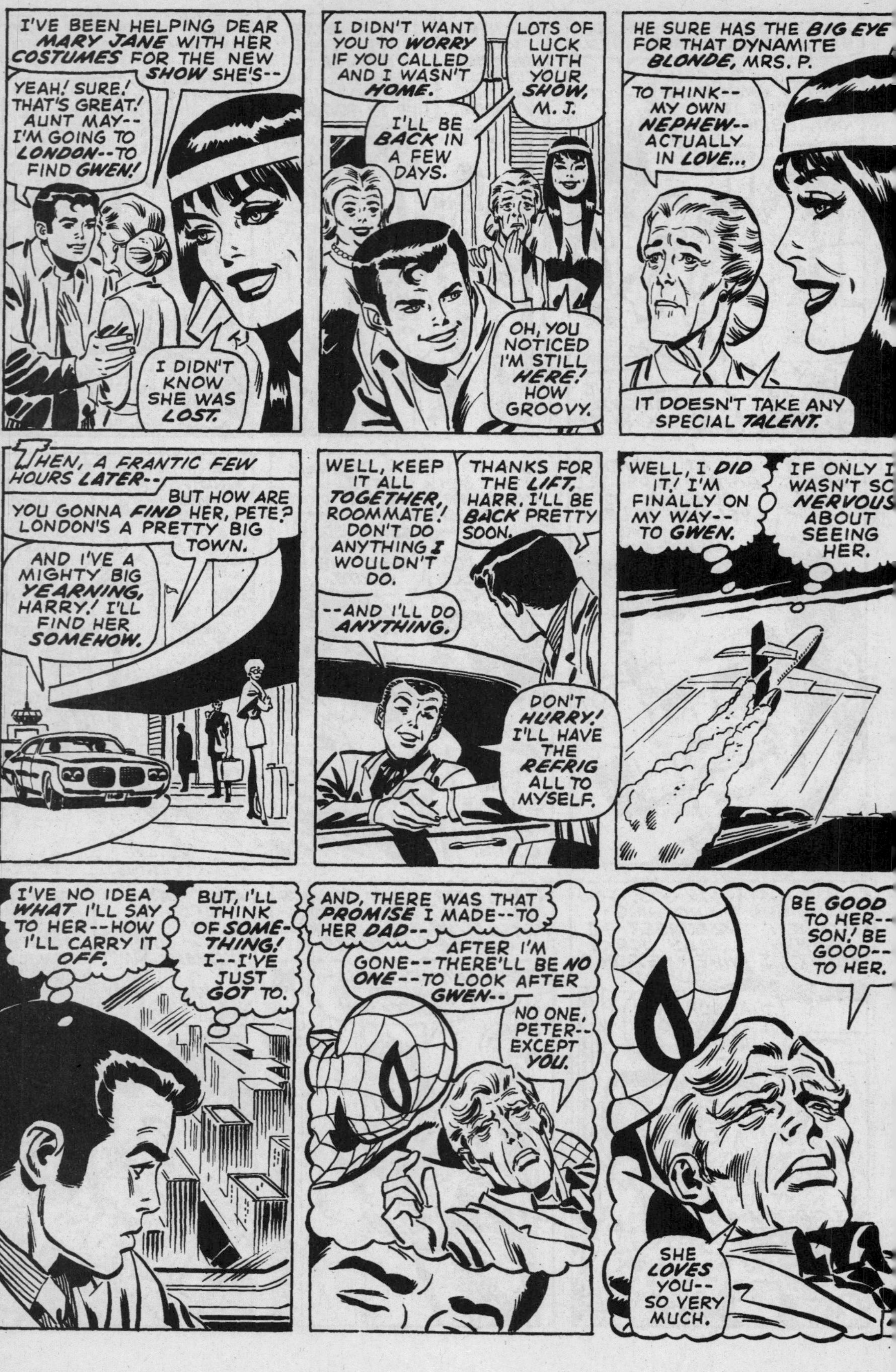
I'VE BEEN HELPING DEAR MARY JANE WITH HER COSTUMES FOR THE NEW SHOW SHE'S--
YEAH! SURE! THAT'S GREAT! AUNT MAY-- I'M GOING TO LONDON--TO FIND GWEN!
I DIDN'T KNOW SHE WAS LOST.
I DIDN'T WANT YOU TO WORRY IF YOU CALLED AND I WASN'T HOME.
LOTS OF LUCK WITH YOUR SHOW, M. J.
I'LL BE BACK IN A FEW DAYS.
OH, YOU NOTICED I'M STILL HERE! HOW GROOVY.
HE SURE HAS THE BIG EYE FOR THAT DYNAMITE BLONDE, MRS. P.
TO THINK-- MY OWN NEPHEW-- ACTUALLY IN LOVE...
IT DOESN'T TAKE ANY SPECIAL TALENT.
THEN, A FRANTIC FEW HOURS LATER--
BUT HOW ARE YOU GONNA FIND HER, PETE? LONDON'S A PRETTY BIG TOWN.
AND I'VE A MIGHTY BIG YEARNING, HARRY! I'LL FIND HER SOMEHOW.
WELL, KEEP IT ALL TOGETHER, ROOMMATE! DON'T DO ANYTHING I WOULDN'T DO.
THANKS FOR THE LIFT, HARR. I'LL BE BACK PRETTY SOON.
--AND I'LL DO ANYTHING.
DON'T HURRY! I'LL HAVE THE REFRIG ALL TO MYSELF.
WELL, I DID IT! I'M FINALLY ON MY WAY-- TO GWEN.
IF ONLY I WASN'T SO NERVOUS ABOUT SEEING HER.
I'VE NO IDEA WHAT I'LL SAY TO HER--HOW I'LL CARRY IT OFF.
BUT, I'LL THINK OF SOME-THING! I--I'VE JUST GOT TO.
AND, THERE WAS THAT PROMISE I MADE--TO HER DAD--
AFTER I'M GONE--THERE'LL BE NO ONE--TO LOOK AFTER GWEN--
NO ONE, PETER-- EXCEPT YOU.
BE GOOD TO HER-- SON! BE GOOD-- TO HER.
SHE LOVES YOU-- SO VERY MUCH.

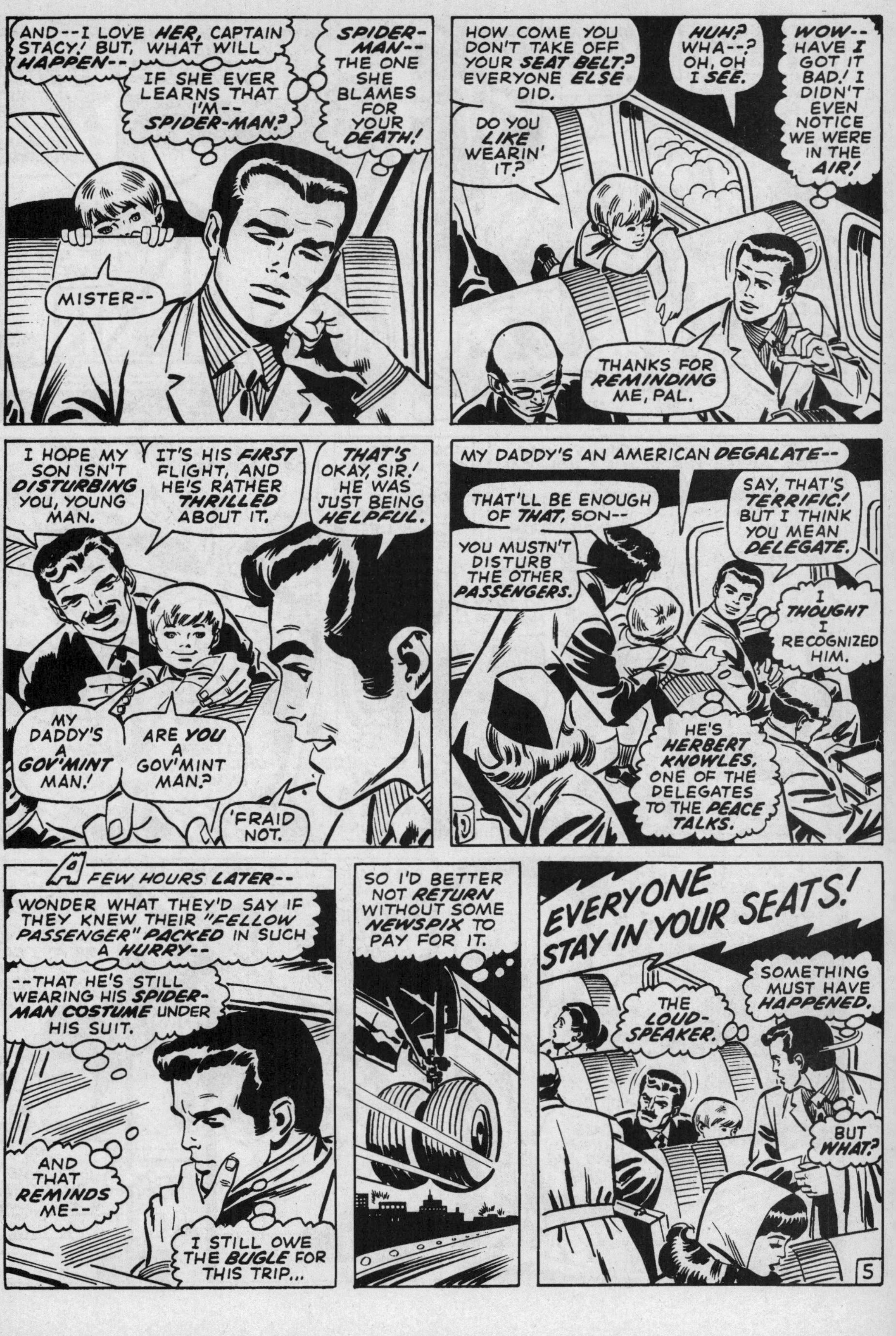
AND--I LOVE HER, CAPTAIN STACY! BUT, WHAT WILL HAPPEN--
IF SHE EVER LEARNS THAT I'M--SPIDER-MAN?
SPIDER-MAN--THE ONE SHE BLAMES FOR YOUR DEATH!
MISTER--
HOW COME YOU DON'T TAKE OFF YOUR SEAT BELT? EVERYONE ELSE DID.
DO YOU LIKE WEARIN' IT?
HUH? WHA--? OH, OH I SEE.
WOW--HAVE I GOT IT BAD! I DIDN'T EVEN NOTICE WE WERE IN THE AIR!
THANKS FOR REMINDING ME, PAL.
I HOPE MY SON ISN'T DISTURBING YOU, YOUNG MAN.
IT'S HIS FIRST FLIGHT, AND HE'S RATHER THRILLED ABOUT IT.
THAT'S OKAY, SIR! HE WAS JUST BEING HELPFUL.
MY DADDY'S A GOV'MINT MAN!
ARE YOU A GOV'MINT MAN?
'FRAID NOT.
MY DADDY'S AN AMERICAN DEGALATE--
THAT'LL BE ENOUGH OF THAT, SON--
YOU MUSTN'T DISTURB THE OTHER PASSENGERS.
SAY, THAT'S TERRIFIC! BUT I THINK YOU MEAN DELEGATE.
I THOUGHT I RECOGNIZED HIM.
HE'S HERBERT KNOWLES, ONE OF THE DELEGATES TO THE PEACE TALKS.
A FEW HOURS LATER--
WONDER WHAT THEY'D SAY IF THEY KNEW THEIR "FELLOW PASSENGER" PACKED IN SUCH A HURRY--
--THAT HE'S STILL WEARING HIS SPIDER-MAN COSTUME UNDER HIS SUIT.
AND THAT REMINDS ME--
I STILL OWE THE BUGLE FOR THIS TRIP...
SO I'D BETTER NOT RETURN WITHOUT SOME NEWSPIX TO PAY FOR IT.
EVERYONE STAY IN YOUR SEATS!
THE LOUD-SPEAKER.
SOMETHING MUST HAVE HAPPENED.
BUT WHAT?

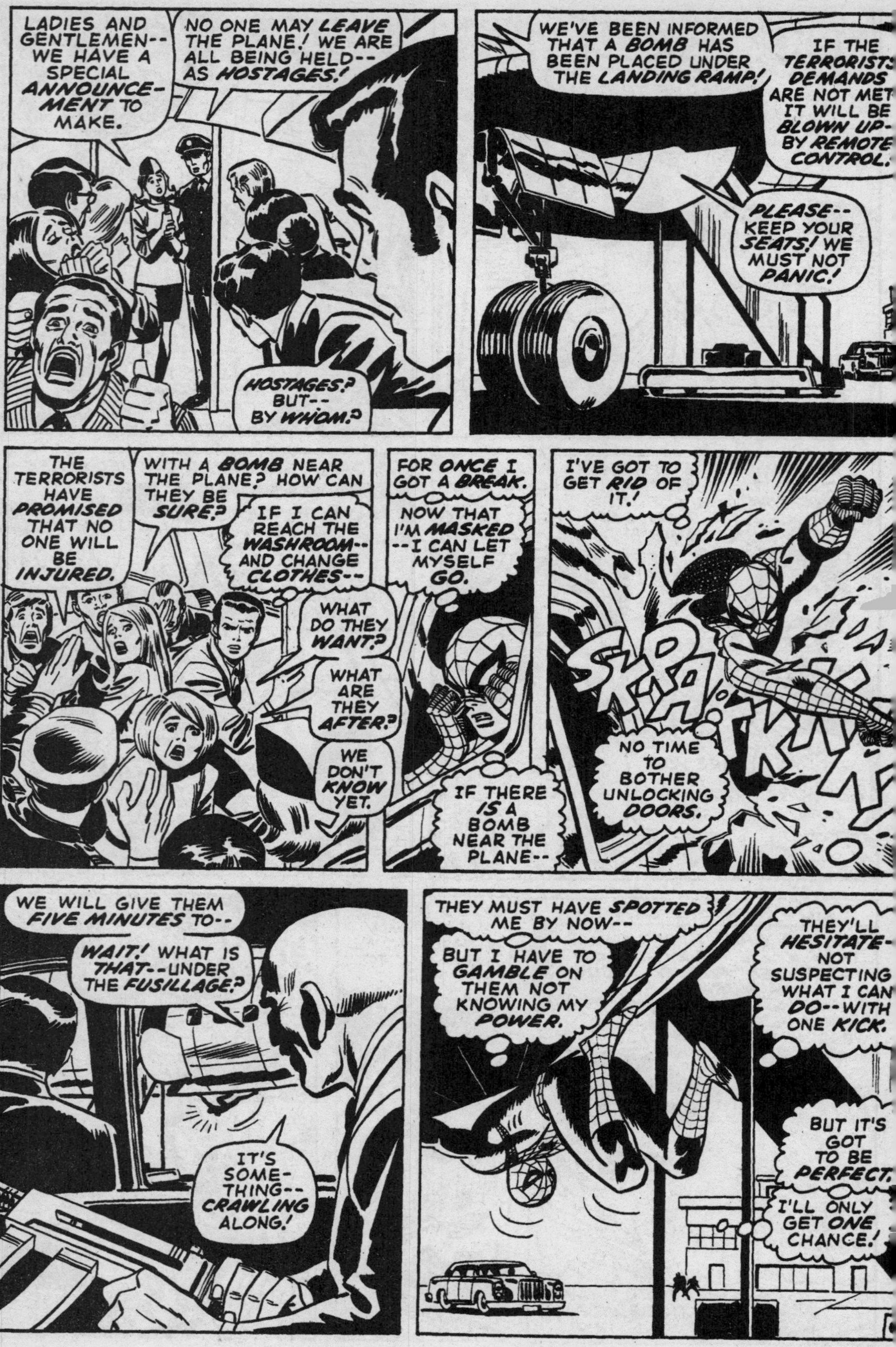
LADIES AND GENTLEMEN-- WE HAVE A SPECIAL ANNOUNCEMENT TO MAKE.
NO ONE MAY LEAVE THE PLANE! WE ARE ALL BEING HELD-- AS HOSTAGES!
HOSTAGES? BUT-- BY WHOM?
WE'VE BEEN INFORMED THAT A BOMB HAS BEEN PLACED UNDER THE LANDING RAMP!
IF THE TERRORISTS DEMANDS ARE NOT MET IT WILL BE BLOWN UP-- BY REMOTE CONTROL.
PLEASE-- KEEP YOUR SEATS! WE MUST NOT PANIC!
THE TERRORISTS HAVE PROMISED THAT NO ONE WILL BE INJURED.
WITH A BOMB NEAR THE PLANE? HOW CAN THEY BE SURE?
IF I CAN REACH THE WASHROOM-- AND CHANGE CLOTHES--
WHAT DO THEY WANT?
WHAT ARE THEY AFTER?
WE DON'T KNOW YET.
FOR ONCE I GOT A BREAK.
NOW THAT I'M MASKED --I CAN LET MYSELF GO.
IF THERE IS A BOMB NEAR THE PLANE--
I'VE GOT TO GET RID OF IT.
SKPAKKK
NO TIME TO BOTHER UNLOCKING DOORS.
WE WILL GIVE THEM FIVE MINUTES TO--
WAIT! WHAT IS THAT--UNDER THE FUSILLAGE?
IT'S SOME-THING-- CRAWLING ALONG!
THEY MUST HAVE SPOTTED ME BY NOW--
BUT I HAVE TO GAMBLE ON THEM NOT KNOWING MY POWER.
THEY'LL HESITATE-- NOT SUSPECTING WHAT I CAN DO--WITH ONE KICK.
BUT IT'S GOT TO BE PERFECT.
I'LL ONLY GET ONE CHANCE!

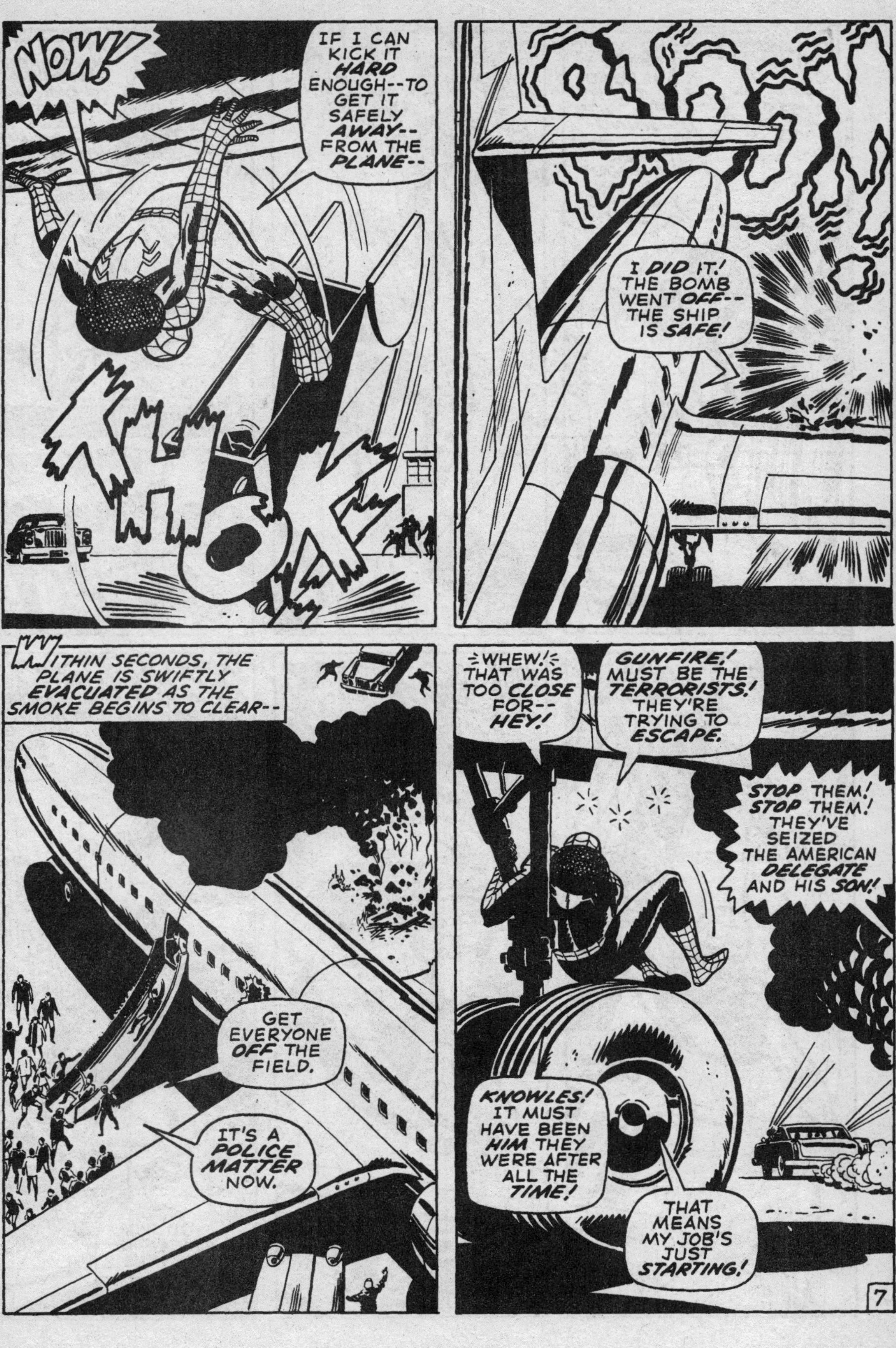
NOW!
IF I CAN KICK IT HARD ENOUGH--TO GET IT SAFELY AWAY--FROM THE PLANE--
I DID IT! THE BOMB WENT OFF--THE SHIP IS SAFE!
WITHIN SECONDS, THE PLANE IS SWIFTLY EVACUATED AS THE SMOKE BEGINS TO CLEAR--
GET EVERYONE OFF THE FIELD.
IT'S A POLICE MATTER NOW.
WHEW! THAT WAS TOO CLOSE FOR-- HEY!
GUNFIRE! MUST BE THE TERRORISTS! THEY'RE TRYING TO ESCAPE.
STOP THEM! STOP THEM! THEY'VE SEIZED THE AMERICAN DELEGATE AND HIS SON!
KNOWLES! IT MUST HAVE BEEN HIM THEY WERE AFTER ALL THE TIME!
THAT MEANS MY JOB'S JUST STARTING!
7

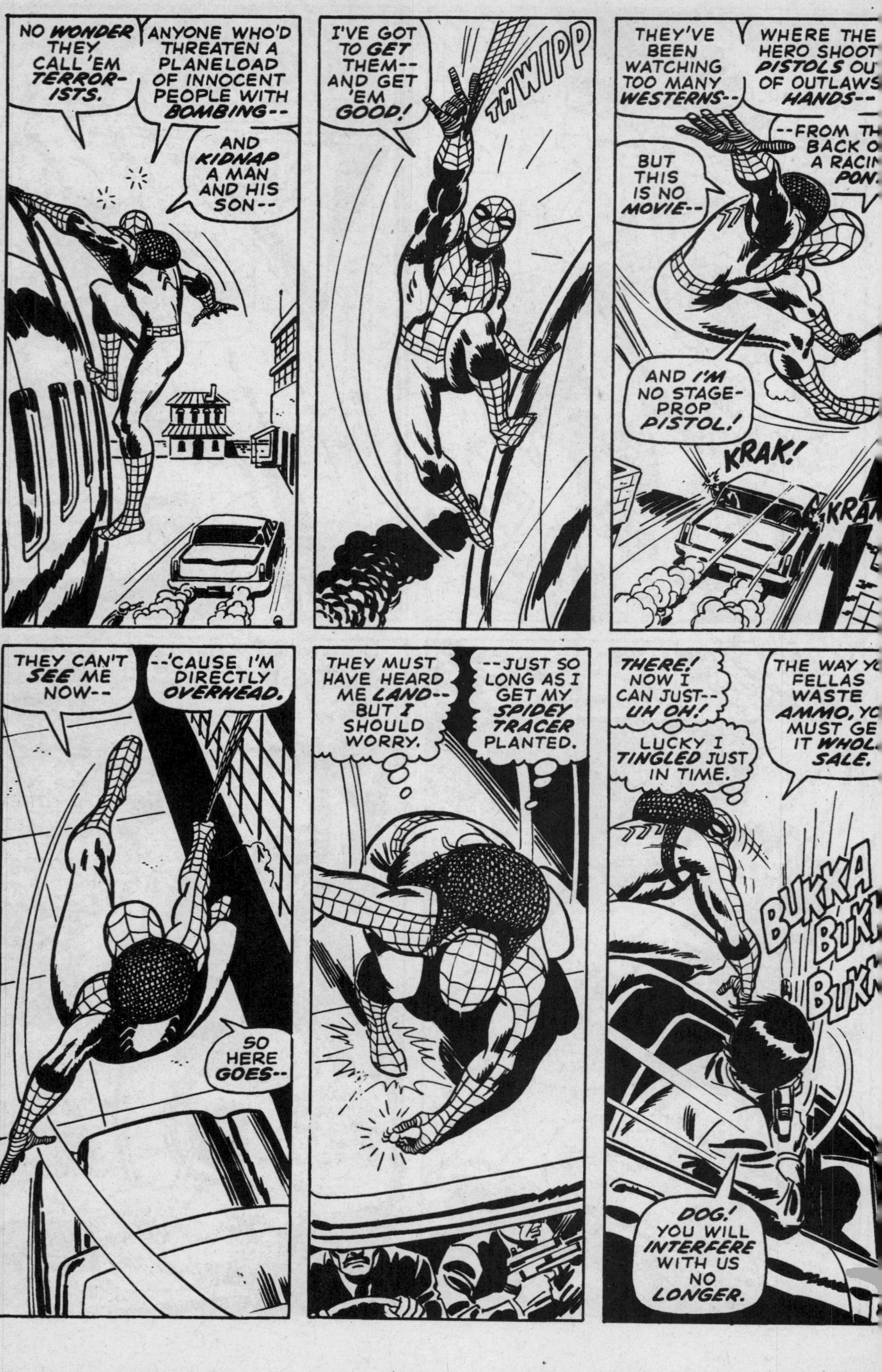
NO WONDER THEY CALL 'EM TERRORISTS.
ANYONE WHO'D THREATEN A PLANELOAD OF INNOCENT PEOPLE WITH BOMBING--
AND KIDNAP A MAN AND HIS SON--
I'VE GOT TO GET THEM-- AND GET 'EM GOOD!
THWIPP
THEY'VE BEEN WATCHING TOO MANY WESTERNS--
WHERE THE HERO SHOOT PISTOLS OUT OF OUTLAWS' HANDS--
--FROM TH BACK O A RACIN PON
BUT THIS IS NO MOVIE--
AND I'M NO STAGE-PROP PISTOL!
KRAK!
KRA
THEY CAN'T SEE ME NOW--
--'CAUSE I'M DIRECTLY OVERHEAD.
SO HERE GOES--
THEY MUST HAVE HEARD ME LAND-- BUT I SHOULD WORRY.
--JUST SO LONG AS I GET MY SPIDEY TRACER PLANTED.
THERE! NOW I CAN JUST-- UH OH!
LUCKY I TINGLED JUST IN TIME.
THE WAY YO FELLAS WASTE AMMO, YO MUST GE IT WHOL SALE.
BUKKA
BUK
BUK
DOG! YOU WILL INTERFERE WITH US NO LONGER.

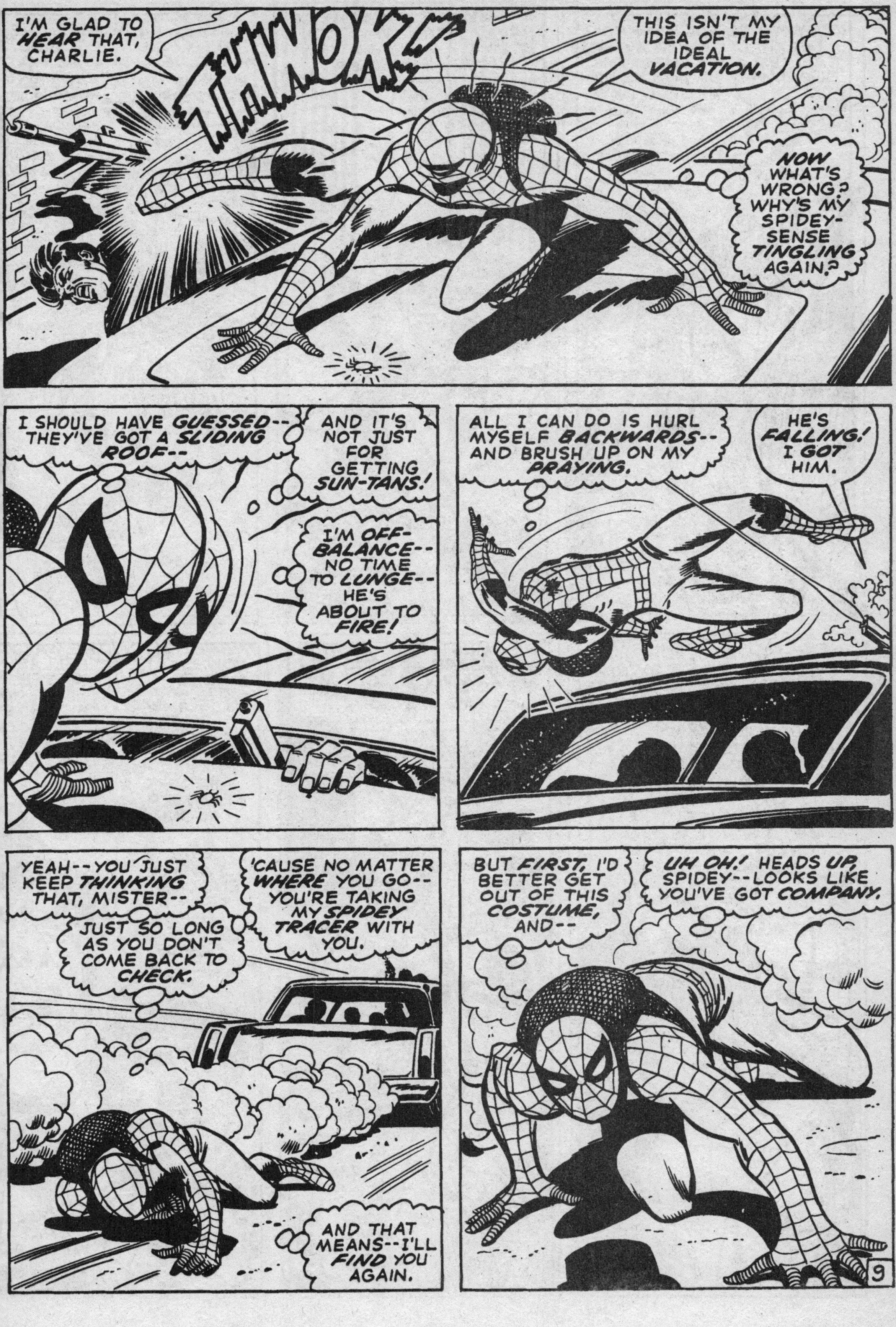
I'M GLAD TO HEAR THAT, CHARLIE.
THWOK!
THIS ISN'T MY IDEA OF THE IDEAL VACATION.
NOW WHAT'S WRONG? WHY'S MY SPIDEY-SENSE TINGLING AGAIN?
I SHOULD HAVE GUESSED-- THEY'VE GOT A SLIDING ROOF--
AND IT'S NOT JUST FOR GETTING SUN-TANS!
I'M OFF-BALANCE-- NO TIME TO LUNGE-- HE'S ABOUT TO FIRE!
ALL I CAN DO IS HURL MYSELF BACKWARDS-- AND BRUSH UP ON MY PRAYING.
HE'S FALLING! I GOT HIM.
YEAH--YOU JUST KEEP THINKING THAT, MISTER--
JUST SO LONG AS YOU DON'T COME BACK TO CHECK.
'CAUSE NO MATTER WHERE YOU GO-- YOU'RE TAKING MY SPIDEY TRACER WITH YOU.
AND THAT MEANS--I'LL FIND YOU AGAIN.
BUT FIRST, I'D BETTER GET OUT OF THIS COSTUME, AND--
UH OH! HEADS UP, SPIDEY--LOOKS LIKE YOU'VE GOT COMPANY.
9

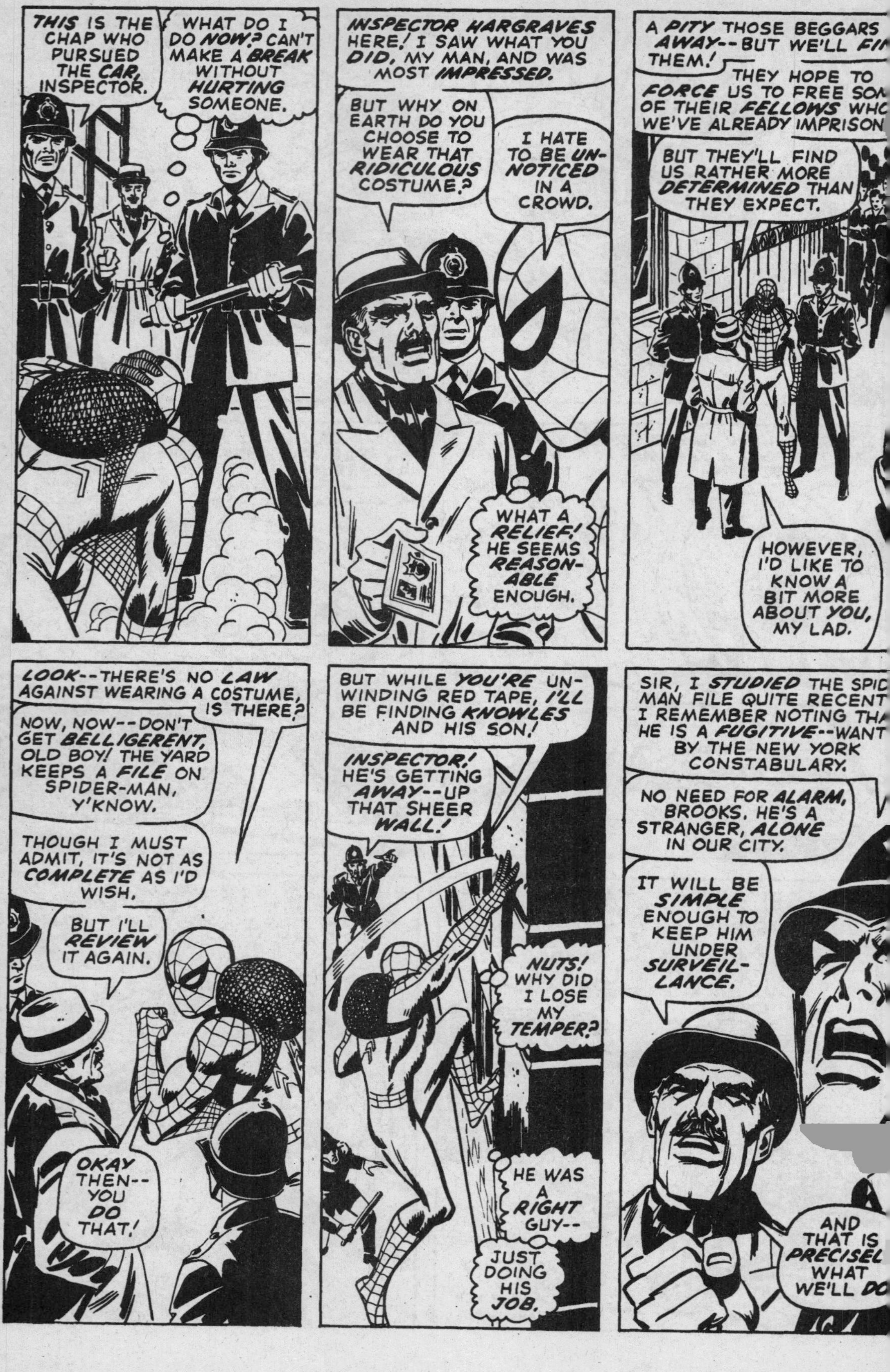
THIS IS THE CHAP WHO PURSUED THE CAR, INSPECTOR.
WHAT DO I DO NOW? CAN'T MAKE A BREAK WITHOUT HURTING SOMEONE.
INSPECTOR HARGRAVES HERE! I SAW WHAT YOU DID, MY MAN, AND WAS MOST IMPRESSED.
BUT WHY ON EARTH DO YOU CHOOSE TO WEAR THAT RIDICULOUS COSTUME?
I HATE TO BE UN-NOTICED IN A CROWD.
WHAT A RELIEF! HE SEEMS REASON-ABLE ENOUGH.
A PITY THOSE BEGGARS AWAY--BUT WE'LL FI
THEM!
THEY HOPE TO FORCE US TO FREE SOM
OF THEIR FELLOWS WHO
WE'VE ALREADY IMPRISON
BUT THEY'LL FIND US RATHER MORE DETERMINED THAN THEY EXPECT.
HOWEVER, I'D LIKE TO KNOW A BIT MORE ABOUT YOU, MY LAD.
LOOK--THERE'S NO LAW AGAINST WEARING A COSTUME, IS THERE?
NOW, NOW--DON'T GET BELLIGERENT, OLD BOY! THE YARD KEEPS A FILE ON SPIDER-MAN, Y'KNOW.
THOUGH I MUST ADMIT, IT'S NOT AS COMPLETE AS I'D WISH.
BUT I'LL REVIEW IT AGAIN.
OKAY THEN--YOU DO THAT!
BUT WHILE YOU'RE UN-WINDING RED TAPE, I'LL BE FINDING KNOWLES AND HIS SON!
INSPECTOR! HE'S GETTING AWAY--UP THAT SHEER WALL!
NUTS! WHY DID I LOSE MY TEMPER?
HE WAS A RIGHT GUY--
JUST DOING HIS JOB.
SIR, I STUDIED THE SPID
MAN FILE QUITE RECENT
I REMEMBER NOTING THA
HE IS A FUGITIVE--WANT
BY THE NEW YORK CONSTABULARY.
NO NEED FOR ALARM, BROOKS. HE'S A STRANGER, ALONE IN OUR CITY.
IT WILL BE SIMPLE ENOUGH TO KEEP HIM UNDER SURVEIL-LANCE.
AND THAT IS PRECISEL
WHAT WE'LL DO

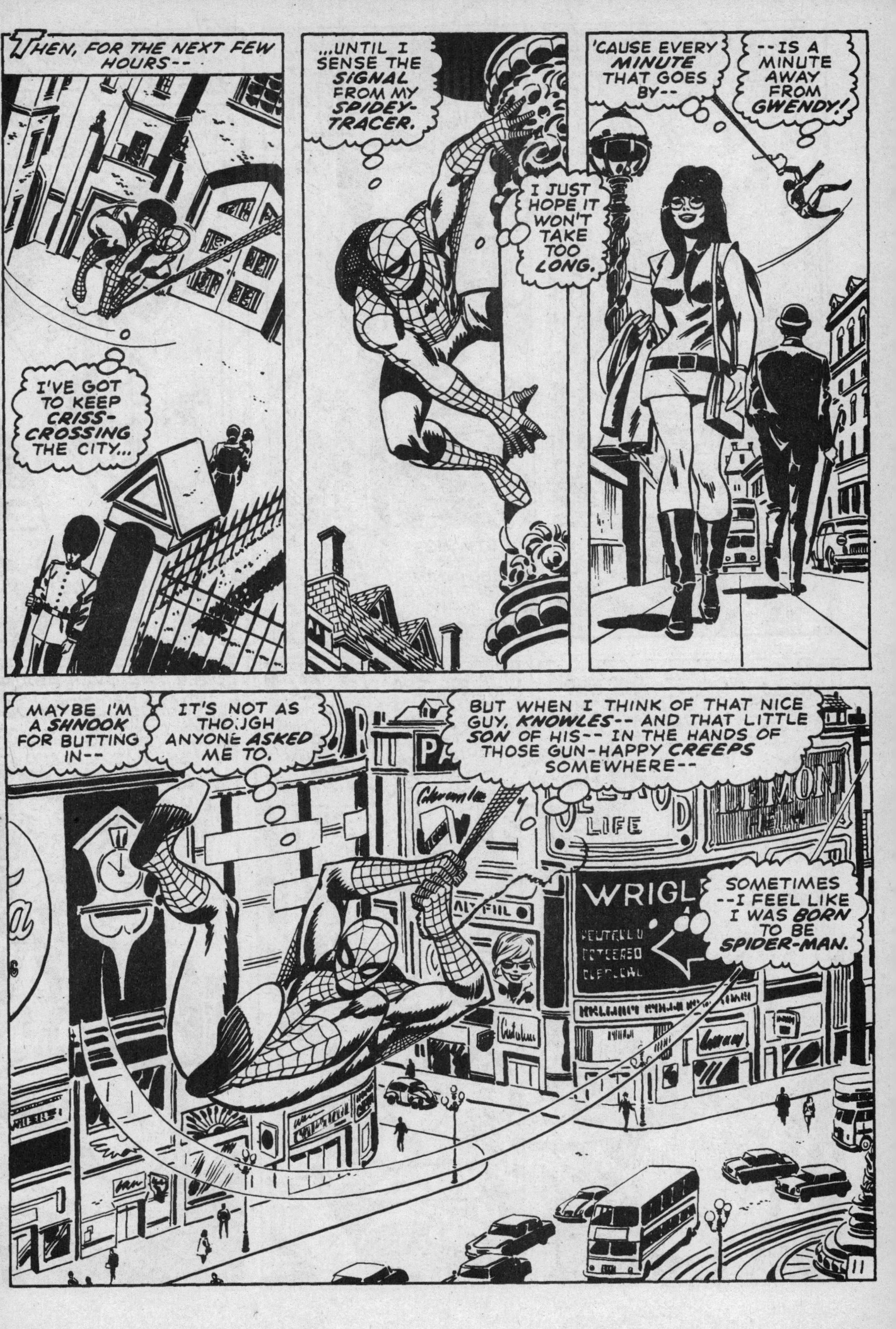
THEN, FOR THE NEXT FEW HOURS--
I'VE GOT TO KEEP CRISS-CROSSING THE CITY...
...UNTIL I SENSE THE SIGNAL FROM MY SPIDEY-TRACER.
I JUST HOPE IT WON'T TAKE TOO LONG.
'CAUSE EVERY MINUTE THAT GOES BY--
--IS A MINUTE AWAY FROM GWENDY!
MAYBE I'M A SHNOOK FOR BUTTING IN--
IT'S NOT AS THOUGH ANYONE ASKED ME TO.
BUT WHEN I THINK OF THAT NICE GUY, KNOWLES-- AND THAT LITTLE SON OF HIS-- IN THE HANDS OF THOSE GUN-HAPPY CREEPS SOMEWHERE--
SOMETIMES --I FEEL LIKE I WAS BORN TO BE SPIDER-MAN.
LIFE
WRIGL
11

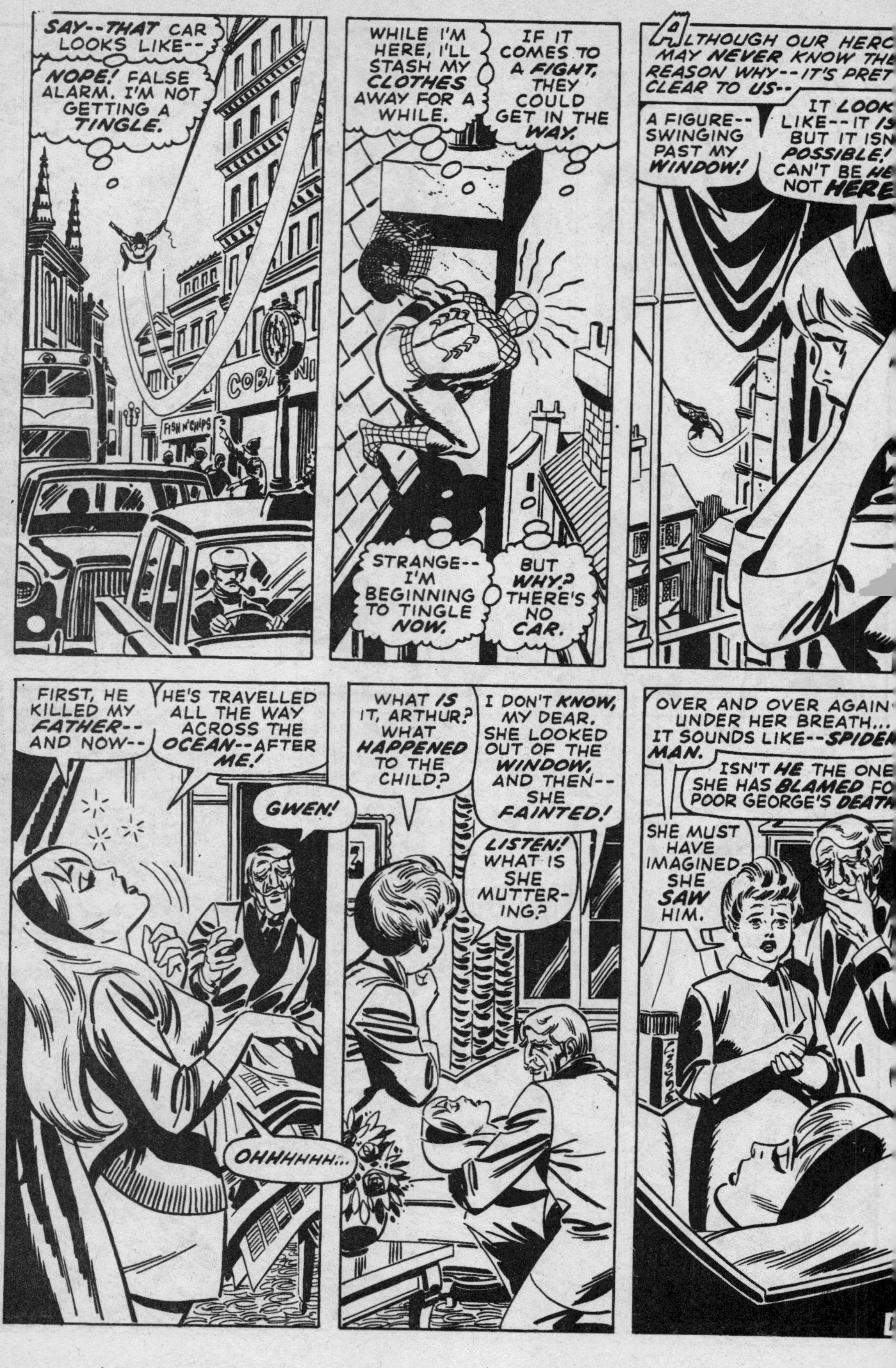

SAY--THAT CAR LOOKS LIKE--
NOPE! FALSE ALARM. I'M NOT GETTING A TINGLE.
FISH N' CHIPS
WHILE I'M HERE, I'LL STASH MY CLOTHES AWAY FOR A WHILE.
IF IT COMES TO A FIGHT, THEY COULD GET IN THE WAY.
STRANGE-- I'M BEGINNING TO TINGLE NOW.
BUT WHY? THERE'S NO CAR.
ALTHOUGH OUR HERC MAY NEVER KNOW THE REASON WHY--IT'S PRET CLEAR TO US--
A FIGURE-- SWINGING PAST MY WINDOW!
IT LOOK LIKE--IT IS BUT IT ISN POSSIBLE! CAN'T BE HE NOT HERE
FIRST, HE KILLED MY FATHER-- AND NOW--
HE'S TRAVELLED ALL THE WAY ACROSS THE OCEAN--AFTER ME!
GWEN!
OHHHHHH...
WHAT IS IT, ARTHUR? WHAT HAPPENED TO THE CHILD?
I DON'T KNOW, MY DEAR. SHE LOOKED OUT OF THE WINDOW, AND THEN-- SHE FAINTED!
LISTEN! WHAT IS SHE MUTTERING?
OVER AND OVER AGAIN UNDER HER BREATH... IT SOUNDS LIKE--SPIDER MAN.
ISN'T HE THE ONE SHE HAS BLAMED FO POOR GEORGE'S DEATH
SHE MUST HAVE IMAGINED SHE SAW HIM.

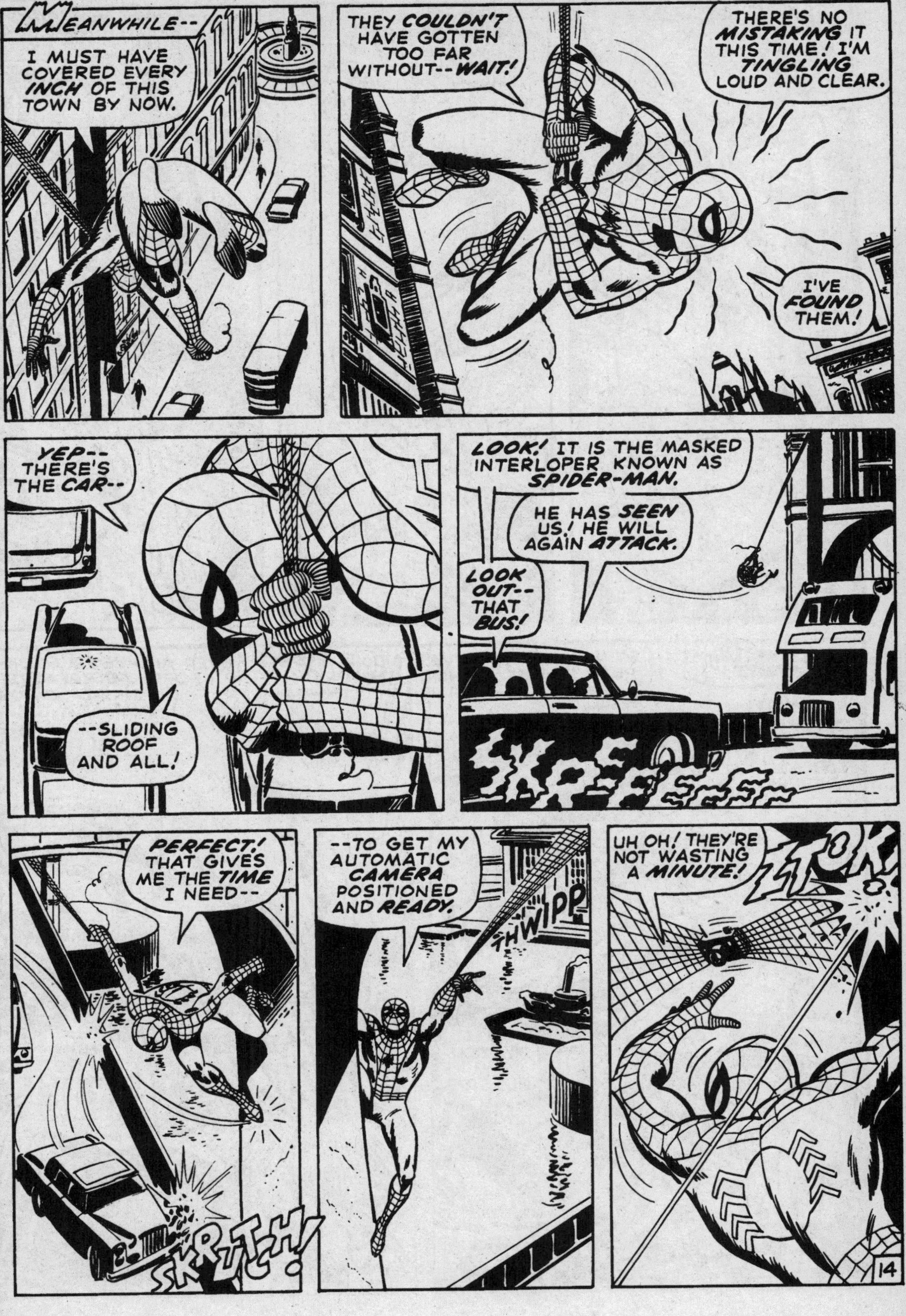
MEANWHILE--
I MUST HAVE COVERED EVERY INCH OF THIS TOWN BY NOW.
THEY COULDN'T HAVE GOTTEN TOO FAR WITHOUT--WAIT!
THERE'S NO MISTAKING IT THIS TIME! I'M TINGLING LOUD AND CLEAR.
I'VE FOUND THEM!
YEP-- THERE'S THE CAR--
--SLIDING ROOF AND ALL!
LOOK! IT IS THE MASKED INTERLOPER KNOWN AS SPIDER-MAN.
HE HAS SEEN US! HE WILL AGAIN ATTACK.
LOOK OUT-- THAT BUS!
SKREEEEE
PERFECT! THAT GIVES ME THE TIME I NEED--
SKRUTCH!
--TO GET MY AUTOMATIC CAMERA POSITIONED AND READY.
THWIPP
UH OH! THEY'RE NOT WASTING A MINUTE!
TOK!
14

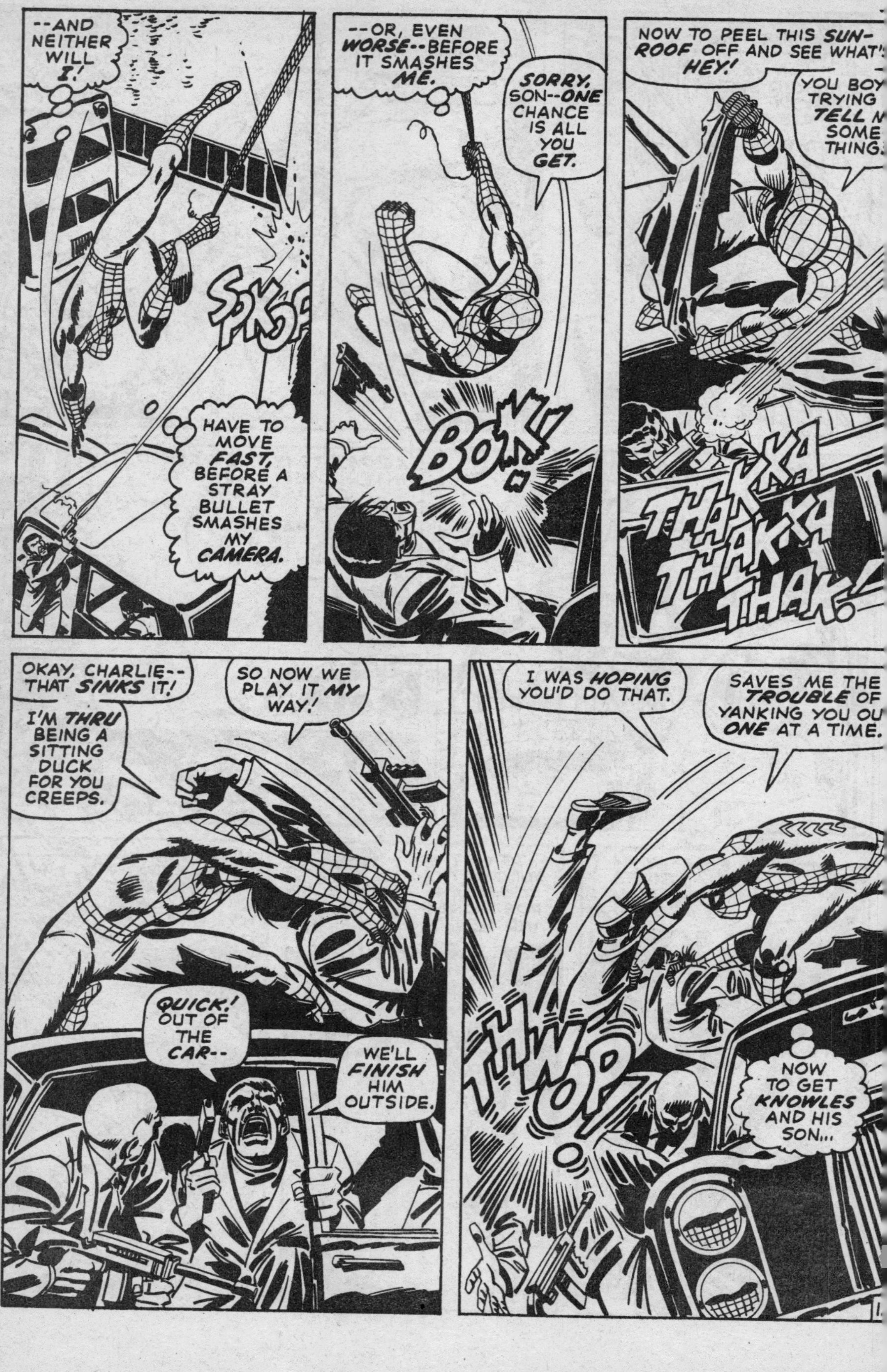
--AND NEITHER WILL I!
SPKOF
HAVE TO MOVE FAST, BEFORE A STRAY BULLET SMASHES MY CAMERA.
--OR, EVEN WORSE--BEFORE IT SMASHES ME.
SORRY, SON--ONE CHANCE IS ALL YOU GET.
BOK!
NOW TO PEEL THIS SUN-ROOF OFF AND SEE WHAT'S
HEY!
YOU BOY TRYING TELL M SOME THINGS
THAKKA THAKKA THAK!
OKAY, CHARLIE--THAT SINKS IT!
I'M THRU BEING A SITTING DUCK FOR YOU CREEPS.
SO NOW WE PLAY IT MY WAY!
QUICK! OUT OF THE CAR--
WE'LL FINISH HIM OUTSIDE.
I WAS HOPING YOU'D DO THAT.
SAVES ME THE TROUBLE OF YANKING YOU OU ONE AT A TIME.
THWOP
NOW TO GET KNOWLES AND HIS SON...

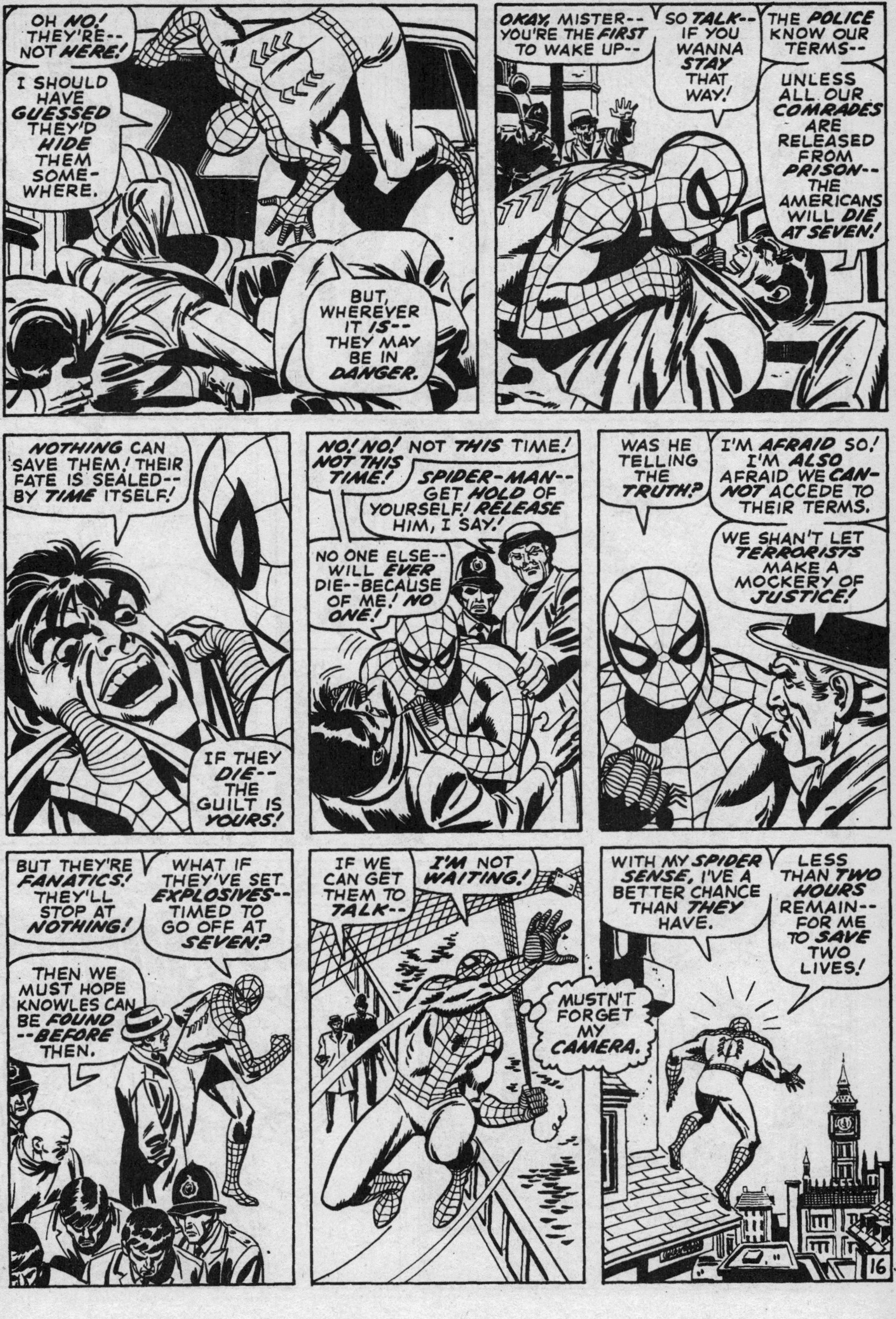
OH NO! THEY'RE-- NOT HERE!
I SHOULD HAVE GUESSED THEY'D HIDE THEM SOME-WHERE.
BUT, WHEREVER IT IS-- THEY MAY BE IN DANGER.
OKAY, MISTER-- YOU'RE THE FIRST TO WAKE UP--
SO TALK-- IF YOU WANNA STAY THAT WAY!
THE POLICE KNOW OUR TERMS--
UNLESS ALL OUR COMRADES ARE RELEASED FROM PRISON-- THE AMERICANS WILL DIE AT SEVEN!
NOTHING CAN SAVE THEM! THEIR FATE IS SEALED-- BY TIME ITSELF!
IF THEY DIE-- THE GUILT IS YOURS!
NO! NO! NOT THIS TIME!
NOT THIS TIME!
SPIDER-MAN-- GET HOLD OF YOURSELF! RELEASE HIM, I SAY!
NO ONE ELSE-- WILL EVER DIE--BECAUSE OF ME! NO ONE!
WAS HE TELLING THE TRUTH?
I'M AFRAID SO! I'M ALSO AFRAID WE CAN-NOT ACCEDE TO THEIR TERMS.
WE SHAN'T LET TERRORISTS MAKE A MOCKERY OF JUSTICE!
BUT THEY'RE FANATICS! THEY'LL STOP AT NOTHING!
WHAT IF THEY'VE SET EXPLOSIVES-- TIMED TO GO OFF AT SEVEN?
THEN WE MUST HOPE KNOWLES CAN BE FOUND --BEFORE THEN.
IF WE CAN GET THEM TO TALK--
I'M NOT WAITING!
MUSTN'T FORGET MY CAMERA.
WITH MY SPIDER SENSE, I'VE A BETTER CHANCE THAN THEY HAVE.
LESS THAN TWO HOURS REMAIN-- FOR ME TO SAVE TWO LIVES!
16

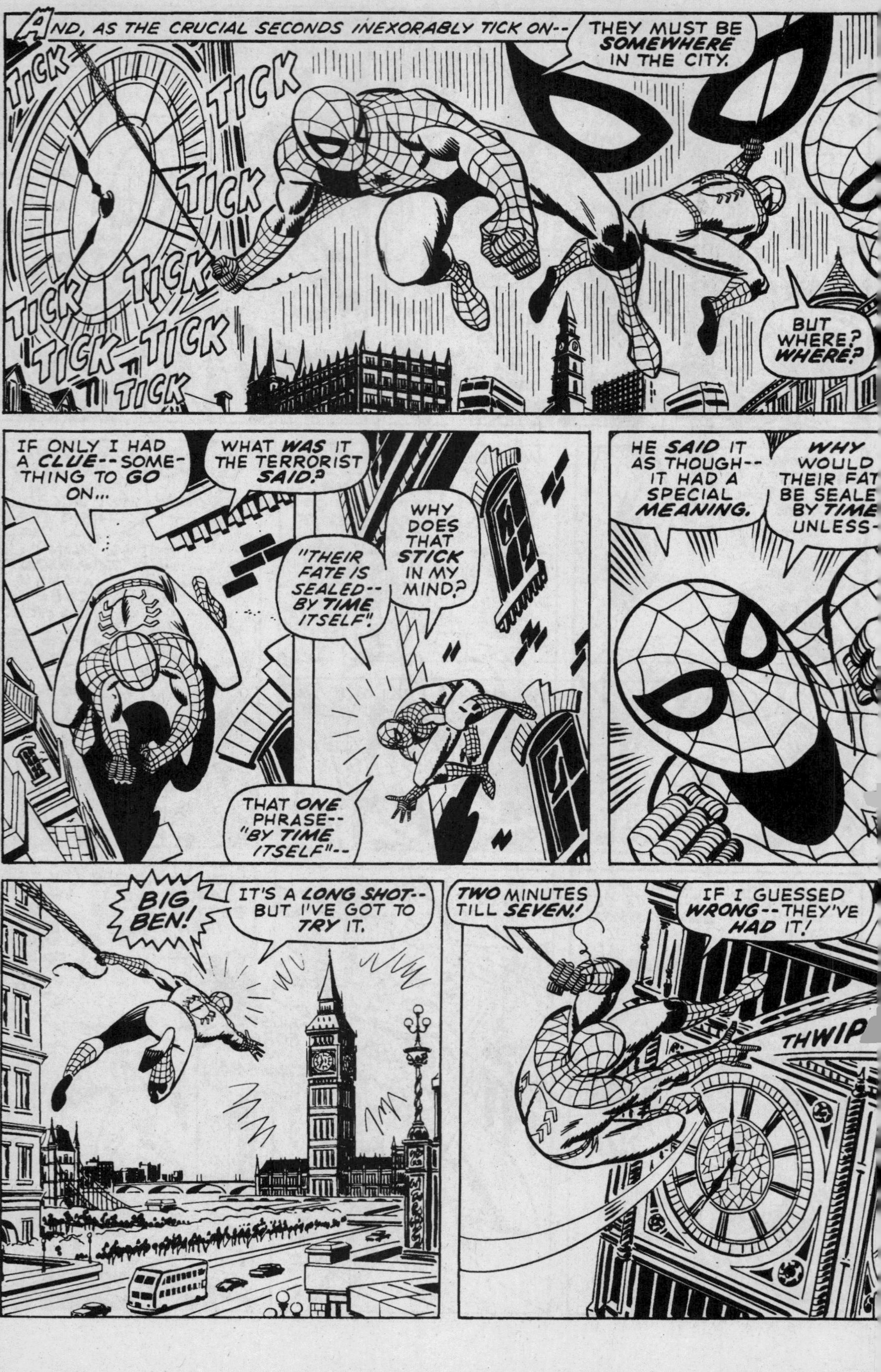
AND, AS THE CRUCIAL SECONDS INEXORABLY TICK ON--
TICK TICK TICK TICK TICK TICK TICK TICK
THEY MUST BE SOMEWHERE IN THE CITY.
BUT WHERE? WHERE?
IF ONLY I HAD A CLUE--SOMETHING TO GO ON...
WHAT WAS IT THE TERRORIST SAID?
"THEIR FATE IS SEALED--BY TIME ITSELF".
WHY DOES THAT STICK IN MY MIND?
THAT ONE PHRASE--"BY TIME ITSELF"--
HE SAID IT AS THOUGH--IT HAD A SPECIAL MEANING.
WHY WOULD THEIR FAT BE SEALE BY TIME UNLESS-
BIG BEN!
IT'S A LONG SHOT--BUT I'VE GOT TO TRY IT.
TWO MINUTES TILL SEVEN!
IF I GUESSED WRONG--THEY'VE HAD IT!
THWIP

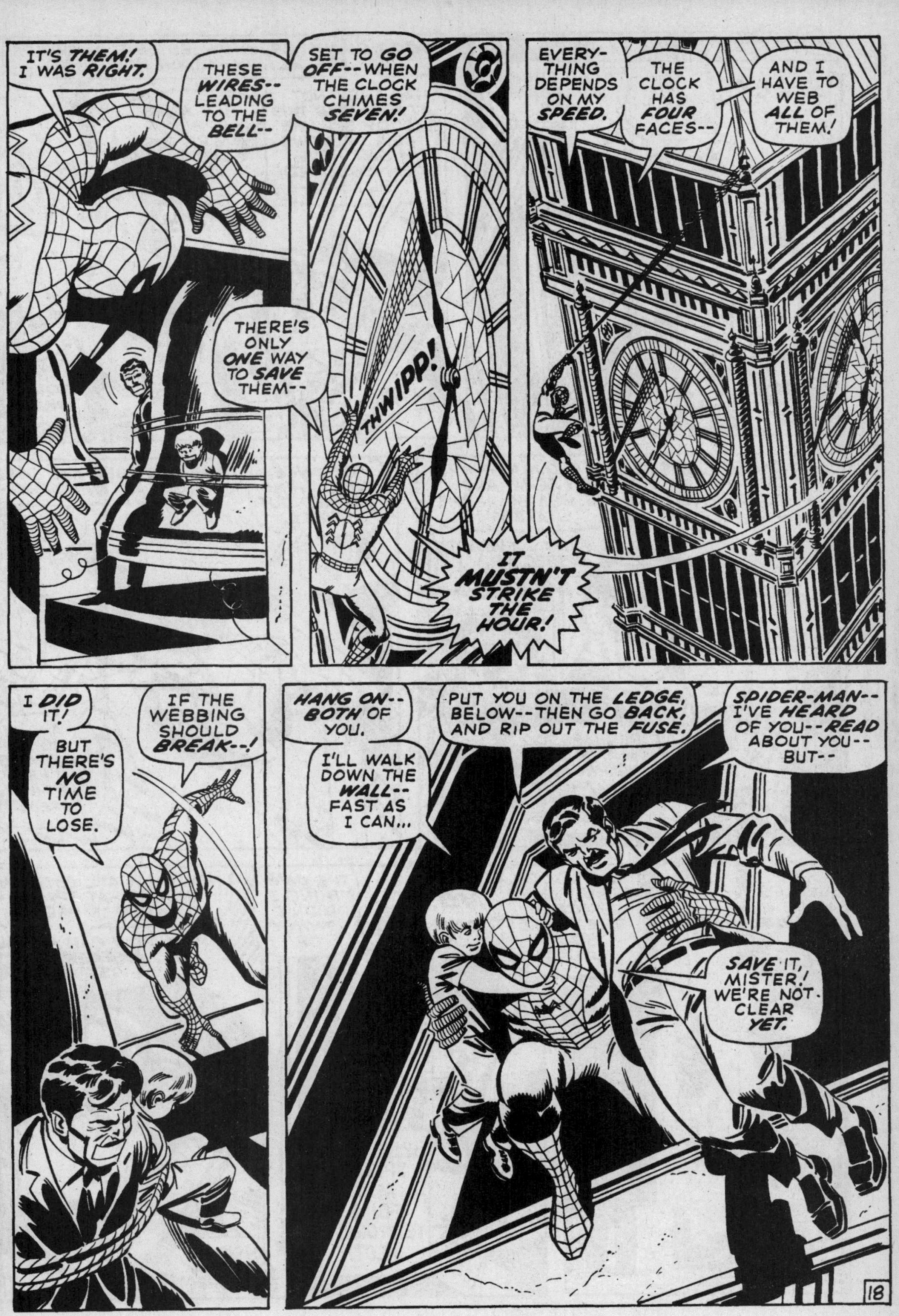
IT'S THEM! I WAS RIGHT.
THESE WIRES--LEADING TO THE BELL--
SET TO GO OFF--WHEN THE CLOCK CHIMES SEVEN!
THERE'S ONLY ONE WAY TO SAVE THEM--
THWIPP!
EVERY-THING DEPENDS ON MY SPEED.
THE CLOCK HAS FOUR FACES--
AND I HAVE TO WEB ALL OF THEM!
IT MUSTN'T STRIKE THE HOUR!
I DID IT!
BUT THERE'S NO TIME TO LOSE.
IF THE WEBBING SHOULD BREAK--!
HANG ON--BOTH OF YOU.
I'LL WALK DOWN THE WALL--FAST AS I CAN...
PUT YOU ON THE LEDGE, BELOW--THEN GO BACK, AND RIP OUT THE FUSE.
SPIDER-MAN--I'VE HEARD OF YOU--READ ABOUT YOU--BUT--
SAVE IT, MISTER! WE'RE NOT CLEAR YET.
18

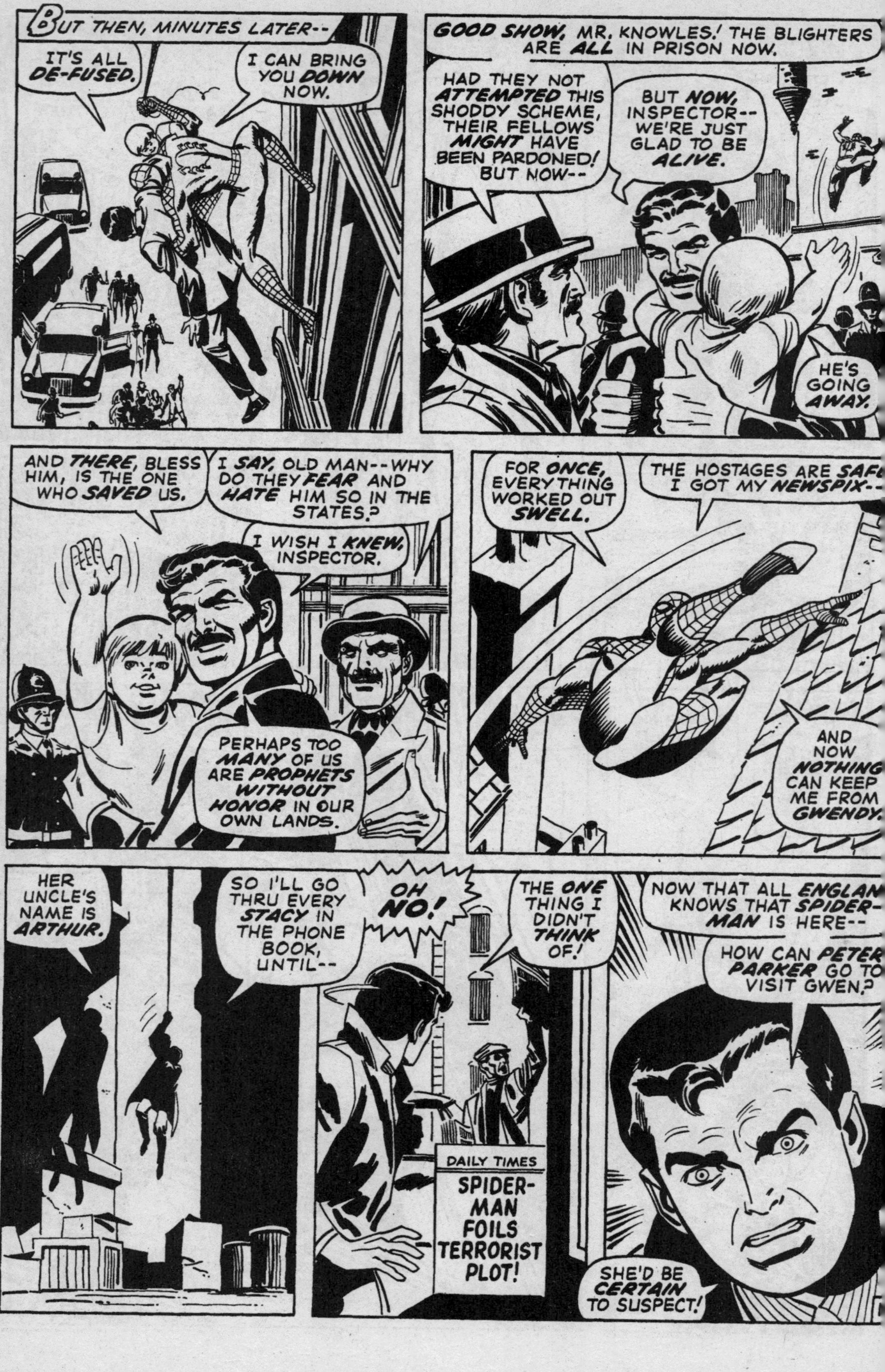
BUT THEN, MINUTES LATER--
IT'S ALL DE-FUSED.
I CAN BRING YOU DOWN NOW.
GOOD SHOW, MR. KNOWLES! THE BLIGHTERS ARE ALL IN PRISON NOW.
HAD THEY NOT ATTEMPTED THIS SHODDY SCHEME, THEIR FELLOWS MIGHT HAVE BEEN PARDONED! BUT NOW--
BUT NOW, INSPECTOR-- WE'RE JUST GLAD TO BE ALIVE.
HE'S GOING AWAY.
AND THERE, BLESS HIM, IS THE ONE WHO SAVED US.
I SAY, OLD MAN--WHY DO THEY FEAR AND HATE HIM SO IN THE STATES?
I WISH I KNEW, INSPECTOR.
PERHAPS TOO MANY OF US ARE PROPHETS WITHOUT HONOR IN OUR OWN LANDS.
FOR ONCE, EVERYTHING WORKED OUT SWELL.
THE HOSTAGES ARE SAFE I GOT MY NEWSPIX--
AND NOW NOTHING CAN KEEP ME FROM GWENDY.
HER UNCLE'S NAME IS ARTHUR.
SO I'LL GO THRU EVERY STACY IN THE PHONE BOOK, UNTIL--
OH NO!
THE ONE THING I DIDN'T THINK OF!
DAILY TIMES
SPIDER-MAN FOILS TERRORIST PLOT!
NOW THAT ALL ENGLAN KNOWS THAT SPIDER-MAN IS HERE--
HOW CAN PETER PARKER GO TO VISIT GWEN?
SHE'D BE CERTAIN TO SUSPECT!

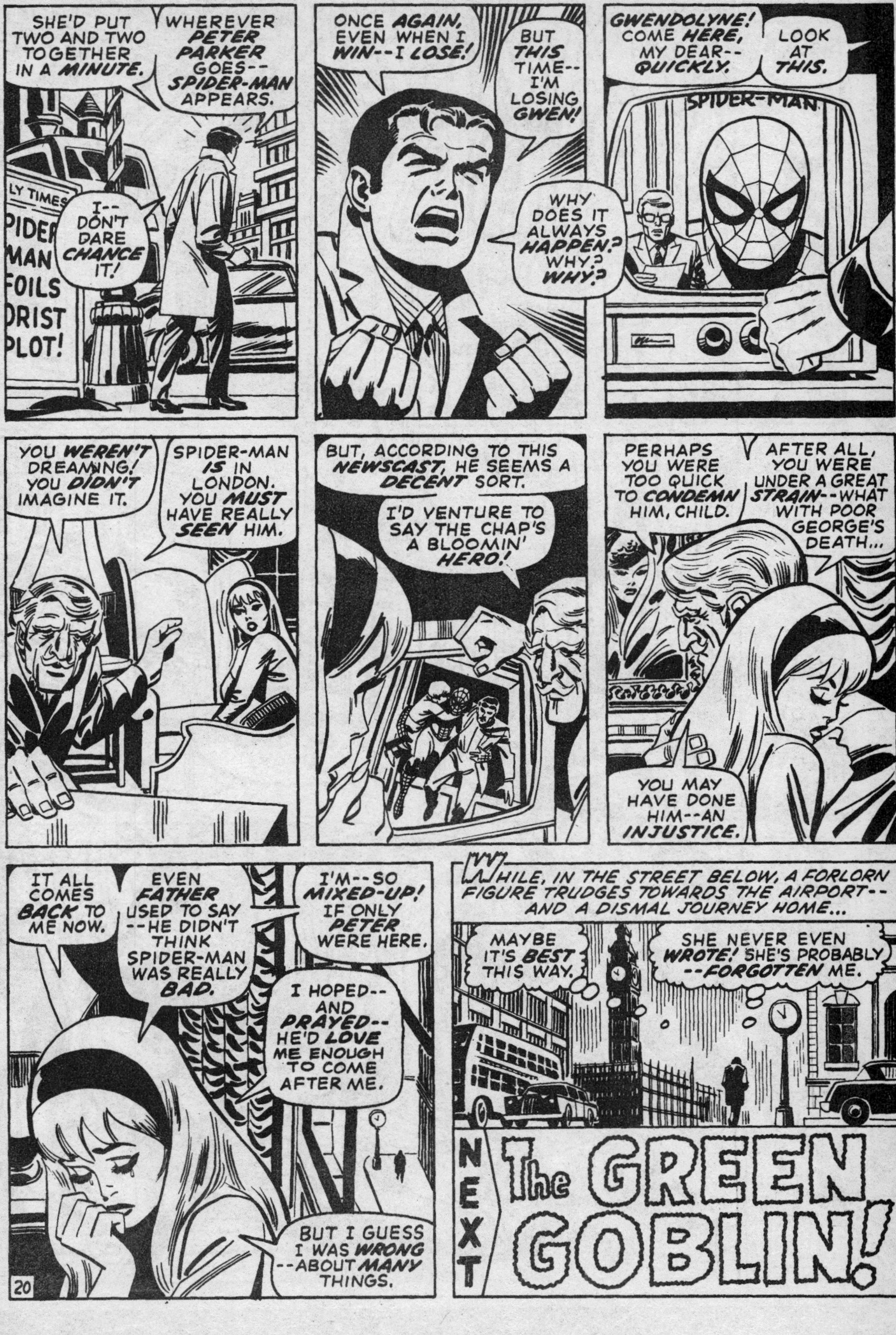

SHE'D PUT TWO AND TWO TOGETHER IN A MINUTE.
WHEREVER PETER PARKER GOES-- SPIDER-MAN APPEARS.
I-- DON'T DARE CHANCE IT!
...LY TIMES
...PIDER MAN FOILS ...ORIST PLOT!
ONCE AGAIN, EVEN WHEN I WIN--I LOSE!
BUT THIS TIME-- I'M LOSING GWEN!
WHY DOES IT ALWAYS HAPPEN? WHY? WHY?
GWENDOLYNE! COME HERE, MY DEAR-- QUICKLY.
LOOK AT THIS.
SPIDER-MAN
YOU WEREN'T DREAMING! YOU DIDN'T IMAGINE IT.
SPIDER-MAN IS IN LONDON. YOU MUST HAVE REALLY SEEN HIM.
BUT, ACCORDING TO THIS NEWSCAST, HE SEEMS A DECENT SORT.
I'D VENTURE TO SAY THE CHAP'S A BLOOMIN' HERO!
PERHAPS YOU WERE TOO QUICK TO CONDEMN HIM, CHILD.
AFTER ALL, YOU WERE UNDER A GREAT STRAIN--WHAT WITH POOR GEORGE'S DEATH...
YOU MAY HAVE DONE HIM--AN INJUSTICE.
IT ALL COMES BACK TO ME NOW.
EVEN FATHER USED TO SAY --HE DIDN'T THINK SPIDER-MAN WAS REALLY BAD.
I'M--SO MIXED-UP! IF ONLY PETER WERE HERE.
I HOPED-- AND PRAYED-- HE'D LOVE ME ENOUGH TO COME AFTER ME.
BUT I GUESS I WAS WRONG --ABOUT MANY THINGS.
20
WHILE, IN THE STREET BELOW, A FORLORN FIGURE TRUDGES TOWARDS THE AIRPORT-- AND A DISMAL JOURNEY HOME...
MAYBE IT'S BEST THIS WAY.
SHE NEVER EVEN WROTE! SHE'S PROBABLY --FORGOTTEN ME.
NEXT
The GREEN GOBLIN!

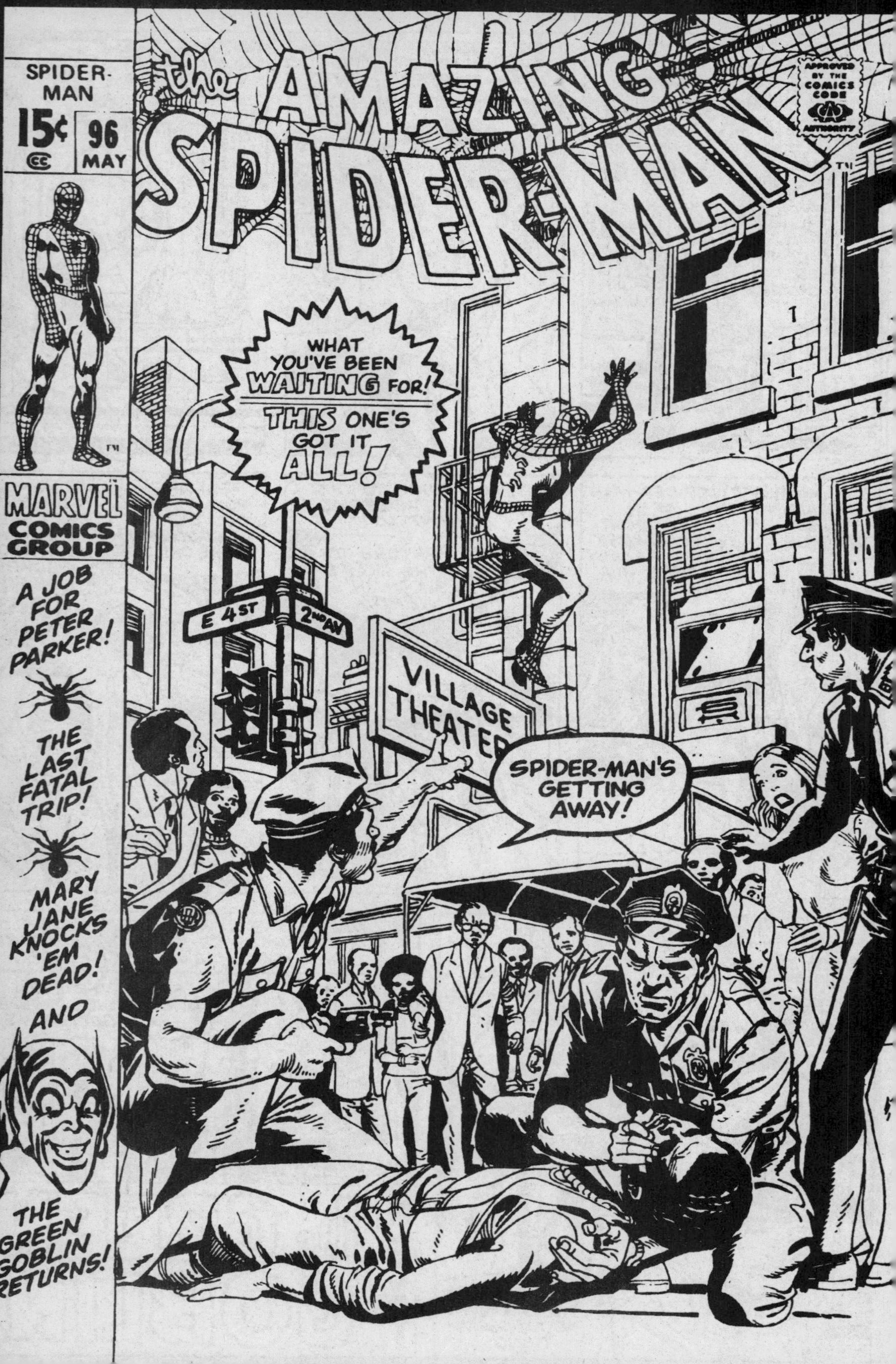

SPIDER-MAN
15¢
96
MAY
the AMAZING SPIDER-MAN
APPROVED BY THE COMICS CODE AUTHORITY
MARVEL COMICS GROUP
A JOB FOR PETER PARKER!
THE LAST FATAL TRIP!
MARY JANE KNOCKS 'EM DEAD!
AND
THE GREEN GOBLIN RETURNS!
WHAT YOU'VE BEEN WAITING FOR!
THIS ONE'S GOT IT ALL!
E 4ST
2ND AV
VILLAGE THEATER
SPIDER-MAN'S GETTING AWAY!

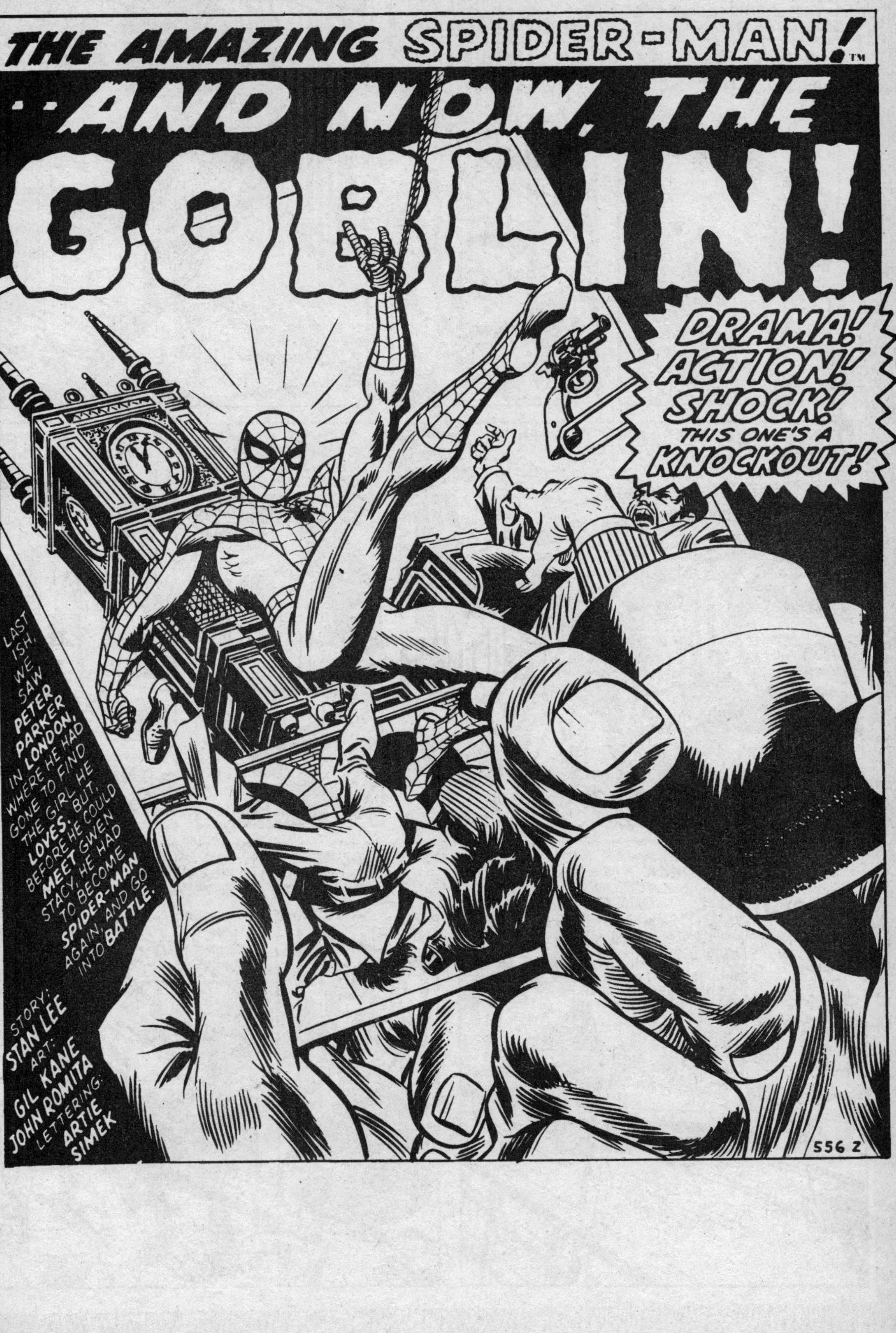
THE AMAZING SPIDER-MAN!™
--AND NOW, THE GOBLIN!
DRAMA! ACTION! SHOCK! THIS ONE'S A KNOCKOUT!
LAST ISH, WE SAW PETER PARKER IN LONDON, WHERE HE HAD GONE TO FIND THE GIRL HE LOVES. BUT, BEFORE HE COULD MEET GWEN STACY, HE HAD TO BECOME SPIDER-MAN AGAIN, AND GO INTO BATTLE.
STORY: STAN LEE
ART: GIL KANE JOHN ROMITA
LETTERING: ARTIE SIMEK
556 2

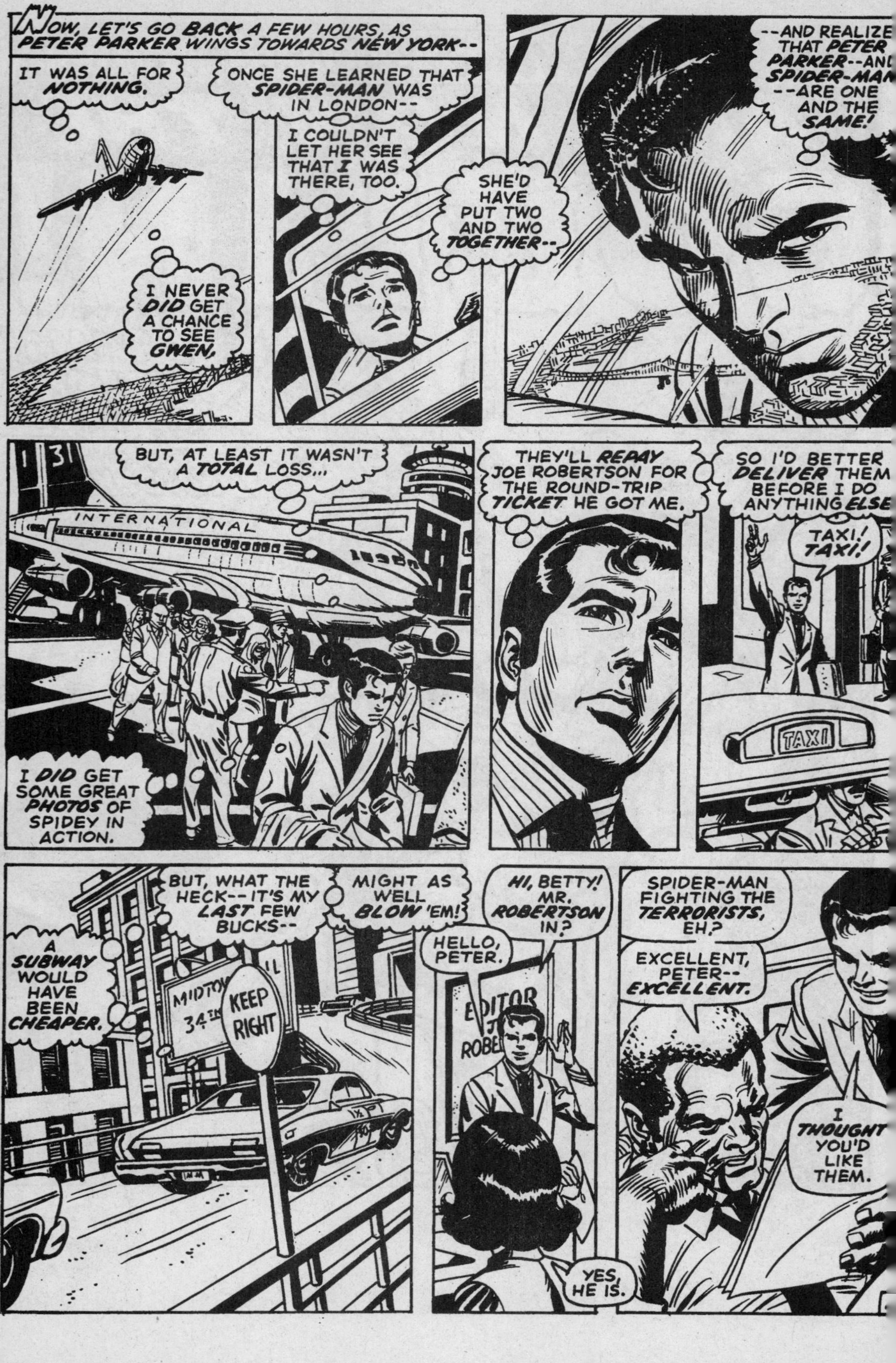
NOW, LET'S GO BACK A FEW HOURS, AS PETER PARKER WINGS TOWARDS NEW YORK--
IT WAS ALL FOR NOTHING.
I NEVER DID GET A CHANCE TO SEE GWEN.
ONCE SHE LEARNED THAT SPIDER-MAN WAS IN LONDON--
I COULDN'T LET HER SEE THAT I WAS THERE, TOO.
SHE'D HAVE PUT TWO AND TWO TOGETHER--
--AND REALIZE THAT PETER PARKER--AND SPIDER-MAN --ARE ONE AND THE SAME!
BUT, AT LEAST IT WASN'T A TOTAL LOSS...
INTERNATIONAL
I DID GET SOME GREAT PHOTOS OF SPIDEY IN ACTION.
THEY'LL REPAY JOE ROBERTSON FOR THE ROUND-TRIP TICKET HE GOT ME.
SO I'D BETTER DELIVER THEM BEFORE I DO ANYTHING ELSE
TAXI! TAXI!
TAXI
A SUBWAY WOULD HAVE BEEN CHEAPER.
BUT, WHAT THE HECK-- IT'S MY LAST FEW BUCKS--
MIGHT AS WELL BLOW 'EM!
KEEP RIGHT
HI, BETTY! MR. ROBERTSON IN?
HELLO, PETER.
YES, HE IS.
SPIDER-MAN FIGHTING THE TERRORISTS, EH?
EXCELLENT, PETER-- EXCELLENT.
I THOUGHT YOU'D LIKE THEM.

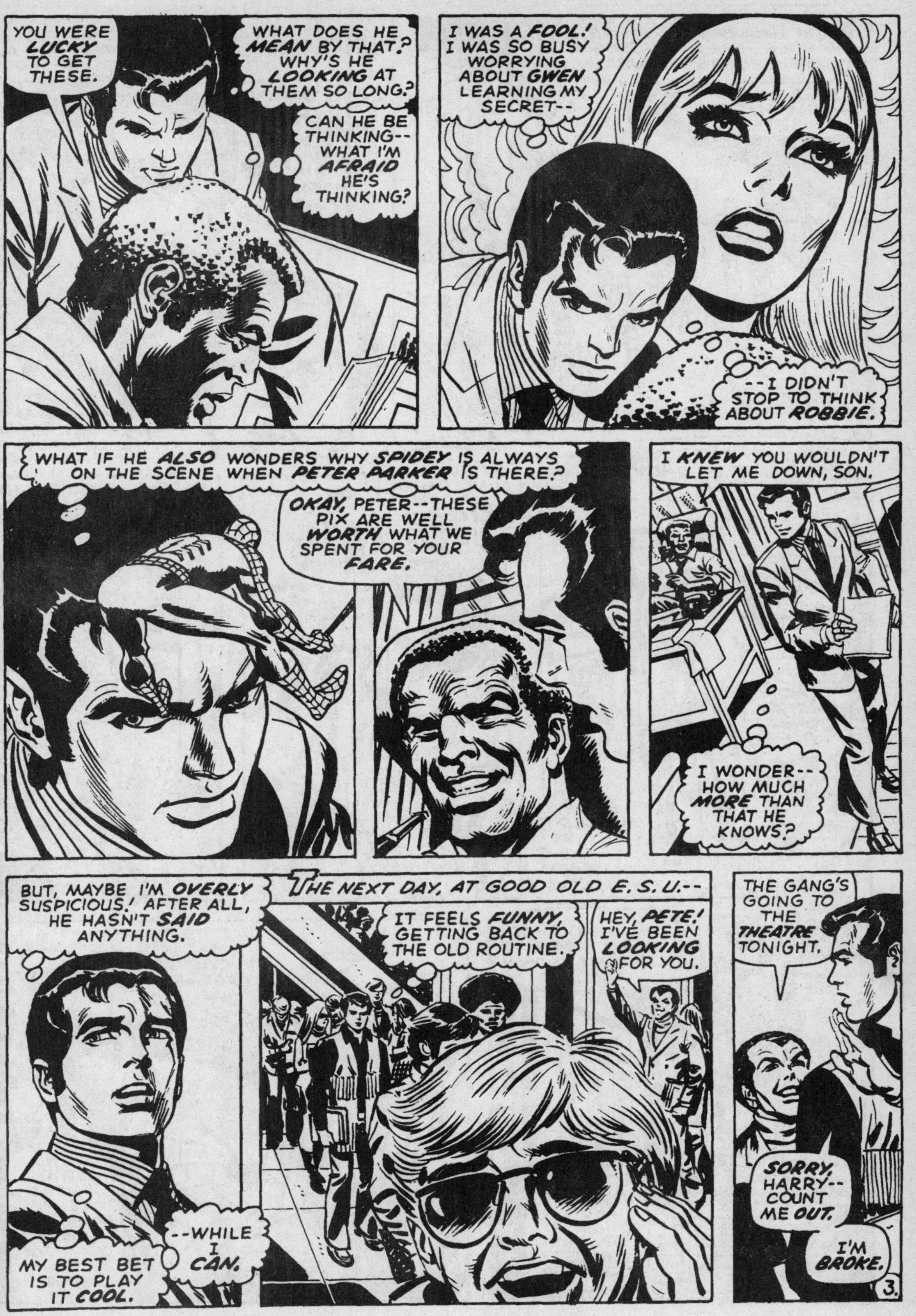
YOU WERE LUCKY TO GET THESE.
WHAT DOES HE MEAN BY THAT? WHY'S HE LOOKING AT THEM SO LONG?
CAN HE BE THINKING-- WHAT I'M AFRAID HE'S THINKING?
I WAS A FOOL! I WAS SO BUSY WORRYING ABOUT GWEN LEARNING MY SECRET--
--I DIDN'T STOP TO THINK ABOUT ROBBIE.
WHAT IF HE ALSO WONDERS WHY SPIDEY IS ALWAYS ON THE SCENE WHEN PETER PARKER IS THERE?
OKAY, PETER--THESE PIX ARE WELL WORTH WHAT WE SPENT FOR YOUR FARE.
I KNEW YOU WOULDN'T LET ME DOWN, SON.
I WONDER-- HOW MUCH MORE THAN THAT HE KNOWS?
BUT, MAYBE I'M OVERLY SUSPICIOUS! AFTER ALL, HE HASN'T SAID ANYTHING.
MY BEST BET IS TO PLAY IT COOL.
--WHILE I CAN.
THE NEXT DAY, AT GOOD OLD E. S. U.--
IT FEELS FUNNY, GETTING BACK TO THE OLD ROUTINE.
HEY, PETE! I'VE BEEN LOOKING FOR YOU.
THE GANG'S GOING TO THE THEATRE TONIGHT.
SORRY, HARRY-- COUNT ME OUT.
I'M BROKE.
3.

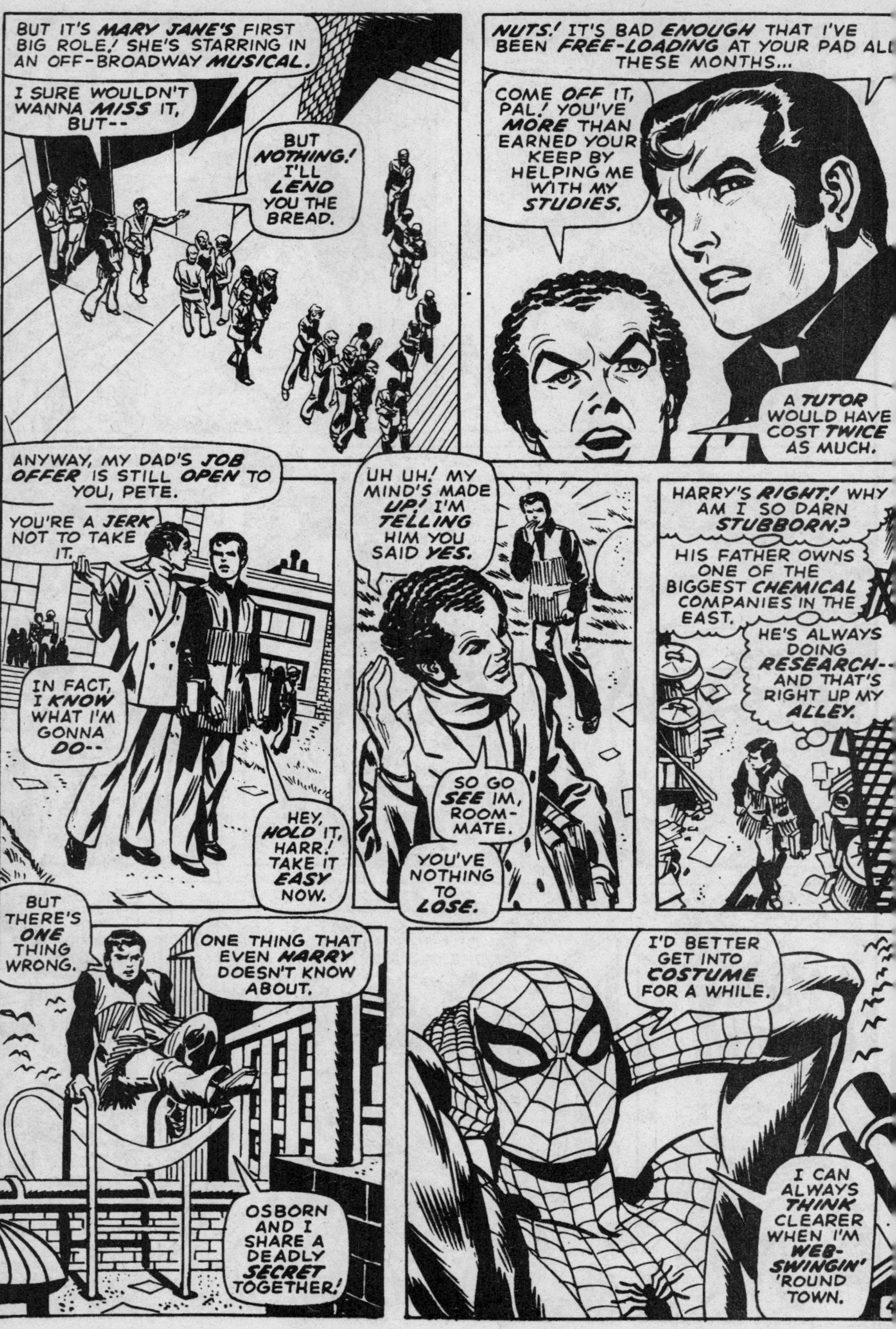

BUT IT'S MARY JANE'S FIRST BIG ROLE! SHE'S STARRING IN AN OFF-BROADWAY MUSICAL.
I SURE WOULDN'T WANNA MISS IT, BUT--
BUT NOTHING! I'LL LEND YOU THE BREAD.
NUTS! IT'S BAD ENOUGH THAT I'VE BEEN FREE-LOADING AT YOUR PAD ALL THESE MONTHS...
COME OFF IT, PAL! YOU'VE MORE THAN EARNED YOUR KEEP BY HELPING ME WITH MY STUDIES.
A TUTOR WOULD HAVE COST TWICE AS MUCH.
ANYWAY, MY DAD'S JOB OFFER IS STILL OPEN TO YOU, PETE.
YOU'RE A JERK NOT TO TAKE IT.
IN FACT, I KNOW WHAT I'M GONNA DO--
HEY, HOLD IT, HARR! TAKE IT EASY NOW.
UH UH! MY MIND'S MADE UP! I'M TELLING HIM YOU SAID YES.
SO GO SEE IM, ROOM-MATE.
YOU'VE NOTHING TO LOSE.
HARRY'S RIGHT! WHY AM I SO DARN STUBBORN?
HIS FATHER OWNS ONE OF THE BIGGEST CHEMICAL COMPANIES IN THE EAST.
HE'S ALWAYS DOING RESEARCH-- AND THAT'S RIGHT UP MY ALLEY.
BUT THERE'S ONE THING WRONG.
ONE THING THAT EVEN HARRY DOESN'T KNOW ABOUT.
OSBORN AND I SHARE A DEADLY SECRET TOGETHER!
I'D BETTER GET INTO COSTUME FOR A WHILE.
I CAN ALWAYS THINK CLEARER WHEN I'M WEB-SWINGIN' 'ROUND TOWN.

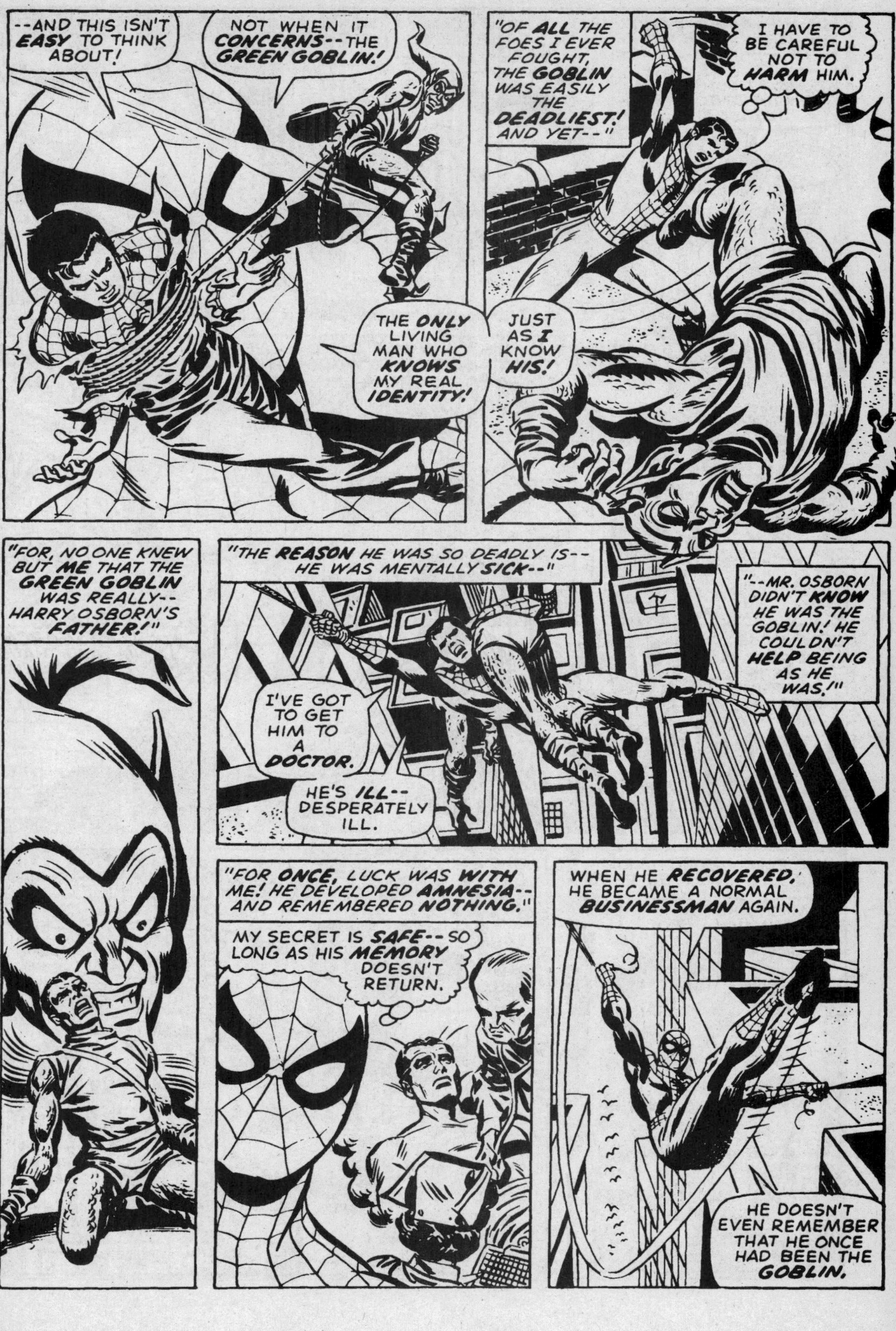

--AND THIS ISN'T EASY TO THINK ABOUT!
NOT WHEN IT CONCERNS--THE GREEN GOBLIN!
THE ONLY LIVING MAN WHO KNOWS MY REAL IDENTITY!
"OF ALL THE FOES I EVER FOUGHT, THE GOBLIN WAS EASILY THE DEADLIEST! AND YET--"
I HAVE TO BE CAREFUL NOT TO HARM HIM.
JUST AS I KNOW HIS!
"FOR, NO ONE KNEW BUT ME THAT THE GREEN GOBLIN WAS REALLY--HARRY OSBORN'S FATHER!"
"THE REASON HE WAS SO DEADLY IS--HE WAS MENTALLY SICK--"
"--MR. OSBORN DIDN'T KNOW HE WAS THE GOBLIN! HE COULDN'T HELP BEING AS HE WAS."
I'VE GOT TO GET HIM TO A DOCTOR.
HE'S ILL--DESPERATELY ILL.
"FOR ONCE, LUCK WAS WITH ME! HE DEVELOPED AMNESIA--AND REMEMBERED NOTHING."
MY SECRET IS SAFE--SO LONG AS HIS MEMORY DOESN'T RETURN.
WHEN HE RECOVERED, HE BECAME A NORMAL BUSINESSMAN AGAIN.
HE DOESN'T EVEN REMEMBER THAT HE ONCE HAD BEEN THE GOBLIN.

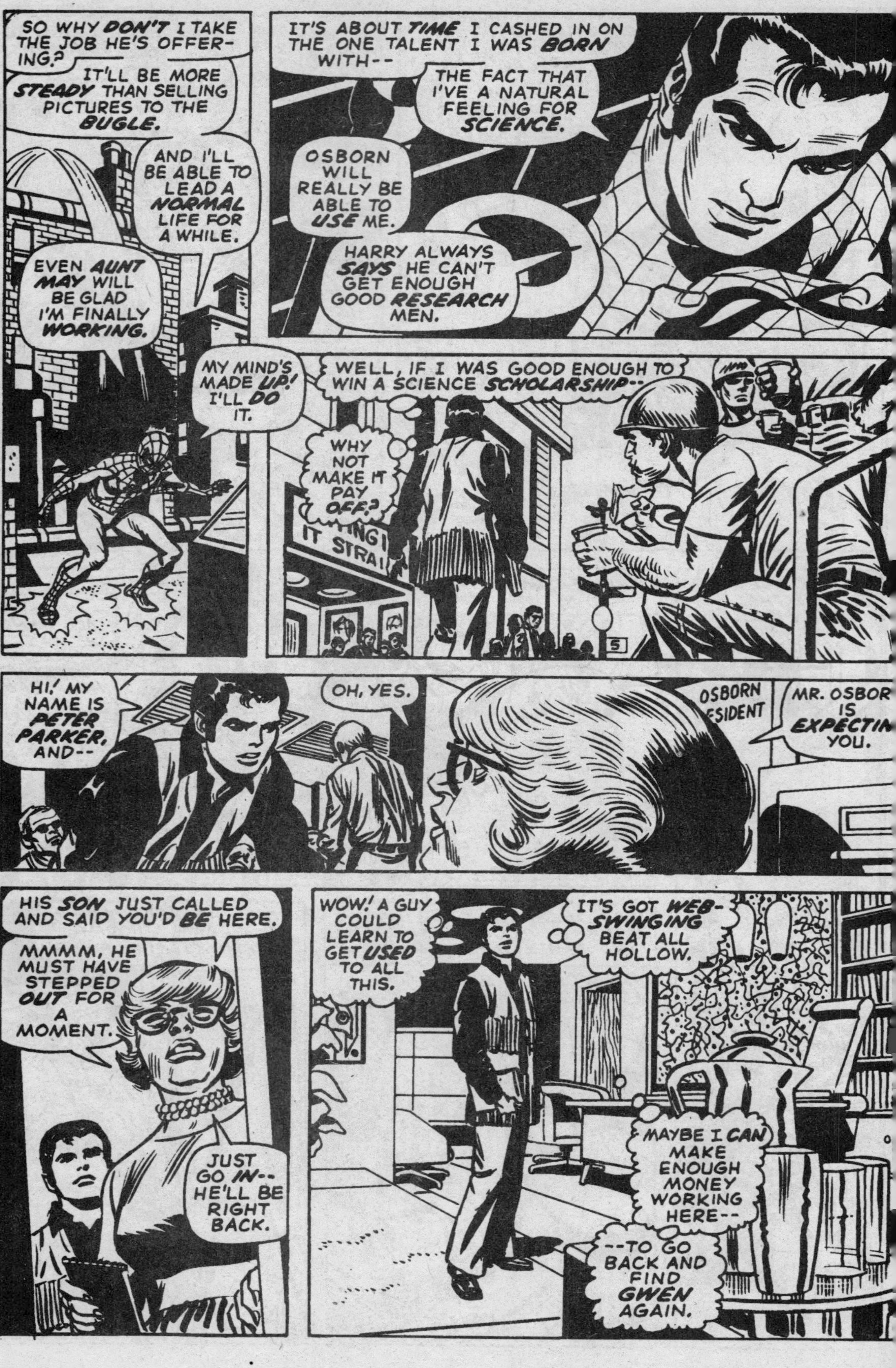
SO WHY DON'T I TAKE THE JOB HE'S OFFERING?
IT'LL BE MORE STEADY THAN SELLING PICTURES TO THE BUGLE.
AND I'LL BE ABLE TO LEAD A NORMAL LIFE FOR A WHILE.
EVEN AUNT MAY WILL BE GLAD I'M FINALLY WORKING.
IT'S ABOUT TIME I CASHED IN ON THE ONE TALENT I WAS BORN WITH--
THE FACT THAT I'VE A NATURAL FEELING FOR SCIENCE.
OSBORN WILL REALLY BE ABLE TO USE ME.
HARRY ALWAYS SAYS HE CAN'T GET ENOUGH GOOD RESEARCH MEN.
MY MIND'S MADE UP! I'LL DO IT.
WELL, IF I WAS GOOD ENOUGH TO WIN A SCIENCE SCHOLARSHIP--
WHY NOT MAKE IT PAY OFF?
5
HI! MY NAME IS PETER PARKER, AND--
OH, YES.
OSBORN
MR. OSBOR IS EXPECTIN YOU.
HIS SON JUST CALLED AND SAID YOU'D BE HERE.
MMMM, HE MUST HAVE STEPPED OUT FOR A MOMENT.
JUST GO IN-- HE'LL BE RIGHT BACK.
WOW! A GUY COULD LEARN TO GET USED TO ALL THIS.
IT'S GOT WEB-SWINGING BEAT ALL HOLLOW.
MAYBE I CAN MAKE ENOUGH MONEY WORKING HERE--
--TO GO BACK AND FIND GWEN AGAIN.

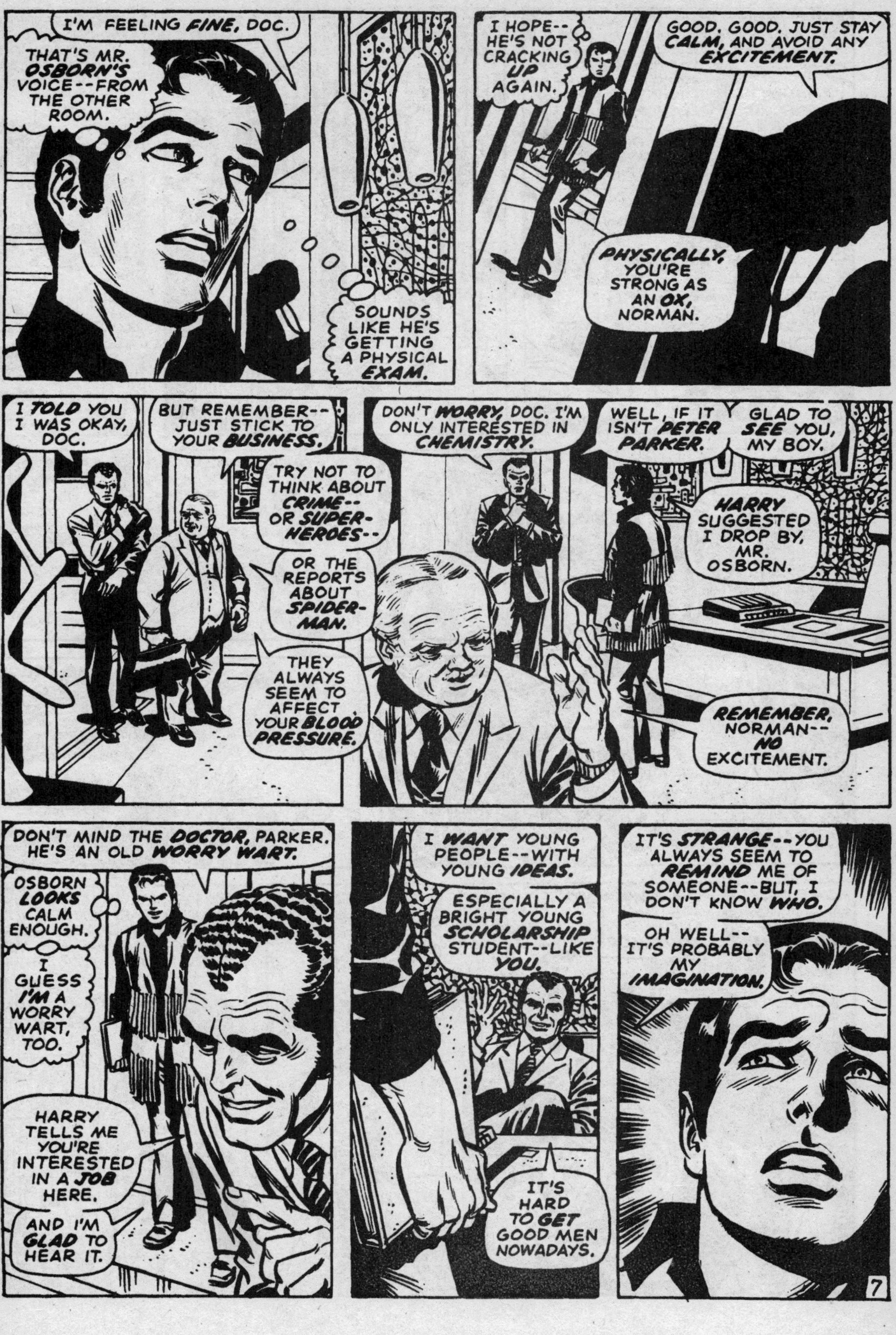
I'M FEELING FINE, DOC.
THAT'S MR. OSBORN'S VOICE--FROM THE OTHER ROOM.
SOUNDS LIKE HE'S GETTING A PHYSICAL EXAM.
I HOPE--HE'S NOT CRACKING UP AGAIN.
GOOD. GOOD. JUST STAY CALM, AND AVOID ANY EXCITEMENT.
PHYSICALLY, YOU'RE STRONG AS AN OX, NORMAN.
I TOLD YOU I WAS OKAY, DOC.
BUT REMEMBER--JUST STICK TO YOUR BUSINESS.
TRY NOT TO THINK ABOUT CRIME--OR SUPER-HEROES--
OR THE REPORTS ABOUT SPIDER-MAN.
THEY ALWAYS SEEM TO AFFECT YOUR BLOOD PRESSURE.
DON'T WORRY, DOC. I'M ONLY INTERESTED IN CHEMISTRY.
WELL, IF IT ISN'T PETER PARKER.
GLAD TO SEE YOU, MY BOY.
HARRY SUGGESTED I DROP BY, MR. OSBORN.
REMEMBER, NORMAN--NO EXCITEMENT.
DON'T MIND THE DOCTOR, PARKER. HE'S AN OLD WORRY WART.
OSBORN LOOKS CALM ENOUGH.
I GUESS I'M A WORRY WART, TOO.
HARRY TELLS ME YOU'RE INTERESTED IN A JOB HERE.
AND I'M GLAD TO HEAR IT.
I WANT YOUNG PEOPLE--WITH YOUNG IDEAS.
ESPECIALLY A BRIGHT YOUNG SCHOLARSHIP STUDENT--LIKE YOU.
IT'S HARD TO GET GOOD MEN NOWADAYS.
IT'S STRANGE--YOU ALWAYS SEEM TO REMIND ME OF SOMEONE--BUT, I DON'T KNOW WHO.
OH WELL--IT'S PROBABLY MY IMAGINATION.
7

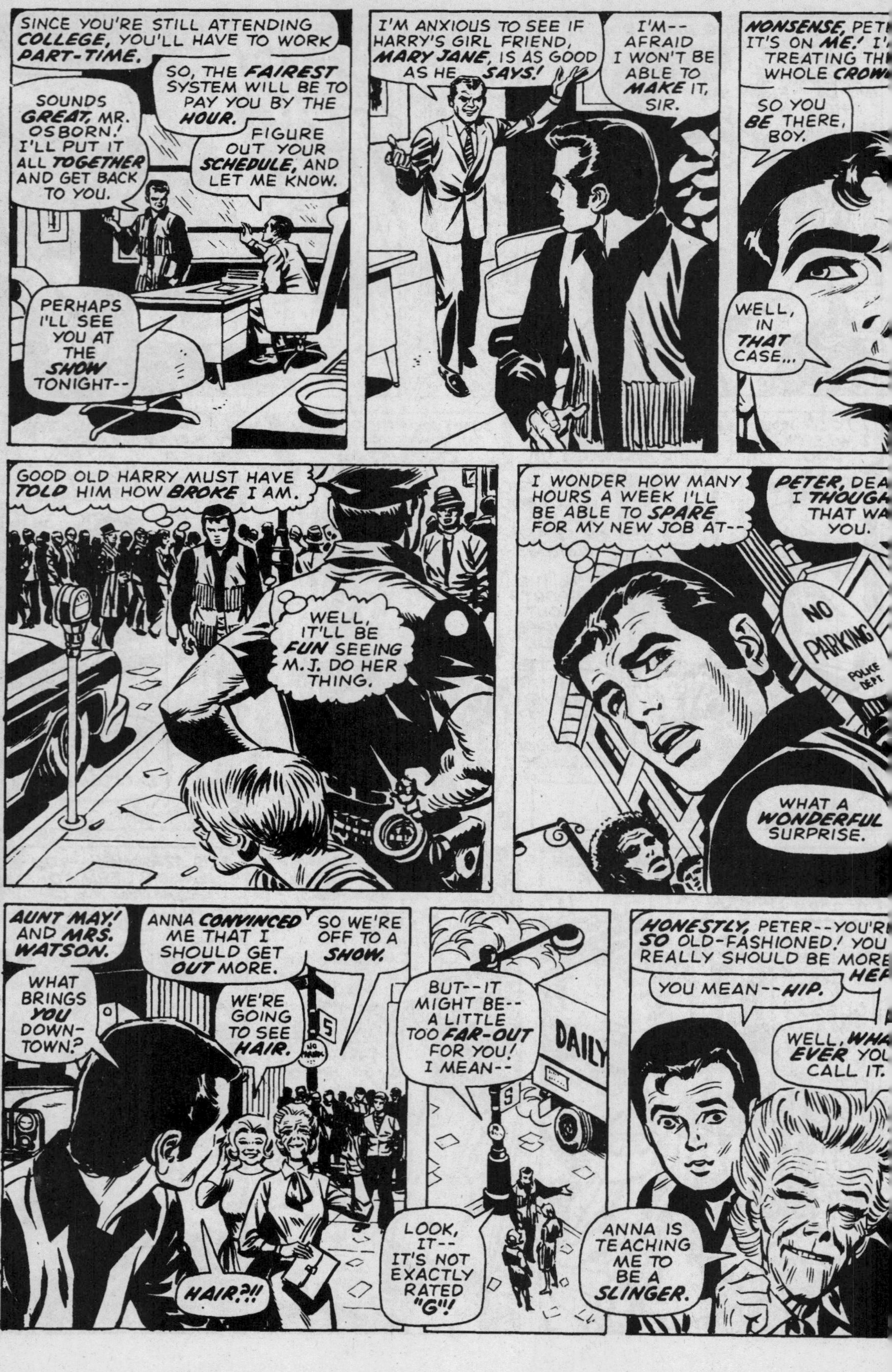

SINCE YOU'RE STILL ATTENDING COLLEGE, YOU'LL HAVE TO WORK PART-TIME.
SO, THE FAIREST SYSTEM WILL BE TO PAY YOU BY THE HOUR.
SOUNDS GREAT, MR. OSBORN! I'LL PUT IT ALL TOGETHER AND GET BACK TO YOU.
FIGURE OUT YOUR SCHEDULE, AND LET ME KNOW.
PERHAPS I'LL SEE YOU AT THE SHOW TONIGHT--
I'M ANXIOUS TO SEE IF HARRY'S GIRL FRIEND, MARY JANE, IS AS GOOD AS HE SAYS!
I'M-- AFRAID I WON'T BE ABLE TO MAKE IT, SIR.
NONSENSE, PETE IT'S ON ME! I' TREATING TH WHOLE CROW
SO YOU BE THERE, BOY.
WELL, IN THAT CASE...
GOOD OLD HARRY MUST HAVE TOLD HIM HOW BROKE I AM.
WELL, IT'LL BE FUN SEEING M.J. DO HER THING.
I WONDER HOW MANY HOURS A WEEK I'LL BE ABLE TO SPARE FOR MY NEW JOB AT--
PETER, DEA I THOUGH THAT WA YOU.
NO PARKING POLICE DEPT.
WHAT A WONDERFUL SURPRISE.
AUNT MAY! AND MRS. WATSON.
WHAT BRINGS YOU DOWN-TOWN?
ANNA CONVINCED ME THAT I SHOULD GET OUT MORE.
SO WE'RE OFF TO A SHOW.
WE'RE GOING TO SEE HAIR.
HAIR?!!
BUT--IT MIGHT BE-- A LITTLE TOO FAR-OUT FOR YOU! I MEAN--
DAILY
LOOK, IT-- IT'S NOT EXACTLY RATED "G"!
HONESTLY, PETER--YOU'R SO OLD-FASHIONED! YOU REALLY SHOULD BE MORE HEP
YOU MEAN--HIP.
WELL, WHA EVER YO CALL IT.
ANNA IS TEACHING ME TO BE A SLINGER.

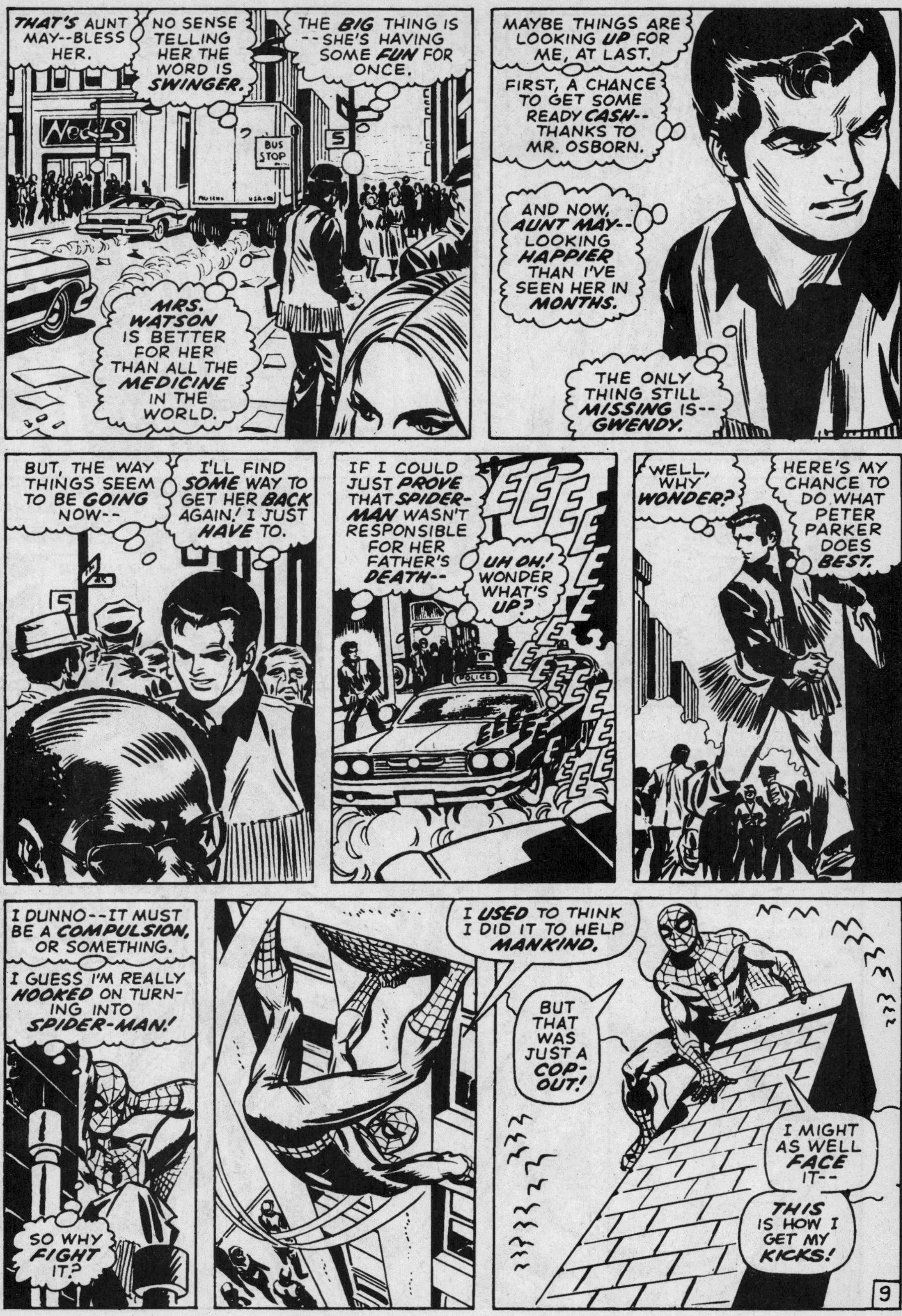
THAT'S AUNT MAY--BLESS HER.
NO SENSE TELLING HER THE WORD IS SWINGER.
THE BIG THING IS --SHE'S HAVING SOME FUN FOR ONCE.
BUS STOP
MRS. WATSON IS BETTER FOR HER THAN ALL THE MEDICINE IN THE WORLD.
MAYBE THINGS ARE LOOKING UP FOR ME, AT LAST.
FIRST, A CHANCE TO GET SOME READY CASH-- THANKS TO MR. OSBORN.
AND NOW, AUNT MAY-- LOOKING HAPPIER THAN I'VE SEEN HER IN MONTHS.
THE ONLY THING STILL MISSING IS-- GWENDY.
BUT, THE WAY THINGS SEEM TO BE GOING NOW--
I'LL FIND SOME WAY TO GET HER BACK AGAIN! I JUST HAVE TO.
IF I COULD JUST PROVE THAT SPIDER-MAN WASN'T RESPONSIBLE FOR HER FATHER'S DEATH--
EEEEEEEEEEEEEEEEEEE
UH OH! WONDER WHAT'S UP?
POLICE
WELL, WHY WONDER?
HERE'S MY CHANCE TO DO WHAT PETER PARKER DOES BEST.
I DUNNO--IT MUST BE A COMPULSION, OR SOMETHING.
I GUESS I'M REALLY HOOKED ON TURNING INTO SPIDER-MAN!
SO WHY FIGHT IT?
I USED TO THINK I DID IT TO HELP MANKIND.
BUT THAT WAS JUST A COP-OUT!
I MIGHT AS WELL FACE IT--
THIS IS HOW I GET MY KICKS!

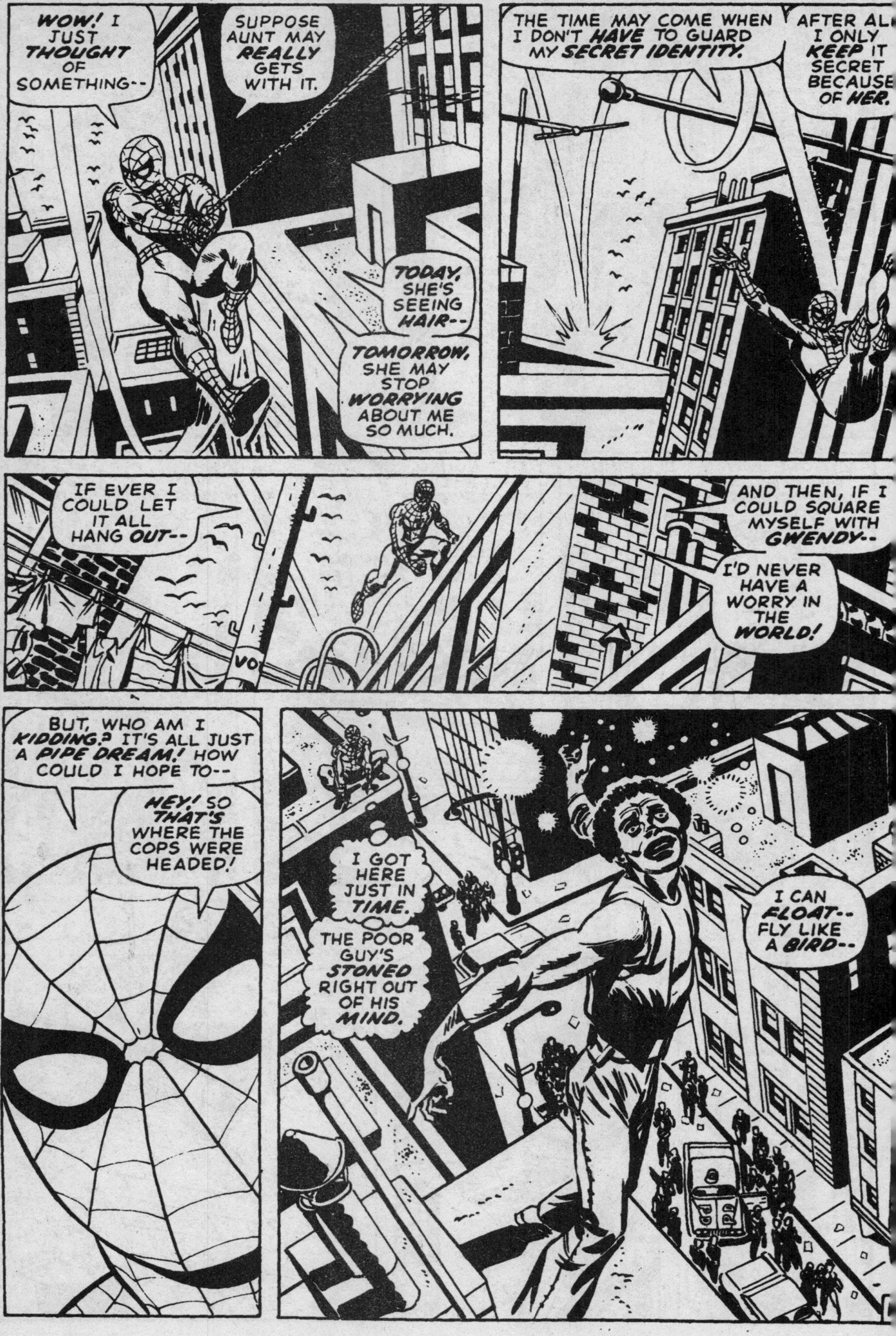

WOW! I JUST THOUGHT OF SOMETHING--
SUPPOSE AUNT MAY REALLY GETS WITH IT.
TODAY, SHE'S SEEING HAIR--
TOMORROW, SHE MAY STOP WORRYING ABOUT ME SO MUCH.
THE TIME MAY COME WHEN I DON'T HAVE TO GUARD MY SECRET IDENTITY.
AFTER AL I ONLY KEEP IT SECRET BECAUSE OF HER.
IF EVER I COULD LET IT ALL HANG OUT--
AND THEN, IF I COULD SQUARE MYSELF WITH GWENDY--
I'D NEVER HAVE A WORRY IN THE WORLD!
BUT, WHO AM I KIDDING? IT'S ALL JUST A PIPE DREAM! HOW COULD I HOPE TO--
HEY! SO THAT'S WHERE THE COPS WERE HEADED!
I GOT HERE JUST IN TIME.
THE POOR GUY'S STONED RIGHT OUT OF HIS MIND.
I CAN FLOAT-- FLY LIKE A BIRD--

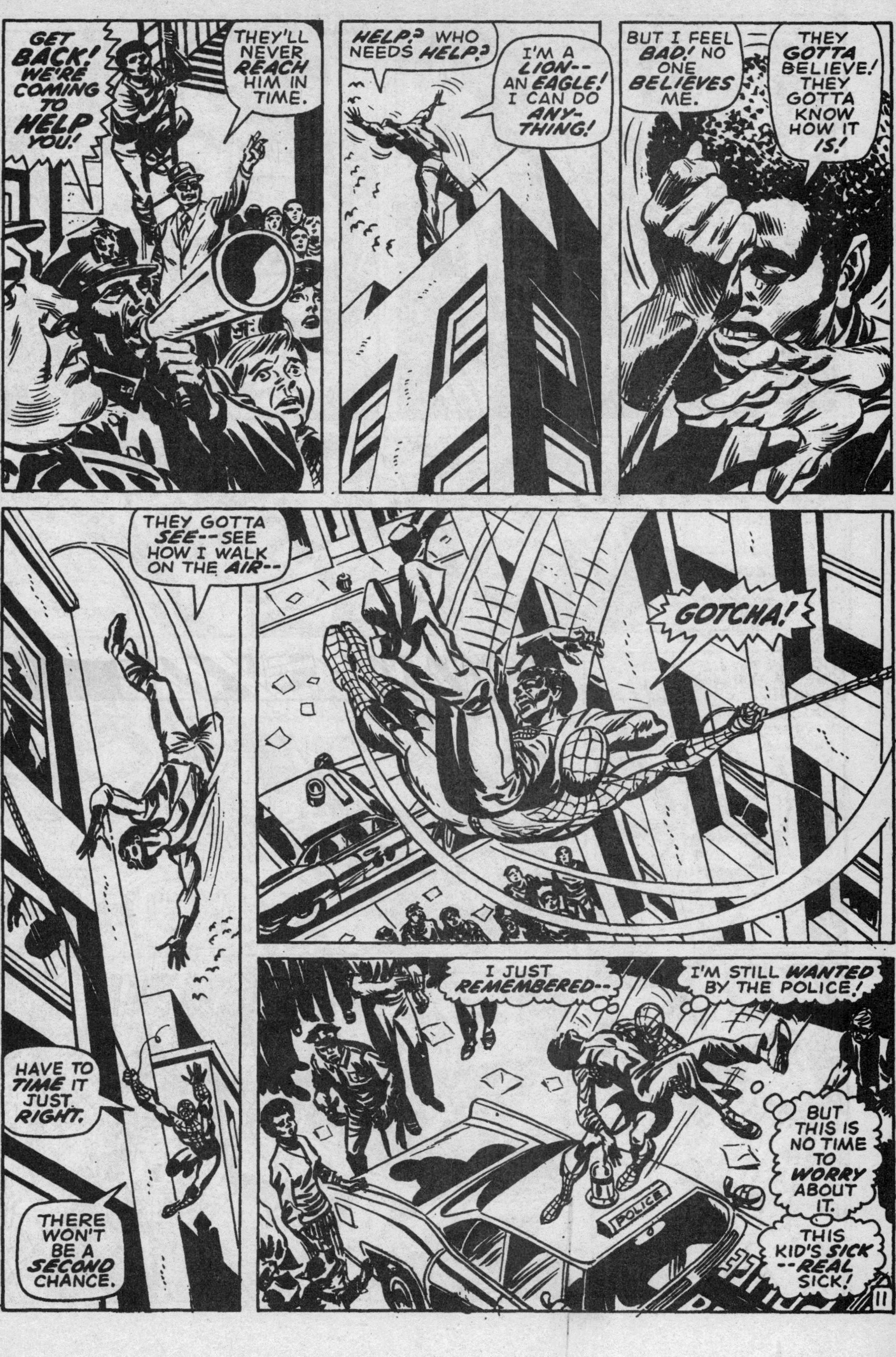
GET BACK! WE'RE COMING TO HELP YOU!
THEY'LL NEVER REACH HIM IN TIME.
HELP? WHO NEEDS HELP?
I'M A LION-- AN EAGLE! I CAN DO ANY-THING!
BUT I FEEL BAD! NO ONE BELIEVES ME.
THEY GOTTA BELIEVE! THEY GOTTA KNOW HOW IT IS!
THEY GOTTA SEE--SEE HOW I WALK ON THE AIR--
HAVE TO TIME IT JUST RIGHT.
THERE WON'T BE A SECOND CHANCE.
GOTCHA!
I JUST REMEMBERED--
I'M STILL WANTED BY THE POLICE!
BUT THIS IS NO TIME TO WORRY ABOUT IT.
THIS KID'S SICK --REAL SICK!
POLICE
11

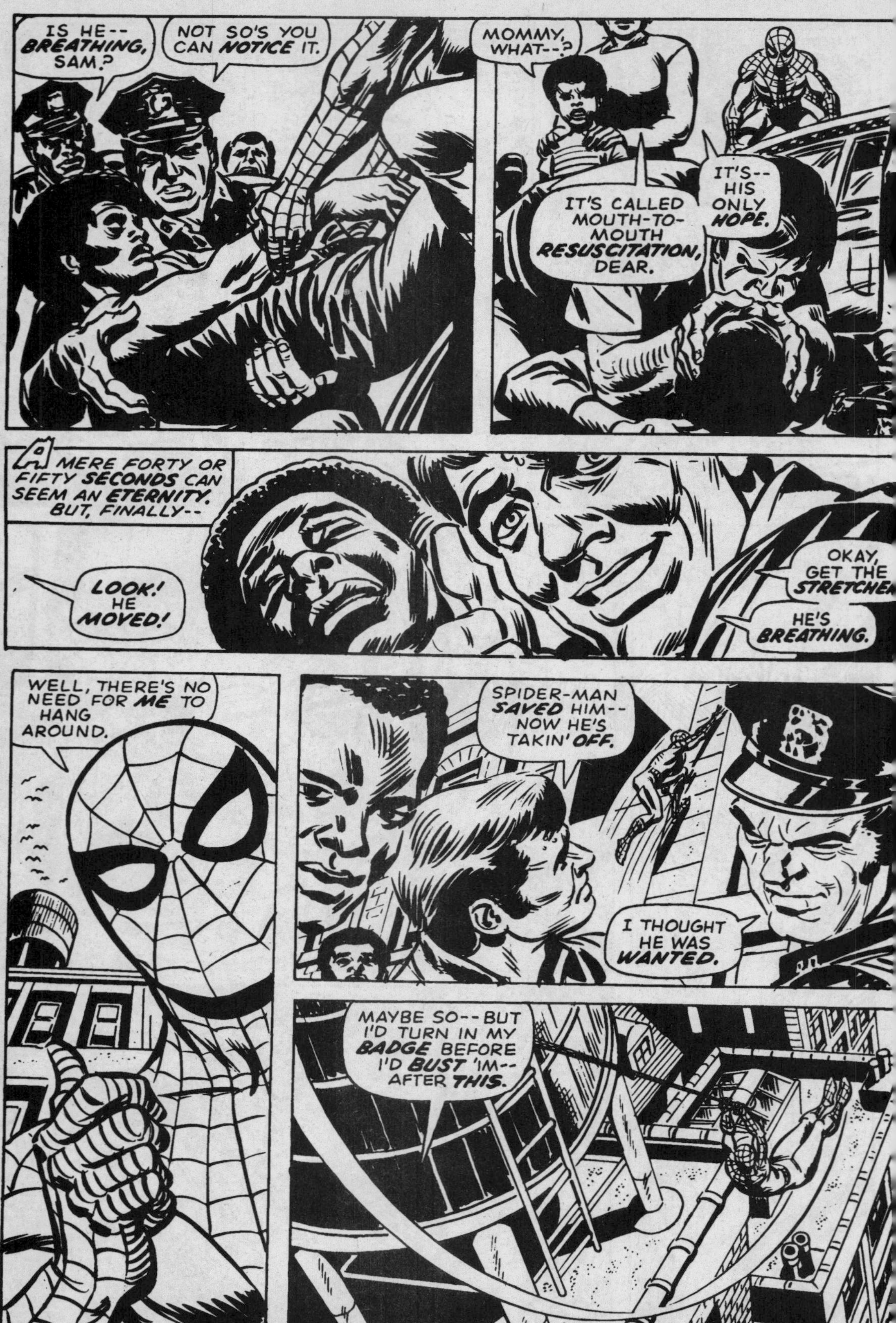

IS HE-- BREATHING, SAM?
NOT SO'S YOU CAN NOTICE IT.
MOMMY, WHAT--?
IT'S CALLED MOUTH-TO-MOUTH RESUSCITATION, DEAR.
IT'S-- HIS ONLY HOPE.
A MERE FORTY OR FIFTY SECONDS CAN SEEM AN ETERNITY. BUT, FINALLY--
LOOK! HE MOVED!
OKAY, GET THE STRETCHER
HE'S BREATHING.
WELL, THERE'S NO NEED FOR ME TO HANG AROUND.
SPIDER-MAN SAVED HIM-- NOW HE'S TAKIN' OFF.
I THOUGHT HE WAS WANTED.
MAYBE SO-- BUT I'D TURN IN MY BADGE BEFORE I'D BUST 'IM-- AFTER THIS.

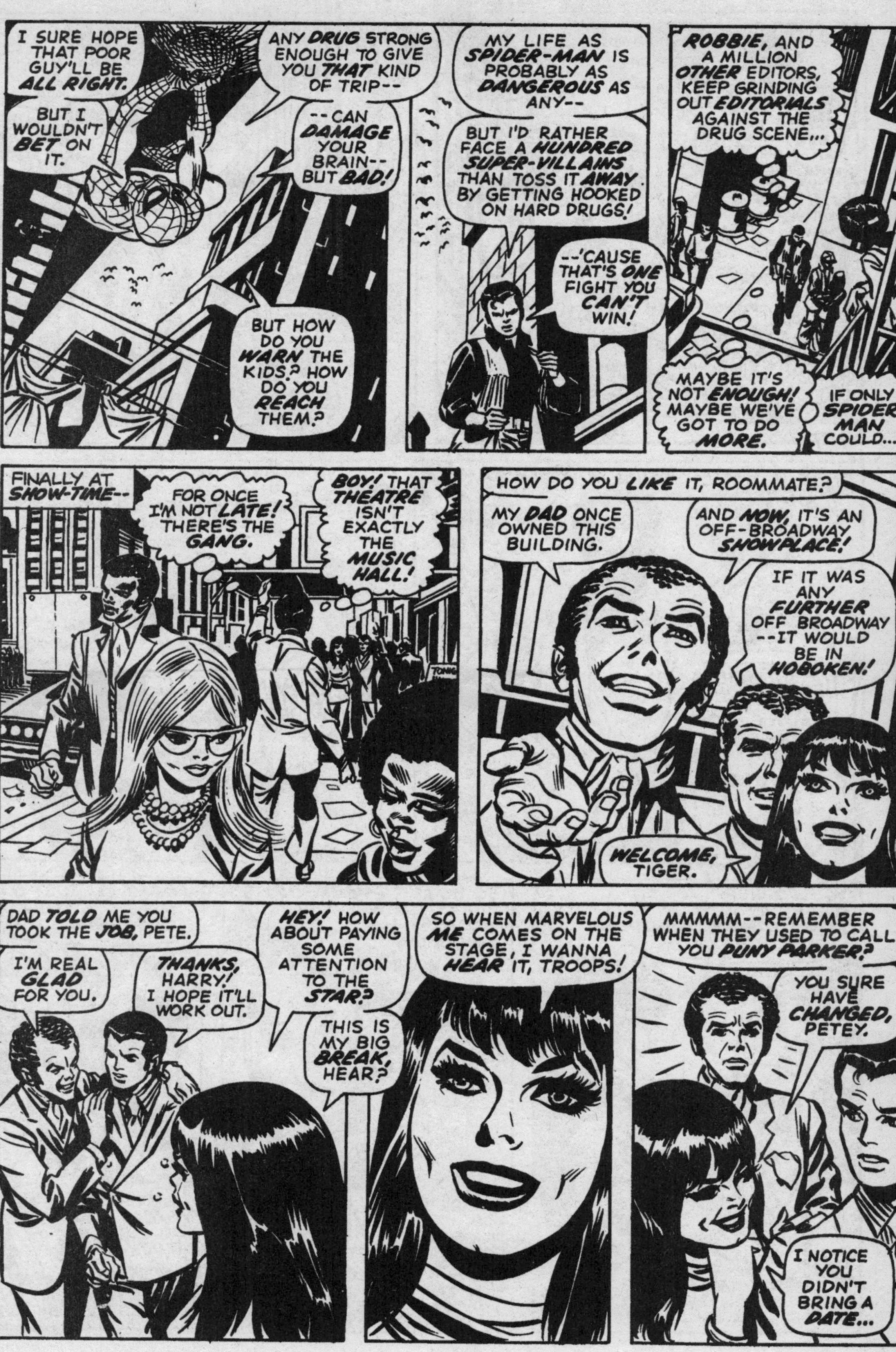
I SURE HOPE THAT POOR GUY'LL BE ALL RIGHT.
BUT I WOULDN'T BET ON IT.
ANY DRUG STRONG ENOUGH TO GIVE YOU THAT KIND OF TRIP--
--CAN DAMAGE YOUR BRAIN--BUT BAD!
BUT HOW DO YOU WARN THE KIDS? HOW DO YOU REACH THEM?
MY LIFE AS SPIDER-MAN IS PROBABLY AS DANGEROUS AS ANY--
BUT I'D RATHER FACE A HUNDRED SUPER-VILLAINS THAN TOSS IT AWAY BY GETTING HOOKED ON HARD DRUGS!
--'CAUSE THAT'S ONE FIGHT YOU CAN'T WIN!
ROBBIE, AND A MILLION OTHER EDITORS, KEEP GRINDING OUT EDITORIALS AGAINST THE DRUG SCENE...
MAYBE IT'S NOT ENOUGH! MAYBE WE'VE GOT TO DO MORE.
IF ONLY SPIDER-MAN COULD...
FINALLY AT SHOW-TIME--
FOR ONCE I'M NOT LATE! THERE'S THE GANG.
BOY! THAT THEATRE ISN'T EXACTLY THE MUSIC HALL!
HOW DO YOU LIKE IT, ROOMMATE?
MY DAD ONCE OWNED THIS BUILDING.
AND NOW, IT'S AN OFF-BROADWAY SHOWPLACE!
IF IT WAS ANY FURTHER OFF BROADWAY --IT WOULD BE IN HOBOKEN!
WELCOME, TIGER.
DAD TOLD ME YOU TOOK THE JOB, PETE.
I'M REAL GLAD FOR YOU.
THANKS, HARRY! I HOPE IT'LL WORK OUT.
HEY! HOW ABOUT PAYING SOME ATTENTION TO THE STAR?
THIS IS MY BIG BREAK, HEAR?
SO WHEN MARVELOUS ME COMES ON THE STAGE, I WANNA HEAR IT, TROOPS!
MMMMM--REMEMBER WHEN THEY USED TO CALL YOU PUNY PARKER?
YOU SURE HAVE CHANGED, PETEY.
I NOTICE YOU DIDN'T BRING A DATE...

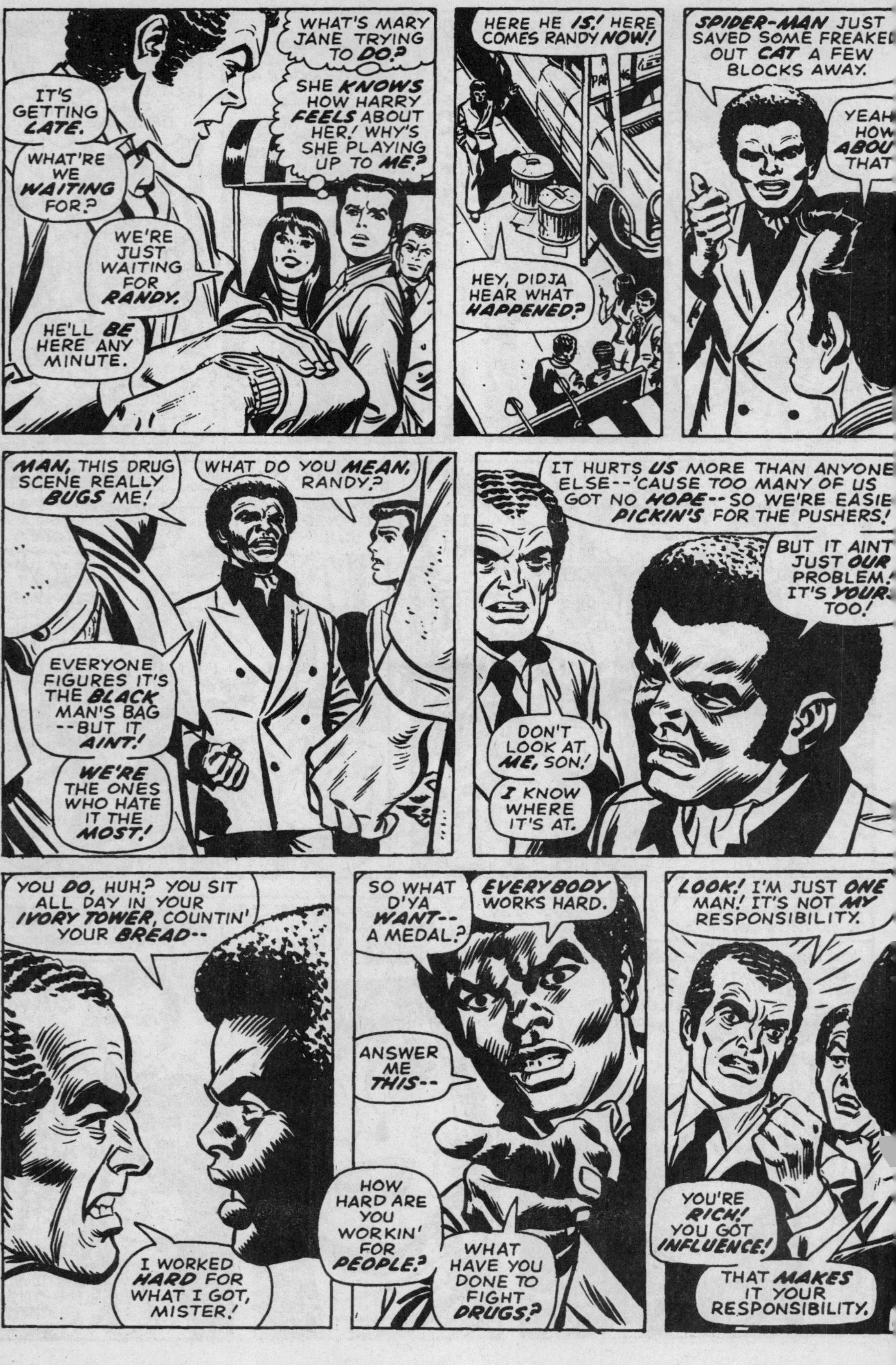
WHAT'S MARY JANE TRYING TO DO?
SHE KNOWS HOW HARRY FEELS ABOUT HER! WHY'S SHE PLAYING UP TO ME?
IT'S GETTING LATE.
WHAT'RE WE WAITING FOR?
WE'RE JUST WAITING FOR RANDY.
HE'LL BE HERE ANY MINUTE.
HERE HE IS! HERE COMES RANDY NOW!
HEY, DIDJA HEAR WHAT HAPPENED?
SPIDER-MAN JUST SAVED SOME FREAKE OUT CAT A FEW BLOCKS AWAY.
YEAH HOW ABOU THAT
MAN, THIS DRUG SCENE REALLY BUGS ME!
WHAT DO YOU MEAN, RANDY?
EVERYONE FIGURES IT'S THE BLACK MAN'S BAG --BUT IT AINT!
WE'RE THE ONES WHO HATE IT THE MOST!
IT HURTS US MORE THAN ANYONE ELSE--'CAUSE TOO MANY OF US GOT NO HOPE--SO WE'RE EASIE PICKIN'S FOR THE PUSHERS!
BUT IT AINT JUST OUR PROBLEM. IT'S YOUR TOO!
DON'T LOOK AT ME, SON!
I KNOW WHERE IT'S AT.
YOU DO, HUH? YOU SIT ALL DAY IN YOUR IVORY TOWER, COUNTIN' YOUR BREAD--
I WORKED HARD FOR WHAT I GOT, MISTER!
SO WHAT D'YA WANT-- A MEDAL?
EVERYBODY WORKS HARD.
ANSWER ME THIS--
HOW HARD ARE YOU WORKIN' FOR PEOPLE?
WHAT HAVE YOU DONE TO FIGHT DRUGS?
LOOK! I'M JUST ONE MAN! IT'S NOT MY RESPONSIBILITY.
YOU'RE RICH! YOU GOT INFLUENCE!
THAT MAKES IT YOUR RESPONSIBILITY.

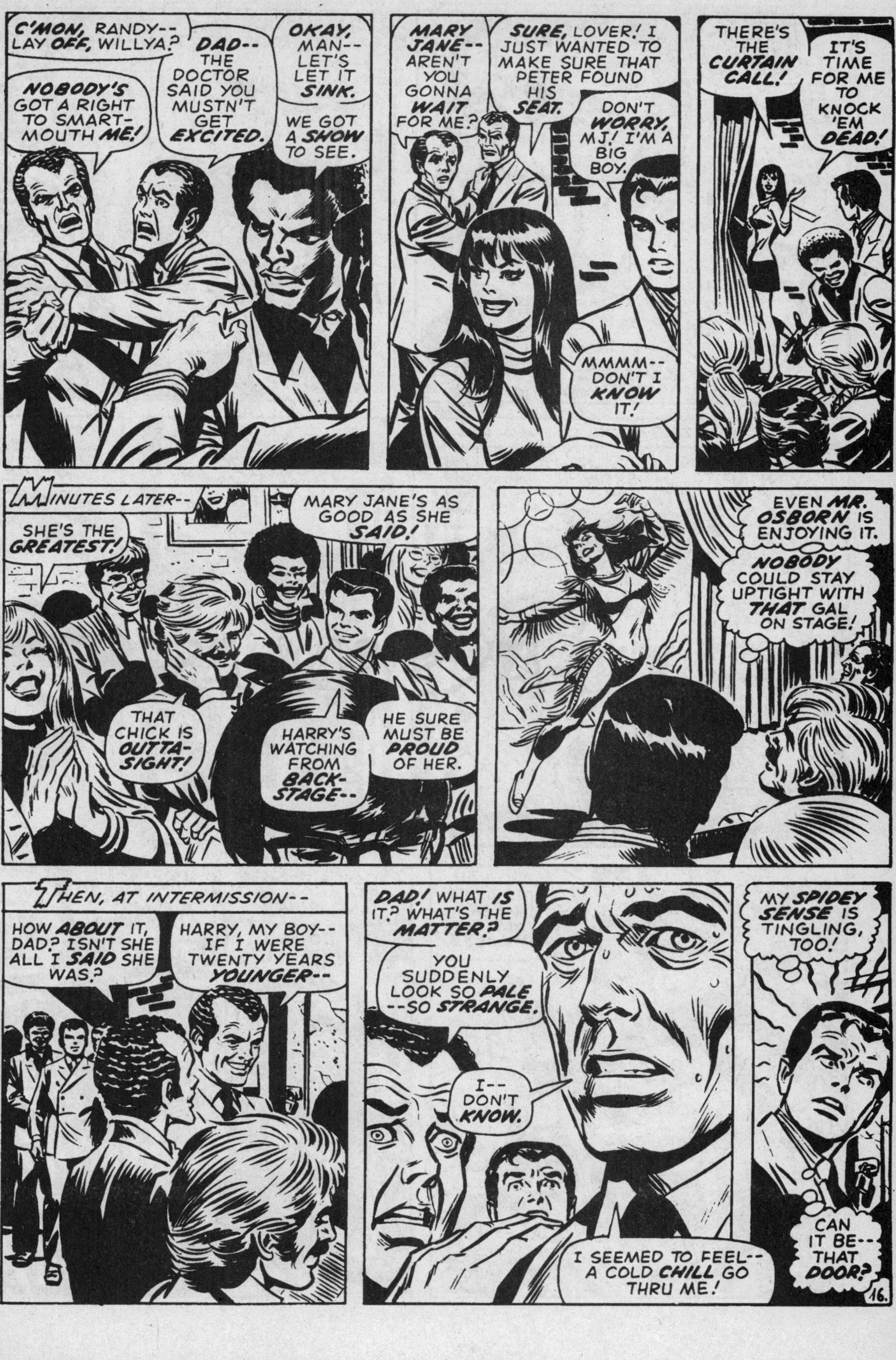
C'MON, RANDY-- LAY OFF, WILLYA?
NOBODY'S GOT A RIGHT TO SMART-MOUTH ME!
DAD-- THE DOCTOR SAID YOU MUSTN'T GET EXCITED.
OKAY, MAN-- LET'S LET IT SINK.
WE GOT A SHOW TO SEE.
MARY JANE-- AREN'T YOU GONNA WAIT FOR ME?
SURE, LOVER! I JUST WANTED TO MAKE SURE THAT PETER FOUND HIS SEAT.
DON'T WORRY, MJ! I'M A BIG BOY.
MMMM-- DON'T I KNOW IT!
THERE'S THE CURTAIN CALL!
IT'S TIME FOR ME TO KNOCK 'EM DEAD!
MINUTES LATER--
SHE'S THE GREATEST!
MARY JANE'S AS GOOD AS SHE SAID!
THAT CHICK IS OUTTA-SIGHT!
HARRY'S WATCHING FROM BACK-STAGE--
HE SURE MUST BE PROUD OF HER.
EVEN MR. OSBORN IS ENJOYING IT.
NOBODY COULD STAY UPTIGHT WITH THAT GAL ON STAGE!
THEN, AT INTERMISSION--
HOW ABOUT IT, DAD? ISN'T SHE ALL I SAID SHE WAS?
HARRY, MY BOY-- IF I WERE TWENTY YEARS YOUNGER--
DAD! WHAT IS IT? WHAT'S THE MATTER?
YOU SUDDENLY LOOK SO PALE --SO STRANGE.
I-- DON'T KNOW.
I SEEMED TO FEEL-- A COLD CHILL GO THRU ME!
MY SPIDEY SENSE IS TINGLING, TOO!
CAN IT BE-- THAT DOOR?
16.

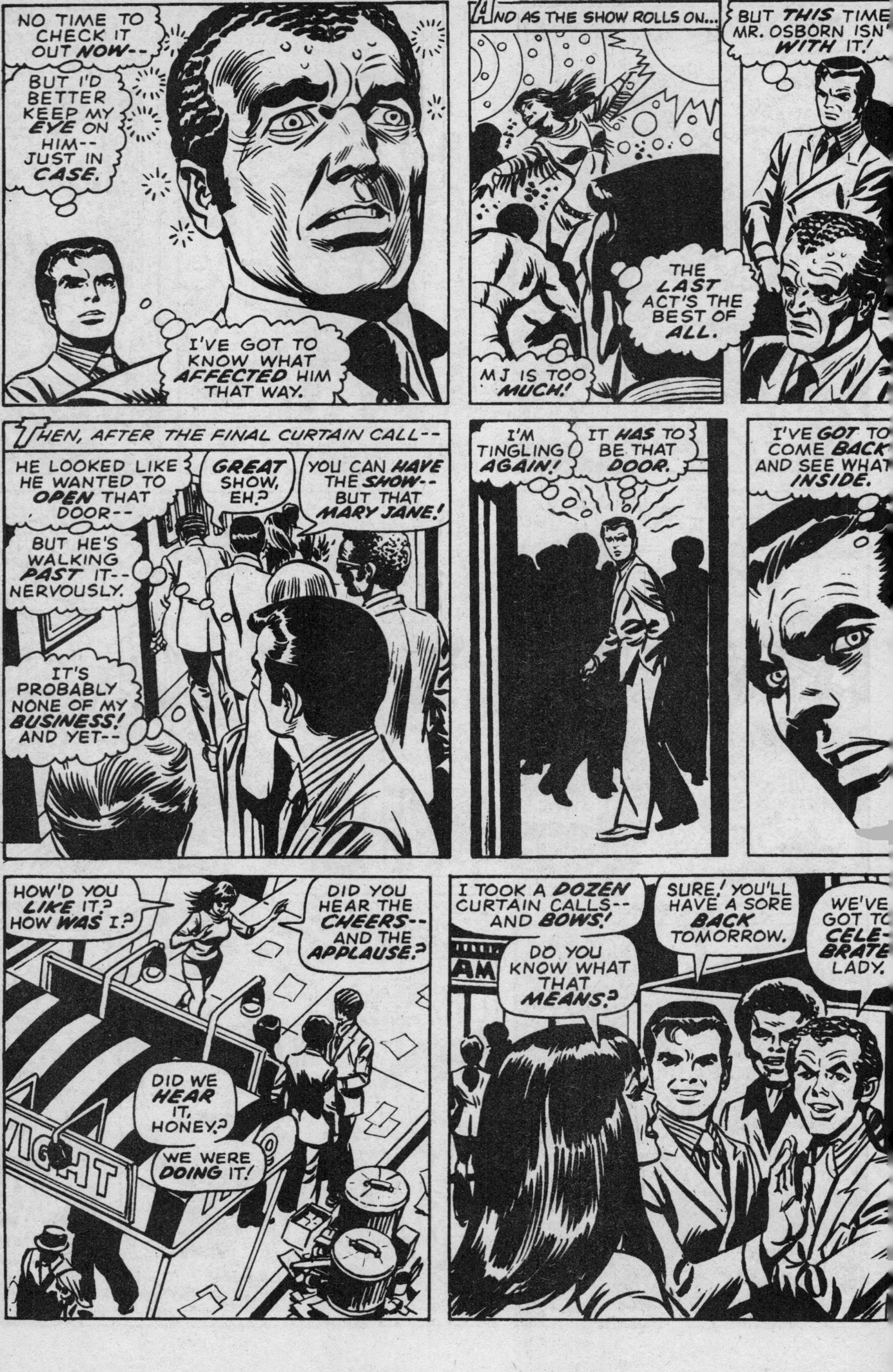
NO TIME TO CHECK IT OUT NOW--
BUT I'D BETTER KEEP MY EYE ON HIM-- JUST IN CASE.
I'VE GOT TO KNOW WHAT AFFECTED HIM THAT WAY.
AND AS THE SHOW ROLLS ON...
THE LAST ACT'S THE BEST OF ALL.
MJ IS TOO MUCH!
BUT THIS TIME MR. OSBORN ISN' WITH IT!
THEN, AFTER THE FINAL CURTAIN CALL--
HE LOOKED LIKE HE WANTED TO OPEN THAT DOOR--
BUT HE'S WALKING PAST IT-- NERVOUSLY.
GREAT SHOW, EH?
YOU CAN HAVE THE SHOW-- BUT THAT MARY JANE!
IT'S PROBABLY NONE OF MY BUSINESS! AND YET--
I'M TINGLING AGAIN!
IT HAS TO BE THAT DOOR.
I'VE GOT TO COME BACK AND SEE WHAT INSIDE.
HOW'D YOU LIKE IT? HOW WAS I?
DID YOU HEAR THE CHEERS-- AND THE APPLAUSE?
DID WE HEAR IT, HONEY?
WE WERE DOING IT!
I TOOK A DOZEN CURTAIN CALLS-- AND BOWS!
SURE! YOU'LL HAVE A SORE BACK TOMORROW.
DO YOU KNOW WHAT THAT MEANS?
WE'VE GOT TO CELE- BRATE LADY.

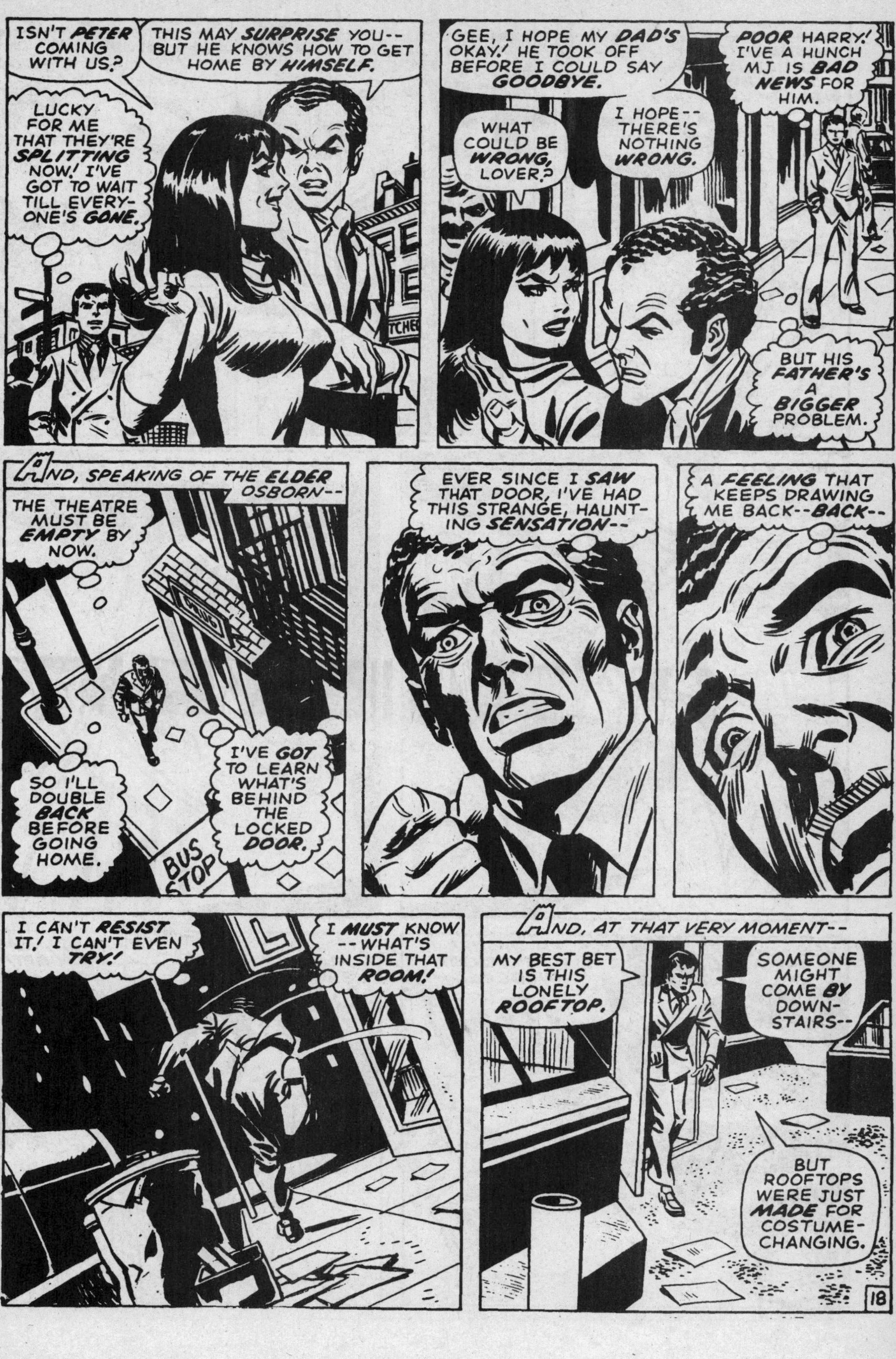
ISN'T PETER COMING WITH US?
THIS MAY SURPRISE YOU-- BUT HE KNOWS HOW TO GET HOME BY HIMSELF.
LUCKY FOR ME THAT THEY'RE SPLITTING NOW! I'VE GOT TO WAIT TILL EVERY-ONE'S GONE.
GEE, I HOPE MY DAD'S OKAY! HE TOOK OFF BEFORE I COULD SAY GOODBYE.
WHAT COULD BE WRONG, LOVER?
I HOPE-- THERE'S NOTHING WRONG.
POOR HARRY! I'VE A HUNCH MJ IS BAD NEWS FOR HIM.
BUT HIS FATHER'S A BIGGER PROBLEM.
AND, SPEAKING OF THE ELDER OSBORN--
THE THEATRE MUST BE EMPTY BY NOW.
SO I'LL DOUBLE BACK BEFORE GOING HOME.
I'VE GOT TO LEARN WHAT'S BEHIND THE LOCKED DOOR.
BUS STOP
EVER SINCE I SAW THAT DOOR, I'VE HAD THIS STRANGE, HAUNT-ING SENSATION--
A FEELING THAT KEEPS DRAWING ME BACK--BACK--
I CAN'T RESIST IT! I CAN'T EVEN TRY!
I MUST KNOW --WHAT'S INSIDE THAT ROOM!
AND, AT THAT VERY MOMENT--
MY BEST BET IS THIS LONELY ROOFTOP.
SOMEONE MIGHT COME BY DOWN-STAIRS--
BUT ROOFTOPS WERE JUST MADE FOR COSTUME-CHANGING.
18

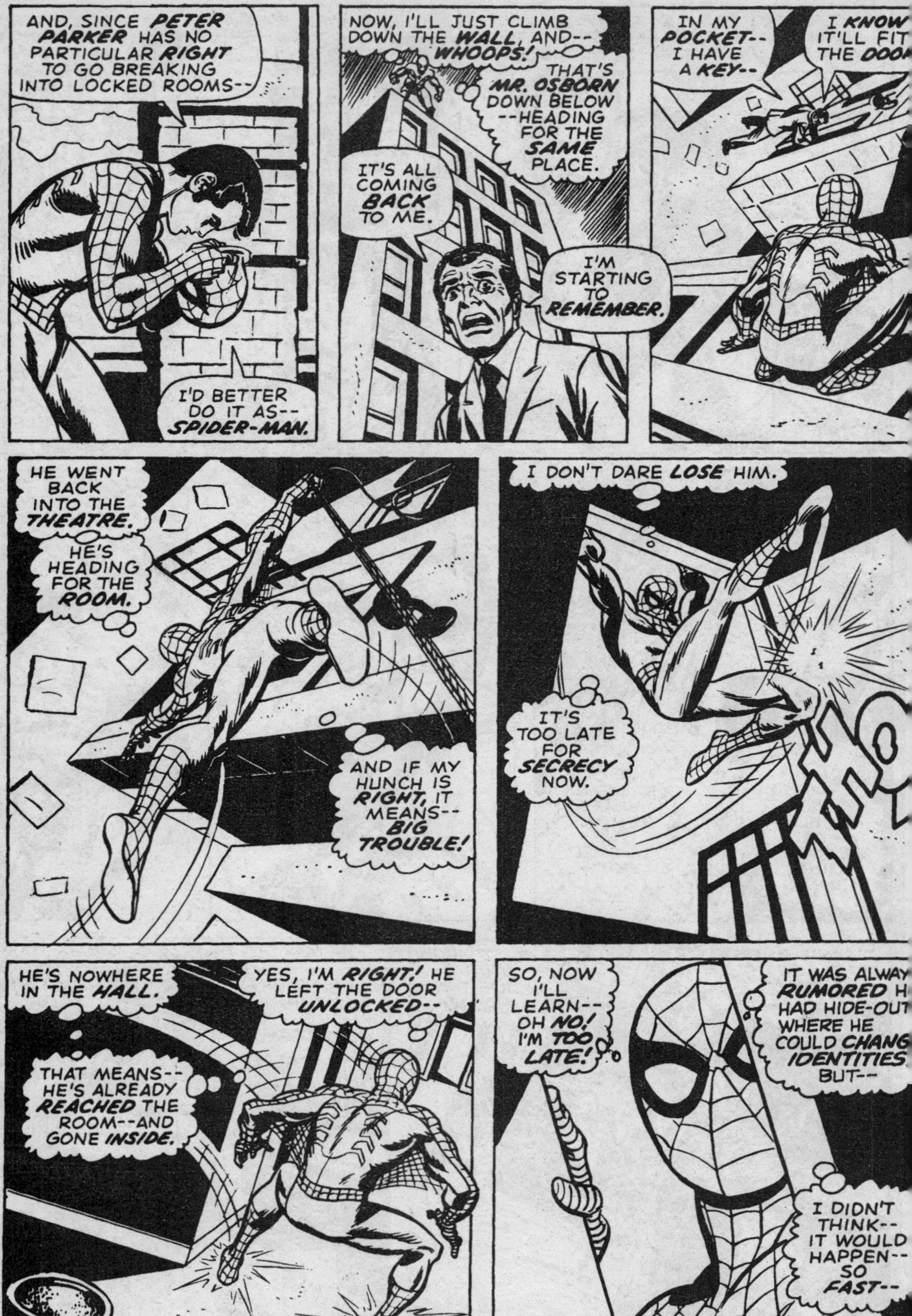
AND, SINCE PETER PARKER HAS NO PARTICULAR RIGHT TO GO BREAKING INTO LOCKED ROOMS--
I'D BETTER DO IT AS-- SPIDER-MAN.
NOW, I'LL JUST CLIMB DOWN THE WALL, AND-- WHOOPS!
THAT'S MR. OSBORN DOWN BELOW --HEADING FOR THE SAME PLACE.
IT'S ALL COMING BACK TO ME.
I'M STARTING TO REMEMBER.
IN MY POCKET-- I HAVE A KEY--
I KNOW IT'LL FIT THE DOO
HE WENT BACK INTO THE THEATRE.
HE'S HEADING FOR THE ROOM.
AND IF MY HUNCH IS RIGHT, IT MEANS-- BIG TROUBLE!
I DON'T DARE LOSE HIM.
IT'S TOO LATE FOR SECRECY NOW.
HE'S NOWHERE IN THE HALL.
YES, I'M RIGHT! HE LEFT THE DOOR UNLOCKED--
THAT MEANS-- HE'S ALREADY REACHED THE ROOM--AND GONE INSIDE.
SO, NOW I'LL LEARN-- OH NO! I'M TOO LATE!
IT WAS ALWAY RUMORED H HAD HIDE-OUT WHERE HE COULD CHANG IDENTITIES BUT--
I DIDN'T THINK-- IT WOULD HAPPEN-- SO FAST--

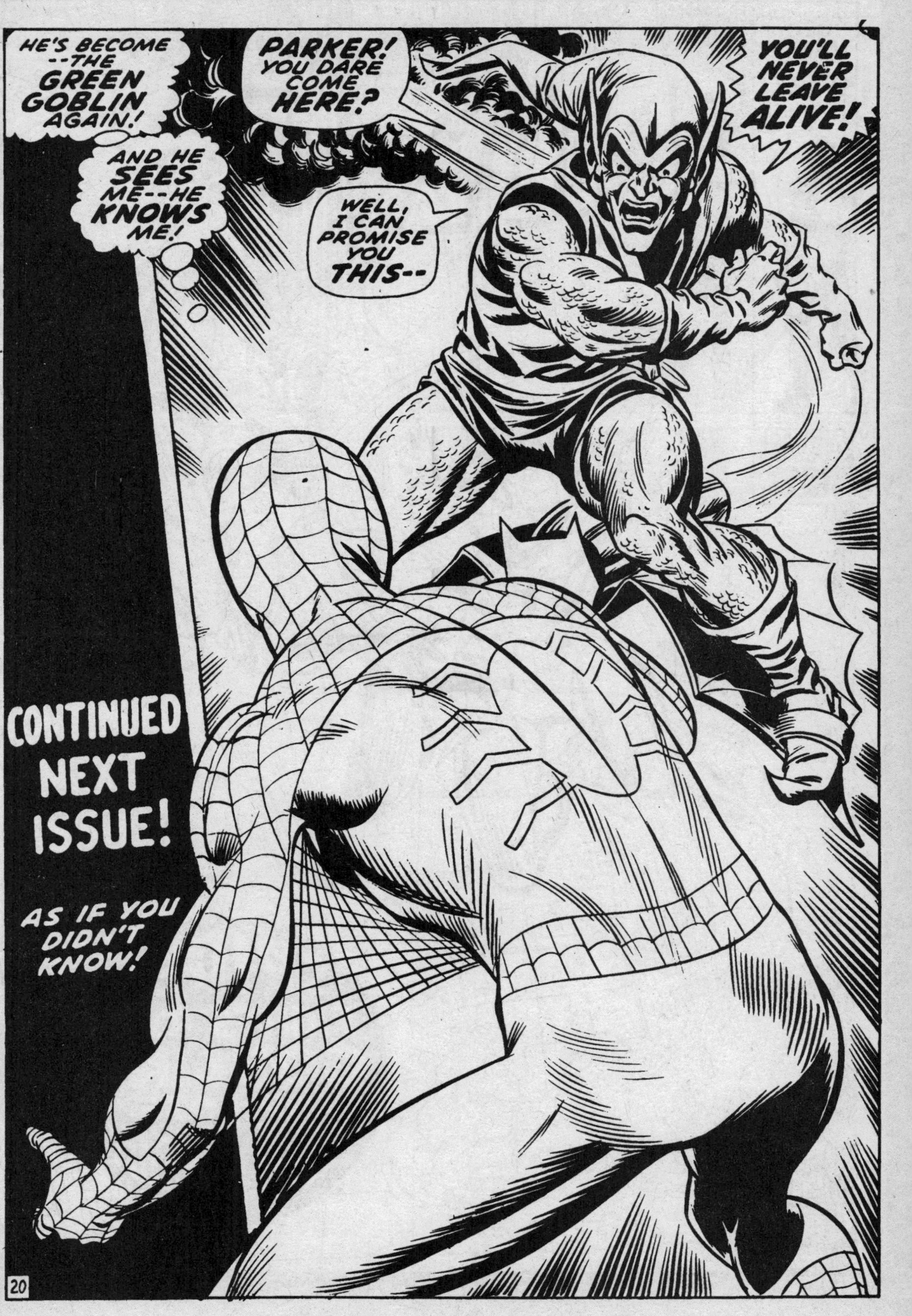
HE'S BECOME --THE GREEN GOBLIN AGAIN!
AND HE SEES ME--HE KNOWS ME!
PARKER! YOU DARE COME HERE?
WELL, I CAN PROMISE YOU THIS--
YOU'LL NEVER LEAVE ALIVE!
CONTINUED NEXT ISSUE!
AS IF YOU DIDN'T KNOW!

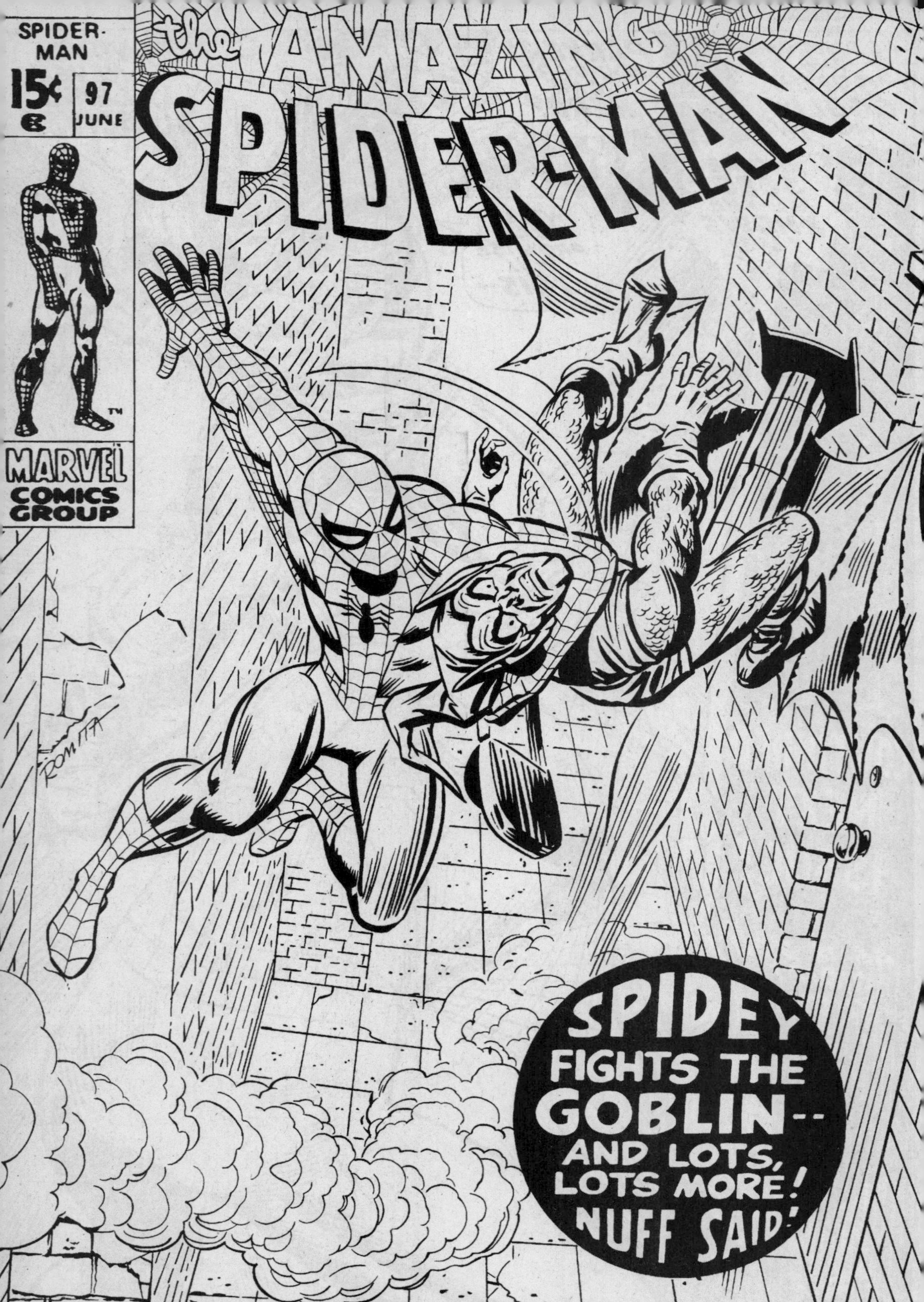
SPIDER-MAN
15¢
97
JUNE
the AMAZING
SPIDER-MAN
MARVEL
COMICS GROUP
ROMITA
SPIDEY
FIGHTS THE
GOBLIN--
AND LOTS,
LOTS MORE!
NUFF SAID!

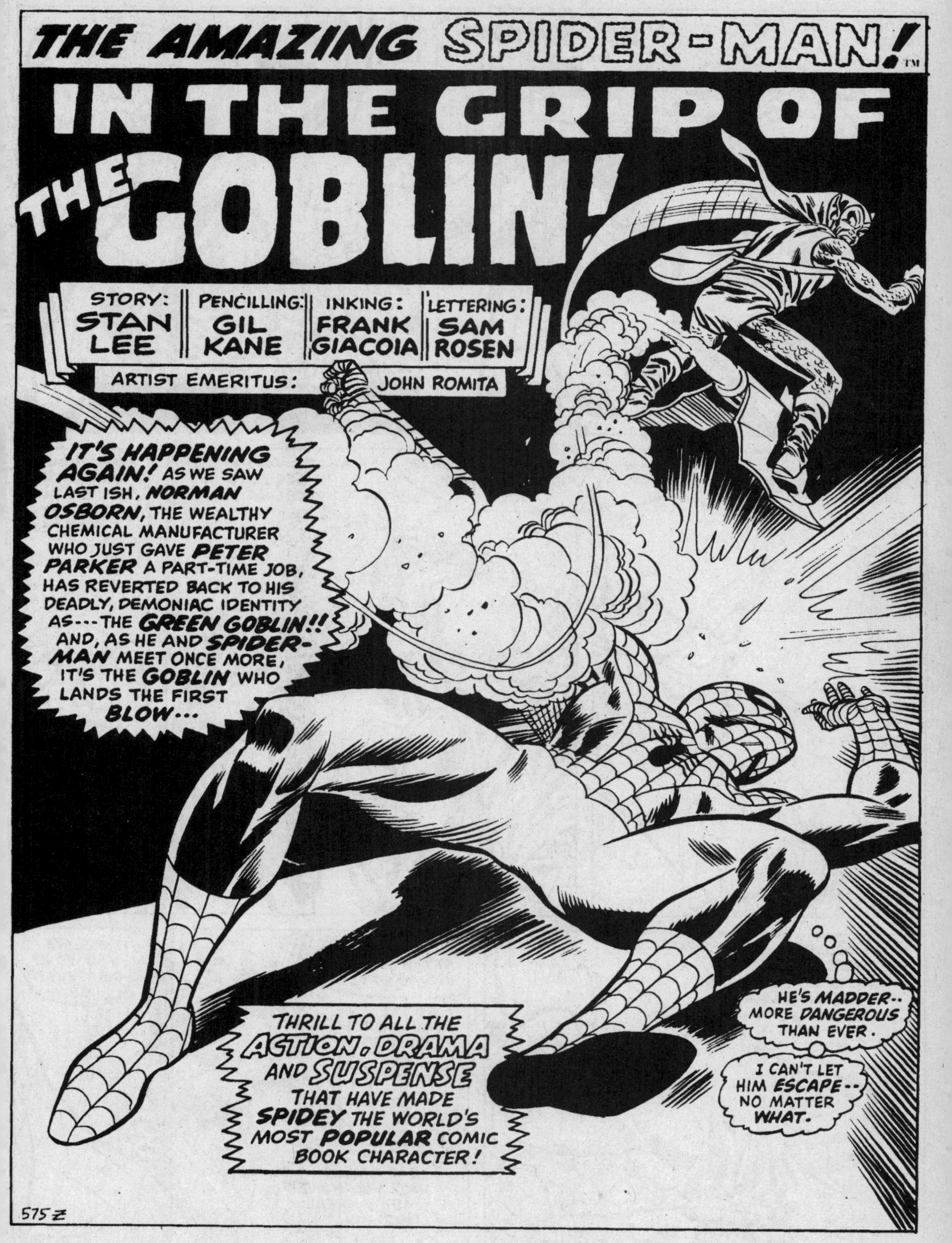
THE AMAZING SPIDER-MAN!
IN THE GRIP OF THE GOBLIN!
STORY: STAN LEE
PENCILLING: GIL KANE
INKING: FRANK GIACOIA
LETTERING: SAM ROSEN
ARTIST EMERITUS: JOHN ROMITA
IT'S HAPPENING AGAIN! AS WE SAW LAST ISH, NORMAN OSBORN, THE WEALTHY CHEMICAL MANUFACTURER WHO JUST GAVE PETER PARKER A PART-TIME JOB, HAS REVERTED BACK TO HIS DEADLY, DEMONIAC IDENTITY AS--- THE GREEN GOBLIN!! AND, AS HE AND SPIDER-MAN MEET ONCE MORE, IT'S THE GOBLIN WHO LANDS THE FIRST BLOW...
THRILL TO ALL THE ACTION, DRAMA AND SUSPENSE THAT HAVE MADE SPIDEY THE WORLD'S MOST POPULAR COMIC BOOK CHARACTER!
HE'S MADDER-- MORE DANGEROUS THAN EVER.
I CAN'T LET HIM ESCAPE-- NO MATTER WHAT.
575 Z

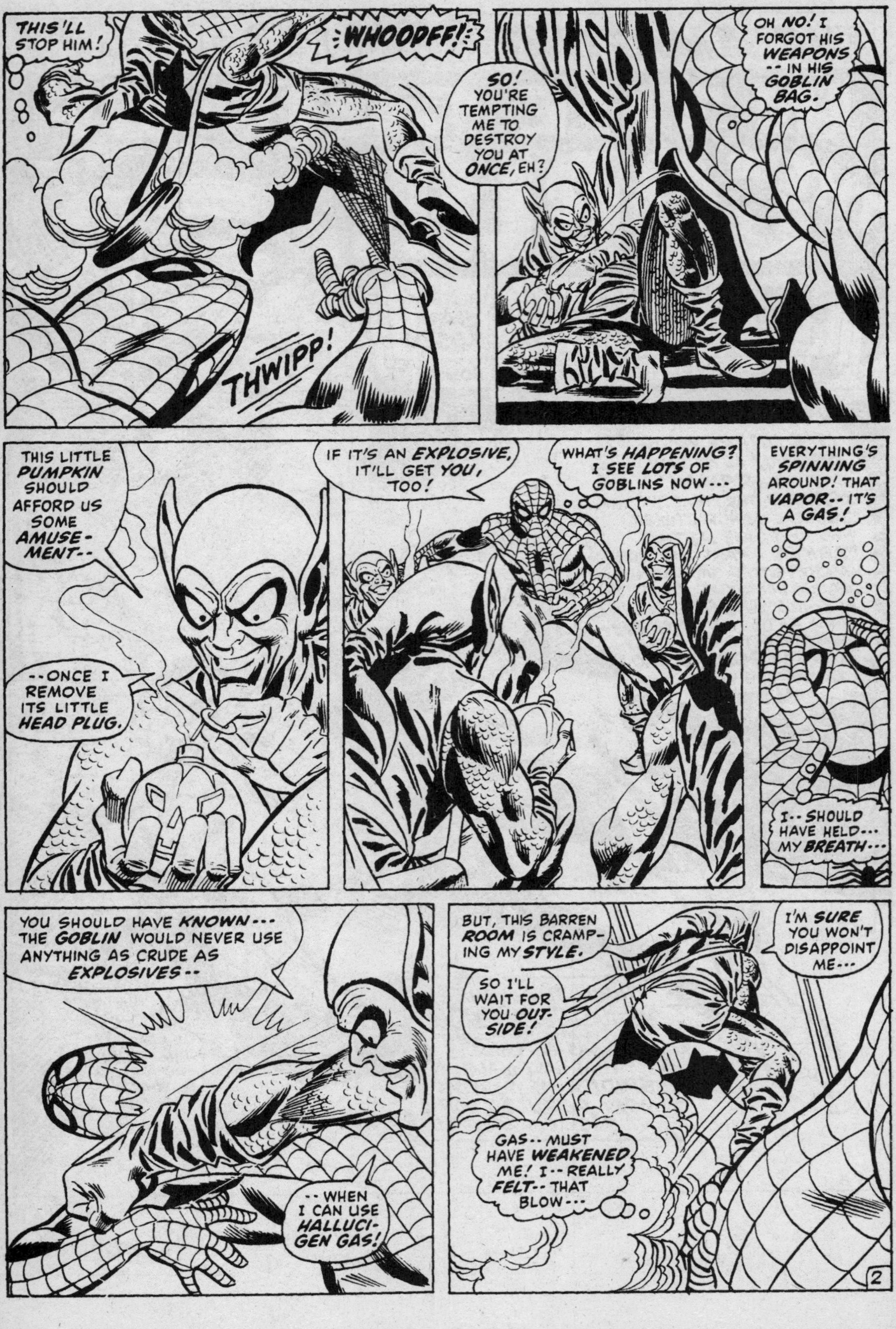
THIS'LL STOP HIM!
WHOODFF!
THWIPP!
SO! YOU'RE TEMPTING ME TO DESTROY YOU AT ONCE, EH?
OH NO! I FORGOT HIS WEAPONS -- IN HIS GOBLIN BAG.
THIS LITTLE PUMPKIN SHOULD AFFORD US SOME AMUSE-MENT--
--ONCE I REMOVE ITS LITTLE HEAD PLUG.
IF IT'S AN EXPLOSIVE, IT'LL GET YOU, TOO!
WHAT'S HAPPENING? I SEE LOTS OF GOBLINS NOW...
EVERYTHING'S SPINNING AROUND! THAT VAPOR-- IT'S A GAS!
I-- SHOULD HAVE HELD... MY BREATH...
YOU SHOULD HAVE KNOWN--- THE GOBLIN WOULD NEVER USE ANYTHING AS CRUDE AS EXPLOSIVES--
--WHEN I CAN USE HALLUCI-GEN GAS!
BUT, THIS BARREN ROOM IS CRAMP-ING MY STYLE.
SO I'LL WAIT FOR YOU OUT-SIDE!
I'M SURE YOU WON'T DISAPPOINT ME...
GAS-- MUST HAVE WEAKENED ME! I-- REALLY FELT-- THAT BLOW---
2

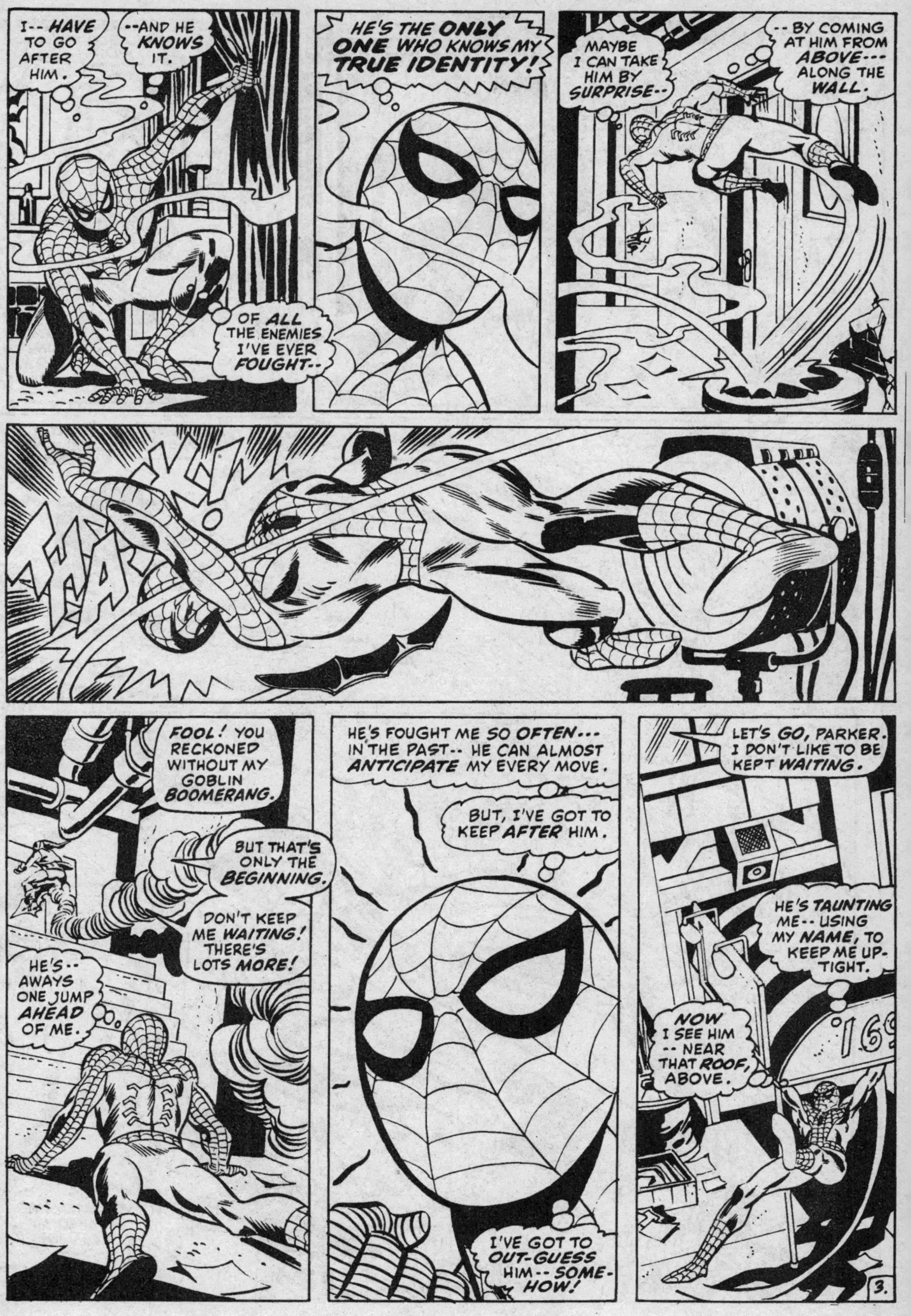
I-- HAVE TO GO AFTER HIM.
--AND HE KNOWS IT.
OF ALL THE ENEMIES I'VE EVER FOUGHT--
HE'S THE ONLY ONE WHO KNOWS MY TRUE IDENTITY!
MAYBE I CAN TAKE HIM BY SURPRISE--
-- BY COMING AT HIM FROM ABOVE--- ALONG THE WALL.
FOOL! YOU RECKONED WITHOUT MY GOBLIN BOOMERANG.
BUT THAT'S ONLY THE BEGINNING.
DON'T KEEP ME WAITING! THERE'S LOTS MORE!
HE'S-- AWAYS ONE JUMP AHEAD OF ME.
HE'S FOUGHT ME SO OFTEN... IN THE PAST-- HE CAN ALMOST ANTICIPATE MY EVERY MOVE.
BUT, I'VE GOT TO KEEP AFTER HIM.
I'VE GOT TO OUT-GUESS HIM-- SOME-HOW!
LET'S GO, PARKER. I DON'T LIKE TO BE KEPT WAITING.
HE'S TAUNTING ME-- USING MY NAME, TO KEEP ME UP-TIGHT.
NOW I SEE HIM -- NEAR THAT ROOF, ABOVE.

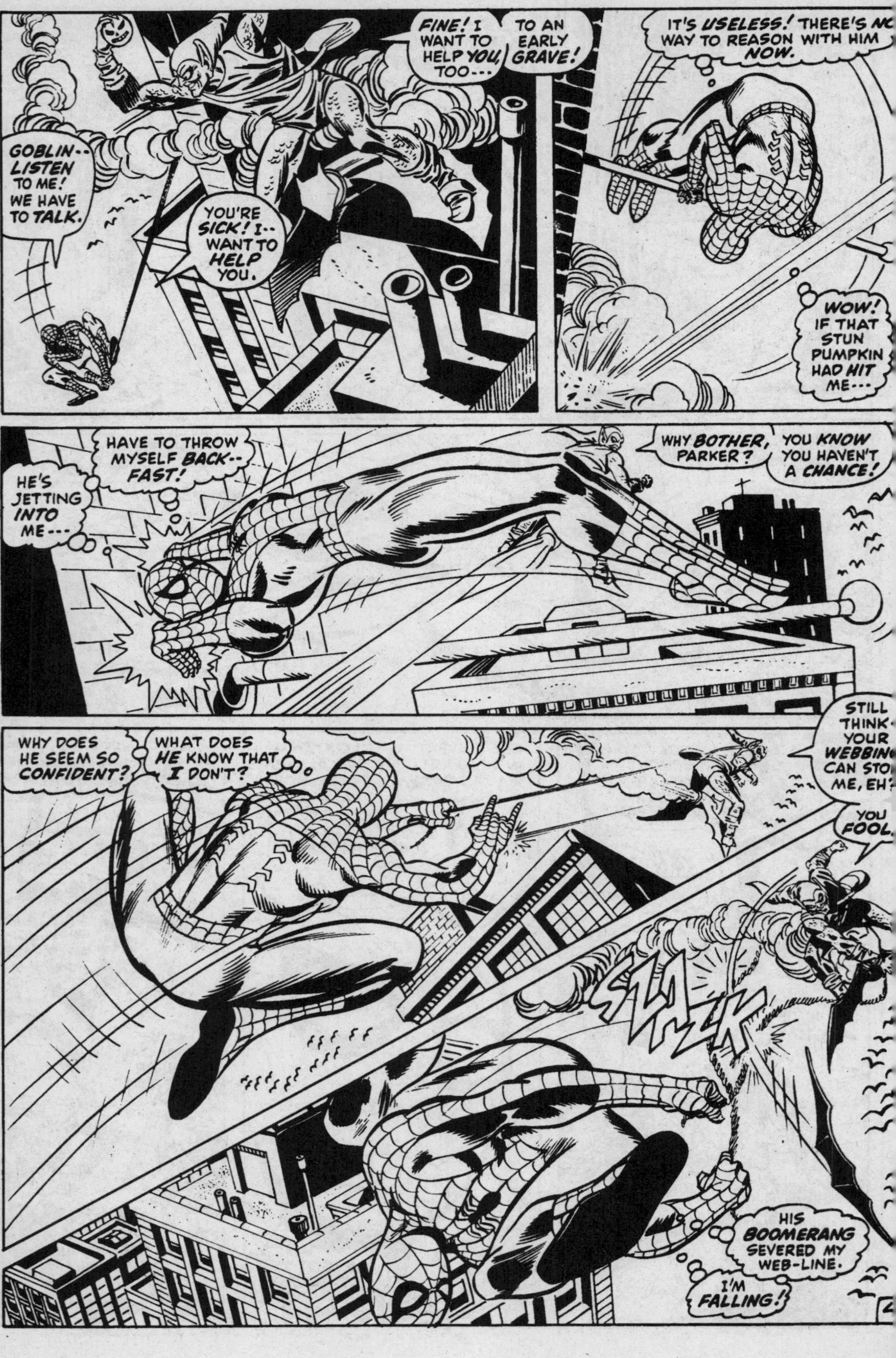

GOBLIN-- LISTEN TO ME! WE HAVE TO TALK.
FINE! I WANT TO HELP YOU, TOO---
TO AN EARLY GRAVE!
YOU'RE SICK! I-- WANT TO HELP YOU.
IT'S USELESS! THERE'S NO WAY TO REASON WITH HIM NOW.
WOW! IF THAT STUN PUMPKIN HAD HIT ME---
HE'S JETTING INTO ME---
HAVE TO THROW MYSELF BACK-- FAST!
WHY BOTHER, PARKER?
YOU KNOW YOU HAVEN'T A CHANCE!
WHY DOES HE SEEM SO CONFIDENT?
WHAT DOES HE KNOW THAT I DON'T?
STILL THINK YOUR WEBBING CAN STOP ME, EH?
YOU FOOL.
SLAZK
HIS BOOMERANG SEVERED MY WEB-LINE.
I'M FALLING!

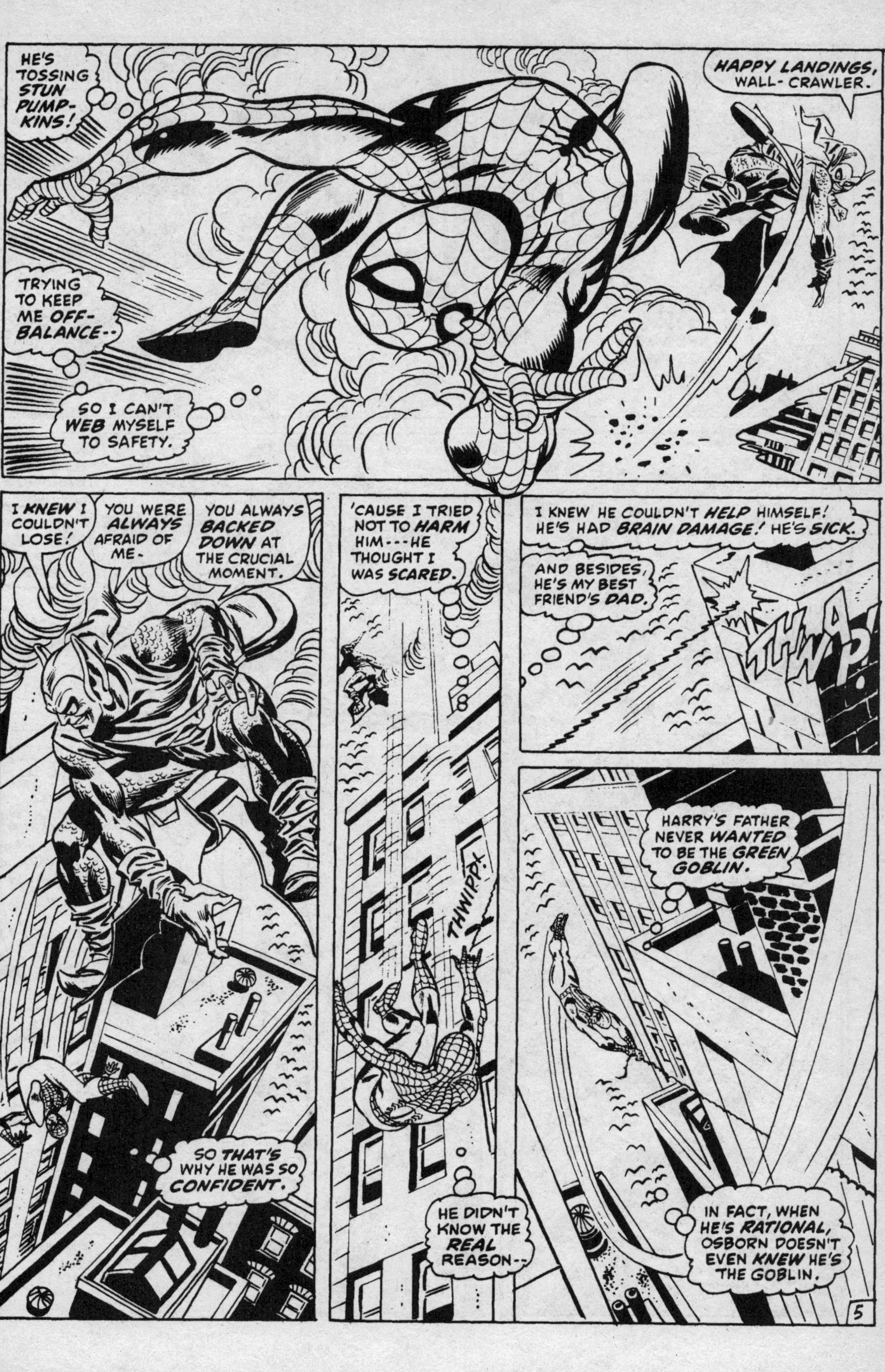
HE'S TOSSING STUN PUMP-KINS!
TRYING TO KEEP ME OFF-BALANCE--
SO I CAN'T WEB MYSELF TO SAFETY.
HAPPY LANDINGS, WALL-CRAWLER.
I KNEW I COULDN'T LOSE!
YOU WERE ALWAYS AFRAID OF ME-
YOU ALWAYS BACKED DOWN AT THE CRUCIAL MOMENT.
SO THAT'S WHY HE WAS SO CONFIDENT.
'CAUSE I TRIED NOT TO HARM HIM---HE THOUGHT I WAS SCARED.
THWIPP!
HE DIDN'T KNOW THE REAL REASON--
I KNEW HE COULDN'T HELP HIMSELF! HE'S HAD BRAIN DAMAGE! HE'S SICK.
AND BESIDES, HE'S MY BEST FRIEND'S DAD.
THWAP!
HARRY'S FATHER NEVER WANTED TO BE THE GREEN GOBLIN.
IN FACT, WHEN HE'S RATIONAL, OSBORN DOESN'T EVEN KNEW HE'S THE GOBLIN.
5

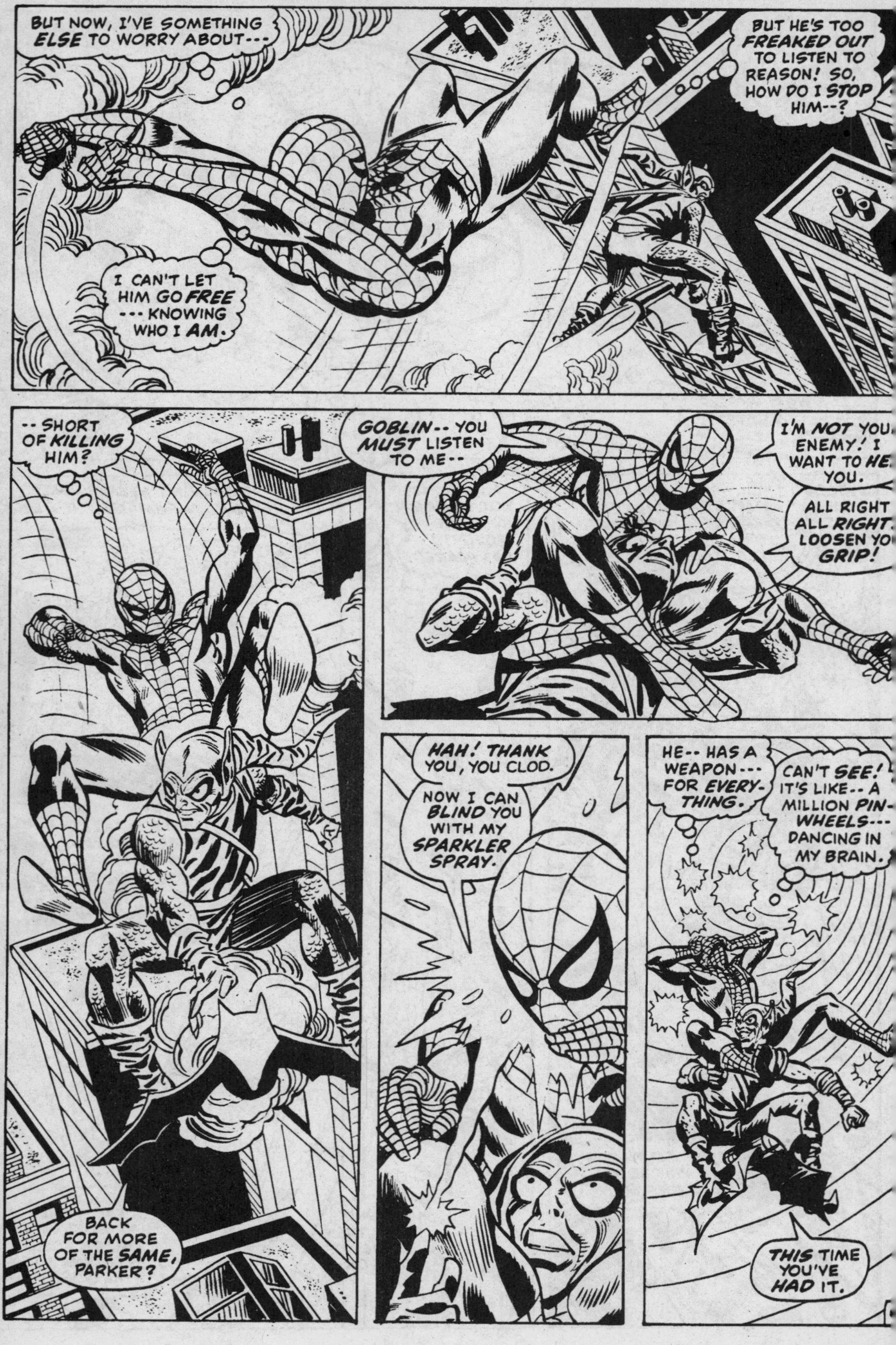

BUT NOW, I'VE SOMETHING ELSE TO WORRY ABOUT---
I CAN'T LET HIM GO FREE --- KNOWING WHO I AM.
BUT HE'S TOO FREAKED OUT TO LISTEN TO REASON! SO, HOW DO I STOP HIM--?
-- SHORT OF KILLING HIM?
BACK FOR MORE OF THE SAME, PARKER?
GOBLIN -- YOU MUST LISTEN TO ME --
ALL RIGHT ALL RIGHT.
GRIP!
HAH! THANK YOU, YOU CLOD.
NOW I CAN BLIND YOU WITH MY SPARKLER SPRAY.
HE -- HAS A WEAPON --- FOR EVERY-THING.
IT'S LIKE -- A MILLION PIN-WHEELS --- DANCING IN MY BRAIN.
THIS TIME YOU'VE HAD IT.

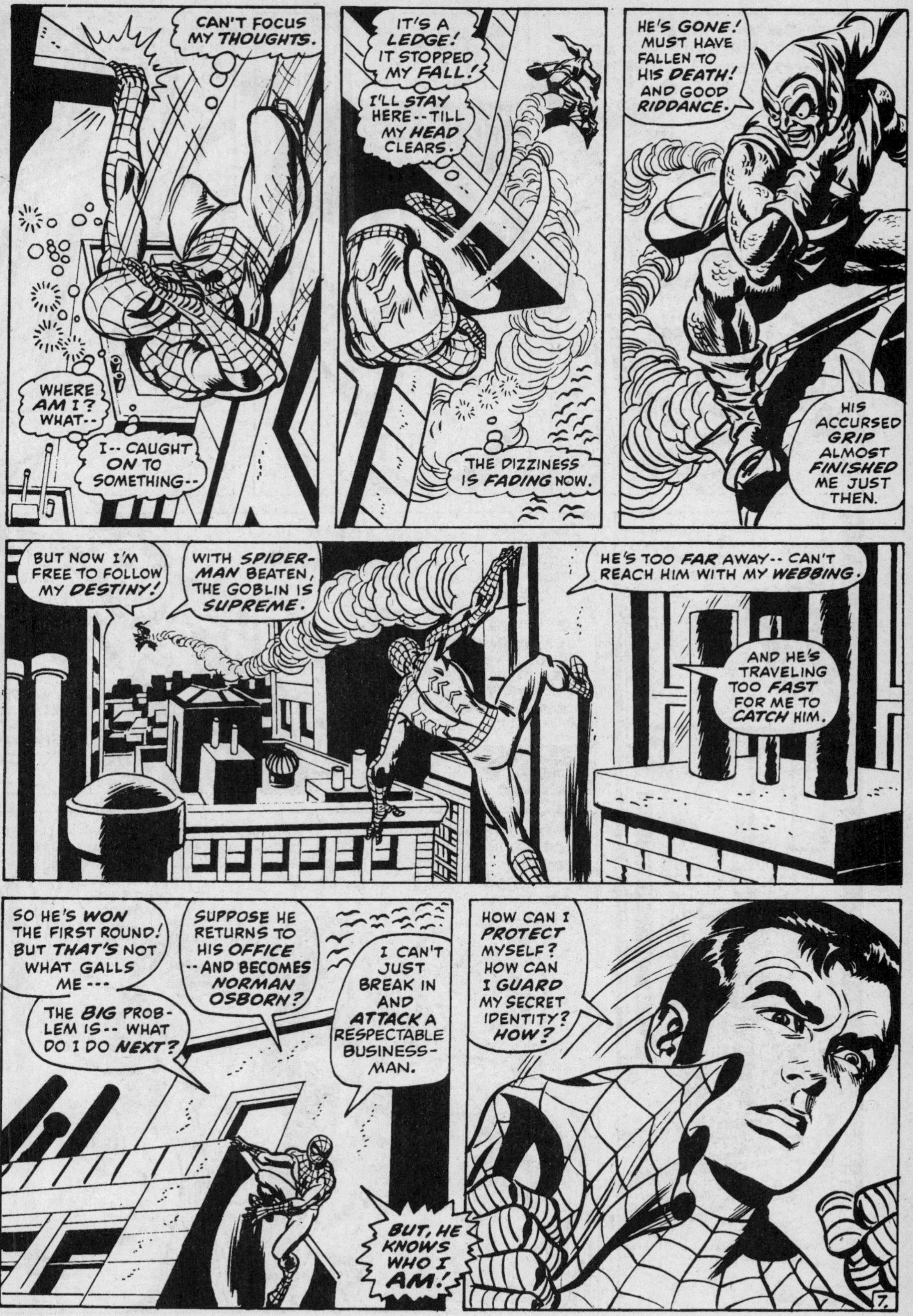
CAN'T FOCUS MY THOUGHTS.
WHERE AM I? WHAT--
I--CAUGHT ON TO SOMETHING--
IT'S A LEDGE! IT STOPPED MY FALL!
I'LL STAY HERE--TILL MY HEAD CLEARS.
THE DIZZINESS IS FADING NOW.
HE'S GONE! MUST HAVE FALLEN TO HIS DEATH! AND GOOD RIDDANCE.
HIS ACCURSED GRIP ALMOST FINISHED ME JUST THEN.
BUT NOW I'M FREE TO FOLLOW MY DESTINY!
WITH SPIDER-MAN BEATEN, THE GOBLIN IS SUPREME.
HE'S TOO FAR AWAY--CAN'T REACH HIM WITH MY WEBBING.
AND HE'S TRAVELING TOO FAST FOR ME TO CATCH HIM.
SO HE'S WON THE FIRST ROUND! BUT THAT'S NOT WHAT GALLS ME---
THE BIG PROBLEM IS--WHAT DO I DO NEXT?
SUPPOSE HE RETURNS TO HIS OFFICE --AND BECOMES NORMAN OSBORN?
I CAN'T JUST BREAK IN AND ATTACK A RESPECTABLE BUSINESS-MAN.
BUT, HE KNOWS WHO I AM!
HOW CAN I PROTECT MYSELF? HOW CAN I GUARD MY SECRET IDENTITY? HOW?
7.

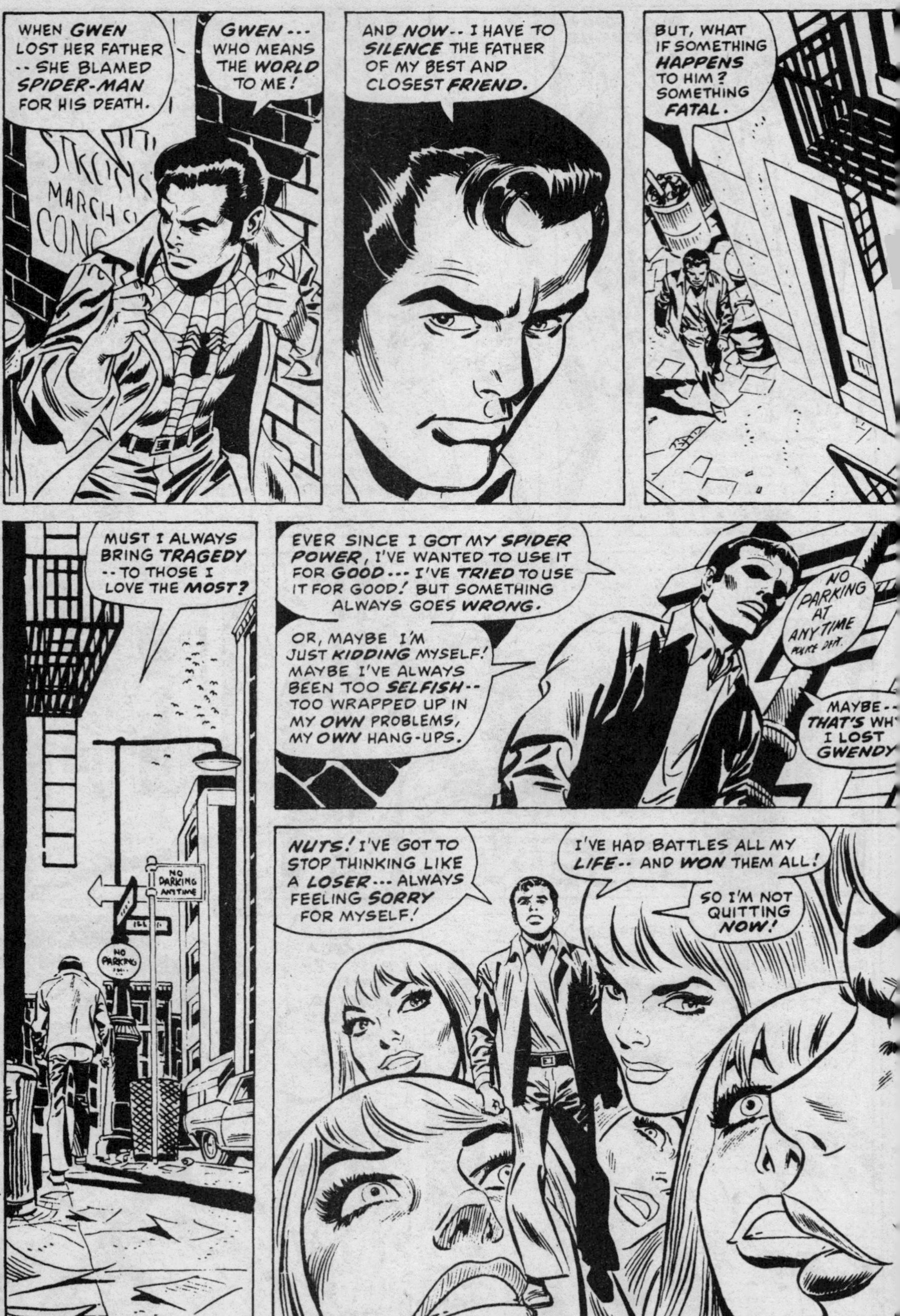

WHEN GWEN LOST HER FATHER -- SHE BLAMED SPIDER-MAN FOR HIS DEATH.
GWEN -- WHO MEANS THE WORLD TO ME!
AND NOW -- I HAVE TO SILENCE THE FATHER OF MY BEST AND CLOSEST FRIEND.
BUT, WHAT IF SOMETHING HAPPENS TO HIM? SOMETHING FATAL.
MUST I ALWAYS BRING TRAGEDY -- TO THOSE I LOVE THE MOST?
NO PARKING ANYTIME
NO PARKING
EVER SINCE I GOT MY SPIDER POWER, I'VE WANTED TO USE IT FOR GOOD --- I'VE TRIED TO USE IT FOR GOOD! BUT SOMETHING ALWAYS GOES WRONG.
OR, MAYBE I'M JUST KIDDING MYSELF! MAYBE I'VE ALWAYS BEEN TOO SELFISH -- TOO WRAPPED UP IN MY OWN PROBLEMS, MY OWN HANG-UPS.
NO PARKING AT ANY TIME POLICE DEPT.
MAYBE -- THAT'S WHY I LOST GWENDY
NUTS! I'VE GOT TO STOP THINKING LIKE A LOSER --- ALWAYS FEELING SORRY FOR MYSELF!
I'VE HAD BATTLES ALL MY LIFE -- AND WON THEM ALL!
SO I'M NOT QUITTING NOW!

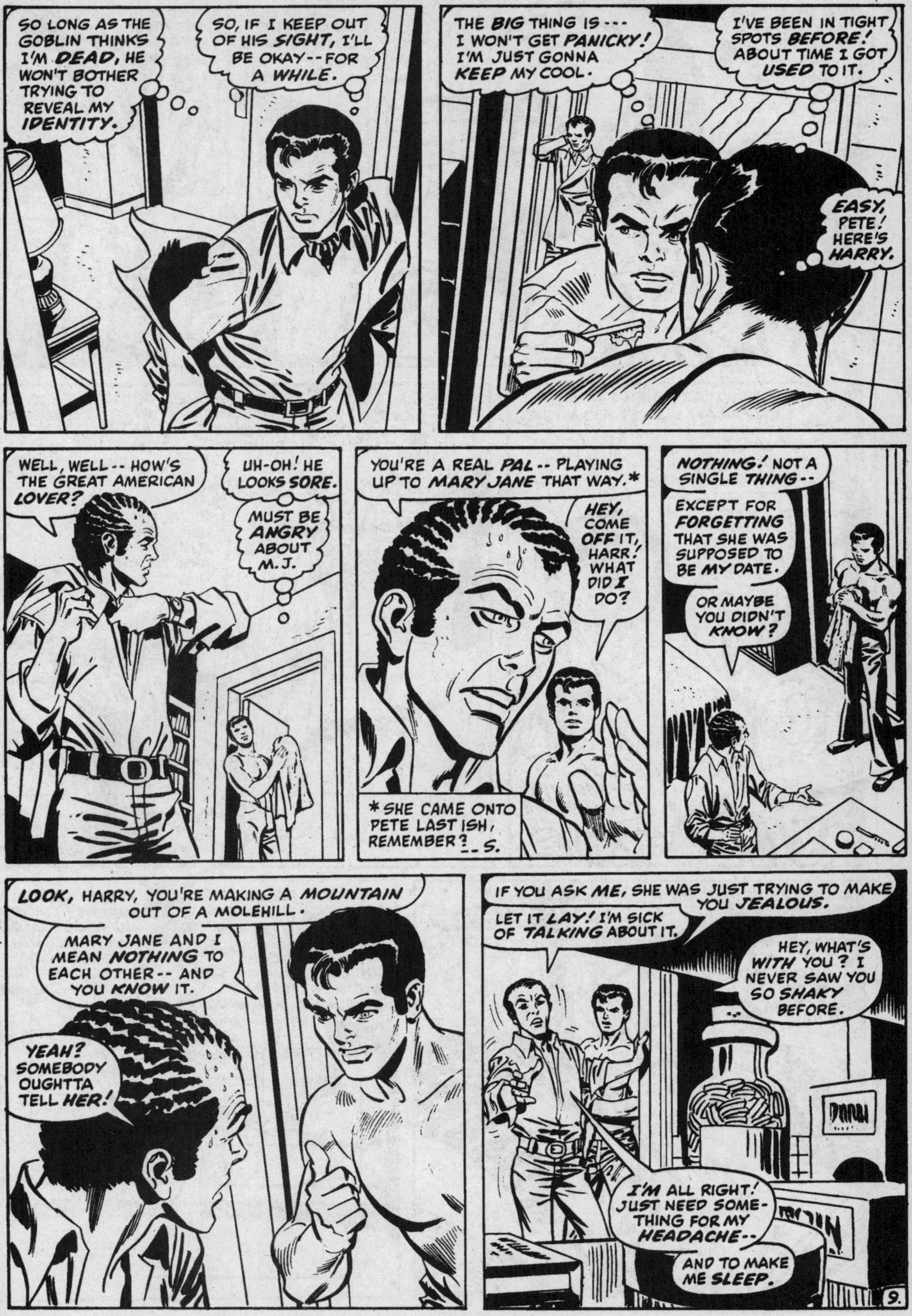

SO LONG AS THE GOBLIN THINKS I'M DEAD, HE WON'T BOTHER TRYING TO REVEAL MY IDENTITY.
SO, IF I KEEP OUT OF HIS SIGHT, I'LL BE OKAY--FOR A WHILE.
THE BIG THING IS--- I WON'T GET PANICKY! I'M JUST GONNA KEEP MY COOL.
I'VE BEEN IN TIGHT SPOTS BEFORE! ABOUT TIME I GOT USED TO IT.
EASY, PETE! HERE'S HARRY.
WELL, WELL-- HOW'S THE GREAT AMERICAN LOVER?
UH-OH! HE LOOKS SORE.
MUST BE ANGRY ABOUT M.J.
YOU'RE A REAL PAL-- PLAYING UP TO MARY JANE THAT WAY.*
HEY, COME OFF IT, HARR! WHAT DID I DO?
* SHE CAME ONTO PETE LAST ISH, REMEMBER? -- S.
NOTHING! NOT A SINGLE THING--
EXCEPT FOR FORGETTING THAT SHE WAS SUPPOSED TO BE MY DATE.
OR MAYBE YOU DIDN'T KNOW?
LOOK, HARRY, YOU'RE MAKING A MOUNTAIN OUT OF A MOLEHILL.
MARY JANE AND I MEAN NOTHING TO EACH OTHER-- AND YOU KNOW IT.
YEAH? SOMEBODY OUGHTTA TELL HER!
IF YOU ASK ME, SHE WAS JUST TRYING TO MAKE YOU JEALOUS.
LET IT LAY! I'M SICK OF TALKING ABOUT IT.
HEY, WHAT'S WITH YOU? I NEVER SAW YOU SO SHAKY BEFORE.
I'M ALL RIGHT! JUST NEED SOME-THING FOR MY HEADACHE--
AND TO MAKE ME SLEEP.
9.

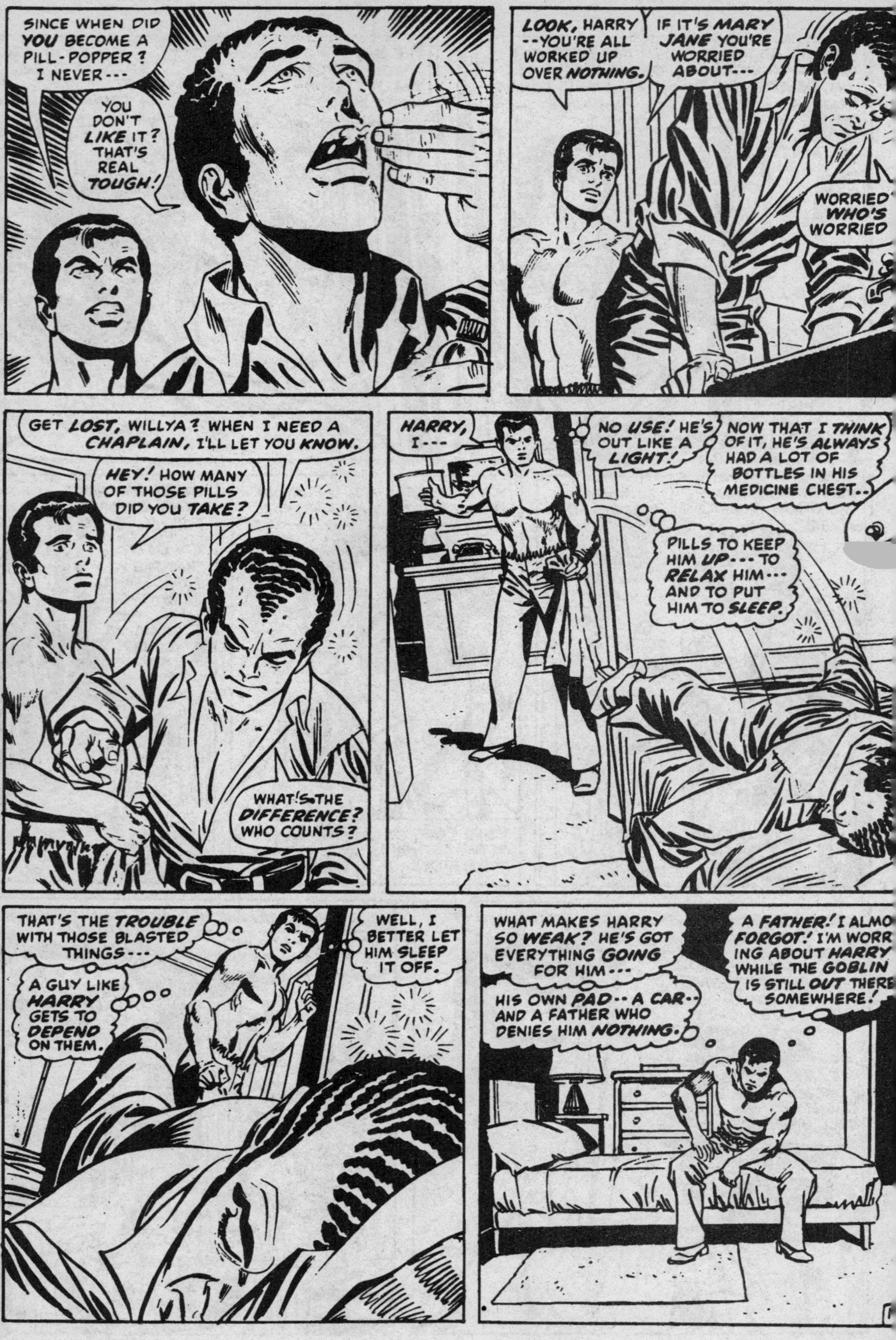
SINCE WHEN DID YOU BECOME A PILL-POPPER? I NEVER---
YOU DON'T LIKE IT? THAT'S REAL TOUGH!
LOOK, HARRY --YOU'RE ALL WORKED UP OVER NOTHING.
IF IT'S MARY JANE YOU'RE WORRIED ABOUT---
WORRIED WHO'S WORRIED
GET LOST, WILLYA? WHEN I NEED A CHAPLAIN, I'LL LET YOU KNOW.
HEY! HOW MANY OF THOSE PILLS DID YOU TAKE?
WHAT'S THE DIFFERENCE? WHO COUNTS?
HARRY, I---
NO USE! HE'S OUT LIKE A LIGHT!
NOW THAT I THINK OF IT, HE'S ALWAYS HAD A LOT OF BOTTLES IN HIS MEDICINE CHEST..
PILLS TO KEEP HIM UP--- TO RELAX HIM--- AND TO PUT HIM TO SLEEP.
THAT'S THE TROUBLE WITH THOSE BLASTED THINGS---
A GUY LIKE HARRY GETS TO DEPEND ON THEM.
WELL, I BETTER LET HIM SLEEP IT OFF.
WHAT MAKES HARRY SO WEAK? HE'S GOT EVERYTHING GOING FOR HIM---
HIS OWN PAD-- A CAR-- AND A FATHER WHO DENIES HIM NOTHING.
A FATHER! I ALMO FORGOT! I'M WORR ING ABOUT HARRY WHILE THE GOBLIN IS STILL OUT THERE SOMEWHERE!

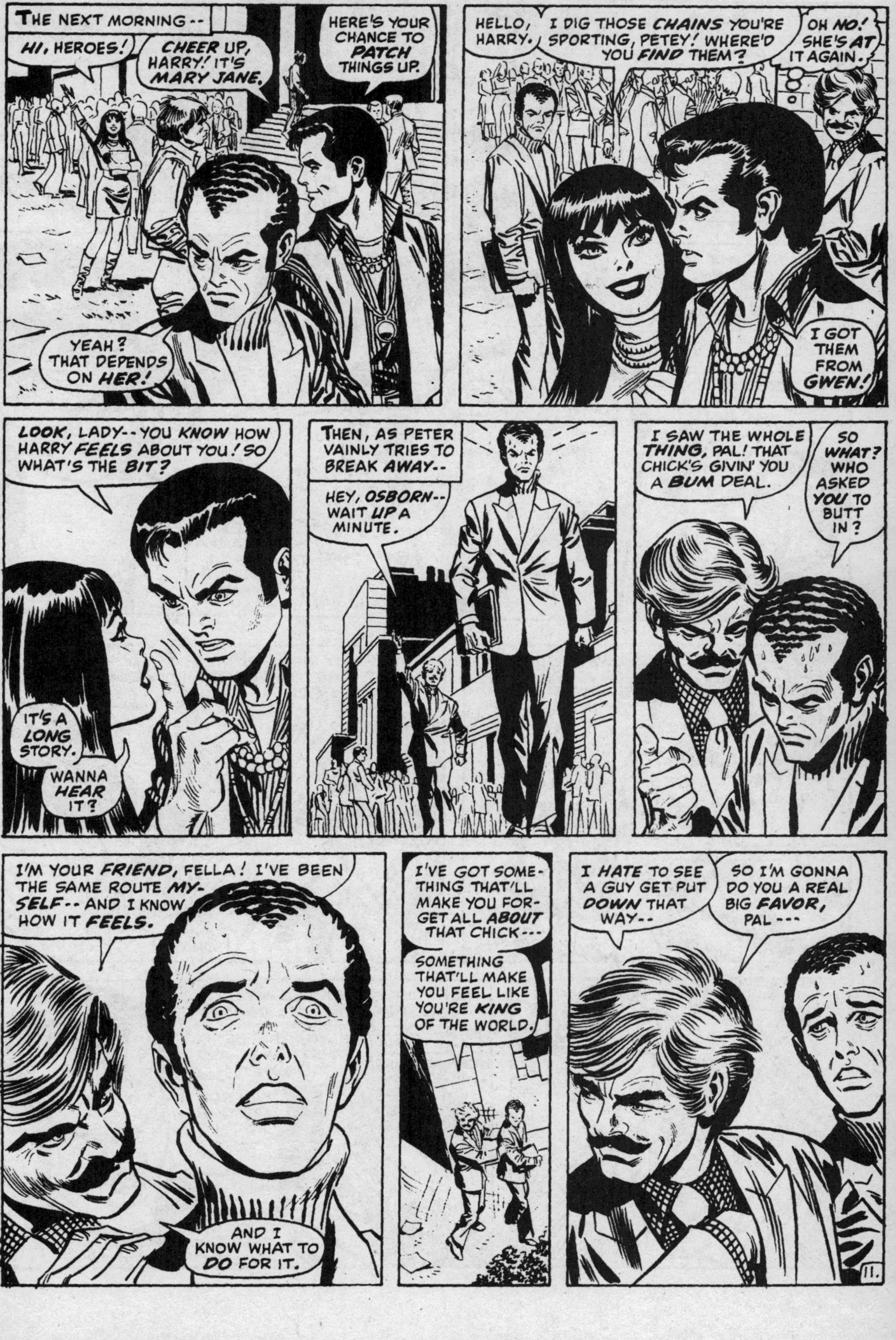
THE NEXT MORNING--
HI, HEROES!
CHEER UP, HARRY! IT'S MARY JANE.
HERE'S YOUR CHANCE TO PATCH THINGS UP.
YEAH? THAT DEPENDS ON HER!
HELLO, HARRY.
I DIG THOSE CHAINS YOU'RE SPORTING, PETEY! WHERE'D YOU FIND THEM?
OH NO! SHE'S AT IT AGAIN.
I GOT THEM FROM GWEN!
LOOK, LADY--YOU KNOW HOW HARRY FEELS ABOUT YOU! SO WHAT'S THE BIT?
IT'S A LONG STORY.
WANNA HEAR IT?
THEN, AS PETER VAINLY TRIES TO BREAK AWAY--
HEY, OSBORN--WAIT UP A MINUTE.
I SAW THE WHOLE THING, PAL! THAT CHICK'S GIVIN' YOU A BUM DEAL.
SO WHAT? WHO ASKED YOU TO BUTT IN?
I'M YOUR FRIEND, FELLA! I'VE BEEN THE SAME ROUTE MYSELF--AND I KNOW HOW IT FEELS.
AND I KNOW WHAT TO DO FOR IT.
I'VE GOT SOMETHING THAT'LL MAKE YOU FORGET ALL ABOUT THAT CHICK---
SOMETHING THAT'LL MAKE YOU FEEL LIKE YOU'RE KING OF THE WORLD.
I HATE TO SEE A GUY GET PUT DOWN THAT WAY--
SO I'M GONNA DO YOU A REAL BIG FAVOR, PAL---
11.

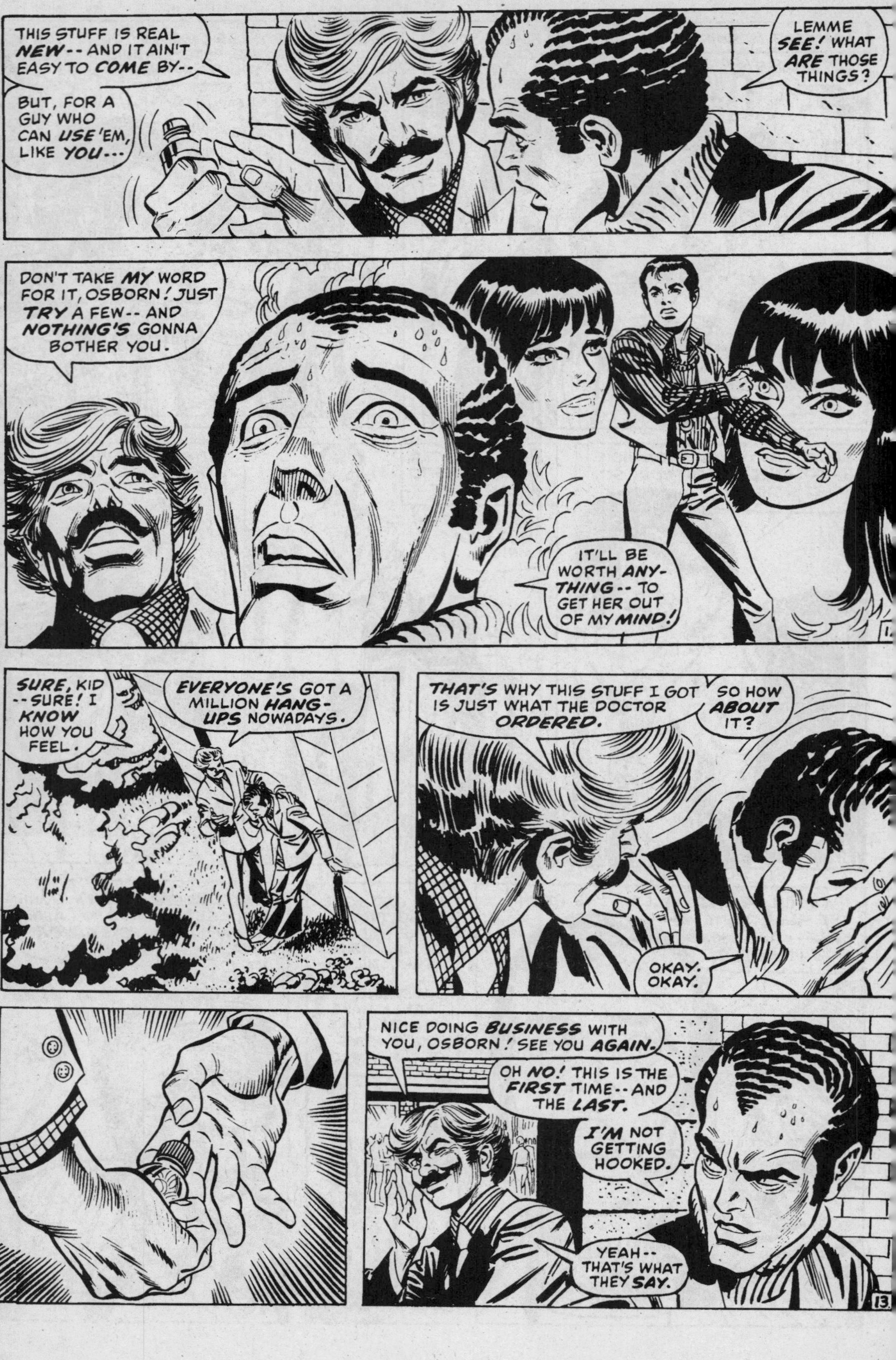

THIS STUFF IS REAL NEW-- AND IT AIN'T EASY TO COME BY--
BUT, FOR A GUY WHO CAN USE 'EM, LIKE YOU...
LEMME SEE! WHAT ARE THOSE THINGS?
DON'T TAKE MY WORD FOR IT, OSBORN! JUST TRY A FEW-- AND NOTHING'S GONNA BOTHER YOU.
IT'LL BE WORTH ANY-THING-- TO GET HER OUT OF MY MIND!
SURE, KID --SURE! I KNOW HOW YOU FEEL.
EVERYONE'S GOT A MILLION HANG-UPS NOWADAYS.
THAT'S WHY THIS STUFF I GOT IS JUST WHAT THE DOCTOR ORDERED.
SO HOW ABOUT IT?
OKAY. OKAY.
NICE DOING BUSINESS WITH YOU, OSBORN! SEE YOU AGAIN.
OH NO! THIS IS THE FIRST TIME-- AND THE LAST.
I'M NOT GETTING HOOKED.
YEAH-- THAT'S WHAT THEY SAY.
13

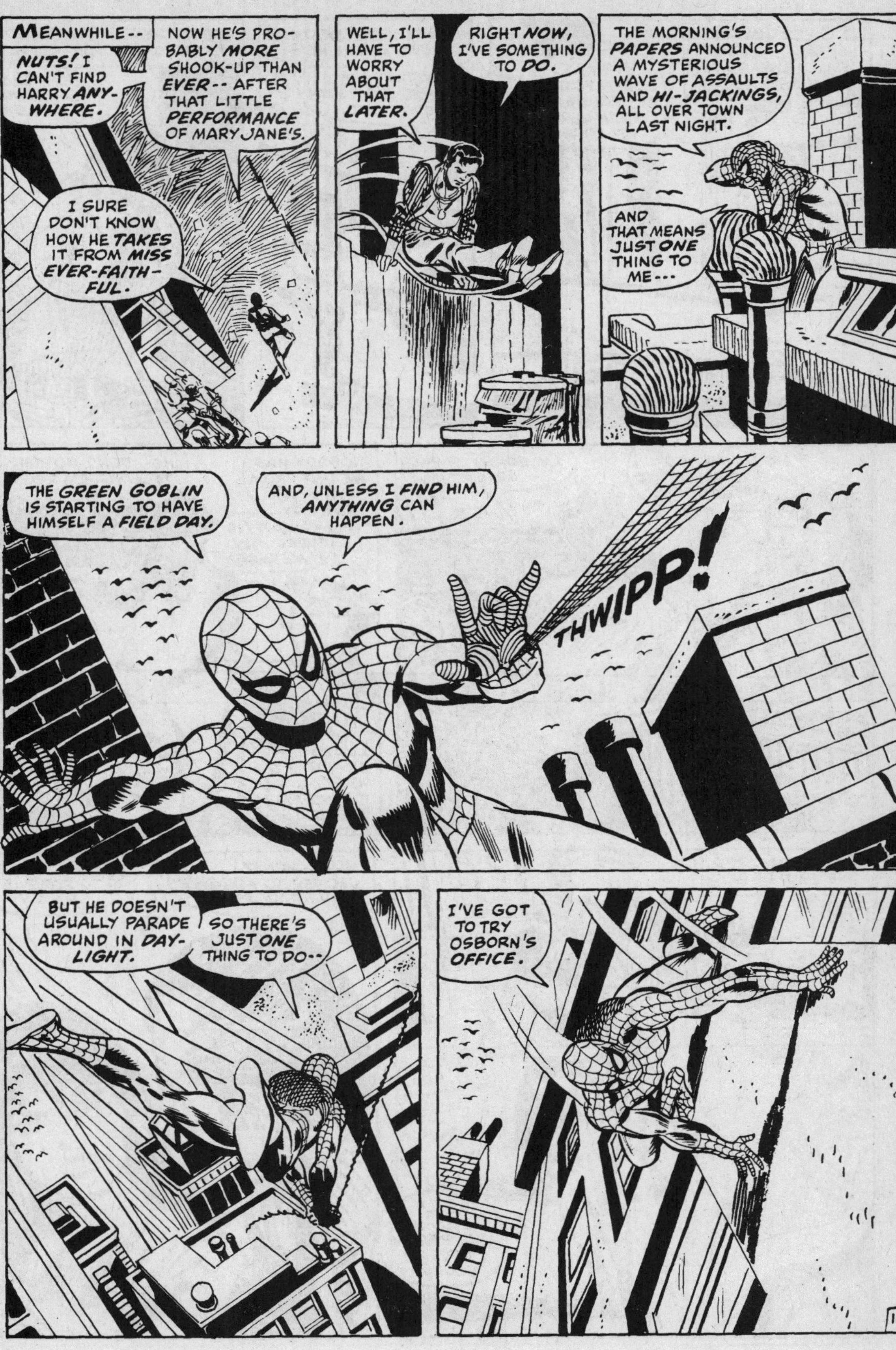
MEANWHILE--
NUTS! I CAN'T FIND HARRY ANYWHERE.
NOW HE'S PROBABLY MORE SHOOK-UP THAN EVER-- AFTER THAT LITTLE PERFORMANCE OF MARY JANE'S.
I SURE DON'T KNOW HOW HE TAKES IT FROM MISS EVER-FAITHFUL.
WELL, I'LL HAVE TO WORRY ABOUT THAT LATER.
RIGHT NOW, I'VE SOMETHING TO DO.
THE MORNING'S PAPERS ANNOUNCED A MYSTERIOUS WAVE OF ASSAULTS AND HI-JACKINGS, ALL OVER TOWN LAST NIGHT.
AND THAT MEANS JUST ONE THING TO ME---
THE GREEN GOBLIN IS STARTING TO HAVE HIMSELF A FIELD DAY.
AND, UNLESS I FIND HIM, ANYTHING CAN HAPPEN.
THWIPP!
BUT HE DOESN'T USUALLY PARADE AROUND IN DAYLIGHT.
SO THERE'S JUST ONE THING TO DO--
I'VE GOT TO TRY OSBORN'S OFFICE.
14

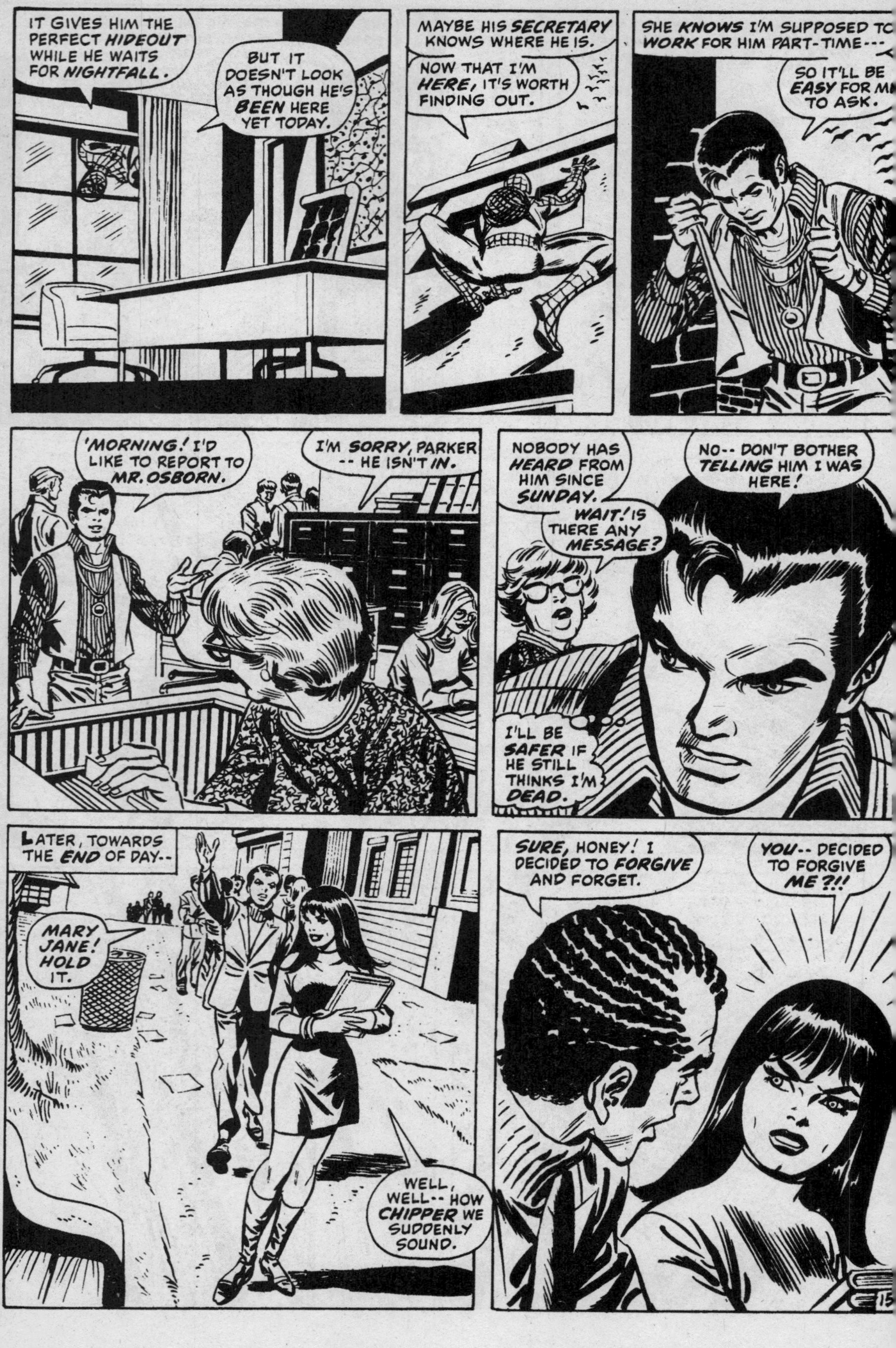
IT GIVES HIM THE PERFECT HIDEOUT WHILE HE WAITS FOR NIGHTFALL.
BUT IT DOESN'T LOOK AS THOUGH HE'S BEEN HERE YET TODAY.
MAYBE HIS SECRETARY KNOWS WHERE HE IS.
NOW THAT I'M HERE, IT'S WORTH FINDING OUT.
SHE KNOWS I'M SUPPOSED TO WORK FOR HIM PART-TIME---
SO IT'LL BE EASY FOR ME TO ASK.
'MORNING! I'D LIKE TO REPORT TO MR. OSBORN.
I'M SORRY, PARKER -- HE ISN'T IN.
NOBODY HAS HEARD FROM HIM SINCE SUNDAY.
NO-- DON'T BOTHER TELLING HIM I WAS HERE!
WAIT! IS THERE ANY MESSAGE?
I'LL BE SAFER IF HE STILL THINKS I'M DEAD.
LATER, TOWARDS THE END OF DAY--
MARY JANE! HOLD IT.
WELL, WELL-- HOW CHIPPER WE SUDDENLY SOUND.
SURE, HONEY! I DECIDED TO FORGIVE AND FORGET.
YOU-- DECIDED TO FORGIVE ME?!!
15

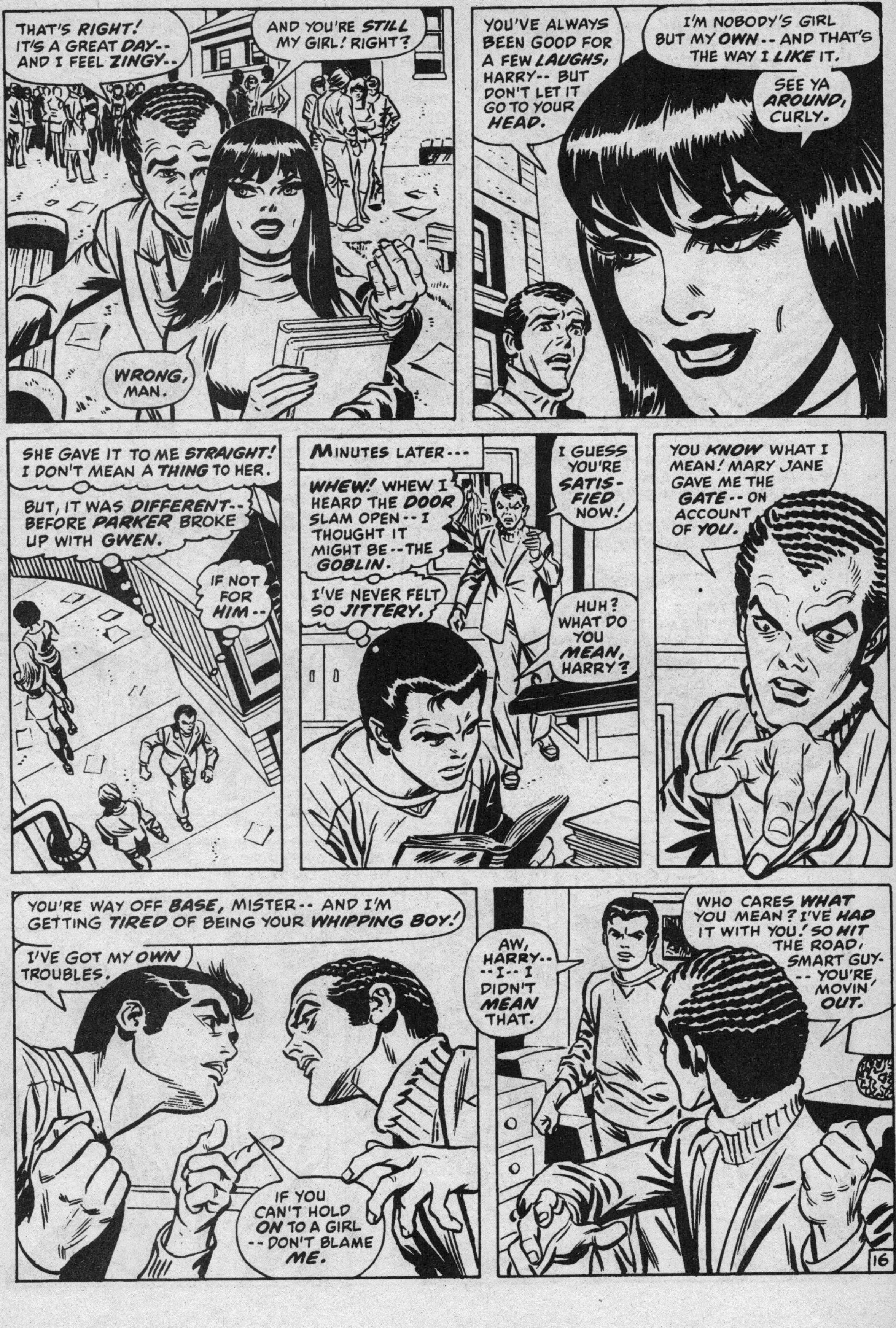
THAT'S RIGHT! IT'S A GREAT DAY-- AND I FEEL ZINGY--
AND YOU'RE STILL MY GIRL! RIGHT?
WRONG, MAN.
YOU'VE ALWAYS BEEN GOOD FOR A FEW LAUGHS, HARRY-- BUT DON'T LET IT GO TO YOUR HEAD.
I'M NOBODY'S GIRL BUT MY OWN-- AND THAT'S THE WAY I LIKE IT.
SEE YA AROUND, CURLY.
SHE GAVE IT TO ME STRAIGHT! I DON'T MEAN A THING TO HER.
BUT, IT WAS DIFFERENT-- BEFORE PARKER BROKE UP WITH GWEN.
IF NOT FOR HIM--
MINUTES LATER---
WHEW! WHEW I HEARD THE DOOR SLAM OPEN-- I THOUGHT IT MIGHT BE--THE GOBLIN.
I'VE NEVER FELT SO JITTERY.
I GUESS YOU'RE SATIS-FIED NOW!
HUH? WHAT DO YOU MEAN, HARRY?
YOU KNOW WHAT I MEAN! MARY JANE GAVE ME THE GATE-- ON ACCOUNT OF YOU.
YOU'RE WAY OFF BASE, MISTER-- AND I'M GETTING TIRED OF BEING YOUR WHIPPING BOY!
I'VE GOT MY OWN TROUBLES.
IF YOU CAN'T HOLD ON TO A GIRL --DON'T BLAME ME.
AW, HARRY-- --I-- I DIDN'T MEAN THAT.
WHO CARES WHAT YOU MEAN? I'VE HAD IT WITH YOU! SO HIT THE ROAD, SMART GUY-- --YOU'RE MOVIN' OUT.
16

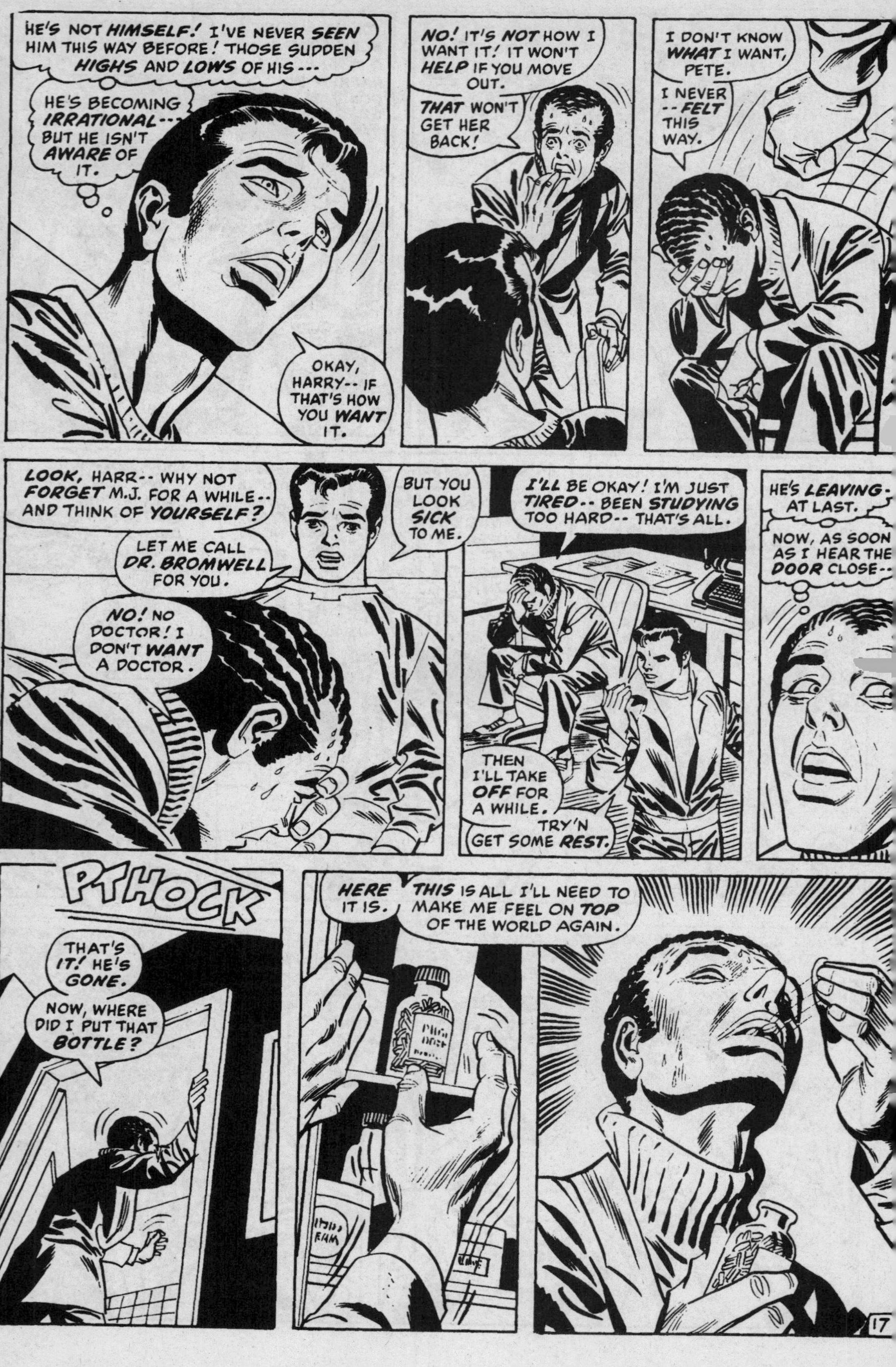
HE'S NOT HIMSELF! I'VE NEVER SEEN HIM THIS WAY BEFORE! THOSE SUDDEN HIGHS AND LOWS OF HIS---
HE'S BECOMING IRRATIONAL--- BUT HE ISN'T AWARE OF IT.
OKAY, HARRY-- IF THAT'S HOW YOU WANT IT.
NO! IT'S NOT HOW I WANT IT! IT WON'T HELP IF YOU MOVE OUT.
THAT WON'T GET HER BACK!
I DON'T KNOW WHAT I WANT, PETE.
I NEVER --FELT THIS WAY.
LOOK, HARR-- WHY NOT FORGET M.J. FOR A WHILE-- AND THINK OF YOURSELF?
LET ME CALL DR. BROMWELL FOR YOU.
NO! NO DOCTOR! I DON'T WANT A DOCTOR.
BUT YOU LOOK SICK TO ME.
I'LL BE OKAY! I'M JUST TIRED-- BEEN STUDYING TOO HARD-- THAT'S ALL.
THEN I'LL TAKE OFF FOR A WHILE.
TRY'N GET SOME REST.
HE'S LEAVING-- AT LAST.
NOW, AS SOON AS I HEAR THE DOOR CLOSE--
PTHOCK
THAT'S IT! HE'S GONE.
NOW, WHERE DID I PUT THAT BOTTLE?
HERE IT IS.
THIS IS ALL I'LL NEED TO MAKE ME FEEL ON TOP OF THE WORLD AGAIN.
17

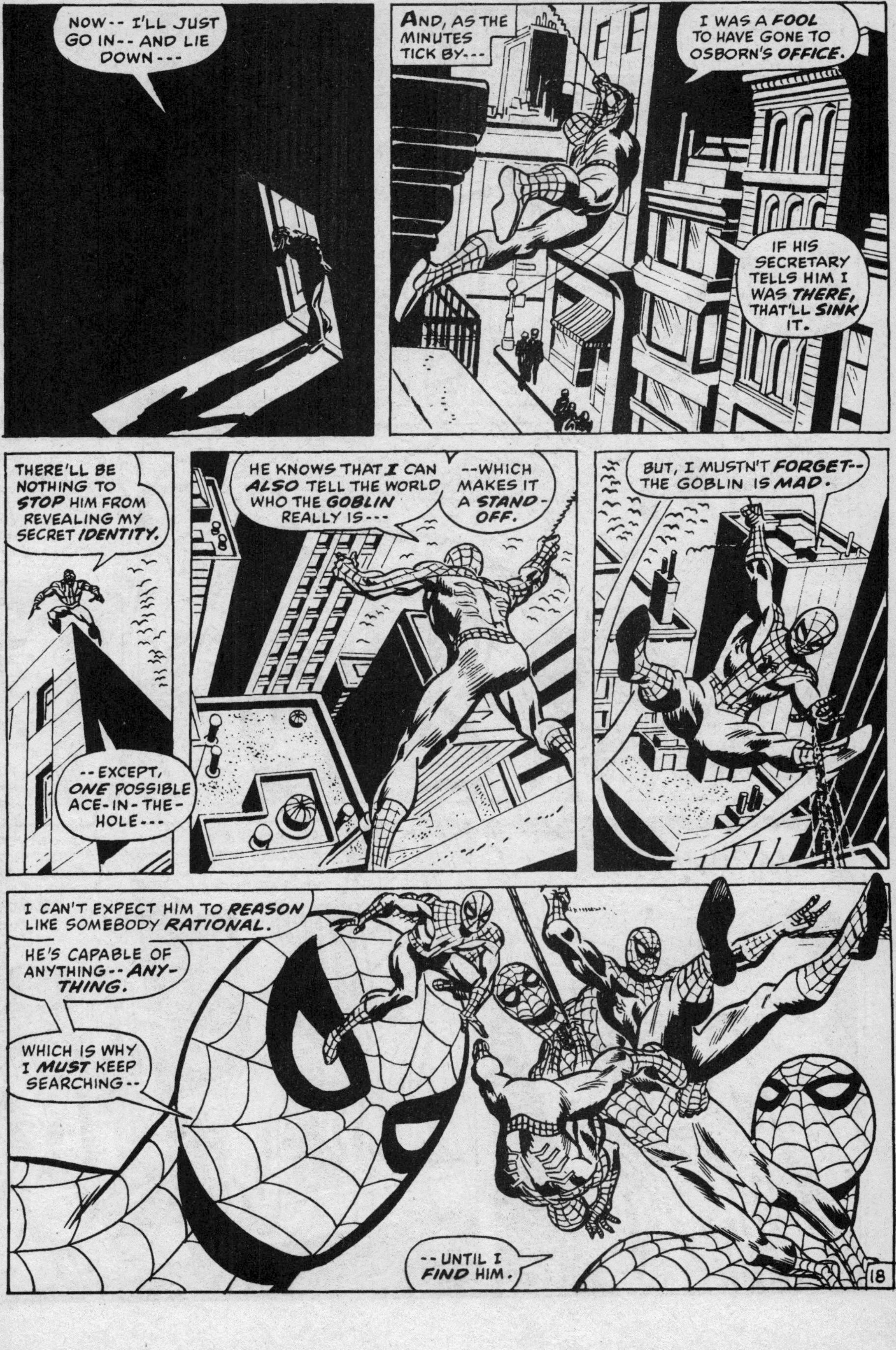
NOW-- I'LL JUST GO IN-- AND LIE DOWN---
AND, AS THE MINUTES TICK BY---
I WAS A FOOL TO HAVE GONE TO OSBORN'S OFFICE.
IF HIS SECRETARY TELLS HIM I WAS THERE, THAT'LL SINK IT.
THERE'LL BE NOTHING TO STOP HIM FROM REVEALING MY SECRET IDENTITY.
--EXCEPT, ONE POSSIBLE ACE-IN-THE-HOLE---
HE KNOWS THAT I CAN ALSO TELL THE WORLD WHO THE GOBLIN REALLY IS---
--WHICH MAKES IT A STAND-OFF.
BUT, I MUSTN'T FORGET-- THE GOBLIN IS MAD.
I CAN'T EXPECT HIM TO REASON LIKE SOMEBODY RATIONAL.
HE'S CAPABLE OF ANYTHING-- ANY-THING.
WHICH IS WHY I MUST KEEP SEARCHING--
--UNTIL I FIND HIM.
18

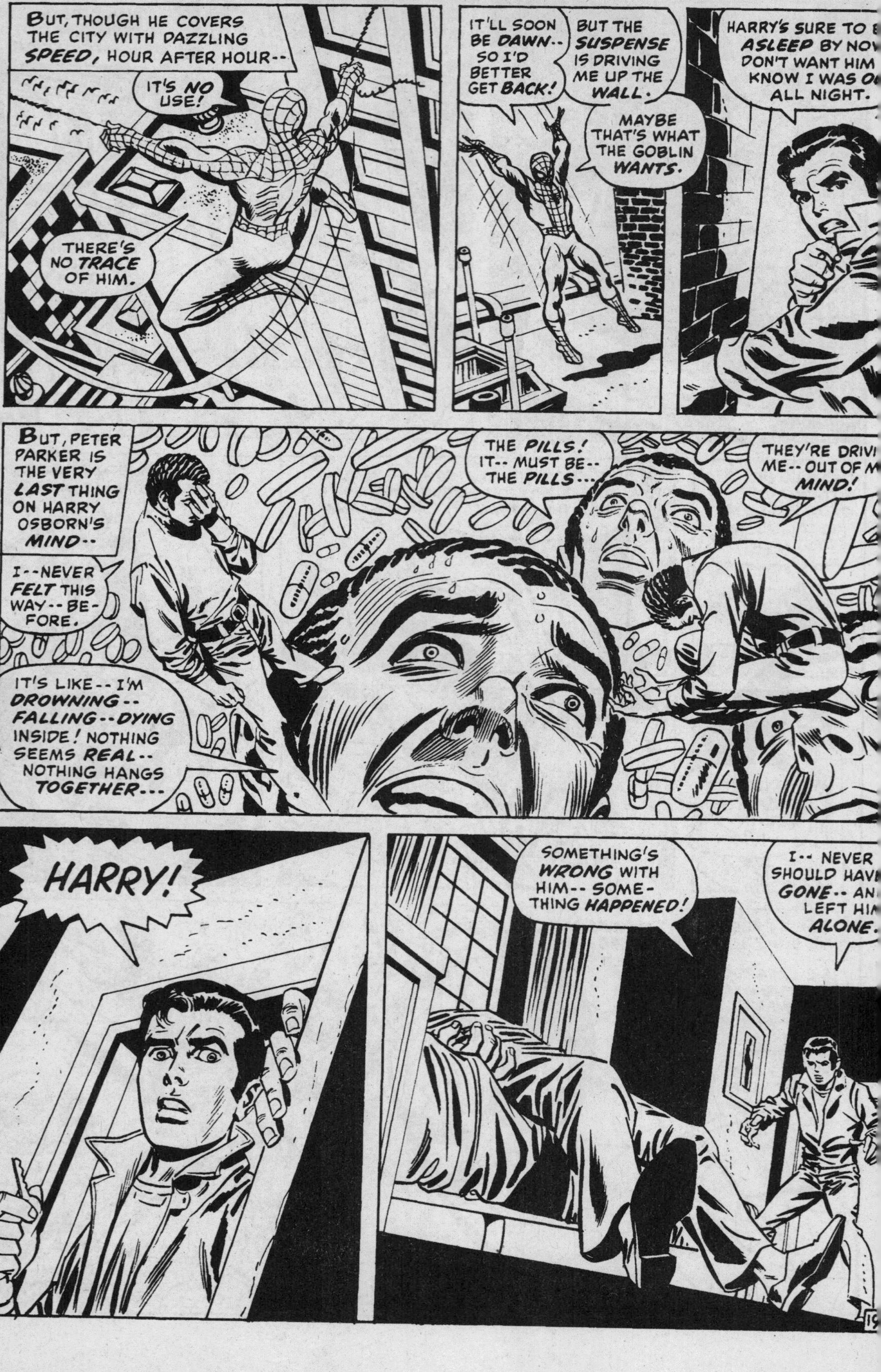
BUT, THOUGH HE COVERS THE CITY WITH DAZZLING SPEED, HOUR AFTER HOUR--
IT'S NO USE!
THERE'S NO TRACE OF HIM.
IT'LL SOON BE DAWN-- SO I'D BETTER GET BACK!
BUT THE SUSPENSE IS DRIVING ME UP THE WALL.
MAYBE THAT'S WHAT THE GOBLIN WANTS.
HARRY'S SURE TO B ASLEEP BY NOW DON'T WANT HIM KNOW I WAS O ALL NIGHT.
BUT, PETER PARKER IS THE VERY LAST THING ON HARRY OSBORN'S MIND--
I--NEVER FELT THIS WAY--BE- FORE.
IT'S LIKE-- I'M DROWNING-- FALLING--DYING INSIDE! NOTHING SEEMS REAL-- NOTHING HANGS TOGETHER---
THE PILLS! IT-- MUST BE-- THE PILLS---
THEY'RE DRIVI ME-- OUT OF M MIND!
HARRY!
SOMETHING'S WRONG WITH HIM-- SOME- THING HAPPENED!
I-- NEVER SHOULD HAV GONE-- AN LEFT HI ALONE.

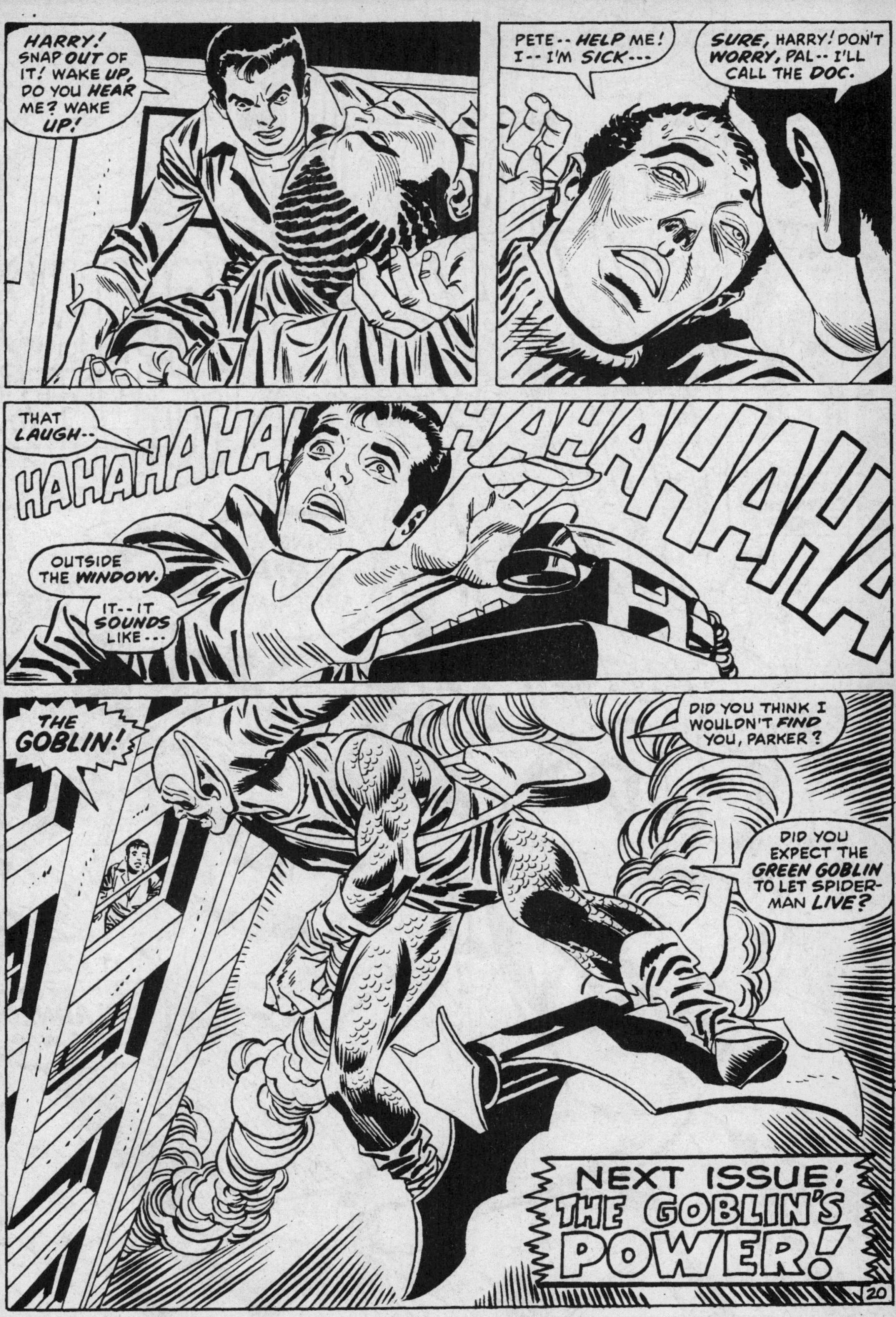

HARRY! SNAP OUT OF IT! WAKE UP, DO YOU HEAR ME? WAKE UP!
PETE-- HELP ME! I-- I'M SICK---
SURE, HARRY! DON'T WORRY, PAL-- I'LL CALL THE DOC.
THAT LAUGH--
HAHAHAHAHAHAHAHAHAHA
OUTSIDE THE WINDOW.
IT-- IT SOUNDS LIKE---
THE GOBLIN!
DID YOU THINK I WOULDN'T FIND YOU, PARKER?
DID YOU EXPECT THE GREEN GOBLIN TO LET SPIDER-MAN LIVE?
NEXT ISSUE: THE GOBLIN'S POWER!
20

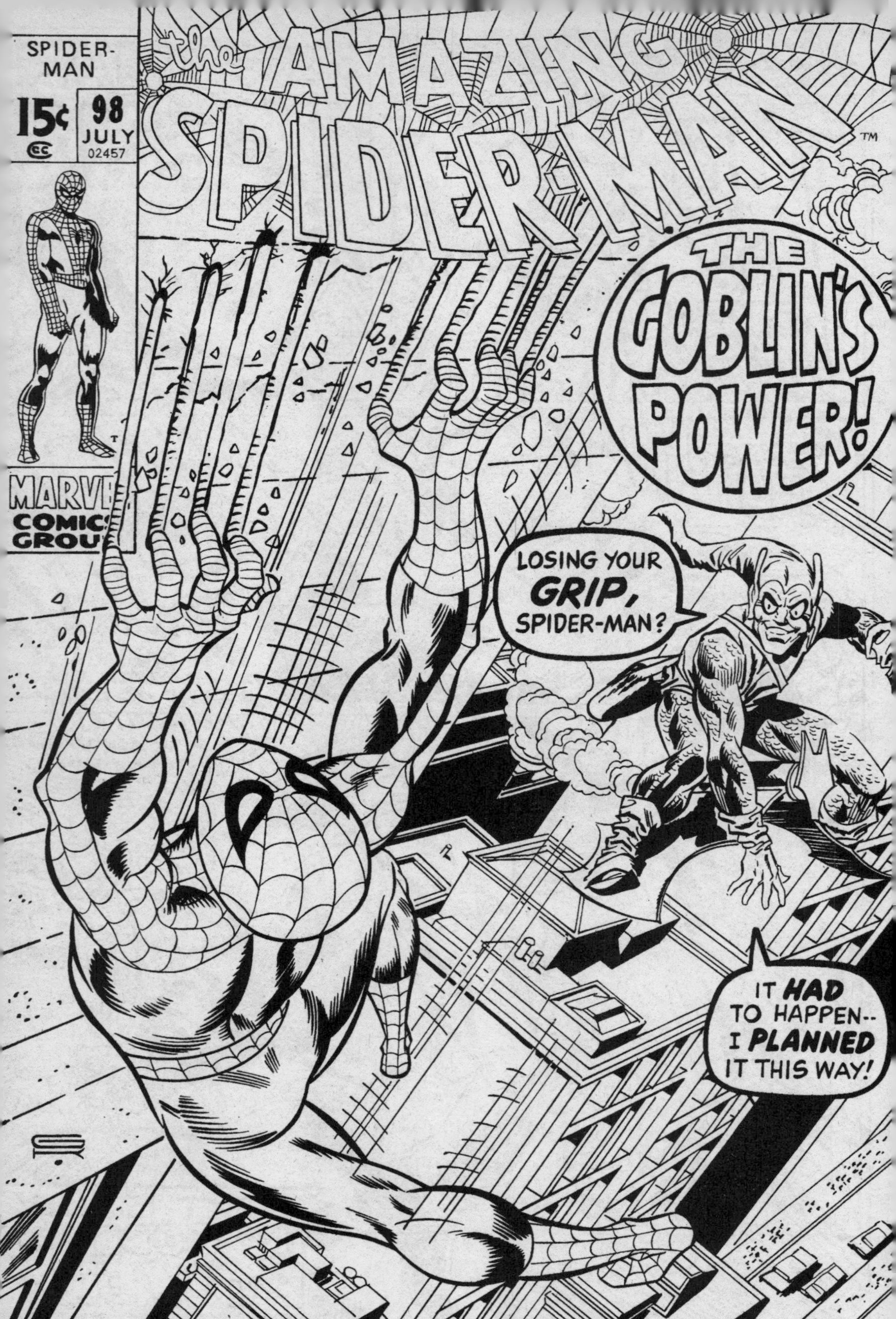
SPIDER-MAN
15¢
98
JULY
02457
the AMAZING SPIDER-MAN
MARVEL COMICS GROUP
THE GOBLIN'S POWER!
LOSING YOUR GRIP, SPIDER-MAN?
IT HAD TO HAPPEN-- I PLANNED IT THIS WAY!

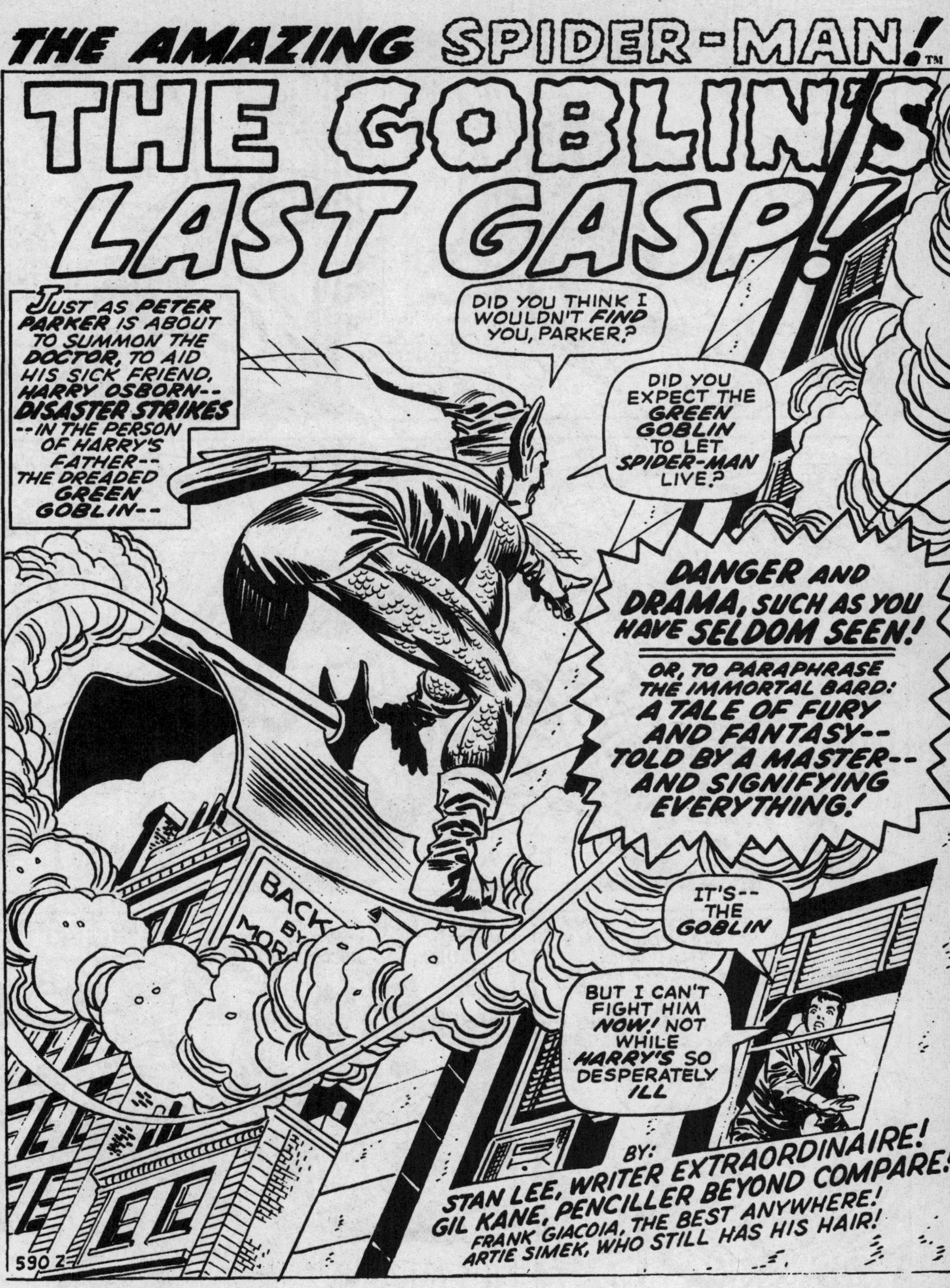
THE AMAZING SPIDER-MAN!™
THE GOBLIN'S LAST GASP!
JUST AS PETER PARKER IS ABOUT TO SUMMON THE DOCTOR, TO AID HIS SICK FRIEND, HARRY OSBORN--DISASTER STRIKES --IN THE PERSON OF HARRY'S FATHER-- THE DREADED GREEN GOBLIN--
DID YOU THINK I WOULDN'T FIND YOU, PARKER?
DID YOU EXPECT THE GREEN GOBLIN TO LET SPIDER-MAN LIVE?
DANGER AND DRAMA, SUCH AS YOU HAVE SELDOM SEEN!
OR, TO PARAPHRASE THE IMMORTAL BARD: A TALE OF FURY AND FANTASY-- TOLD BY A MASTER-- AND SIGNIFYING EVERYTHING!
BACK BY MOR
IT'S-- THE GOBLIN
BUT I CAN'T FIGHT HIM NOW! NOT WHILE HARRY'S SO DESPERATELY ILL
BY:
STAN LEE, WRITER EXTRAORDINAIRE!
GIL KANE, PENCILLER BEYOND COMPARE!
FRANK GIACOIA, THE BEST ANYWHERE!
ARTIE SIMEK, WHO STILL HAS HIS HAIR!
590 2

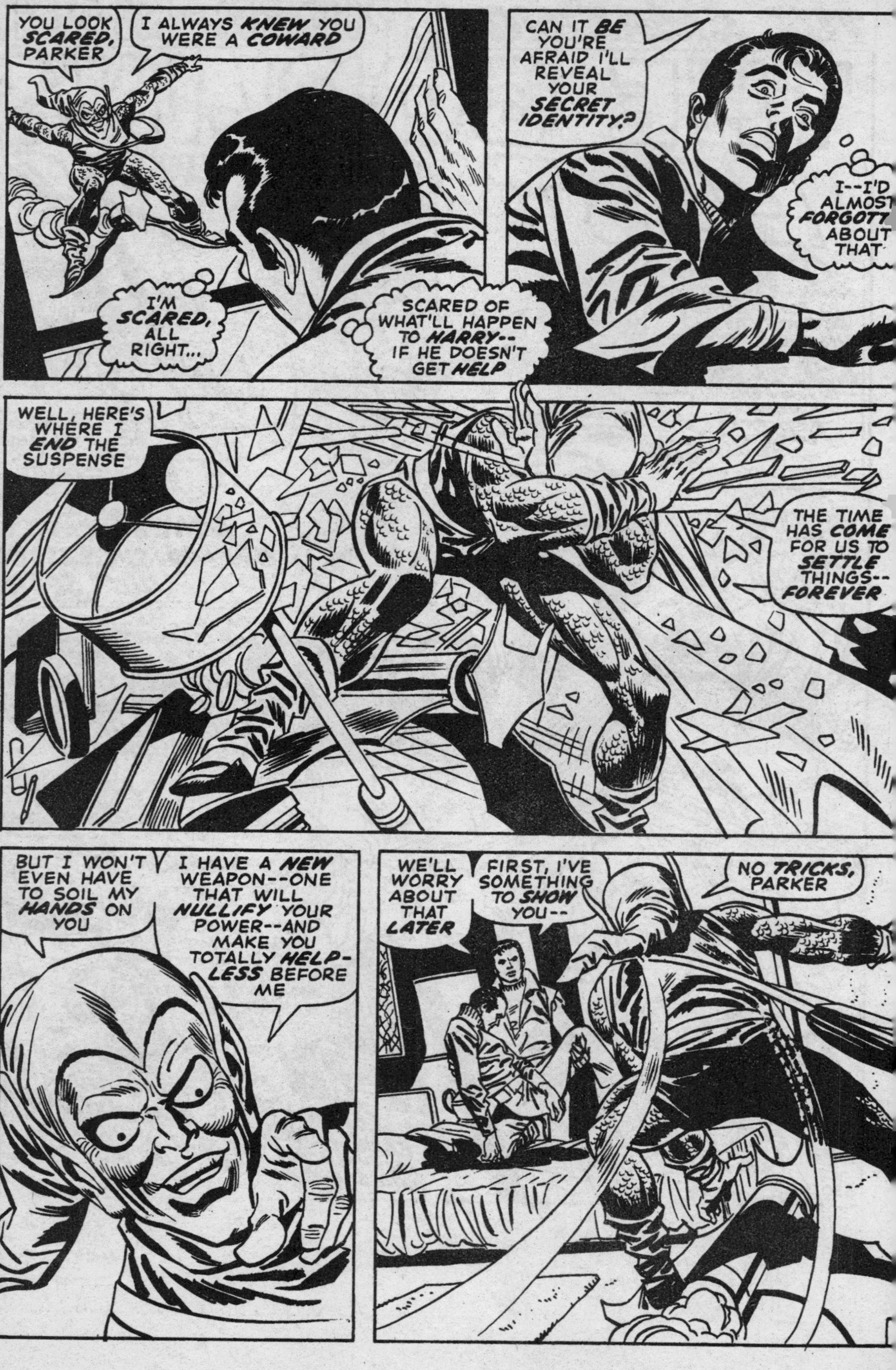
YOU LOOK SCARED, PARKER
I ALWAYS KNEW YOU WERE A COWARD
I'M SCARED, ALL RIGHT...
SCARED OF WHAT'LL HAPPEN TO HARRY-- IF HE DOESN'T GET HELP
CAN IT BE YOU'RE AFRAID I'LL REVEAL YOUR SECRET IDENTITY?
I--I'D ALMOST FORGOTT ABOUT THAT
WELL, HERE'S WHERE I END THE SUSPENSE
THE TIME HAS COME FOR US TO SETTLE THINGS-- FOREVER
BUT I WON'T EVEN HAVE TO SOIL MY HANDS ON YOU
I HAVE A NEW WEAPON--ONE THAT WILL NULLIFY YOUR POWER--AND MAKE YOU TOTALLY HELP-LESS BEFORE ME
WE'LL WORRY ABOUT THAT LATER
FIRST, I'VE SOMETHING TO SHOW YOU--
NO TRICKS, PARKER

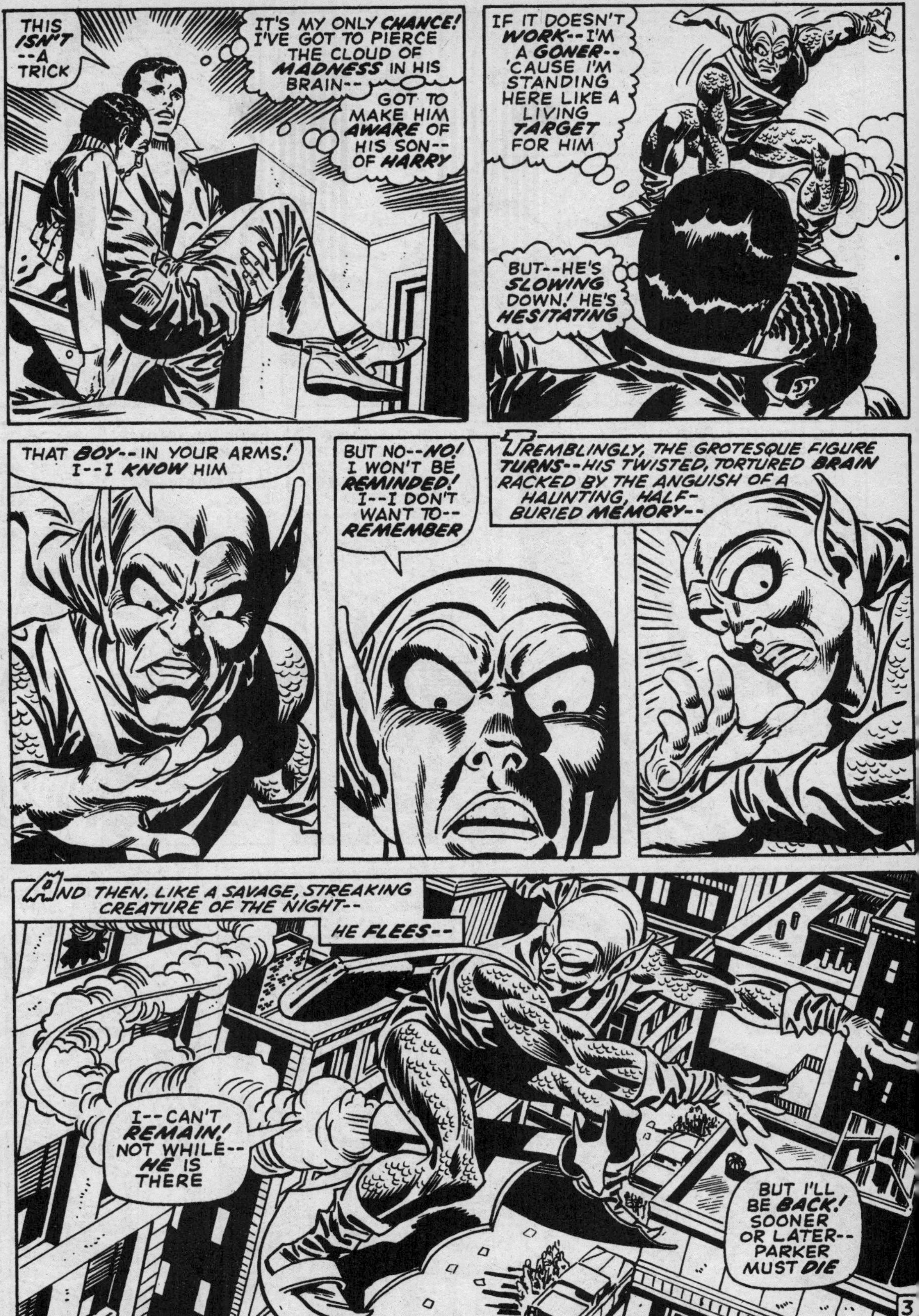

THIS ISN'T --A TRICK
IT'S MY ONLY CHANCE! I'VE GOT TO PIERCE THE CLOUD OF MADNESS IN HIS BRAIN--
GOT TO MAKE HIM AWARE OF HIS SON-- OF HARRY
IF IT DOESN'T WORK--I'M A GONER--'CAUSE I'M STANDING HERE LIKE A LIVING TARGET FOR HIM
BUT--HE'S SLOWING DOWN! HE'S HESITATING
THAT BOY--IN YOUR ARMS! I--I KNOW HIM
BUT NO--NO! I WON'T BE REMINDED! I--I DON'T WANT TO--REMEMBER
TREMBLINGLY, THE GROTESQUE FIGURE TURNS--HIS TWISTED, TORTURED BRAIN RACKED BY THE ANGUISH OF A HAUNTING, HALF-BURIED MEMORY--
AND THEN, LIKE A SAVAGE, STREAKING CREATURE OF THE NIGHT--
HE FLEES--
I--CAN'T REMAIN! NOT WHILE--HE IS THERE
BUT I'LL BE BACK! SOONER OR LATER--PARKER MUST DIE
3

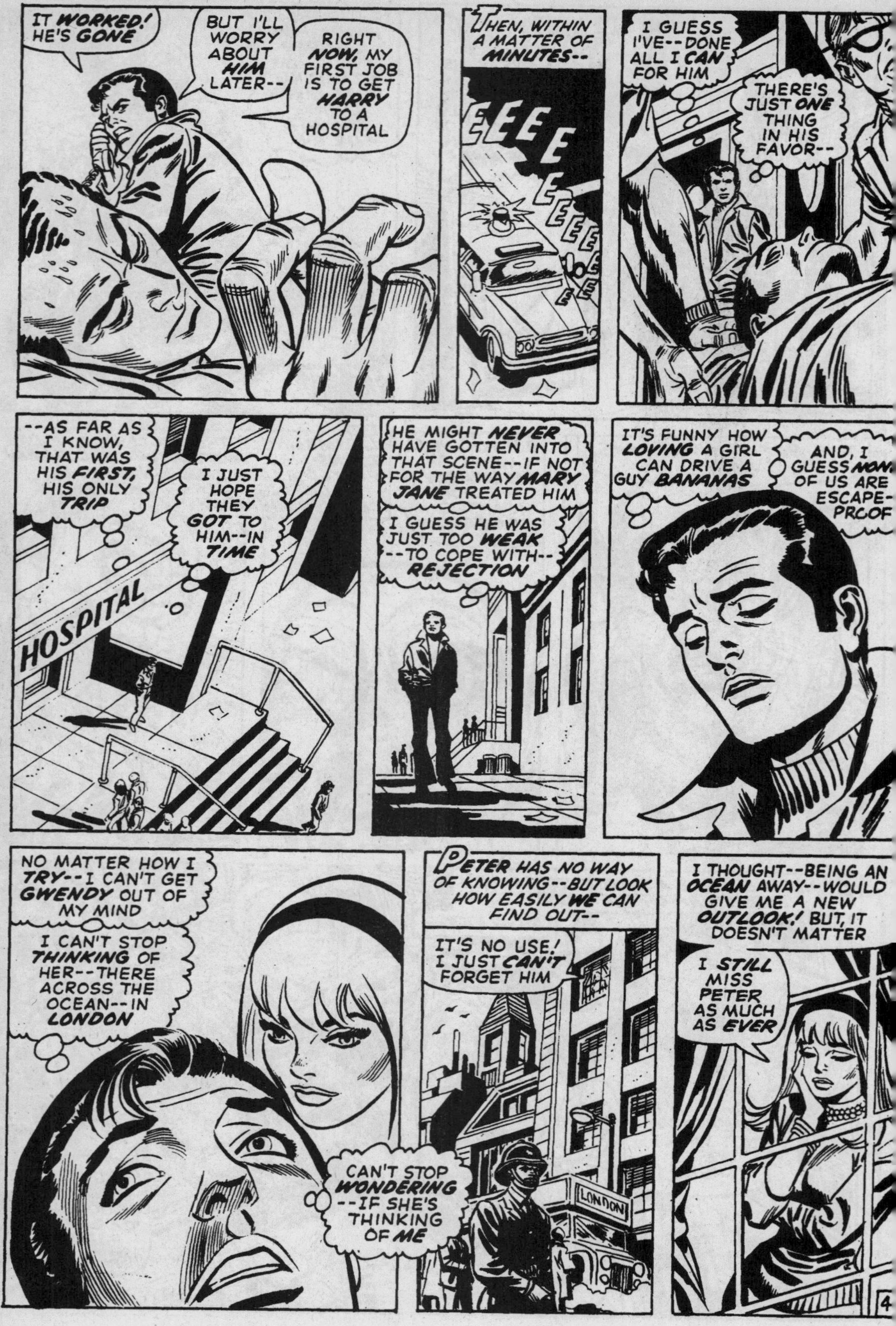
IT WORKED! HE'S GONE
BUT I'LL WORRY ABOUT HIM LATER--
RIGHT NOW, MY FIRST JOB IS TO GET HARRY TO A HOSPITAL
THEN, WITHIN A MATTER OF MINUTES--
EEEEEEEEEEEEE
I GUESS I'VE--DONE ALL I CAN FOR HIM
THERE'S JUST ONE THING IN HIS FAVOR--
--AS FAR AS I KNOW, THAT WAS HIS FIRST, HIS ONLY TRIP
I JUST HOPE THEY GOT TO HIM--IN TIME
HOSPITAL
HE MIGHT NEVER HAVE GOTTEN INTO THAT SCENE--IF NOT FOR THE WAY MARY JANE TREATED HIM
I GUESS HE WAS JUST TOO WEAK --TO COPE WITH-- REJECTION
IT'S FUNNY HOW LOVING A GIRL CAN DRIVE A GUY BANANAS
AND, I GUESS NONE OF US ARE ESCAPE-PROOF
NO MATTER HOW I TRY--I CAN'T GET GWENDY OUT OF MY MIND
I CAN'T STOP THINKING OF HER--THERE ACROSS THE OCEAN--IN LONDON
CAN'T STOP WONDERING --IF SHE'S THINKING OF ME
PETER HAS NO WAY OF KNOWING--BUT LOOK HOW EASILY WE CAN FIND OUT--
IT'S NO USE! I JUST CAN'T FORGET HIM
LONDON
I THOUGHT--BEING AN OCEAN AWAY--WOULD GIVE ME A NEW OUTLOOK! BUT, IT DOESN'T MATTER
I STILL MISS PETER AS MUCH AS EVER
4

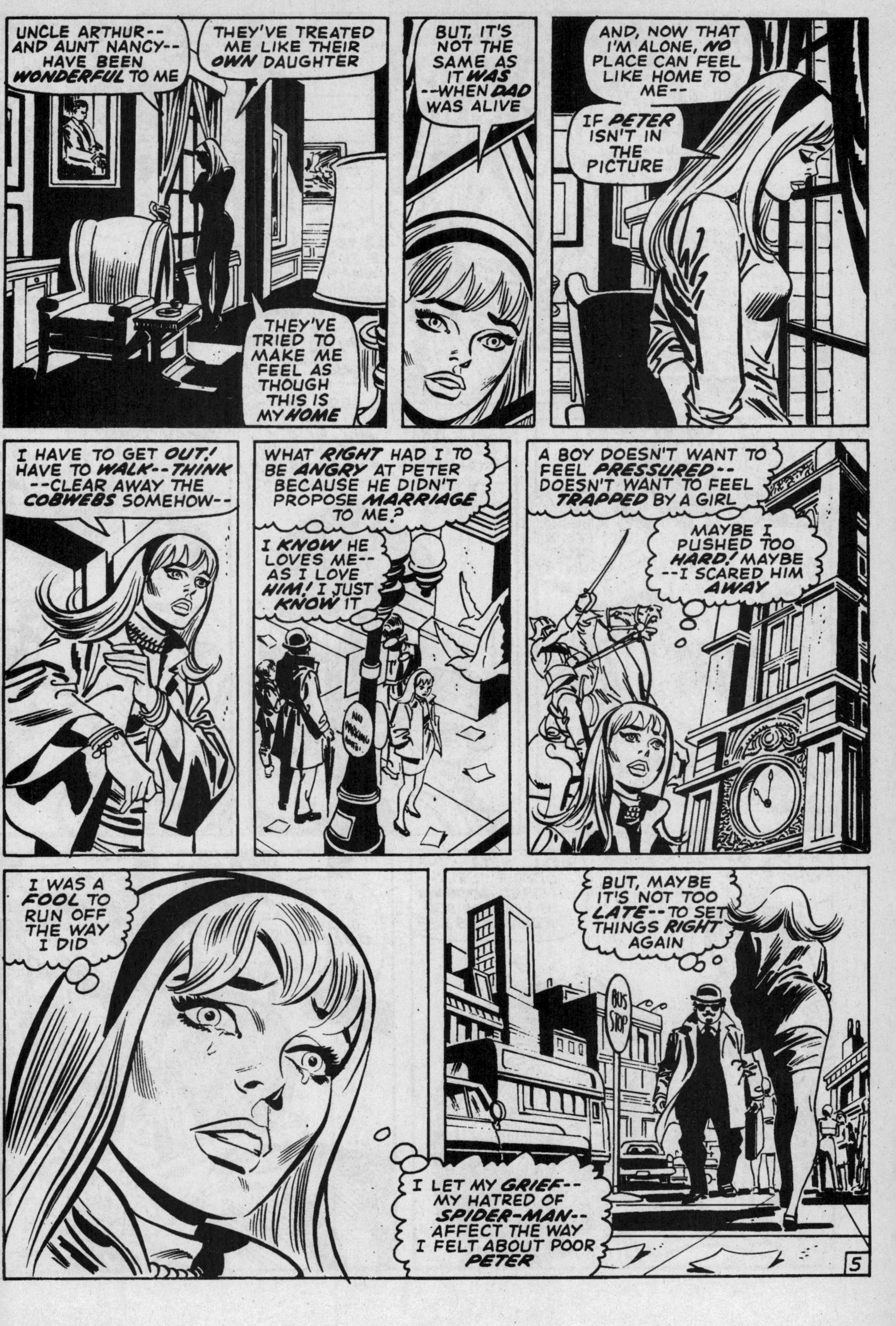
UNCLE ARTHUR-- AND AUNT NANCY-- HAVE BEEN WONDERFUL TO ME
THEY'VE TREATED ME LIKE THEIR OWN DAUGHTER
THEY'VE TRIED TO MAKE ME FEEL AS THOUGH THIS IS MY HOME
BUT, IT'S NOT THE SAME AS IT WAS --WHEN DAD WAS ALIVE
AND, NOW THAT I'M ALONE, NO PLACE CAN FEEL LIKE HOME TO ME--
IF PETER ISN'T IN THE PICTURE
I HAVE TO GET OUT! HAVE TO WALK--THINK --CLEAR AWAY THE COBWEBS SOMEHOW--
WHAT RIGHT HAD I TO BE ANGRY AT PETER BECAUSE HE DIDN'T PROPOSE MARRIAGE TO ME?
I KNOW HE LOVES ME-- AS I LOVE HIM! I JUST KNOW IT
NO PARKING
A BOY DOESN'T WANT TO FEEL PRESSURED-- DOESN'T WANT TO FEEL TRAPPED BY A GIRL
MAYBE I PUSHED TOO HARD! MAYBE --I SCARED HIM AWAY
I WAS A FOOL TO RUN OFF THE WAY I DID
BUT, MAYBE IT'S NOT TOO LATE--TO SET THINGS RIGHT AGAIN
BUS STOP
I LET MY GRIEF-- MY HATRED OF SPIDER-MAN-- AFFECT THE WAY I FELT ABOUT POOR PETER
5

SEE YA AROUND, PARKER

WISH I COULD FIND *MARY JANE*

YEAH-- SURE

AND NOW THAT THE LONGEST SOLILOQUEYS SINCE *HAMLET* HAVE DRAWN TO AN END, LET'S GET THINGS *ROLLING* AGAIN AS WE REJOIN OUR HERO, LEAVING GOOD OL' *E.S.U.* AFTER CLASSES--

M.J. WOULD BE JUST WHAT HARRY *NEEDS* TO CHEER HIM UP AT THE *HOSPITAL*

POOR GU I HOPE H GETTIN ALON OKAY

HEY, MAN--I WANNA *TALK* TO YOU

GO AHEAD! IT'S A *FREE* COUNTRY

THAT'S WHAT I *LIKE*--A SENSAHUMOR

I BEEN WAIT- ING FOR YOUR *PAL*, HARRY OSBORN! KNOW WHERE HE *IS?*

YEAH, I KNOW

OKAY, THEN! TELL 'IM I *GOT* SOME- THING FOR HIM

BUT I CAN'T WAIT FOREVER

SO *YOU'RE* THE CREEP WHO SOLD HIM THOSE *PILLS,* HUH?

WELL, WELL--THE LITTLE CURLY- HAIRED *GOODNIK* IS LOOKIN' FOR *TROUBLE,* IS HE?

LET'S SEE IF I CAN *OBLIGE* YA, SONNY--

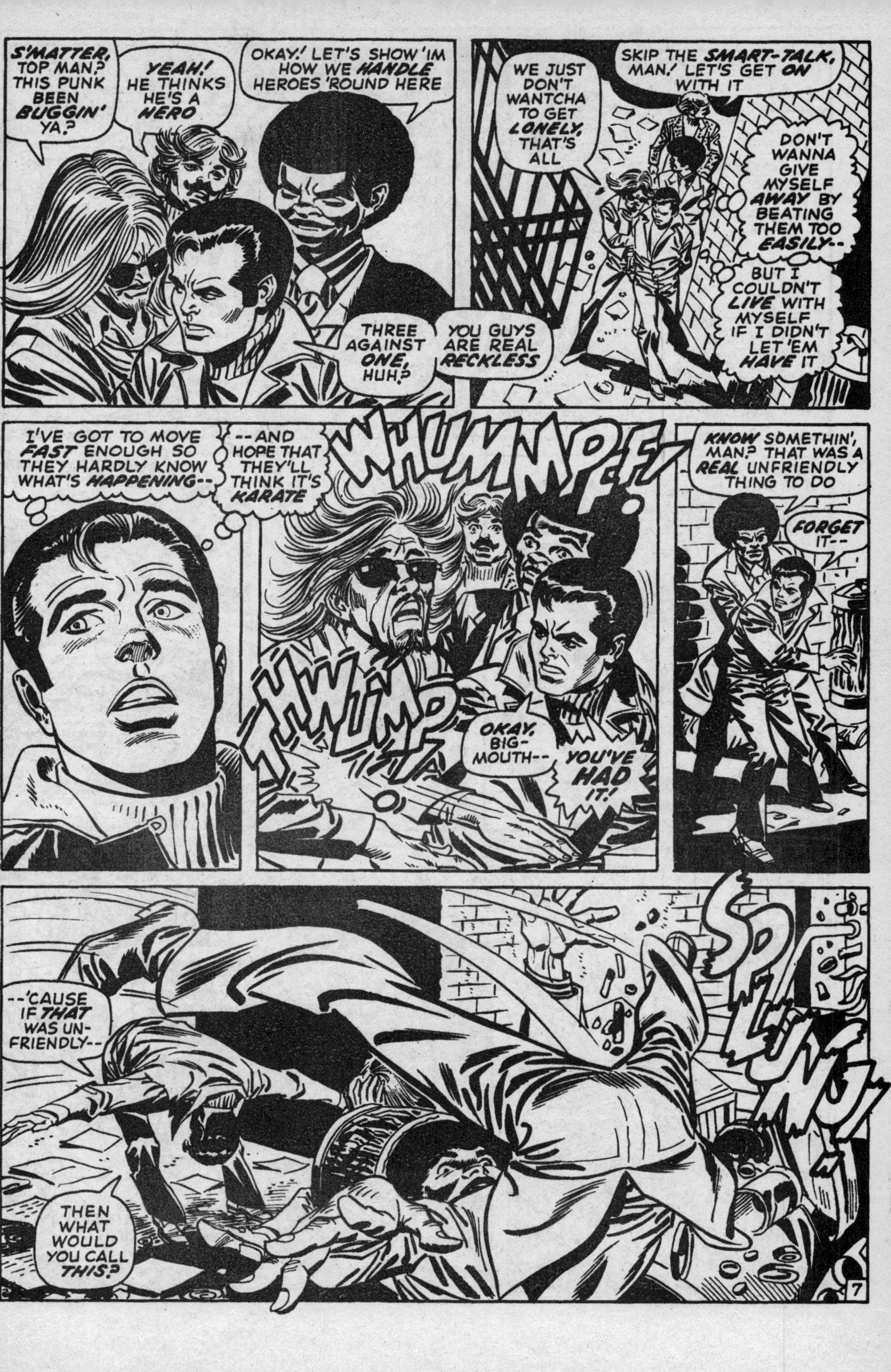
S'MATTER, TOP MAN? THIS PUNK BEEN BUGGIN' YA?
YEAH! HE THINKS HE'S A HERO
OKAY! LET'S SHOW 'IM HOW WE HANDLE HEROES 'ROUND HERE
THREE AGAINST ONE, HUH?
YOU GUYS ARE REAL RECKLESS
WE JUST DON'T WANTCHA TO GET LONELY, THAT'S ALL
SKIP THE SMART-TALK, MAN! LET'S GET ON WITH IT
DON'T WANNA GIVE MYSELF AWAY BY BEATING THEM TOO EASILY--
BUT I COULDN'T LIVE WITH MYSELF IF I DIDN'T LET 'EM HAVE IT
I'VE GOT TO MOVE FAST ENOUGH SO THEY HARDLY KNOW WHAT'S HAPPENING--
--AND HOPE THAT THEY'LL THINK IT'S KARATE
WHUMMPFF!
HWUMP
OKAY, BIG-MOUTH--
YOU'VE HAD IT!
KNOW SOMETHIN', MAN? THAT WAS A REAL UNFRIENDLY THING TO DO
FORGET IT--
--'CAUSE IF THAT WAS UN-FRIENDLY--
THEN WHAT WOULD YOU CALL THIS?
SPLUNG

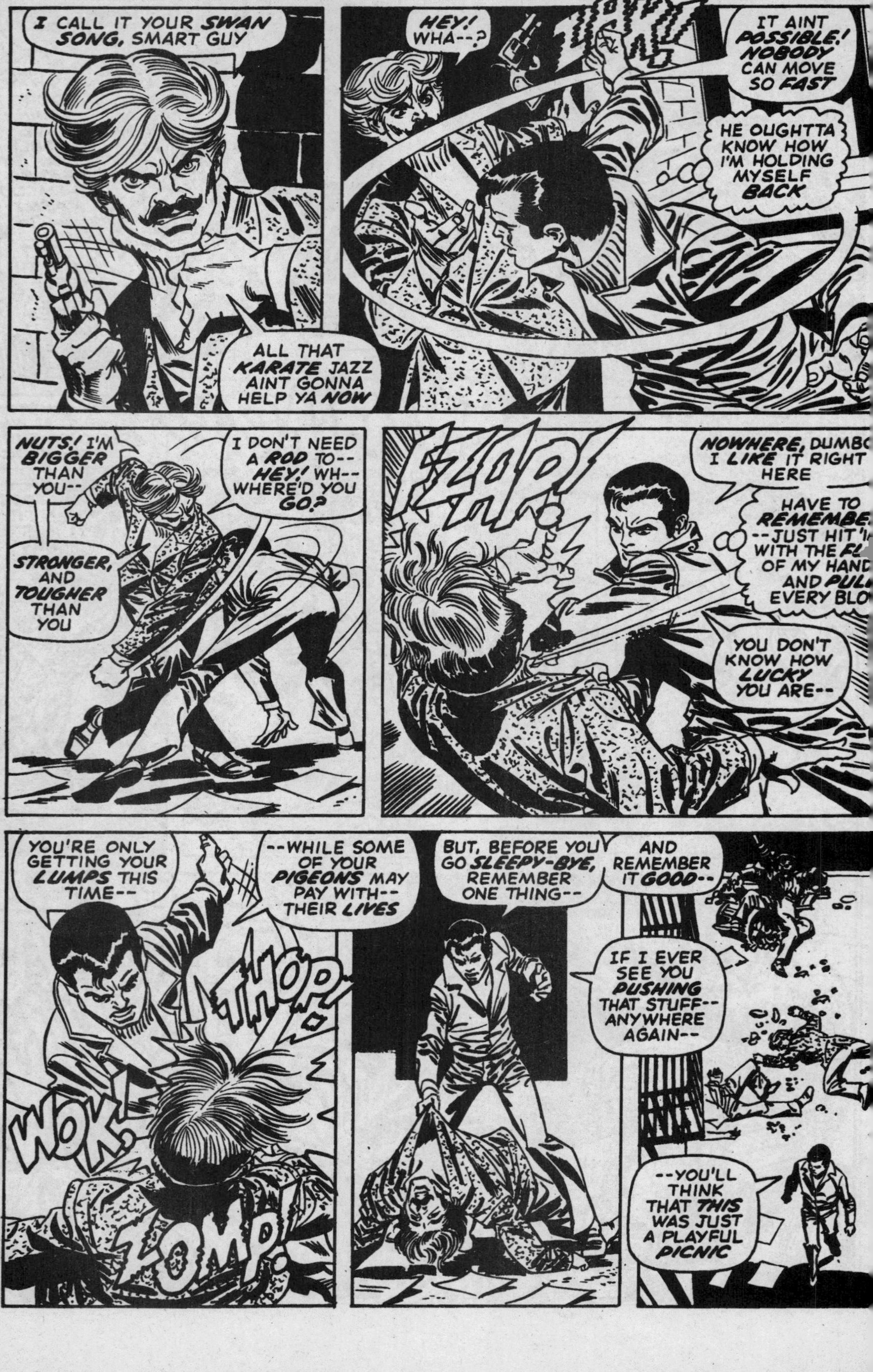
I CALL IT YOUR SWAN SONG, SMART GUY
ALL THAT KARATE JAZZ AINT GONNA HELP YA NOW
HEY! WHA--?
IT AINT POSSIBLE! NOBODY CAN MOVE SO FAST
HE OUGHTTA KNOW HOW I'M HOLDING MYSELF BACK
NUTS! I'M BIGGER THAN YOU--
STRONGER, AND TOUGHER THAN YOU
I DON'T NEED A ROD TO-- HEY! WH-- WHERE'D YOU GO?
FZAP!
NOWHERE, DUMB I LIKE IT RIGHT HERE
HAVE TO
YOU DON'T KNOW HOW LUCKY YOU ARE--
YOU'RE ONLY GETTING YOUR LUMPS THIS TIME--
--WHILE SOME OF YOUR PIGEONS MAY PAY WITH-- THEIR LIVES
THOP!
WOK!
ZOMP!
BUT, BEFORE YOU GO SLEEPY-BYE, REMEMBER ONE THING--
AND REMEMBER IT GOOD--
IF I EVER SEE YOU PUSHING THAT STUFF-- ANYWHERE AGAIN--
--YOU'LL THINK THAT THIS WAS JUST A PLAYFUL PICNIC

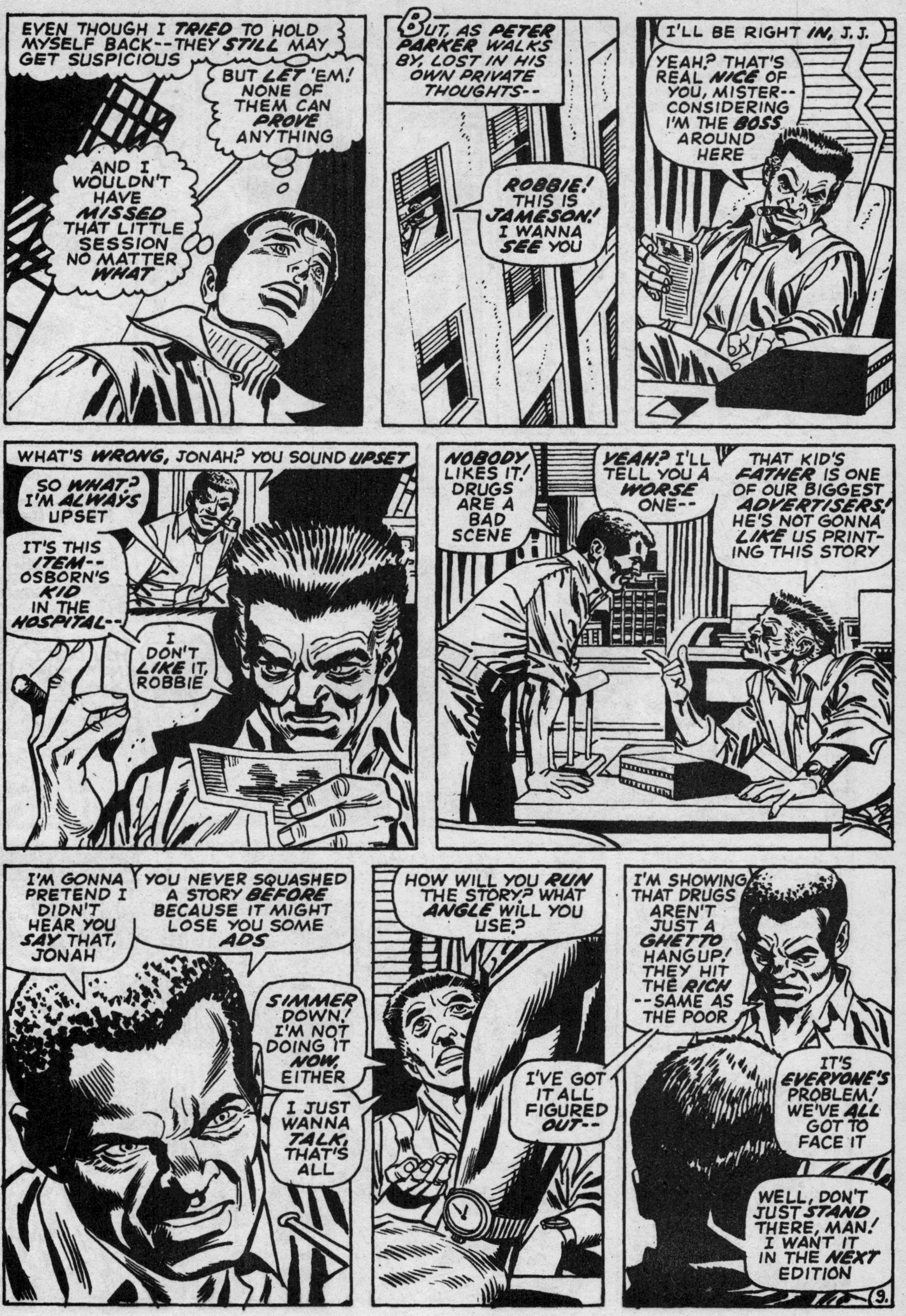

EVEN THOUGH I TRIED TO HOLD MYSELF BACK--THEY STILL MAY GET SUSPICIOUS
BUT LET 'EM! NONE OF THEM CAN PROVE ANYTHING
AND I WOULDN'T HAVE MISSED THAT LITTLE SESSION NO MATTER WHAT
BUT, AS PETER PARKER WALKS BY, LOST IN HIS OWN PRIVATE THOUGHTS--
ROBBIE! THIS IS JAMESON! I WANNA SEE YOU
I'LL BE RIGHT IN, J.J.
YEAH? THAT'S REAL NICE OF YOU, MISTER--CONSIDERING I'M THE BOSS AROUND HERE
WHAT'S WRONG, JONAH? YOU SOUND UPSET
SO WHAT? I'M ALWAYS UPSET
IT'S THIS ITEM--OSBORN'S KID IN THE HOSPITAL--
I DON'T LIKE IT, ROBBIE
NOBODY LIKES IT! DRUGS ARE A BAD SCENE
YEAH? I'LL TELL YOU A WORSE ONE--
THAT KID'S FATHER IS ONE OF OUR BIGGEST ADVERTISERS! HE'S NOT GONNA LIKE US PRINTING THIS STORY
I'M GONNA PRETEND I DIDN'T HEAR YOU SAY THAT, JONAH
YOU NEVER SQUASHED A STORY BEFORE BECAUSE IT MIGHT LOSE YOU SOME ADS
SIMMER DOWN! I'M NOT DOING IT NOW, EITHER
I JUST WANNA TALK, THAT'S ALL
HOW WILL YOU RUN THE STORY? WHAT ANGLE WILL YOU USE?
I'VE GOT IT ALL FIGURED OUT--
I'M SHOWING THAT DRUGS AREN'T JUST A GHETTO HANGUP! THEY HIT THE RICH--SAME AS THE POOR
IT'S EVERYONE'S PROBLEM! WE'VE ALL GOT TO FACE IT
WELL, DON'T JUST STAND THERE, MAN! I WANT IT IN THE NEXT EDITION
9.

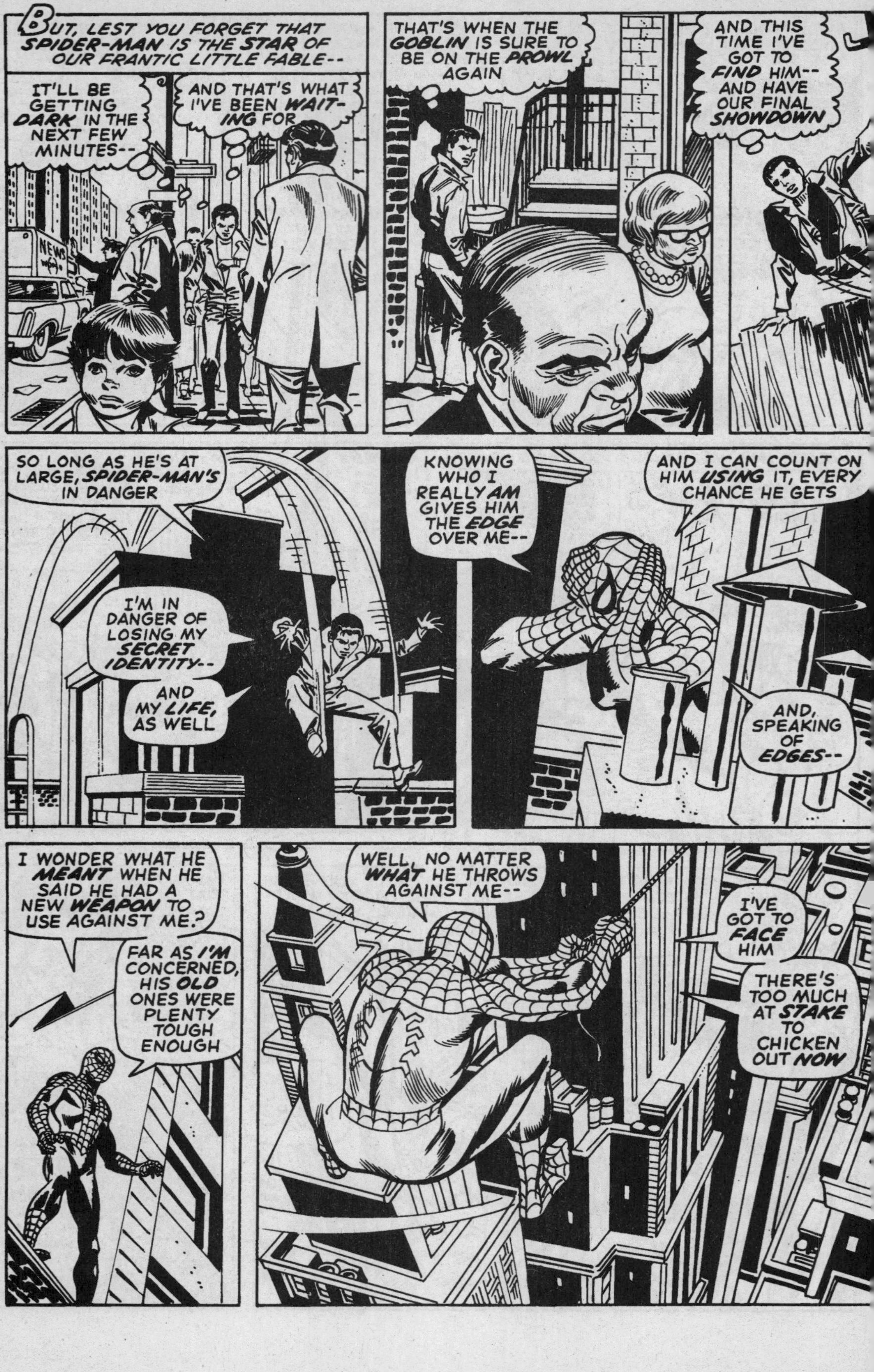
BUT, LEST YOU FORGET THAT SPIDER-MAN IS THE STAR OF OUR FRANTIC LITTLE FABLE--
IT'LL BE GETTING DARK IN THE NEXT FEW MINUTES--
AND THAT'S WHAT I'VE BEEN WAITING FOR
NEWS
THAT'S WHEN THE GOBLIN IS SURE TO BE ON THE PROWL AGAIN
AND THIS TIME I'VE GOT TO FIND HIM-- AND HAVE OUR FINAL SHOWDOWN
SO LONG AS HE'S AT LARGE, SPIDER-MAN'S IN DANGER
I'M IN DANGER OF LOSING MY SECRET IDENTITY--
AND MY LIFE, AS WELL
KNOWING WHO I REALLY AM GIVES HIM THE EDGE OVER ME--
AND I CAN COUNT ON HIM USING IT, EVERY CHANCE HE GETS
AND, SPEAKING OF EDGES--
I WONDER WHAT HE MEANT WHEN HE SAID HE HAD A NEW WEAPON TO USE AGAINST ME?
FAR AS I'M CONCERNED, HIS OLD ONES WERE PLENTY TOUGH ENOUGH
WELL, NO MATTER WHAT HE THROWS AGAINST ME--
I'VE GOT TO FACE HIM
THERE'S TOO MUCH AT STAKE TO CHICKEN OUT NOW

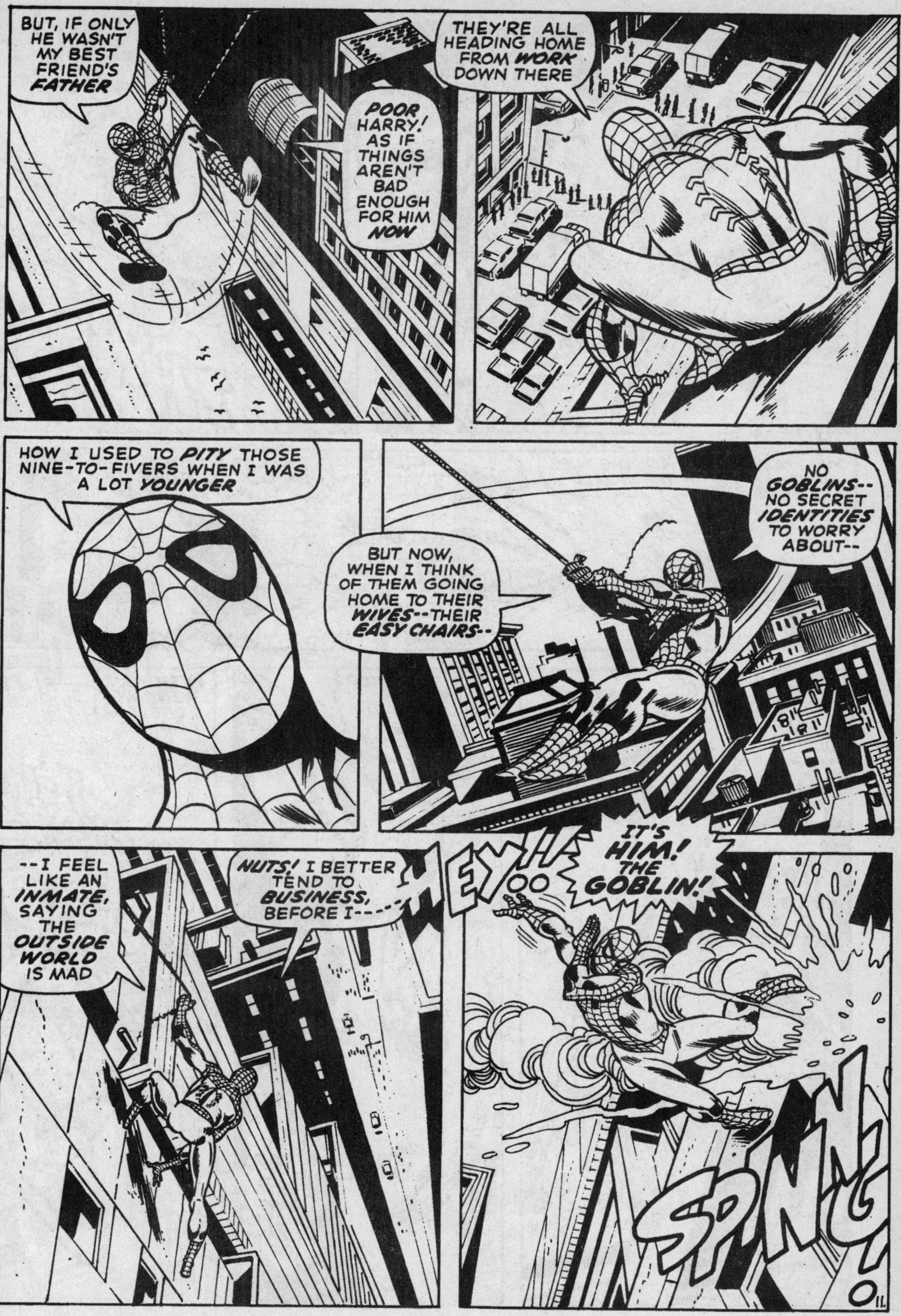
BUT, IF ONLY HE WASN'T MY BEST FRIEND'S FATHER
POOR HARRY! AS IF THINGS AREN'T BAD ENOUGH FOR HIM NOW
THEY'RE ALL HEADING HOME FROM WORK DOWN THERE
HOW I USED TO PITY THOSE NINE-TO-FIVERS WHEN I WAS A LOT YOUNGER
BUT NOW, WHEN I THINK OF THEM GOING HOME TO THEIR WIVES--THEIR EASY CHAIRS--
NO GOBLINS--NO SECRET IDENTITIES TO WORRY ABOUT--
--I FEEL LIKE AN INMATE, SAYING THE OUTSIDE WORLD IS MAD
NUTS! I BETTER TEND TO BUSINESS, BEFORE I----
HEY!
IT'S HIM! THE GOBLIN!
SPANG
11.

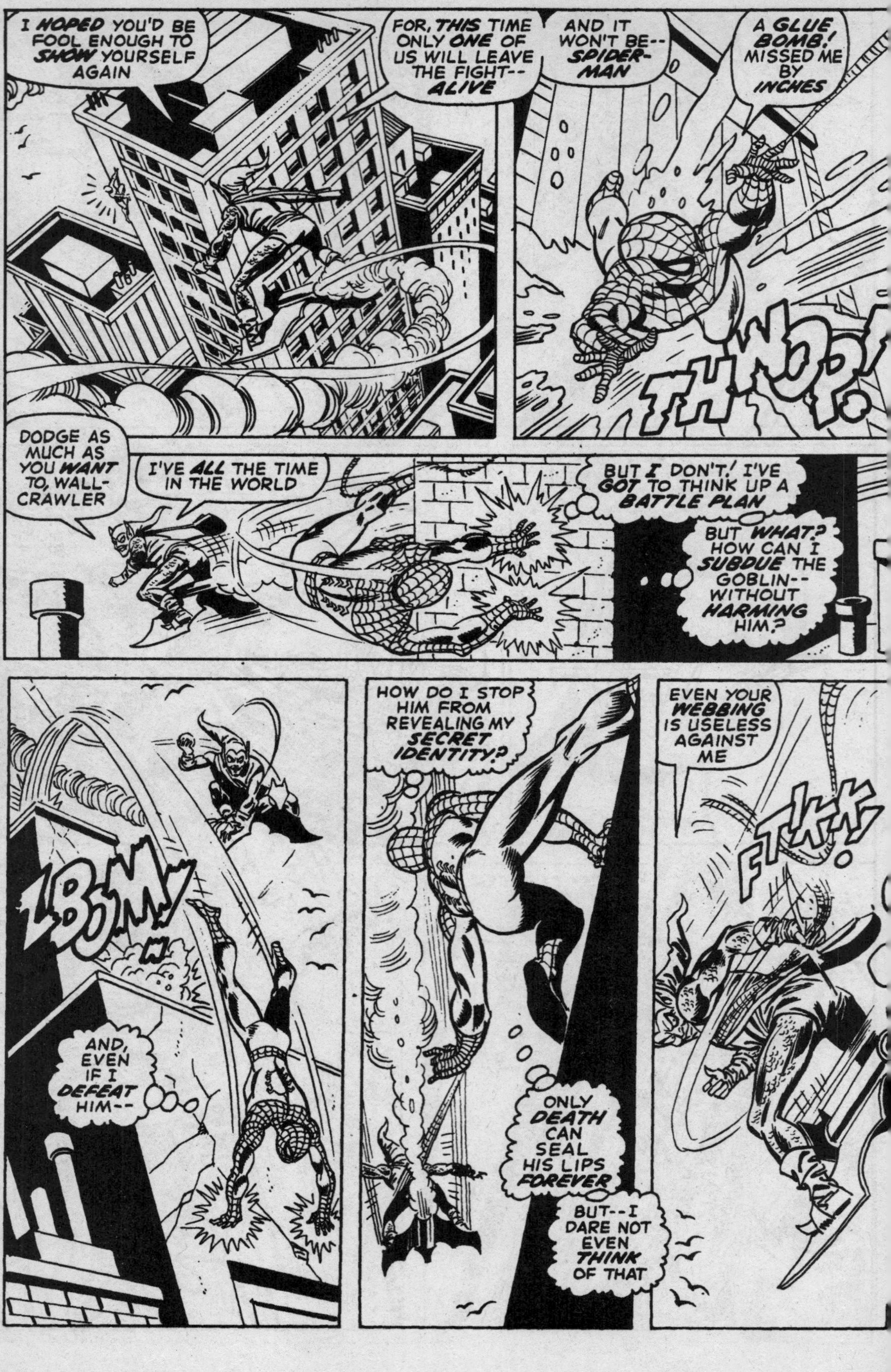
I HOPED YOU'D BE FOOL ENOUGH TO SHOW YOURSELF AGAIN
FOR, THIS TIME ONLY ONE OF US WILL LEAVE THE FIGHT--ALIVE
AND IT WON'T BE--SPIDER-MAN
A GLUE BOMB! MISSED ME BY INCHES
THWOPP!
DODGE AS MUCH AS YOU WANT TO, WALL-CRAWLER
I'VE ALL THE TIME IN THE WORLD
BUT I DON'T! I'VE GOT TO THINK UP A BATTLE PLAN
BUT WHAT? HOW CAN I SUBDUE THE GOBLIN--WITHOUT HARMING HIM?
BOOM
AND, EVEN IF I DEFEAT HIM--
HOW DO I STOP HIM FROM REVEALING MY SECRET IDENTITY?
ONLY DEATH CAN SEAL HIS LIPS FOREVER
BUT--I DARE NOT EVEN THINK OF THAT
EVEN YOUR WEBBING IS USELESS AGAINST ME
FTIKK!

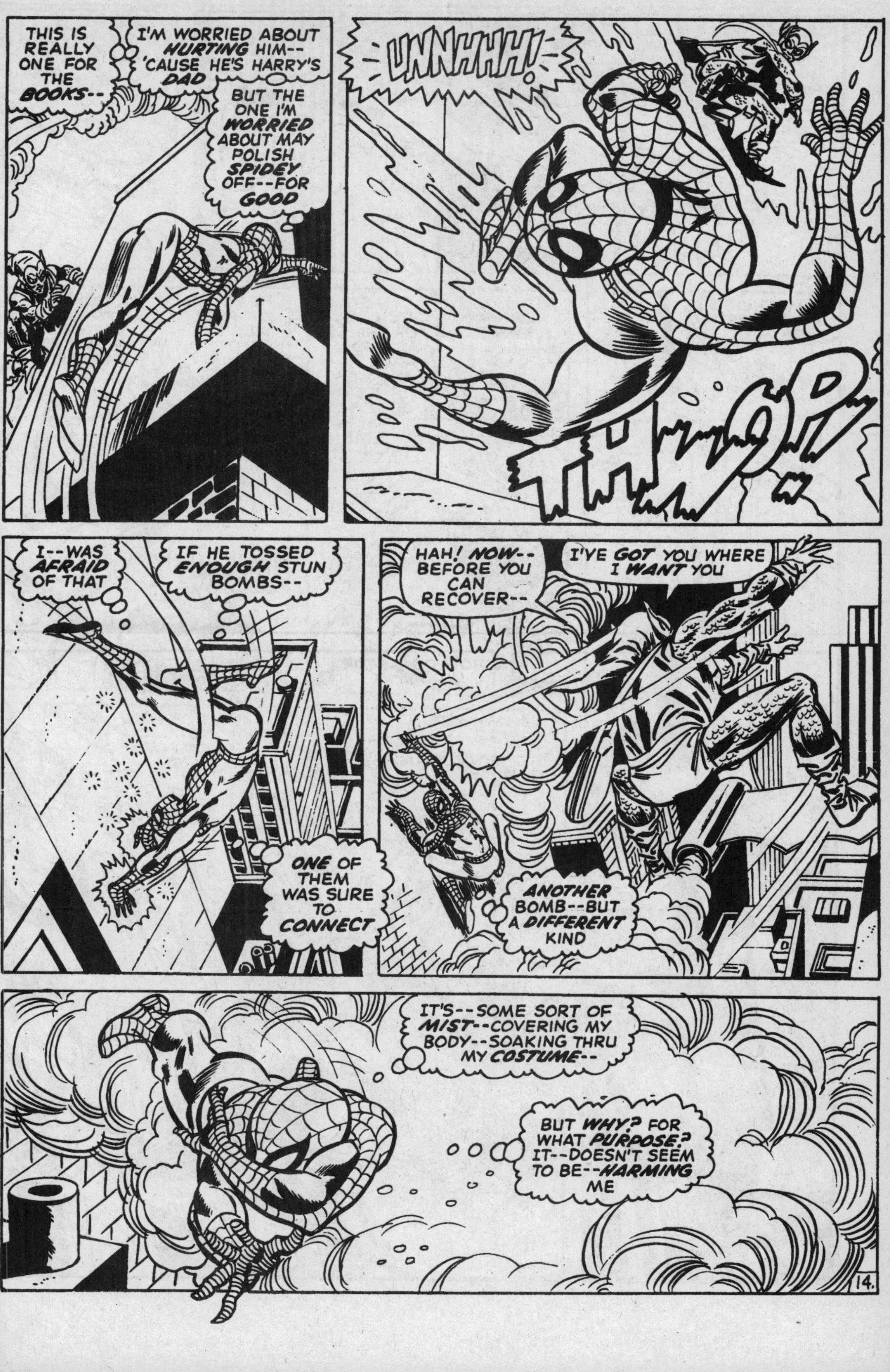
THIS IS REALLY ONE FOR THE BOOKS--
I'M WORRIED ABOUT HURTING HIM--'CAUSE HE'S HARRY'S DAD
BUT THE ONE I'M WORRIED ABOUT MAY POLISH SPIDEY OFF--FOR GOOD
UNNHHH!
THWOP!
I--WAS AFRAID OF THAT
IF HE TOSSED ENOUGH STUN BOMBS--
ONE OF THEM WAS SURE TO CONNECT
HAH! NOW--BEFORE YOU CAN RECOVER--
I'VE GOT YOU WHERE I WANT YOU
ANOTHER BOMB--BUT A DIFFERENT KIND
IT'S--SOME SORT OF MIST--COVERING MY BODY--SOAKING THRU MY COSTUME--
BUT WHY? FOR WHAT PURPOSE? IT--DOESN'T SEEM TO BE--HARMING ME

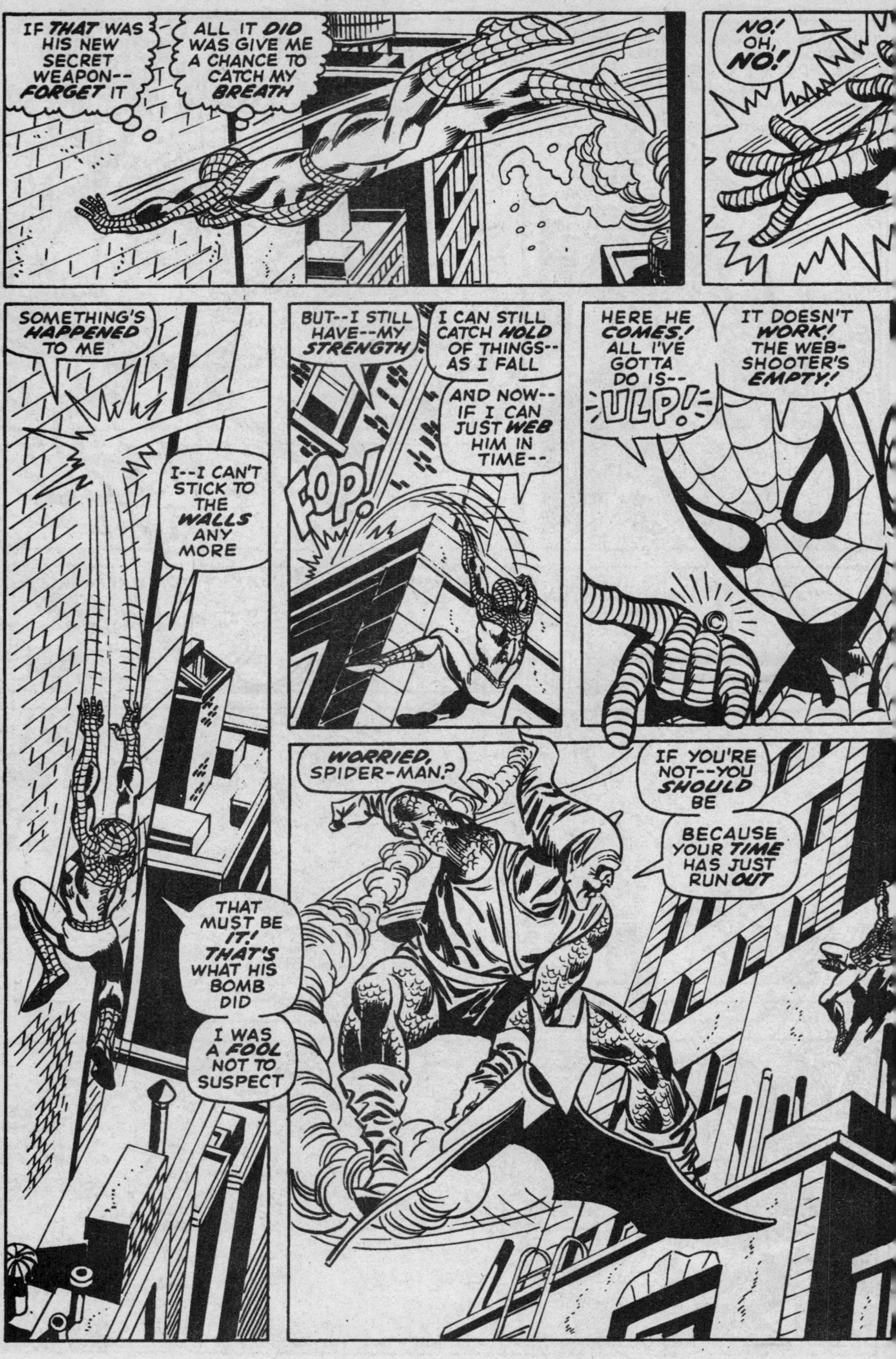
IF THAT WAS HIS NEW SECRET WEAPON-- FORGET IT
ALL IT DID WAS GIVE ME A CHANCE TO CATCH MY BREATH
NO! OH, NO!
SOMETHING'S HAPPENED TO ME
I--I CAN'T STICK TO THE WALLS ANY MORE
THAT MUST BE IT! THAT'S WHAT HIS BOMB DID
I WAS A FOOL NOT TO SUSPECT
BUT--I STILL HAVE--MY STRENGTH
I CAN STILL CATCH HOLD OF THINGS-- AS I FALL
AND NOW-- IF I CAN JUST WEB HIM IN TIME--
FOP!
HERE HE COMES! ALL I'VE GOTTA DO IS--
ULP!
IT DOESN'T WORK! THE WEB-SHOOTER'S EMPTY!
WORRIED, SPIDER-MAN?
IF YOU'RE NOT--YOU SHOULD BE
BECAUSE YOUR TIME HAS JUST RUN OUT

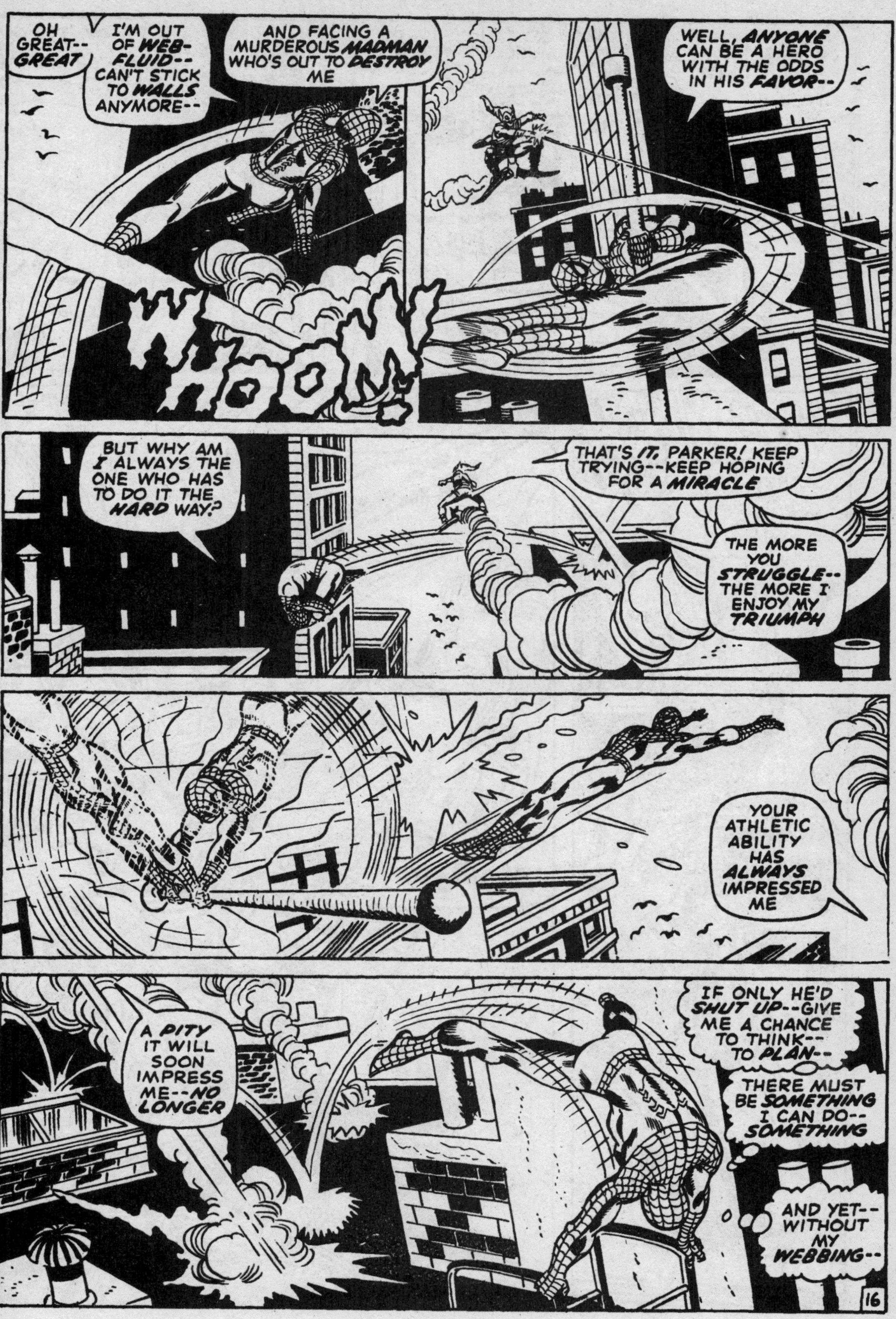
OH GREAT-- GREAT
I'M OUT OF WEB-FLUID-- CAN'T STICK TO WALLS ANYMORE--
AND FACING A MURDEROUS MADMAN WHO'S OUT TO DESTROY ME
WELL, ANYONE CAN BE A HERO WITH THE ODDS IN HIS FAVOR--
WHOOM!
BUT WHY AM I ALWAYS THE ONE WHO HAS TO DO IT THE HARD WAY?
THAT'S IT, PARKER! KEEP TRYING--KEEP HOPING FOR A MIRACLE
THE MORE YOU STRUGGLE-- THE MORE I ENJOY MY TRIUMPH
YOUR ATHLETIC ABILITY HAS ALWAYS IMPRESSED ME
A PITY IT WILL SOON IMPRESS ME--NO LONGER
IF ONLY HE'D SHUT UP--GIVE ME A CHANCE TO THINK-- TO PLAN--
THERE MUST BE SOMETHING I CAN DO-- SOMETHING
AND YET-- WITHOUT MY WEBBING--
16

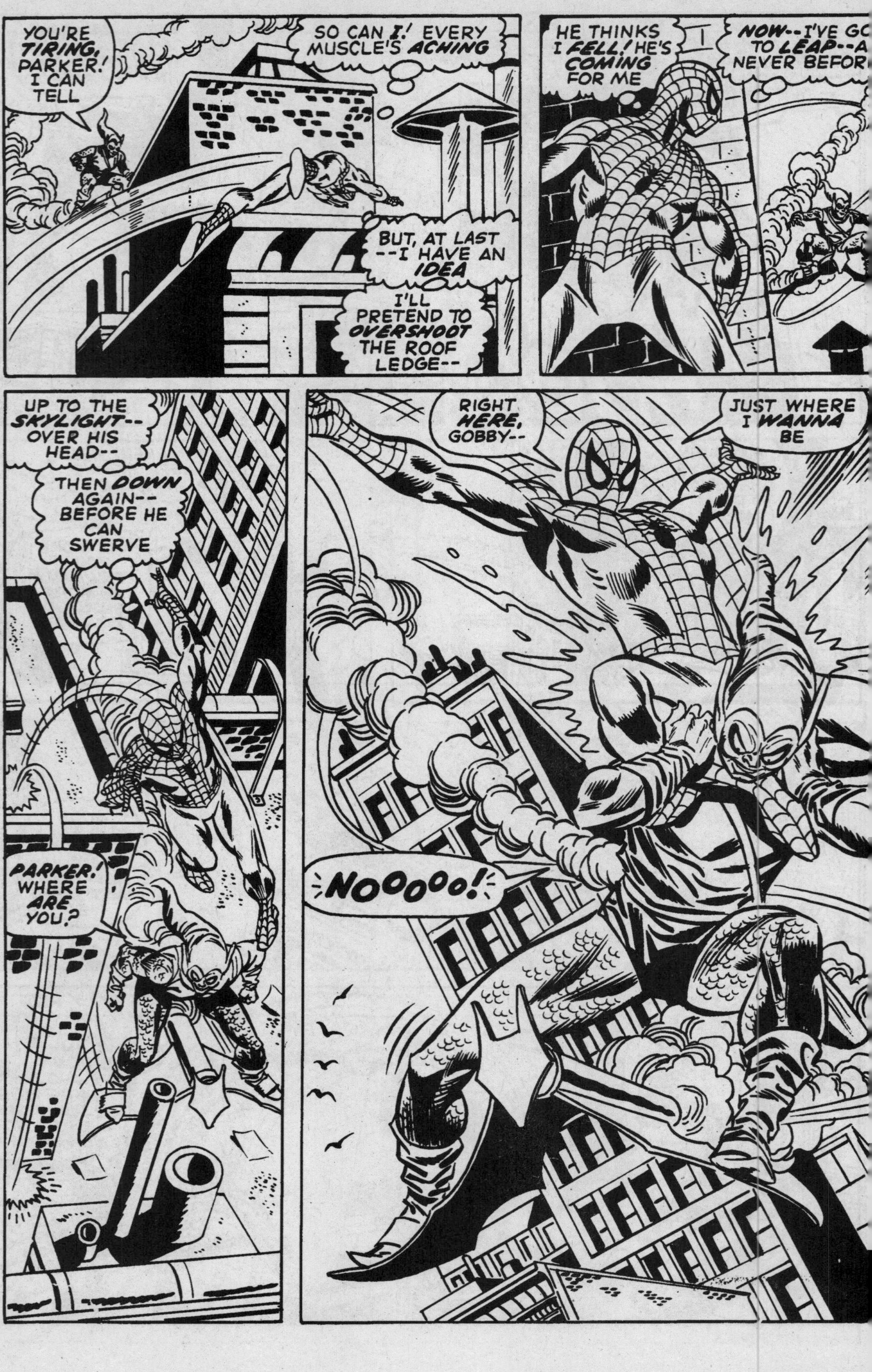
YOU'RE TIRING, PARKER! I CAN TELL
SO CAN I! EVERY MUSCLE'S ACHING
BUT, AT LAST --I HAVE AN IDEA
I'LL PRETEND TO OVERSHOOT THE ROOF LEDGE--
HE THINKS I FELL! HE'S COMING FOR ME
NOW--I'VE GO TO LEAP--A NEVER BEFOR
UP TO THE SKYLIGHT-- OVER HIS HEAD--
THEN DOWN AGAIN-- BEFORE HE CAN SWERVE
PARKER! WHERE ARE YOU?
RIGHT HERE, GOBBY--
JUST WHERE I WANNA BE
NOOOOOO!

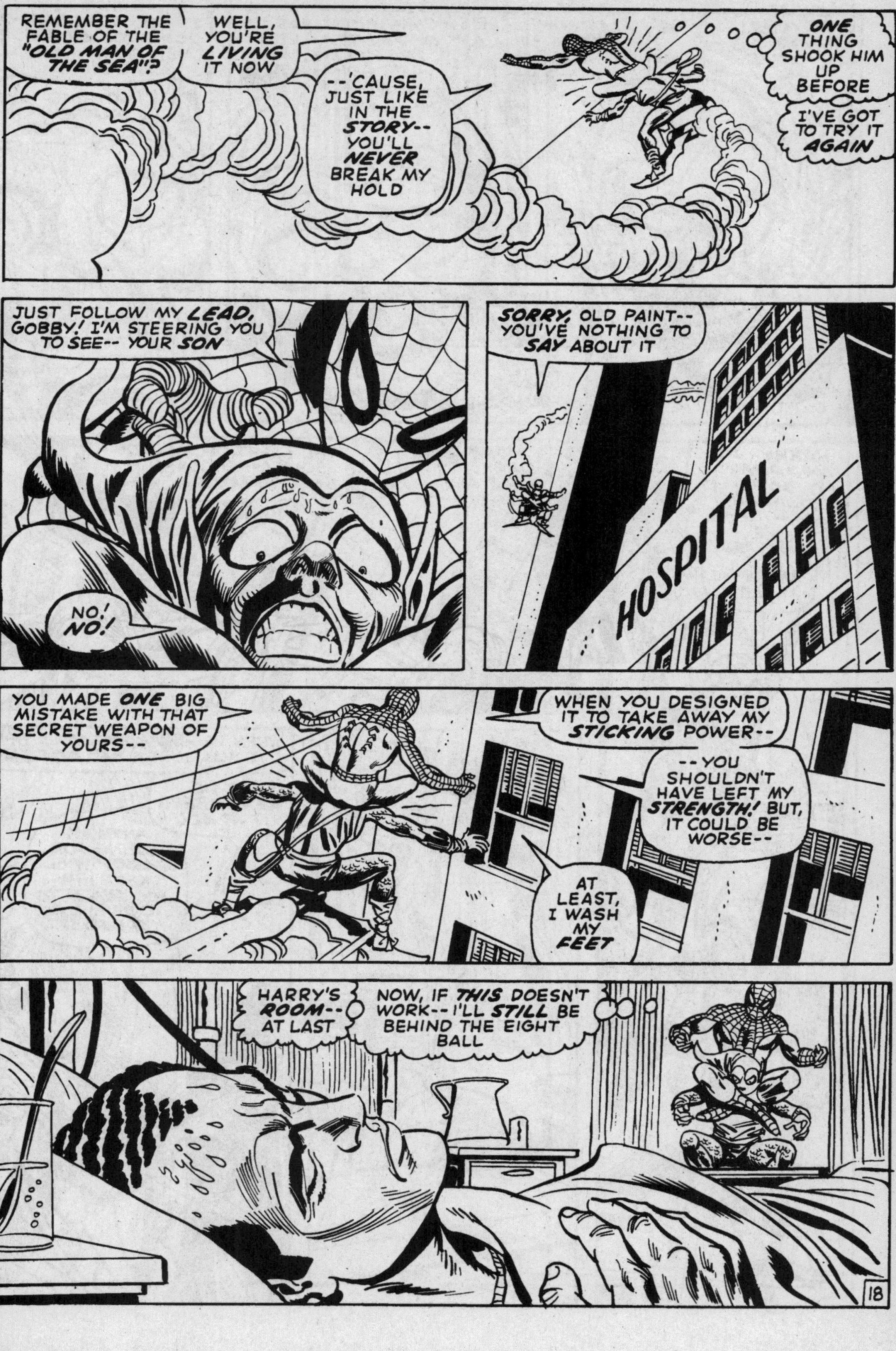

REMEMBER THE FABLE OF THE "OLD MAN OF THE SEA"?
WELL, YOU'RE LIVING IT NOW
--'CAUSE, JUST LIKE IN THE STORY-- YOU'LL NEVER BREAK MY HOLD
ONE THING SHOOK HIM UP BEFORE
I'VE GOT TO TRY IT AGAIN
JUST FOLLOW MY LEAD, GOBBY! I'M STEERING YOU TO SEE-- YOUR SON
NO! NO!
SORRY, OLD PAINT-- YOU'VE NOTHING TO SAY ABOUT IT
HOSPITAL
YOU MADE ONE BIG MISTAKE WITH THAT SECRET WEAPON OF YOURS--
WHEN YOU DESIGNED IT TO TAKE AWAY MY STICKING POWER--
--YOU SHOULDN'T HAVE LEFT MY STRENGTH! BUT, IT COULD BE WORSE--
AT LEAST, I WASH MY FEET
HARRY'S ROOM-- AT LAST
NOW, IF THIS DOESN'T WORK-- I'LL STILL BE BEHIND THE EIGHT BALL
18

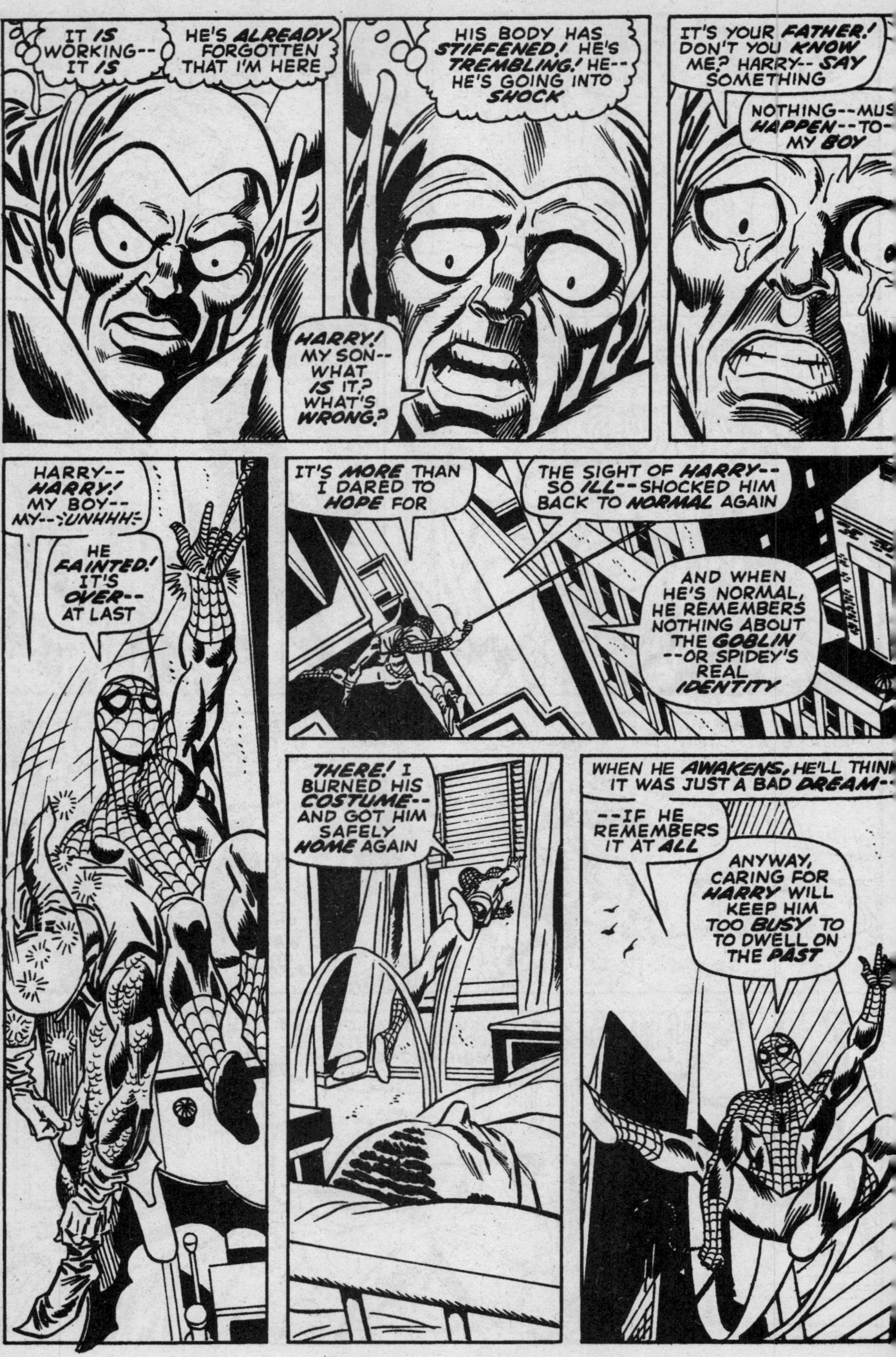
IT IS WORKING-- IT IS
HE'S ALREADY FORGOTTEN THAT I'M HERE
HIS BODY HAS STIFFENED! HE'S TREMBLING! HE-- HE'S GOING INTO SHOCK
HARRY! MY SON-- WHAT IS IT? WHAT'S WRONG?
IT'S YOUR FATHER! DON'T YOU KNOW ME? HARRY-- SAY SOMETHING
NOTHING--MUS HAPPEN--TO-- MY BOY
HARRY-- HARRY! MY BOY-- MY--UNHHH!
HE FAINTED! IT'S OVER-- AT LAST
IT'S MORE THAN I DARED TO HOPE FOR
THE SIGHT OF HARRY-- SO ILL--SHOCKED HIM BACK TO NORMAL AGAIN
AND WHEN HE'S NORMAL, HE REMEMBERS NOTHING ABOUT THE GOBLIN --OR SPIDEY'S REAL IDENTITY
THERE! I BURNED HIS COSTUME-- AND GOT HIM SAFELY HOME AGAIN
WHEN HE AWAKENS, HE'LL THINK IT WAS JUST A BAD DREAM--
--IF HE REMEMBERS IT AT ALL
ANYWAY, CARING FOR HARRY WILL KEEP HIM TOO BUSY TO TO DWELL ON THE PAST

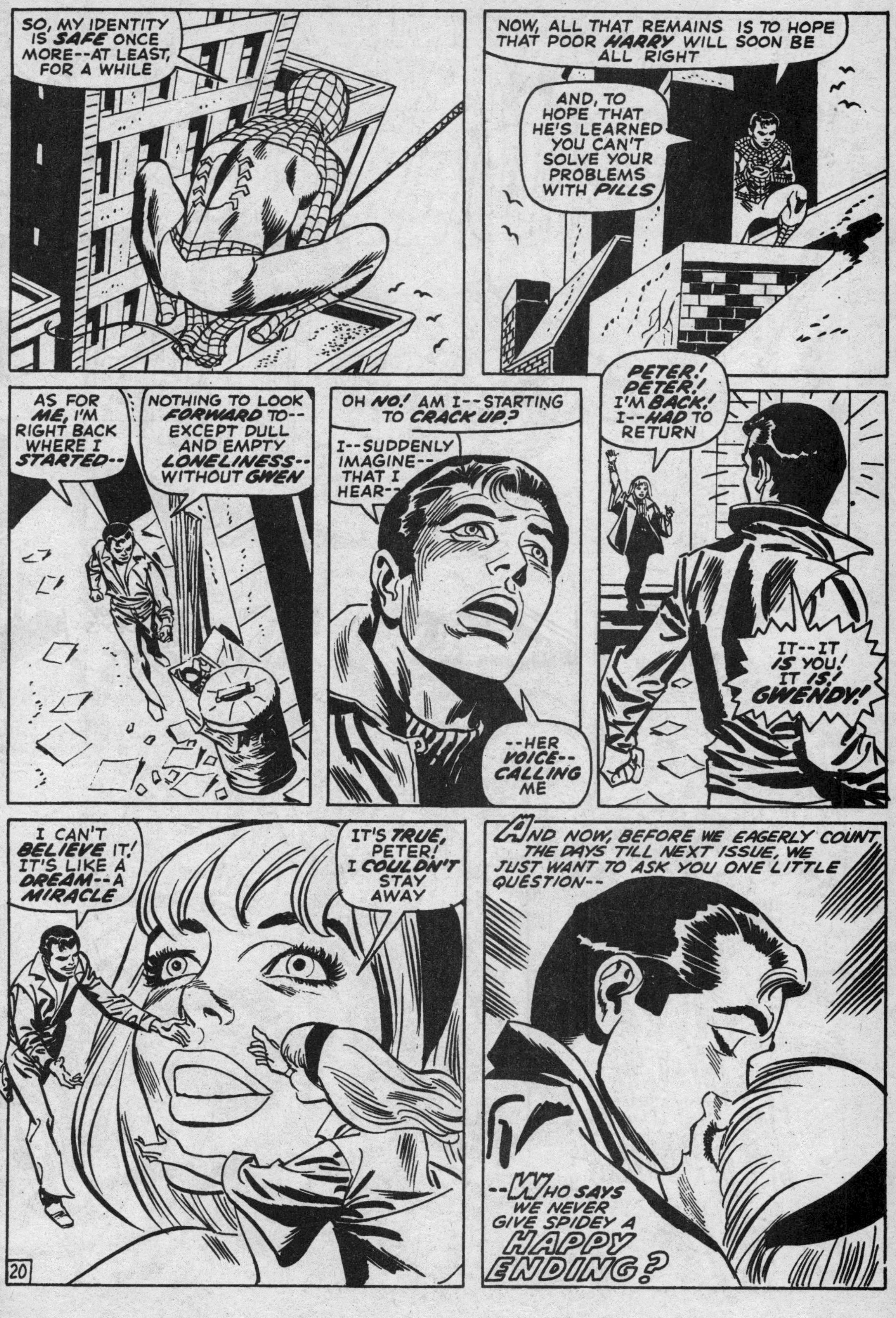
SO, MY IDENTITY IS SAFE ONCE MORE--AT LEAST, FOR A WHILE
NOW, ALL THAT REMAINS IS TO HOPE THAT POOR HARRY WILL SOON BE ALL RIGHT
AND, TO HOPE THAT HE'S LEARNED YOU CAN'T SOLVE YOUR PROBLEMS WITH PILLS
AS FOR ME, I'M RIGHT BACK WHERE I STARTED--
NOTHING TO LOOK FORWARD TO--EXCEPT DULL AND EMPTY LONELINESS--WITHOUT GWEN
OH NO! AM I--STARTING TO CRACK UP?
I--SUDDENLY IMAGINE--THAT I HEAR--
--HER VOICE--CALLING ME
PETER! PETER! I'M BACK! I--HAD TO RETURN
IT--IT IS YOU! IT IS! GWENDY!
I CAN'T BELIEVE IT! IT'S LIKE A DREAM--A MIRACLE
IT'S TRUE, PETER! I COULDN'T STAY AWAY
AND NOW, BEFORE WE EAGERLY COUNT THE DAYS TILL NEXT ISSUE, WE JUST WANT TO ASK YOU ONE LITTLE QUESTION--
--WHO SAYS WE NEVER GIVE SPIDEY A HAPPY ENDING?
20

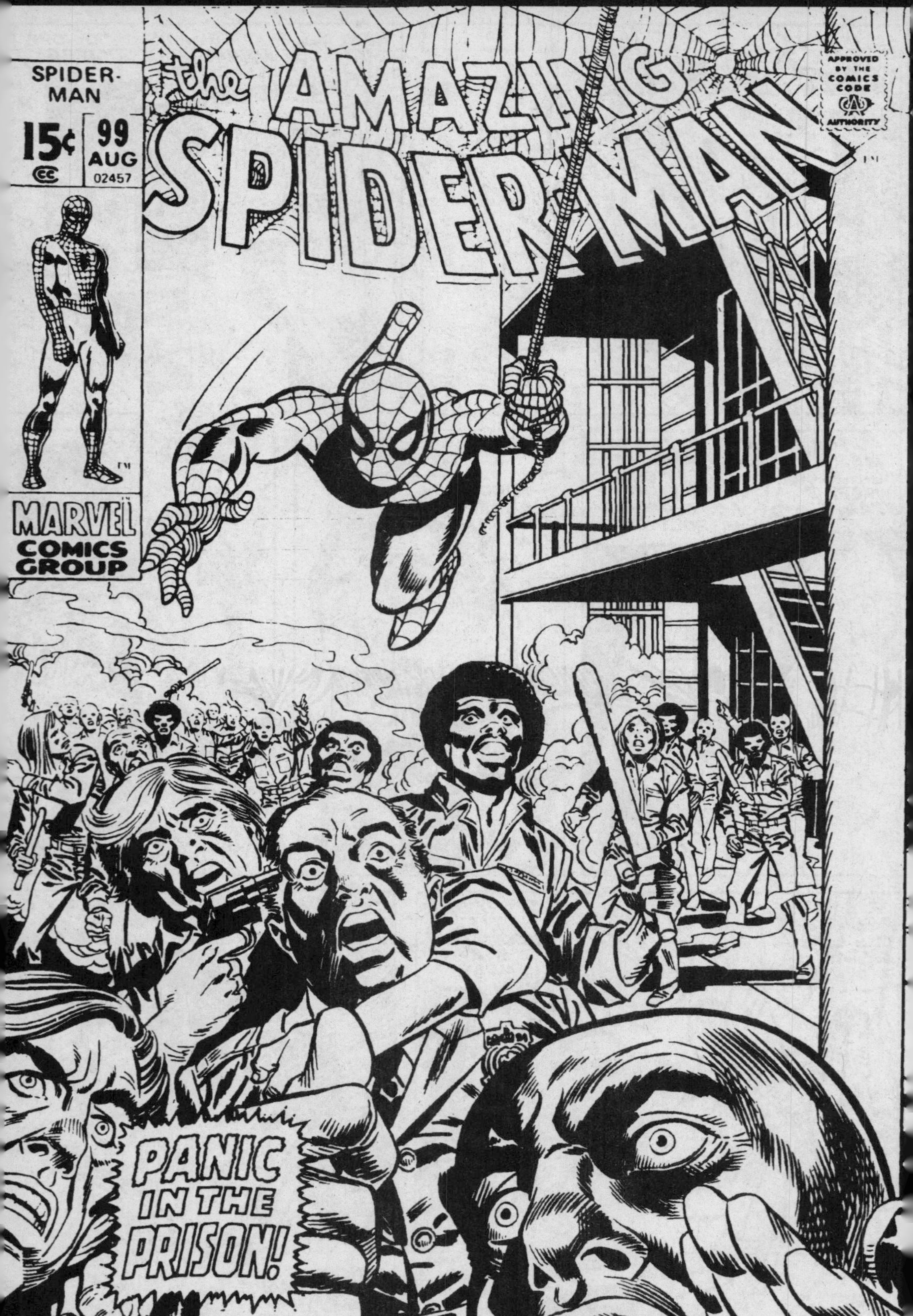
SPIDER-MAN
15¢
99
AUG
02457
the AMAZING SPIDER-MAN
APPROVED BY THE COMICS CODE AUTHORITY
MARVEL COMICS GROUP
PANIC IN THE PRISON!

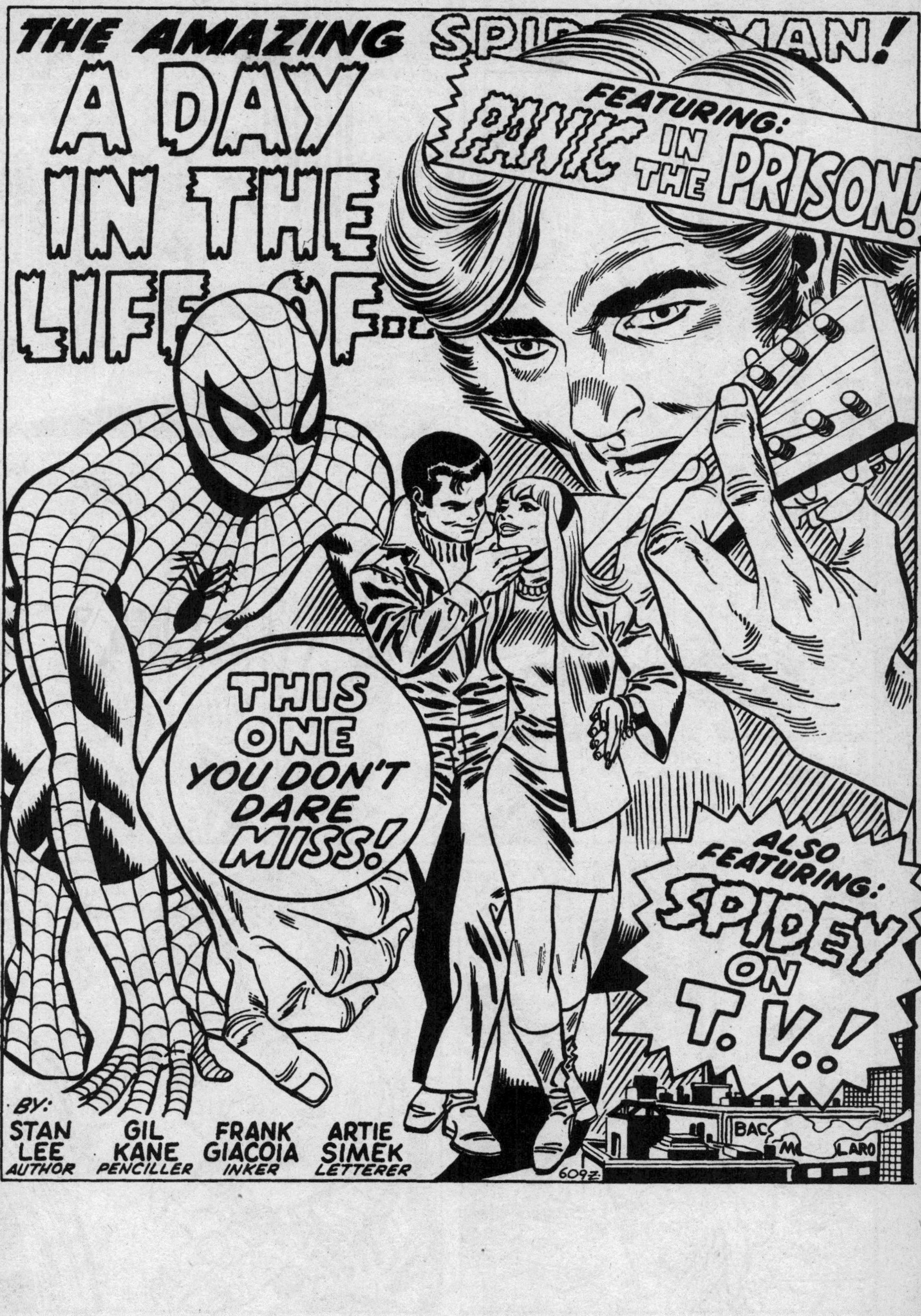
THE AMAZING SPIDER-MAN!
A DAY IN THE LIFE OF...
FEATURING: PANIC IN THE PRISON!
THIS ONE YOU DON'T DARE MISS!
ALSO FEATURING: SPIDEY ON T.V.!
BY: STAN LEE AUTHOR GIL KANE PENCILLER FRANK GIACOIA INKER ARTIE SIMEK LETTERER
609Z

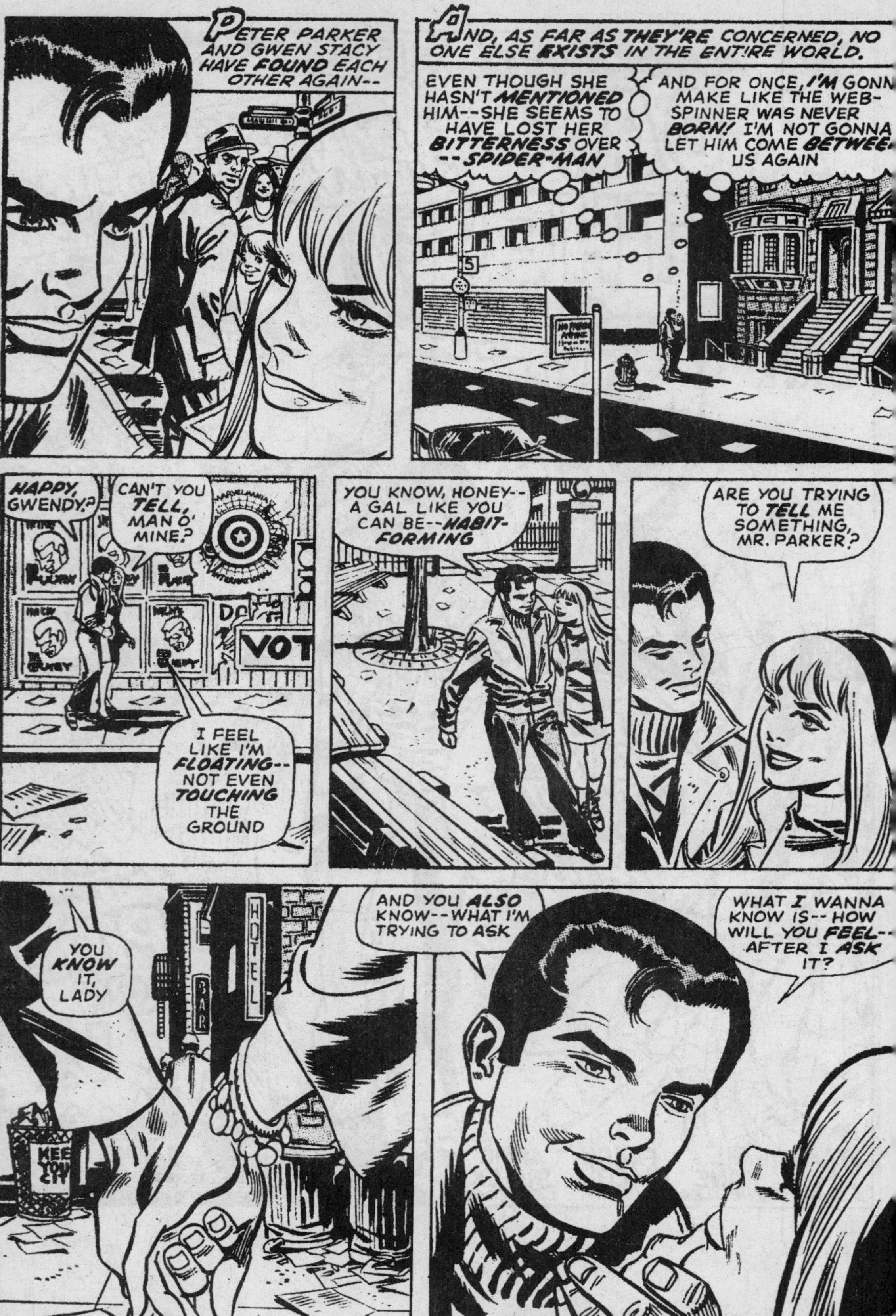
PETER PARKER AND GWEN STACY HAVE FOUND EACH OTHER AGAIN--
AND, AS FAR AS THEY'RE CONCERNED, NO ONE ELSE EXISTS IN THE ENTIRE WORLD.
EVEN THOUGH SHE HASN'T MENTIONED HIM--SHE SEEMS TO HAVE LOST HER BITTERNESS OVER --SPIDER-MAN
AND FOR ONCE, I'M GONN MAKE LIKE THE WEB-SPINNER WAS NEVER BORN! I'M NOT GONNA LET HIM COME BETWEE US AGAIN
HAPPY, GWENDY?
CAN'T YOU TELL, MAN O' MINE?
I FEEL LIKE I'M FLOATING--NOT EVEN TOUCHING THE GROUND
VOT
YOU KNOW, HONEY--A GAL LIKE YOU CAN BE--HABIT-FORMING
ARE YOU TRYING TO TELL ME SOMETHING, MR. PARKER?
YOU KNOW IT, LADY
HOTEL
BAR
AND YOU ALSO KNOW--WHAT I'M TRYING TO ASK
WHAT I WANNA KNOW IS--HOW WILL YOU FEEL--AFTER I ASK IT?
2

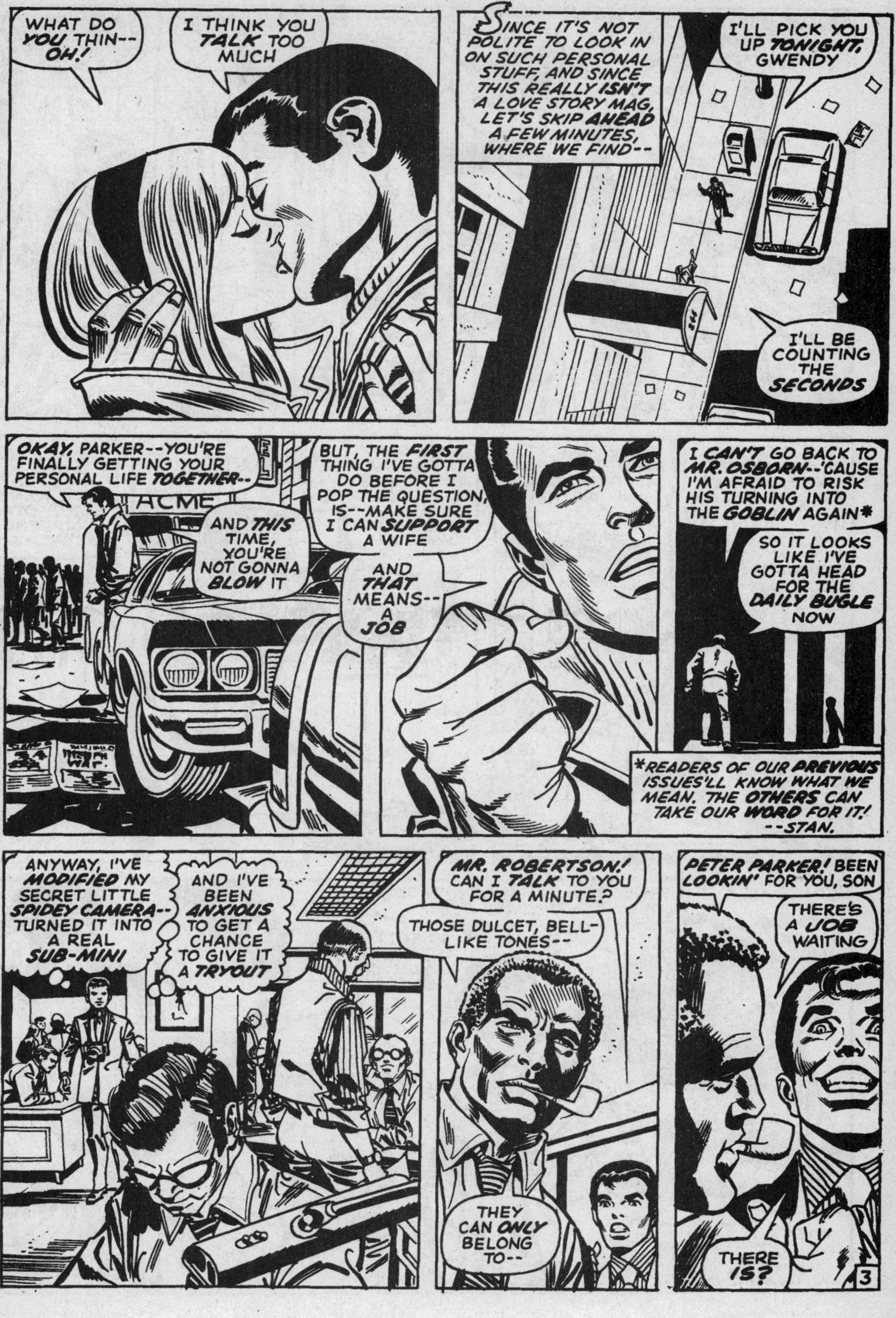
WHAT DO YOU THIN--OH!
I THINK YOU TALK TOO MUCH
SINCE IT'S NOT POLITE TO LOOK IN ON SUCH PERSONAL STUFF, AND SINCE THIS REALLY ISN'T A LOVE STORY MAG, LET'S SKIP AHEAD A FEW MINUTES, WHERE WE FIND--
I'LL PICK YOU UP TONIGHT, GWENDY
I'LL BE COUNTING THE SECONDS
OKAY, PARKER--YOU'RE FINALLY GETTING YOUR PERSONAL LIFE TOGETHER--
ACME
AND THIS TIME, YOU'RE NOT GONNA BLOW IT
BUT, THE FIRST THING I'VE GOTTA DO BEFORE I POP THE QUESTION, IS--MAKE SURE I CAN SUPPORT A WIFE
AND THAT MEANS--A JOB
I CAN'T GO BACK TO MR. OSBORN--'CAUSE I'M AFRAID TO RISK HIS TURNING INTO THE GOBLIN AGAIN*
SO IT LOOKS LIKE I'VE GOTTA HEAD FOR THE DAILY BUGLE NOW
*READERS OF OUR PREVIOUS ISSUES'LL KNOW WHAT WE MEAN. THE OTHERS CAN TAKE OUR WORD FOR IT! --STAN.
ANYWAY, I'VE MODIFIED MY SECRET LITTLE SPIDEY CAMERA--TURNED IT INTO A REAL SUB-MINI
AND I'VE BEEN ANXIOUS TO GET A CHANCE TO GIVE IT A TRYOUT
MR. ROBERTSON! CAN I TALK TO YOU FOR A MINUTE?
THOSE DULCET, BELL-LIKE TONES--
THEY CAN ONLY BELONG TO--
PETER PARKER! BEEN LOOKIN' FOR YOU, SON
THERE'S A JOB WAITING
THERE IS?
3

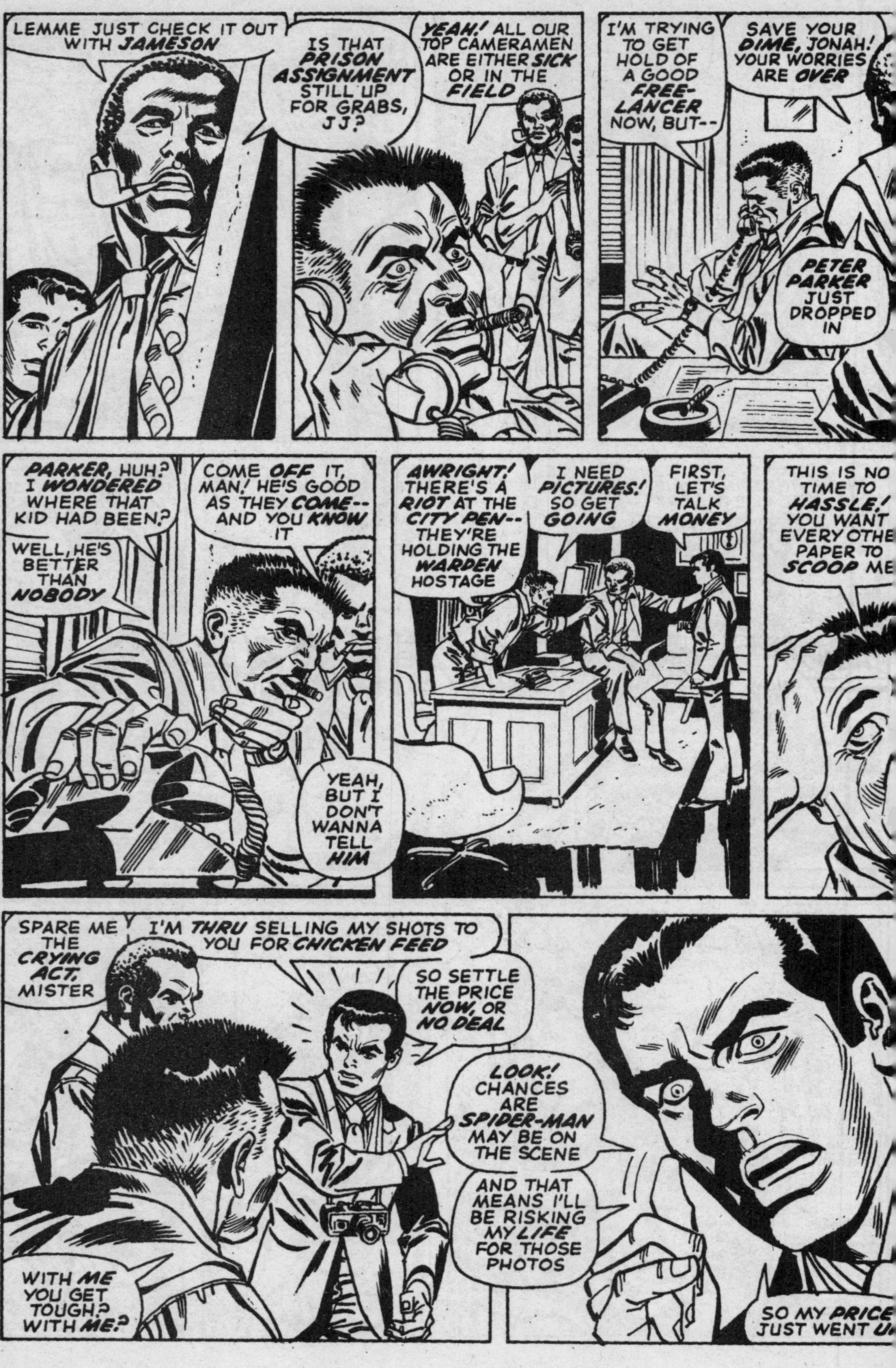

LEMME JUST CHECK IT OUT WITH JAMESON
IS THAT PRISON ASSIGNMENT STILL UP FOR GRABS, JJ?
YEAH! ALL OUR TOP CAMERAMEN ARE EITHER SICK OR IN THE FIELD
I'M TRYING TO GET HOLD OF A GOOD FREE-LANCER NOW, BUT--
SAVE YOUR DIME, JONAH! YOUR WORRIES ARE OVER
PETER PARKER JUST DROPPED IN
PARKER, HUH? I WONDERED WHERE THAT KID HAD BEEN?
WELL, HE'S BETTER THAN NOBODY
COME OFF IT, MAN! HE'S GOOD AS THEY COME-- AND YOU KNOW IT
YEAH, BUT I DON'T WANNA TELL HIM
AWRIGHT! THERE'S A RIOT AT THE CITY PEN-- THEY'RE HOLDING THE WARDEN HOSTAGE
I NEED PICTURES! SO GET GOING
FIRST, LET'S TALK MONEY
THIS IS NO TIME TO HASSLE! YOU WANT EVERY OTHE PAPER TO SCOOP ME
SPARE ME THE CRYING ACT, MISTER
I'M THRU SELLING MY SHOTS TO YOU FOR CHICKEN FEED
SO SETTLE THE PRICE NOW, OR NO DEAL
LOOK! CHANCES ARE SPIDER-MAN MAY BE ON THE SCENE
AND THAT MEANS I'LL BE RISKING MY LIFE FOR THOSE PHOTOS
WITH ME YOU GET TOUGH? WITH ME?
SO MY PRICE JUST WENT U

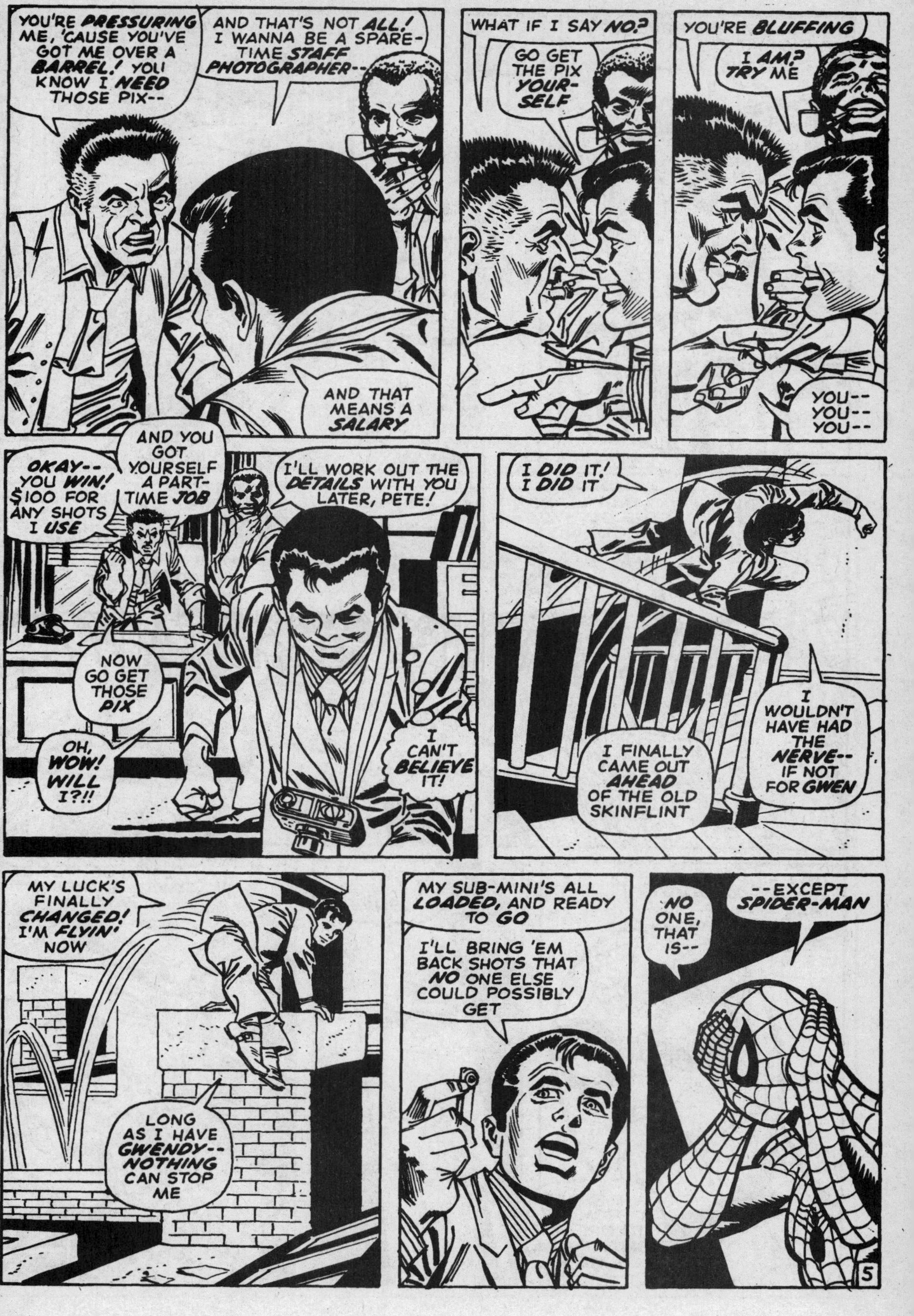
YOU'RE PRESSURING ME, 'CAUSE YOU'VE GOT ME OVER A BARREL! YOU KNOW I NEED THOSE PIX--
AND THAT'S NOT ALL! I WANNA BE A SPARE-TIME STAFF PHOTOGRAPHER--
AND THAT MEANS A SALARY
WHAT IF I SAY NO?
GO GET THE PIX YOURSELF
YOU'RE BLUFFING
I AM? TRY ME
YOU-- YOU-- YOU--
OKAY-- YOU WIN! $100 FOR ANY SHOTS I USE
AND YOU GOT YOURSELF A PART-TIME JOB
I'LL WORK OUT THE DETAILS WITH YOU LATER, PETE!
NOW GO GET THOSE PIX
OH, WOW! WILL I?!!
I CAN'T BELIEVE IT!
I DID IT! I DID IT
I FINALLY CAME OUT AHEAD OF THE OLD SKINFLINT
I WOULDN'T HAVE HAD THE NERVE-- IF NOT FOR GWEN
MY LUCK'S FINALLY CHANGED! I'M FLYIN' NOW
LONG AS I HAVE GWENDY-- NOTHING CAN STOP ME
MY SUB-MINI'S ALL LOADED, AND READY TO GO
I'LL BRING 'EM BACK SHOTS THAT NO ONE ELSE COULD POSSIBLY GET
NO ONE, THAT IS--
--EXCEPT SPIDER-MAN
5

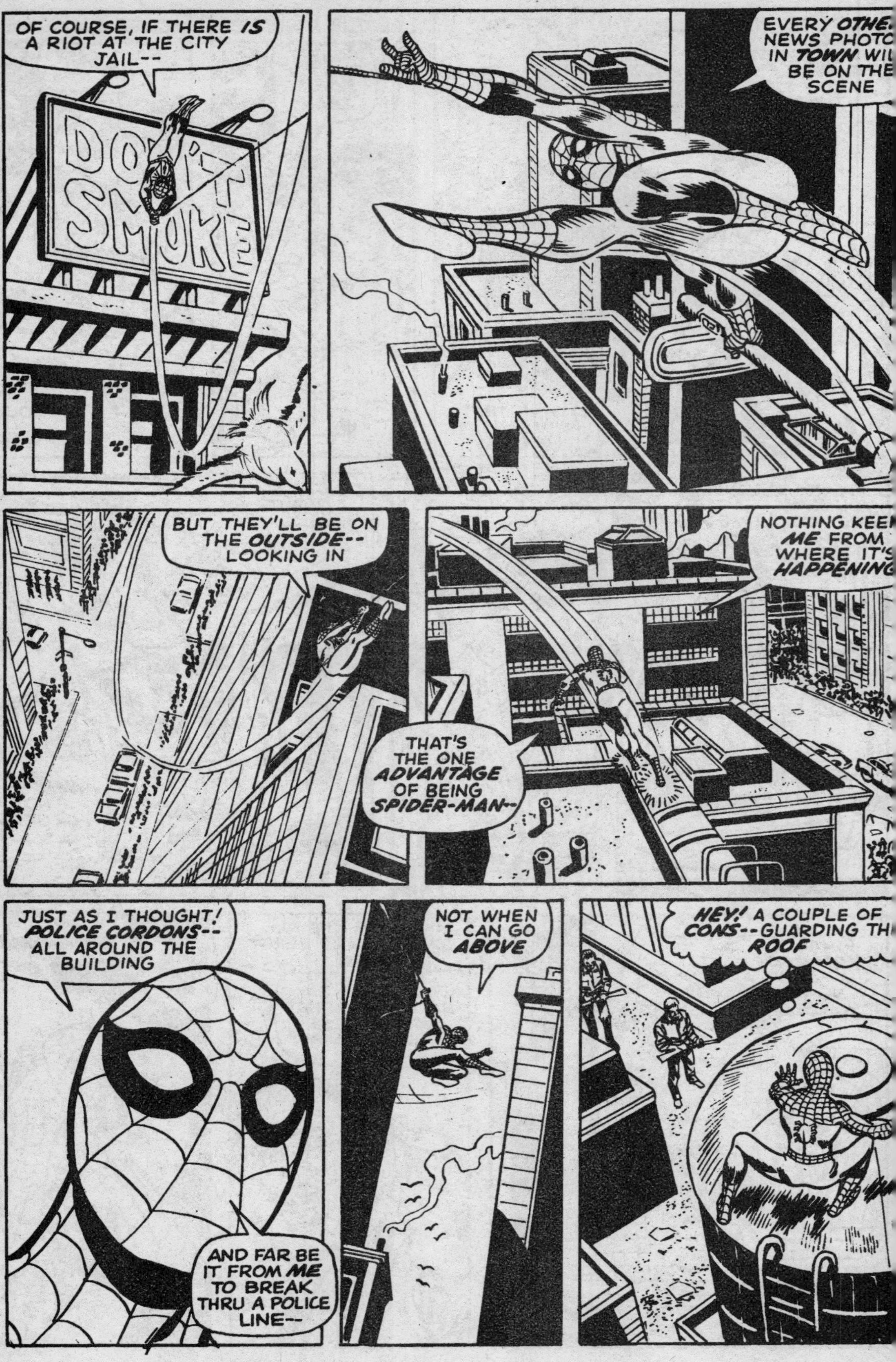
OF COURSE, IF THERE *IS* A RIOT AT THE CITY JAIL--
DON'T SMOKE
EVERY *OTHE* NEWS PHOTO IN *TOWN* WIL BE ON THE SCENE
BUT THEY'LL BE ON THE *OUTSIDE*-- LOOKING IN
NOTHING KEE *ME* FROM WHERE IT'S *HAPPENING*
THAT'S THE ONE *ADVANTAGE* OF BEING *SPIDER-MAN*--
JUST AS I THOUGHT! *POLICE CORDONS*-- ALL AROUND THE BUILDING
AND FAR BE IT FROM *ME* TO BREAK THRU A POLICE LINE--
NOT WHEN I CAN GO *ABOVE*
HEY! A COUPLE OF *CONS*--GUARDING TH *ROOF*

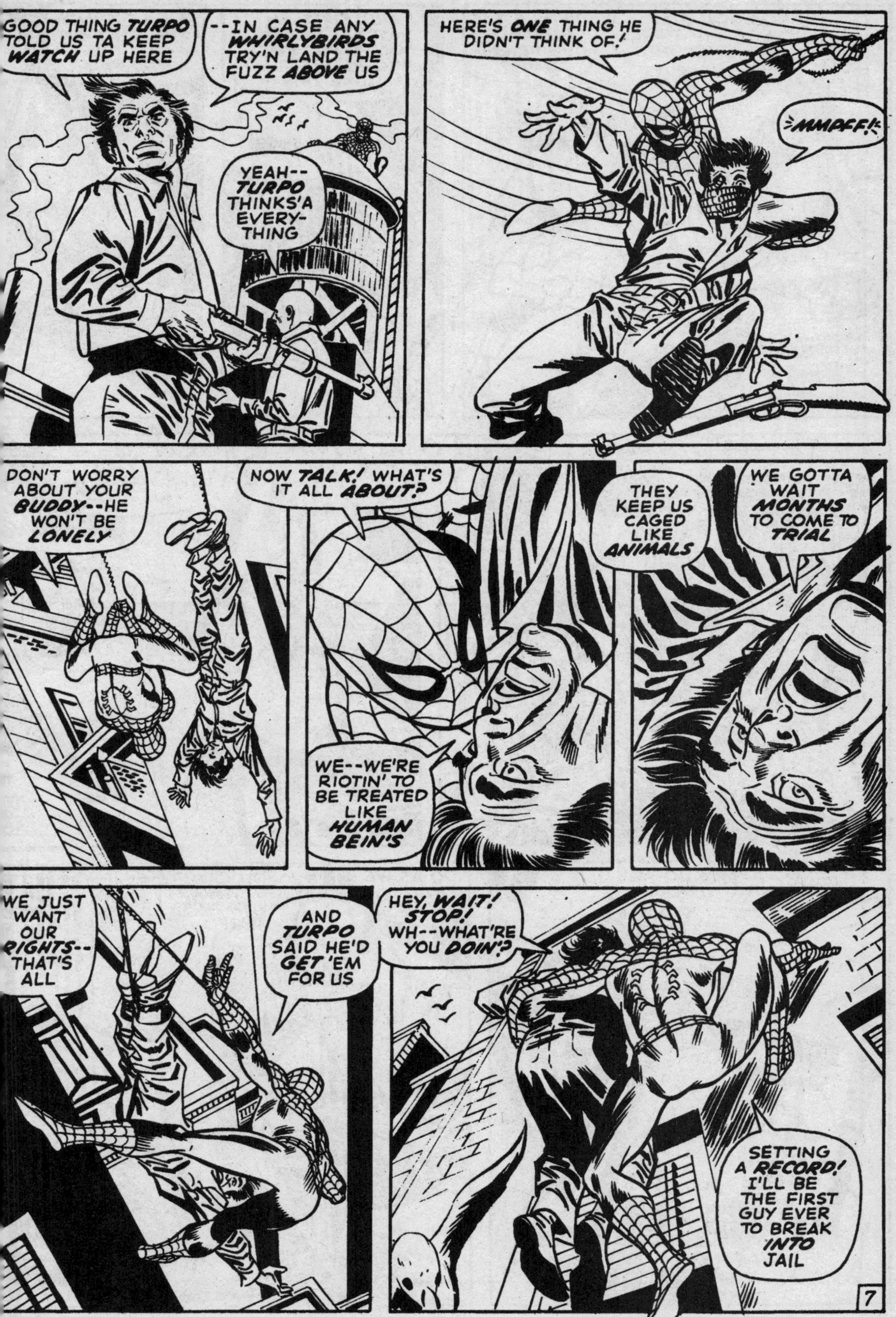
GOOD THING TURPO TOLD US TA KEEP WATCH UP HERE
--IN CASE ANY WHIRLYBIRDS TRY'N LAND THE FUZZ ABOVE US
YEAH-- TURPO THINKS'A EVERY-THING
HERE'S ONE THING HE DIDN'T THINK OF!
MMPFF!
DON'T WORRY ABOUT YOUR BUDDY--HE WON'T BE LONELY
NOW TALK! WHAT'S IT ALL ABOUT?
WE--WE'RE RIOTIN' TO BE TREATED LIKE HUMAN BEIN'S
THEY KEEP US CAGED LIKE ANIMALS
WE GOTTA WAIT MONTHS TO COME TO TRIAL
WE JUST WANT OUR RIGHTS--THAT'S ALL
AND TURPO SAID HE'D GET 'EM FOR US
HEY, WAIT! STOP! WH--WHAT'RE YOU DOIN'?
SETTING A RECORD! I'LL BE THE FIRST GUY EVER TO BREAK INTO JAIL
7

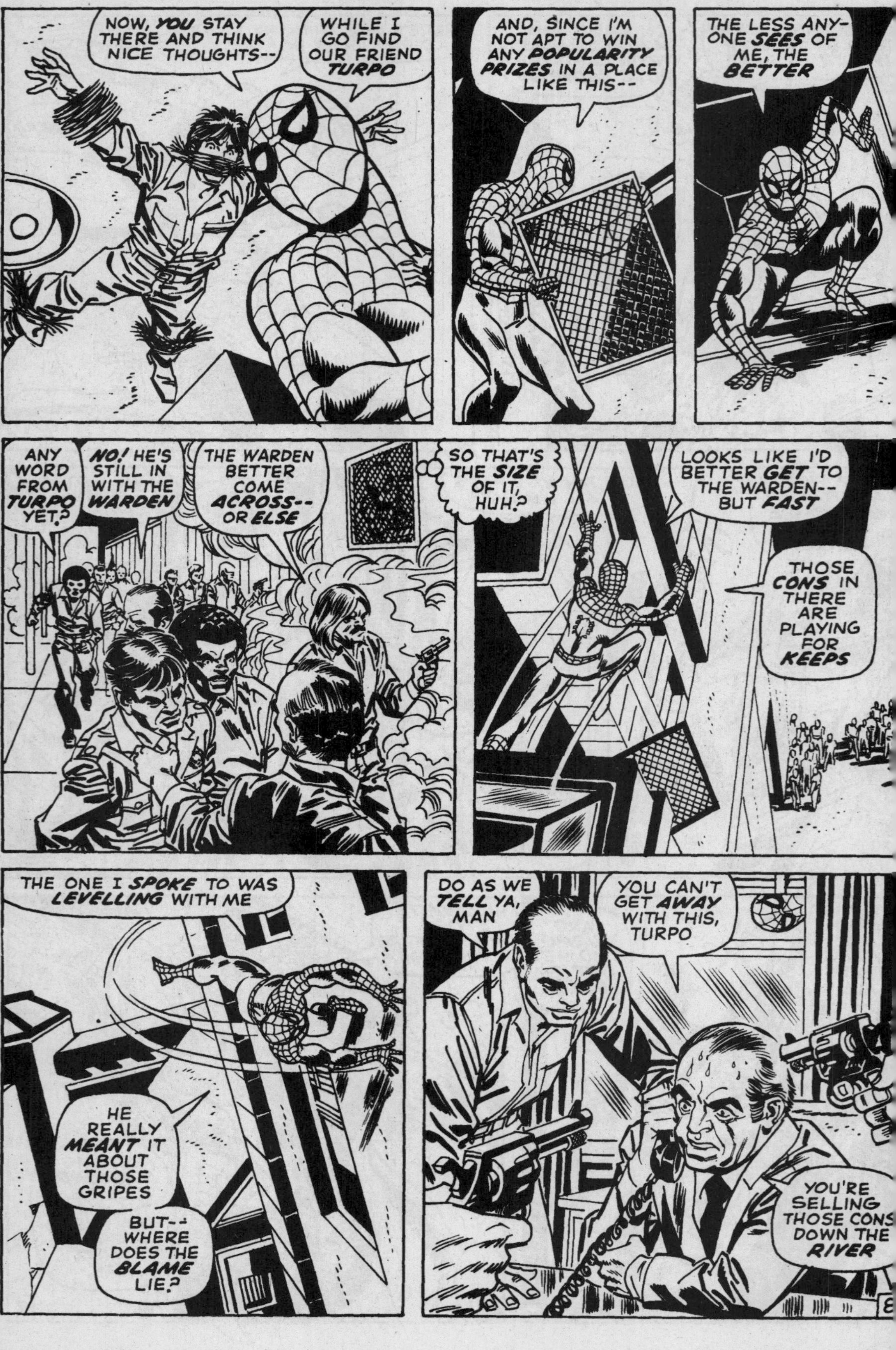
NOW, YOU STAY THERE AND THINK NICE THOUGHTS--
WHILE I GO FIND OUR FRIEND TURPO
AND, SINCE I'M NOT APT TO WIN ANY POPULARITY PRIZES IN A PLACE LIKE THIS--
THE LESS ANY-ONE SEES OF ME, THE BETTER
ANY WORD FROM TURPO YET?
NO! HE'S STILL IN WITH THE WARDEN
THE WARDEN BETTER COME ACROSS-- OR ELSE
SO THAT'S THE SIZE OF IT, HUH?
LOOKS LIKE I'D BETTER GET TO THE WARDEN-- BUT FAST
THOSE CONS IN THERE ARE PLAYING FOR KEEPS
THE ONE I SPOKE TO WAS LEVELLING WITH ME
HE REALLY MEANT IT ABOUT THOSE GRIPES
BUT-- WHERE DOES THE BLAME LIE?
DO AS WE TELL YA, MAN
YOU CAN'T GET AWAY WITH THIS, TURPO
YOU'RE SELLING THOSE CONS DOWN THE RIVER
8

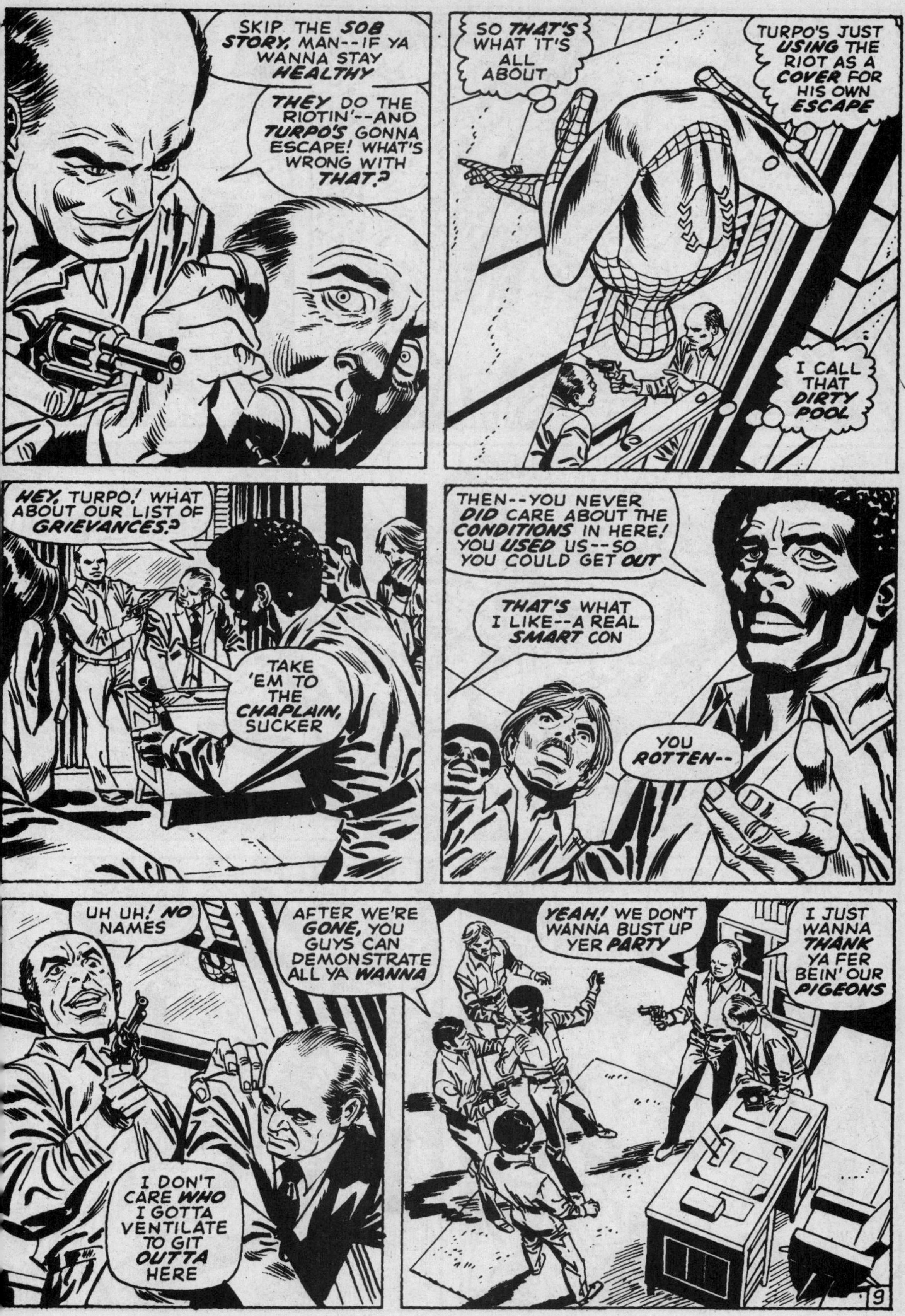

SKIP THE SOB STORY, MAN--IF YA WANNA STAY HEALTHY
THEY DO THE RIOTIN'--AND TURPO'S GONNA ESCAPE! WHAT'S WRONG WITH THAT?
SO THAT'S WHAT IT'S ALL ABOUT
TURPO'S JUST USING THE RIOT AS A COVER FOR HIS OWN ESCAPE
I CALL THAT DIRTY POOL
HEY, TURPO! WHAT ABOUT OUR LIST OF GRIEVANCES?
TAKE 'EM TO THE CHAPLAIN, SUCKER
THEN--YOU NEVER DID CARE ABOUT THE CONDITIONS IN HERE! YOU USED US--SO YOU COULD GET OUT
THAT'S WHAT I LIKE--A REAL SMART CON
YOU ROTTEN--
UH UH! NO NAMES
I DON'T CARE WHO I GOTTA VENTILATE TO GIT OUTTA HERE
AFTER WE'RE GONE, YOU GUYS CAN DEMONSTRATE ALL YA WANNA
YEAH! WE DON'T WANNA BUST UP YER PARTY
I JUST WANNA THANK YA FER BEIN' OUR PIGEONS
9

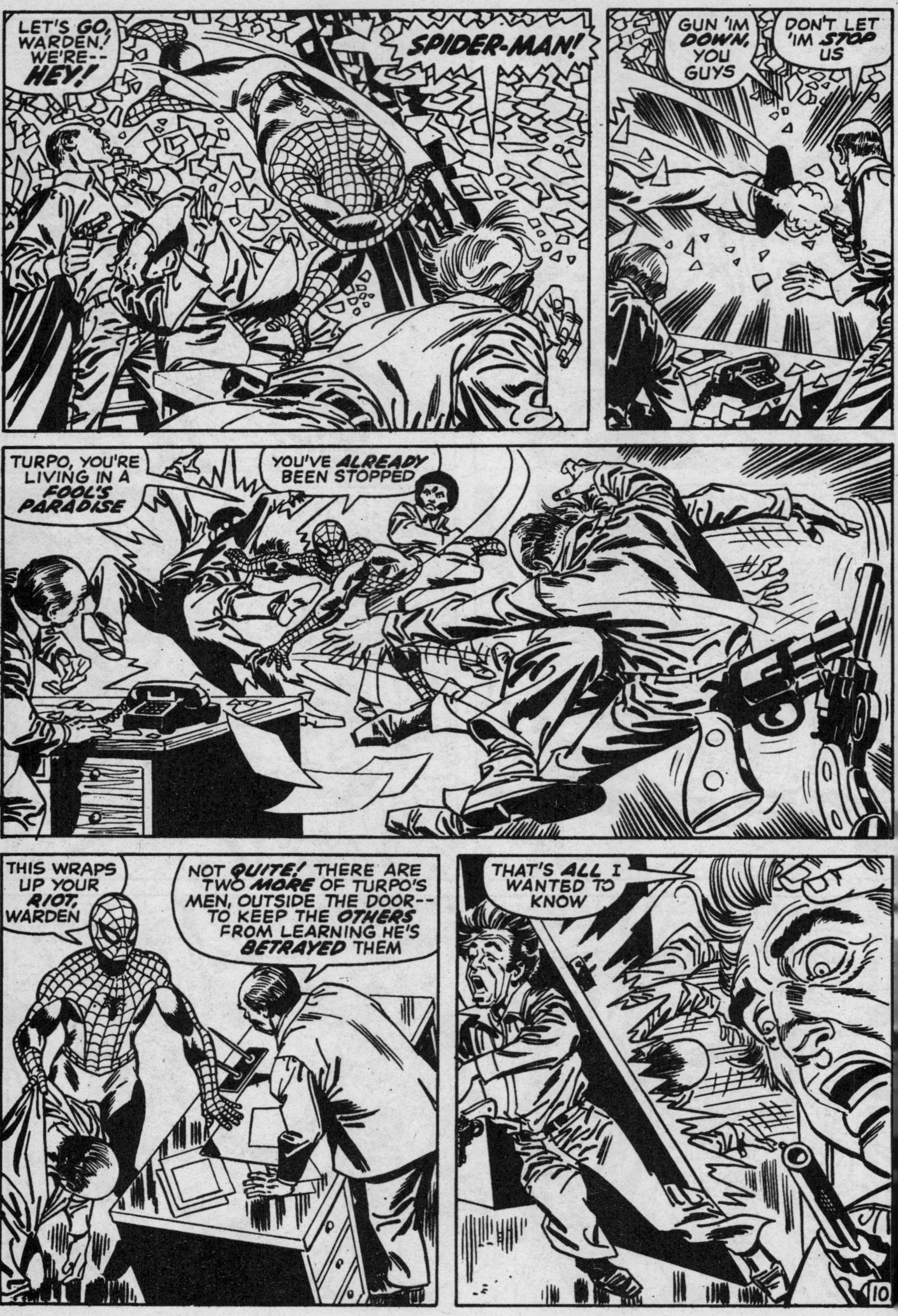

LET'S GO, WARDEN! WE'RE-- HEY!
SPIDER-MAN!
GUN 'IM DOWN, YOU GUYS
DON'T LET 'IM STOP US
TURPO, YOU'RE LIVING IN A FOOL'S PARADISE
YOU'VE ALREADY BEEN STOPPED
THIS WRAPS UP YOUR RIOT, WARDEN
NOT QUITE! THERE ARE TWO MORE OF TURPO'S MEN, OUTSIDE THE DOOR-- TO KEEP THE OTHERS FROM LEARNING HE'S BETRAYED THEM
THAT'S ALL I WANTED TO KNOW

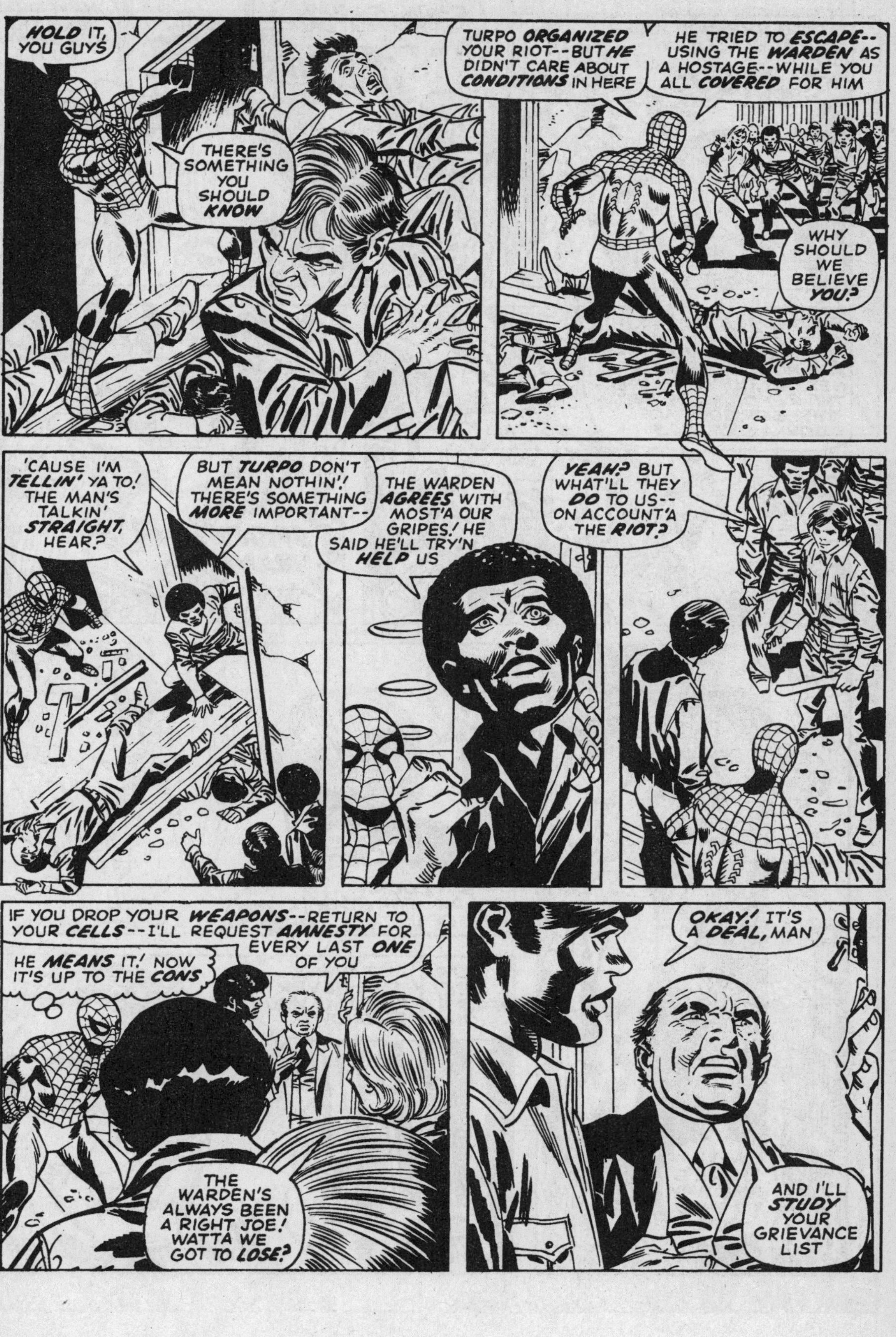

HOLD IT, YOU GUYS
THERE'S SOMETHING YOU SHOULD KNOW
TURPO ORGANIZED YOUR RIOT--BUT HE DIDN'T CARE ABOUT CONDITIONS IN HERE
HE TRIED TO ESCAPE--USING THE WARDEN AS A HOSTAGE--WHILE YOU ALL COVERED FOR HIM
WHY SHOULD WE BELIEVE YOU?
'CAUSE I'M TELLIN' YA TO! THE MAN'S TALKIN' STRAIGHT, HEAR?
BUT TURPO DON'T MEAN NOTHIN'! THERE'S SOMETHING MORE IMPORTANT--
THE WARDEN AGREES WITH MOST'A OUR GRIPES! HE SAID HE'LL TRY'N HELP US
YEAH? BUT WHAT'LL THEY DO TO US--ON ACCOUNT'A THE RIOT?
IF YOU DROP YOUR WEAPONS--RETURN TO YOUR CELLS--I'LL REQUEST AMNESTY FOR EVERY LAST ONE OF YOU
HE MEANS IT! NOW IT'S UP TO THE CONS
THE WARDEN'S ALWAYS BEEN A RIGHT JOE! WATTA WE GOT TO LOSE?
OKAY! IT'S A DEAL, MAN
AND I'LL STUDY YOUR GRIEVANCE LIST

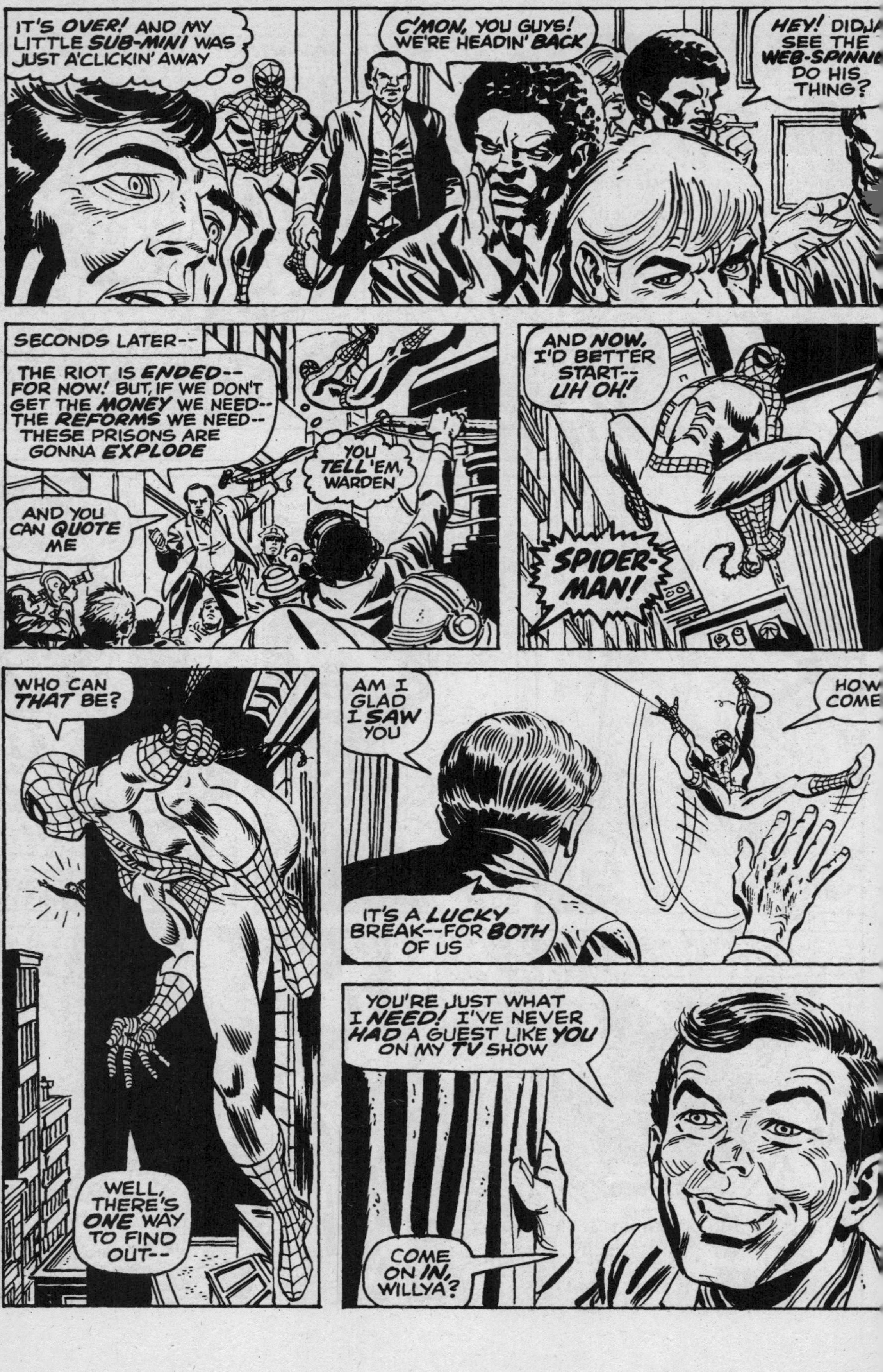
IT'S OVER! AND MY LITTLE SUB-MINI WAS JUST A'CLICKIN' AWAY
C'MON, YOU GUYS! WE'RE HEADIN' BACK
HEY! DIDJA SEE THE WEB-SPINN DO HIS THING?
SECONDS LATER--
THE RIOT IS ENDED-- FOR NOW! BUT, IF WE DON'T GET THE MONEY WE NEED-- THE REFORMS WE NEED-- THESE PRISONS ARE GONNA EXPLODE
YOU TELL 'EM, WARDEN
AND YOU CAN QUOTE ME
AND NOW, I'D BETTER START-- UH OH!
SPIDER-MAN!
WHO CAN THAT BE?
WELL, THERE'S ONE WAY TO FIND OUT--
AM I GLAD I SAW YOU
HOW COME
IT'S A LUCKY BREAK--FOR BOTH OF US
YOU'RE JUST WHAT I NEED! I'VE NEVER HAD A GUEST LIKE YOU ON MY TV SHOW
COME ON IN, WILLYA?

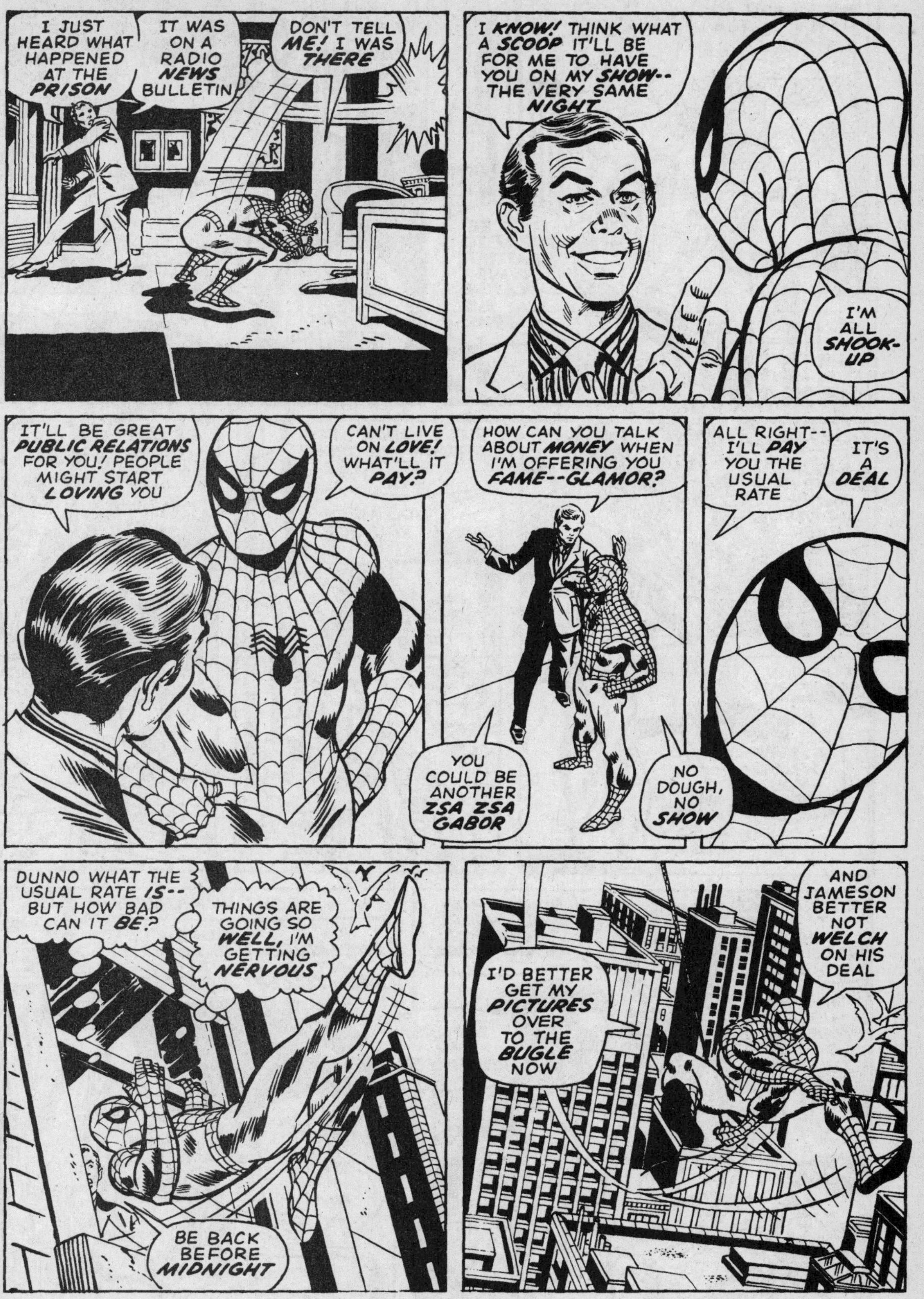
I JUST HEARD WHAT HAPPENED AT THE PRISON
IT WAS ON A RADIO NEWS BULLETIN
DON'T TELL ME! I WAS THERE
I KNOW! THINK WHAT A SCOOP IT'LL BE FOR ME TO HAVE YOU ON MY SHOW-- THE VERY SAME NIGHT
I'M ALL SHOOK-UP
IT'LL BE GREAT PUBLIC RELATIONS FOR YOU! PEOPLE MIGHT START LOVING YOU
CAN'T LIVE ON LOVE! WHAT'LL IT PAY?
HOW CAN YOU TALK ABOUT MONEY WHEN I'M OFFERING YOU FAME--GLAMOR?
YOU COULD BE ANOTHER ZSA ZSA GABOR
NO DOUGH, NO SHOW
ALL RIGHT-- I'LL PAY YOU THE USUAL RATE
IT'S A DEAL
DUNNO WHAT THE USUAL RATE IS-- BUT HOW BAD CAN IT BE?
THINGS ARE GOING SO WELL, I'M GETTING NERVOUS
BE BACK BEFORE MIDNIGHT
I'D BETTER GET MY PICTURES OVER TO THE BUGLE NOW
AND JAMESON BETTER NOT WELCH ON HIS DEAL

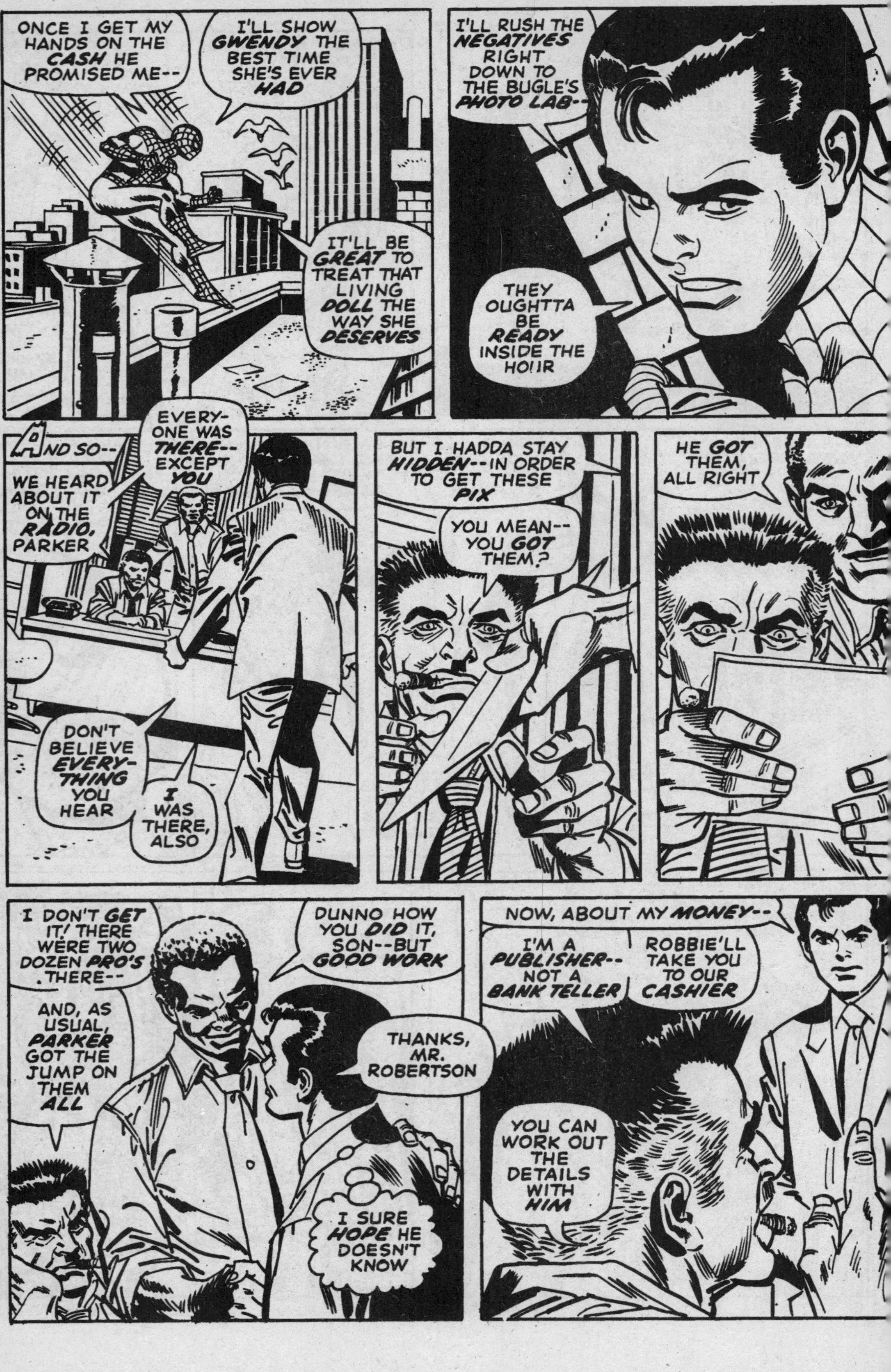

ONCE I GET MY HANDS ON THE CASH HE PROMISED ME--
I'LL SHOW GWENDY THE BEST TIME SHE'S EVER HAD
IT'LL BE GREAT TO TREAT THAT LIVING DOLL THE WAY SHE DESERVES
I'LL RUSH THE NEGATIVES RIGHT DOWN TO THE BUGLE'S PHOTO LAB--
THEY OUGHTTA BE READY INSIDE THE HOUR
AND SO--
WE HEARD ABOUT IT ON THE RADIO, PARKER
EVERY-ONE WAS THERE--EXCEPT YOU
DON'T BELIEVE EVERY-THING YOU HEAR
I WAS THERE, ALSO
BUT I HADDA STAY HIDDEN--IN ORDER TO GET THESE PIX
YOU MEAN-- YOU GOT THEM?
HE GOT THEM, ALL RIGHT
I DON'T GET IT! THERE WERE TWO DOZEN PRO'S THERE--
AND, AS USUAL, PARKER GOT THE JUMP ON THEM ALL
DUNNO HOW YOU DID IT, SON--BUT GOOD WORK
THANKS, MR. ROBERTSON
I SURE HOPE HE DOESN'T KNOW
NOW, ABOUT MY MONEY--
I'M A PUBLISHER-- NOT A BANK TELLER
ROBBIE'LL TAKE YOU TO OUR CASHIER
YOU CAN WORK OUT THE DETAILS WITH HIM

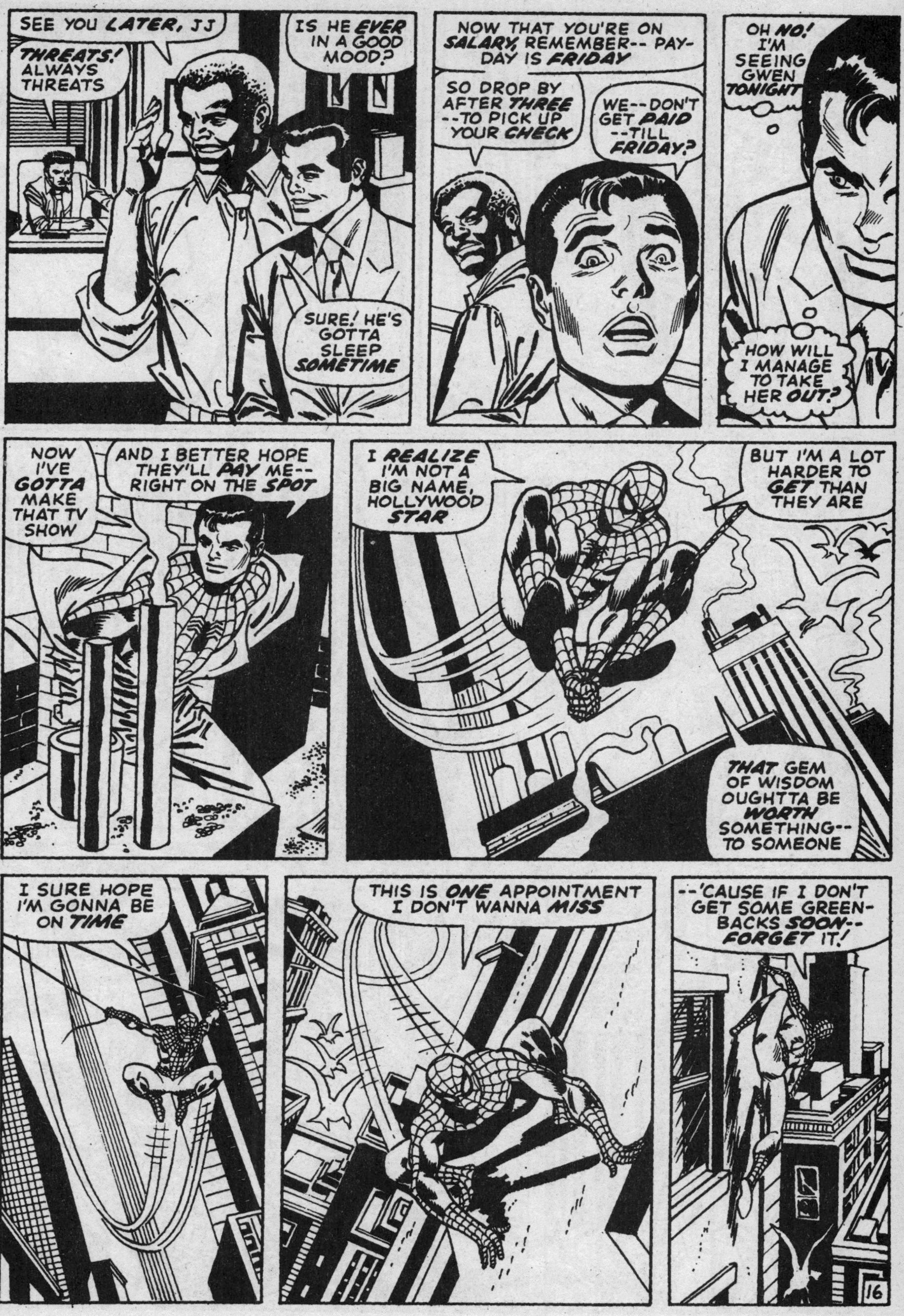
SEE YOU LATER, JJ
THREATS! ALWAYS THREATS
IS HE EVER IN A GOOD MOOD?
SURE! HE'S GOTTA SLEEP SOMETIME
NOW THAT YOU'RE ON SALARY, REMEMBER-- PAY-DAY IS FRIDAY
SO DROP BY AFTER THREE --TO PICK UP YOUR CHECK
WE--DON'T GET PAID --TILL FRIDAY?
OH NO! I'M SEEING GWEN TONIGHT
HOW WILL I MANAGE TO TAKE HER OUT?
NOW I'VE GOTTA MAKE THAT TV SHOW
AND I BETTER HOPE THEY'LL PAY ME-- RIGHT ON THE SPOT
I REALIZE I'M NOT A BIG NAME, HOLLYWOOD STAR
BUT I'M A LOT HARDER TO GET THAN THEY ARE
THAT GEM OF WISDOM OUGHTTA BE WORTH SOMETHING-- TO SOMEONE
I SURE HOPE I'M GONNA BE ON TIME
THIS IS ONE APPOINTMENT I DON'T WANNA MISS
--'CAUSE IF I DON'T GET SOME GREEN-BACKS SOON-- FORGET IT!
16

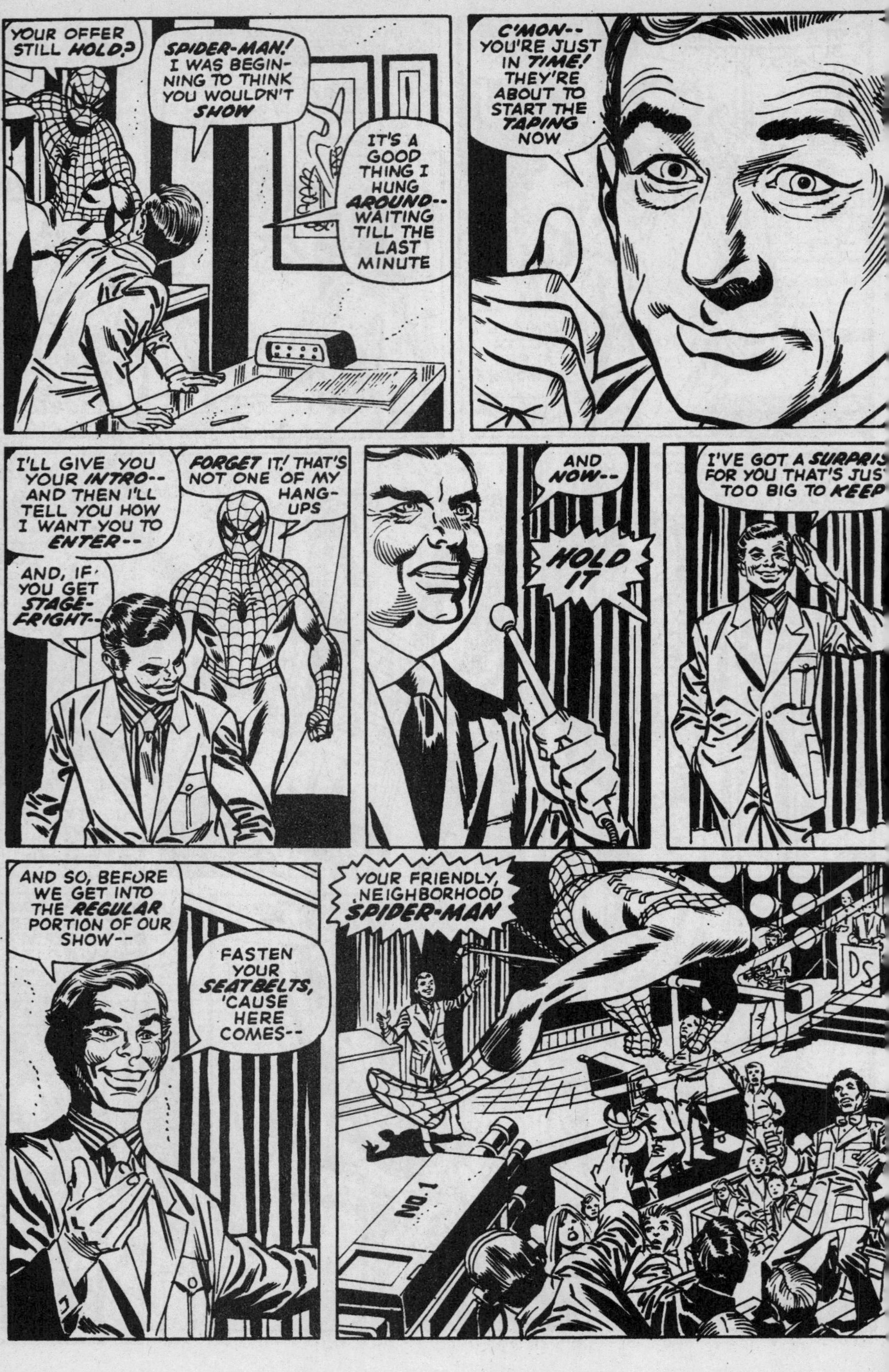
YOUR OFFER STILL HOLD?
SPIDER-MAN! I WAS BEGINNING TO THINK YOU WOULDN'T SHOW
IT'S A GOOD THING I HUNG AROUND-- WAITING TILL THE LAST MINUTE
C'MON-- YOU'RE JUST IN TIME! THEY'RE ABOUT TO START THE TAPING NOW
I'LL GIVE YOU YOUR INTRO-- AND THEN I'LL TELL YOU HOW I WANT YOU TO ENTER--
AND, IF YOU GET STAGE-FRIGHT--
FORGET IT! THAT'S NOT ONE OF MY HANG-UPS
AND NOW--
HOLD IT
I'VE GOT A SURPRIS FOR YOU THAT'S JUST TOO BIG TO KEEP
AND SO, BEFORE WE GET INTO THE REGULAR PORTION OF OUR SHOW--
FASTEN YOUR SEATBELTS, 'CAUSE HERE COMES--
YOUR FRIENDLY, NEIGHBORHOOD SPIDER-MAN
DS
NO. 1

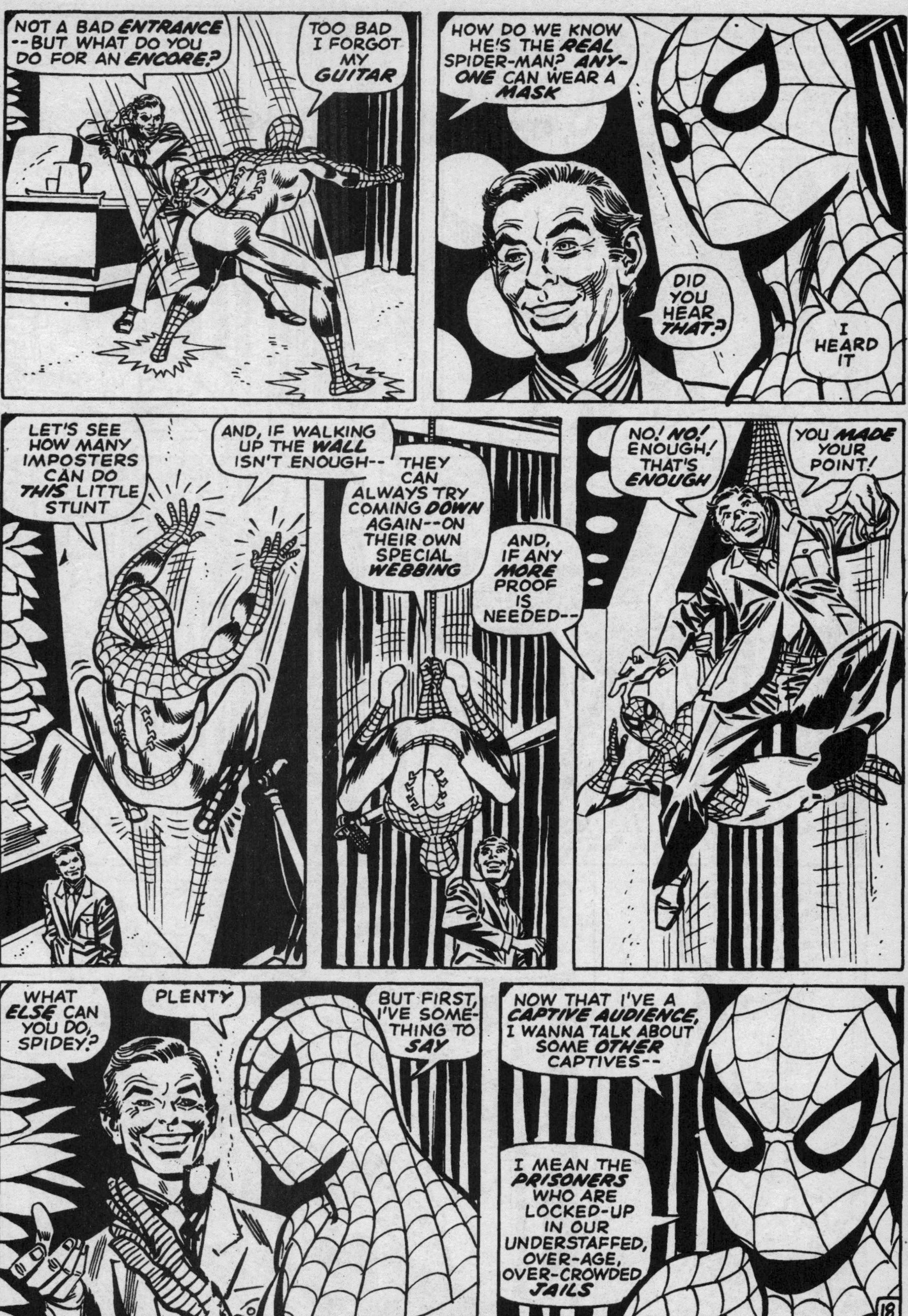
NOT A BAD ENTRANCE --BUT WHAT DO YOU DO FOR AN ENCORE?
TOO BAD I FORGOT MY GUITAR
HOW DO WE KNOW HE'S THE REAL SPIDER-MAN? ANY-ONE CAN WEAR A MASK
DID YOU HEAR THAT?
I HEARD IT
LET'S SEE HOW MANY IMPOSTERS CAN DO THIS LITTLE STUNT
AND, IF WALKING UP THE WALL ISN'T ENOUGH--
THEY CAN ALWAYS TRY COMING DOWN AGAIN--ON THEIR OWN SPECIAL WEBBING
AND, IF ANY MORE PROOF IS NEEDED--
NO! NO! ENOUGH! THAT'S ENOUGH
YOU MADE YOUR POINT!
WHAT ELSE CAN YOU DO, SPIDEY?
PLENTY
BUT FIRST, I'VE SOME-THING TO SAY
NOW THAT I'VE A CAPTIVE AUDIENCE, I WANNA TALK ABOUT SOME OTHER CAPTIVES--
I MEAN THE PRISONERS WHO ARE LOCKED-UP IN OUR UNDERSTAFFED, OVER-AGE, OVER-CROWDED JAILS
18

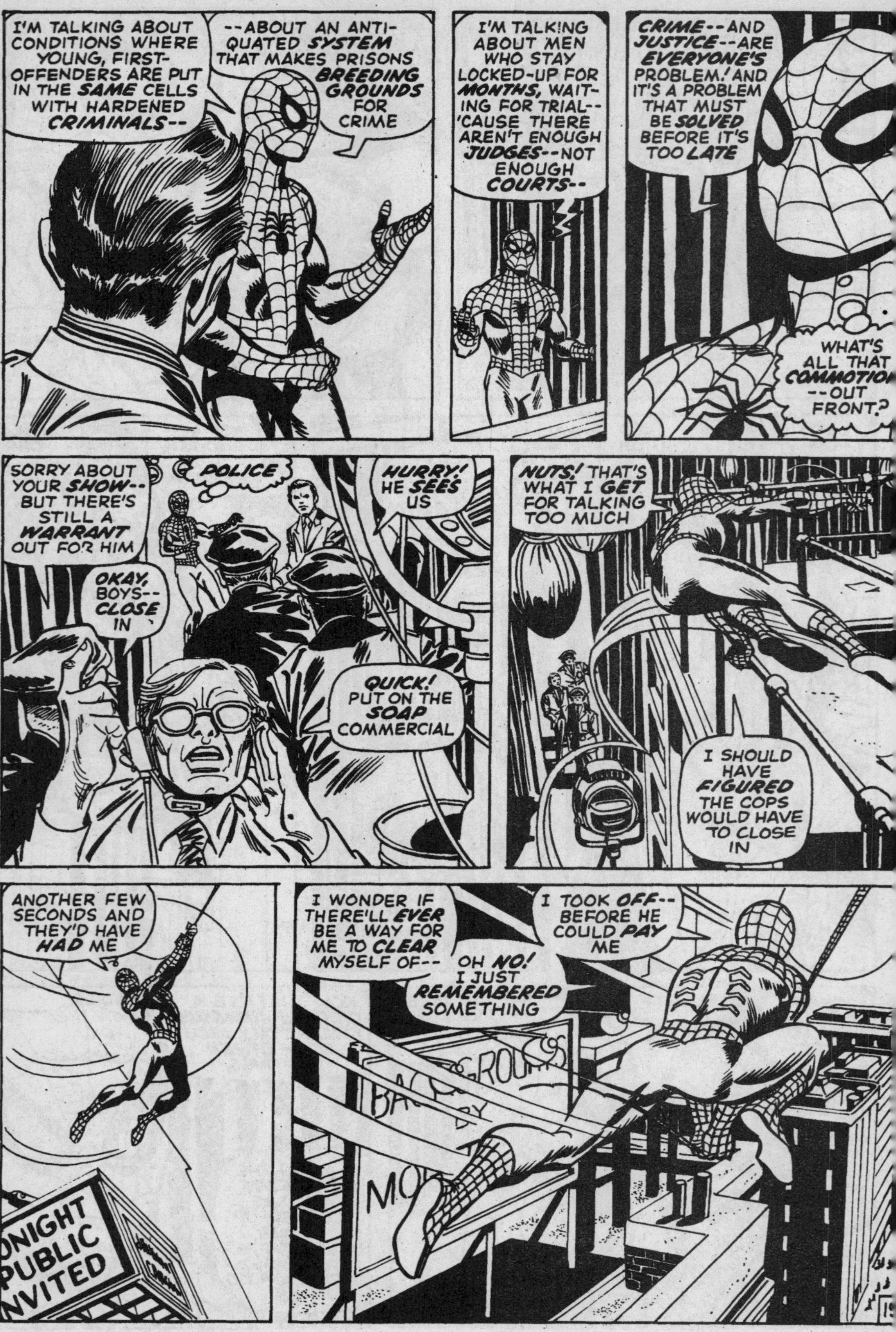
I'M TALKING ABOUT CONDITIONS WHERE YOUNG, FIRST-OFFENDERS ARE PUT IN THE SAME CELLS WITH HARDENED CRIMINALS--
--ABOUT AN ANTI-QUATED SYSTEM THAT MAKES PRISONS BREEDING GROUNDS FOR CRIME
I'M TALKING ABOUT MEN WHO STAY LOCKED-UP FOR MONTHS, WAITING FOR TRIAL--'CAUSE THERE AREN'T ENOUGH JUDGES--NOT ENOUGH COURTS--
CRIME--AND JUSTICE--ARE EVERYONE'S PROBLEM! AND IT'S A PROBLEM THAT MUST BE SOLVED BEFORE IT'S TOO LATE
WHAT'S ALL THAT COMMOTION --OUT FRONT?
SORRY ABOUT YOUR SHOW--BUT THERE'S STILL A WARRANT OUT FOR HIM
POLICE
HURRY! HE SEES US
OKAY, BOYS--CLOSE IN
QUICK! PUT ON THE SOAP COMMERCIAL
NUTS! THAT'S WHAT I GET FOR TALKING TOO MUCH
I SHOULD HAVE FIGURED THE COPS WOULD HAVE TO CLOSE IN
ANOTHER FEW SECONDS AND THEY'D HAVE HAD ME
ONIGHT
PUBLIC
NVITED
I WONDER IF THERE'LL EVER BE A WAY FOR ME TO CLEAR MYSELF OF--
I TOOK OFF--BEFORE HE COULD PAY ME
OH NO! I JUST REMEMBERED SOMETHING

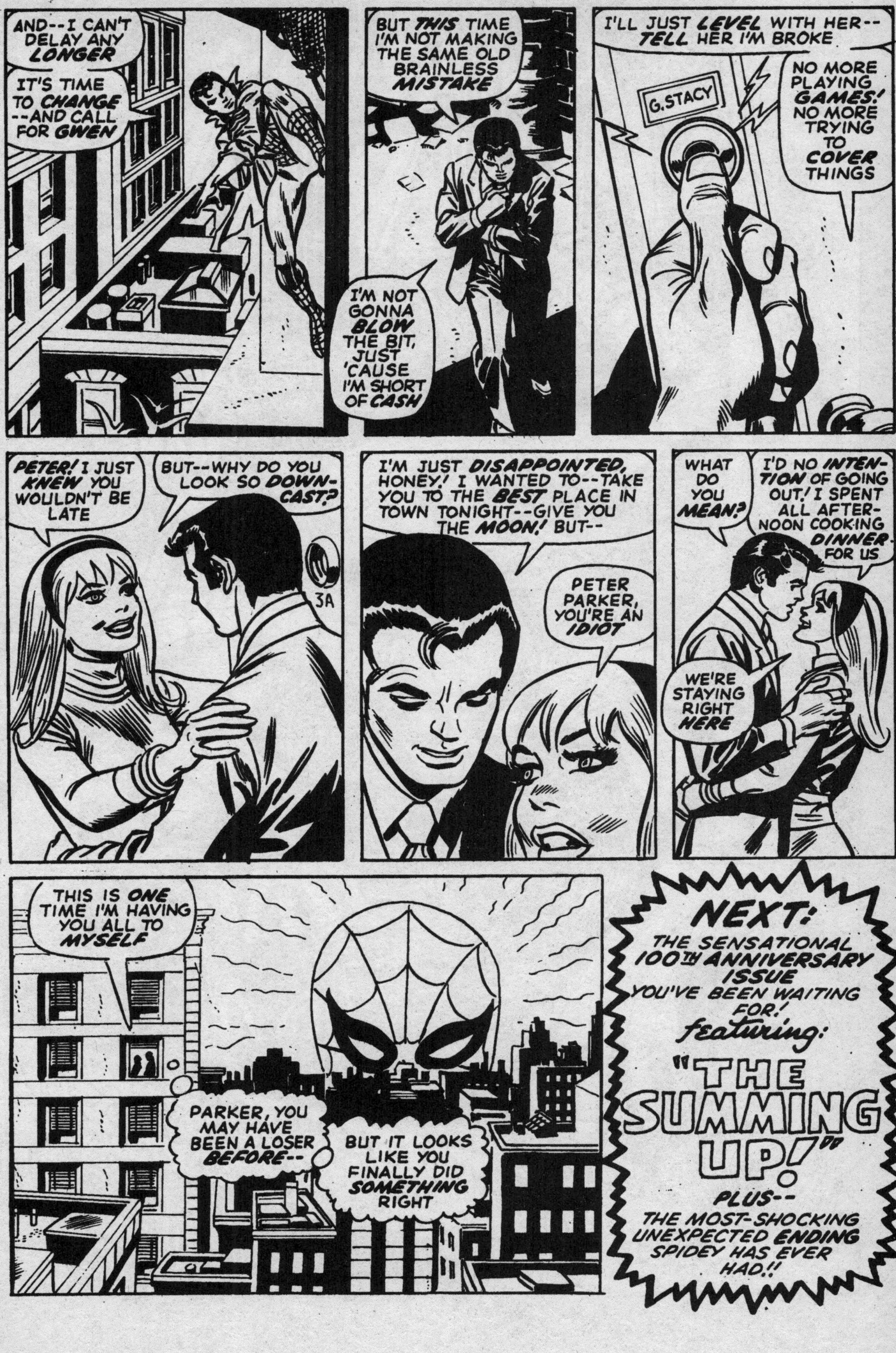

AND--I CAN'T DELAY ANY LONGER
IT'S TIME TO CHANGE --AND CALL FOR GWEN
BUT THIS TIME I'M NOT MAKING THE SAME OLD BRAINLESS MISTAKE
I'M NOT GONNA BLOW THE BIT, JUST 'CAUSE I'M SHORT OF CASH
I'LL JUST LEVEL WITH HER--TELL HER I'M BROKE
G. STACY
NO MORE PLAYING GAMES! NO MORE TRYING TO COVER THINGS
PETER! I JUST KNEW YOU WOULDN'T BE LATE
BUT--WHY DO YOU LOOK SO DOWN-CAST?
3A
I'M JUST DISAPPOINTED, HONEY! I WANTED TO--TAKE YOU TO THE BEST PLACE IN TOWN TONIGHT--GIVE YOU THE MOON! BUT--
PETER PARKER, YOU'RE AN IDIOT
WHAT DO YOU MEAN?
I'D NO INTENTION OF GOING OUT! I SPENT ALL AFTER-NOON COOKING DINNER FOR US
WE'RE STAYING RIGHT HERE
THIS IS ONE TIME I'M HAVING YOU ALL TO MYSELF
PARKER, YOU MAY HAVE BEEN A LOSER BEFORE--
BUT IT LOOKS LIKE YOU FINALLY DID SOMETHING RIGHT
NEXT: THE SENSATIONAL 100TH ANNIVERSARY ISSUE YOU'VE BEEN WAITING FOR! featuring: "THE SUMMING UP!"
PLUS-- THE MOST-SHOCKING UNEXPECTED ENDING SPIDEY HAS EVER HAD!!

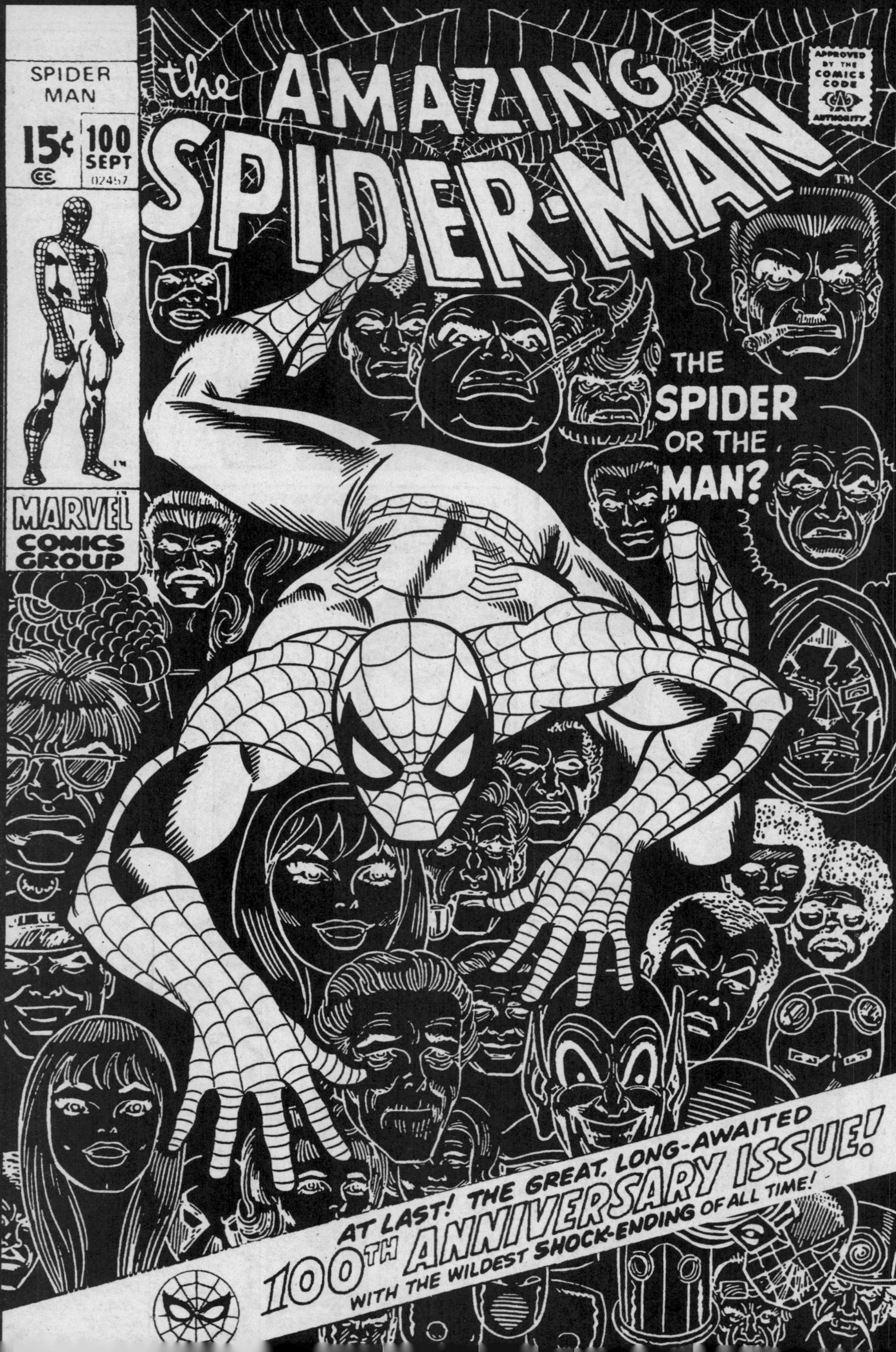
SPIDER MAN
15¢
100
SEPT
02457
MARVEL COMICS GROUP
APPROVED BY THE COMICS CODE AUTHORITY
the AMAZING SPIDER-MAN
THE SPIDER OR THE MAN?
AT LAST! THE GREAT, LONG-AWAITED
100TH ANNIVERSARY ISSUE!
WITH THE WILDEST SHOCK-ENDING OF ALL TIME!

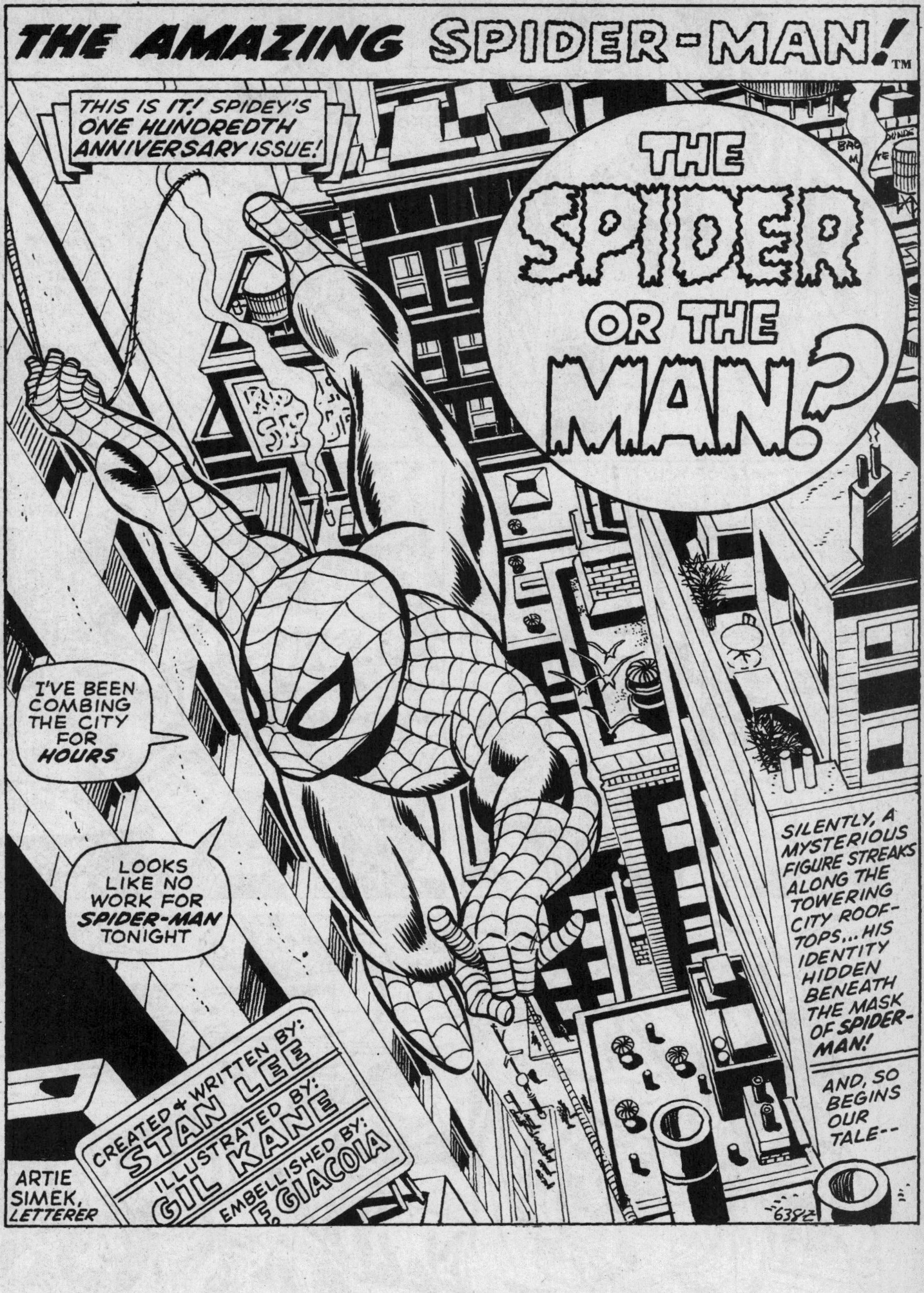
THE AMAZING SPIDER-MAN!™
THIS IS IT! SPIDEY'S ONE HUNDREDTH ANNIVERSARY ISSUE!
THE SPIDER OR THE MAN?
I'VE BEEN COMBING THE CITY FOR HOURS
LOOKS LIKE NO WORK FOR SPIDER-MAN TONIGHT
SILENTLY, A MYSTERIOUS FIGURE STREAKS ALONG THE TOWERING CITY ROOF-TOPS... HIS IDENTITY HIDDEN BENEATH THE MASK OF SPIDER-MAN!
AND, SO BEGINS OUR TALE--
CREATED & WRITTEN BY: STAN LEE
ILLUSTRATED BY: GIL KANE
EMBELLISHED BY: F. GIACOIA
ARTIE SIMEK, LETTERER

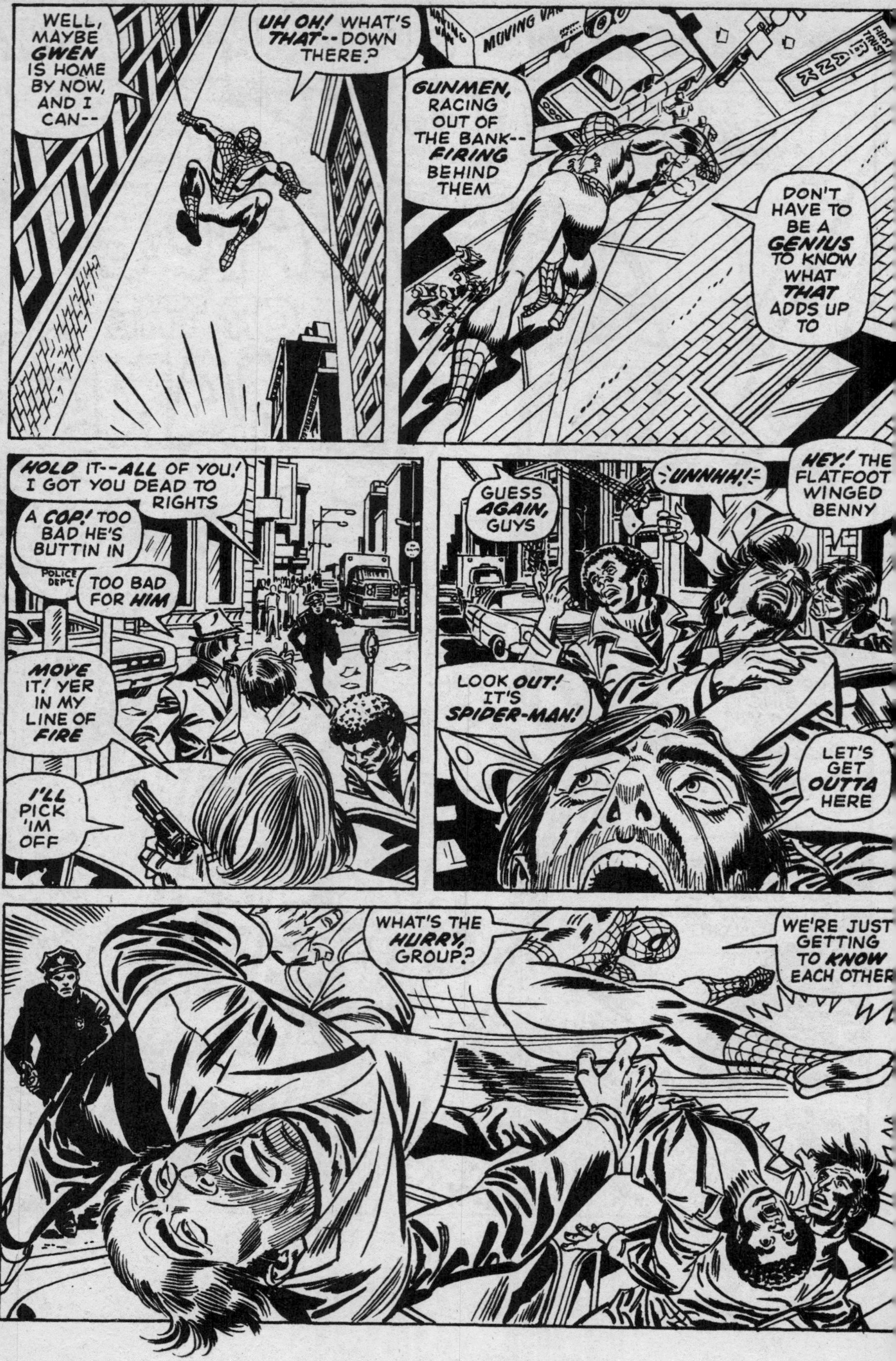

WELL, MAYBE GWEN IS HOME BY NOW, AND I CAN--
UH OH! WHAT'S THAT--DOWN THERE?
MOVING VAN
GUNMEN, RACING OUT OF THE BANK--FIRING BEHIND THEM
DON'T HAVE TO BE A GENIUS TO KNOW WHAT THAT ADDS UP TO
HOLD IT--ALL OF YOU! I GOT YOU DEAD TO RIGHTS
A COP! TOO BAD HE'S BUTTIN IN
POLICE DEPT.
TOO BAD FOR HIM
MOVE IT! YER IN MY LINE OF FIRE
I'LL PICK 'IM OFF
GUESS AGAIN, GUYS
UNNHH!
HEY! THE FLATFOOT WINGED BENNY
LOOK OUT! IT'S SPIDER-MAN!
LET'S GET OUTTA HERE
WHAT'S THE HURRY, GROUP?
WE'RE JUST GETTING TO KNOW EACH OTHER

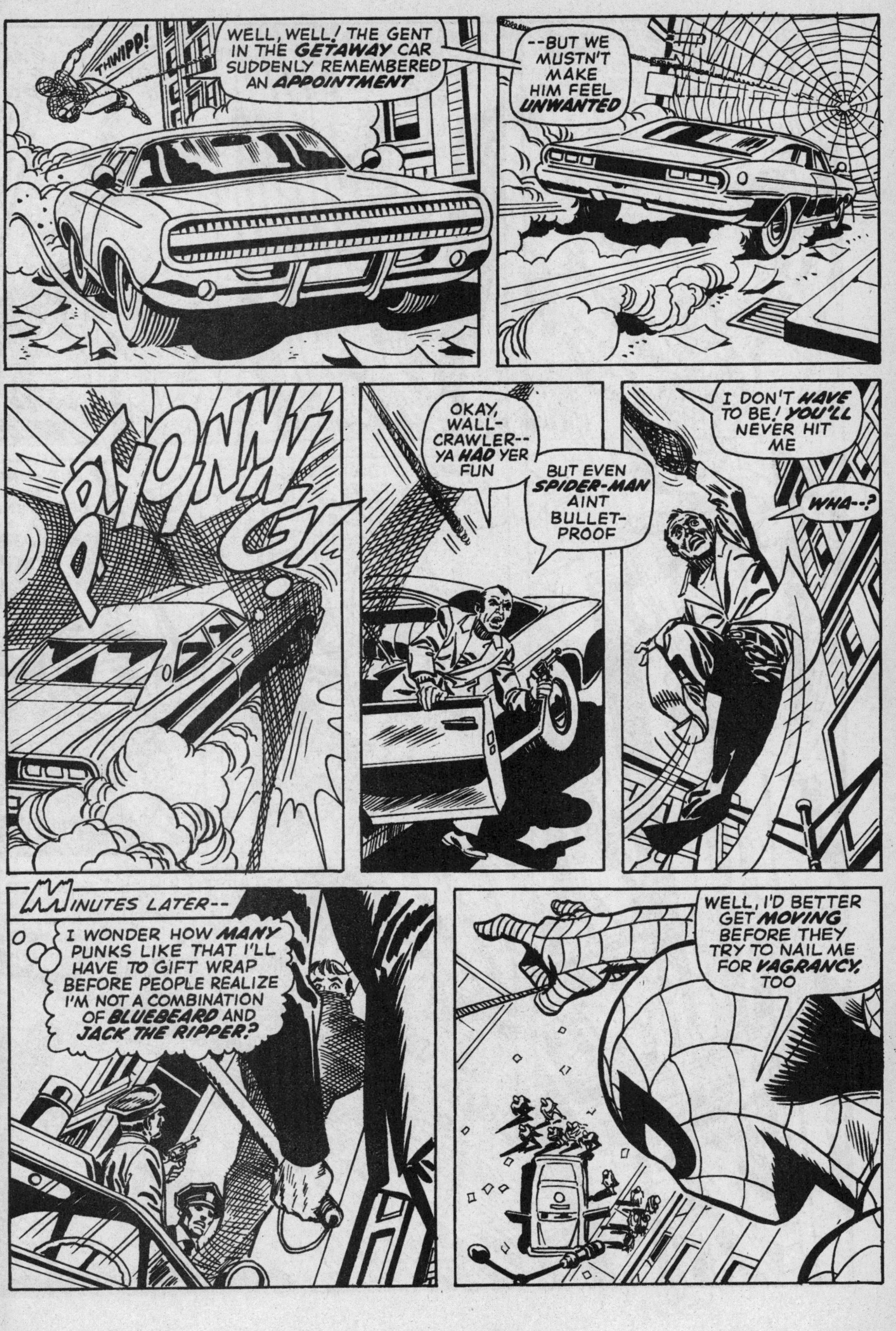
THWIPP!
WELL, WELL! THE GENT IN THE GETAWAY CAR SUDDENLY REMEMBERED AN APPOINTMENT
--BUT WE MUSTN'T MAKE HIM FEEL UNWANTED
P'TYONNNG!
OKAY, WALL-CRAWLER--YA HAD YER FUN
BUT EVEN SPIDER-MAN AINT BULLET-PROOF
I DON'T HAVE TO BE! YOU'LL NEVER HIT ME
WHA--?
MINUTES LATER--
I WONDER HOW MANY PUNKS LIKE THAT I'LL HAVE TO GIFT WRAP BEFORE PEOPLE REALIZE I'M NOT A COMBINATION OF BLUEBEARD AND JACK THE RIPPER?
WELL, I'D BETTER GET MOVING BEFORE THEY TRY TO NAIL ME FOR VAGRANCY, TOO

IT'S FUNNY--I DIDN'T GET AS MUCH OF A *CHARGE* OUT OF TACKLING THOSE JOKERS AS I *USED* TO

EVEN SWINGING AROUND *TOWN* THIS WAY ISN'T THE SAME OLD *KICK*

I MIGHT AS WELL *FACE* IT--

I'M JUST PLAIN *BORED*

I *USED* TO THINK I WAS A MILLION TIMES BETTER OFF THAN *THEY* ARE-- DOWN THERE

BUT *NOW*-- I'M BEGINNING TO *WONDER*

MADISON

NO KING

AT LEAST THEY'RE REALLY *LIVING*

WHILE *I* SEEM TO SPEND MY TIME WATCHING LIFE FROM THE *SIDELINES*

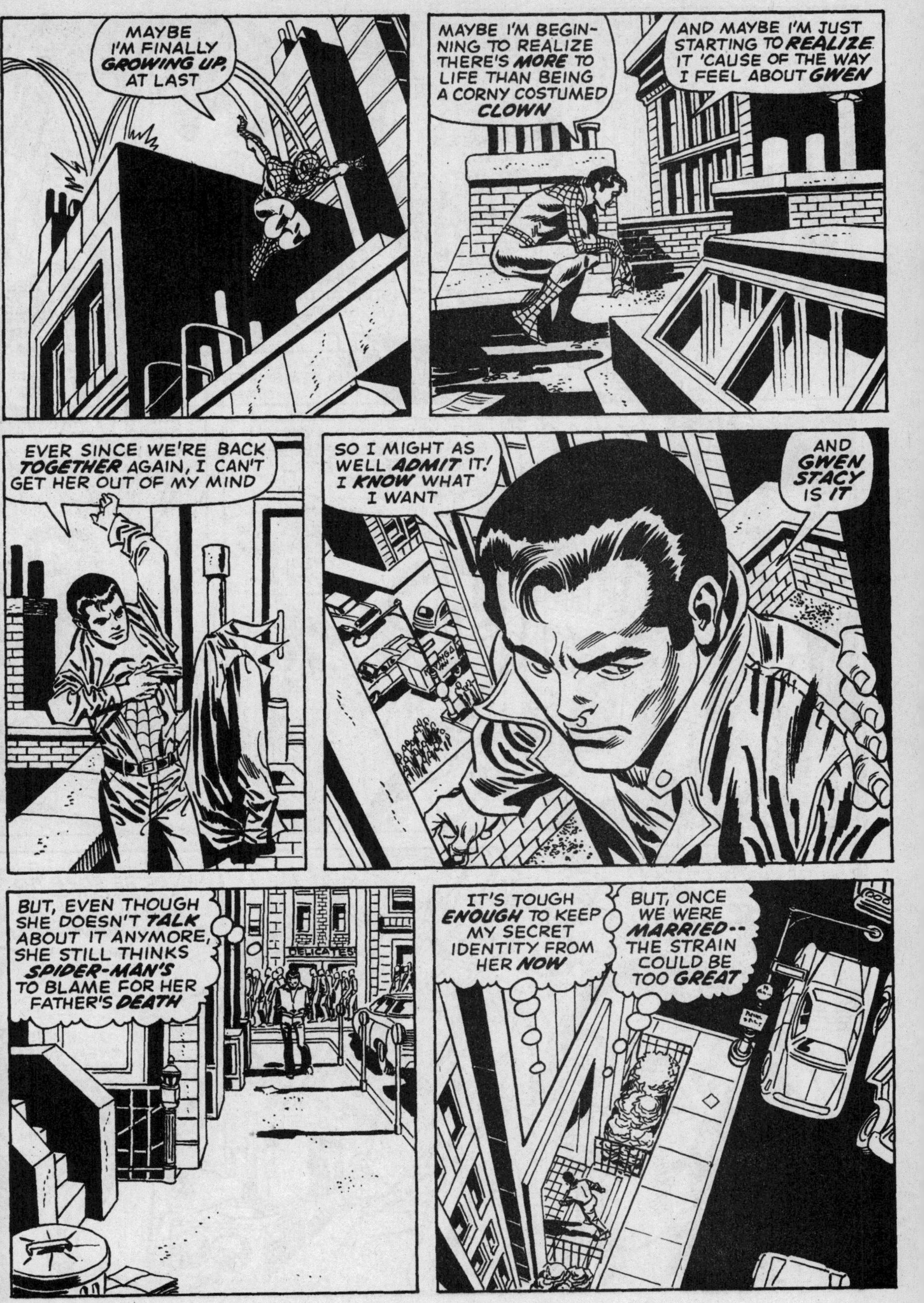
MAYBE I'M FINALLY GROWING UP, AT LAST
MAYBE I'M BEGINNING TO REALIZE THERE'S MORE TO LIFE THAN BEING A CORNY COSTUMED CLOWN
AND MAYBE I'M JUST STARTING TO REALIZE IT 'CAUSE OF THE WAY I FEEL ABOUT GWEN
EVER SINCE WE'RE BACK TOGETHER AGAIN, I CAN'T GET HER OUT OF MY MIND
SO I MIGHT AS WELL ADMIT IT! I KNOW WHAT I WANT
AND GWEN STACY IS IT
BUT, EVEN THOUGH SHE DOESN'T TALK ABOUT IT ANYMORE, SHE STILL THINKS SPIDER-MAN'S TO BLAME FOR HER FATHER'S DEATH
DELICATES
IT'S TOUGH ENOUGH TO KEEP MY SECRET IDENTITY FROM HER NOW
BUT, ONCE WE WERE MARRIED-- THE STRAIN COULD BE TOO GREAT

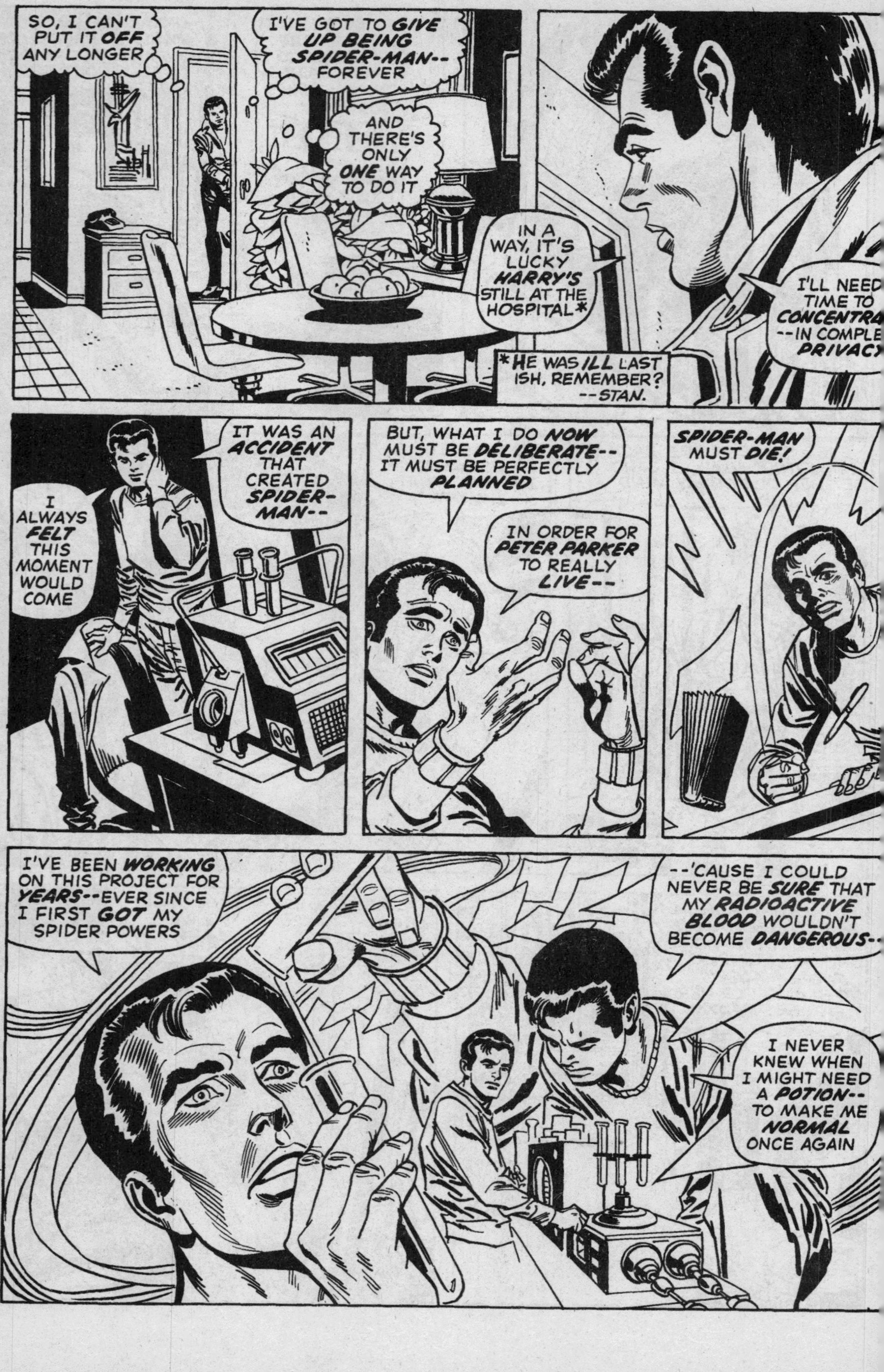

SO, I CAN'T PUT IT OFF ANY LONGER
I'VE GOT TO GIVE UP BEING SPIDER-MAN-- FOREVER
AND THERE'S ONLY ONE WAY TO DO IT
IN A WAY, IT'S LUCKY HARRY'S STILL AT THE HOSPITAL*
*HE WAS ILL LAST ISH, REMEMBER? --STAN.
I'LL NEED TIME TO CONCENTRA --IN COMPLE PRIVACY
I ALWAYS FELT THIS MOMENT WOULD COME
IT WAS AN ACCIDENT THAT CREATED SPIDER-MAN--
BUT, WHAT I DO NOW MUST BE DELIBERATE-- IT MUST BE PERFECTLY PLANNED
IN ORDER FOR PETER PARKER TO REALLY LIVE--
SPIDER-MAN MUST DIE!
I'VE BEEN WORKING ON THIS PROJECT FOR YEARS--EVER SINCE I FIRST GOT MY SPIDER POWERS
--'CAUSE I COULD NEVER BE SURE THAT MY RADIOACTIVE BLOOD WOULDN'T BECOME DANGEROUS--
I NEVER KNEW WHEN I MIGHT NEED A POTION-- TO MAKE ME NORMAL ONCE AGAIN

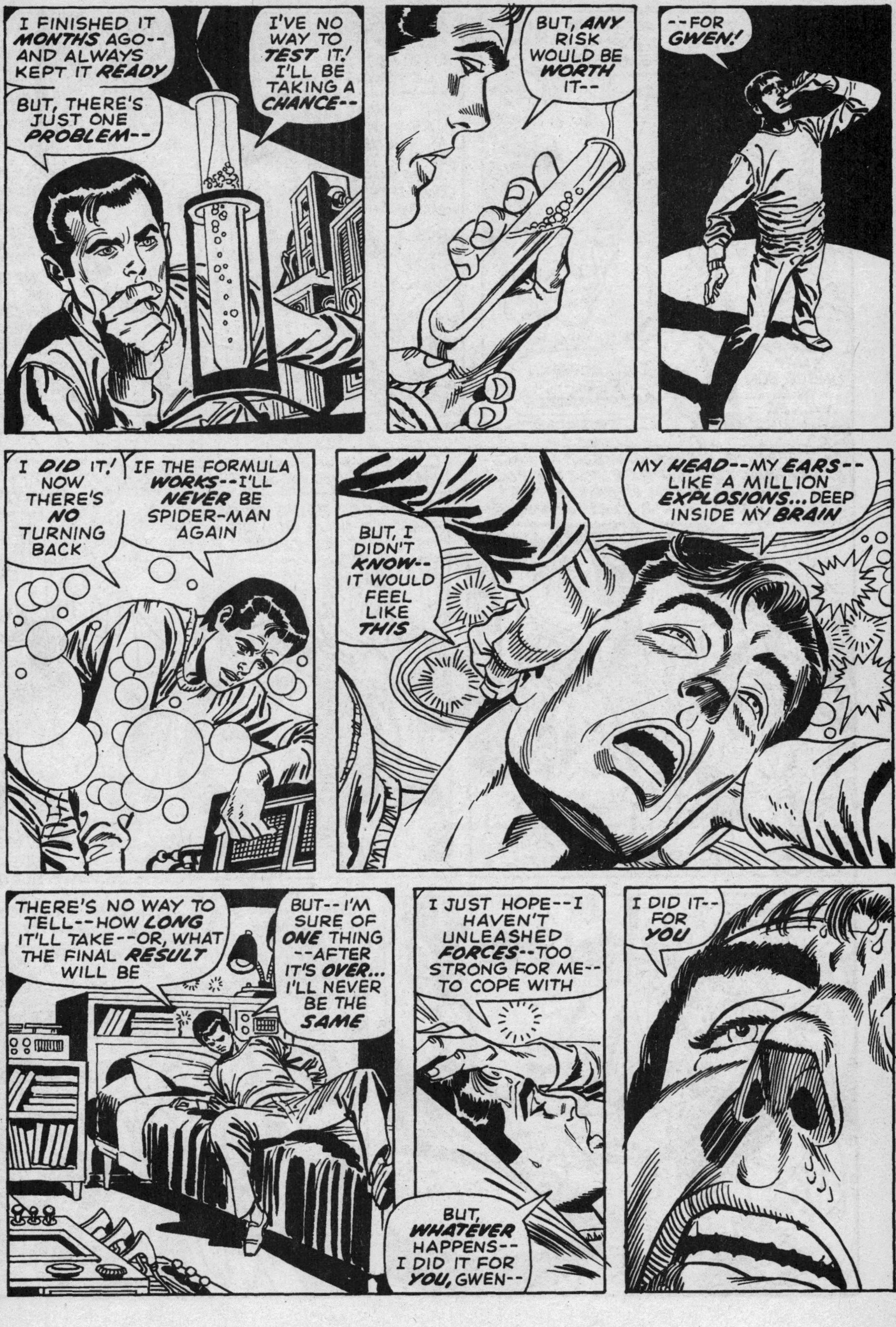
I FINISHED IT MONTHS AGO--AND ALWAYS KEPT IT READY
BUT, THERE'S JUST ONE PROBLEM--
I'VE NO WAY TO TEST IT! I'LL BE TAKING A CHANCE--
BUT, ANY RISK WOULD BE WORTH IT--
--FOR GWEN!
I DID IT! NOW THERE'S NO TURNING BACK
IF THE FORMULA WORKS--I'LL NEVER BE SPIDER-MAN AGAIN
MY HEAD--MY EARS--LIKE A MILLION EXPLOSIONS...DEEP INSIDE MY BRAIN
BUT, I DIDN'T KNOW--IT WOULD FEEL LIKE THIS
THERE'S NO WAY TO TELL--HOW LONG IT'LL TAKE--OR, WHAT THE FINAL RESULT WILL BE
BUT--I'M SURE OF ONE THING--AFTER IT'S OVER... I'LL NEVER BE THE SAME
I JUST HOPE--I HAVEN'T UNLEASHED FORCES--TOO STRONG FOR ME--TO COPE WITH
BUT, WHATEVER HAPPENS--I DID IT FOR YOU, GWEN--
I DID IT--FOR YOU

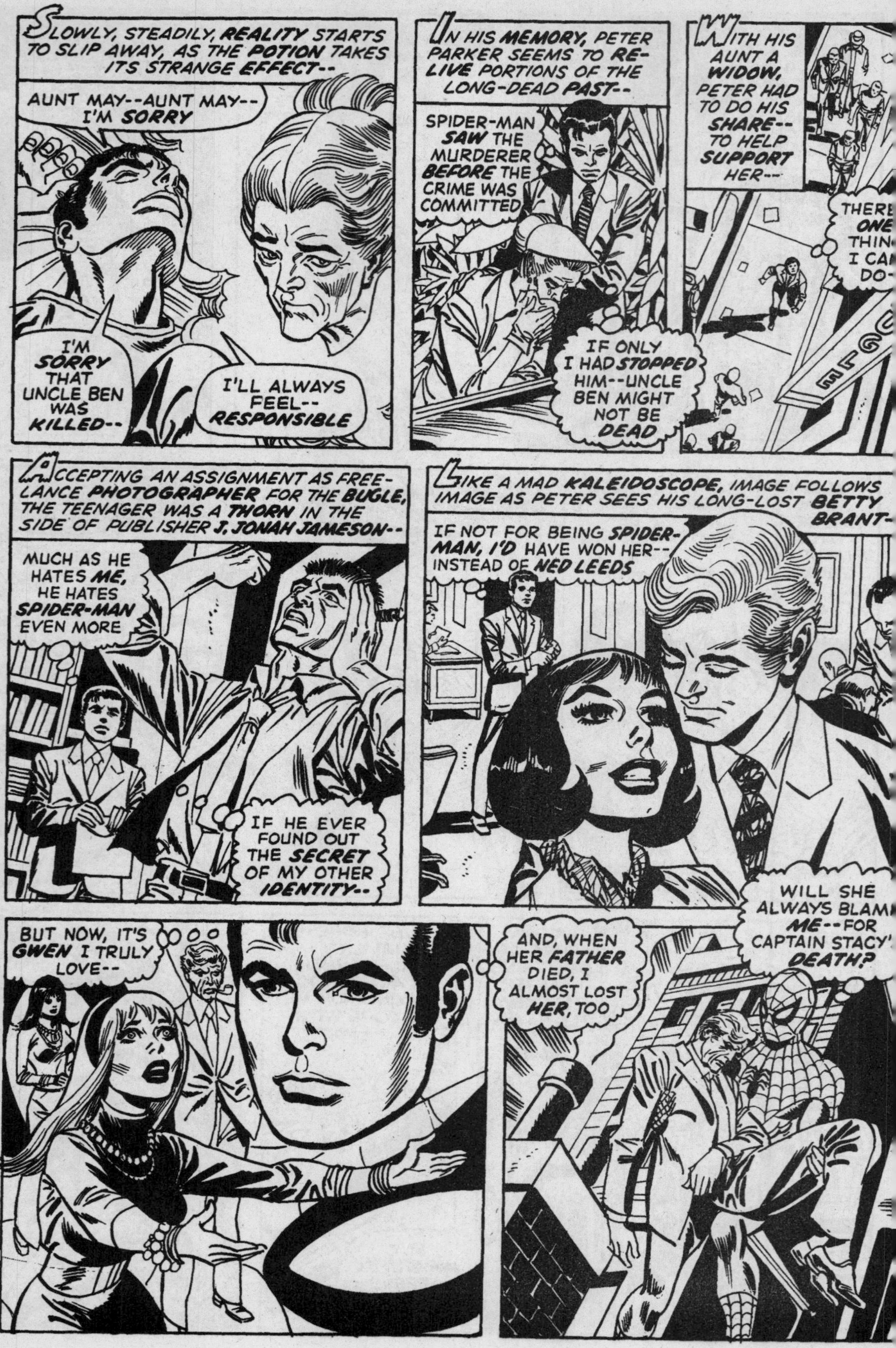
SLOWLY, STEADILY, REALITY STARTS TO SLIP AWAY, AS THE POTION TAKES ITS STRANGE EFFECT--
AUNT MAY--AUNT MAY-- I'M SORRY
I'M SORRY THAT UNCLE BEN WAS KILLED--
I'LL ALWAYS FEEL-- RESPONSIBLE
IN HIS MEMORY, PETER PARKER SEEMS TO RE-LIVE PORTIONS OF THE LONG-DEAD PAST--
SPIDER-MAN SAW THE MURDERER BEFORE THE CRIME WAS COMMITTED
IF ONLY I HAD STOPPED HIM--UNCLE BEN MIGHT NOT BE DEAD
WITH HIS AUNT A WIDOW, PETER HAD TO DO HIS SHARE-- TO HELP SUPPORT HER--
ACCEPTING AN ASSIGNMENT AS FREE-LANCE PHOTOGRAPHER FOR THE BUGLE, THE TEENAGER WAS A THORN IN THE SIDE OF PUBLISHER J. JONAH JAMESON--
MUCH AS HE HATES ME, HE HATES SPIDER-MAN EVEN MORE
IF HE EVER FOUND OUT THE SECRET OF MY OTHER IDENTITY--
LIKE A MAD KALEIDOSCOPE, IMAGE FOLLOWS IMAGE AS PETER SEES HIS LONG-LOST BETTY BRANT--
IF NOT FOR BEING SPIDER-MAN, I'D HAVE WON HER-- INSTEAD OF NED LEEDS
BUT NOW, IT'S GWEN I TRULY LOVE--
AND, WHEN HER FATHER DIED, I ALMOST LOST HER, TOO
WILL SHE ALWAYS BLAM ME--FOR CAPTAIN STACY' DEATH?

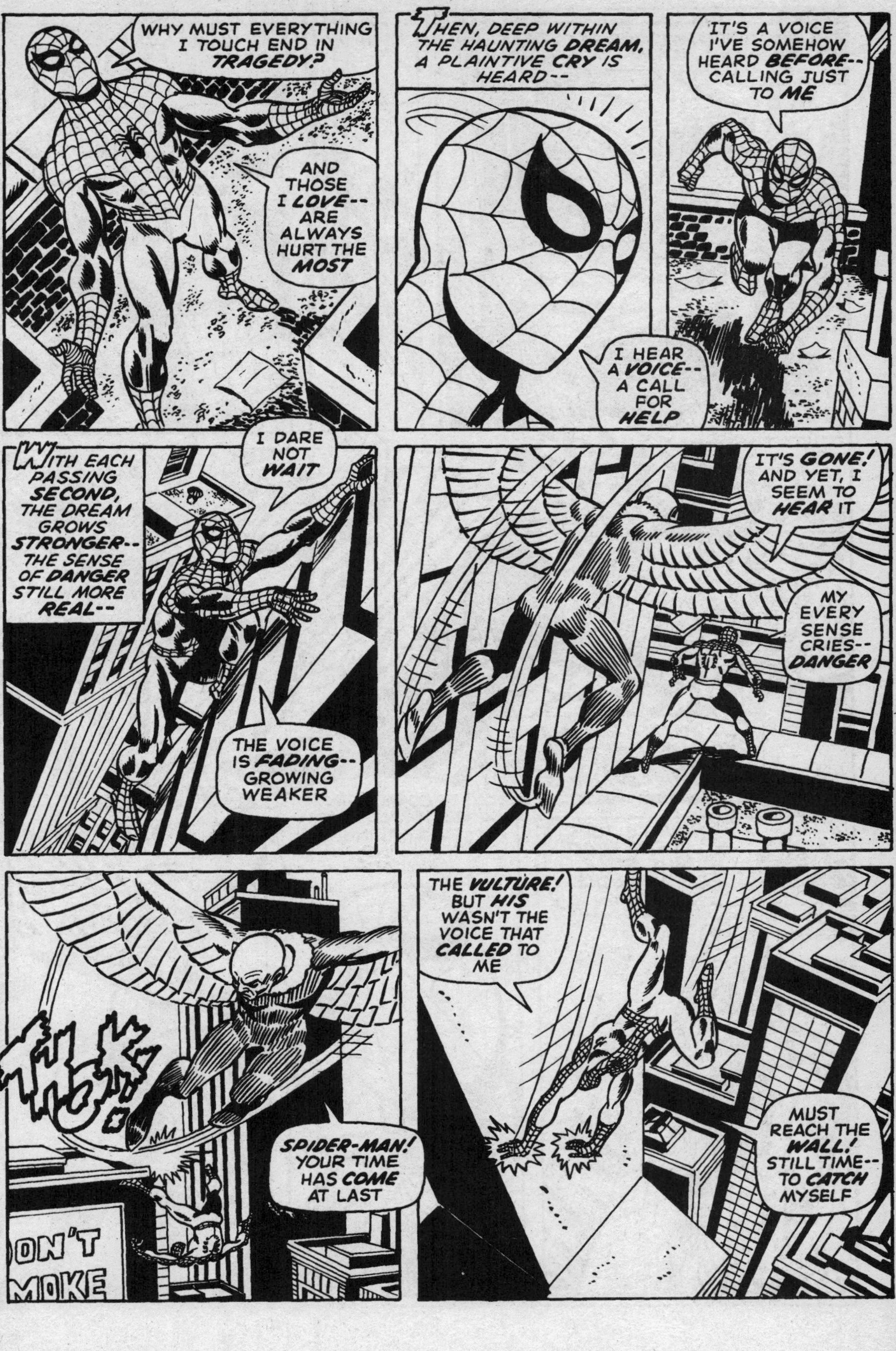
WHY MUST EVERYTHING I TOUCH END IN TRAGEDY?
AND THOSE I LOVE-- ARE ALWAYS HURT THE MOST
THEN, DEEP WITHIN THE HAUNTING DREAM, A PLAINTIVE CRY IS HEARD--
I HEAR A VOICE-- A CALL FOR HELP
IT'S A VOICE I'VE SOMEHOW HEARD BEFORE-- CALLING JUST TO ME
WITH EACH PASSING SECOND, THE DREAM GROWS STRONGER-- THE SENSE OF DANGER STILL MORE REAL--
I DARE NOT WAIT
THE VOICE IS FADING-- GROWING WEAKER
IT'S GONE! AND YET, I SEEM TO HEAR IT
MY EVERY SENSE CRIES-- DANGER
THOK!
SPIDER-MAN! YOUR TIME HAS COME AT LAST
DON'T
MOKE
THE VULTURE! BUT HIS WASN'T THE VOICE THAT CALLED TO ME
MUST REACH THE WALL! STILL TIME-- TO CATCH MYSELF

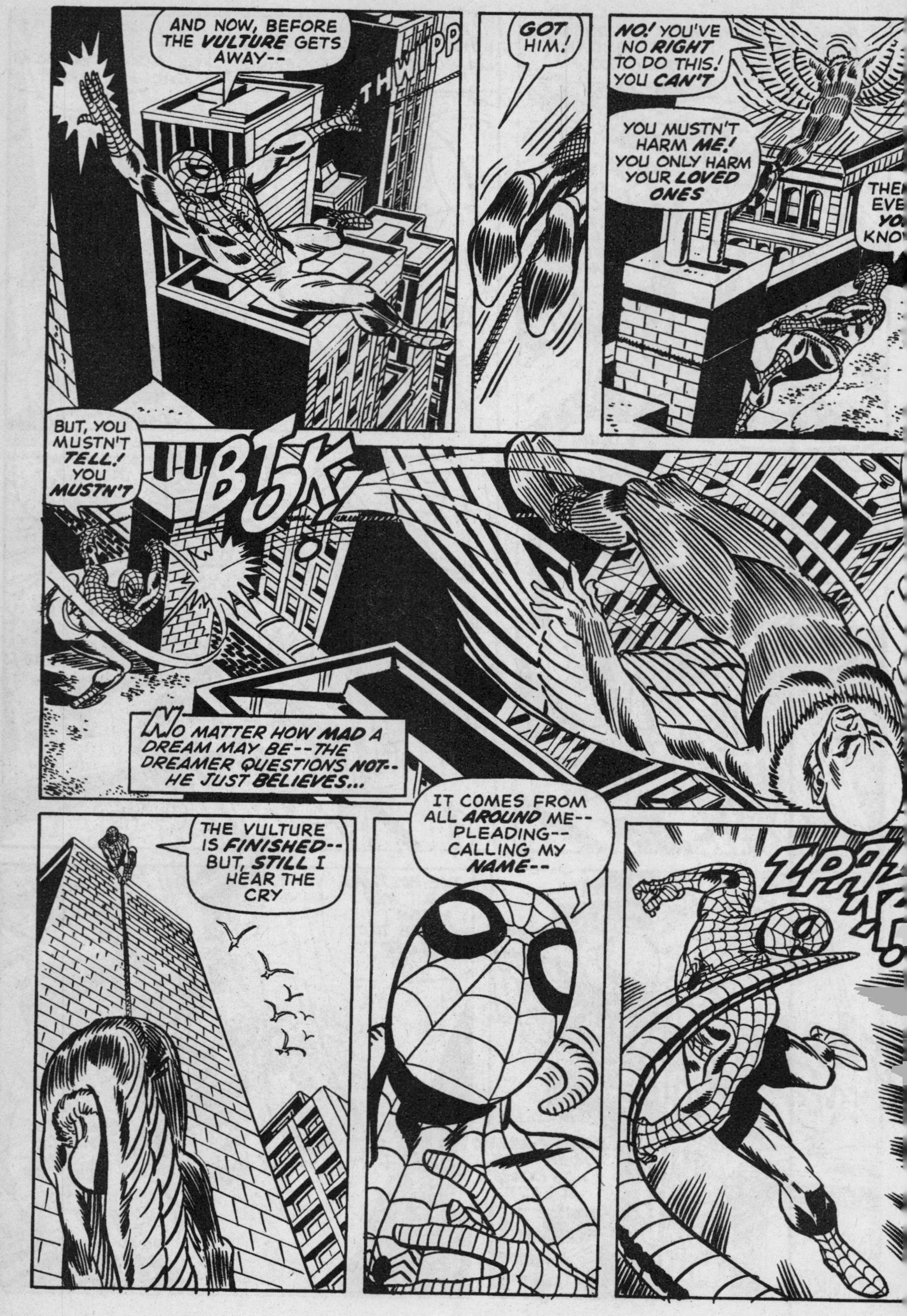

AND NOW, BEFORE THE VULTURE GETS AWAY--
THWIPP
GOT HIM!
NO! YOU'VE NO RIGHT TO DO THIS! YOU CAN'T
YOU MUSTN'T HARM ME! YOU ONLY HARM YOUR LOVED ONES
BUT, YOU MUSTN'T TELL! YOU MUSTN'T
BTOK!
NO MATTER HOW MAD A DREAM MAY BE--THE DREAMER QUESTIONS NOT--HE JUST BELIEVES...
THE VULTURE IS FINISHED--BUT, STILL I HEAR THE CRY
IT COMES FROM ALL AROUND ME--PLEADING--CALLING MY NAME--

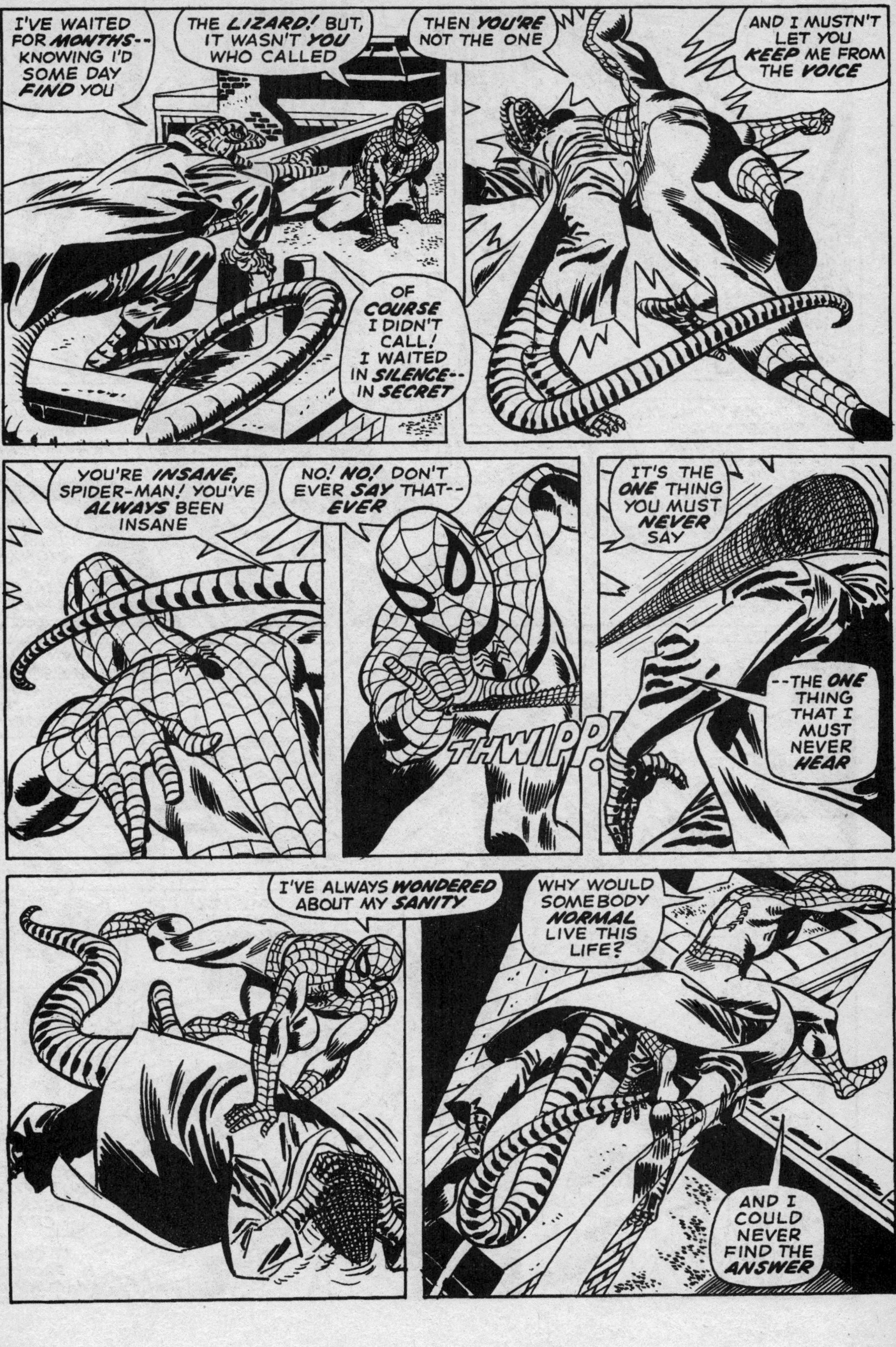
I'VE WAITED FOR MONTHS-- KNOWING I'D SOME DAY FIND YOU
THE LIZARD! BUT, IT WASN'T YOU WHO CALLED
OF COURSE I DIDN'T CALL! I WAITED IN SILENCE-- IN SECRET
THEN YOU'RE NOT THE ONE
AND I MUSTN'T LET YOU KEEP ME FROM THE VOICE
YOU'RE INSANE, SPIDER-MAN! YOU'VE ALWAYS BEEN INSANE
NO! NO! DON'T EVER SAY THAT-- EVER
THWIPP!
IT'S THE ONE THING YOU MUST NEVER SAY
--THE ONE THING THAT I MUST NEVER HEAR
I'VE ALWAYS WONDERED ABOUT MY SANITY
WHY WOULD SOMEBODY NORMAL LIVE THIS LIFE?
AND I COULD NEVER FIND THE ANSWER

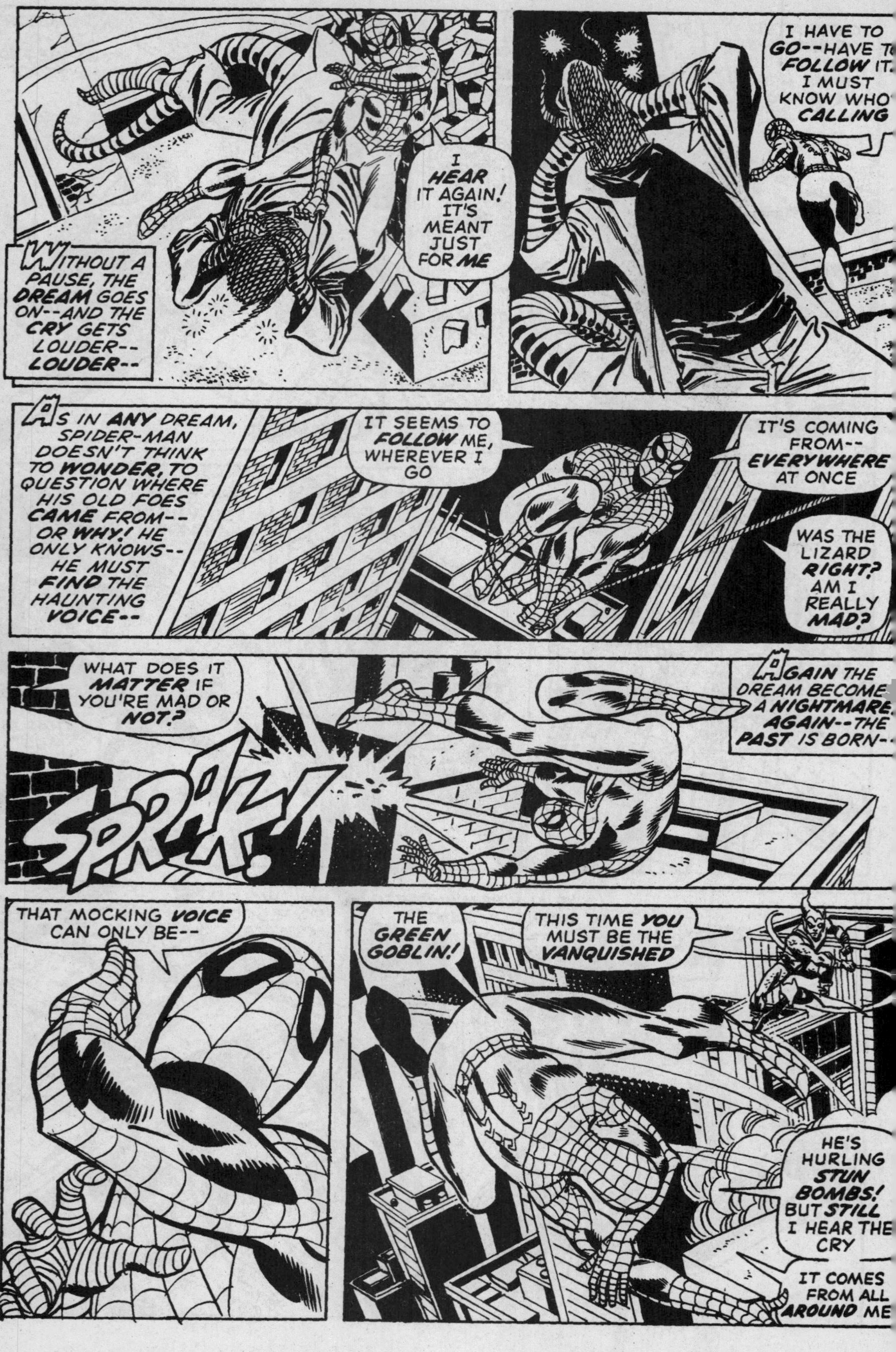
WITHOUT A PAUSE, THE DREAM GOES ON--AND THE CRY GETS LOUDER--LOUDER--
I HEAR IT AGAIN! IT'S MEANT JUST FOR ME
I HAVE TO GO--HAVE TO FOLLOW IT. I MUST KNOW WHO CALLING
AS IN ANY DREAM, SPIDER-MAN DOESN'T THINK TO WONDER, TO QUESTION WHERE HIS OLD FOES CAME FROM--OR WHY! HE ONLY KNOWS--HE MUST FIND THE HAUNTING VOICE--
IT SEEMS TO FOLLOW ME, WHEREVER I GO
IT'S COMING FROM--EVERYWHERE AT ONCE
WAS THE LIZARD RIGHT? AM I REALLY MAD?
WHAT DOES IT MATTER IF YOU'RE MAD OR NOT?
AGAIN THE DREAM BECOME A NIGHTMARE AGAIN--THE PAST IS BORN--
SPRAK!
THAT MOCKING VOICE CAN ONLY BE--
THE GREEN GOBLIN!
THIS TIME YOU MUST BE THE VANQUISHED
HE'S HURLING STUN BOMBS! BUT STILL I HEAR THE CRY
IT COMES FROM ALL AROUND ME

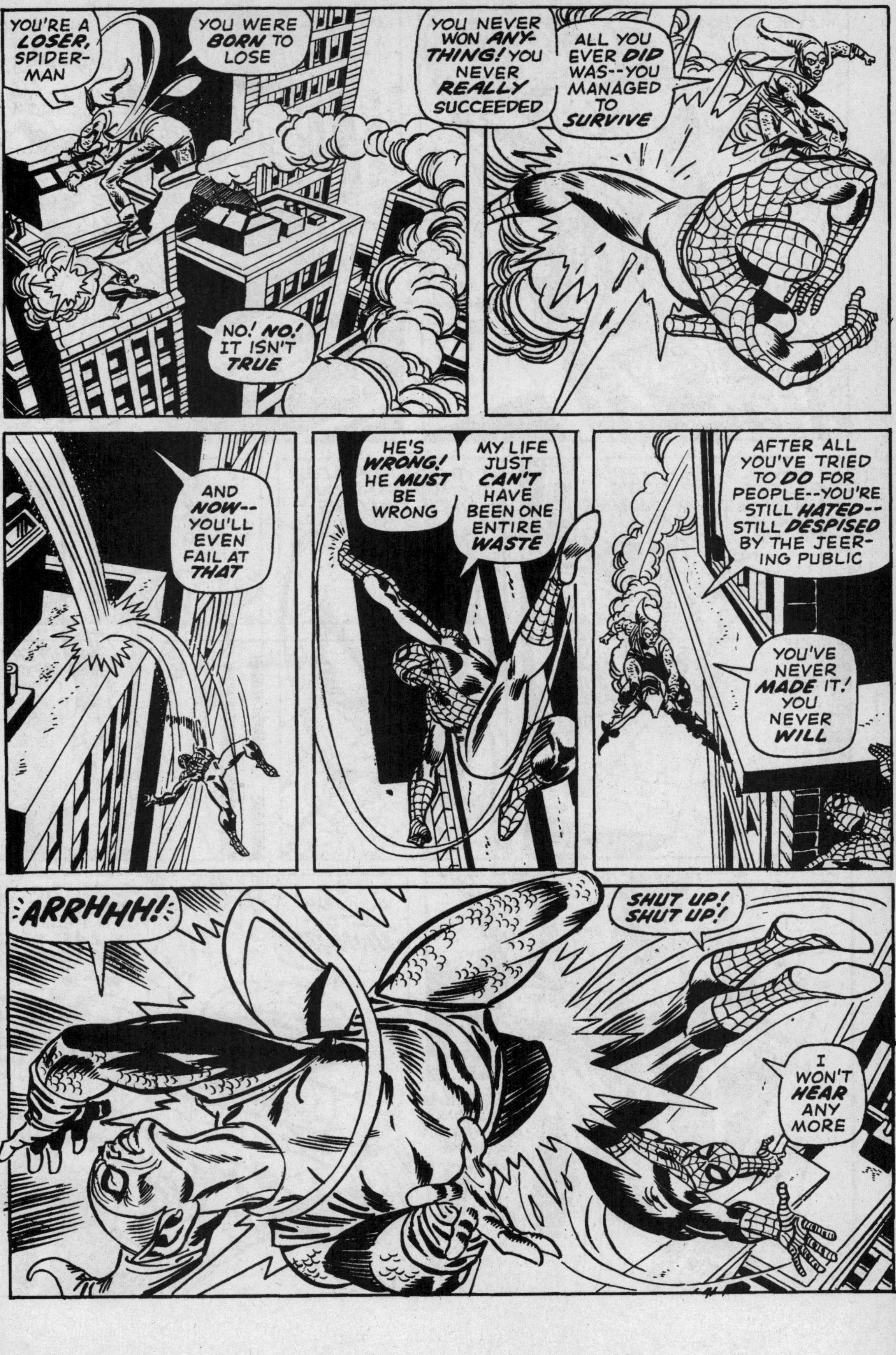
YOU'RE A LOSER, SPIDER-MAN
YOU WERE BORN TO LOSE
NO! NO! IT ISN'T TRUE
YOU NEVER WON ANYTHING! YOU NEVER REALLY SUCCEEDED
ALL YOU EVER DID WAS--YOU MANAGED TO SURVIVE
AND NOW--YOU'LL EVEN FAIL AT THAT
HE'S WRONG! HE MUST BE WRONG
MY LIFE JUST CAN'T HAVE BEEN ONE ENTIRE WASTE
AFTER ALL YOU'VE TRIED TO DO FOR PEOPLE--YOU'RE STILL HATED--STILL DESPISED BY THE JEERING PUBLIC
YOU'VE NEVER MADE IT! YOU NEVER WILL
ARRHHH!
SHUT UP! SHUT UP!
I WON'T HEAR ANY MORE

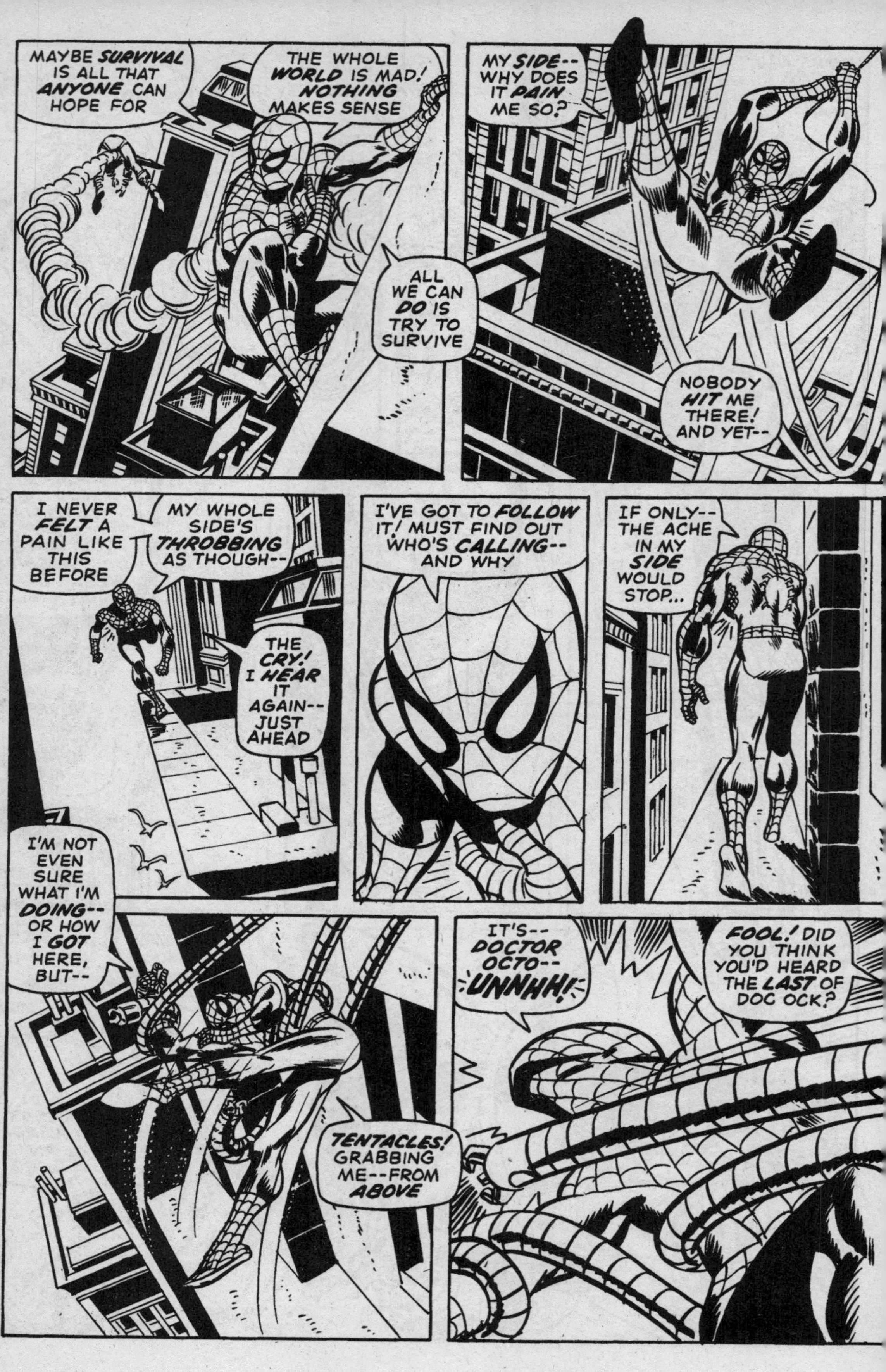
MAYBE SURVIVAL IS ALL THAT ANYONE CAN HOPE FOR
THE WHOLE WORLD IS MAD! NOTHING MAKES SENSE
ALL WE CAN DO IS TRY TO SURVIVE
MY SIDE-- WHY DOES IT PAIN ME SO?
NOBODY HIT ME THERE! AND YET--
I NEVER FELT A PAIN LIKE THIS BEFORE
MY WHOLE SIDE'S THROBBING AS THOUGH--
THE CRY! I HEAR IT AGAIN-- JUST AHEAD
I'VE GOT TO FOLLOW IT! MUST FIND OUT WHO'S CALLING-- AND WHY
IF ONLY-- THE ACHE IN MY SIDE WOULD STOP...
I'M NOT EVEN SURE WHAT I'M DOING-- OR HOW I GOT HERE, BUT--
TENTACLES! GRABBING ME--FROM ABOVE
IT'S-- DOCTOR OCTO-- UNNHH!
FOOL! DID YOU THINK YOU'D HEARD THE LAST OF DOC OCK?

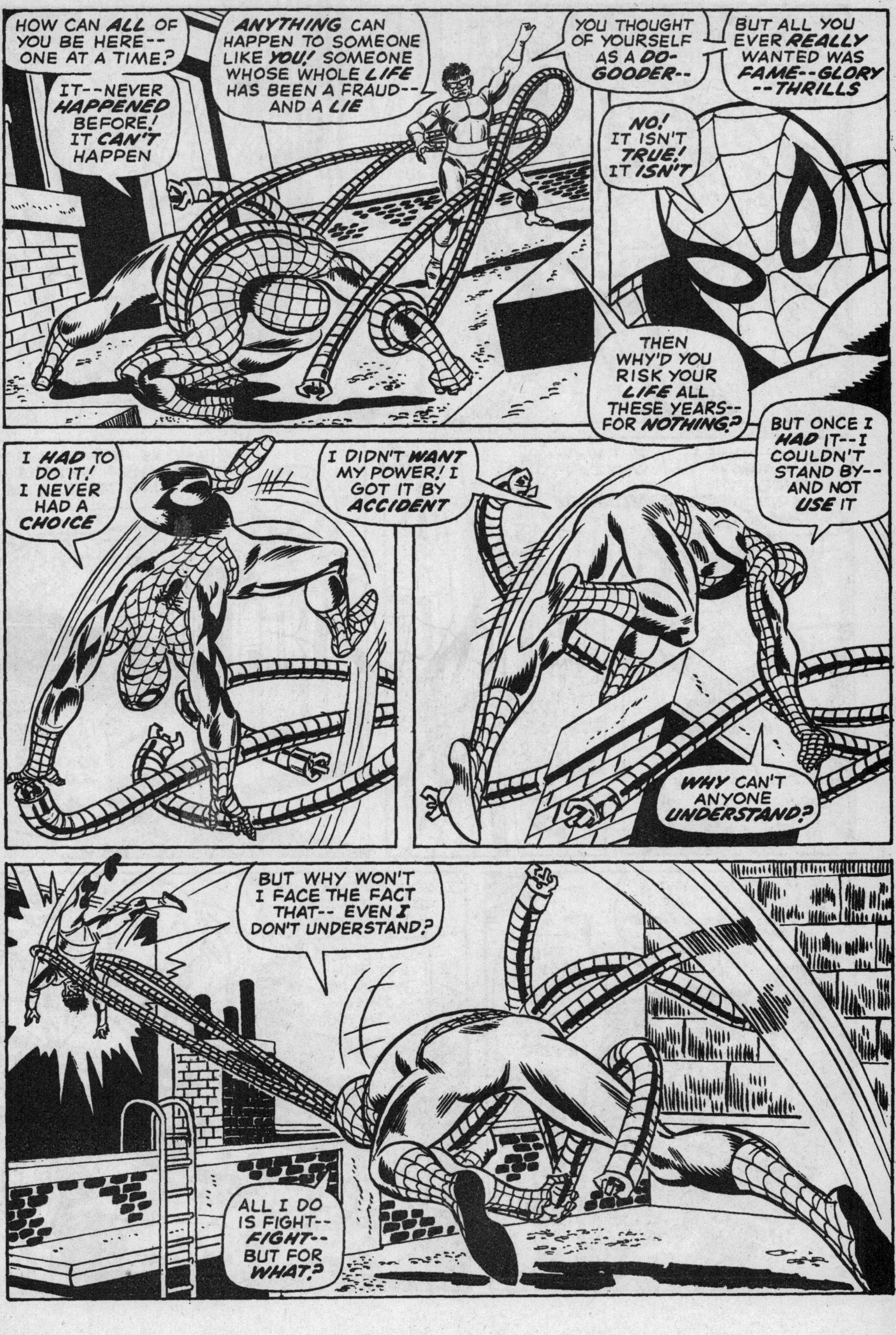
HOW CAN ALL OF YOU BE HERE-- ONE AT A TIME?
ANYTHING CAN HAPPEN TO SOMEONE LIKE YOU! SOMEONE WHOSE WHOLE LIFE HAS BEEN A FRAUD-- AND A LIE
IT--NEVER HAPPENED BEFORE! IT CAN'T HAPPEN
YOU THOUGHT OF YOURSELF AS A DO-GOODER--
BUT ALL YOU EVER REALLY WANTED WAS FAME--GLORY --THRILLS
NO! IT ISN'T TRUE! IT ISN'T
THEN WHY'D YOU RISK YOUR LIFE ALL THESE YEARS-- FOR NOTHING?
I HAD TO DO IT! I NEVER HAD A CHOICE
I DIDN'T WANT MY POWER! I GOT IT BY ACCIDENT
BUT ONCE I HAD IT--I COULDN'T STAND BY-- AND NOT USE IT
WHY CAN'T ANYONE UNDERSTAND?
BUT WHY WON'T I FACE THE FACT THAT-- EVEN I DON'T UNDERSTAND?
ALL I DO IS FIGHT-- FIGHT-- BUT FOR WHAT?

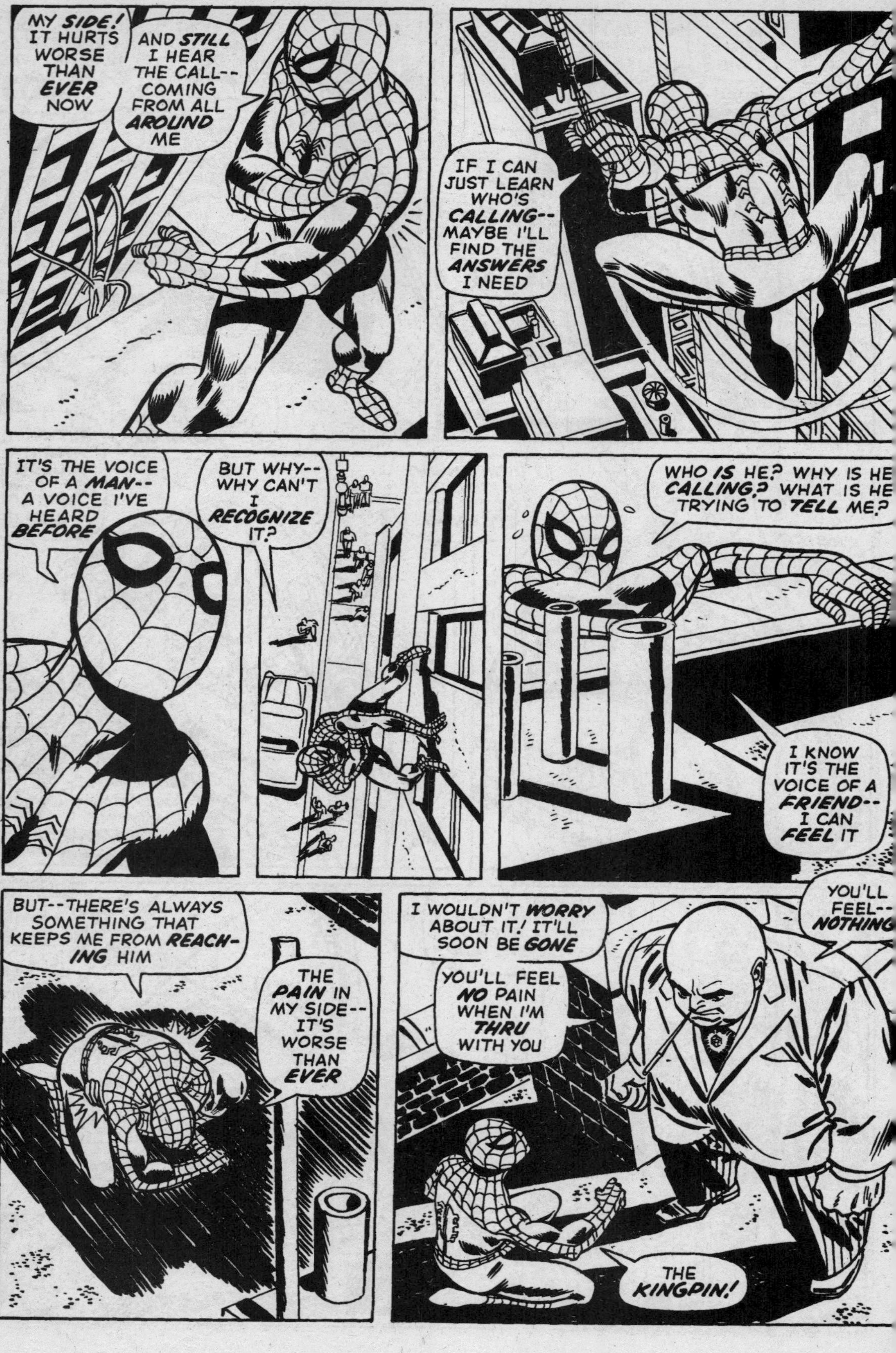

MY SIDE! IT HURTS WORSE THAN EVER NOW
AND STILL I HEAR THE CALL-- COMING FROM ALL AROUND ME
IF I CAN JUST LEARN WHO'S CALLING-- MAYBE I'LL FIND THE ANSWERS I NEED
IT'S THE VOICE OF A MAN-- A VOICE I'VE HEARD BEFORE
BUT WHY-- WHY CAN'T I RECOGNIZE IT?
WHO IS HE? WHY IS HE CALLING? WHAT IS HE TRYING TO TELL ME?
I KNOW IT'S THE VOICE OF A FRIEND-- I CAN FEEL IT
BUT--THERE'S ALWAYS SOMETHING THAT KEEPS ME FROM REACHING HIM
THE PAIN IN MY SIDE-- IT'S WORSE THAN EVER
I WOULDN'T WORRY ABOUT IT! IT'LL SOON BE GONE
YOU'LL FEEL NO PAIN WHEN I'M THRU WITH YOU
YOU'LL FEEL-- NOTHING
THE KINGPIN!

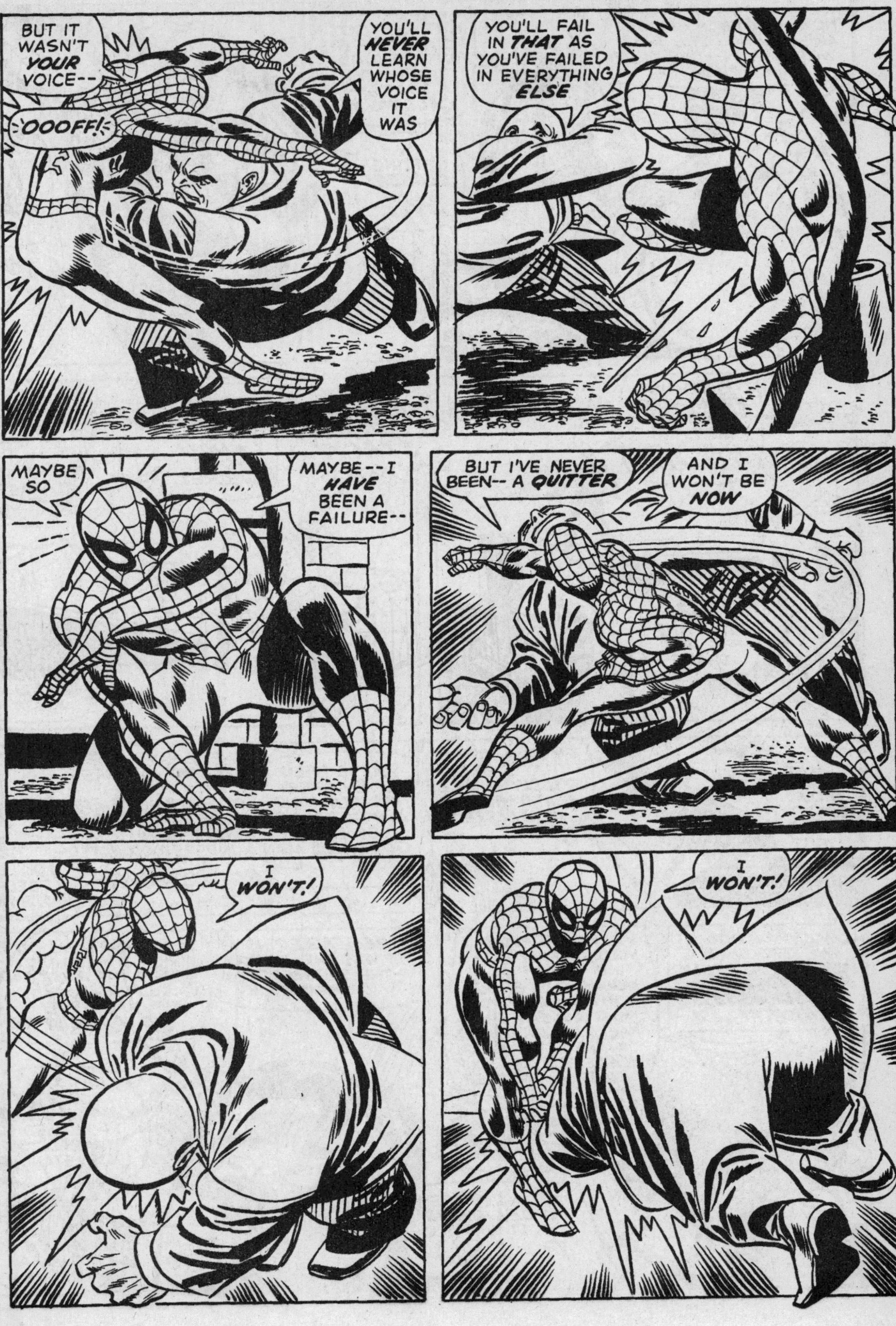
BUT IT WASN'T YOUR VOICE--
OOOFF!
YOU'LL NEVER LEARN WHOSE VOICE IT WAS
YOU'LL FAIL IN THAT AS YOU'VE FAILED IN EVERYTHING ELSE
MAYBE SO
MAYBE--I HAVE BEEN A FAILURE--
BUT I'VE NEVER BEEN-- A QUITTER
AND I WON'T BE NOW
I WON'T!
I WON'T!

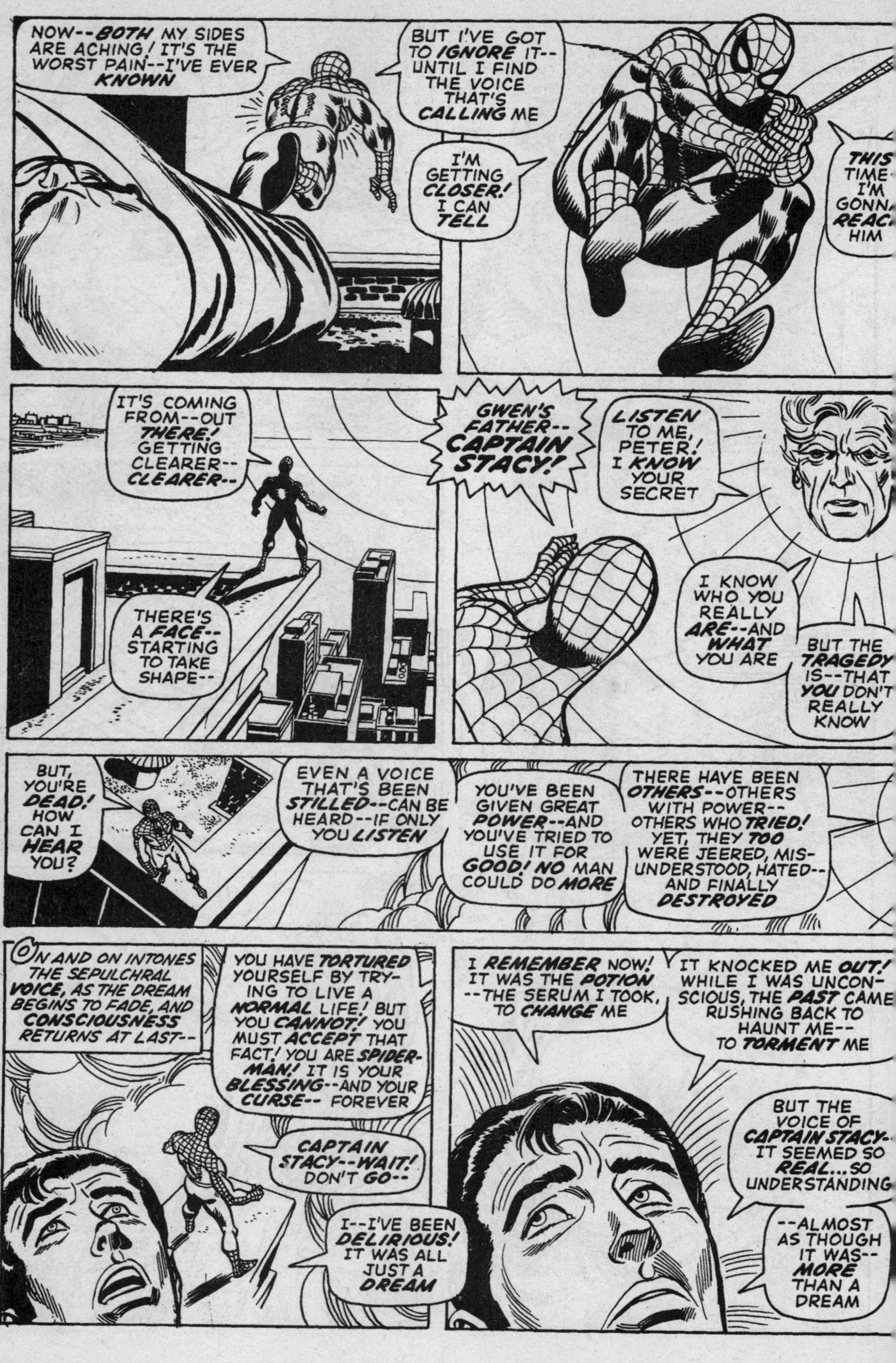
NOW--BOTH MY SIDES ARE ACHING! IT'S THE WORST PAIN--I'VE EVER KNOWN
BUT I'VE GOT TO IGNORE IT--UNTIL I FIND THE VOICE THAT'S CALLING ME
I'M GETTING CLOSER! I CAN TELL
THIS TIME I'M GONN REAC HIM
IT'S COMING FROM--OUT THERE! GETTING CLEARER--CLEARER--
THERE'S A FACE--STARTING TO TAKE SHAPE--
GWEN'S FATHER--CAPTAIN STACY!
LISTEN TO ME, PETER! I KNOW YOUR SECRET
I KNOW WHO YOU REALLY ARE--AND WHAT YOU ARE
BUT THE TRAGEDY IS--THAT YOU DON'T REALLY KNOW
BUT, YOU'RE DEAD! HOW CAN I HEAR YOU?
EVEN A VOICE THAT'S BEEN STILLED--CAN BE HEARD--IF ONLY YOU LISTEN
YOU'VE BEEN GIVEN GREAT POWER--AND YOU'VE TRIED TO USE IT FOR GOOD! NO MAN COULD DO MORE
THERE HAVE BEEN OTHERS--OTHERS WITH POWER--OTHERS WHO TRIED! YET, THEY TOO WERE JEERED, MISUNDERSTOOD, HATED--AND FINALLY DESTROYED
ON AND ON INTONES THE SEPULCHRAL VOICE, AS THE DREAM BEGINS TO FADE, AND CONSCIOUSNESS RETURNS AT LAST--
YOU HAVE TORTURED YOURSELF BY TRYING TO LIVE A NORMAL LIFE! BUT YOU CANNOT! YOU MUST ACCEPT THAT FACT! YOU ARE SPIDER-MAN! IT IS YOUR BLESSING--AND YOUR CURSE-- FOREVER
CAPTAIN STACY--WAIT! DON'T GO--
I--I'VE BEEN DELIRIOUS! IT WAS ALL JUST A DREAM
I REMEMBER NOW! IT WAS THE POTION--THE SERUM I TOOK, TO CHANGE ME
IT KNOCKED ME OUT! WHILE I WAS UNCONSCIOUS, THE PAST CAME RUSHING BACK TO HAUNT ME--TO TORMENT ME
BUT THE VOICE OF CAPTAIN STACY--IT SEEMED SO REAL...SO UNDERSTANDING
--ALMOST AS THOUGH IT WAS--MORE THAN A DREAM

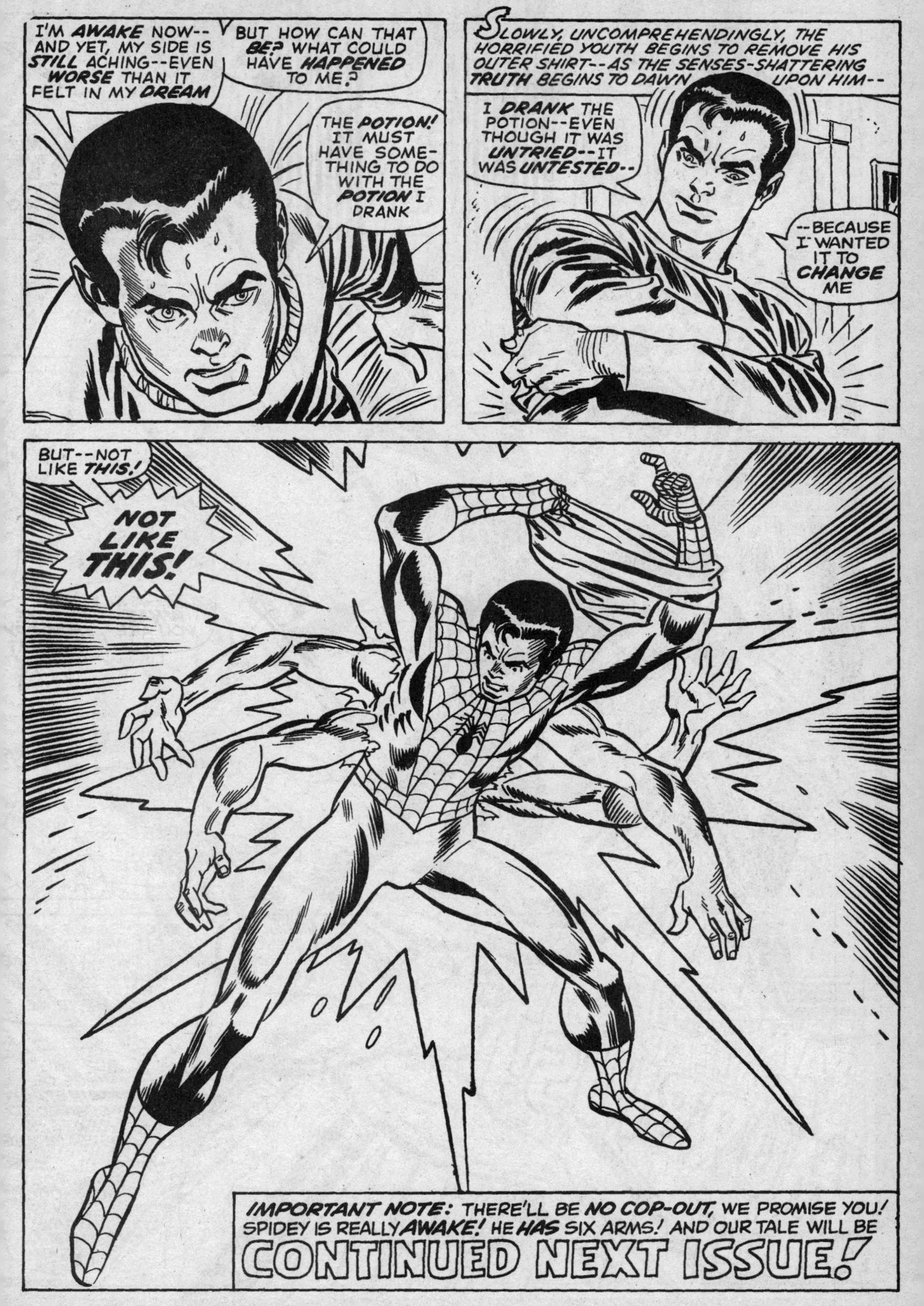
I'M AWAKE NOW--AND YET, MY SIDE IS STILL ACHING--EVEN WORSE THAN IT FELT IN MY DREAM
BUT HOW CAN THAT BE? WHAT COULD HAVE HAPPENED TO ME?
THE POTION! IT MUST HAVE SOMETHING TO DO WITH THE POTION I DRANK
SLOWLY, UNCOMPREHENDINGLY, THE HORRIFIED YOUTH BEGINS TO REMOVE HIS OUTER SHIRT--AS THE SENSES-SHATTERING TRUTH BEGINS TO DAWN UPON HIM--
I DRANK THE POTION--EVEN THOUGH IT WAS UNTRIED--IT WAS UNTESTED--
--BECAUSE I WANTED IT TO CHANGE ME
BUT--NOT LIKE THIS!
NOT LIKE THIS!
IMPORTANT NOTE: THERE'LL BE NO COP-OUT, WE PROMISE YOU! SPIDEY IS REALLY AWAKE! HE HAS SIX ARMS! AND OUR TALE WILL BE
CONTINUED NEXT ISSUE!

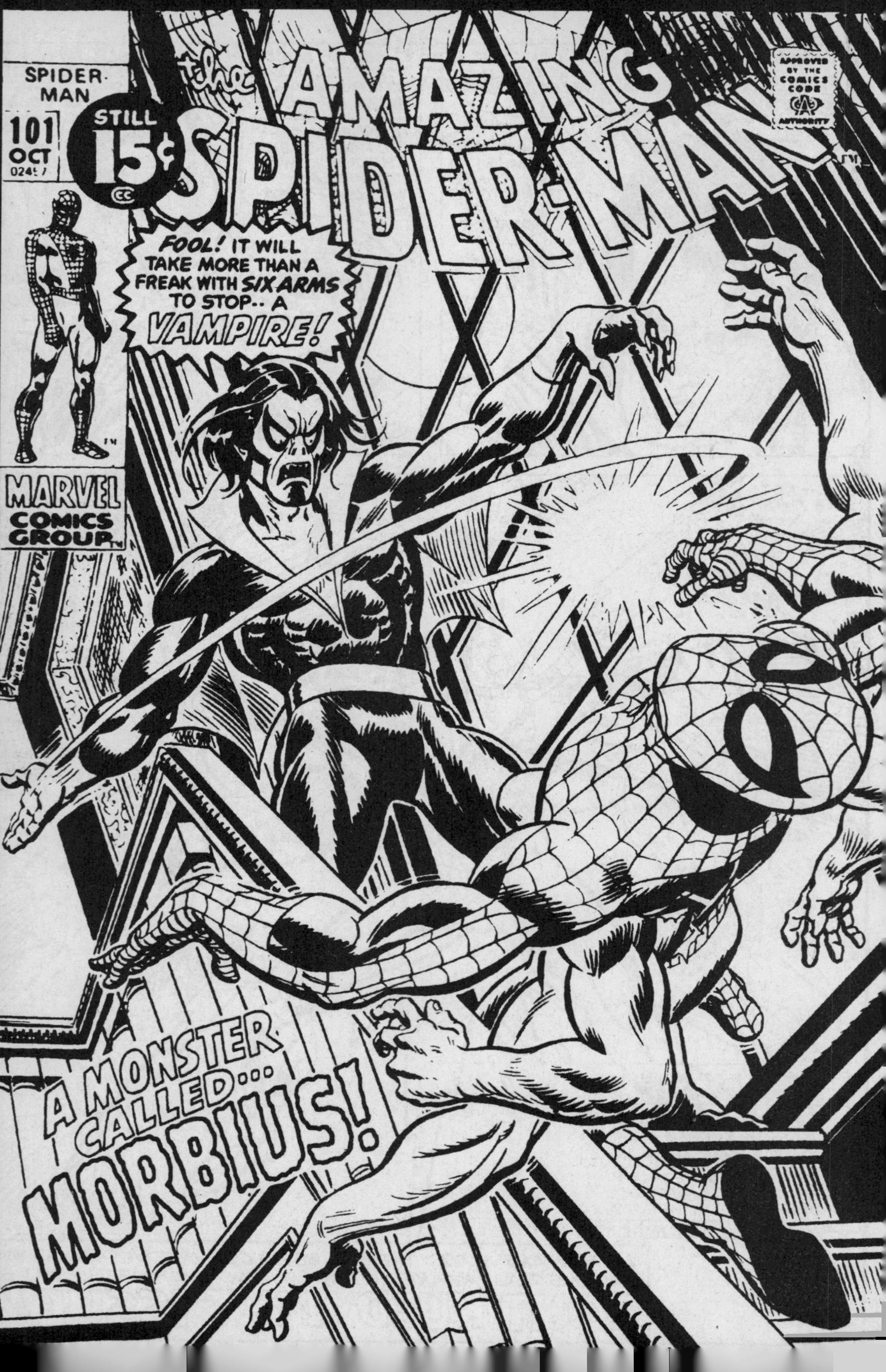
SPIDER-MAN
101
OCT
STILL 15¢
the AMAZING SPIDER-MAN
APPROVED BY THE COMICS CODE AUTHORITY
FOOL! IT WILL TAKE MORE THAN A FREAK WITH SIX ARMS TO STOP-- A VAMPIRE!
MARVEL COMICS GROUP
A MONSTER CALLED... MORBIUS!

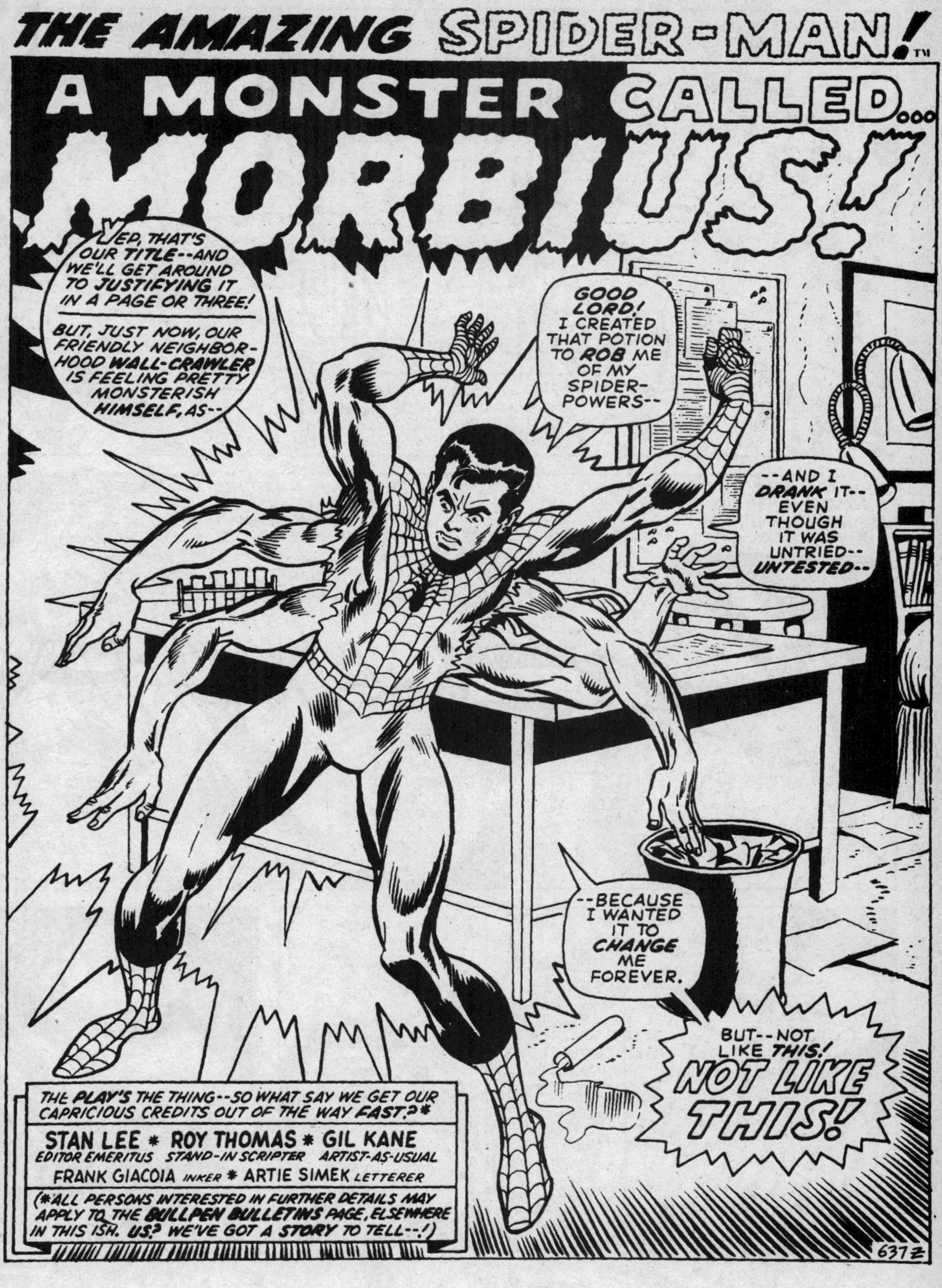
THE AMAZING SPIDER-MAN!™
A MONSTER CALLED... MORBIUS!
YEP, THAT'S OUR TITLE--AND WE'LL GET AROUND TO JUSTIFYING IT IN A PAGE OR THREE!
BUT, JUST NOW, OUR FRIENDLY NEIGHBOR-HOOD WALL-CRAWLER IS FEELING PRETTY MONSTERISH HIMSELF, AS--
GOOD LORD! I CREATED THAT POTION TO ROB ME OF MY SPIDER-POWERS--
--AND I DRANK IT--EVEN THOUGH IT WAS UNTRIED--UNTESTED--
--BECAUSE I WANTED IT TO CHANGE ME FOREVER.
BUT--NOT LIKE THIS! NOT LIKE THIS!
THE PLAY'S THE THING--SO WHAT SAY WE GET OUR CAPRICIOUS CREDITS OUT OF THE WAY FAST?*
STAN LEE * ROY THOMAS * GIL KANE
EDITOR EMERITUS STAND-IN SCRIPTER ARTIST-AS-USUAL
FRANK GIACOIA INKER * ARTIE SIMEK LETTERER
(*ALL PERSONS INTERESTED IN FURTHER DETAILS MAY APPLY TO THE BULLPEN BULLETINS PAGE, ELSEWHERE IN THIS ISH. US? WE'VE GOT A STORY TO TELL--!)
637Z

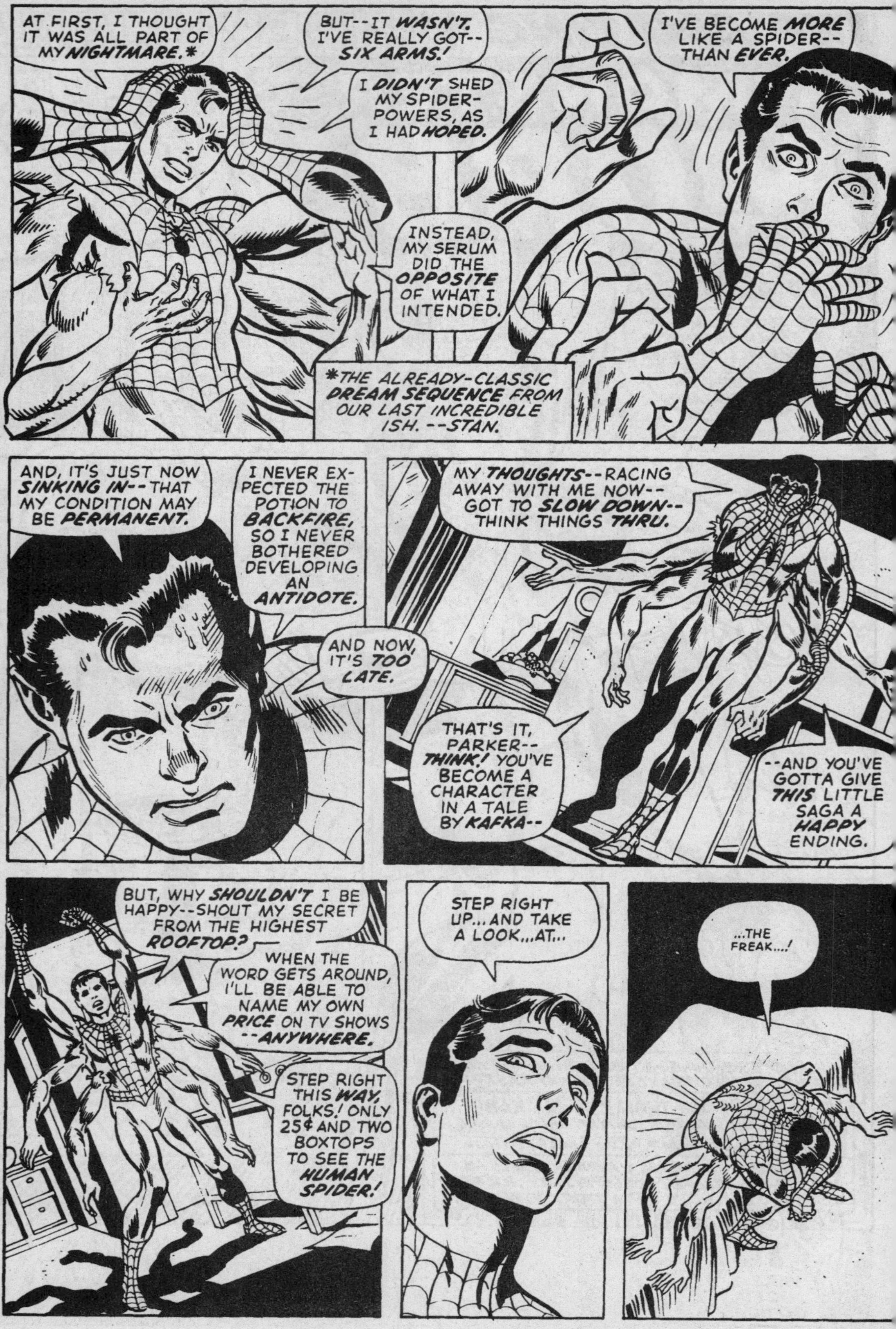
AT FIRST, I THOUGHT IT WAS ALL PART OF MY NIGHTMARE.*
BUT--IT WASN'T. I'VE REALLY GOT--SIX ARMS!
I DIDN'T SHED MY SPIDER-POWERS, AS I HAD HOPED.
INSTEAD, MY SERUM DID THE OPPOSITE OF WHAT I INTENDED.
I'VE BECOME MORE LIKE A SPIDER--THAN EVER.
*THE ALREADY-CLASSIC DREAM SEQUENCE FROM OUR LAST INCREDIBLE ISH. --STAN.
AND, IT'S JUST NOW SINKING IN--THAT MY CONDITION MAY BE PERMANENT.
I NEVER EXPECTED THE POTION TO BACKFIRE, SO I NEVER BOTHERED DEVELOPING AN ANTIDOTE.
AND NOW, IT'S TOO LATE.
MY THOUGHTS--RACING AWAY WITH ME NOW--GOT TO SLOW DOWN--THINK THINGS THRU.
THAT'S IT, PARKER--THINK! YOU'VE BECOME A CHARACTER IN A TALE BY KAFKA--
--AND YOU'VE GOTTA GIVE THIS LITTLE SAGA A HAPPY ENDING.
BUT, WHY SHOULDN'T I BE HAPPY--SHOUT MY SECRET FROM THE HIGHEST ROOFTOP?
WHEN THE WORD GETS AROUND, I'LL BE ABLE TO NAME MY OWN PRICE ON TV SHOWS --ANYWHERE.
STEP RIGHT THIS WAY, FOLKS! ONLY 25¢ AND TWO BOXTOPS TO SEE THE HUMAN SPIDER!
STEP RIGHT UP...AND TAKE A LOOK...AT...
...THE FREAK...!

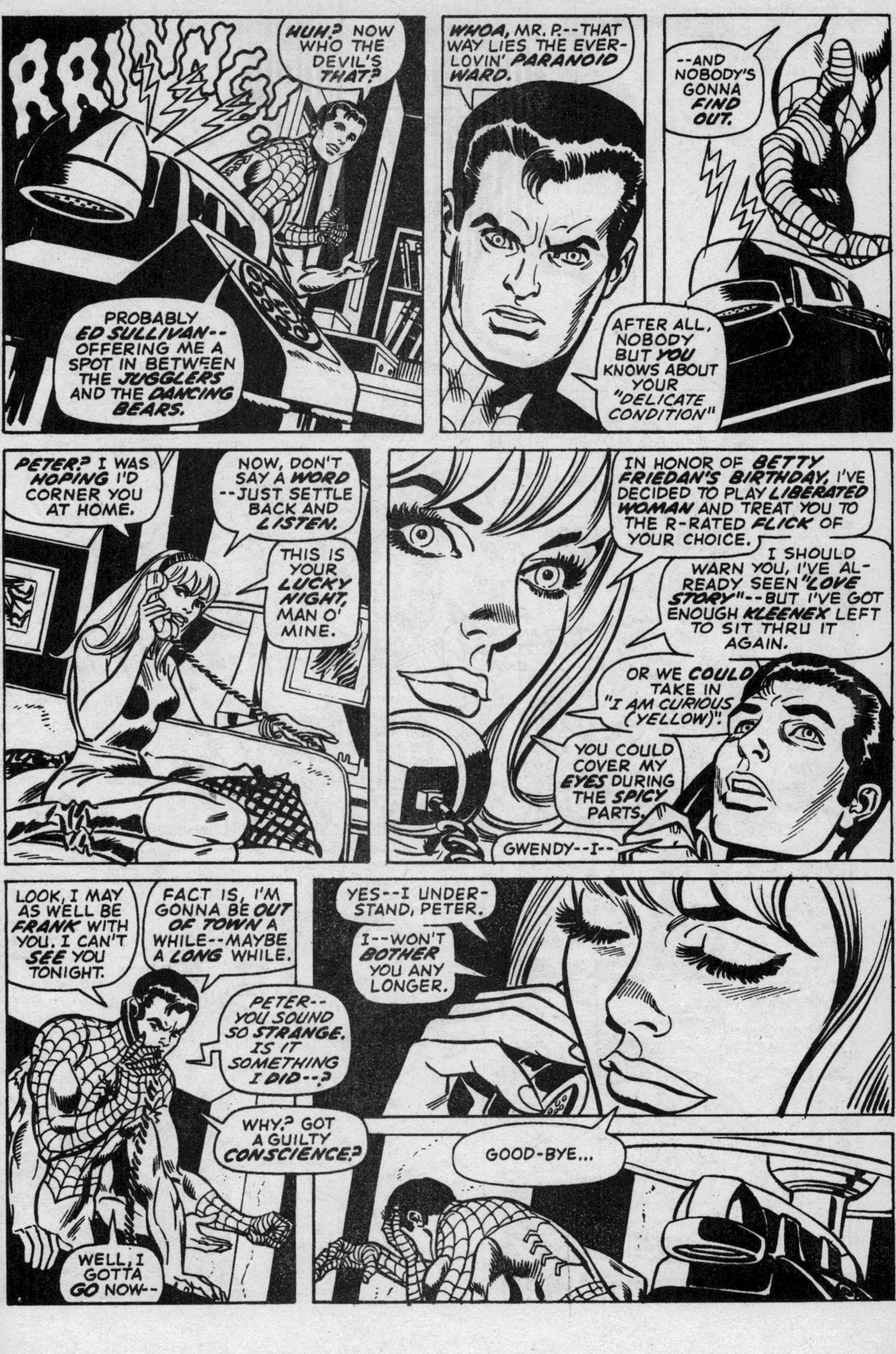
HUH? NOW WHO THE DEVIL'S THAT?
PROBABLY ED SULLIVAN--OFFERING ME A SPOT IN BETWEEN THE JUGGLERS AND THE DANCING BEARS.
WHOA, MR. P.--THAT WAY LIES THE EVER-LOVIN' PARANOID WARD.
AFTER ALL, NOBODY BUT YOU KNOWS ABOUT YOUR "DELICATE CONDITION"
--AND NOBODY'S GONNA FIND OUT.
PETER? I WAS HOPING I'D CORNER YOU AT HOME.
NOW, DON'T SAY A WORD --JUST SETTLE BACK AND LISTEN.
THIS IS YOUR LUCKY NIGHT, MAN O' MINE.
IN HONOR OF BETTY FRIEDAN'S BIRTHDAY, I'VE DECIDED TO PLAY LIBERATED WOMAN AND TREAT YOU TO THE R-RATED FLICK OF YOUR CHOICE.
I SHOULD WARN YOU, I'VE AL-READY SEEN "LOVE STORY"--BUT I'VE GOT ENOUGH KLEENEX LEFT TO SIT THRU IT AGAIN.
OR WE COULD TAKE IN "I AM CURIOUS (YELLOW)".
YOU COULD COVER MY EYES DURING THE SPICY PARTS.
GWENDY--I--
LOOK, I MAY AS WELL BE FRANK WITH YOU. I CAN'T SEE YOU TONIGHT.
FACT IS, I'M GONNA BE OUT OF TOWN A WHILE--MAYBE A LONG WHILE.
PETER--YOU SOUND SO STRANGE. IS IT SOMETHING I DID--?
WHY? GOT A GUILTY CONSCIENCE?
WELL, I GOTTA GO NOW--
YES--I UNDER-STAND, PETER.
I--WON'T BOTHER YOU ANY LONGER.
GOOD-BYE...

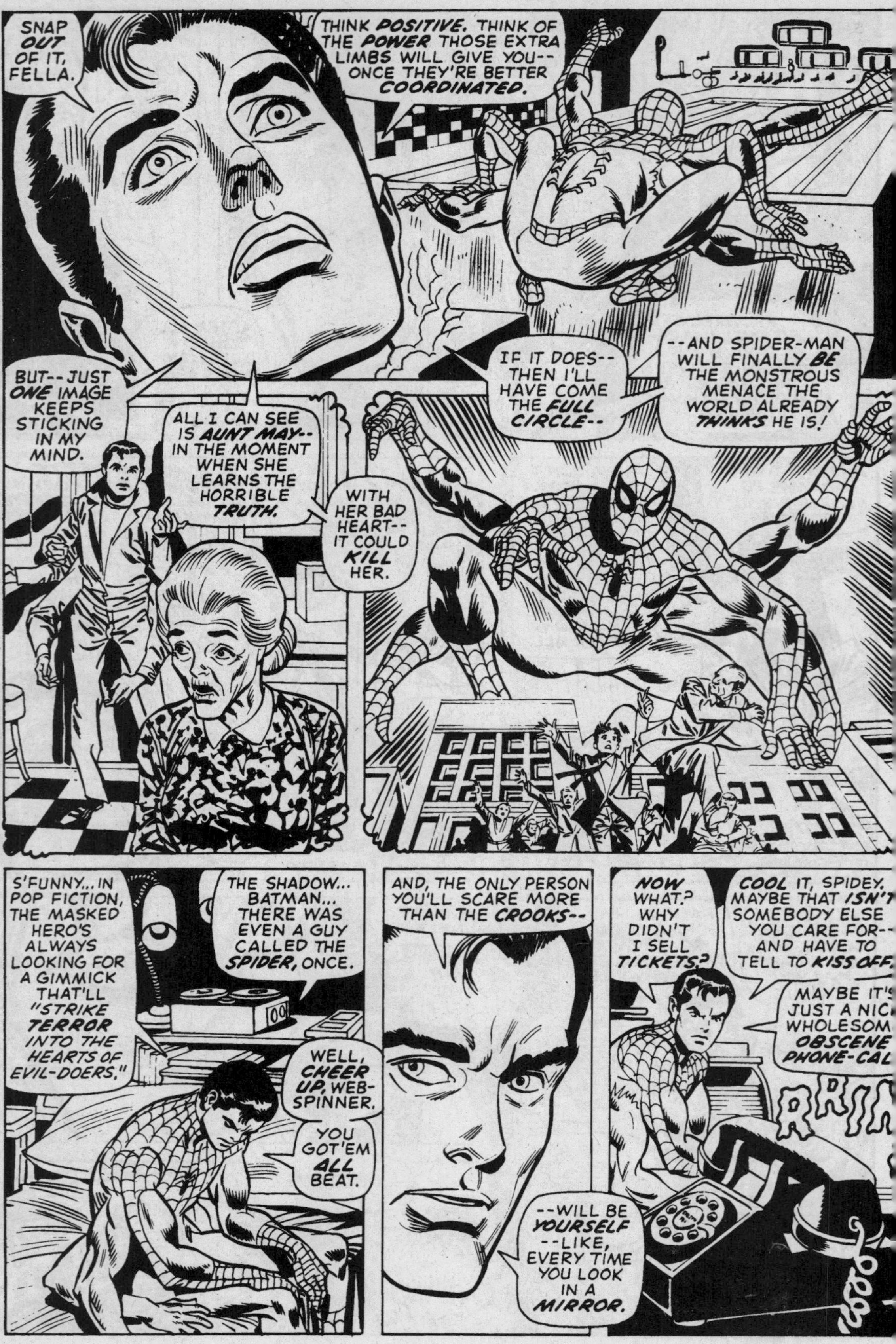
SNAP OUT OF IT, FELLA.
THINK POSITIVE. THINK OF THE POWER THOSE EXTRA LIMBS WILL GIVE YOU-- ONCE THEY'RE BETTER COORDINATED.
BUT-- JUST ONE IMAGE KEEPS STICKING IN MY MIND.
ALL I CAN SEE IS AUNT MAY-- IN THE MOMENT WHEN SHE LEARNS THE HORRIBLE TRUTH.
WITH HER BAD HEART-- IT COULD KILL HER.
IF IT DOES-- THEN I'LL HAVE COME THE FULL CIRCLE--
--AND SPIDER-MAN WILL FINALLY BE THE MONSTROUS MENACE THE WORLD ALREADY THINKS HE IS!
S'FUNNY... IN POP FICTION, THE MASKED HERO'S ALWAYS LOOKING FOR A GIMMICK THAT'LL "STRIKE TERROR INTO THE HEARTS OF EVIL-DOERS."
THE SHADOW... BATMAN... THERE WAS EVEN A GUY CALLED THE SPIDER, ONCE.
WELL, CHEER UP, WEB-SPINNER.
YOU GOT'EM ALL BEAT.
AND, THE ONLY PERSON YOU'LL SCARE MORE THAN THE CROOKS--
--WILL BE YOURSELF --LIKE, EVERY TIME YOU LOOK IN A MIRROR.
NOW WHAT? WHY DIDN'T I SELL TICKETS?
COOL IT, SPIDEY. MAYBE THAT ISN'T SOMEBODY ELSE YOU CARE FOR-- AND HAVE TO TELL TO KISS OFF.
MAYBE IT'S JUST A NIC WHOLESOM OBSCENE PHONE-CAL
RRIN

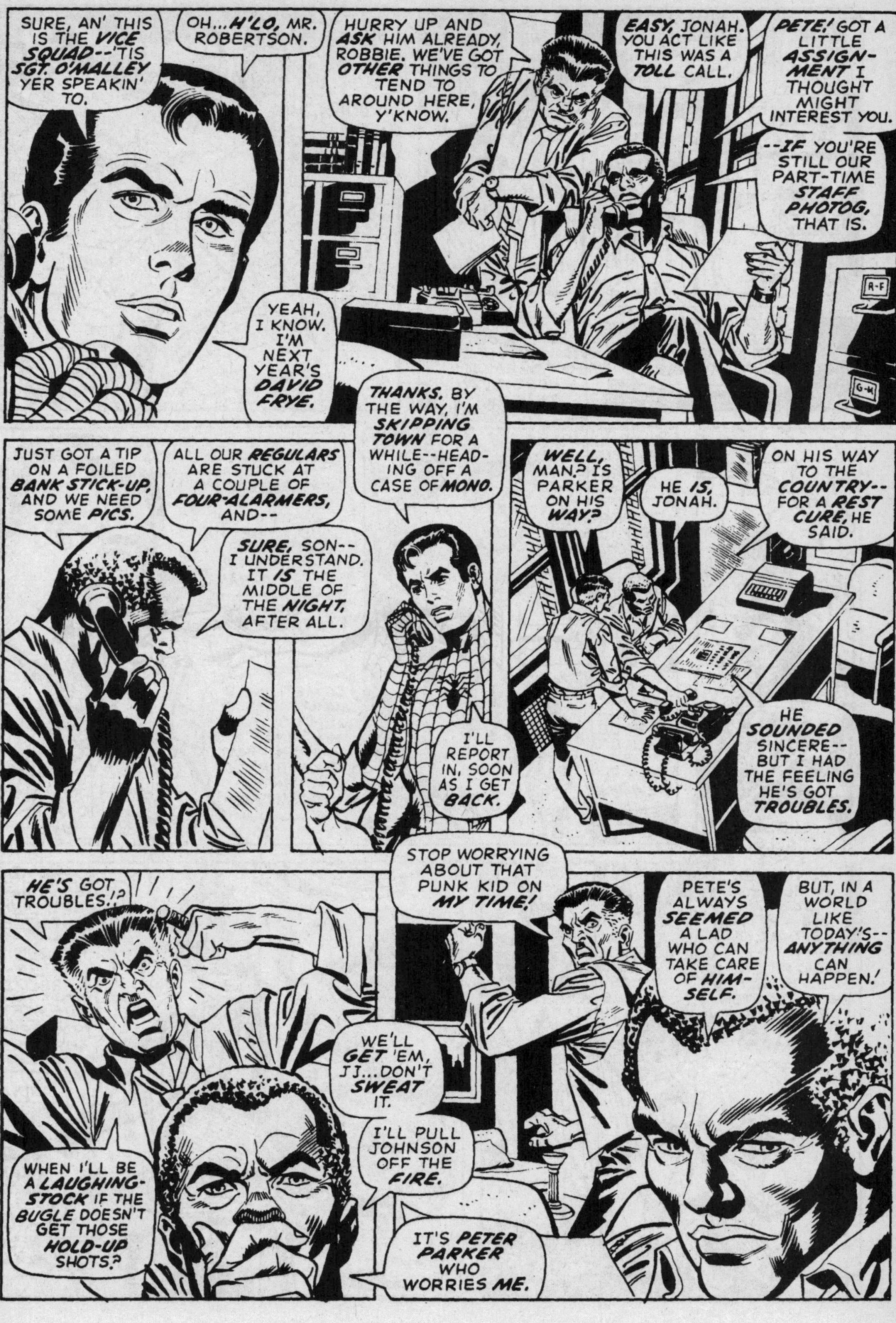
SURE, AN' THIS IS THE VICE SQUAD--'TIS SGT. O'MALLEY YER SPEAKIN' TO.
OH...H'LO, MR. ROBERTSON.
HURRY UP AND ASK HIM ALREADY, ROBBIE. WE'VE GOT OTHER THINGS TO TEND TO AROUND HERE, Y'KNOW.
EASY, JONAH. YOU ACT LIKE THIS WAS A TOLL CALL.
PETE! GOT A LITTLE ASSIGNMENT I THOUGHT MIGHT INTEREST YOU.
--IF YOU'RE STILL OUR PART-TIME STAFF PHOTOG, THAT IS.
YEAH, I KNOW. I'M NEXT YEAR'S DAVID FRYE.
R-F
G-K
JUST GOT A TIP ON A FOILED BANK STICK-UP, AND WE NEED SOME PICS.
ALL OUR REGULARS ARE STUCK AT A COUPLE OF FOUR-ALARMERS, AND--
SURE, SON--I UNDERSTAND. IT IS THE MIDDLE OF THE NIGHT, AFTER ALL.
THANKS. BY THE WAY, I'M SKIPPING TOWN FOR A WHILE--HEADING OFF A CASE OF MONO.
I'LL REPORT IN, SOON AS I GET BACK.
WELL, MAN? IS PARKER ON HIS WAY?
HE IS, JONAH.
ON HIS WAY TO THE COUNTRY--FOR A REST CURE, HE SAID.
HE SOUNDED SINCERE--BUT I HAD THE FEELING HE'S GOT TROUBLES.
HE'S GOT TROUBLES!?
WHEN I'LL BE A LAUGHING-STOCK IF THE BUGLE DOESN'T GET THOSE HOLD-UP SHOTS?
WE'LL GET 'EM, JJ...DON'T SWEAT IT.
I'LL PULL JOHNSON OFF THE FIRE.
STOP WORRYING ABOUT THAT PUNK KID ON MY TIME!
IT'S PETER PARKER WHO WORRIES ME.
PETE'S ALWAYS SEEMED A LAD WHO CAN TAKE CARE OF HIMSELF.
BUT, IN A WORLD LIKE TODAY'S--ANYTHING CAN HAPPEN!

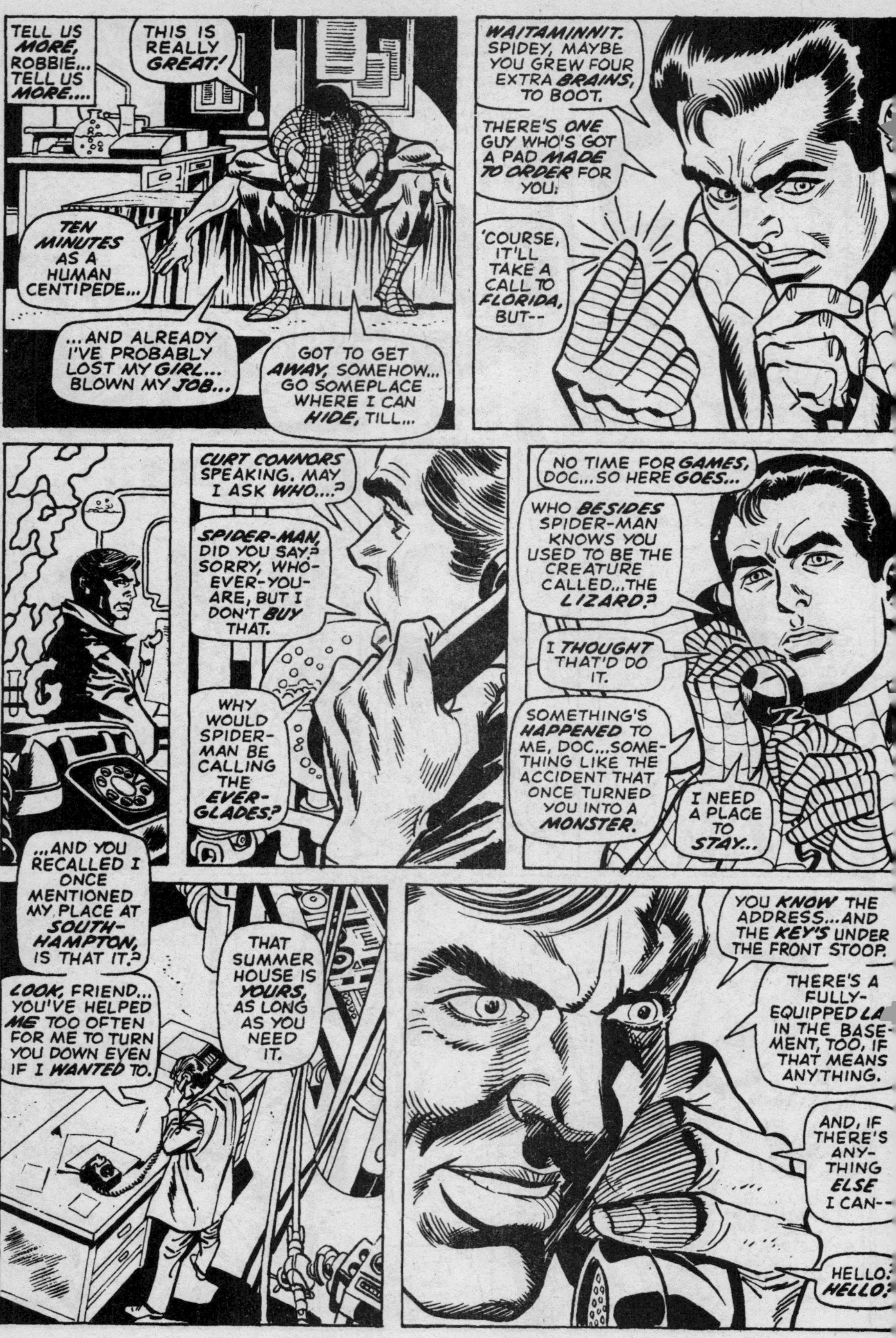
TELL US MORE, ROBBIE... TELL US MORE....
THIS IS REALLY GREAT!
TEN MINUTES AS A HUMAN CENTIPEDE...
...AND ALREADY I'VE PROBABLY LOST MY GIRL... BLOWN MY JOB...
GOT TO GET AWAY, SOMEHOW... GO SOMEPLACE WHERE I CAN HIDE, TILL...
WAITAMINNIT. SPIDEY, MAYBE YOU GREW FOUR EXTRA BRAINS, TO BOOT.
THERE'S ONE GUY WHO'S GOT A PAD MADE TO ORDER FOR YOU.
'COURSE, IT'LL TAKE A CALL TO FLORIDA, BUT--
CURT CONNORS SPEAKING. MAY I ASK WHO....?
SPIDER-MAN, DID YOU SAY? SORRY, WHO-EVER-YOU-ARE, BUT I DON'T BUY THAT.
WHY WOULD SPIDER-MAN BE CALLING THE EVER-GLADES?
NO TIME FOR GAMES, DOC...SO HERE GOES...
WHO BESIDES SPIDER-MAN KNOWS YOU USED TO BE THE CREATURE CALLED...THE LIZARD?
I THOUGHT THAT'D DO IT.
SOMETHING'S HAPPENED TO ME, DOC...SOME-THING LIKE THE ACCIDENT THAT ONCE TURNED YOU INTO A MONSTER.
I NEED A PLACE TO STAY...
...AND YOU RECALLED I ONCE MENTIONED MY PLACE AT SOUTH-HAMPTON, IS THAT IT?
LOOK, FRIEND... YOU'VE HELPED ME TOO OFTEN FOR ME TO TURN YOU DOWN EVEN IF I WANTED TO.
THAT SUMMER HOUSE IS YOURS, AS LONG AS YOU NEED IT.
YOU KNOW THE ADDRESS...AND THE KEY'S UNDER THE FRONT STOOP.
THERE'S A FULLY-EQUIPPED LAB IN THE BASE-MENT, TOO, IF THAT MEANS ANYTHING.
AND, IF THERE'S ANY-THING ELSE I CAN--
HELLO? HELLO?

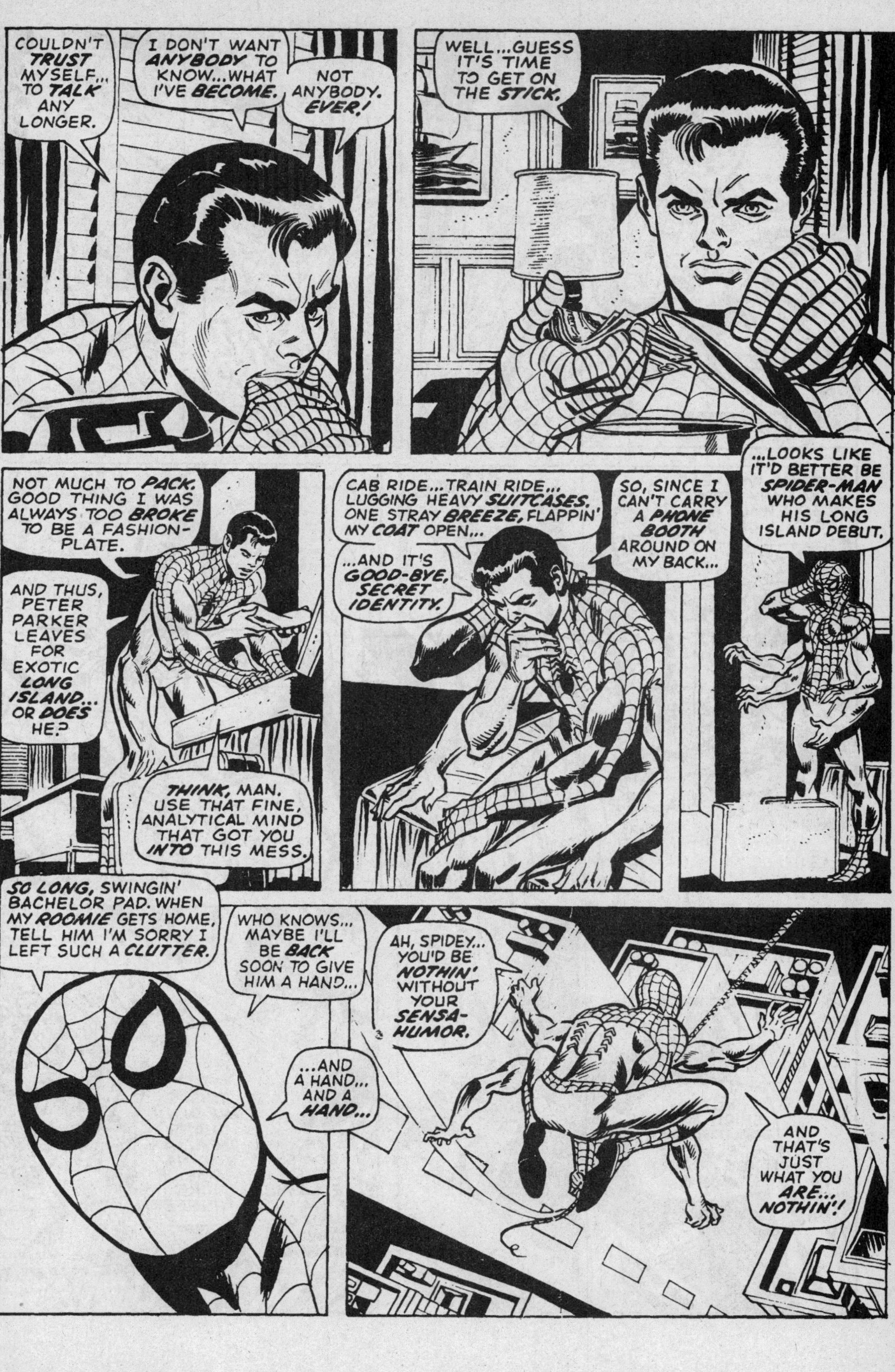
COULDN'T TRUST MYSELF... TO TALK ANY LONGER.
I DON'T WANT ANYBODY TO KNOW... WHAT I'VE BECOME.
NOT ANYBODY. EVER!
WELL... GUESS IT'S TIME TO GET ON THE STICK.
NOT MUCH TO PACK. GOOD THING I WAS ALWAYS TOO BROKE TO BE A FASHION-PLATE.
AND THUS, PETER PARKER LEAVES FOR EXOTIC LONG ISLAND... OR DOES HE?
THINK, MAN. USE THAT FINE, ANALYTICAL MIND THAT GOT YOU INTO THIS MESS.
CAB RIDE... TRAIN RIDE... LUGGING HEAVY SUITCASES. ONE STRAY BREEZE, FLAPPIN' MY COAT OPEN...
...AND IT'S GOOD-BYE, SECRET IDENTITY.
SO, SINCE I CAN'T CARRY A PHONE BOOTH AROUND ON MY BACK...
...LOOKS LIKE IT'D BETTER BE SPIDER-MAN WHO MAKES HIS LONG ISLAND DEBUT.
SO LONG, SWINGIN' BACHELOR PAD. WHEN MY ROOMIE GETS HOME, TELL HIM I'M SORRY I LEFT SUCH A CLUTTER.
WHO KNOWS... MAYBE I'LL BE BACK SOON TO GIVE HIM A HAND...
...AND A HAND... AND A HAND...
AH, SPIDEY... YOU'D BE NOTHIN' WITHOUT YOUR SENSA-HUMOR.
AND THAT'S JUST WHAT YOU ARE... NOTHIN'!

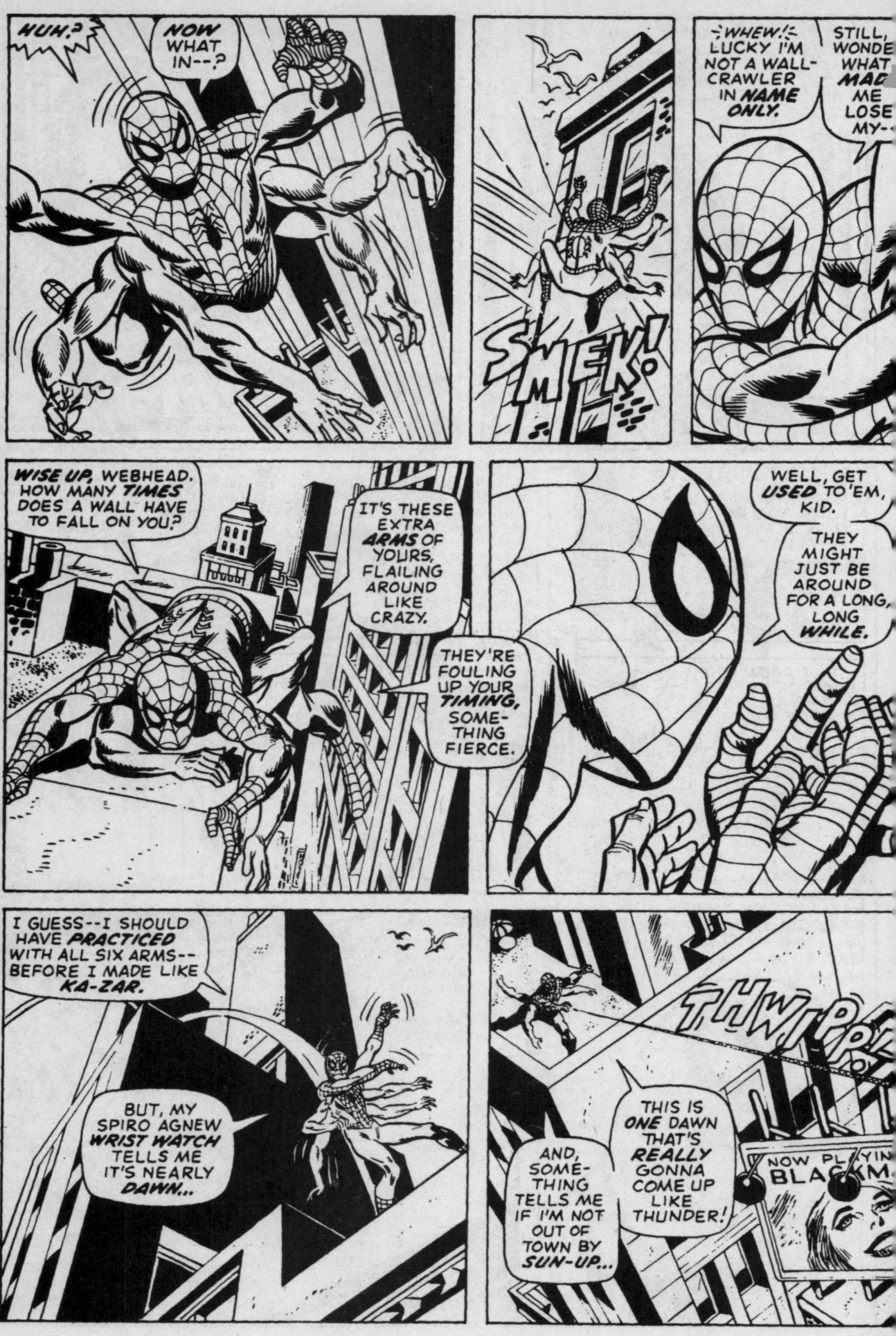
HUH?
NOW WHAT IN--?
SMEK!
WHEW! LUCKY I'M NOT A WALL-CRAWLER IN NAME ONLY.
STILL, WONDE WHAT MAD ME LOSE MY--
WISE UP, WEBHEAD. HOW MANY TIMES DOES A WALL HAVE TO FALL ON YOU?
IT'S THESE EXTRA ARMS OF YOURS, FLAILING AROUND LIKE CRAZY.
THEY'RE FOULING UP YOUR TIMING, SOME-THING FIERCE.
WELL, GET USED TO 'EM, KID.
THEY MIGHT JUST BE AROUND FOR A LONG, LONG WHILE.
I GUESS--I SHOULD HAVE PRACTICED WITH ALL SIX ARMS--BEFORE I MADE LIKE KA-ZAR.
BUT, MY SPIRO AGNEW WRIST WATCH TELLS ME IT'S NEARLY DAWN...
THWIPP
THIS IS ONE DAWN THAT'S REALLY GONNA COME UP LIKE THUNDER!
AND, SOME-THING TELLS ME IF I'M NOT OUT OF TOWN BY SUN-UP...
NOW PLAYIN BLACKM

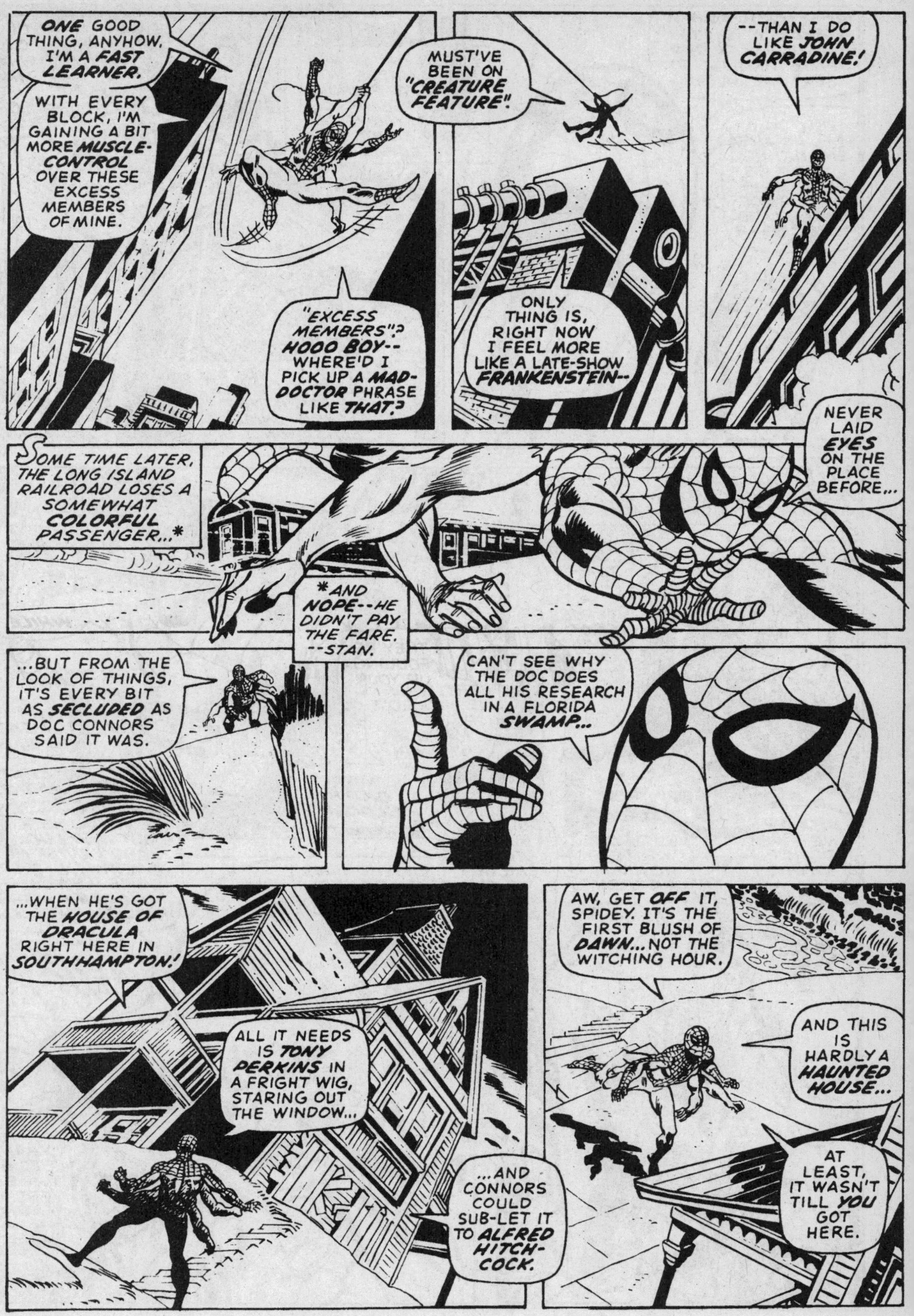
ONE GOOD THING, ANYHOW, I'M A FAST LEARNER.
WITH EVERY BLOCK, I'M GAINING A BIT MORE MUSCLE-CONTROL OVER THESE EXCESS MEMBERS OF MINE.
"EXCESS MEMBERS"? HOOO BOY-- WHERE'D I PICK UP A MAD-DOCTOR PHRASE LIKE THAT?
MUST'VE BEEN ON "CREATURE FEATURE".
ONLY THING IS, RIGHT NOW I FEEL MORE LIKE A LATE-SHOW FRANKENSTEIN--
--THAN I DO LIKE JOHN CARRADINE!
SOME TIME LATER, THE LONG ISLAND RAILROAD LOSES A SOMEWHAT COLORFUL PASSENGER...*
NEVER LAID EYES ON THE PLACE BEFORE...
*AND NOPE--HE DIDN'T PAY THE FARE. --STAN.
...BUT FROM THE LOOK OF THINGS, IT'S EVERY BIT AS SECLUDED AS DOC CONNORS SAID IT WAS.
CAN'T SEE WHY THE DOC DOES ALL HIS RESEARCH IN A FLORIDA SWAMP...
...WHEN HE'S GOT THE HOUSE OF DRACULA RIGHT HERE IN SOUTHHAMPTON!
ALL IT NEEDS IS TONY PERKINS IN A FRIGHT WIG, STARING OUT THE WINDOW...
...AND CONNORS COULD SUB-LET IT TO ALFRED HITCH-COCK.
AW, GET OFF IT, SPIDEY. IT'S THE FIRST BLUSH OF DAWN... NOT THE WITCHING HOUR.
AND THIS IS HARDLY A HAUNTED HOUSE...
AT LEAST, IT WASN'T TILL YOU GOT HERE.

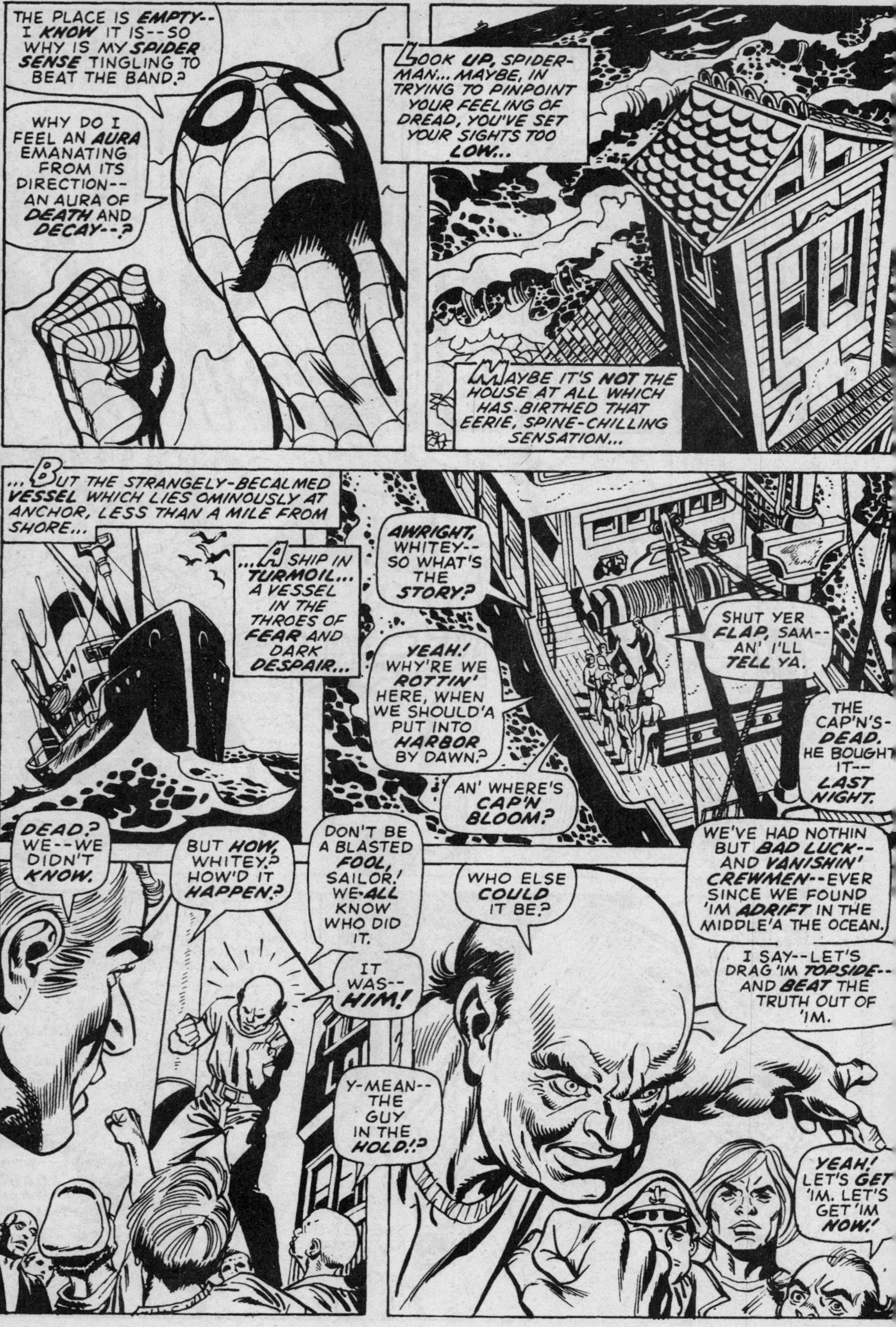
THE PLACE IS EMPTY-- I KNOW IT IS--SO WHY IS MY SPIDER SENSE TINGLING TO BEAT THE BAND?
WHY DO I FEEL AN AURA EMANATING FROM ITS DIRECTION-- AN AURA OF DEATH AND DECAY--?
LOOK UP, SPIDER-MAN... MAYBE, IN TRYING TO PINPOINT YOUR FEELING OF DREAD, YOU'VE SET YOUR SIGHTS TOO LOW...
MAYBE IT'S NOT THE HOUSE AT ALL WHICH HAS BIRTHED THAT EERIE, SPINE-CHILLING SENSATION...
...BUT THE STRANGELY-BECALMED VESSEL WHICH LIES OMINOUSLY AT ANCHOR, LESS THAN A MILE FROM SHORE...
...A SHIP IN TURMOIL... A VESSEL IN THE THROES OF FEAR AND DARK DESPAIR...
AWRIGHT, WHITEY-- SO WHAT'S THE STORY?
YEAH! WHY'RE WE ROTTIN' HERE, WHEN WE SHOULD'A PUT INTO HARBOR BY DAWN?
AN' WHERE'S CAP'N BLOOM?
SHUT YER FLAP, SAM-- AN' I'LL TELL YA.
THE CAP'N'S DEAD. HE BOUGHT IT-- LAST NIGHT.
DEAD? WE--WE DIDN'T KNOW.
BUT HOW, WHITEY? HOW'D IT HAPPEN?
DON'T BE A BLASTED FOOL, SAILOR! WE ALL KNOW WHO DID IT.
IT WAS-- HIM!
Y-MEAN-- THE GUY IN THE HOLD!?
WHO ELSE COULD IT BE?
WE'VE HAD NOTHIN BUT BAD LUCK-- AND VANISHIN' CREWMEN--EVER SINCE WE FOUND 'IM ADRIFT IN THE MIDDLE'A THE OCEAN.
I SAY--LET'S DRAG 'IM TOPSIDE-- AND BEAT THE TRUTH OUT OF 'IM.
YEAH! LET'S GET 'IM. LET'S GET 'IM NOW!

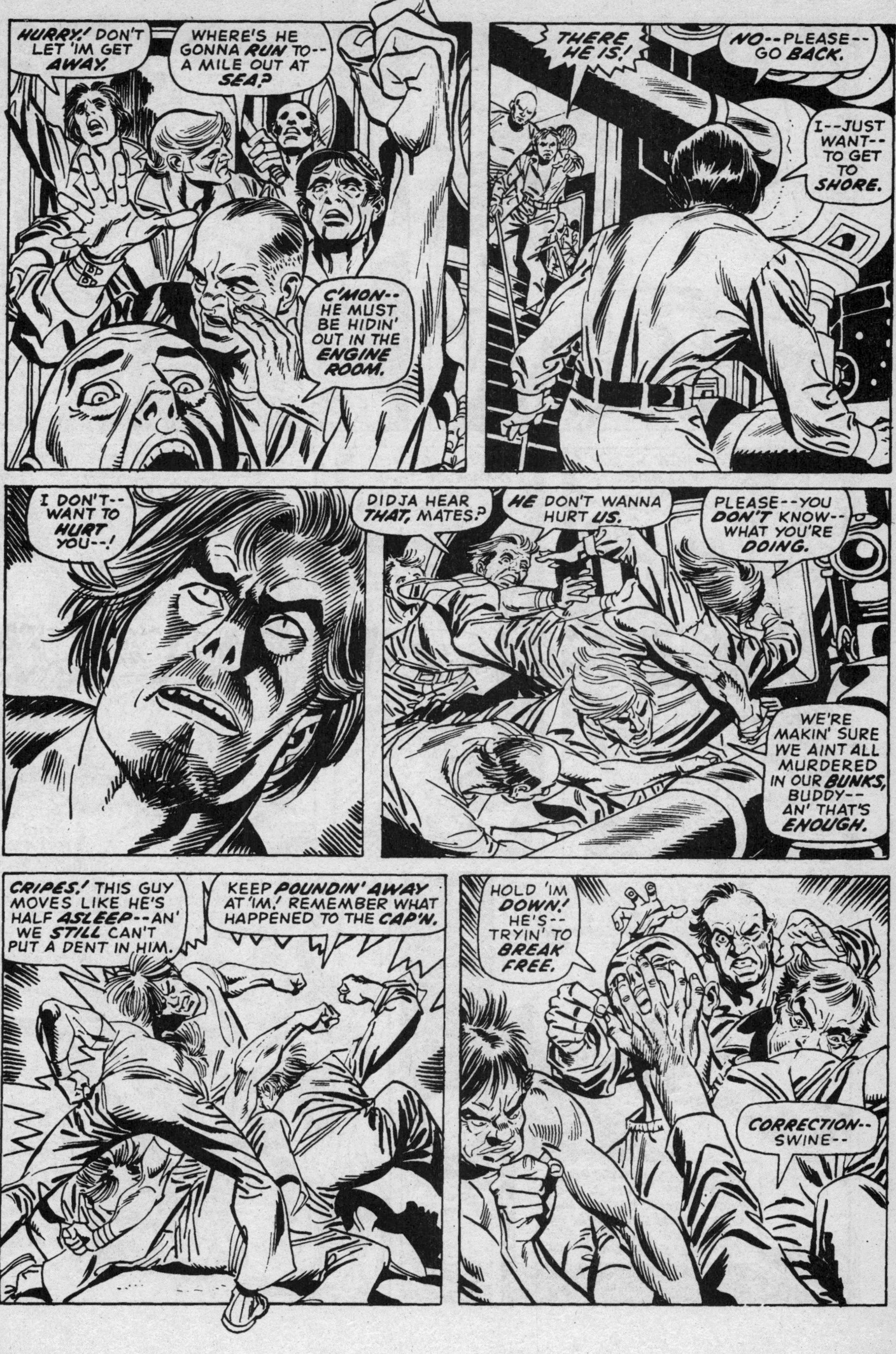
HURRY! DON'T LET 'IM GET AWAY.
WHERE'S HE GONNA RUN TO-- A MILE OUT AT SEA?
C'MON-- HE MUST BE HIDIN' OUT IN THE ENGINE ROOM.
THERE HE IS!
NO--PLEASE-- GO BACK.
I--JUST WANT-- TO GET TO SHORE.
I DON'T-- WANT TO HURT YOU--!
DIDJA HEAR THAT, MATES?
HE DON'T WANNA HURT US.
PLEASE--YOU DON'T KNOW-- WHAT YOU'RE DOING.
WE'RE MAKIN' SURE WE AINT ALL MURDERED IN OUR BUNKS, BUDDY-- AN' THAT'S ENOUGH.
CRIPES! THIS GUY MOVES LIKE HE'S HALF ASLEEP--AN' WE STILL CAN'T PUT A DENT IN HIM.
KEEP POUNDIN' AWAY AT 'IM! REMEMBER WHAT HAPPENED TO THE CAP'N.
HOLD 'IM DOWN! HE'S-- TRYIN' TO BREAK FREE.
CORRECTION-- SWINE--

--I AM FREE!

STOP HIM! HE'S GETTIN' AWAY!

YOU STOP 'IM! HE MOVES LIKE A BLASTED STREAK OF LIGHTNIN'!

THE POO[R] BLIND FOOLS

IF THEY BUT KNE[W] HOW SLO[W] MY MOVE[-]MENTS SEEM TO ME...

...OR HOW HEAVY, HOW LEADEN MY LIMBS....!

AH, BUT WHEN IT GETS DARK...WHEN IT'S NIGHT...A NIGHT LIKE LAST NIGHT...

NO! I MUST NOT THINK OF THAT. THE MEMORIES-- WOULD DRIVE ME MAD.

IT WAS A DREAM. IT HAD TO BE A DREAM.

BUT-- IT WAS NOT.

HE RAN DOWN THIS WAY.

WE CAN'T PULL INTO PORT TILL WE FIND THAT CREEP-- OR HE'LL ESCAPE.

IF ON[LY] I DARE[D] GIVE MYSEL[F] UP.

BUT MY WILL IS TOO WEAK. TOO WEAK

THUS, IN THE HEAT OF THE DAY, THE MYSTERIOUS FUGITIVE MANAGES-- HOW, HE KNOWS NOT-- TO ELUDE THE FEARFULLY-SEARCHING CREWMEN...

"HE'S FALLEN OVERBOARD," THEY SAY...AND SLAP EACH OTHER ON THE BACK... AND FINALLY TURN IN, FOR ONE LAST SLEEP BEFORE ENTERING PORT...

YES... ONE LAST SLEEP...

FOR, THAT NIGHT, BENEATH THE MOON'S EERIE, WHITISH GLOW...

I AM ALMOST AS GREAT A FOOL AS THE[Y].

TO EASE A MOMENT'S ANGUISH, I NEARLY SURREN-DERED MYSELF TO THEIR TENDER MERCIES.

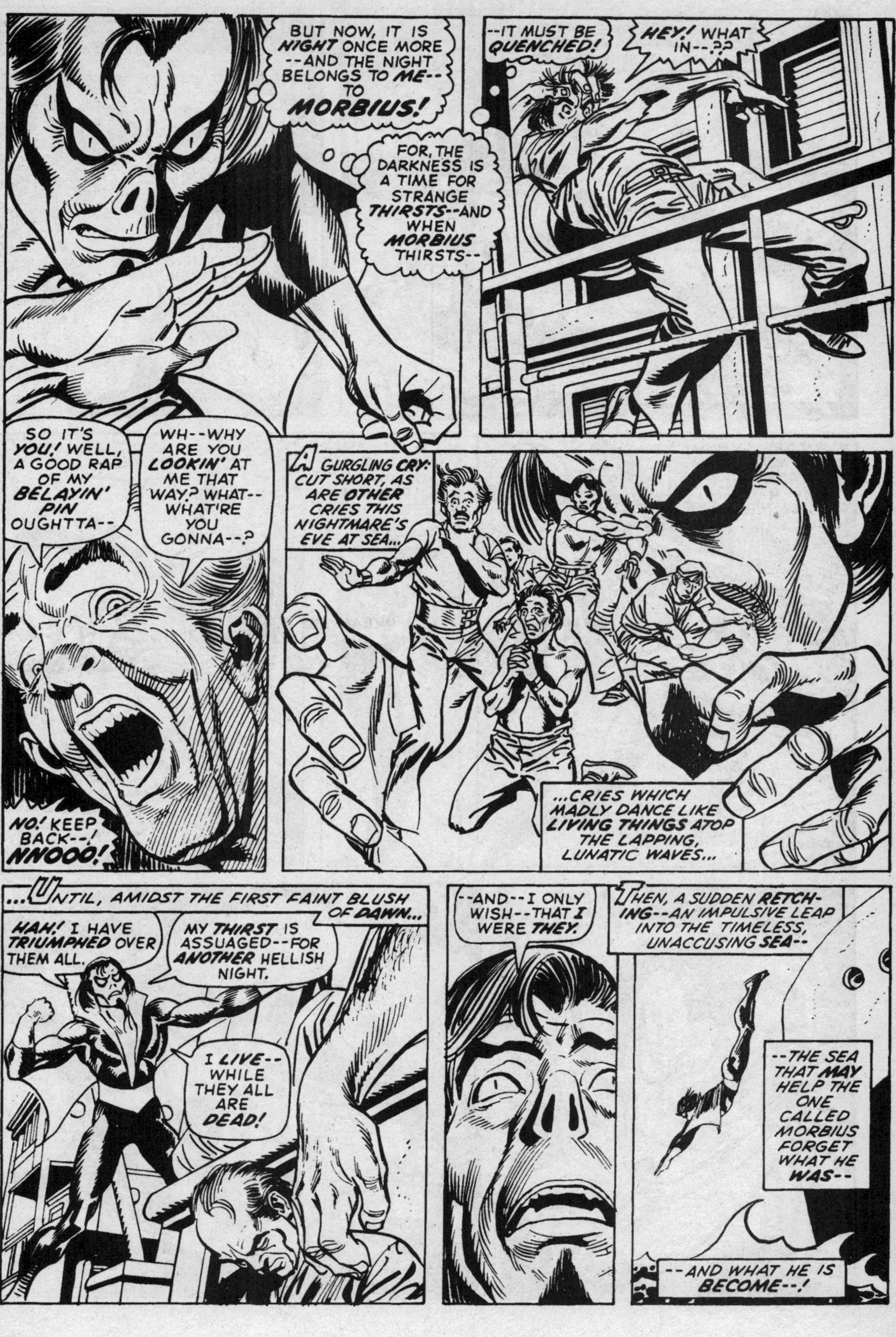
BUT NOW, IT IS NIGHT ONCE MORE --AND THE NIGHT BELONGS TO ME-- TO MORBIUS!
FOR, THE DARKNESS IS A TIME FOR STRANGE THIRSTS--AND WHEN MORBIUS THIRSTS--
--IT MUST BE QUENCHED!
HEY! WHAT IN--??
SO IT'S YOU! WELL, A GOOD RAP OF MY BELAYIN' PIN OUGHTTA--
WH--WHY ARE YOU LOOKIN' AT ME THAT WAY? WHAT--WHAT'RE YOU GONNA--?
NO! KEEP BACK--! NNOOO!
A GURGLING CRY: CUT SHORT, AS ARE OTHER CRIES THIS NIGHTMARE'S EVE AT SEA...
...CRIES WHICH MADLY DANCE LIKE LIVING THINGS ATOP THE LAPPING, LUNATIC WAVES...
...UNTIL, AMIDST THE FIRST FAINT BLUSH OF DAWN...
HAH! I HAVE TRIUMPHED OVER THEM ALL.
MY THIRST IS ASSUAGED--FOR ANOTHER HELLISH NIGHT.
I LIVE--WHILE THEY ALL ARE DEAD!
--AND--I ONLY WISH--THAT I WERE THEY.
THEN, A SUDDEN RETCHING--AN IMPULSIVE LEAP INTO THE TIMELESS, UNACCUSING SEA--
--THE SEA THAT MAY HELP THE ONE CALLED MORBIUS FORGET WHAT HE WAS--
--AND WHAT HE IS BECOME--!

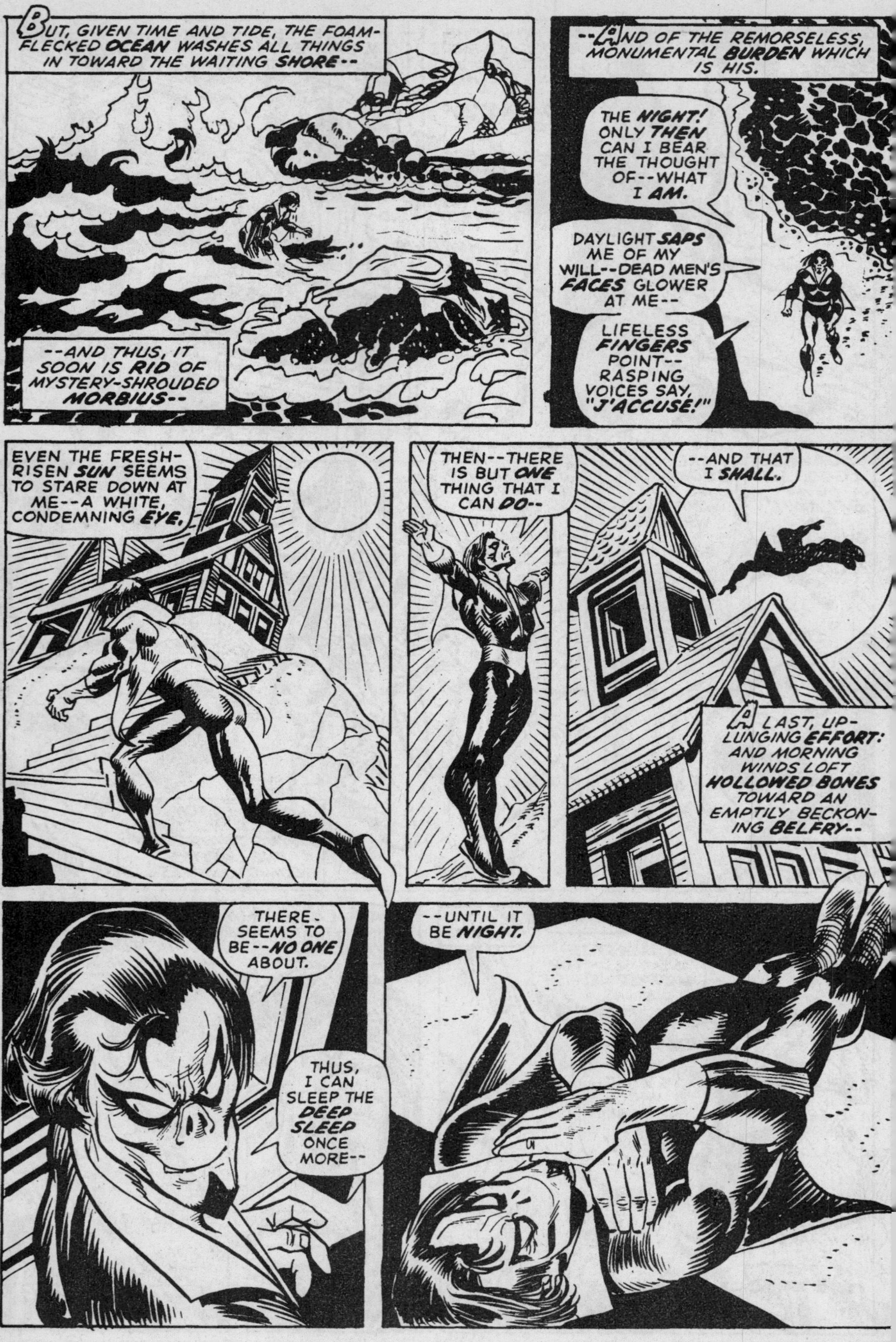

BUT, GIVEN TIME AND TIDE, THE FOAM-FLECKED OCEAN WASHES ALL THINGS IN TOWARD THE WAITING SHORE--
--AND THUS, IT SOON IS RID OF MYSTERY-SHROUDED MORBIUS--
--AND OF THE REMORSELESS, MONUMENTAL BURDEN WHICH IS HIS.
THE NIGHT! ONLY THEN CAN I BEAR THE THOUGHT OF--WHAT I AM.
DAYLIGHT SAPS ME OF MY WILL--DEAD MEN'S FACES GLOWER AT ME--
LIFELESS FINGERS POINT--RASPING VOICES SAY, "J'ACCUSE!"
EVEN THE FRESH-RISEN SUN SEEMS TO STARE DOWN AT ME--A WHITE, CONDEMNING EYE.
THEN--THERE IS BUT ONE THING THAT I CAN DO--
--AND THAT I SHALL.
A LAST, UP-LUNGING EFFORT: AND MORNING WINDS LOFT HOLLOWED BONES TOWARD AN EMPTILY BECKONING BELFRY--
THERE-SEEMS TO BE--NO ONE ABOUT.
THUS, I CAN SLEEP THE DEEP SLEEP ONCE MORE--
--UNTIL IT BE NIGHT.

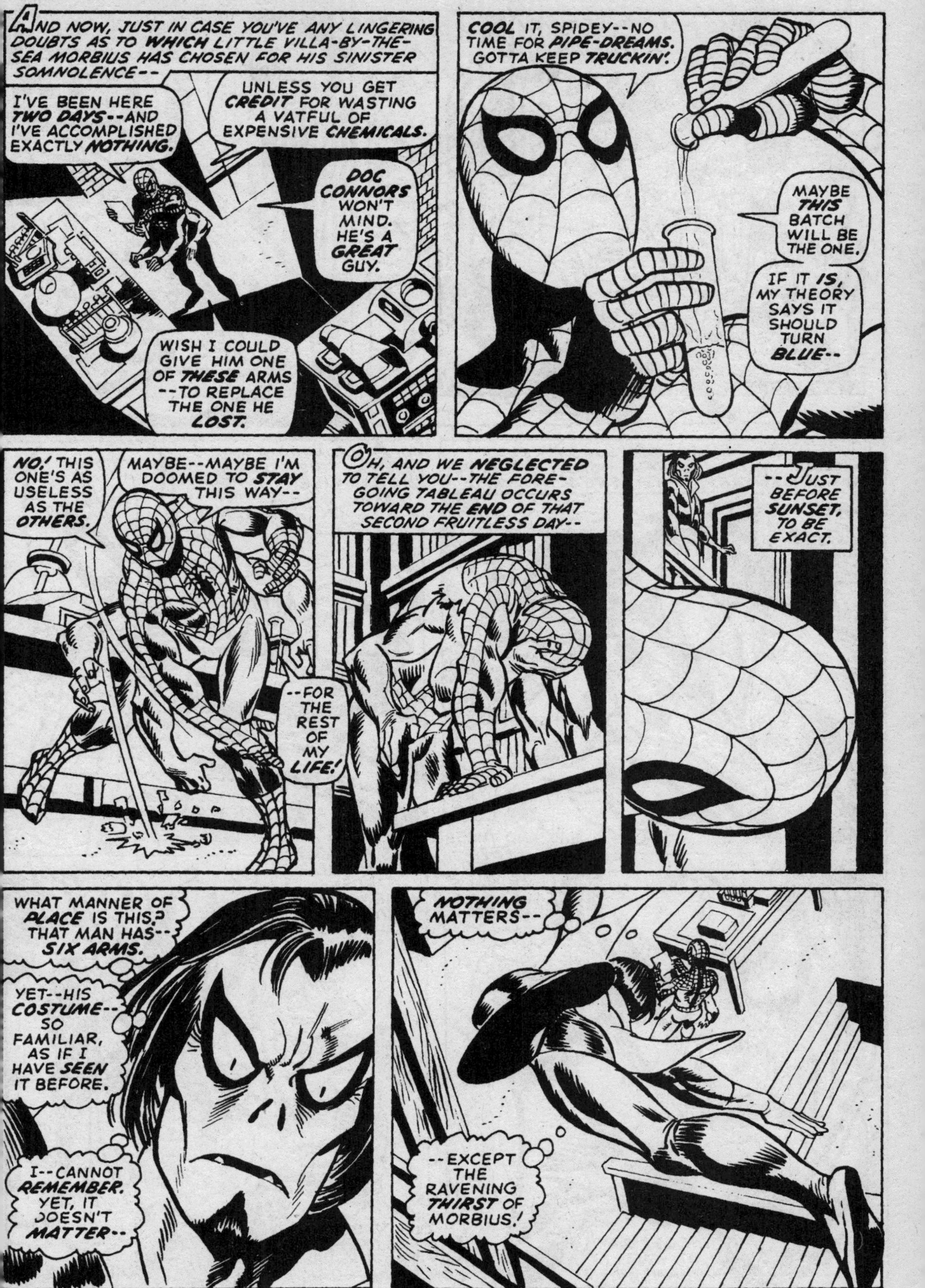

AND NOW, JUST IN CASE YOU'VE ANY LINGERING DOUBTS AS TO WHICH LITTLE VILLA-BY-THE-SEA MORBIUS HAS CHOSEN FOR HIS SINISTER SOMNOLENCE--
I'VE BEEN HERE TWO DAYS--AND I'VE ACCOMPLISHED EXACTLY NOTHING.
UNLESS YOU GET CREDIT FOR WASTING A VATFUL OF EXPENSIVE CHEMICALS.
DOC CONNORS WON'T MIND. HE'S A GREAT GUY.
WISH I COULD GIVE HIM ONE OF THESE ARMS --TO REPLACE THE ONE HE LOST.
COOL IT, SPIDEY--NO TIME FOR PIPE-DREAMS. GOTTA KEEP TRUCKIN'.
MAYBE THIS BATCH WILL BE THE ONE.
IF IT IS, MY THEORY SAYS IT SHOULD TURN BLUE--
NO! THIS ONE'S AS USELESS AS THE OTHERS.
MAYBE--MAYBE I'M DOOMED TO STAY THIS WAY--
--FOR THE REST OF MY LIFE!
OH, AND WE NEGLECTED TO TELL YOU--THE FORE-GOING TABLEAU OCCURS TOWARD THE END OF THAT SECOND FRUITLESS DAY--
--JUST BEFORE SUNSET, TO BE EXACT.
WHAT MANNER OF PLACE IS THIS? THAT MAN HAS--SIX ARMS.
YET--HIS COSTUME--SO FAMILIAR, AS IF I HAVE SEEN IT BEFORE.
I--CANNOT REMEMBER. YET, IT DOESN'T MATTER--
NOTHING MATTERS--
--EXCEPT THE RAVENING THIRST OF MORBIUS!

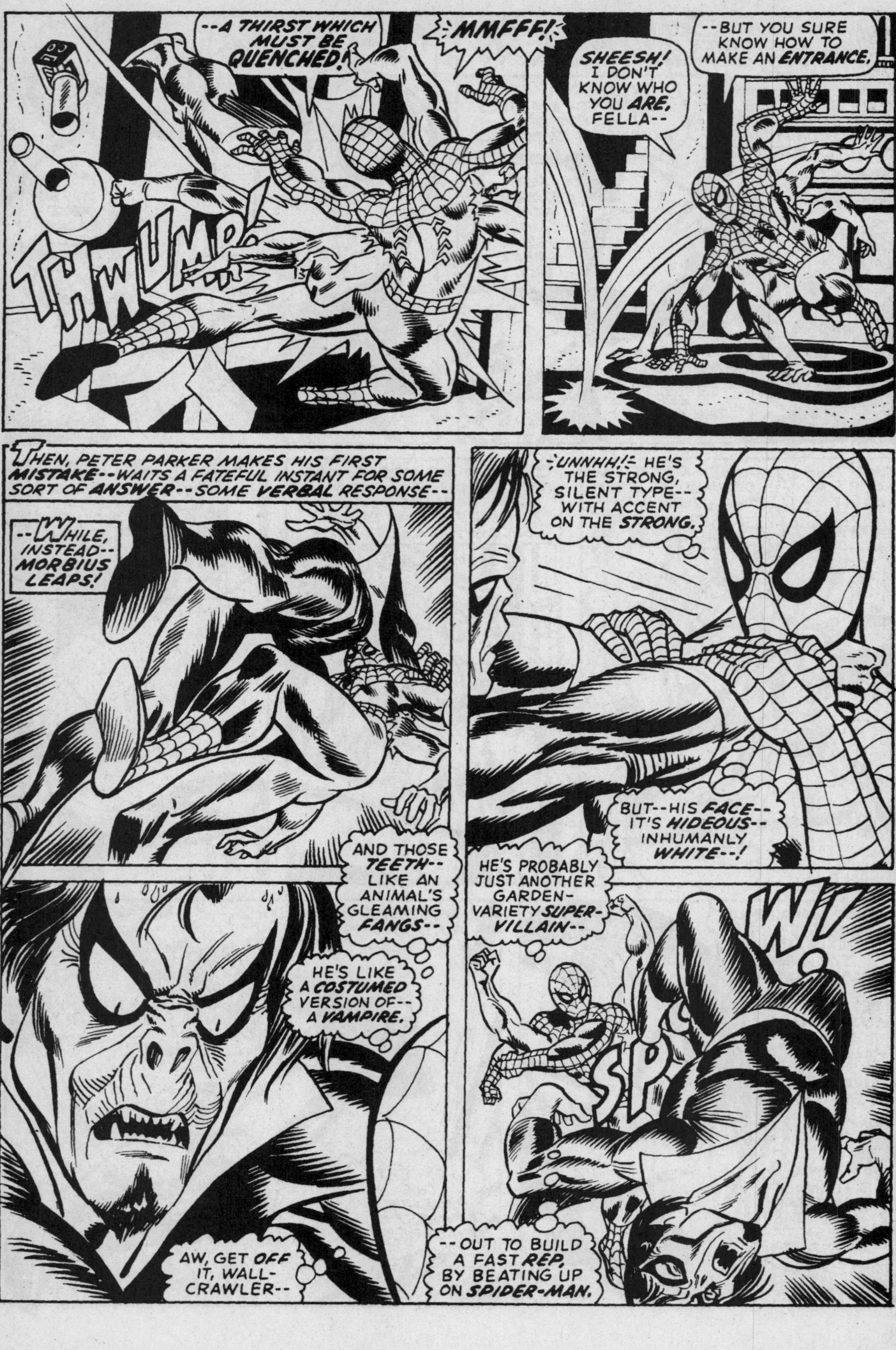

--A THIRST WHICH MUST BE QUENCHED!
MMFFF!
THWUMP
SHEESH! I DON'T KNOW WHO YOU ARE, FELLA--
--BUT YOU SURE KNOW HOW TO MAKE AN ENTRANCE.
THEN, PETER PARKER MAKES HIS FIRST MISTAKE--WAITS A FATEFUL INSTANT FOR SOME SORT OF ANSWER--SOME VERBAL RESPONSE--
--WHILE, INSTEAD--MORBIUS LEAPS!
UNNHH! HE'S THE STRONG, SILENT TYPE--WITH ACCENT ON THE STRONG.
BUT--HIS FACE--IT'S HIDEOUS--INHUMANLY WHITE--!
AND THOSE TEETH--LIKE AN ANIMAL'S GLEAMING FANGS--
HE'S LIKE A COSTUMED VERSION OF--A VAMPIRE.
AW, GET OFF IT, WALL-CRAWLER--
HE'S PROBABLY JUST ANOTHER GARDEN-VARIETY SUPER-VILLAIN--
--OUT TO BUILD A FAST REP, BY BEATING UP ON SPIDER-MAN.

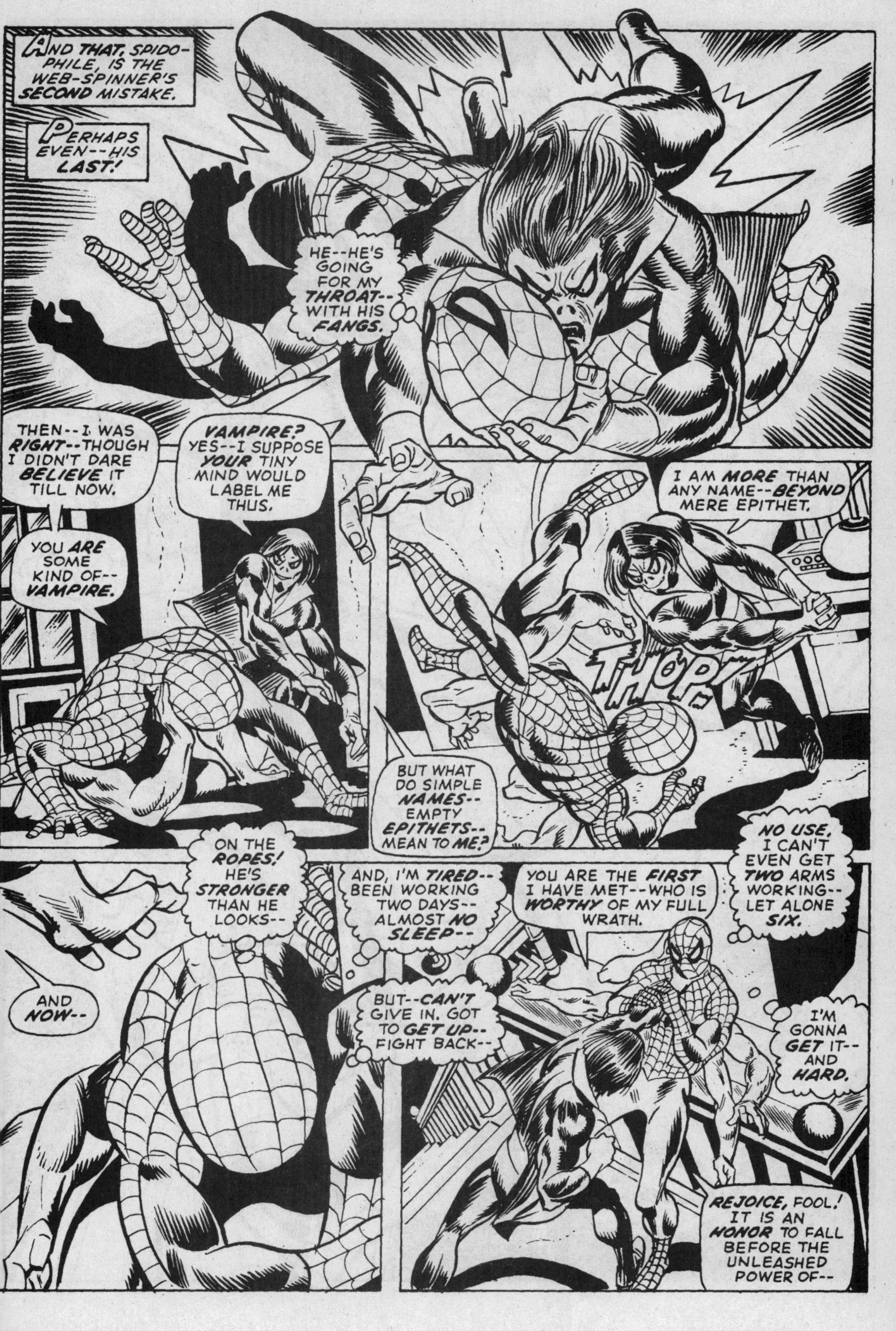
AND THAT, SPIDO-PHILE, IS THE WEB-SPINNER'S SECOND MISTAKE.
PERHAPS EVEN--HIS LAST!
HE--HE'S GOING FOR MY THROAT--WITH HIS FANGS.
THEN--I WAS RIGHT--THOUGH I DIDN'T DARE BELIEVE IT TILL NOW.
YOU ARE SOME KIND OF--VAMPIRE.
VAMPIRE? YES--I SUPPOSE YOUR TINY MIND WOULD LABEL ME THUS.
I AM MORE THAN ANY NAME--BEYOND MERE EPITHET.
THOP!
BUT WHAT DO SIMPLE NAMES--EMPTY EPITHETS--MEAN TO ME?
ON THE ROPES! HE'S STRONGER THAN HE LOOKS--
AND, I'M TIRED--BEEN WORKING TWO DAYS--ALMOST NO SLEEP--
AND NOW--
BUT--CAN'T GIVE IN. GOT TO GET UP--FIGHT BACK--
YOU ARE THE FIRST I HAVE MET--WHO IS WORTHY OF MY FULL WRATH.
NO USE. I CAN'T EVEN GET TWO ARMS WORKING--LET ALONE SIX.
I'M GONNA GET IT--AND HARD.
REJOICE, FOOL! IT IS AN HONOR TO FALL BEFORE THE UNLEASHED POWER OF--

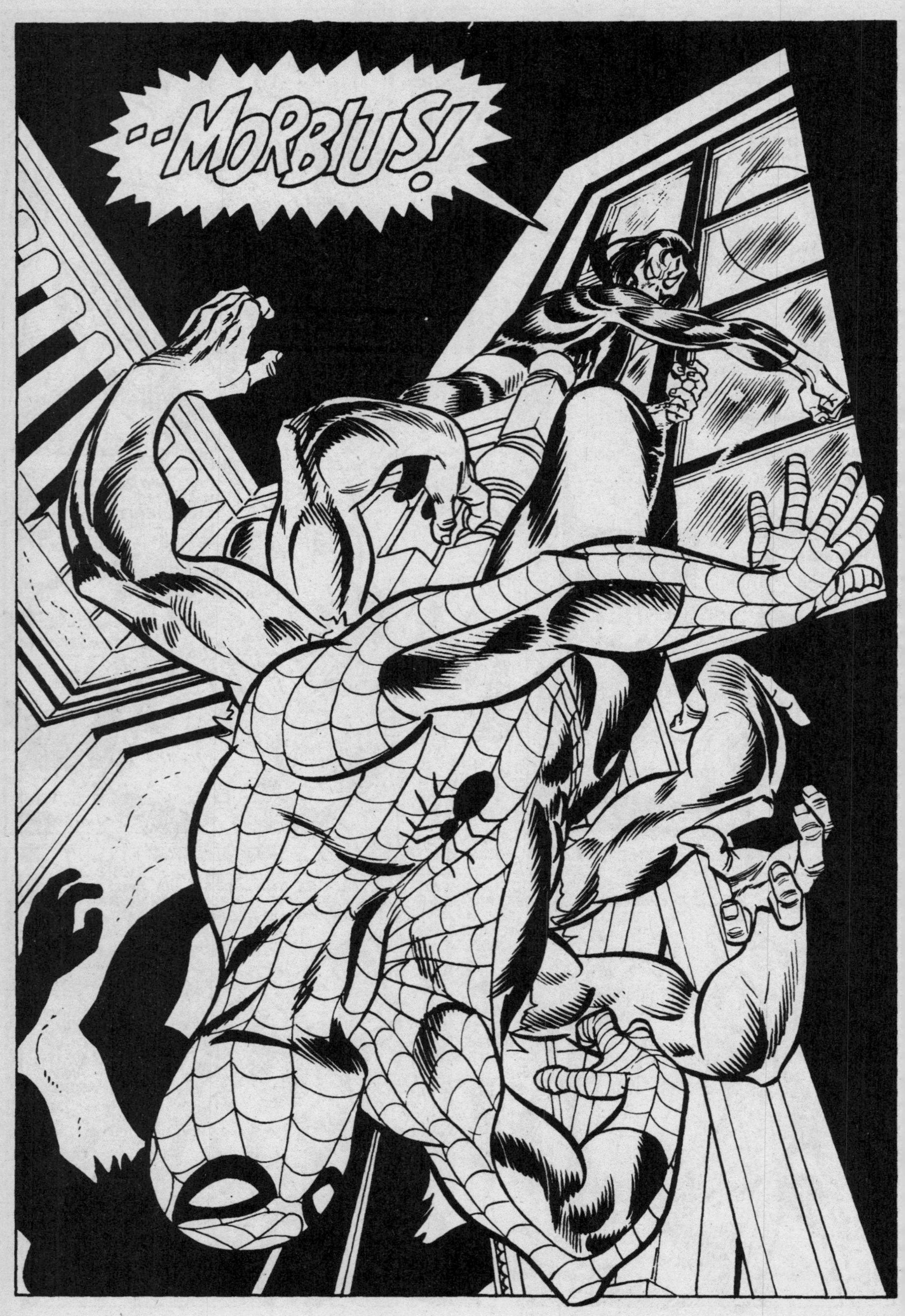
--MORBIUS!

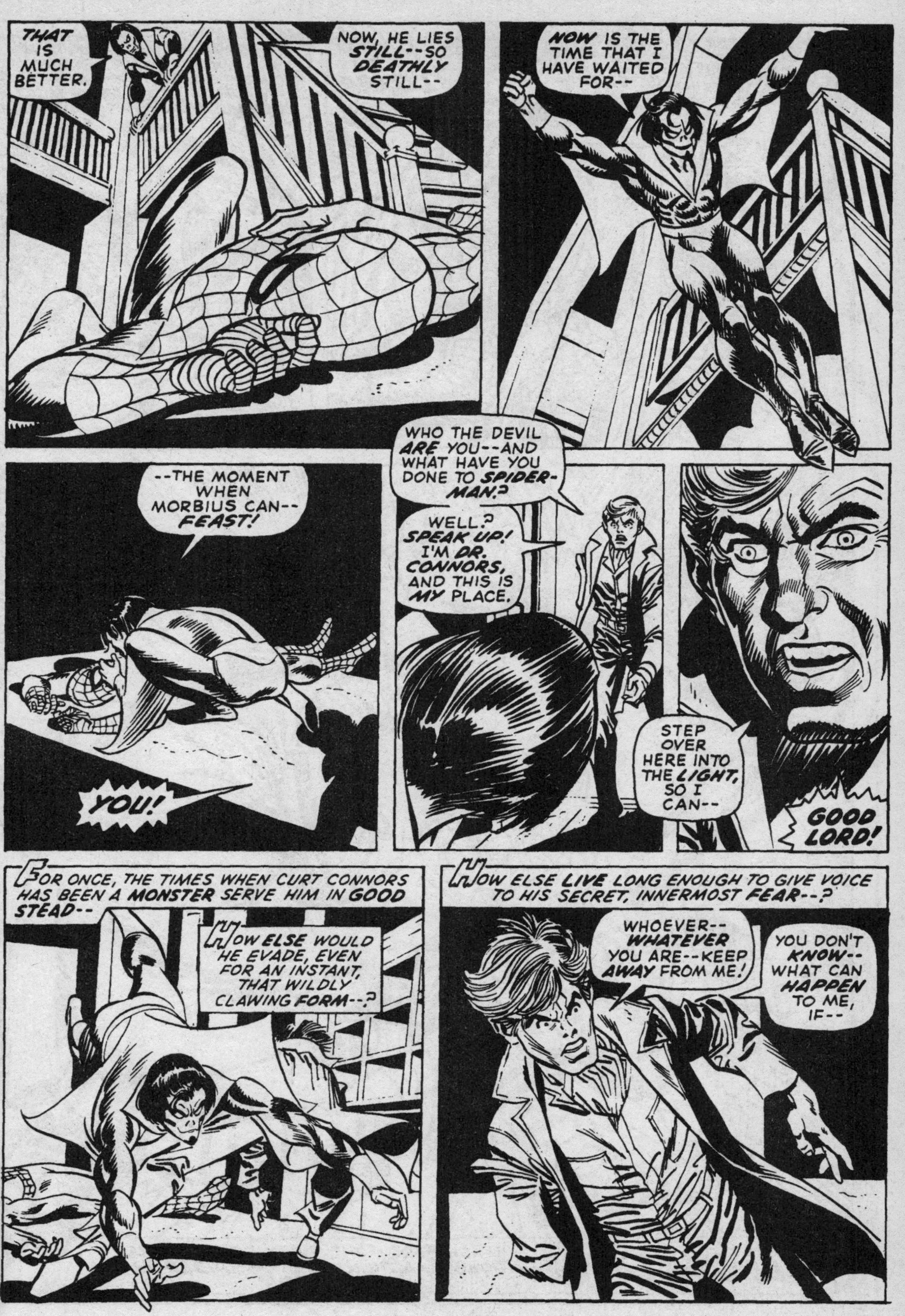

THAT IS MUCH BETTER.
NOW, HE LIES STILL--SO DEATHLY STILL--
NOW IS THE TIME THAT I HAVE WAITED FOR--
--THE MOMENT WHEN MORBIUS CAN--FEAST!
YOU!
WHO THE DEVIL ARE YOU--AND WHAT HAVE YOU DONE TO SPIDER-MAN?
WELL? SPEAK UP! I'M DR. CONNORS, AND THIS IS MY PLACE.
STEP OVER HERE INTO THE LIGHT, SO I CAN--
GOOD LORD!
FOR ONCE, THE TIMES WHEN CURT CONNORS HAS BEEN A MONSTER SERVE HIM IN GOOD STEAD--
HOW ELSE WOULD HE EVADE, EVEN FOR AN INSTANT, THAT WILDLY CLAWING FORM--?
HOW ELSE LIVE LONG ENOUGH TO GIVE VOICE TO HIS SECRET, INNERMOST FEAR--?
WHOEVER--WHATEVER YOU ARE--KEEP AWAY FROM ME!
YOU DON'T KNOW--WHAT CAN HAPPEN TO ME, IF--

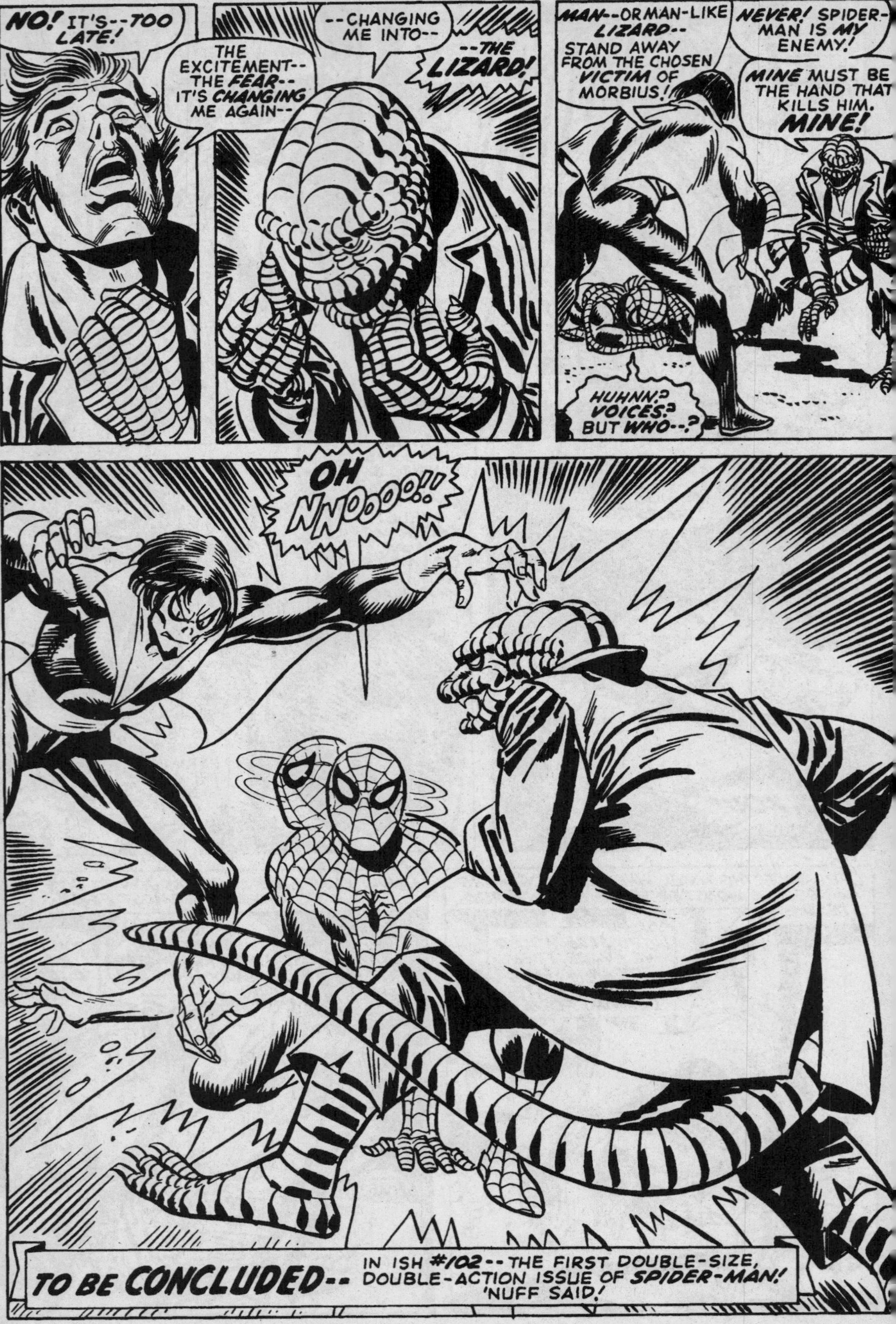
NO! IT'S--TOO LATE!
THE EXCITEMENT--THE FEAR--IT'S CHANGING ME AGAIN--
--CHANGING ME INTO--
--THE LIZARD!
MAN--OR MAN-LIKE LIZARD--STAND AWAY FROM THE CHOSEN VICTIM OF MORBIUS!
NEVER! SPIDER-MAN IS MY ENEMY!
MINE MUST BE THE HAND THAT KILLS HIM. MINE!
HUHNN? VOICES? BUT WHO--?
OH NNOOOO!!
TO BE CONCLUDED-- IN ISH #102--THE FIRST DOUBLE-SIZE, DOUBLE-ACTION ISSUE OF SPIDER-MAN! 'NUFF SAID!

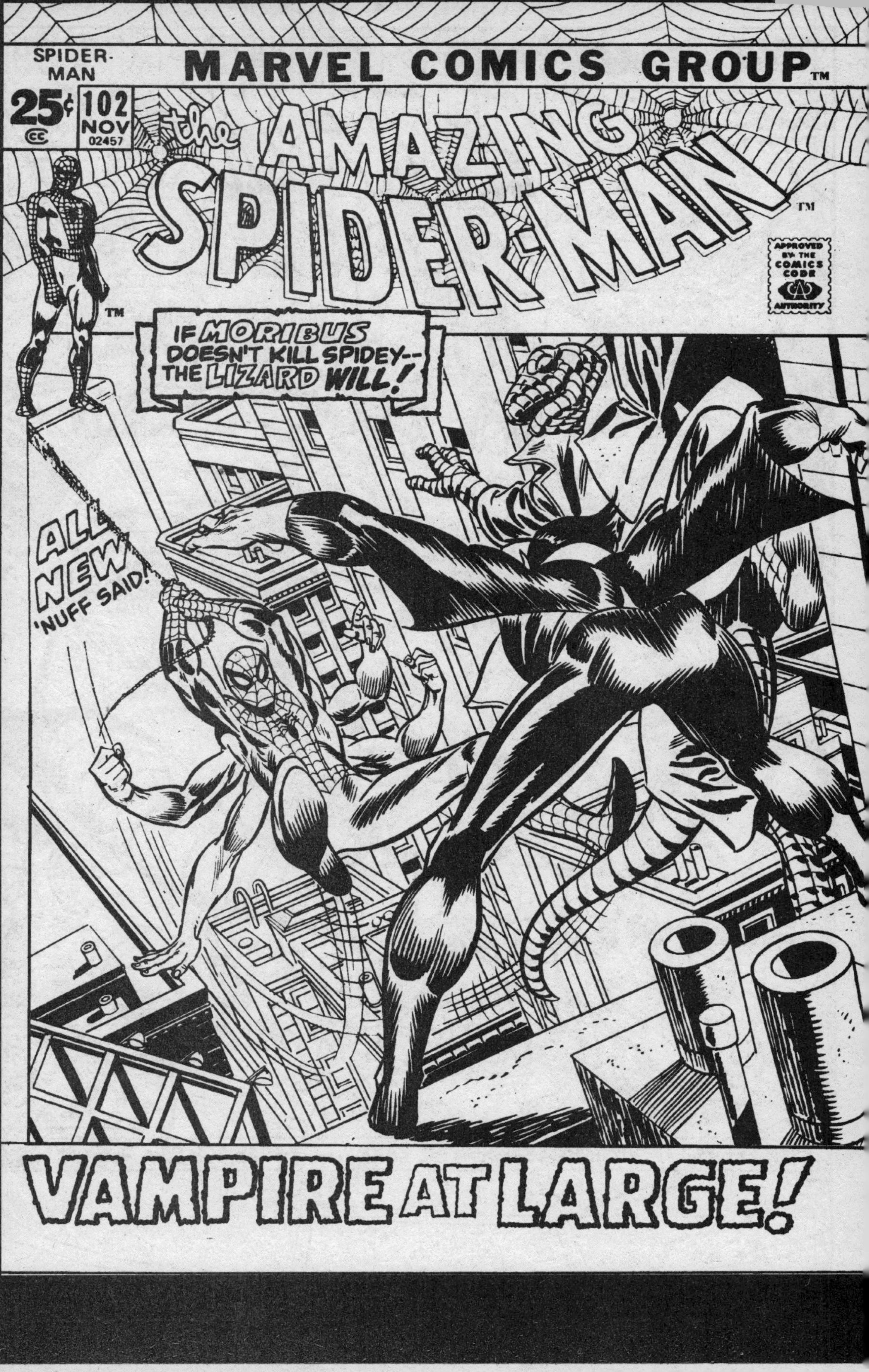
SPIDER-MAN
MARVEL COMICS GROUP™
25¢ CC
102 NOV 02457
the AMAZING SPIDER-MAN™
APPROVED BY THE COMICS CODE AUTHORITY
IF MORIBUS DOESN'T KILL SPIDEY-- THE LIZARD WILL!
ALL NEW 'NUFF SAID!
VAMPIRE AT LARGE!

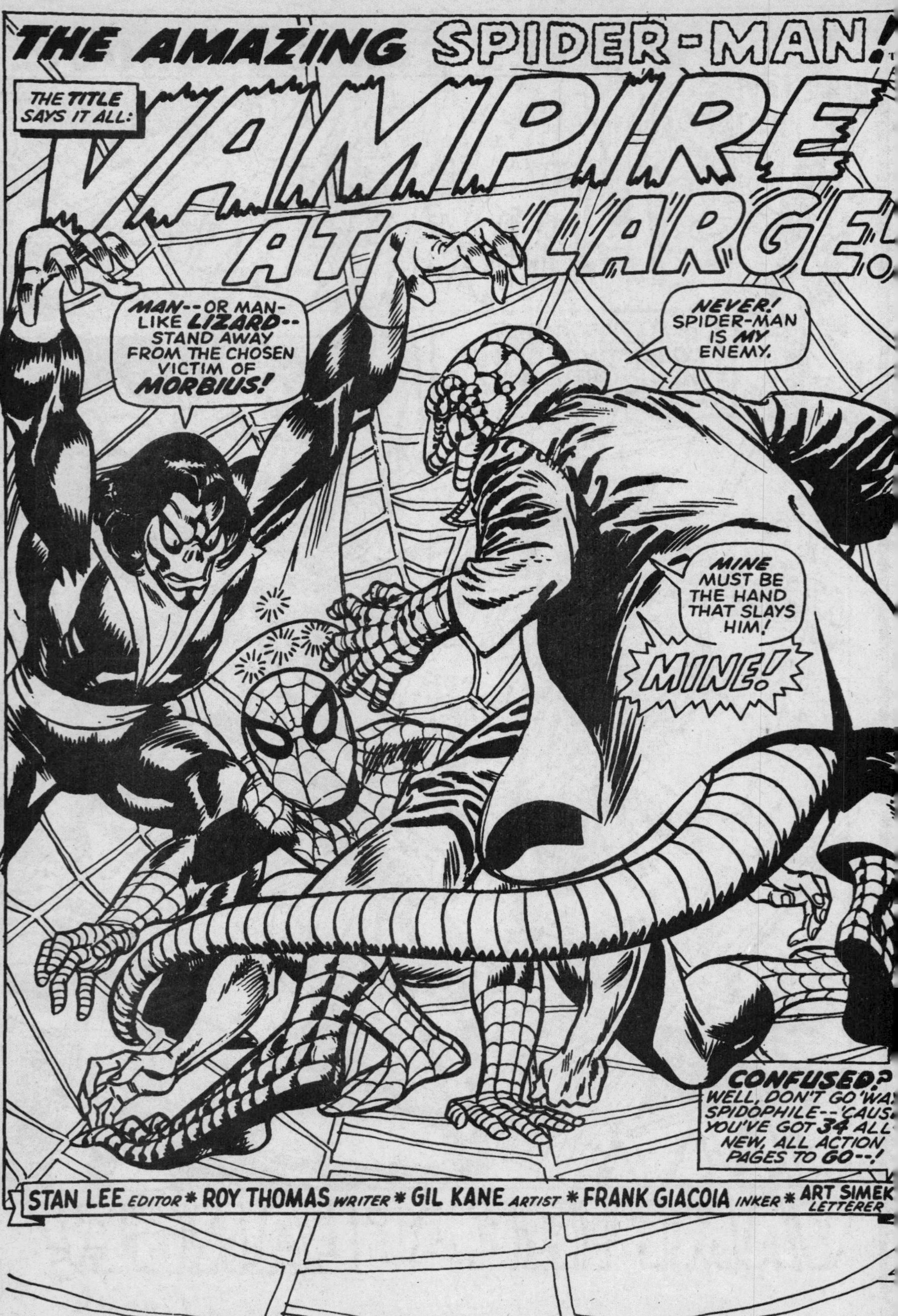
THE AMAZING SPIDER-MAN!
THE TITLE SAYS IT ALL:
VAMPIRE AT LARGE!
MAN--OR MAN-LIKE LIZARD--STAND AWAY FROM THE CHOSEN VICTIM OF MORBIUS!
NEVER! SPIDER-MAN IS MY ENEMY.
MINE MUST BE THE HAND THAT SLAYS HIM!
MINE!
CONFUSED? WELL, DON'T GO 'WA SPIDOPHILE--'CAUS YOU'VE GOT 34 ALL NEW, ALL ACTION PAGES TO GO--!
STAN LEE EDITOR * ROY THOMAS WRITER * GIL KANE ARTIST * FRANK GIACOIA INKER * ART SIMEK LETTERER

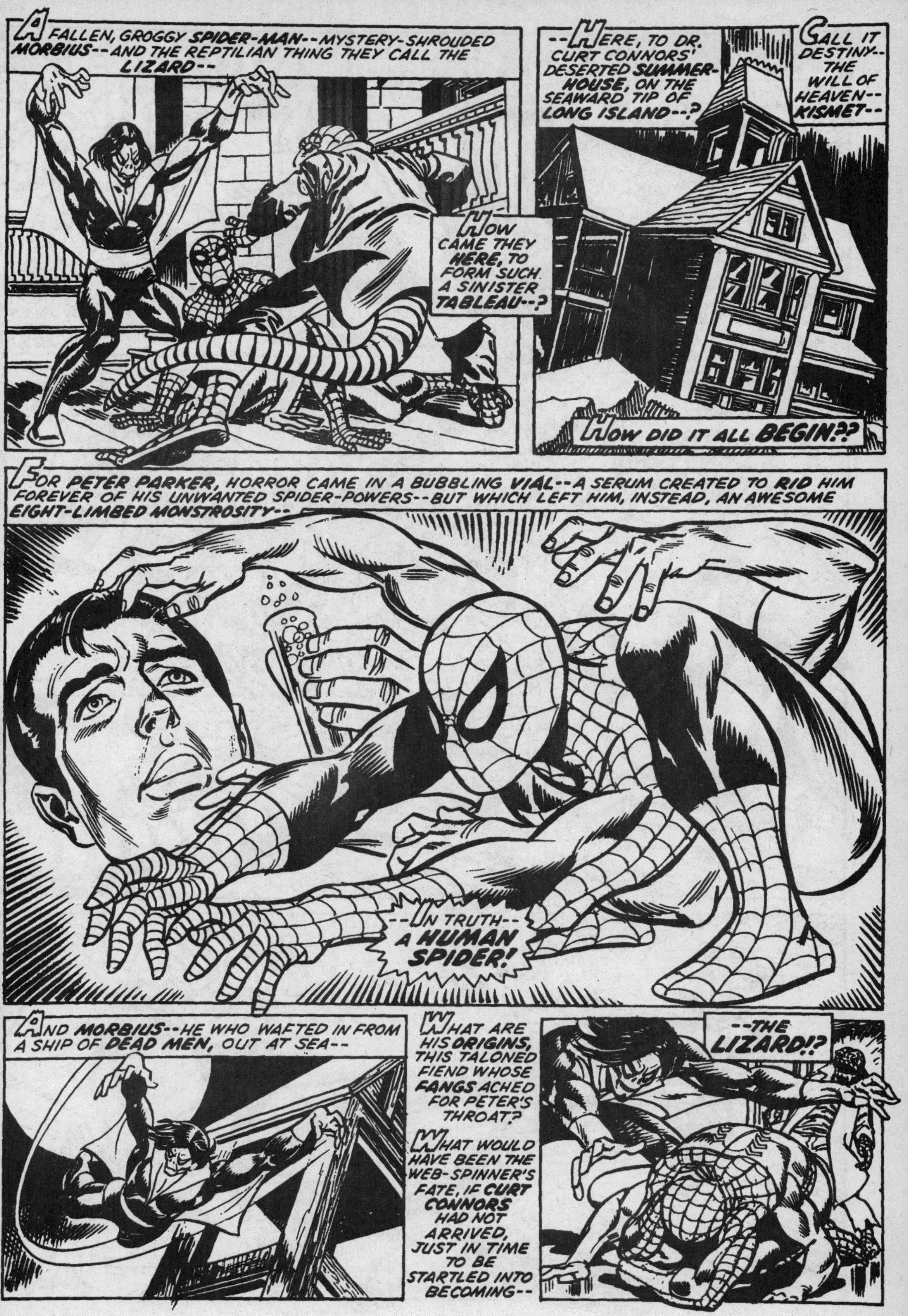
A FALLEN, GROGGY SPIDER-MAN--MYSTERY-SHROUDED MORBIUS--AND THE REPTILIAN THING THEY CALL THE LIZARD--
HOW CAME THEY HERE, TO FORM SUCH A SINISTER TABLEAU--?
--HERE, TO DR. CURT CONNORS' DESERTED SUMMER-HOUSE, ON THE SEAWARD TIP OF LONG ISLAND--?
CALL IT DESTINY--THE WILL OF HEAVEN--KISMET--
HOW DID IT ALL BEGIN??
FOR PETER PARKER, HORROR CAME IN A BUBBLING VIAL--A SERUM CREATED TO RID HIM FOREVER OF HIS UNWANTED SPIDER-POWERS--BUT WHICH LEFT HIM, INSTEAD, AN AWESOME EIGHT-LIMBED MONSTROSITY--
--IN TRUTH--A HUMAN SPIDER!
AND MORBIUS--HE WHO WAFTED IN FROM A SHIP OF DEAD MEN, OUT AT SEA--
WHAT ARE HIS ORIGINS, THIS TALONED FIEND WHOSE FANGS ACHED FOR PETER'S THROAT?
WHAT WOULD HAVE BEEN THE WEB-SPINNER'S FATE, IF CURT CONNORS HAD NOT ARRIVED, JUST IN TIME TO BE STARTLED INTO BECOMING--
--THE LIZARD!?

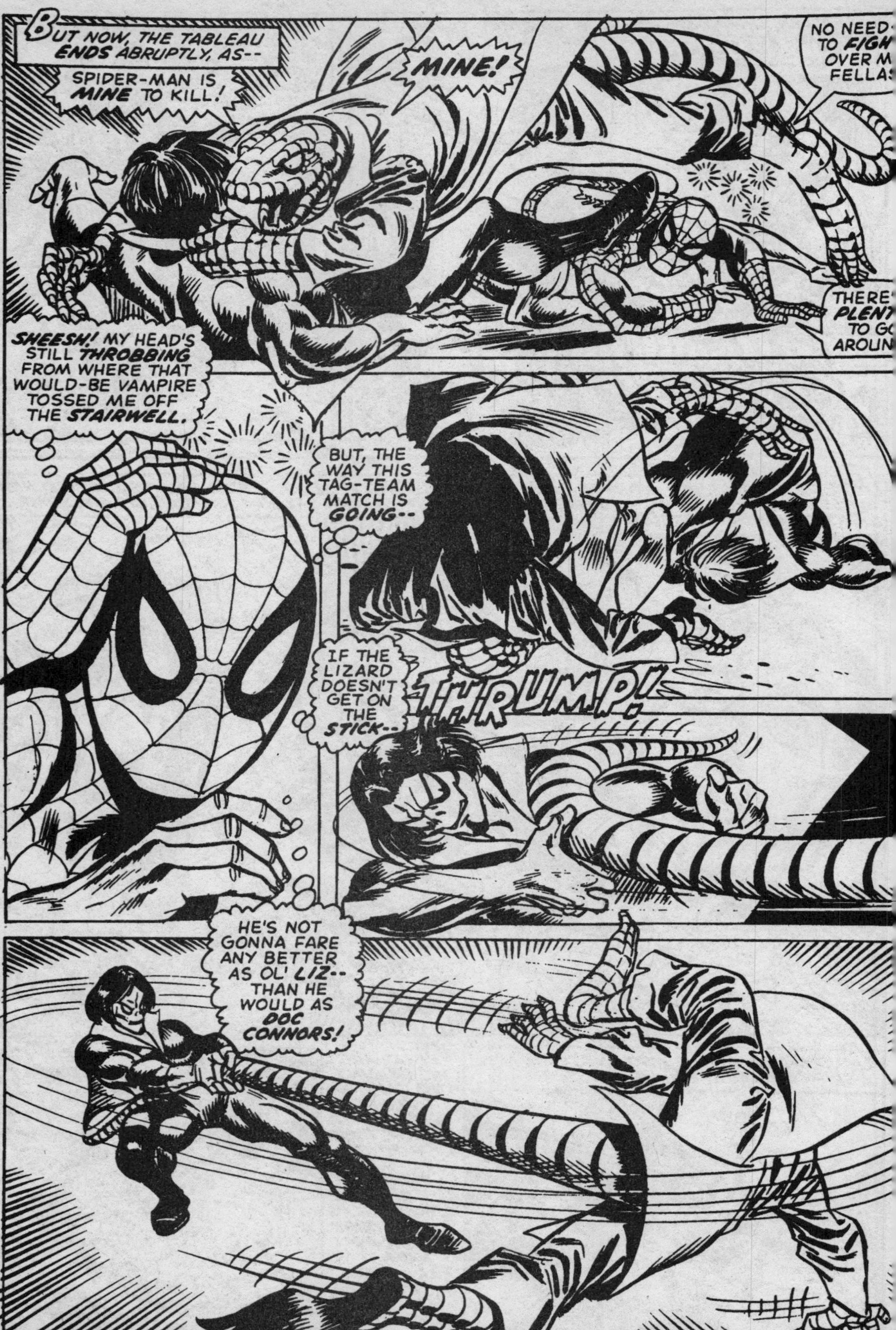
BUT NOW, THE TABLEAU ENDS ABRUPTLY, AS--
SPIDER-MAN IS MINE TO KILL!
MINE!
NO NEED-- TO FIGH OVER M FELLAS
THERE' PLENT TO GO AROUN
SHEESH! MY HEAD'S STILL THROBBING FROM WHERE THAT WOULD-BE VAMPIRE TOSSED ME OFF THE STAIRWELL.
BUT, THE WAY THIS TAG-TEAM MATCH IS GOING--
IF THE LIZARD DOESN'T GET ON THE STICK--
THRUMP!
HE'S NOT GONNA FARE ANY BETTER AS OL' LIZ-- THAN HE WOULD AS DOC CONNORS!

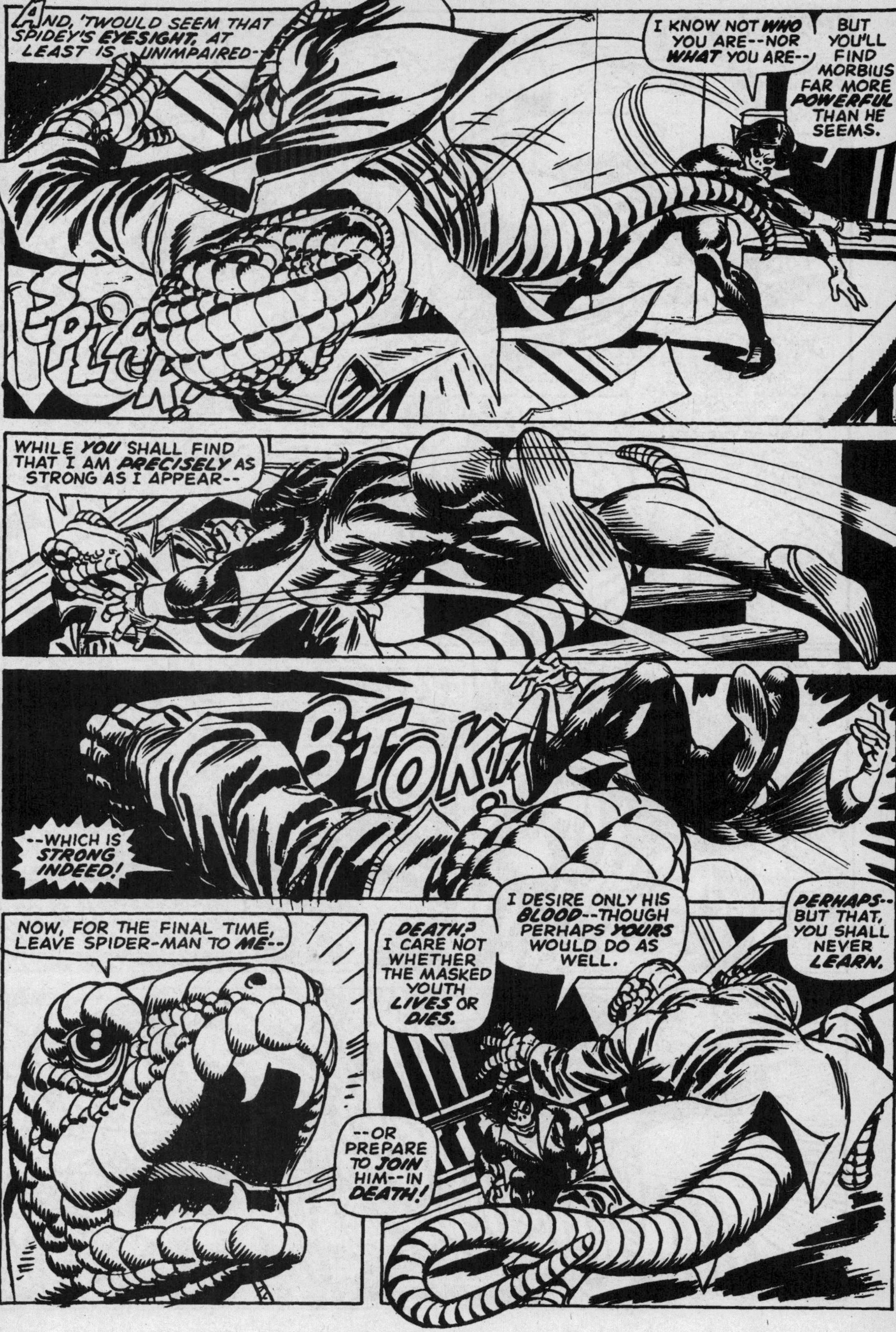
AND, 'TWOULD SEEM THAT SPIDEY'S EYESIGHT, AT LEAST IS UNIMPAIRED--
I KNOW NOT WHO YOU ARE--NOR WHAT YOU ARE--
BUT YOU'LL FIND MORBIUS FAR MORE POWERFUL THAN HE SEEMS.
SPLAK!
WHILE YOU SHALL FIND THAT I AM PRECISELY AS STRONG AS I APPEAR--
BTOK!
--WHICH IS STRONG INDEED!
NOW, FOR THE FINAL TIME, LEAVE SPIDER-MAN TO ME--
--OR PREPARE TO JOIN HIM--IN DEATH!
DEATH? I CARE NOT WHETHER THE MASKED YOUTH LIVES OR DIES.
I DESIRE ONLY HIS BLOOD--THOUGH PERHAPS YOURS WOULD DO AS WELL.
PERHAPS-- BUT THAT, YOU SHALL NEVER LEARN.

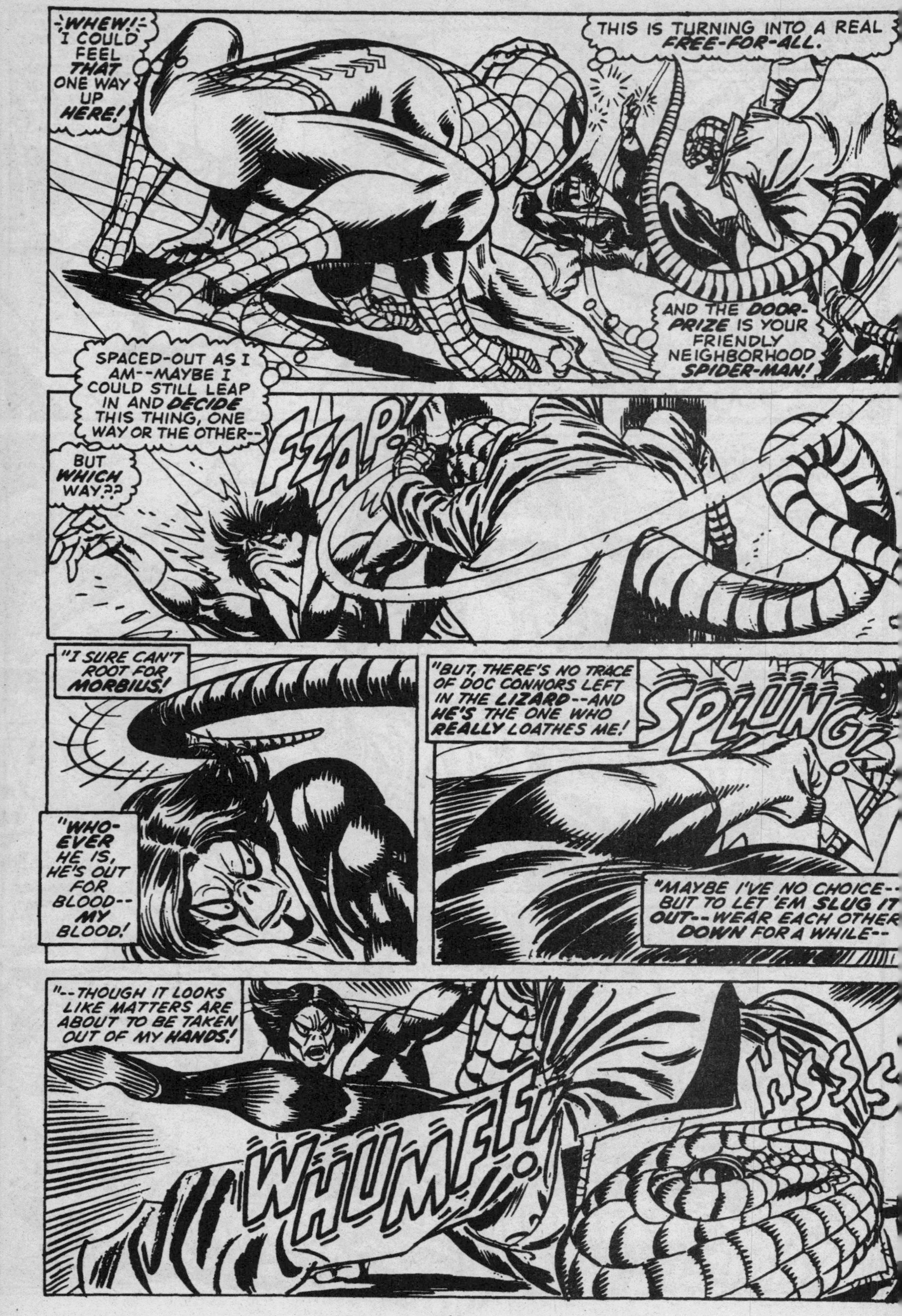

-WHEW!- I COULD FEEL THAT ONE WAY UP HERE!
THIS IS TURNING INTO A REAL FREE-FOR-ALL.
AND THE DOOR-PRIZE IS YOUR FRIENDLY NEIGHBORHOOD SPIDER-MAN!
SPACED-OUT AS I AM--MAYBE I COULD STILL LEAP IN AND DECIDE THIS THING, ONE WAY OR THE OTHER--
BUT WHICH WAY??
FZAP!
"I SURE CAN'T ROOT FOR MORBIUS!
"WHO-EVER HE IS, HE'S OUT FOR BLOOD--MY BLOOD!
"BUT, THERE'S NO TRACE OF DOC CONNORS LEFT IN THE LIZARD--AND HE'S THE ONE WHO REALLY LOATHES ME!
SPLUNG!
"MAYBE I'VE NO CHOICE--BUT TO LET 'EM SLUG IT OUT--WEAR EACH OTHER DOWN FOR A WHILE--
"--THOUGH IT LOOKS LIKE MATTERS ARE ABOUT TO BE TAKEN OUT OF MY HANDS!
WHUMFF!
HSSS

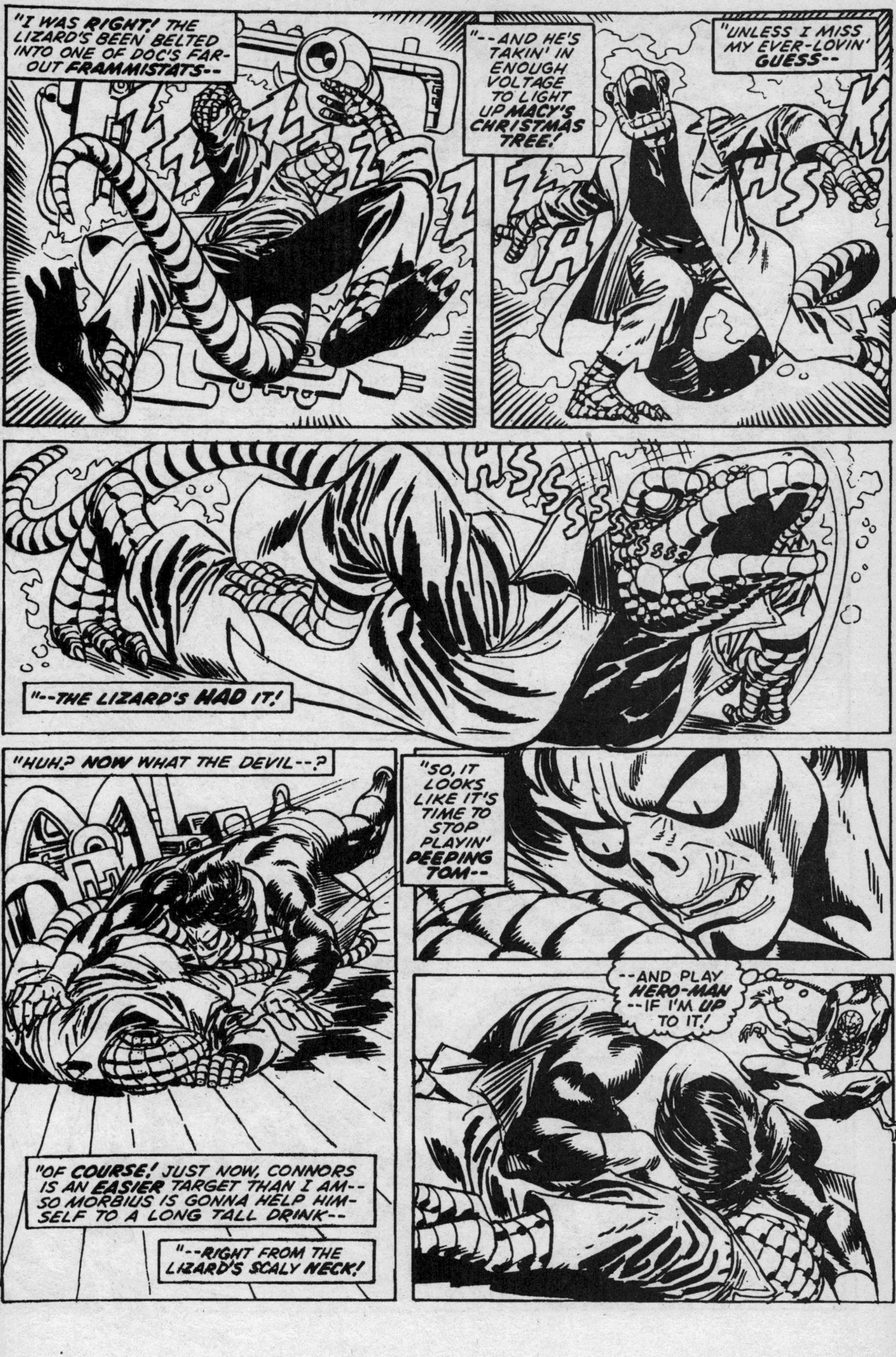
"I WAS RIGHT! THE LIZARD'S BEEN BELTED INTO ONE OF DOC'S FAR-OUT FRAMMISTATS--
"--AND HE'S TAKIN' IN ENOUGH VOLTAGE TO LIGHT UP MACY'S CHRISTMAS TREE!
"UNLESS I MISS MY EVER-LOVIN' GUESS--
"--THE LIZARD'S HAD IT!
"HUH? NOW WHAT THE DEVIL--?
"OF COURSE! JUST NOW, CONNORS IS AN EASIER TARGET THAN I AM--SO MORBIUS IS GONNA HELP HIMSELF TO A LONG TALL DRINK--
"--RIGHT FROM THE LIZARD'S SCALY NECK!
"SO, IT LOOKS LIKE IT'S TIME TO STOP PLAYIN' PEEPING TOM--
--AND PLAY HERO-MAN --IF I'M UP TO IT!

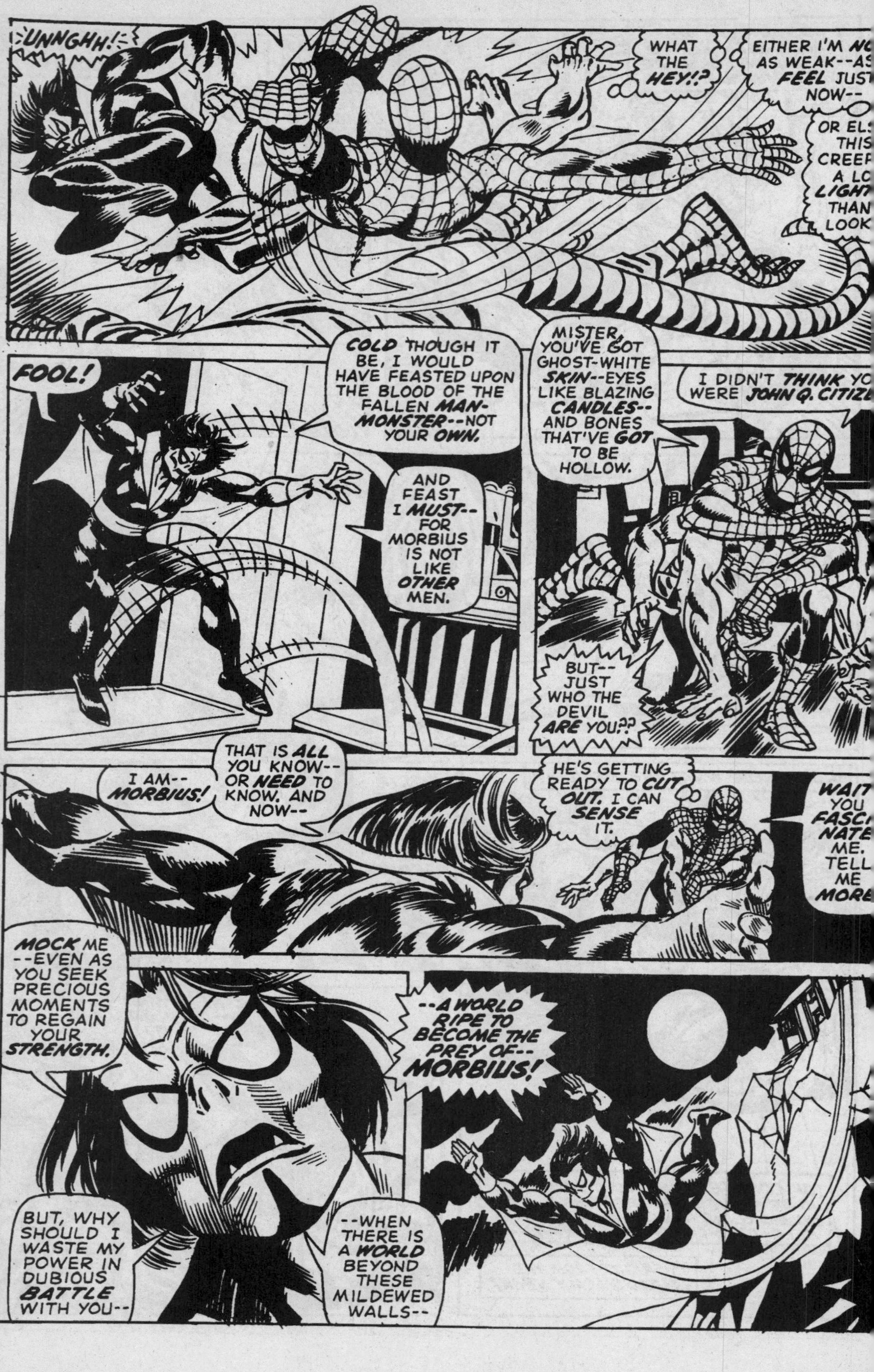
UNNGHH!
WHAT THE HEY!?
EITHER I'M NO AS WEAK--AS FEEL JUS NOW--
OR ELS THIS CREEP A LO LIGHT THAN LOOK
FOOL!
COLD THOUGH IT BE, I WOULD HAVE FEASTED UPON THE BLOOD OF THE FALLEN MAN-MONSTER--NOT YOUR OWN.
AND FEAST I MUST--FOR MORBIUS IS NOT LIKE OTHER MEN.
MISTER, YOU'VE GOT GHOST-WHITE SKIN--EYES LIKE BLAZING CANDLES--AND BONES THAT'VE GOT TO BE HOLLOW.
I DIDN'T THINK YO WERE JOHN Q. CITIZ
BUT--JUST WHO THE DEVIL ARE YOU??
I AM--MORBIUS!
THAT IS ALL YOU KNOW--OR NEED TO KNOW. AND NOW--
HE'S GETTING READY TO CUT OUT. I CAN SENSE IT.
WAIT YOU FASC NATE ME. TELL ME MORE
MOCK ME--EVEN AS YOU SEEK PRECIOUS MOMENTS TO REGAIN YOUR STRENGTH.
BUT, WHY SHOULD I WASTE MY POWER IN DUBIOUS BATTLE WITH YOU--
--WHEN THERE IS A WORLD BEYOND THESE MILDEWED WALLS--
--A WORLD RIPE TO BECOME THE PREY OF--MORBIUS!

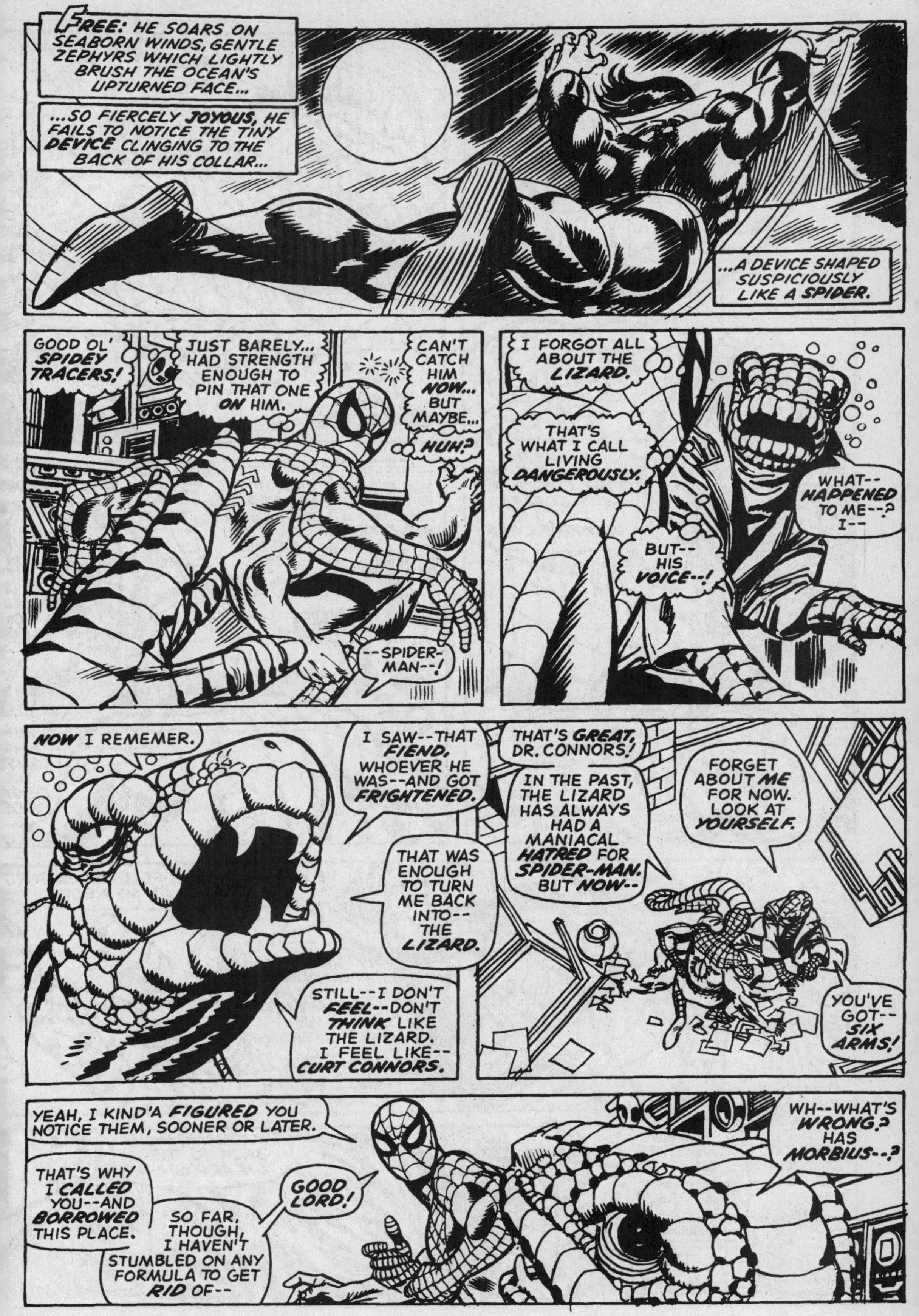
FREE: HE SOARS ON SEABORN WINDS, GENTLE ZEPHYRS WHICH LIGHTLY BRUSH THE OCEAN'S UPTURNED FACE...
...SO FIERCELY JOYOUS, HE FAILS TO NOTICE THE TINY DEVICE CLINGING TO THE BACK OF HIS COLLAR...
...A DEVICE SHAPED SUSPICIOUSLY LIKE A SPIDER.
GOOD OL' SPIDEY TRACERS!
JUST BARELY... HAD STRENGTH ENOUGH TO PIN THAT ONE ON HIM.
CAN'T CATCH HIM NOW... BUT MAYBE...
HUH?
--SPIDER-MAN--!
I FORGOT ALL ABOUT THE LIZARD.
THAT'S WHAT I CALL LIVING DANGEROUSLY.
WHAT--HAPPENED TO ME--? I--
BUT--HIS VOICE--!
NOW I REMEMER.
I SAW--THAT FIEND, WHOEVER HE WAS--AND GOT FRIGHTENED.
THAT WAS ENOUGH TO TURN ME BACK INTO--THE LIZARD.
STILL--I DON'T FEEL--DON'T THINK LIKE THE LIZARD. I FEEL LIKE--CURT CONNORS.
THAT'S GREAT, DR. CONNORS!
IN THE PAST, THE LIZARD HAS ALWAYS HAD A MANIACAL HATRED FOR SPIDER-MAN. BUT NOW--
FORGET ABOUT ME FOR NOW. LOOK AT YOURSELF.
YOU'VE GOT--SIX ARMS!
YEAH, I KIND'A FIGURED YOU NOTICE THEM, SOONER OR LATER.
THAT'S WHY I CALLED YOU--AND BORROWED THIS PLACE.
SO FAR, THOUGH, I HAVEN'T STUMBLED ON ANY FORMULA TO GET RID OF--
GOOD LORD!
WH--WHAT'S WRONG? HAS MORBIUS--?

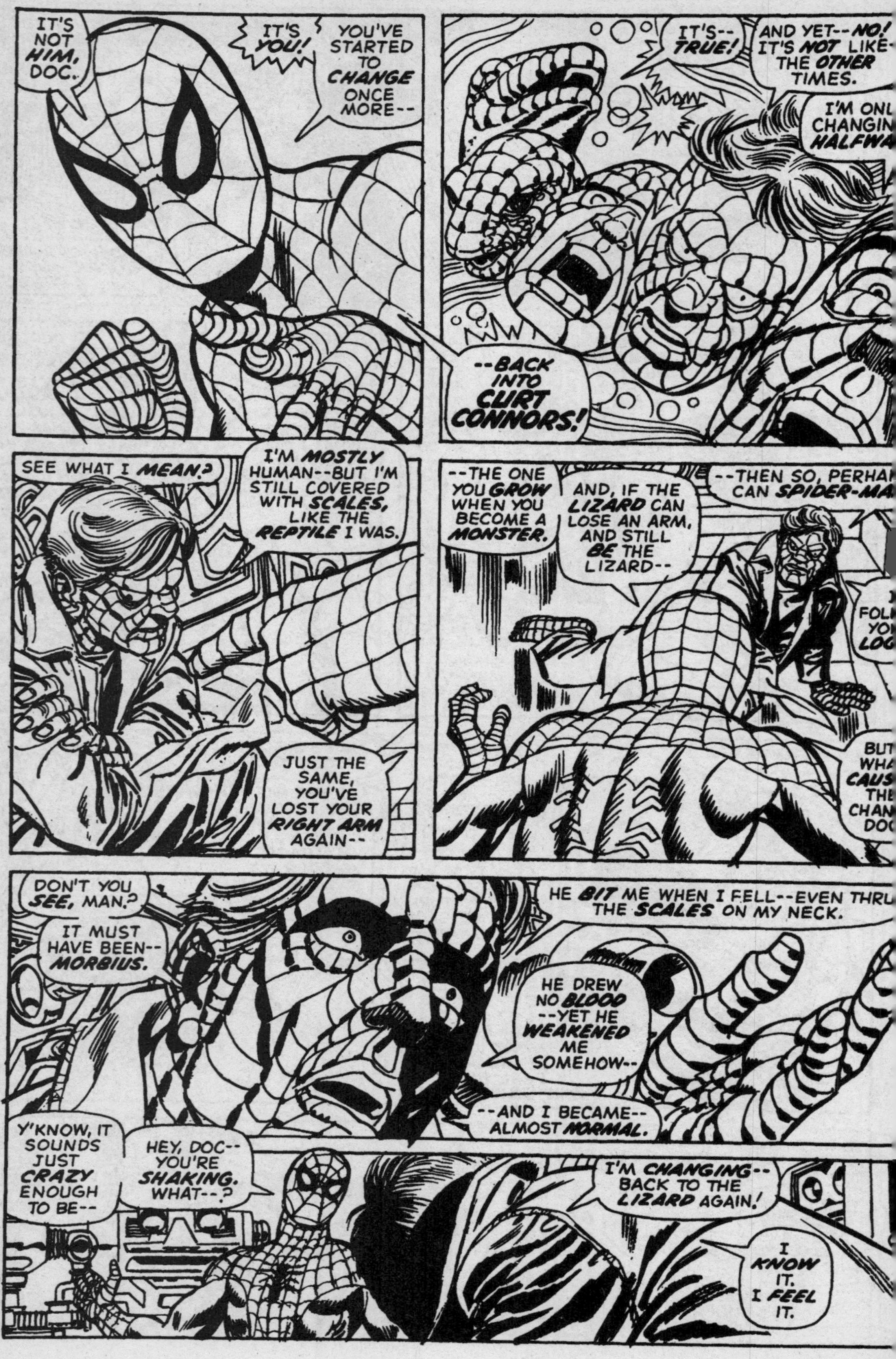

IT'S NOT HIM, DOC..
IT'S YOU!
YOU'VE STARTED TO CHANGE ONCE MORE--
IT'S-- TRUE!
AND YET-- NO! IT'S NOT LIKE THE OTHER TIMES.
I'M ONL CHANGIN HALFWA
--BACK INTO CURT CONNORS!
SEE WHAT I MEAN?
I'M MOSTLY HUMAN--BUT I'M STILL COVERED WITH SCALES, LIKE THE REPTILE I WAS.
JUST THE SAME, YOU'VE LOST YOUR RIGHT ARM AGAIN--
--THE ONE YOU GROW WHEN YOU BECOME A MONSTER.
AND, IF THE LIZARD CAN LOSE AN ARM, AND STILL BE THE LIZARD--
--THEN SO, PERHA CAN SPIDER-MA
DON'T YOU SEE, MAN?
IT MUST HAVE BEEN-- MORBIUS.
HE BIT ME WHEN I FELL--EVEN THRU THE SCALES ON MY NECK.
HE DREW NO BLOOD --YET HE WEAKENED ME SOMEHOW--
--AND I BECAME-- ALMOST NORMAL.
Y'KNOW, IT SOUNDS JUST CRAZY ENOUGH TO BE--
HEY, DOC-- YOU'RE SHAKING. WHAT--?
I'M CHANGING-- BACK TO THE LIZARD AGAIN!
I KNOW IT. I FEEL IT.

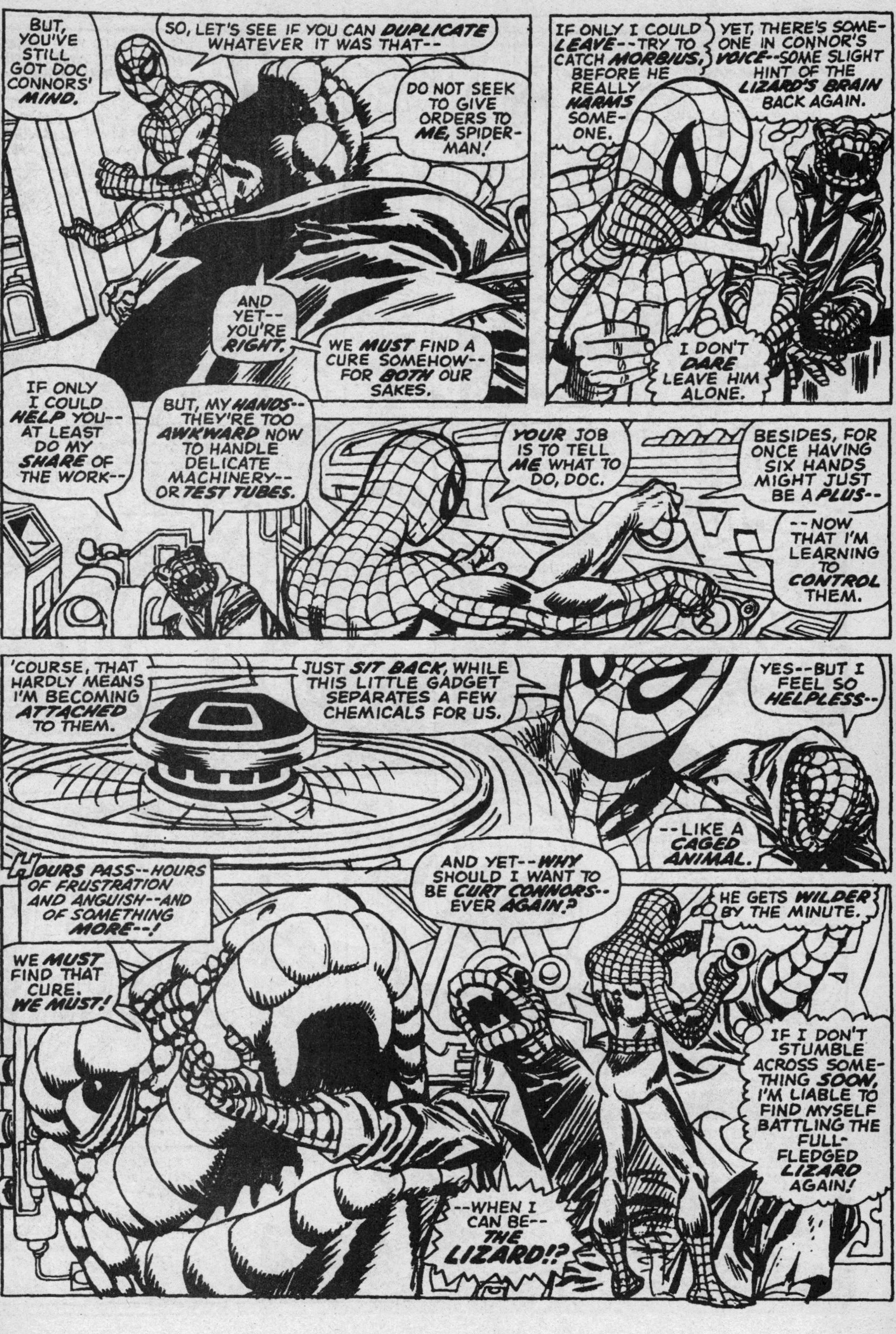

BUT, YOU'VE STILL GOT DOC CONNORS' MIND.
SO, LET'S SEE IF YOU CAN DUPLICATE WHATEVER IT WAS THAT--
DO NOT SEEK TO GIVE ORDERS TO ME, SPIDER-MAN!
AND YET-- YOU'RE RIGHT.
WE MUST FIND A CURE SOMEHOW-- FOR BOTH OUR SAKES.
IF ONLY I COULD LEAVE--TRY TO CATCH MORBIUS, BEFORE HE REALLY HARMS SOME-ONE.
YET, THERE'S SOME-ONE IN CONNOR'S VOICE--SOME SLIGHT HINT OF THE LIZARD'S BRAIN BACK AGAIN.
I DON'T DARE LEAVE HIM ALONE.
IF ONLY I COULD HELP YOU-- AT LEAST DO MY SHARE OF THE WORK--
BUT, MY HANDS-- THEY'RE TOO AWKWARD NOW TO HANDLE DELICATE MACHINERY-- OR TEST TUBES.
YOUR JOB IS TO TELL ME WHAT TO DO, DOC.
BESIDES, FOR ONCE HAVING SIX HANDS MIGHT JUST BE A PLUS--
--NOW THAT I'M LEARNING TO CONTROL THEM.
'COURSE, THAT HARDLY MEANS I'M BECOMING ATTACHED TO THEM.
JUST SIT BACK, WHILE THIS LITTLE GADGET SEPARATES A FEW CHEMICALS FOR US.
YES--BUT I FEEL SO HELPLESS--
--LIKE A CAGED ANIMAL.
HOURS PASS--HOURS OF FRUSTRATION AND ANGUISH--AND OF SOMETHING MORE--!
WE MUST FIND THAT CURE. WE MUST!
AND YET--WHY SHOULD I WANT TO BE CURT CONNORS-- EVER AGAIN?
HE GETS WILDER BY THE MINUTE.
IF I DON'T STUMBLE ACROSS SOME-THING SOON, I'M LIABLE TO FIND MYSELF BATTLING THE FULL-FLEDGED LIZARD AGAIN!
--WHEN I CAN BE-- THE LIZARD!?

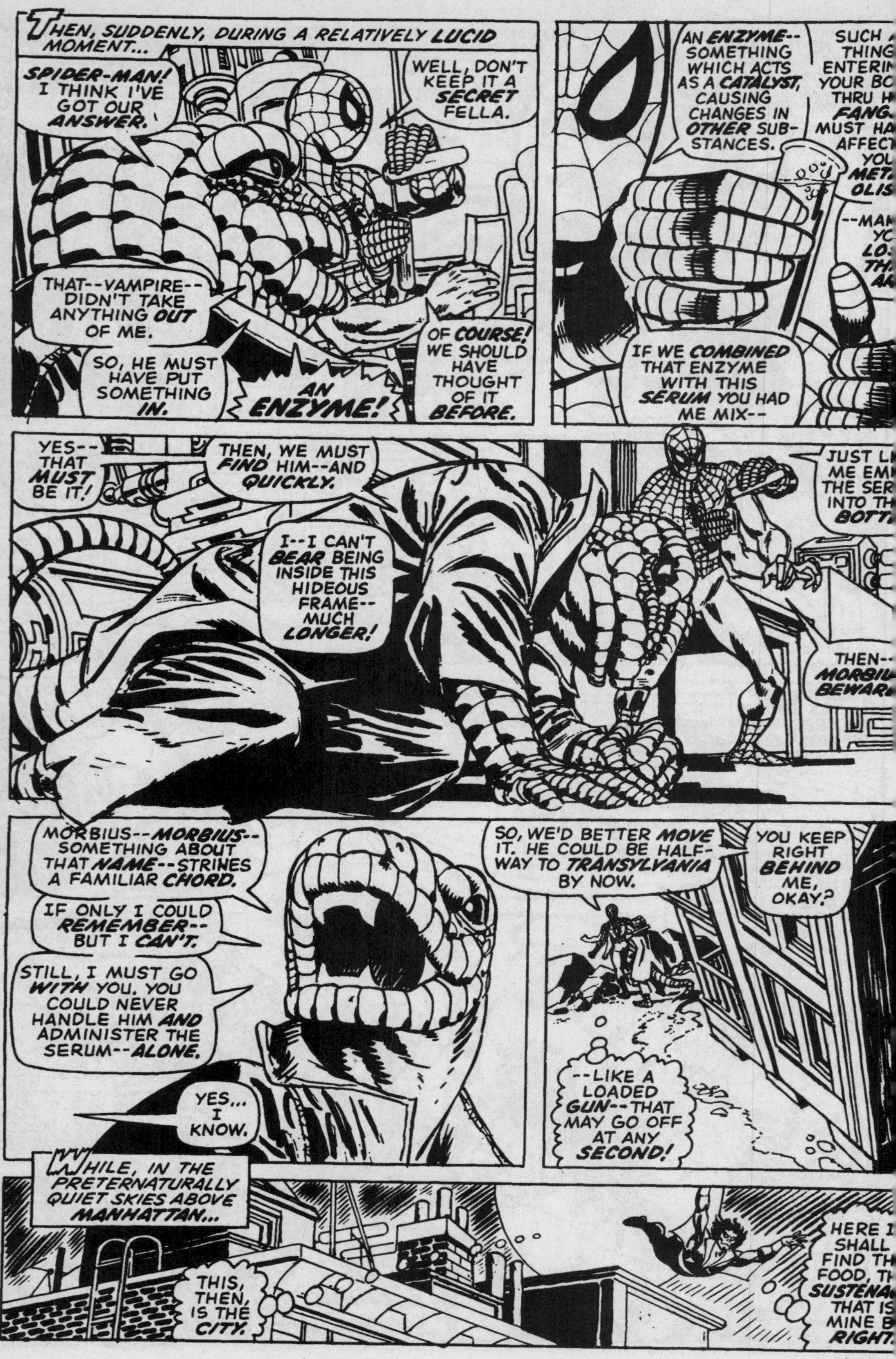
THEN, SUDDENLY, DURING A RELATIVELY LUCID MOMENT...
SPIDER-MAN! I THINK I'VE GOT OUR ANSWER.
WELL, DON'T KEEP IT A SECRET FELLA.
THAT--VAMPIRE--DIDN'T TAKE ANYTHING OUT OF ME.
SO, HE MUST HAVE PUT SOMETHING IN.
AN ENZYME!
OF COURSE! WE SHOULD HAVE THOUGHT OF IT BEFORE.
AN ENZYME--SOMETHING WHICH ACTS AS A CATALYST, CAUSING CHANGES IN OTHER SUBSTANCES.
IF WE COMBINED THAT ENZYME WITH THIS SERUM YOU HAD ME MIX--
YES--THAT MUST BE IT!
THEN, WE MUST FIND HIM--AND QUICKLY.
I--I CAN'T BEAR BEING INSIDE THIS HIDEOUS FRAME--MUCH LONGER!
MORBIUS--MORBIUS--SOMETHING ABOUT THAT NAME--STRINES A FAMILIAR CHORD.
IF ONLY I COULD REMEMBER--BUT I CAN'T.
STILL, I MUST GO WITH YOU. YOU COULD NEVER HANDLE HIM AND ADMINISTER THE SERUM--ALONE.
YES... I KNOW.
SO, WE'D BETTER MOVE IT. HE COULD BE HALF-WAY TO TRANSYLVANIA BY NOW.
YOU KEEP RIGHT BEHIND ME, OKAY?
--LIKE A LOADED GUN--THAT MAY GO OFF AT ANY SECOND!
WHILE, IN THE PRETERNATURALLY QUIET SKIES ABOVE MANHATTAN...
THIS, THEN, IS THE CITY.

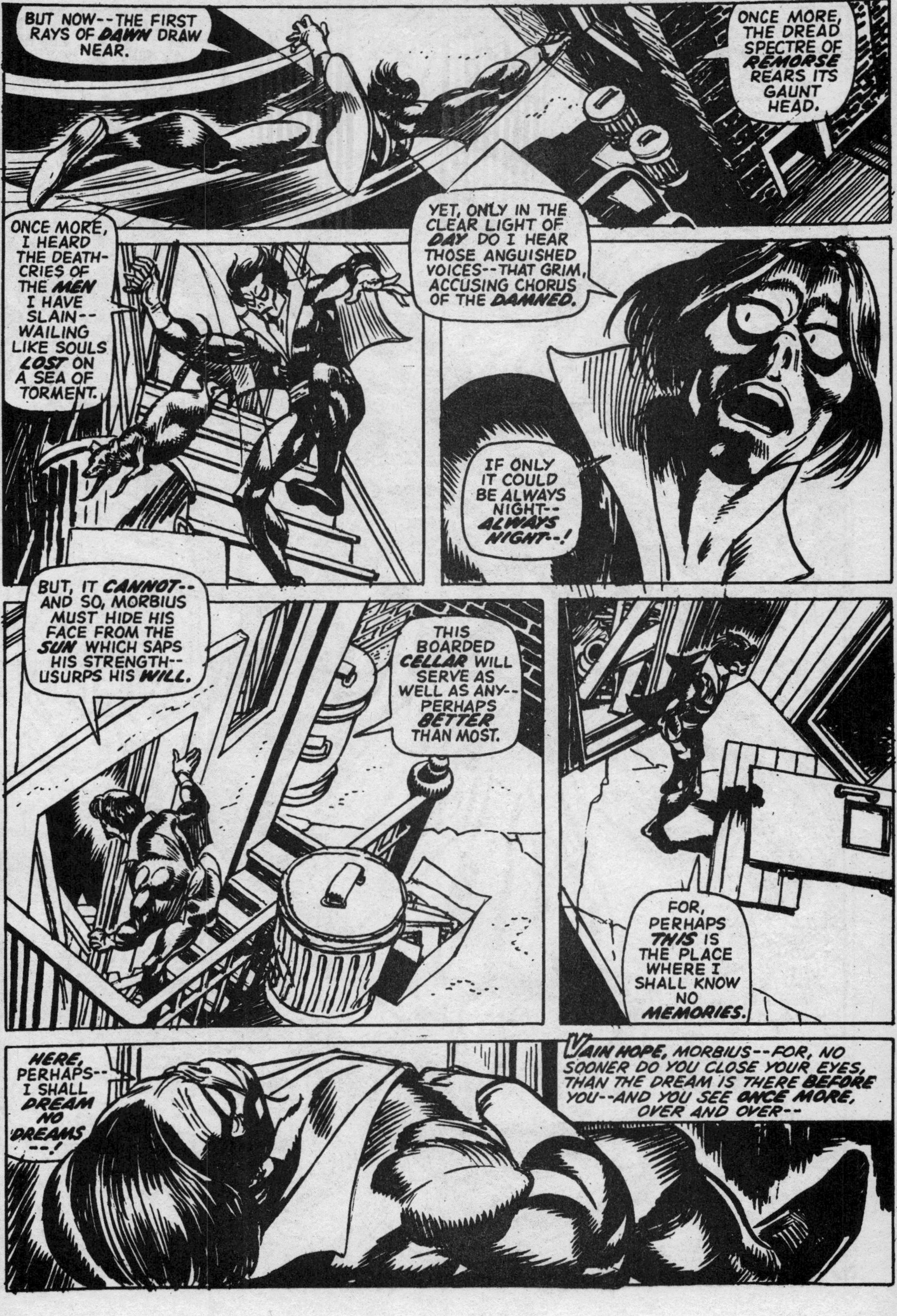

BUT NOW--THE FIRST RAYS OF DAWN DRAW NEAR.
ONCE MORE, THE DREAD SPECTRE OF REMORSE REARS ITS GAUNT HEAD.
ONCE MORE, I HEARD THE DEATH-CRIES OF THE MEN I HAVE SLAIN--WAILING LIKE SOULS LOST ON A SEA OF TORMENT.
YET, ONLY IN THE CLEAR LIGHT OF DAY DO I HEAR THOSE ANGUISHED VOICES--THAT GRIM, ACCUSING CHORUS OF THE DAMNED.
IF ONLY IT COULD BE ALWAYS NIGHT--ALWAYS NIGHT--!
BUT, IT CANNOT--AND SO, MORBIUS MUST HIDE HIS FACE FROM THE SUN WHICH SAPS HIS STRENGTH--USURPS HIS WILL.
THIS BOARDED CELLAR WILL SERVE AS WELL AS ANY--PERHAPS BETTER THAN MOST.
FOR, PERHAPS THIS IS THE PLACE WHERE I SHALL KNOW NO MEMORIES.
HERE, PERHAPS--I SHALL DREAM NO DREAMS--!
VAIN HOPE, MORBIUS--FOR, NO SOONER DO YOU CLOSE YOUR EYES, THAN THE DREAM IS THERE BEFORE YOU--AND YOU SEE ONCE MORE, OVER AND OVER--

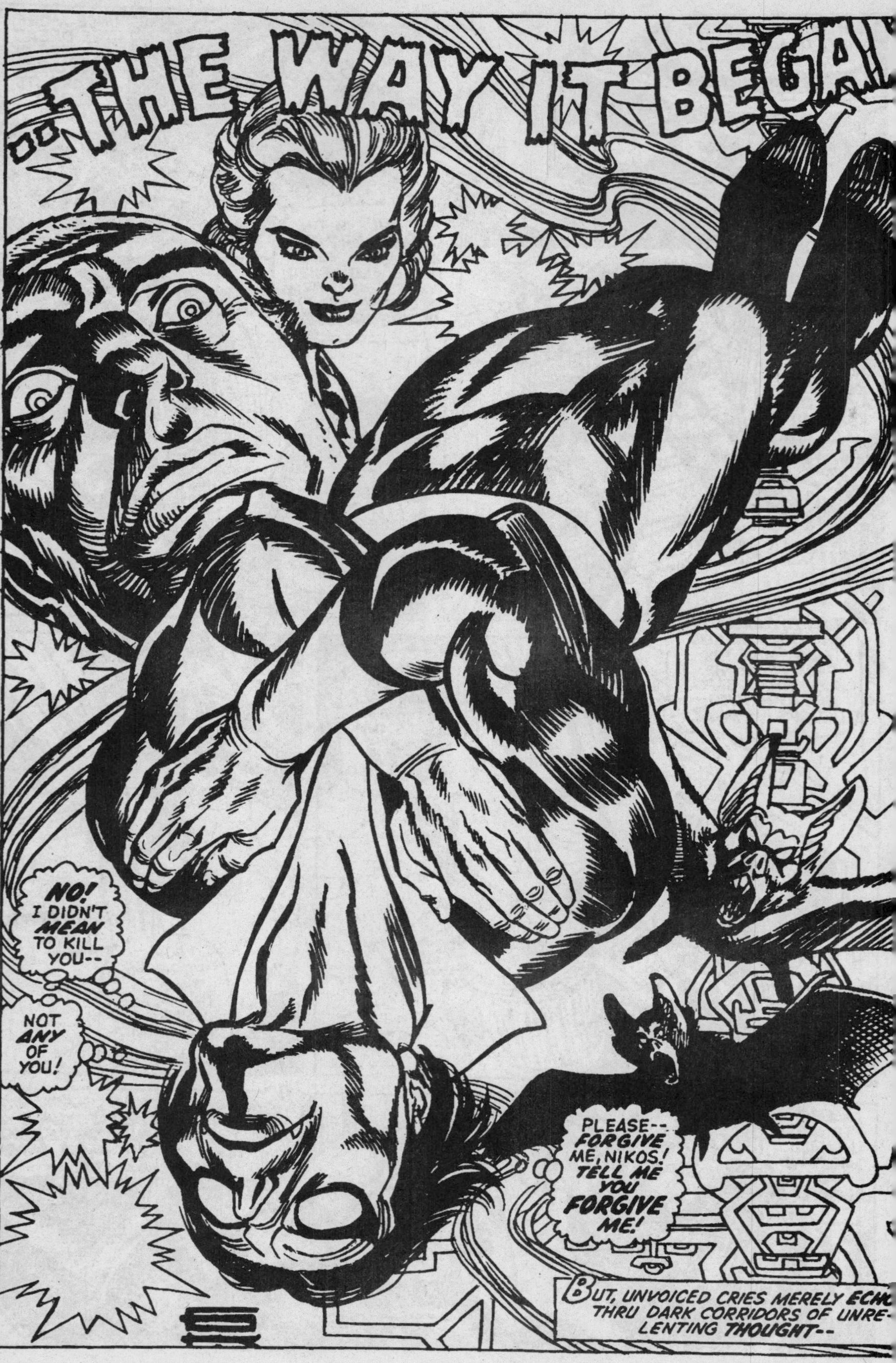
..THE WAY IT BEGAN
NO! I DIDN'T MEAN TO KILL YOU--
NOT ANY OF YOU!
PLEASE-- FORGIVE ME, NIKOS! TELL ME YOU FORGIVE ME!
BUT, UNVOICED CRIES MERELY ECHO THRU DARK CORRIDORS OF UNRE-LENTING THOUGHT--

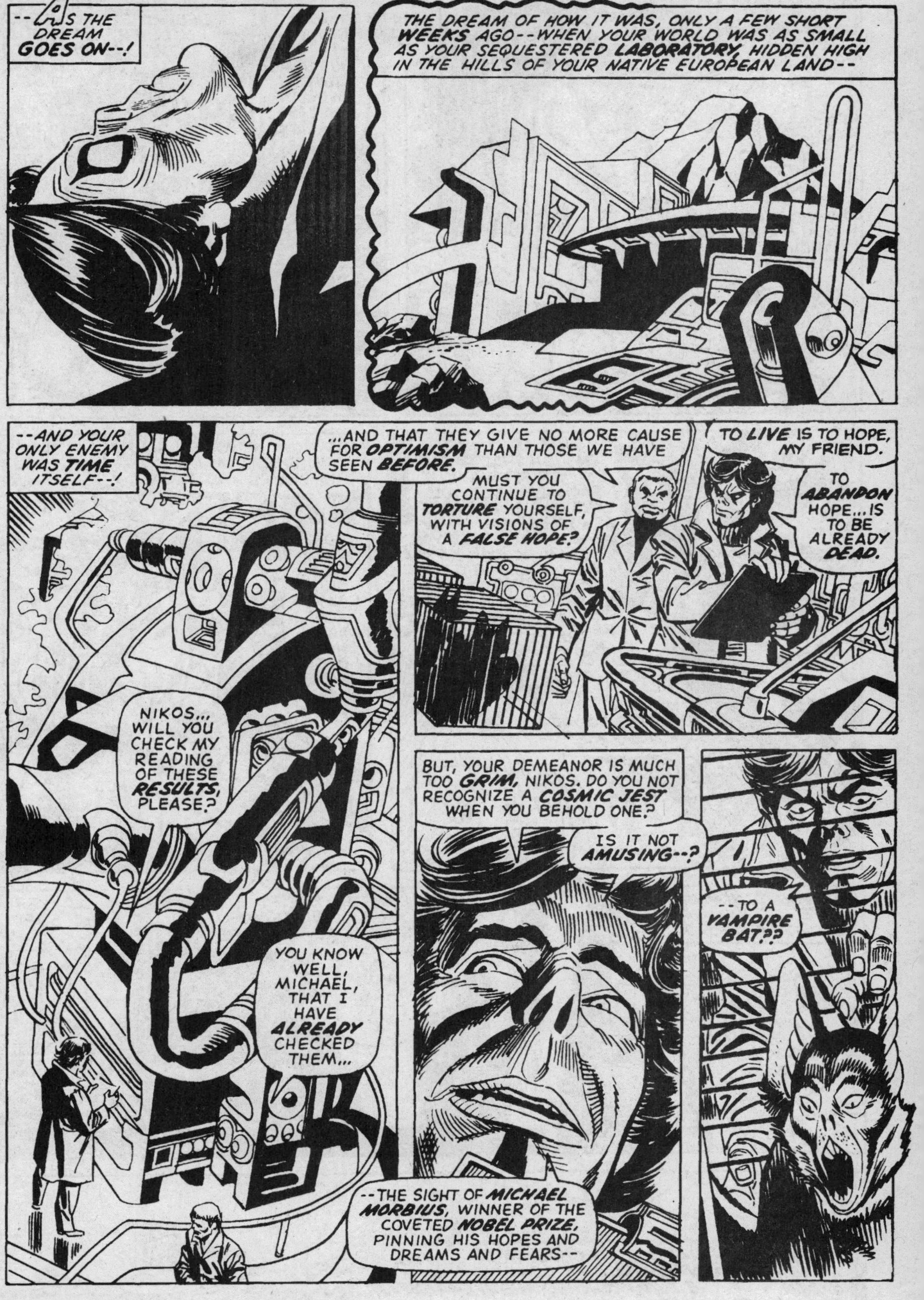
--AS THE DREAM GOES ON--!
THE DREAM OF HOW IT WAS, ONLY A FEW SHORT WEEKS AGO--WHEN YOUR WORLD WAS AS SMALL AS YOUR SEQUESTERED LABORATORY, HIDDEN HIGH IN THE HILLS OF YOUR NATIVE EUROPEAN LAND--
--AND YOUR ONLY ENEMY WAS TIME ITSELF--!
NIKOS... WILL YOU CHECK MY READING OF THESE RESULTS, PLEASE?
YOU KNOW WELL, MICHAEL, THAT I HAVE ALREADY CHECKED THEM...
...AND THAT THEY GIVE NO MORE CAUSE FOR OPTIMISM THAN THOSE WE HAVE SEEN BEFORE.
MUST YOU CONTINUE TO TORTURE YOURSELF, WITH VISIONS OF A FALSE HOPE?
TO LIVE IS TO HOPE, MY FRIEND.
TO ABANDON HOPE... IS TO BE ALREADY DEAD.
BUT, YOUR DEMEANOR IS MUCH TOO GRIM, NIKOS. DO YOU NOT RECOGNIZE A COSMIC JEST WHEN YOU BEHOLD ONE?
IS IT NOT AMUSING--?
--THE SIGHT OF MICHAEL MORBIUS, WINNER OF THE COVETED NOBEL PRIZE, PINNING HIS HOPES AND DREAMS AND FEARS--
--TO A VAMPIRE BAT??

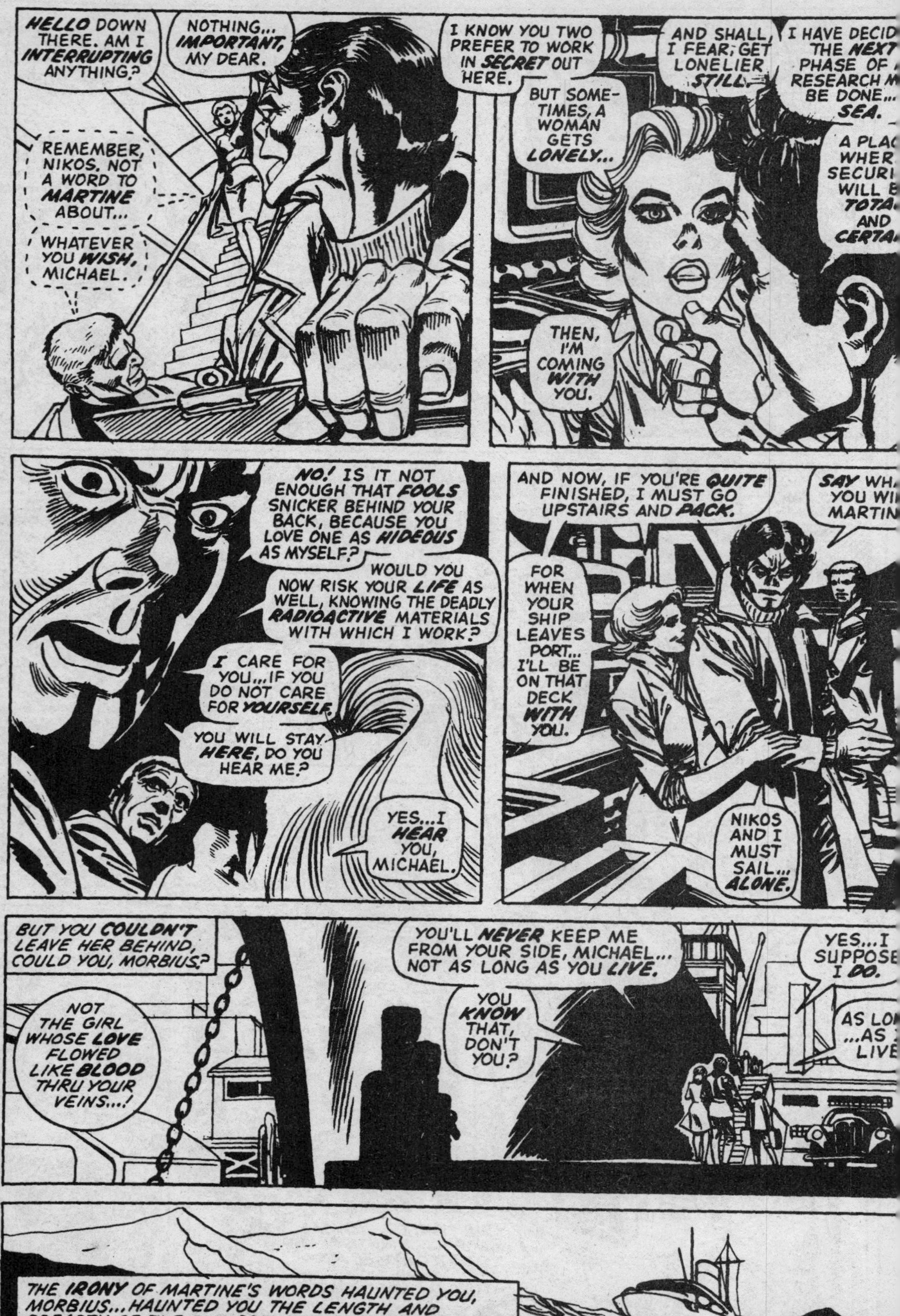

HELLO DOWN THERE. AM I INTERRUPTING ANYTHING?
NOTHING... IMPORTANT, MY DEAR.
REMEMBER, NIKOS. NOT A WORD TO MARTINE ABOUT...
WHATEVER YOU WISH, MICHAEL.
I KNOW YOU TWO PREFER TO WORK IN SECRET OUT HERE.
BUT SOMETIMES, A WOMAN GETS LONELY...
AND SHALL, I FEAR, GET LONELIER STILL.
I HAVE DECID THE NEXT PHASE OF RESEARCH M BE DONE... SEA.
A PLAC WHER SECURI WILL B TOTA AND CERTA
THEN, I'M COMING WITH YOU.
NO! IS IT NOT ENOUGH THAT FOOLS SNICKER BEHIND YOUR BACK, BECAUSE YOU LOVE ONE AS HIDEOUS AS MYSELF?
WOULD YOU NOW RISK YOUR LIFE AS WELL, KNOWING THE DEADLY RADIOACTIVE MATERIALS WITH WHICH I WORK?
I CARE FOR YOU...IF YOU DO NOT CARE FOR YOURSELF.
YOU WILL STAY HERE, DO YOU HEAR ME?
YES...I HEAR YOU, MICHAEL.
AND NOW, IF YOU'RE QUITE FINISHED, I MUST GO UPSTAIRS AND PACK.
FOR WHEN YOUR SHIP LEAVES PORT... I'LL BE ON THAT DECK WITH YOU.
SAY WH YOU WI MARTIN
NIKOS AND I MUST SAIL... ALONE.
BUT YOU COULDN'T LEAVE HER BEHIND, COULD YOU, MORBIUS?
NOT THE GIRL WHOSE LOVE FLOWED LIKE BLOOD THRU YOUR VEINS...!
YOU'LL NEVER KEEP ME FROM YOUR SIDE, MICHAEL... NOT AS LONG AS YOU LIVE.
YOU KNOW THAT, DON'T YOU?
YES...I SUPPOSE I DO.
AS LO ...AS LIVE
THE IRONY OF MARTINE'S WORDS HAUNTED YOU, MORBIUS...HAUNTED YOU THE LENGTH AND BREADTH OF THE SUN-DRENCHED MEDITERRANEAN...

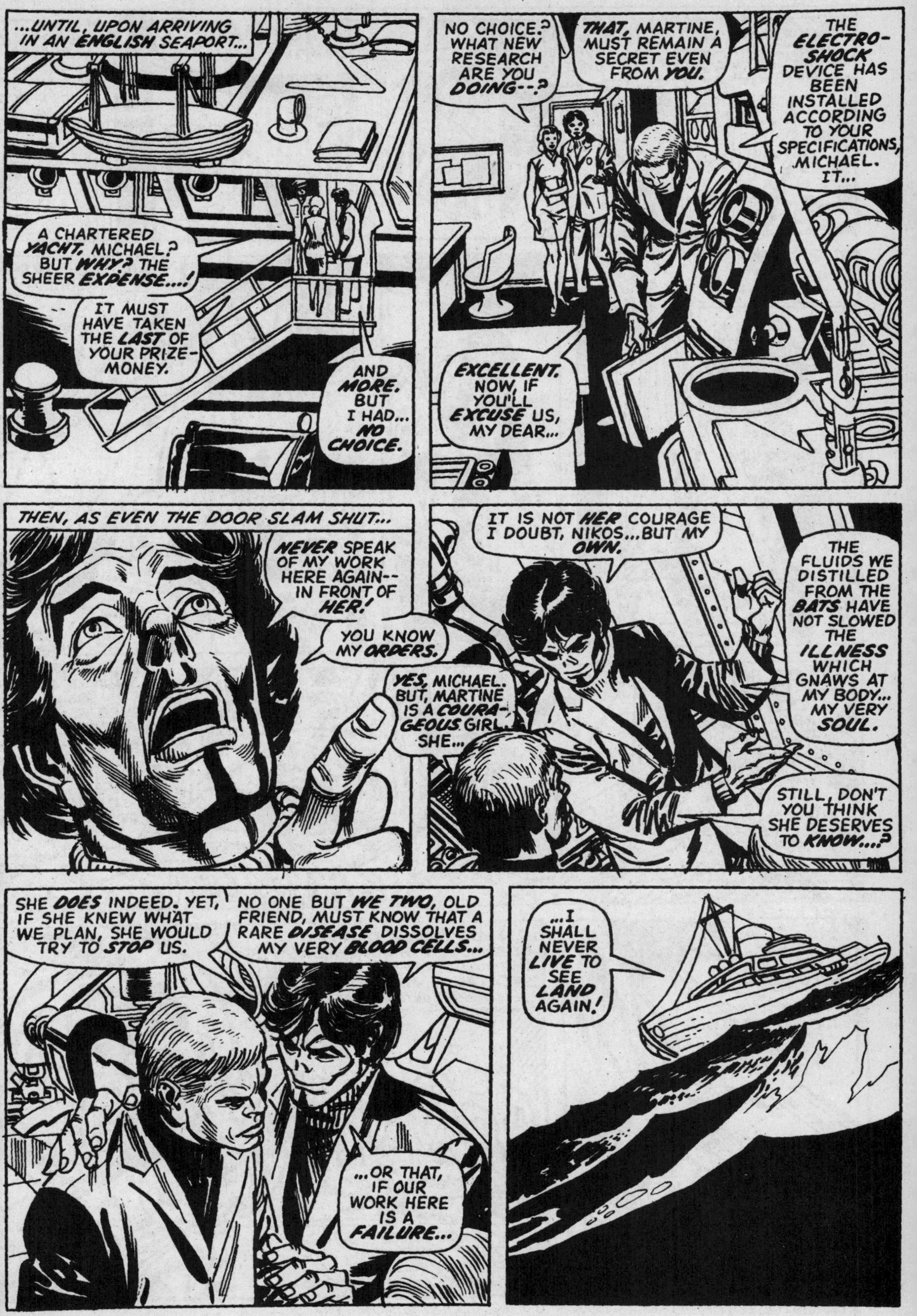
...UNTIL, UPON ARRIVING IN AN ENGLISH SEAPORT...
A CHARTERED YACHT, MICHAEL? BUT WHY? THE SHEER EXPENSE...!
IT MUST HAVE TAKEN THE LAST OF YOUR PRIZE-MONEY.
AND MORE. BUT I HAD... NO CHOICE.
NO CHOICE? WHAT NEW RESEARCH ARE YOU DOING--?
THAT, MARTINE, MUST REMAIN A SECRET EVEN FROM YOU.
THE ELECTRO-SHOCK DEVICE HAS BEEN INSTALLED ACCORDING TO YOUR SPECIFICATIONS, MICHAEL. IT...
EXCELLENT. NOW, IF YOU'LL EXCUSE US, MY DEAR...
THEN, AS EVEN THE DOOR SLAM SHUT...
NEVER SPEAK OF MY WORK HERE AGAIN-- IN FRONT OF HER!
YOU KNOW MY ORDERS.
YES, MICHAEL. BUT, MARTINE IS A COURAGEOUS GIRL. SHE...
IT IS NOT HER COURAGE I DOUBT, NIKOS...BUT MY OWN.
THE FLUIDS WE DISTILLED FROM THE BATS HAVE NOT SLOWED THE ILLNESS WHICH GNAWS AT MY BODY... MY VERY SOUL.
STILL, DON'T YOU THINK SHE DESERVES TO KNOW...?
SHE DOES INDEED. YET, IF SHE KNEW WHAT WE PLAN, SHE WOULD TRY TO STOP US.
NO ONE BUT WE TWO, OLD FRIEND, MUST KNOW THAT A RARE DISEASE DISSOLVES MY VERY BLOOD CELLS...
...OR THAT, IF OUR WORK HERE IS A FAILURE...
...I SHALL NEVER LIVE TO SEE LAND AGAIN!

HOW *HARD* IT WAS, MORBIUS, THAT *NIGHT*...THAT *FINAL* NIGHT...WITH *HER*....!

PLEASE *FORGIVE* MARTINE, IF I LEAVE YOU *EARLY* THIS EVENING.

THERE ARE ROUTINE MATTERS I MUST CHECK IN THE *LABORATORY* BELOW.

OF COURSE. I UNDERSTAND MY LOVE.

BUT, DO NOT WORK *TOO* LONG. YOU SEEM...SO *PALE.*

DOES SHE *SUSPECT,* OLD FRIEND?

I... THINK *NOT.*

YET, WE MUST *HURRY,* MY TIME GROWS *SHORT.*

UNLESS THIS SHOCK-TREATMENT *SUCCEEDS*...AGAINST ALL HOPE, ALL *ODDS*...

...I'LL MEASURE OUT MY LIFE IN *DAYS*...PERHAPS *HOURS!*

I KNOW, MICHAEL.

BUT, *ELECTRICAL* CREATION OF BLOOD-CELLS IS SOMETHING NEVER BEFORE *ATTEMPTED*...LET ALONE *ACHIEVED.*

IF ONLY WE HAD TIME TO GAUGE ALL POSSIBLE *RESULTS*...ALL POTENTIAL *SIDE EFFECTS*...

AND YET, AS YOU *SAY*... WE HAVE *NO CHOICE.*

FOR, *WHAT* SIDE-EFFECT COULD POSSIBLY BE WORSE THAN-- *DEATH?*

DID YOU *SENSE* IT THEN, MORBIUS--IN THAT *MOMENT?* DID YOU GLIMPSE THE UN-SPEAKABLE *ANSWER* TO NIKOS' QUESTION...

ARRRRRRRR-RRR!

...IN THAT SINGLE, SEARING *INSTANT* WHEN TIME AND SPACE WERE SWALLOWED IN THE GAPING MAW OF *PAIN--?*

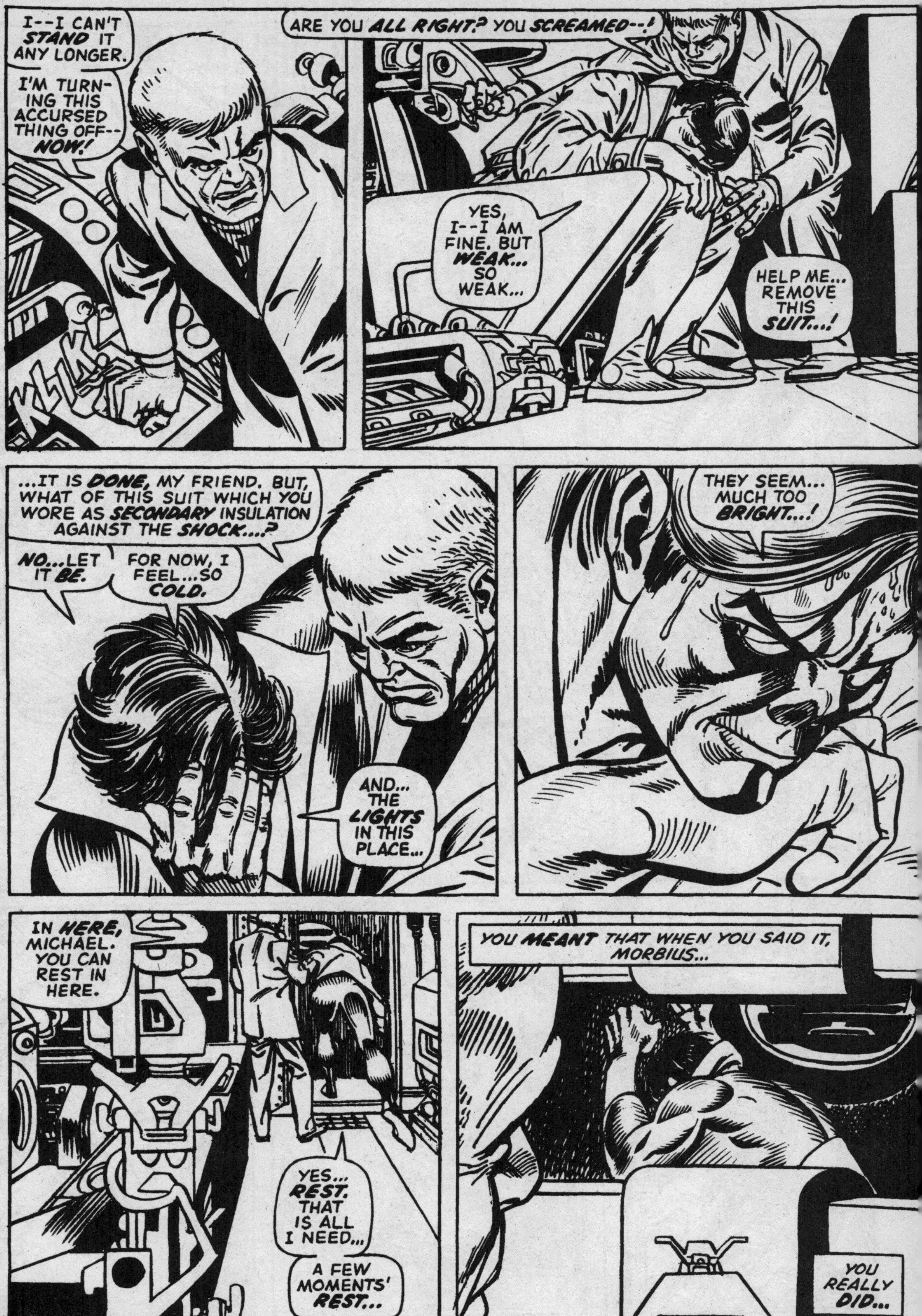

I--I CAN'T STAND IT ANY LONGER.
I'M TURNING THIS ACCURSED THING OFF--NOW!
KLIK
ARE YOU ALL RIGHT? YOU SCREAMED--!
YES, I--I AM FINE. BUT WEAK... SO WEAK...
HELP ME... REMOVE THIS SUIT...!
...IT IS DONE, MY FRIEND. BUT, WHAT OF THIS SUIT WHICH YOU WORE AS SECONDARY INSULATION AGAINST THE SHOCK...?
NO...LET IT BE.
FOR NOW, I FEEL...SO COLD.
AND... THE LIGHTS IN THIS PLACE...
THEY SEEM... MUCH TOO BRIGHT...!
IN HERE, MICHAEL. YOU CAN REST IN HERE.
YES... REST. THAT IS ALL I NEED...
A FEW MOMENTS' REST...
YOU MEANT THAT WHEN YOU SAID IT, MORBIUS...
YOU REALLY DID...

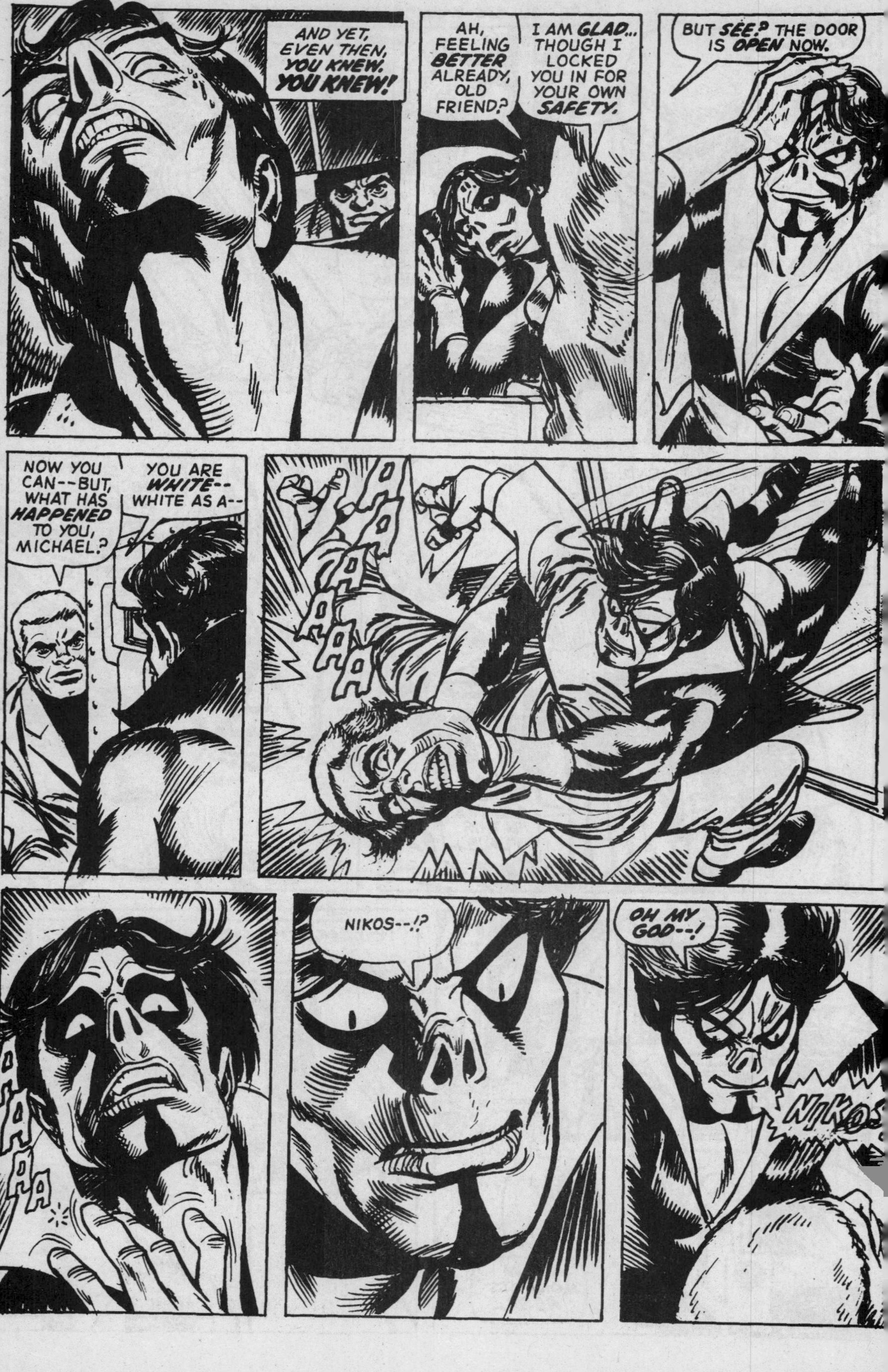
AND YET, EVEN THEN, YOU KNEW. YOU KNEW!
AH, FEELING BETTER ALREADY, OLD FRIEND?
I AM GLAD... THOUGH I LOCKED YOU IN FOR YOUR OWN SAFETY.
BUT SEE? THE DOOR IS OPEN NOW.
NOW YOU CAN--BUT, WHAT HAS HAPPENED TO YOU, MICHAEL?
YOU ARE WHITE-- WHITE AS A--
NIKOS--!?
OH MY GOD--!
NIKOS

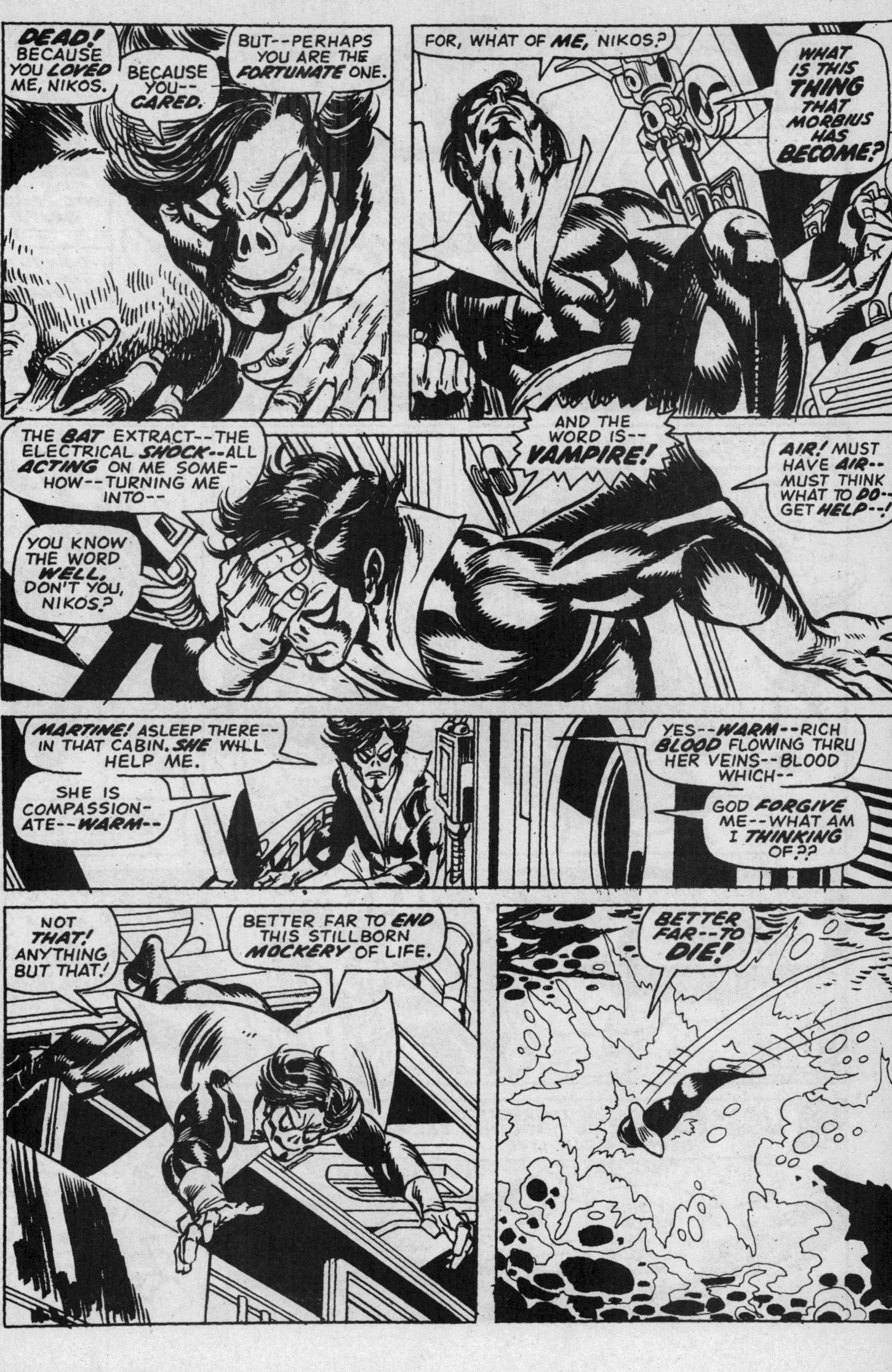
DEAD! BECAUSE YOU LOVED ME, NIKOS.
BECAUSE YOU-- CARED.
BUT--PERHAPS YOU ARE THE FORTUNATE ONE.
FOR, WHAT OF ME, NIKOS?
WHAT IS THIS THING THAT MORBIUS HAS BECOME?
THE BAT EXTRACT--THE ELECTRICAL SHOCK--ALL ACTING ON ME SOME-HOW--TURNING ME INTO--
YOU KNOW THE WORD WELL, DON'T YOU, NIKOS?
AND THE WORD IS-- VAMPIRE!
AIR! MUST HAVE AIR-- MUST THINK WHAT TO DO-- GET HELP--!
MARTINE! ASLEEP THERE-- IN THAT CABIN. SHE WILL HELP ME.
SHE IS COMPASSION-ATE--WARM--
YES--WARM--RICH BLOOD FLOWING THRU HER VEINS--BLOOD WHICH--
GOD FORGIVE ME--WHAT AM I THINKING OF??
NOT THAT! ANYTHING BUT THAT!
BETTER FAR TO END THIS STILLBORN MOCKERY OF LIFE.
BETTER FAR--TO DIE!

YES, MORBIUS--EVEN HERE, IN YOUR TOO-VIVID *DREAM WORLD*, YOU KNOW THAT YOU GLIMPSED THE TRUTH IN THAT FLEETING INSTANT--!

BETTER TO PERISH--TO FILL YOUR STRAINING LUNGS WITH WATER, AND SINK DEEP INTO A LIQUID GRAVE--

--THAN TO LIVE THE LIFE OF THE DAMNED!

YET, EVEN *AMONG* THE DAMNED, THE LUST FOR *LIVING* IS A SURGING *TIDAL WAVE*--

--AND IN ITS RELENTLESS WAKE ARE SUBMERGED THE HUMAN INSTINCTS WHICH BIRTHED THE SELFLESS ACT--

--SUBMERGED, DROWNED --TILL ONLY THE BEAST REMAINS--

--THE BEAST WHICH KICKS AND CLAWS AND *CAREENS* ITS FRANTIC WAY TO THE SURFACE--

AIR! AT LAST!

I WAS A *FOOL* TO LEAP OVERBOARD--TO SACRIFICE *MYSELF*, SO THAT OTHER, *LESSER* BEINGS MIGHT LIVE.

THE SHIP WHICH WAS MINE IS *GONE* NOW--

BUT THERE WILL BE *OTHER* SHIPS--

--OTHER PREY FOR MORBIUS!

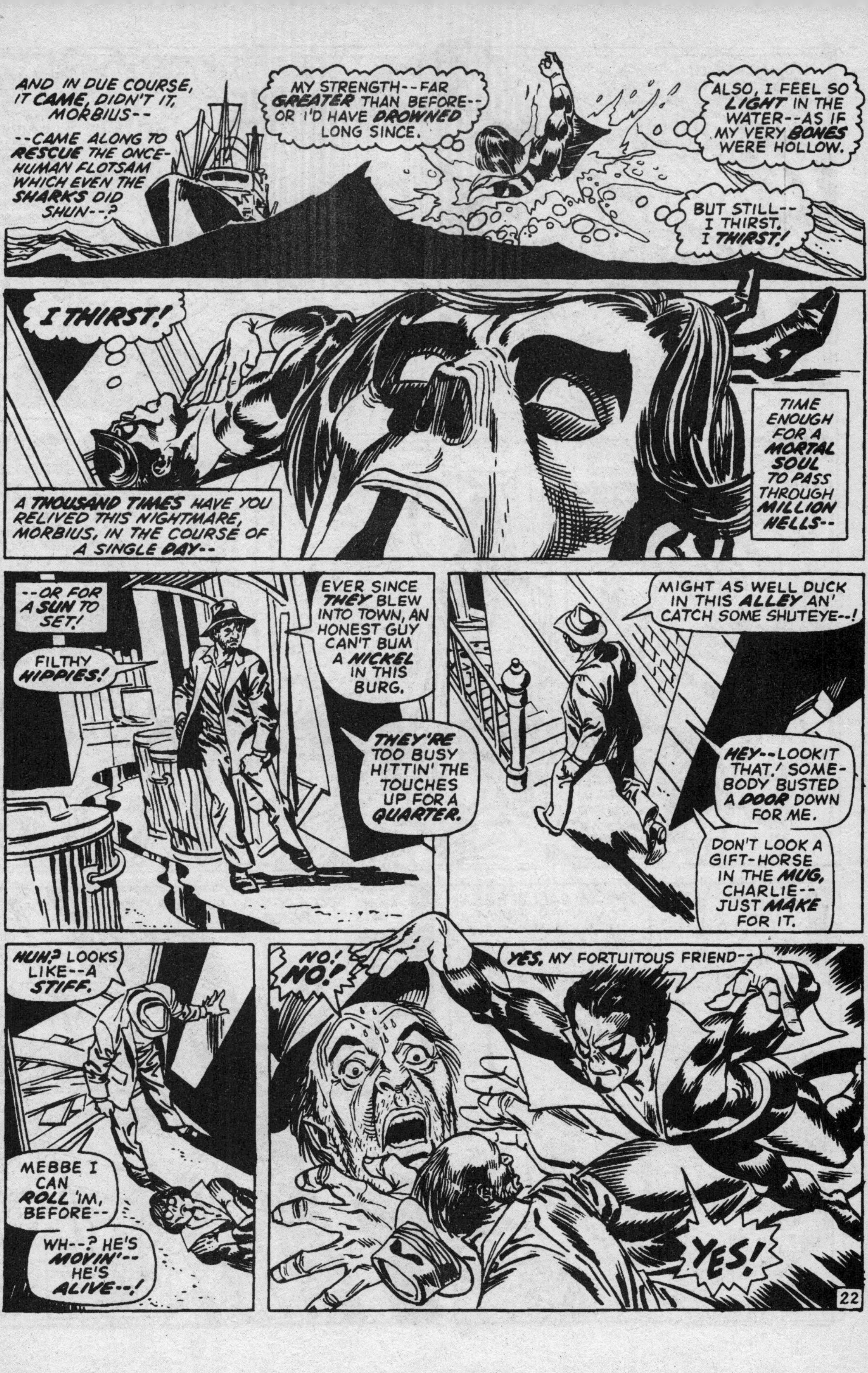
AND IN DUE COURSE, IT CAME, DIDN'T IT, MORBIUS--
--CAME ALONG TO RESCUE THE ONCE-HUMAN FLOTSAM WHICH EVEN THE SHARKS DID SHUN--?
MY STRENGTH--FAR GREATER THAN BEFORE--OR I'D HAVE DROWNED LONG SINCE.
ALSO, I FEEL SO LIGHT IN THE WATER--AS IF MY VERY BONES WERE HOLLOW.
BUT STILL--I THIRST. I THIRST!
I THIRST!
A THOUSAND TIMES HAVE YOU RELIVED THIS NIGHTMARE, MORBIUS, IN THE COURSE OF A SINGLE DAY--
TIME ENOUGH FOR A MORTAL SOUL TO PASS THROUGH MILLION HELLS--
--OR FOR A SUN TO SET!
FILTHY HIPPIES!
EVER SINCE THEY BLEW INTO TOWN, AN HONEST GUY CAN'T BUM A NICKEL IN THIS BURG.
THEY'RE TOO BUSY HITTIN' THE TOUCHES UP FOR A QUARTER.
MIGHT AS WELL DUCK IN THIS ALLEY AN' CATCH SOME SHUTEYE--!
HEY--LOOKIT THAT! SOMEBODY BUSTED A DOOR DOWN FOR ME.
DON'T LOOK A GIFT-HORSE IN THE MUG, CHARLIE--JUST MAKE FOR IT.
HUH? LOOKS LIKE--A STIFF.
MEBBE I CAN ROLL 'IM, BEFORE--
WH--? HE'S MOVIN'--HE'S ALIVE--!
NO! NO!
YES, MY FORTUITOUS FRIEND--
YES!

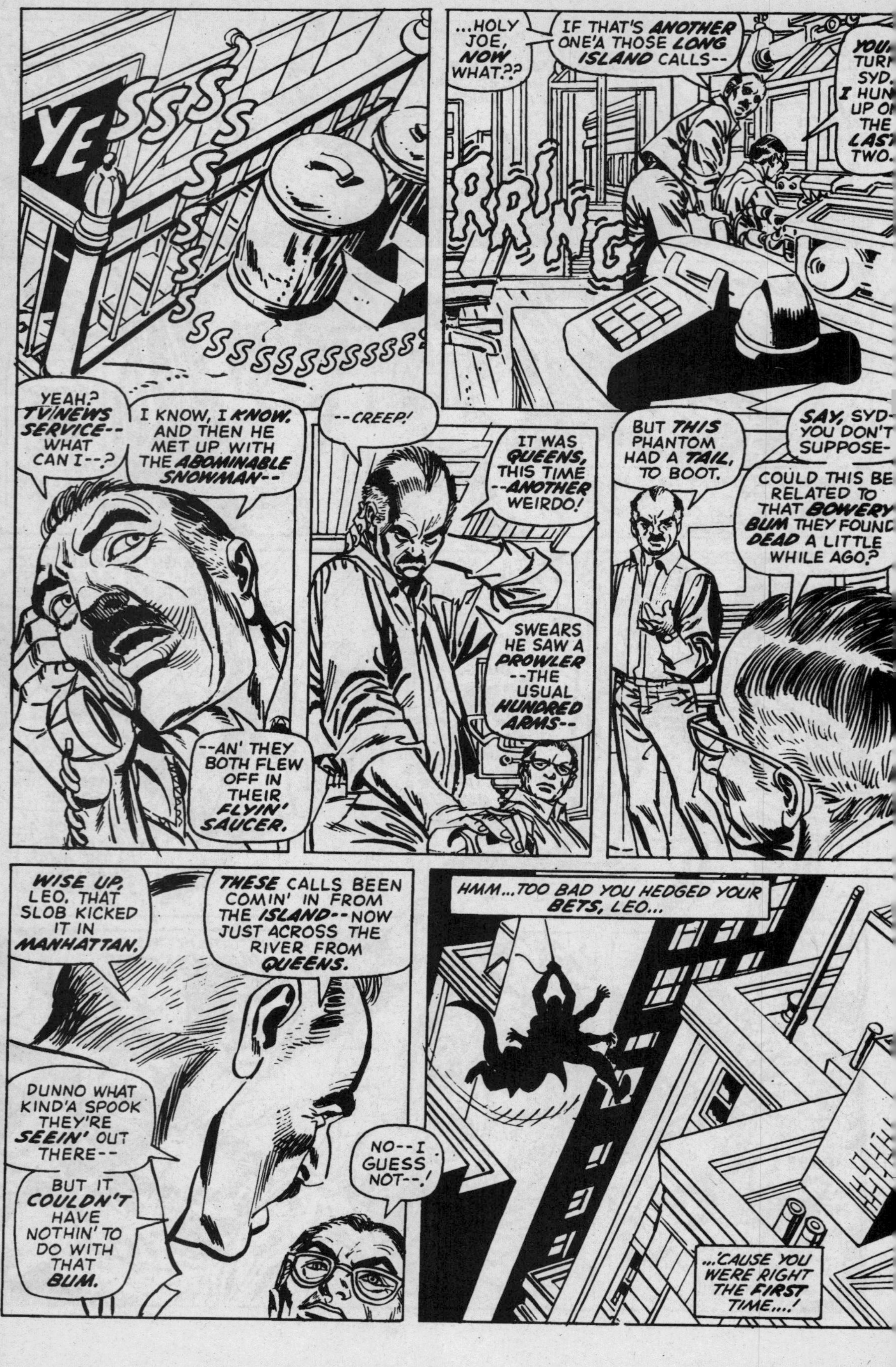
YESSSSSSSSSSSSSSSSSS
...HOLY JOE, NOW WHAT??
IF THAT'S ANOTHER ONE'A THOSE LONG ISLAND CALLS--
RRING
YEAH? TV/NEWS SERVICE--WHAT CAN I--?
I KNOW, I KNOW. AND THEN HE MET UP WITH THE ABOMINABLE SNOWMAN--
--AN' THEY BOTH FLEW OFF IN THEIR FLYIN' SAUCER.
--CREEP!
IT WAS QUEENS, THIS TIME --ANOTHER WEIRDO!
SWEARS HE SAW A PROWLER --THE USUAL HUNDRED ARMS--
BUT THIS PHANTOM HAD A TAIL, TO BOOT.
SAY, SYD-YOU DON'T SUPPOSE-
COULD THIS BE RELATED TO THAT BOWERY BUM THEY FOUND DEAD A LITTLE WHILE AGO?
WISE UP, LEO. THAT SLOB KICKED IT IN MANHATTAN.
THESE CALLS BEEN COMIN' IN FROM THE ISLAND--NOW JUST ACROSS THE RIVER FROM QUEENS.
DUNNO WHAT KIND'A SPOOK THEY'RE SEEIN' OUT THERE--
BUT IT COULDN'T HAVE NOTHIN' TO DO WITH THAT BUM.
NO--I GUESS NOT--!
HMM...TOO BAD YOU HEDGED YOUR BETS, LEO...
...'CAUSE YOU WERE RIGHT THE FIRST TIME....!

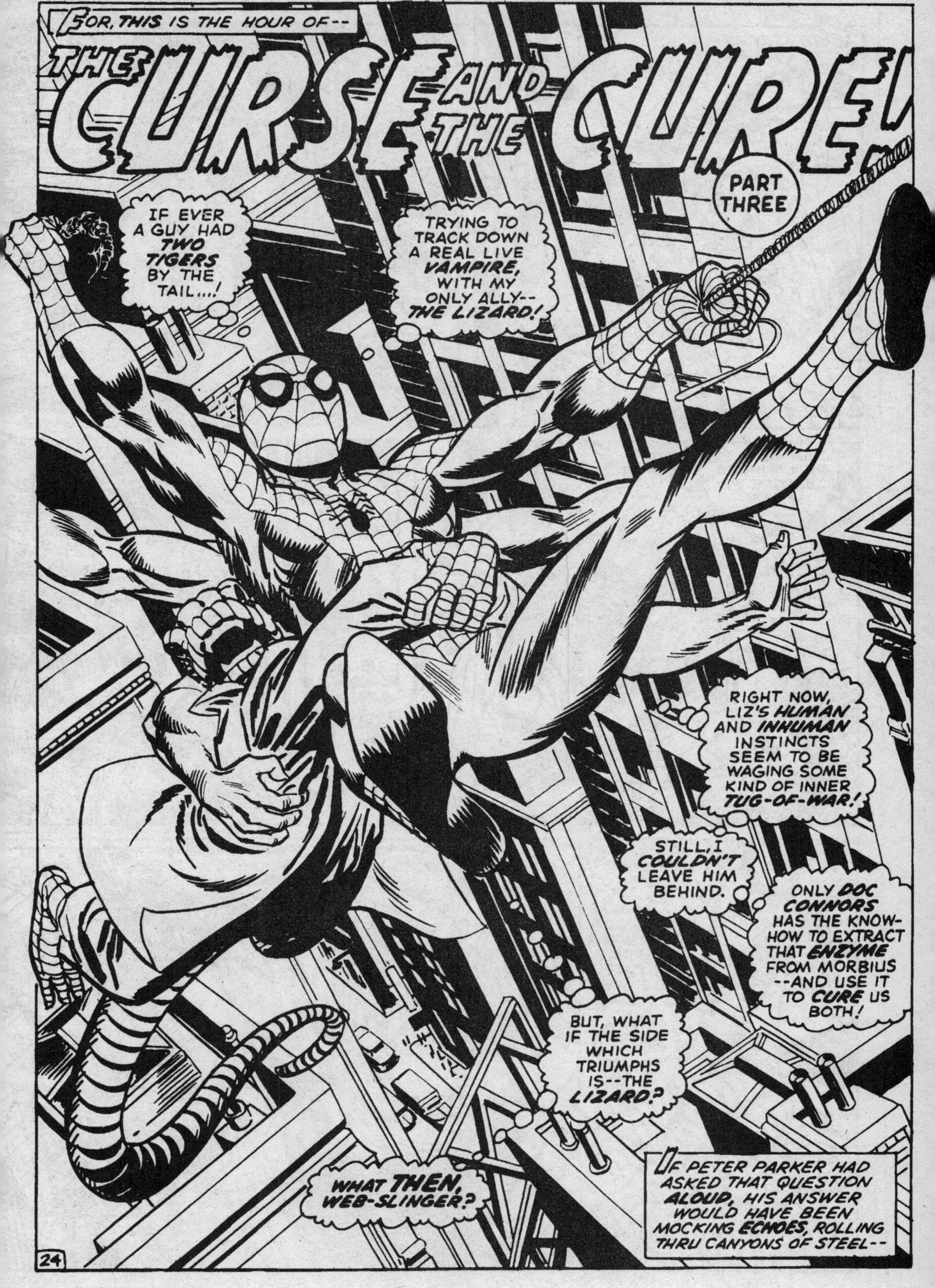
FOR, THIS IS THE HOUR OF--
THE CURSE AND THE CURE!
PART THREE
IF EVER A GUY HAD TWO TIGERS BY THE TAIL...!
TRYING TO TRACK DOWN A REAL LIVE VAMPIRE, WITH MY ONLY ALLY-- THE LIZARD!
RIGHT NOW, LIZ'S HUMAN AND INHUMAN INSTINCTS SEEM TO BE WAGING SOME KIND OF INNER TUG-OF-WAR!
STILL, I COULDN'T LEAVE HIM BEHIND.
ONLY DOC CONNORS HAS THE KNOW-HOW TO EXTRACT THAT ENZYME FROM MORBIUS --AND USE IT TO CURE US BOTH!
BUT, WHAT IF THE SIDE WHICH TRIUMPHS IS--THE LIZARD?
WHAT THEN, WEB-SLINGER?
IF PETER PARKER HAD ASKED THAT QUESTION ALOUD, HIS ANSWER WOULD HAVE BEEN MOCKING ECHOES, ROLLING THRU CANYONS OF STEEL--
24

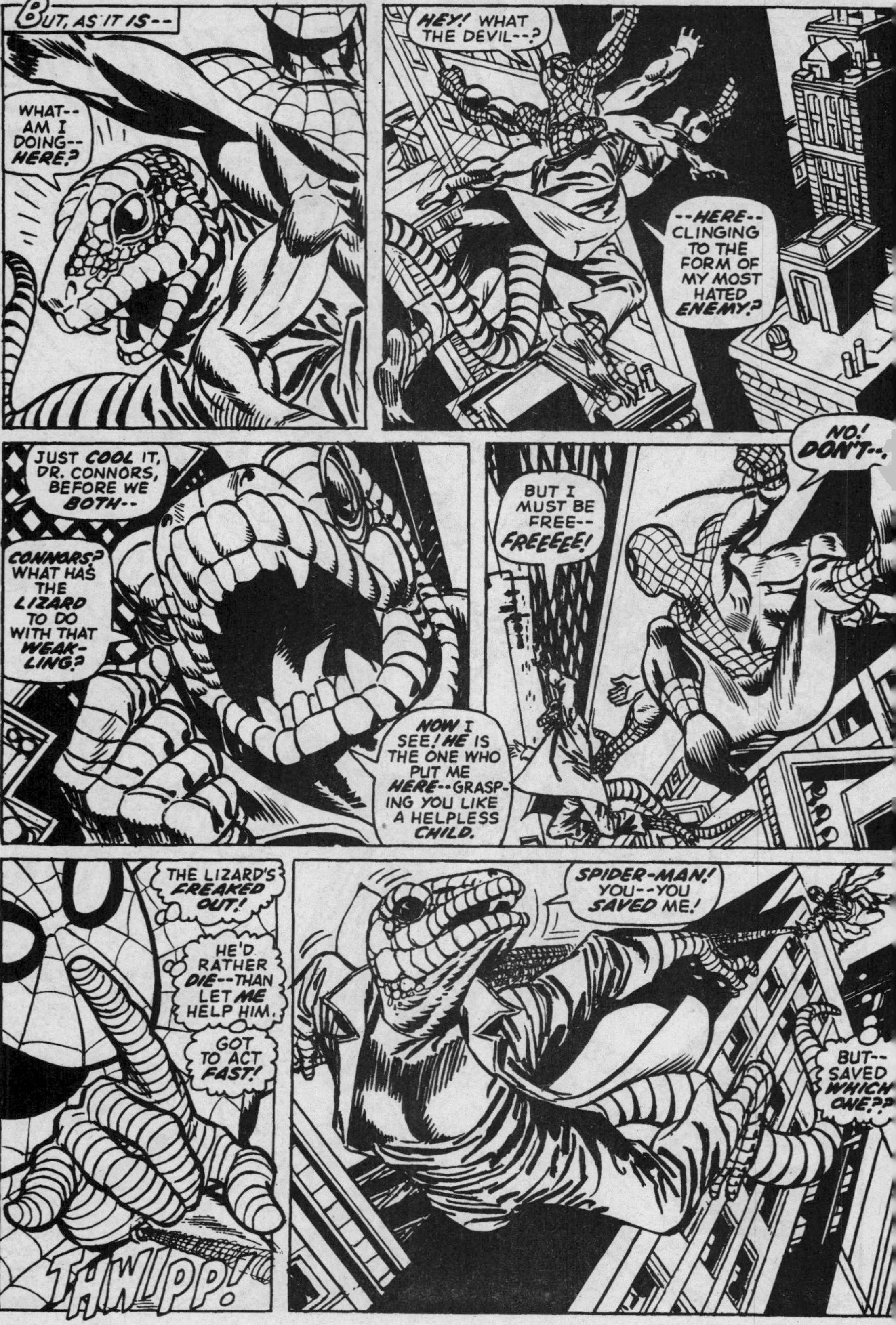
BUT, AS IT IS--
WHAT-- AM I DOING-- HERE?
HEY! WHAT THE DEVIL--?
--HERE-- CLINGING TO THE FORM OF MY MOST HATED ENEMY?
JUST COOL IT, DR. CONNORS, BEFORE WE BOTH--
CONNORS? WHAT HAS THE LIZARD TO DO WITH THAT WEAK-LING?
BUT I MUST BE FREE-- FREEEEE!
NO! DON'T--.
NOW I SEE! HE IS THE ONE WHO PUT ME HERE--GRASP-ING YOU LIKE A HELPLESS CHILD.
THE LIZARD'S FREAKED OUT!
HE'D RATHER DIE--THAN LET ME HELP HIM.
GOT TO ACT FAST!
THWIPP!
SPIDER-MAN! YOU--YOU SAVED ME!
BUT-- SAVED WHICH ONE??

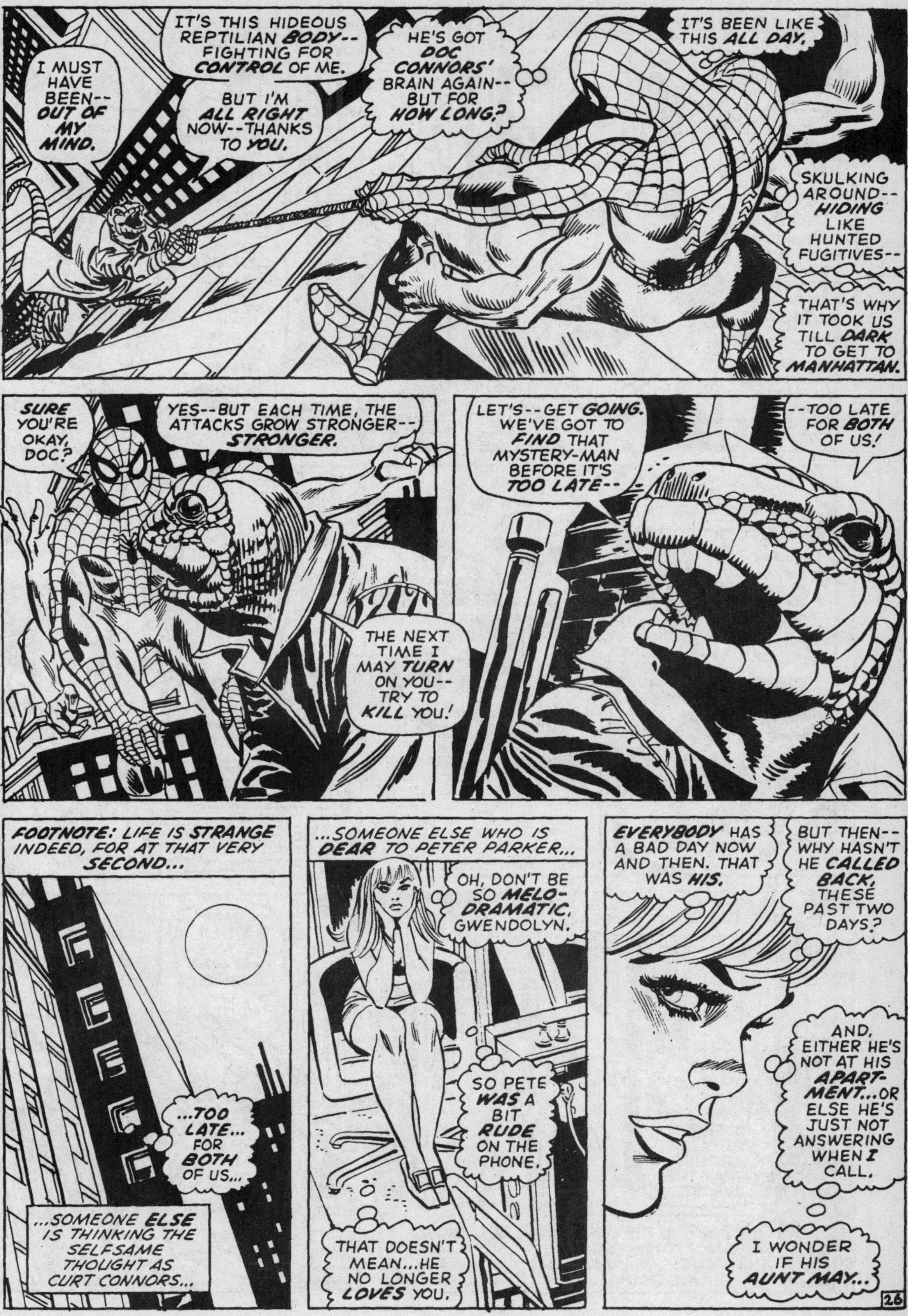
I MUST HAVE BEEN--OUT OF MY MIND.
IT'S THIS HIDEOUS REPTILIAN BODY--FIGHTING FOR CONTROL OF ME.
BUT I'M ALL RIGHT NOW--THANKS TO YOU.
HE'S GOT DOC CONNORS' BRAIN AGAIN--BUT FOR HOW LONG?
IT'S BEEN LIKE THIS ALL DAY.
SKULKING AROUND--HIDING LIKE HUNTED FUGITIVES--
THAT'S WHY IT TOOK US TILL DARK TO GET TO MANHATTAN.
SURE YOU'RE OKAY, DOC?
YES--BUT EACH TIME, THE ATTACKS GROW STRONGER--STRONGER.
THE NEXT TIME I MAY TURN ON YOU--TRY TO KILL YOU!
LET'S--GET GOING. WE'VE GOT TO FIND THAT MYSTERY-MAN BEFORE IT'S TOO LATE--
--TOO LATE FOR BOTH OF US!
FOOTNOTE: LIFE IS STRANGE INDEED, FOR AT THAT VERY SECOND...
...TOO LATE... FOR BOTH OF US...
...SOMEONE ELSE IS THINKING THE SELFSAME THOUGHT AS CURT CONNORS...
...SOMEONE ELSE WHO IS DEAR TO PETER PARKER...
OH, DON'T BE SO MELO-DRAMATIC, GWENDOLYN.
SO PETE WAS A BIT RUDE ON THE PHONE.
THAT DOESN'T MEAN...HE NO LONGER LOVES YOU.
EVERYBODY HAS A BAD DAY NOW AND THEN. THAT WAS HIS.
BUT THEN--WHY HASN'T HE CALLED BACK, THESE PAST TWO DAYS?
AND, EITHER HE'S NOT AT HIS APART-MENT...OR ELSE HE'S JUST NOT ANSWERING WHEN I CALL.
I WONDER IF HIS AUNT MAY...
26

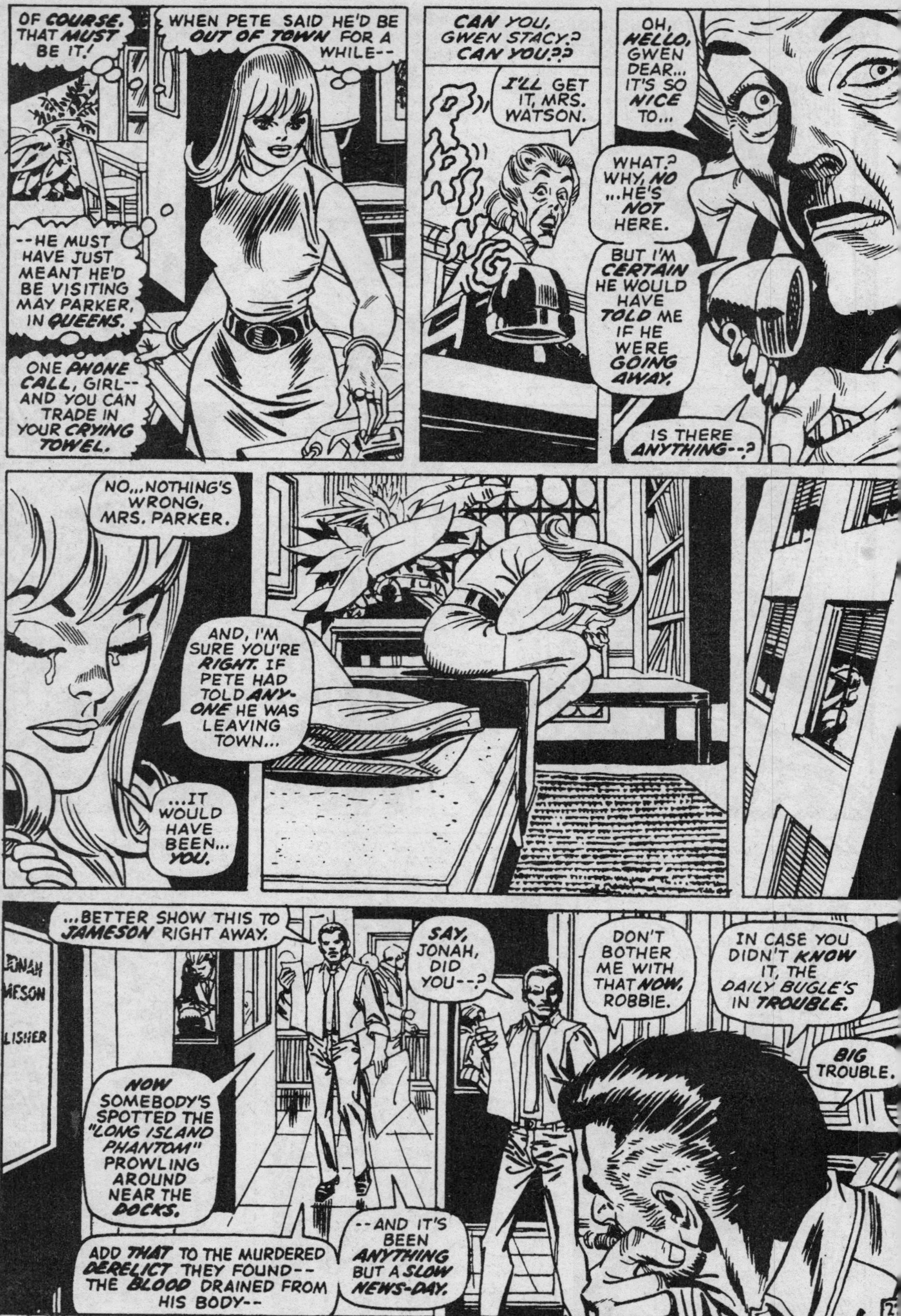
OF COURSE. THAT MUST BE IT!
WHEN PETE SAID HE'D BE OUT OF TOWN FOR A WHILE--
--HE MUST HAVE JUST MEANT HE'D BE VISITING MAY PARKER, IN QUEENS.
ONE PHONE CALL, GIRL-- AND YOU CAN TRADE IN YOUR CRYING TOWEL.
CAN YOU, GWEN STACY? CAN YOU??
I'LL GET IT, MRS. WATSON.
OH, HELLO, GWEN DEAR... IT'S SO NICE TO...
WHAT? WHY, NO ...HE'S NOT HERE.
BUT I'M CERTAIN HE WOULD HAVE TOLD ME IF HE WERE GOING AWAY.
IS THERE ANYTHING--?
NO... NOTHING'S WRONG, MRS. PARKER.
AND, I'M SURE YOU'RE RIGHT. IF PETE HAD TOLD ANY-ONE HE WAS LEAVING TOWN...
...IT WOULD HAVE BEEN... YOU.
...BETTER SHOW THIS TO JAMESON RIGHT AWAY.
NOW SOMEBODY'S SPOTTED THE "LONG ISLAND PHANTOM" PROWLING AROUND NEAR THE DOCKS.
ADD THAT TO THE MURDERED DERELICT THEY FOUND-- THE BLOOD DRAINED FROM HIS BODY--
--AND IT'S BEEN ANYTHING BUT A SLOW NEWS-DAY.
SAY, JONAH, DID YOU--?
DON'T BOTHER ME WITH THAT NOW, ROBBIE.
IN CASE YOU DIDN'T KNOW IT, THE DAILY BUGLE'S IN TROUBLE.
BIG TROUBLE.

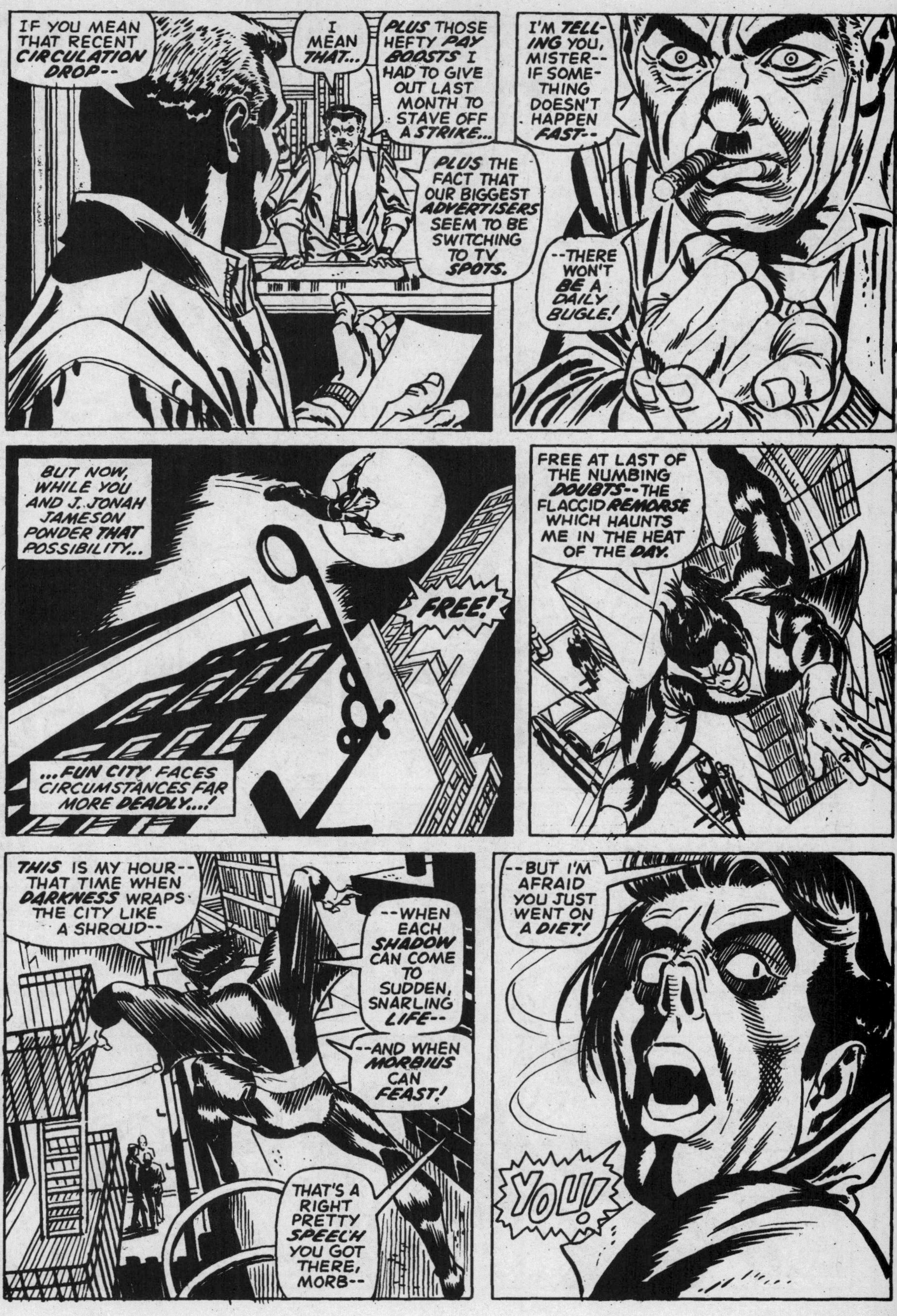
IF YOU MEAN THAT RECENT CIRCULATION DROP--
I MEAN THAT...
PLUS THOSE HEFTY PAY BOOSTS I HAD TO GIVE OUT LAST MONTH TO STAVE OFF A STRIKE...
PLUS THE FACT THAT OUR BIGGEST ADVERTISERS SEEM TO BE SWITCHING TO TV SPOTS.
I'M TELLING YOU, MISTER-- IF SOMETHING DOESN'T HAPPEN FAST--
--THERE WON'T BE A DAILY BUGLE!
BUT NOW, WHILE YOU AND J. JONAH JAMESON PONDER THAT POSSIBILITY...
FREE!
...FUN CITY FACES CIRCUMSTANCES FAR MORE DEADLY...!
FREE AT LAST OF THE NUMBING DOUBTS--THE FLACCID REMORSE WHICH HAUNTS ME IN THE HEAT OF THE DAY.
THIS IS MY HOUR-- THAT TIME WHEN DARKNESS WRAPS THE CITY LIKE A SHROUD--
--WHEN EACH SHADOW CAN COME TO SUDDEN, SNARLING LIFE--
--AND WHEN MORBIUS CAN FEAST!
THAT'S A RIGHT PRETTY SPEECH YOU GOT THERE, MORB--
--BUT I'M AFRAID YOU JUST WENT ON A DIET!
YOU!

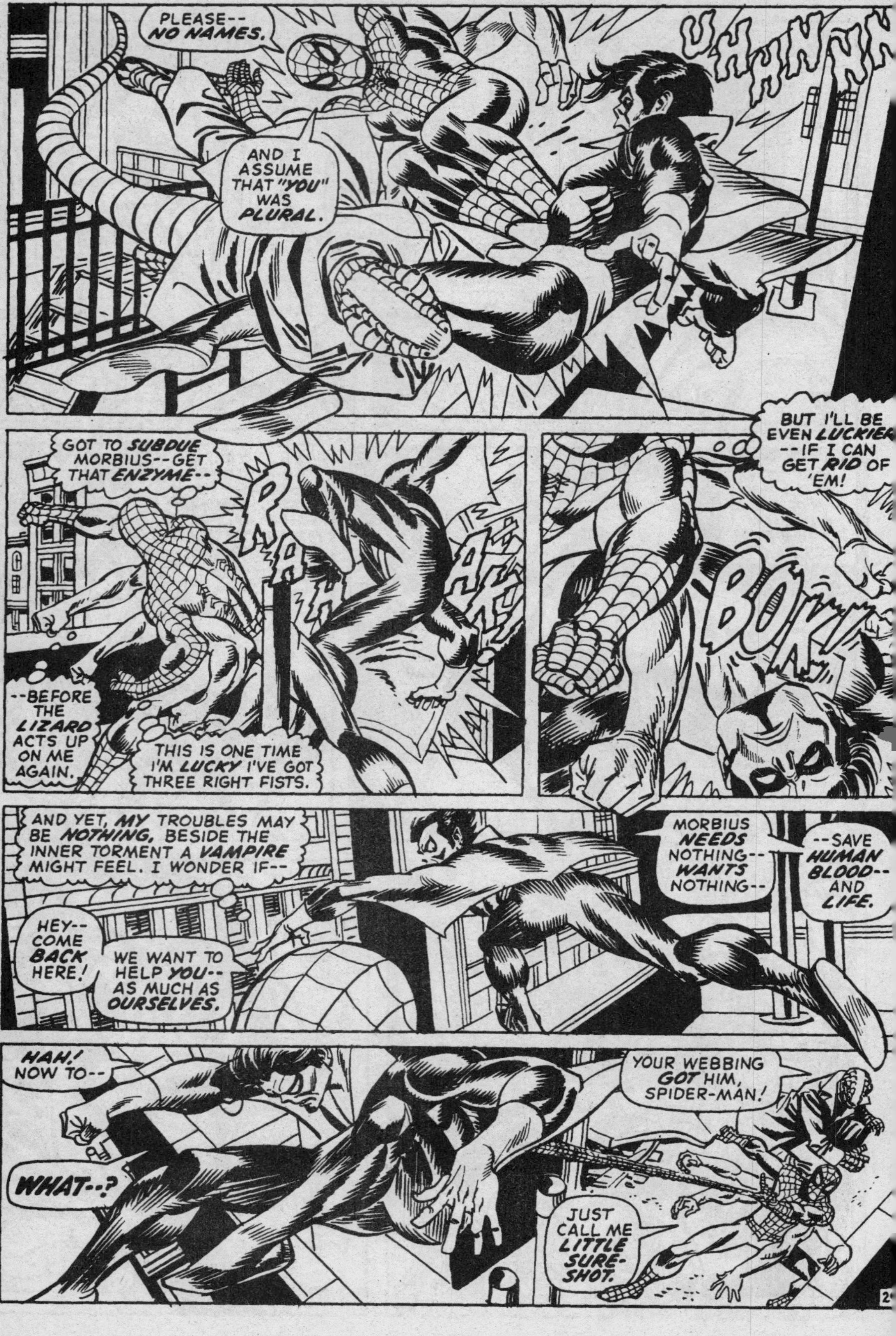
PLEASE--
NO NAMES.
UHHNNH
AND I ASSUME THAT "YOU" WAS PLURAL.
GOT TO SUBDUE MORBIUS--GET THAT ENZYME--
--BEFORE THE LIZARD ACTS UP ON ME AGAIN.
RAH
AK
THIS IS ONE TIME I'M LUCKY I'VE GOT THREE RIGHT FISTS.
BUT I'LL BE EVEN LUCKIER --IF I CAN GET RID OF 'EM!
BOK!
AND YET, MY TROUBLES MAY BE NOTHING, BESIDE THE INNER TORMENT A VAMPIRE MIGHT FEEL. I WONDER IF--
HEY--COME BACK HERE!
WE WANT TO HELP YOU--AS MUCH AS OURSELVES.
MORBIUS NEEDS NOTHING--WANTS NOTHING--
--SAVE HUMAN BLOOD--AND LIFE.
HAH! NOW TO--
WHAT--?
YOUR WEBBING GOT HIM, SPIDER-MAN!
JUST CALL ME LITTLE SURE-SHOT.

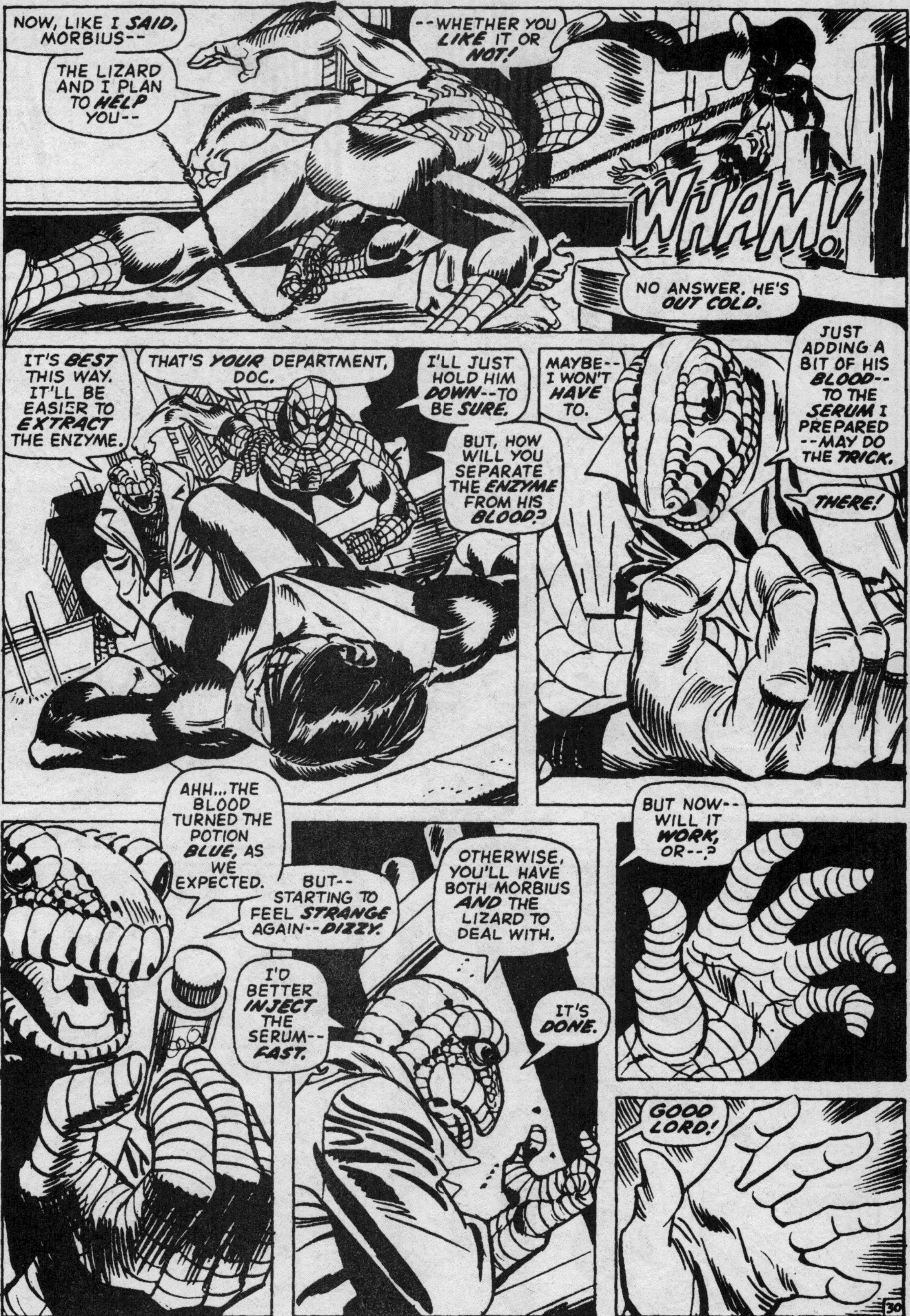

NOW, LIKE I SAID, MORBIUS--
THE LIZARD AND I PLAN TO HELP YOU--
--WHETHER YOU LIKE IT OR NOT!
WHAM!
NO ANSWER. HE'S OUT COLD.
IT'S BEST THIS WAY. IT'LL BE EASIER TO EXTRACT THE ENZYME.
THAT'S YOUR DEPARTMENT, DOC.
I'LL JUST HOLD HIM DOWN--TO BE SURE.
BUT, HOW WILL YOU SEPARATE THE ENZYME FROM HIS BLOOD?
MAYBE-- I WON'T HAVE TO.
JUST ADDING A BIT OF HIS BLOOD-- TO THE SERUM I PREPARED --MAY DO THE TRICK.
THERE!
AHH...THE BLOOD TURNED THE POTION BLUE, AS WE EXPECTED.
BUT-- STARTING TO FEEL STRANGE AGAIN--DIZZY.
I'D BETTER INJECT THE SERUM-- FAST.
OTHERWISE, YOU'LL HAVE BOTH MORBIUS AND THE LIZARD TO DEAL WITH.
IT'S DONE.
BUT NOW-- WILL IT WORK, OR--?
GOOD LORD!
30

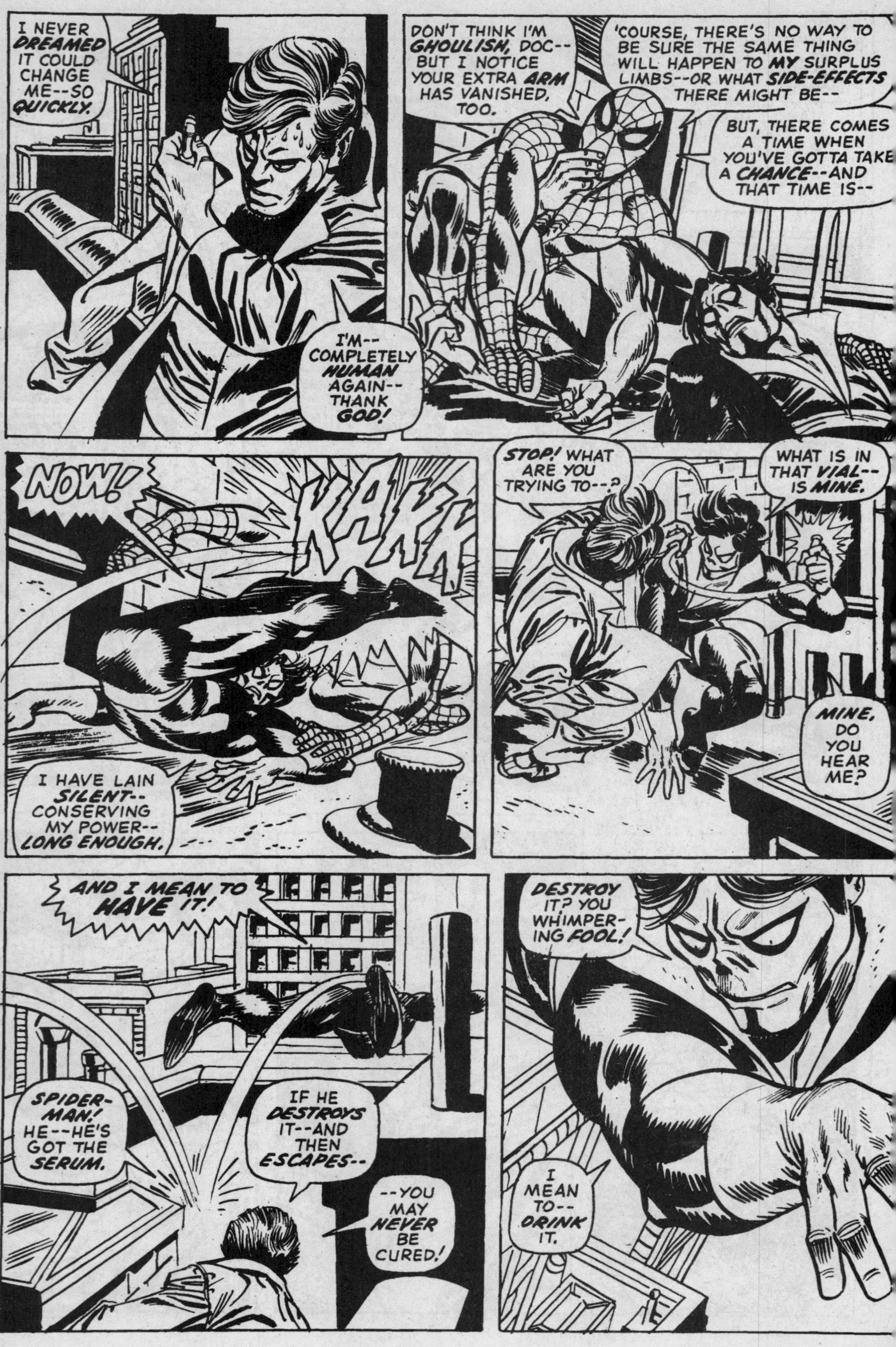

I NEVER DREAMED IT COULD CHANGE ME--SO QUICKLY.
I'M--COMPLETELY HUMAN AGAIN--THANK GOD!
DON'T THINK I'M GHOULISH, DOC--BUT I NOTICE YOUR EXTRA ARM HAS VANISHED, TOO.
'COURSE, THERE'S NO WAY TO BE SURE THE SAME THING WILL HAPPEN TO MY SURPLUS LIMBS--OR WHAT SIDE-EFFECTS THERE MIGHT BE--
BUT, THERE COMES A TIME WHEN YOU'VE GOTTA TAKE A CHANCE--AND THAT TIME IS--
NOW!
KAKK
I HAVE LAIN SILENT--CONSERVING MY POWER--LONG ENOUGH.
STOP! WHAT ARE YOU TRYING TO--?
WHAT IS IN THAT VIAL--IS MINE.
MINE, DO YOU HEAR ME?
AND I MEAN TO HAVE IT!
SPIDER-MAN! HE--HE'S GOT THE SERUM.
IF HE DESTROYS IT--AND THEN ESCAPES--
--YOU MAY NEVER BE CURED!
DESTROY IT? YOU WHIMPER-ING FOOL!
I MEAN TO--DRINK IT.

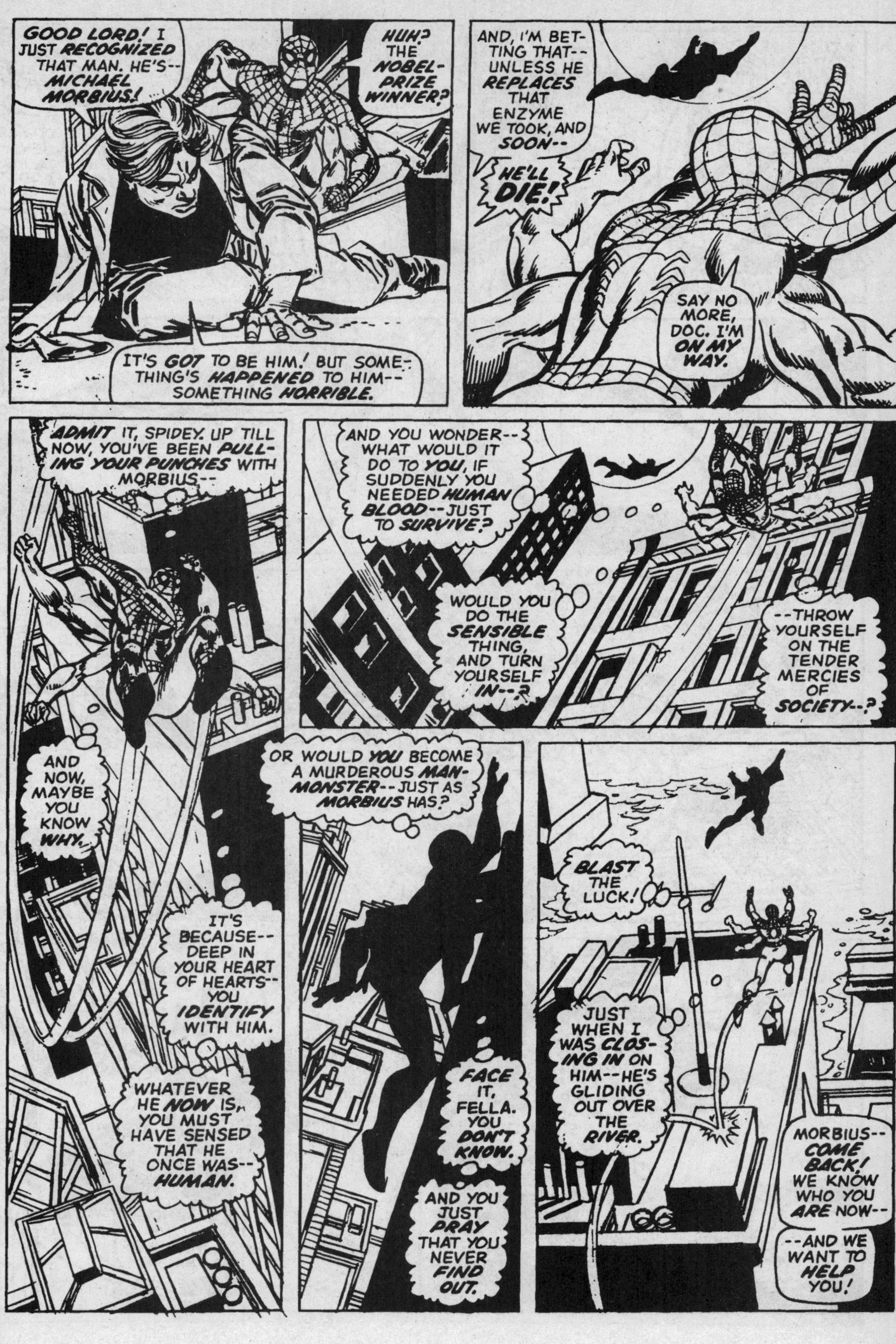
GOOD LORD! I JUST RECOGNIZED THAT MAN. HE'S-- MICHAEL MORBIUS!
HUH? THE NOBEL-PRIZE WINNER?
IT'S GOT TO BE HIM! BUT SOMETHING'S HAPPENED TO HIM-- SOMETHING HORRIBLE.
AND, I'M BETTING THAT-- UNLESS HE REPLACES THAT ENZYME WE TOOK, AND SOON--
HE'LL DIE!
SAY NO MORE, DOC. I'M ON MY WAY.
ADMIT IT, SPIDEY. UP TILL NOW, YOU'VE BEEN PULLING YOUR PUNCHES WITH MORBIUS--
AND NOW, MAYBE YOU KNOW WHY.
IT'S BECAUSE-- DEEP IN YOUR HEART OF HEARTS-- YOU IDENTIFY WITH HIM.
WHATEVER HE NOW IS, YOU MUST HAVE SENSED THAT HE ONCE WAS-- HUMAN.
AND YOU WONDER-- WHAT WOULD IT DO TO YOU, IF SUDDENLY YOU NEEDED HUMAN BLOOD-- JUST TO SURVIVE?
WOULD YOU DO THE SENSIBLE THING, AND TURN YOURSELF IN--?
--THROW YOURSELF ON THE TENDER MERCIES OF SOCIETY--?
OR WOULD YOU BECOME A MURDEROUS MAN-MONSTER-- JUST AS MORBIUS HAS?
FACE IT, FELLA. YOU DON'T KNOW.
AND YOU JUST PRAY THAT YOU NEVER FIND OUT.
BLAST THE LUCK!
JUST WHEN I WAS CLOSING IN ON HIM--HE'S GLIDING OUT OVER THE RIVER.
MORBIUS-- COME BACK! WE KNOW WHO YOU ARE NOW--
--AND WE WANT TO HELP YOU!

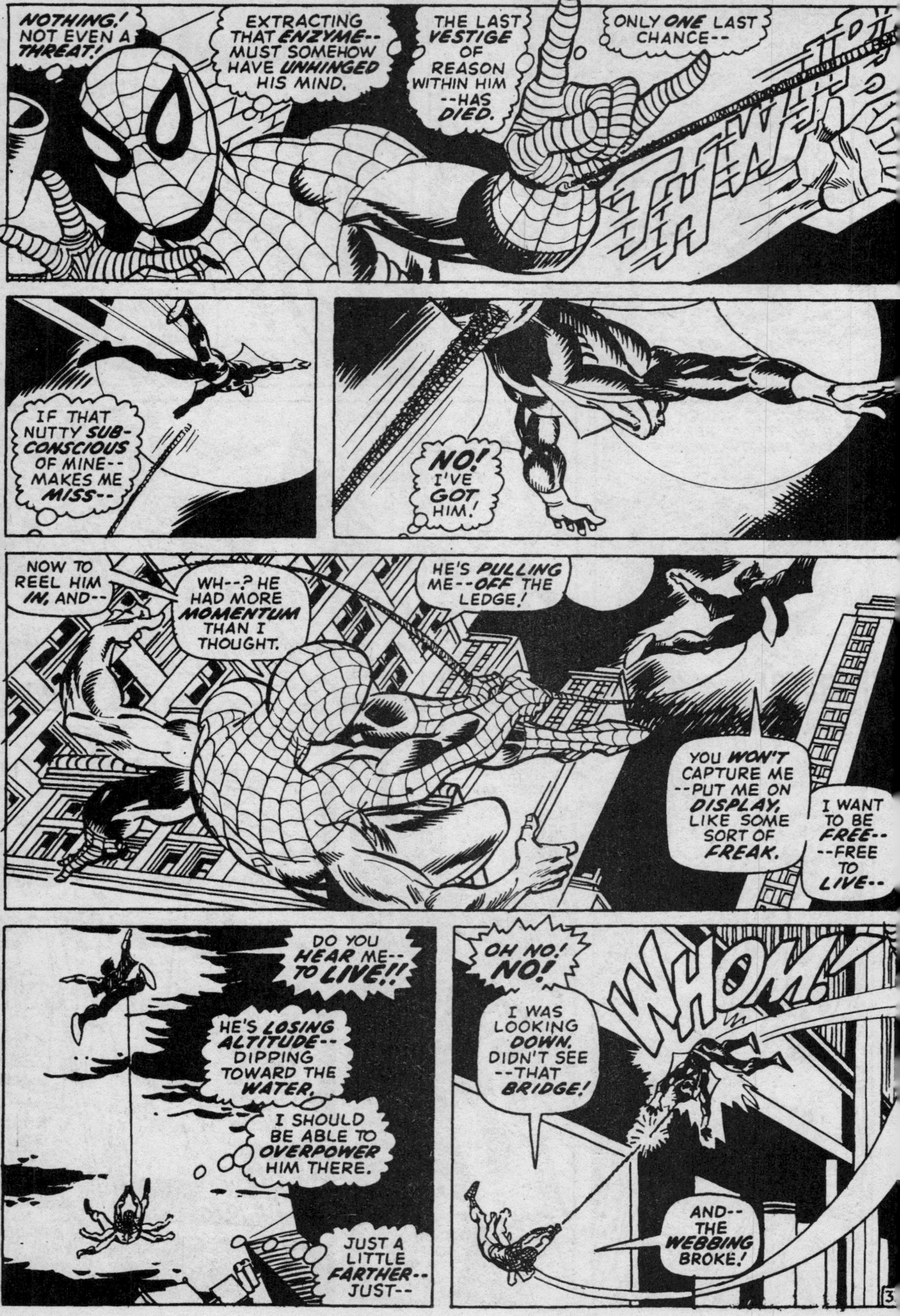
NOTHING! NOT EVEN A THREAT!
EXTRACTING THAT ENZYME-- MUST SOMEHOW HAVE UNHINGED HIS MIND.
THE LAST VESTIGE OF REASON WITHIN HIM --HAS DIED.
ONLY ONE LAST CHANCE--
THWAP
IF THAT NUTTY SUB-CONSCIOUS OF MINE-- MAKES ME MISS--
NO! I'VE GOT HIM!
NOW TO REEL HIM IN, AND--
WH--? HE HAD MORE MOMENTUM THAN I THOUGHT.
HE'S PULLING ME--OFF THE LEDGE!
YOU WON'T CAPTURE ME --PUT ME ON DISPLAY, LIKE SOME SORT OF FREAK.
I WANT TO BE FREE-- --FREE TO LIVE--
DO YOU HEAR ME-- TO LIVE!!
HE'S LOSING ALTITUDE-- DIPPING TOWARD THE WATER.
I SHOULD BE ABLE TO OVERPOWER HIM THERE.
JUST A LITTLE FARTHER-- JUST--
OH NO! NO!
WHOM!
I WAS LOOKING DOWN. DIDN'T SEE --THAT BRIDGE!
AND-- THE WEBBING BROKE!

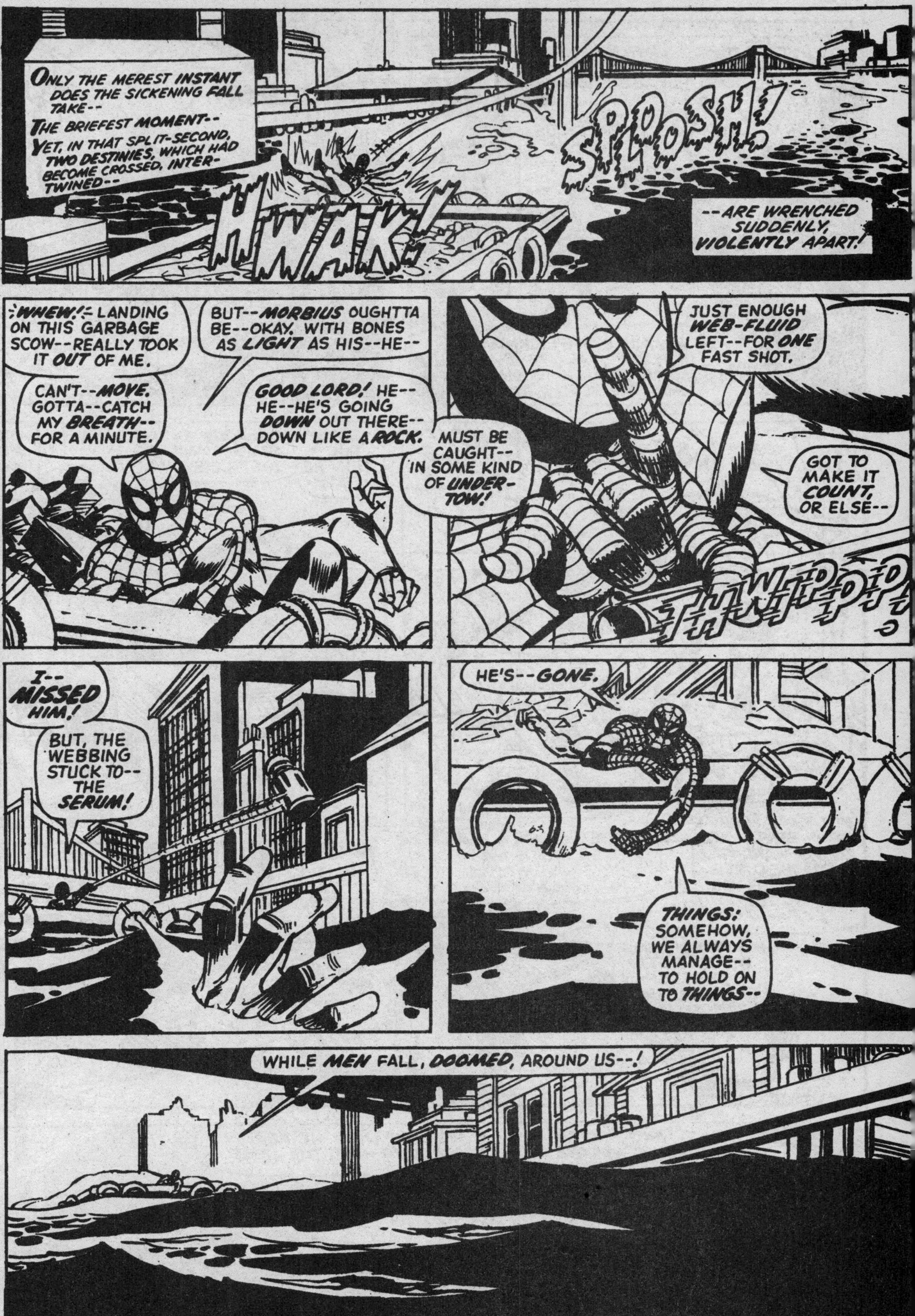
ONLY THE MEREST INSTANT DOES THE SICKENING FALL TAKE-- THE BRIEFEST MOMENT-- YET, IN THAT SPLIT-SECOND, TWO DESTINIES, WHICH HAD BECOME CROSSED, INTER-TWINED--
HWAK!
SPLOSH!
--ARE WRENCHED SUDDENLY, VIOLENTLY APART!
WHEW! LANDING ON THIS GARBAGE SCOW--REALLY TOOK IT OUT OF ME.
CAN'T--MOVE. GOTTA--CATCH MY BREATH-- FOR A MINUTE.
BUT--MORBIUS OUGHTTA BE--OKAY, WITH BONES AS LIGHT AS HIS--HE--
GOOD LORD! HE-- HE--HE'S GOING DOWN OUT THERE-- DOWN LIKE A ROCK.
MUST BE CAUGHT-- IN SOME KIND OF UNDER-TOW!
JUST ENOUGH WEB-FLUID LEFT--FOR ONE FAST SHOT.
GOT TO MAKE IT COUNT, OR ELSE--
THWIPPP
I-- MISSED HIM!
BUT, THE WEBBING STUCK TO-- THE SERUM!
HE'S--GONE.
THINGS: SOMEHOW, WE ALWAYS MANAGE-- TO HOLD ON TO THINGS--
WHILE MEN FALL, DOOMED, AROUND US--!

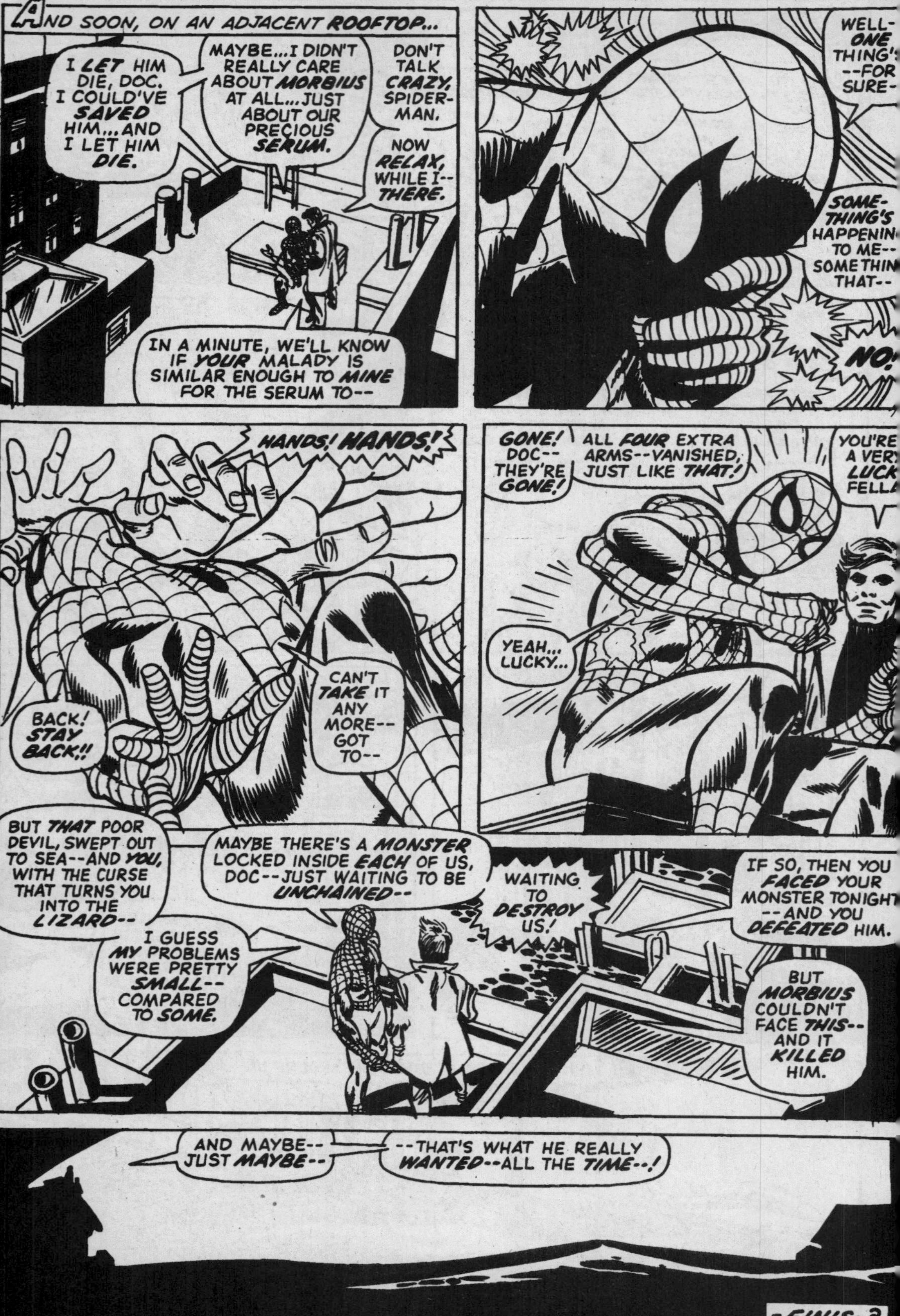

AND SOON, ON AN ADJACENT ROOFTOP...
I LET HIM DIE, DOC. I COULD'VE SAVED HIM... AND I LET HIM DIE.
MAYBE... I DIDN'T REALLY CARE ABOUT MORBIUS AT ALL... JUST ABOUT OUR PRECIOUS SERUM.
DON'T TALK CRAZY, SPIDER-MAN.
NOW RELAX, WHILE I-- THERE.
IN A MINUTE, WE'LL KNOW IF YOUR MALADY IS SIMILAR ENOUGH TO MINE FOR THE SERUM TO--
WELL-- ONE THING'S --FOR SURE-
SOME-THING'S HAPPENIN TO ME-- SOMETHIN THAT--
NO
HANDS! HANDS!
BACK! STAY BACK!!
CAN'T TAKE IT ANY MORE-- GOT TO--
GONE! DOC-- THEY'RE GONE!
ALL FOUR EXTRA ARMS--VANISHED, JUST LIKE THAT!
YOU'RE A VERY LUCK FELLA
YEAH... LUCKY...
BUT THAT POOR DEVIL, SWEPT OUT TO SEA--AND YOU, WITH THE CURSE THAT TURNS YOU INTO THE LIZARD--
I GUESS MY PROBLEMS WERE PRETTY SMALL-- COMPARED TO SOME.
MAYBE THERE'S A MONSTER LOCKED INSIDE EACH OF US, DOC--JUST WAITING TO BE UNCHAINED--
WAITING TO DESTROY US!
IF SO, THEN YOU FACED YOUR MONSTER TONIGHT --AND YOU DEFEATED HIM.
BUT MORBIUS COULDN'T FACE THIS-- AND IT KILLED HIM.
AND MAYBE-- JUST MAYBE--
--THAT'S WHAT HE REALLY WANTED--ALL THE TIME--!
-FINIS-?

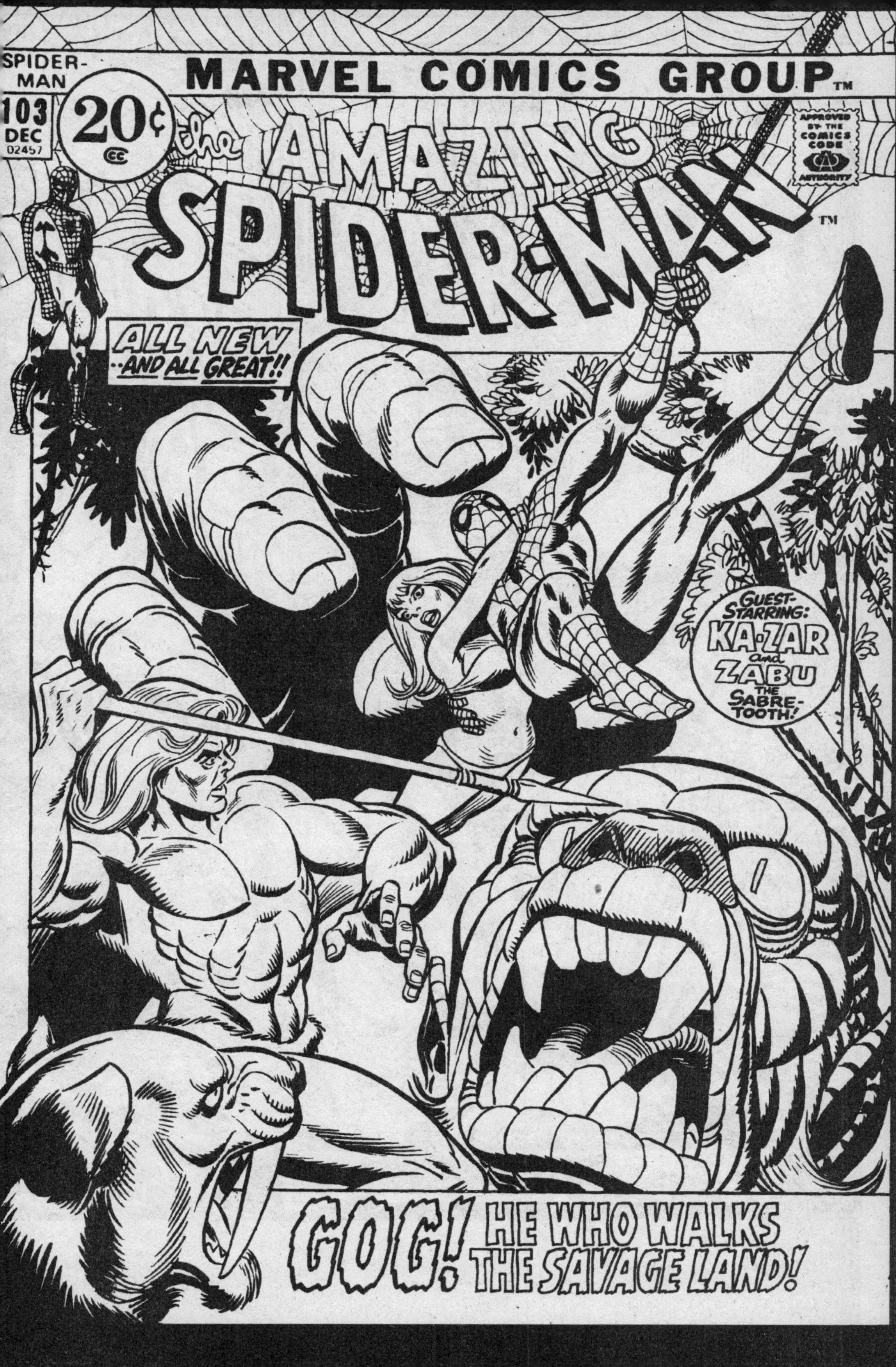

SPIDER-MAN
103
DEC
02457
20¢
CC
MARVEL COMICS GROUP
APPROVED BY THE COMICS CODE AUTHORITY
the AMAZING SPIDER-MAN
ALL NEW ..AND ALL GREAT!!
GUEST-STARRING: KA-ZAR and ZABU THE SABRE-TOOTH!
GOG! HE WHO WALKS THE SAVAGE LAND!

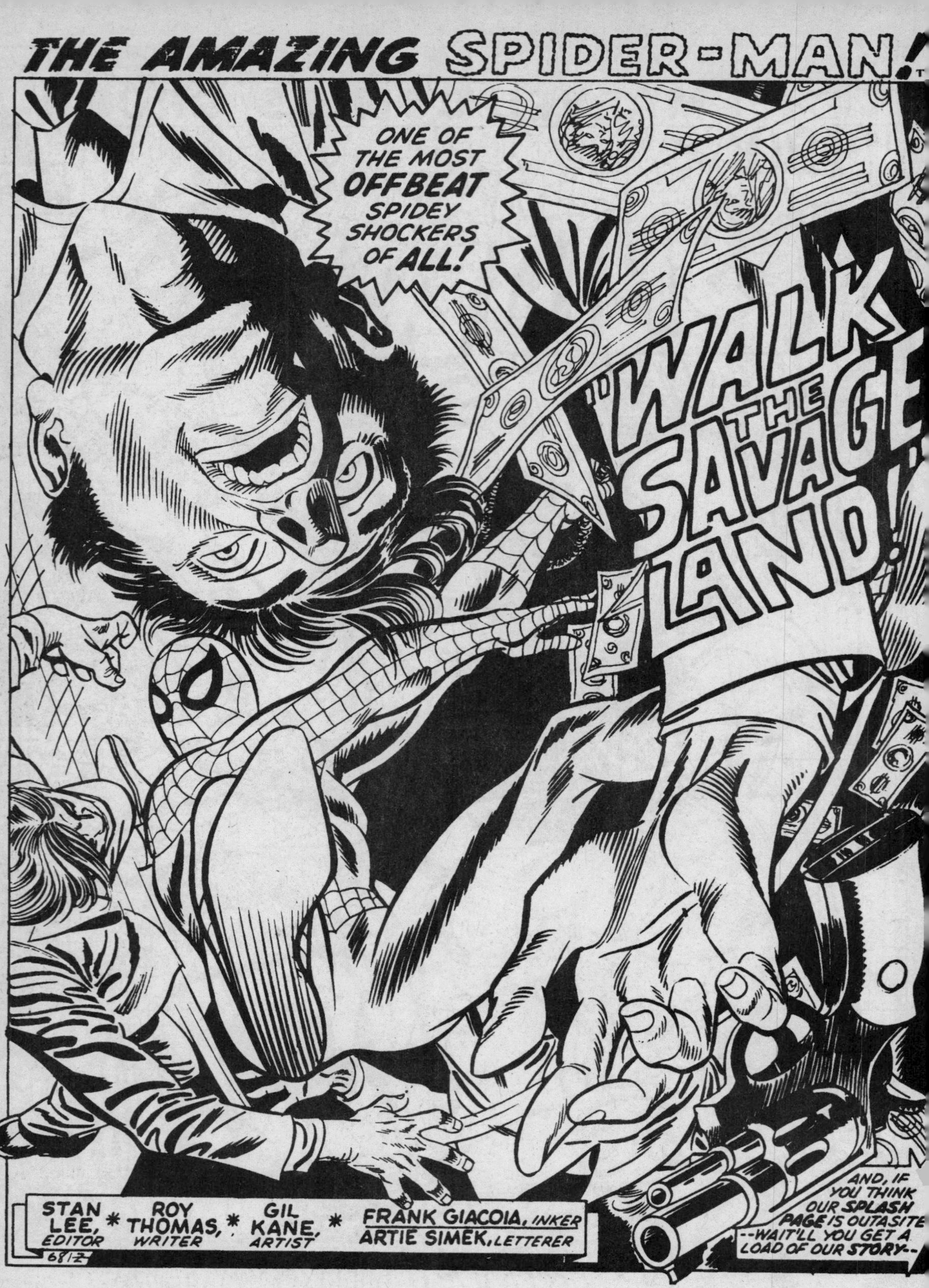
THE AMAZING SPIDER-MAN!
ONE OF THE MOST OFFBEAT SPIDEY SHOCKERS OF ALL!
"WALK THE SAVAGE LAND!"
STAN LEE, EDITOR * ROY THOMAS, WRITER * GIL KANE, ARTIST * FRANK GIACOIA, INKER
ARTIE SIMEK, LETTERER
AND, IF YOU THINK OUR SPLASH PAGE IS OUTASITE --WAIT'LL YOU GET A LOAD OF OUR STORY--

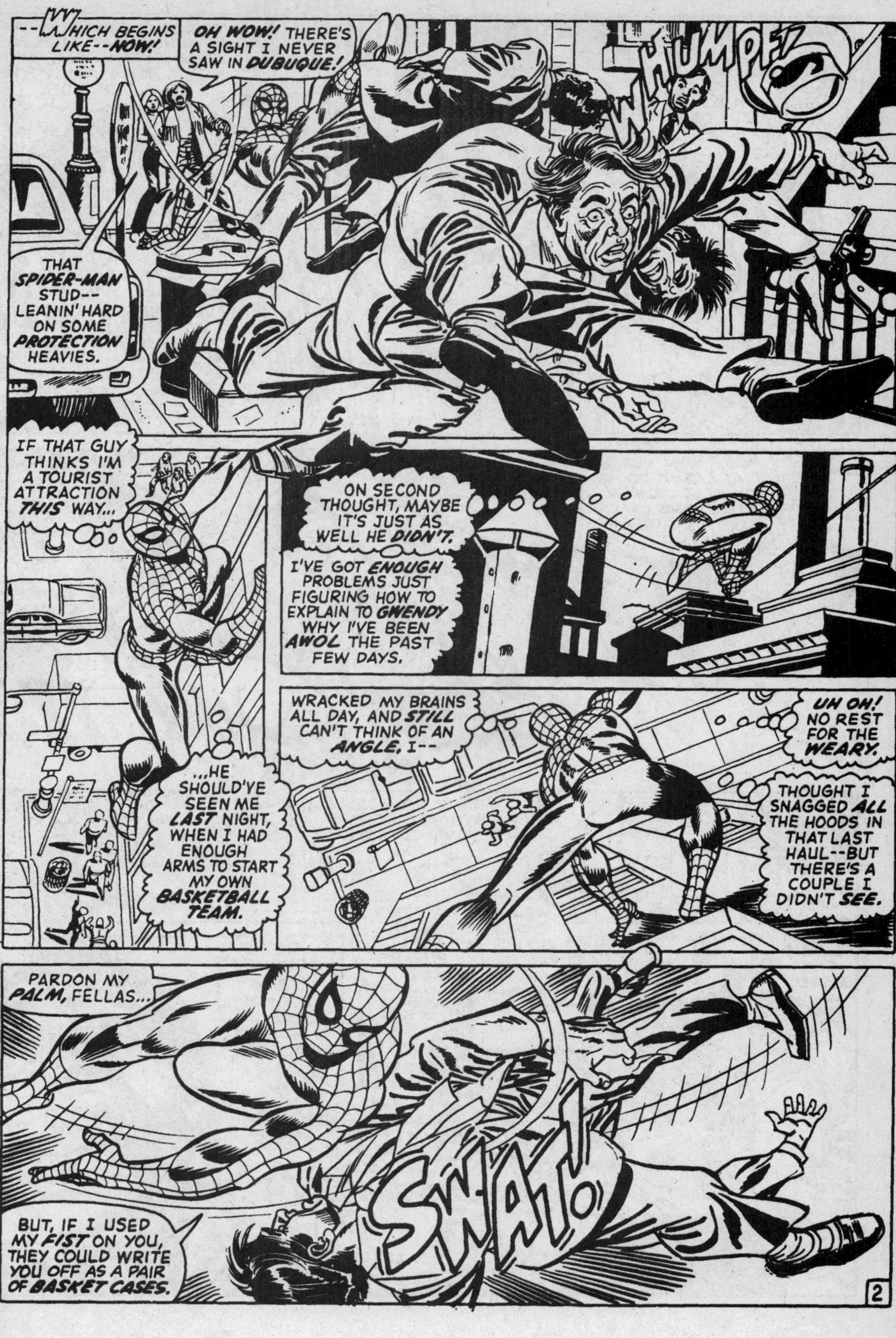
--WHICH BEGINS LIKE--NOW!
OH WOW! THERE'S A SIGHT I NEVER SAW IN DUBUQUE!
WHUMPF!
THAT SPIDER-MAN STUD-- LEANIN' HARD ON SOME PROTECTION HEAVIES.
IF THAT GUY THINKS I'M A TOURIST ATTRACTION THIS WAY...
...HE SHOULD'VE SEEN ME LAST NIGHT, WHEN I HAD ENOUGH ARMS TO START MY OWN BASKETBALL TEAM.
ON SECOND THOUGHT, MAYBE IT'S JUST AS WELL HE DIDN'T.
I'VE GOT ENOUGH PROBLEMS JUST FIGURING HOW TO EXPLAIN TO GWENDY WHY I'VE BEEN AWOL THE PAST FEW DAYS.
WRACKED MY BRAINS ALL DAY, AND STILL CAN'T THINK OF AN ANGLE, I--
UH OH! NO REST FOR THE WEARY.
THOUGHT I SNAGGED ALL THE HOODS IN THAT LAST HAUL--BUT THERE'S A COUPLE I DIDN'T SEE.
PARDON MY PALM, FELLAS...
SWAT!
BUT, IF I USED MY FIST ON YOU, THEY COULD WRITE YOU OFF AS A PAIR OF BASKET CASES.
2

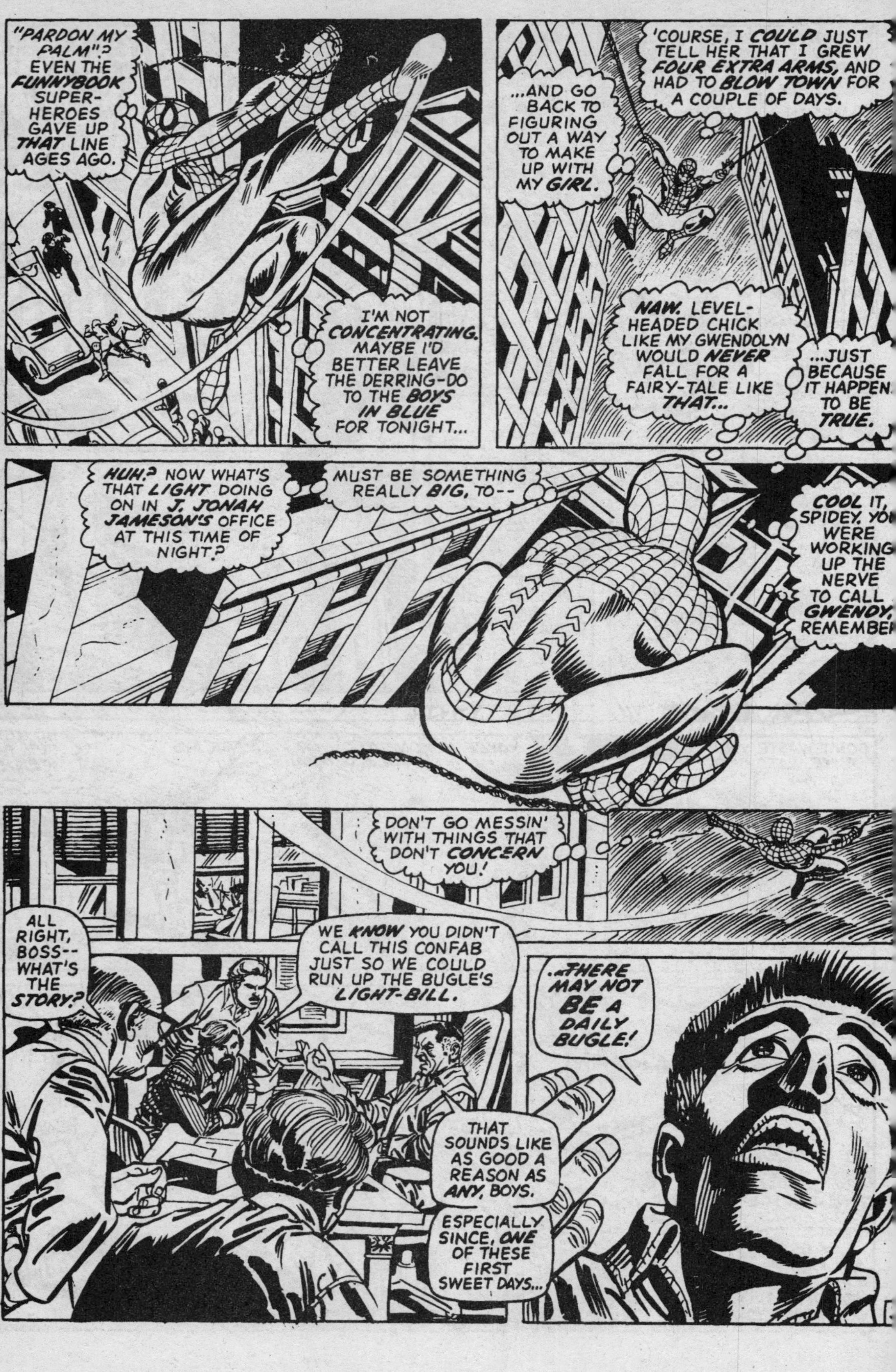

"PARDON MY PALM"? EVEN THE FUNNYBOOK SUPER-HEROES GAVE UP THAT LINE AGES AGO.
I'M NOT CONCENTRATING. MAYBE I'D BETTER LEAVE THE DERRING-DO TO THE BOYS IN BLUE FOR TONIGHT...
...AND GO BACK TO FIGURING OUT A WAY TO MAKE UP WITH MY GIRL.
'COURSE, I COULD JUST TELL HER THAT I GREW FOUR EXTRA ARMS, AND HAD TO BLOW TOWN FOR A COUPLE OF DAYS.
NAW. LEVEL-HEADED CHICK LIKE MY GWENDOLYN WOULD NEVER FALL FOR A FAIRY-TALE LIKE THAT...
...JUST BECAUSE IT HAPPEN TO BE TRUE.
HUH? NOW WHAT'S THAT LIGHT DOING ON IN J. JONAH JAMESON'S OFFICE AT THIS TIME OF NIGHT?
MUST BE SOMETHING REALLY BIG, TO--
COOL IT, SPIDEY. YO WERE WORKING UP THE NERVE TO CALL GWENDY, REMEMBE
DON'T GO MESSIN' WITH THINGS THAT DON'T CONCERN YOU!
ALL RIGHT, BOSS--WHAT'S THE STORY?
WE KNOW YOU DIDN'T CALL THIS CONFAB JUST SO WE COULD RUN UP THE BUGLE'S LIGHT-BILL.
...THERE MAY NOT BE A DAILY BUGLE!
THAT SOUNDS LIKE AS GOOD A REASON AS ANY, BOYS.
ESPECIALLY SINCE, ONE OF THESE FIRST SWEET DAYS...

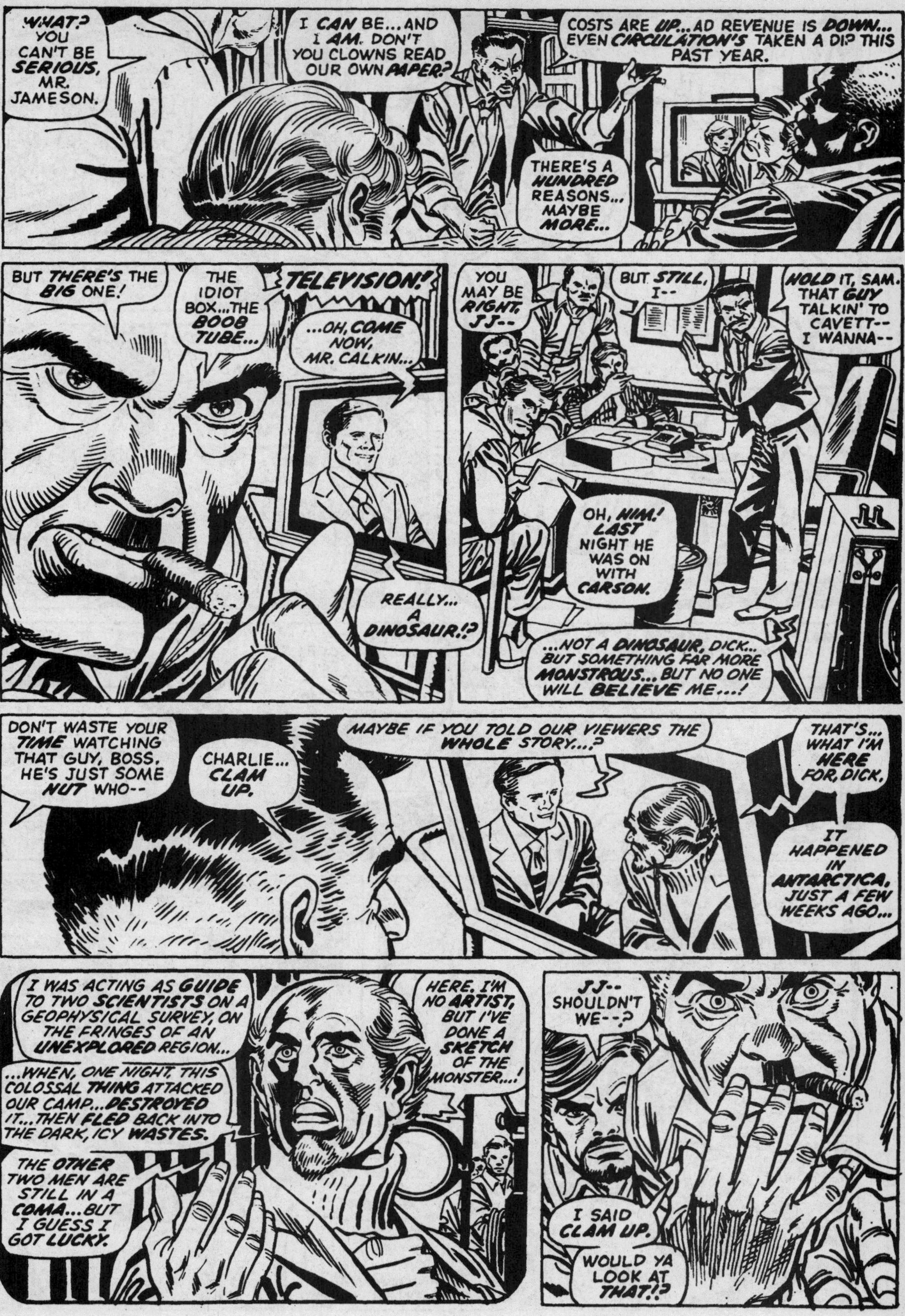
WHAT? YOU CAN'T BE SERIOUS, MR. JAMESON.
I CAN BE... AND I AM. DON'T YOU CLOWNS READ OUR OWN PAPER?
COSTS ARE UP... AD REVENUE IS DOWN... EVEN CIRCULATION'S TAKEN A DIP THIS PAST YEAR.
THERE'S A HUNDRED REASONS... MAYBE MORE...
BUT THERE'S THE BIG ONE!
THE IDIOT BOX... THE BOOB TUBE...
TELEVISION!
...OH, COME NOW, MR. CALKIN...
REALLY... A DINOSAUR!?
YOU MAY BE RIGHT, JJ--
BUT STILL, I--
HOLD IT, SAM. THAT GUY TALKIN' TO CAVETT-- I WANNA--
OH, NIM! LAST NIGHT HE WAS ON WITH CARSON.
...NOT A DINOSAUR, DICK... BUT SOMETHING FAR MORE MONSTROUS... BUT NO ONE WILL BELIEVE ME...!
DON'T WASTE YOUR TIME WATCHING THAT GUY, BOSS. HE'S JUST SOME NUT WHO--
CHARLIE... CLAM UP.
MAYBE IF YOU TOLD OUR VIEWERS THE WHOLE STORY...?
THAT'S... WHAT I'M HERE FOR, DICK.
IT HAPPENED IN ANTARCTICA, JUST A FEW WEEKS AGO...
I WAS ACTING AS GUIDE TO TWO SCIENTISTS ON A GEOPHYSICAL SURVEY, ON THE FRINGES OF AN UNEXPLORED REGION...
...WHEN, ONE NIGHT, THIS COLOSSAL THING ATTACKED OUR CAMP... DESTROYED IT... THEN FLED BACK INTO THE DARK, ICY WASTES.
THE OTHER TWO MEN ARE STILL IN A COMA... BUT I GUESS I GOT LUCKY.
HERE. I'M NO ARTIST, BUT I'VE DONE A SKETCH OF THE MONSTER...!
JJ-- SHOULDN'T WE--?
I SAID CLAM UP.
WOULD YA LOOK AT THAT!?

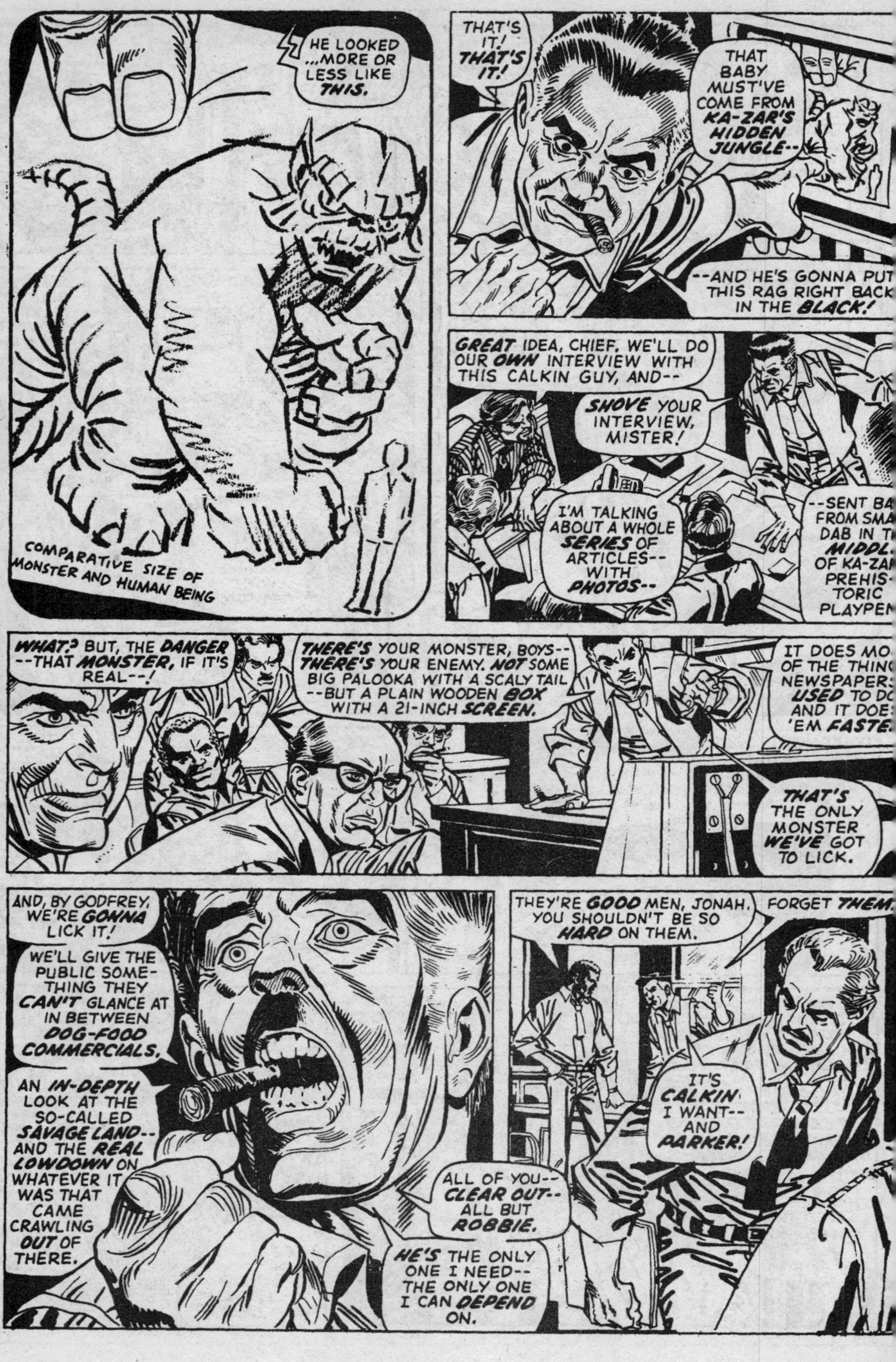
HE LOOKED ...MORE OR LESS LIKE THIS.
COMPARATIVE SIZE OF MONSTER AND HUMAN BEING
THAT'S IT! THAT'S IT!
THAT BABY MUST'VE COME FROM KA-ZAR'S HIDDEN JUNGLE--
--AND HE'S GONNA PUT THIS RAG RIGHT BACK IN THE BLACK!
GREAT IDEA, CHIEF. WE'LL DO OUR OWN INTERVIEW WITH THIS CALKIN GUY, AND--
SHOVE YOUR INTERVIEW, MISTER!
I'M TALKING ABOUT A WHOLE SERIES OF ARTICLES--WITH PHOTOS--
WHAT? BUT, THE DANGER --THAT MONSTER, IF IT'S REAL--!
THERE'S YOUR MONSTER, BOYS--THERE'S YOUR ENEMY. NOT SOME BIG PALOOKA WITH A SCALY TAIL --BUT A PLAIN WOODEN BOX WITH A 21-INCH SCREEN.
THAT'S THE ONLY MONSTER WE'VE GOT TO LICK.
AND, BY GODFREY, WE'RE GONNA LICK IT!
WE'LL GIVE THE PUBLIC SOMETHING THEY CAN'T GLANCE AT IN BETWEEN DOG-FOOD COMMERCIALS.
AN IN-DEPTH LOOK AT THE SO-CALLED SAVAGE LAND--AND THE REAL LOWDOWN ON WHATEVER IT WAS THAT CAME CRAWLING OUT OF THERE.
ALL OF YOU--CLEAR OUT--ALL BUT ROBBIE.
HE'S THE ONLY ONE I NEED--THE ONLY ONE I CAN DEPEND ON.
THEY'RE GOOD MEN, JONAH. YOU SHOULDN'T BE SO HARD ON THEM.
IT'S CALKIN I WANT--AND PARKER!

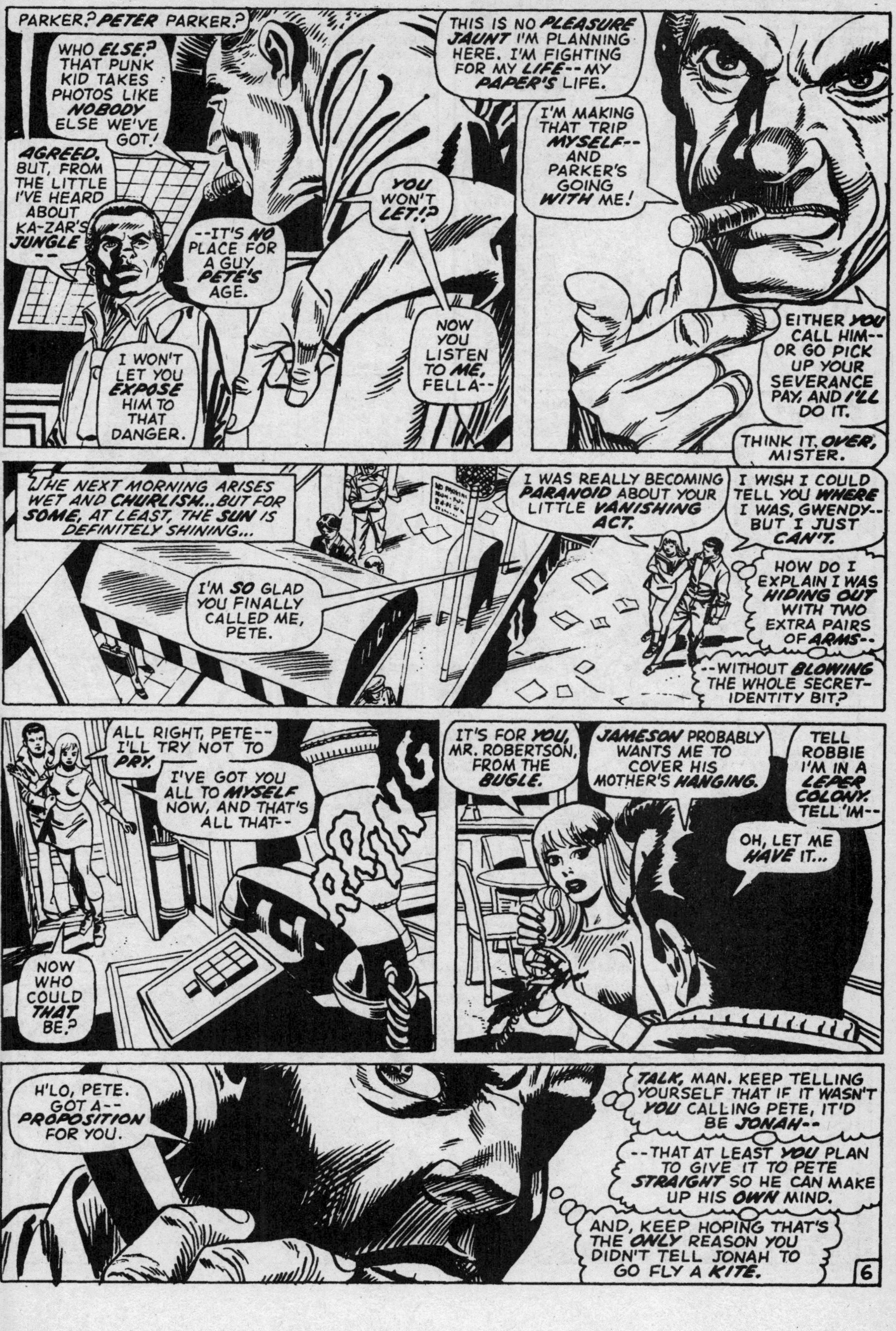
PARKER? PETER PARKER?
WHO ELSE? THAT PUNK KID TAKES PHOTOS LIKE NOBODY ELSE WE'VE GOT!
AGREED. BUT, FROM THE LITTLE I'VE HEARD ABOUT KA-ZAR'S JUNGLE --
--IT'S NO PLACE FOR A GUY PETE'S AGE.
I WON'T LET YOU EXPOSE HIM TO THAT DANGER.
YOU WON'T LET!?
NOW YOU LISTEN TO ME, FELLA--
THIS IS NO PLEASURE JAUNT I'M PLANNING HERE. I'M FIGHTING FOR MY LIFE--MY PAPER'S LIFE.
I'M MAKING THAT TRIP MYSELF--AND PARKER'S GOING WITH ME!
EITHER YOU CALL HIM--OR GO PICK UP YOUR SEVERANCE PAY, AND I'LL DO IT.
THINK IT OVER, MISTER.
THE NEXT MORNING ARISES WET AND CHURLISH...BUT FOR SOME, AT LEAST, THE SUN IS DEFINITELY SHINING...
I'M SO GLAD YOU FINALLY CALLED ME, PETE.
I WAS REALLY BECOMING PARANOID ABOUT YOUR LITTLE VANISHING ACT.
I WISH I COULD TELL YOU WHERE I WAS, GWENDY--BUT I JUST CAN'T.
HOW DO I EXPLAIN I WAS HIDING OUT WITH TWO EXTRA PAIRS OF ARMS--
--WITHOUT BLOWING THE WHOLE SECRET-IDENTITY BIT?
ALL RIGHT, PETE--I'LL TRY NOT TO PRY.
I'VE GOT YOU ALL TO MYSELF NOW, AND THAT'S ALL THAT--
BRING
NOW WHO COULD THAT BE?
IT'S FOR YOU, MR. ROBERTSON, FROM THE BUGLE.
JAMESON PROBABLY WANTS ME TO COVER HIS MOTHER'S HANGING.
TELL ROBBIE I'M IN A LEPER COLONY. TELL 'IM--
OH, LET ME HAVE IT...
H'LO, PETE. GOT A--PROPOSITION FOR YOU.
TALK, MAN. KEEP TELLING YOURSELF THAT IF IT WASN'T YOU CALLING PETE, IT'D BE JONAH--
--THAT AT LEAST YOU PLAN TO GIVE IT TO PETE STRAIGHT SO HE CAN MAKE UP HIS OWN MIND.
AND, KEEP HOPING THAT'S THE ONLY REASON YOU DIDN'T TELL JONAH TO GO FLY A KITE.
6

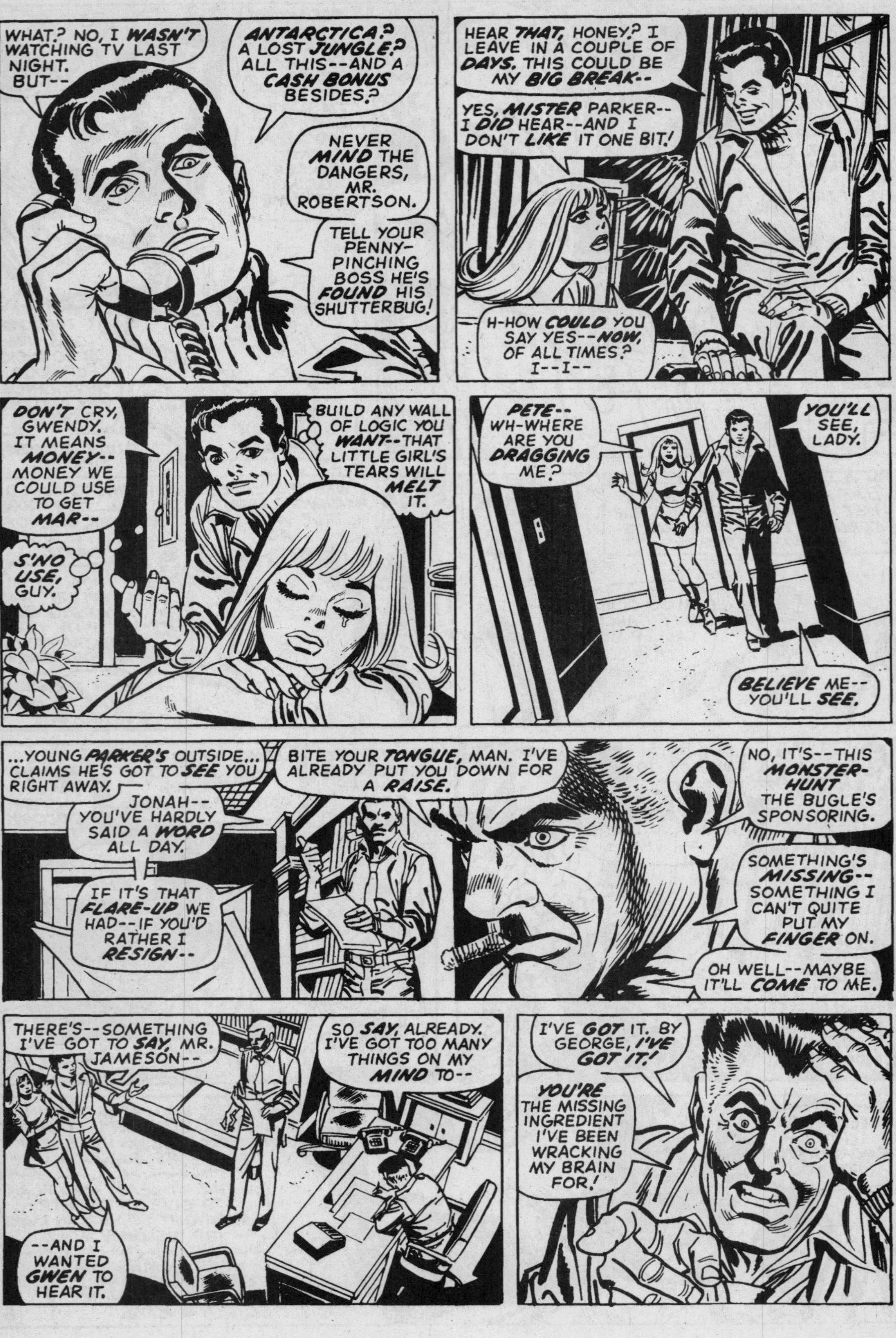
WHAT? NO, I WASN'T WATCHING TV LAST NIGHT. BUT--
ANTARCTICA? A LOST JUNGLE? ALL THIS--AND A CASH BONUS BESIDES?
NEVER MIND THE DANGERS, MR. ROBERTSON.
TELL YOUR PENNY-PINCHING BOSS HE'S FOUND HIS SHUTTERBUG!
HEAR THAT, HONEY? I LEAVE IN A COUPLE OF DAYS. THIS COULD BE MY BIG BREAK--
YES, MISTER PARKER--I DID HEAR--AND I DON'T LIKE IT ONE BIT!
H-HOW COULD YOU SAY YES--NOW, OF ALL TIMES? I--I--
DON'T CRY, GWENDY. IT MEANS MONEY--MONEY WE COULD USE TO GET MAR--
BUILD ANY WALL OF LOGIC YOU WANT--THAT LITTLE GIRL'S TEARS WILL MELT IT.
S'NO USE, GUY.
PETE--WH-WHERE ARE YOU DRAGGING ME?
YOU'LL SEE, LADY.
BELIEVE ME--YOU'LL SEE.
...YOUNG PARKER'S OUTSIDE... CLAIMS HE'S GOT TO SEE YOU RIGHT AWAY.
JONAH--YOU'VE HARDLY SAID A WORD ALL DAY.
IF IT'S THAT FLARE-UP WE HAD--IF YOU'D RATHER I RESIGN--
BITE YOUR TONGUE, MAN. I'VE ALREADY PUT YOU DOWN FOR A RAISE.
NO, IT'S--THIS MONSTER-HUNT THE BUGLE'S SPONSORING.
SOMETHING'S MISSING--SOMETHING I CAN'T QUITE PUT MY FINGER ON.
OH WELL--MAYBE IT'LL COME TO ME.
THERE'S--SOMETHING I'VE GOT TO SAY, MR. JAMESON--
--AND I WANTED GWEN TO HEAR IT.
SO SAY, ALREADY. I'VE GOT TOO MANY THINGS ON MY MIND TO--
I'VE GOT IT. BY GEORGE, I'VE GOT IT!
YOU'RE THE MISSING INGREDIENT I'VE BEEN WRACKING MY BRAIN FOR!

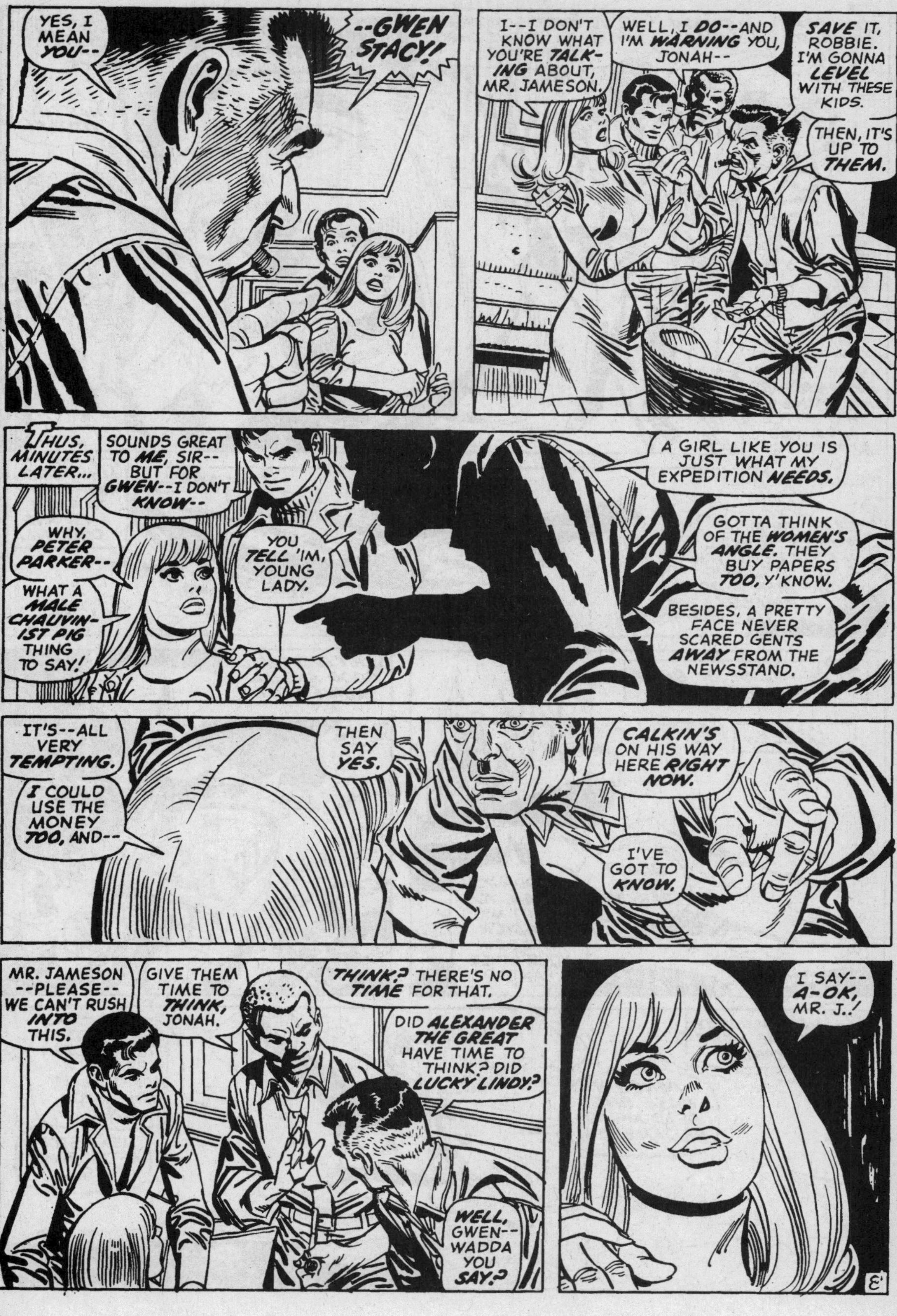

YES, I MEAN YOU--
--GWEN STACY!
I--I DON'T KNOW WHAT YOU'RE TALKING ABOUT, MR. JAMESON.
WELL, I DO--AND I'M WARNING YOU, JONAH--
SAVE IT, ROBBIE. I'M GONNA LEVEL WITH THESE KIDS.
THEN, IT'S UP TO THEM.
THUS, MINUTES LATER...
SOUNDS GREAT TO ME, SIR--BUT FOR GWEN--I DON'T KNOW--
WHY, PETER PARKER--
WHAT A MALE CHAUVINIST PIG THING TO SAY!
YOU TELL 'IM, YOUNG LADY.
A GIRL LIKE YOU IS JUST WHAT MY EXPEDITION NEEDS.
GOTTA THINK OF THE WOMEN'S ANGLE. THEY BUY PAPERS TOO, Y'KNOW.
BESIDES, A PRETTY FACE NEVER SCARED GENTS AWAY FROM THE NEWSSTAND.
IT'S--ALL VERY TEMPTING.
I COULD USE THE MONEY TOO, AND--
THEN SAY YES.
CALKIN'S ON HIS WAY HERE RIGHT NOW.
I'VE GOT TO KNOW.
MR. JAMESON--PLEASE--WE CAN'T RUSH INTO THIS.
GIVE THEM TIME TO THINK, JONAH.
THINK? THERE'S NO TIME FOR THAT.
DID ALEXANDER THE GREAT HAVE TIME TO THINK? DID LUCKY LINDY?
WELL, GWEN--WADDA YOU SAY?
I SAY--A-OK, MR. J.!
3

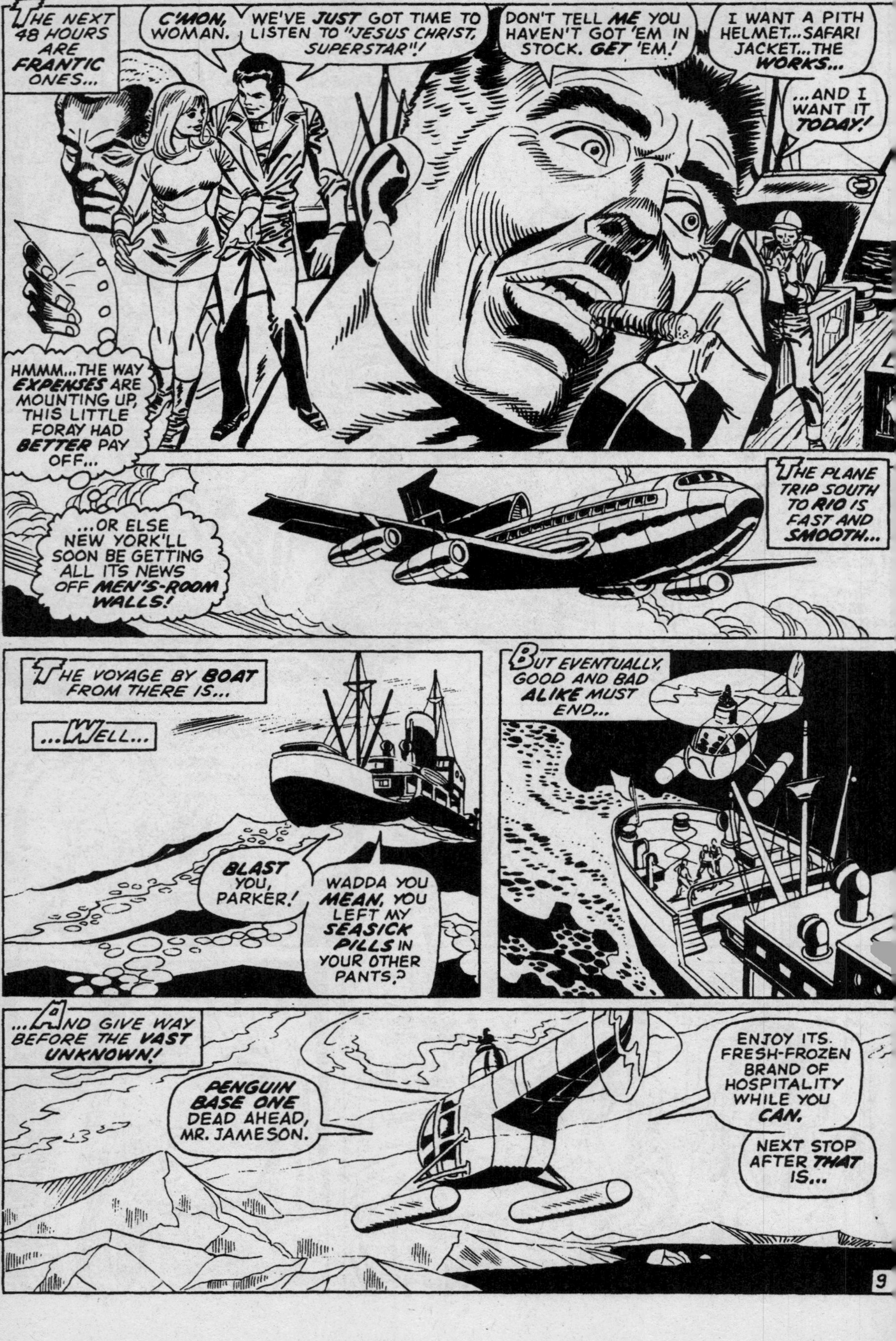
THE NEXT 48 HOURS ARE FRANTIC ONES...
C'MON, WOMAN.
WE'VE JUST GOT TIME TO LISTEN TO "JESUS CHRIST, SUPERSTAR"!
DON'T TELL ME YOU HAVEN'T GOT 'EM IN STOCK. GET 'EM!
I WANT A PITH HELMET...SAFARI JACKET...THE WORKS...
...AND I WANT IT TODAY!
HMMM...THE WAY EXPENSES ARE MOUNTING UP, THIS LITTLE FORAY HAD BETTER PAY OFF...
...OR ELSE NEW YORK'LL SOON BE GETTING ALL ITS NEWS OFF MEN'S-ROOM WALLS!
THE PLANE TRIP SOUTH TO RIO IS FAST AND SMOOTH...
THE VOYAGE BY BOAT FROM THERE IS...
...WELL...
BLAST YOU, PARKER!
WADDA YOU MEAN, YOU LEFT MY SEASICK PILLS IN YOUR OTHER PANTS?
BUT EVENTUALLY, GOOD AND BAD ALIKE MUST END...
...AND GIVE WAY BEFORE THE VAST UNKNOWN!
PENGUIN BASE ONE DEAD AHEAD, MR. JAMESON.
ENJOY ITS FRESH-FROZEN BRAND OF HOSPITALITY WHILE YOU CAN.
NEXT STOP AFTER THAT IS...

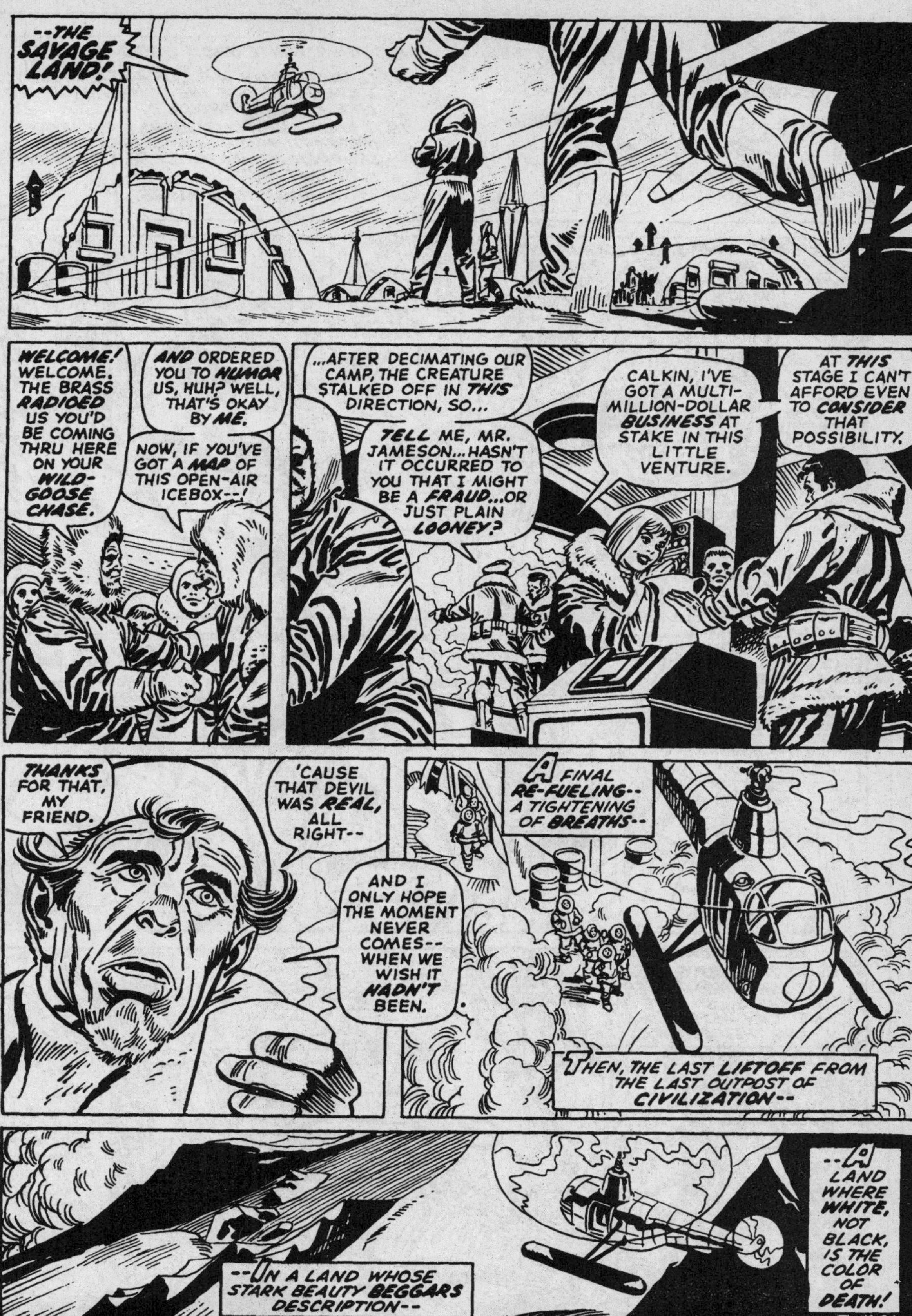
--THE SAVAGE LAND!
WELCOME! WELCOME. THE BRASS RADIOED US YOU'D BE COMING THRU HERE ON YOUR WILD-GOOSE CHASE.
AND ORDERED YOU TO HUMOR US, HUH? WELL, THAT'S OKAY BY ME.
NOW, IF YOU'VE GOT A MAP OF THIS OPEN-AIR ICEBOX--!
...AFTER DECIMATING OUR CAMP, THE CREATURE STALKED OFF IN THIS DIRECTION, SO...
TELL ME, MR. JAMESON... HASN'T IT OCCURRED TO YOU THAT I MIGHT BE A FRAUD... OR JUST PLAIN LOONEY?
CALKIN, I'VE GOT A MULTI-MILLION-DOLLAR BUSINESS AT STAKE IN THIS LITTLE VENTURE.
AT THIS STAGE I CAN'T AFFORD EVEN TO CONSIDER THAT POSSIBILITY.
THANKS FOR THAT, MY FRIEND.
'CAUSE THAT DEVIL WAS REAL, ALL RIGHT--
AND I ONLY HOPE THE MOMENT NEVER COMES-- WHEN WE WISH IT HADN'T BEEN.
A FINAL RE-FUELING-- A TIGHTENING OF BREATHS--
THEN, THE LAST LIFTOFF FROM THE LAST OUTPOST OF CIVILIZATION--
--ON A LAND WHOSE STARK BEAUTY BEGGARS DESCRIPTION--
--A LAND WHERE WHITE, NOT BLACK, IS THE COLOR OF DEATH!
10.

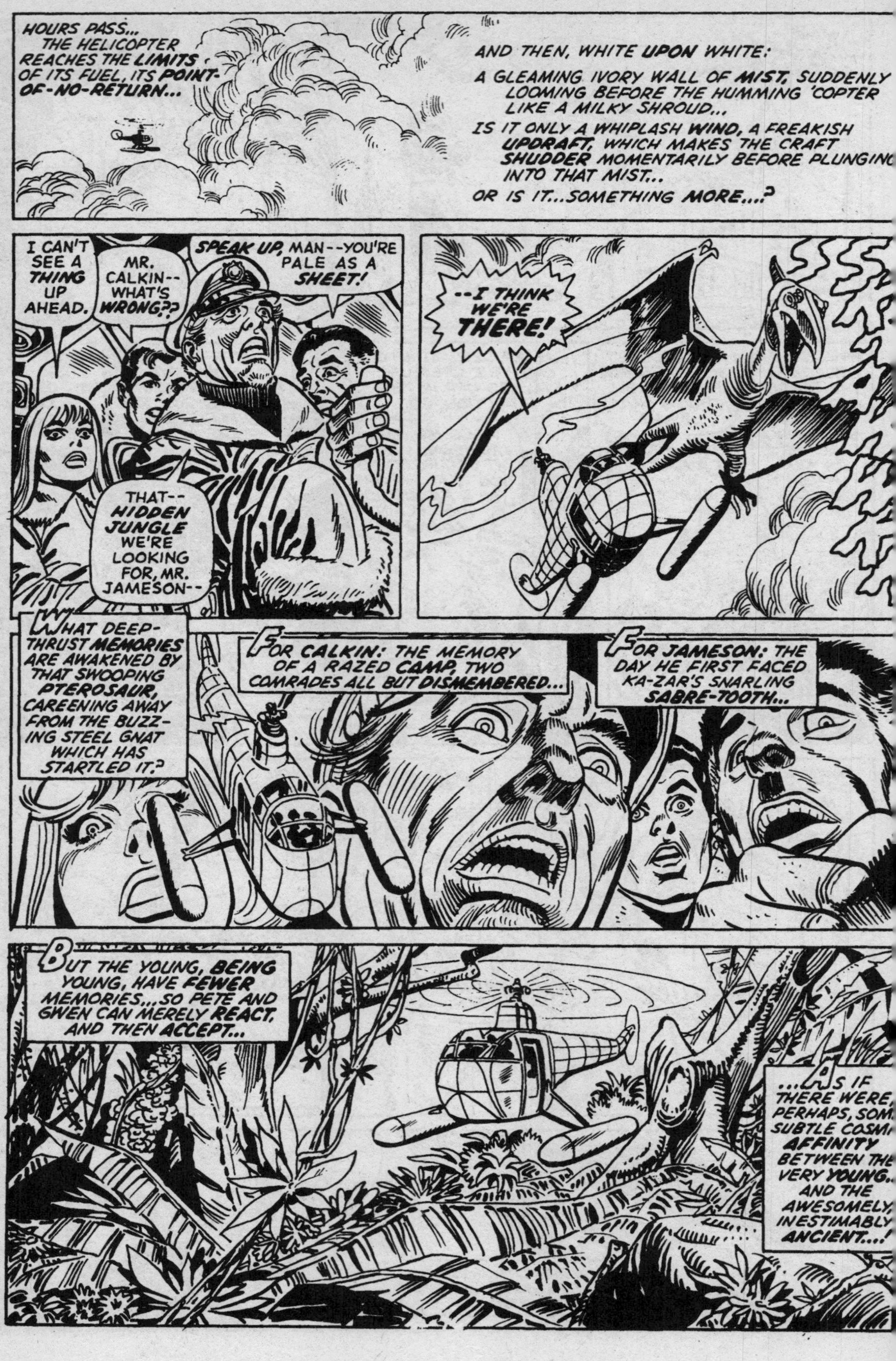

HOURS PASS... THE HELICOPTER REACHES THE LIMITS OF ITS FUEL, ITS POINT-OF-NO-RETURN...
AND THEN, WHITE UPON WHITE:
A GLEAMING IVORY WALL OF MIST, SUDDENLY LOOMING BEFORE THE HUMMING 'COPTER LIKE A MILKY SHROUD...
IS IT ONLY A WHIPLASH WIND, A FREAKISH UPDRAFT, WHICH MAKES THE CRAFT SHUDDER MOMENTARILY BEFORE PLUNGING INTO THAT MIST...
OR IS IT...SOMETHING MORE...?
I CAN'T SEE A THING UP AHEAD.
MR. CALKIN-- WHAT'S WRONG??
SPEAK UP, MAN--YOU'RE PALE AS A SHEET!
THAT-- HIDDEN JUNGLE WE'RE LOOKING FOR, MR. JAMESON--
--I THINK WE'RE THERE!
WHAT DEEP-THRUST MEMORIES ARE AWAKENED BY THAT SWOOPING PTEROSAUR, CAREENING AWAY FROM THE BUZZING STEEL GNAT WHICH HAS STARTLED IT?
FOR CALKIN: THE MEMORY OF A RAZED CAMP, TWO COMRADES ALL BUT DISMEMBERED...
FOR JAMESON: THE DAY HE FIRST FACED KA-ZAR'S SNARLING SABRE-TOOTH...
BUT THE YOUNG, BEING YOUNG, HAVE FEWER MEMORIES...SO PETE AND GWEN CAN MERELY REACT. AND THEN ACCEPT...
...AS IF THERE WERE, PERHAPS, SOME SUBTLE COSMIC AFFINITY BETWEEN THE VERY YOUNG... AND THE AWESOMELY, INESTIMABLY ANCIENT...!

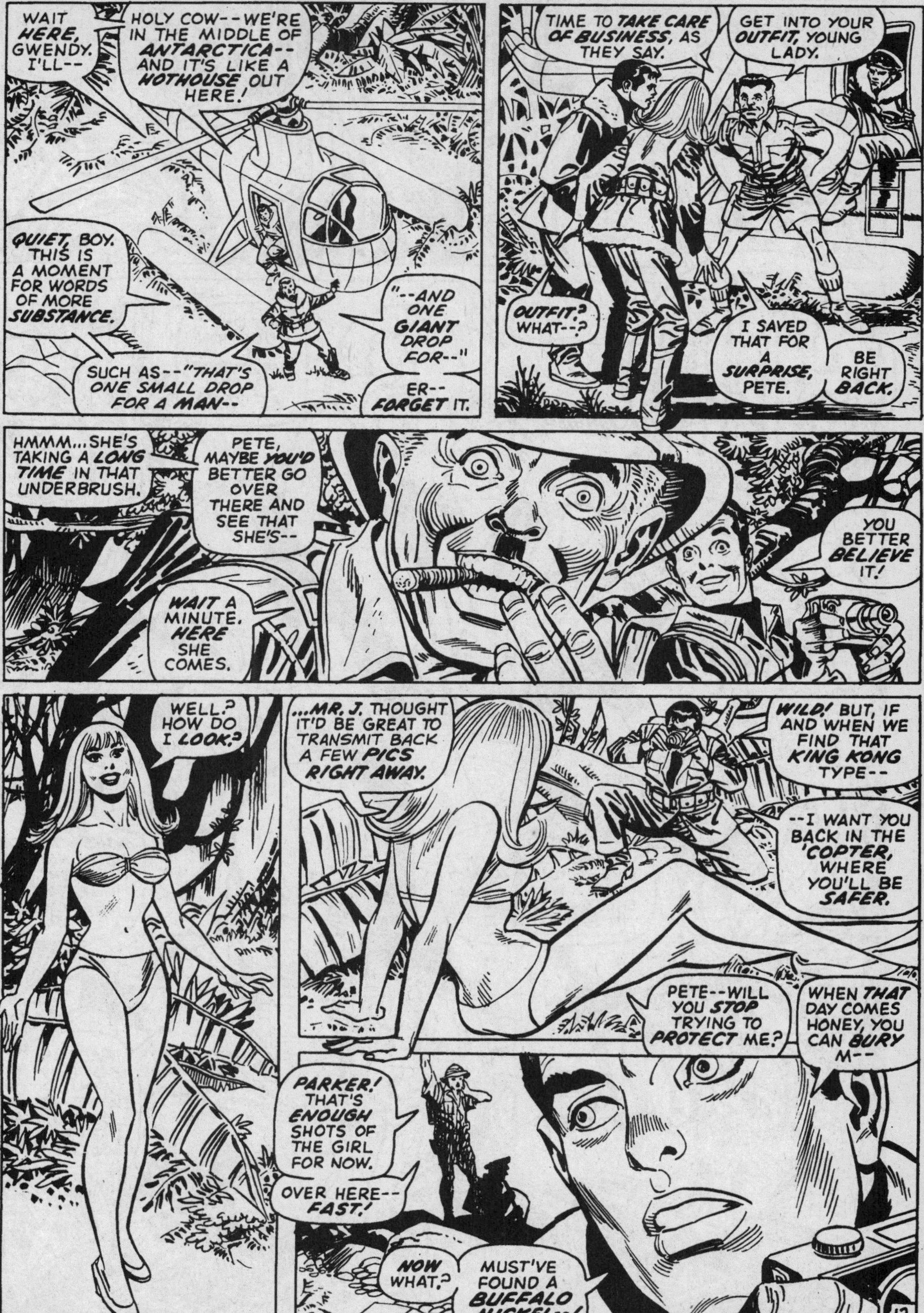

WAIT HERE, GWENDY. I'LL--
HOLY COW--WE'RE IN THE MIDDLE OF ANTARCTICA--AND IT'S LIKE A HOTHOUSE OUT HERE!
QUIET, BOY. THIS IS A MOMENT FOR WORDS OF MORE SUBSTANCE.
SUCH AS--"THAT'S ONE SMALL DROP FOR A MAN--
"--AND ONE GIANT DROP FOR--"
ER-- FORGET IT.
TIME TO TAKE CARE OF BUSINESS, AS THEY SAY.
GET INTO YOUR OUTFIT, YOUNG LADY.
OUTFIT? WHAT--?
I SAVED THAT FOR A SURPRISE, PETE.
BE RIGHT BACK.
HMMM... SHE'S TAKING A LONG TIME IN THAT UNDERBRUSH.
PETE, MAYBE YOU'D BETTER GO OVER THERE AND SEE THAT SHE'S--
WAIT A MINUTE. HERE SHE COMES.
YOU BETTER BELIEVE IT!
WELL? HOW DO I LOOK?
...MR. J. THOUGHT IT'D BE GREAT TO TRANSMIT BACK A FEW PICS RIGHT AWAY.
WILD! BUT, IF AND WHEN WE FIND THAT KING KONG TYPE--
--I WANT YOU BACK IN THE 'COPTER, WHERE YOU'LL BE SAFER.
PETE--WILL YOU STOP TRYING TO PROTECT ME?
WHEN THAT DAY COMES HONEY, YOU CAN BURY M--
PARKER! THAT'S ENOUGH SHOTS OF THE GIRL FOR NOW.
OVER HERE--FAST!
NOW WHAT?
MUST'VE FOUND A BUFFALO NICKEL--!
12

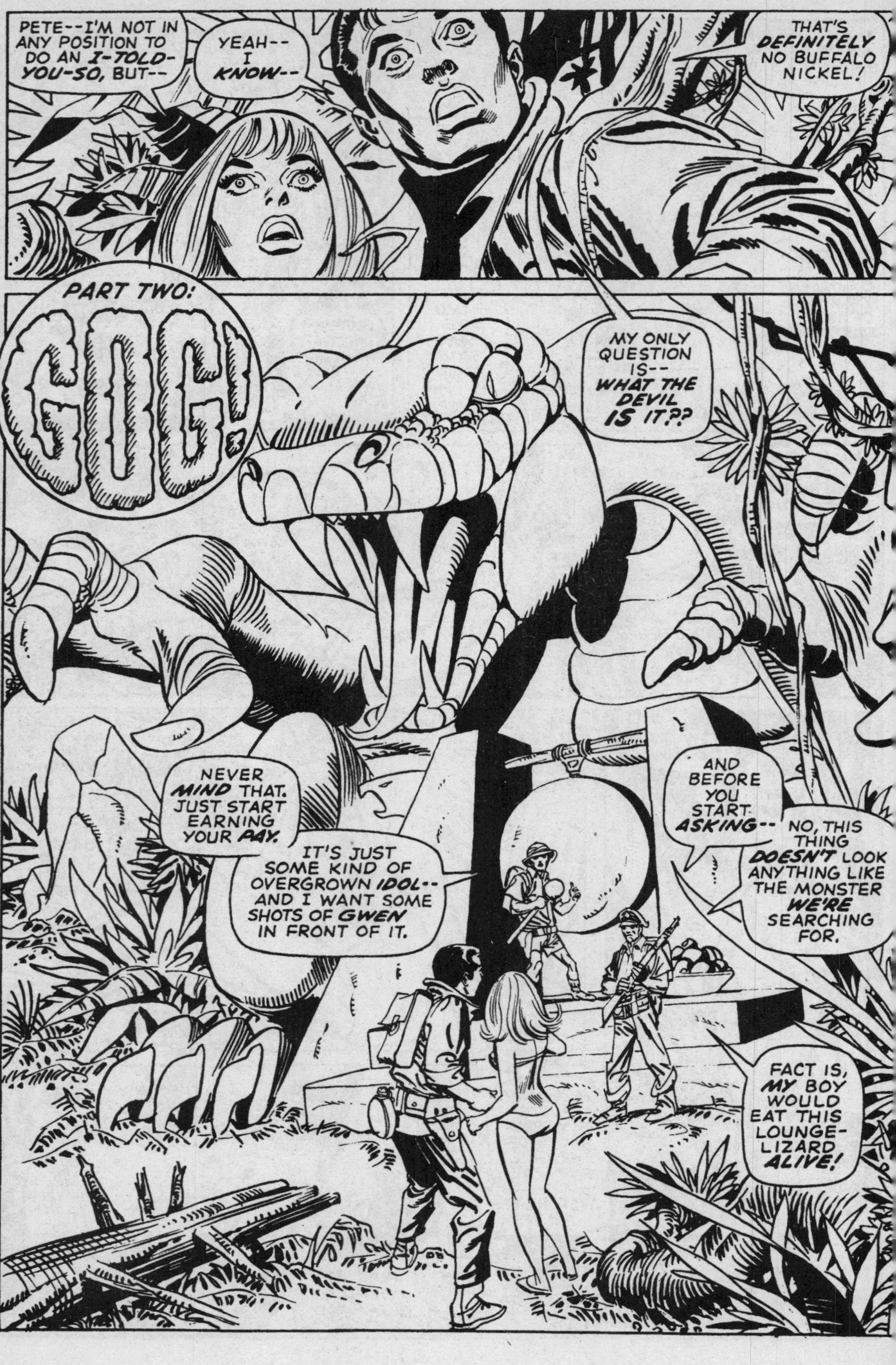

PETE--I'M NOT IN ANY POSITION TO DO AN I-TOLD-YOU-SO, BUT--
YEAH-- I KNOW--
THAT'S DEFINITELY NO BUFFALO NICKEL!
PART TWO: GOG!
MY ONLY QUESTION IS-- WHAT THE DEVIL IS IT??
NEVER MIND THAT. JUST START EARNING YOUR PAY.
IT'S JUST SOME KIND OF OVERGROWN IDOL-- AND I WANT SOME SHOTS OF GWEN IN FRONT OF IT.
AND BEFORE YOU START ASKING--
NO, THIS THING DOESN'T LOOK ANYTHING LIKE THE MONSTER WE'RE SEARCHING FOR.
FACT IS, MY BOY WOULD EAT THIS LOUNGE-LIZARD ALIVE!

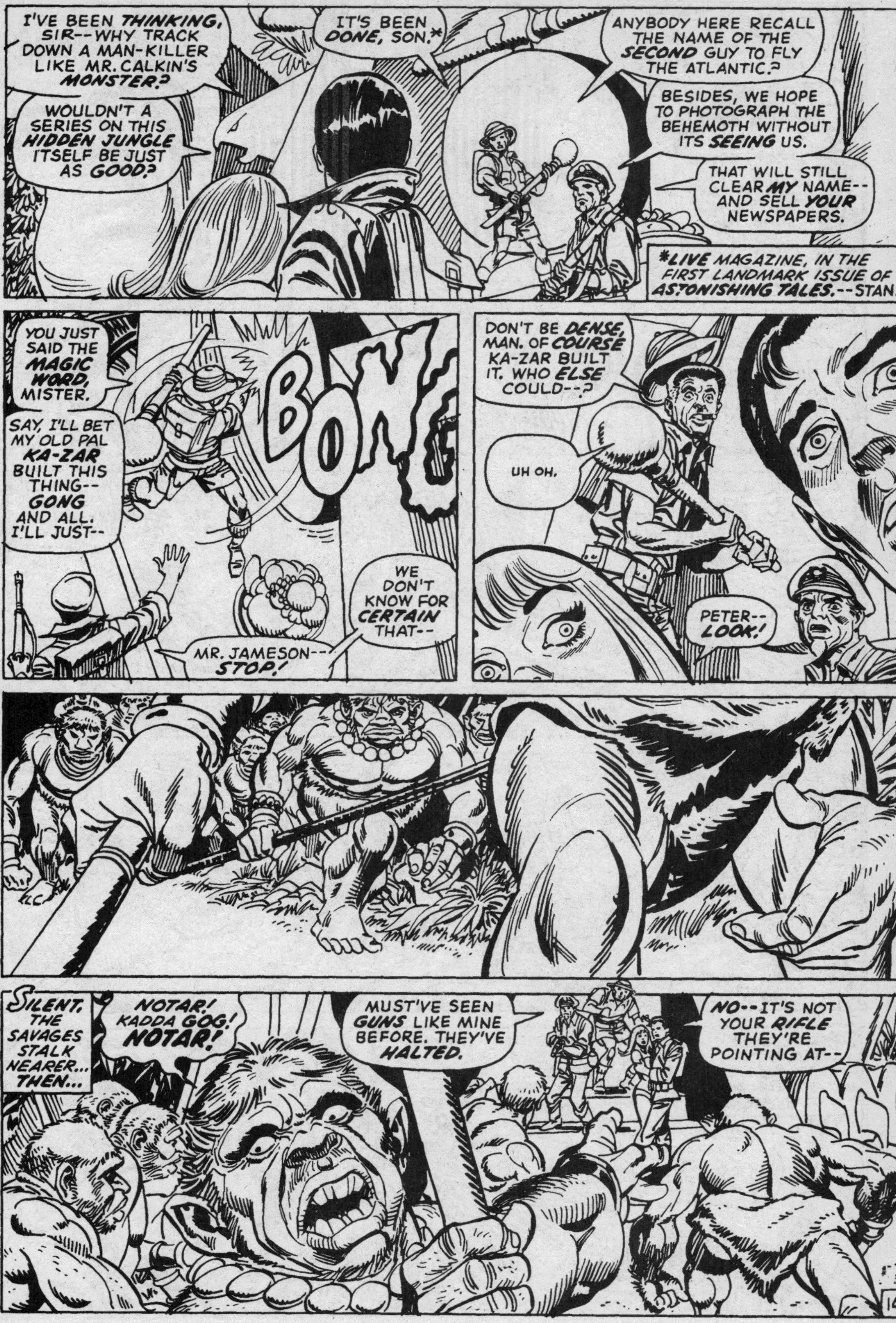

I'VE BEEN THINKING, SIR--WHY TRACK DOWN A MAN-KILLER LIKE MR. CALKIN'S MONSTER?
WOULDN'T A SERIES ON THIS HIDDEN JUNGLE ITSELF BE JUST AS GOOD?
IT'S BEEN DONE, SON.*
ANYBODY HERE RECALL THE NAME OF THE SECOND GUY TO FLY THE ATLANTIC?
BESIDES, WE HOPE TO PHOTOGRAPH THE BEHEMOTH WITHOUT ITS SEEING US.
THAT WILL STILL CLEAR MY NAME--AND SELL YOUR NEWSPAPERS.
*LIVE MAGAZINE, IN THE FIRST LANDMARK ISSUE OF ASTONISHING TALES.--STAN.
YOU JUST SAID THE MAGIC WORD, MISTER.
SAY, I'LL BET MY OLD PAL KA-ZAR BUILT THIS THING--GONG AND ALL. I'LL JUST--
BONG
MR. JAMESON--STOP!
WE DON'T KNOW FOR CERTAIN THAT--
DON'T BE DENSE, MAN. OF COURSE KA-ZAR BUILT IT. WHO ELSE COULD--?
UH OH.
PETER--LOOK!
SILENT, THE SAVAGES STALK NEARER... THEN...
NOTAR! KADDA GOG! NOTAR!
MUST'VE SEEN GUNS LIKE MINE BEFORE. THEY'VE HALTED.
NO--IT'S NOT YOUR RIFLE THEY'RE POINTING AT--

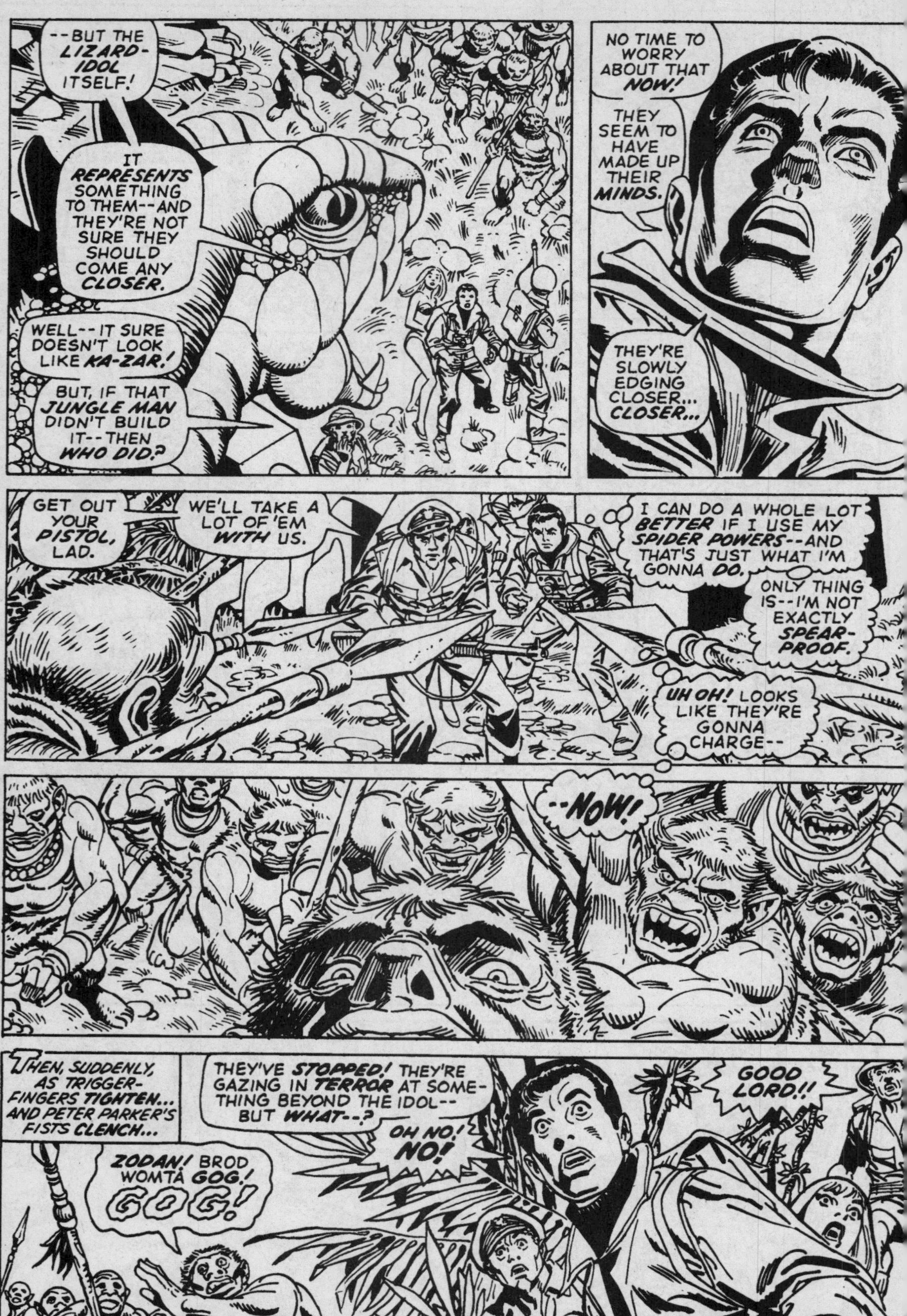
--BUT THE LIZARD-IDOL ITSELF!
IT REPRESENTS SOMETHING TO THEM--AND THEY'RE NOT SURE THEY SHOULD COME ANY CLOSER.
WELL--IT SURE DOESN'T LOOK LIKE KA-ZAR!
BUT, IF THAT JUNGLE MAN DIDN'T BUILD IT--THEN WHO DID?
NO TIME TO WORRY ABOUT THAT NOW!
THEY SEEM TO HAVE MADE UP THEIR MINDS.
THEY'RE SLOWLY EDGING CLOSER... CLOSER...
GET OUT YOUR PISTOL, LAD.
WE'LL TAKE A LOT OF 'EM WITH US.
I CAN DO A WHOLE LOT BETTER IF I USE MY SPIDER POWERS--AND THAT'S JUST WHAT I'M GONNA DO.
ONLY THING IS--I'M NOT EXACTLY SPEAR-PROOF.
UH OH! LOOKS LIKE THEY'RE GONNA CHARGE--
--NOW!
THEN, SUDDENLY, AS TRIGGER-FINGERS TIGHTEN... AND PETER PARKER'S FISTS CLENCH...
THEY'VE STOPPED! THEY'RE GAZING IN TERROR AT SOMETHING BEYOND THE IDOL--BUT WHAT--?
GOOD LORD!!
OH NO! NO!
ZODAN! BROD WOMTA GOG! GOG!

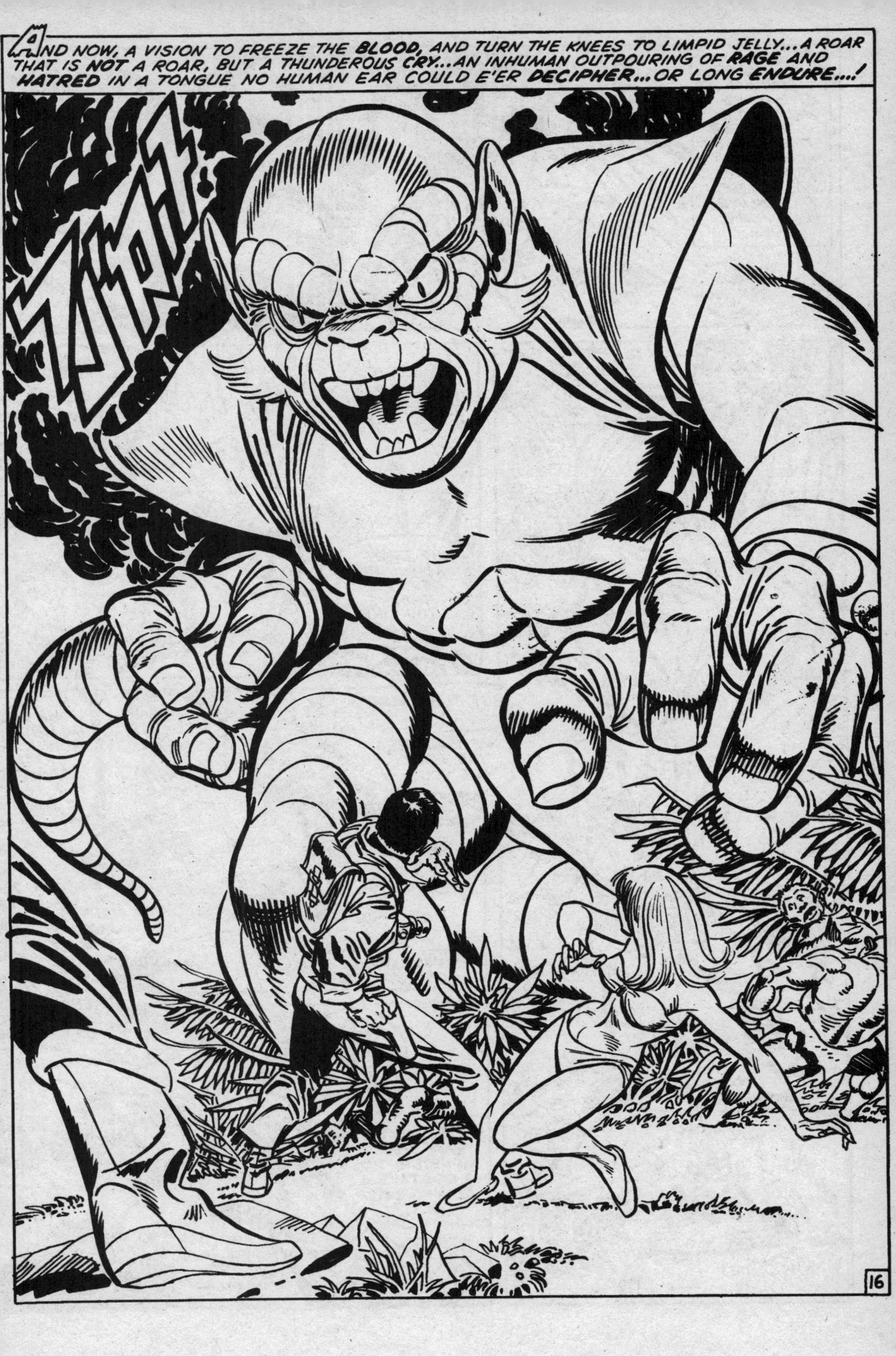
AND NOW, A VISION TO FREEZE THE BLOOD, AND TURN THE KNEES TO LIMPID JELLY... A ROAR THAT IS NOT A ROAR, BUT A THUNDEROUS CRY... AN INHUMAN OUTPOURING OF RAGE AND HATRED IN A TONGUE NO HUMAN EAR COULD E'ER DECIPHER... OR LONG ENDURE...!

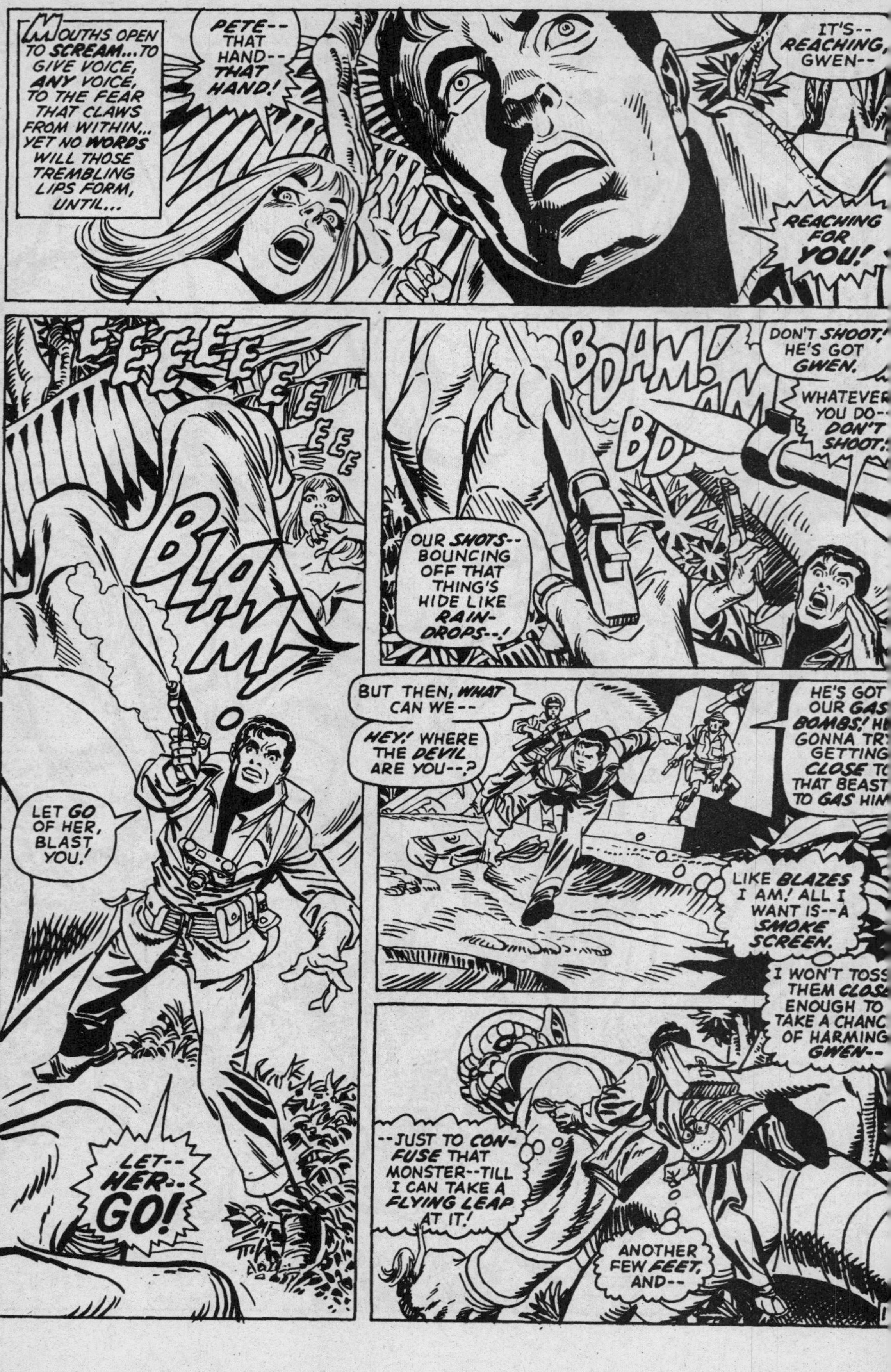
MOUTHS OPEN TO SCREAM...TO GIVE VOICE, ANY VOICE, TO THE FEAR THAT CLAWS FROM WITHIN... YET NO WORDS WILL THOSE TREMBLING LIPS FORM, UNTIL...
PETE-- THAT HAND-- THAT HAND!
IT'S-- REACHING, GWEN--
REACHING FOR YOU!
EEEEEEEEEE
BLAM
LET GO OF HER, BLAST YOU!
LET-- HER-- GO!
BDAM! BDAM!
DON'T SHOOT! HE'S GOT GWEN.
WHATEVER YOU DO-- DON'T SHOOT!
OUR SHOTS-- BOUNCING OFF THAT THING'S HIDE LIKE RAIN-DROPS--!
BUT THEN, WHAT CAN WE--
HEY! WHERE THE DEVIL ARE YOU--?
HE'S GOT OUR GAS BOMBS! HE GONNA TRY GETTING CLOSE TO THAT BEAST TO GAS HIM
LIKE BLAZES I AM! ALL I WANT IS--A SMOKE SCREEN.
I WON'T TOSS THEM CLOSE ENOUGH TO TAKE A CHANCE OF HARMING GWEN--
--JUST TO CONFUSE THAT MONSTER--TILL I CAN TAKE A FLYING LEAP AT IT!
ANOTHER FEW FEET, AND--

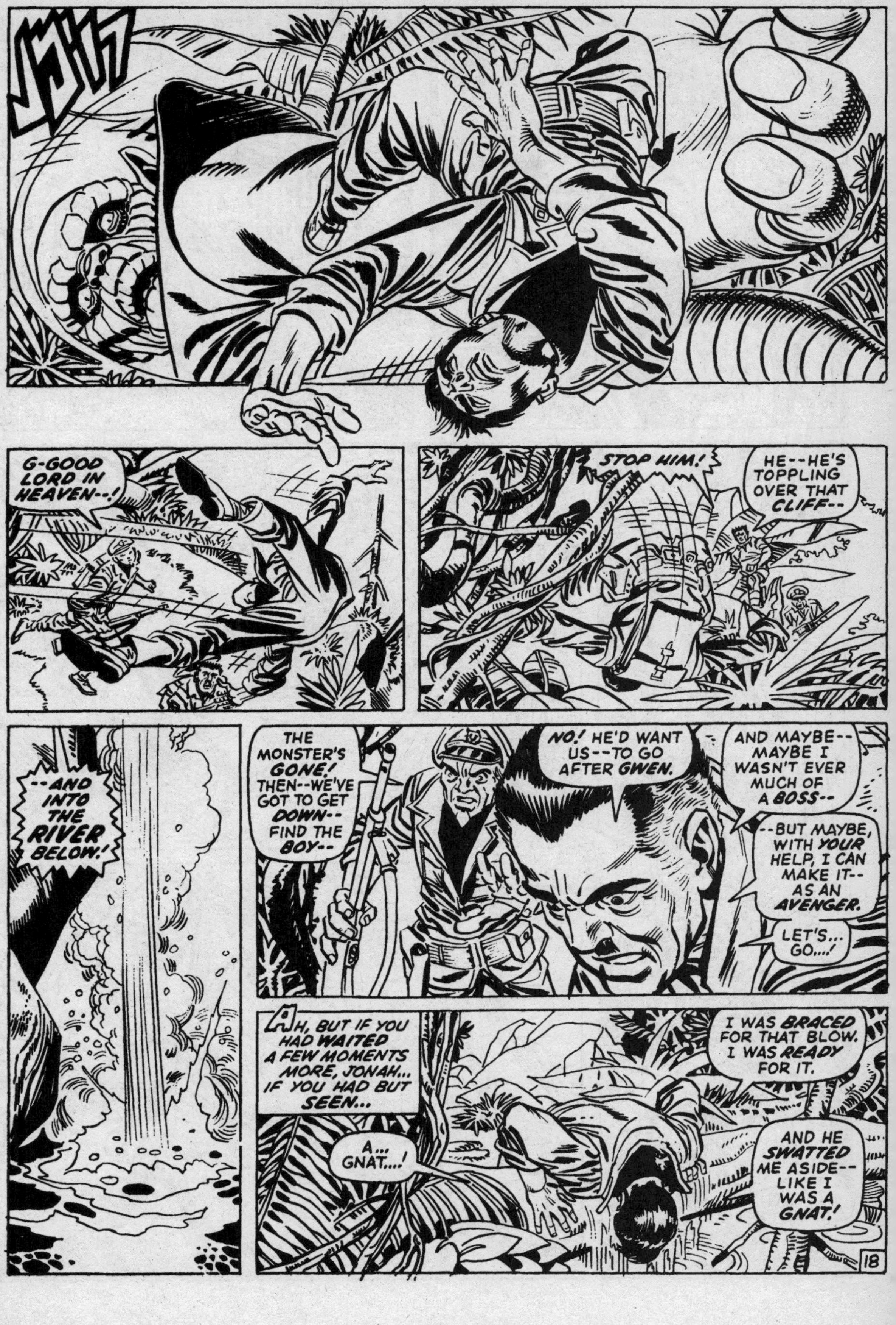

G-GOOD LORD IN HEAVEN--!
STOP HIM!
HE--HE'S TOPPLING OVER THAT CLIFF--
--AND INTO THE RIVER BELOW!
THE MONSTER'S GONE! THEN--WE'VE GOT TO GET DOWN--FIND THE BOY--
NO! HE'D WANT US--TO GO AFTER GWEN.
AND MAYBE--MAYBE I WASN'T EVER MUCH OF A BOSS--
--BUT MAYBE, WITH YOUR HELP, I CAN MAKE IT--AS AN AVENGER.
LET'S... GO...!
AH, BUT IF YOU HAD WAITED A FEW MOMENTS MORE, JONAH... IF YOU HAD BUT SEEN...
I WAS BRACED FOR THAT BLOW. I WAS READY FOR IT.
A... GNAT...!
AND HE SWATTED ME ASIDE--LIKE I WAS A GNAT!
18

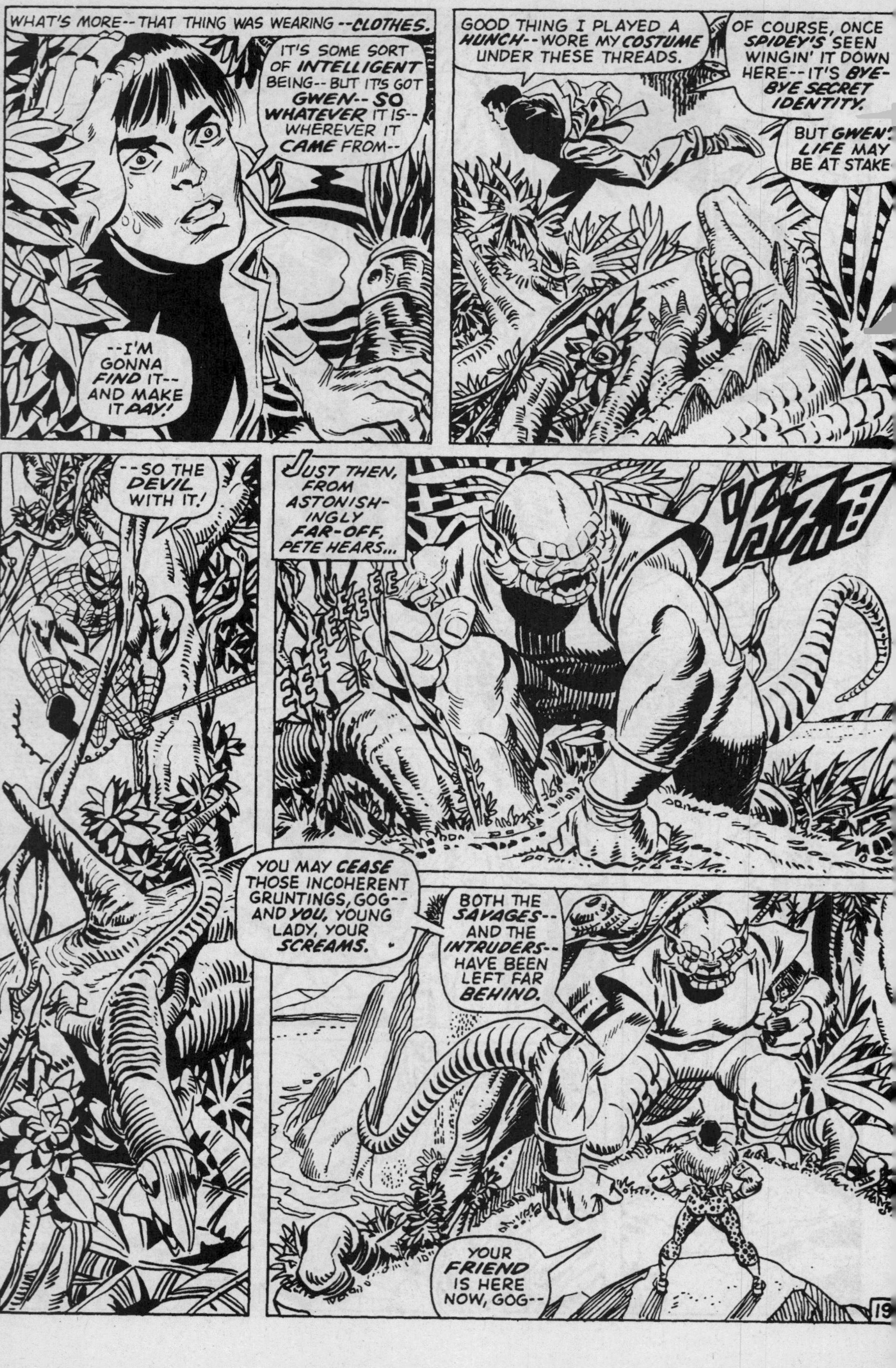
WHAT'S MORE--THAT THING WAS WEARING--CLOTHES.
IT'S SOME SORT OF INTELLIGENT BEING--BUT IT'S GOT GWEN--SO WHATEVER IT IS--WHEREVER IT CAME FROM--
--I'M GONNA FIND IT--AND MAKE IT PAY!
GOOD THING I PLAYED A HUNCH--WORE MY COSTUME UNDER THESE THREADS.
OF COURSE, ONCE SPIDEY'S SEEN WINGIN' IT DOWN HERE--IT'S BYE-BYE SECRET IDENTITY.
BUT GWEN'S LIFE MAY BE AT STAKE
--SO THE DEVIL WITH IT!
JUST THEN, FROM ASTONISH-INGLY FAR-OFF, PETE HEARS...
EEEEEE
YOU MAY CEASE THOSE INCOHERENT GRUNTINGS, GOG--AND YOU, YOUNG LADY, YOUR SCREAMS.
BOTH THE SAVAGES--AND THE INTRUDERS--HAVE BEEN LEFT FAR BEHIND.
YOUR FRIEND IS HERE NOW, GOG--
19

Panel 1:
--YOUR FRIEND-- --KRAVEN THE HUNTER!

Y-YOU!

BUT-- WHAT ARE YOU DOING HERE-- IN THIS PLACE?

AND, WHY DID THIS MONSTER BRING ME HERE-- BUT NOT PETE --NOT THE OTHERS?

Panel 2:
BECAUSE YOU ARE FAR MORE APPEALING THAN THEY, MISS STACY--OR MAY I CALL YOU GWEN?

WITH GOG'S HELP, I'M CARVING OUT A KINGDOM DOWN HERE.

AND WHAT GOOD A KINGDOM--

--WITHOUT A QUEEN--?

Panel 3:
AND NOW, WHILE THE FULL IMPACT OF THAT LITTLE BON MOT SINKS IN...

THE TRACKS LEAD THAT WAY, MR. JAMESON.

THEN, THAT'S WHERE WE'RE GOING.

COME ON!

Panel 4:
CAREFUL, SIR. ANYTHING MIGHT LIE WAITING IN THERE.

THERE'S A STORY THIS WAY, CALKIN-- A STORY, AND A HELPLESS GIRL.

NOTHING'S GONNA STOP ME FROM FINDING BOTH OF THEM.

AND I MEAN NOTH--

Panel 5:
--ING--!

20

Panel 1:
TH-THEN AGAIN--M-MAYBE THE MONSTER DOUBLED BACK TH-THIS WAY--!

JAMESON! WHAT THE DEVIL--?

RUN FOR YOUR LIFE, MAN! THERE'S A SABRETOOTH TIGER IN THAT GRASS!

Panel 2:
AND, WHERE GREAT-FANGED ZABU IS SEEN--

--CAN THE LORD OF THE SAVAGE LAND BE FAR AWAY?

KA-ZAR!

Panel 3:
I, UH--I KNEW YOU'D BE SOMEWHERE AROUND HERE, OLD BUDDY.

DO NOT WASTE WORDS, JONAH JAMESON.

FACT IS, I--I WAS JUST RUNNING OFF TO FIND YOU--YES, I--

WHY ARE YOU HERE--IN KA-ZAR'S HIDDEN JUNGLE?

Panel 4:
WE CAME HERE SEEKING A MONSTER--ONE WHOM THE SAVAGES SEEM TO CALL GOG.

IT--IT MADE OFF WITH A GIRL WE BROUGHT ALONG--AND STALKED OFF THAT WAY.

GOG--YES, KA-ZAR HAS HEARD THE SWAMP-MEN'S DRUMS TELL OF SUCH A BEAST.

Panel 5:
KA-ZAR WILL FIND THE GIRL FOR YOU.

THEN, YOU SHALL LEAVE THIS LAND FOREVER!

RRR

Panel 6:
HASTEN, ZABU--LAST OF THE MIGHTY LONGTOOTHS!

THE THING OF WHICH THE DRUMS HAVE SPOKEN IS A MENACE TO ALL WHO DWELL IN THE JUNGLE.

A MENACE WHICH KA-ZAR MUST FIND--AND PURGE!

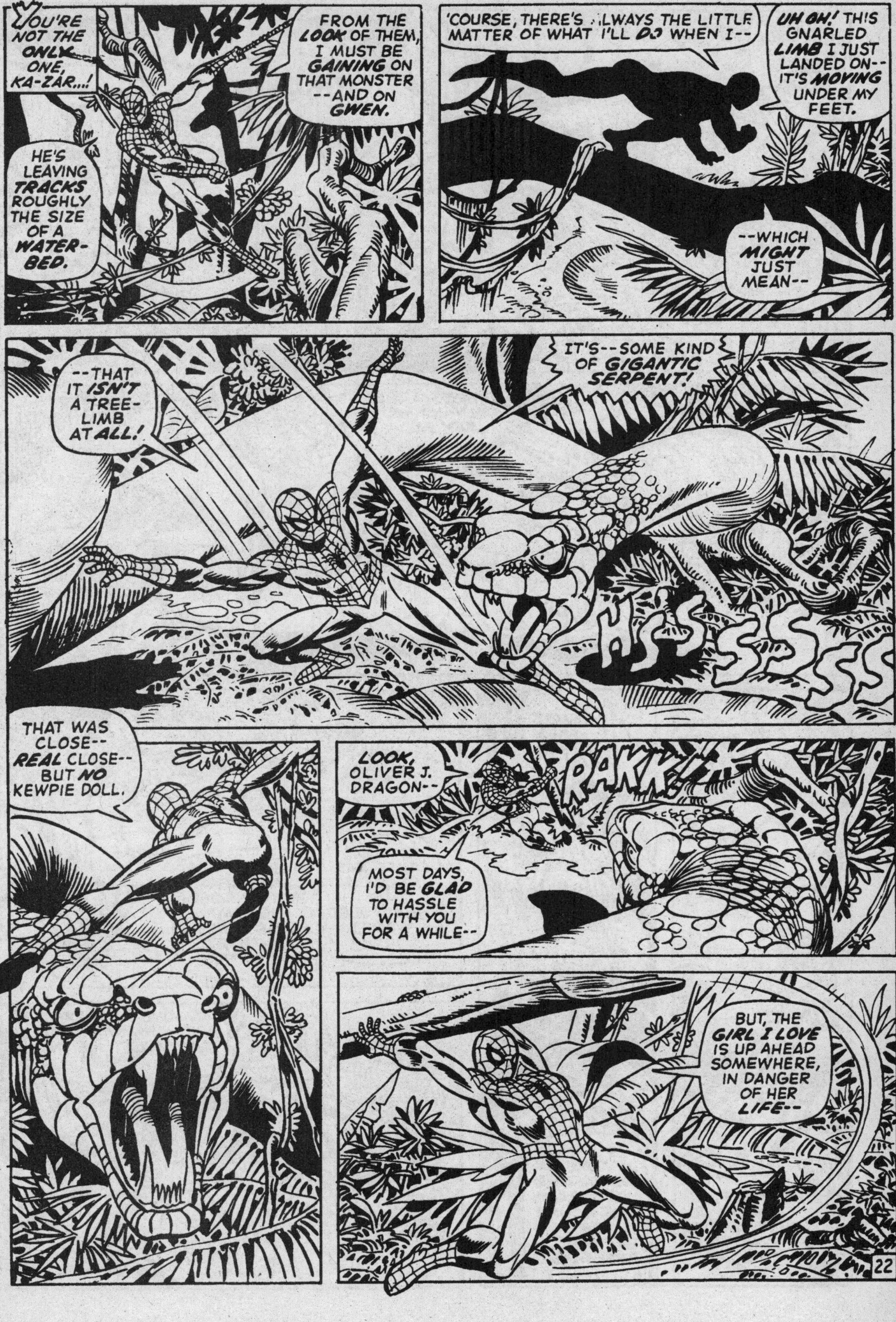
YOU'RE NOT THE ONLY ONE, KA-ZAR...!
FROM THE LOOK OF THEM, I MUST BE GAINING ON THAT MONSTER --AND ON GWEN.
HE'S LEAVING TRACKS ROUGHLY THE SIZE OF A WATER-BED.
'COURSE, THERE'S ALWAYS THE LITTLE MATTER OF WHAT I'LL DO WHEN I--
UH OH! THIS GNARLED LIMB I JUST LANDED ON--IT'S MOVING UNDER MY FEET.
--WHICH MIGHT JUST MEAN--
--THAT IT ISN'T A TREE-LIMB AT ALL!
IT'S--SOME KIND OF GIGANTIC SERPENT!
HSSSSSS
THAT WAS CLOSE--REAL CLOSE--BUT NO KEWPIE DOLL.
LOOK, OLIVER J. DRAGON--
RAKK!
MOST DAYS, I'D BE GLAD TO HASSLE WITH YOU FOR A WHILE--
BUT, THE GIRL I LOVE IS UP AHEAD SOMEWHERE, IN DANGER OF HER LIFE--
22

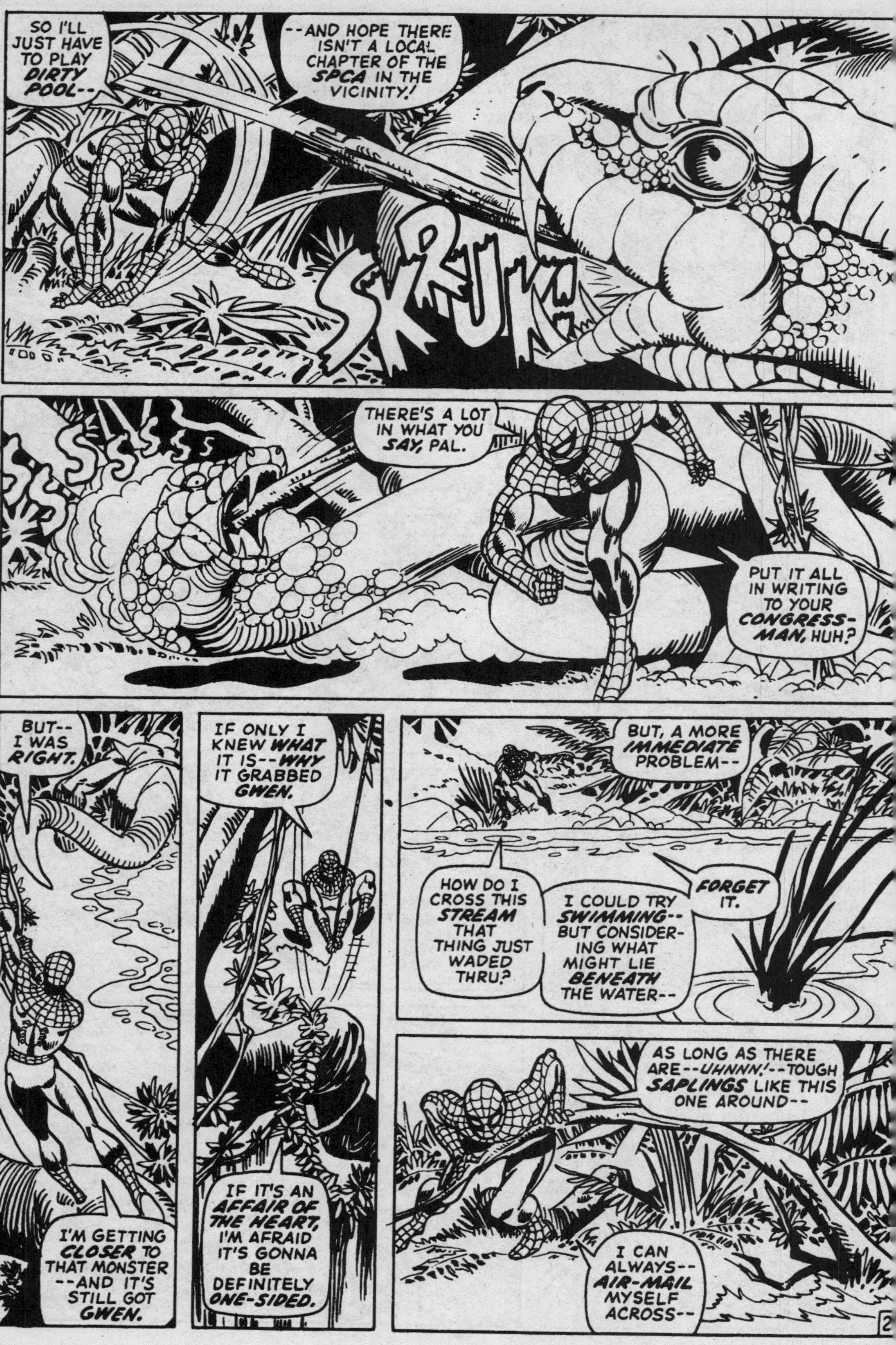
SO I'LL JUST HAVE TO PLAY DIRTY POOL--
--AND HOPE THERE ISN'T A LOCAL CHAPTER OF THE SPCA IN THE VICINITY!
SKRUK!
THERE'S A LOT IN WHAT YOU SAY, PAL.
PUT IT ALL IN WRITING TO YOUR CONGRESS-MAN, HUH?
BUT-- I WAS RIGHT.
I'M GETTING CLOSER TO THAT MONSTER --AND IT'S STILL GOT GWEN.
IF ONLY I KNEW WHAT IT IS--WHY IT GRABBED GWEN.
IF IT'S AN AFFAIR OF THE HEART, I'M AFRAID IT'S GONNA BE DEFINITELY ONE-SIDED.
BUT, A MORE IMMEDIATE PROBLEM--
HOW DO I CROSS THIS STREAM THAT THING JUST WADED THRU?
I COULD TRY SWIMMING-- BUT CONSIDER-ING WHAT MIGHT LIE BENEATH THE WATER--
FORGET IT.
AS LONG AS THERE ARE--UHHNNN!--TOUGH SAPLINGS LIKE THIS ONE AROUND--
I CAN ALWAYS-- AIR-MAIL MYSELF ACROSS--
2

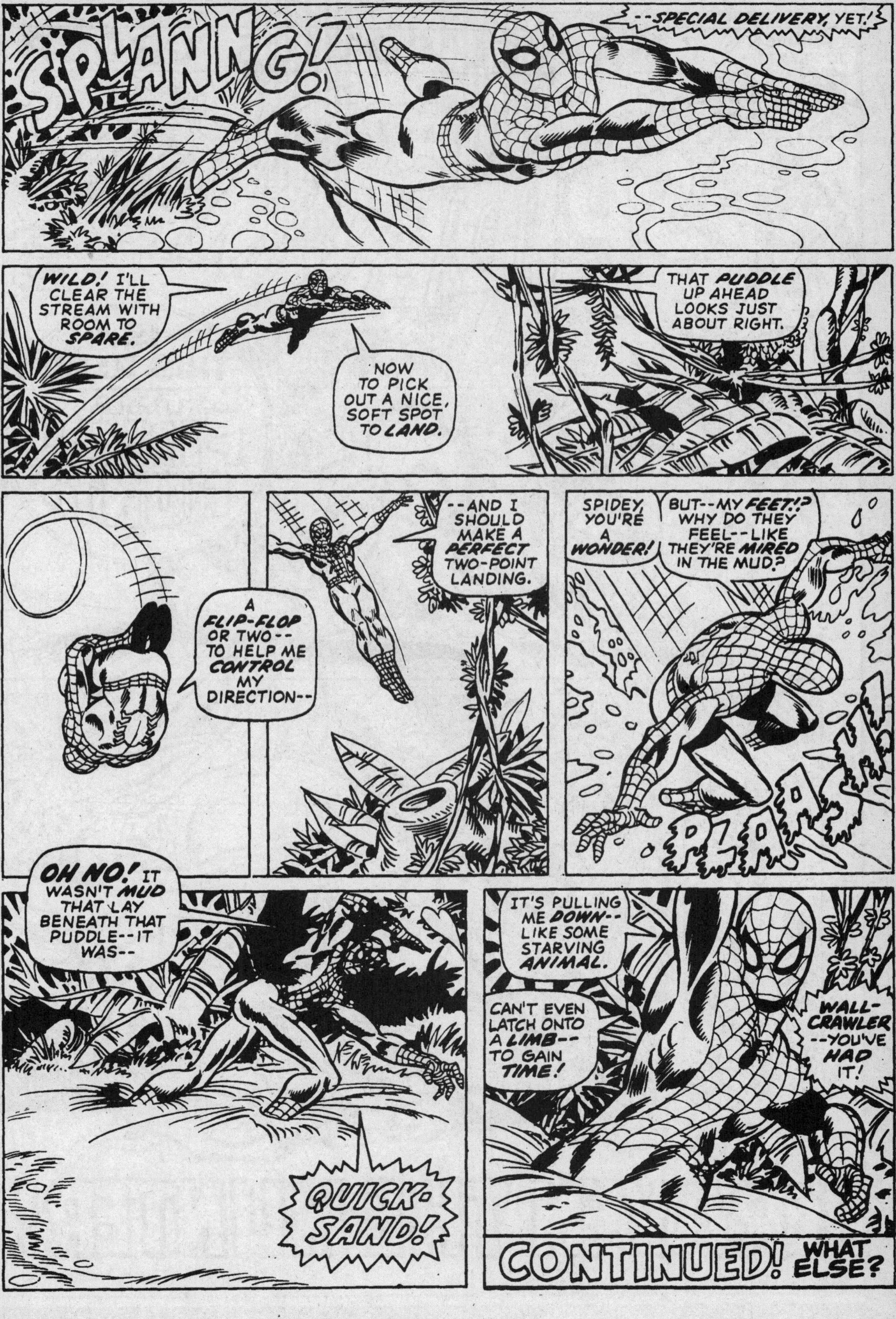
SPLANNG!
--SPECIAL DELIVERY, YET!
WILD! I'LL CLEAR THE STREAM WITH ROOM TO SPARE.
NOW TO PICK OUT A NICE, SOFT SPOT TO LAND.
THAT PUDDLE UP AHEAD LOOKS JUST ABOUT RIGHT.
A FLIP-FLOP OR TWO--TO HELP ME CONTROL MY DIRECTION--
--AND I SHOULD MAKE A PERFECT TWO-POINT LANDING.
SPIDEY, YOU'RE A WONDER!
BUT--MY FEET!? WHY DO THEY FEEL--LIKE THEY'RE MIRED IN THE MUD?
PLASH
OH NO! IT WASN'T MUD THAT LAY BENEATH THAT PUDDLE--IT WAS--
QUICK-SAND!
IT'S PULLING ME DOWN--LIKE SOME STARVING ANIMAL.
CAN'T EVEN LATCH ONTO A LIMB--TO GAIN TIME!
WALL-CRAWLER--YOU'VE HAD IT!
CONTINUED! WHAT ELSE?

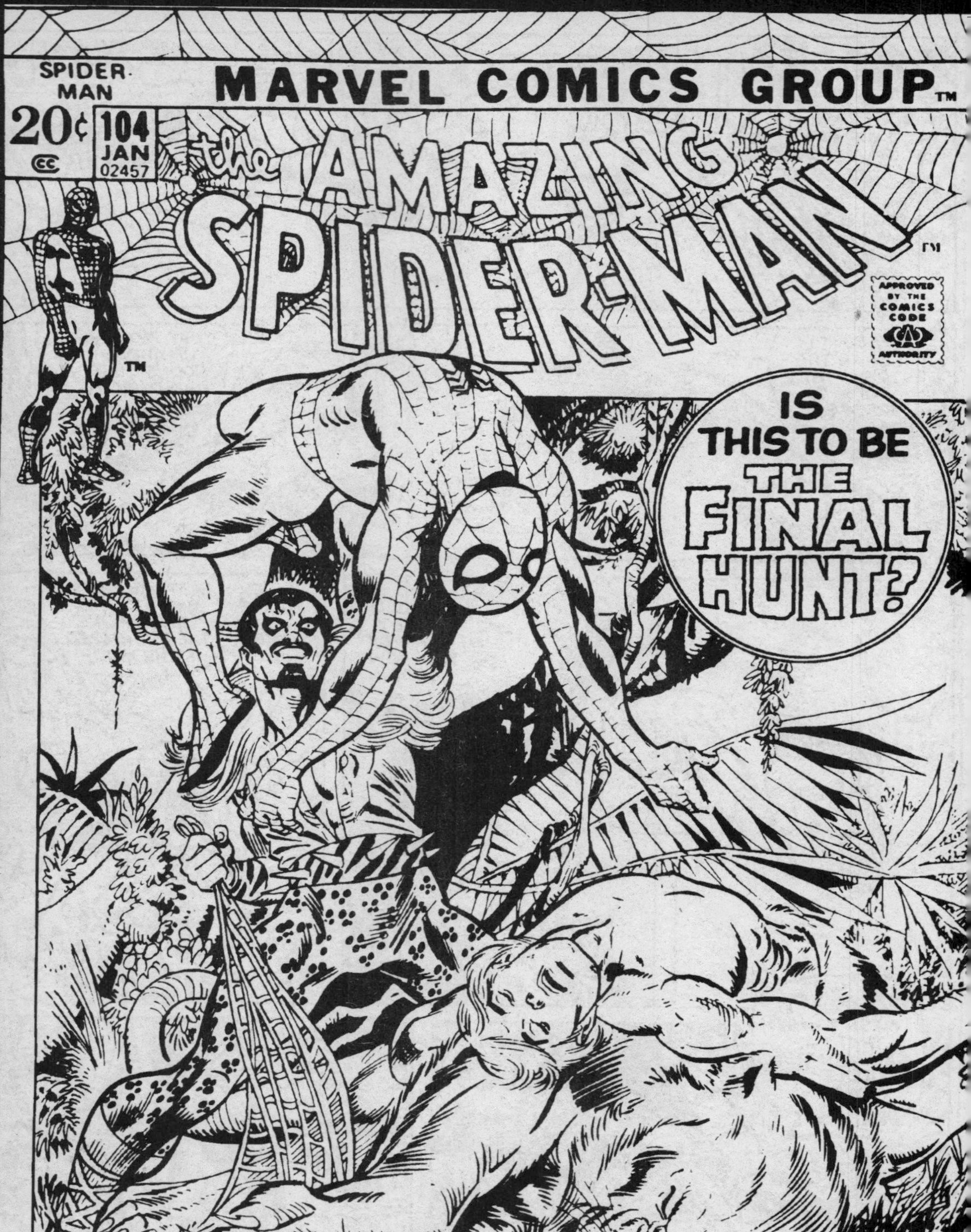
SPIDER-MAN
MARVEL COMICS GROUP™
20¢
104
JAN
02457
the AMAZING SPIDER-MAN™
APPROVED BY THE COMICS CODE AUTHORITY
IS THIS TO BE THE FINAL HUNT?
KRAVEN THE HUNTER!

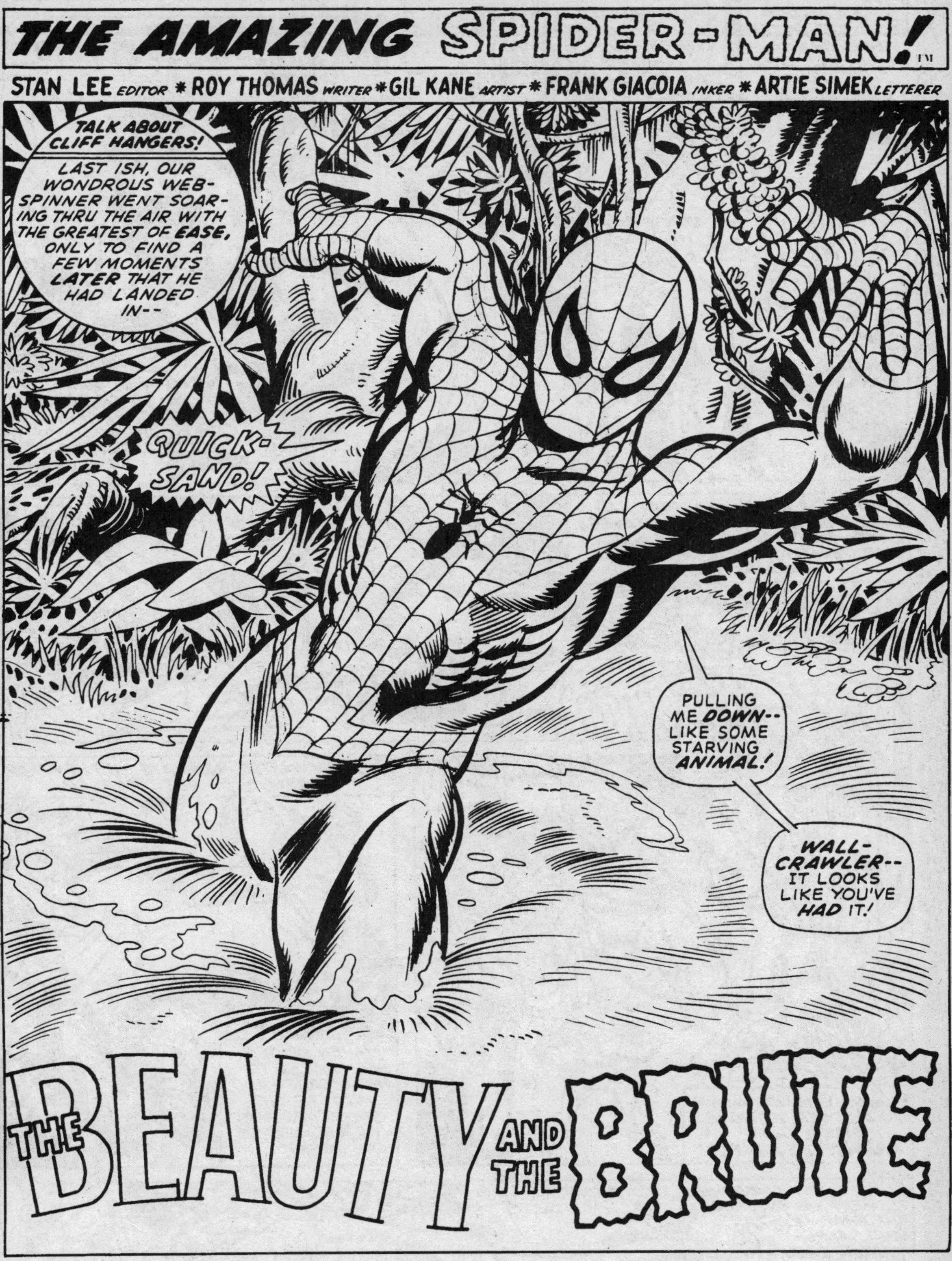
THE AMAZING SPIDER-MAN! TM
STAN LEE EDITOR * ROY THOMAS WRITER * GIL KANE ARTIST * FRANK GIACOIA INKER * ARTIE SIMEK LETTERER
TALK ABOUT CLIFF HANGERS!
LAST ISH, OUR WONDROUS WEB-SPINNER WENT SOARING THRU THE AIR WITH THE GREATEST OF EASE, ONLY TO FIND A FEW MOMENTS LATER THAT HE HAD LANDED IN--
QUICK-SAND!
PULLING ME DOWN--LIKE SOME STARVING ANIMAL!
WALL-CRAWLER--IT LOOKS LIKE YOU'VE HAD IT!
THE BEAUTY AND THE BRUTE

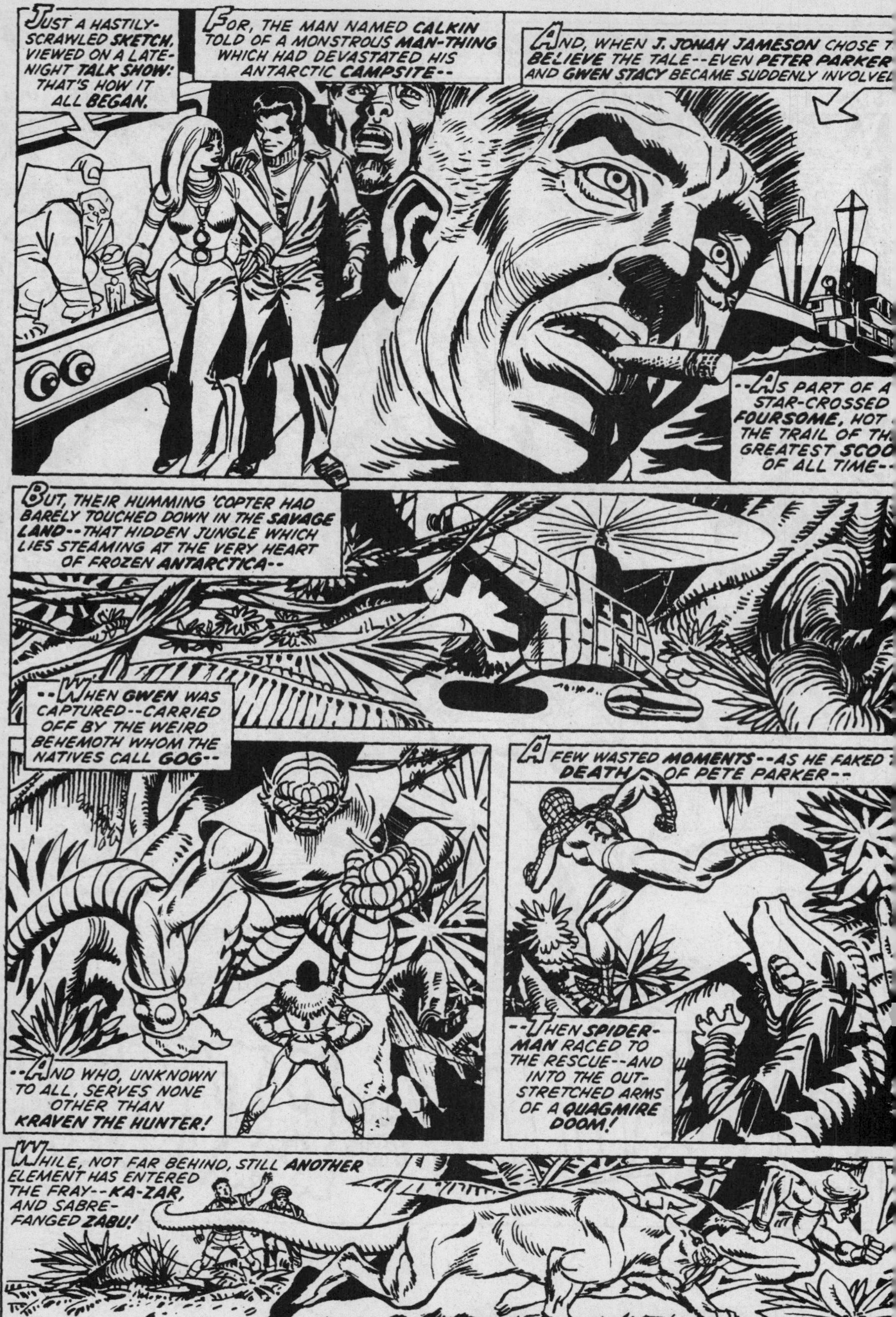
JUST A HASTILY-SCRAWLED SKETCH, VIEWED ON A LATE-NIGHT TALK SHOW: THAT'S HOW IT ALL BEGAN.
FOR, THE MAN NAMED CALKIN TOLD OF A MONSTROUS MAN-THING WHICH HAD DEVASTATED HIS ANTARCTIC CAMPSITE--
AND, WHEN J. JONAH JAMESON CHOSE T BELIEVE THE TALE--EVEN PETER PARKER AND GWEN STACY BECAME SUDDENLY INVOLVE
--AS PART OF A STAR-CROSSED FOURSOME, HOT THE TRAIL OF TH GREATEST SCOO OF ALL TIME--
BUT, THEIR HUMMING 'COPTER HAD BARELY TOUCHED DOWN IN THE SAVAGE LAND--THAT HIDDEN JUNGLE WHICH LIES STEAMING AT THE VERY HEART OF FROZEN ANTARCTICA--
--WHEN GWEN WAS CAPTURED--CARRIED OFF BY THE WEIRD BEHEMOTH WHOM THE NATIVES CALL GOG--
--AND WHO, UNKNOWN TO ALL, SERVES NONE OTHER THAN KRAVEN THE HUNTER!
A FEW WASTED MOMENTS--AS HE FAKED DEATH OF PETE PARKER--
--THEN SPIDER-MAN RACED TO THE RESCUE--AND INTO THE OUT-STRETCHED ARMS OF A QUAGMIRE DOOM!
WHILE, NOT FAR BEHIND, STILL ANOTHER ELEMENT HAS ENTERED THE FRAY--KA-ZAR, AND SABRE-FANGED ZABU!

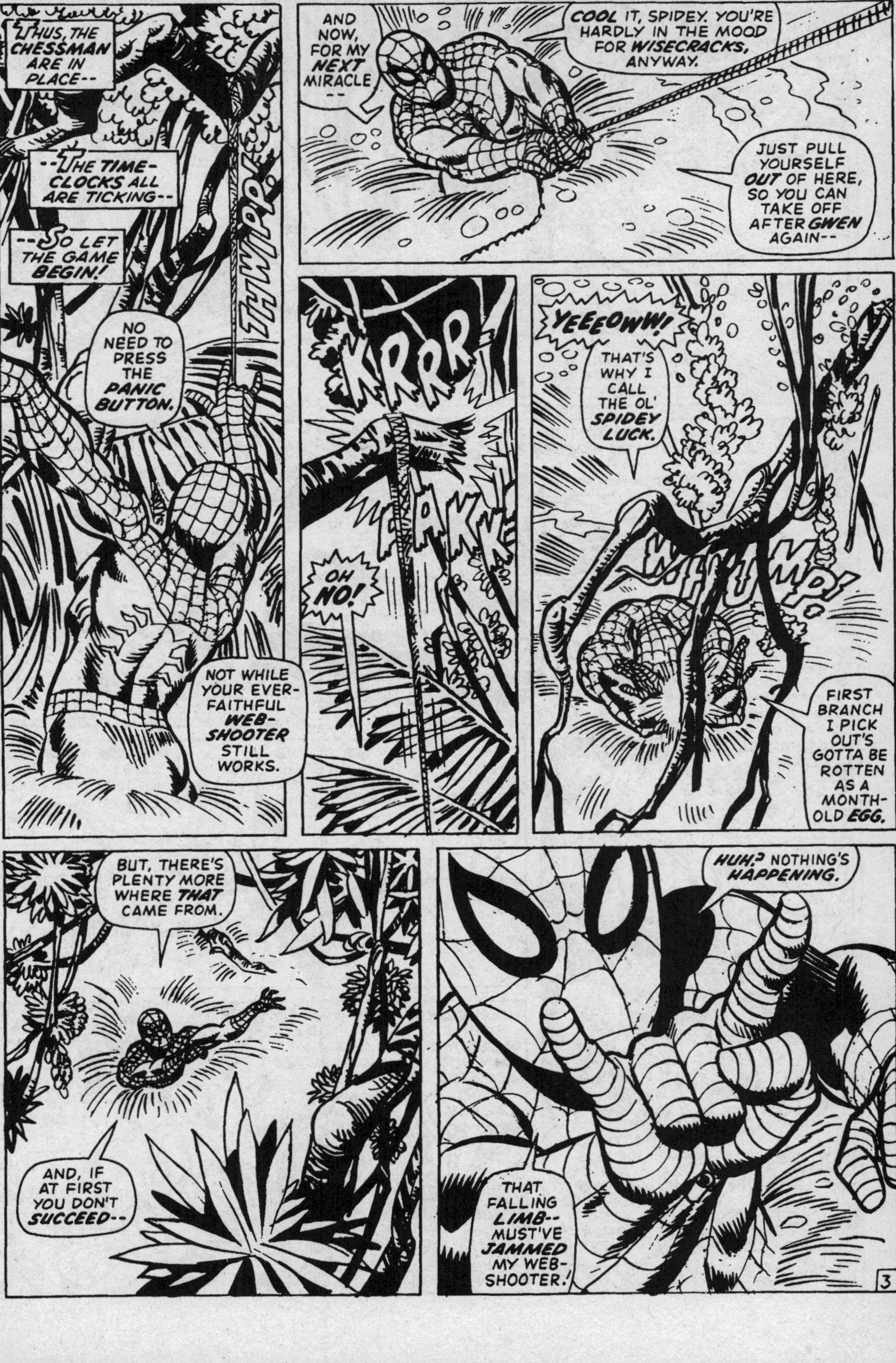

THUS, THE CHESSMAN ARE IN PLACE--
--THE TIME-CLOCKS ALL ARE TICKING--
--SO LET THE GAME BEGIN!
THWIPP!
NO NEED TO PRESS THE PANIC BUTTON.
NOT WHILE YOUR EVER-FAITHFUL WEB-SHOOTER STILL WORKS.
AND NOW, FOR MY NEXT MIRACLE --
COOL IT, SPIDEY. YOU'RE HARDLY IN THE MOOD FOR WISECRACKS, ANYWAY.
JUST PULL YOURSELF OUT OF HERE, SO YOU CAN TAKE OFF AFTER GWEN AGAIN--
KRRR
RAKK
OH NO!
YEEEOWW!
THAT'S WHY I CALL THE OL' SPIDEY LUCK.
WHUMP!
FIRST BRANCH I PICK OUT'S GOTTA BE ROTTEN AS A MONTH-OLD EGG.
BUT, THERE'S PLENTY MORE WHERE THAT CAME FROM.
AND, IF AT FIRST YOU DON'T SUCCEED--
HUH? NOTHING'S HAPPENING.
THAT FALLING LIMB--MUST'VE JAMMED MY WEB-SHOOTER!

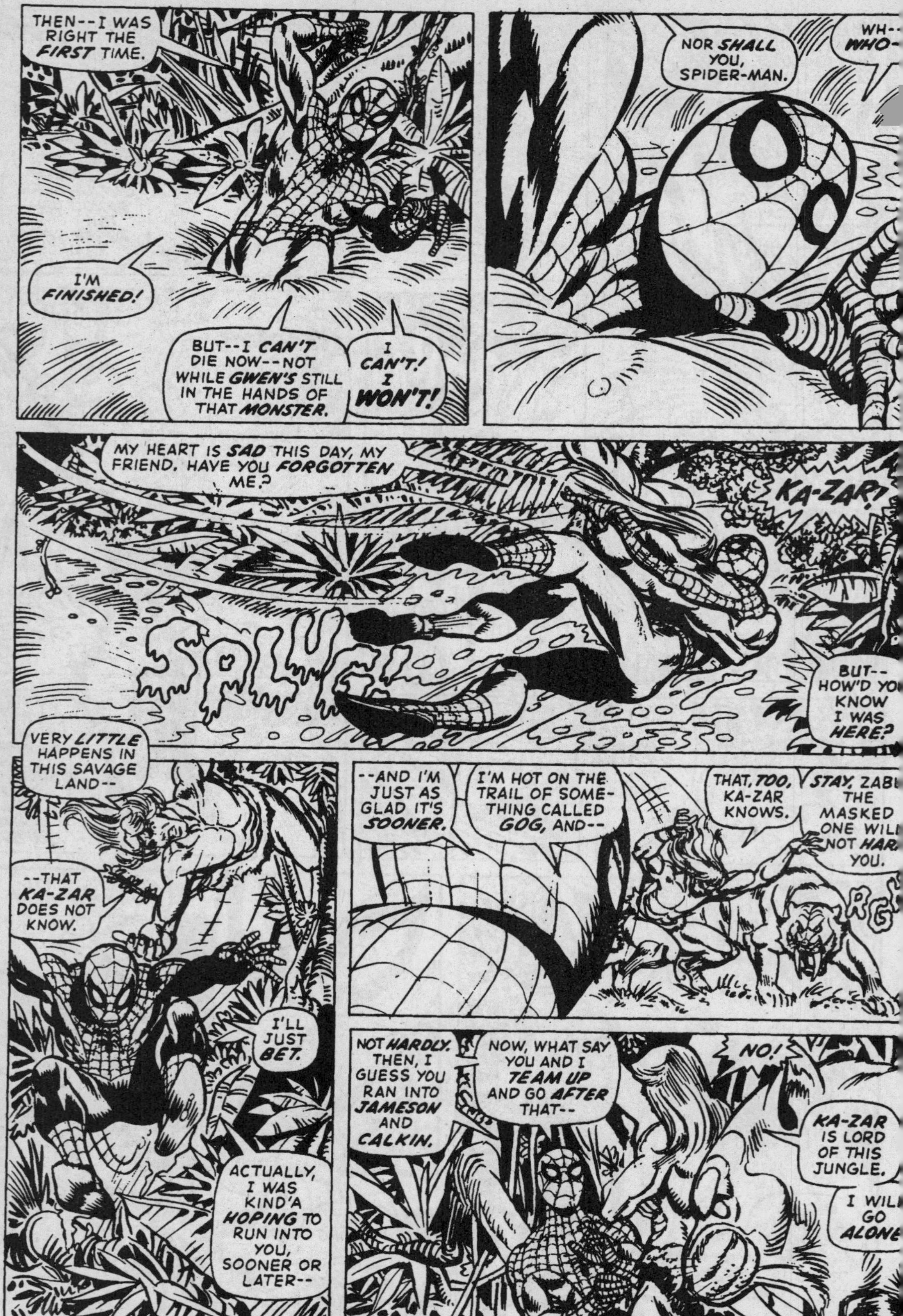

THEN--I WAS RIGHT THE FIRST TIME.
I'M FINISHED!
BUT--I CAN'T DIE NOW--NOT WHILE GWEN'S STILL IN THE HANDS OF THAT MONSTER.
I CAN'T! I WON'T!
NOR SHALL YOU, SPIDER-MAN.
WH-- WHO-
MY HEART IS SAD THIS DAY, MY FRIEND. HAVE YOU FORGOTTEN ME?
KA-ZAR!
SPLUG!
BUT-- HOW'D YO KNOW I WAS HERE?
VERY LITTLE HAPPENS IN THIS SAVAGE LAND--
--THAT KA-ZAR DOES NOT KNOW.
I'LL JUST BET.
ACTUALLY, I WAS KIND'A HOPING TO RUN INTO YOU, SOONER OR LATER--
--AND I'M JUST AS GLAD IT'S SOONER.
I'M HOT ON THE TRAIL OF SOMETHING CALLED GOG, AND--
THAT, TOO, KA-ZAR KNOWS.
STAY, ZABU THE MASKED ONE WIL NOT HAR YOU.
NOT HARDLY. THEN, I GUESS YOU RAN INTO JAMESON AND CALKIN.
NOW, WHAT SAY YOU AND I TEAM UP AND GO AFTER THAT--
NO!
KA-ZAR IS LORD OF THIS JUNGLE.
I WIL GO ALONE

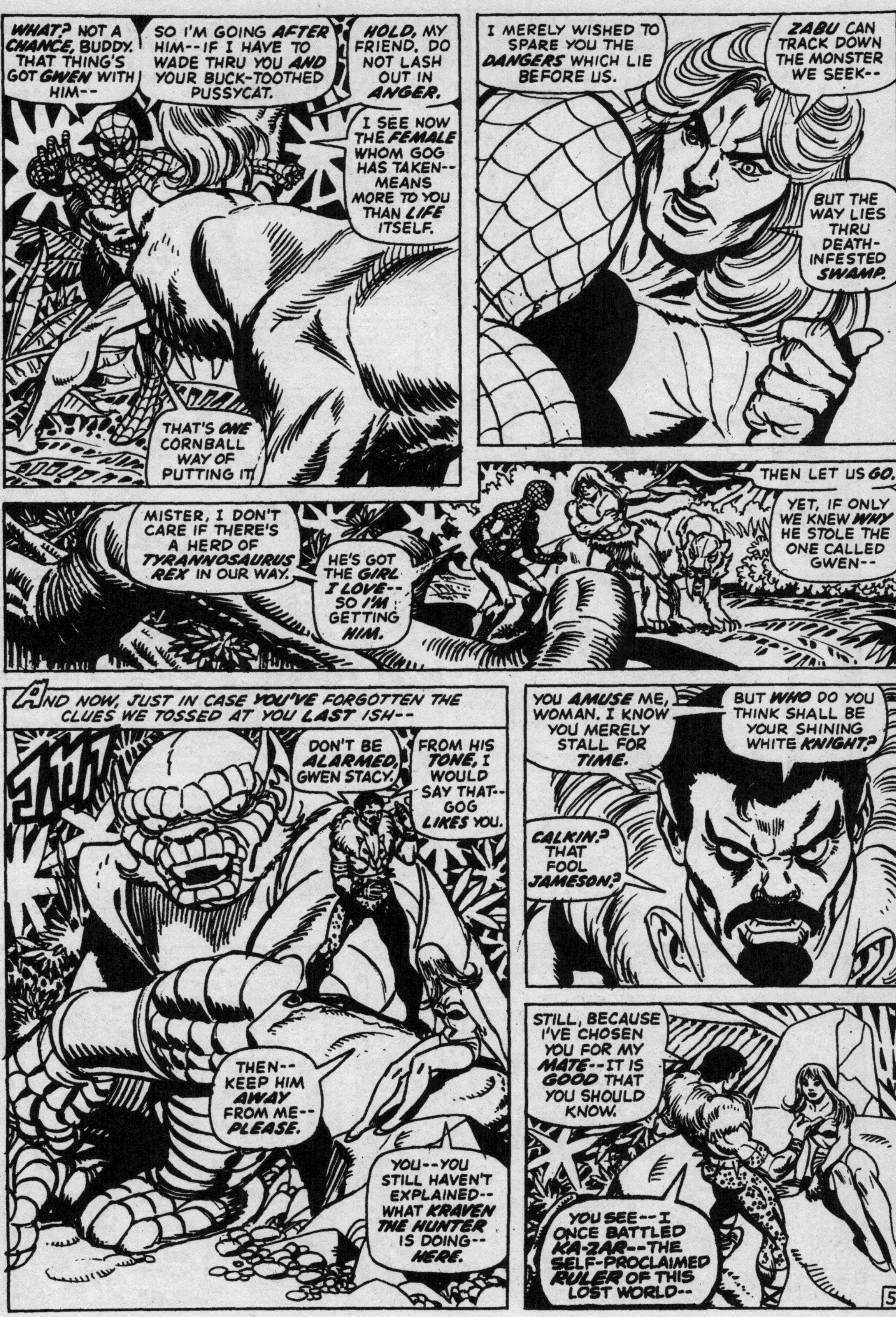

WHAT? NOT A CHANCE, BUDDY. THAT THING'S GOT GWEN WITH HIM--
SO I'M GOING AFTER HIM--IF I HAVE TO WADE THRU YOU AND YOUR BUCK-TOOTHED PUSSYCAT.
HOLD, MY FRIEND. DO NOT LASH OUT IN ANGER.
I SEE NOW THE FEMALE WHOM GOG HAS TAKEN--MEANS MORE TO YOU THAN LIFE ITSELF.
THAT'S ONE CORNBALL WAY OF PUTTING IT.
I MERELY WISHED TO SPARE YOU THE DANGERS WHICH LIE BEFORE US.
ZABU CAN TRACK DOWN THE MONSTER WE SEEK--
BUT THE WAY LIES THRU DEATH-INFESTED SWAMP.
MISTER, I DON'T CARE IF THERE'S A HERD OF TYRANNOSAURUS REX IN OUR WAY.
HE'S GOT THE GIRL I LOVE--SO I'M GETTING HIM.
THEN LET US GO.
YET, IF ONLY WE KNEW WHY HE STOLE THE ONE CALLED GWEN--
AND NOW, JUST IN CASE YOU'VE FORGOTTEN THE CLUES WE TOSSED AT YOU LAST ISH--
DON'T BE ALARMED, GWEN STACY.
FROM HIS TONE, I WOULD SAY THAT--GOG LIKES YOU.
THEN--KEEP HIM AWAY FROM ME--PLEASE.
YOU--YOU STILL HAVEN'T EXPLAINED--WHAT KRAVEN THE HUNTER IS DOING--HERE.
YOU AMUSE ME, WOMAN. I KNOW YOU MERELY STALL FOR TIME.
BUT WHO DO YOU THINK SHALL BE YOUR SHINING WHITE KNIGHT?
CALKIN? THAT FOOL JAMESON?
STILL, BECAUSE I'VE CHOSEN YOU FOR MY MATE--IT IS GOOD THAT YOU SHOULD KNOW.
YOU SEE--I ONCE BATTLED KA-ZAR--THE SELF-PROCLAIMED RULER OF THIS LOST WORLD--
5

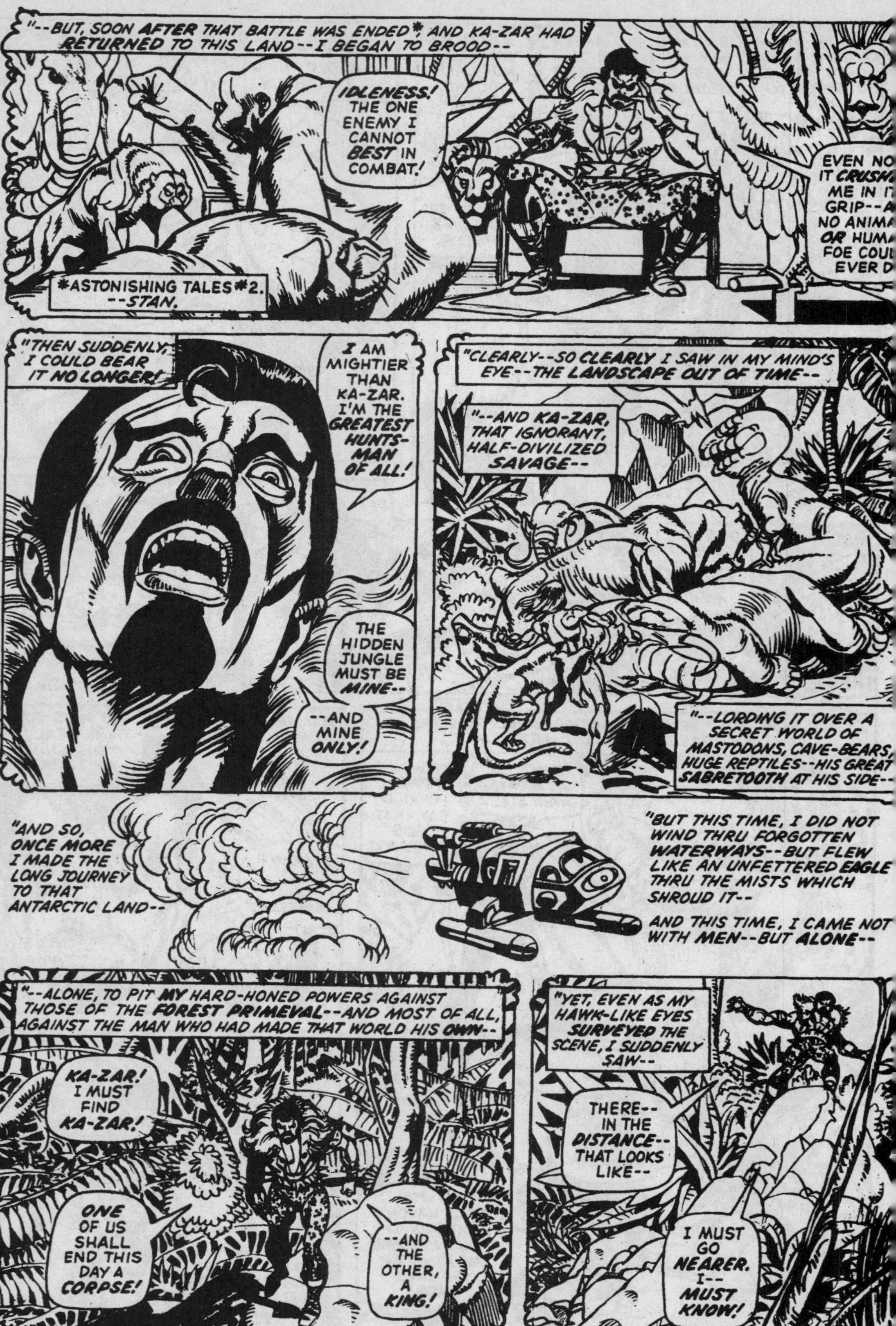
"--BUT, SOON AFTER THAT BATTLE WAS ENDED*, AND KA-ZAR HAD RETURNED TO THIS LAND--I BEGAN TO BROOD--
IDLENESS! THE ONE ENEMY I CANNOT BEST IN COMBAT!
EVEN NO IT CRUSH ME IN IT GRIP--A NO ANIMA OR HUMA FOE COUL EVER D
*ASTONISHING TALES #2. --STAN.
"THEN SUDDENLY, I COULD BEAR IT NO LONGER!
I AM MIGHTIER THAN KA-ZAR. I'M THE GREATEST HUNTS-MAN OF ALL!
THE HIDDEN JUNGLE MUST BE MINE--
--AND MINE ONLY!
"CLEARLY--SO CLEARLY I SAW IN MY MIND'S EYE--THE LANDSCAPE OUT OF TIME--
"--AND KA-ZAR, THAT IGNORANT, HALF-DIVILIZED SAVAGE--
"--LORDING IT OVER A SECRET WORLD OF MASTODONS, CAVE-BEARS, HUGE REPTILES--HIS GREAT SABRETOOTH AT HIS SIDE--
"AND SO, ONCE MORE I MADE THE LONG JOURNEY TO THAT ANTARCTIC LAND--
"BUT THIS TIME, I DID NOT WIND THRU FORGOTTEN WATERWAYS--BUT FLEW LIKE AN UNFETTERED EAGLE THRU THE MISTS WHICH SHROUD IT--
AND THIS TIME, I CAME NOT WITH MEN--BUT ALONE--
"--ALONE, TO PIT MY HARD-HONED POWERS AGAINST THOSE OF THE FOREST PRIMEVAL--AND MOST OF ALL, AGAINST THE MAN WHO HAD MADE THAT WORLD HIS OWN--
KA-ZAR! I MUST FIND KA-ZAR!
ONE OF US SHALL END THIS DAY A CORPSE!
--AND THE OTHER, A KING!
"YET, EVEN AS MY HAWK-LIKE EYES SURVEYED THE SCENE, I SUDDENLY SAW--
THERE-- IN THE DISTANCE-- THAT LOOKS LIKE--
I MUST GO NEARER. I-- MUST KNOW!

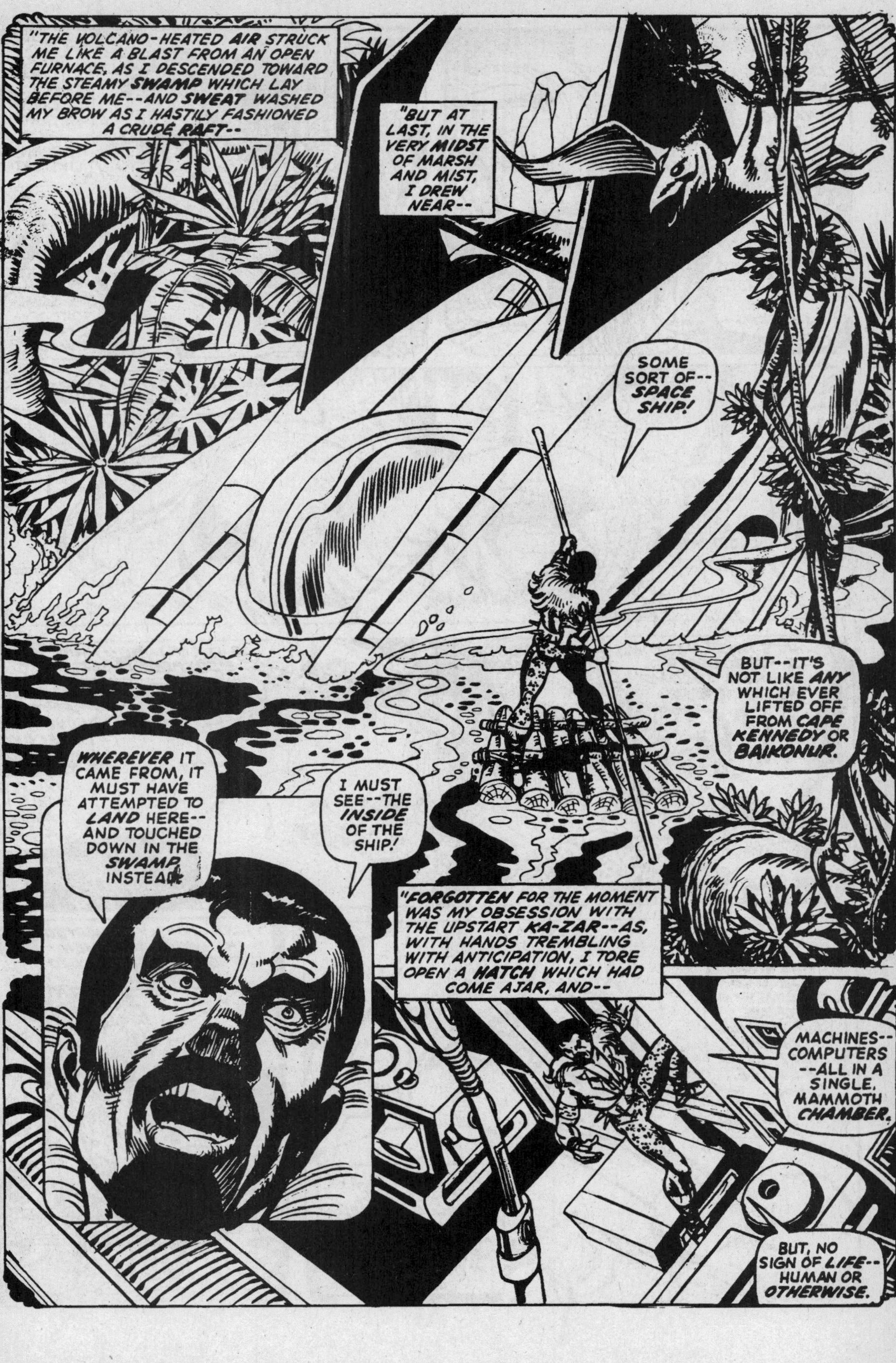
"THE VOLCANO-HEATED AIR STRUCK ME LIKE A BLAST FROM AN OPEN FURNACE, AS I DESCENDED TOWARD THE STEAMY SWAMP WHICH LAY BEFORE ME--AND SWEAT WASHED MY BROW AS I HASTILY FASHIONED A CRUDE RAFT--
"BUT AT LAST, IN THE VERY MIDST OF MARSH AND MIST, I DREW NEAR--
SOME SORT OF-- SPACE SHIP!
BUT--IT'S NOT LIKE ANY WHICH EVER LIFTED OFF FROM CAPE KENNEDY OR BAIKONUR.
WHEREVER IT CAME FROM, IT MUST HAVE ATTEMPTED TO LAND HERE-- AND TOUCHED DOWN IN THE SWAMP INSTEAD!
I MUST SEE--THE INSIDE OF THE SHIP!
"FORGOTTEN FOR THE MOMENT WAS MY OBSESSION WITH THE UPSTART KA-ZAR--AS, WITH HANDS TREMBLING WITH ANTICIPATION, I TORE OPEN A HATCH WHICH HAD COME AJAR, AND--
MACHINES-- COMPUTERS --ALL IN A SINGLE, MAMMOTH CHAMBER.
BUT, NO SIGN OF LIFE-- HUMAN OR OTHERWISE.

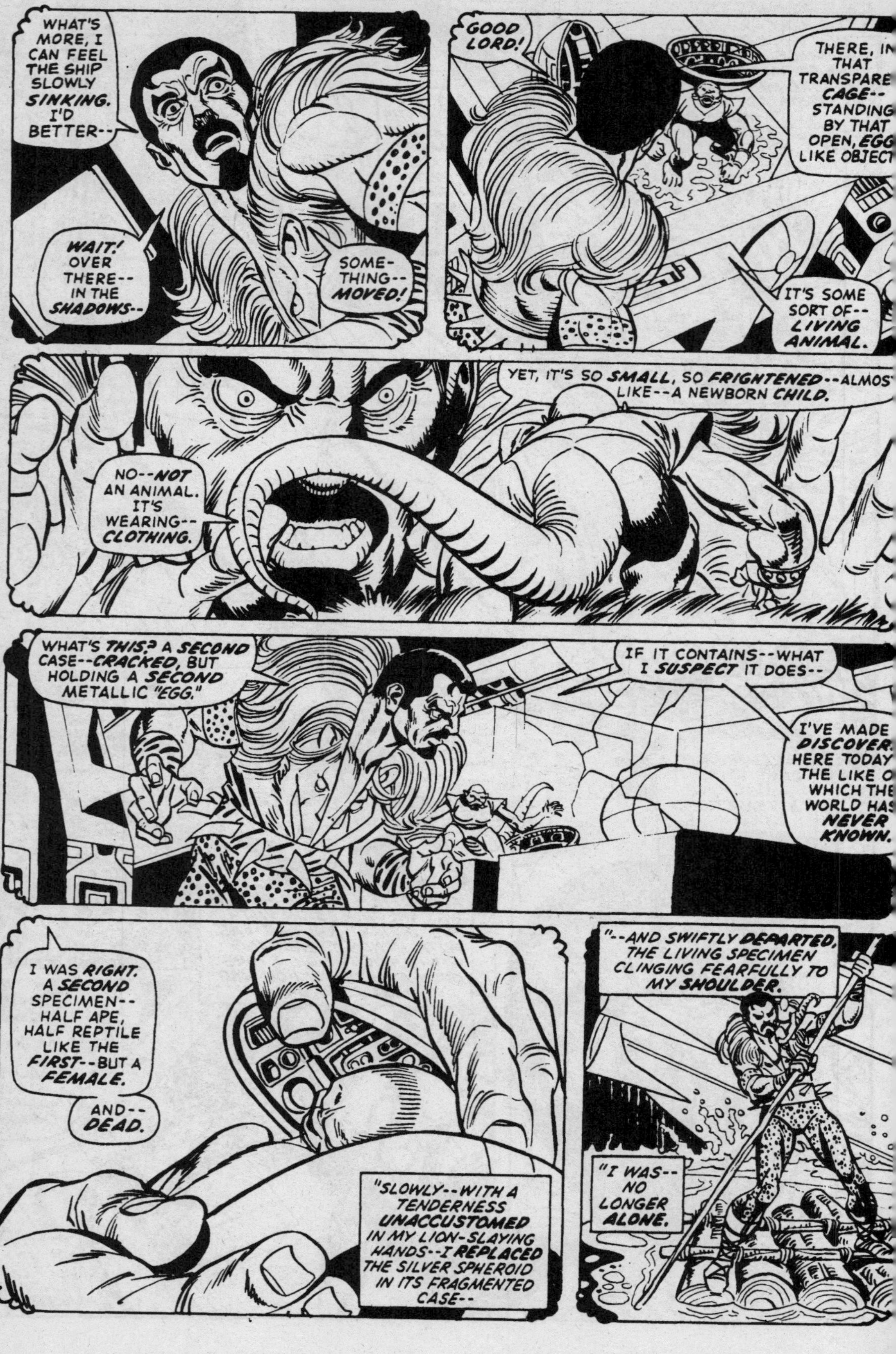
WHAT'S MORE, I CAN FEEL THE SHIP SLOWLY SINKING. I'D BETTER--
WAIT! OVER THERE-- IN THE SHADOWS--
SOME-THING--MOVED!
GOOD LORD!
THERE, IN THAT TRANSPARE CAGE-- STANDING BY THAT OPEN, EGG LIKE OBJECT
IT'S SOME SORT OF-- LIVING ANIMAL.
YET, IT'S SO SMALL, SO FRIGHTENED--ALMOST LIKE--A NEWBORN CHILD.
NO--NOT AN ANIMAL. IT'S WEARING-- CLOTHING.
WHAT'S THIS? A SECOND CASE--CRACKED, BUT HOLDING A SECOND METALLIC "EGG."
IF IT CONTAINS--WHAT I SUSPECT IT DOES--
I'VE MADE DISCOVER HERE TODAY THE LIKE O WHICH THE WORLD HAS NEVER KNOWN.
I WAS RIGHT. A SECOND SPECIMEN-- HALF APE, HALF REPTILE LIKE THE FIRST--BUT A FEMALE.
AND-- DEAD.
"SLOWLY--WITH A TENDERNESS UNACCUSTOMED IN MY LION-SLAYING HANDS--I REPLACED THE SILVER SPHEROID IN ITS FRAGMENTED CASE--
"--AND SWIFTLY DEPARTED, THE LIVING SPECIMEN CLINGING FEARFULLY TO MY SHOULDER.
"I WAS-- NO LONGER ALONE.

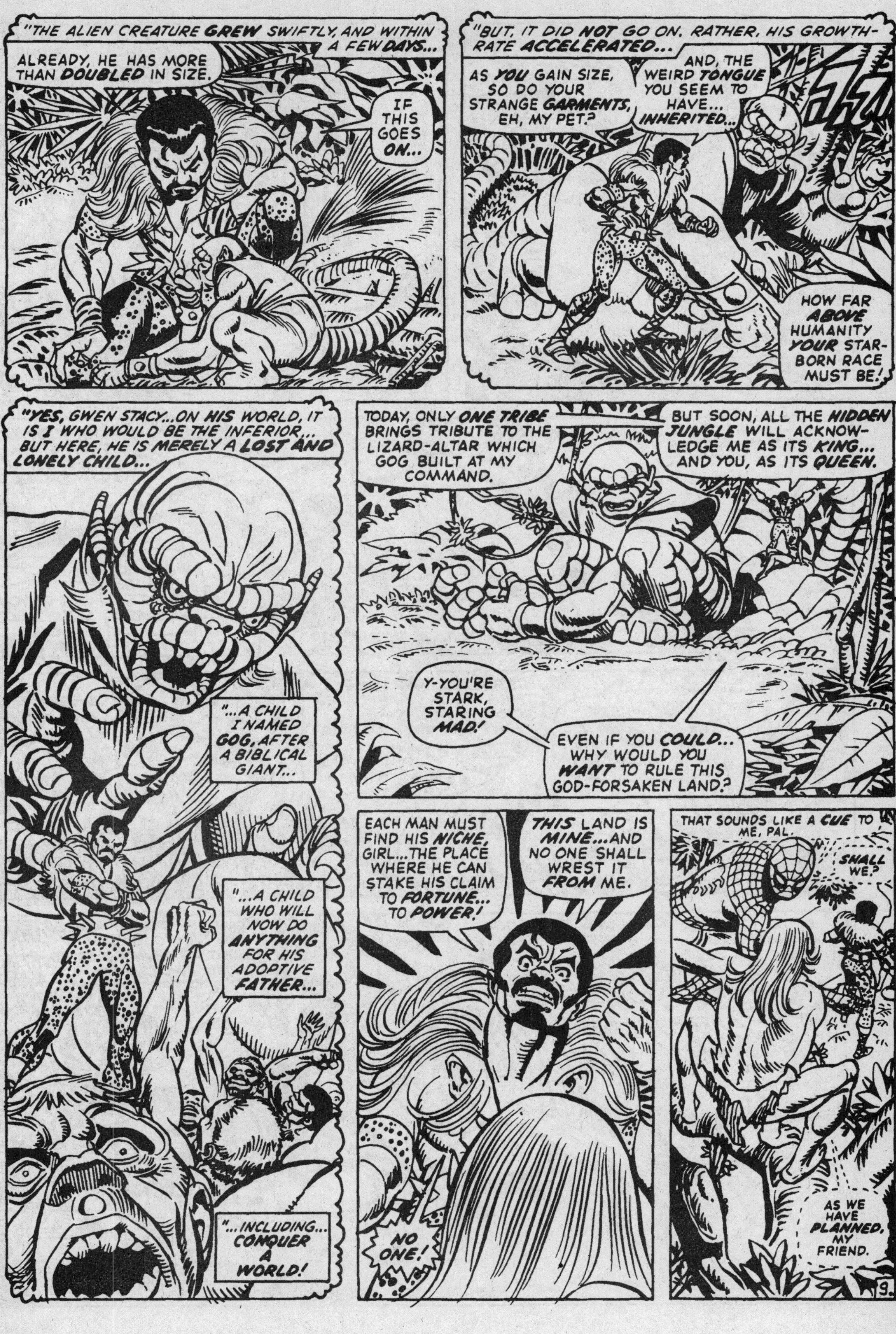
"THE ALIEN CREATURE GREW SWIFTLY, AND WITHIN A FEW DAYS...
ALREADY, HE HAS MORE THAN DOUBLED IN SIZE.
IF THIS GOES ON...
"BUT, IT DID NOT GO ON. RATHER, HIS GROWTH-RATE ACCELERATED...
AS YOU GAIN SIZE, SO DO YOUR STRANGE GARMENTS, EH, MY PET?
AND, THE WEIRD TONGUE YOU SEEM TO HAVE... INHERITED...
HOW FAR ABOVE HUMANITY YOUR STAR-BORN RACE MUST BE!
"YES, GWEN STACY...ON HIS WORLD, IT IS I WHO WOULD BE THE INFERIOR... BUT HERE, HE IS MERELY A LOST AND LONELY CHILD...
"...A CHILD I NAMED GOG, AFTER A BIBLICAL GIANT...
"...A CHILD WHO WILL NOW DO ANYTHING FOR HIS ADOPTIVE FATHER...
"...INCLUDING... CONQUER A WORLD!
TODAY, ONLY ONE TRIBE BRINGS TRIBUTE TO THE LIZARD-ALTAR WHICH GOG BUILT AT MY COMMAND.
BUT SOON, ALL THE HIDDEN JUNGLE WILL ACKNOWLEDGE ME AS ITS KING... AND YOU, AS ITS QUEEN.
Y-YOU'RE STARK, STARING MAD!
EVEN IF YOU COULD... WHY WOULD YOU WANT TO RULE THIS GOD-FORSAKEN LAND?
EACH MAN MUST FIND HIS NICHE, GIRL...THE PLACE WHERE HE CAN STAKE HIS CLAIM TO FORTUNE... TO POWER!
THIS LAND IS MINE...AND NO ONE SHALL WREST IT FROM ME.
NO ONE!
THAT SOUNDS LIKE A CUE TO ME, PAL.
SHALL WE?
AS WE HAVE PLANNED, MY FRIEND.
9

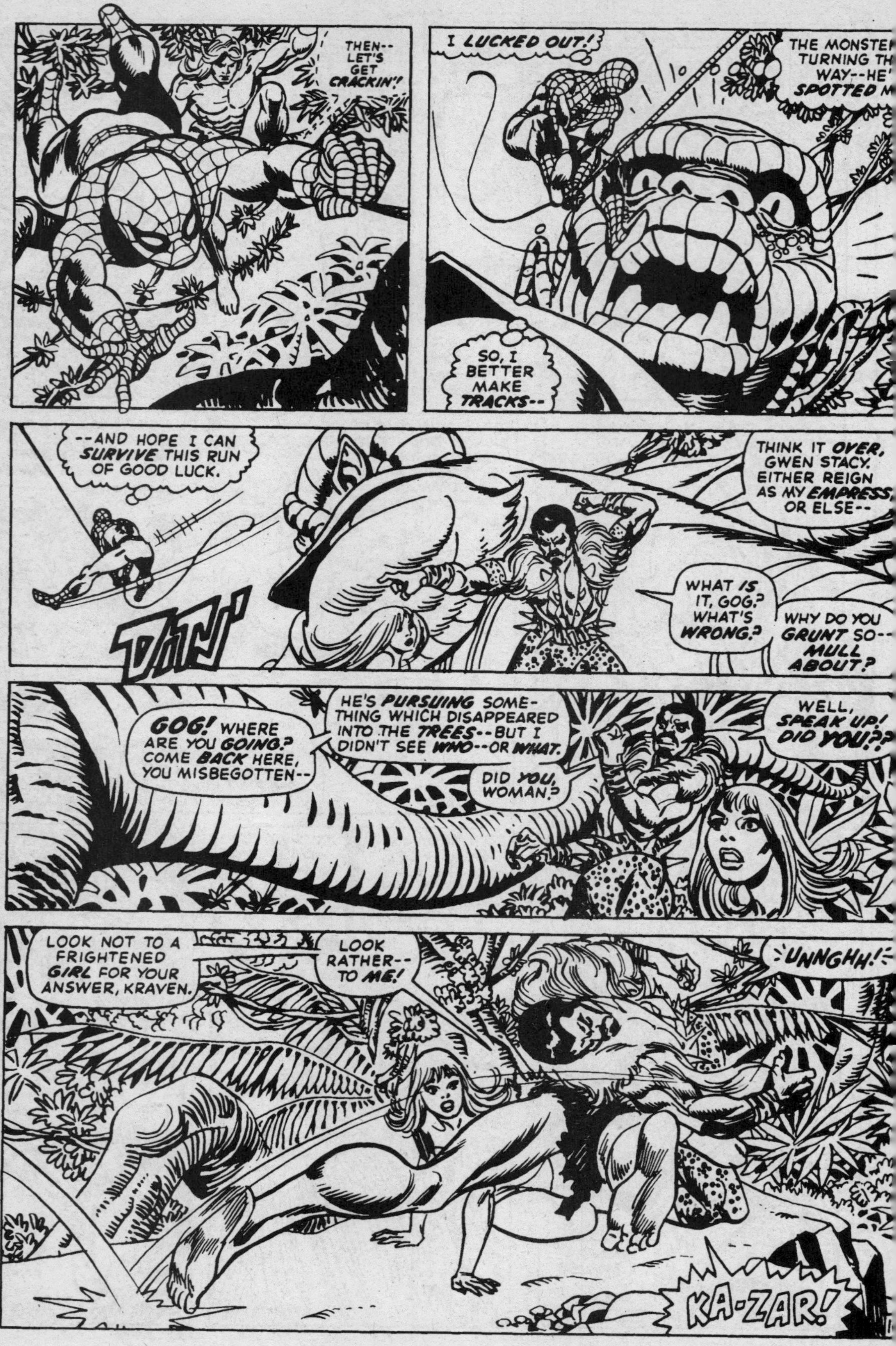
THEN--
LET'S
GET
CRACKIN'!
I LUCKED OUT!
THE MONSTE
TURNING TH
WAY--HE'
SPOTTED M
SO, I
BETTER
MAKE
TRACKS--
--AND HOPE I CAN
SURVIVE THIS RUN
OF GOOD LUCK.
THINK IT OVER,
GWEN STACY.
EITHER REIGN
AS MY EMPRESS,
OR ELSE--
WHAT IS
IT, GOG?
WHAT'S
WRONG?
WHY DO YOU
GRUNT SO--
MULL
ABOUT?
GOG! WHERE
ARE YOU GOING?
COME BACK HERE,
YOU MISBEGOTTEN--
HE'S PURSUING SOME-
THING WHICH DISAPPEARED
INTO THE TREES--BUT I
DIDN'T SEE WHO--OR WHAT.
DID YOU,
WOMAN?
WELL,
SPEAK UP!
DID YOU??
LOOK NOT TO A
FRIGHTENED
GIRL FOR YOUR
ANSWER, KRAVEN.
LOOK
RATHER--
TO ME!
UNNGHH!
KA-ZAR!

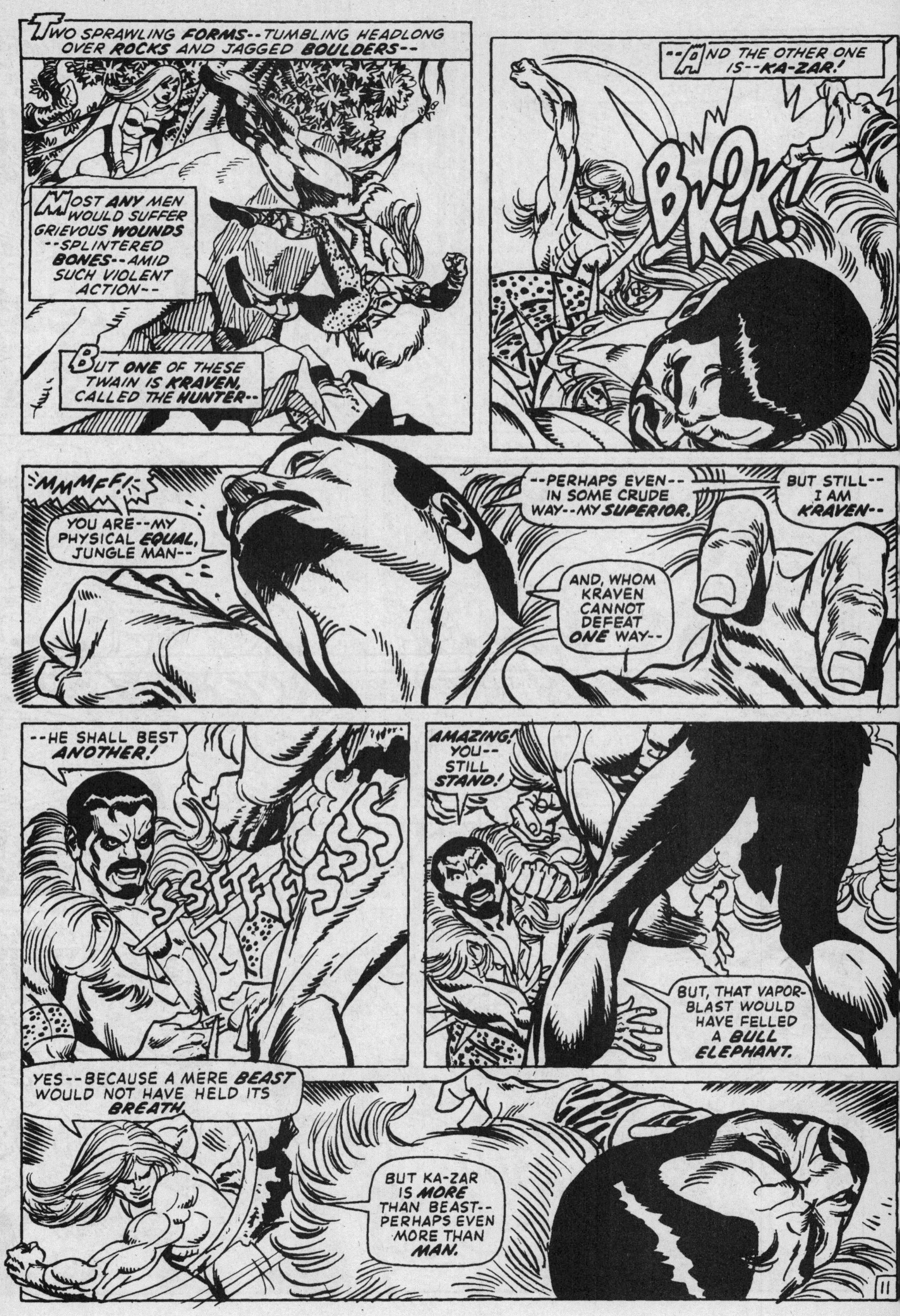

TWO SPRAWLING FORMS--TUMBLING HEADLONG OVER ROCKS AND JAGGED BOULDERS--
MOST ANY MEN WOULD SUFFER GRIEVOUS WOUNDS --SPLINTERED BONES--AMID SUCH VIOLENT ACTION--
BUT ONE OF THESE TWAIN IS KRAVEN, CALLED THE HUNTER--
--AND THE OTHER ONE IS--KA-ZAR!
BKOK!
MMMFF!
YOU ARE--MY PHYSICAL EQUAL, JUNGLE MAN--
--PERHAPS EVEN--IN SOME CRUDE WAY--MY SUPERIOR.
BUT STILL--I AM KRAVEN--
AND, WHOM KRAVEN CANNOT DEFEAT ONE WAY--
--HE SHALL BEST ANOTHER!
SSFFSSS
AMAZING! YOU--STILL STAND!
BUT, THAT VAPOR-BLAST WOULD HAVE FELLED A BULL ELEPHANT.
YES--BECAUSE A MERE BEAST WOULD NOT HAVE HELD ITS BREATH.
BUT KA-ZAR IS MORE THAN BEAST--PERHAPS EVEN MORE THAN MAN.
11

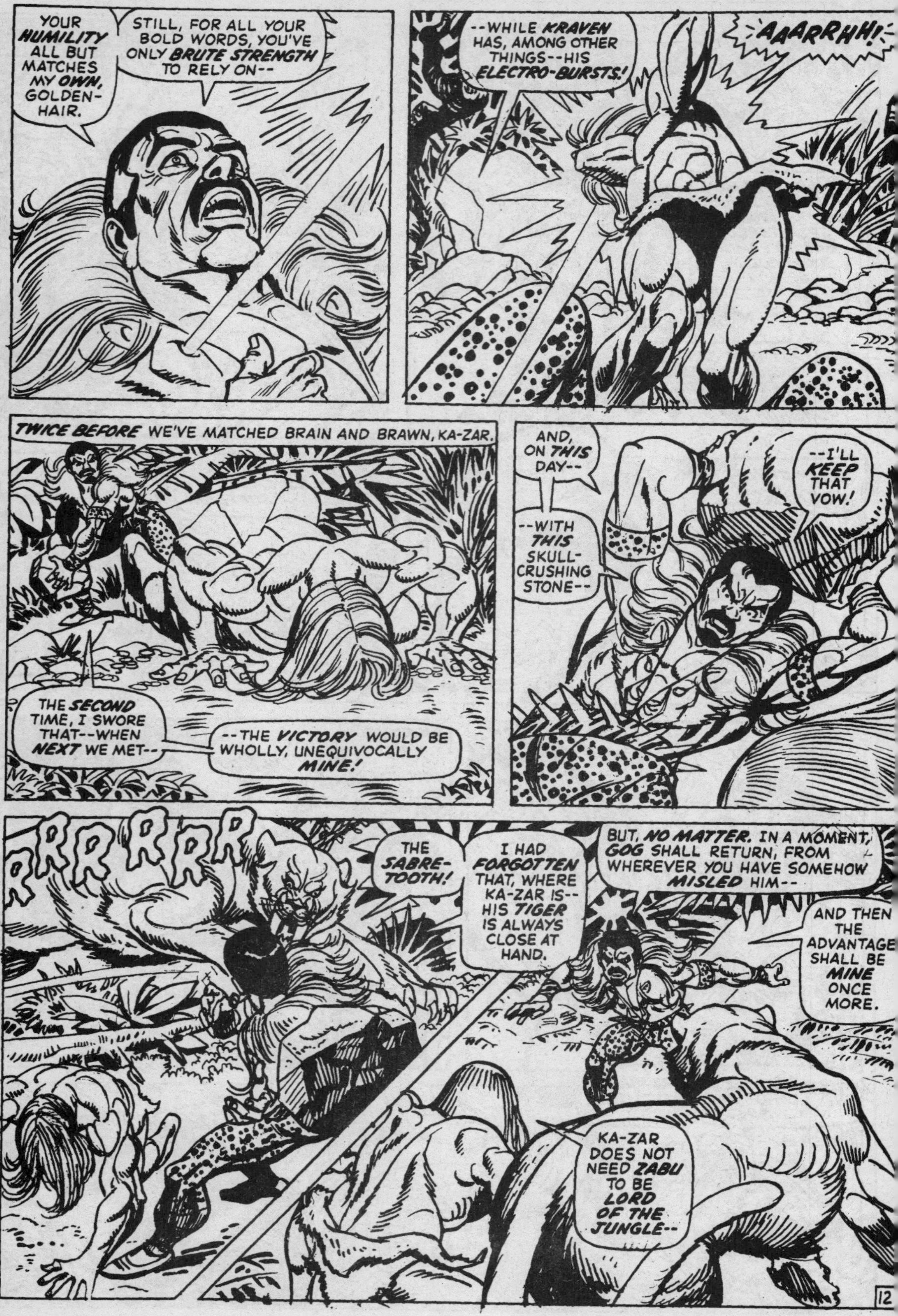
YOUR HUMILITY ALL BUT MATCHES MY OWN, GOLDEN-HAIR.
STILL, FOR ALL YOUR BOLD WORDS, YOU'VE ONLY BRUTE STRENGTH TO RELY ON--
--WHILE KRAVEN HAS, AMONG OTHER THINGS--HIS ELECTRO-BURSTS!
AAARRHH!
TWICE BEFORE WE'VE MATCHED BRAIN AND BRAWN, KA-ZAR.
THE SECOND TIME, I SWORE THAT--WHEN NEXT WE MET--
--THE VICTORY WOULD BE WHOLLY, UNEQUIVOCALLY MINE!
AND, ON THIS DAY--
--WITH THIS SKULL-CRUSHING STONE--
--I'LL KEEP THAT VOW!
RRRRRR
THE SABRE-TOOTH!
I HAD FORGOTTEN THAT, WHERE KA-ZAR IS--HIS TIGER IS ALWAYS CLOSE AT HAND.
BUT, NO MATTER. IN A MOMENT, GOG SHALL RETURN, FROM WHEREVER YOU HAVE SOMEHOW MISLED HIM--
AND THEN THE ADVANTAGE SHALL BE MINE ONCE MORE.
KA-ZAR DOES NOT NEED ZABU TO BE LORD OF THE JUNGLE--
12

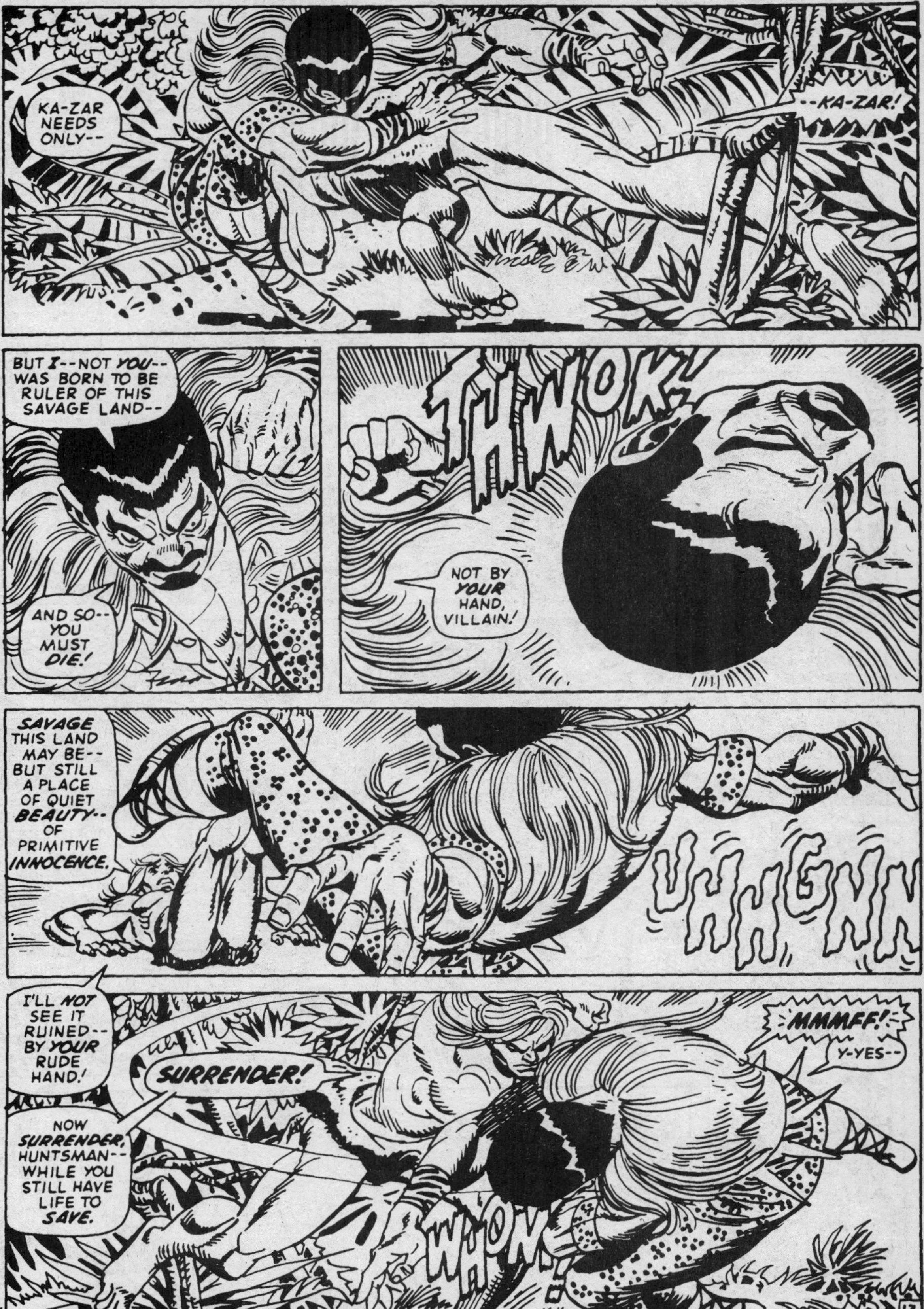
KA-ZAR NEEDS ONLY--
--KA-ZAR!
BUT I--NOT YOU--WAS BORN TO BE RULER OF THIS SAVAGE LAND--
AND SO--YOU MUST DIE!
THWOK!
NOT BY YOUR HAND, VILLAIN!
SAVAGE THIS LAND MAY BE--BUT STILL A PLACE OF QUIET BEAUTY--OF PRIMITIVE INNOCENCE.
UHHGNN
I'LL NOT SEE IT RUINED--BY YOUR RUDE HAND!
SURRENDER!
NOW SURRENDER, HUNTSMAN--WHILE YOU STILL HAVE LIFE TO SAVE.
MMMFF!
Y-YES--
WHOM!
13

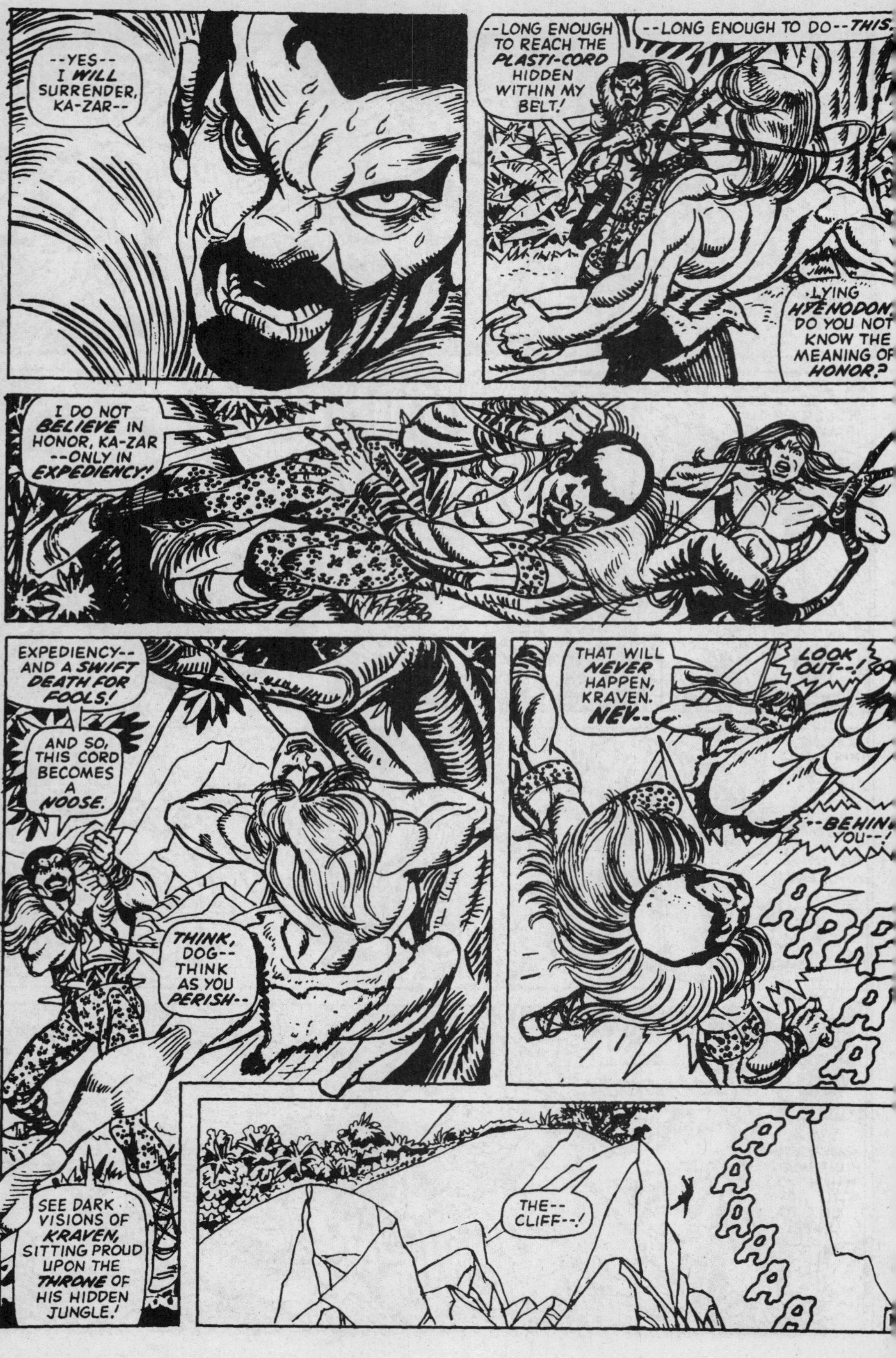
--YES-- I WILL SURRENDER, KA-ZAR--
--LONG ENOUGH TO REACH THE PLASTI-CORD HIDDEN WITHIN MY BELT!
--LONG ENOUGH TO DO--THIS.
LYING HYENODON, DO YOU NOT KNOW THE MEANING OF HONOR?
I DO NOT BELIEVE IN HONOR, KA-ZAR --ONLY IN EXPEDIENCY!
EXPEDIENCY--AND A SWIFT DEATH FOR FOOLS!
AND SO, THIS CORD BECOMES A NOOSE.
THINK, DOG--THINK AS YOU PERISH--
SEE DARK VISIONS OF KRAVEN, SITTING PROUD UPON THE THRONE OF HIS HIDDEN JUNGLE!
THAT WILL NEVER HAPPEN, KRAVEN. NEV--
LOOK OUT--!
--BEHIN YOU--!
AAAAAAA
THE--CLIFF--!
AAAAAAAA

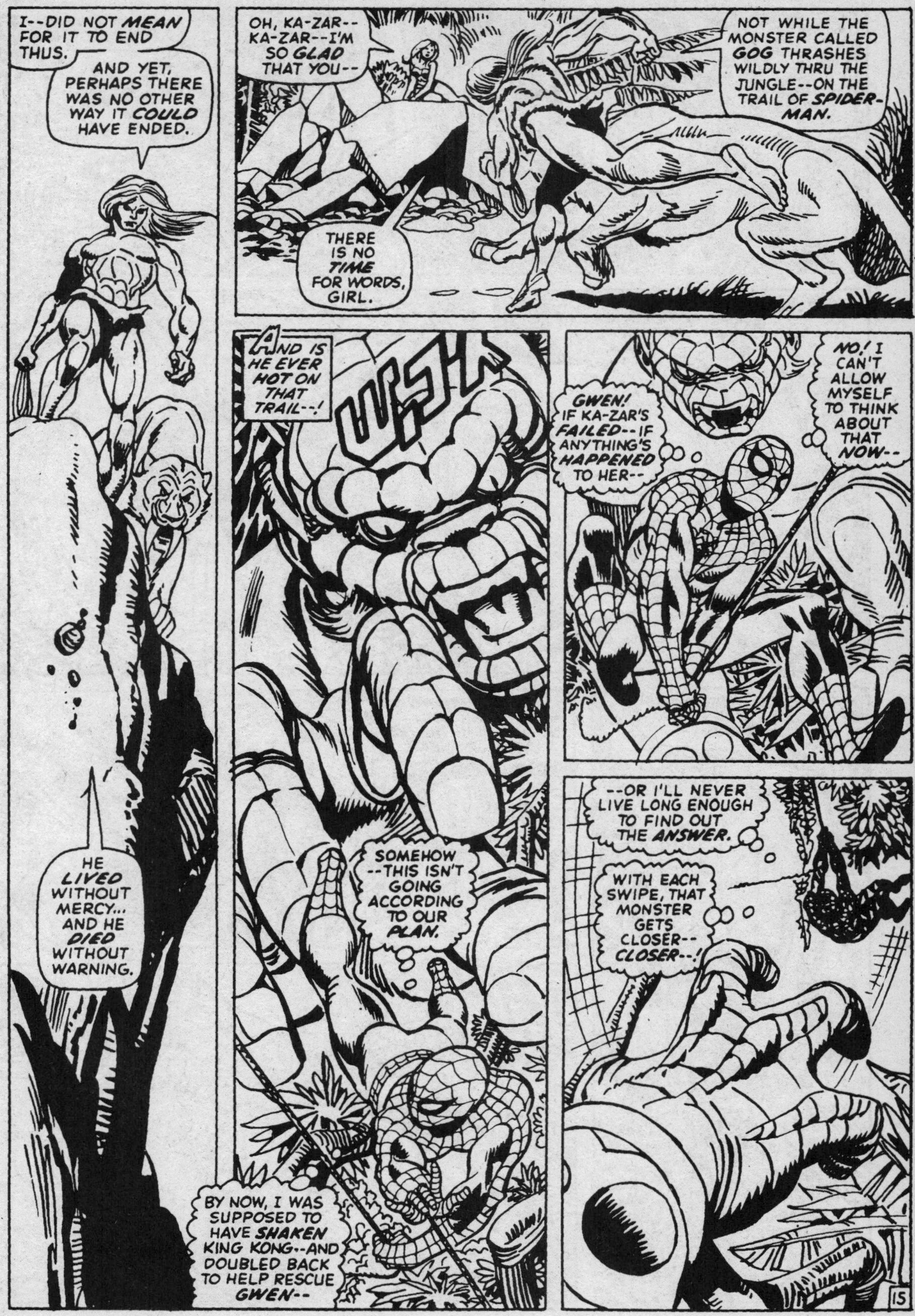

I--DID NOT MEAN FOR IT TO END THUS.
AND YET, PERHAPS THERE WAS NO OTHER WAY IT COULD HAVE ENDED.
HE LIVED WITHOUT MERCY... AND HE DIED WITHOUT WARNING.
OH, KA-ZAR-- KA-ZAR--I'M SO GLAD THAT YOU--
THERE IS NO TIME FOR WORDS, GIRL.
NOT WHILE THE MONSTER CALLED GOG THRASHES WILDLY THRU THE JUNGLE--ON THE TRAIL OF SPIDER-MAN.
AND IS HE EVER HOT ON THAT TRAIL--!
WSSH
SOMEHOW --THIS ISN'T GOING ACCORDING TO OUR PLAN.
BY NOW, I WAS SUPPOSED TO HAVE SHAKEN KING KONG--AND DOUBLED BACK TO HELP RESCUE GWEN--
GWEN! IF KA-ZAR'S FAILED--IF ANYTHING'S HAPPENED TO HER--
NO! I CAN'T ALLOW MYSELF TO THINK ABOUT THAT NOW--
--OR I'LL NEVER LIVE LONG ENOUGH TO FIND OUT THE ANSWER.
WITH EACH SWIPE, THAT MONSTER GETS CLOSER-- CLOSER--!
15

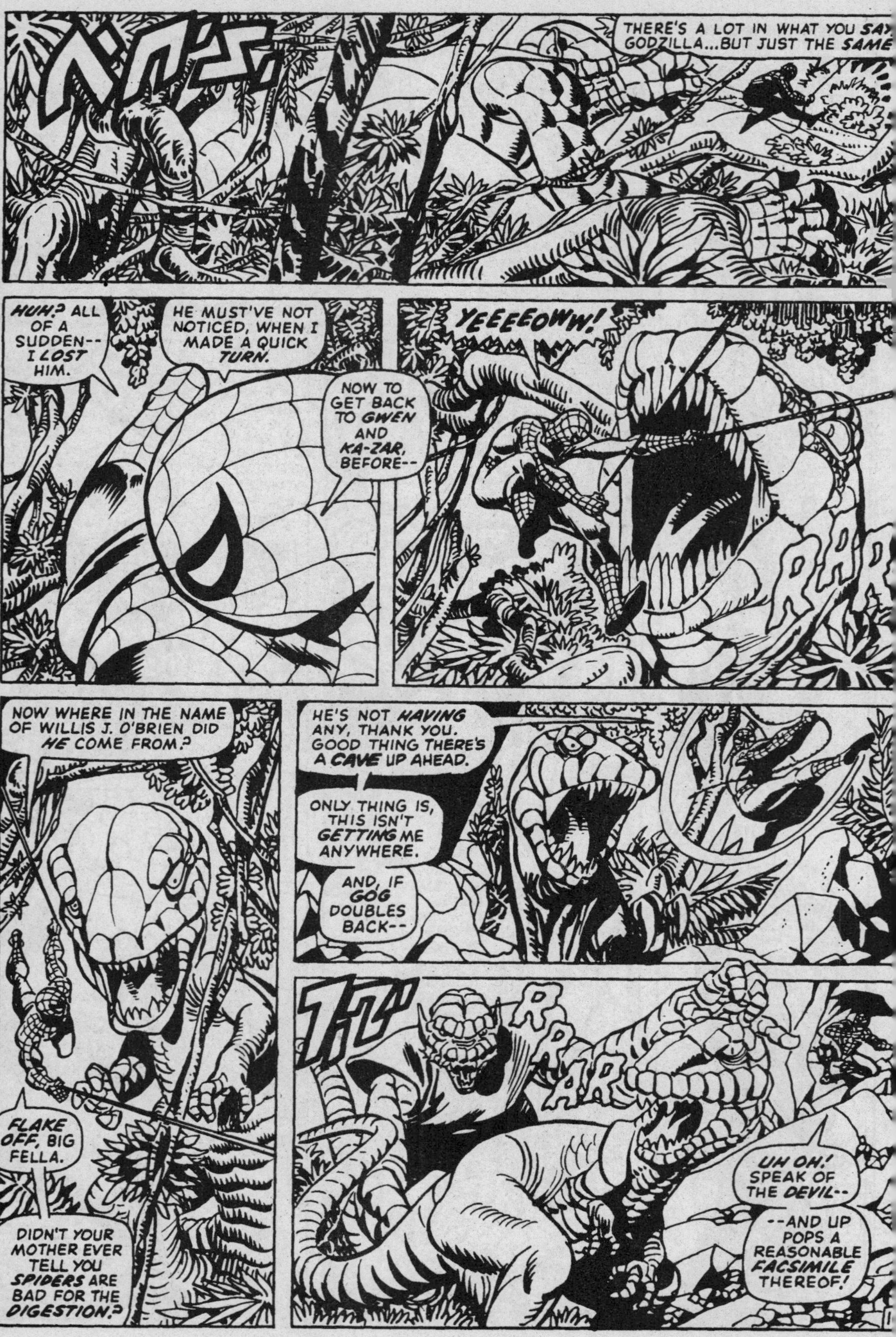

THERE'S A LOT IN WHAT YOU SAY, GODZILLA...BUT JUST THE SAME
HUH? ALL OF A SUDDEN-- I LOST HIM.
HE MUST'VE NOT NOTICED, WHEN I MADE A QUICK TURN.
NOW TO GET BACK TO GWEN AND KA-ZAR, BEFORE--
YEEEEOWW!
NOW WHERE IN THE NAME OF WILLIS J. O'BRIEN DID HE COME FROM?
FLAKE OFF, BIG FELLA.
DIDN'T YOUR MOTHER EVER TELL YOU SPIDERS ARE BAD FOR THE DIGESTION?
HE'S NOT HAVING ANY, THANK YOU. GOOD THING THERE'S A CAVE UP AHEAD.
ONLY THING IS, THIS ISN'T GETTING ME ANYWHERE.
AND, IF GOG DOUBLES BACK--
RRAR
UH OH! SPEAK OF THE DEVIL--
--AND UP POPS A REASONABLE FACSIMILE THEREOF!

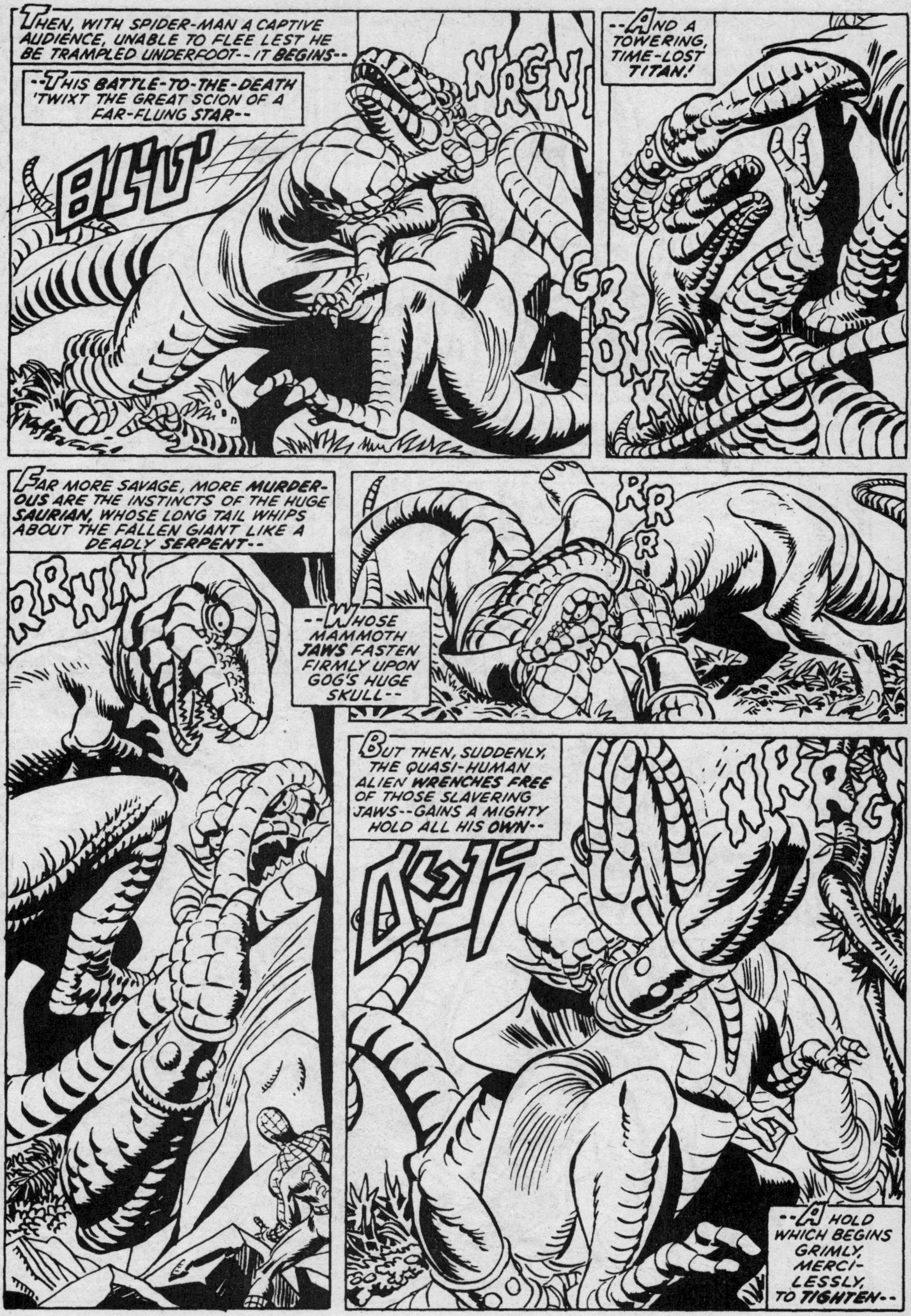
THEN, WITH SPIDER-MAN A CAPTIVE AUDIENCE, UNABLE TO FLEE LEST HE BE TRAMPLED UNDERFOOT-- IT BEGINS--
--THIS BATTLE-TO-THE-DEATH 'TWIXT THE GREAT SCION OF A FAR-FLUNG STAR--
BLUP
NRGN
--AND A TOWERING, TIME-LOST TITAN!
GRONK
FAR MORE SAVAGE, MORE MURDEROUS ARE THE INSTINCTS OF THE HUGE SAURIAN, WHOSE LONG TAIL WHIPS ABOUT THE FALLEN GIANT LIKE A DEADLY SERPENT--
RRHN
--WHOSE MAMMOTH JAWS FASTEN FIRMLY UPON GOG'S HUGE SKULL--
RRR
BUT THEN, SUDDENLY, THE QUASI-HUMAN ALIEN WRENCHES FREE OF THOSE SLAVERING JAWS--GAINS A MIGHTY HOLD ALL HIS OWN--
NRRG
--A HOLD WHICH BEGINS GRIMLY, MERCILESSLY, TO TIGHTEN--

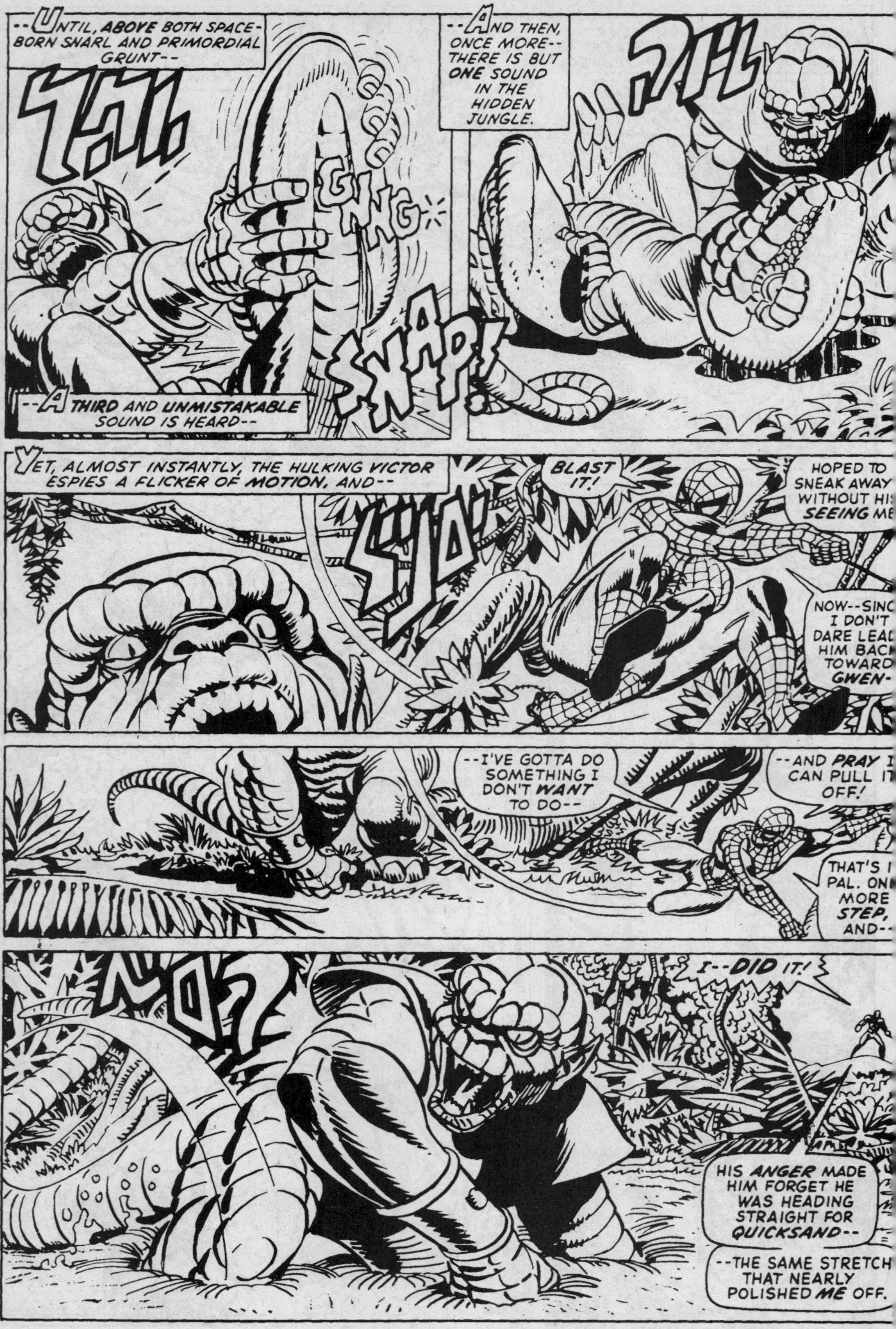
--UNTIL, ABOVE BOTH SPACE-BORN SNARL AND PRIMORDIAL GRUNT--
--A THIRD AND UNMISTAKABLE SOUND IS HEARD--
SNAP!
--AND THEN, ONCE MORE--THERE IS BUT ONE SOUND IN THE HIDDEN JUNGLE.
YET, ALMOST INSTANTLY, THE HULKING VICTOR ESPIES A FLICKER OF MOTION, AND--
BLAST IT!
HOPED TO SNEAK AWAY WITHOUT HIS SEEING ME
NOW--SINC I DON'T DARE LEAD HIM BACK TOWARD GWEN-
--I'VE GOTTA DO SOMETHING I DON'T WANT TO DO--
--AND PRAY I CAN PULL IT OFF!
THAT'S I PAL. ON MORE STEP, AND--
I--DID IT!
HIS ANGER MADE HIM FORGET HE WAS HEADING STRAIGHT FOR QUICKSAND--
--THE SAME STRETCH THAT NEARLY POLISHED ME OFF.

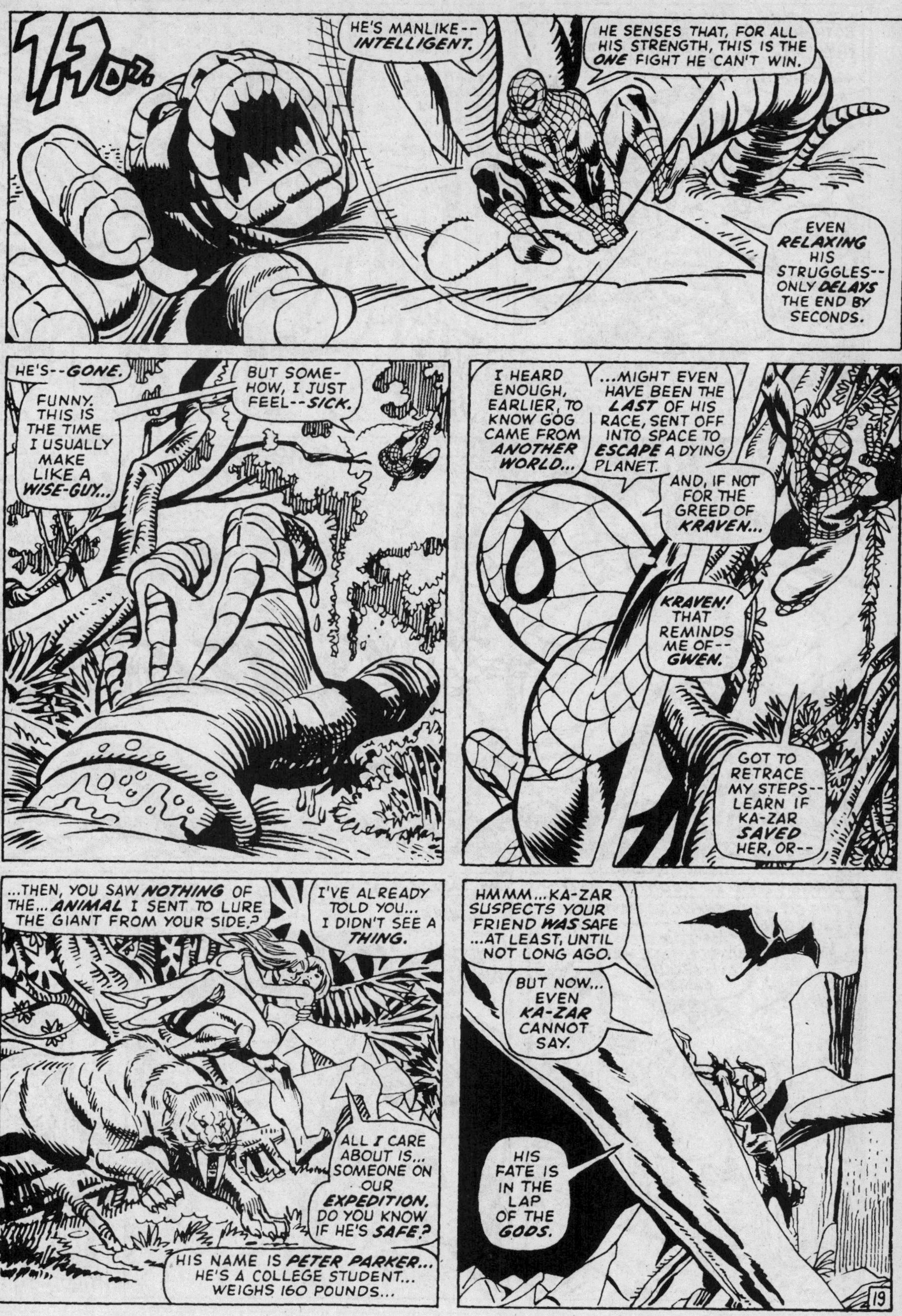

HE'S MANLIKE--INTELLIGENT.
HE SENSES THAT, FOR ALL HIS STRENGTH, THIS IS THE ONE FIGHT HE CAN'T WIN.
EVEN RELAXING HIS STRUGGLES--ONLY DELAYS THE END BY SECONDS.
HE'S--GONE.
FUNNY. THIS IS THE TIME I USUALLY MAKE LIKE A WISE-GUY...
BUT SOME-HOW, I JUST FEEL--SICK.
I HEARD ENOUGH, EARLIER, TO KNOW GOG CAME FROM ANOTHER WORLD...
...MIGHT EVEN HAVE BEEN THE LAST OF HIS RACE, SENT OFF INTO SPACE TO ESCAPE A DYING PLANET.
AND, IF NOT FOR THE GREED OF KRAVEN...
KRAVEN! THAT REMINDS ME OF--GWEN.
GOT TO RETRACE MY STEPS--LEARN IF KA-ZAR SAVED HER, OR--
...THEN, YOU SAW NOTHING OF THE...ANIMAL I SENT TO LURE THE GIANT FROM YOUR SIDE?
I'VE ALREADY TOLD YOU... I DIDN'T SEE A THING.
ALL I CARE ABOUT IS... SOMEONE ON OUR EXPEDITION. DO YOU KNOW IF HE'S SAFE?
HIS NAME IS PETER PARKER... HE'S A COLLEGE STUDENT... WEIGHS 160 POUNDS...
HMMM...KA-ZAR SUSPECTS YOUR FRIEND WAS SAFE ...AT LEAST, UNTIL NOT LONG AGO.
BUT NOW... EVEN KA-ZAR CANNOT SAY.
HIS FATE IS IN THE LAP OF THE GODS.
19

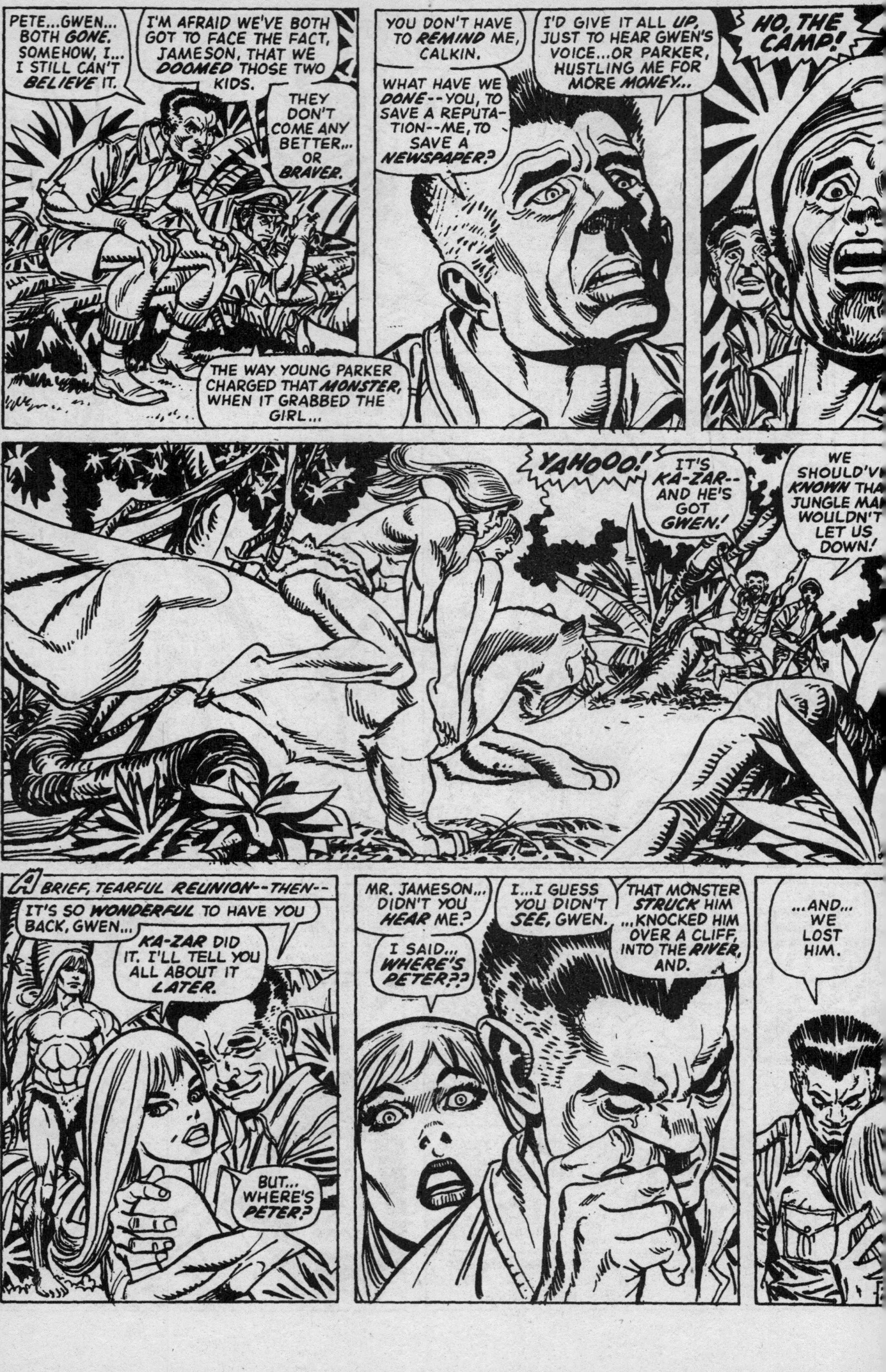
PETE...GWEN... BOTH GONE. SOMEHOW, I... I STILL CAN'T BELIEVE IT.
I'M AFRAID WE'VE BOTH GOT TO FACE THE FACT, JAMESON, THAT WE DOOMED THOSE TWO KIDS.
THEY DON'T COME ANY BETTER... OR BRAVER.
THE WAY YOUNG PARKER CHARGED THAT MONSTER, WHEN IT GRABBED THE GIRL...
YOU DON'T HAVE TO REMIND ME, CALKIN.
WHAT HAVE WE DONE--YOU, TO SAVE A REPUTATION--ME, TO SAVE A NEWSPAPER?
I'D GIVE IT ALL UP, JUST TO HEAR GWEN'S VOICE...OR PARKER, HUSTLING ME FOR MORE MONEY...
HO, THE CAMP!
YAHOOO!
IT'S KA-ZAR-- AND HE'S GOT GWEN!
A BRIEF, TEARFUL REUNION--THEN--
IT'S SO WONDERFUL TO HAVE YOU BACK, GWEN...
KA-ZAR DID IT. I'LL TELL YOU ALL ABOUT IT LATER.
BUT... WHERE'S PETER?
MR. JAMESON... DIDN'T YOU HEAR ME?
I SAID... WHERE'S PETER??
I...I GUESS YOU DIDN'T SEE, GWEN.
THAT MONSTER STRUCK HIM ...KNOCKED HIM OVER A CLIFF, INTO THE RIVER, AND.
...AND... WE LOST HIM.

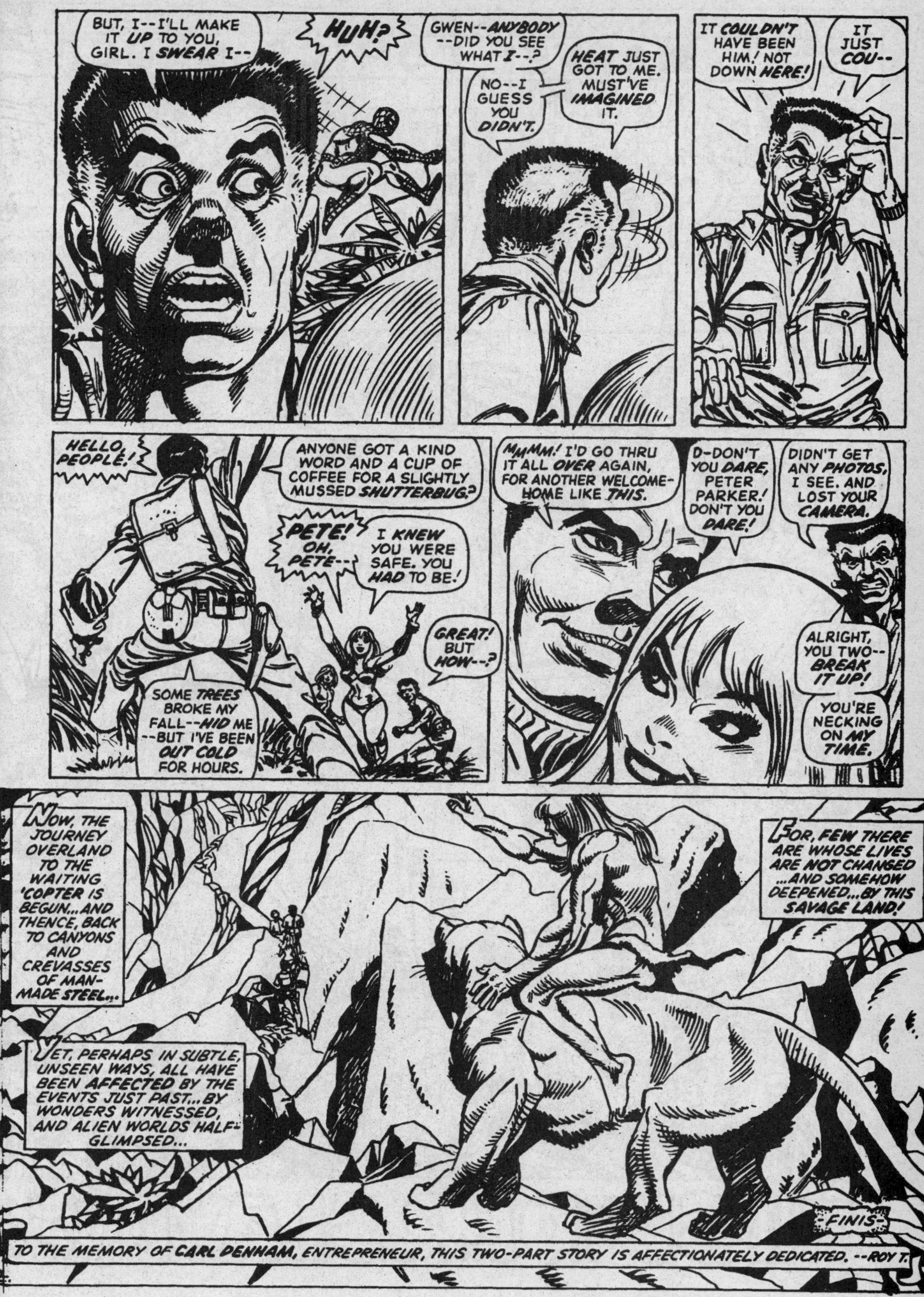
BUT, I--I'LL MAKE IT UP TO YOU, GIRL. I SWEAR I--
HUH?
GWEN--ANYBODY --DID YOU SEE WHAT I--?
NO--I GUESS YOU DIDN'T.
HEAT JUST GOT TO ME. MUST'VE IMAGINED IT.
IT COULDN'T HAVE BEEN HIM! NOT DOWN HERE!
IT JUST COU--
HELLO, PEOPLE!
ANYONE GOT A KIND WORD AND A CUP OF COFFEE FOR A SLIGHTLY MUSSED SHUTTERBUG?
PETE! OH, PETE--
I KNEW YOU WERE SAFE. YOU HAD TO BE!
GREAT! BUT HOW--?
SOME TREES BROKE MY FALL--HID ME --BUT I'VE BEEN OUT COLD FOR HOURS.
MMMM! I'D GO THRU IT ALL OVER AGAIN, FOR ANOTHER WELCOME-HOME LIKE THIS.
D-DON'T YOU DARE, PETER PARKER! DON'T YOU DARE!
DIDN'T GET ANY PHOTOS, I SEE. AND LOST YOUR CAMERA.
ALRIGHT, YOU TWO--BREAK IT UP!
YOU'RE NECKING ON MY TIME.
NOW, THE JOURNEY OVERLAND TO THE WAITING 'COPTER IS BEGUN...AND THENCE, BACK TO CANYONS AND CREVASSES OF MAN-MADE STEEL...
FOR, FEW THERE ARE WHOSE LIVES ARE NOT CHANGED ...AND SOMEHOW DEEPENED...BY THIS SAVAGE LAND!
YET, PERHAPS IN SUBTLE, UNSEEN WAYS, ALL HAVE BEEN AFFECTED BY THE EVENTS JUST PAST...BY WONDERS WITNESSED, AND ALIEN WORLDS HALF-GLIMPSED...
-FINIS-
TO THE MEMORY OF CARL DENHAM, ENTREPRENEUR, THIS TWO-PART STORY IS AFFECTIONATELY DEDICATED. --ROY T.

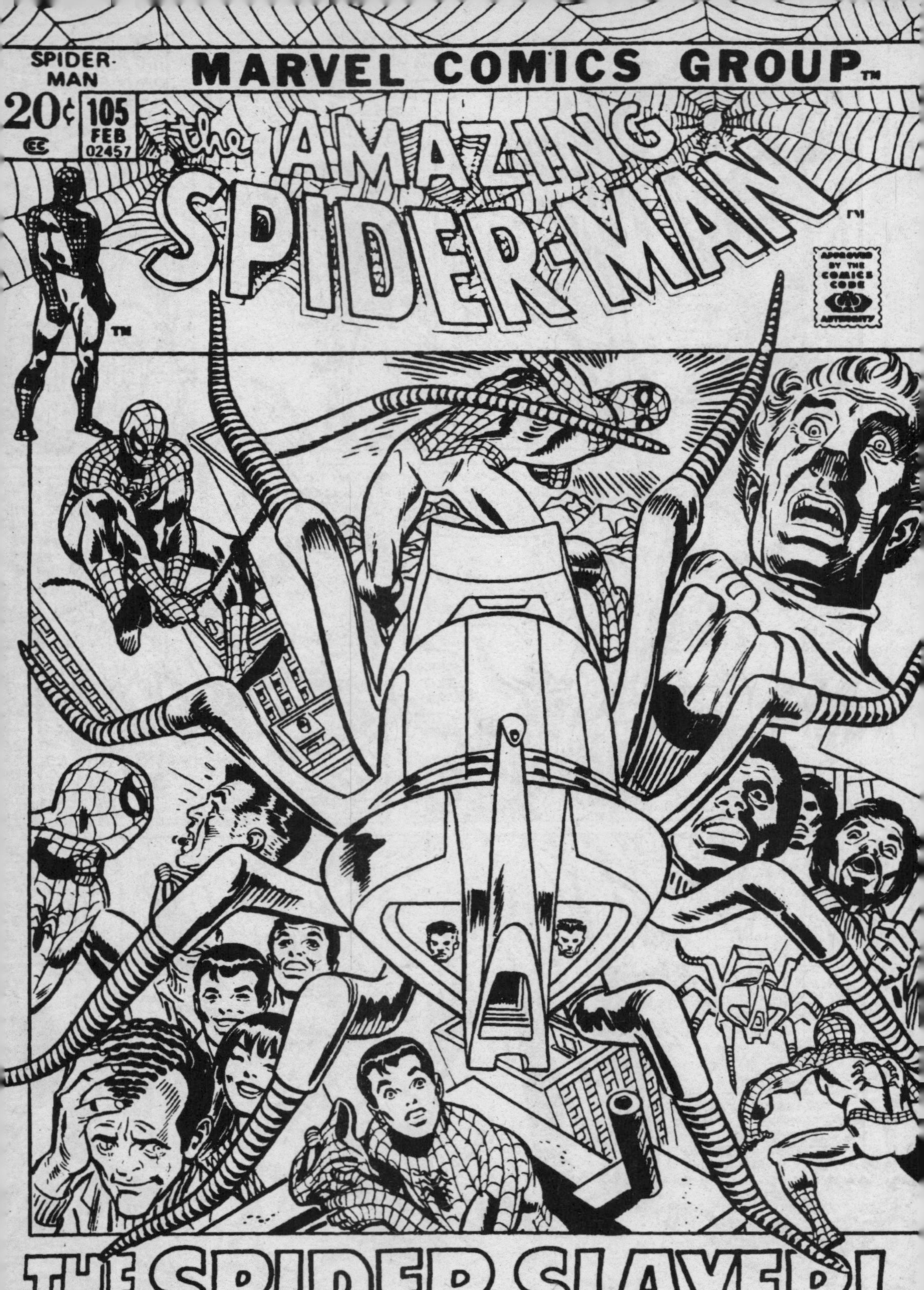

SPIDER-MAN
MARVEL COMICS GROUP
20¢
105 FEB 02457
THE AMAZING SPIDER-MAN
APPROVED BY THE COMICS CODE AUTHORITY
THE SPIDER SLAYER!

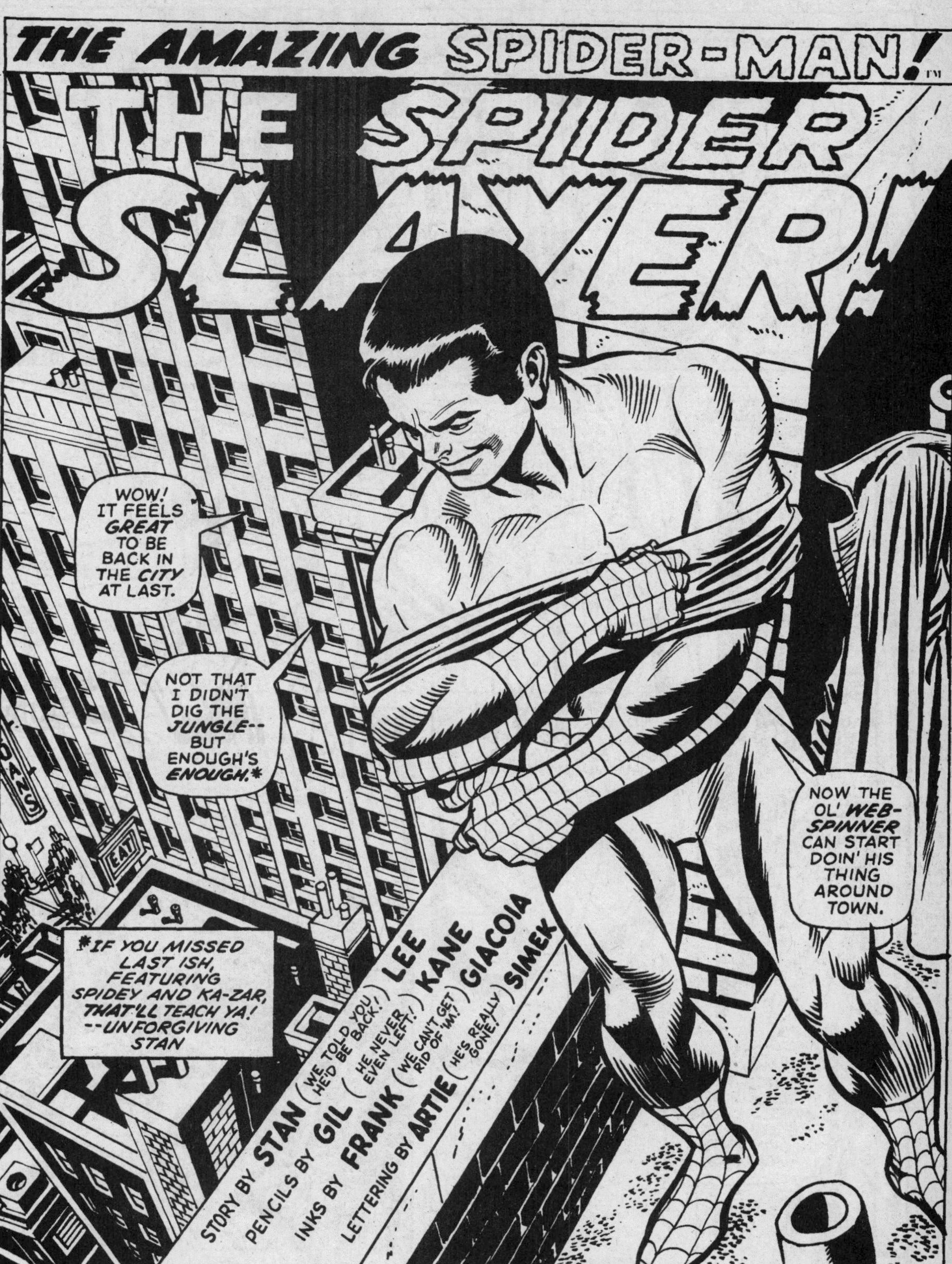
THE AMAZING SPIDER-MAN!
THE SPIDER SLAYER!
WOW! IT FEELS GREAT TO BE BACK IN THE CITY AT LAST.
NOT THAT I DIDN'T DIG THE JUNGLE-- BUT ENOUGH'S ENOUGH!*
NOW THE OL' WEB-SPINNER CAN START DOIN' HIS THING AROUND TOWN.
*IF YOU MISSED LAST ISH, FEATURING SPIDEY AND KA-ZAR, THAT'LL TEACH YA! --UNFORGIVING STAN
STORY BY STAN (WE TOLD YOU HE'D BE BACK!) LEE
PENCILS BY GIL (HE NEVER EVEN LEFT!) KANE
INKS BY FRANK (WE CAN'T GET RID OF 'M!) GIACOIA
LETTERING BY ARTIE (HE'S REALLY GONE!) SIMEK
EAT

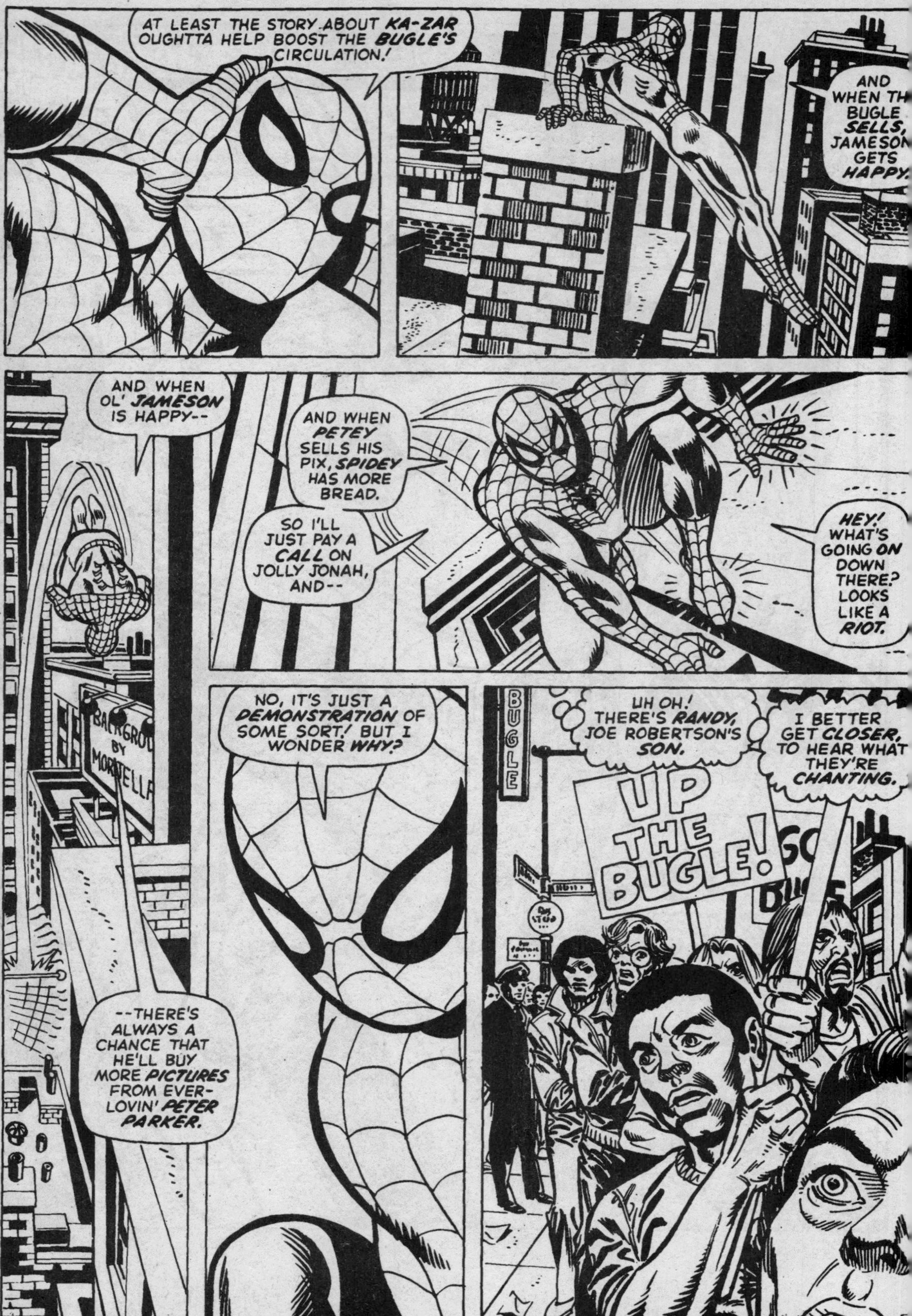

AT LEAST THE STORY ABOUT KA-ZAR OUGHTTA HELP BOOST THE BUGLE'S CIRCULATION!
AND WHEN TH BUGLE SELLS, JAMESON GETS HAPPY.
AND WHEN OL' JAMESON IS HAPPY--
AND WHEN PETEY SELLS HIS PIX, SPIDEY HAS MORE BREAD.
SO I'LL JUST PAY A CALL ON JOLLY JONAH, AND--
HEY! WHAT'S GOING ON DOWN THERE? LOOKS LIKE A RIOT.
--THERE'S ALWAYS A CHANCE THAT HE'LL BUY MORE PICTURES FROM EVER-LOVIN' PETER PARKER.
NO, IT'S JUST A DEMONSTRATION OF SOME SORT! BUT I WONDER WHY?
BUGLE
UH OH! THERE'S RANDY, JOE ROBERTSON'S SON.
I BETTER GET CLOSER, TO HEAR WHAT THEY'RE CHANTING.
UP THE BUGLE!

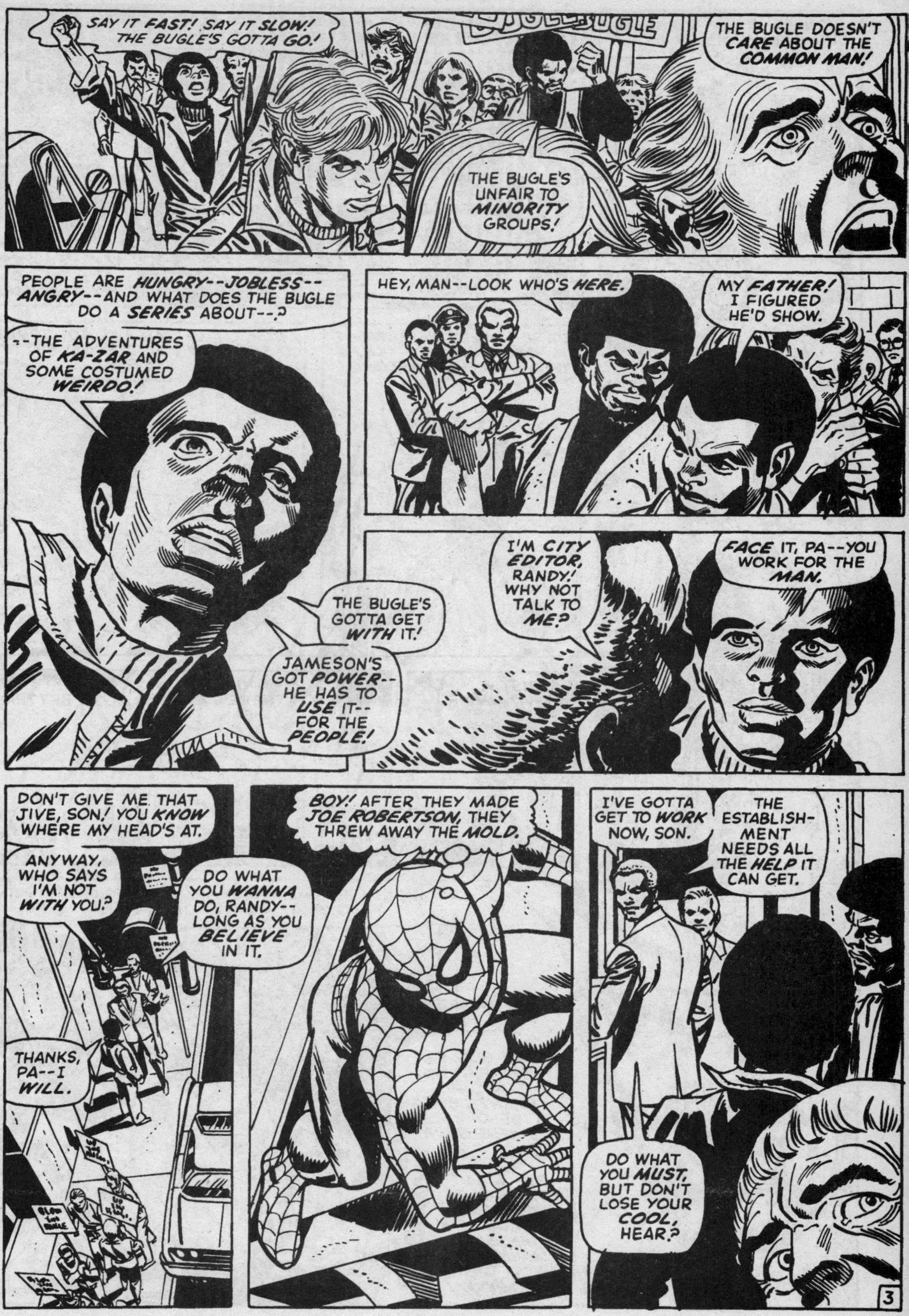

SAY IT FAST! SAY IT SLOW! THE BUGLE'S GOTTA GO!
THE BUGLE DOESN'T CARE ABOUT THE COMMON MAN!
THE BUGLE'S UNFAIR TO MINORITY GROUPS!
PEOPLE ARE HUNGRY--JOBLESS--ANGRY--AND WHAT DOES THE BUGLE DO A SERIES ABOUT--?
--THE ADVENTURES OF KA-ZAR AND SOME COSTUMED WEIRDO!
THE BUGLE'S GOTTA GET WITH IT!
JAMESON'S GOT POWER--HE HAS TO USE IT--FOR THE PEOPLE!
HEY, MAN--LOOK WHO'S HERE.
MY FATHER! I FIGURED HE'D SHOW.
I'M CITY EDITOR, RANDY! WHY NOT TALK TO ME?
FACE IT, PA--YOU WORK FOR THE MAN.
DON'T GIVE ME THAT JIVE, SON! YOU KNOW WHERE MY HEAD'S AT.
ANYWAY, WHO SAYS I'M NOT WITH YOU?
DO WHAT YOU WANNA DO, RANDY--LONG AS YOU BELIEVE IN IT.
THANKS, PA--I WILL.
BOY! AFTER THEY MADE JOE ROBERTSON, THEY THREW AWAY THE MOLD.
I'VE GOTTA GET TO WORK NOW, SON.
THE ESTABLISHMENT NEEDS ALL THE HELP IT CAN GET.
DO WHAT YOU MUST, BUT DON'T LOSE YOUR COOL, HEAR?
3

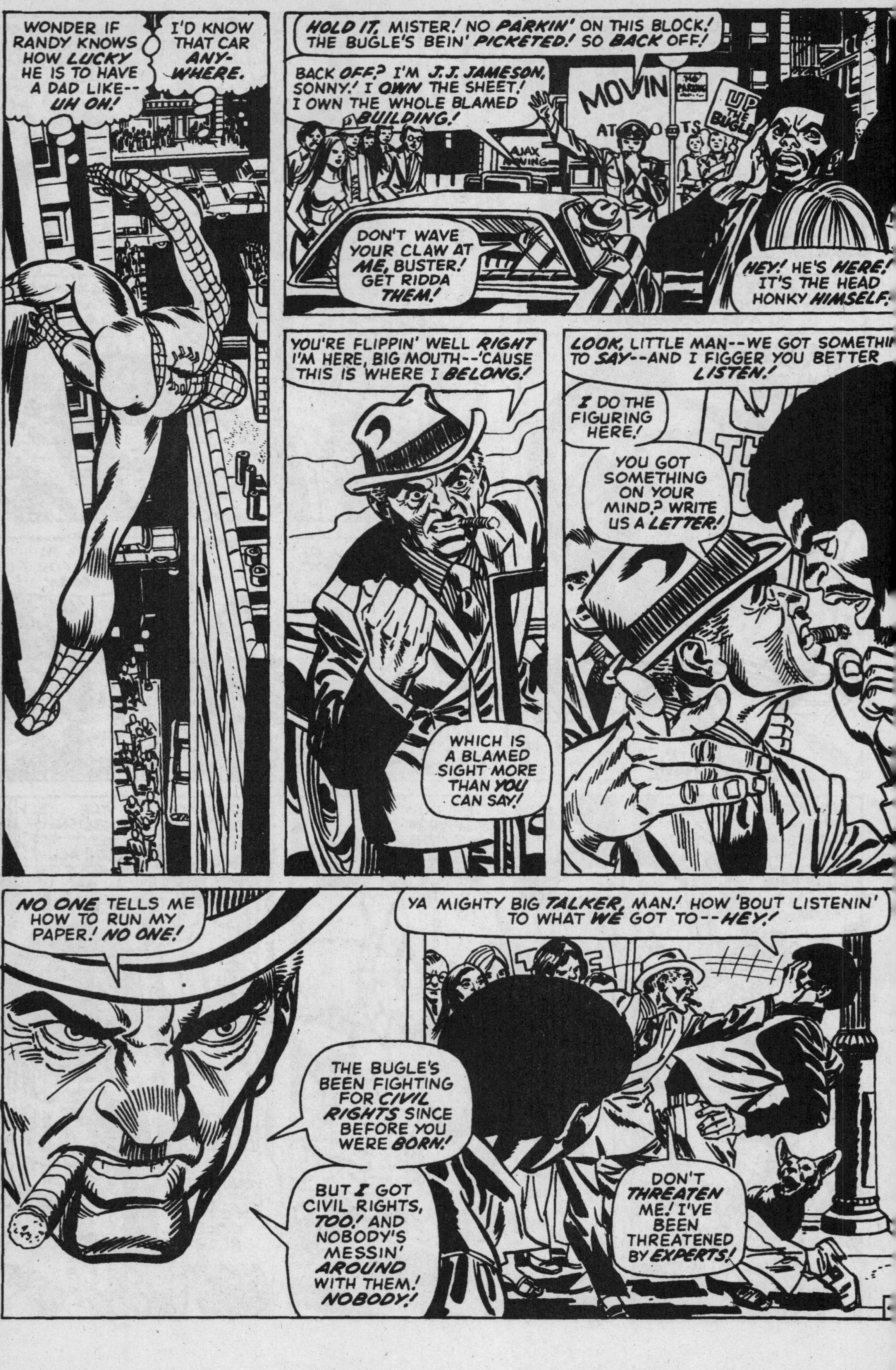
WONDER IF RANDY KNOWS HOW LUCKY HE IS TO HAVE A DAD LIKE-- UH OH!
I'D KNOW THAT CAR ANY-WHERE.
HOLD IT, MISTER! NO PARKIN' ON THIS BLOCK! THE BUGLE'S BEIN' PICKETED! SO BACK OFF!
BACK OFF? I'M J.J. JAMESON, SONNY! I OWN THE SHEET! I OWN THE WHOLE BLAMED BUILDING!
MOVIN
UP THE BUGLE
AJAX
DON'T WAVE YOUR CLAW AT ME, BUSTER! GET RIDDA THEM!
HEY! HE'S HERE! IT'S THE HEAD HONKY HIMSELF.
YOU'RE FLIPPIN' WELL RIGHT I'M HERE, BIG MOUTH--'CAUSE THIS IS WHERE I BELONG!
WHICH IS A BLAMED SIGHT MORE THAN YOU CAN SAY!
LOOK, LITTLE MAN--WE GOT SOMETHIN TO SAY--AND I FIGGER YOU BETTER LISTEN!
I DO THE FIGURING HERE!
YOU GOT SOMETHING ON YOUR MIND? WRITE US A LETTER!
NO ONE TELLS ME HOW TO RUN MY PAPER! NO ONE!
YA MIGHTY BIG TALKER, MAN! HOW 'BOUT LISTENIN' TO WHAT WE GOT TO--HEY!
THE BUGLE'S BEEN FIGHTING FOR CIVIL RIGHTS SINCE BEFORE YOU WERE BORN!
BUT I GOT CIVIL RIGHTS, TOO! AND NOBODY'S MESSIN' AROUND WITH THEM! NOBODY!
DON'T THREATEN ME! I'VE BEEN THREATENED BY EXPERTS!

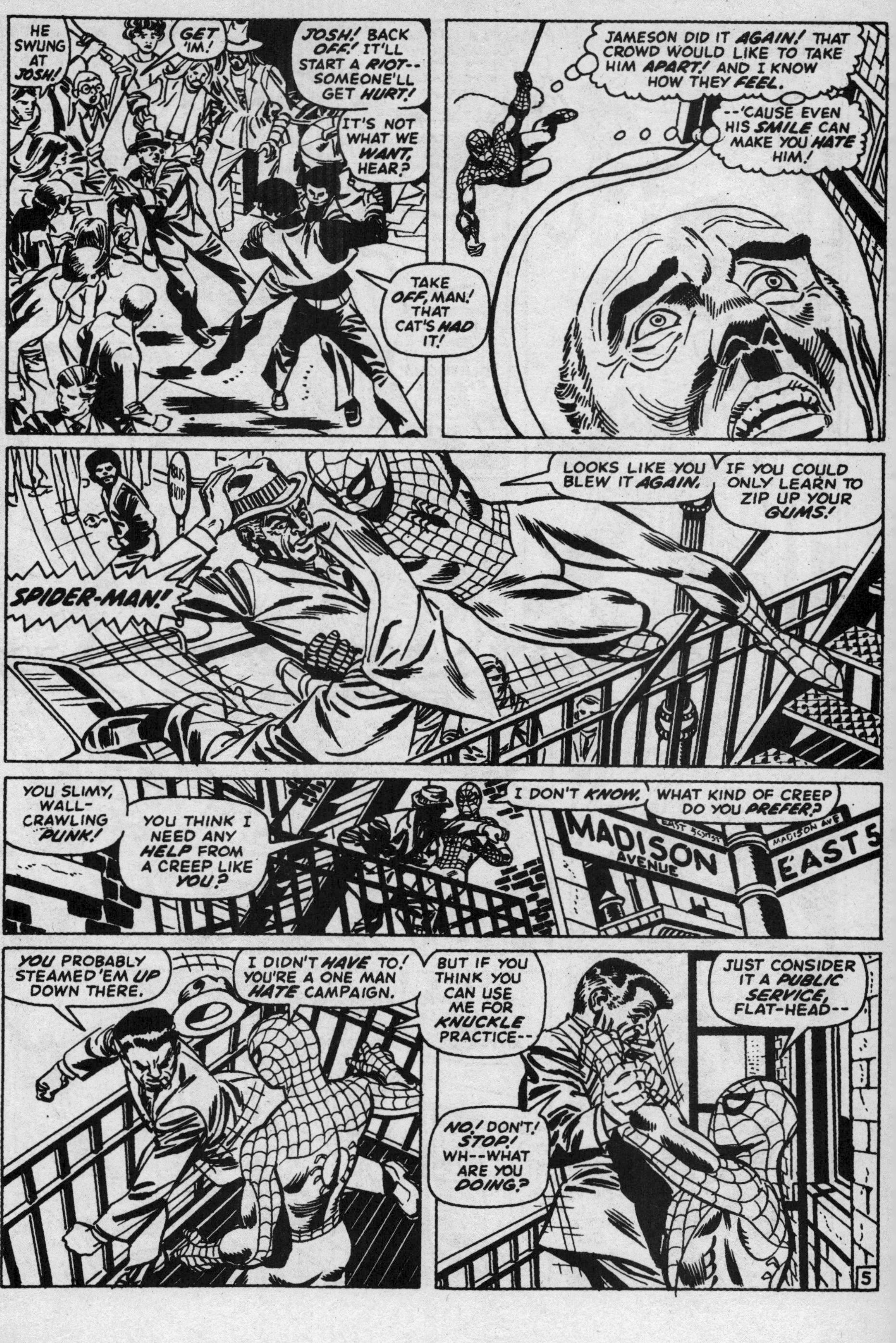
HE SWUNG AT JOSH!
GET 'IM!
JOSH! BACK OFF! IT'LL START A RIOT-- SOMEONE'LL GET HURT!
IT'S NOT WHAT WE WANT, HEAR?
TAKE OFF, MAN! THAT CAT'S HAD IT!
JAMESON DID IT AGAIN! THAT CROWD WOULD LIKE TO TAKE HIM APART! AND I KNOW HOW THEY FEEL.
--'CAUSE EVEN HIS SMILE CAN MAKE YOU HATE HIM!
SPIDER-MAN!
LOOKS LIKE YOU BLEW IT AGAIN.
IF YOU COULD ONLY LEARN TO ZIP UP YOUR GUMS!
YOU SLIMY, WALL-CRAWLING PUNK!
YOU THINK I NEED ANY HELP FROM A CREEP LIKE YOU?
I DON'T KNOW.
WHAT KIND OF CREEP DO YOU PREFER?
MADISON AVENUE
EAST 5
YOU PROBABLY STEAMED 'EM UP DOWN THERE.
I DIDN'T HAVE TO! YOU'RE A ONE MAN HATE CAMPAIGN.
BUT IF YOU THINK YOU CAN USE ME FOR KNUCKLE PRACTICE--
JUST CONSIDER IT A PUBLIC SERVICE, FLAT-HEAD--
NO! DON'T! STOP! WH--WHAT ARE YOU DOING?

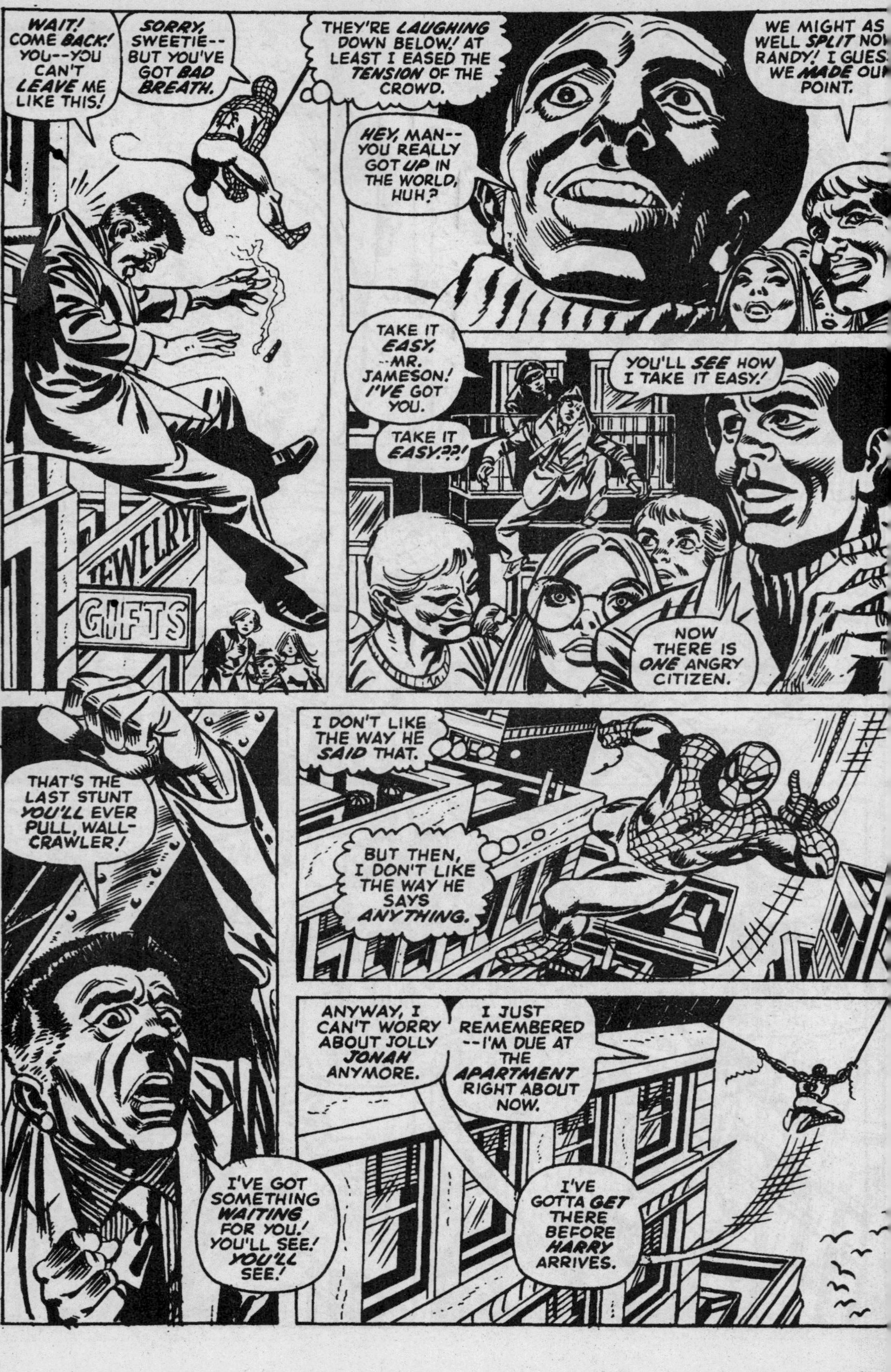
WAIT! COME BACK! YOU--YOU CAN'T LEAVE ME LIKE THIS!
SORRY, SWEETIE--BUT YOU'VE GOT BAD BREATH.
JEWELRY
GIFTS
THEY'RE LAUGHING DOWN BELOW! AT LEAST I EASED THE TENSION OF THE CROWD.
HEY, MAN--YOU REALLY GOT UP IN THE WORLD, HUH?
WE MIGHT AS WELL SPLIT NO RANDY! I GUES WE MADE OU POINT.
TAKE IT EASY, --MR. JAMESON! I'VE GOT YOU.
TAKE IT EASY???!
YOU'LL SEE HOW I TAKE IT EASY!
NOW THERE IS ONE ANGRY CITIZEN.
THAT'S THE LAST STUNT YOU'LL EVER PULL, WALL-CRAWLER!
I'VE GOT SOMETHING WAITING FOR YOU! YOU'LL SEE! YOU'LL SEE!
I DON'T LIKE THE WAY HE SAID THAT.
BUT THEN, I DON'T LIKE THE WAY HE SAYS ANYTHING.
ANYWAY, I CAN'T WORRY ABOUT JOLLY JONAH ANYMORE.
I JUST REMEMBERED --I'M DUE AT THE APARTMENT RIGHT ABOUT NOW.
I'VE GOTTA GET THERE BEFORE HARRY ARRIVES.

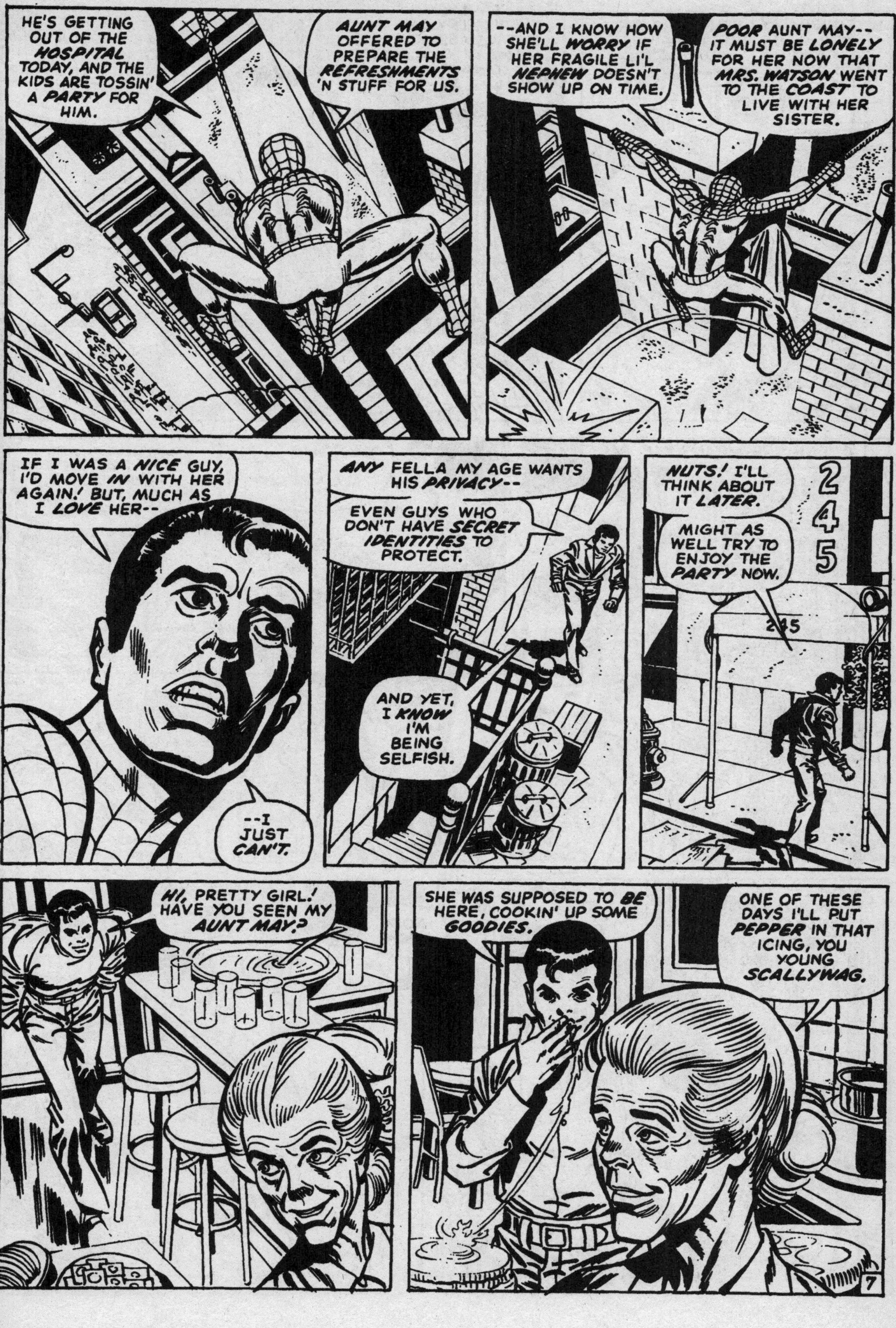
HE'S GETTING OUT OF THE HOSPITAL TODAY, AND THE KIDS ARE TOSSIN' A PARTY FOR HIM.
AUNT MAY OFFERED TO PREPARE THE REFRESHMENTS 'N STUFF FOR US.
--AND I KNOW HOW SHE'LL WORRY IF HER FRAGILE LI'L NEPHEW DOESN'T SHOW UP ON TIME.
POOR AUNT MAY-- IT MUST BE LONELY FOR HER NOW THAT MRS. WATSON WENT TO THE COAST TO LIVE WITH HER SISTER.
IF I WAS A NICE GUY, I'D MOVE IN WITH HER AGAIN! BUT, MUCH AS I LOVE HER--
--I JUST CAN'T.
ANY FELLA MY AGE WANTS HIS PRIVACY--
EVEN GUYS WHO DON'T HAVE SECRET IDENTITIES TO PROTECT.
AND YET, I KNOW I'M BEING SELFISH.
NUTS! I'LL THINK ABOUT IT LATER.
MIGHT AS WELL TRY TO ENJOY THE PARTY NOW.
245
HI, PRETTY GIRL! HAVE YOU SEEN MY AUNT MAY?
SHE WAS SUPPOSED TO BE HERE, COOKIN' UP SOME GOODIES.
ONE OF THESE DAYS I'LL PUT PEPPER IN THAT ICING, YOU YOUNG SCALLYWAG.
7

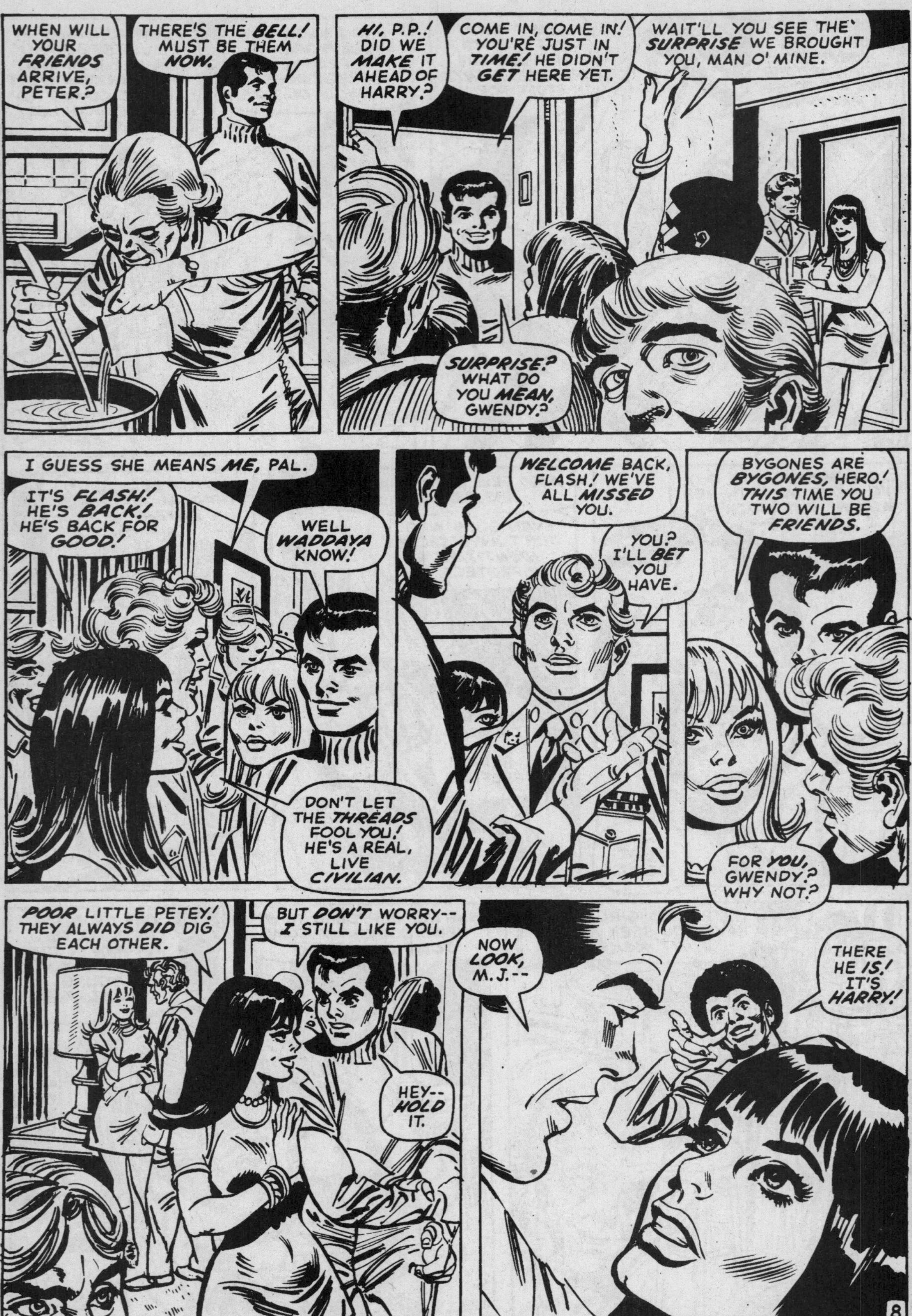

WHEN WILL YOUR FRIENDS ARRIVE, PETER?
THERE'S THE BELL! MUST BE THEM NOW.
HI, P.P.! DID WE MAKE IT AHEAD OF HARRY?
COME IN, COME IN! YOU'RE JUST IN TIME! HE DIDN'T GET HERE YET.
WAIT'LL YOU SEE THE SURPRISE WE BROUGHT YOU, MAN O' MINE.
SURPRISE? WHAT DO YOU MEAN, GWENDY?
I GUESS SHE MEANS ME, PAL.
IT'S FLASH! HE'S BACK! HE'S BACK FOR GOOD!
WELL WADDAYA KNOW!
DON'T LET THE THREADS FOOL YOU! HE'S A REAL, LIVE CIVILIAN.
WELCOME BACK, FLASH! WE'VE ALL MISSED YOU.
YOU? I'LL BET YOU HAVE.
BYGONES ARE BYGONES, HERO! THIS TIME YOU TWO WILL BE FRIENDS.
FOR YOU, GWENDY? WHY NOT?
POOR LITTLE PETEY! THEY ALWAYS DID DIG EACH OTHER.
BUT DON'T WORRY-- I STILL LIKE YOU.
HEY-- HOLD IT.
NOW LOOK, M.J.--
THERE HE IS! IT'S HARRY!
8

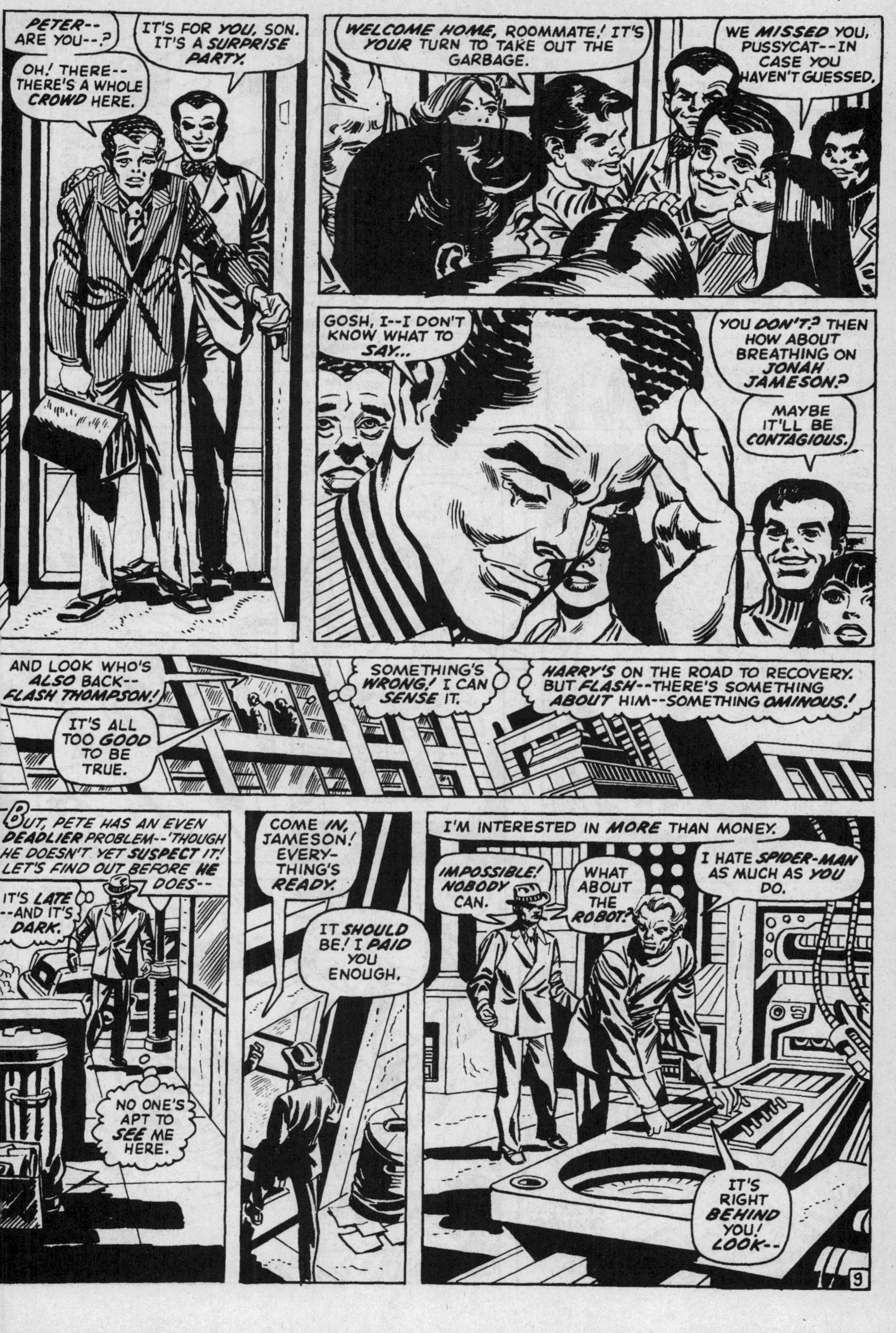
PETER--
ARE YOU--?
OH! THERE--
THERE'S A WHOLE CROWD HERE.
IT'S FOR YOU, SON. IT'S A SURPRISE PARTY.
WELCOME HOME, ROOMMATE! IT'S YOUR TURN TO TAKE OUT THE GARBAGE.
WE MISSED YOU, PUSSYCAT--IN CASE YOU HAVEN'T GUESSED.
GOSH, I--I DON'T KNOW WHAT TO SAY...
YOU DON'T? THEN HOW ABOUT BREATHING ON JONAH JAMESON?
MAYBE IT'LL BE CONTAGIOUS.
AND LOOK WHO'S ALSO BACK--
FLASH THOMPSON!
IT'S ALL TOO GOOD TO BE TRUE.
SOMETHING'S WRONG! I CAN SENSE IT.
HARRY'S ON THE ROAD TO RECOVERY. BUT FLASH--THERE'S SOMETHING ABOUT HIM--SOMETHING OMINOUS!
BUT, PETE HAS AN EVEN DEADLIER PROBLEM--'THOUGH HE DOESN'T YET SUSPECT IT! LET'S FIND OUT BEFORE HE DOES--
IT'S LATE --AND IT'S DARK.
NO ONE'S APT TO SEE ME HERE.
COME IN, JAMESON! EVERY-THING'S READY.
IT SHOULD BE! I PAID YOU ENOUGH.
I'M INTERESTED IN MORE THAN MONEY.
I HATE SPIDER-MAN AS MUCH AS YOU DO.
IMPOSSIBLE! NOBODY CAN.
WHAT ABOUT THE ROBOT?
IT'S RIGHT BEHIND YOU! LOOK--
9

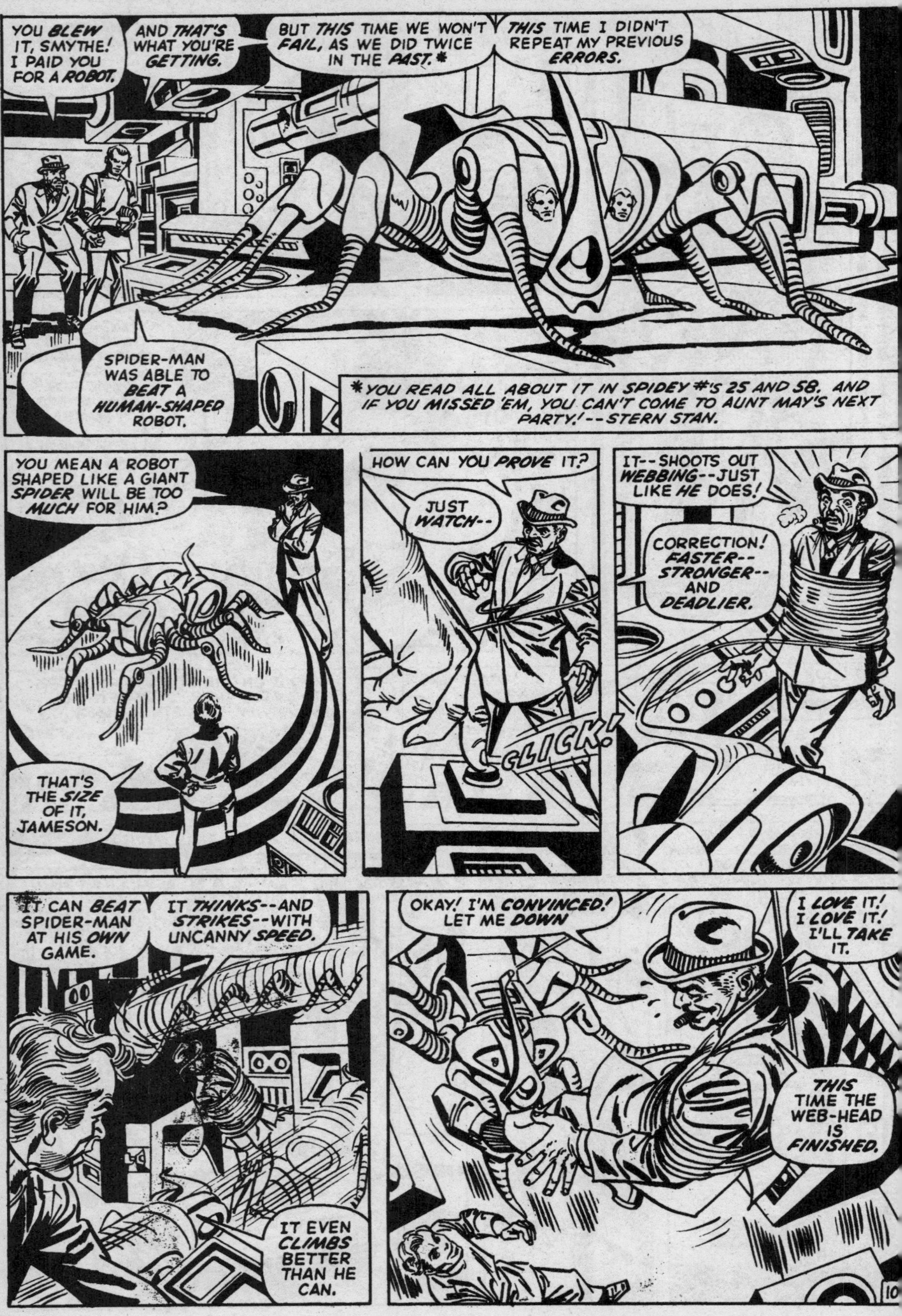

YOU BLEW IT, SMYTHE! I PAID YOU FOR A ROBOT.
AND THAT'S WHAT YOU'RE GETTING.
BUT THIS TIME WE WON'T FAIL, AS WE DID TWICE IN THE PAST.*
THIS TIME I DIDN'T REPEAT MY PREVIOUS ERRORS.
SPIDER-MAN WAS ABLE TO BEAT A HUMAN-SHAPED ROBOT.
*YOU READ ALL ABOUT IT IN SPIDEY #'S 25 AND 58. AND IF YOU MISSED 'EM, YOU CAN'T COME TO AUNT MAY'S NEXT PARTY! --STERN STAN.
YOU MEAN A ROBOT SHAPED LIKE A GIANT SPIDER WILL BE TOO MUCH FOR HIM?
THAT'S THE SIZE OF IT, JAMESON.
HOW CAN YOU PROVE IT?
JUST WATCH--
CLICK!
IT--SHOOTS OUT WEBBING--JUST LIKE HE DOES!
CORRECTION! FASTER--STRONGER--AND DEADLIER.
IT CAN BEAT SPIDER-MAN AT HIS OWN GAME.
IT THINKS--AND STRIKES--WITH UNCANNY SPEED.
IT EVEN CLIMBS BETTER THAN HE CAN.
OKAY! I'M CONVINCED! LET ME DOWN
I LOVE IT! I LOVE IT! I'LL TAKE IT.
THIS TIME THE WEB-HEAD IS FINISHED.
10

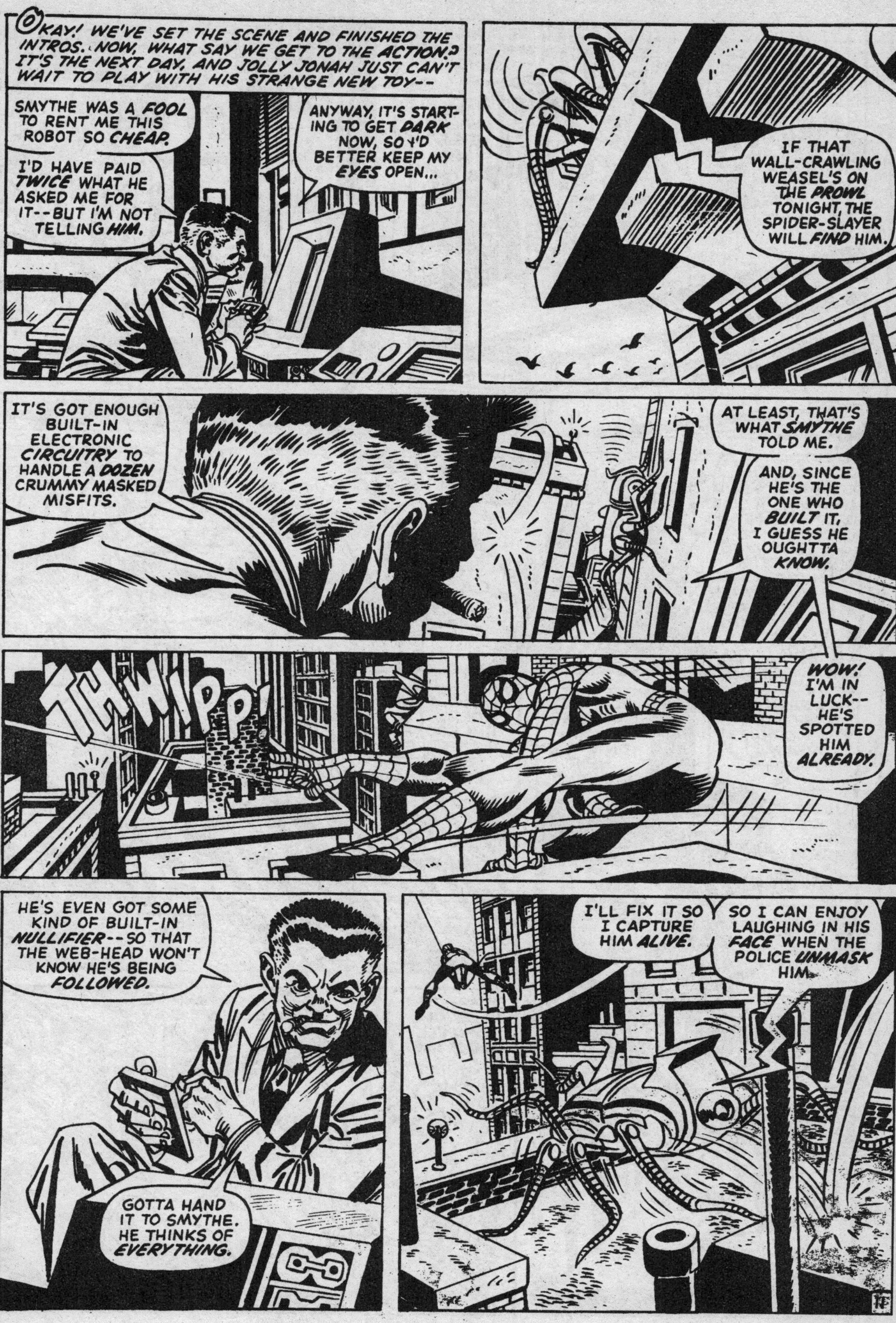
OKAY! WE'VE SET THE SCENE AND FINISHED THE INTROS. NOW, WHAT SAY WE GET TO THE ACTION? IT'S THE NEXT DAY, AND JOLLY JONAH JUST CAN'T WAIT TO PLAY WITH HIS STRANGE NEW TOY--
SMYTHE WAS A FOOL TO RENT ME THIS ROBOT SO CHEAP.
I'D HAVE PAID TWICE WHAT HE ASKED ME FOR IT--BUT I'M NOT TELLING HIM.
ANYWAY, IT'S STARTING TO GET DARK NOW, SO I'D BETTER KEEP MY EYES OPEN...
IF THAT WALL-CRAWLING WEASEL'S ON THE PROWL TONIGHT, THE SPIDER-SLAYER WILL FIND HIM.
IT'S GOT ENOUGH BUILT-IN ELECTRONIC CIRCUITRY TO HANDLE A DOZEN CRUMMY MASKED MISFITS.
AT LEAST, THAT'S WHAT SMYTHE TOLD ME.
AND, SINCE HE'S THE ONE WHO BUILT IT, I GUESS HE OUGHTTA KNOW.
THWIPP!
WOW! I'M IN LUCK--HE'S SPOTTED HIM ALREADY.
HE'S EVEN GOT SOME KIND OF BUILT-IN NULLIFIER--SO THAT THE WEB-HEAD WON'T KNOW HE'S BEING FOLLOWED.
GOTTA HAND IT TO SMYTHE. HE THINKS OF EVERYTHING.
I'LL FIX IT SO I CAPTURE HIM ALIVE.
SO I CAN ENJOY LAUGHING IN HIS FACE WHEN THE POLICE UNMASK HIM.

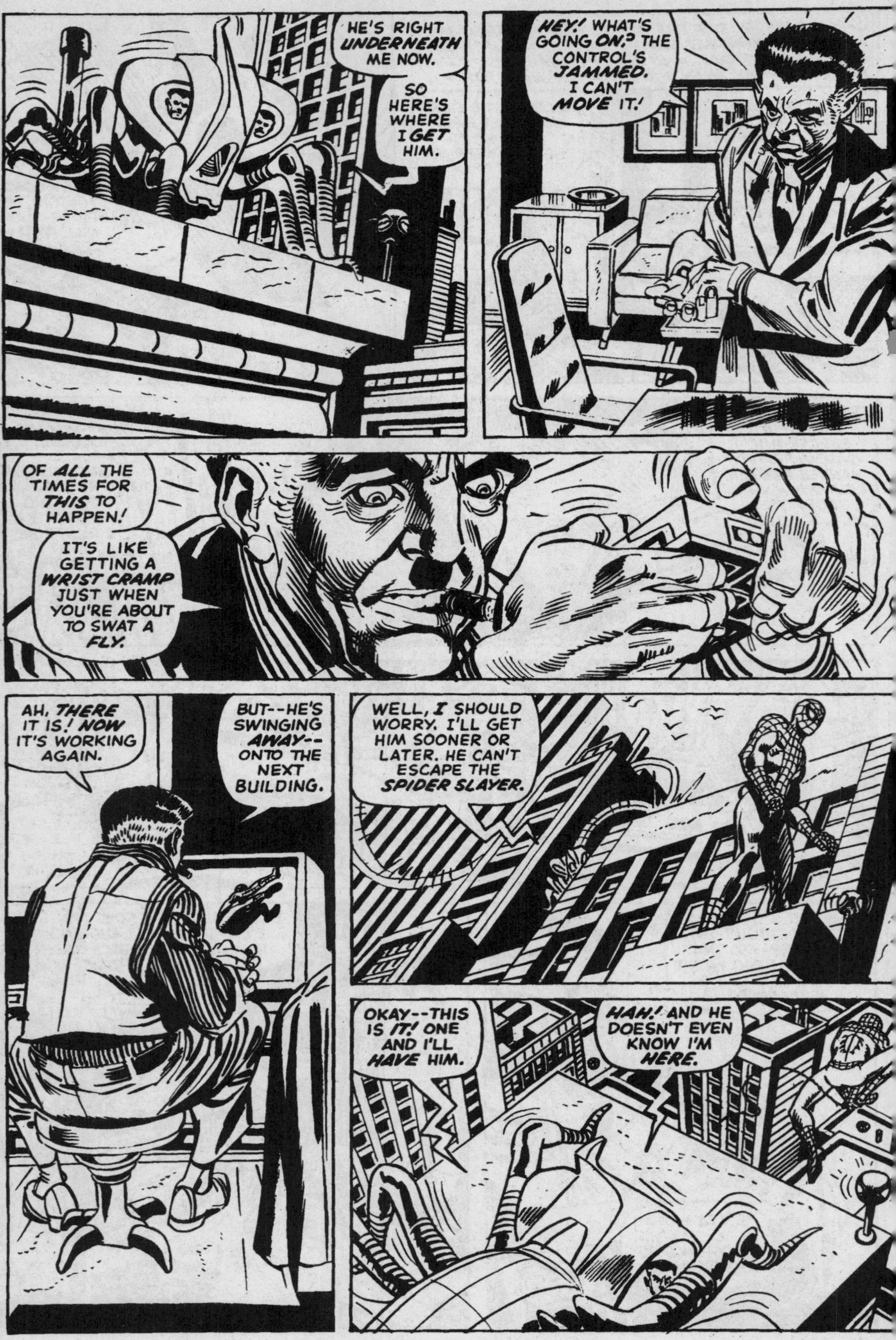
HE'S RIGHT UNDERNEATH ME NOW.
SO HERE'S WHERE I GET HIM.
HEY! WHAT'S GOING ON? THE CONTROL'S JAMMED. I CAN'T MOVE IT!
OF ALL THE TIMES FOR THIS TO HAPPEN!
IT'S LIKE GETTING A WRIST CRAMP JUST WHEN YOU'RE ABOUT TO SWAT A FLY.
AH, THERE IT IS! NOW IT'S WORKING AGAIN.
BUT--HE'S SWINGING AWAY--ONTO THE NEXT BUILDING.
WELL, I SHOULD WORRY. I'LL GET HIM SOONER OR LATER. HE CAN'T ESCAPE THE SPIDER SLAYER.
OKAY--THIS IS IT! ONE AND I'LL HAVE HIM.
HAH! AND HE DOESN'T EVEN KNOW I'M HERE.

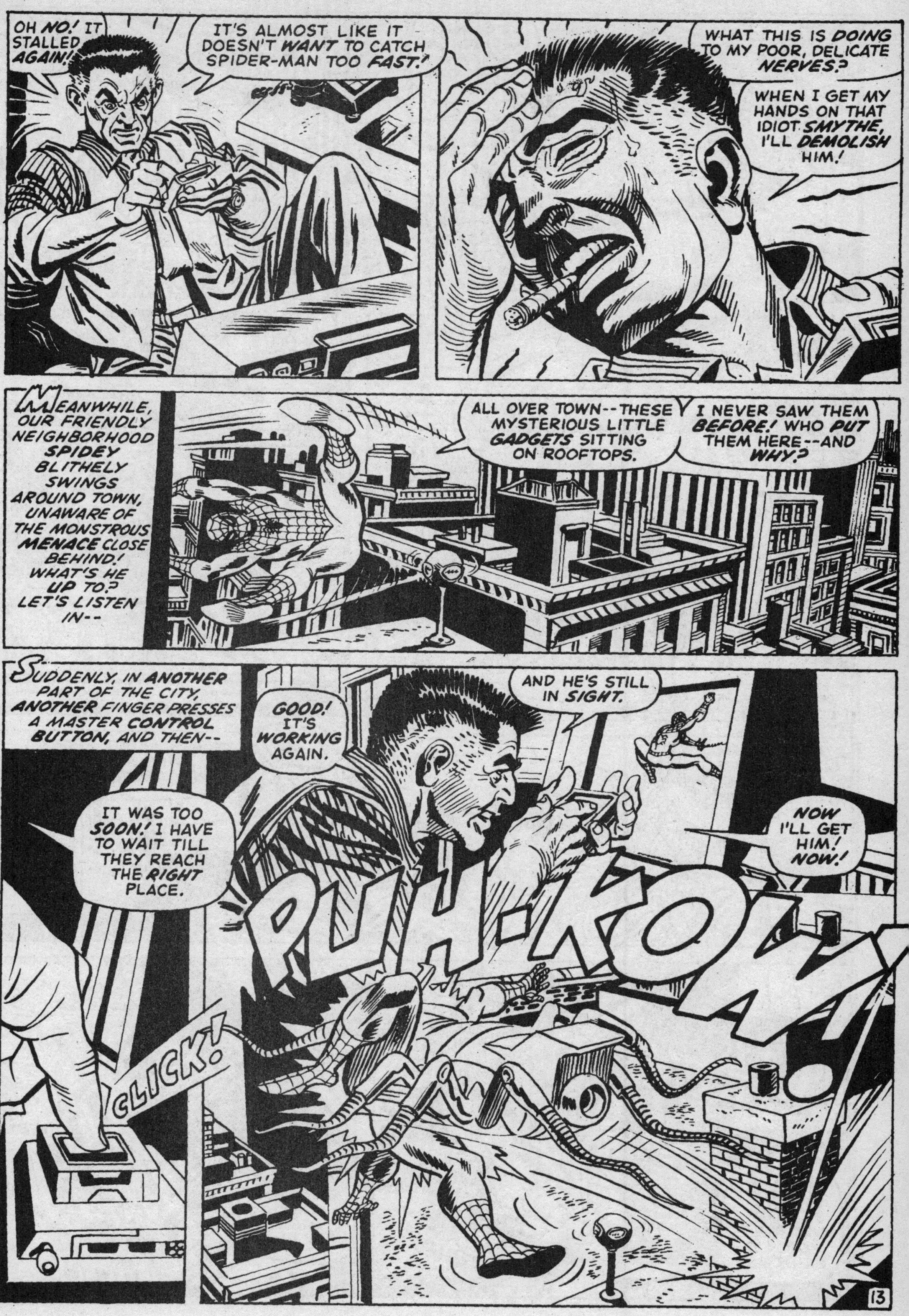

OH NO! IT STALLED AGAIN!
IT'S ALMOST LIKE IT DOESN'T WANT TO CATCH SPIDER-MAN TOO FAST!
WHAT THIS IS DOING TO MY POOR, DELICATE NERVES?
WHEN I GET MY HANDS ON THAT IDIOT SMYTHE, I'LL DEMOLISH HIM!
MEANWHILE, OUR FRIENDLY NEIGHBORHOOD SPIDEY BLITHELY SWINGS AROUND TOWN, UNAWARE OF THE MONSTROUS MENACE CLOSE BEHIND! WHAT'S HE UP TO? LET'S LISTEN IN--
ALL OVER TOWN--THESE MYSTERIOUS LITTLE GADGETS SITTING ON ROOFTOPS.
I NEVER SAW THEM BEFORE! WHO PUT THEM HERE--AND WHY?
SUDDENLY, IN ANOTHER PART OF THE CITY, ANOTHER FINGER PRESSES A MASTER CONTROL BUTTON, AND THEN--
GOOD! IT'S WORKING AGAIN.
AND HE'S STILL IN SIGHT.
IT WAS TOO SOON! I HAVE TO WAIT TILL THEY REACH THE RIGHT PLACE.
NOW I'LL GET HIM! NOW!
PUH-KOW!
CLICK!

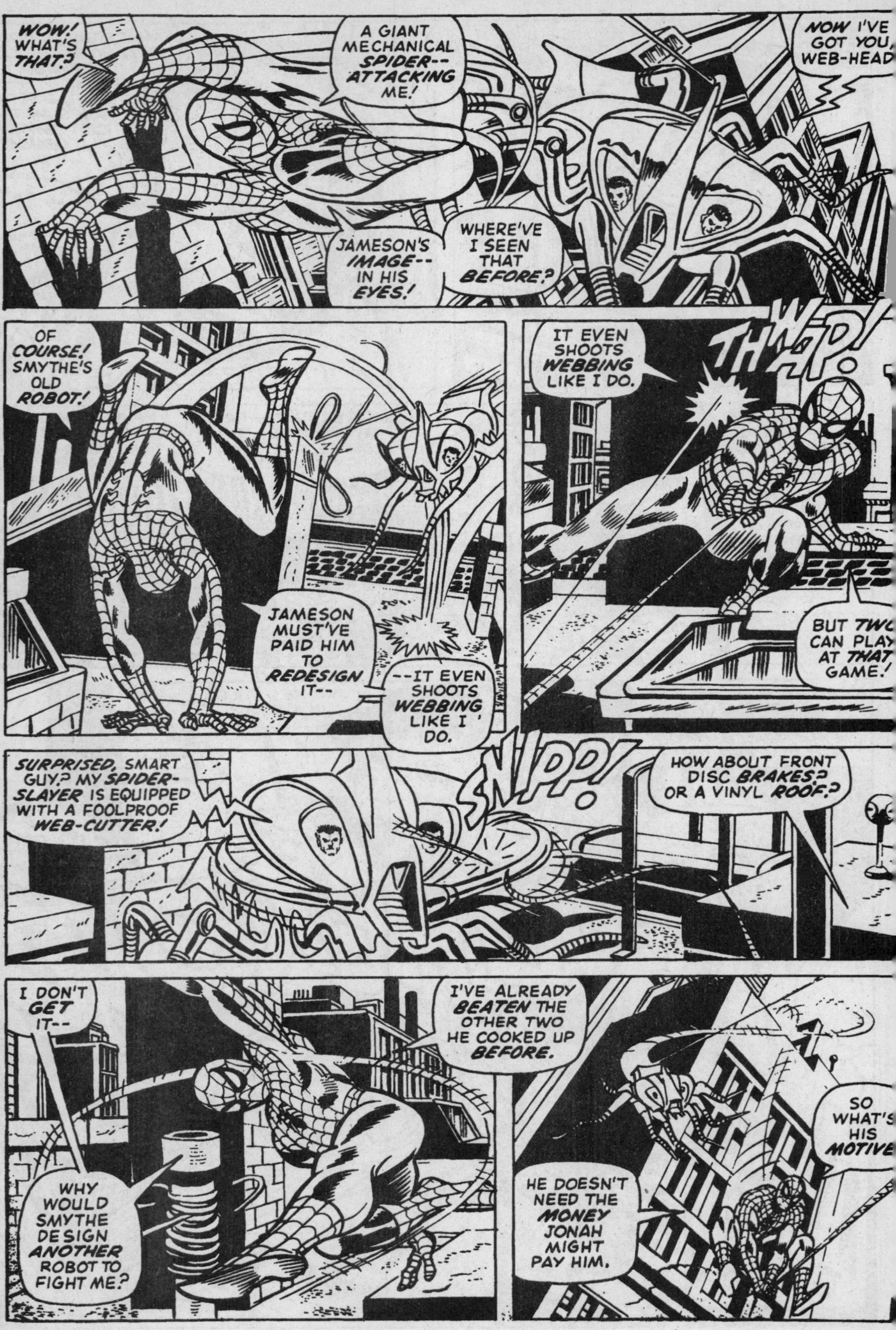
WOW! WHAT'S THAT?
A GIANT MECHANICAL SPIDER-- ATTACKING ME!
NOW I'VE GOT YOU, WEB-HEAD
JAMESON'S IMAGE-- IN HIS EYES!
WHERE'VE I SEEN THAT BEFORE?
OF COURSE! SMYTHE'S OLD ROBOT!
JAMESON MUST'VE PAID HIM TO REDESIGN IT--
--IT EVEN SHOOTS WEBBING LIKE I DO.
THWAP!
IT EVEN SHOOTS WEBBING LIKE I DO.
BUT TWO CAN PLAY AT THAT GAME!
SURPRISED, SMART GUY? MY SPIDER-SLAYER IS EQUIPPED WITH A FOOLPROOF WEB-CUTTER!
SNIPP!
HOW ABOUT FRONT DISC BRAKES? OR A VINYL ROOF?
I DON'T GET IT--
I'VE ALREADY BEATEN THE OTHER TWO HE COOKED UP BEFORE.
WHY WOULD SMYTHE DESIGN ANOTHER ROBOT TO FIGHT ME?
SO WHAT'S HIS MOTIVE
HE DOESN'T NEED THE MONEY JONAH MIGHT PAY HIM.

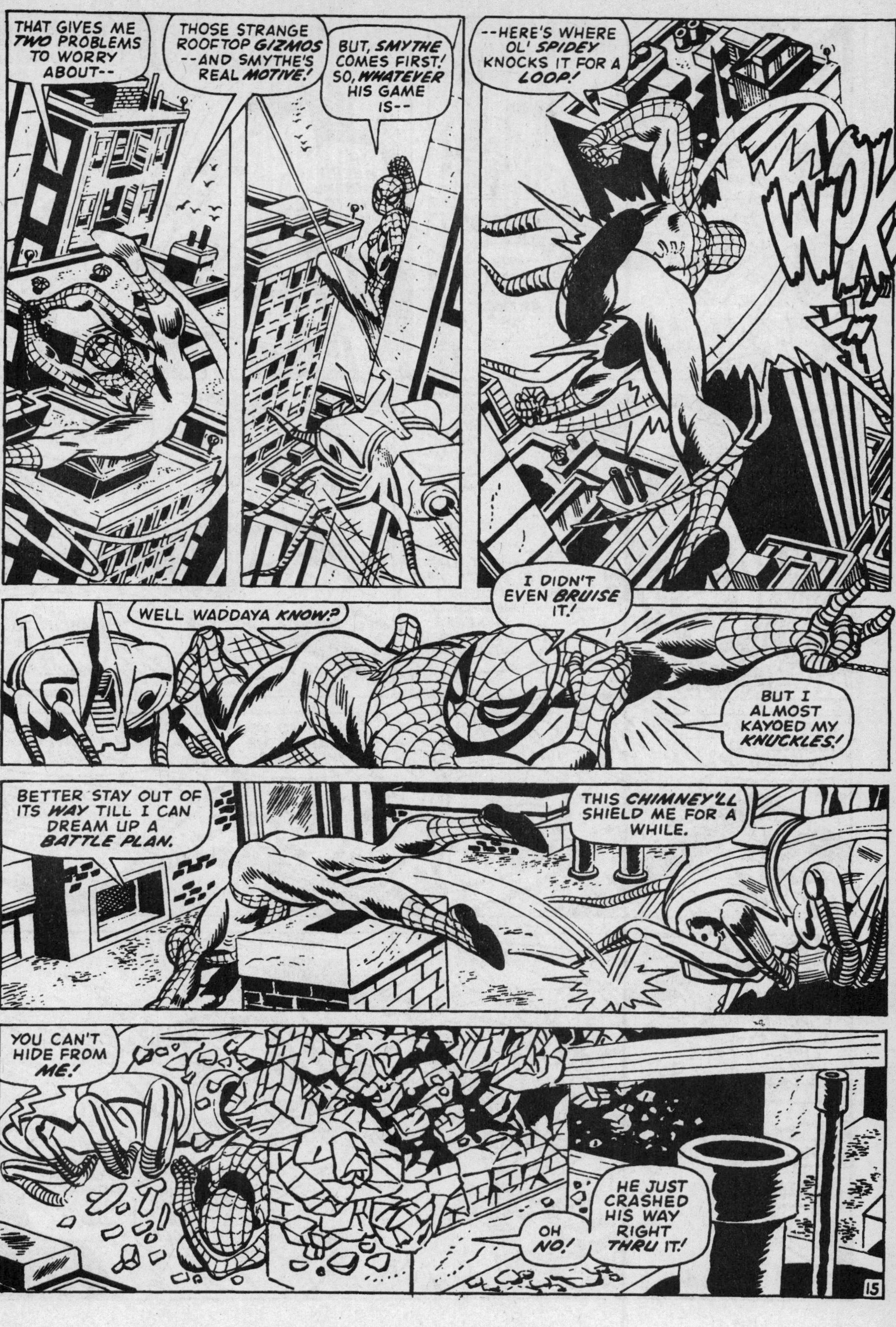
THAT GIVES ME TWO PROBLEMS TO WORRY ABOUT--
THOSE STRANGE ROOFTOP GIZMOS --AND SMYTHE'S REAL MOTIVE!
BUT, SMYTHE COMES FIRST! SO, WHATEVER HIS GAME IS--
--HERE'S WHERE OL' SPIDEY KNOCKS IT FOR A LOOP!
WOK
WELL WADDAYA KNOW?
I DIDN'T EVEN BRUISE IT!
BUT I ALMOST KAYOED MY KNUCKLES!
BETTER STAY OUT OF ITS WAY TILL I CAN DREAM UP A BATTLE PLAN.
THIS CHIMNEY'LL SHIELD ME FOR A WHILE.
YOU CAN'T HIDE FROM ME!
OH NO!
HE JUST CRASHED HIS WAY RIGHT THRU IT!
15

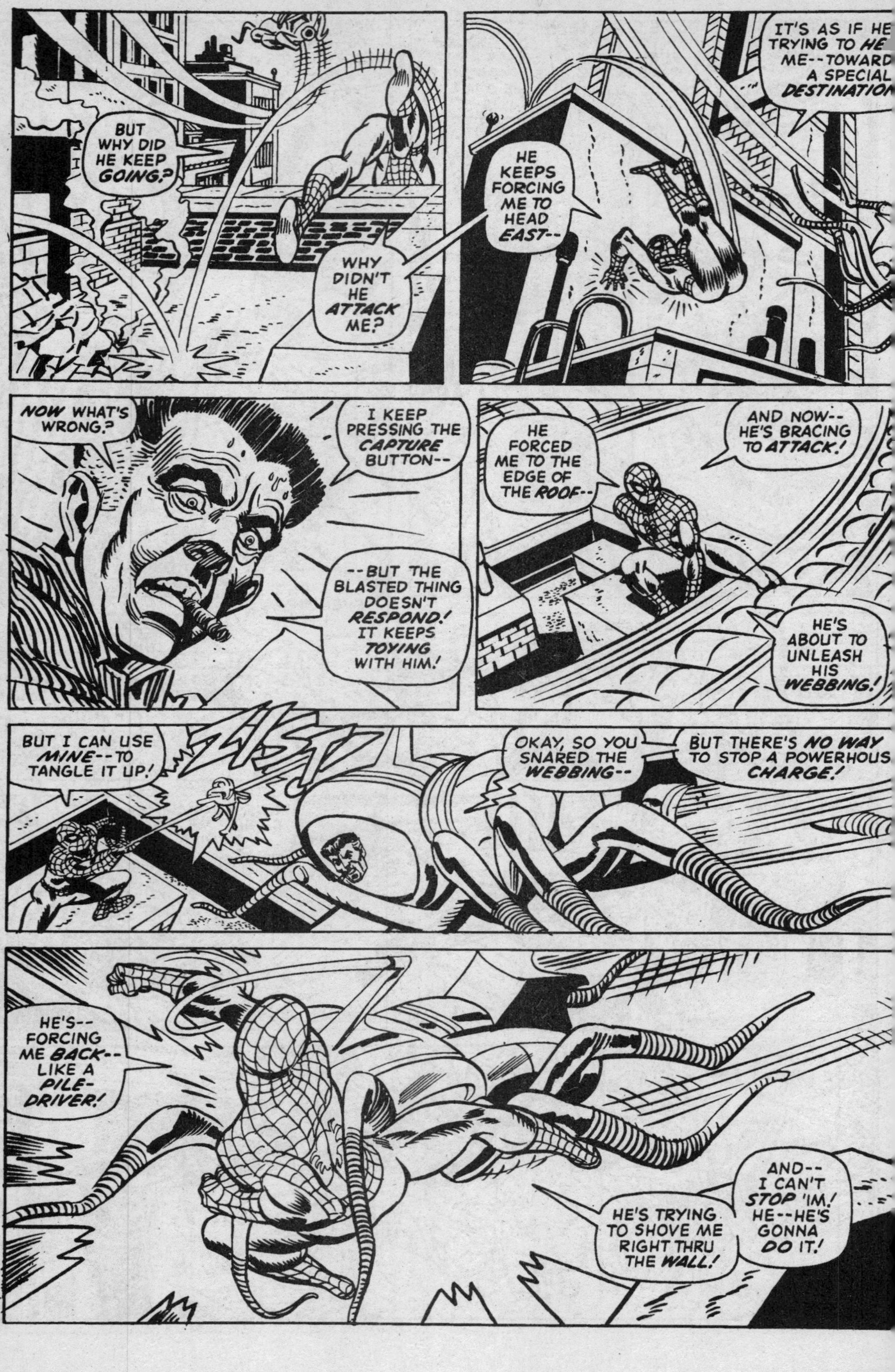
BUT WHY DID HE KEEP GOING?
WHY DIDN'T HE ATTACK ME?
HE KEEPS FORCING ME TO HEAD EAST--
IT'S AS IF HE TRYING TO HE ME--TOWARD A SPECIAL DESTINATION
NOW WHAT'S WRONG?
I KEEP PRESSING THE CAPTURE BUTTON--
--BUT THE BLASTED THING DOESN'T RESPOND! IT KEEPS TOYING WITH HIM!
HE FORCED ME TO THE EDGE OF THE ROOF--
AND NOW--HE'S BRACING TO ATTACK!
HE'S ABOUT TO UNLEASH HIS WEBBING!
BUT I CAN USE MINE--TO TANGLE IT UP!
ZWISST
OKAY, SO YOU SNARED THE WEBBING--
BUT THERE'S NO WAY TO STOP A POWERHOUS CHARGE!
HE'S--FORCING ME BACK--LIKE A PILE-DRIVER!
HE'S TRYING TO SHOVE ME RIGHT THRU THE WALL!
AND--I CAN'T STOP 'IM! HE--HE'S GONNA DO IT!

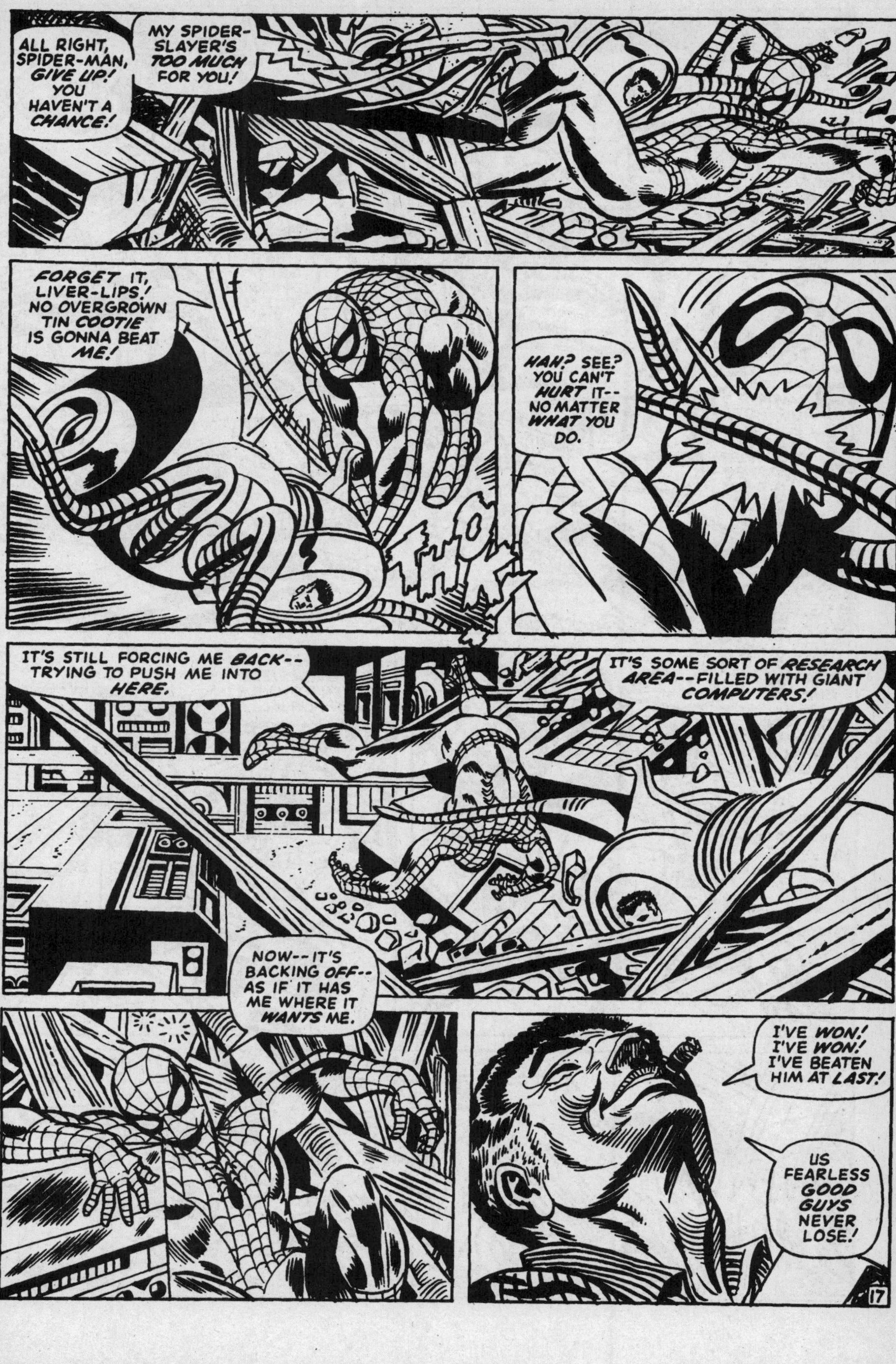
ALL RIGHT, SPIDER-MAN, GIVE UP! YOU HAVEN'T A CHANCE!
MY SPIDER-SLAYER'S TOO MUCH FOR YOU!
FORGET IT, LIVER-LIPS! NO OVERGROWN TIN COOTIE IS GONNA BEAT ME!
THK
HAH? SEE? YOU CAN'T HURT IT-- NO MATTER WHAT YOU DO.
IT'S STILL FORCING ME BACK-- TRYING TO PUSH ME INTO HERE.
IT'S SOME SORT OF RESEARCH AREA--FILLED WITH GIANT COMPUTERS!
NOW--IT'S BACKING OFF-- AS IF IT HAS ME WHERE IT WANTS ME.
I'VE WON! I'VE WON! I'VE BEATEN HIM AT LAST!
US FEARLESS GOOD GUYS NEVER LOSE!
17

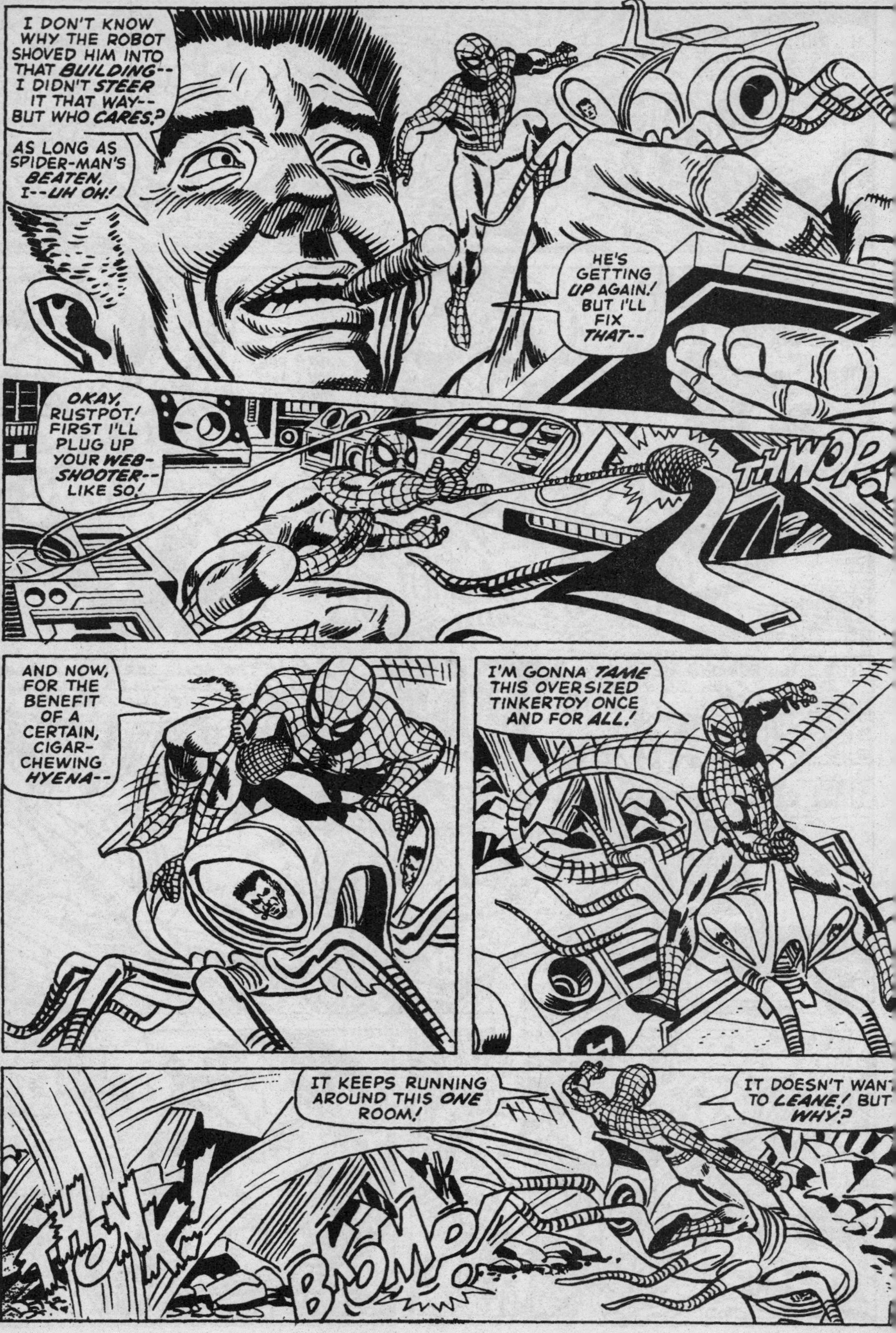
I DON'T KNOW WHY THE ROBOT SHOVED HIM INTO THAT BUILDING-- I DIDN'T STEER IT THAT WAY-- BUT WHO CARES?
AS LONG AS SPIDER-MAN'S BEATEN, I--UH OH!
HE'S GETTING UP AGAIN! BUT I'LL FIX THAT--
OKAY, RUSTPOT! FIRST I'LL PLUG UP YOUR WEB-SHOOTER--LIKE SO!
THWOP
AND NOW, FOR THE BENEFIT OF A CERTAIN, CIGAR-CHEWING HYENA--
I'M GONNA TAME THIS OVERSIZED TINKERTOY ONCE AND FOR ALL!
IT KEEPS RUNNING AROUND THIS ONE ROOM!
IT DOESN'T WANT TO LEANE! BUT WHY?
THONK
BLOMP

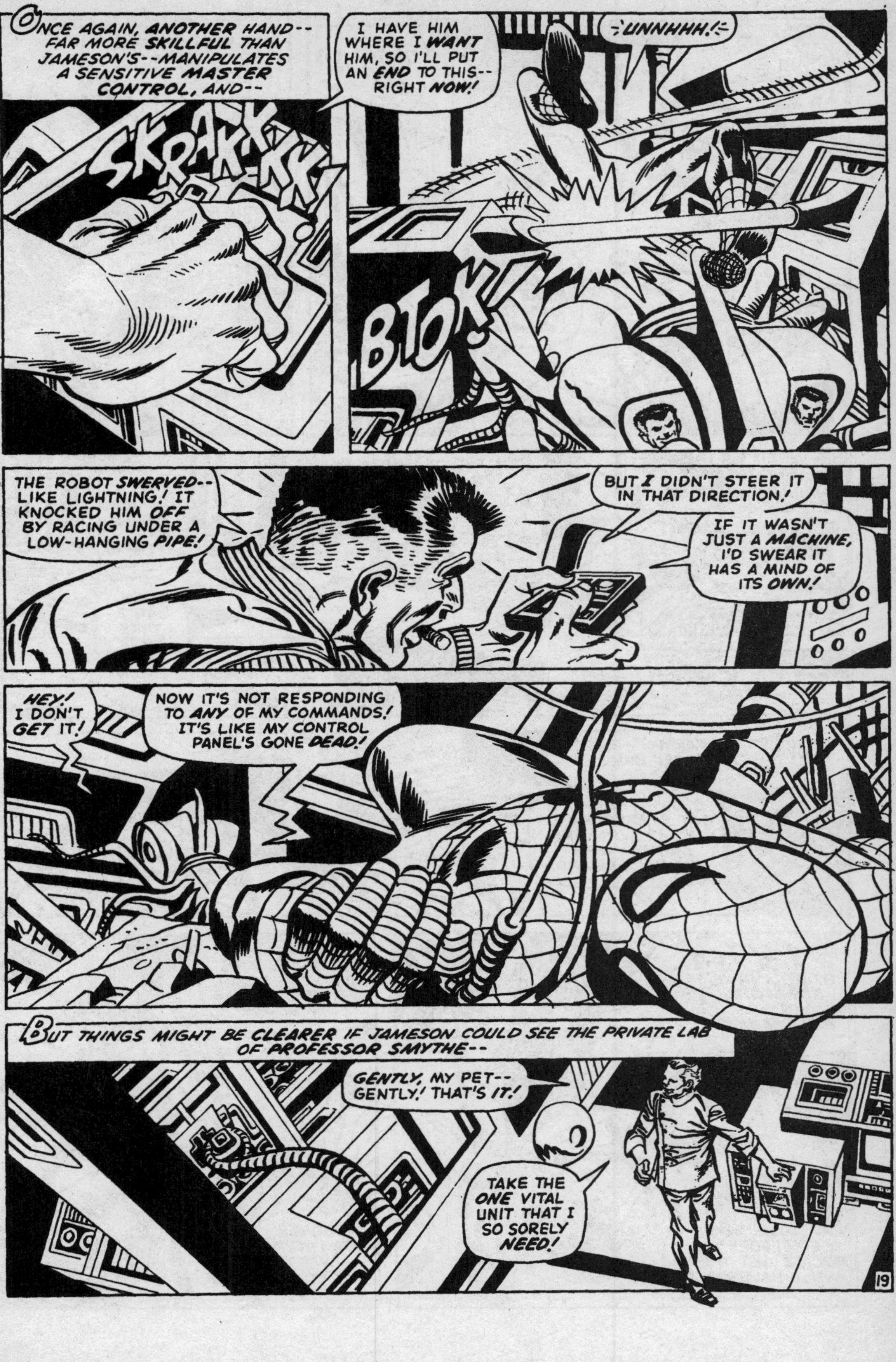
ONCE AGAIN, ANOTHER HAND-- FAR MORE SKILLFUL THAN JAMESON'S--MANIPULATES A SENSITIVE MASTER CONTROL, AND--
SKRAKKKK!
I HAVE HIM WHERE I WANT HIM, SO I'LL PUT AN END TO THIS-- RIGHT NOW!
UNNHHH!
BTOK!
THE ROBOT SWERVED-- LIKE LIGHTNING! IT KNOCKED HIM OFF BY RACING UNDER A LOW-HANGING PIPE!
BUT I DIDN'T STEER IT IN THAT DIRECTION!
IF IT WASN'T JUST A MACHINE, I'D SWEAR IT HAS A MIND OF ITS OWN!
HEY! I DON'T GET IT!
NOW IT'S NOT RESPONDING TO ANY OF MY COMMANDS! IT'S LIKE MY CONTROL PANEL'S GONE DEAD!
BUT THINGS MIGHT BE CLEARER IF JAMESON COULD SEE THE PRIVATE LAB OF PROFESSOR SMYTHE--
GENTLY, MY PET-- GENTLY! THAT'S IT!
TAKE THE ONE VITAL UNIT THAT I SO SORELY NEED!
19

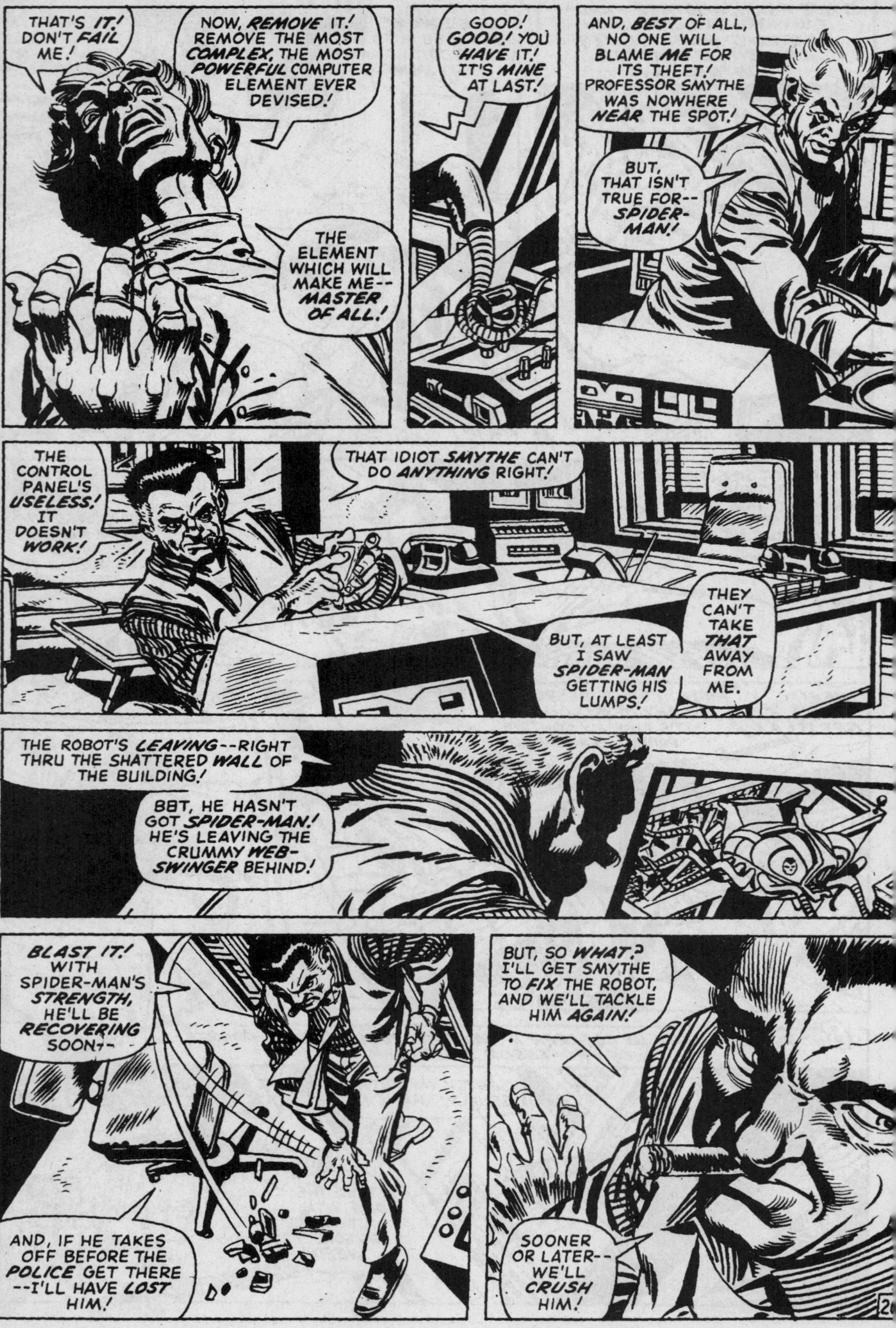
THAT'S IT! DON'T FAIL ME!
NOW, REMOVE IT! REMOVE THE MOST COMPLEX, THE MOST POWERFUL COMPUTER ELEMENT EVER DEVISED!
THE ELEMENT WHICH WILL MAKE ME--MASTER OF ALL!
GOOD! GOOD! YOU HAVE IT! IT'S MINE AT LAST!
AND, BEST OF ALL, NO ONE WILL BLAME ME FOR ITS THEFT! PROFESSOR SMYTHE WAS NOWHERE NEAR THE SPOT!
BUT, THAT ISN'T TRUE FOR--SPIDER-MAN!
THE CONTROL PANEL'S USELESS! IT DOESN'T WORK!
THAT IDIOT SMYTHE CAN'T DO ANYTHING RIGHT!
BUT, AT LEAST I SAW SPIDER-MAN GETTING HIS LUMPS!
THEY CAN'T TAKE THAT AWAY FROM ME.
THE ROBOT'S LEAVING--RIGHT THRU THE SHATTERED WALL OF THE BUILDING!
BBT, HE HASN'T GOT SPIDER-MAN! HE'S LEAVING THE CRUMMY WEB-SWINGER BEHIND!
BLAST IT! WITH SPIDER-MAN'S STRENGTH, HE'LL BE RECOVERING SOON--
AND, IF HE TAKES OFF BEFORE THE POLICE GET THERE --I'LL HAVE LOST HIM!
BUT, SO WHAT? I'LL GET SMYTHE TO FIX THE ROBOT, AND WE'LL TACKLE HIM AGAIN!
SOONER OR LATER--WE'LL CRUSH HIM!
20

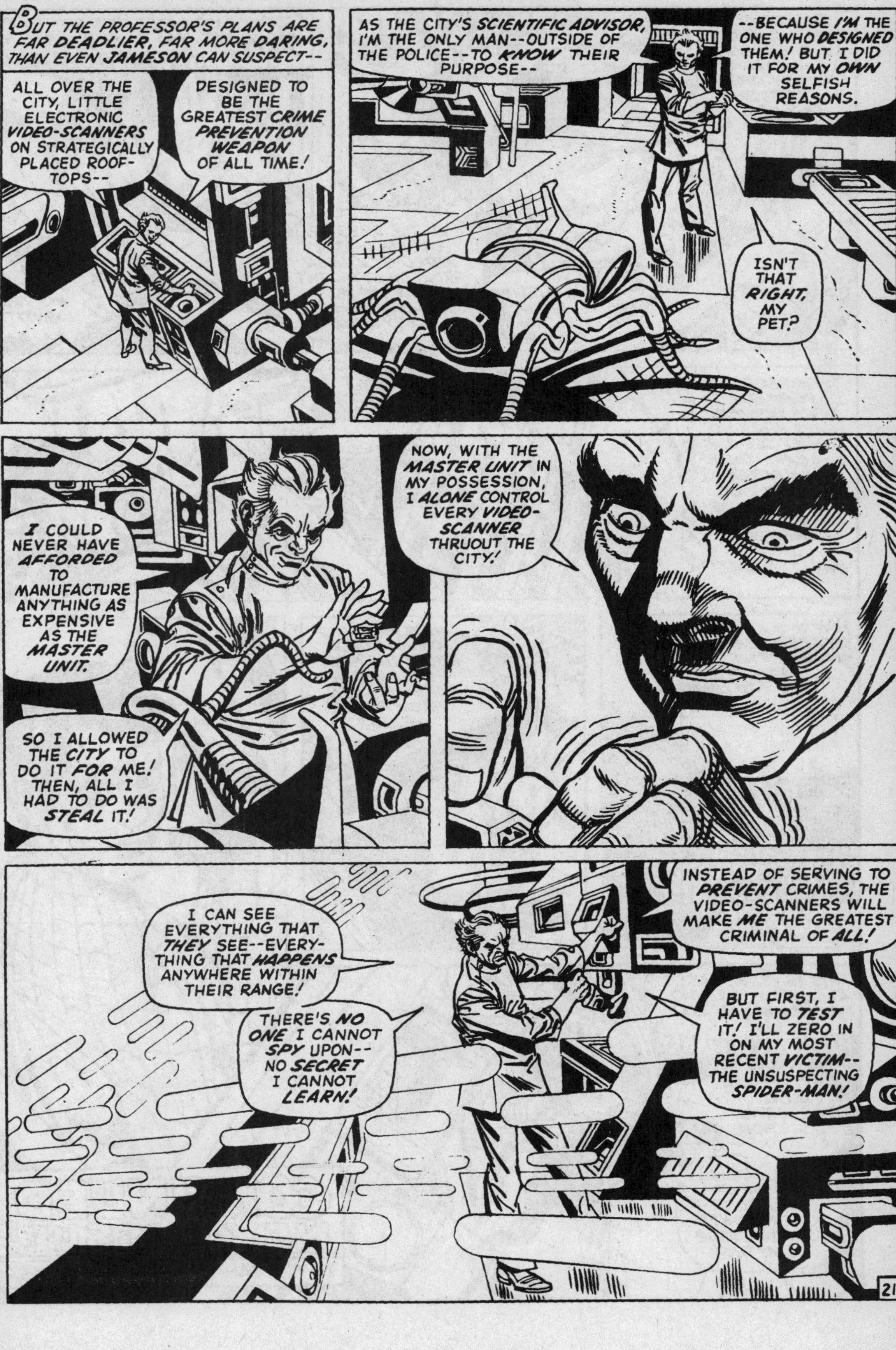

BUT THE PROFESSOR'S PLANS ARE FAR DEADLIER, FAR MORE DARING, THAN EVEN JAMESON CAN SUSPECT--
ALL OVER THE CITY, LITTLE ELECTRONIC VIDEO-SCANNERS ON STRATEGICALLY PLACED ROOF-TOPS--
DESIGNED TO BE THE GREATEST CRIME PREVENTION WEAPON OF ALL TIME!
AS THE CITY'S SCIENTIFIC ADVISOR, I'M THE ONLY MAN--OUTSIDE OF THE POLICE--TO KNOW THEIR PURPOSE--
--BECAUSE I'M THE ONE WHO DESIGNED THEM! BUT I DID IT FOR MY OWN SELFISH REASONS.
ISN'T THAT RIGHT, MY PET?
I COULD NEVER HAVE AFFORDED TO MANUFACTURE ANYTHING AS EXPENSIVE AS THE MASTER UNIT.
SO I ALLOWED THE CITY TO DO IT FOR ME! THEN, ALL I HAD TO DO WAS STEAL IT!
NOW, WITH THE MASTER UNIT IN MY POSSESSION, I ALONE CONTROL EVERY VIDEO-SCANNER THRUOUT THE CITY!
I CAN SEE EVERYTHING THAT THEY SEE--EVERYTHING THAT HAPPENS ANYWHERE WITHIN THEIR RANGE!
THERE'S NO ONE I CANNOT SPY UPON--NO SECRET I CANNOT LEARN!
INSTEAD OF SERVING TO PREVENT CRIMES, THE VIDEO-SCANNERS WILL MAKE ME THE GREATEST CRIMINAL OF ALL!
BUT FIRST, I HAVE TO TEST IT! I'LL ZERO IN ON MY MOST RECENT VICTIM--THE UNSUSPECTING SPIDER-MAN!
21

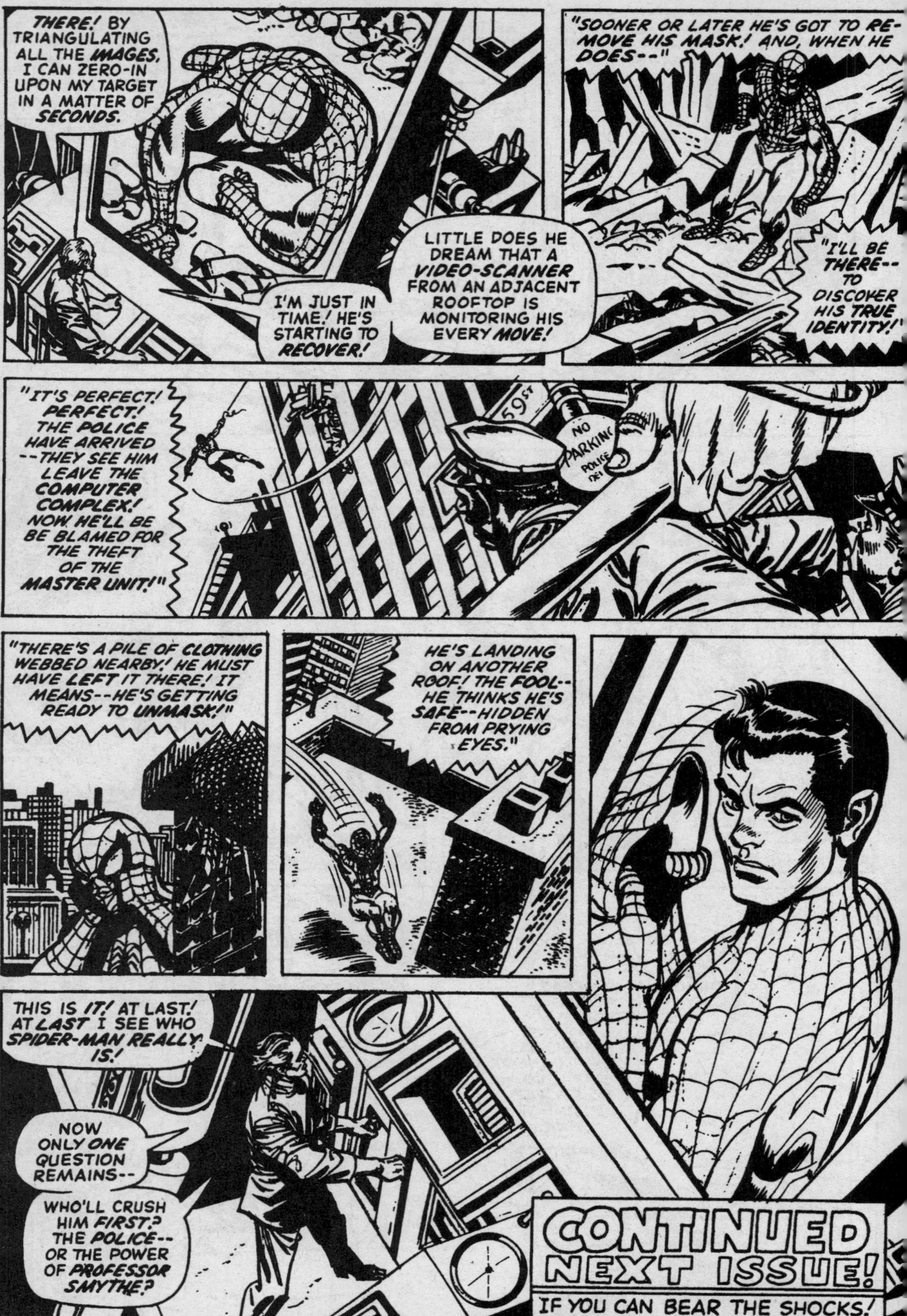
THERE! BY TRIANGULATING ALL THE IMAGES, I CAN ZERO-IN UPON MY TARGET IN A MATTER OF SECONDS.
I'M JUST IN TIME! HE'S STARTING TO RECOVER!
LITTLE DOES HE DREAM THAT A VIDEO-SCANNER FROM AN ADJACENT ROOFTOP IS MONITORING HIS EVERY MOVE!
"SOONER OR LATER HE'S GOT TO REMOVE HIS MASK! AND, WHEN HE DOES--"
"I'LL BE THERE-- TO DISCOVER HIS TRUE IDENTITY!"
"IT'S PERFECT! PERFECT! THE POLICE HAVE ARRIVED --THEY SEE HIM LEAVE THE COMPUTER COMPLEX! NOW HE'LL BE BE BLAMED FOR THE THEFT OF THE MASTER UNIT!"
59ST
NO PARKING POLICE DEPT
"THERE'S A PILE OF CLOTHING WEBBED NEARBY! HE MUST HAVE LEFT IT THERE! IT MEANS--HE'S GETTING READY TO UNMASK!"
HE'S LANDING ON ANOTHER ROOF! THE FOOL--HE THINKS HE'S SAFE--HIDDEN FROM PRYING EYES."
THIS IS IT! AT LAST! AT LAST I SEE WHO SPIDER-MAN REALLY IS!
NOW ONLY ONE QUESTION REMAINS--
WHO'LL CRUSH HIM FIRST? THE POLICE--OR THE POWER OF PROFESSOR SMYTHE?
CONTINUED NEXT ISSUE!
IF YOU CAN BEAR THE SHOCKS!

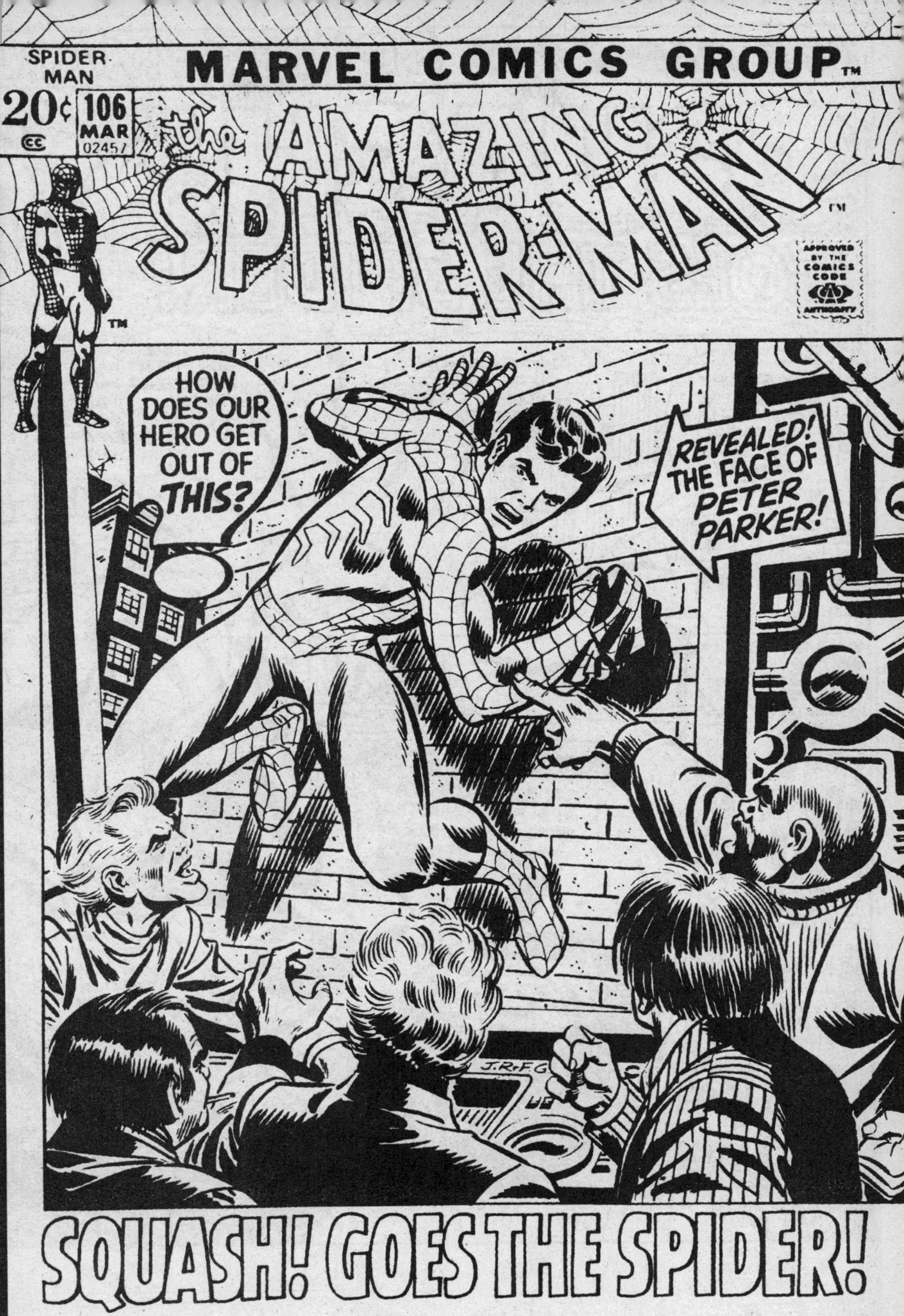
SPIDER-MAN
MARVEL COMICS GROUP
20¢
106
MAR
02457
the AMAZING SPIDER-MAN
APPROVED BY THE COMICS CODE AUTHORITY
HOW DOES OUR HERO GET OUT OF THIS?
REVEALED! THE FACE OF PETER PARKER!
SQUASH! GOES THE SPIDER!

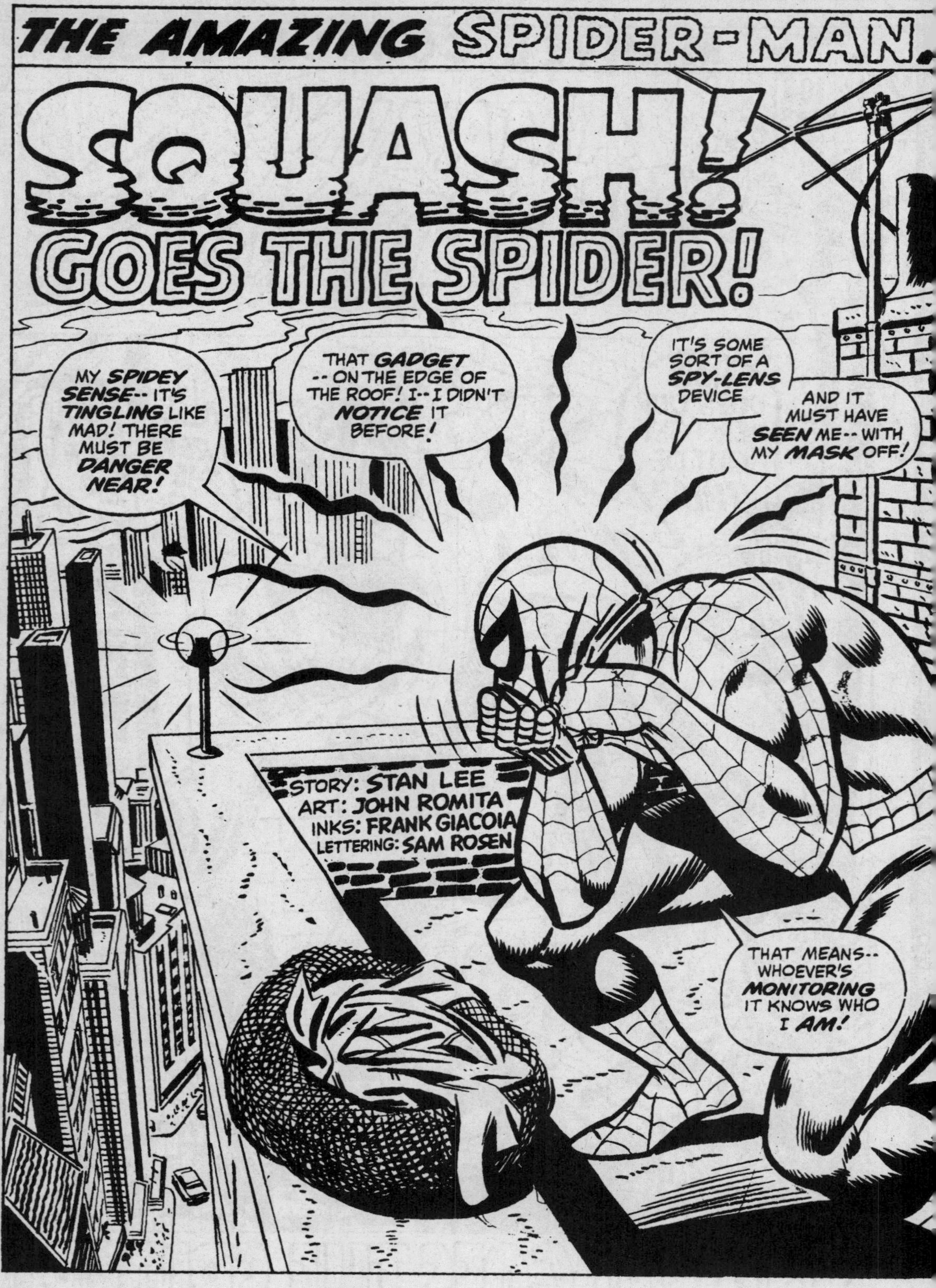
THE AMAZING SPIDER-MAN
SQUASH! GOES THE SPIDER!
MY SPIDEY SENSE-- IT'S TINGLING LIKE MAD! THERE MUST BE DANGER NEAR!
THAT GADGET -- ON THE EDGE OF THE ROOF! I-- I DIDN'T NOTICE IT BEFORE!
IT'S SOME SORT OF A SPY-LENS DEVICE
AND IT MUST HAVE SEEN ME-- WITH MY MASK OFF!
STORY: STAN LEE
ART: JOHN ROMITA
INKS: FRANK GIACOIA
LETTERING: SAM ROSEN
THAT MEANS-- WHOEVER'S MONITORING IT KNOWS WHO I AM!

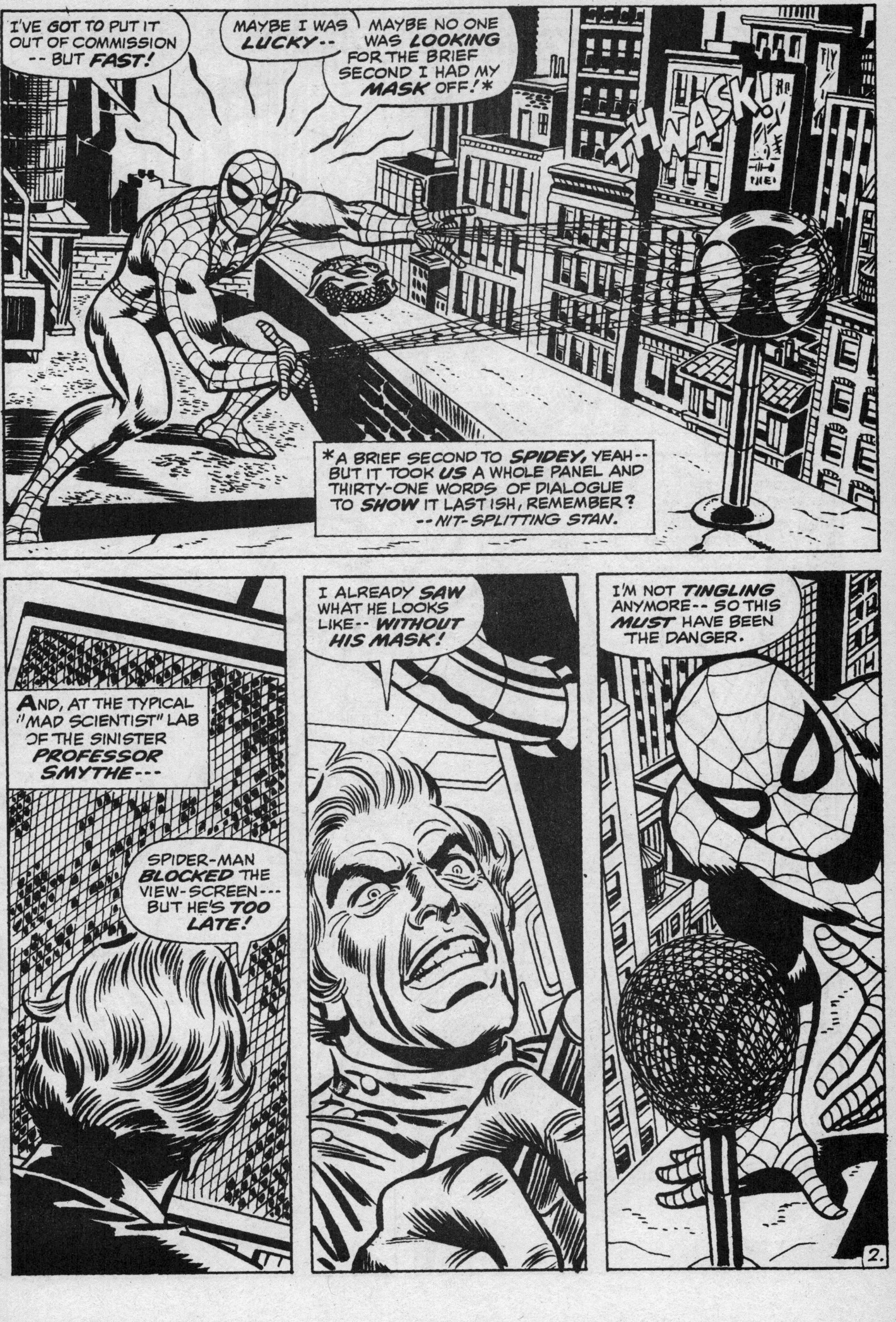
I'VE GOT TO PUT IT OUT OF COMMISSION -- BUT FAST!
MAYBE I WAS LUCKY--
MAYBE NO ONE WAS LOOKING FOR THE BRIEF SECOND I HAD MY MASK OFF!*
THWASK!
*A BRIEF SECOND TO SPIDEY, YEAH-- BUT IT TOOK US A WHOLE PANEL AND THIRTY-ONE WORDS OF DIALOGUE TO SHOW IT LAST ISH, REMEMBER? --NIT-SPLITTING STAN.
AND, AT THE TYPICAL "MAD SCIENTIST" LAB OF THE SINISTER PROFESSOR SMYTHE---
SPIDER-MAN BLOCKED THE VIEW-SCREEN--- BUT HE'S TOO LATE!
I ALREADY SAW WHAT HE LOOKS LIKE-- WITHOUT HIS MASK!
I'M NOT TINGLING ANYMORE-- SO THIS MUST HAVE BEEN THE DANGER.
2.

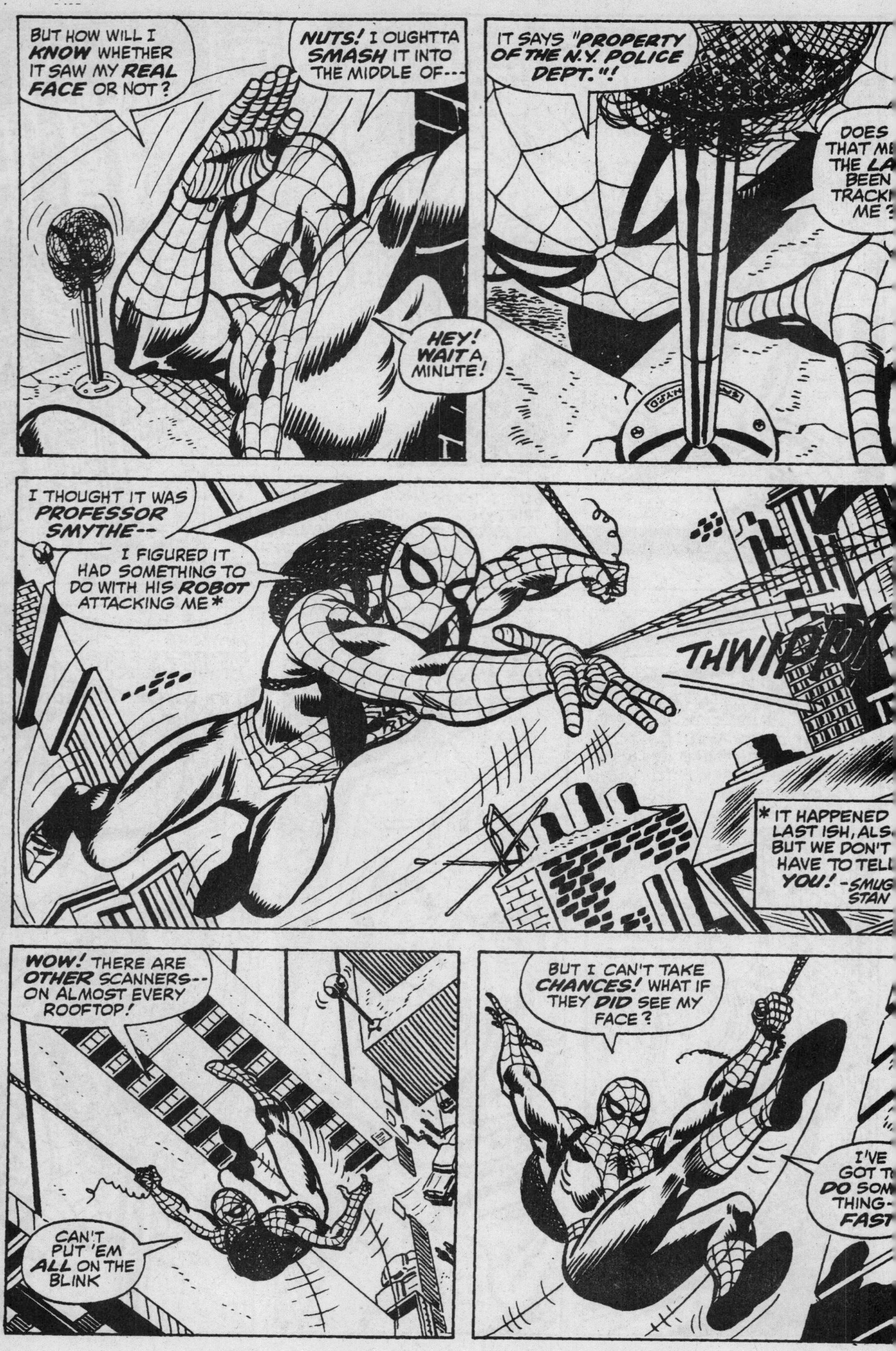

BUT HOW WILL I KNOW WHETHER IT SAW MY REAL FACE OR NOT?
NUTS! I OUGHTTA SMASH IT INTO THE MIDDLE OF---
HEY! WAIT A MINUTE!
IT SAYS "PROPERTY OF THE N.Y. POLICE DEPT."!
DOES THAT ME THE LA BEEN TRACK ME?
I THOUGHT IT WAS PROFESSOR SMYTHE--
I FIGURED IT HAD SOMETHING TO DO WITH HIS ROBOT ATTACKING ME*
THWIPP
* IT HAPPENED LAST ISH, ALS BUT WE DON'T HAVE TO TELL YOU! -SMUG STAN
WOW! THERE ARE OTHER SCANNERS-- ON ALMOST EVERY ROOFTOP!
CAN'T PUT 'EM ALL ON THE BLINK
BUT I CAN'T TAKE CHANCES! WHAT IF THEY DID SEE MY FACE?
I'VE GOT T DO SOM THING- FAST

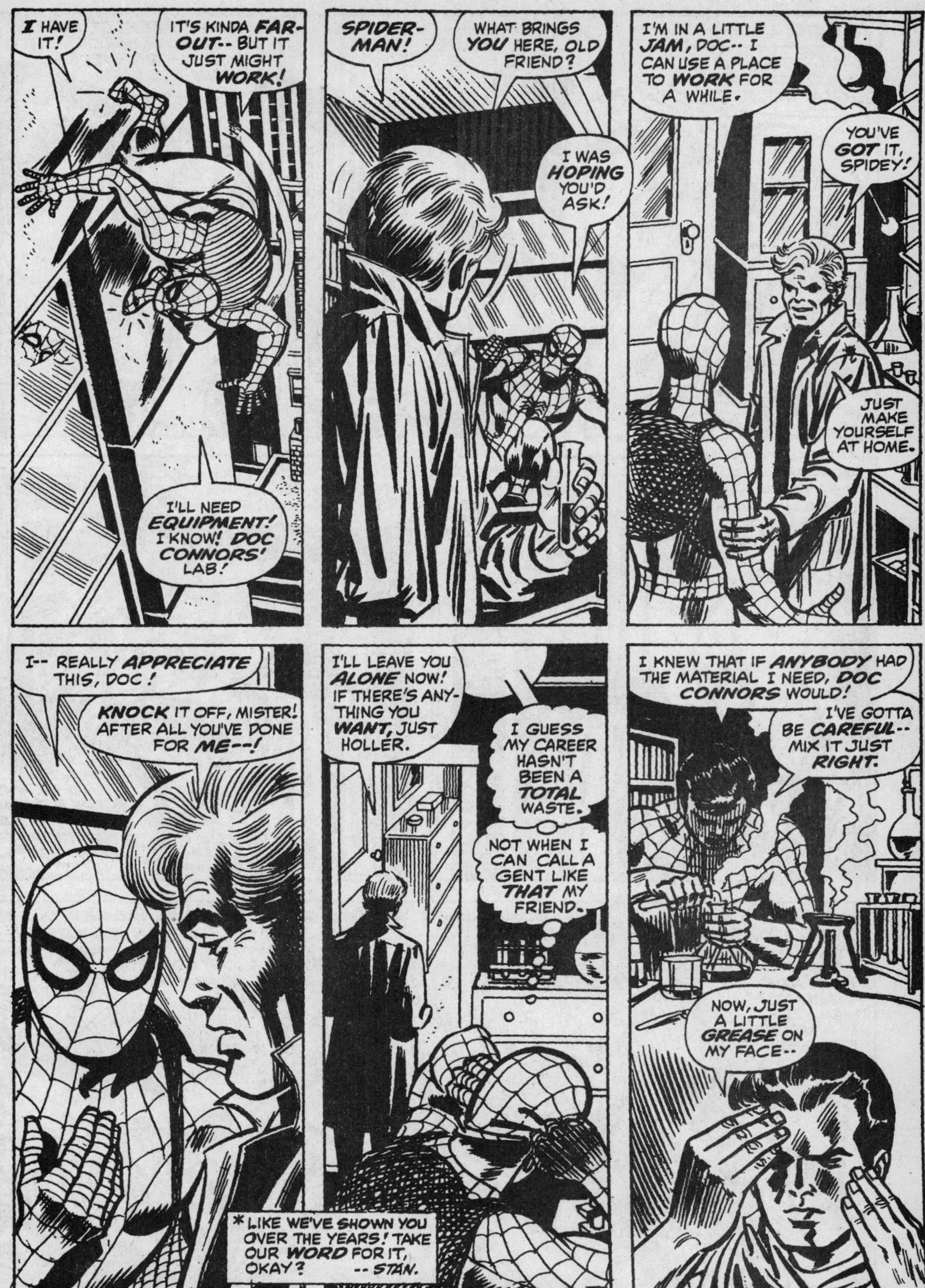
I HAVE IT!
IT'S KINDA FAR-OUT-- BUT IT JUST MIGHT WORK!
I'LL NEED EQUIPMENT! I KNOW! DOC CONNORS' LAB!
SPIDER-MAN!
WHAT BRINGS YOU HERE, OLD FRIEND?
I WAS HOPING YOU'D ASK!
I'M IN A LITTLE JAM, DOC-- I CAN USE A PLACE TO WORK FOR A WHILE.
YOU'VE GOT IT, SPIDEY!
JUST MAKE YOURSELF AT HOME.
I-- REALLY APPRECIATE THIS, DOC!
KNOCK IT OFF, MISTER! AFTER ALL YOU'VE DONE FOR ME--!
I'LL LEAVE YOU ALONE NOW! IF THERE'S ANY-THING YOU WANT, JUST HOLLER.
I GUESS MY CAREER HASN'T BEEN A TOTAL WASTE.
NOT WHEN I CAN CALL A GENT LIKE THAT MY FRIEND.
* LIKE WE'VE SHOWN YOU OVER THE YEARS! TAKE OUR WORD FOR IT, OKAY? -- STAN.
I KNEW THAT IF ANYBODY HAD THE MATERIAL I NEED, DOC CONNORS WOULD!
I'VE GOTTA BE CAREFUL-- MIX IT JUST RIGHT.
NOW, JUST A LITTLE GREASE ON MY FACE--
4

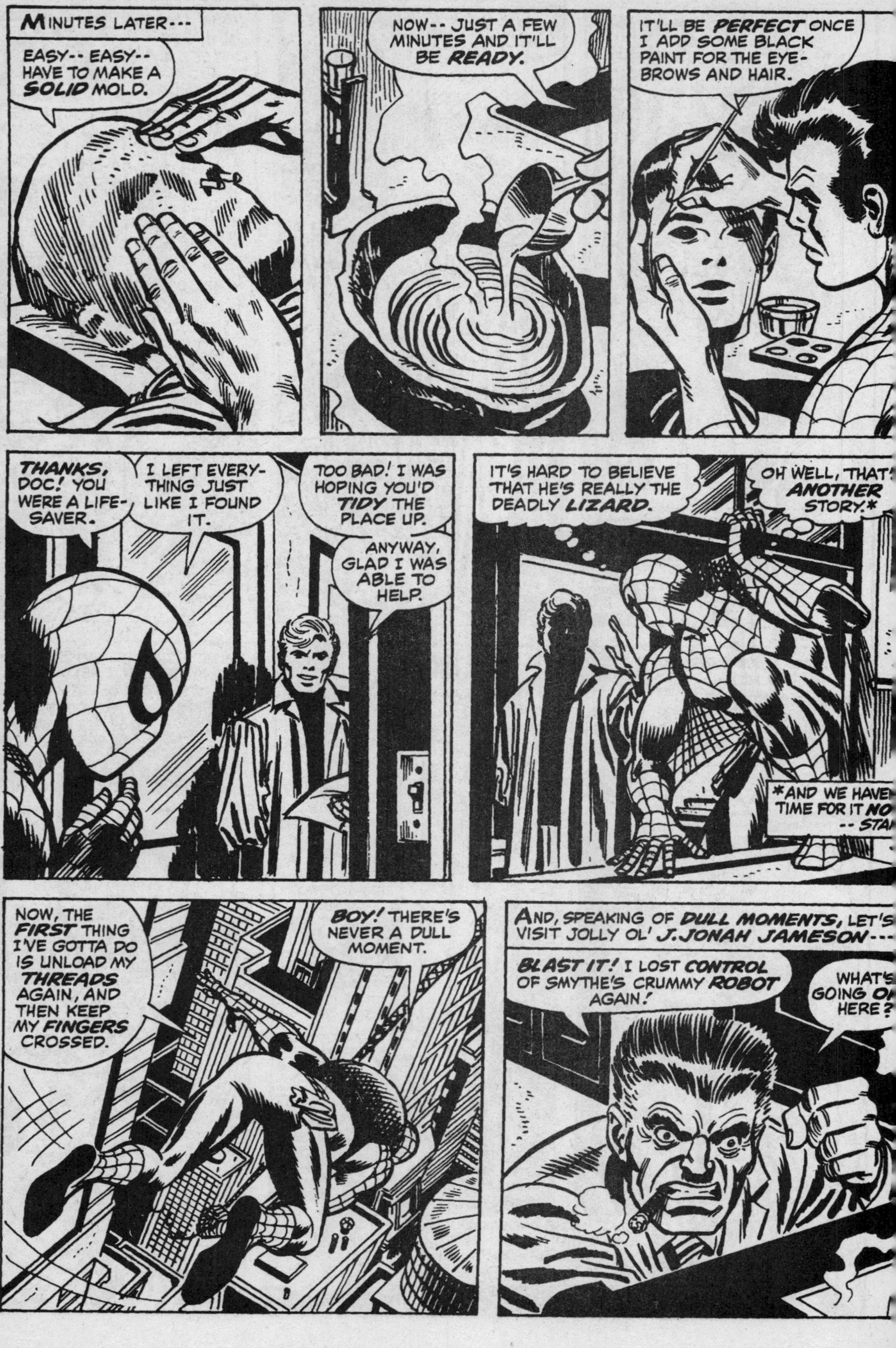
MINUTES LATER---
EASY-- EASY-- HAVE TO MAKE A SOLID MOLD.
NOW-- JUST A FEW MINUTES AND IT'LL BE READY.
IT'LL BE PERFECT ONCE I ADD SOME BLACK PAINT FOR THE EYE-BROWS AND HAIR.
THANKS, DOC! YOU WERE A LIFE-SAVER.
I LEFT EVERY-THING JUST LIKE I FOUND IT.
TOO BAD! I WAS HOPING YOU'D TIDY THE PLACE UP.
ANYWAY, GLAD I WAS ABLE TO HELP.
IT'S HARD TO BELIEVE THAT HE'S REALLY THE DEADLY LIZARD.
OH WELL, THAT'S ANOTHER STORY.*
*AND WE HAVE TIME FOR IT NO -- STA
NOW, THE FIRST THING I'VE GOTTA DO IS UNLOAD MY THREADS AGAIN, AND THEN KEEP MY FINGERS CROSSED.
BOY! THERE'S NEVER A DULL MOMENT.
AND, SPEAKING OF DULL MOMENTS, LET'S VISIT JOLLY OL' J. JONAH JAMESON---
BLAST IT! I LOST CONTROL OF SMYTHE'S CRUMMY ROBOT AGAIN!
WHAT'S GOING O HERE?

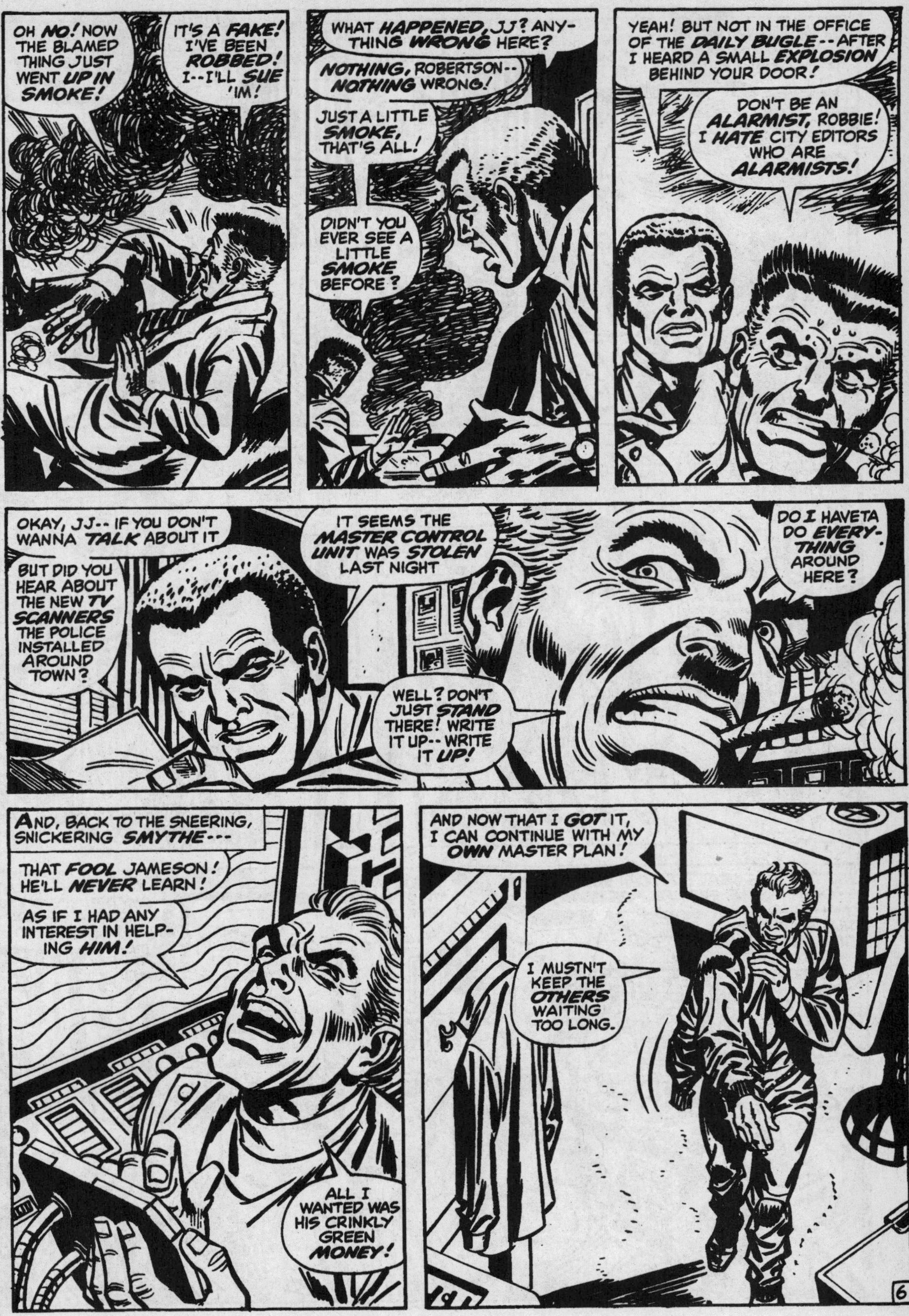
OH NO! NOW THE BLAMED THING JUST WENT UP IN SMOKE!
IT'S A FAKE! I'VE BEEN ROBBED! I--I'LL SUE 'IM!
WHAT HAPPENED, JJ? ANYTHING WRONG HERE?
NOTHING, ROBERTSON-- NOTHING WRONG!
JUST A LITTLE SMOKE, THAT'S ALL!
DIDN'T YOU EVER SEE A LITTLE SMOKE BEFORE?
YEAH! BUT NOT IN THE OFFICE OF THE DAILY BUGLE--AFTER I HEARD A SMALL EXPLOSION BEHIND YOUR DOOR!
DON'T BE AN ALARMIST, ROBBIE! I HATE CITY EDITORS WHO ARE ALARMISTS!
OKAY, JJ-- IF YOU DON'T WANNA TALK ABOUT IT
BUT DID YOU HEAR ABOUT THE NEW TV SCANNERS THE POLICE INSTALLED AROUND TOWN?
IT SEEMS THE MASTER CONTROL UNIT WAS STOLEN LAST NIGHT
DO I HAVETA DO EVERYTHING AROUND HERE?
WELL? DON'T JUST STAND THERE! WRITE IT UP-- WRITE IT UP!
AND, BACK TO THE SNEERING, SNICKERING SMYTHE---
THAT FOOL JAMESON! HE'LL NEVER LEARN!
AS IF I HAD ANY INTEREST IN HELPING HIM!
ALL I WANTED WAS HIS CRINKLY GREEN MONEY!
AND NOW THAT I GOT IT, I CAN CONTINUE WITH MY OWN MASTER PLAN!
I MUSTN'T KEEP THE OTHERS WAITING TOO LONG.
6

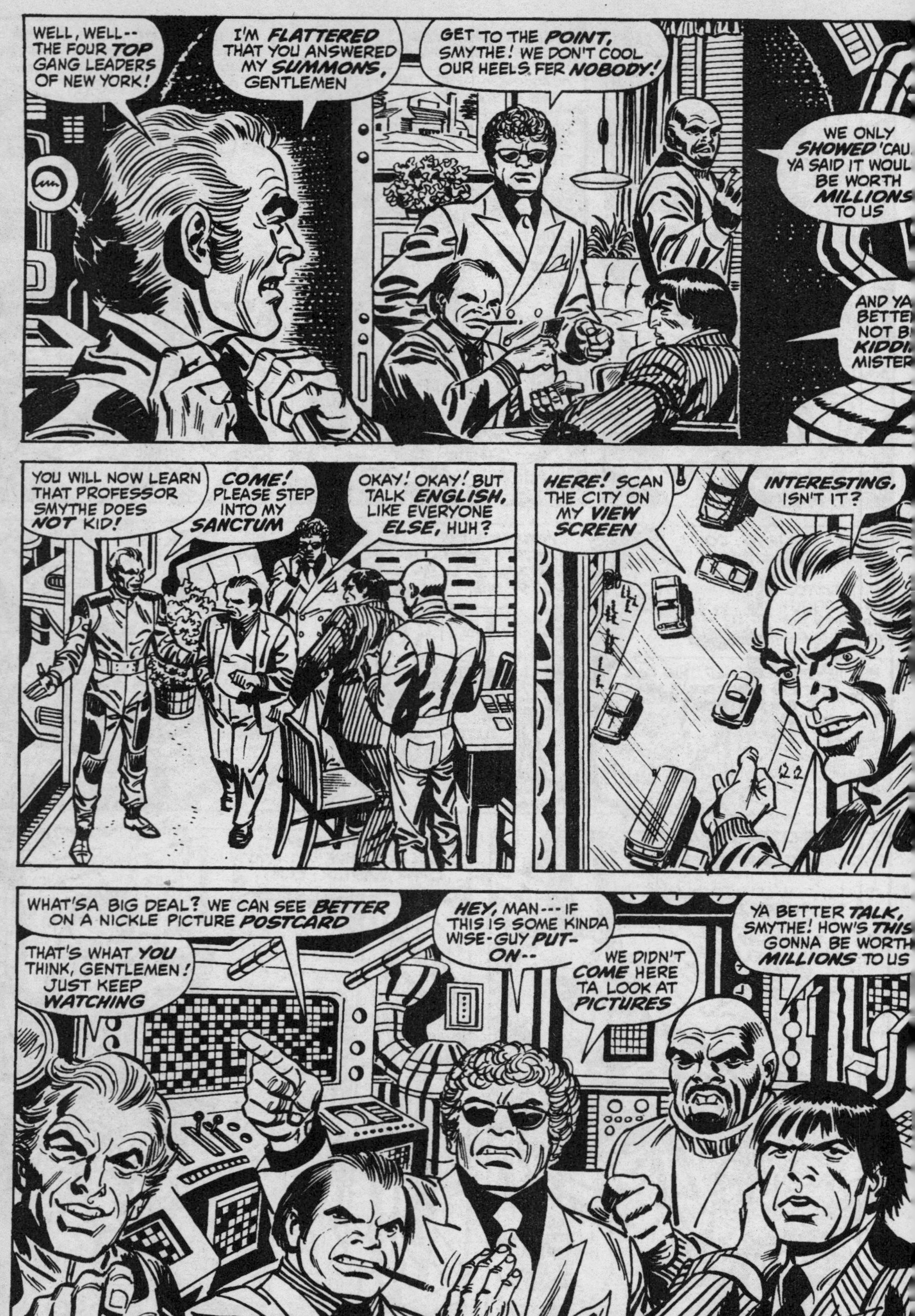

WELL, WELL-- THE FOUR TOP GANG LEADERS OF NEW YORK!
I'M FLATTERED THAT YOU ANSWERED MY SUMMONS, GENTLEMEN
GET TO THE POINT, SMYTHE! WE DON'T COOL OUR HEELS FER NOBODY!
WE ONLY SHOWED 'CAU YA SAID IT WOUL BE WORTH MILLIONS TO US
AND YA BETTE NOT B KIDDI MISTER
YOU WILL NOW LEARN THAT PROFESSOR SMYTHE DOES NOT KID!
COME! PLEASE STEP INTO MY SANCTUM
OKAY! OKAY! BUT TALK ENGLISH, LIKE EVERYONE ELSE, HUH?
HERE! SCAN THE CITY ON MY VIEW SCREEN
INTERESTING, ISN'T IT?
WHAT'SA BIG DEAL? WE CAN SEE BETTER ON A NICKLE PICTURE POSTCARD
THAT'S WHAT YOU THINK, GENTLEMEN! JUST KEEP WATCHING
HEY, MAN--- IF THIS IS SOME KINDA WISE-GUY PUT-ON--
WE DIDN'T COME HERE TA LOOK AT PICTURES
YA BETTER TALK, SMYTHE! HOW'S THIS GONNA BE WORTH MILLIONS TO US

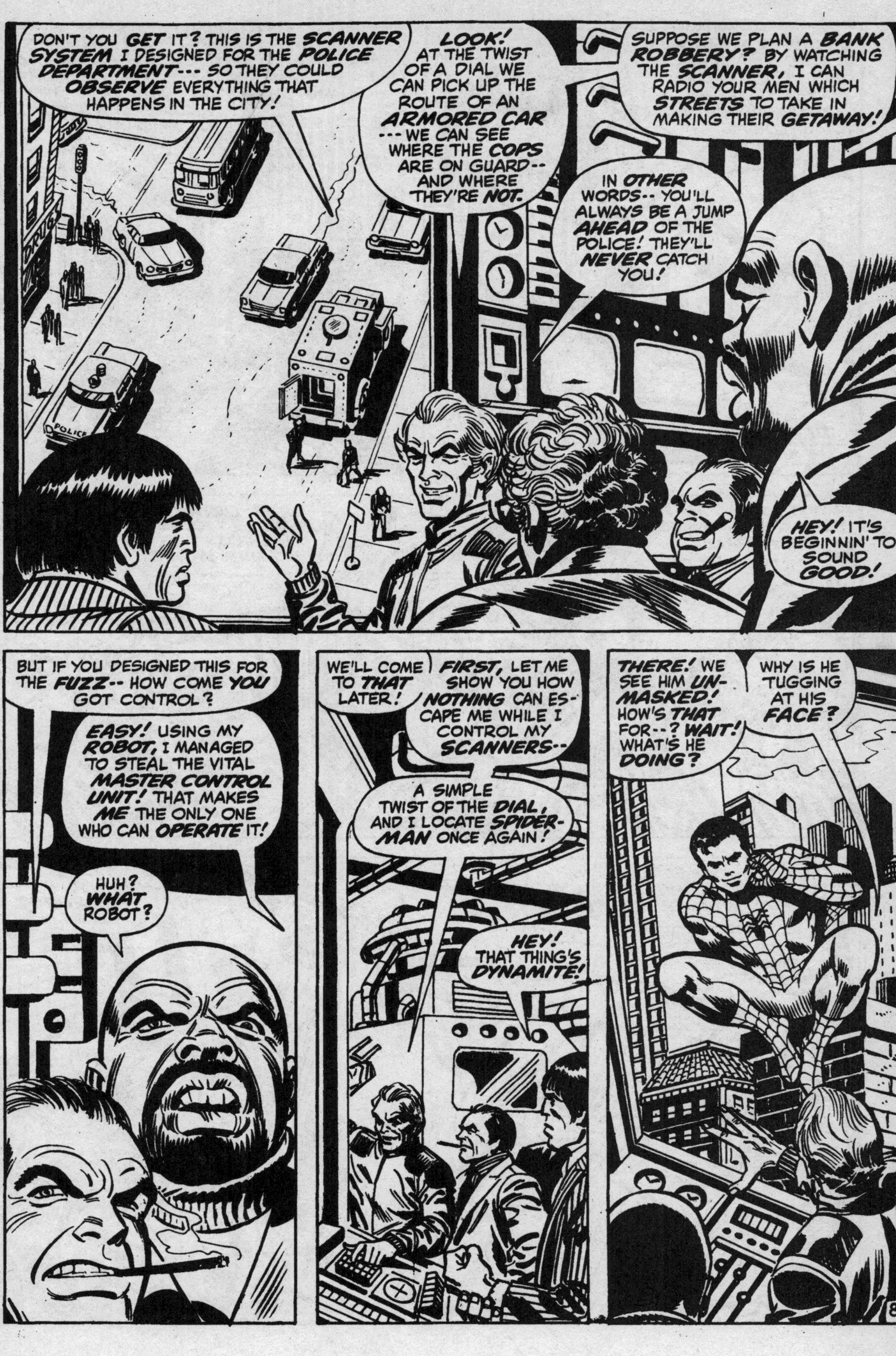

DON'T YOU GET IT? THIS IS THE SCANNER SYSTEM I DESIGNED FOR THE POLICE DEPARTMENT--- SO THEY COULD OBSERVE EVERYTHING THAT HAPPENS IN THE CITY!
LOOK! AT THE TWIST OF A DIAL WE CAN PICK UP THE ROUTE OF AN ARMORED CAR --- WE CAN SEE WHERE THE COPS ARE ON GUARD-- AND WHERE THEY'RE NOT.
SUPPOSE WE PLAN A BANK ROBBERY? BY WATCHING THE SCANNER, I CAN RADIO YOUR MEN WHICH STREETS TO TAKE IN MAKING THEIR GETAWAY!
IN OTHER WORDS-- YOU'LL ALWAYS BE A JUMP AHEAD OF THE POLICE! THEY'LL NEVER CATCH YOU!
HEY! IT'S BEGINNIN' TO SOUND GOOD!
BUT IF YOU DESIGNED THIS FOR THE FUZZ-- HOW COME YOU GOT CONTROL?
EASY! USING MY ROBOT, I MANAGED TO STEAL THE VITAL MASTER CONTROL UNIT! THAT MAKES ME THE ONLY ONE WHO CAN OPERATE IT!
HUH? WHAT ROBOT?
WE'LL COME TO THAT LATER!
FIRST, LET ME SHOW YOU HOW NOTHING CAN ES-CAPE ME WHILE I CONTROL MY SCANNERS--
A SIMPLE TWIST OF THE DIAL, AND I LOCATE SPIDER-MAN ONCE AGAIN!
HEY! THAT THING'S DYNAMITE!
THERE! WE SEE HIM UN-MASKED! HOW'S THAT FOR--? WAIT! WHAT'S HE DOING?
WHY IS HE TUGGING AT HIS FACE?
POLICE
DRUG

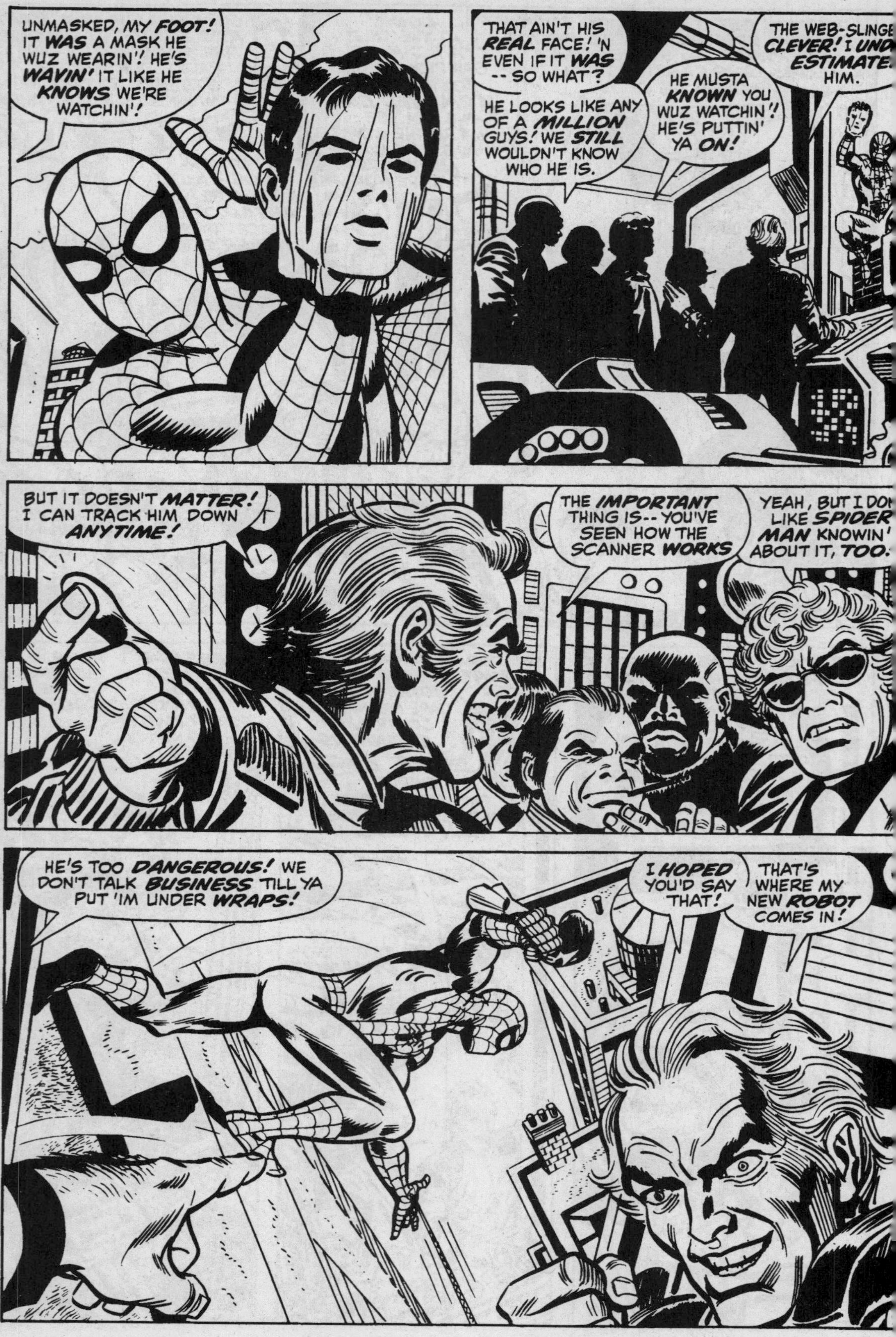
UNMASKED, MY FOOT! IT WAS A MASK HE WUZ WEARIN'! HE'S WAVIN' IT LIKE HE KNOWS WE'RE WATCHIN'!
THAT AIN'T HIS REAL FACE! 'N EVEN IF IT WAS -- SO WHAT?
HE LOOKS LIKE ANY OF A MILLION GUYS! WE STILL WOULDN'T KNOW WHO HE IS.
HE MUSTA KNOWN YOU WUZ WATCHIN'! HE'S PUTTIN' YA ON!
THE WEB-SLINGE CLEVER! I UND ESTIMATE HIM.
BUT IT DOESN'T MATTER! I CAN TRACK HIM DOWN ANYTIME!
THE IMPORTANT THING IS-- YOU'VE SEEN HOW THE SCANNER WORKS
YEAH, BUT I DO LIKE SPIDER MAN KNOWIN' ABOUT IT, TOO.
HE'S TOO DANGEROUS! WE DON'T TALK BUSINESS TILL YA PUT 'IM UNDER WRAPS!
I HOPED YOU'D SAY THAT!
THAT'S WHERE MY NEW ROBOT COMES IN!

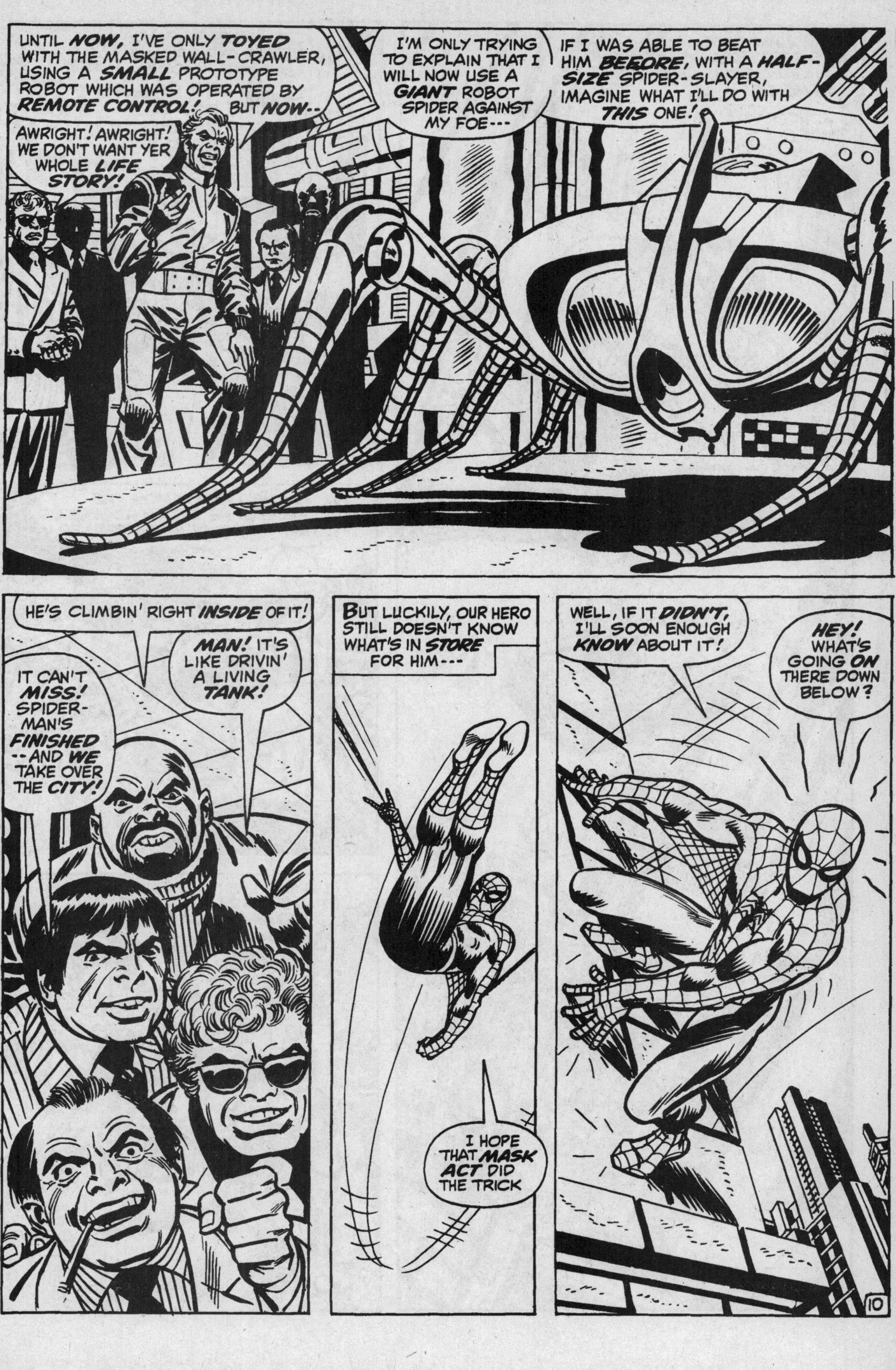
UNTIL NOW, I'VE ONLY TOYED WITH THE MASKED WALL-CRAWLER, USING A SMALL PROTOTYPE ROBOT WHICH WAS OPERATED BY REMOTE CONTROL! BUT NOW--
AWRIGHT! AWRIGHT! WE DON'T WANT YER WHOLE LIFE STORY!
I'M ONLY TRYING TO EXPLAIN THAT I WILL NOW USE A GIANT ROBOT SPIDER AGAINST MY FOE---
IF I WAS ABLE TO BEAT HIM BEFORE, WITH A HALF-SIZE SPIDER-SLAYER, IMAGINE WHAT I'LL DO WITH THIS ONE!
HE'S CLIMBIN' RIGHT INSIDE OF IT!
MAN! IT'S LIKE DRIVIN' A LIVING TANK!
IT CAN'T MISS! SPIDER-MAN'S FINISHED --AND WE TAKE OVER THE CITY!
BUT LUCKILY, OUR HERO STILL DOESN'T KNOW WHAT'S IN STORE FOR HIM---
I HOPE THAT MASK ACT DID THE TRICK
WELL, IF IT DIDN'T, I'LL SOON ENOUGH KNOW ABOUT IT!
HEY! WHAT'S GOING ON THERE DOWN BELOW?
10

THERE'S ANOTHER *PROTEST RALLY* IN FRONT OF THE *BUGLE!*

I WONDER WHAT *THIS* ONE'S ALL ABOUT?

DAILY BUGLE

NO BIG EARS

NO BIG BRO

NO BIG

WELL *WIGGLE MY WEBS* AND CALL ME *SHAKY*-- I CAN'T *BELIEVE* IT!

IT LOOKS LIKE JOLLY JONAH *HIMSELF* IS THE *LEADER* OF THE DEMONSTRATION!

NOW I GET IT! THEY'RE PROTESTING THE *TV SCANNERS* THAT THE POLICE HAVE INSTALLED

SPY 'EYES' VER CITY

DAILY BUGLE

SPY 'EYES' COVER CITY

I GUESS EVEN *J.J.* STILL BELIEVES IN *PRIVACY!*

NO SPIES IN THE SKY!

EYES ON AL

PRIVACY OR ELSE

NO BIG BRO THER

SOUL BROTHER NOT BIG BROTHER

WA UP

OKAY WHAT'RE YO *WAITING* FOR? STAR CHANTIN'

NO BIG

HEY, DAD-- IS THAT FOR *REAL?* OL' *JAMESON* LEADIN' THE PROTESTORS?

YOU BETTER *BELIEVE* IT, RANDY! HE'S A *BUG* ON CIVIL LIBERTIES

--'LONG AS THEY'RE NOT *SPIDER-MAN'S!*

I GUESS *NO ONE* LIKES BEING SPIED UPON-- EVEN IF THE *MOTIVES* ARE GOOD

WOW! I WISH I HAD LOADED MY *CAMERA!*

WHAT A *PICTURE*... JOE ROBERTSON'S SON, *RANDY,* SIDE-BY-SIDE WITH *J. JONAH* HIMSELF!

MAYBE I OUGHTTA SWING DOWN AND SAY HELLO

PRIVACY OR ELSE!

NO BIG BROTHER

WHAT THE HECK-- I'LL LEND THEM MY *MORAL* SUPPORT

RIGHT ON, GANG! I'M *WITH* YOU ALL THE WAY!

SPIDER-MAN!

STOP HIM! DON'T LET HIM *GET* ME!

STAY WAKE

PRIVACY OR ELSE!

NO BIG BROTHER JUST SOUL BROTHER

12

GET YOU? YOU GOTTA BE KIDDING, CHUCKLES! I WOULDN'T TAKE YOU ON A BET!

DON'T BE FLIP WITH ME, PIN-BALL-HEAD!

YOUR DAYS ARE NUMBERED.. AND WE BOTH KNOW IT!

YOU MAY HAVE ESCAPED SMYTHE'S ROBOT LAST TIME, BUT---

AH HAH! I WAS RIGHT! YOU AND THAT SKUNK SMYTHE WERE BEHIND THE ATTACK ON ME!

NO BIG BROTHER!

PRIVACY OR ELSE!

YOU CAN SAY THAT AGAIN!

WHEN YOU FINALLY GET IT, YOU CREEP, I WANT ALL THE CREDIT THAT'S DUE ME!

I'M WITH YOU ALL THE WAY, SWEETIE

I WANT YOU TO GET WHAT'S DUE YOU, TOO!

AND IF I HAVE MY WAY, ONE OF THESE DAYS YOU WILL!

NUTS! WHY DO I EVEN WASTE MY BREATH ON THIS REFUGEE FROM A FUNNY FARM!

I'VE GOT LOTS BIGGER FISH TO FRY!

DON'T LET HIM GET AWAY! CATCH HIM! STOP HIM!

GLAD TO, JAMESON! JUST TELL US HOW

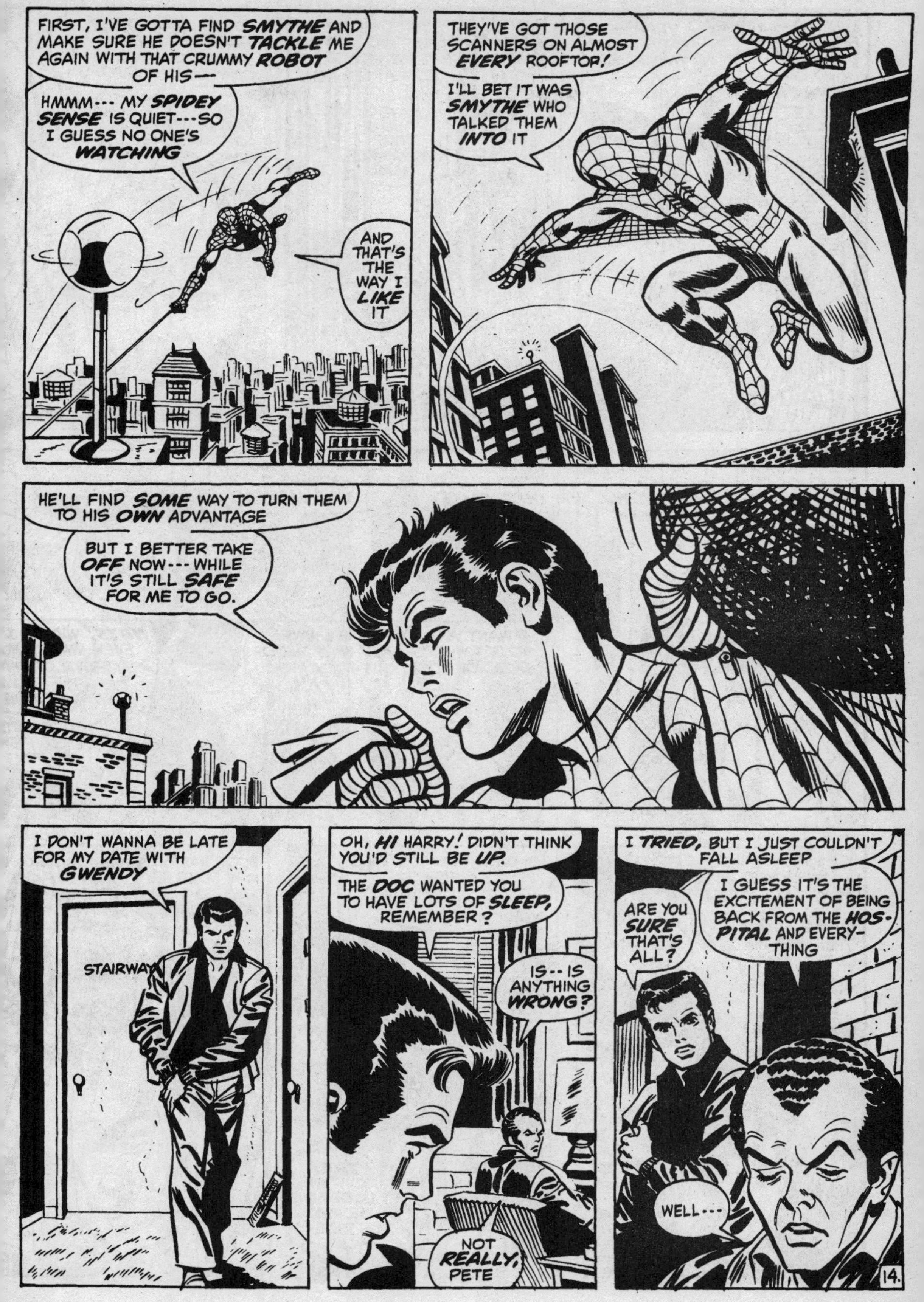
FIRST, I'VE GOTTA FIND SMYTHE AND MAKE SURE HE DOESN'T TACKLE ME AGAIN WITH THAT CRUMMY ROBOT OF HIS---
HMMM--- MY SPIDEY SENSE IS QUIET---SO I GUESS NO ONE'S WATCHING
AND THAT'S THE WAY I LIKE IT
THEY'VE GOT THOSE SCANNERS ON ALMOST EVERY ROOFTOP!
I'LL BET IT WAS SMYTHE WHO TALKED THEM INTO IT
HE'LL FIND SOME WAY TO TURN THEM TO HIS OWN ADVANTAGE
BUT I BETTER TAKE OFF NOW--- WHILE IT'S STILL SAFE FOR ME TO GO.
I DON'T WANNA BE LATE FOR MY DATE WITH GWENDY
STAIRWAY
OH, HI HARRY! DIDN'T THINK YOU'D STILL BE UP.
THE DOC WANTED YOU TO HAVE LOTS OF SLEEP, REMEMBER?
IS--IS ANYTHING WRONG?
NOT REALLY, PETE
I TRIED, BUT I JUST COULDN'T FALL ASLEEP
I GUESS IT'S THE EXCITEMENT OF BEING BACK FROM THE HOS-PITAL AND EVERY-THING
ARE YOU SURE THAT'S ALL?
WELL---
14.

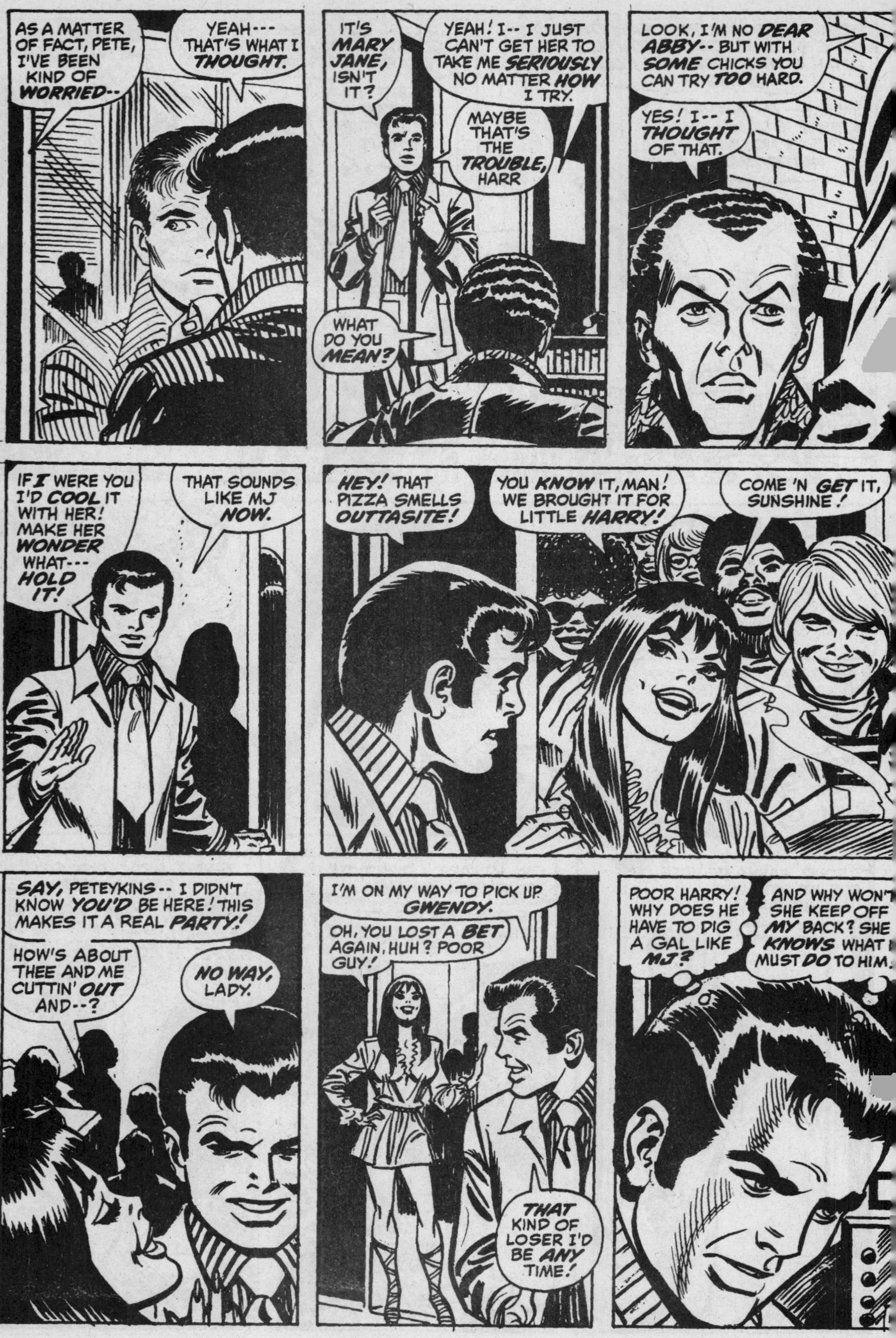
AS A MATTER OF FACT, PETE, I'VE BEEN KIND OF WORRIED--
YEAH--- THAT'S WHAT I THOUGHT.
IT'S MARY JANE, ISN'T IT?
YEAH! I-- I JUST CAN'T GET HER TO TAKE ME SERIOUSLY NO MATTER HOW I TRY.
MAYBE THAT'S THE TROUBLE, HARR
WHAT DO YOU MEAN?
LOOK, I'M NO DEAR ABBY-- BUT WITH SOME CHICKS YOU CAN TRY TOO HARD.
YES! I-- I THOUGHT OF THAT.
IF I WERE YOU I'D COOL IT WITH HER! MAKE HER WONDER WHAT--- HOLD IT!
THAT SOUNDS LIKE MJ NOW.
HEY! THAT PIZZA SMELLS OUTTASITE!
YOU KNOW IT, MAN! WE BROUGHT IT FOR LITTLE HARRY!
COME 'N GET IT, SUNSHINE!
SAY, PETEYKINS-- I DIDN'T KNOW YOU'D BE HERE! THIS MAKES IT A REAL PARTY!
HOW'S ABOUT THEE AND ME CUTTIN' OUT AND--?
NO WAY, LADY.
I'M ON MY WAY TO PICK UP GWENDY.
OH, YOU LOST A BET AGAIN, HUH? POOR GUY!
THAT KIND OF LOSER I'D BE ANY TIME!
POOR HARRY! WHY DOES HE HAVE TO DIG A GAL LIKE MJ?
AND WHY WON'T SHE KEEP OFF MY BACK? SHE KNOWS WHAT I MUST DO TO HIM.

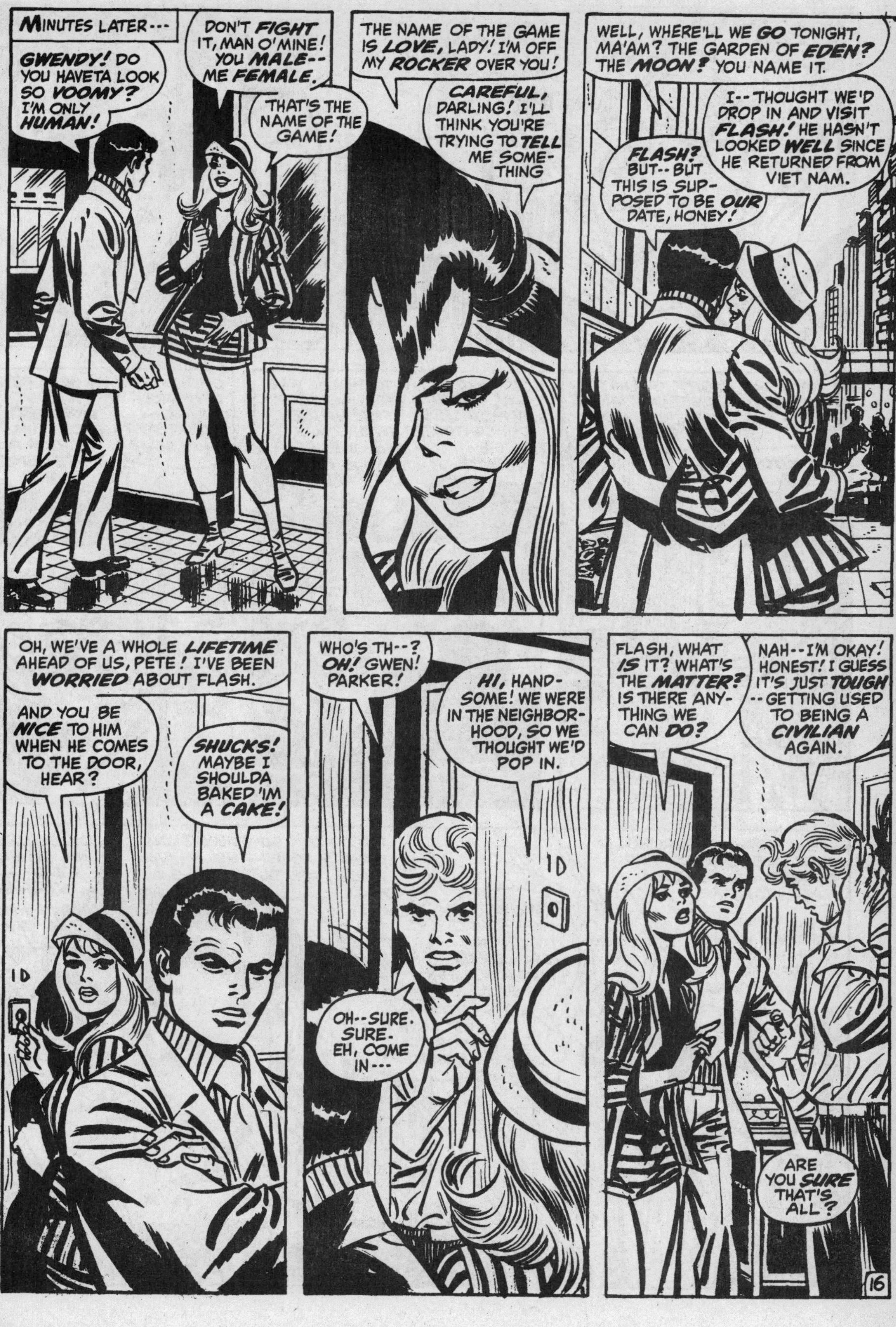
MINUTES LATER---
GWENDY! DO YOU HAVETA LOOK SO VOOMY? I'M ONLY HUMAN!
DON'T FIGHT IT, MAN O'MINE! YOU MALE-- ME FEMALE.
THAT'S THE NAME OF THE GAME!
THE NAME OF THE GAME IS LOVE, LADY! I'M OFF MY ROCKER OVER YOU!
CAREFUL, DARLING! I'LL THINK YOU'RE TRYING TO TELL ME SOME-THING
WELL, WHERE'LL WE GO TONIGHT, MA'AM? THE GARDEN OF EDEN? THE MOON? YOU NAME IT.
I--THOUGHT WE'D DROP IN AND VISIT FLASH! HE HASN'T LOOKED WELL SINCE HE RETURNED FROM VIET NAM.
FLASH? BUT--BUT THIS IS SUP-POSED TO BE OUR DATE, HONEY!
OH, WE'VE A WHOLE LIFETIME AHEAD OF US, PETE! I'VE BEEN WORRIED ABOUT FLASH.
AND YOU BE NICE TO HIM WHEN HE COMES TO THE DOOR, HEAR?
SHUCKS! MAYBE I SHOULDA BAKED 'IM A CAKE!
1D
WHO'S TH--? OH! GWEN! PARKER!
HI, HAND-SOME! WE WERE IN THE NEIGHBOR-HOOD, SO WE THOUGHT WE'D POP IN.
1D
OH--SURE. SURE. EH, COME IN---
FLASH, WHAT IS IT? WHAT'S THE MATTER? IS THERE ANY-THING WE CAN DO?
NAH--I'M OKAY! HONEST! I GUESS IT'S JUST TOUGH --GETTING USED TO BEING A CIVILIAN AGAIN.
ARE YOU SURE THAT'S ALL?
16

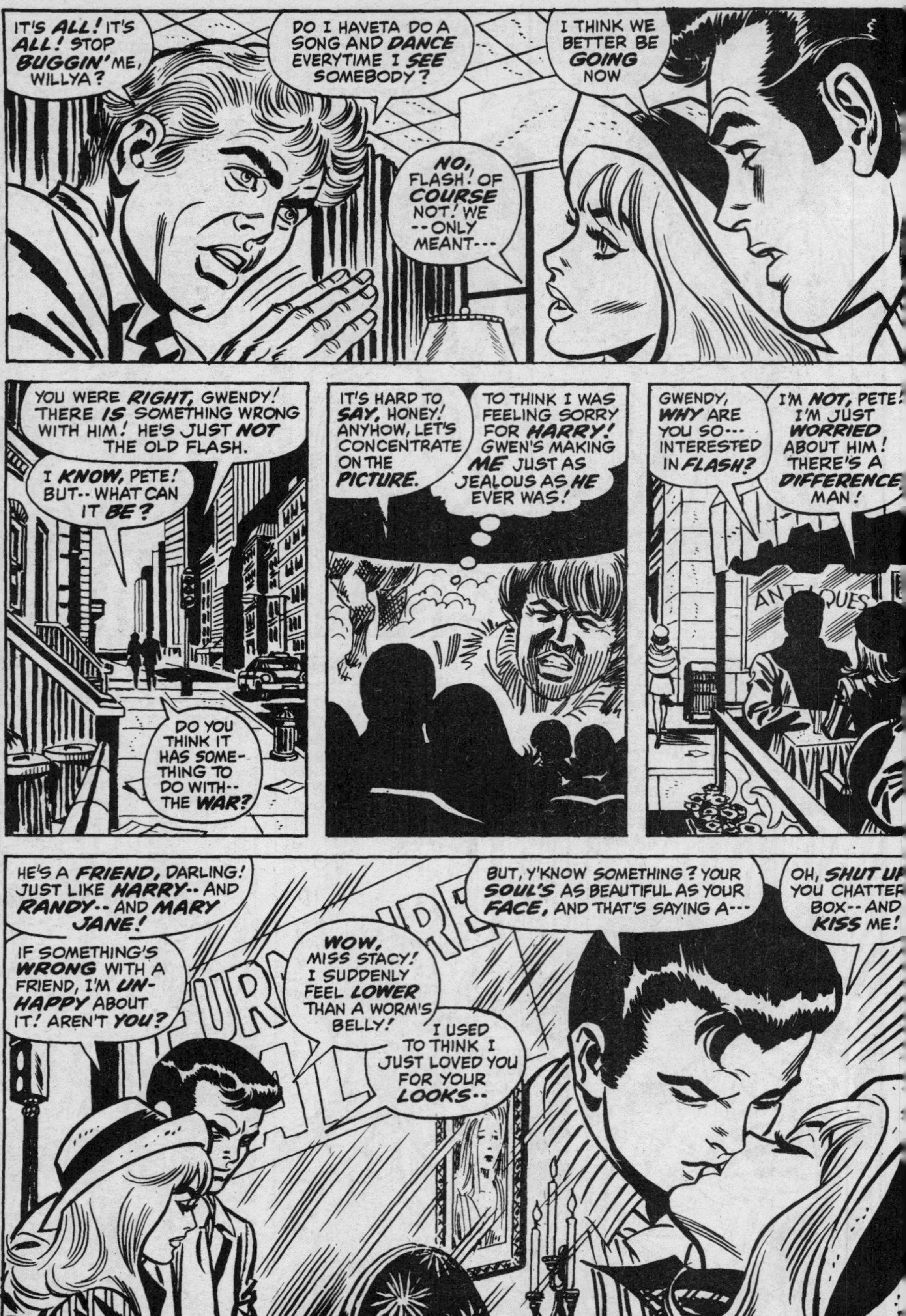
IT'S ALL! IT'S ALL! STOP BUGGIN' ME, WILLYA?
DO I HAVETA DO A SONG AND DANCE EVERYTIME I SEE SOMEBODY?
I THINK WE BETTER BE GOING NOW
NO, FLASH! OF COURSE NOT! WE --ONLY MEANT---
YOU WERE RIGHT, GWENDY! THERE IS SOMETHING WRONG WITH HIM! HE'S JUST NOT THE OLD FLASH.
I KNOW, PETE! BUT-- WHAT CAN IT BE?
DO YOU THINK IT HAS SOMETHING TO DO WITH-- THE WAR?
IT'S HARD TO SAY, HONEY! ANYHOW, LET'S CONCENTRATE ON THE PICTURE.
TO THINK I WAS FEELING SORRY FOR HARRY! GWEN'S MAKING ME JUST AS JEALOUS AS HE EVER WAS!
GWENDY, WHY ARE YOU SO--- INTERESTED IN FLASH?
I'M NOT, PETE! I'M JUST WORRIED ABOUT HIM! THERE'S A DIFFERENCE MAN!
ANTIQUES
HE'S A FRIEND, DARLING! JUST LIKE HARRY-- AND RANDY-- AND MARY JANE!
IF SOMETHING'S WRONG WITH A FRIEND, I'M UNHAPPY ABOUT IT! AREN'T YOU?
WOW, MISS STACY! I SUDDENLY FEEL LOWER THAN A WORM'S BELLY!
I USED TO THINK I JUST LOVED YOU FOR YOUR LOOKS--
BUT, Y'KNOW SOMETHING? YOUR SOUL'S AS BEAUTIFUL AS YOUR FACE, AND THAT'S SAYING A---
OH, SHUT UP YOU CHATTER BOX-- AND KISS ME!

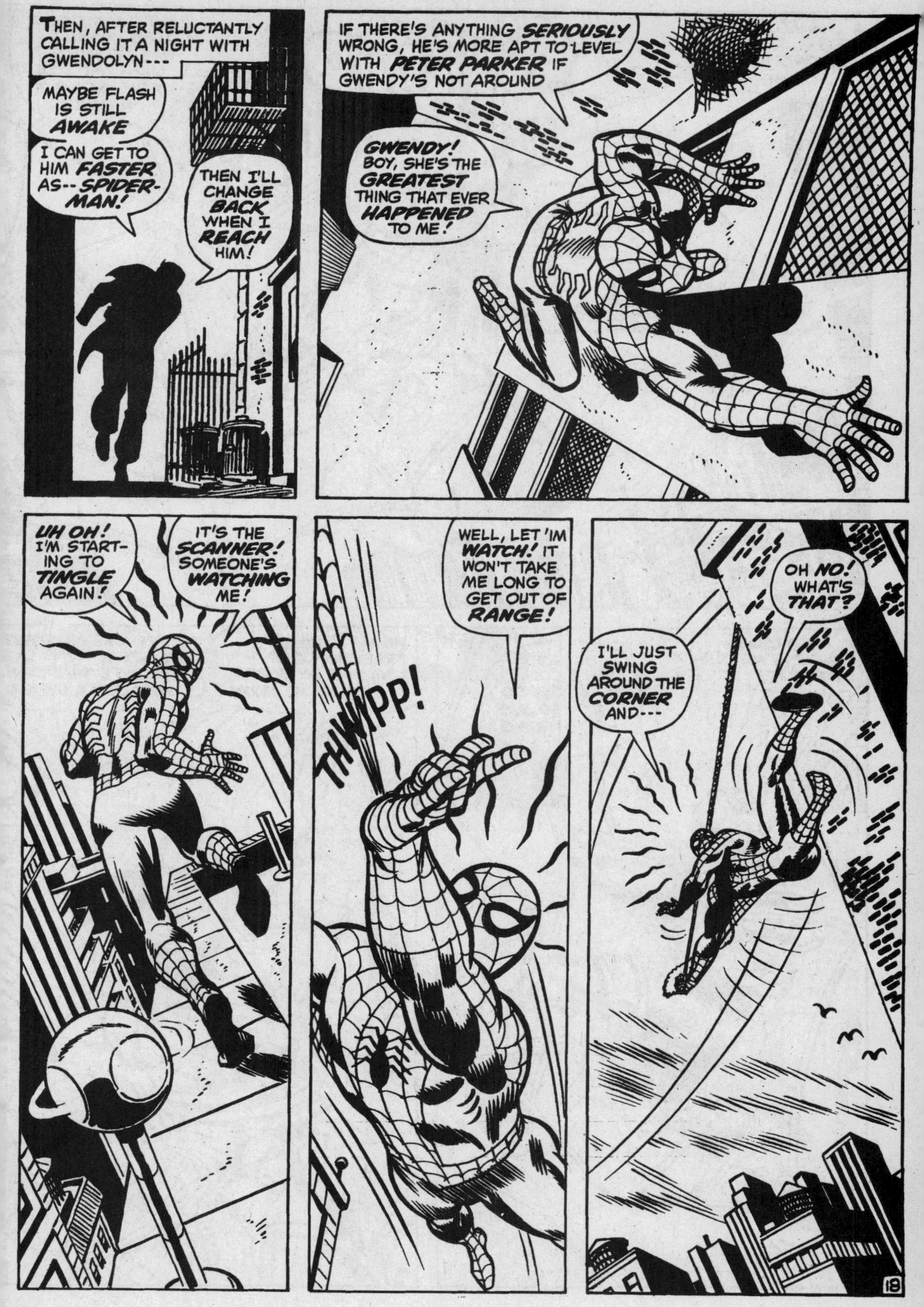
THEN, AFTER RELUCTANTLY CALLING IT A NIGHT WITH GWENDOLYN---
MAYBE FLASH IS STILL AWAKE
I CAN GET TO HIM FASTER AS--SPIDER-MAN!
THEN I'LL CHANGE BACK WHEN I REACH HIM!
IF THERE'S ANYTHING SERIOUSLY WRONG, HE'S MORE APT TO LEVEL WITH PETER PARKER IF GWENDY'S NOT AROUND
GWENDY! BOY, SHE'S THE GREATEST THING THAT EVER HAPPENED TO ME!
UH OH! I'M STARTING TO TINGLE AGAIN!
IT'S THE SCANNER! SOMEONE'S WATCHING ME!
WELL, LET 'IM WATCH! IT WON'T TAKE ME LONG TO GET OUT OF RANGE!
THWIPP!
I'LL JUST SWING AROUND THE CORNER AND---
OH NO! WHAT'S THAT?
18

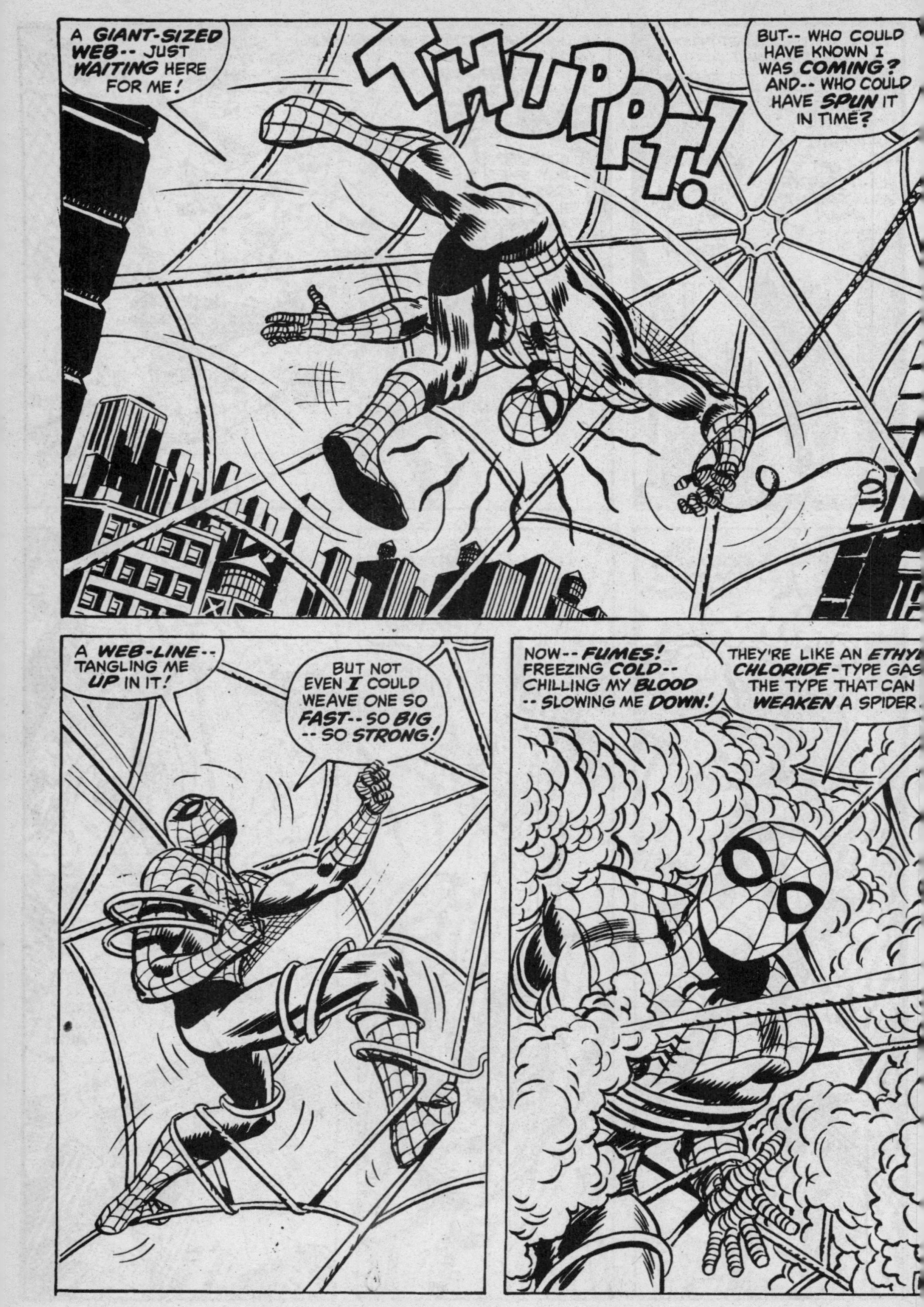
A GIANT-SIZED WEB-- JUST WAITING HERE FOR ME!
THUPPT!
BUT-- WHO COULD HAVE KNOWN I WAS COMING? AND-- WHO COULD HAVE SPUN IT IN TIME?
A WEB-LINE-- TANGLING ME UP IN IT!
BUT NOT EVEN I COULD WEAVE ONE SO FAST-- SO BIG -- SO STRONG!
NOW-- FUMES! FREEZING COLD-- CHILLING MY BLOOD -- SLOWING ME DOWN!
THEY'RE LIKE AN ETHY CHLORIDE-TYPE GAS THE TYPE THAT CAN WEAKEN A SPIDER

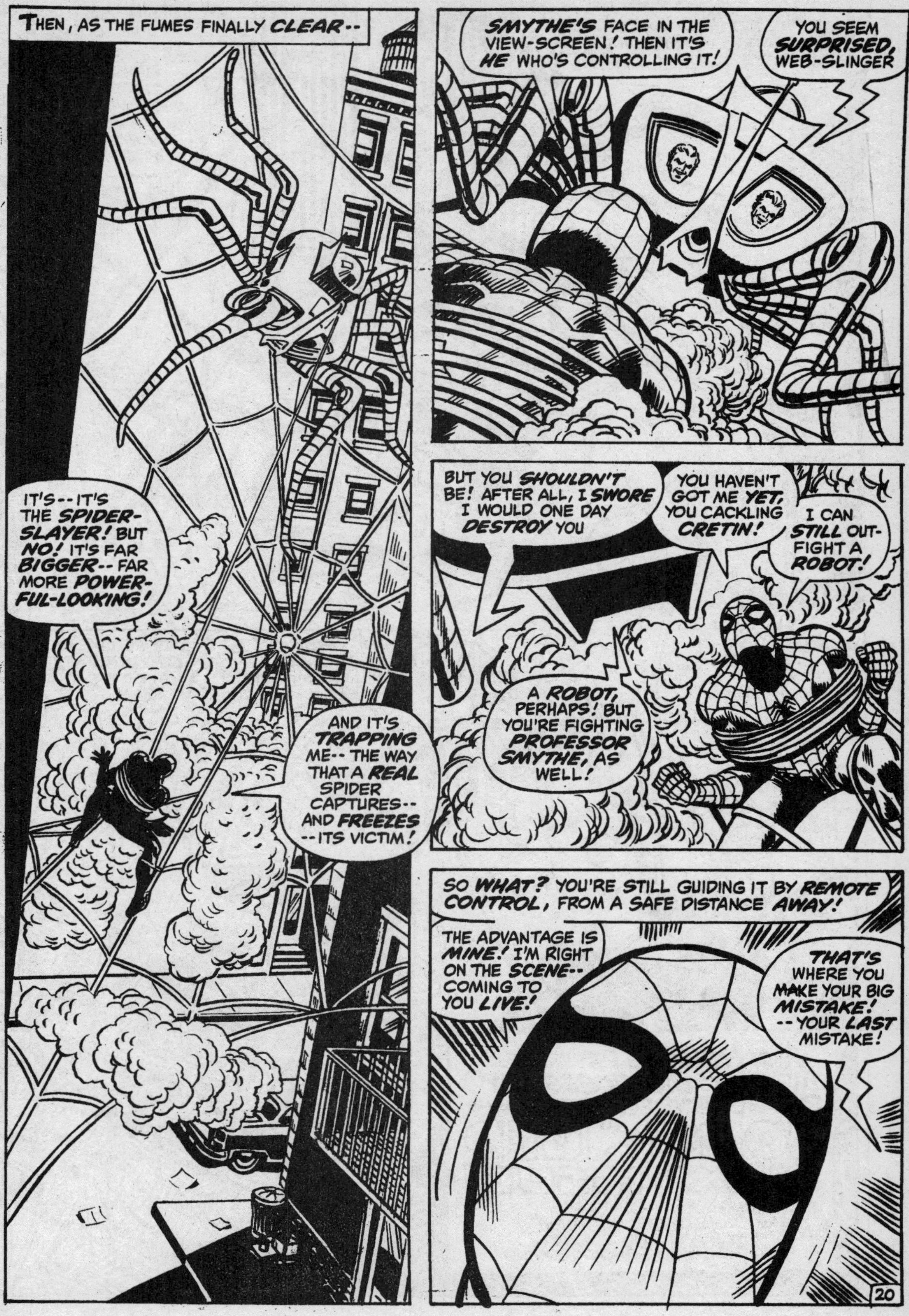
THEN, AS THE FUMES FINALLY CLEAR--
IT'S--IT'S THE SPIDER-SLAYER! BUT NO! IT'S FAR BIGGER--FAR MORE POWERFUL-LOOKING!
AND IT'S TRAPPING ME--THE WAY THAT A REAL SPIDER CAPTURES--AND FREEZES--ITS VICTIM!
SMYTHE'S FACE IN THE VIEW-SCREEN! THEN IT'S HE WHO'S CONTROLLING IT!
YOU SEEM SURPRISED, WEB-SLINGER
BUT YOU SHOULDN'T BE! AFTER ALL, I SWORE I WOULD ONE DAY DESTROY YOU
YOU HAVEN'T GOT ME YET, YOU CACKLING CRETIN!
I CAN STILL OUT-FIGHT A ROBOT!
A ROBOT, PERHAPS! BUT YOU'RE FIGHTING PROFESSOR SMYTHE, AS WELL!
SO WHAT? YOU'RE STILL GUIDING IT BY REMOTE CONTROL, FROM A SAFE DISTANCE AWAY!
THE ADVANTAGE IS MINE! I'M RIGHT ON THE SCENE--COMING TO YOU LIVE!
THAT'S WHERE YOU MAKE YOUR BIG MISTAKE! --YOUR LAST MISTAKE!
20

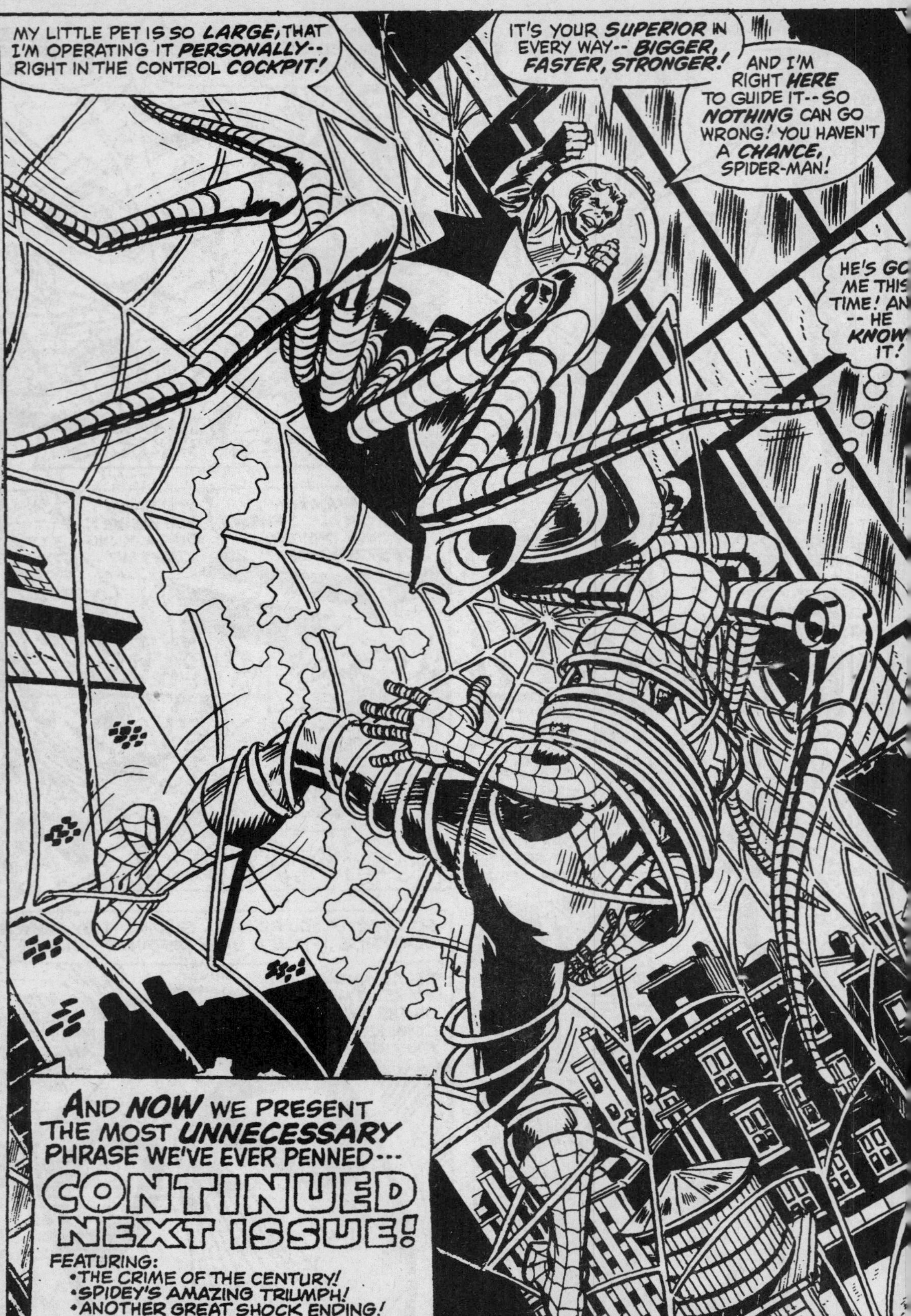
MY LITTLE PET IS SO LARGE, THAT I'M OPERATING IT PERSONALLY-- RIGHT IN THE CONTROL COCKPIT!
IT'S YOUR SUPERIOR IN EVERY WAY-- BIGGER, FASTER, STRONGER!
AND I'M RIGHT HERE TO GUIDE IT--SO NOTHING CAN GO WRONG! YOU HAVEN'T A CHANCE, SPIDER-MAN!
HE'S GO ME THIS TIME! AN -- HE KNOW IT!
AND NOW WE PRESENT THE MOST UNNECESSARY PHRASE WE'VE EVER PENNED---
CONTINUED NEXT ISSUE!
FEATURING:
•THE CRIME OF THE CENTURY!
•SPIDEY'S AMAZING TRIUMPH!
•ANOTHER GREAT SHOCK ENDING!

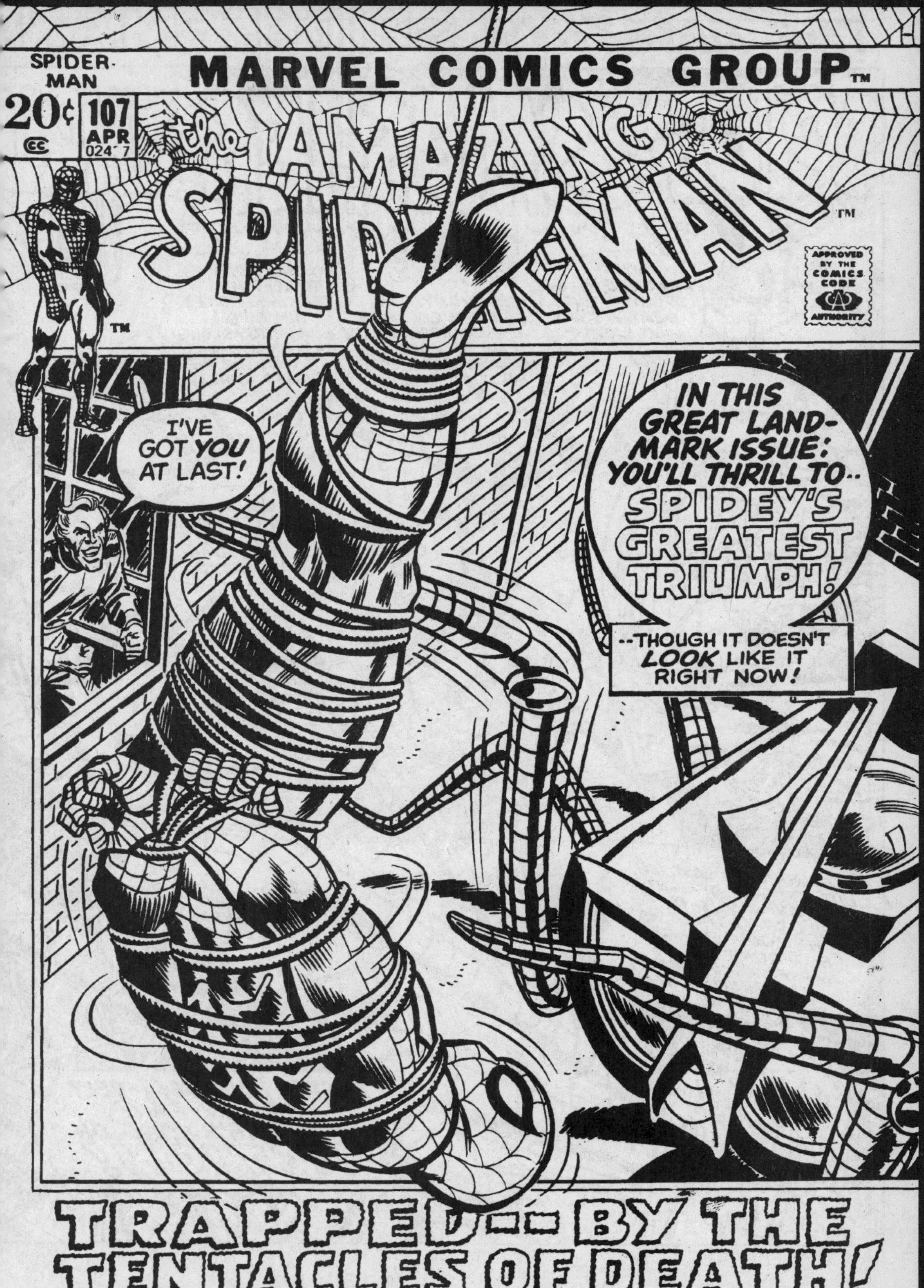
SPIDER-MAN
MARVEL COMICS GROUP™
20¢ 107 APR 02447
the AMAZING SPIDER-MAN™
APPROVED BY THE COMICS CODE AUTHORITY
I'VE GOT YOU AT LAST!
IN THIS GREAT LAND-MARK ISSUE: YOU'LL THRILL TO.. SPIDEY'S GREATEST TRIUMPH!
--THOUGH IT DOESN'T LOOK LIKE IT RIGHT NOW!
TRAPPED-- BY THE TENTACLES OF DEATH!

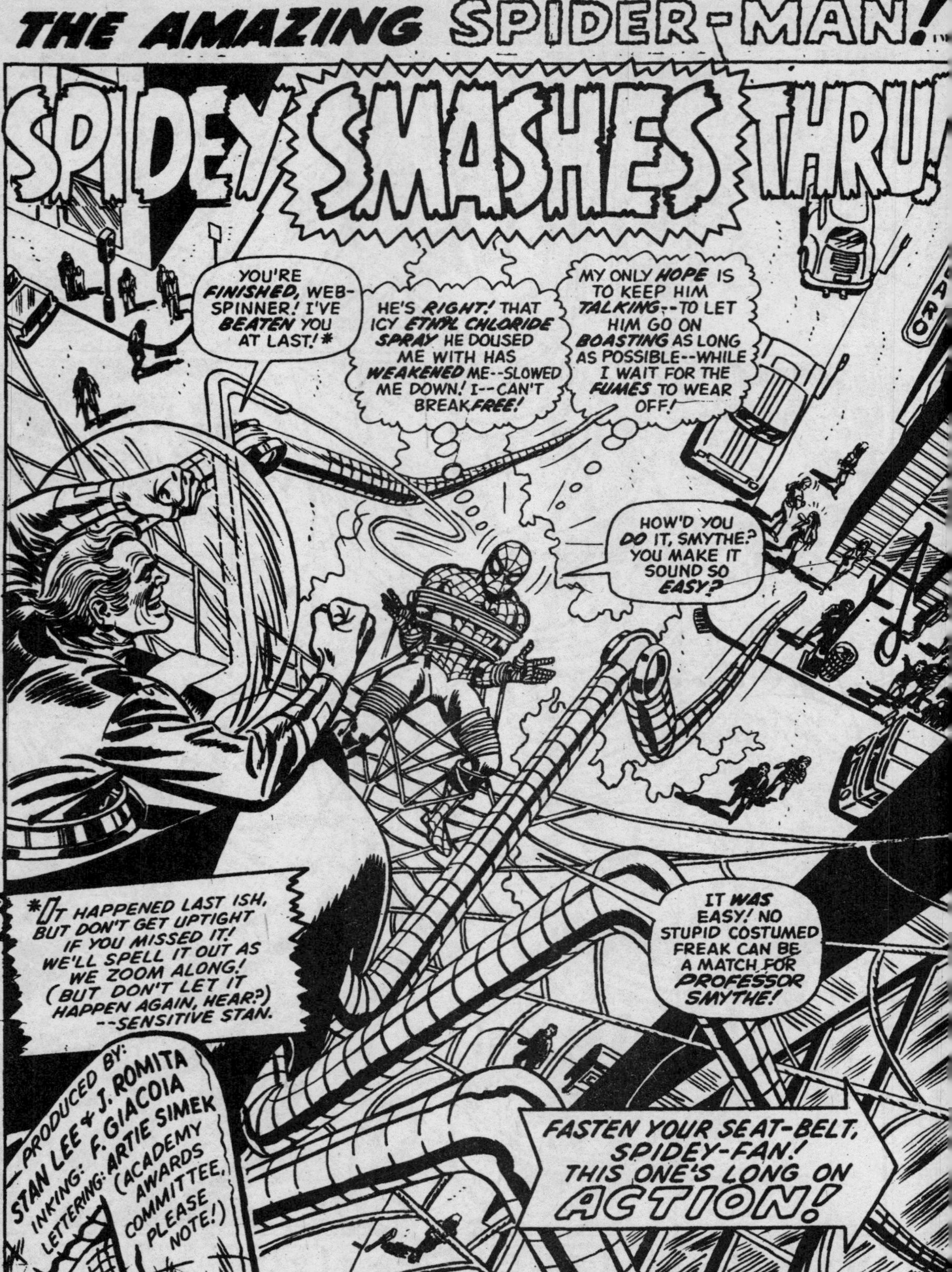

THE AMAZING SPIDER-MAN!
SPIDEY SMASHES THRU!
YOU'RE FINISHED, WEB-SPINNER! I'VE BEATEN YOU AT LAST!*
HE'S RIGHT! THAT ICY ETHYL CHLORIDE SPRAY HE DOUSED ME WITH HAS WEAKENED ME--SLOWED ME DOWN! I--CAN'T BREAK FREE!
MY ONLY HOPE IS TO KEEP HIM TALKING--TO LET HIM GO ON BOASTING AS LONG AS POSSIBLE--WHILE I WAIT FOR THE FUMES TO WEAR OFF!
HOW'D YOU DO IT, SMYTHE? YOU MAKE IT SOUND SO EASY?
IT WAS EASY! NO STUPID COSTUMED FREAK CAN BE A MATCH FOR PROFESSOR SMYTHE!
*IT HAPPENED LAST ISH, BUT DON'T GET UPTIGHT IF YOU MISSED IT! WE'LL SPELL IT OUT AS WE ZOOM ALONG! (BUT DON'T LET IT HAPPEN AGAIN, HEAR?) --SENSITIVE STAN.
PRODUCED BY: STAN LEE & J. ROMITA INKING: F. GIACOIA LETTERING: ARTIE SIMEK (ACADEMY AWARDS COMMITTEE, PLEASE NOTE!)
FASTEN YOUR SEAT-BELT, SPIDEY-FAN! THIS ONE'S LONG ON ACTION!

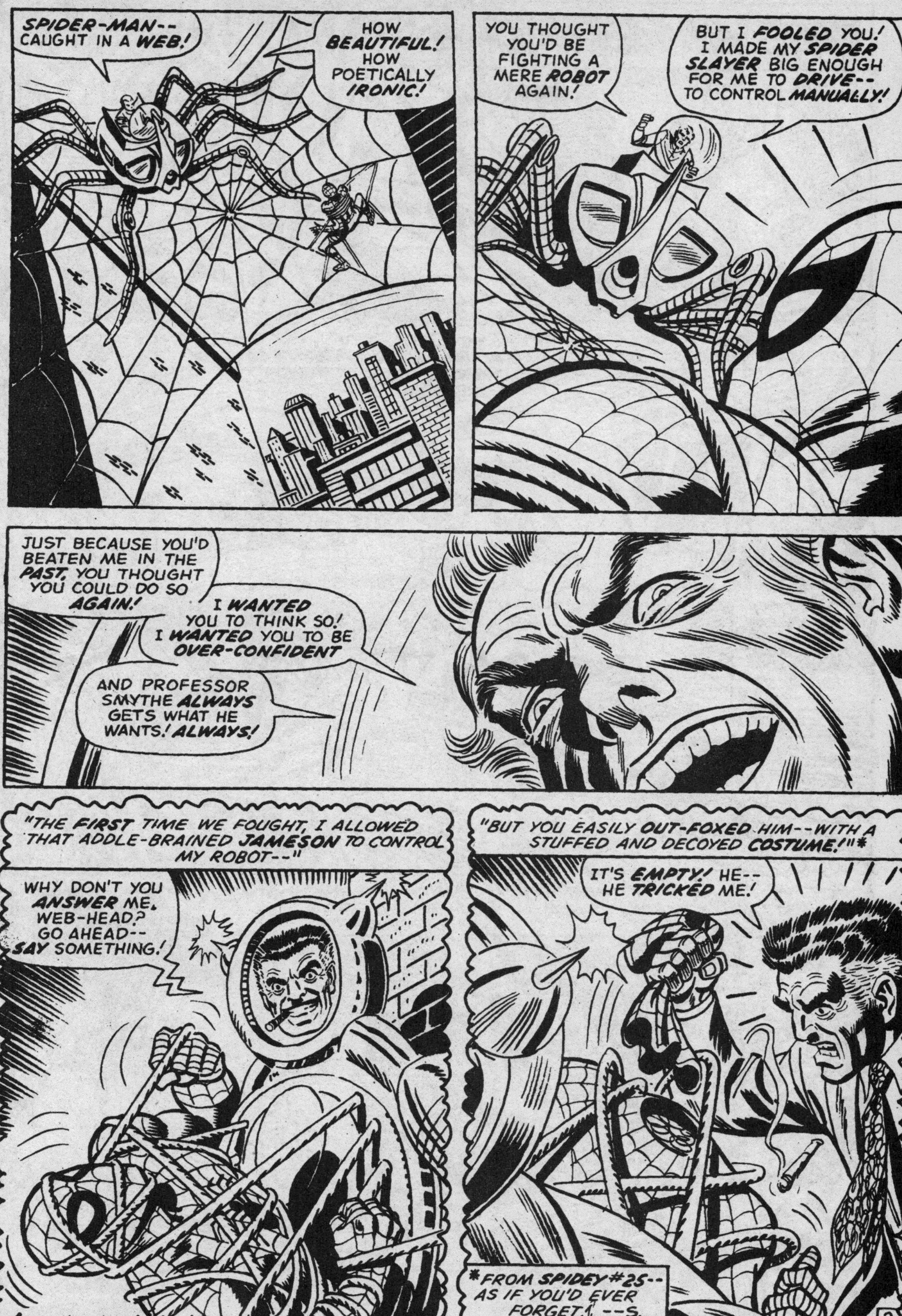
SPIDER-MAN-- CAUGHT IN A WEB!
HOW BEAUTIFUL! HOW POETICALLY IRONIC!
YOU THOUGHT YOU'D BE FIGHTING A MERE ROBOT AGAIN!
BUT I FOOLED YOU! I MADE MY SPIDER SLAYER BIG ENOUGH FOR ME TO DRIVE-- TO CONTROL MANUALLY!
JUST BECAUSE YOU'D BEATEN ME IN THE PAST, YOU THOUGHT YOU COULD DO SO AGAIN!
I WANTED YOU TO THINK SO! I WANTED YOU TO BE OVER-CONFIDENT
AND PROFESSOR SMYTHE ALWAYS GETS WHAT HE WANTS! ALWAYS!
"THE FIRST TIME WE FOUGHT, I ALLOWED THAT ADDLE-BRAINED JAMESON TO CONTROL MY ROBOT--"
WHY DON'T YOU ANSWER ME, WEB-HEAD? GO AHEAD-- SAY SOMETHING!
"BUT YOU EASILY OUT-FOXED HIM--WITH A STUFFED AND DECOYED COSTUME!"*
IT'S EMPTY! HE-- HE TRICKED ME!
*FROM SPIDEY #25-- AS IF YOU'D EVER FORGET.! --S.
2

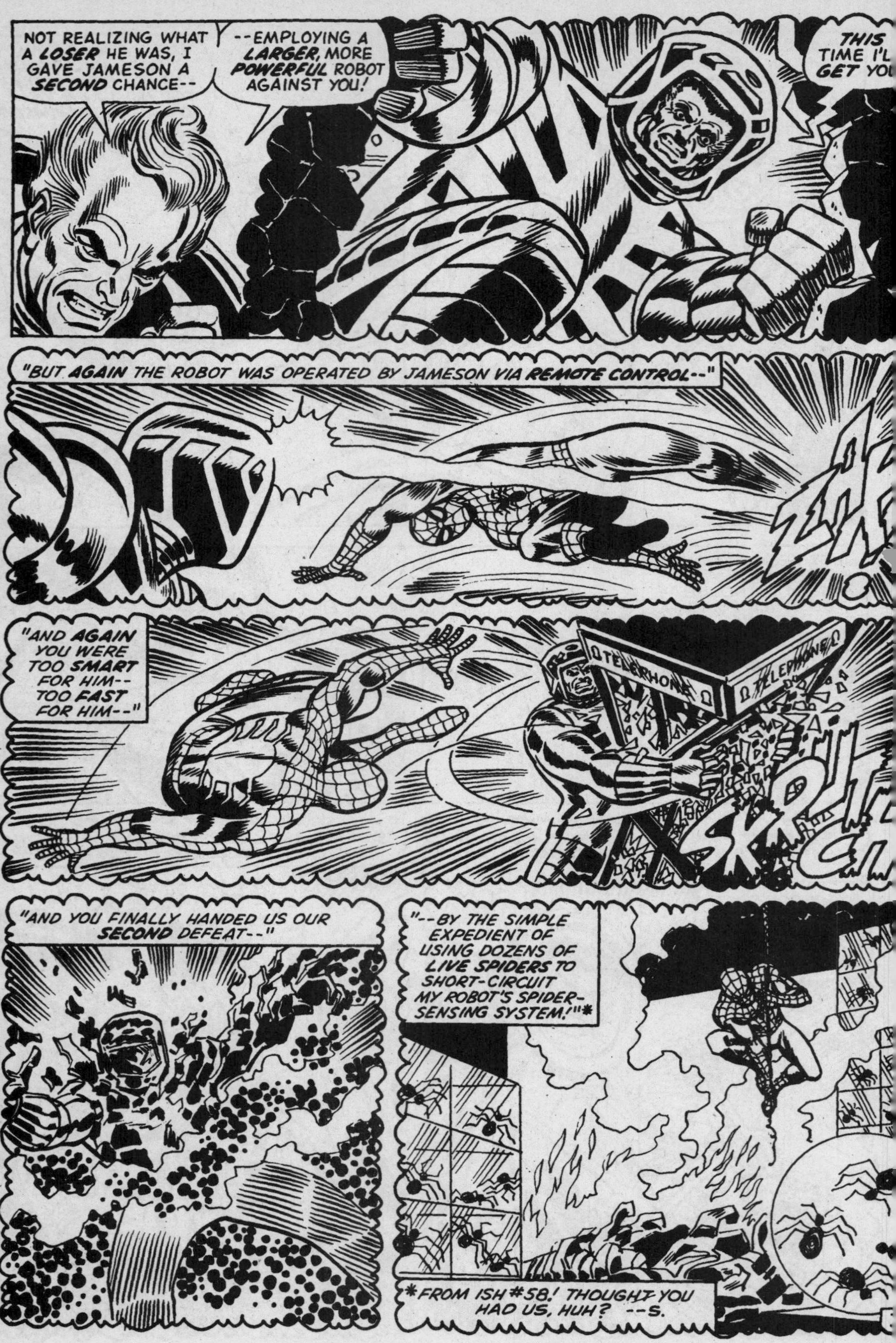
NOT REALIZING WHAT A LOSER HE WAS, I GAVE JAMESON A SECOND CHANCE--
--EMPLOYING A LARGER, MORE POWERFUL ROBOT AGAINST YOU!
THIS TIME I'L GET YO
"BUT AGAIN THE ROBOT WAS OPERATED BY JAMESON VIA REMOTE CONTROL--"
"AND AGAIN YOU WERE TOO SMART FOR HIM-- TOO FAST FOR HIM--"
TELEPHONE
TELEPHONE
"AND YOU FINALLY HANDED US OUR SECOND DEFEAT--"
"--BY THE SIMPLE EXPEDIENT OF USING DOZENS OF LIVE SPIDERS TO SHORT-CIRCUIT MY ROBOT'S SPIDER-SENSING SYSTEM!"*
*FROM ISH #58! THOUGHT YOU HAD US, HUH? --S.

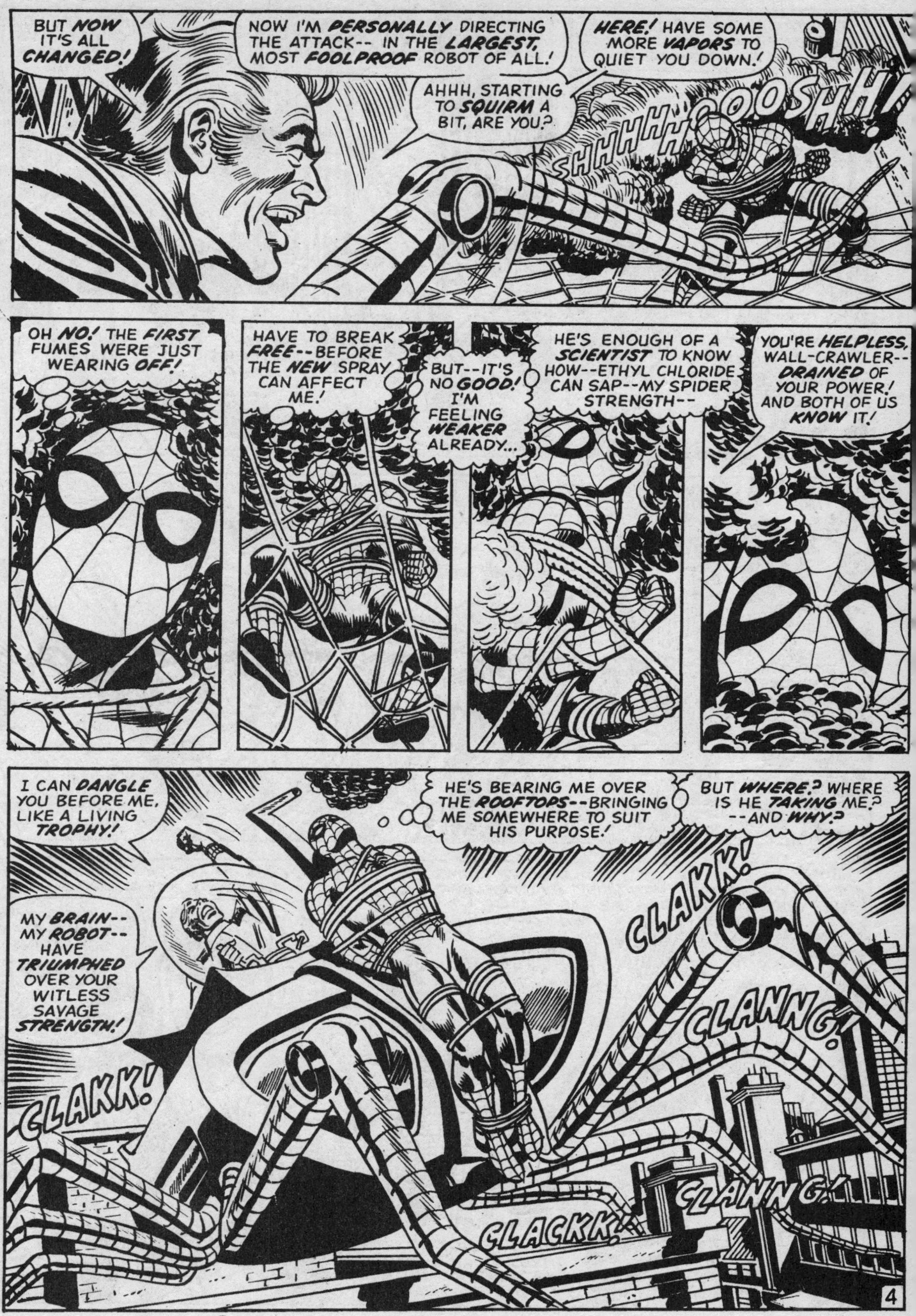

BUT NOW IT'S ALL CHANGED!
NOW I'M PERSONALLY DIRECTING THE ATTACK-- IN THE LARGEST, MOST FOOLPROOF ROBOT OF ALL!
HERE! HAVE SOME MORE VAPORS TO QUIET YOU DOWN!
AHHH, STARTING TO SQUIRM A BIT, ARE YOU?
SHHHHHOOOSHH!
OH NO! THE FIRST FUMES WERE JUST WEARING OFF!
HAVE TO BREAK FREE--BEFORE THE NEW SPRAY CAN AFFECT ME!
BUT--IT'S NO GOOD! I'M FEELING WEAKER ALREADY...
HE'S ENOUGH OF A SCIENTIST TO KNOW HOW--ETHYL CHLORIDE CAN SAP--MY SPIDER STRENGTH--
YOU'RE HELPLESS, WALL-CRAWLER--DRAINED OF YOUR POWER! AND BOTH OF US KNOW IT!
I CAN DANGLE YOU BEFORE ME, LIKE A LIVING TROPHY!
HE'S BEARING ME OVER THE ROOFTOPS--BRINGING ME SOMEWHERE TO SUIT HIS PURPOSE!
BUT WHERE? WHERE IS HE TAKING ME? --AND WHY?
MY BRAIN-- MY ROBOT-- HAVE TRIUMPHED OVER YOUR WITLESS SAVAGE STRENGTH!
CLAKK!
CLANNG!
CLAKK!
CLANNG!
CLACKK!
4

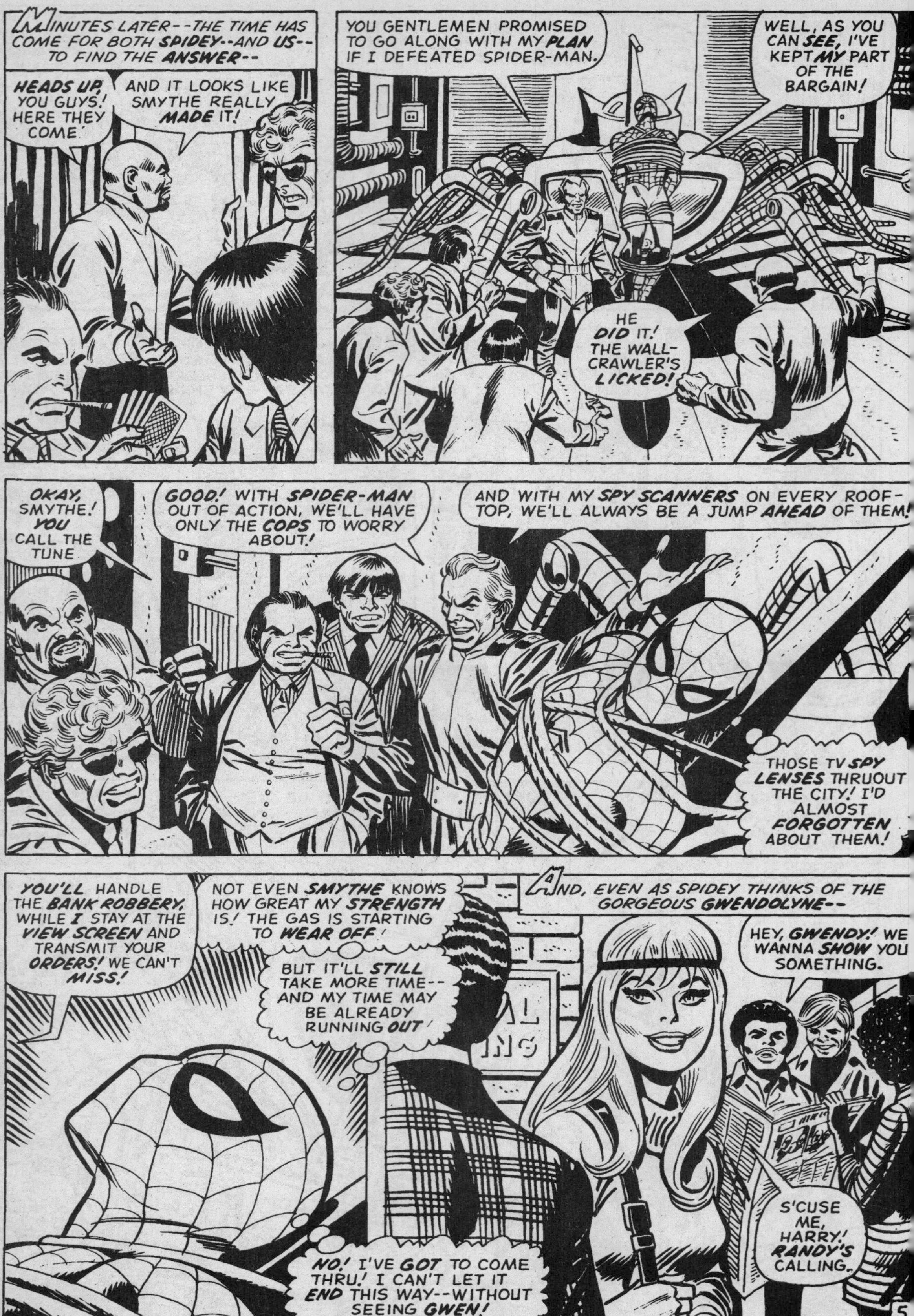
MINUTES LATER--THE TIME HAS COME FOR BOTH SPIDEY--AND US--TO FIND THE ANSWER--
HEADS UP, YOU GUYS! HERE THEY COME!
AND IT LOOKS LIKE SMYTHE REALLY MADE IT!
YOU GENTLEMEN PROMISED TO GO ALONG WITH MY PLAN IF I DEFEATED SPIDER-MAN.
WELL, AS YOU CAN SEE, I'VE KEPT MY PART OF THE BARGAIN!
HE DID IT! THE WALL-CRAWLER'S LICKED!
OKAY, SMYTHE! YOU CALL THE TUNE
GOOD! WITH SPIDER-MAN OUT OF ACTION, WE'LL HAVE ONLY THE COPS TO WORRY ABOUT!
AND WITH MY SPY SCANNERS ON EVERY ROOF-TOP, WE'LL ALWAYS BE A JUMP AHEAD OF THEM!
THOSE TV SPY LENSES THRUOUT THE CITY! I'D ALMOST FORGOTTEN ABOUT THEM!
YOU'LL HANDLE THE BANK ROBBERY, WHILE I STAY AT THE VIEW SCREEN AND TRANSMIT YOUR ORDERS! WE CAN'T MISS!
NOT EVEN SMYTHE KNOWS HOW GREAT MY STRENGTH IS! THE GAS IS STARTING TO WEAR OFF!
BUT IT'LL STILL TAKE MORE TIME--AND MY TIME MAY BE ALREADY RUNNING OUT!
NO! I'VE GOT TO COME THRU! I CAN'T LET IT END THIS WAY--WITHOUT SEEING GWEN!
AND, EVEN AS SPIDEY THINKS OF THE GORGEOUS GWENDOLYNE--
HEY, GWENDY! WE WANNA SHOW YOU SOMETHING.
S'CUSE ME, HARRY! RANDY'S CALLING.
5

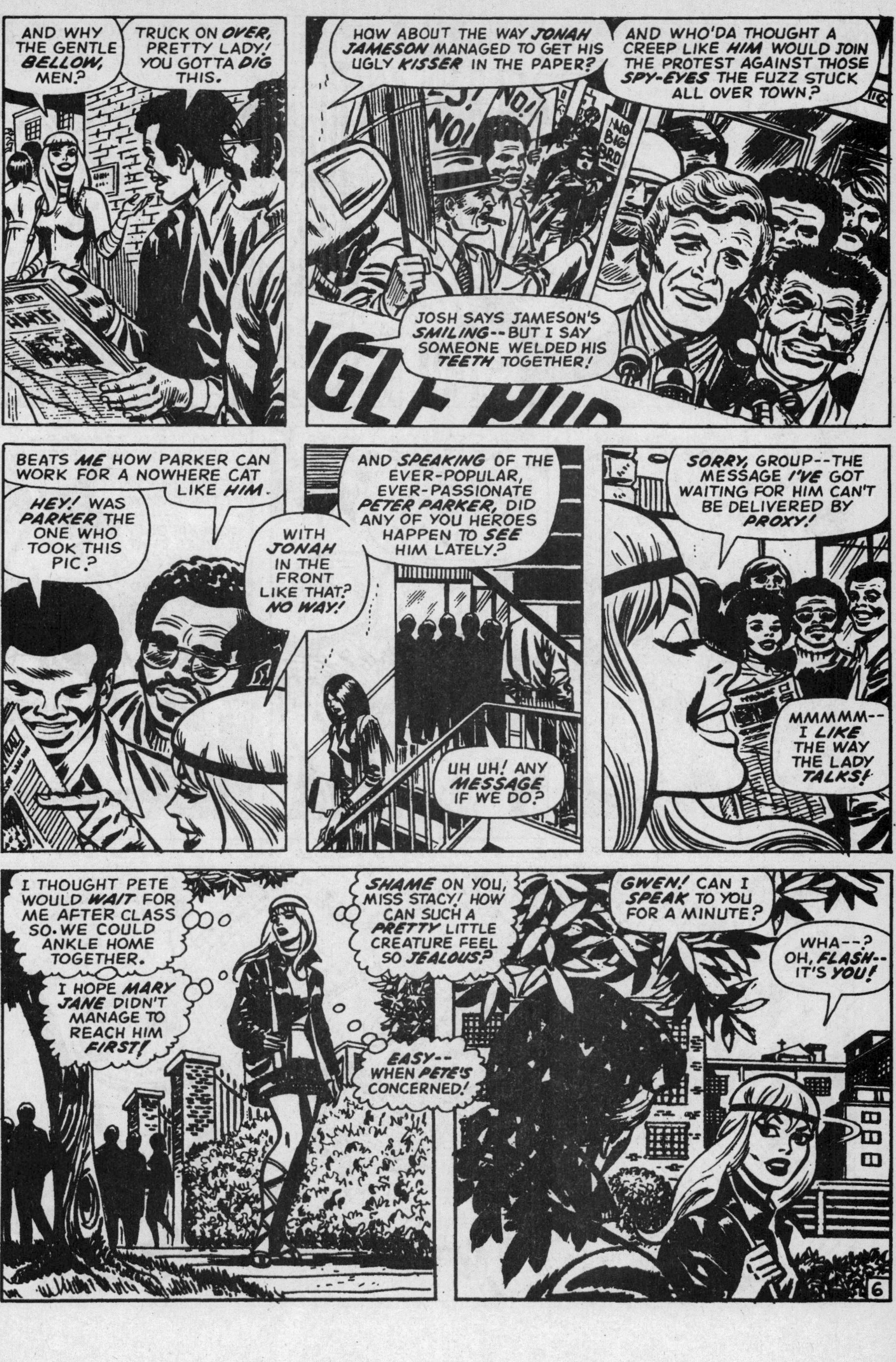
AND WHY THE GENTLE BELLOW, MEN?
TRUCK ON OVER, PRETTY LADY! YOU GOTTA DIG THIS.
HOW ABOUT THE WAY JONAH JAMESON MANAGED TO GET HIS UGLY KISSER IN THE PAPER?
AND WHO'DA THOUGHT A CREEP LIKE HIM WOULD JOIN THE PROTEST AGAINST THOSE SPY-EYES THE FUZZ STUCK ALL OVER TOWN?
NO!
NO!
NO BIG BRO
JOSH SAYS JAMESON'S SMILING--BUT I SAY SOMEONE WELDED HIS TEETH TOGETHER!
BEATS ME HOW PARKER CAN WORK FOR A NOWHERE CAT LIKE HIM.
HEY! WAS PARKER THE ONE WHO TOOK THIS PIC?
WITH JONAH IN THE FRONT LIKE THAT? NO WAY!
AND SPEAKING OF THE EVER-POPULAR, EVER-PASSIONATE PETER PARKER, DID ANY OF YOU HEROES HAPPEN TO SEE HIM LATELY?
UH UH! ANY MESSAGE IF WE DO?
SORRY, GROUP--THE MESSAGE I'VE GOT WAITING FOR HIM CAN'T BE DELIVERED BY PROXY!
MMMMM--I LIKE THE WAY THE LADY TALKS!
I THOUGHT PETE WOULD WAIT FOR ME AFTER CLASS SO WE COULD ANKLE HOME TOGETHER.
I HOPE MARY JANE DIDN'T MANAGE TO REACH HIM FIRST!
SHAME ON YOU, MISS STACY! HOW CAN SUCH A PRETTY LITTLE CREATURE FEEL SO JEALOUS?
EASY--WHEN PETE'S CONCERNED!
GWEN! CAN I SPEAK TO YOU FOR A MINUTE?
WHA--? OH, FLASH--IT'S YOU!
6

I JUST WANTED TO *APOLOGIZE*--FOR THE WAY I *ACTED* YESTERDAY--WHEN YOU AND *PARKER* CAME TO SEE ME*

IT'S ALL RIGHT, FLASH! YOU DON'T *HAVE* TO--

*YOU *GUESSED* IT: LAST ISH!--S.

I *DO* HAVE TO! I *WANT* TO!

AFTER ALL, GWEN--YOU KNOW HOW I *FEEL* ABOUT YOU--

I FEEL THE SAME *WAY*, FLASH! WE'RE *FRIENDS*--I WANT US TO *STAY* THAT WAY.

THAT'S--NOT WHAT I *MEAN*! YOU'RE *MORE* TO ME--THAN JUST A *FRIEND.*

WHAT--ARE YOU TRYING TO *SAY*?

NO--DON'T ANSWER! JUST *LISTEN!*

YOU KNOW HOW *PETER* AND I *FEEL* ABOUT EACH OTHER! IT'S FOR *REAL*, FLASH!

BUT, I'VE A FEELING THERE'S SOMETHING *ELSE*--

THERE'S SOMETHING YOU'RE NOT *TELLING* ME!

I *CAN'T*, GWEN! I *WANT* TO, BUT I *CAN'T* TELL YOU--CAN'T TELL *ANYONE!*

IF YOU'RE IN *TROUBLE*--IF THERE'S ANY WAY PETER AND I CAN *HELP*--

PETER AND YOU! PETER AND YOU!

WOW--IF ONLY IT WERE THAT *SIMPLE!*

BUT, SPEAKING OF *TROUBLE*, LET'S RETURN TO THE GUY WHO WROTE THE *BOOK*--

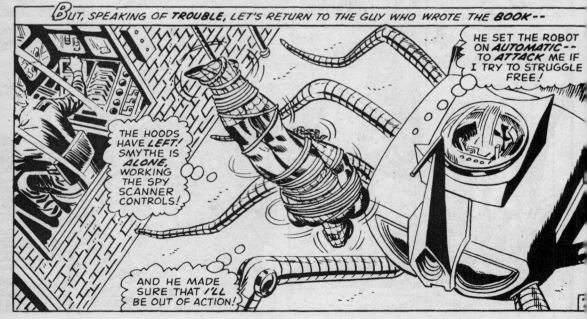

HE SET THE ROBOT ON *AUTOMATIC*--TO *ATTACK* ME IF I TRY TO STRUGGLE FREE!

THE HOODS HAVE *LEFT!* SMYTHE IS *ALONE*, WORKING THE SPY SCANNER CONTROLS!

AND HE MADE SURE THAT *I'LL* BE OUT OF ACTION!

BUT I MUSTN'T LOSE MY COOL! I'VE BEEN IN *TOUGHER* SPOTS THAN *THIS* BEFORE--

THOUGH I CAN'T REMEMBER *WHEN!*

SMYTHE'S SO SURE I'M *TRAPPED*, HE DOESN'T EVEN BOTHER TO TURN AROUND!

CAN YOU ALL *HEAR* ME? GOOD! GOOD! THE COAST IS *CLEAR!* I'M MONITORING YOUR ENTIRE *ROUTE!*

JUST FOLLOW MY RADIO *INSTRUCTIONS*, AND THE BANK'S MILLIONS WILL BE *OURS!*

SMYTHE'S A *GENIUS!* ONCE WE HEIST THE *BANK*, HE'LL TELL US WHICH *STREETS* TO TAKE TO AVOID THE *FUZZ!*

YEAH! WITH HIM WATCHIN' 'EM THRU THEM *SPY SCANNERS*, IT'LL BE A *BREEZE!*

SO FAR SO *GOOD*, SMYTHE! WE'RE READIN' YA LOUD 'N CLEAR!

REMEMBER, FOLLOW MY ORDERS *EXACTLY!*

THIS TIME THERE WILL BE *NO* SLIP UP! I'VE *SEEN* TO THAT!

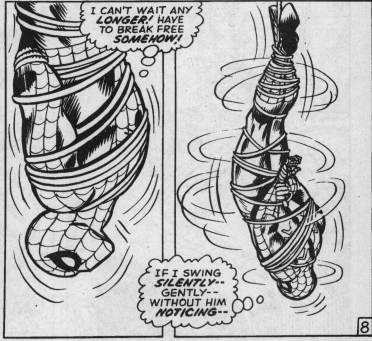

I CAN'T WAIT ANY *LONGER!* HAVE TO BREAK FREE *SOMEHOW!*

IF I SWING *SILENTLY-- GENTLY-- WITHOUT HIM *NOTICING--*

8

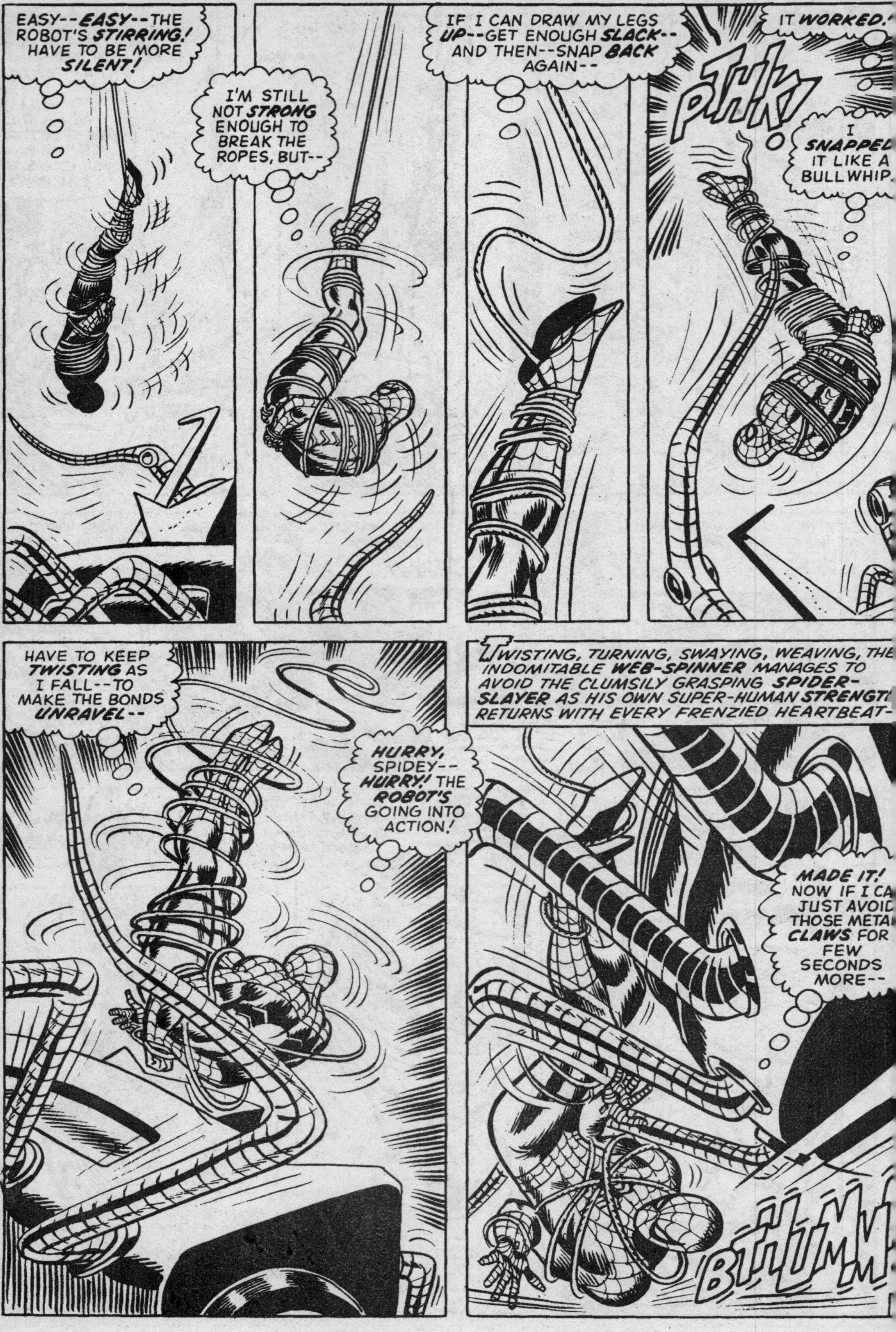
EASY--EASY--THE ROBOT'S STIRRING! HAVE TO BE MORE SILENT!
I'M STILL NOT STRONG ENOUGH TO BREAK THE ROPES, BUT--
IF I CAN DRAW MY LEGS UP--GET ENOUGH SLACK--AND THEN--SNAP BACK AGAIN--
IT WORKED.
PTHK!
I SNAPPED IT LIKE A BULLWHIP.
HAVE TO KEEP TWISTING AS I FALL--TO MAKE THE BONDS UNRAVEL--
HURRY, SPIDEY--HURRY! THE ROBOT'S GOING INTO ACTION!
TWISTING, TURNING, SWAYING, WEAVING, THE INDOMITABLE WEB-SPINNER MANAGES TO AVOID THE CLUMSILY GRASPING SPIDER-SLAYER AS HIS OWN SUPER-HUMAN STRENGTH RETURNS WITH EVERY FRENZIED HEARTBEAT--
MADE IT! NOW IF I CAN JUST AVOID THOSE METAL CLAWS FOR FEW SECONDS MORE--
BTHUMM

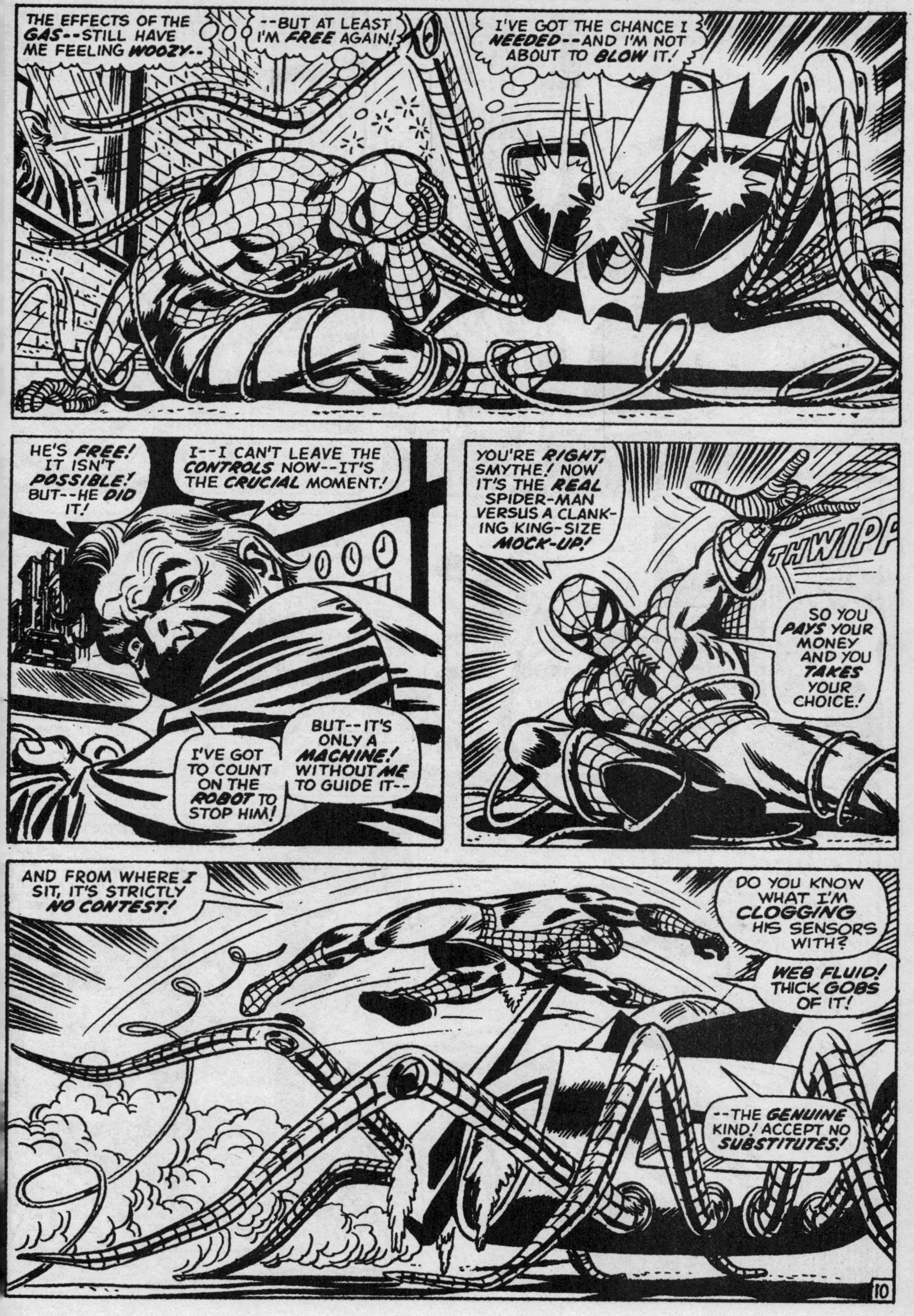
THE EFFECTS OF THE GAS--STILL HAVE ME FEELING WOOZY--
--BUT AT LEAST I'M FREE AGAIN!
I'VE GOT THE CHANCE I NEEDED--AND I'M NOT ABOUT TO BLOW IT!
HE'S FREE! IT ISN'T POSSIBLE! BUT--HE DID IT!
I--I CAN'T LEAVE THE CONTROLS NOW--IT'S THE CRUCIAL MOMENT!
I'VE GOT TO COUNT ON THE ROBOT TO STOP HIM!
BUT--IT'S ONLY A MACHINE! WITHOUT ME TO GUIDE IT--
YOU'RE RIGHT, SMYTHE! NOW IT'S THE REAL SPIDER-MAN VERSUS A CLANKING KING-SIZE MOCK-UP!
THWIPP
SO YOU PAYS YOUR MONEY AND YOU TAKES YOUR CHOICE!
AND FROM WHERE I SIT, IT'S STRICTLY NO CONTEST!
DO YOU KNOW WHAT I'M CLOGGING HIS SENSORS WITH?
WEB FLUID! THICK GOBS OF IT!
--THE GENUINE KIND! ACCEPT NO SUBSTITUTES!

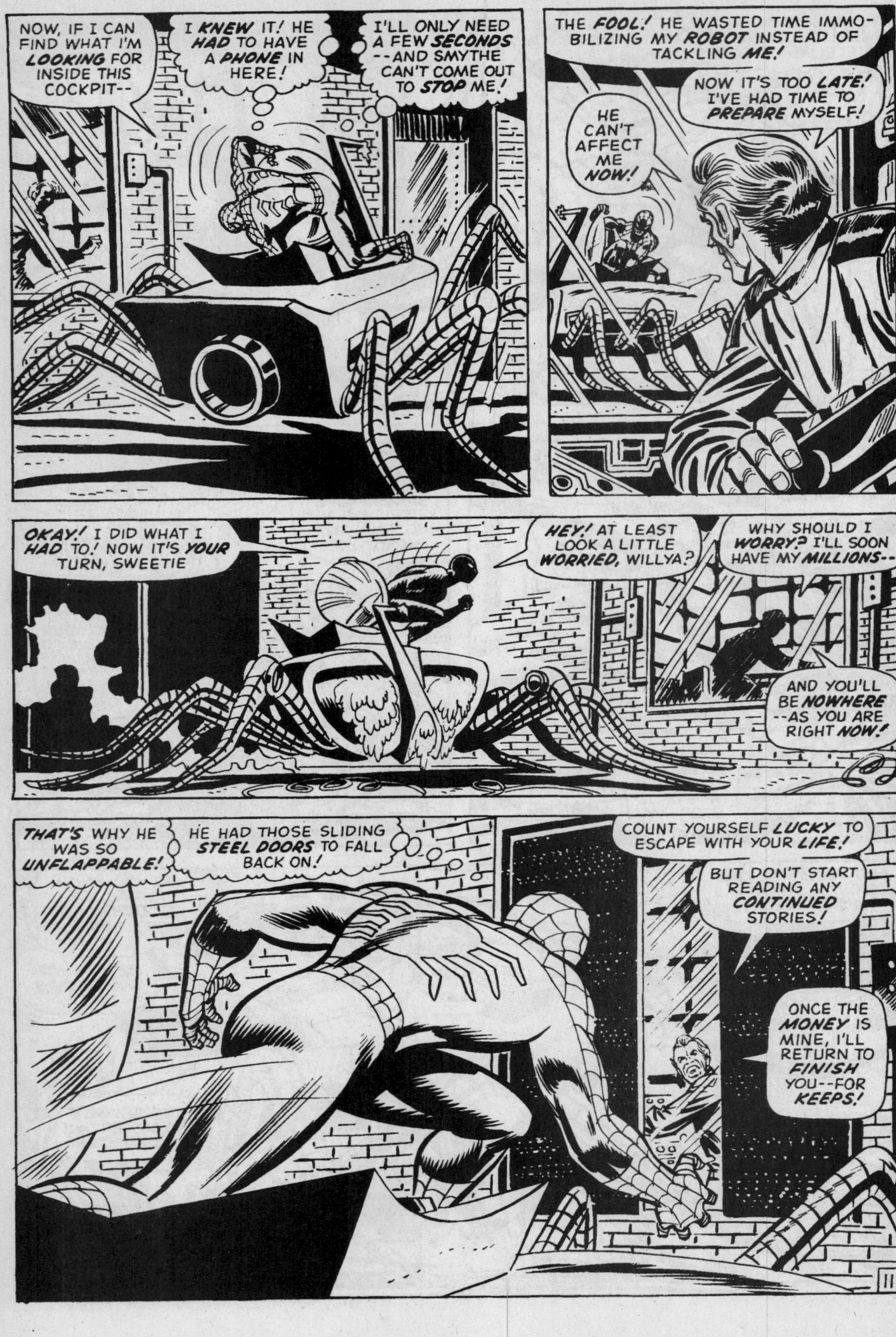
NOW, IF I CAN FIND WHAT I'M LOOKING FOR INSIDE THIS COCKPIT--
I KNEW IT! HE HAD TO HAVE A PHONE IN HERE!
I'LL ONLY NEED A FEW SECONDS --AND SMYTHE CAN'T COME OUT TO STOP ME!
THE FOOL! HE WASTED TIME IMMOBILIZING MY ROBOT INSTEAD OF TACKLING ME!
NOW IT'S TOO LATE! I'VE HAD TIME TO PREPARE MYSELF!
HE CAN'T AFFECT ME NOW!
OKAY! I DID WHAT I HAD TO! NOW IT'S YOUR TURN, SWEETIE
HEY! AT LEAST LOOK A LITTLE WORRIED, WILLYA?
WHY SHOULD I WORRY? I'LL SOON HAVE MY MILLIONS--
AND YOU'LL BE NOWHERE --AS YOU ARE RIGHT NOW!
THAT'S WHY HE WAS SO UNFLAPPABLE!
HE HAD THOSE SLIDING STEEL DOORS TO FALL BACK ON!
COUNT YOURSELF LUCKY TO ESCAPE WITH YOUR LIFE!
BUT DON'T START READING ANY CONTINUED STORIES!
ONCE THE MONEY IS MINE, I'LL RETURN TO FINISH YOU--FOR KEEPS!
11

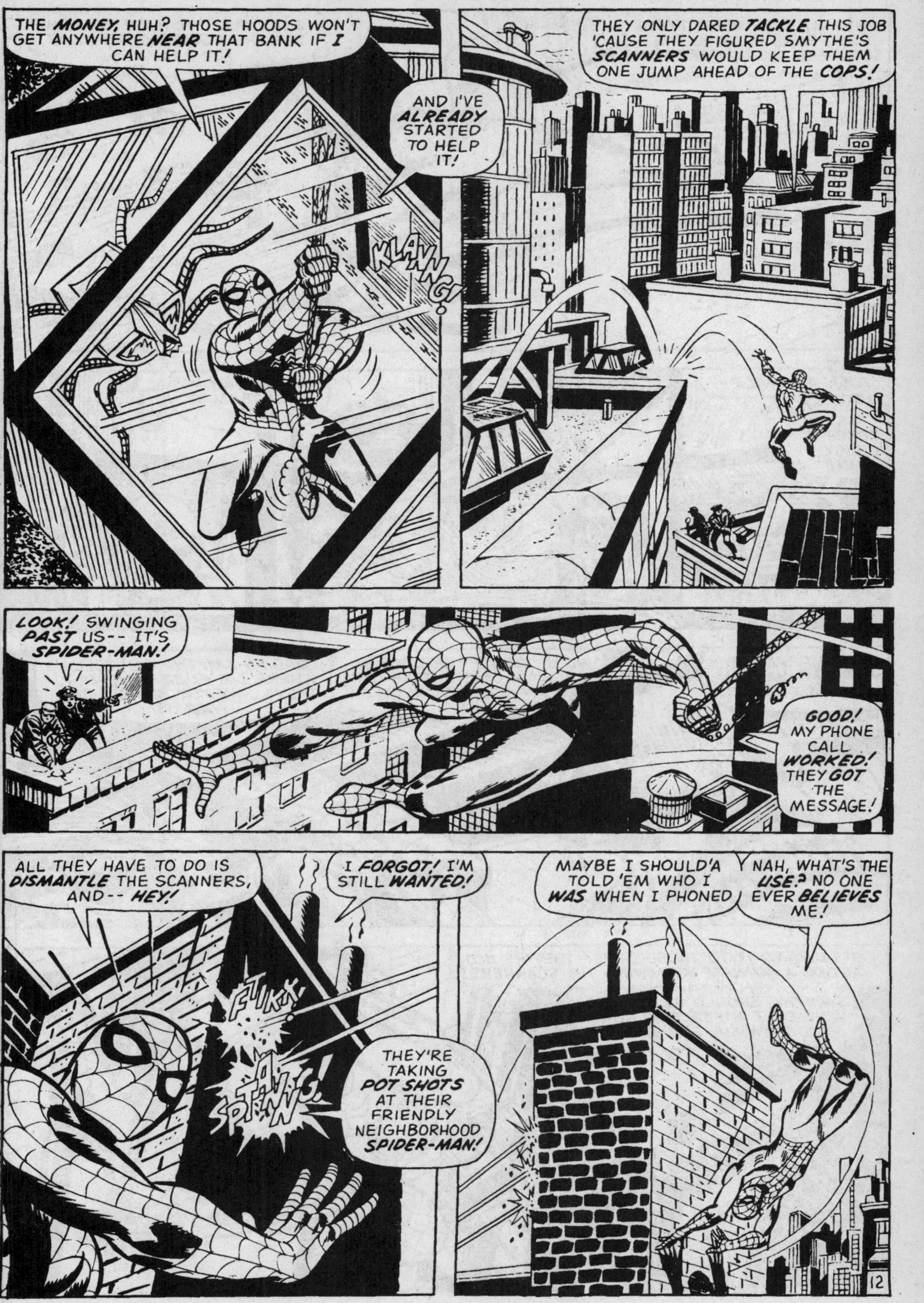
THE MONEY, HUH? THOSE HOODS WON'T GET ANYWHERE NEAR THAT BANK IF I CAN HELP IT!
AND I'VE ALREADY STARTED TO HELP IT!
KLANNG!
THEY ONLY DARED TACKLE THIS JOB 'CAUSE THEY FIGURED SMYTHE'S SCANNERS WOULD KEEP THEM ONE JUMP AHEAD OF THE COPS!
LOOK! SWINGING PAST US-- IT'S SPIDER-MAN!
GOOD! MY PHONE CALL WORKED! THEY GOT THE MESSAGE!
ALL THEY HAVE TO DO IS DISMANTLE THE SCANNERS, AND-- HEY!
I FORGOT! I'M STILL WANTED!
THEY'RE TAKING POT SHOTS AT THEIR FRIENDLY NEIGHBORHOOD SPIDER-MAN!
MAYBE I SHOULD'A TOLD 'EM WHO I WAS WHEN I PHONED
NAH, WHAT'S THE USE? NO ONE EVER BELIEVES ME!
12

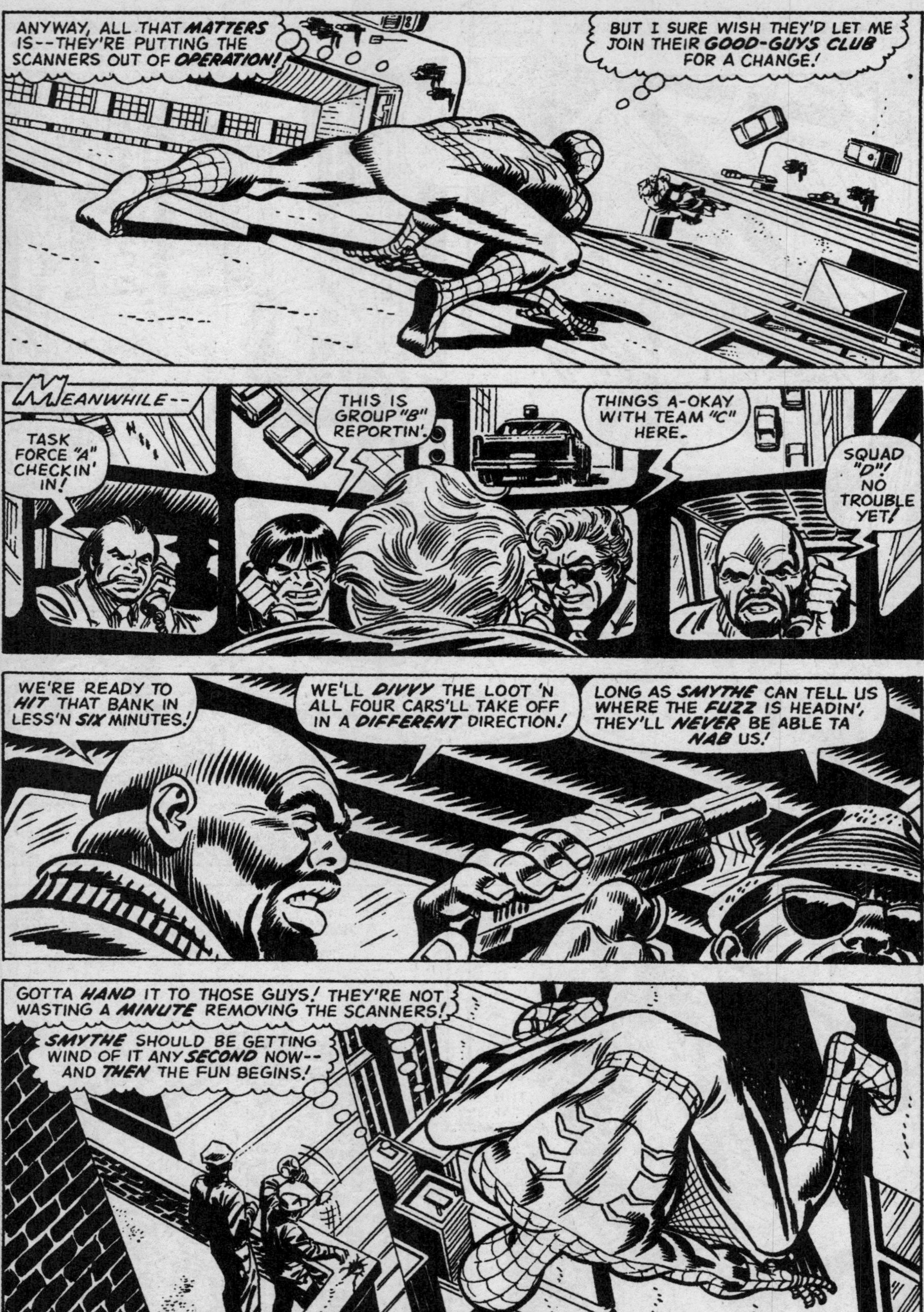
ANYWAY, ALL THAT MATTERS IS--THEY'RE PUTTING THE SCANNERS OUT OF OPERATION!
BUT I SURE WISH THEY'D LET ME JOIN THEIR GOOD-GUYS CLUB FOR A CHANGE!
MEANWHILE--
TASK FORCE "A" CHECKIN' IN!
THIS IS GROUP "B" REPORTIN'.
THINGS A-OKAY WITH TEAM "C" HERE.
SQUAD "D"! NO TROUBLE YET!
WE'RE READY TO HIT THAT BANK IN LESS'N SIX MINUTES!
WE'LL DIVVY THE LOOT 'N ALL FOUR CARS'LL TAKE OFF IN A DIFFERENT DIRECTION!
LONG AS SMYTHE CAN TELL US WHERE THE FUZZ IS HEADIN', THEY'LL NEVER BE ABLE TA NAB US!
GOTTA HAND IT TO THOSE GUYS! THEY'RE NOT WASTING A MINUTE REMOVING THE SCANNERS!
SMYTHE SHOULD BE GETTING WIND OF IT ANY SECOND NOW-- AND THEN THE FUN BEGINS!
13

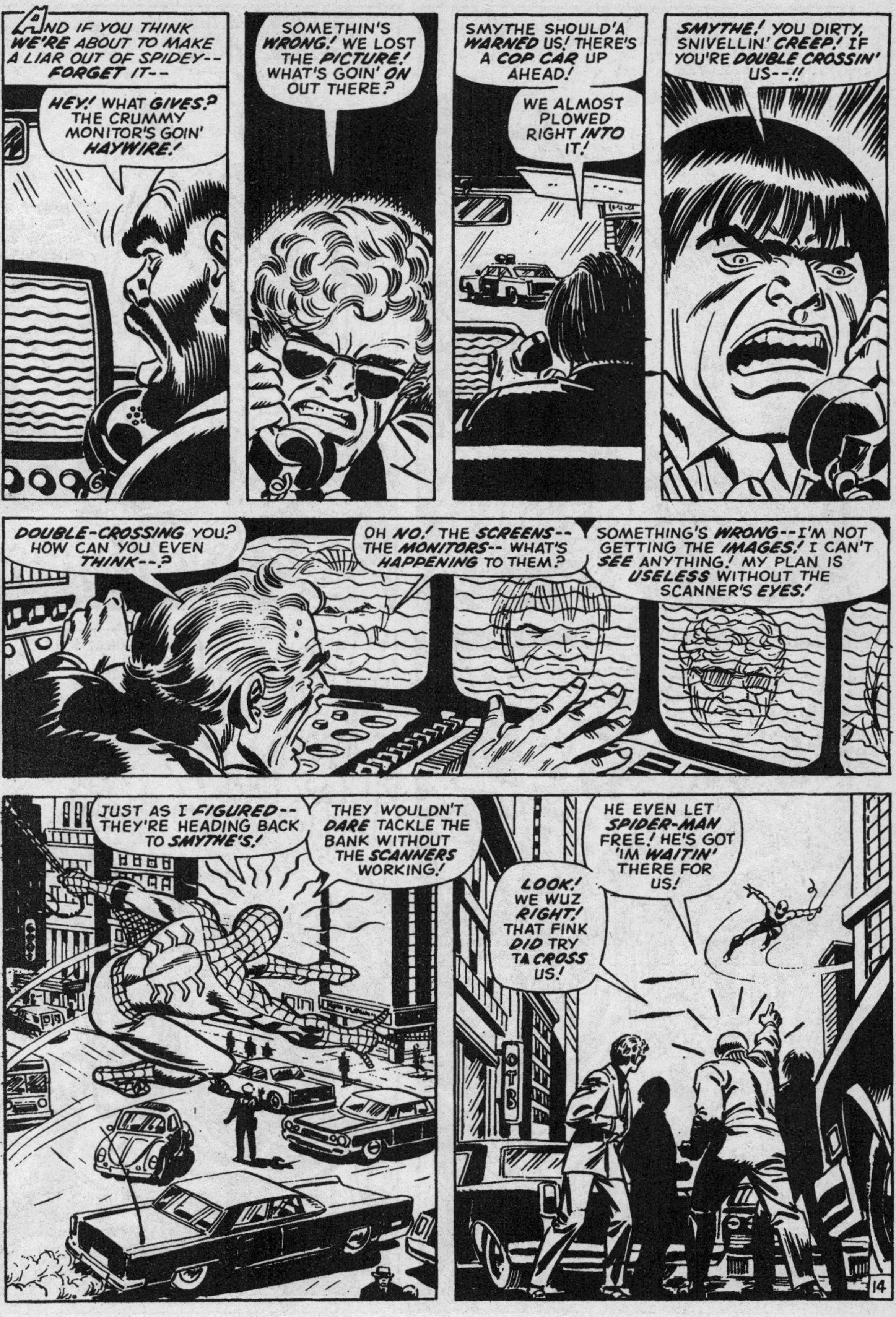

AND IF YOU THINK WE'RE ABOUT TO MAKE A LIAR OUT OF SPIDEY-- FORGET IT--
HEY! WHAT GIVES? THE CRUMMY MONITOR'S GOIN' HAYWIRE!
SOMETHIN'S WRONG! WE LOST THE PICTURE! WHAT'S GOIN' ON OUT THERE?
SMYTHE SHOULD'A WARNED US! THERE'S A COP CAR UP AHEAD!
WE ALMOST PLOWED RIGHT INTO IT!
SMYTHE! YOU DIRTY, SNIVELLIN' CREEP! IF YOU'RE DOUBLE CROSSIN' US--!!
DOUBLE-CROSSING YOU? HOW CAN YOU EVEN THINK--?
OH NO! THE SCREENS-- THE MONITORS-- WHAT'S HAPPENING TO THEM?
SOMETHING'S WRONG--I'M NOT GETTING THE IMAGES! I CAN'T SEE ANYTHING! MY PLAN IS USELESS WITHOUT THE SCANNER'S EYES!
JUST AS I FIGURED-- THEY'RE HEADING BACK TO SMYTHE'S!
THEY WOULDN'T DARE TACKLE THE BANK WITHOUT THE SCANNERS WORKING!
HE EVEN LET SPIDER-MAN FREE! HE'S GOT 'IM WAITIN' THERE FOR US!
LOOK! WE WUZ RIGHT! THAT FINK DID TRY TA CROSS US!
OTB
14

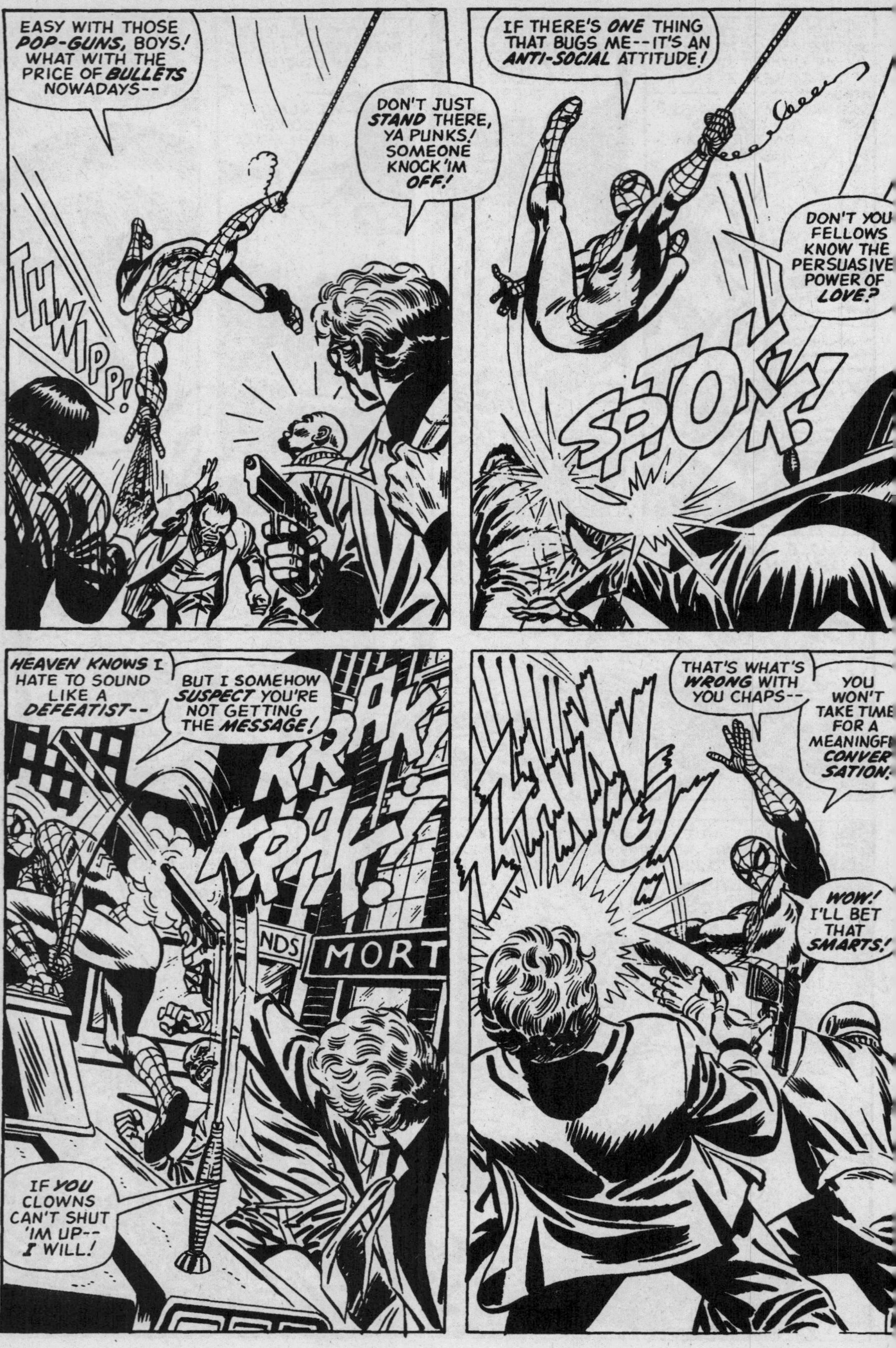
EASY WITH THOSE POP-GUNS, BOYS! WHAT WITH THE PRICE OF BULLETS NOWADAYS--
DON'T JUST STAND THERE, YA PUNKS! SOMEONE KNOCK 'IM OFF!
THWIPP!
IF THERE'S ONE THING THAT BUGS ME--IT'S AN ANTI-SOCIAL ATTITUDE!
DON'T YOU FELLOWS KNOW THE PERSUASIVE POWER OF LOVE?
SPTOK!
HEAVEN KNOWS I HATE TO SOUND LIKE A DEFEATIST--
BUT I SOMEHOW SUSPECT YOU'RE NOT GETTING THE MESSAGE!
KRAK!
KRAK!
NDS
MORT
IF YOU CLOWNS CAN'T SHUT 'IM UP-- I WILL!
THAT'S WHAT'S WRONG WITH YOU CHAPS--
YOU WON'T TAKE TIME FOR A MEANINGF CONVER SATION!
WOW! I'LL BET THAT SMARTS!

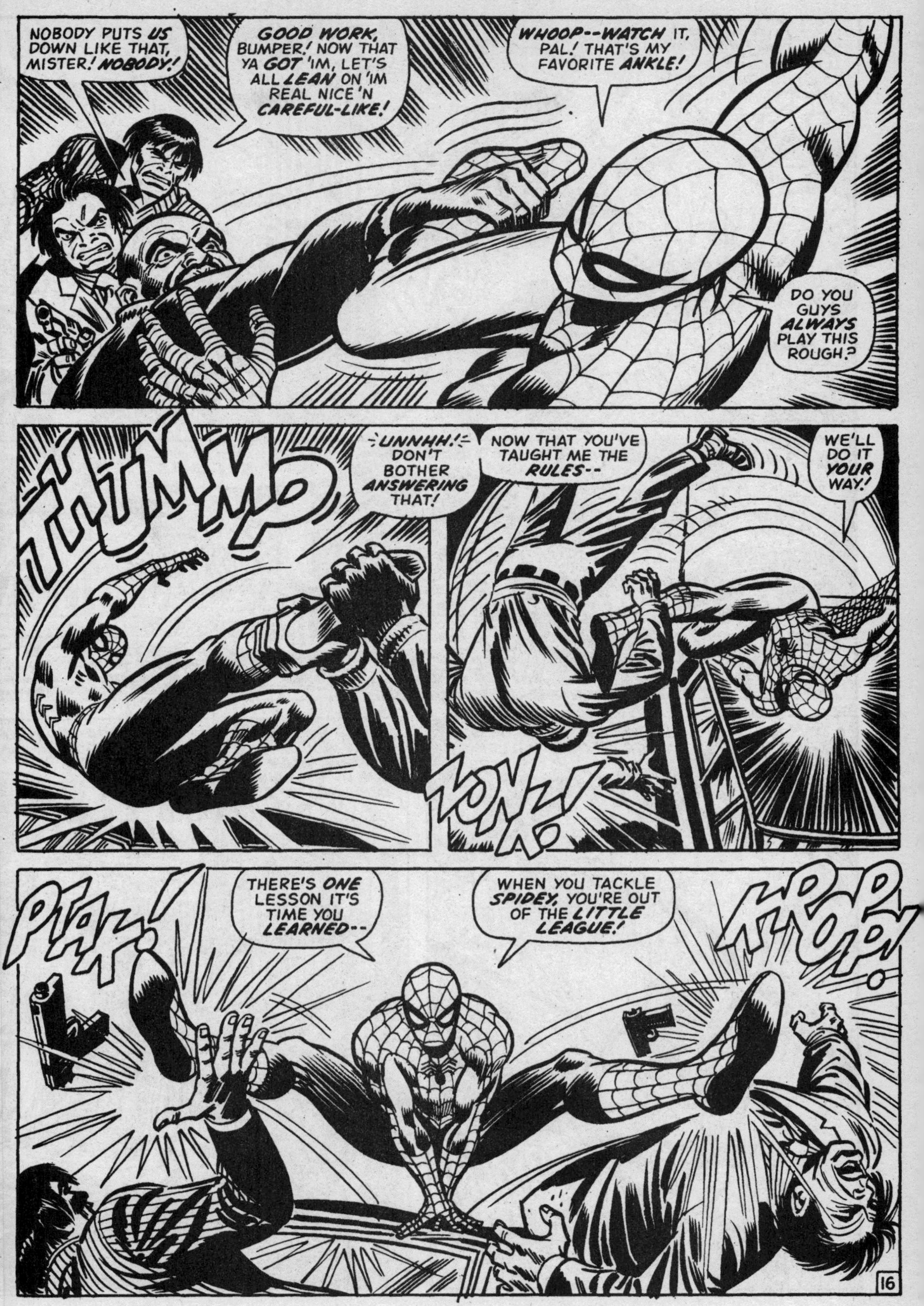
NOBODY PUTS US DOWN LIKE THAT, MISTER! NOBODY!
GOOD WORK, BUMPER! NOW THAT YA GOT 'IM, LET'S ALL LEAN ON 'IM REAL NICE 'N CAREFUL-LIKE!
WHOOP--WATCH IT, PAL! THAT'S MY FAVORITE ANKLE!
DO YOU GUYS ALWAYS PLAY THIS ROUGH?
THUMMP
-UNNHH!- DON'T BOTHER ANSWERING THAT!
NOW THAT YOU'VE TAUGHT ME THE RULES--
WE'LL DO IT YOUR WAY!
TONK!
PTAK!
THERE'S ONE LESSON IT'S TIME YOU LEARNED--
WHEN YOU TACKLE SPIDEY, YOU'RE OUT OF THE LITTLE LEAGUE!
KROPP!
16

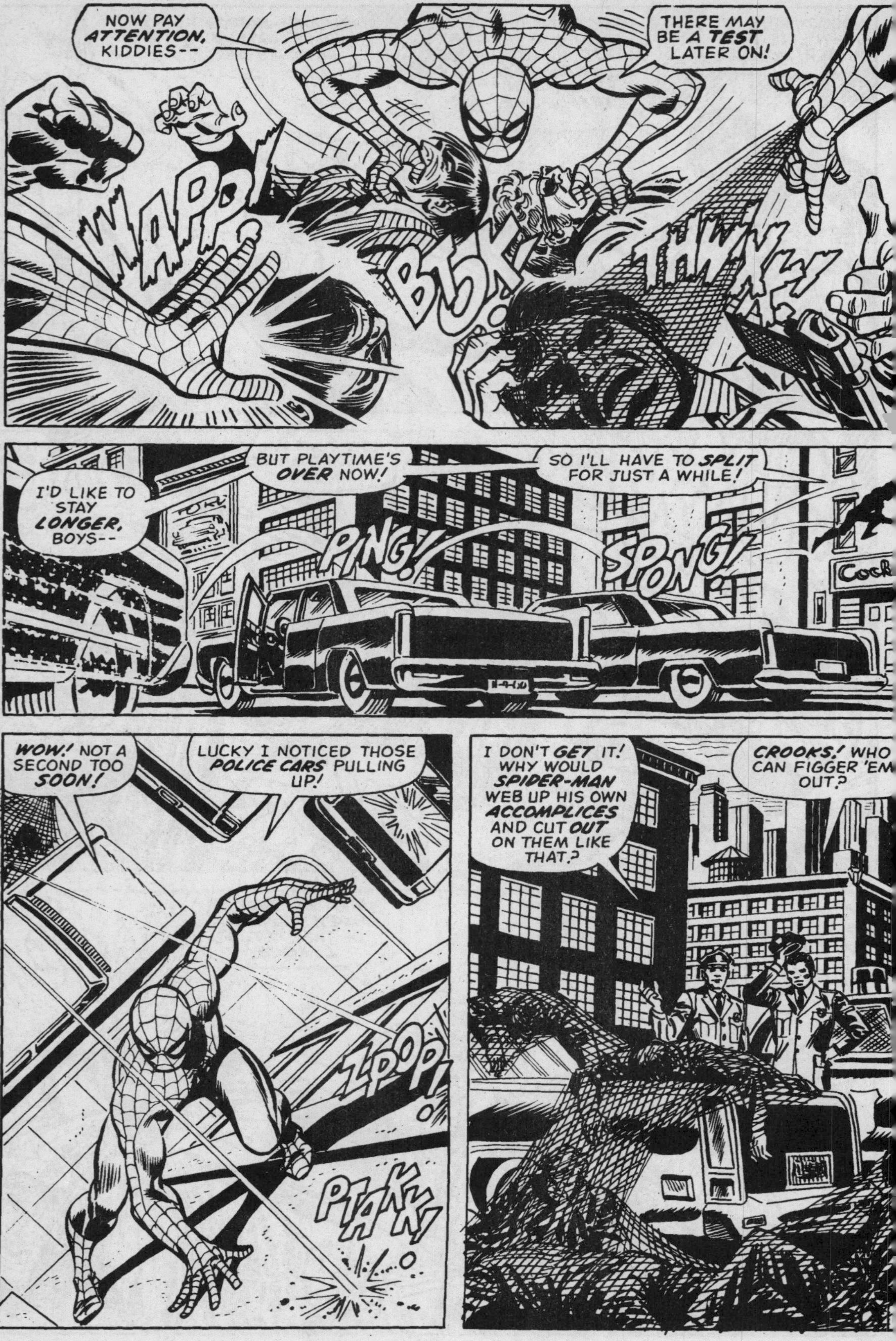
NOW PAY ATTENTION, KIDDIES--
THERE MAY BE A TEST LATER ON!
WAPP!
BTSK!
THWKK!
I'D LIKE TO STAY LONGER, BOYS--
BUT PLAYTIME'S OVER NOW!
SO I'LL HAVE TO SPLIT FOR JUST A WHILE!
PING!
SPONG!
WOW! NOT A SECOND TOO SOON!
LUCKY I NOTICED THOSE POLICE CARS PULLING UP!
ZPOP!
PTAKK!
I DON'T GET IT! WHY WOULD SPIDER-MAN WEB UP HIS OWN ACCOMPLICES AND CUT OUT ON THEM LIKE THAT?
CROOKS! WHO CAN FIGGER 'EM OUT?

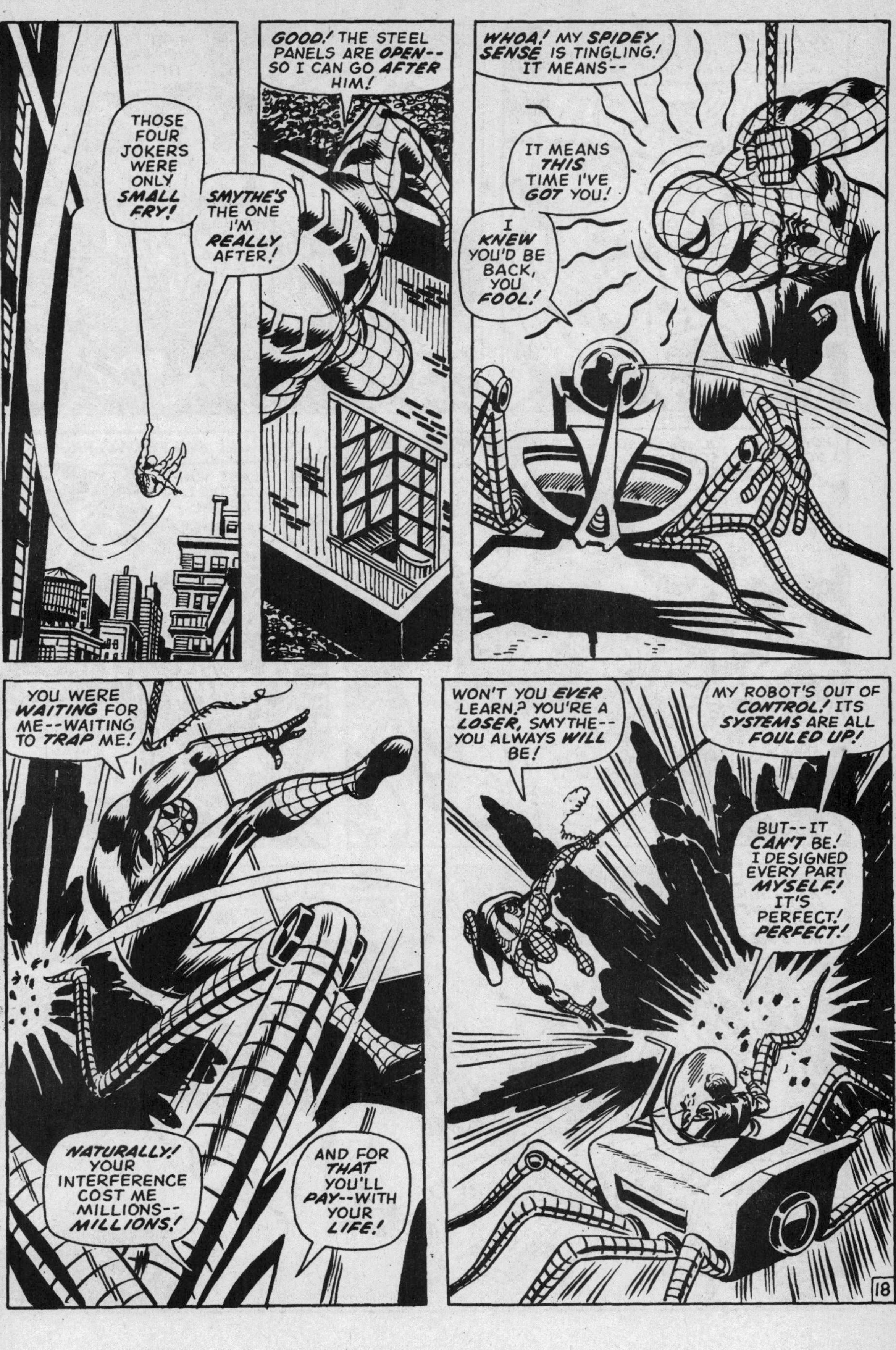
THOSE FOUR JOKERS WERE ONLY SMALL FRY!
SMYTHE'S THE ONE I'M REALLY AFTER!
GOOD! THE STEEL PANELS ARE OPEN-- SO I CAN GO AFTER HIM!
WHOA! MY SPIDEY SENSE IS TINGLING! IT MEANS--
IT MEANS THIS TIME I'VE GOT YOU!
I KNEW YOU'D BE BACK, YOU FOOL!
YOU WERE WAITING FOR ME--WAITING TO TRAP ME!
NATURALLY! YOUR INTERFERENCE COST ME MILLIONS-- MILLIONS!
AND FOR THAT YOU'LL PAY--WITH YOUR LIFE!
WON'T YOU EVER LEARN? YOU'RE A LOSER, SMYTHE-- YOU ALWAYS WILL BE!
MY ROBOT'S OUT OF CONTROL! ITS SYSTEMS ARE ALL FOULED UP!
BUT--IT CAN'T BE! I DESIGNED EVERY PART MYSELF! IT'S PERFECT! PERFECT!
18

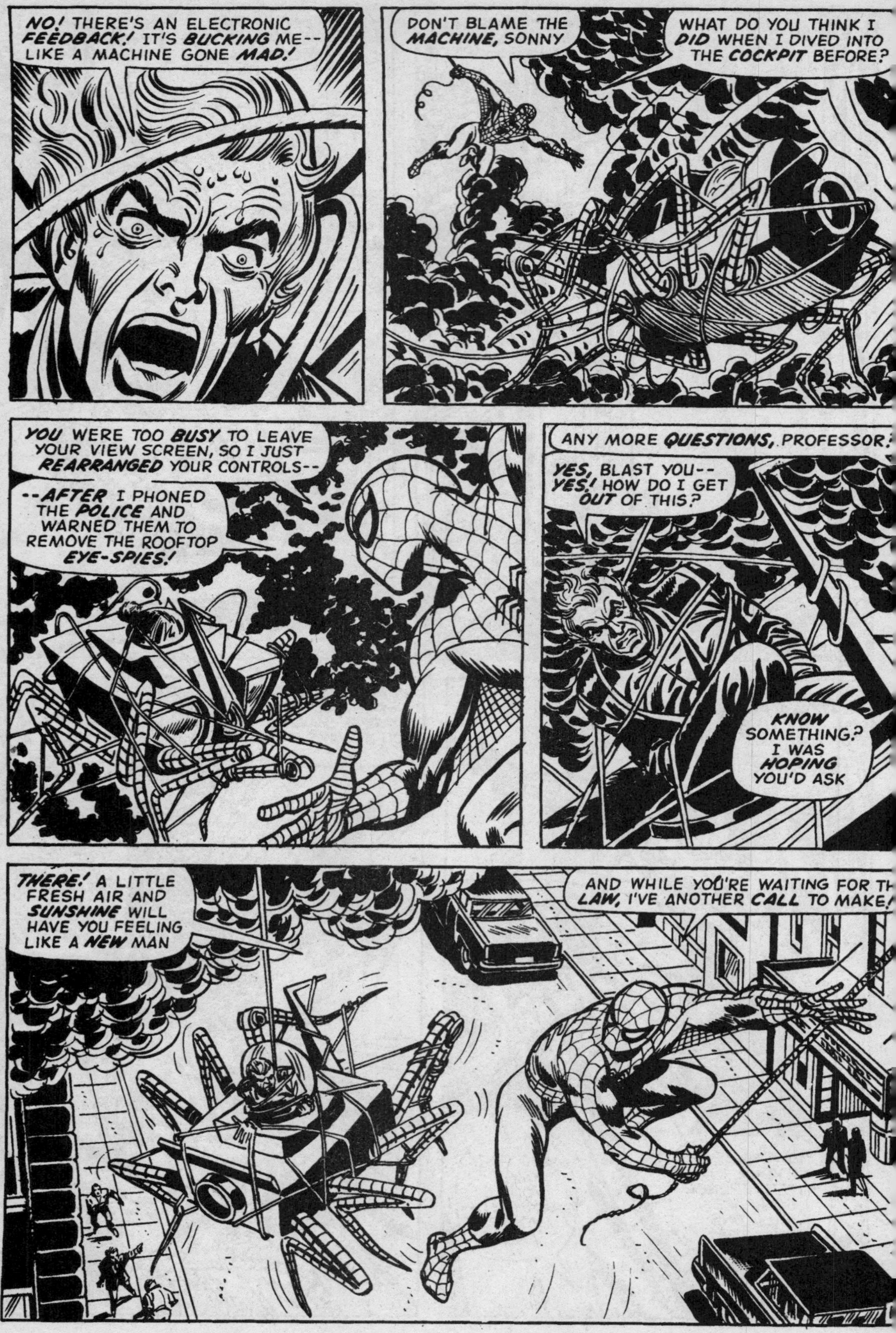

NO! THERE'S AN ELECTRONIC FEEDBACK! IT'S BUCKING ME-- LIKE A MACHINE GONE MAD!
DON'T BLAME THE MACHINE, SONNY
WHAT DO YOU THINK I DID WHEN I DIVED INTO THE COCKPIT BEFORE?
YOU WERE TOO BUSY TO LEAVE YOUR VIEW SCREEN, SO I JUST REARRANGED YOUR CONTROLS--
--AFTER I PHONED THE POLICE AND WARNED THEM TO REMOVE THE ROOFTOP EYE-SPIES!
ANY MORE QUESTIONS, PROFESSOR?
YES, BLAST YOU-- YES! HOW DO I GET OUT OF THIS?
KNOW SOMETHING? I WAS HOPING YOU'D ASK
THERE! A LITTLE FRESH AIR AND SUNSHINE WILL HAVE YOU FEELING LIKE A NEW MAN
AND WHILE YOU'RE WAITING FOR TH LAW, I'VE ANOTHER CALL TO MAKE!

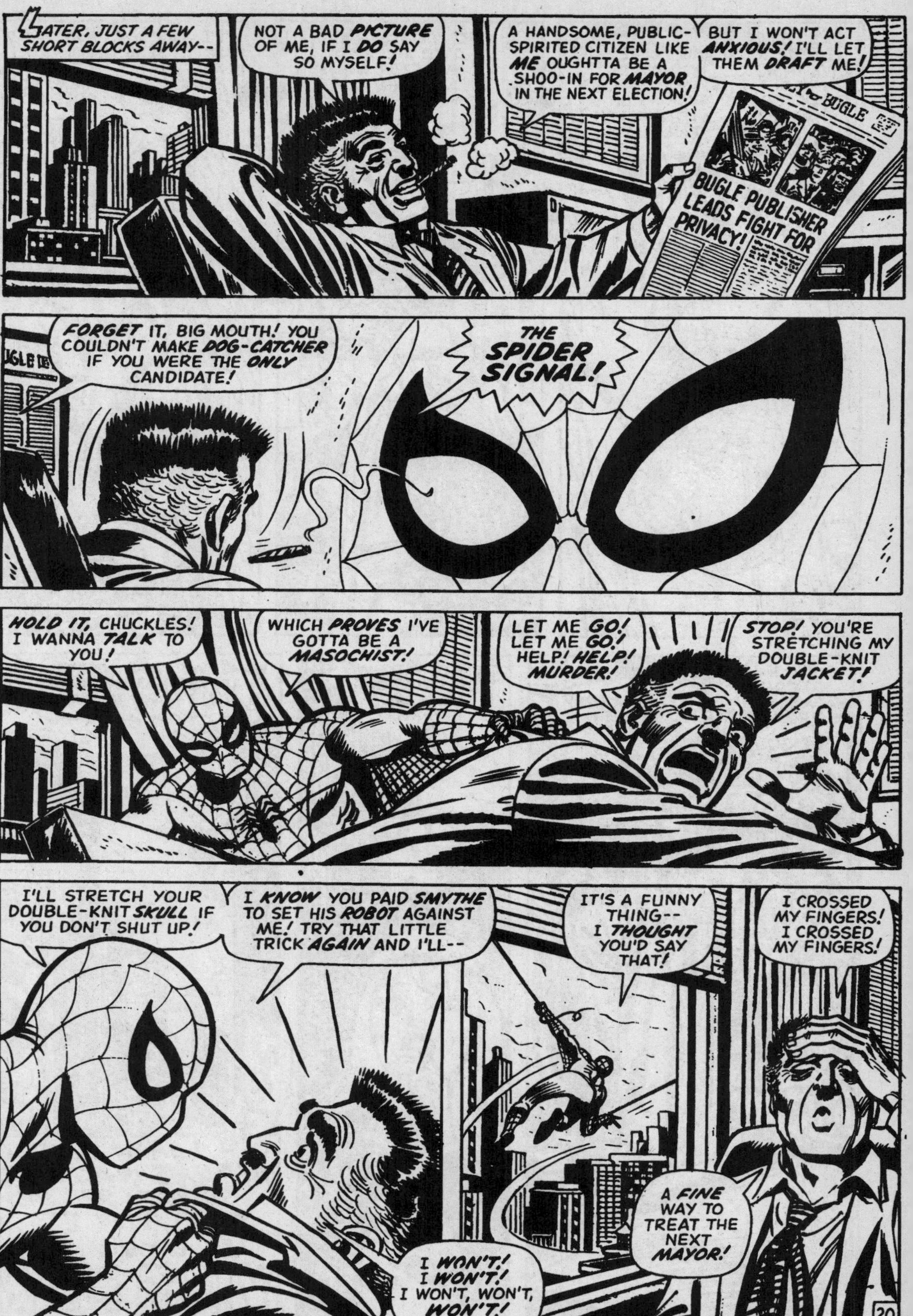
LATER, JUST A FEW SHORT BLOCKS AWAY--
NOT A BAD PICTURE OF ME, IF I DO SAY SO MYSELF!
A HANDSOME, PUBLIC-SPIRITED CITIZEN LIKE ME OUGHTTA BE A SHOO-IN FOR MAYOR IN THE NEXT ELECTION!
BUT I WON'T ACT ANXIOUS! I'LL LET THEM DRAFT ME!
BUGLE
BUGLE PUBLISHER LEADS FIGHT FOR PRIVACY!
FORGET IT, BIG MOUTH! YOU COULDN'T MAKE DOG-CATCHER IF YOU WERE THE ONLY CANDIDATE!
THE SPIDER SIGNAL!
HOLD IT, CHUCKLES! I WANNA TALK TO YOU!
WHICH PROVES I'VE GOTTA BE A MASOCHIST!
LET ME GO! LET ME GO! HELP! HELP! MURDER!
STOP! YOU'RE STRETCHING MY DOUBLE-KNIT JACKET!
I'LL STRETCH YOUR DOUBLE-KNIT SKULL IF YOU DON'T SHUT UP!
I KNOW YOU PAID SMYTHE TO SET HIS ROBOT AGAINST ME! TRY THAT LITTLE TRICK AGAIN AND I'LL--
I WON'T! I WON'T! I WON'T, WON'T, WON'T!
IT'S A FUNNY THING-- I THOUGHT YOU'D SAY THAT!
I CROSSED MY FINGERS! I CROSSED MY FINGERS!
A FINE WAY TO TREAT THE NEXT MAYOR!
20

Panel 1: IT SURE IS *GREAT* TO HAVE THINGS TURN OUT *OKAY* FOR A CHANGE!

NOW THERE'S NOTHING TO *STOP* ME FROM PICKING UP WITH *GWENDY* ONCE AGAIN!

~*AFTER* I CHANGE INTO MY *CIVVIES*, THAT IS!

Panel 2: SO I'LL JUST LATCH ONTO A NEARBY *ROOFTOP*, AND-- OH NO! *NO!*

Panel 3: IT'S *HER*-- WALKING ARM-IN-ARM WITH *FLASH!* THEY'RE AS *COZY* AS--

WAIT! THAT CAR!-- PULLING UP *NEXT* TO THEM! FLASH LOOKS *SCARED!*

Panel 4: YOU'LL HAVE TO COME *ALONG* WITH ME, THOMPSON!

YEAH, I *KNOW!* I'VE BEEN-- WAITING!

Panel 5: GWEN'S WATCHING THEM DRIVE OFF! SHE--SHE'S CRYING!

Panel 6: WHATEVER THIS *MEANS*-- WHATEVER HAS HAPPENED TO *FLASH*--AND TO *GWENDY*--

I'VE GOT A FEELING THAT THINGS'LL NEVER BE THE *SAME* AGAIN!

NEXT: LEARN WHAT IT *MEANS* IN A STARTLING SPIDEY SPECIAL-- **BACK TO VIET NAM!**

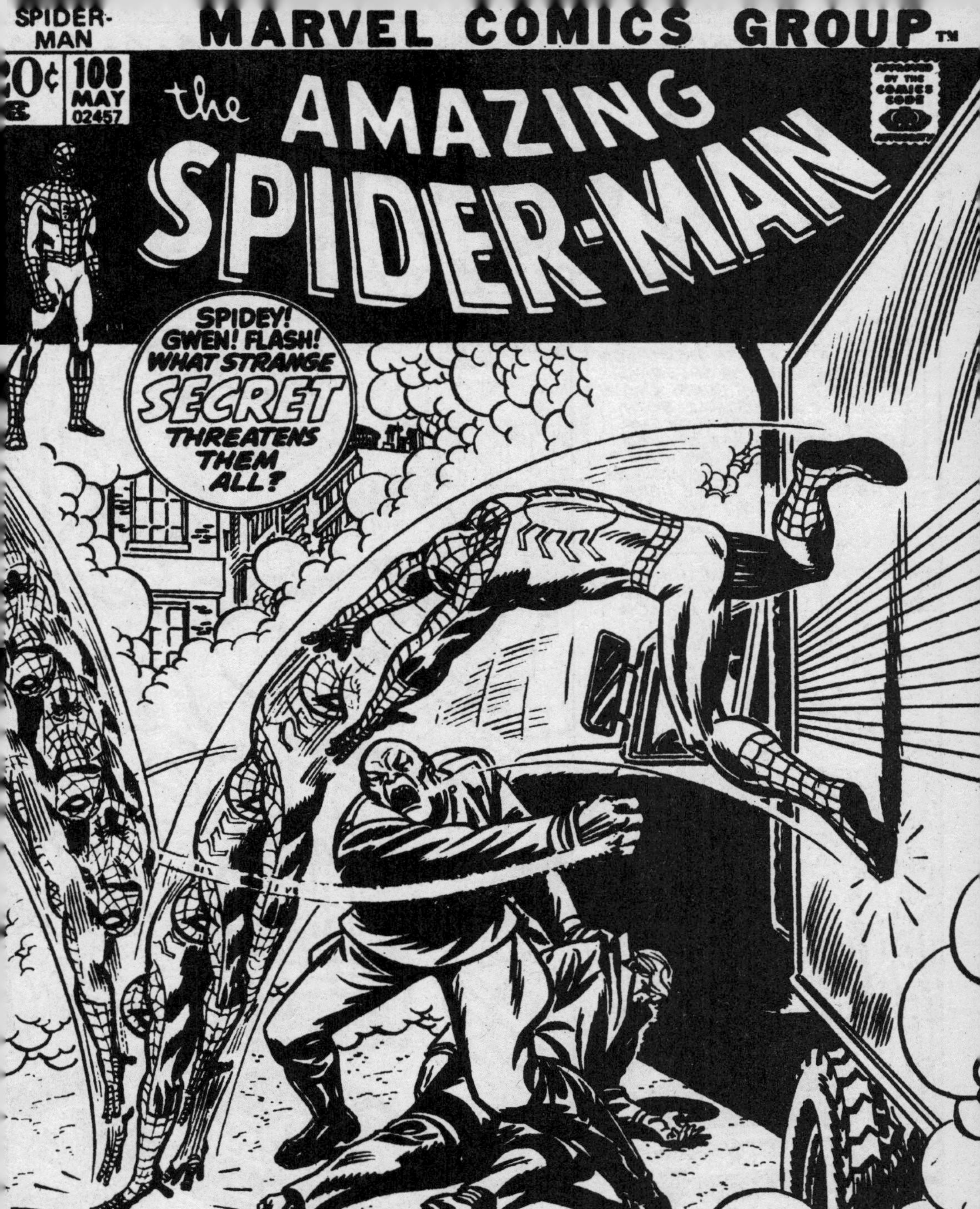
SPIDER-MAN
MARVEL COMICS GROUP™
20¢
108 MAY 02457
the AMAZING SPIDER-MAN
SPIDEY! GWEN! FLASH! WHAT STRANGE SECRET THREATENS THEM ALL?
ROMITA
NEW! UNEXPECTED! STARTLING!
MARKED FOR MURDER!

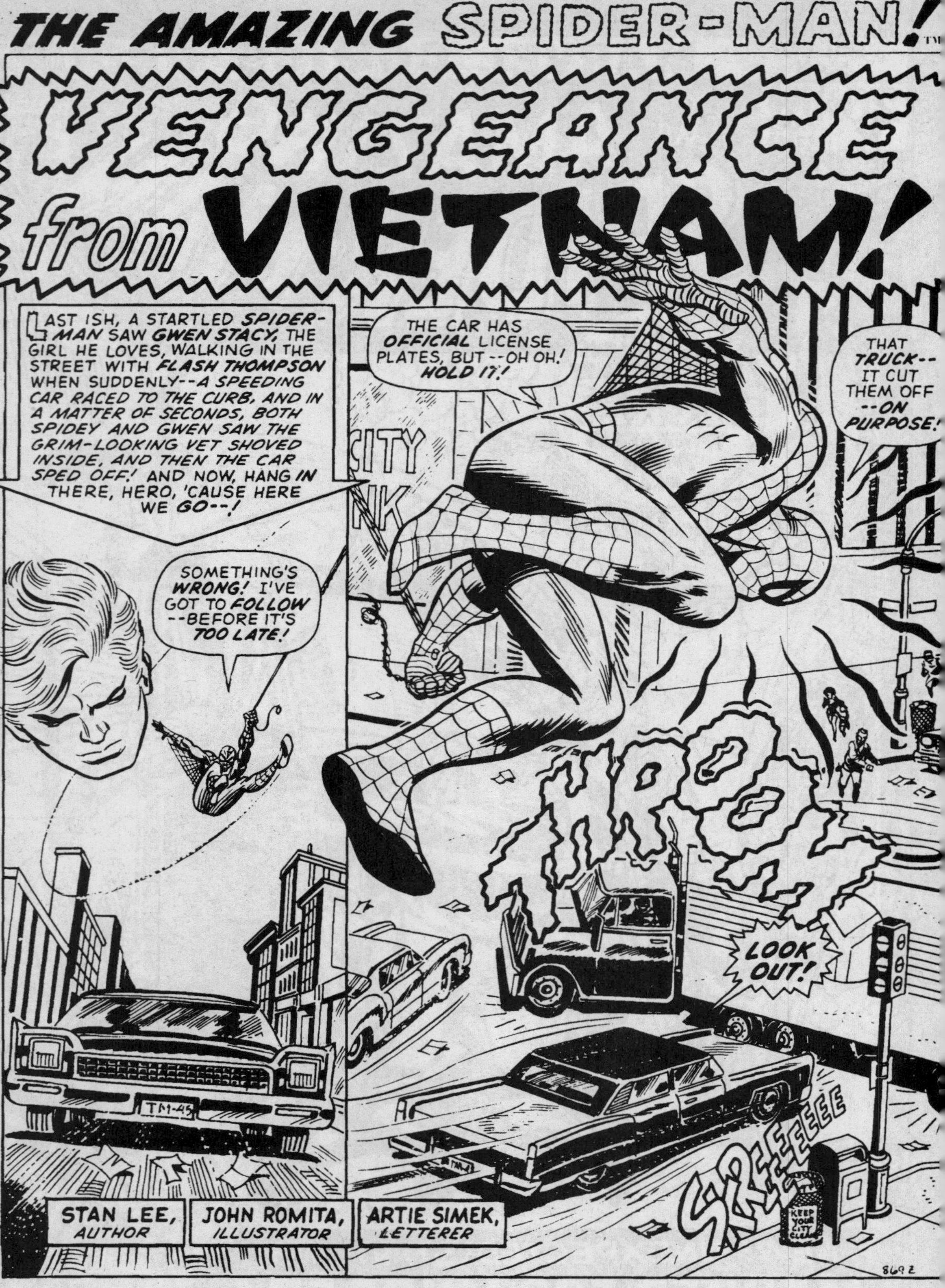
THE AMAZING SPIDER-MAN!
VENGEANCE from VIETNAM!
LAST ISH, A STARTLED SPIDER-MAN SAW GWEN STACY, THE GIRL HE LOVES, WALKING IN THE STREET WITH FLASH THOMPSON WHEN SUDDENLY--A SPEEDING CAR RACED TO THE CURB, AND IN A MATTER OF SECONDS, BOTH SPIDEY AND GWEN SAW THE GRIM-LOOKING VET SHOVED INSIDE, AND THEN THE CAR SPED OFF! AND NOW, HANG IN THERE, HERO, 'CAUSE HERE WE GO--!
SOMETHING'S WRONG! I'VE GOT TO FOLLOW --BEFORE IT'S TOO LATE!
TM-45
THE CAR HAS OFFICIAL LICENSE PLATES, BUT --OH OH! HOLD IT!
THAT TRUCK-- IT CUT THEM OFF --ON PURPOSE!
CITY
LOOK OUT!
STAN LEE, AUTHOR
JOHN ROMITA, ILLUSTRATOR
ARTIE SIMEK, LETTERER

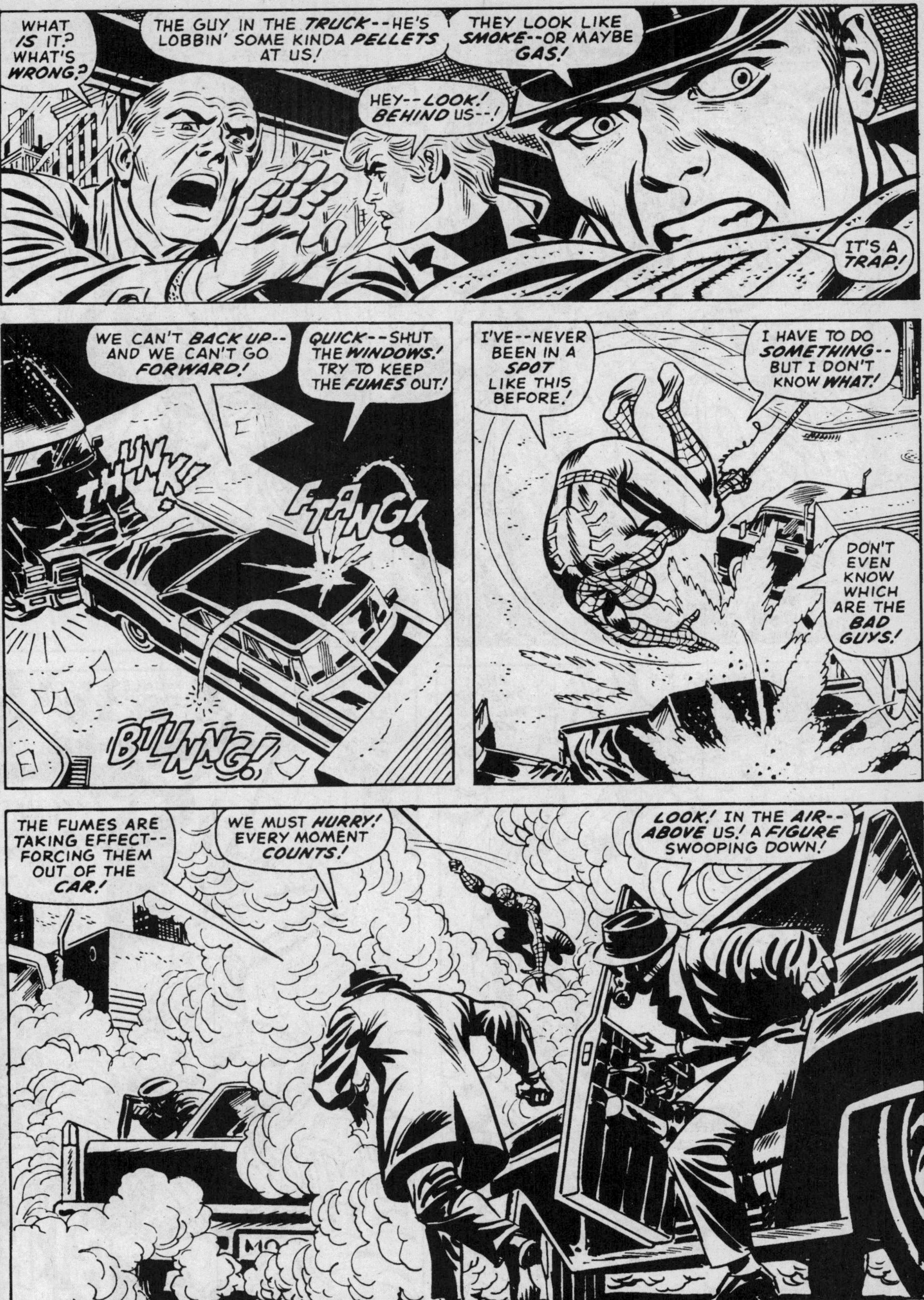
WHAT IS IT? WHAT'S WRONG?
THE GUY IN THE TRUCK--HE'S LOBBIN' SOME KINDA PELLETS AT US!
THEY LOOK LIKE SMOKE--OR MAYBE GAS!
HEY--LOOK! BEHIND US--!
IT'S A TRAP!
WE CAN'T BACK UP--AND WE CAN'T GO FORWARD!
QUICK--SHUT THE WINDOWS! TRY TO KEEP THE FUMES OUT!
THUNK!
FTANG!
BTUNNG!
I'VE--NEVER BEEN IN A SPOT LIKE THIS BEFORE!
I HAVE TO DO SOMETHING--BUT I DON'T KNOW WHAT!
DON'T EVEN KNOW WHICH ARE THE BAD GUYS!
THE FUMES ARE TAKING EFFECT--FORCING THEM OUT OF THE CAR!
WE MUST HURRY! EVERY MOMENT COUNTS!
LOOK! IN THE AIR--ABOVE US! A FIGURE SWOOPING DOWN!
2

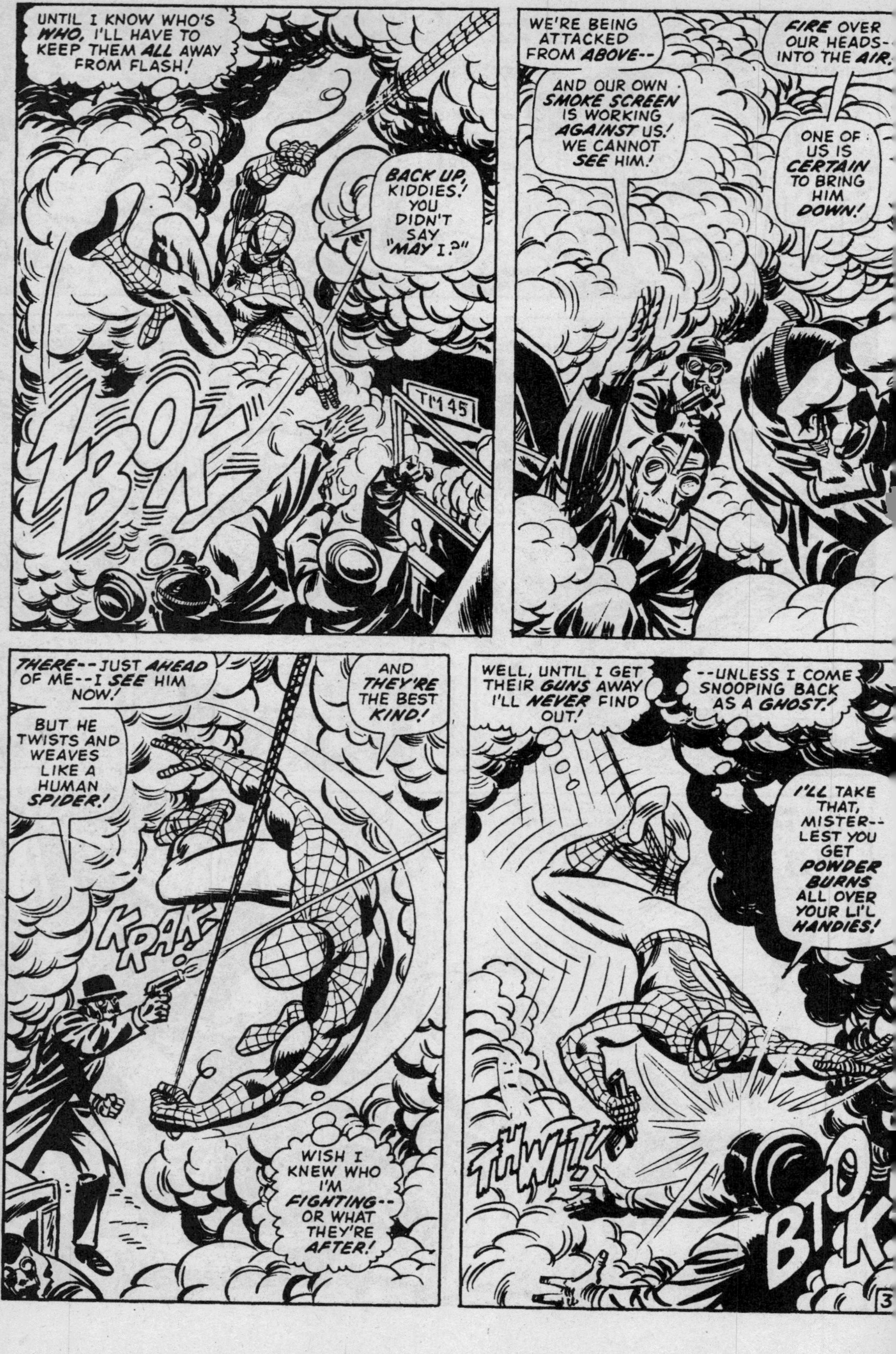
UNTIL I KNOW WHO'S WHO, I'LL HAVE TO KEEP THEM ALL AWAY FROM FLASH!
BACK UP, KIDDIES! YOU DIDN'T SAY "MAY I?"
ZBOK
TM 45
WE'RE BEING ATTACKED FROM ABOVE--
AND OUR OWN SMOKE SCREEN IS WORKING AGAINST US! WE CANNOT SEE HIM!
FIRE OVER OUR HEADS-- INTO THE AIR.
ONE OF US IS CERTAIN TO BRING HIM DOWN!
THERE--JUST AHEAD OF ME--I SEE HIM NOW!
BUT HE TWISTS AND WEAVES LIKE A HUMAN SPIDER!
AND THEY'RE THE BEST KIND!
KRAK
WISH I KNEW WHO I'M FIGHTING--OR WHAT THEY'RE AFTER!
WELL, UNTIL I GET THEIR GUNS AWAY I'LL NEVER FIND OUT!
--UNLESS I COME SNOOPING BACK AS A GHOST!
I'LL TAKE THAT, MISTER--LEST YOU GET POWDER BURNS ALL OVER YOUR LI'L HANDIES!
THWIT
BTOK
3

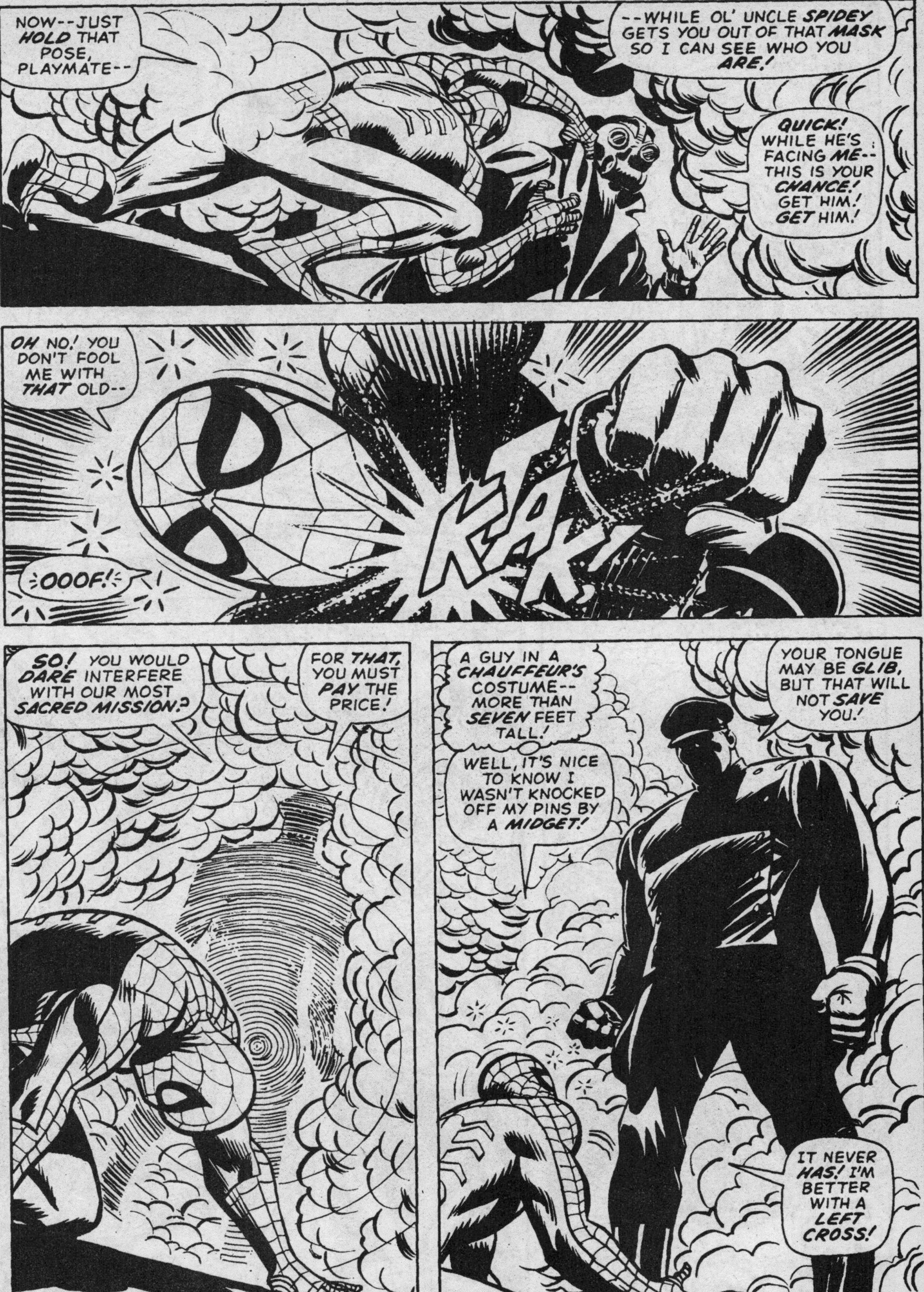
NOW--JUST HOLD THAT POSE, PLAYMATE--
--WHILE OL' UNCLE SPIDEY GETS YOU OUT OF THAT MASK SO I CAN SEE WHO YOU ARE!
QUICK! WHILE HE'S FACING ME-- THIS IS YOUR CHANCE! GET HIM! GET HIM!
OH NO! YOU DON'T FOOL ME WITH THAT OLD--
KTAK!
OOOF!
SO! YOU WOULD DARE INTERFERE WITH OUR MOST SACRED MISSION?
FOR THAT, YOU MUST PAY THE PRICE!
A GUY IN A CHAUFFEUR'S COSTUME-- MORE THAN SEVEN FEET TALL!
WELL, IT'S NICE TO KNOW I WASN'T KNOCKED OFF MY PINS BY A MIDGET!
YOUR TONGUE MAY BE GLIB, BUT THAT WILL NOT SAVE YOU!
IT NEVER HAS! I'M BETTER WITH A LEFT CROSS!
4

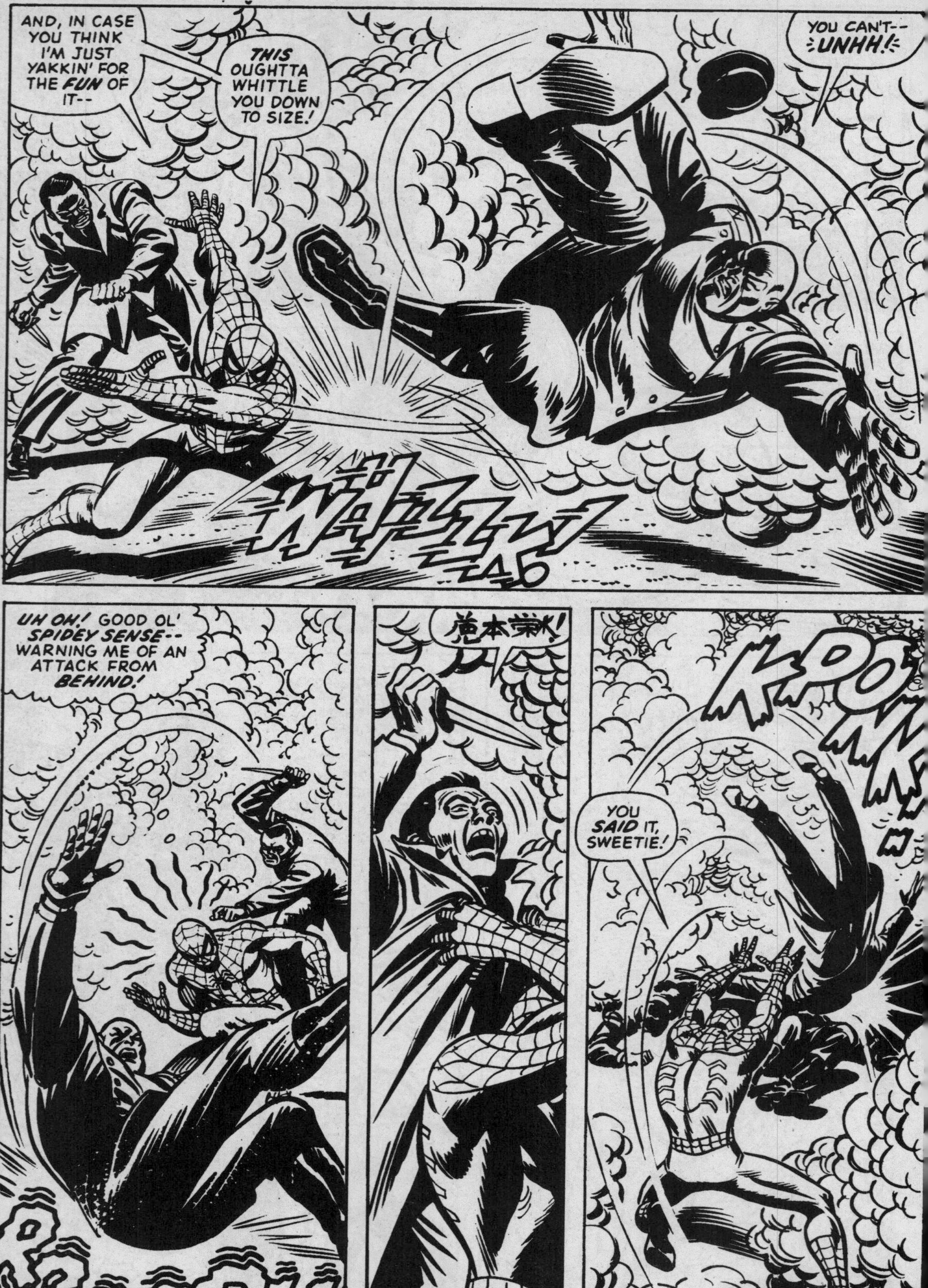
AND, IN CASE YOU THINK I'M JUST YAKKIN' FOR THE FUN OF IT--
THIS OUGHTTA WHITTLE YOU DOWN TO SIZE!
YOU CAN'T-- UNHH!
UH OH! GOOD OL' SPIDEY SENSE-- WARNING ME OF AN ATTACK FROM BEHIND!
YOU SAID IT, SWEETIE!

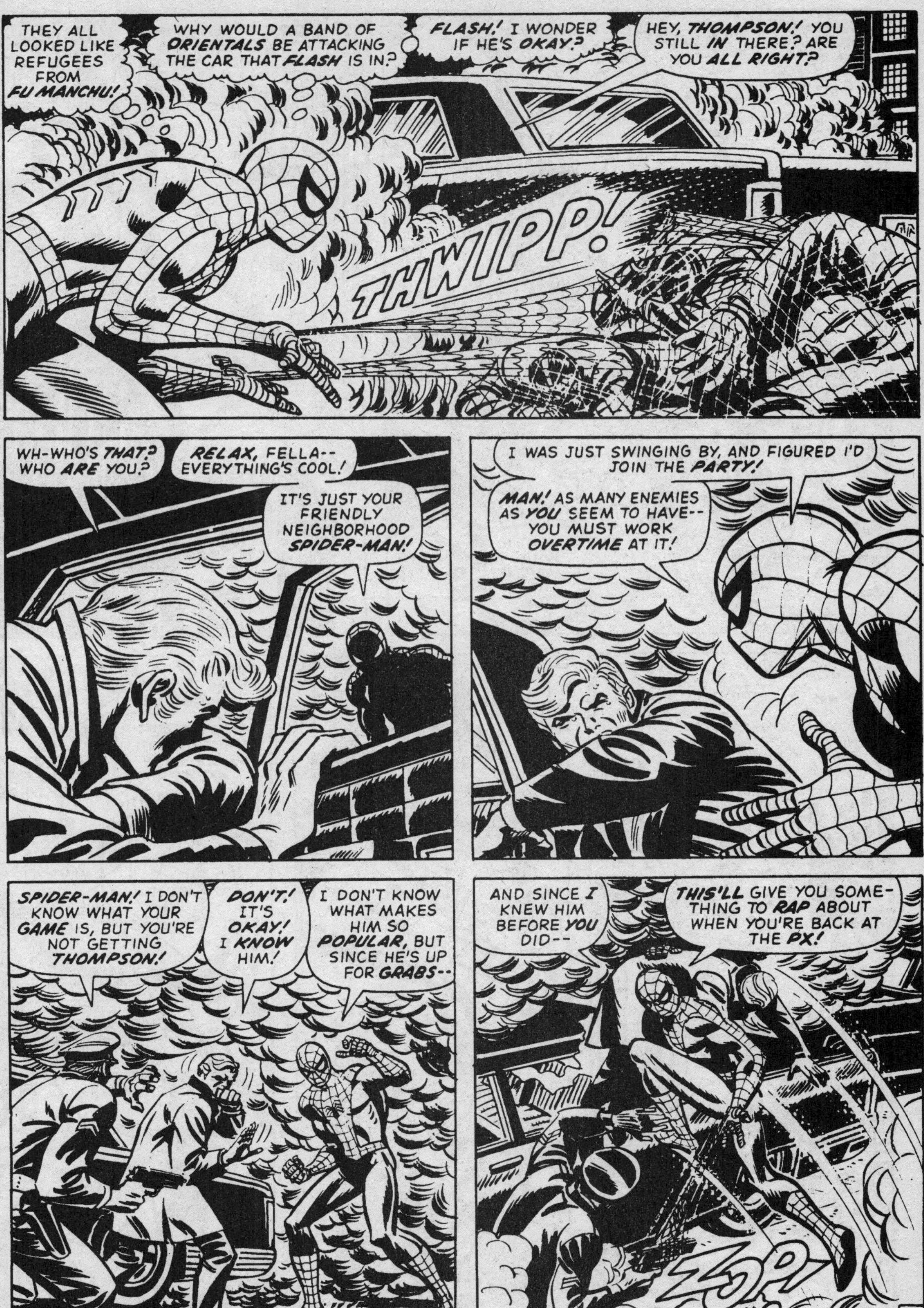
THEY ALL LOOKED LIKE REFUGEES FROM FU MANCHU!
WHY WOULD A BAND OF ORIENTALS BE ATTACKING THE CAR THAT FLASH IS IN?
FLASH! I WONDER IF HE'S OKAY?
HEY, THOMPSON! YOU STILL IN THERE? ARE YOU ALL RIGHT?
THWIPP!
WH-WHO'S THAT? WHO ARE YOU?
RELAX, FELLA-- EVERYTHING'S COOL!
IT'S JUST YOUR FRIENDLY NEIGHBORHOOD SPIDER-MAN!
I WAS JUST SWINGING BY, AND FIGURED I'D JOIN THE PARTY!
MAN! AS MANY ENEMIES AS YOU SEEM TO HAVE-- YOU MUST WORK OVERTIME AT IT!
SPIDER-MAN! I DON'T KNOW WHAT YOUR GAME IS, BUT YOU'RE NOT GETTING THOMPSON!
DON'T! IT'S OKAY! I KNOW HIM!
I DON'T KNOW WHAT MAKES HIM SO POPULAR, BUT SINCE HE'S UP FOR GRABS--
AND SINCE I KNEW HIM BEFORE YOU DID--
THIS'LL GIVE YOU SOMETHING TO RAP ABOUT WHEN YOU'RE BACK AT THE PX!
ZOP!
6

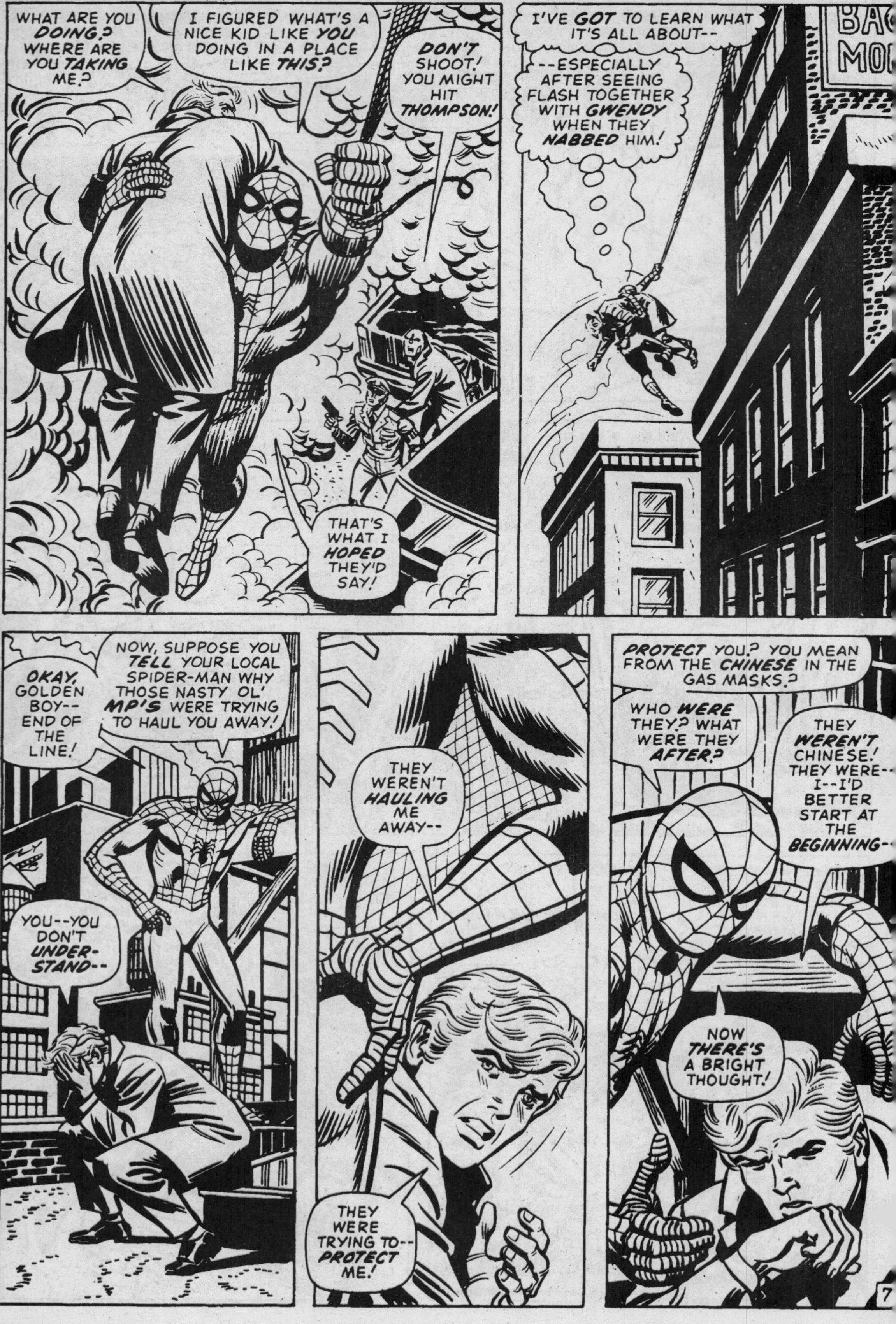

WHAT ARE YOU DOING? WHERE ARE YOU TAKING ME?
I FIGURED WHAT'S A NICE KID LIKE YOU DOING IN A PLACE LIKE THIS?
DON'T SHOOT! YOU MIGHT HIT THOMPSON!
THAT'S WHAT I HOPED THEY'D SAY!
I'VE GOT TO LEARN WHAT IT'S ALL ABOUT--
--ESPECIALLY AFTER SEEING FLASH TOGETHER WITH GWENDY WHEN THEY NABBED HIM!
OKAY, GOLDEN BOY--END OF THE LINE!
NOW, SUPPOSE YOU TELL YOUR LOCAL SPIDER-MAN WHY THOSE NASTY OL' MP'S WERE TRYING TO HAUL YOU AWAY!
YOU--YOU DON'T UNDER-STAND--
THEY WEREN'T HAULING ME AWAY--
THEY WERE TRYING TO--PROTECT ME!
PROTECT YOU? YOU MEAN FROM THE CHINESE IN THE GAS MASKS?
WHO WERE THEY? WHAT WERE THEY AFTER?
THEY WEREN'T CHINESE! THEY WERE--I--I'D BETTER START AT THE BEGINNING--
NOW THERE'S A BRIGHT THOUGHT!

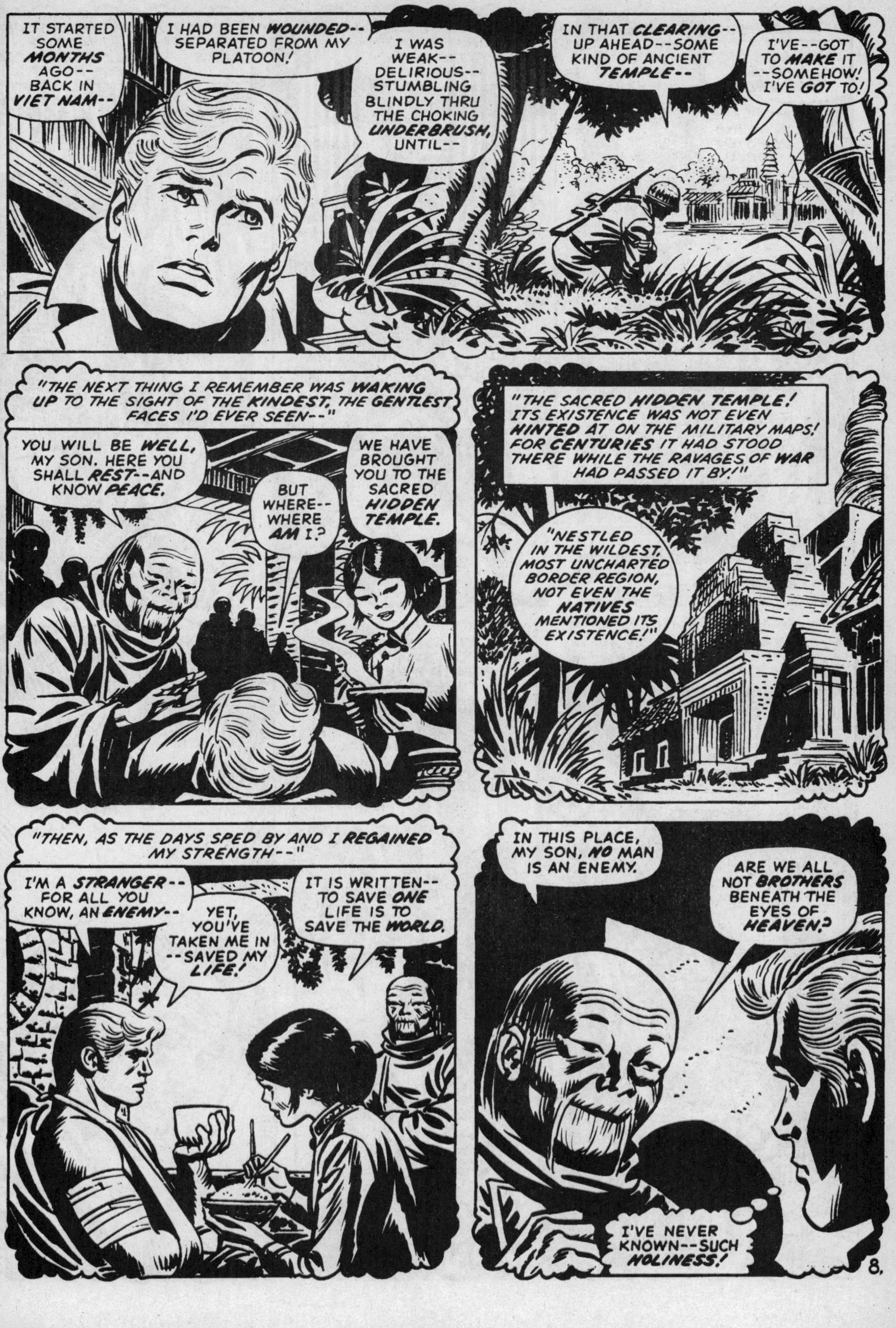

IT STARTED SOME MONTHS AGO-- BACK IN VIET NAM--
I HAD BEEN WOUNDED-- SEPARATED FROM MY PLATOON!
I WAS WEAK-- DELIRIOUS-- STUMBLING BLINDLY THRU THE CHOKING UNDERBRUSH, UNTIL--
IN THAT CLEARING-- UP AHEAD--SOME KIND OF ANCIENT TEMPLE--
I'VE--GOT TO MAKE IT --SOMEHOW! I'VE GOT TO!
"THE NEXT THING I REMEMBER WAS WAKING UP TO THE SIGHT OF THE KINDEST, THE GENTLEST FACES I'D EVER SEEN--"
YOU WILL BE WELL, MY SON. HERE YOU SHALL REST--AND KNOW PEACE.
BUT WHERE-- WHERE AM I?
WE HAVE BROUGHT YOU TO THE SACRED HIDDEN TEMPLE.
"THE SACRED HIDDEN TEMPLE! ITS EXISTENCE WAS NOT EVEN HINTED AT ON THE MILITARY MAPS! FOR CENTURIES IT HAD STOOD THERE WHILE THE RAVAGES OF WAR HAD PASSED IT BY!"
"NESTLED IN THE WILDEST, MOST UNCHARTED BORDER REGION, NOT EVEN THE NATIVES MENTIONED ITS EXISTENCE!"
"THEN, AS THE DAYS SPED BY AND I REGAINED MY STRENGTH--"
I'M A STRANGER-- FOR ALL YOU KNOW, AN ENEMY--
YET, YOU'VE TAKEN ME IN --SAVED MY LIFE!
IT IS WRITTEN-- TO SAVE ONE LIFE IS TO SAVE THE WORLD.
IN THIS PLACE, MY SON, NO MAN IS AN ENEMY.
ARE WE ALL NOT BROTHERS BENEATH THE EYES OF HEAVEN?
I'VE NEVER KNOWN--SUCH HOLINESS!

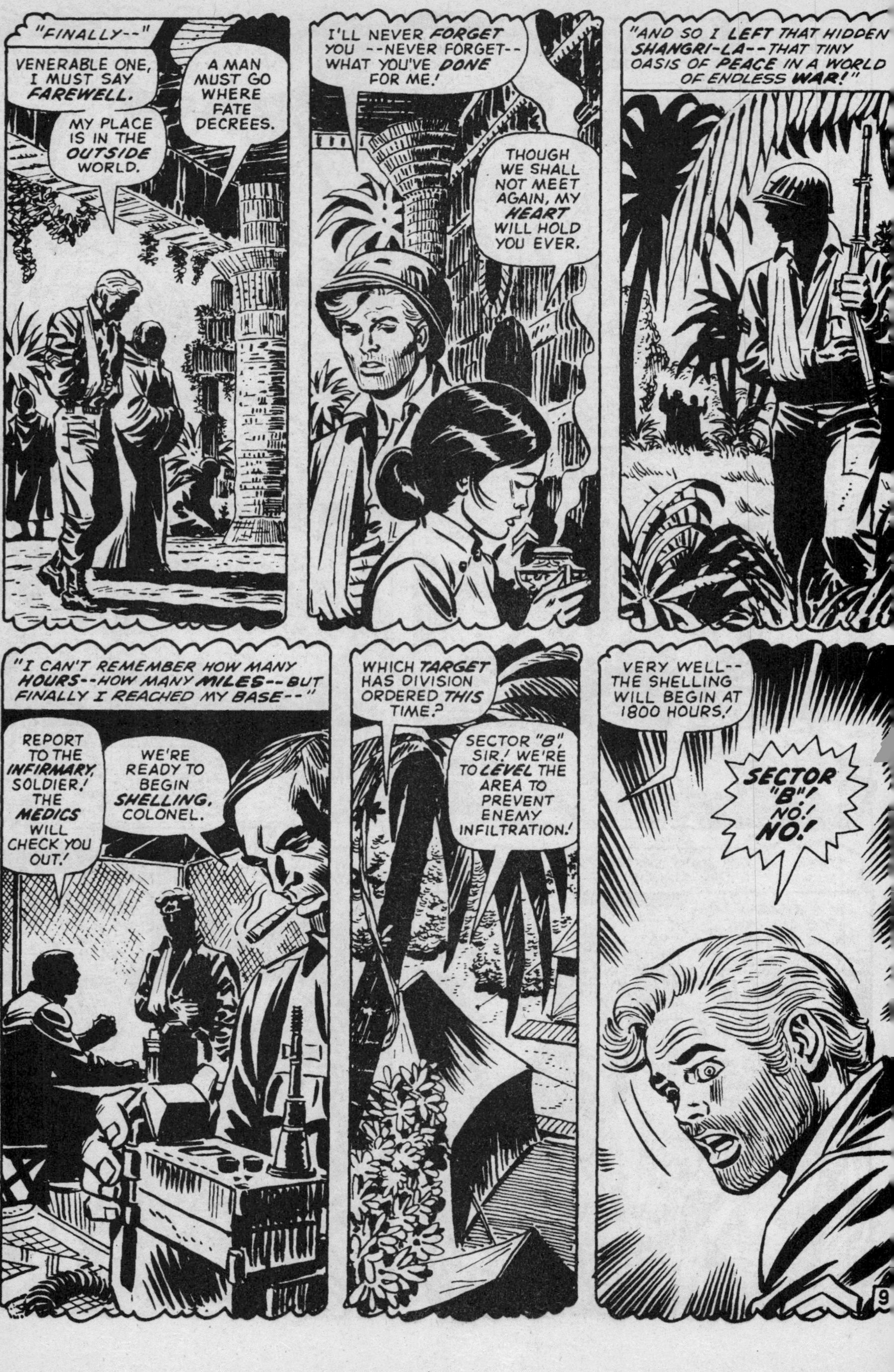
"FINALLY--"
VENERABLE ONE, I MUST SAY FAREWELL.
MY PLACE IS IN THE OUTSIDE WORLD.
A MAN MUST GO WHERE FATE DECREES.
I'LL NEVER FORGET YOU --NEVER FORGET-- WHAT YOU'VE DONE FOR ME!
THOUGH WE SHALL NOT MEET AGAIN, MY HEART WILL HOLD YOU EVER.
"AND SO I LEFT THAT HIDDEN SHANGRI-LA--THAT TINY OASIS OF PEACE IN A WORLD OF ENDLESS WAR!"
"I CAN'T REMEMBER HOW MANY HOURS--HOW MANY MILES--BUT FINALLY I REACHED MY BASE--"
REPORT TO THE INFIRMARY, SOLDIER! THE MEDICS WILL CHECK YOU OUT!
WE'RE READY TO BEGIN SHELLING, COLONEL.
WHICH TARGET HAS DIVISION ORDERED THIS TIME?
SECTOR "B", SIR! WE'RE TO LEVEL THE AREA TO PREVENT ENEMY INFILTRATION!
VERY WELL-- THE SHELLING WILL BEGIN AT 1800 HOURS!
SECTOR "B"! NO! NO!
9

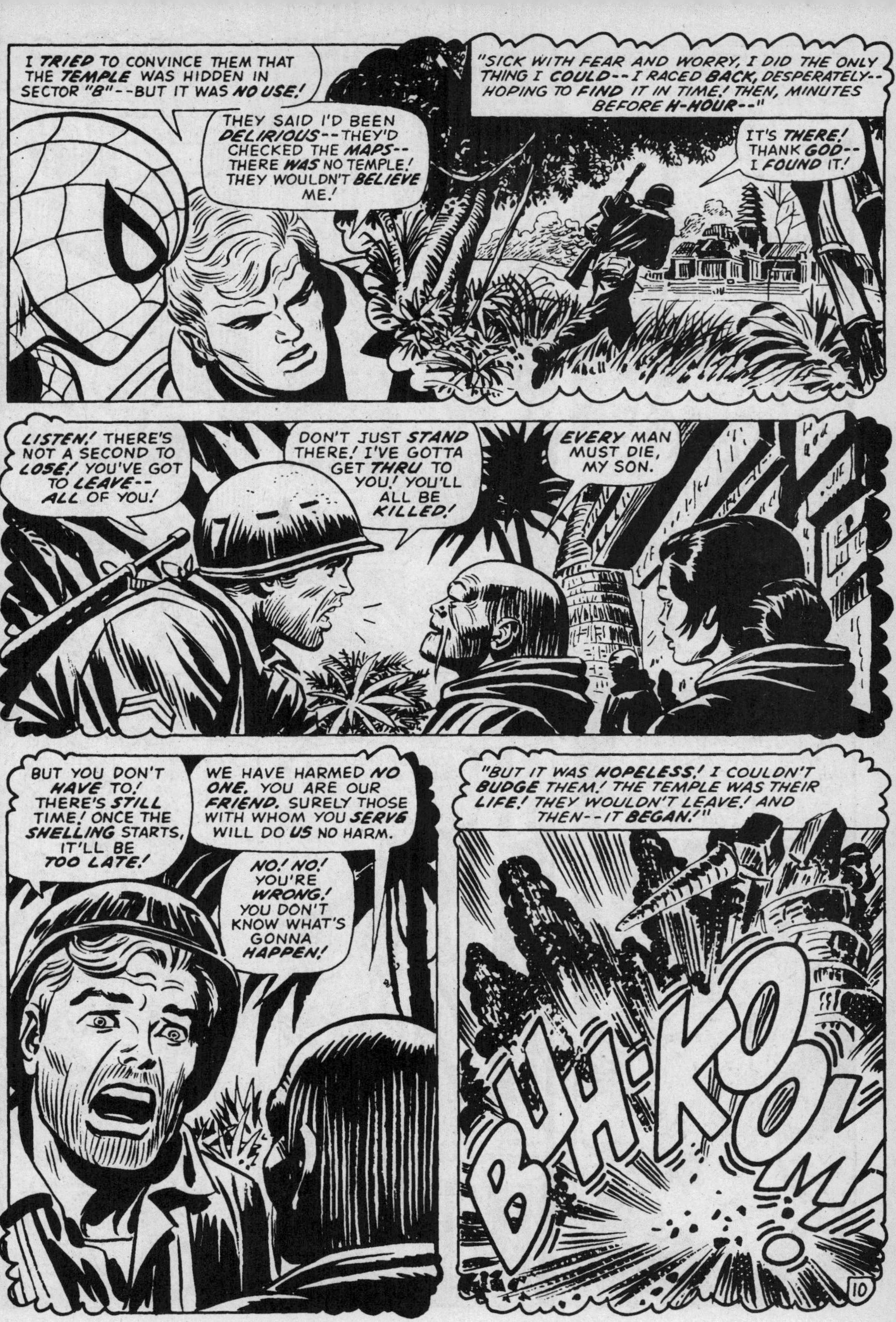
I TRIED TO CONVINCE THEM THAT THE TEMPLE WAS HIDDEN IN SECTOR "B"--BUT IT WAS NO USE!
THEY SAID I'D BEEN DELIRIOUS--THEY'D CHECKED THE MAPS--THERE WAS NO TEMPLE! THEY WOULDN'T BELIEVE ME!
"SICK WITH FEAR AND WORRY, I DID THE ONLY THING I COULD--I RACED BACK, DESPERATELY--HOPING TO FIND IT IN TIME! THEN, MINUTES BEFORE H-HOUR--"
IT'S THERE! THANK GOD--I FOUND IT!
LISTEN! THERE'S NOT A SECOND TO LOSE! YOU'VE GOT TO LEAVE--ALL OF YOU!
DON'T JUST STAND THERE! I'VE GOTTA GET THRU TO YOU! YOU'LL ALL BE KILLED!
EVERY MAN MUST DIE, MY SON.
BUT YOU DON'T HAVE TO! THERE'S STILL TIME! ONCE THE SHELLING STARTS, IT'LL BE TOO LATE!
WE HAVE HARMED NO ONE. YOU ARE OUR FRIEND. SURELY THOSE WITH WHOM YOU SERVE WILL DO US NO HARM.
NO! NO! YOU'RE WRONG! YOU DON'T KNOW WHAT'S GONNA HAPPEN!
"BUT IT WAS HOPELESS! I COULDN'T BUDGE THEM! THE TEMPLE WAS THEIR LIFE! THEY WOULDN'T LEAVE! AND THEN--IT BEGAN!"
BUH-KOOM!
10

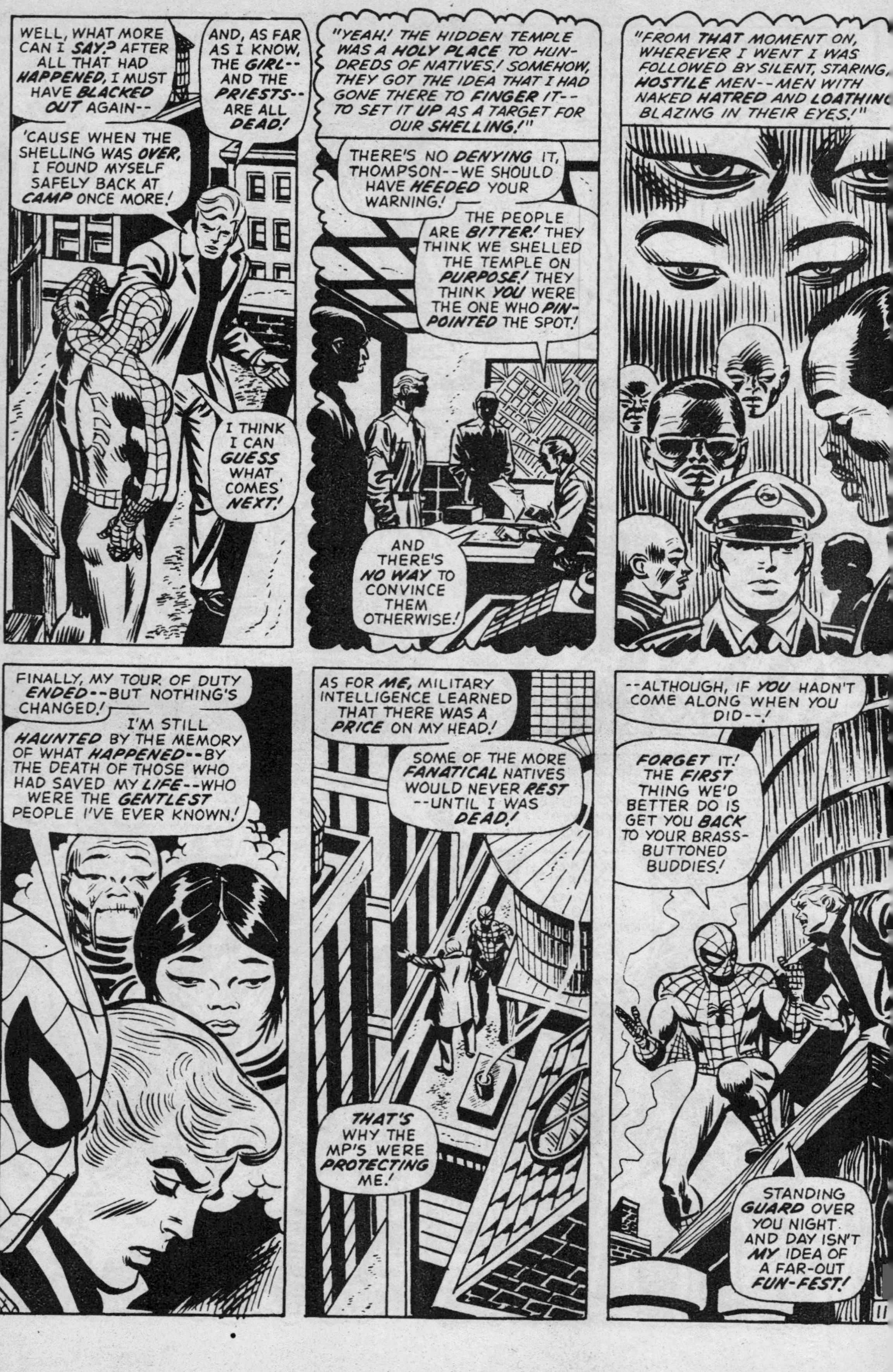
WELL, WHAT MORE CAN I SAY? AFTER ALL THAT HAD HAPPENED, I MUST HAVE BLACKED OUT AGAIN--
AND, AS FAR AS I KNOW, THE GIRL-- AND THE PRIESTS-- ARE ALL DEAD!
'CAUSE WHEN THE SHELLING WAS OVER, I FOUND MYSELF SAFELY BACK AT CAMP ONCE MORE!
I THINK I CAN GUESS WHAT COMES NEXT!
"YEAH! THE HIDDEN TEMPLE WAS A HOLY PLACE TO HUNDREDS OF NATIVES! SOMEHOW, THEY GOT THE IDEA THAT I HAD GONE THERE TO FINGER IT-- TO SET IT UP AS A TARGET FOR OUR SHELLING!"
THERE'S NO DENYING IT, THOMPSON--WE SHOULD HAVE HEEDED YOUR WARNING!
THE PEOPLE ARE BITTER! THEY THINK WE SHELLED THE TEMPLE ON PURPOSE! THEY THINK YOU WERE THE ONE WHO PIN-POINTED THE SPOT!
AND THERE'S NO WAY TO CONVINCE THEM OTHERWISE!
"FROM THAT MOMENT ON, WHEREVER I WENT I WAS FOLLOWED BY SILENT, STARING, HOSTILE MEN--MEN WITH NAKED HATRED AND LOATHING BLAZING IN THEIR EYES!"
FINALLY, MY TOUR OF DUTY ENDED--BUT NOTHING'S CHANGED!
I'M STILL HAUNTED BY THE MEMORY OF WHAT HAPPENED--BY THE DEATH OF THOSE WHO HAD SAVED MY LIFE--WHO WERE THE GENTLEST PEOPLE I'VE EVER KNOWN!
AS FOR ME, MILITARY INTELLIGENCE LEARNED THAT THERE WAS A PRICE ON MY HEAD!
SOME OF THE MORE FANATICAL NATIVES WOULD NEVER REST --UNTIL I WAS DEAD!
THAT'S WHY THE MP'S WERE PROTECTING ME!
--ALTHOUGH, IF YOU HADN'T COME ALONG WHEN YOU DID--!
FORGET IT! THE FIRST THING WE'D BETTER DO IS GET YOU BACK TO YOUR BRASS-BUTTONED BUDDIES!
STANDING GUARD OVER YOU NIGHT AND DAY ISN'T MY IDEA OF A FAR-OUT FUN-FEST!
11

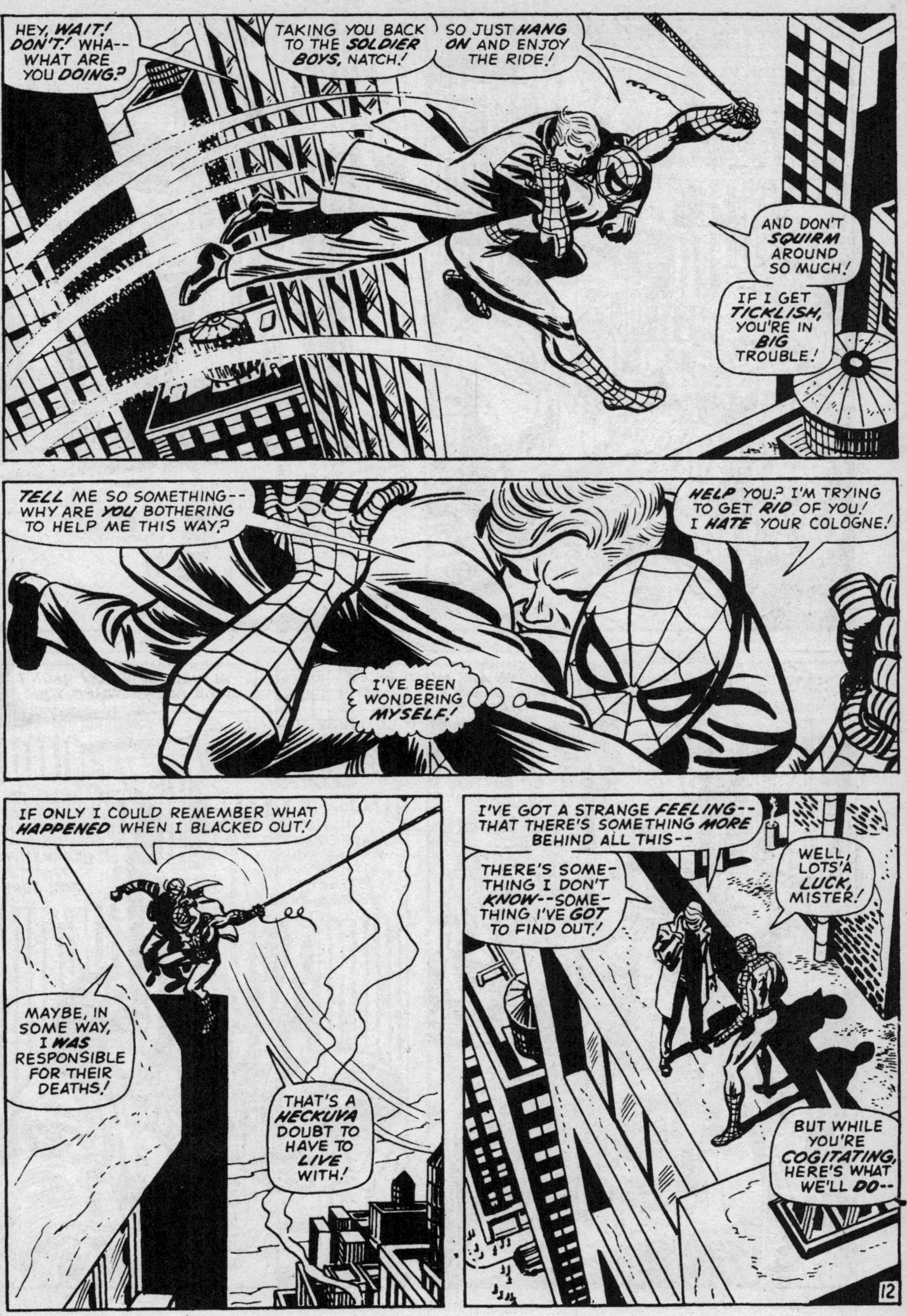
HEY, WAIT! DON'T! WHA-- WHAT ARE YOU DOING?
TAKING YOU BACK TO THE SOLDIER BOYS, NATCH!
SO JUST HANG ON AND ENJOY THE RIDE!
AND DON'T SQUIRM AROUND SO MUCH!
IF I GET TICKLISH, YOU'RE IN BIG TROUBLE!
TELL ME SO SOMETHING-- WHY ARE YOU BOTHERING TO HELP ME THIS WAY?
HELP YOU? I'M TRYING TO GET RID OF YOU! I HATE YOUR COLOGNE!
I'VE BEEN WONDERING MYSELF!
IF ONLY I COULD REMEMBER WHAT HAPPENED WHEN I BLACKED OUT!
MAYBE, IN SOME WAY, I WAS RESPONSIBLE FOR THEIR DEATHS!
THAT'S A HECKUVA DOUBT TO HAVE TO LIVE WITH!
I'VE GOT A STRANGE FEELING-- THAT THERE'S SOMETHING MORE BEHIND ALL THIS--
THERE'S SOMETHING I DON'T KNOW--SOMETHING I'VE GOT TO FIND OUT!
WELL, LOTS'A LUCK, MISTER!
BUT WHILE YOU'RE COGITATING, HERE'S WHAT WE'LL DO--
12

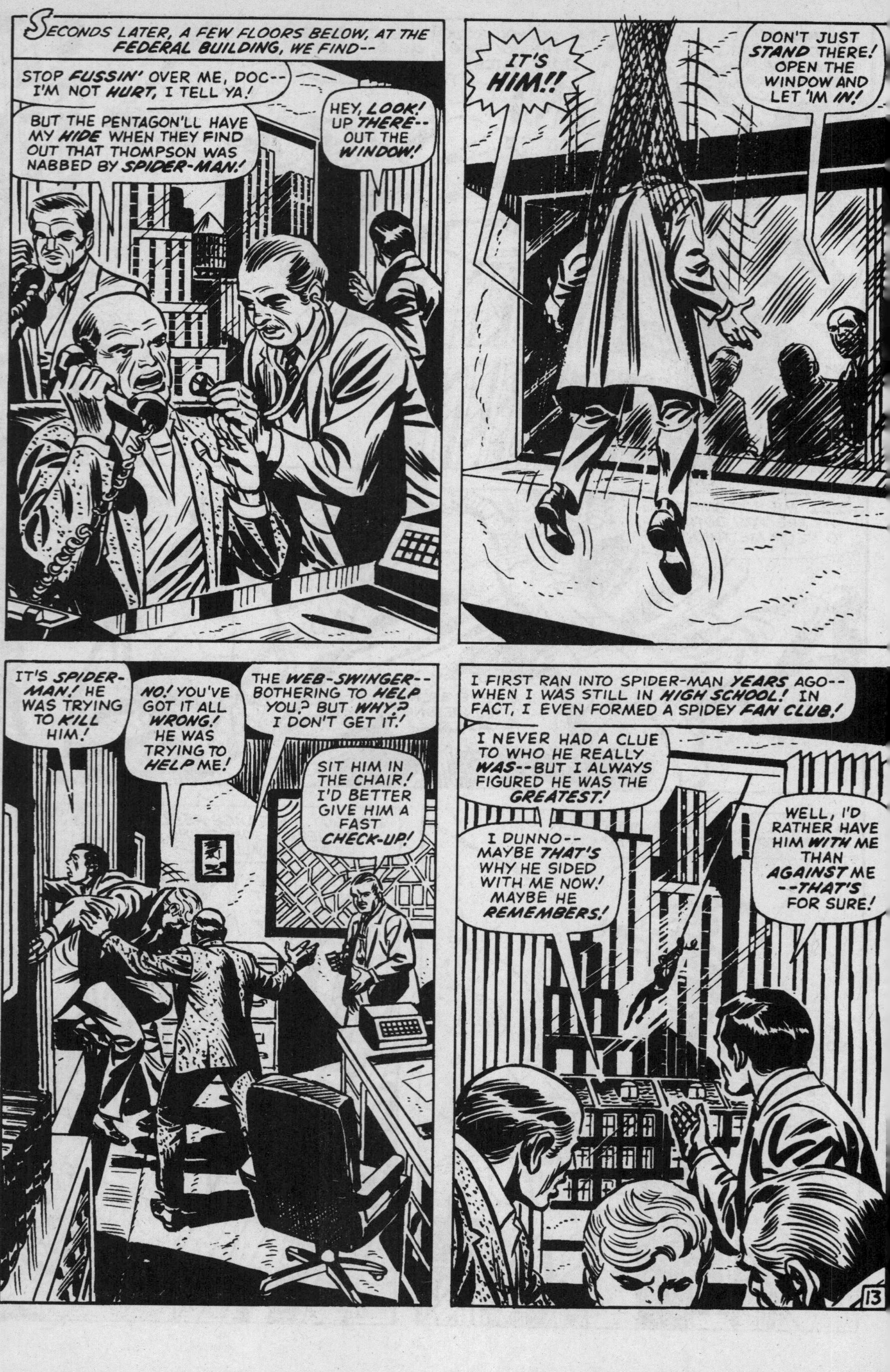
SECONDS LATER, A FEW FLOORS BELOW, AT THE FEDERAL BUILDING, WE FIND--
STOP FUSSIN' OVER ME, DOC-- I'M NOT HURT, I TELL YA!
BUT THE PENTAGON'LL HAVE MY HIDE WHEN THEY FIND OUT THAT THOMPSON WAS NABBED BY SPIDER-MAN!
HEY, LOOK! UP THERE-- OUT THE WINDOW!
IT'S HIM!!
DON'T JUST STAND THERE! OPEN THE WINDOW AND LET 'IM IN!
IT'S SPIDER-MAN! HE WAS TRYING TO KILL HIM!
NO! YOU'VE GOT IT ALL WRONG! HE WAS TRYING TO HELP ME!
THE WEB-SWINGER-- BOTHERING TO HELP YOU? BUT WHY? I DON'T GET IT!
SIT HIM IN THE CHAIR! I'D BETTER GIVE HIM A FAST CHECK-UP!
I FIRST RAN INTO SPIDER-MAN YEARS AGO-- WHEN I WAS STILL IN HIGH SCHOOL! IN FACT, I EVEN FORMED A SPIDEY FAN CLUB!
I NEVER HAD A CLUE TO WHO HE REALLY WAS-- BUT I ALWAYS FIGURED HE WAS THE GREATEST!
I DUNNO-- MAYBE THAT'S WHY HE SIDED WITH ME NOW! MAYBE HE REMEMBERS!
WELL, I'D RATHER HAVE HIM WITH ME THAN AGAINST ME --THAT'S FOR SURE!
13

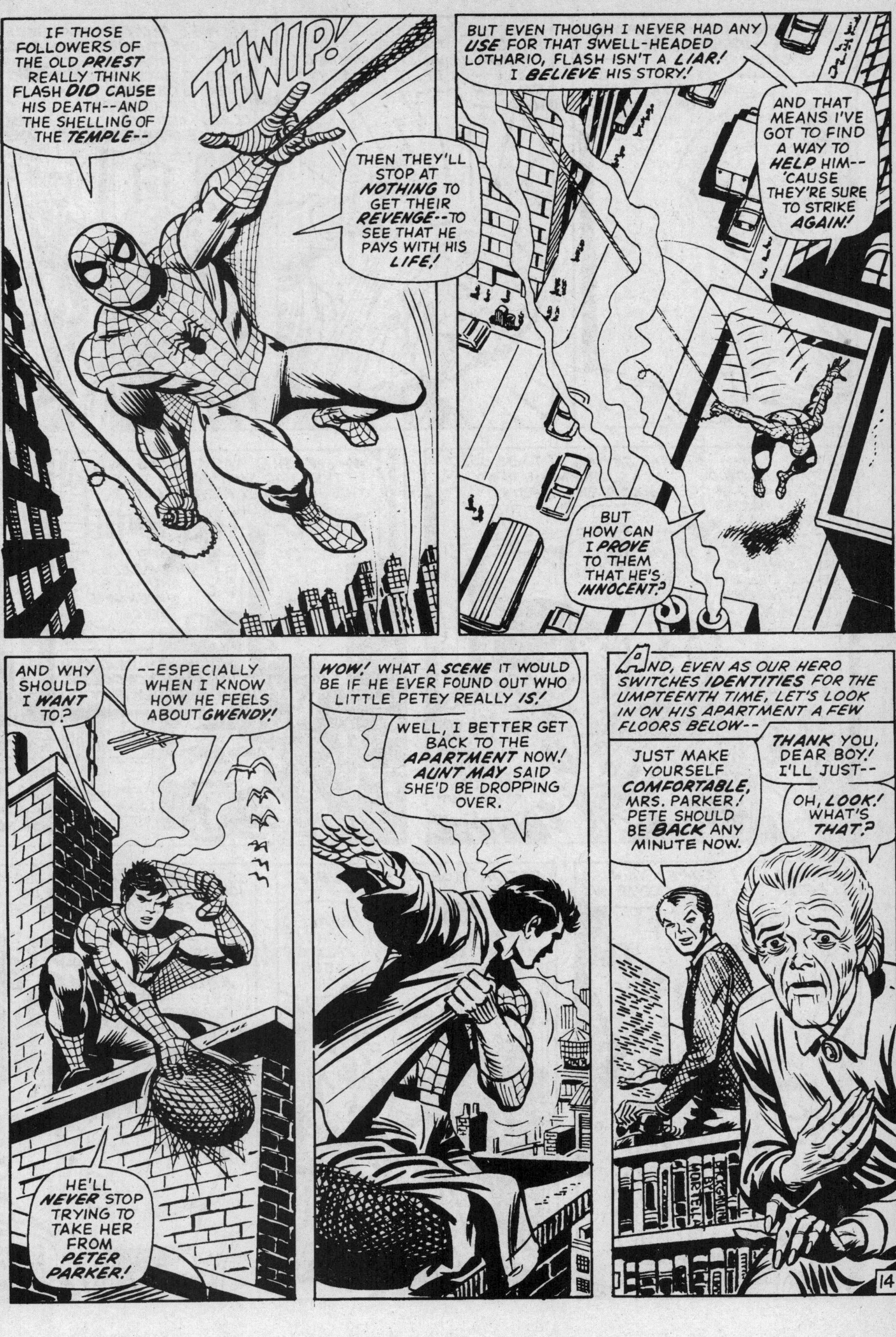
IF THOSE FOLLOWERS OF THE OLD PRIEST REALLY THINK FLASH DID CAUSE HIS DEATH--AND THE SHELLING OF THE TEMPLE--
THWIP!
THEN THEY'LL STOP AT NOTHING TO GET THEIR REVENGE--TO SEE THAT HE PAYS WITH HIS LIFE!
BUT EVEN THOUGH I NEVER HAD ANY USE FOR THAT SWELL-HEADED LOTHARIO, FLASH ISN'T A LIAR! I BELIEVE HIS STORY!
AND THAT MEANS I'VE GOT TO FIND A WAY TO HELP HIM--'CAUSE THEY'RE SURE TO STRIKE AGAIN!
BUT HOW CAN I PROVE TO THEM THAT HE'S INNOCENT?
AND WHY SHOULD I WANT TO?
--ESPECIALLY WHEN I KNOW HOW HE FEELS ABOUT GWENDY!
HE'LL NEVER STOP TRYING TO TAKE HER FROM PETER PARKER!
WOW! WHAT A SCENE IT WOULD BE IF HE EVER FOUND OUT WHO LITTLE PETEY REALLY IS!
WELL, I BETTER GET BACK TO THE APARTMENT NOW! AUNT MAY SAID SHE'D BE DROPPING OVER.
AND, EVEN AS OUR HERO SWITCHES IDENTITIES FOR THE UMPTEENTH TIME, LET'S LOOK IN ON HIS APARTMENT A FEW FLOORS BELOW--
JUST MAKE YOURSELF COMFORTABLE, MRS. PARKER! PETE SHOULD BE BACK ANY MINUTE NOW.
THANK YOU, DEAR BOY! I'LL JUST--
OH, LOOK! WHAT'S THAT?
14

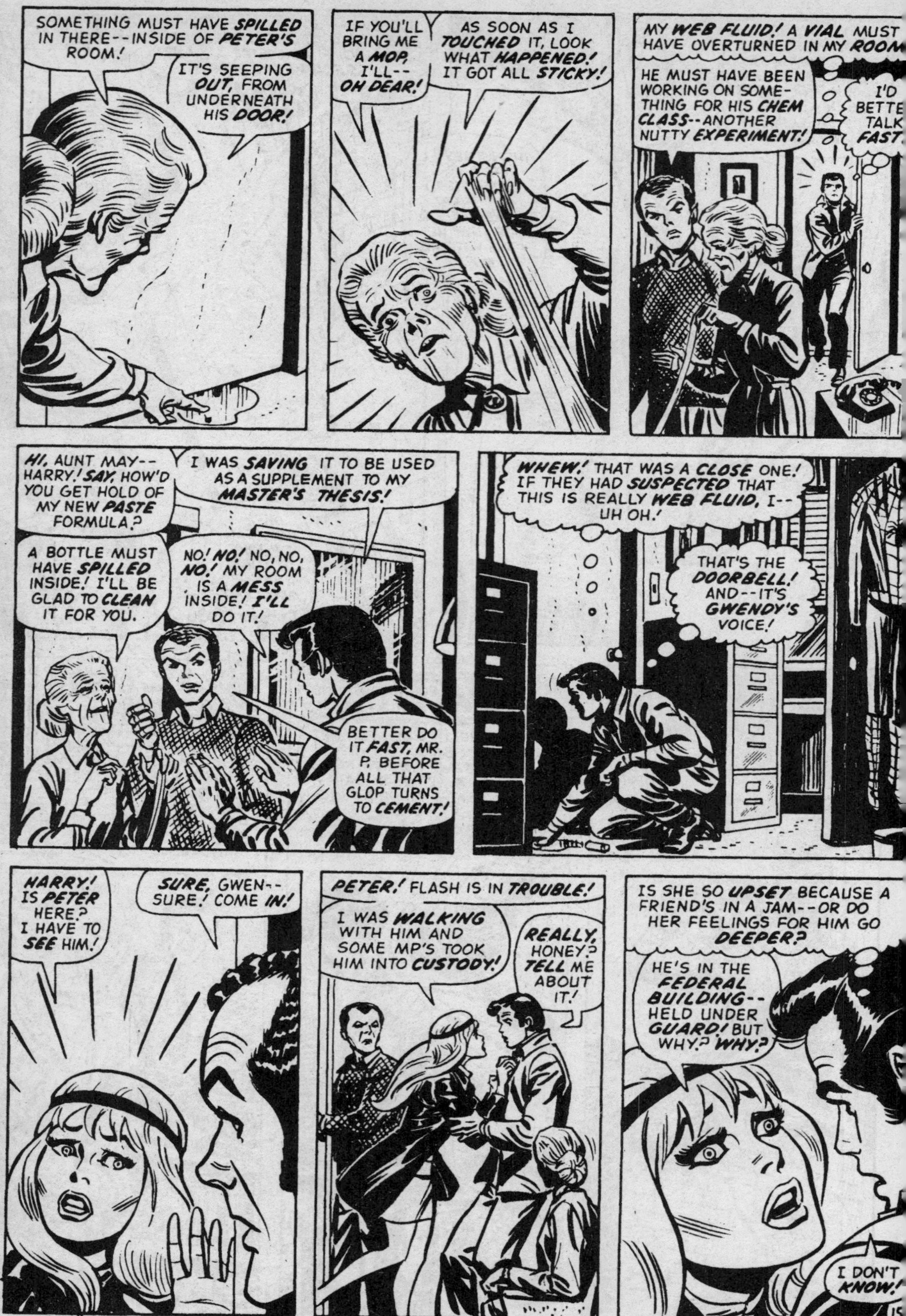
SOMETHING MUST HAVE SPILLED IN THERE--INSIDE OF PETER'S ROOM!
IT'S SEEPING OUT, FROM UNDERNEATH HIS DOOR!
IF YOU'LL BRING ME A MOP, I'LL-- OH DEAR!
AS SOON AS I TOUCHED IT, LOOK WHAT HAPPENED! IT GOT ALL STICKY!
MY WEB FLUID! A VIAL MUST HAVE OVERTURNED IN MY ROOM
HE MUST HAVE BEEN WORKING ON SOMETHING FOR HIS CHEM CLASS--ANOTHER NUTTY EXPERIMENT!
HI, AUNT MAY-- HARRY! SAY, HOW'D YOU GET HOLD OF MY NEW PASTE FORMULA?
I WAS SAVING IT TO BE USED AS A SUPPLEMENT TO MY MASTER'S THESIS!
A BOTTLE MUST HAVE SPILLED INSIDE! I'LL BE GLAD TO CLEAN IT FOR YOU.
NO! NO! NO, NO, NO! MY ROOM IS A MESS INSIDE! I'LL DO IT!
BETTER DO IT FAST, MR. P. BEFORE ALL THAT GLOP TURNS TO CEMENT!
WHEW! THAT WAS A CLOSE ONE! IF THEY HAD SUSPECTED THAT THIS IS REALLY WEB FLUID, I-- UH OH!
THAT'S THE DOORBELL! AND--IT'S GWENDY'S VOICE!
HARRY! IS PETER HERE? I HAVE TO SEE HIM!
SURE, GWEN-- SURE! COME IN!
PETER! FLASH IS IN TROUBLE!
I WAS WALKING WITH HIM AND SOME MP'S TOOK HIM INTO CUSTODY!
REALLY, HONEY? TELL ME ABOUT IT!
IS SHE SO UPSET BECAUSE A FRIEND'S IN A JAM--OR DO HER FEELINGS FOR HIM GO DEEPER?
HE'S IN THE FEDERAL BUILDING--HELD UNDER GUARD! BUT WHY? WHY?
I DON'T KNOW!

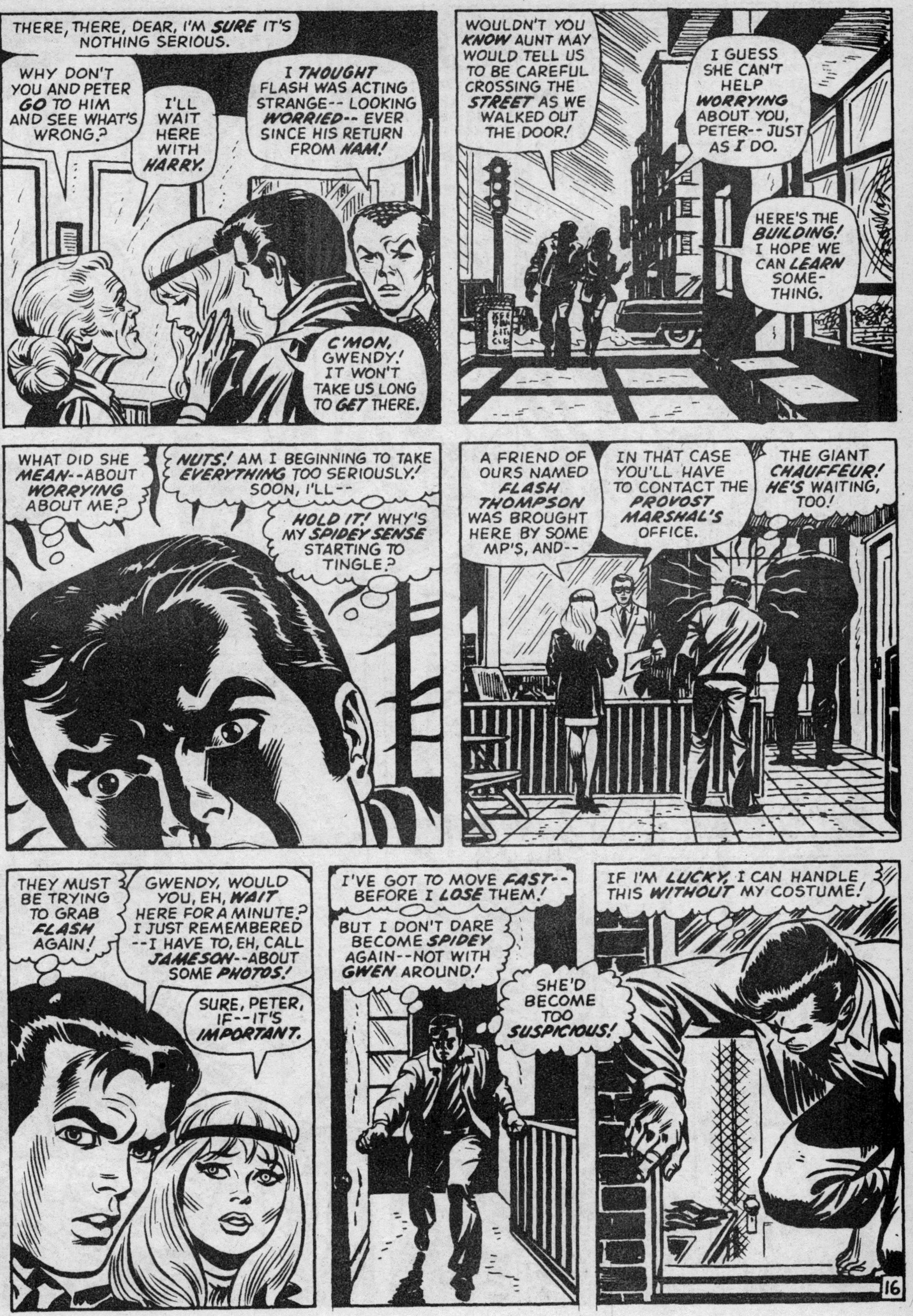
THERE, THERE, DEAR, I'M SURE IT'S NOTHING SERIOUS.
WHY DON'T YOU AND PETER GO TO HIM AND SEE WHAT'S WRONG?
I'LL WAIT HERE WITH HARRY.
I THOUGHT FLASH WAS ACTING STRANGE-- LOOKING WORRIED-- EVER SINCE HIS RETURN FROM NAM!
C'MON, GWENDY! IT WON'T TAKE US LONG TO GET THERE.
WOULDN'T YOU KNOW AUNT MAY WOULD TELL US TO BE CAREFUL CROSSING THE STREET AS WE WALKED OUT THE DOOR!
I GUESS SHE CAN'T HELP WORRYING ABOUT YOU, PETER-- JUST AS I DO.
HERE'S THE BUILDING! I HOPE WE CAN LEARN SOME-THING.
WHAT DID SHE MEAN--ABOUT WORRYING ABOUT ME?
NUTS! AM I BEGINNING TO TAKE EVERYTHING TOO SERIOUSLY! SOON, I'LL--
HOLD IT! WHY'S MY SPIDEY SENSE STARTING TO TINGLE?
A FRIEND OF OURS NAMED FLASH THOMPSON WAS BROUGHT HERE BY SOME MP'S, AND--
IN THAT CASE YOU'LL HAVE TO CONTACT THE PROVOST MARSHAL'S OFFICE.
THE GIANT CHAUFFEUR! HE'S WAITING, TOO!
THEY MUST BE TRYING TO GRAB FLASH AGAIN!
GWENDY, WOULD YOU, EH, WAIT HERE FOR A MINUTE? I JUST REMEMBERED --I HAVE TO, EH, CALL JAMESON--ABOUT SOME PHOTOS!
SURE, PETER, IF--IT'S IMPORTANT.
I'VE GOT TO MOVE FAST-- BEFORE I LOSE THEM!
BUT I DON'T DARE BECOME SPIDEY AGAIN--NOT WITH GWEN AROUND!
SHE'D BECOME TOO SUSPICIOUS!
IF I'M LUCKY, I CAN HANDLE THIS WITHOUT MY COSTUME!

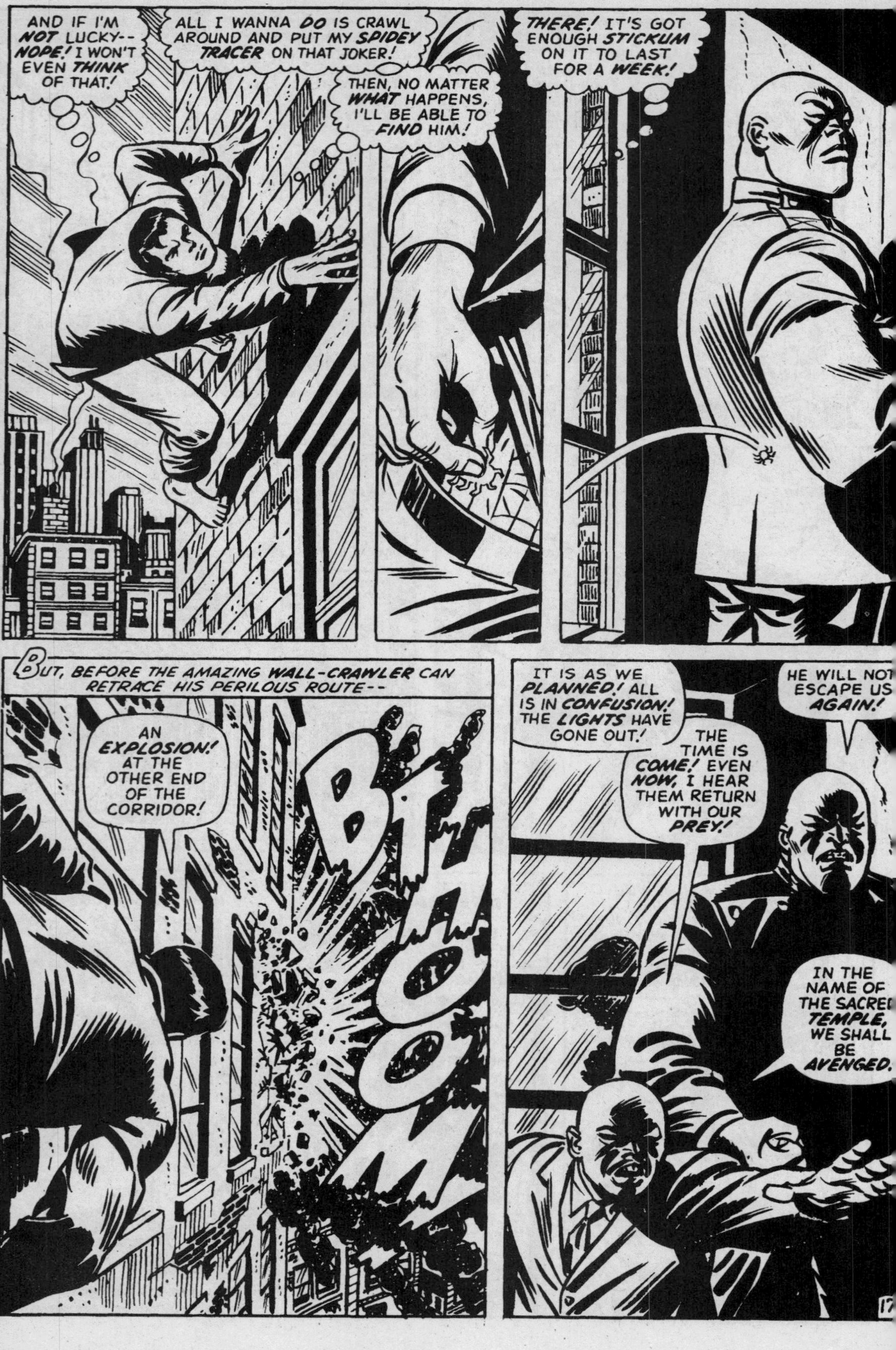
AND IF I'M NOT LUCKY-- NOPE! I WON'T EVEN THINK OF THAT!
ALL I WANNA DO IS CRAWL AROUND AND PUT MY SPIDEY TRACER ON THAT JOKER!
THEN, NO MATTER WHAT HAPPENS, I'LL BE ABLE TO FIND HIM!
THERE! IT'S GOT ENOUGH STICKUM ON IT TO LAST FOR A WEEK!
BUT, BEFORE THE AMAZING WALL-CRAWLER CAN RETRACE HIS PERILOUS ROUTE--
AN EXPLOSION! AT THE OTHER END OF THE CORRIDOR!
BTHOOOM
IT IS AS WE PLANNED! ALL IS IN CONFUSION! THE LIGHTS HAVE GONE OUT!
THE TIME IS COME! EVEN NOW, I HEAR THEM RETURN WITH OUR PREY!
HE WILL NOT ESCAPE US AGAIN!
IN THE NAME OF THE SACRED TEMPLE, WE SHALL BE AVENGED.
17

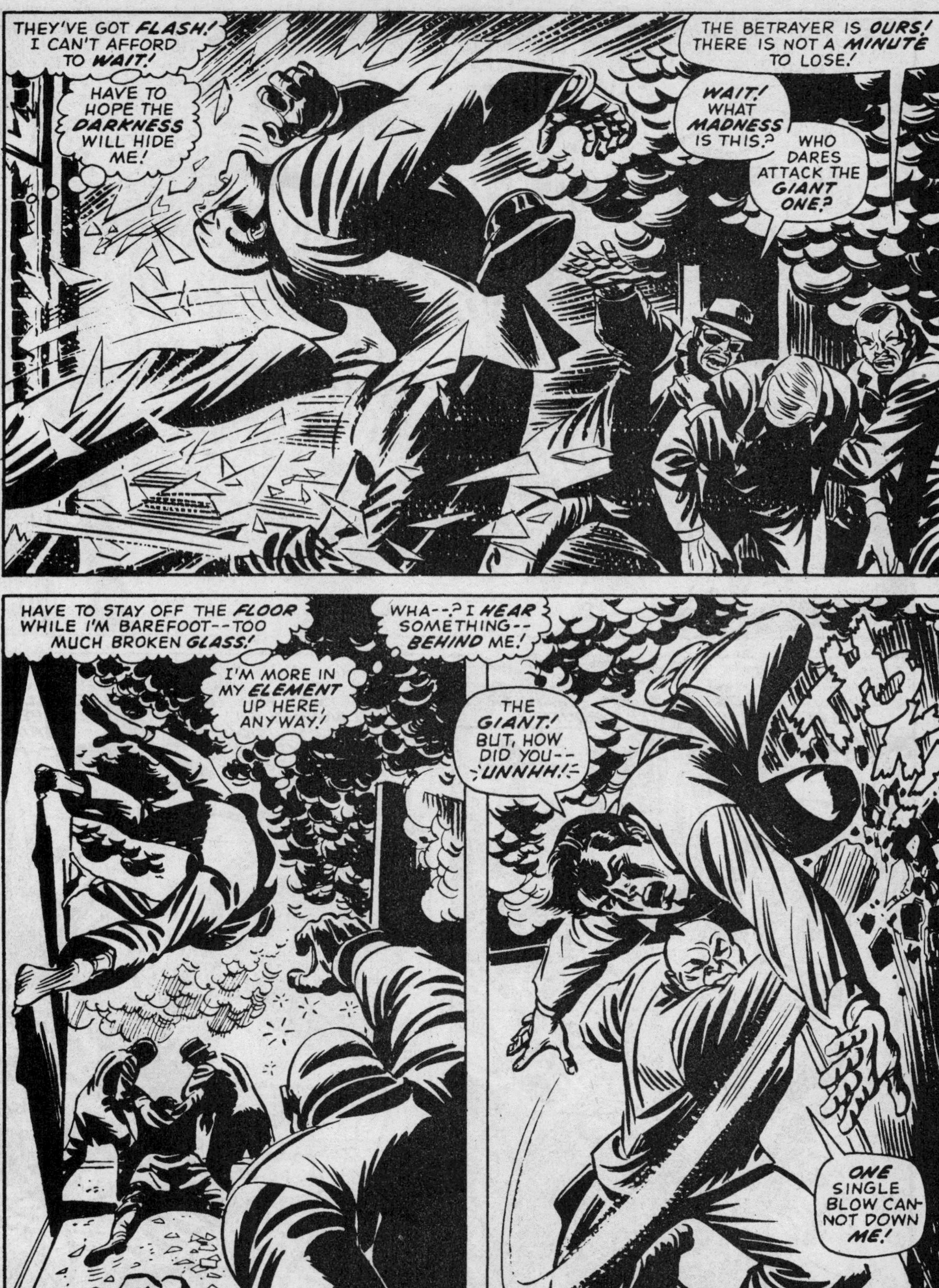
THEY'VE GOT FLASH! I CAN'T AFFORD TO WAIT!
HAVE TO HOPE THE DARKNESS WILL HIDE ME!
THE BETRAYER IS OURS! THERE IS NOT A MINUTE TO LOSE!
WAIT! WHAT MADNESS IS THIS?
WHO DARES ATTACK THE GIANT ONE?
HAVE TO STAY OFF THE FLOOR WHILE I'M BAREFOOT--TOO MUCH BROKEN GLASS!
I'M MORE IN MY ELEMENT UP HERE, ANYWAY!
WHA--? I HEAR SOMETHING--BEHIND ME!
THE GIANT! BUT, HOW DID YOU-- UNNHH!
ONE SINGLE BLOW CANNOT DOWN ME!
18

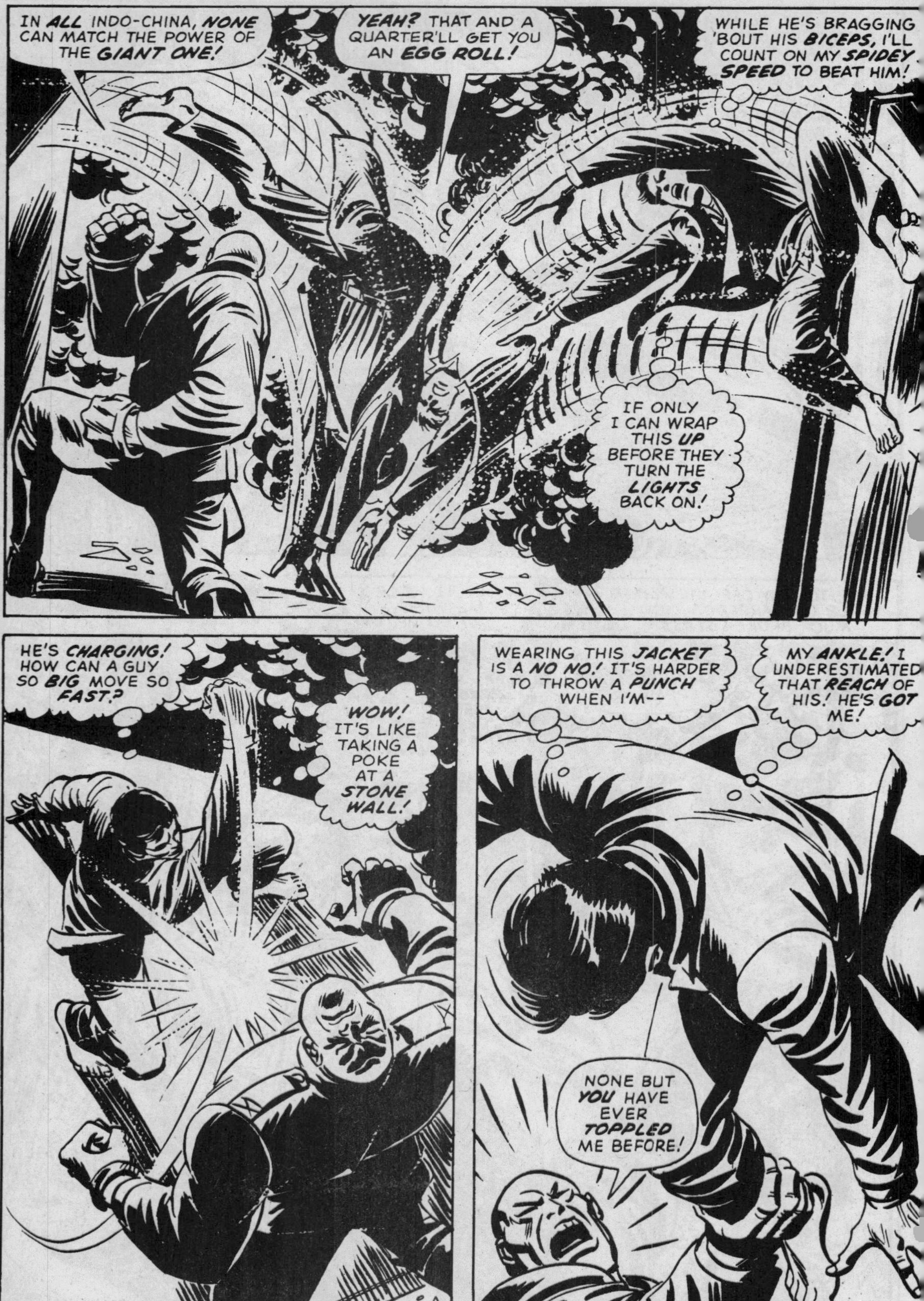
IN ALL INDO-CHINA, NONE CAN MATCH THE POWER OF THE GIANT ONE!
YEAH? THAT AND A QUARTER'LL GET YOU AN EGG ROLL!
WHILE HE'S BRAGGING 'BOUT HIS BICEPS, I'LL COUNT ON MY SPIDEY SPEED TO BEAT HIM!
IF ONLY I CAN WRAP THIS UP BEFORE THEY TURN THE LIGHTS BACK ON!
HE'S CHARGING! HOW CAN A GUY SO BIG MOVE SO FAST?
WOW! IT'S LIKE TAKING A POKE AT A STONE WALL!
WEARING THIS JACKET IS A NO NO! IT'S HARDER TO THROW A PUNCH WHEN I'M--
MY ANKLE! I UNDERESTIMATED THAT REACH OF HIS! HE'S GOT ME!
NONE BUT YOU HAVE EVER TOPPLED ME BEFORE!
19

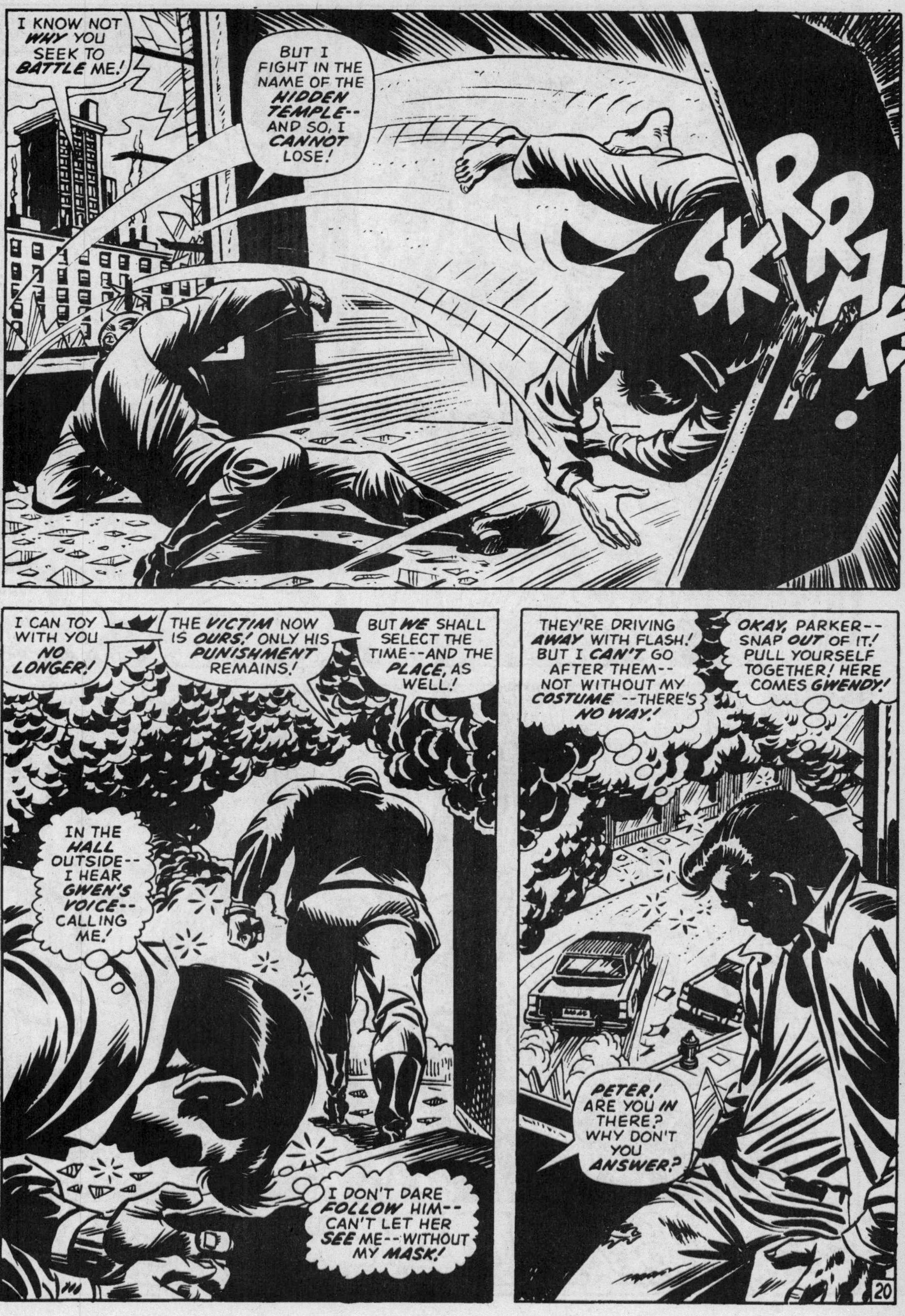

I KNOW NOT WHY YOU SEEK TO BATTLE ME!
BUT I FIGHT IN THE NAME OF THE HIDDEN TEMPLE-- AND SO, I CANNOT LOSE!
SKRRAKK!
I CAN TOY WITH YOU NO LONGER!
THE VICTIM NOW IS OURS! ONLY HIS PUNISHMENT REMAINS!
BUT WE SHALL SELECT THE TIME--AND THE PLACE, AS WELL!
IN THE HALL OUTSIDE-- I HEAR GWEN'S VOICE-- CALLING ME!
I DON'T DARE FOLLOW HIM-- CAN'T LET HER SEE ME--WITHOUT MY MASK!
THEY'RE DRIVING AWAY WITH FLASH! BUT I CAN'T GO AFTER THEM-- NOT WITHOUT MY COSTUME --THERE'S NO WAY!
OKAY, PARKER-- SNAP OUT OF IT! PULL YOURSELF TOGETHER! HERE COMES GWENDY!
PETER! ARE YOU IN THERE? WHY DON'T YOU ANSWER?
20

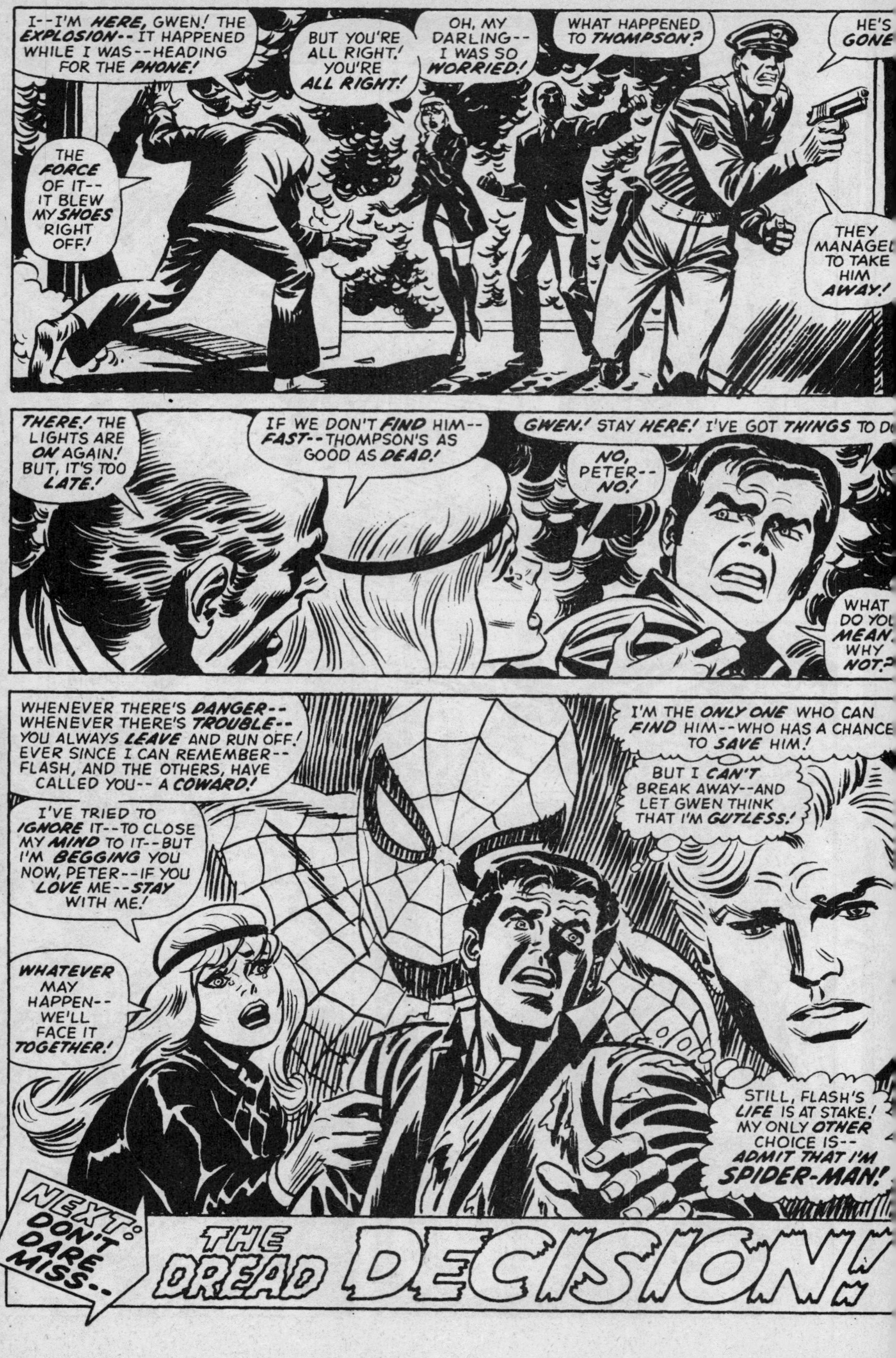
I--I'M HERE, GWEN! THE EXPLOSION-- IT HAPPENED WHILE I WAS--HEADING FOR THE PHONE!
BUT YOU'RE ALL RIGHT! YOU'RE ALL RIGHT!
OH, MY DARLING-- I WAS SO WORRIED!
WHAT HAPPENED TO THOMPSON?
HE'S GONE
THE FORCE OF IT-- IT BLEW MY SHOES RIGHT OFF!
THEY MANAGED TO TAKE HIM AWAY!
THERE! THE LIGHTS ARE ON AGAIN! BUT, IT'S TOO LATE!
IF WE DON'T FIND HIM-- FAST--THOMPSON'S AS GOOD AS DEAD!
GWEN! STAY HERE! I'VE GOT THINGS TO DO
NO, PETER-- NO!
WHAT DO YOU MEAN, WHY NOT?
WHENEVER THERE'S DANGER-- WHENEVER THERE'S TROUBLE-- YOU ALWAYS LEAVE AND RUN OFF! EVER SINCE I CAN REMEMBER-- FLASH, AND THE OTHERS, HAVE CALLED YOU-- A COWARD!
I'VE TRIED TO IGNORE IT--TO CLOSE MY MIND TO IT--BUT I'M BEGGING YOU NOW, PETER--IF YOU LOVE ME--STAY WITH ME!
WHATEVER MAY HAPPEN-- WE'LL FACE IT TOGETHER!
I'M THE ONLY ONE WHO CAN FIND HIM--WHO HAS A CHANCE TO SAVE HIM!
BUT I CAN'T BREAK AWAY--AND LET GWEN THINK THAT I'M GUTLESS!
STILL, FLASH'S LIFE IS AT STAKE! MY ONLY OTHER CHOICE IS-- ADMIT THAT I'M SPIDER-MAN!
NEXT: DON'T DARE MISS..
THE DREAD DECISION!

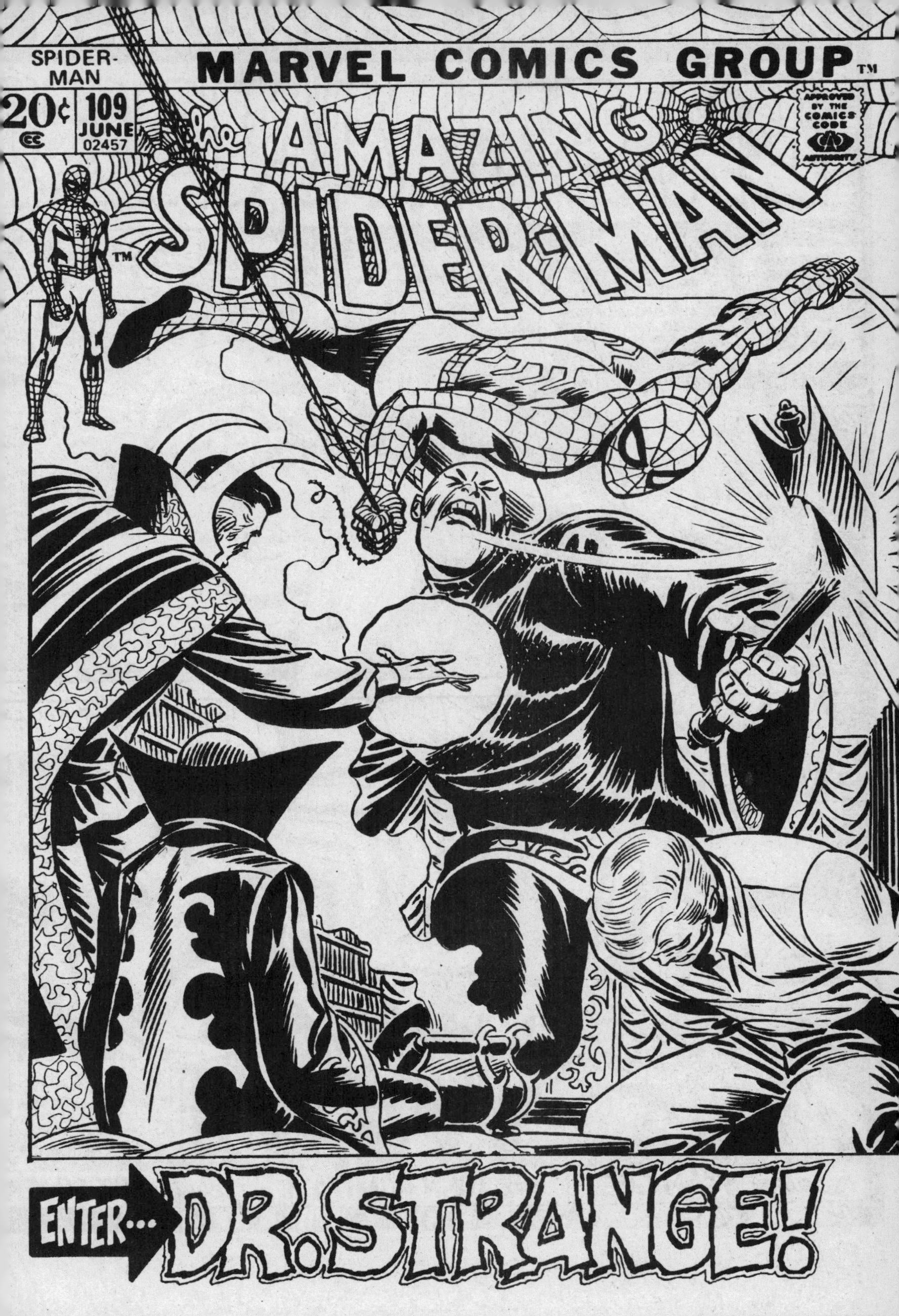
SPIDER-MAN
MARVEL COMICS GROUP™
20¢
109
JUNE
02457
the AMAZING SPIDER-MAN™
APPROVED BY THE COMICS CODE AUTHORITY
ENTER... DR. STRANGE!

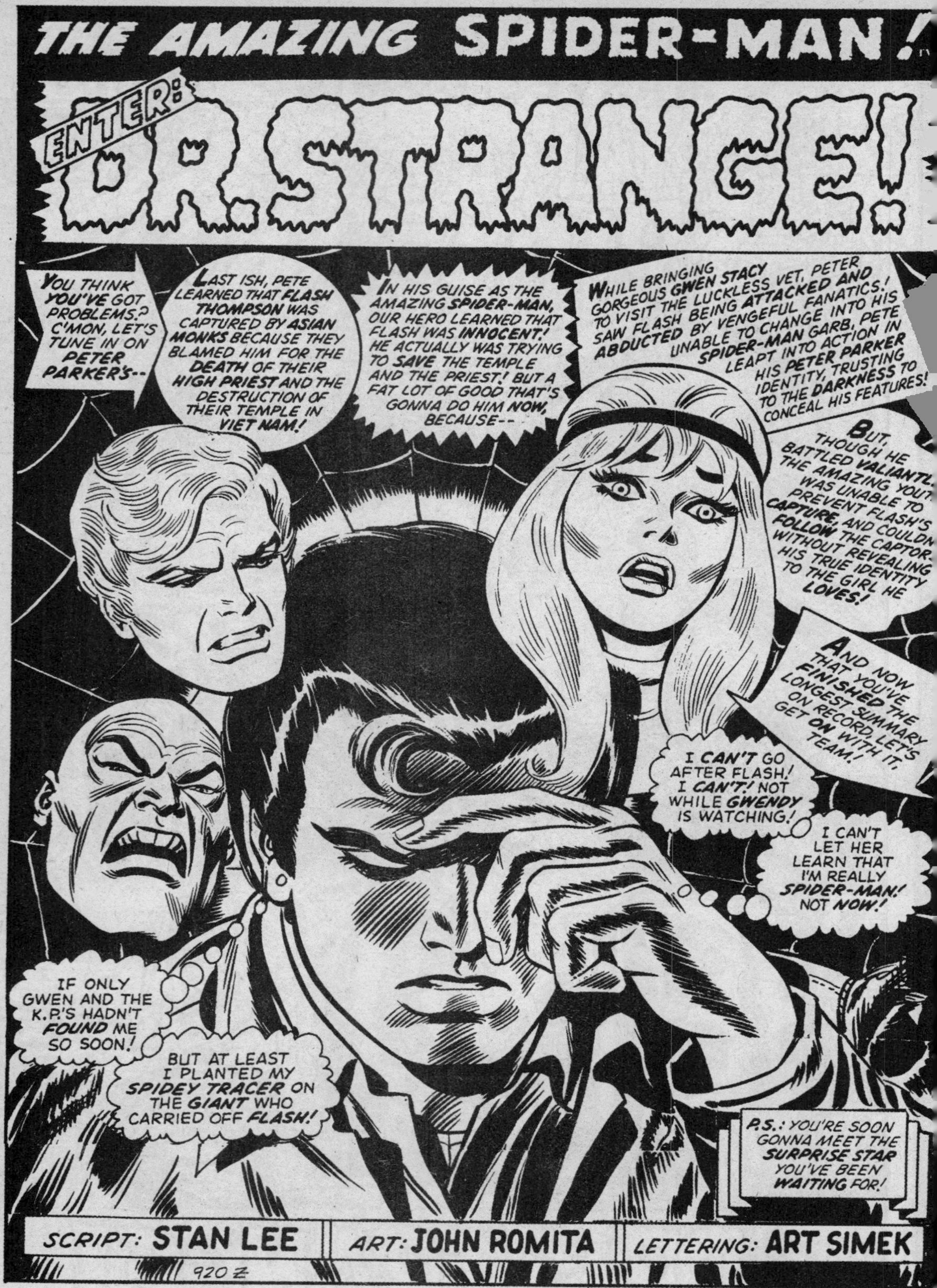
THE AMAZING SPIDER-MAN!
ENTER: DR. STRANGE!
YOU THINK YOU'VE GOT PROBLEMS?? C'MON, LET'S TUNE IN ON PETER PARKER'S--
LAST ISH, PETE LEARNED THAT FLASH THOMPSON WAS CAPTURED BY ASIAN MONKS BECAUSE THEY BLAMED HIM FOR THE DEATH OF THEIR HIGH PRIEST AND THE DESTRUCTION OF THEIR TEMPLE IN VIET NAM!
IN HIS GUISE AS THE AMAZING SPIDER-MAN, OUR HERO LEARNED THAT FLASH WAS INNOCENT! HE ACTUALLY WAS TRYING TO SAVE THE TEMPLE AND THE PRIEST! BUT A FAT LOT OF GOOD THAT'S GONNA DO HIM NOW, BECAUSE--
WHILE BRINGING GORGEOUS GWEN STACY TO VISIT THE LUCKLESS VET, PETER SAW FLASH BEING ATTACKED AND ABDUCTED BY VENGEFUL FANATICS! UNABLE TO CHANGE INTO HIS SPIDER-MAN GARB, PETE LEAPT INTO ACTION IN HIS PETER PARKER IDENTITY, TRUSTING TO THE DARKNESS TO CONCEAL HIS FEATURES!
BUT, THOUGH HE BATTLED VALIANTL THE AMAZING YOUT WAS UNABLE TO PREVENT FLASH'S CAPTURE, AND COULDN FOLLOW THE CAPTOR- WITHOUT REVEALING HIS TRUE IDENTITY TO THE GIRL HE LOVES!
AND NOW THAT YOU'VE FINISHED THE LONGEST SUMMARY ON RECORD, LET'S GET ON WITH IT, TEAM!
I CAN'T GO AFTER FLASH! I CAN'T! NOT WHILE GWENDY IS WATCHING!
I CAN'T LET HER LEARN THAT I'M REALLY SPIDER-MAN! NOT NOW!
IF ONLY GWEN AND THE K.P.'S HADN'T FOUND ME SO SOON!
BUT AT LEAST I PLANTED MY SPIDEY TRACER ON THE GIANT WHO CARRIED OFF FLASH!
P.S.: YOU'RE SOON GONNA MEET THE SURPRISE STAR YOU'VE BEEN WAITING FOR!
SCRIPT: STAN LEE
ART: JOHN ROMITA
LETTERING: ART SIMEK
920 Z

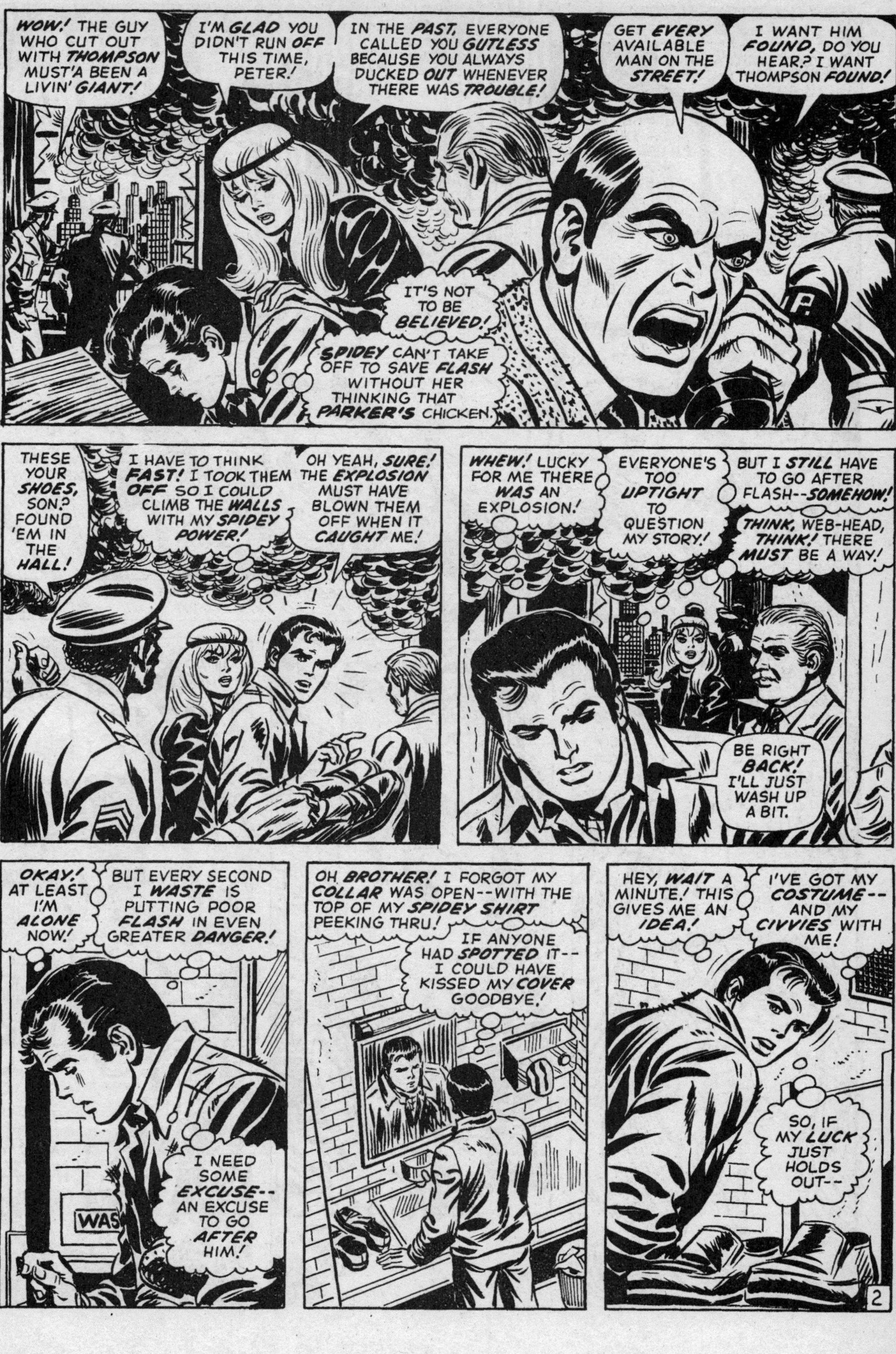
WOW! THE GUY WHO CUT OUT WITH THOMPSON MUST'A BEEN A LIVIN' GIANT!
I'M GLAD YOU DIDN'T RUN OFF THIS TIME, PETER!
IN THE PAST, EVERYONE CALLED YOU GUTLESS BECAUSE YOU ALWAYS DUCKED OUT WHENEVER THERE WAS TROUBLE!
GET EVERY AVAILABLE MAN ON THE STREET!
I WANT HIM FOUND, DO YOU HEAR? I WANT THOMPSON FOUND!
IT'S NOT TO BE BELIEVED!
SPIDEY CAN'T TAKE OFF TO SAVE FLASH WITHOUT HER THINKING THAT PARKER'S CHICKEN.
THESE YOUR SHOES, SON? FOUND 'EM IN THE HALL!
I HAVE TO THINK FAST! I TOOK THEM OFF SO I COULD CLIMB THE WALLS WITH MY SPIDEY POWER!
OH YEAH, SURE! THE EXPLOSION MUST HAVE BLOWN THEM OFF WHEN IT CAUGHT ME!
WHEW! LUCKY FOR ME THERE WAS AN EXPLOSION!
EVERYONE'S TOO UPTIGHT TO QUESTION MY STORY!
BUT I STILL HAVE TO GO AFTER FLASH--SOMEHOW!
THINK, WEB-HEAD, THINK! THERE MUST BE A WAY!
BE RIGHT BACK! I'LL JUST WASH UP A BIT.
OKAY! AT LEAST I'M ALONE NOW!
BUT EVERY SECOND I WASTE IS PUTTING POOR FLASH IN EVEN GREATER DANGER!
I NEED SOME EXCUSE-- AN EXCUSE TO GO AFTER HIM!
WAS
OH BROTHER! I FORGOT MY COLLAR WAS OPEN--WITH THE TOP OF MY SPIDEY SHIRT PEEKING THRU!
IF ANYONE HAD SPOTTED IT-- I COULD HAVE KISSED MY COVER GOODBYE!
HEY, WAIT A MINUTE! THIS GIVES ME AN IDEA!
I'VE GOT MY COSTUME-- AND MY CIVVIES WITH ME!
SO, IF MY LUCK JUST HOLDS OUT--
2

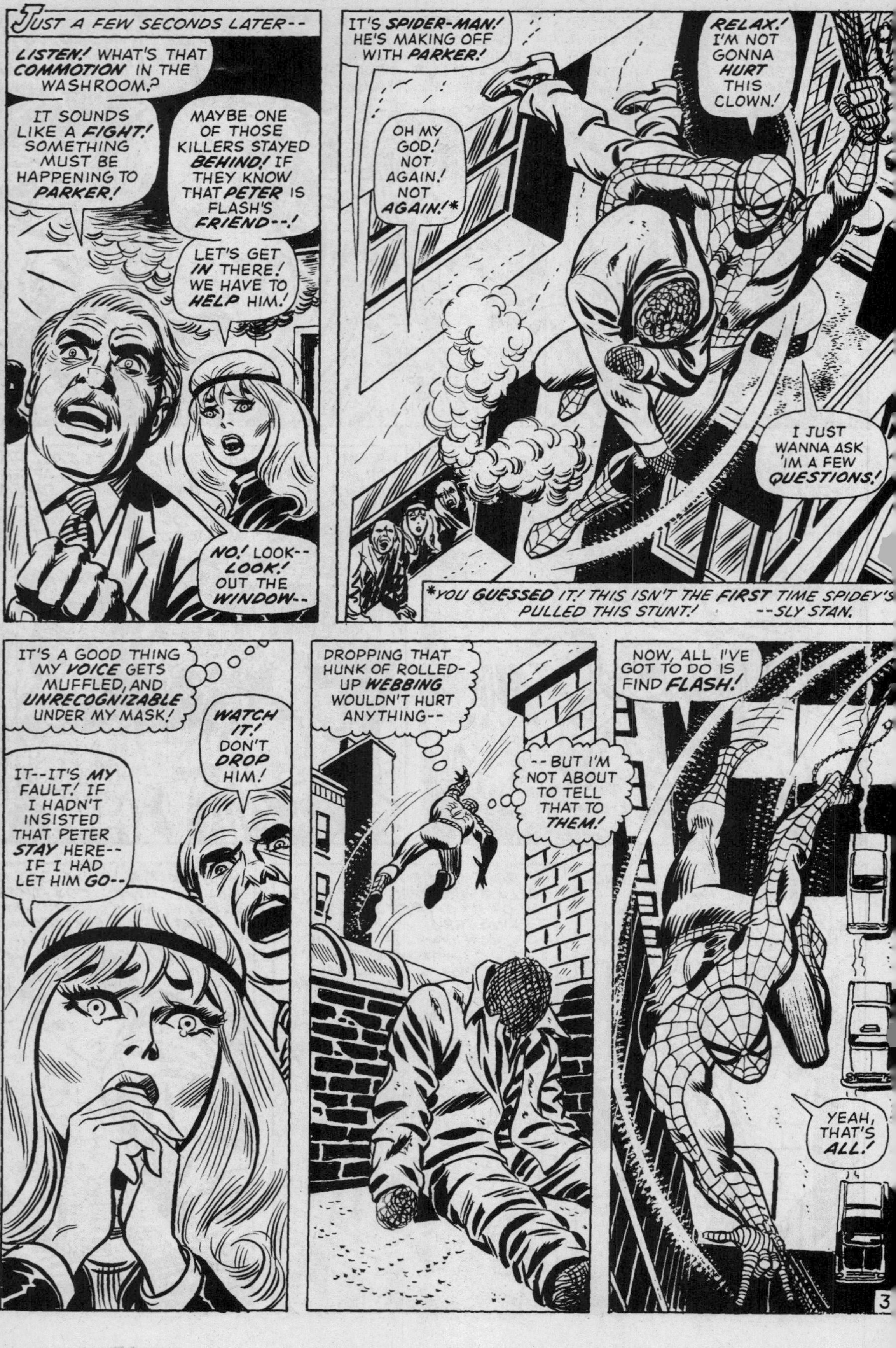
JUST A FEW SECONDS LATER--
LISTEN! WHAT'S THAT COMMOTION IN THE WASHROOM?
IT SOUNDS LIKE A FIGHT! SOMETHING MUST BE HAPPENING TO PARKER!
MAYBE ONE OF THOSE KILLERS STAYED BEHIND! IF THEY KNOW THAT PETER IS FLASH'S FRIEND--!
LET'S GET IN THERE! WE HAVE TO HELP HIM!
NO! LOOK-- LOOK! OUT THE WINDOW--
IT'S SPIDER-MAN! HE'S MAKING OFF WITH PARKER!
OH MY GOD! NOT AGAIN! NOT AGAIN!*
RELAX! I'M NOT GONNA HURT THIS CLOWN!
I JUST WANNA ASK 'IM A FEW QUESTIONS!
*YOU GUESSED IT! THIS ISN'T THE FIRST TIME SPIDEY'S PULLED THIS STUNT! --SLY STAN.
IT'S A GOOD THING MY VOICE GETS MUFFLED, AND UNRECOGNIZABLE UNDER MY MASK!
WATCH IT! DON'T DROP HIM!
IT--IT'S MY FAULT! IF I HADN'T INSISTED THAT PETER STAY HERE-- IF I HAD LET HIM GO--
DROPPING THAT HUNK OF ROLLED-UP WEBBING WOULDN'T HURT ANYTHING--
--BUT I'M NOT ABOUT TO TELL THAT TO THEM!
NOW, ALL I'VE GOT TO DO IS FIND FLASH!
YEAH, THAT'S ALL!
3

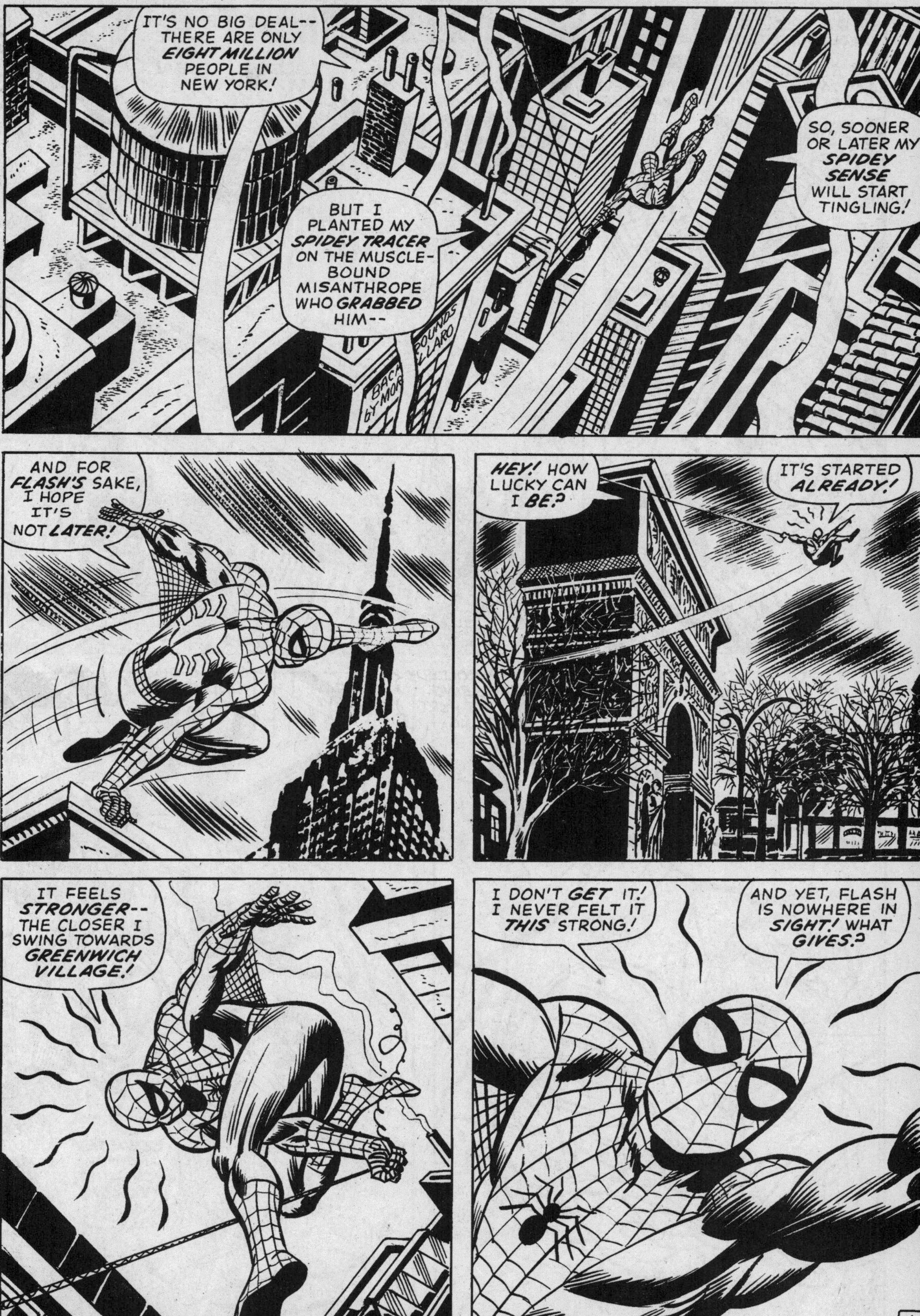
IT'S NO BIG DEAL-- THERE ARE ONLY EIGHT MILLION PEOPLE IN NEW YORK!
BUT I PLANTED MY SPIDEY TRACER ON THE MUSCLE-BOUND MISANTHROPE WHO GRABBED HIM--
SO, SOONER OR LATER MY SPIDEY SENSE WILL START TINGLING!
AND FOR FLASH'S SAKE, I HOPE IT'S NOT LATER!
HEY! HOW LUCKY CAN I BE?
IT'S STARTED ALREADY!
IT FEELS STRONGER-- THE CLOSER I SWING TOWARDS GREENWICH VILLAGE!
I DON'T GET IT! I NEVER FELT IT THIS STRONG!
AND YET, FLASH IS NOWHERE IN SIGHT! WHAT GIVES?
4

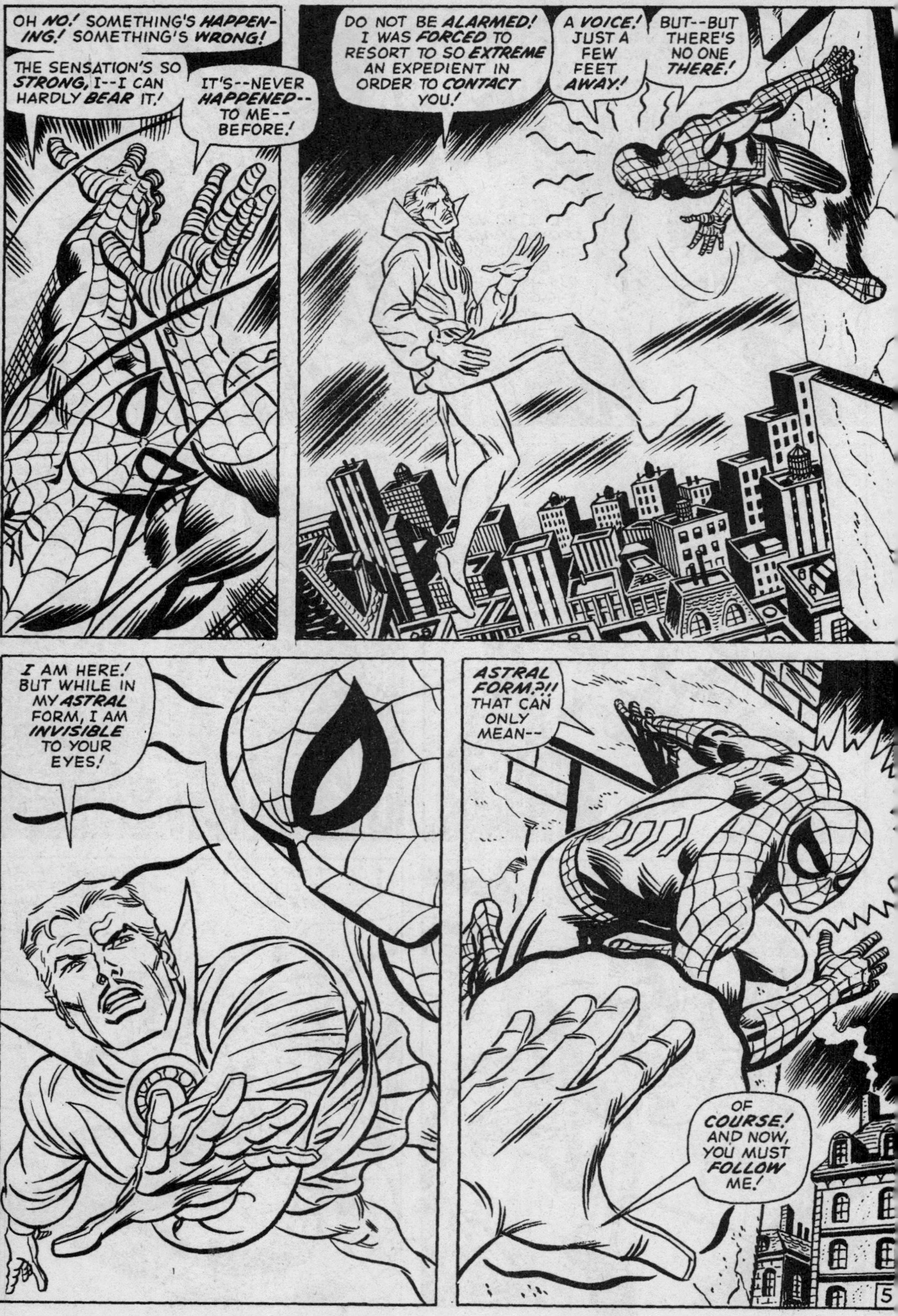
OH NO! SOMETHING'S HAPPENING! SOMETHING'S WRONG!
THE SENSATION'S SO STRONG, I--I CAN HARDLY BEAR IT!
IT'S--NEVER HAPPENED-- TO ME-- BEFORE!
DO NOT BE ALARMED! I WAS FORCED TO RESORT TO SO EXTREME AN EXPEDIENT IN ORDER TO CONTACT YOU!
A VOICE! JUST A FEW FEET AWAY!
BUT--BUT THERE'S NO ONE THERE!
I AM HERE! BUT WHILE IN MY ASTRAL FORM, I AM INVISIBLE TO YOUR EYES!
ASTRAL FORM?!! THAT CAN ONLY MEAN--
OF COURSE! AND NOW, YOU MUST FOLLOW ME!
5

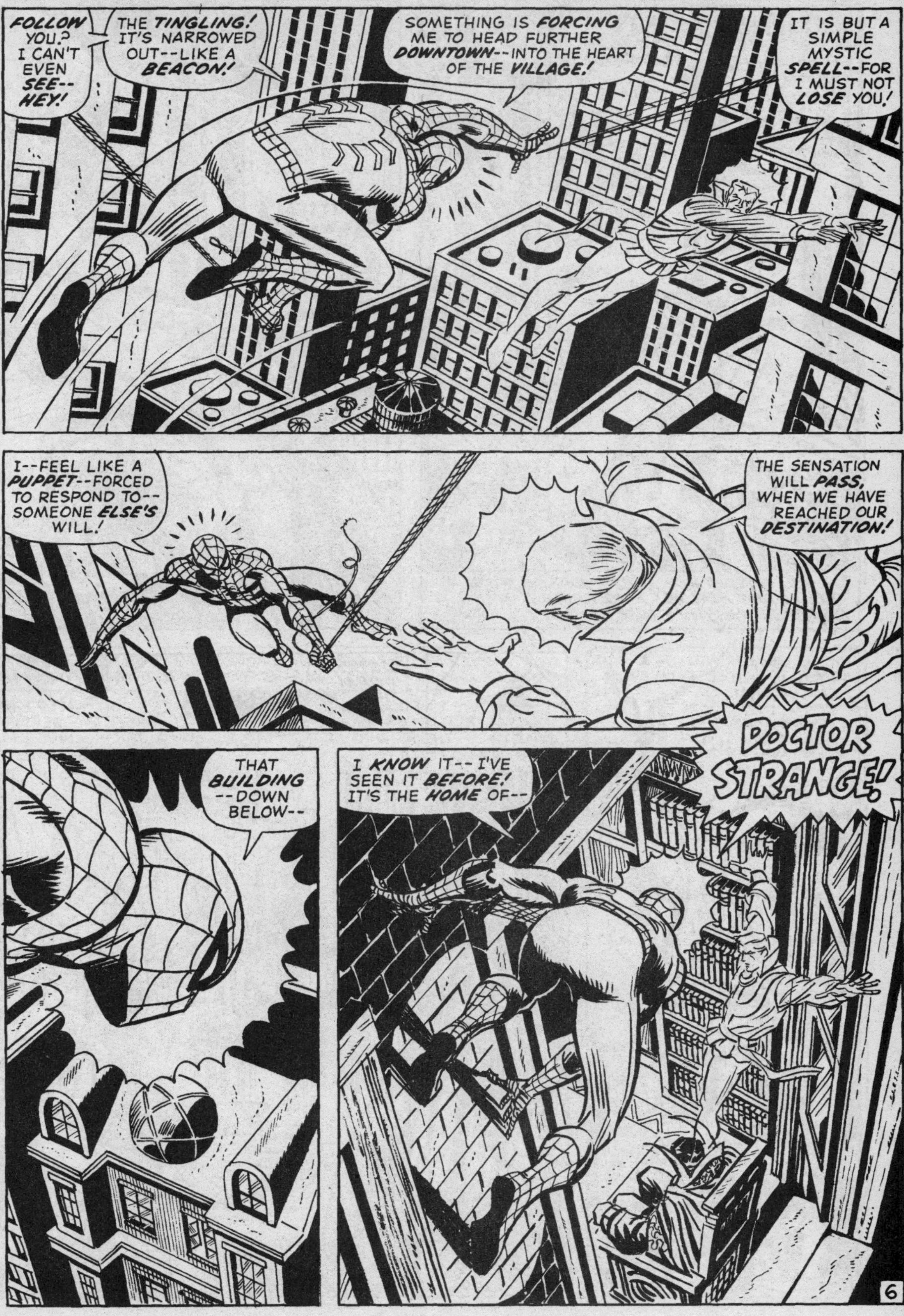
FOLLOW YOU..? I CAN'T EVEN SEE-- HEY!
THE TINGLING! IT'S NARROWED OUT--LIKE A BEACON!
SOMETHING IS FORCING ME TO HEAD FURTHER DOWNTOWN--INTO THE HEART OF THE VILLAGE!
IT IS BUT A SIMPLE MYSTIC SPELL--FOR I MUST NOT LOSE YOU!
I--FEEL LIKE A PUPPET--FORCED TO RESPOND TO--SOMEONE ELSE'S WILL!
THE SENSATION WILL PASS, WHEN WE HAVE REACHED OUR DESTINATION!
THAT BUILDING --DOWN BELOW--
I KNOW IT-- I'VE SEEN IT BEFORE! IT'S THE HOME OF--
DOCTOR STRANGE!
6

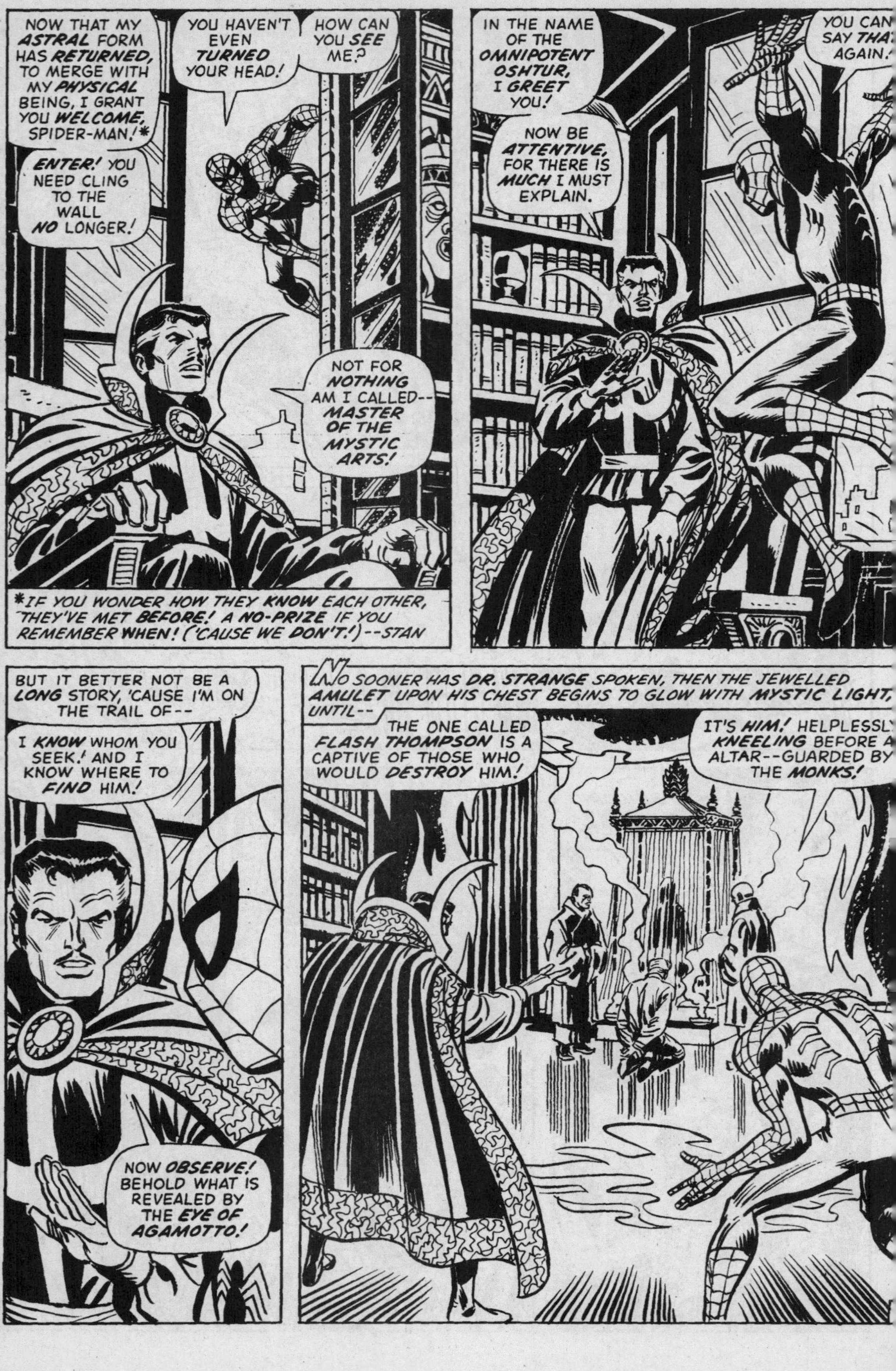
NOW THAT MY ASTRAL FORM HAS RETURNED, TO MERGE WITH MY PHYSICAL BEING, I GRANT YOU WELCOME, SPIDER-MAN!*
ENTER! YOU NEED CLING TO THE WALL NO LONGER!
YOU HAVEN'T EVEN TURNED YOUR HEAD!
HOW CAN YOU SEE ME?
NOT FOR NOTHING AM I CALLED--MASTER OF THE MYSTIC ARTS!
*IF YOU WONDER HOW THEY KNOW EACH OTHER, THEY'VE MET BEFORE! A NO-PRIZE IF YOU REMEMBER WHEN! ('CAUSE WE DON'T!) --STAN
IN THE NAME OF THE OMNIPOTENT OSHTUR, I GREET YOU!
NOW BE ATTENTIVE, FOR THERE IS MUCH I MUST EXPLAIN.
YOU CAN SAY THA AGAIN.
BUT IT BETTER NOT BE A LONG STORY, 'CAUSE I'M ON THE TRAIL OF--
I KNOW WHOM YOU SEEK! AND I KNOW WHERE TO FIND HIM!
NOW OBSERVE! BEHOLD WHAT IS REVEALED BY THE EYE OF AGAMOTTO!
NO SOONER HAS DR. STRANGE SPOKEN, THEN THE JEWELLED AMULET UPON HIS CHEST BEGINS TO GLOW WITH MYSTIC LIGHT, UNTIL--
THE ONE CALLED FLASH THOMPSON IS A CAPTIVE OF THOSE WHO WOULD DESTROY HIM!
IT'S HIM! HELPLESSL KNEELING BEFORE A ALTAR--GUARDED BY THE MONKS!

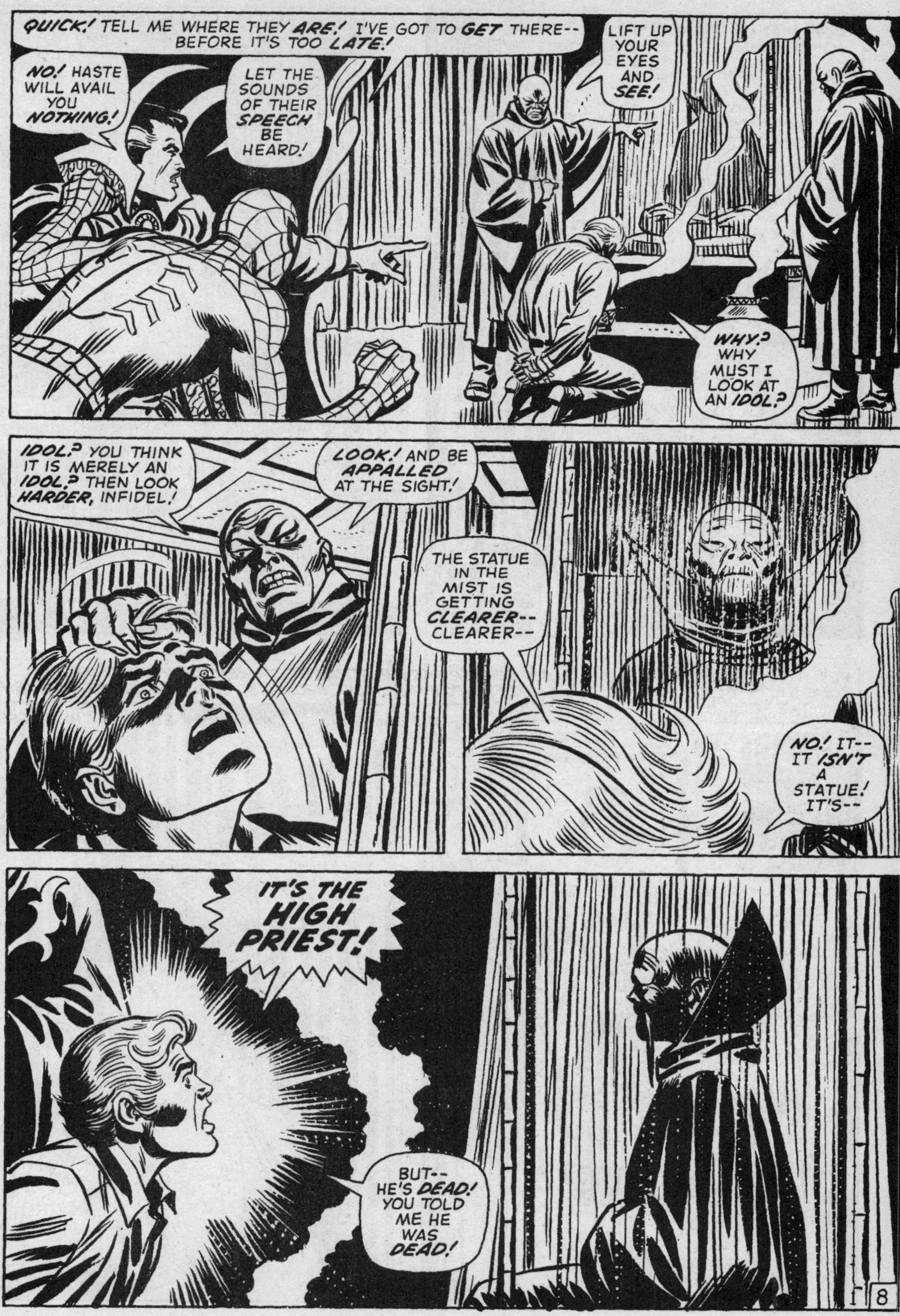
QUICK! TELL ME WHERE THEY ARE! I'VE GOT TO GET THERE-- BEFORE IT'S TOO LATE!
NO! HASTE WILL AVAIL YOU NOTHING!
LET THE SOUNDS OF THEIR SPEECH BE HEARD!
LIFT UP YOUR EYES AND SEE!
WHY? WHY MUST I LOOK AT AN IDOL?
IDOL? YOU THINK IT IS MERELY AN IDOL? THEN LOOK HARDER, INFIDEL!
LOOK! AND BE APPALLED AT THE SIGHT!
THE STATUE IN THE MIST IS GETTING CLEARER-- CLEARER--
NO! IT-- IT ISN'T A STATUE! IT'S--
IT'S THE HIGH PRIEST!
BUT-- HE'S DEAD! YOU TOLD ME HE WAS DEAD!
8

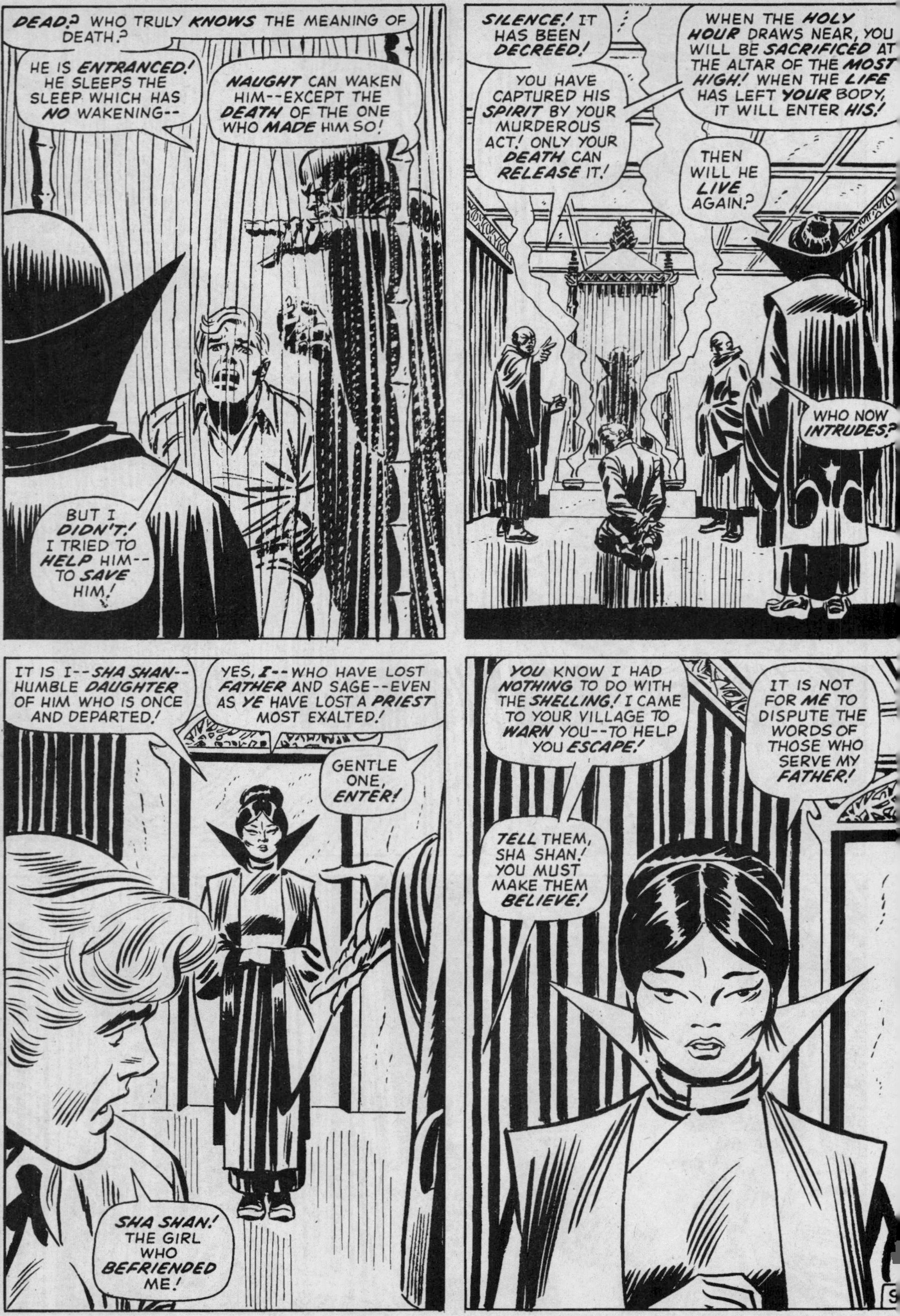
DEAD? WHO TRULY KNOWS THE MEANING OF DEATH?
HE IS ENTRANCED! HE SLEEPS THE SLEEP WHICH HAS NO WAKENING--
NAUGHT CAN WAKEN HIM--EXCEPT THE DEATH OF THE ONE WHO MADE HIM SO!
BUT I DIDN'T! I TRIED TO HELP HIM--TO SAVE HIM!
SILENCE! IT HAS BEEN DECREED!
YOU HAVE CAPTURED HIS SPIRIT BY YOUR MURDEROUS ACT! ONLY YOUR DEATH CAN RELEASE IT!
WHEN THE HOLY HOUR DRAWS NEAR, YOU WILL BE SACRIFICED AT THE ALTAR OF THE MOST HIGH! WHEN THE LIFE HAS LEFT YOUR BODY, IT WILL ENTER HIS!
THEN WILL HE LIVE AGAIN?
WHO NOW INTRUDES?
IT IS I--SHA SHAN--HUMBLE DAUGHTER OF HIM WHO IS ONCE AND DEPARTED!
YES, I--WHO HAVE LOST FATHER AND SAGE--EVEN AS YE HAVE LOST A PRIEST MOST EXALTED!
GENTLE ONE, ENTER!
SHA SHAN! THE GIRL WHO BEFRIENDED ME!
YOU KNOW I HAD NOTHING TO DO WITH THE SHELLING! I CAME TO YOUR VILLAGE TO WARN YOU--TO HELP YOU ESCAPE!
IT IS NOT FOR ME TO DISPUTE THE WORDS OF THOSE WHO SERVE MY FATHER!
TELL THEM, SHA SHAN! YOU MUST MAKE THEM BELIEVE!
9

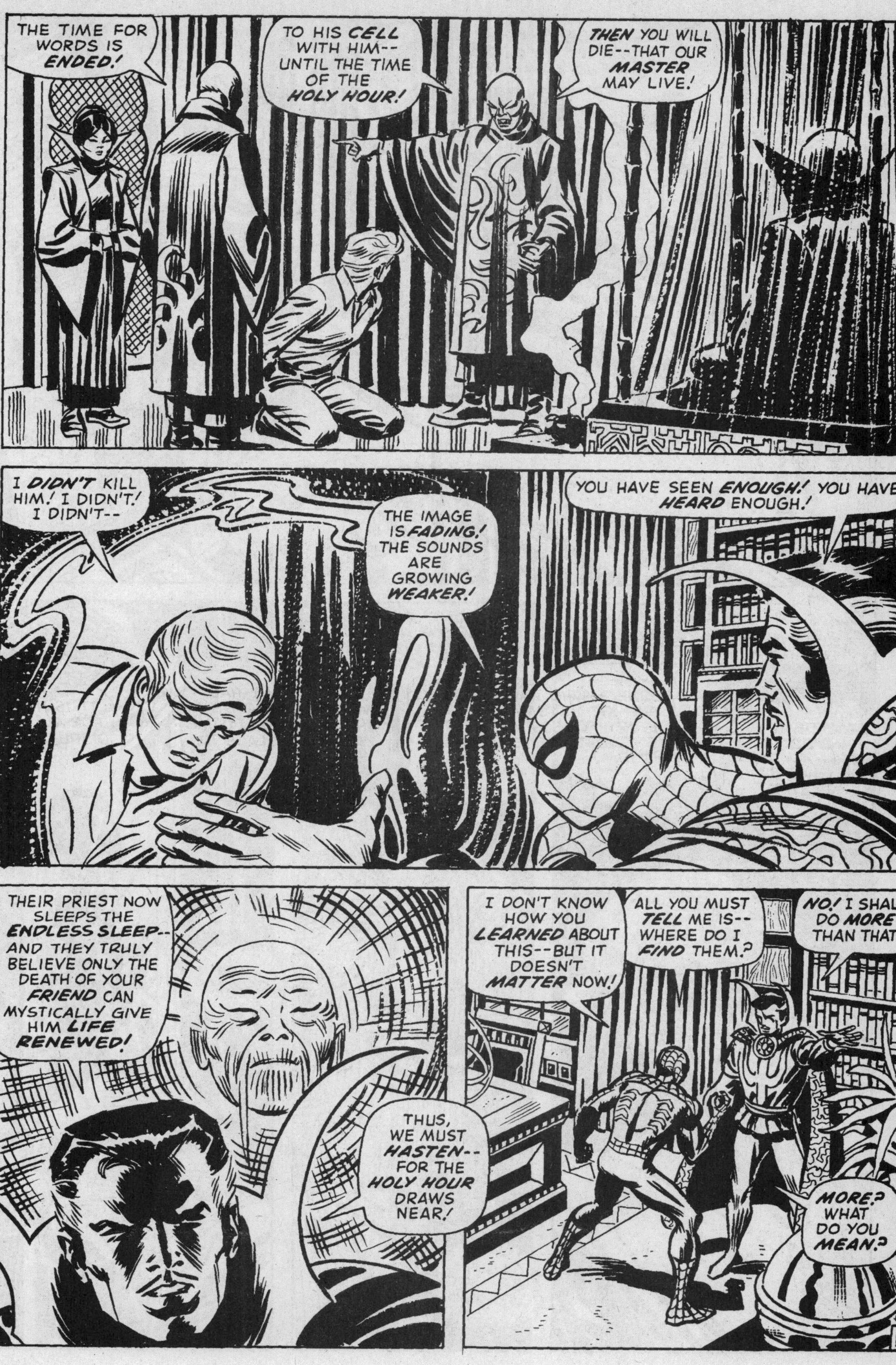
THE TIME FOR WORDS IS ENDED!
TO HIS CELL WITH HIM-- UNTIL THE TIME OF THE HOLY HOUR!
THEN YOU WILL DIE--THAT OUR MASTER MAY LIVE!
I DIDN'T KILL HIM! I DIDN'T! I DIDN'T--
THE IMAGE IS FADING! THE SOUNDS ARE GROWING WEAKER!
YOU HAVE SEEN ENOUGH! YOU HAVE HEARD ENOUGH!
THEIR PRIEST NOW SLEEPS THE ENDLESS SLEEP-- AND THEY TRULY BELIEVE ONLY THE DEATH OF YOUR FRIEND CAN MYSTICALLY GIVE HIM LIFE RENEWED!
THUS, WE MUST HASTEN-- FOR THE HOLY HOUR DRAWS NEAR!
I DON'T KNOW HOW YOU LEARNED ABOUT THIS--BUT IT DOESN'T MATTER NOW!
ALL YOU MUST TELL ME IS-- WHERE DO I FIND THEM?
NO! I SHALL DO MORE THAN THAT--
MORE? WHAT DO YOU MEAN?
10

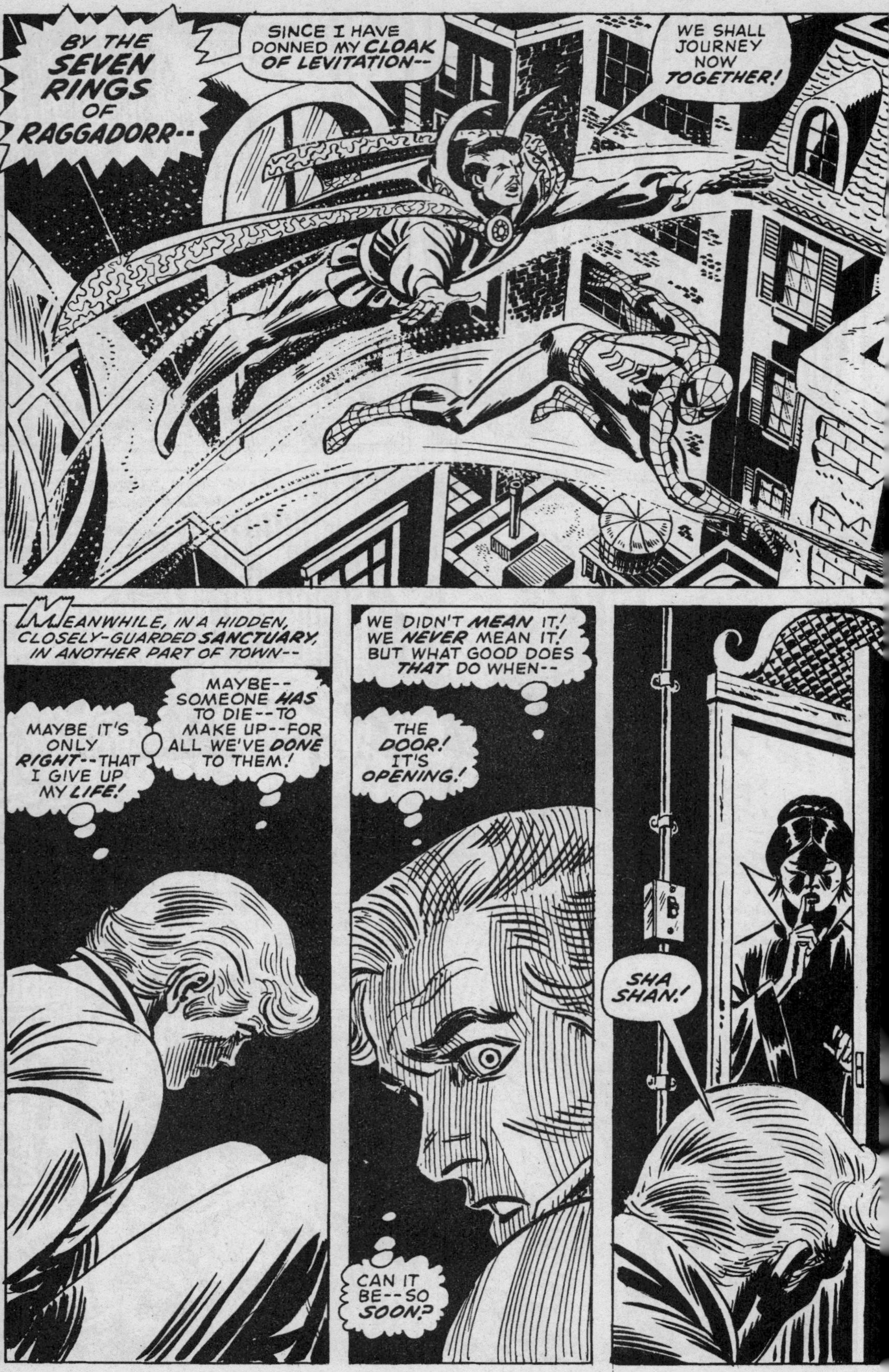
BY THE SEVEN RINGS OF RAGGADORR--
SINCE I HAVE DONNED MY CLOAK OF LEVITATION--
WE SHALL JOURNEY NOW TOGETHER!
MEANWHILE, IN A HIDDEN, CLOSELY-GUARDED SANCTUARY, IN ANOTHER PART OF TOWN--
MAYBE IT'S ONLY RIGHT--THAT I GIVE UP MY LIFE!
MAYBE-- SOMEONE HAS TO DIE--TO MAKE UP--FOR ALL WE'VE DONE TO THEM!
WE DIDN'T MEAN IT! WE NEVER MEAN IT! BUT WHAT GOOD DOES THAT DO WHEN--
THE DOOR! IT'S OPENING!
CAN IT BE--SO SOON?
SHA SHAN!

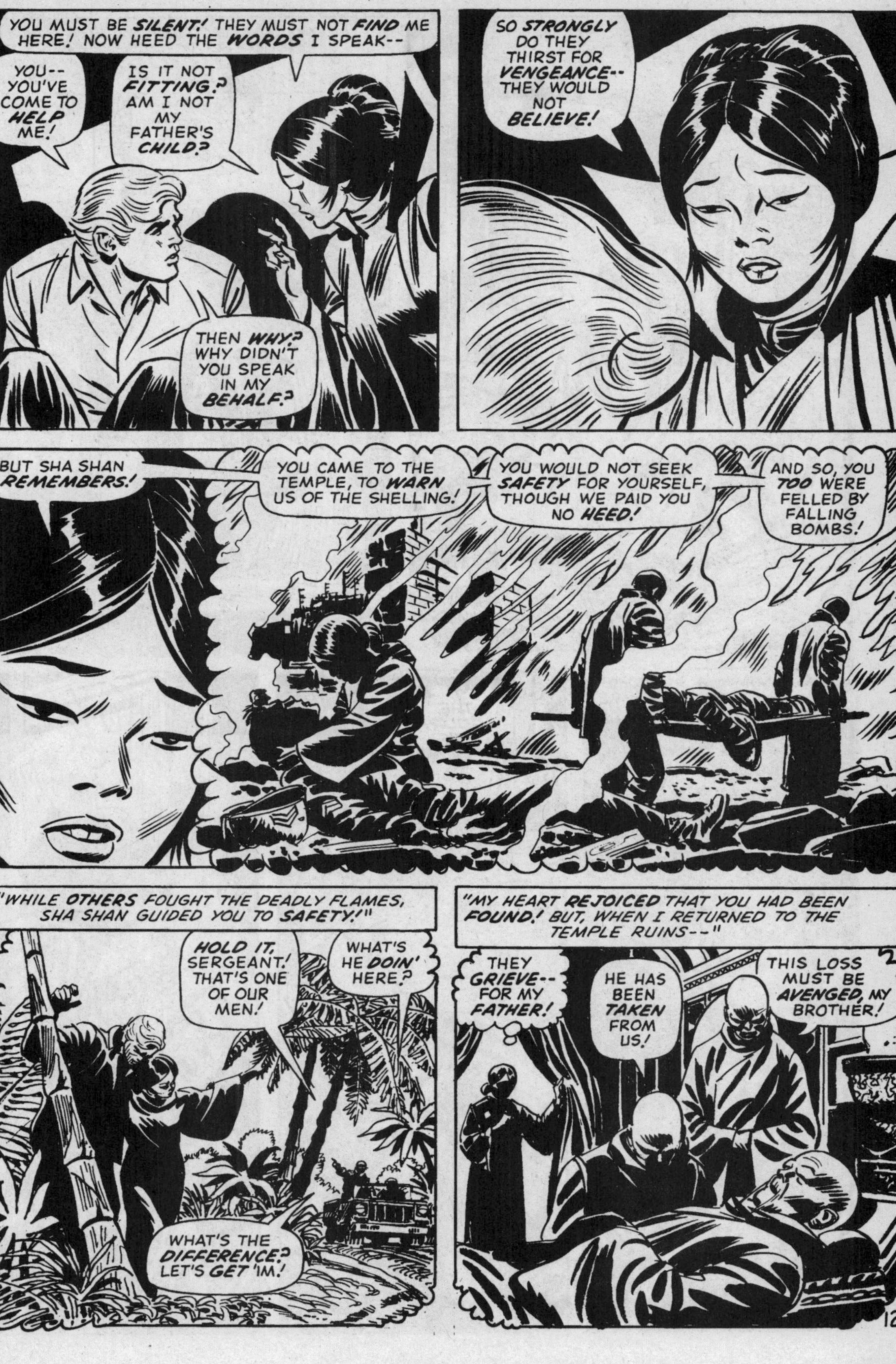
YOU MUST BE SILENT! THEY MUST NOT FIND ME HERE! NOW HEED THE WORDS I SPEAK--
YOU-- YOU'VE COME TO HELP ME!
IS IT NOT FITTING? AM I NOT MY FATHER'S CHILD?
THEN WHY? WHY DIDN'T YOU SPEAK IN MY BEHALF?
SO STRONGLY DO THEY THIRST FOR VENGEANCE-- THEY WOULD NOT BELIEVE!
BUT SHA SHAN REMEMBERS!
YOU CAME TO THE TEMPLE, TO WARN US OF THE SHELLING!
YOU WOULD NOT SEEK SAFETY FOR YOURSELF, THOUGH WE PAID YOU NO HEED!
AND SO, YOU TOO WERE FELLED BY FALLING BOMBS!
"WHILE OTHERS FOUGHT THE DEADLY FLAMES, SHA SHAN GUIDED YOU TO SAFETY!"
HOLD IT, SERGEANT! THAT'S ONE OF OUR MEN!
WHAT'S HE DOIN' HERE?
WHAT'S THE DIFFERENCE? LET'S GET 'IM!
"MY HEART REJOICED THAT YOU HAD BEEN FOUND! BUT, WHEN I RETURNED TO THE TEMPLE RUINS--"
THEY GRIEVE-- FOR MY FATHER!
HE HAS BEEN TAKEN FROM US!
THIS LOSS MUST BE AVENGED, MY BROTHER!

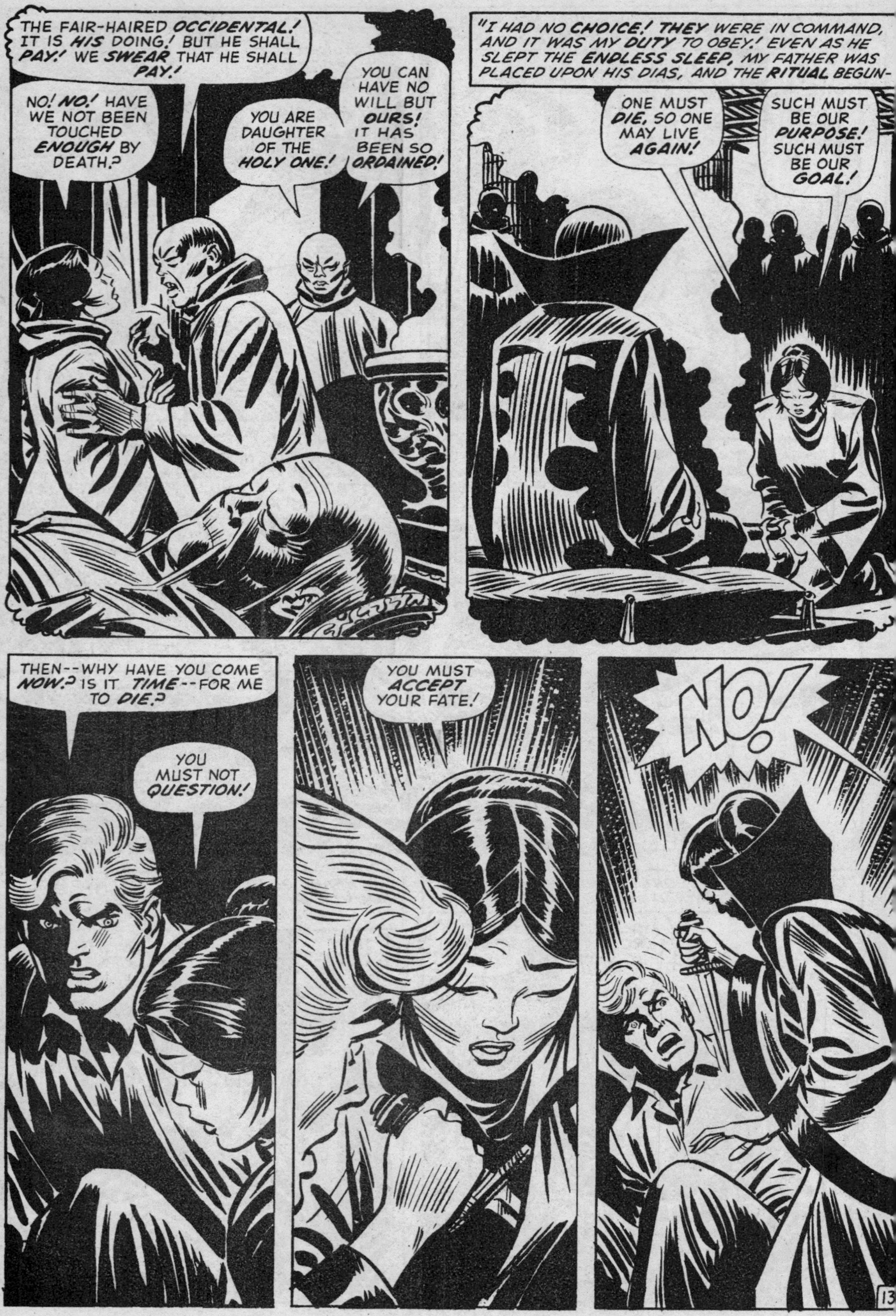

THE FAIR-HAIRED OCCIDENTAL! IT IS HIS DOING! BUT HE SHALL PAY! WE SWEAR THAT HE SHALL PAY!
NO! NO! HAVE WE NOT BEEN TOUCHED ENOUGH BY DEATH?
YOU ARE DAUGHTER OF THE HOLY ONE!
YOU CAN HAVE NO WILL BUT OURS! IT HAS BEEN SO ORDAINED!
"I HAD NO CHOICE! THEY WERE IN COMMAND, AND IT WAS MY DUTY TO OBEY! EVEN AS HE SLEPT THE ENDLESS SLEEP, MY FATHER WAS PLACED UPON HIS DIAS, AND THE RITUAL BEGUN-
ONE MUST DIE, SO ONE MAY LIVE AGAIN!
SUCH MUST BE OUR PURPOSE! SUCH MUST BE OUR GOAL!
THEN--WHY HAVE YOU COME NOW? IS IT TIME--FOR ME TO DIE?
YOU MUST NOT QUESTION!
YOU MUST ACCEPT YOUR FATE!
NO!

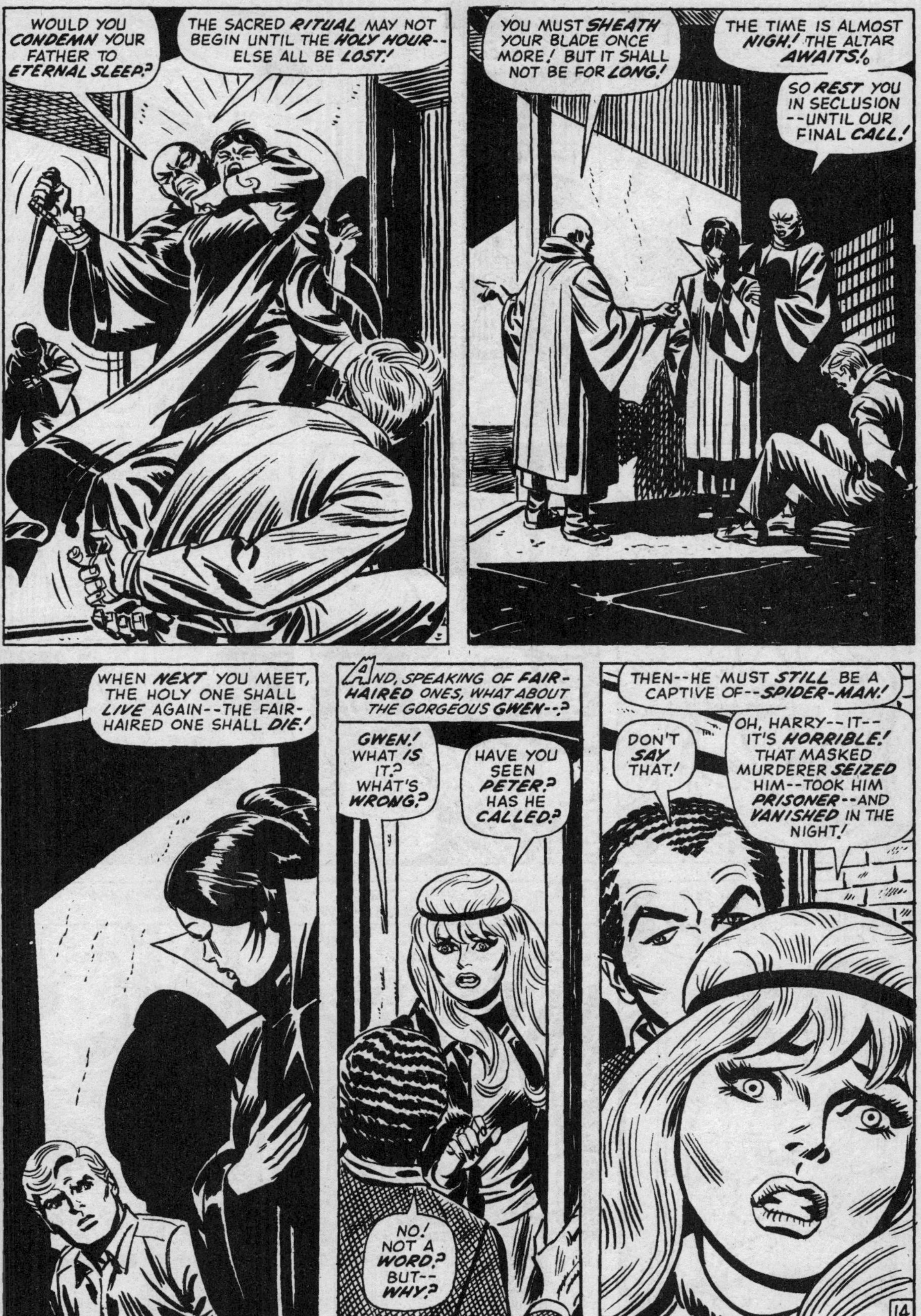
WOULD YOU CONDEMN YOUR FATHER TO ETERNAL SLEEP?
THE SACRED RITUAL MAY NOT BEGIN UNTIL THE HOLY HOUR-- ELSE ALL BE LOST!
YOU MUST SHEATH YOUR BLADE ONCE MORE! BUT IT SHALL NOT BE FOR LONG!
THE TIME IS ALMOST NIGH! THE ALTAR AWAITS!
SO REST YOU IN SECLUSION --UNTIL OUR FINAL CALL!
WHEN NEXT YOU MEET, THE HOLY ONE SHALL LIVE AGAIN--THE FAIR-HAIRED ONE SHALL DIE!
AND, SPEAKING OF FAIR-HAIRED ONES, WHAT ABOUT THE GORGEOUS GWEN--?
GWEN! WHAT IS IT? WHAT'S WRONG?
HAVE YOU SEEN PETER? HAS HE CALLED?
NO! NOT A WORD? BUT-- WHY?
THEN--HE MUST STILL BE A CAPTIVE OF--SPIDER-MAN!
DON'T SAY THAT!
OH, HARRY--IT-- IT'S HORRIBLE! THAT MASKED MURDERER SEIZED HIM--TOOK HIM PRISONER--AND VANISHED IN THE NIGHT!
14

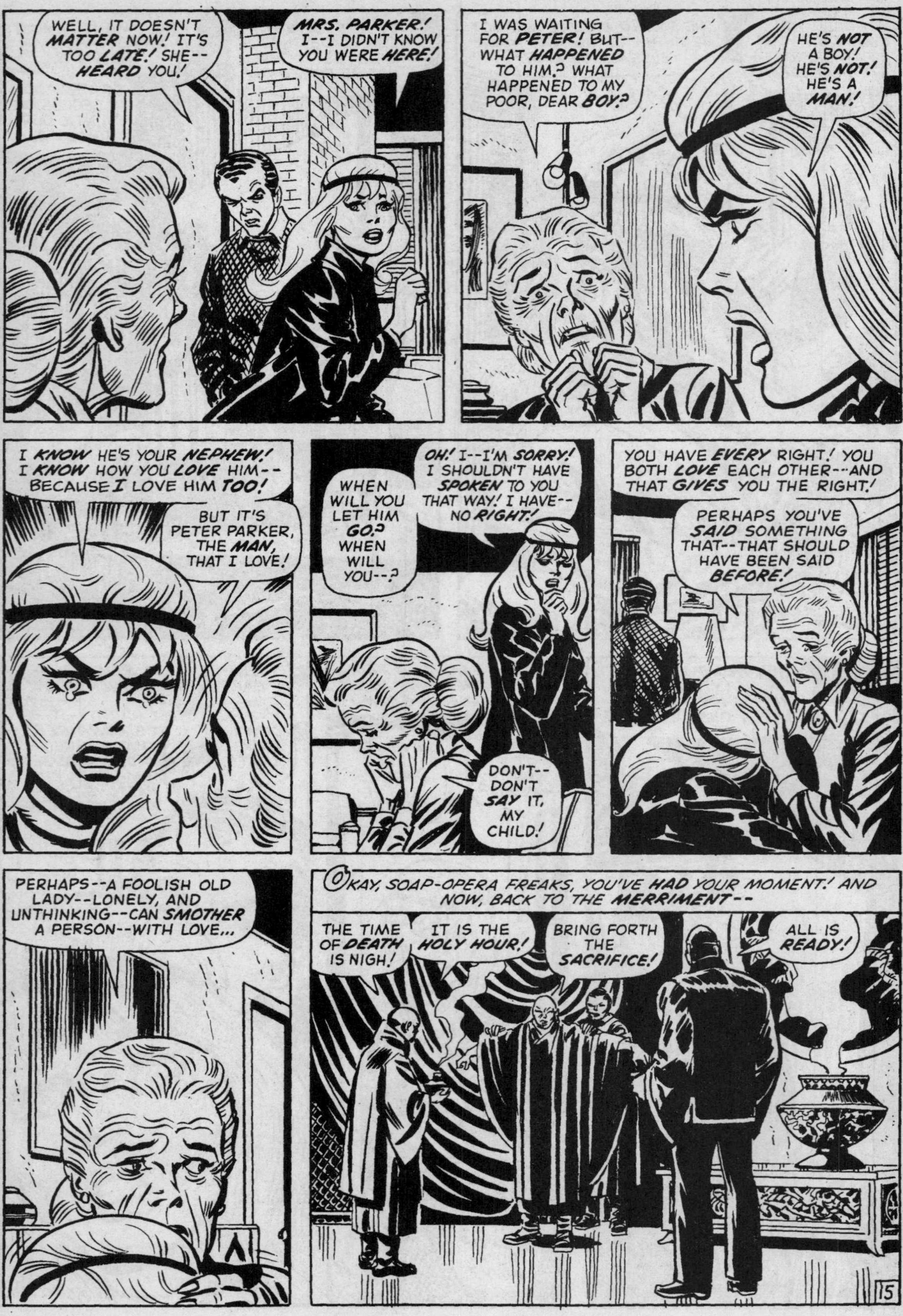
WELL, IT DOESN'T MATTER NOW! IT'S TOO LATE! SHE--HEARD YOU!
MRS. PARKER! I--I DIDN'T KNOW YOU WERE HERE!
I WAS WAITING FOR PETER! BUT--WHAT HAPPENED TO HIM? WHAT HAPPENED TO MY POOR, DEAR BOY?
HE'S NOT A BOY! HE'S NOT! HE'S A MAN!
I KNOW HE'S YOUR NEPHEW! I KNOW HOW YOU LOVE HIM--BECAUSE I LOVE HIM TOO!
BUT IT'S PETER PARKER, THE MAN, THAT I LOVE!
WHEN WILL YOU LET HIM GO? WHEN WILL YOU--?
OH! I--I'M SORRY! I SHOULDN'T HAVE SPOKEN TO YOU THAT WAY! I HAVE--NO RIGHT!
DON'T--DON'T SAY IT, MY CHILD!
YOU HAVE EVERY RIGHT! YOU BOTH LOVE EACH OTHER--AND THAT GIVES YOU THE RIGHT!
PERHAPS YOU'VE SAID SOMETHING THAT--THAT SHOULD HAVE BEEN SAID BEFORE!
PERHAPS--A FOOLISH OLD LADY--LONELY, AND UNTHINKING--CAN SMOTHER A PERSON--WITH LOVE...
OKAY, SOAP-OPERA FREAKS, YOU'VE HAD YOUR MOMENT! AND NOW, BACK TO THE MERRIMENT--
THE TIME OF DEATH IS NIGH!
IT IS THE HOLY HOUR!
BRING FORTH THE SACRIFICE!
ALL IS READY!
15

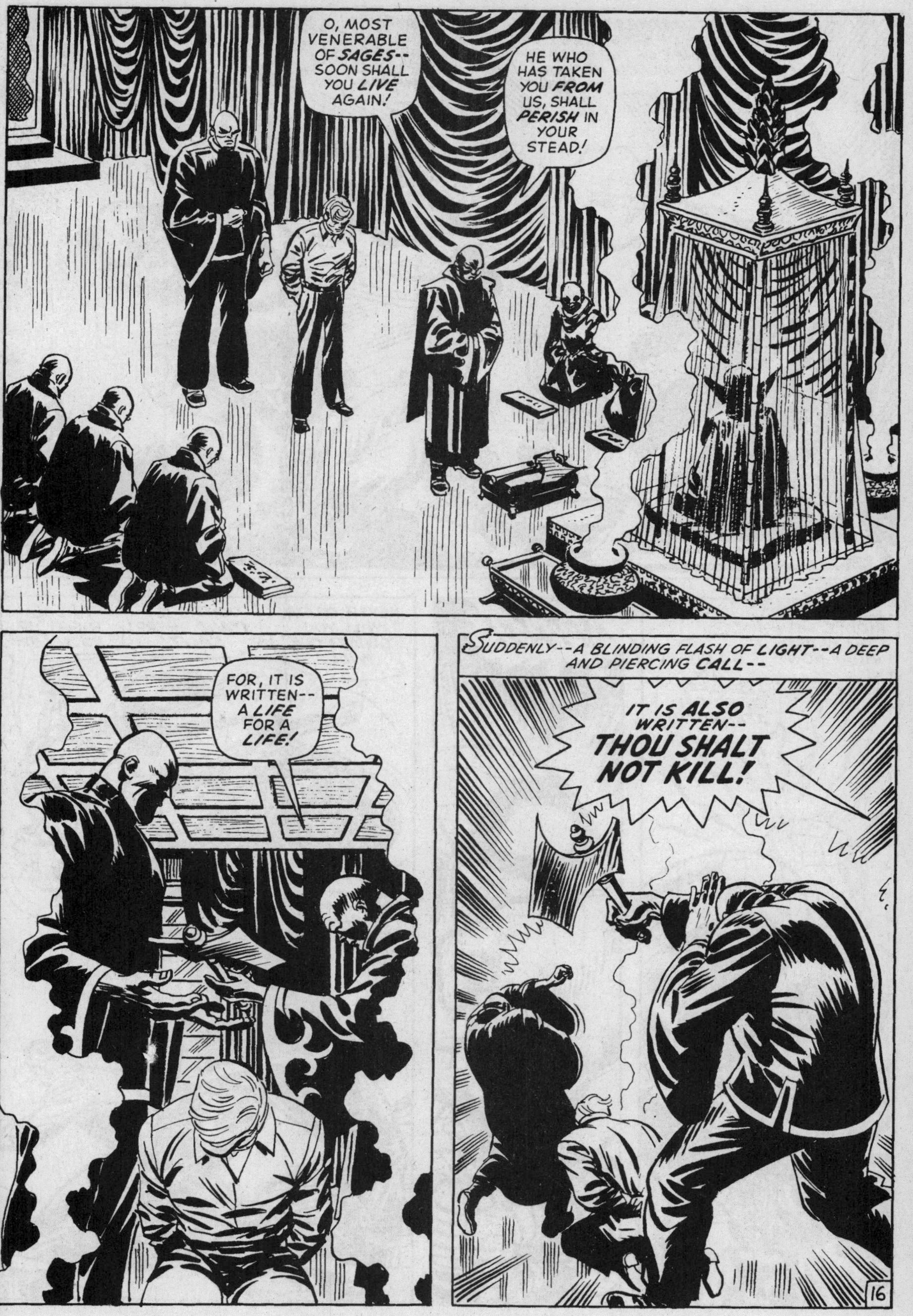

O, MOST VENERABLE OF SAGES-- SOON SHALL YOU LIVE AGAIN!
HE WHO HAS TAKEN YOU FROM US, SHALL PERISH IN YOUR STEAD!
FOR, IT IS WRITTEN-- A LIFE FOR A LIFE!
SUDDENLY--A BLINDING FLASH OF LIGHT--A DEEP AND PIERCING CALL--
IT IS ALSO WRITTEN-- THOU SHALT NOT KILL!
16

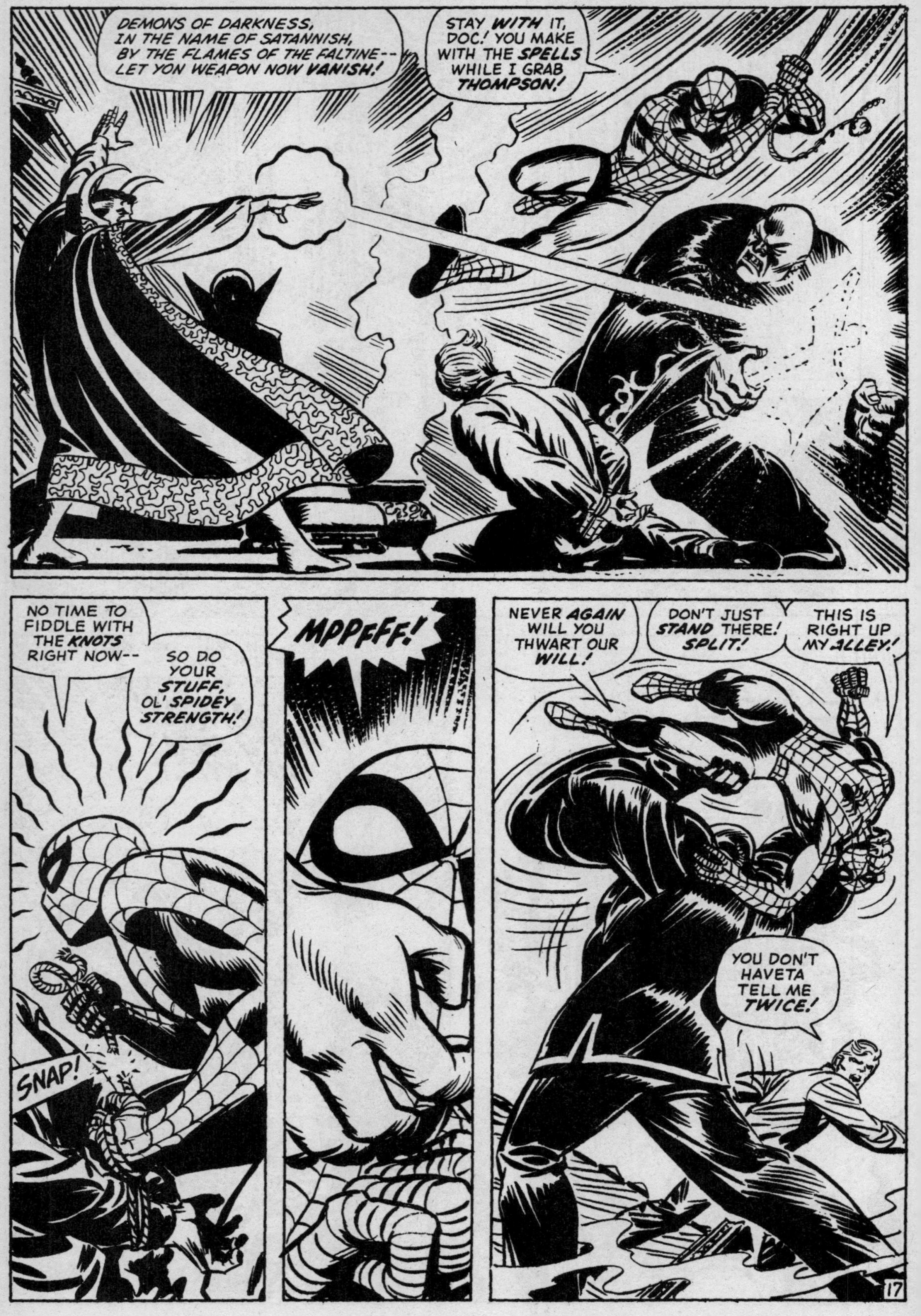
DEMONS OF DARKNESS, IN THE NAME OF SATANNISH, BY THE FLAMES OF THE FALTINE-- LET YON WEAPON NOW VANISH!
STAY WITH IT, DOC! YOU MAKE WITH THE SPELLS WHILE I GRAB THOMPSON!
NO TIME TO FIDDLE WITH THE KNOTS RIGHT NOW--
SO DO YOUR STUFF, OL' SPIDEY STRENGTH!
SNAP!
MPPFFF!
NEVER AGAIN WILL YOU THWART OUR WILL!
DON'T JUST STAND THERE! SPLIT!
THIS IS RIGHT UP MY ALLEY!
YOU DON'T HAVETA TELL ME TWICE!
17

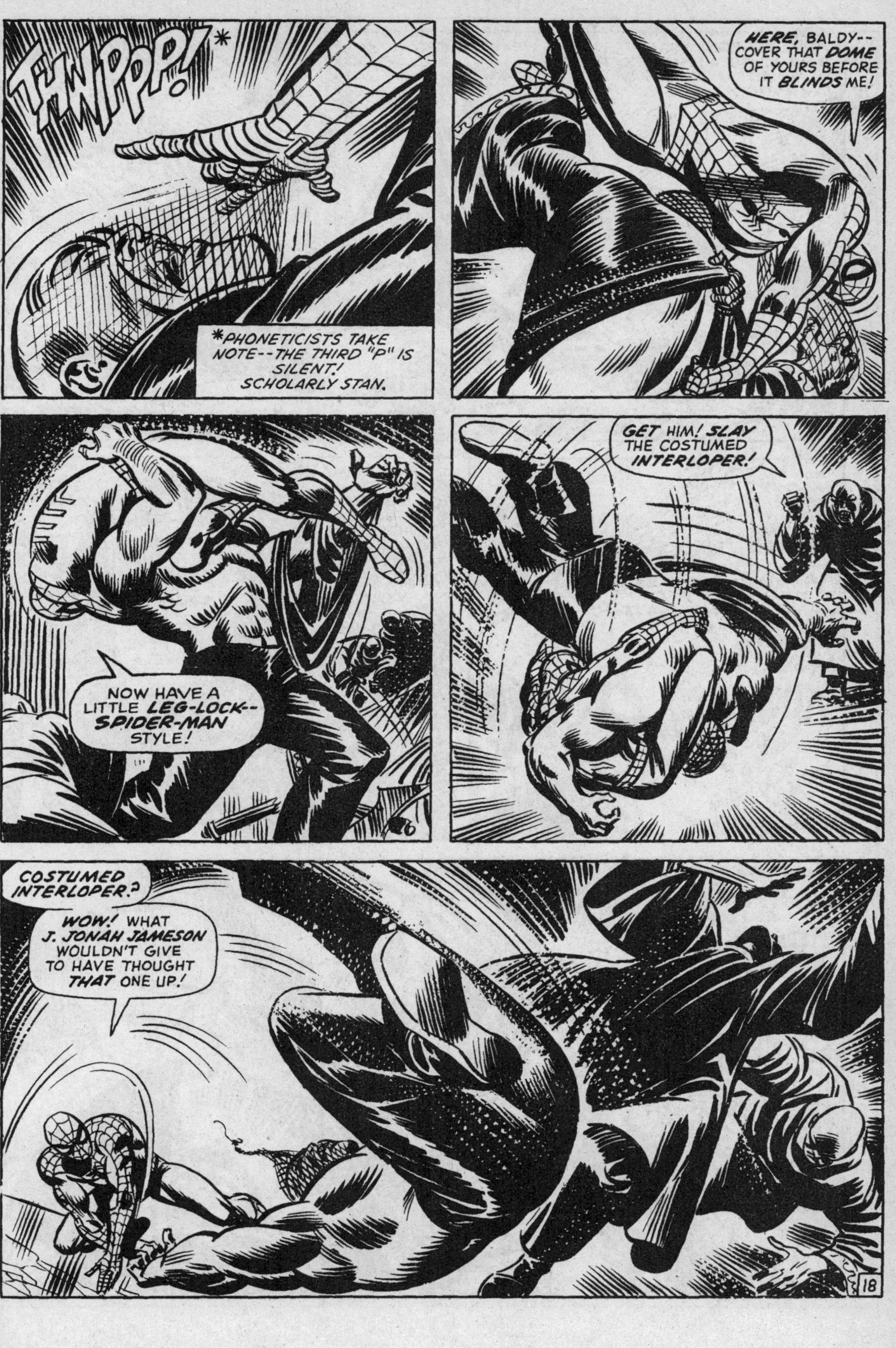
THWIPPP!*
*PHONETICISTS TAKE NOTE--THE THIRD "P" IS SILENT! SCHOLARLY STAN.
HERE, BALDY-- COVER THAT DOME OF YOURS BEFORE IT BLINDS ME!
NOW HAVE A LITTLE LEG-LOCK-- SPIDER-MAN STYLE!
GET HIM! SLAY THE COSTUMED INTERLOPER!
COSTUMED INTERLOPER?
WOW! WHAT J. JONAH JAMESON WOULDN'T GIVE TO HAVE THOUGHT THAT ONE UP!
18

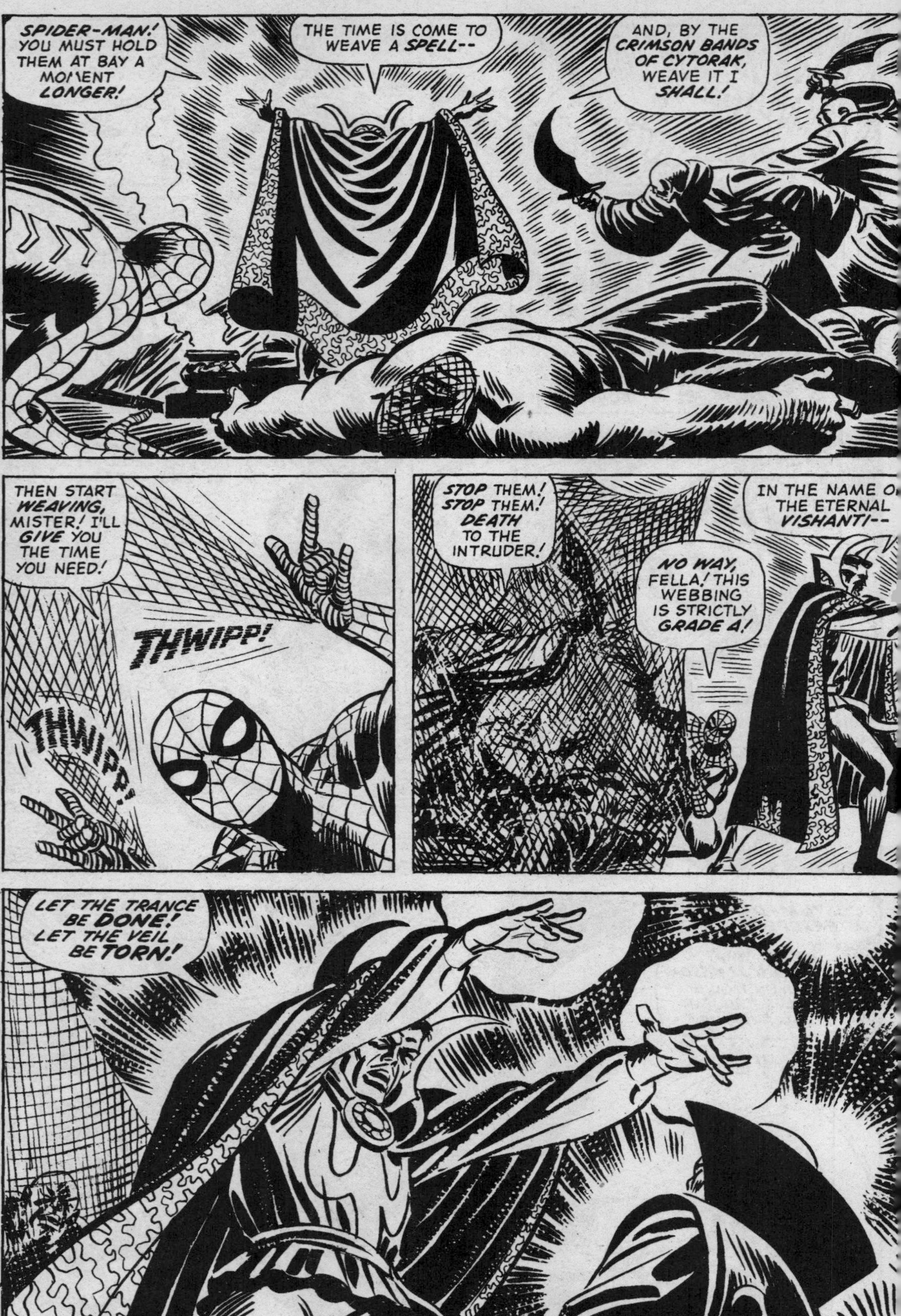
SPIDER-MAN! YOU MUST HOLD THEM AT BAY A MOMENT LONGER!
THE TIME IS COME TO WEAVE A SPELL--
AND, BY THE CRIMSON BANDS OF CYTORAK, WEAVE IT I SHALL!
THEN START WEAVING, MISTER! I'LL GIVE YOU THE TIME YOU NEED!
THWIPP!
THWIPP!
THWIPP!
STOP THEM! STOP THEM! DEATH TO THE INTRUDER!
IN THE NAME O THE ETERNAL VISHANTI!--
NO WAY, FELLA! THIS WEBBING IS STRICTLY GRADE A!
LET THE TRANCE BE DONE! LET THE VEIL BE TORN!

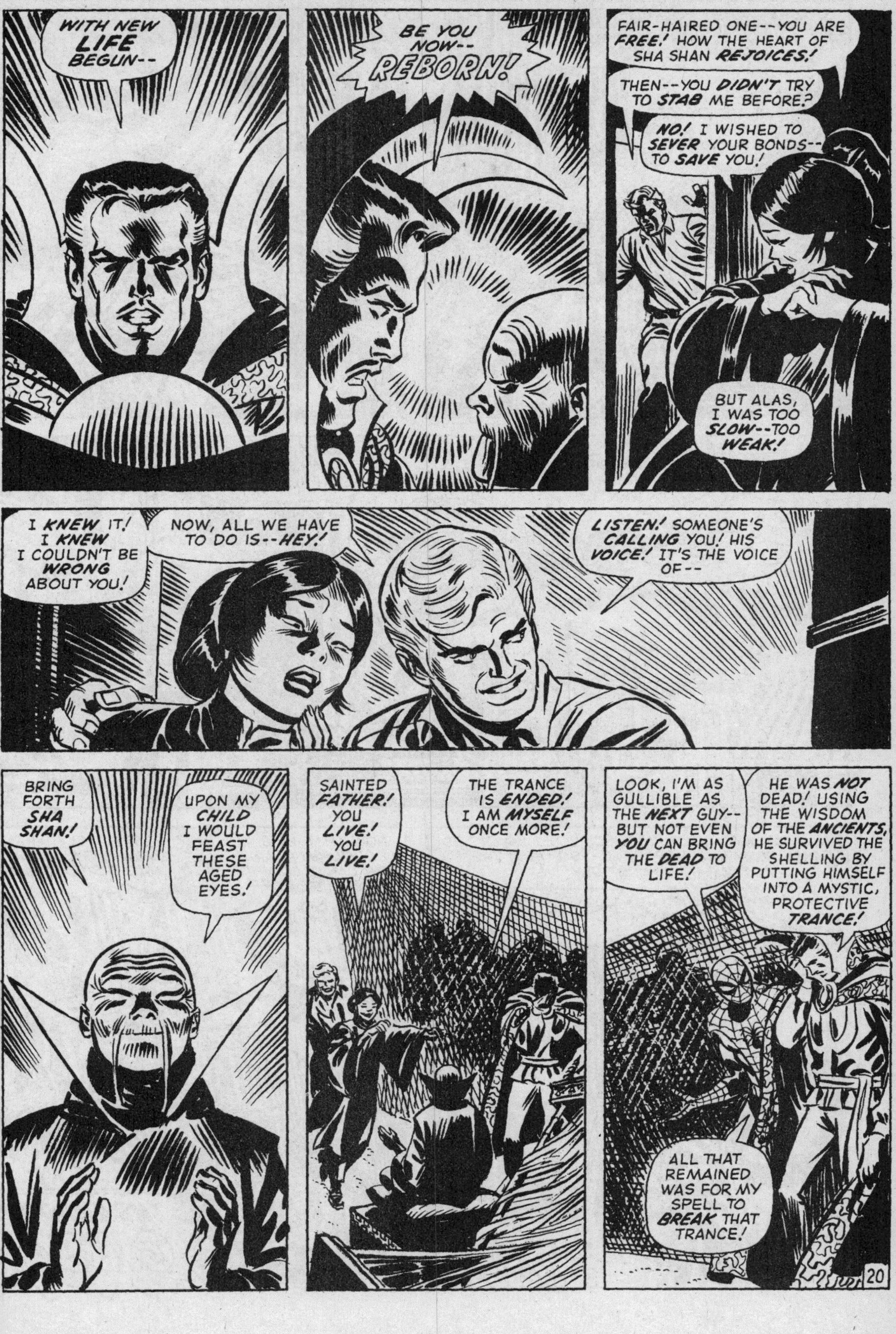
WITH NEW LIFE BEGUN--
BE YOU NOW-- REBORN!
FAIR-HAIRED ONE--YOU ARE FREE! HOW THE HEART OF SHA SHAN REJOICES!
THEN--YOU DIDN'T TRY TO STAB ME BEFORE?
NO! I WISHED TO SEVER YOUR BONDS-- TO SAVE YOU!
BUT ALAS, I WAS TOO SLOW--TOO WEAK!
I KNEW IT! I KNEW I COULDN'T BE WRONG ABOUT YOU!
NOW, ALL WE HAVE TO DO IS--HEY!
LISTEN! SOMEONE'S CALLING YOU! HIS VOICE! IT'S THE VOICE OF--
BRING FORTH SHA SHAN!
UPON MY CHILD I WOULD FEAST THESE AGED EYES!
SAINTED FATHER! YOU LIVE! YOU LIVE!
THE TRANCE IS ENDED! I AM MYSELF ONCE MORE!
LOOK, I'M AS GULLIBLE AS THE NEXT GUY-- BUT NOT EVEN YOU CAN BRING THE DEAD TO LIFE!
HE WAS NOT DEAD! USING THE WISDOM OF THE ANCIENTS, HE SURVIVED THE SHELLING BY PUTTING HIMSELF INTO A MYSTIC, PROTECTIVE TRANCE!
ALL THAT REMAINED WAS FOR MY SPELL TO BREAK THAT TRANCE!
20

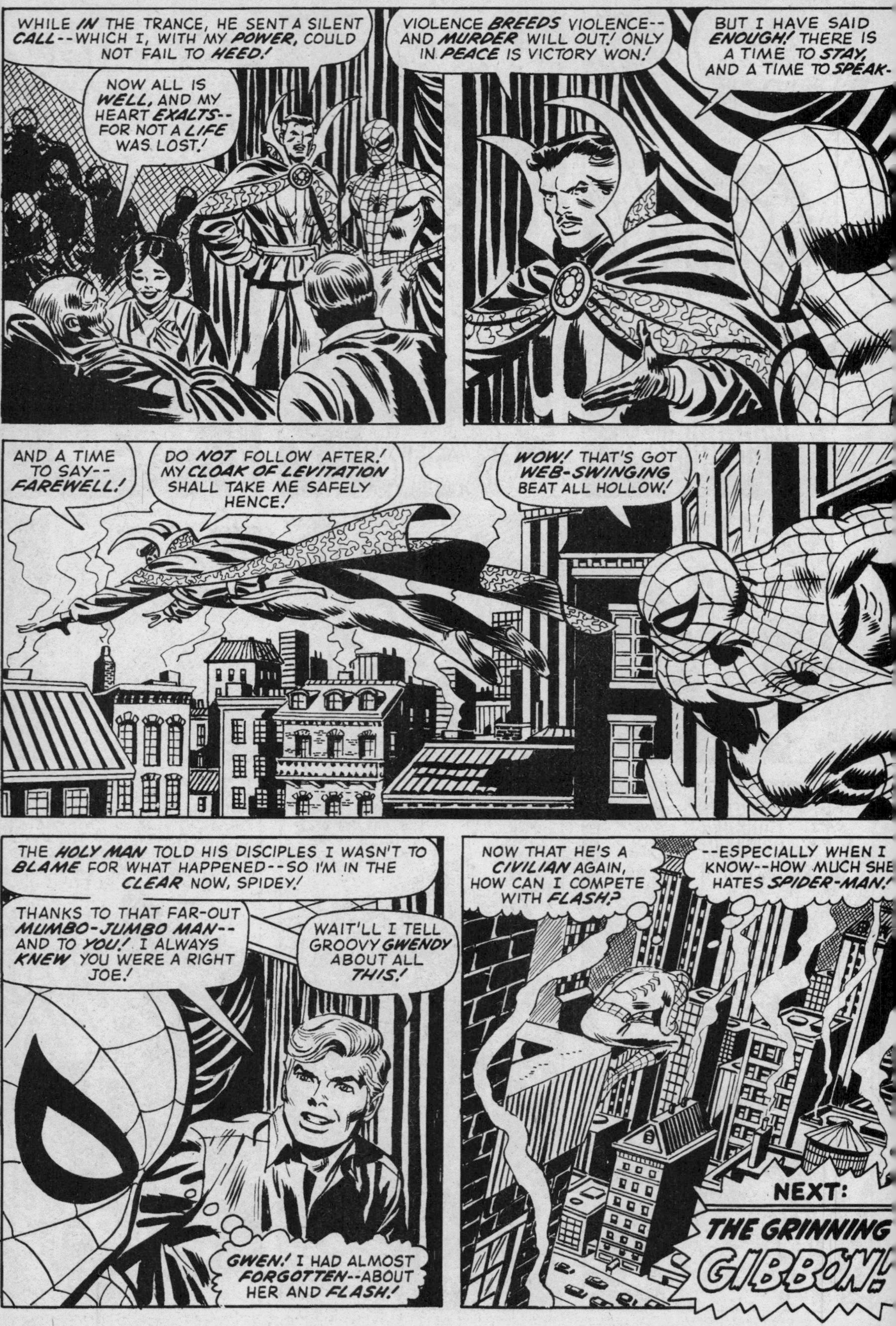
WHILE IN THE TRANCE, HE SENT A SILENT CALL--WHICH I, WITH MY POWER, COULD NOT FAIL TO HEED!
NOW ALL IS WELL, AND MY HEART EXALTS--FOR NOT A LIFE WAS LOST!
VIOLENCE BREEDS VIOLENCE--AND MURDER WILL OUT! ONLY IN PEACE IS VICTORY WON!
BUT I HAVE SAID ENOUGH! THERE IS A TIME TO STAY, AND A TIME TO SPEAK-
AND A TIME TO SAY--FAREWELL!
DO NOT FOLLOW AFTER! MY CLOAK OF LEVITATION SHALL TAKE ME SAFELY HENCE!
WOW! THAT'S GOT WEB-SWINGING BEAT ALL HOLLOW!
THE HOLY MAN TOLD HIS DISCIPLES I WASN'T TO BLAME FOR WHAT HAPPENED--SO I'M IN THE CLEAR NOW, SPIDEY!
THANKS TO THAT FAR-OUT MUMBO-JUMBO MAN--AND TO YOU! I ALWAYS KNEW YOU WERE A RIGHT JOE!
WAIT'LL I TELL GROOVY GWENDY ABOUT ALL THIS!
GWEN! I HAD ALMOST FORGOTTEN--ABOUT HER AND FLASH!
NOW THAT HE'S A CIVILIAN AGAIN, HOW CAN I COMPETE WITH FLASH?
--ESPECIALLY WHEN I KNOW--HOW MUCH SHE HATES SPIDER-MAN!
NEXT:
THE GRINNING GIBBON!

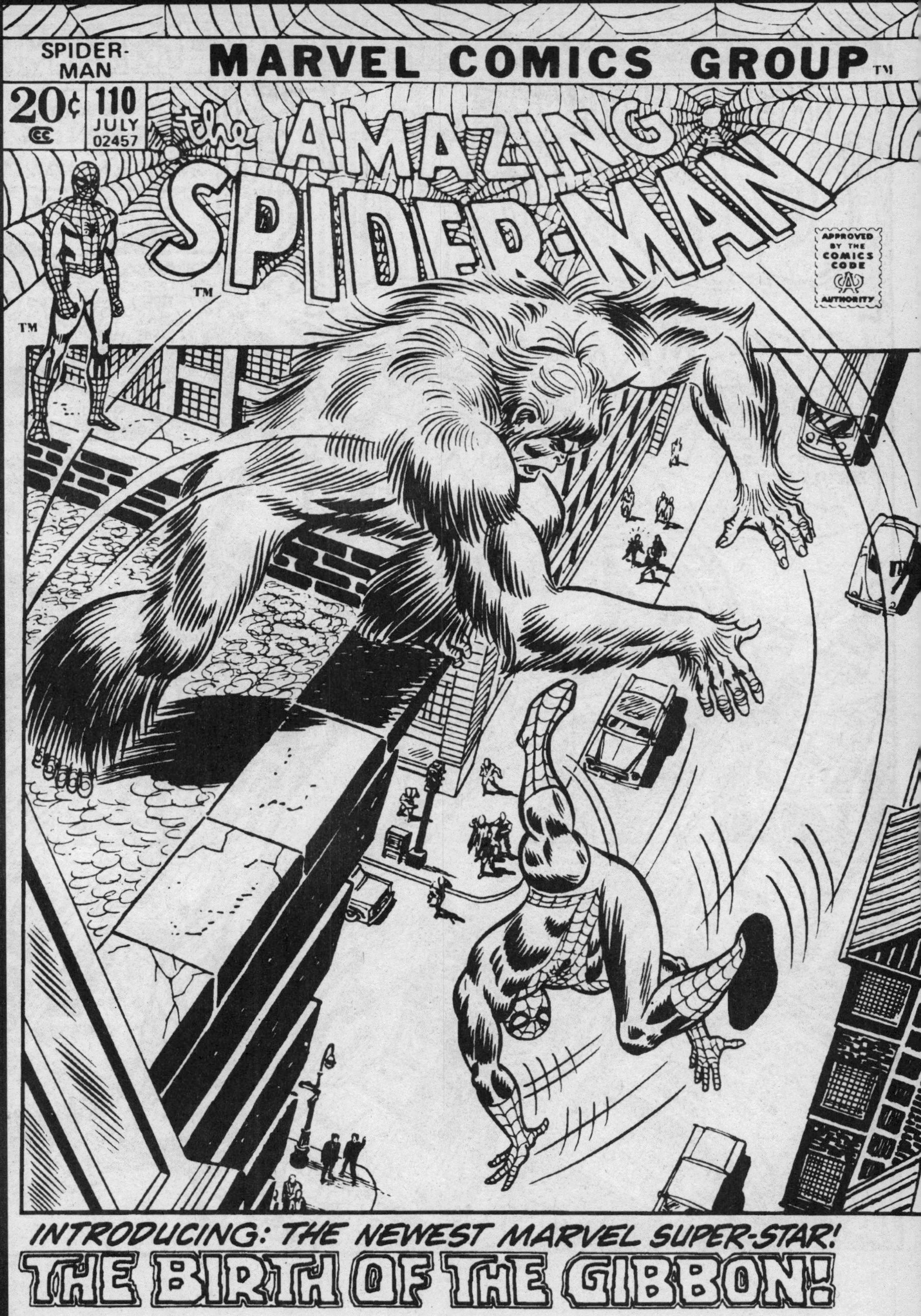

SPIDER-MAN
MARVEL COMICS GROUP
20¢
110
JULY
02457
the AMAZING SPIDER-MAN
APPROVED BY THE COMICS CODE AUTHORITY
INTRODUCING: THE NEWEST MARVEL SUPER-STAR!
THE BIRTH OF THE GIBBON!

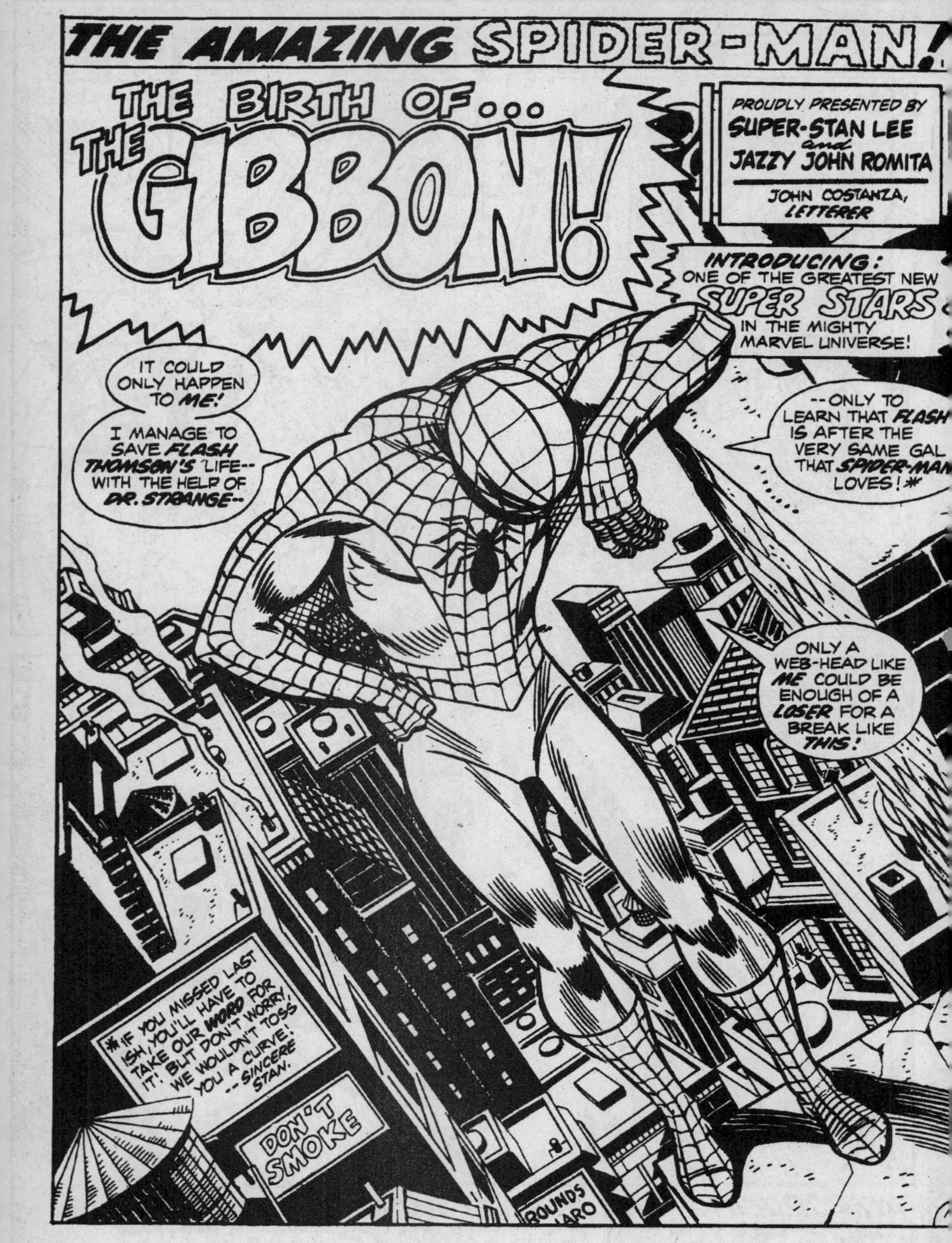

THE AMAZING SPIDER-MAN!
THE BIRTH OF... THE GIBBON!
PROUDLY PRESENTED BY SUPER-STAN LEE and JAZZY JOHN ROMITA
JOHN COSTANZA, LETTERER
INTRODUCING: ONE OF THE GREATEST NEW SUPER STARS IN THE MIGHTY MARVEL UNIVERSE!
IT COULD ONLY HAPPEN TO ME!
I MANAGE TO SAVE FLASH THOMSON'S LIFE-- WITH THE HELP OF DR. STRANGE--
--ONLY TO LEARN THAT FLASH IS AFTER THE VERY SAME GAL THAT SPIDER-MAN LOVES!*
ONLY A WEB-HEAD LIKE ME COULD BE ENOUGH OF A LOSER FOR A BREAK LIKE THIS!
*IF YOU MISSED LAST ISH, YOU'LL HAVE TO TAKE OUR WORD FOR IT! BUT DON'T WORRY, WE WOULDN'T TOSS YOU A CURVE! --SINCERE STAN.
DON'T SMOKE

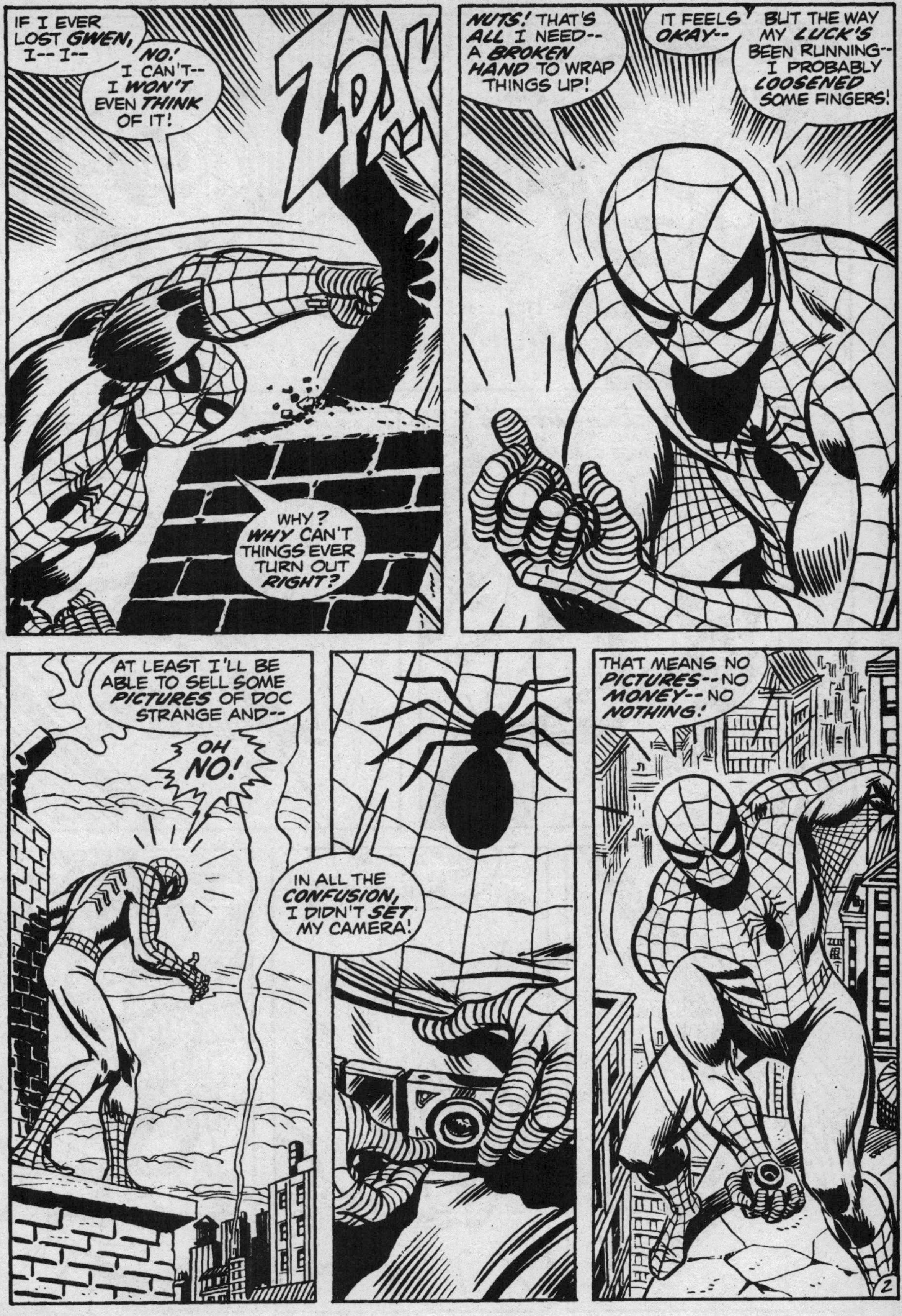

IF I EVER LOST GWEN, I-- I--
NO! I CAN'T-- I WON'T EVEN THINK OF IT!
ZPAK
WHY? WHY CAN'T THINGS EVER TURN OUT RIGHT?
NUTS! THAT'S ALL I NEED-- A BROKEN HAND TO WRAP THINGS UP!
IT FEELS OKAY--
BUT THE WAY MY LUCK'S BEEN RUNNING-- I PROBABLY LOOSENED SOME FINGERS!
AT LEAST I'LL BE ABLE TO SELL SOME PICTURES OF DOC STRANGE AND--
OH NO!
IN ALL THE CONFUSION, I DIDN'T SET MY CAMERA!
THAT MEANS NO PICTURES-- NO MONEY-- NO NOTHING!
2

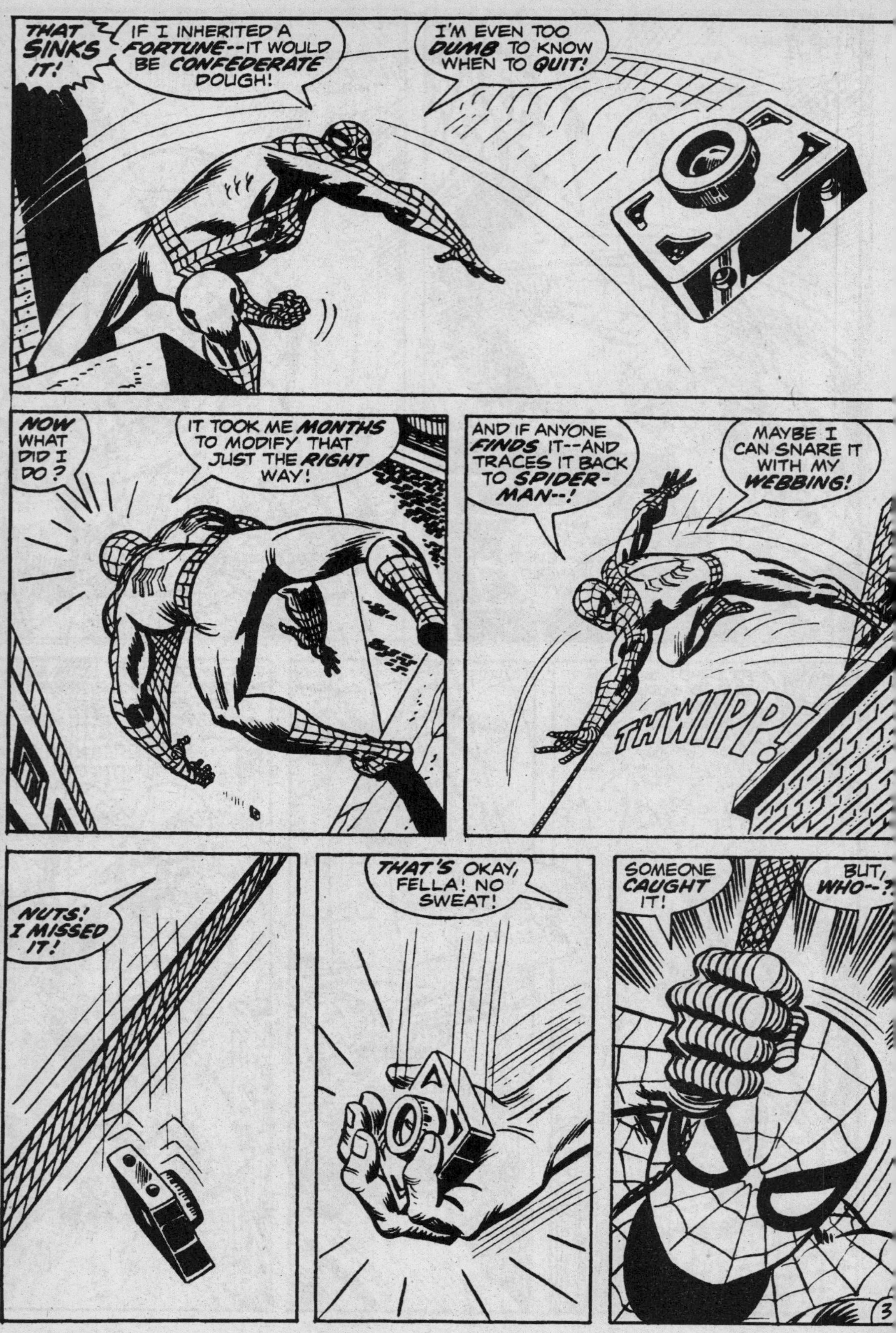
THAT SINKS IT!
IF I INHERITED A FORTUNE--IT WOULD BE CONFEDERATE DOUGH!
I'M EVEN TOO DUMB TO KNOW WHEN TO QUIT!
NOW WHAT DID I DO?
IT TOOK ME MONTHS TO MODIFY THAT JUST THE RIGHT WAY!
AND IF ANYONE FINDS IT--AND TRACES IT BACK TO SPIDER-MAN--!
MAYBE I CAN SNARE IT WITH MY WEBBING!
THWIPP!
NUTS! I MISSED IT!
THAT'S OKAY, FELLA! NO SWEAT!
A
SOMEONE CAUGHT IT!
BUT, WHO--?
3

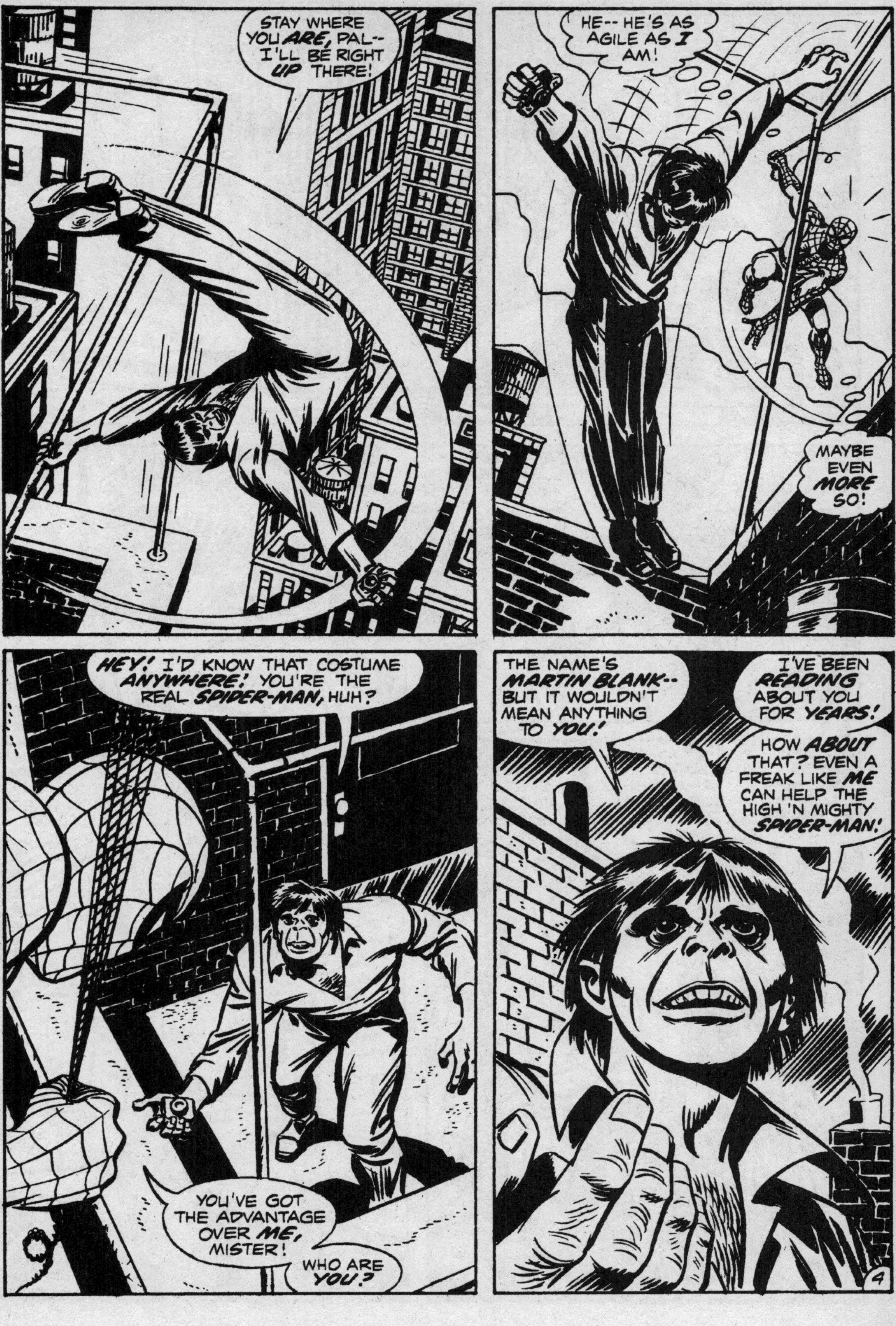
STAY WHERE YOU ARE, PAL-- I'LL BE RIGHT UP THERE!
HE-- HE'S AS AGILE AS I AM!
MAYBE EVEN MORE SO!
HEY! I'D KNOW THAT COSTUME ANYWHERE! YOU'RE THE REAL SPIDER-MAN, HUH?
YOU'VE GOT THE ADVANTAGE OVER ME, MISTER!
WHO ARE YOU?
THE NAME'S MARTIN BLANK-- BUT IT WOULDN'T MEAN ANYTHING TO YOU!
I'VE BEEN READING ABOUT YOU FOR YEARS!
HOW ABOUT THAT? EVEN A FREAK LIKE ME CAN HELP THE HIGH 'N MIGHTY SPIDER-MAN!
4

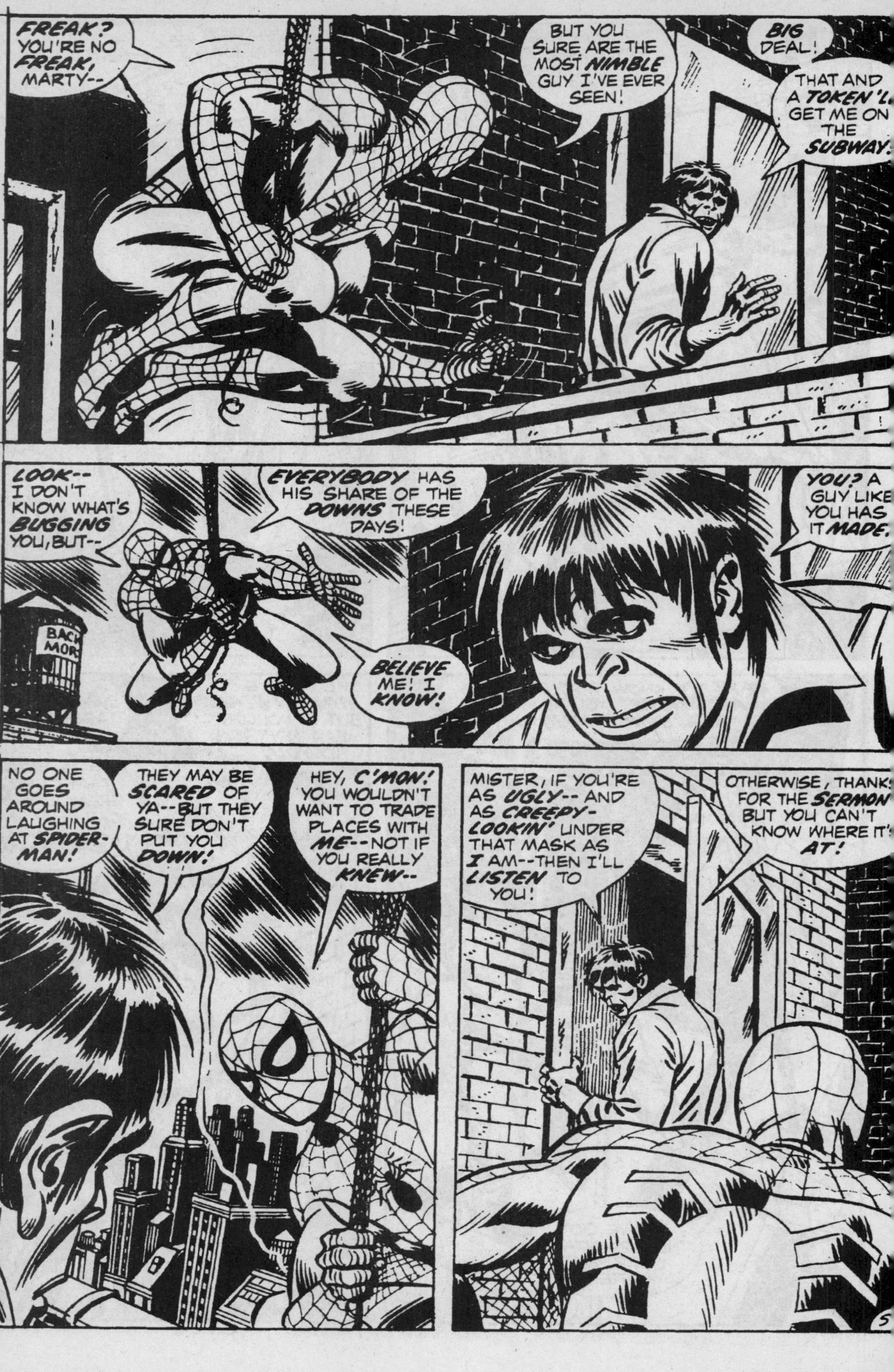
FREAK? YOU'RE NO FREAK, MARTY--
BUT YOU SURE ARE THE MOST NIMBLE GUY I'VE EVER SEEN!
BIG DEAL!
THAT AND A TOKEN'L GET ME ON THE SUBWAY!
LOOK-- I DON'T KNOW WHAT'S BUGGING YOU, BUT--
EVERYBODY HAS HIS SHARE OF THE DOWNS THESE DAYS!
BELIEVE ME! I KNOW!
YOU? A GUY LIKE YOU HAS IT MADE.
BACK MORE
NO ONE GOES AROUND LAUGHING AT SPIDER-MAN!
THEY MAY BE SCARED OF YA--BUT THEY SURE DON'T PUT YOU DOWN!
HEY, C'MON! YOU WOULDN'T WANT TO TRADE PLACES WITH ME--NOT IF YOU REALLY KNEW--
MISTER, IF YOU'RE AS UGLY-- AND AS CREEPY-LOOKIN' UNDER THAT MASK AS I AM--THEN I'LL LISTEN TO YOU!
OTHERWISE, THANKS FOR THE SERMON BUT YOU CAN'T KNOW WHERE IT' AT!
5

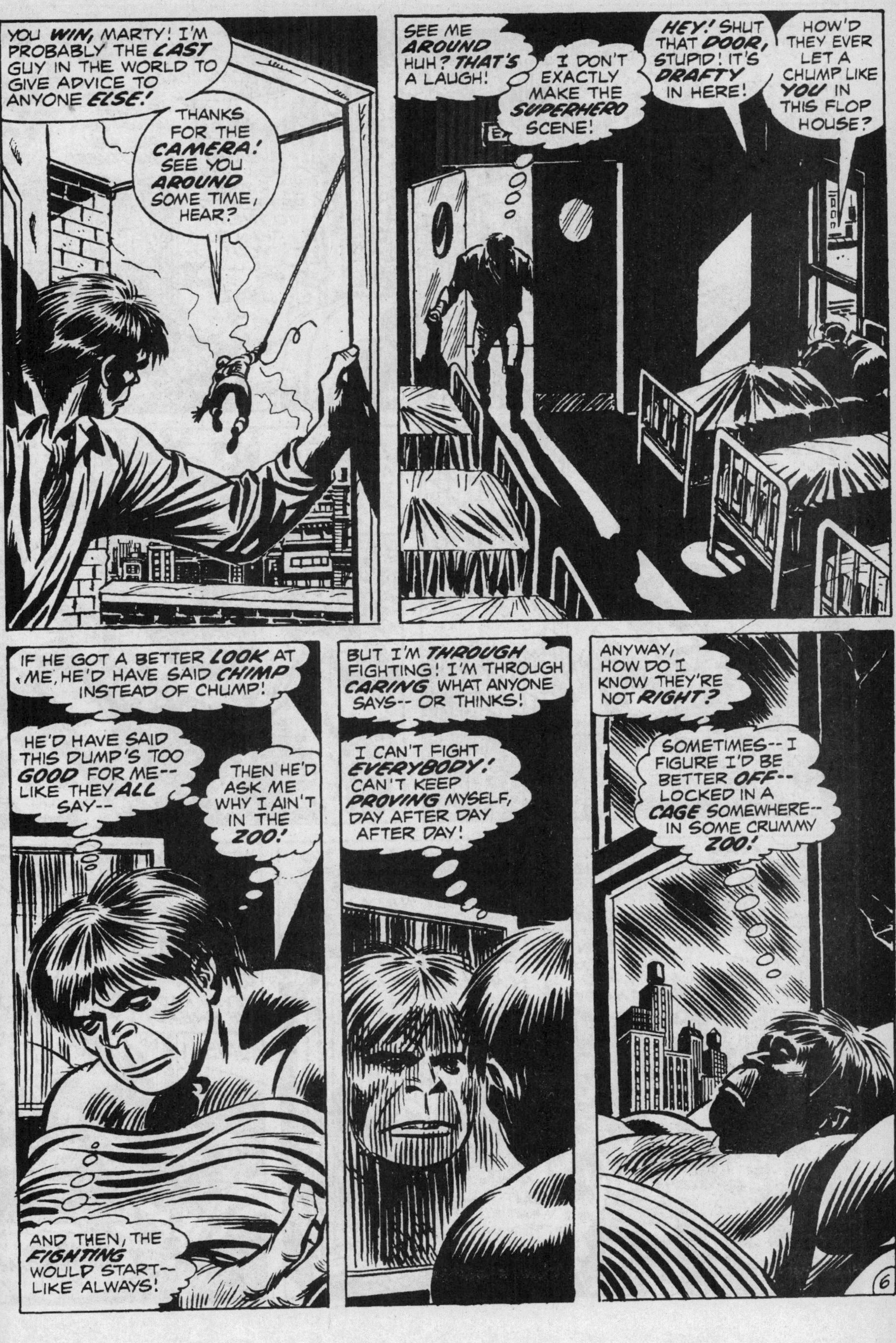
YOU WIN, MARTY! I'M PROBABLY THE LAST GUY IN THE WORLD TO GIVE ADVICE TO ANYONE ELSE!
THANKS FOR THE CAMERA! SEE YOU AROUND SOME TIME, HEAR?
SEE ME AROUND HUH? THAT'S A LAUGH!
I DON'T EXACTLY MAKE THE SUPERHERO SCENE!
HEY! SHUT THAT DOOR, STUPID! IT'S DRAFTY IN HERE!
HOW'D THEY EVER LET A CHUMP LIKE YOU IN THIS FLOP HOUSE?
IF HE GOT A BETTER LOOK AT ME, HE'D HAVE SAID CHIMP INSTEAD OF CHUMP!
HE'D HAVE SAID THIS DUMP'S TOO GOOD FOR ME-- LIKE THEY ALL SAY--
THEN HE'D ASK ME WHY I AIN'T IN THE ZOO!
AND THEN, THE FIGHTING WOULD START-- LIKE ALWAYS!
BUT I'M THROUGH FIGHTING! I'M THROUGH CARING WHAT ANYONE SAYS-- OR THINKS!
I CAN'T FIGHT EVERYBODY! CAN'T KEEP PROVING MYSELF, DAY AFTER DAY AFTER DAY!
ANYWAY, HOW DO I KNOW THEY'RE NOT RIGHT?
SOMETIMES-- I FIGURE I'D BE BETTER OFF-- LOCKED IN A CAGE SOMEWHERE-- IN SOME CRUMMY ZOO!
6

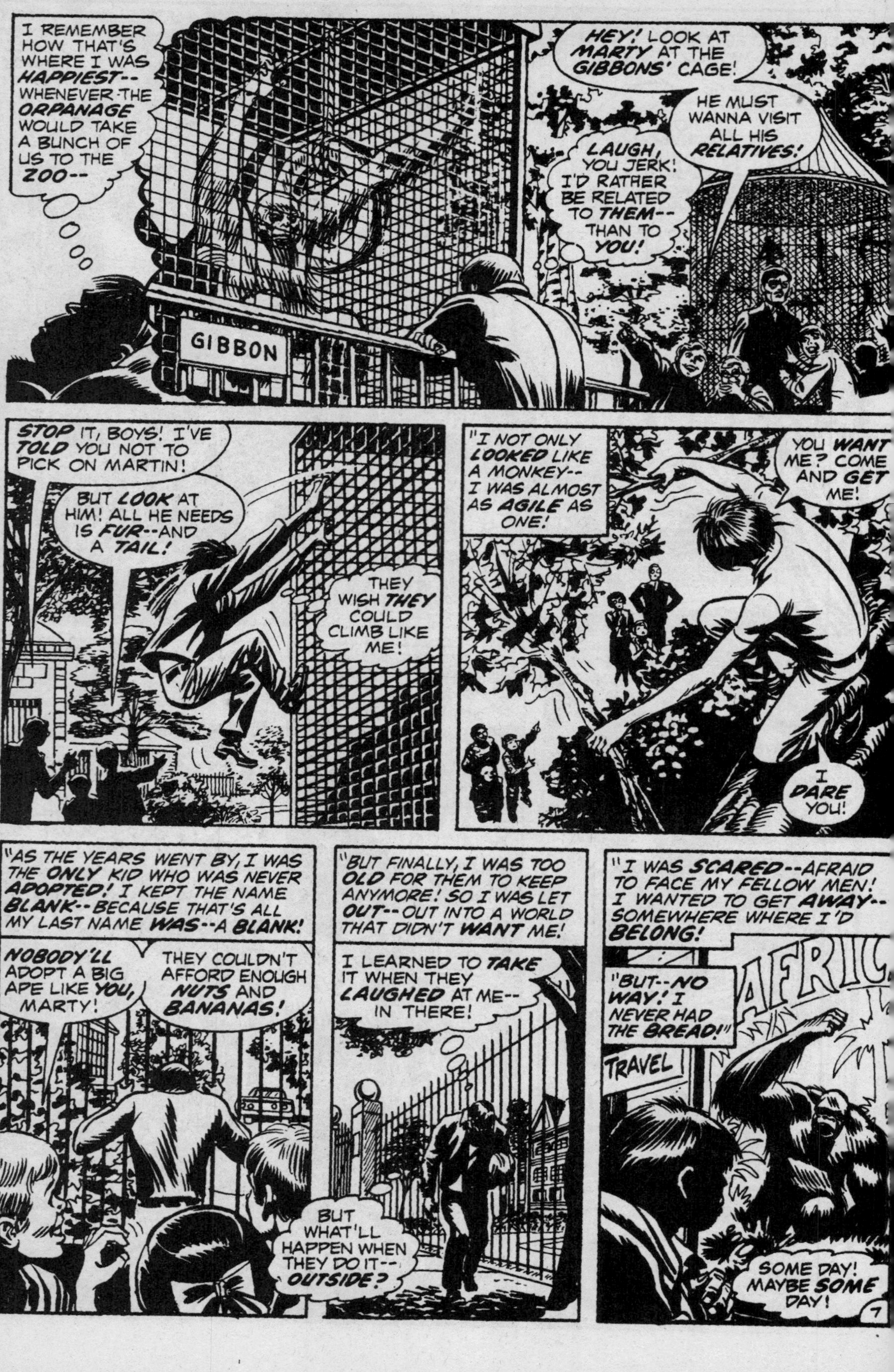
I REMEMBER HOW THAT'S WHERE I WAS HAPPIEST-- WHENEVER THE ORPANAGE WOULD TAKE A BUNCH OF US TO THE ZOO--
GIBBON
HEY! LOOK AT MARTY AT THE GIBBONS' CAGE!
HE MUST WANNA VISIT ALL HIS RELATIVES!
LAUGH, YOU JERK! I'D RATHER BE RELATED TO THEM-- THAN TO YOU!
STOP IT, BOYS! I'VE TOLD YOU NOT TO PICK ON MARTIN!
BUT LOOK AT HIM! ALL HE NEEDS IS FUR--AND A TAIL!
THEY WISH THEY COULD CLIMB LIKE ME!
"I NOT ONLY LOOKED LIKE A MONKEY-- I WAS ALMOST AS AGILE AS ONE!
YOU WANT ME? COME AND GET ME!
I DARE YOU!
"AS THE YEARS WENT BY, I WAS THE ONLY KID WHO WAS NEVER ADOPTED! I KEPT THE NAME BLANK--BECAUSE THAT'S ALL MY LAST NAME WAS--A BLANK!
NOBODY'LL ADOPT A BIG APE LIKE YOU, MARTY!
THEY COULDN'T AFFORD ENOUGH NUTS AND BANANAS!
"BUT FINALLY, I WAS TOO OLD FOR THEM TO KEEP ANYMORE! SO I WAS LET OUT--OUT INTO A WORLD THAT DIDN'T WANT ME!
I LEARNED TO TAKE IT WHEN THEY LAUGHED AT ME-- IN THERE!
BUT WHAT'LL HAPPEN WHEN THEY DO IT-- OUTSIDE?
"I WAS SCARED--AFRAID TO FACE MY FELLOW MEN! I WANTED TO GET AWAY-- SOMEWHERE WHERE I'D BELONG!
"BUT--NO WAY! I NEVER HAD THE BREAD!"
AFRIC
TRAVEL
SOME DAY! MAYBE SOME DAY!
7

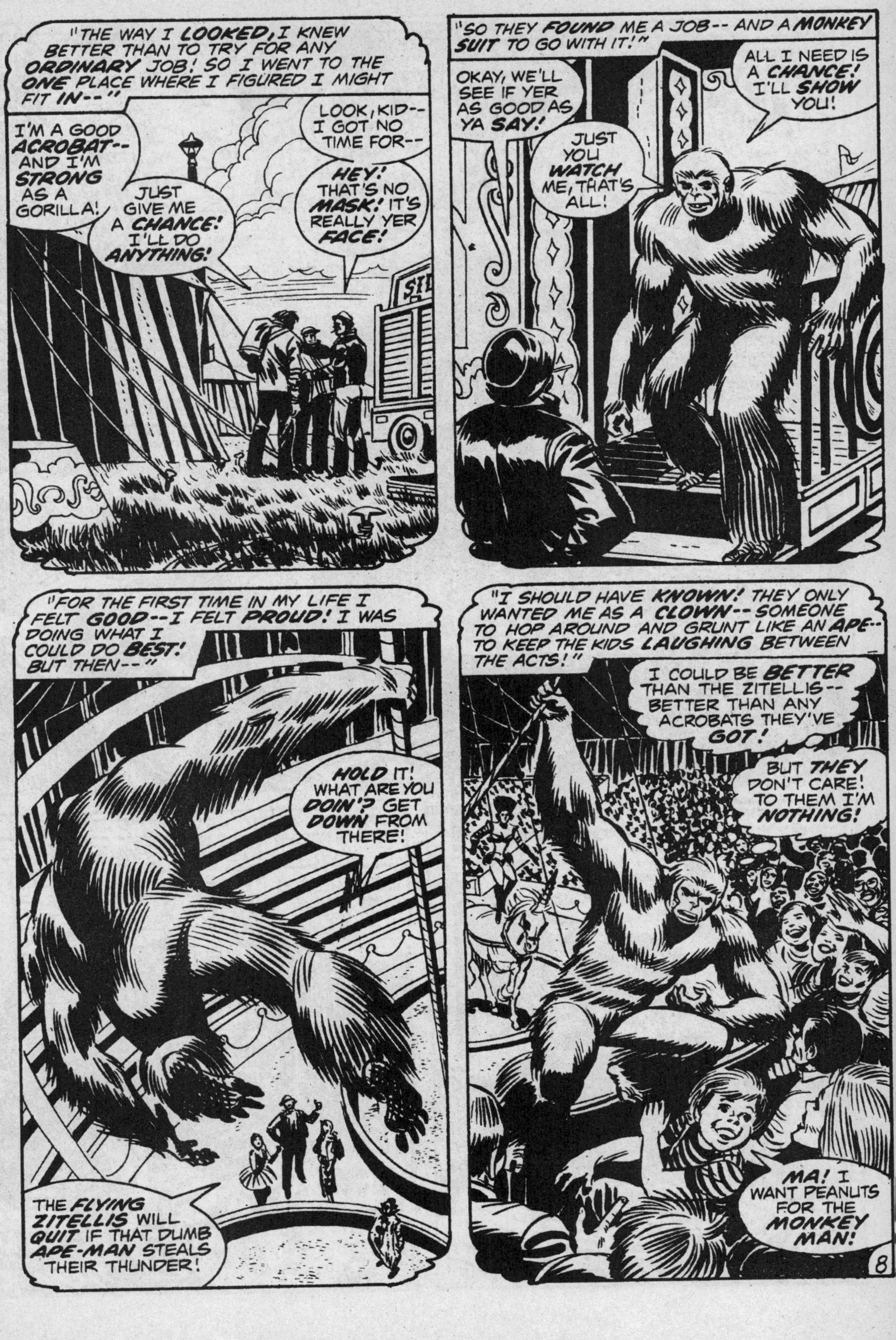
"THE WAY I LOOKED, I KNEW BETTER THAN TO TRY FOR ANY ORDINARY JOB! SO I WENT TO THE ONE PLACE WHERE I FIGURED I MIGHT FIT IN--"
I'M A GOOD ACROBAT-- AND I'M STRONG AS A GORILLA!
JUST GIVE ME A CHANCE! I'LL DO ANYTHING!
LOOK, KID-- I GOT NO TIME FOR--
HEY! THAT'S NO MASK! IT'S REALLY YER FACE!
"SO THEY FOUND ME A JOB-- AND A MONKEY SUIT TO GO WITH IT!"
OKAY, WE'LL SEE IF YER AS GOOD AS YA SAY!
JUST YOU WATCH ME, THAT'S ALL!
ALL I NEED IS A CHANCE! I'LL SHOW YOU!
"FOR THE FIRST TIME IN MY LIFE I FELT GOOD--I FELT PROUD! I WAS DOING WHAT I COULD DO BEST! BUT THEN--"
HOLD IT! WHAT ARE YOU DOIN'? GET DOWN FROM THERE!
THE FLYING ZITELLIS WILL QUIT IF THAT DUMB APE-MAN STEALS THEIR THUNDER!
"I SHOULD HAVE KNOWN! THEY ONLY WANTED ME AS A CLOWN-- SOMEONE TO HOP AROUND AND GRUNT LIKE AN APE-- TO KEEP THE KIDS LAUGHING BETWEEN THE ACTS!"
I COULD BE BETTER THAN THE ZITELLIS-- BETTER THAN ANY ACROBATS THEY'VE GOT!
BUT THEY DON'T CARE! TO THEM I'M NOTHING!
MA! I WANT PEANUTS FOR THE MONKEY MAN!
8

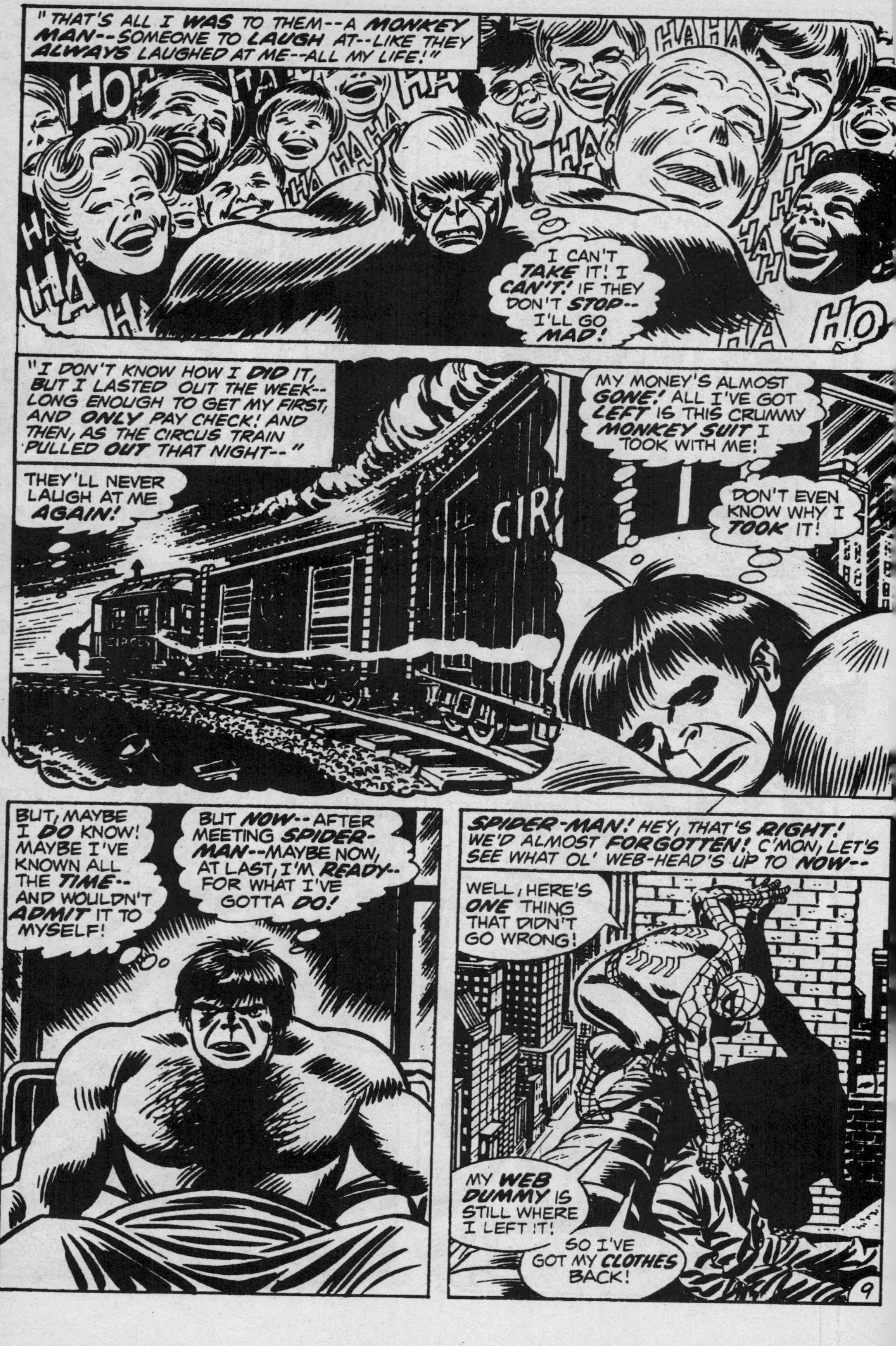
"THAT'S ALL I WAS TO THEM--A MONKEY MAN--SOMEONE TO LAUGH AT--LIKE THEY ALWAYS LAUGHED AT ME--ALL MY LIFE!"
HO
HA HA
HA HA
HA
HA HA
HA HA
HA
HO
I CAN'T TAKE IT! I CAN'T! IF THEY DON'T STOP--I'LL GO MAD!
HO
HA
"I DON'T KNOW HOW I DID IT, BUT I LASTED OUT THE WEEK--LONG ENOUGH TO GET MY FIRST, AND ONLY PAY CHECK! AND THEN, AS THE CIRCUS TRAIN PULLED OUT THAT NIGHT--"
THEY'LL NEVER LAUGH AT ME AGAIN!
CIR
MY MONEY'S ALMOST GONE! ALL I'VE GOT LEFT IS THIS CRUMMY MONKEY SUIT I TOOK WITH ME!
DON'T EVEN KNOW WHY I TOOK IT!
BUT, MAYBE I DO KNOW! MAYBE I'VE KNOWN ALL THE TIME--AND WOULDN'T ADMIT IT TO MYSELF!
BUT NOW--AFTER MEETING SPIDER-MAN--MAYBE NOW, AT LAST, I'M READY--FOR WHAT I'VE GOTTA DO!
SPIDER-MAN! HEY, THAT'S RIGHT! WE'D ALMOST FORGOTTEN! C'MON, LET'S SEE WHAT OL' WEB-HEAD'S UP TO NOW--
WELL, HERE'S ONE THING THAT DIDN'T GO WRONG!
MY WEB DUMMY IS STILL WHERE I LEFT IT!
SO I'VE GOT MY CLOTHES BACK!
9

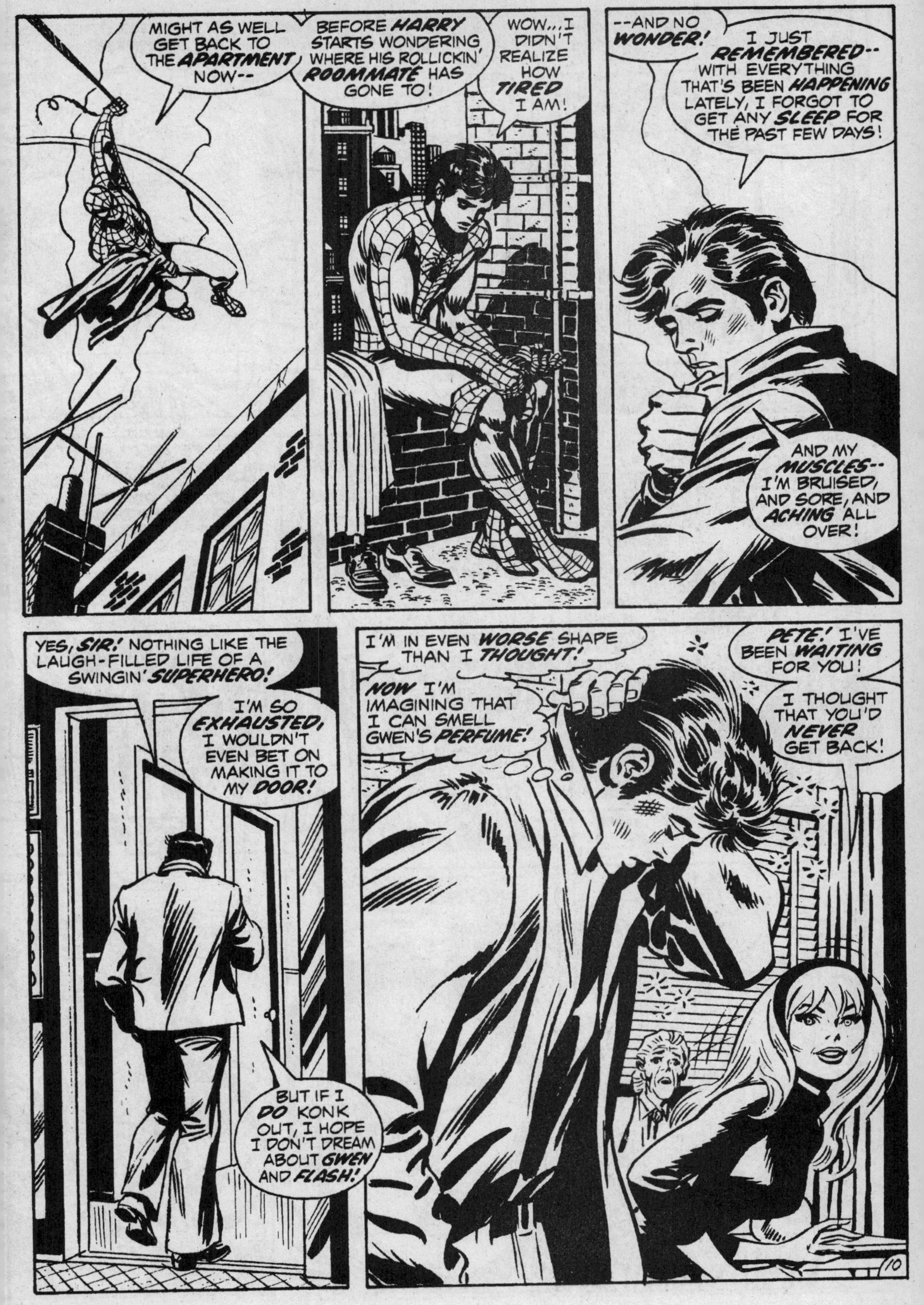
MIGHT AS WELL GET BACK TO THE APARTMENT NOW--
BEFORE HARRY STARTS WONDERING WHERE HIS ROLLICKIN' ROOMMATE HAS GONE TO!
WOW...I DIDN'T REALIZE HOW TIRED I AM!
--AND NO WONDER!
I JUST REMEMBERED-- WITH EVERYTHING THAT'S BEEN HAPPENING LATELY, I FORGOT TO GET ANY SLEEP FOR THE PAST FEW DAYS!
AND MY MUSCLES-- I'M BRUISED, AND SORE, AND ACHING ALL OVER!
YES, SIR! NOTHING LIKE THE LAUGH-FILLED LIFE OF A SWINGIN' SUPERHERO!
I'M SO EXHAUSTED, I WOULDN'T EVEN BET ON MAKING IT TO MY DOOR!
BUT IF I DO KONK OUT, I HOPE I DON'T DREAM ABOUT GWEN AND FLASH!
I'M IN EVEN WORSE SHAPE THAN I THOUGHT!
NOW I'M IMAGINING THAT I CAN SMELL GWEN'S PERFUME!
PETE! I'VE BEEN WAITING FOR YOU!
I THOUGHT THAT YOU'D NEVER GET BACK!
10

GWENDY! I THOUGHT YOU'D BE WITH--I MEAN, I DIDN'T EXPECT TO FIND--

I GUESS FLASH HASN'T HAD A CHANCE TO CALL HER YET!

YOU WERE GONE SO LONG! WE WERE SO WORRIED ABOUT YOU!

YOU POOR BOY! I'VE NEVER SEEN YOU LOOKING SO TIRED BEFORE!

YOUR CLOTHES ARE [SO?] WRINKLED--AND A[LL] THOS[E] BRUISE[S] ON Y[OUR] FA[CE]

IT'S THAT HORRIBLE SPIDER-MAN, ISN'T IT?

I HEARD HOW HE ATTACKED YOU! BUT WHY? WHY, PETER?

IT WAS THE ONLY WAY I COULD SET IT UP--SO NO ONE WOULD SUSPECT THAT WE'RE BOTH THE SAME ONE! BUT HOW DO I TELL THAT TO POOR AUNT MAY?

MRS. PARKER-- YOU PROMISED!

DON'T YOU REMEMBER? YOU PROMISED TO STOP TREATING PETER LIKE A CHILD--TO STOP BABYING HIM!

OH, DEAR! I DID IT AGAIN! AND-- I TRIED NOT TO!

AW, THAT'S OKAY, AUNT MAY!

NO, PETER DEAR--IT'S NOT OKAY!

I--DON'T KNOW WHAT THEY'RE TALKING ABOUT! AND MY HEAD-- IT'S ACHING SO THAT I CAN'T EVEN THINK!

GWENDOLYN'S RIGHT! I'VE BEEN TOO MATERNAL--TOO POSSESSIVE ALL THESE YEARS!

GWENDY, WHAT IS IT? WHAT'S HAPPENED TO AUNT MAY?

IT'S MY FAULT, PETER! I TOLD HER SHE SHOULDN'T TRY TO CODDLE YOU SO MUCH--

BUT I DIDN'T MEAN TO HURT HER--TO MAKE HER FEEL GUILTY!

I JUST DID IT FOR YOUR SAKE, BECAUSE--

PETE! WHAT IS IT? WHAT'S WRONG?

IT'S--ALL RIGHT, GWEN--I'M JUST--TIRED!

CAN'T KEEP MY EYES OPEN--ANY LONGER!

PETE!

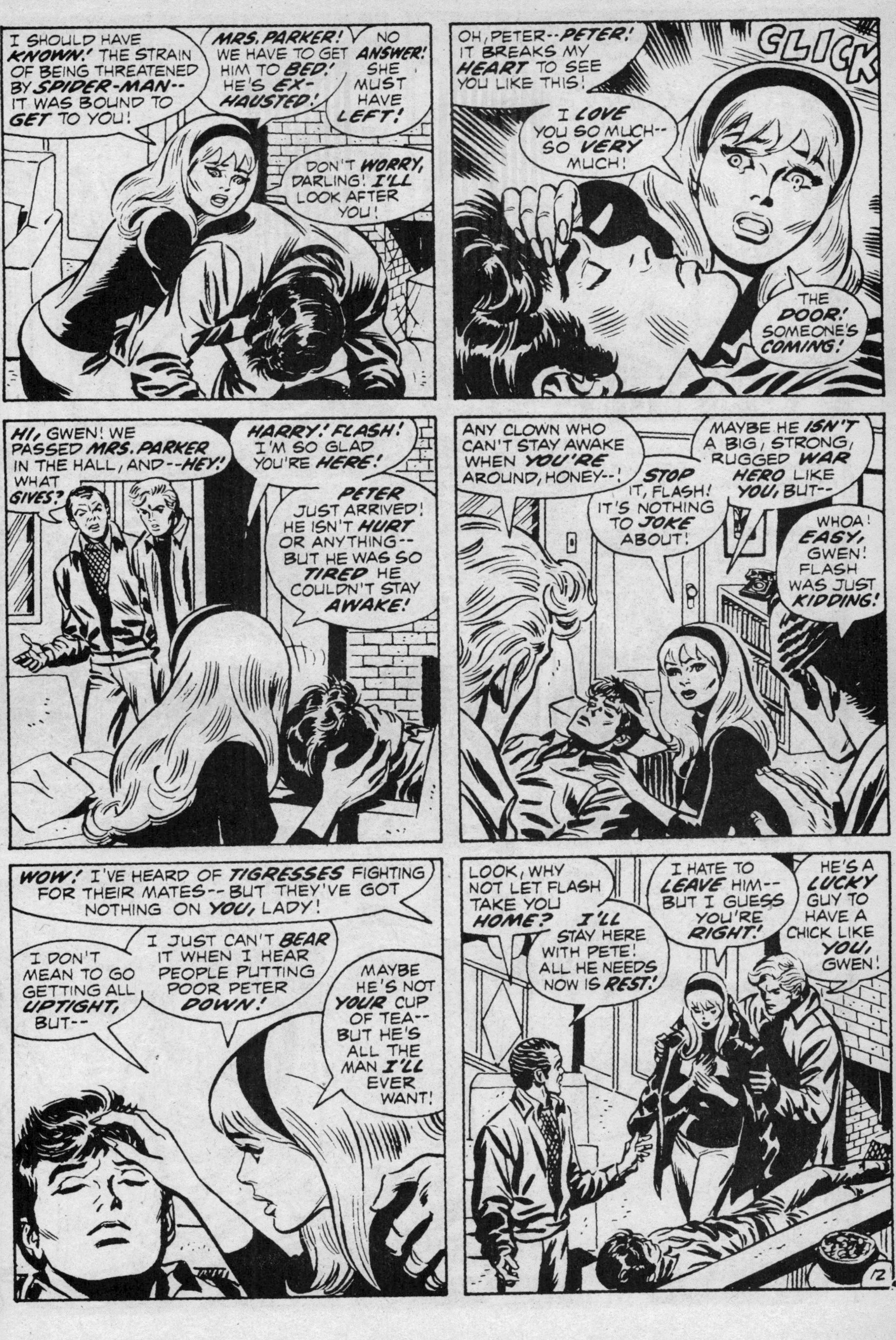
I SHOULD HAVE KNOWN! THE STRAIN OF BEING THREATENED BY SPIDER-MAN-- IT WAS BOUND TO GET TO YOU!
MRS. PARKER! WE HAVE TO GET HIM TO BED! HE'S EX-HAUSTED!
NO ANSWER! SHE MUST HAVE LEFT!
DON'T WORRY, DARLING! I'LL LOOK AFTER YOU!
OH, PETER--PETER! IT BREAKS MY HEART TO SEE YOU LIKE THIS!
CLICK
I LOVE YOU SO MUCH-- SO VERY MUCH!
THE DOOR! SOMEONE'S COMING!
HI, GWEN! WE PASSED MRS. PARKER IN THE HALL, AND--HEY! WHAT GIVES?
HARRY! FLASH! I'M SO GLAD YOU'RE HERE!
PETER JUST ARRIVED! HE ISN'T HURT OR ANYTHING-- BUT HE WAS SO TIRED HE COULDN'T STAY AWAKE!
ANY CLOWN WHO CAN'T STAY AWAKE WHEN YOU'RE AROUND, HONEY--!
MAYBE HE ISN'T A BIG, STRONG, RUGGED WAR HERO LIKE YOU, BUT--
STOP IT, FLASH! IT'S NOTHING TO JOKE ABOUT!
WHOA! EASY, GWEN! FLASH WAS JUST KIDDING!
WOW! I'VE HEARD OF TIGRESSES FIGHTING FOR THEIR MATES--BUT THEY'VE GOT NOTHING ON YOU, LADY!
I DON'T MEAN TO GO GETTING ALL UPTIGHT, BUT--
I JUST CAN'T BEAR IT WHEN I HEAR PEOPLE PUTTING POOR PETER DOWN!
MAYBE HE'S NOT YOUR CUP OF TEA-- BUT HE'S ALL THE MAN I'LL EVER WANT!
LOOK, WHY NOT LET FLASH TAKE YOU HOME? I'LL STAY HERE WITH PETE! ALL HE NEEDS NOW IS REST!
I HATE TO LEAVE HIM-- BUT I GUESS YOU'RE RIGHT!
HE'S A LUCKY GUY TO HAVE A CHICK LIKE YOU, GWEN!
12

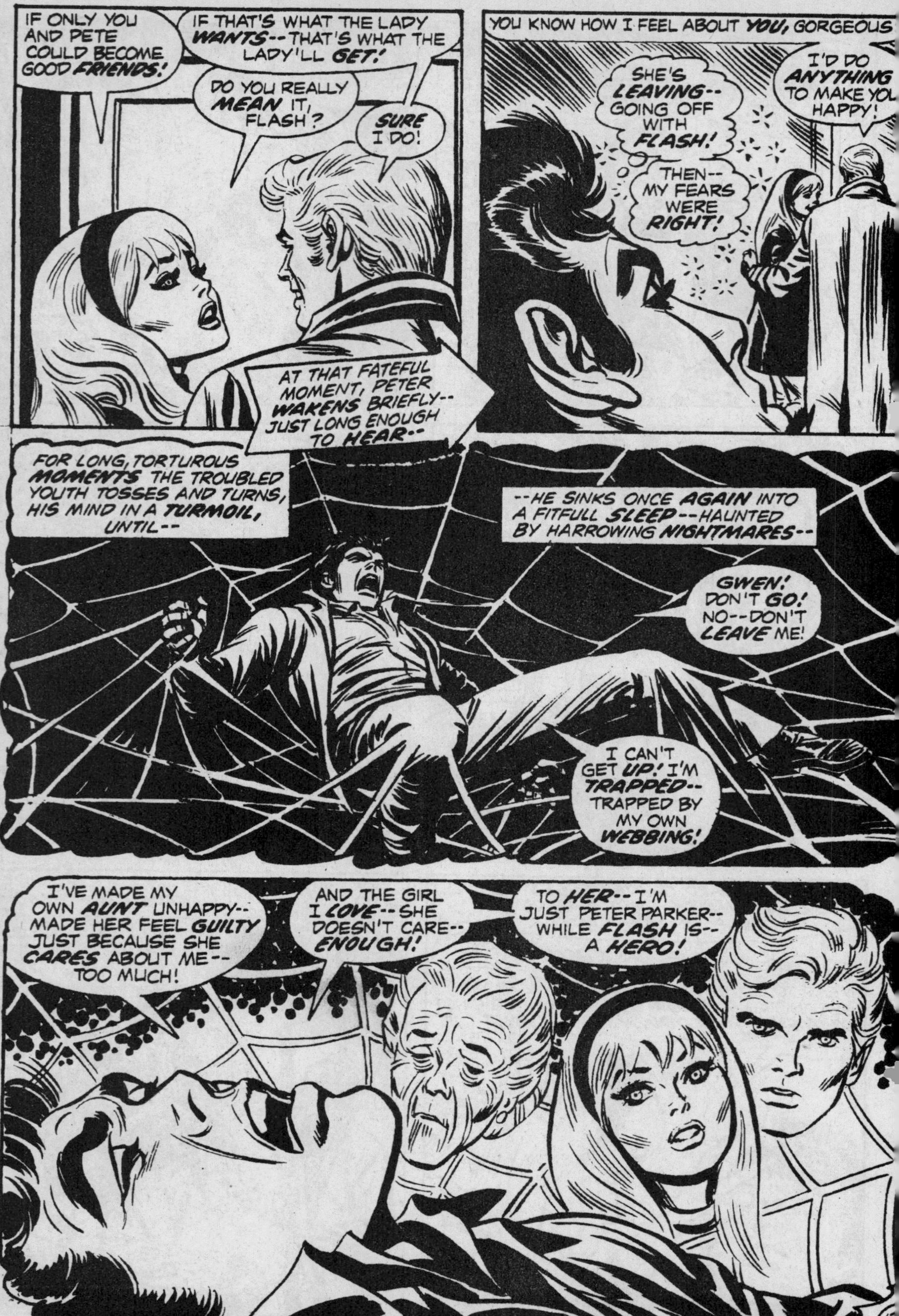
IF ONLY YOU AND PETE COULD BECOME GOOD FRIENDS!
IF THAT'S WHAT THE LADY WANTS--THAT'S WHAT THE LADY'LL GET!
DO YOU REALLY MEAN IT, FLASH?
SURE I DO!
AT THAT FATEFUL MOMENT, PETER WAKENS BRIEFLY--JUST LONG ENOUGH TO HEAR--
YOU KNOW HOW I FEEL ABOUT YOU, GORGEOUS
I'D DO ANYTHING TO MAKE YOU HAPPY!
SHE'S LEAVING--GOING OFF WITH FLASH!
THEN--MY FEARS WERE RIGHT!
FOR LONG, TORTUROUS MOMENTS THE TROUBLED YOUTH TOSSES AND TURNS, HIS MIND IN A TURMOIL, UNTIL--
--HE SINKS ONCE AGAIN INTO A FITFULL SLEEP--HAUNTED BY HARROWING NIGHTMARES--
GWEN! DON'T GO! NO--DON'T LEAVE ME!
I CAN'T GET UP! I'M TRAPPED--TRAPPED BY MY OWN WEBBING!
I'VE MADE MY OWN AUNT UNHAPPY--MADE HER FEEL GUILTY JUST BECAUSE SHE CARES ABOUT ME--TOO MUCH!
AND THE GIRL I LOVE--SHE DOESN'T CARE--ENOUGH!
TO HER--I'M JUST PETER PARKER--WHILE FLASH IS--A HERO!
13

I'm *LOSING* her! I *KNOW* it! I *KNOW* it! And I can't get her *BACK!*

Just as I'm losing *AUNT MAY!*

WHY MUST I *HURT* ALL THOSE I *LOVE* -- OR HAVE THEM HURT *ME?*

WHY? WHY? WHY? WHY? WHY?

PETER! WAKE *UP!* EVERYTHING'S *OKAY!* C'MON, FELLA--SNAP *OUT* OF IT!

THE *WEB!* IT'S *GONE!* I--I CAN *MOVE* AGAIN!

I--I'M *FREE!*

MAN! YOU MUST HAVE JUST HAD THE *GRAND-DADDY* OF ALL *NIGHTMARES!*

I DON'T KNOW WHAT YOU WERE *YELLING* ABOUT, BUT YOU COULD PROBABLY *SELL* IT TO ALFRED HITCHCOCK!

A *NIGHTMARE?* YOU MEAN--I WAS JUST--*DREAMING?*

WHAT WOULD *YOU* CALL IT WHEN A GUY ROLLS AND TURNS AND MUMBLES FOR ALMOST *TWELVE HOURS* -- BETWEEN *SNORES,* THAT IS -- WITH HIS *EYES* TIGHTLY CLOSED?

TWELVE HOURS? IT FEELS LIKE I *JUST* HIT THE COUCH!

BOY, I *MUST* HAVE BEEN TIRED!

FEELING *OKAY* NOW?

OH *GREAT!* CONSIDERING I JUST LOST MY *GIRL!*

14

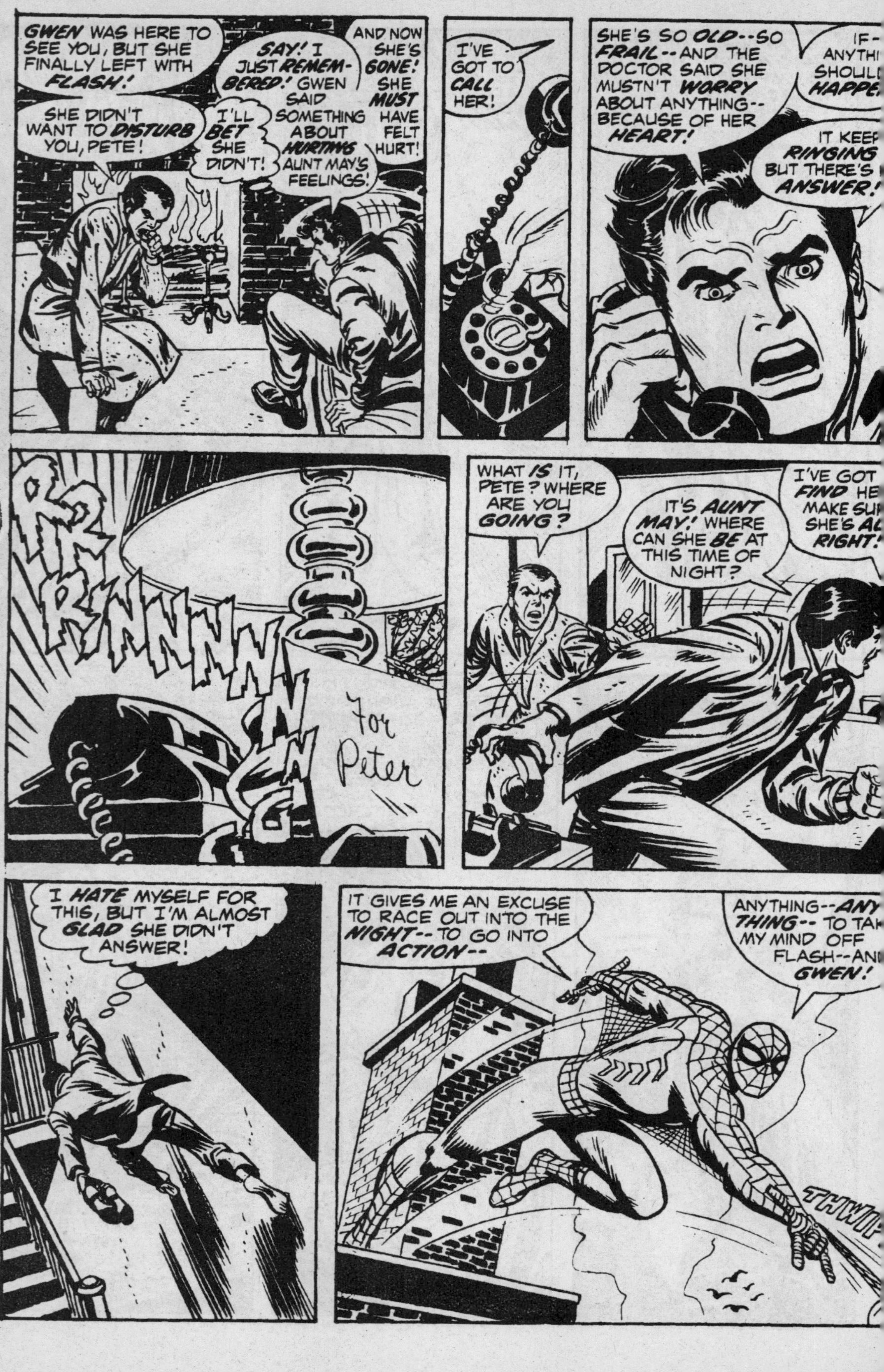
GWEN WAS HERE TO SEE YOU, BUT SHE FINALLY LEFT WITH FLASH!
SHE DIDN'T WANT TO DISTURB YOU, PETE!
I'LL BET SHE DIDN'T!
SAY! I JUST REMEMBERED! GWEN SAID SOMETHING ABOUT HURTING AUNT MAY'S FEELINGS!
AND NOW SHE'S GONE! SHE MUST HAVE FELT HURT!
I'VE GOT TO CALL HER!
SHE'S SO OLD--SO FRAIL--AND THE DOCTOR SAID SHE MUSTN'T WORRY ABOUT ANYTHING--BECAUSE OF HER HEART!
IF-- ANYTHI SHOUL HAPPE
IT KEEP RINGING BUT THERE'S ANSWER!
RRRINNNNNNN
For Peter
WHAT IS IT, PETE? WHERE ARE YOU GOING?
IT'S AUNT MAY! WHERE CAN SHE BE AT THIS TIME OF NIGHT?
I'VE GOT FIND HE MAKE SU SHE'S AL RIGHT!
I HATE MYSELF FOR THIS, BUT I'M ALMOST GLAD SHE DIDN'T ANSWER!
IT GIVES ME AN EXCUSE TO RACE OUT INTO THE NIGHT--TO GO INTO ACTION--
ANYTHING--ANY THING--TO TAK MY MIND OFF FLASH--AN GWEN!
THWIP

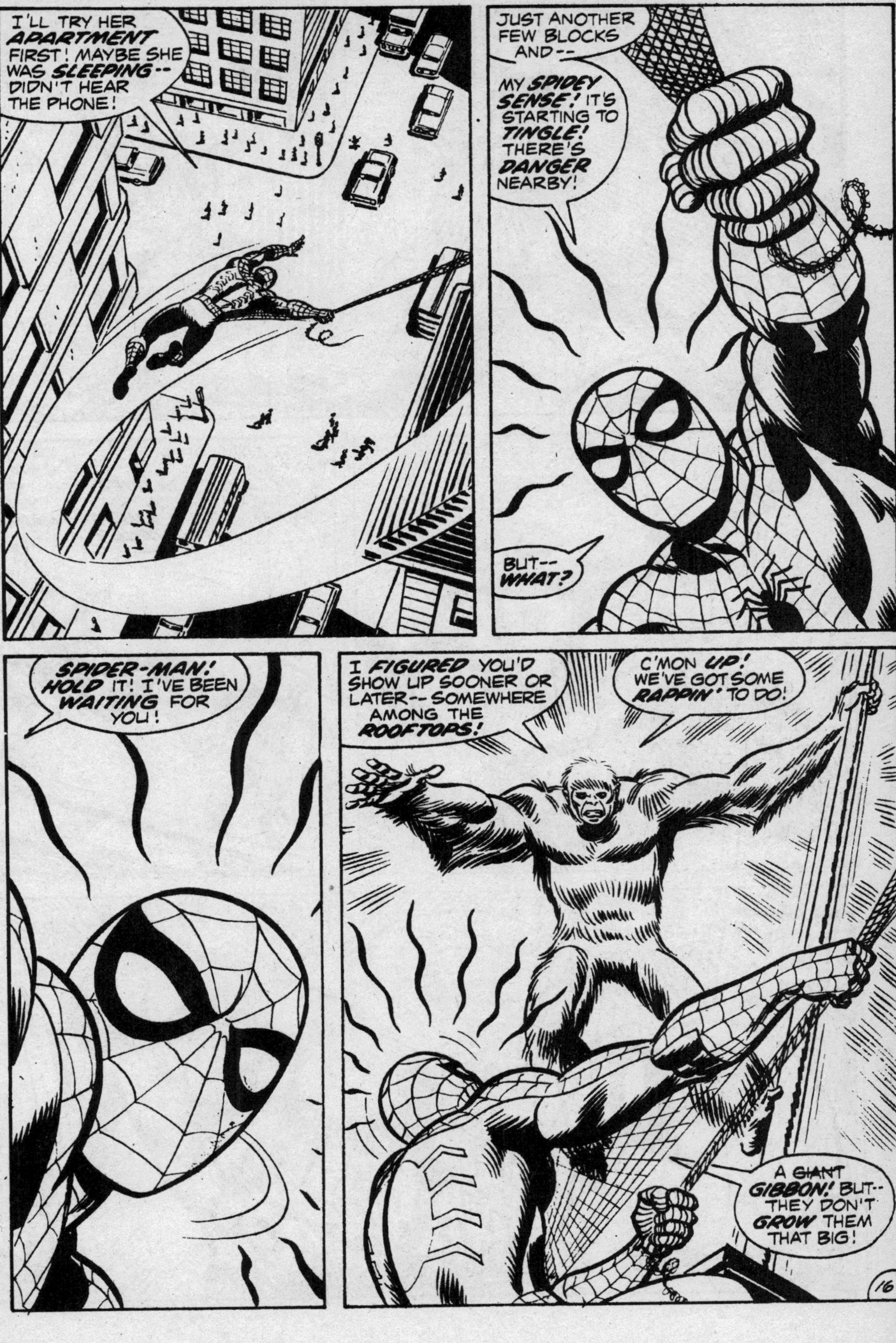
I'LL TRY HER APARTMENT FIRST! MAYBE SHE WAS SLEEPING-- DIDN'T HEAR THE PHONE!
JUST ANOTHER FEW BLOCKS AND--
MY SPIDEY SENSE! IT'S STARTING TO TINGLE! THERE'S DANGER NEARBY!
BUT-- WHAT?
SPIDER-MAN! HOLD IT! I'VE BEEN WAITING FOR YOU!
I FIGURED YOU'D SHOW UP SOONER OR LATER-- SOMEWHERE AMONG THE ROOFTOPS!
C'MON UP! WE'VE GOT SOME RAPPIN' TO DO!
A GIANT GIBBON! BUT-- THEY DON'T GROW THEM THAT BIG!

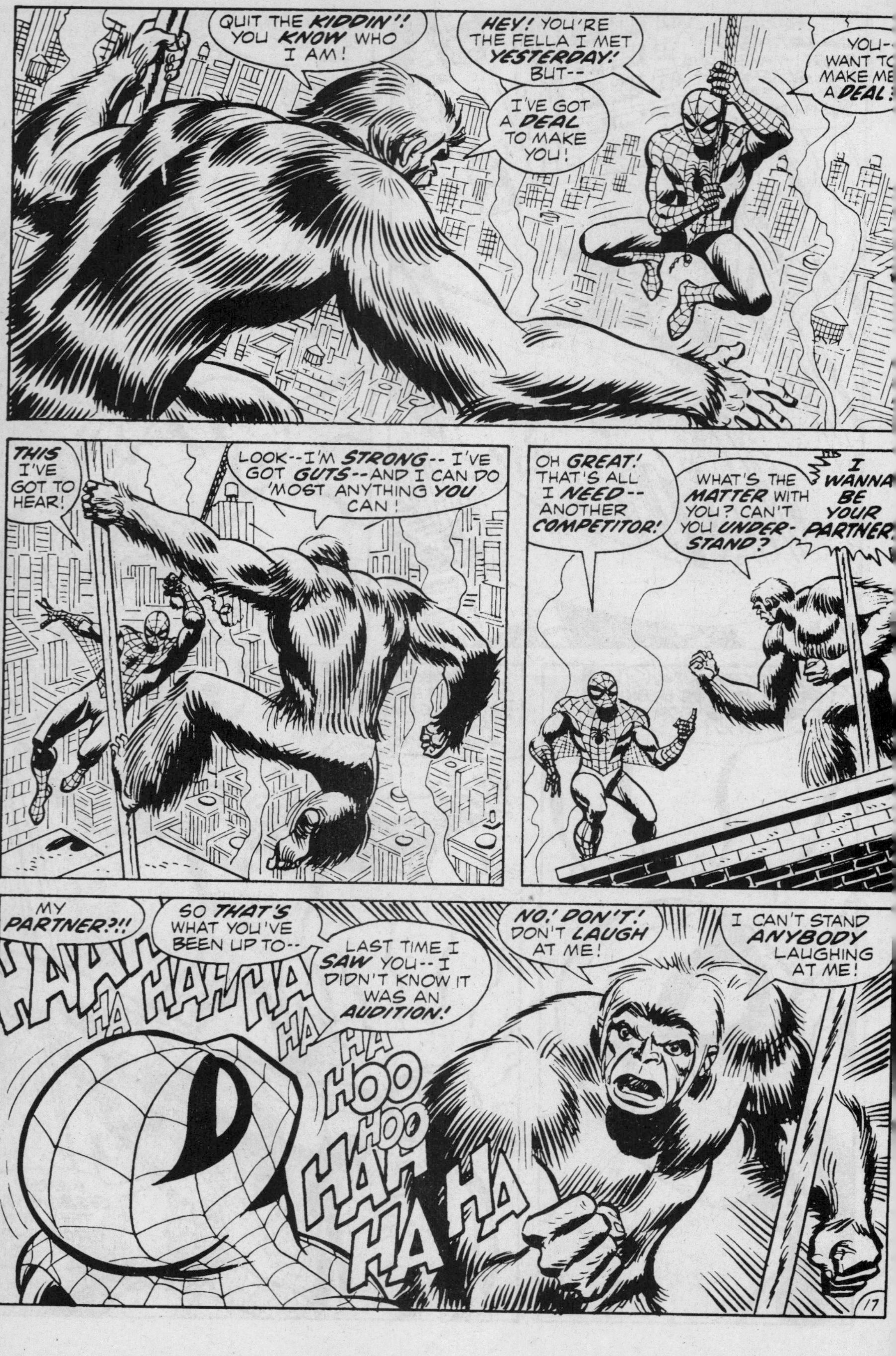
QUIT THE KIDDIN'! YOU KNOW WHO I AM!
HEY! YOU'RE THE FELLA I MET YESTERDAY! BUT--
I'VE GOT A DEAL TO MAKE YOU!
YOU-- WANT TO MAKE ME A DEAL?
THIS I'VE GOT TO HEAR!
LOOK--I'M STRONG-- I'VE GOT GUTS--AND I CAN DO 'MOST ANYTHING YOU CAN!
OH GREAT! THAT'S ALL I NEED-- ANOTHER COMPETITOR!
WHAT'S THE MATTER WITH YOU? CAN'T YOU UNDER-STAND?
I WANNA BE YOUR PARTNER!
MY PARTNER?!!
HAH HA HAH HA HA HA HOO HOO HAH HA HA
SO THAT'S WHAT YOU'VE BEEN UP TO--
LAST TIME I SAW YOU--I DIDN'T KNOW IT WAS AN AUDITION!
NO! DON'T! DON'T LAUGH AT ME!
I CAN'T STAND ANYBODY LAUGHING AT ME!
17

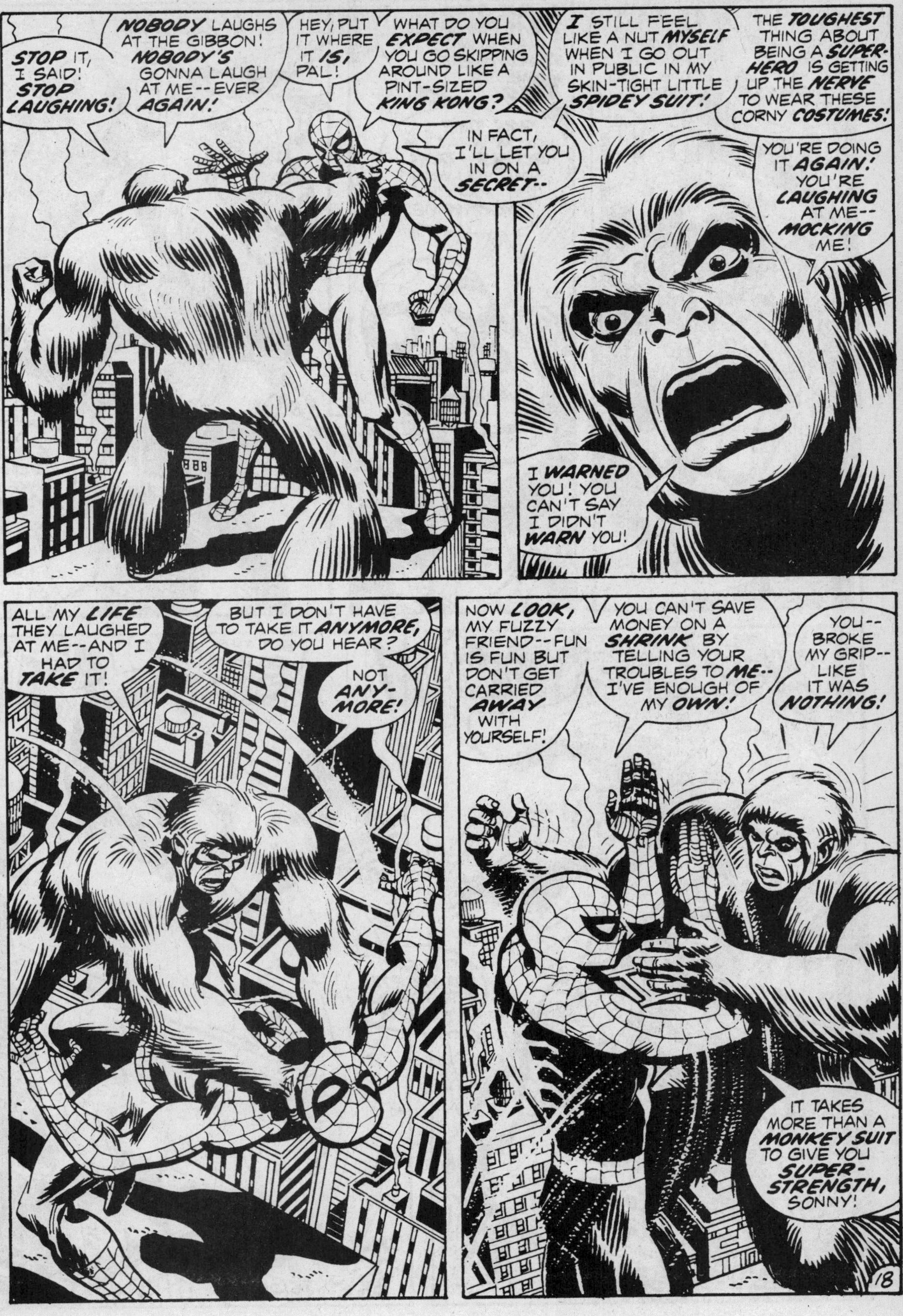

STOP IT, I SAID! STOP LAUGHING!
NOBODY LAUGHS AT THE GIBBON! NOBODY'S GONNA LAUGH AT ME--EVER AGAIN!
HEY, PUT IT WHERE IT IS, PAL!
WHAT DO YOU EXPECT WHEN YOU GO SKIPPING AROUND LIKE A PINT-SIZED KING KONG?
IN FACT, I'LL LET YOU IN ON A SECRET--
I STILL FEEL LIKE A NUT MYSELF WHEN I GO OUT IN PUBLIC IN MY SKIN-TIGHT LITTLE SPIDEY SUIT!
THE TOUGHEST THING ABOUT BEING A SUPER-HERO IS GETTING UP THE NERVE TO WEAR THESE CORNY COSTUMES!
YOU'RE DOING IT AGAIN! YOU'RE LAUGHING AT ME--MOCKING ME!
I WARNED YOU! YOU CAN'T SAY I DIDN'T WARN YOU!
ALL MY LIFE THEY LAUGHED AT ME--AND I HAD TO TAKE IT!
BUT I DON'T HAVE TO TAKE IT ANYMORE, DO YOU HEAR?
NOT ANYMORE!
NOW LOOK, MY FUZZY FRIEND--FUN IS FUN BUT DON'T GET CARRIED AWAY WITH YOURSELF!
YOU CAN'T SAVE MONEY ON A SHRINK BY TELLING YOUR TROUBLES TO ME-- I'VE ENOUGH OF MY OWN!
YOU--BROKE MY GRIP--LIKE IT WAS NOTHING!
IT TAKES MORE THAN A MONKEY SUIT TO GIVE YOU SUPER-STRENGTH, SONNY!
18

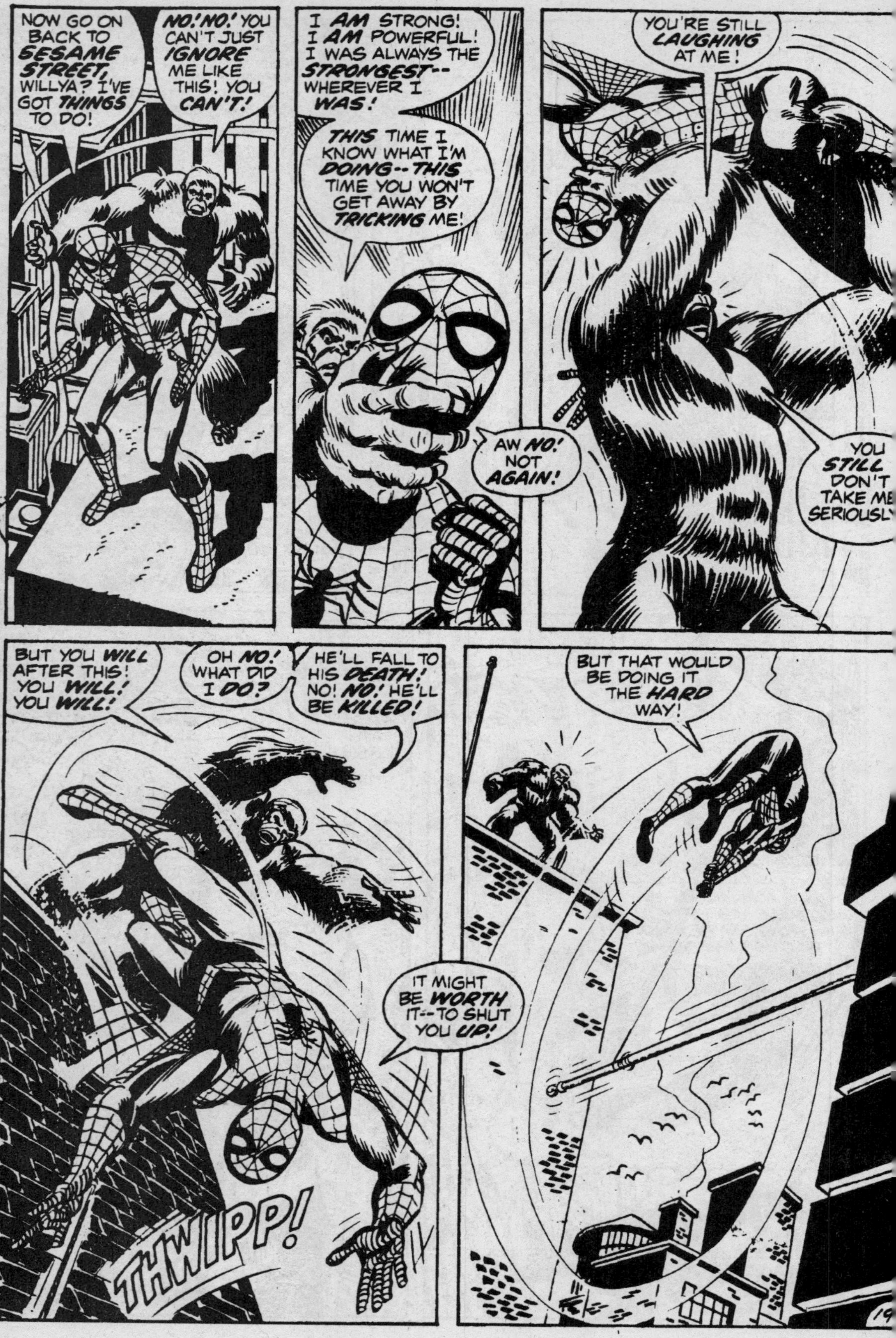
NOW GO ON BACK TO SESAME STREET, WILLYA? I'VE GOT THINGS TO DO!
NO! NO! YOU CAN'T JUST IGNORE ME LIKE THIS! YOU CAN'T!
I AM STRONG! I AM POWERFUL! I WAS ALWAYS THE STRONGEST--WHEREVER I WAS!
THIS TIME I KNOW WHAT I'M DOING--THIS TIME YOU WON'T GET AWAY BY TRICKING ME!
AW NO! NOT AGAIN!
YOU'RE STILL LAUGHING AT ME!
YOU STILL DON'T TAKE ME SERIOUSLY
BUT YOU WILL AFTER THIS! YOU WILL! YOU WILL!
OH NO! WHAT DID I DO?
HE'LL FALL TO HIS DEATH! NO! NO! HE'LL BE KILLED!
IT MIGHT BE WORTH IT--TO SHUT YOU UP!
THWIPP!
BUT THAT WOULD BE DOING IT THE HARD WAY!

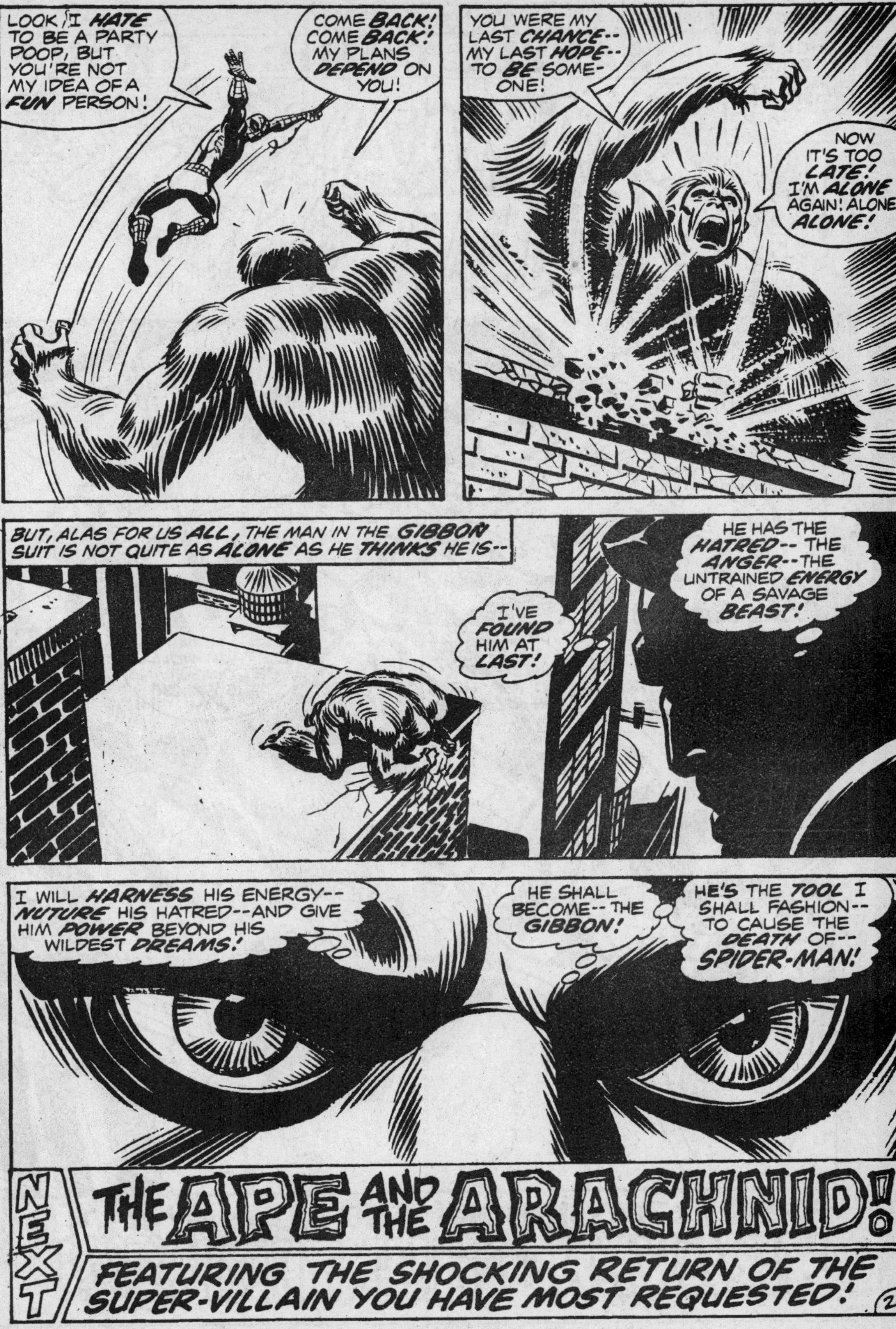
LOOK, I HATE TO BE A PARTY POOP, BUT YOU'RE NOT MY IDEA OF A FUN PERSON!
COME BACK! COME BACK! MY PLANS DEPEND ON YOU!
YOU WERE MY LAST CHANCE-- MY LAST HOPE-- TO BE SOME-ONE!
NOW IT'S TOO LATE! I'M ALONE AGAIN! ALONE! ALONE!
BUT, ALAS FOR US ALL, THE MAN IN THE GIBBON SUIT IS NOT QUITE AS ALONE AS HE THINKS HE IS--
I'VE FOUND HIM AT LAST!
HE HAS THE HATRED-- THE ANGER-- THE UNTRAINED ENERGY OF A SAVAGE BEAST!
I WILL HARNESS HIS ENERGY-- NUTURE HIS HATRED--AND GIVE HIM POWER BEYOND HIS WILDEST DREAMS!
HE SHALL BECOME-- THE GIBBON!
HE'S THE TOOL I SHALL FASHION-- TO CAUSE THE DEATH OF-- SPIDER-MAN!
NEXT
THE APE AND THE ARACHNID!
FEATURING THE SHOCKING RETURN OF THE SUPER-VILLAIN YOU HAVE MOST REQUESTED!
20

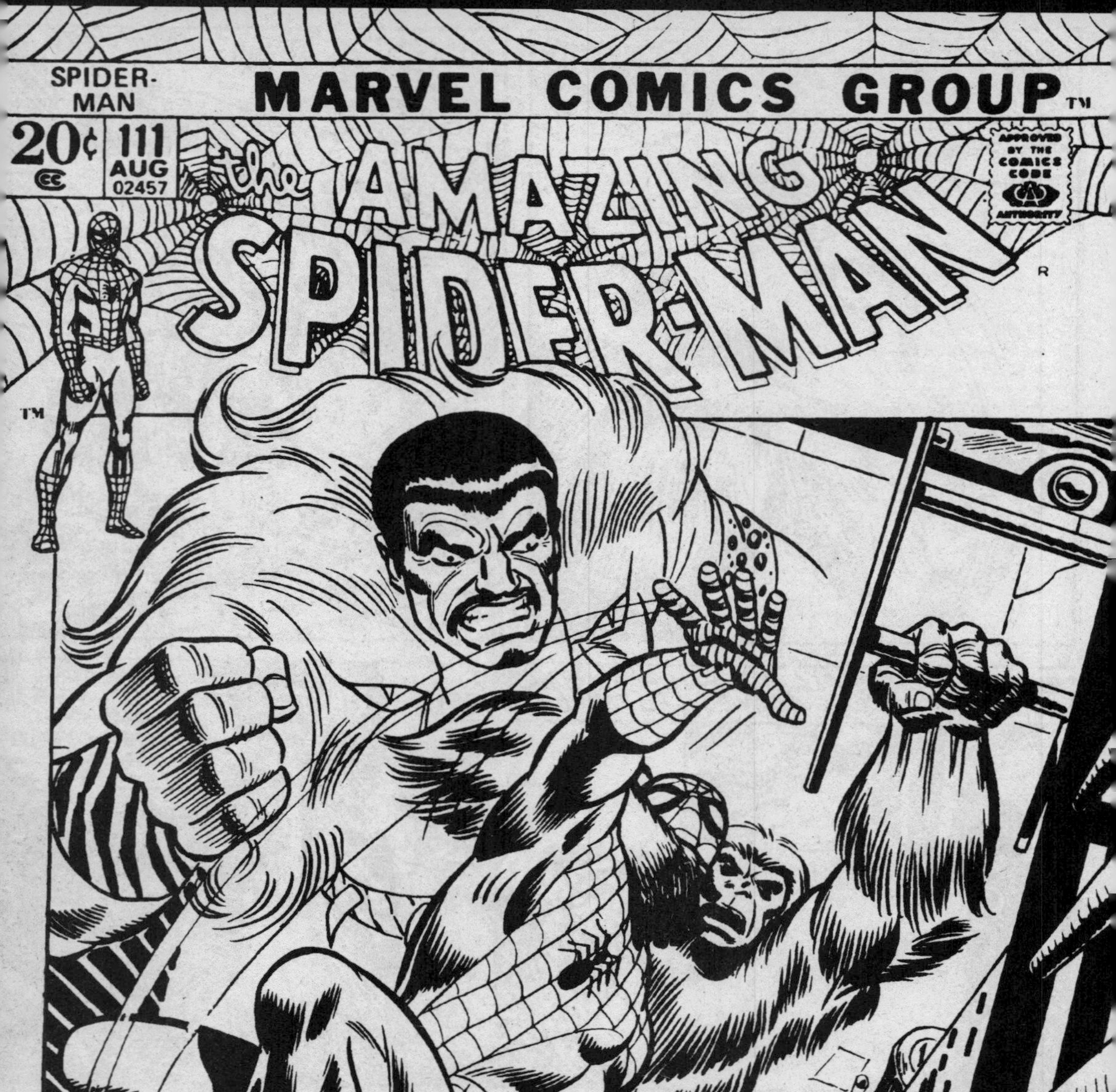

SPIDER-MAN
MARVEL COMICS GROUP
20¢
111
AUG
02457
APPROVED BY THE COMICS CODE AUTHORITY
THE AMAZING SPIDER-MAN
SPIDEY! THE GIBBON! AND NOW---
KRAVEN THE HUNTER!
IT'S ACTION ALL THE WAY!

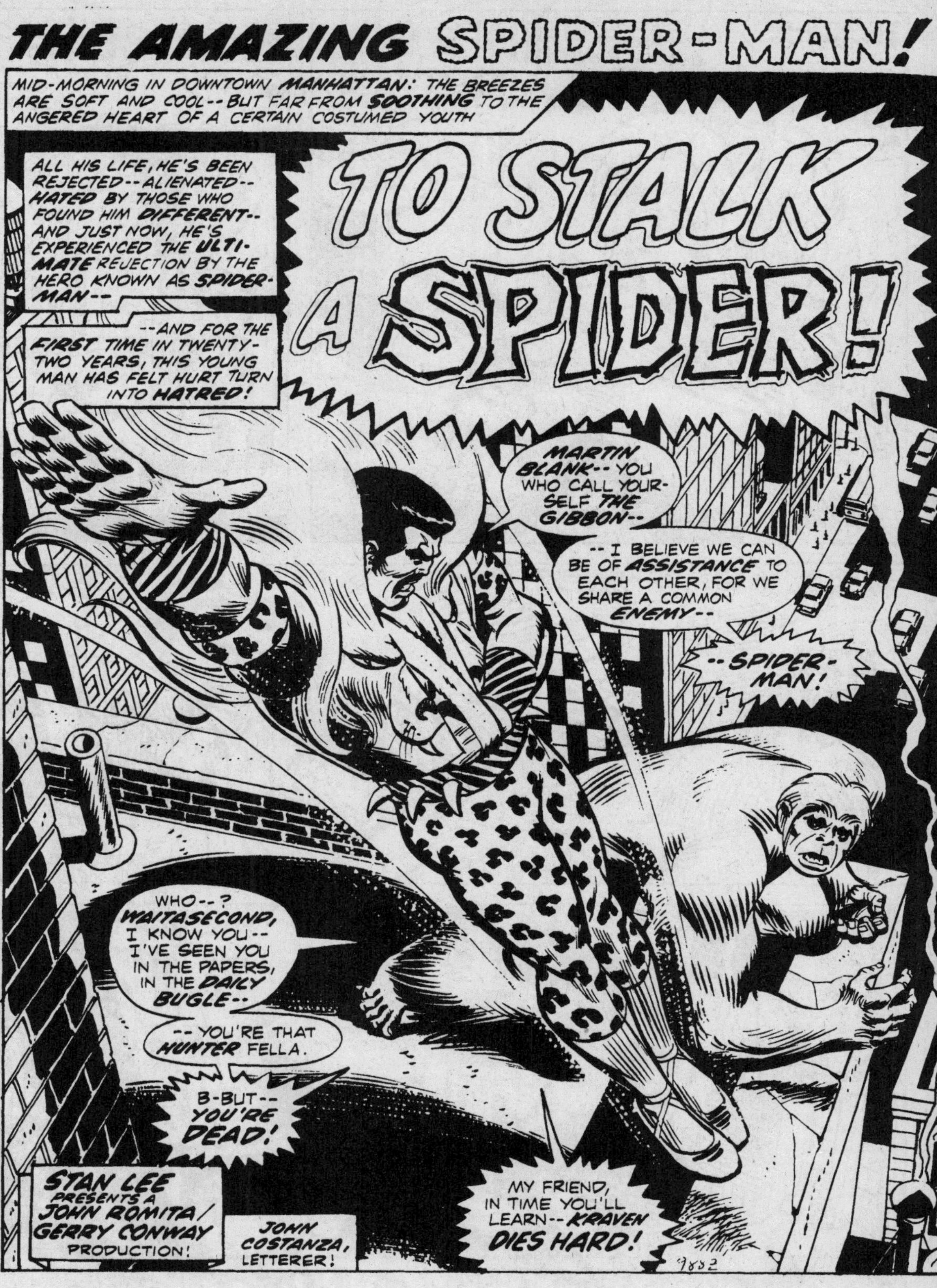

THE AMAZING SPIDER-MAN!
MID-MORNING IN DOWNTOWN MANHATTAN: THE BREEZES ARE SOFT AND COOL--BUT FAR FROM SOOTHING TO THE ANGERED HEART OF A CERTAIN COSTUMED YOUTH
ALL HIS LIFE, HE'S BEEN REJECTED--ALIENATED--HATED BY THOSE WHO FOUND HIM DIFFERENT--AND JUST NOW, HE'S EXPERIENCED THE ULTIMATE REJECTION BY THE HERO KNOWN AS SPIDER-MAN--
--AND FOR THE FIRST TIME IN TWENTY-TWO YEARS, THIS YOUNG MAN HAS FELT HURT TURN INTO HATRED!
TO STALK A SPIDER!
MARTIN BLANK--YOU WHO CALL YOURSELF THE GIBBON--
--I BELIEVE WE CAN BE OF ASSISTANCE TO EACH OTHER, FOR WE SHARE A COMMON ENEMY--
--SPIDER-MAN!
WHO--? WAITASECOND, I KNOW YOU--I'VE SEEN YOU IN THE PAPERS, IN THE DAILY BUGLE--
--YOU'RE THAT HUNTER FELLA.
B-BUT--YOU'RE DEAD!
MY FRIEND, IN TIME YOU'LL LEARN--KRAVEN DIES HARD!
STAN LEE PRESENTS A JOHN ROMITA/GERRY CONWAY PRODUCTION!
JOHN COSTANZA, LETTERER!

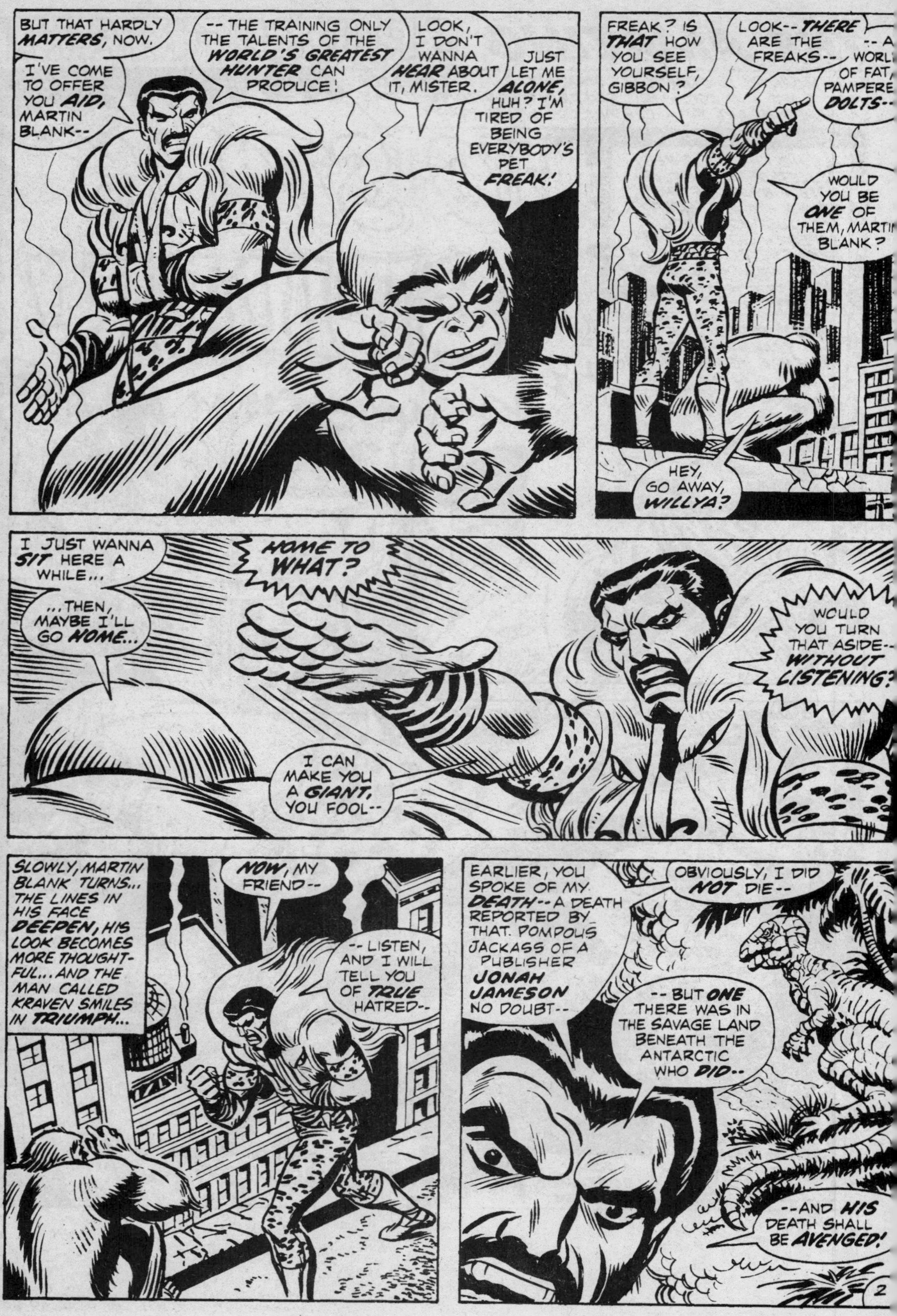

BUT THAT HARDLY MATTERS, NOW.
I'VE COME TO OFFER YOU AID, MARTIN BLANK--
-- THE TRAINING ONLY THE TALENTS OF THE WORLD'S GREATEST HUNTER CAN PRODUCE!
LOOK, I DON'T WANNA HEAR ABOUT IT, MISTER.
JUST LET ME ALONE, HUH? I'M TIRED OF BEING EVERYBODY'S PET FREAK!
FREAK? IS THAT HOW YOU SEE YOURSELF, GIBBON?
LOOK-- THERE ARE THE FREAKS--
-- A WORL OF FAT, PAMPERE DOLTS--
WOULD YOU BE ONE OF THEM, MARTIN BLANK?
HEY, GO AWAY, WILLYA?
I JUST WANNA SIT HERE A WHILE...
...THEN, MAYBE I'LL GO HOME...
HOME TO WHAT?
WOULD YOU TURN THAT ASIDE-- WITHOUT LISTENING?
I CAN MAKE YOU A GIANT, YOU FOOL--
SLOWLY, MARTIN BLANK TURNS... THE LINES IN HIS FACE DEEPEN, HIS LOOK BECOMES MORE THOUGHT-FUL... AND THE MAN CALLED KRAVEN SMILES IN TRIUMPH...
NOW, MY FRIEND--
-- LISTEN, AND I WILL TELL YOU OF TRUE HATRED--
EARLIER, YOU SPOKE OF MY DEATH-- A DEATH REPORTED BY THAT POMPOUS JACKASS OF A PUBLISHER JONAH JAMESON NO DOUBT--
OBVIOUSLY, I DID NOT DIE--
-- BUT ONE THERE WAS IN THE SAVAGE LAND BENEATH THE ANTARCTIC WHO DID--
--AND HIS DEATH SHALL BE AVENGED!
2

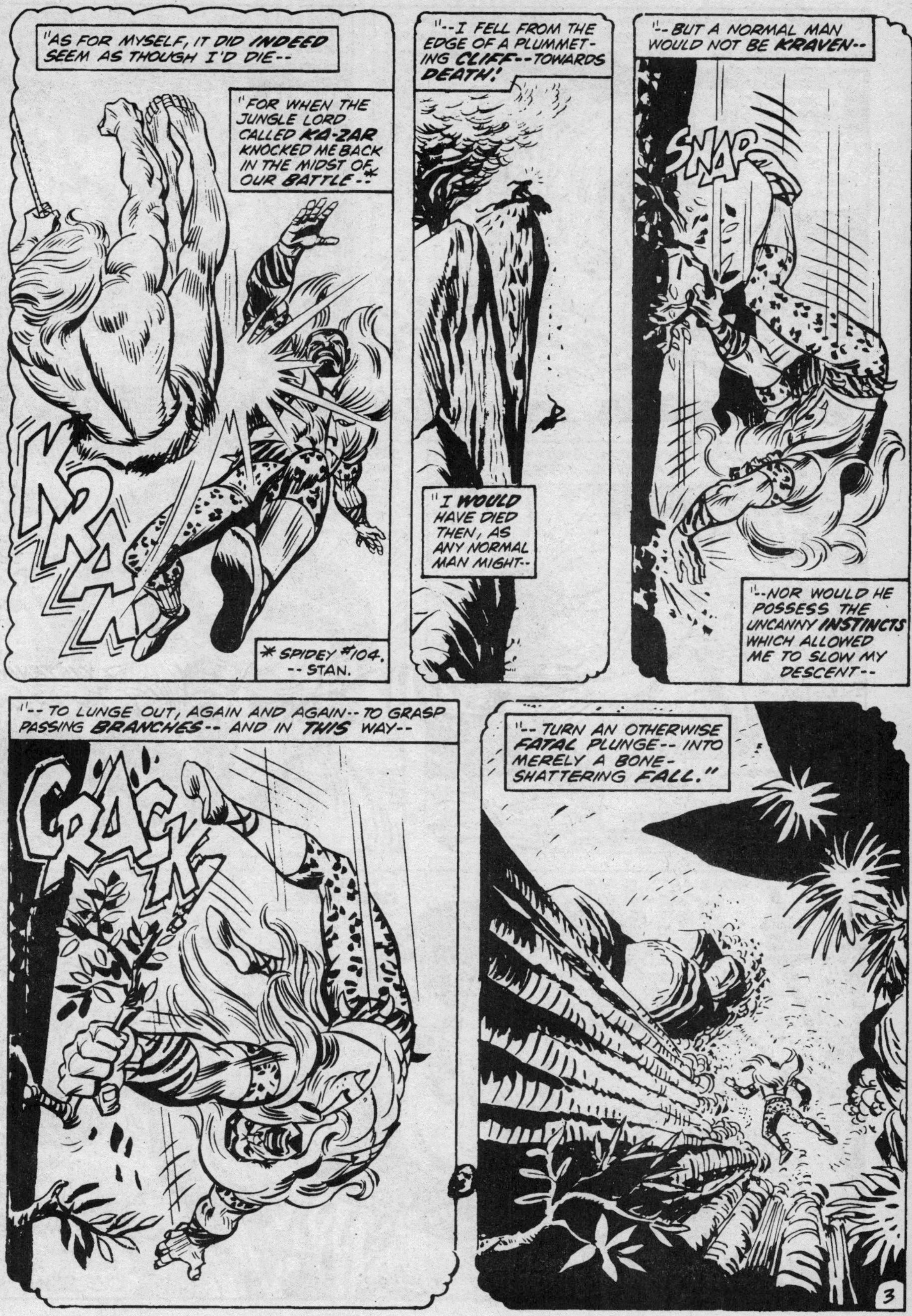
"AS FOR MYSELF, IT DID INDEED SEEM AS THOUGH I'D DIE--
"FOR WHEN THE JUNGLE LORD CALLED KA-ZAR KNOCKED ME BACK IN THE MIDST OF OUR BATTLE--*
KRAKK
* SPIDEY #104. --STAN.
"--I FELL FROM THE EDGE OF A PLUMMETING CLIFF--TOWARDS DEATH!
"I WOULD HAVE DIED THEN, AS ANY NORMAL MAN MIGHT--
"--BUT A NORMAL MAN WOULD NOT BE KRAVEN--
SNAP
"--NOR WOULD HE POSSESS THE UNCANNY INSTINCTS WHICH ALLOWED ME TO SLOW MY DESCENT--
"--TO LUNGE OUT, AGAIN AND AGAIN--TO GRASP PASSING BRANCHES-- AND IN THIS WAY--
CRACK
"--TURN AN OTHERWISE FATAL PLUNGE-- INTO MERELY A BONE-SHATTERING FALL."
3

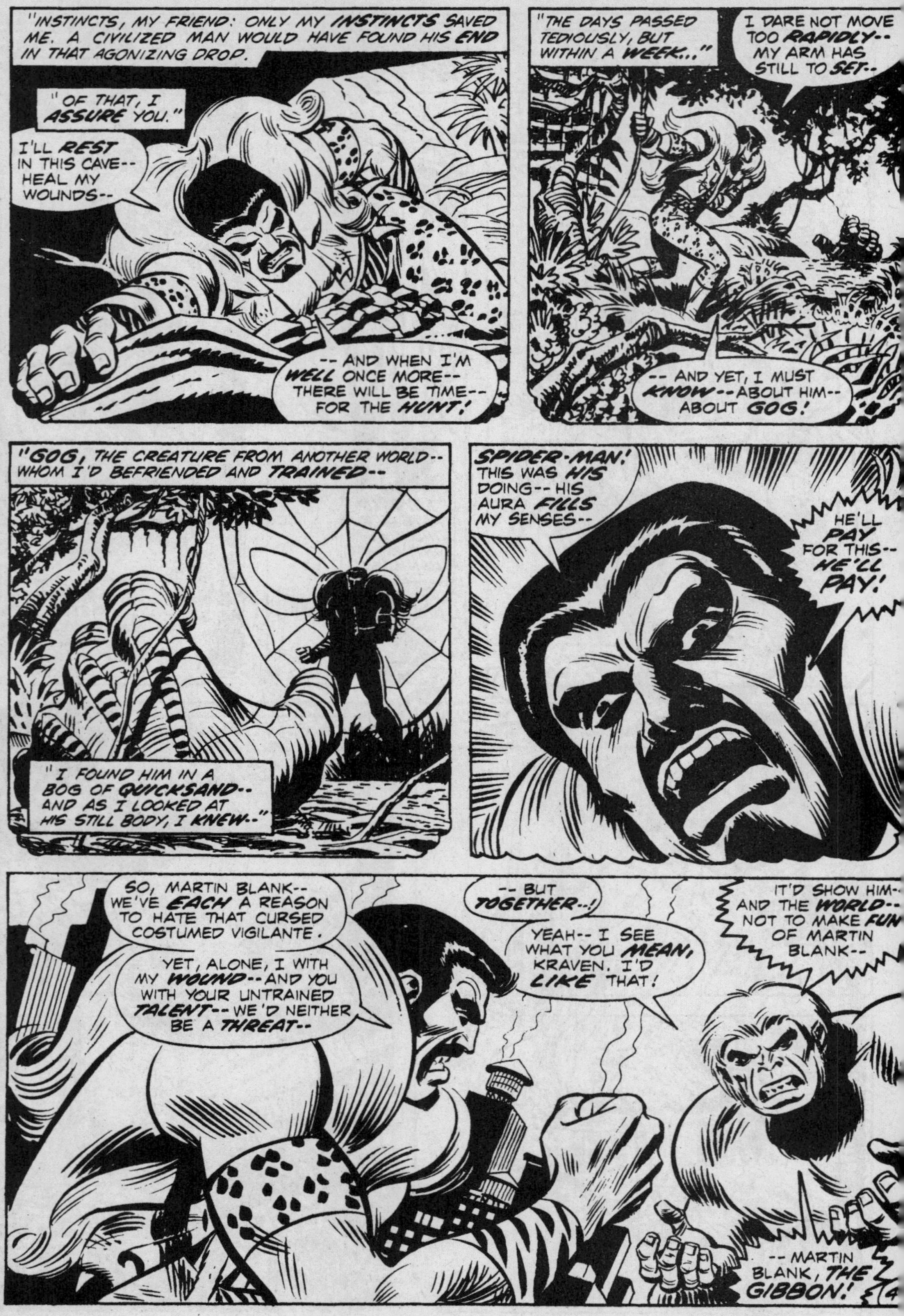
"INSTINCTS, MY FRIEND: ONLY MY INSTINCTS SAVED ME. A CIVILIZED MAN WOULD HAVE FOUND HIS END IN THAT AGONIZING DROP.
"OF THAT, I ASSURE YOU."
I'LL REST IN THIS CAVE-- HEAL MY WOUNDS--
-- AND WHEN I'M WELL ONCE MORE-- THERE WILL BE TIME-- FOR THE HUNT!
"THE DAYS PASSED TEDIOUSLY, BUT WITHIN A WEEK..."
I DARE NOT MOVE TOO RAPIDLY-- MY ARM HAS STILL TO SET--
-- AND YET, I MUST KNOW-- ABOUT HIM-- ABOUT GOG!
"GOG, THE CREATURE FROM ANOTHER WORLD-- WHOM I'D BEFRIENDED AND TRAINED--
"I FOUND HIM IN A BOG OF QUICKSAND-- AND AS I LOOKED AT HIS STILL BODY, I KNEW--"
SPIDER-MAN! THIS WAS HIS DOING-- HIS AURA FILLS MY SENSES--
HE'LL PAY FOR THIS-- HE'LL PAY!
SO, MARTIN BLANK-- WE'VE EACH A REASON TO HATE THAT CURSED COSTUMED VIGILANTE.
YET, ALONE, I WITH MY WOUND-- AND YOU WITH YOUR UNTRAINED TALENT-- WE'D NEITHER BE A THREAT--
-- BUT TOGETHER--!
YEAH-- I SEE WHAT YOU MEAN, KRAVEN. I'D LIKE THAT!
IT'D SHOW HIM-- AND THE WORLD-- NOT TO MAKE FUN OF MARTIN BLANK--
-- MARTIN BLANK, THE GIBBON!
4

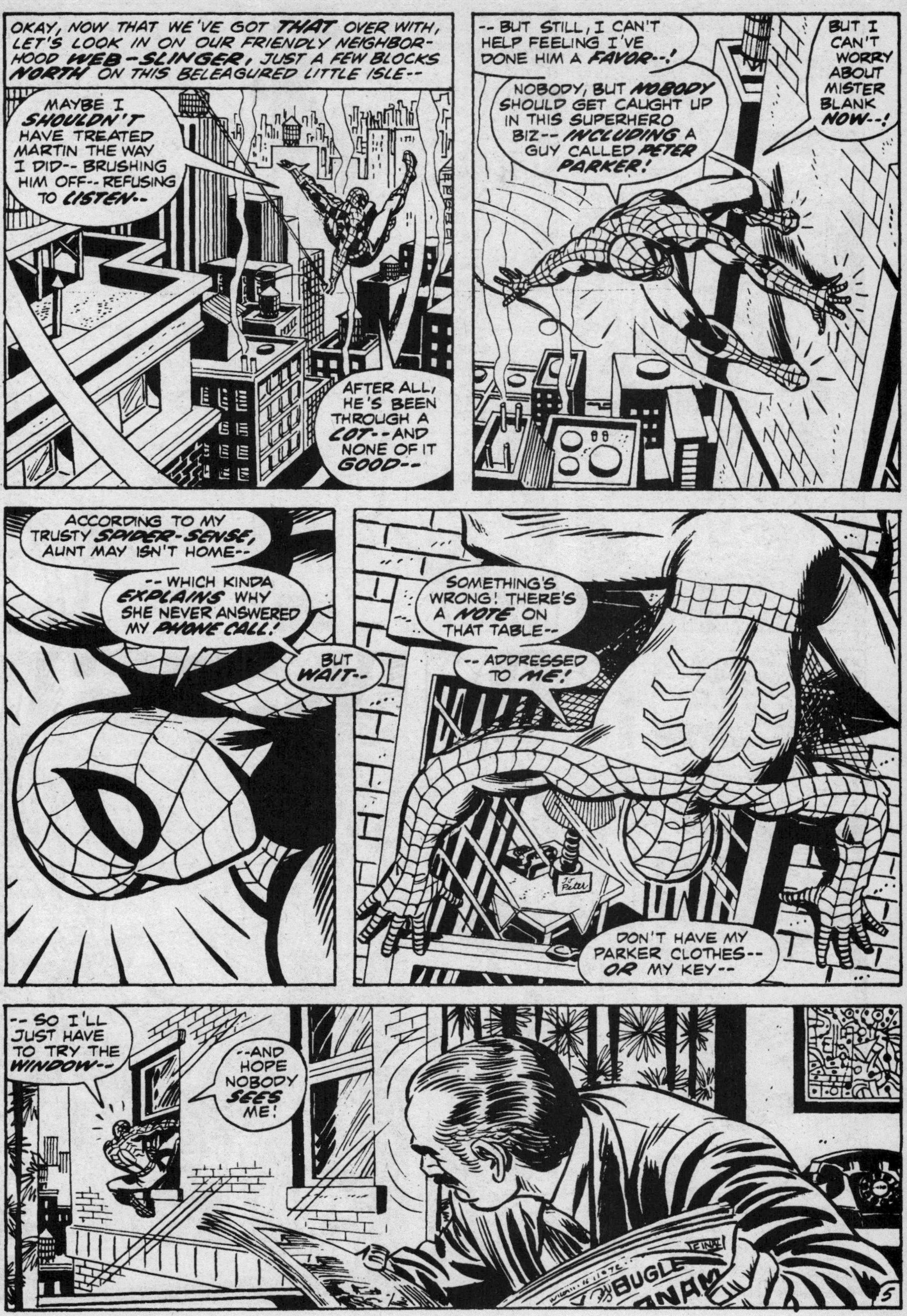

OKAY, NOW THAT WE'VE GOT THAT OVER WITH, LET'S LOOK IN ON OUR FRIENDLY NEIGHBORHOOD WEB-SLINGER, JUST A FEW BLOCKS NORTH ON THIS BELEAGURED LITTLE ISLE--
MAYBE I SHOULDN'T HAVE TREATED MARTIN THE WAY I DID-- BRUSHING HIM OFF--REFUSING TO LISTEN--
AFTER ALL, HE'S BEEN THROUGH A LOT--AND NONE OF IT GOOD--
--BUT STILL, I CAN'T HELP FEELING I'VE DONE HIM A FAVOR--!
NOBODY, BUT NOBODY SHOULD GET CAUGHT UP IN THIS SUPERHERO BIZ--INCLUDING A GUY CALLED PETER PARKER!
BUT I CAN'T WORRY ABOUT MISTER BLANK NOW--!
ACCORDING TO MY TRUSTY SPIDER-SENSE, AUNT MAY ISN'T HOME--
--WHICH KINDA EXPLAINS WHY SHE NEVER ANSWERED MY PHONE CALL!
BUT WAIT--
SOMETHING'S WRONG! THERE'S A NOTE ON THAT TABLE--
--ADDRESSED TO ME!
DON'T HAVE MY PARKER CLOTHES-- OR MY KEY--
--SO I'LL JUST HAVE TO TRY THE WINDOW--
--AND HOPE NOBODY SEES ME!
BUGLE
5

GWEN MENTIONED SOMETHING ABOUT HOW SHE'D *HURT* AUNT MAY'S FEELINGS--

--TOLD HER SHE'D BEEN TOO *POSSESSIVE* WITH ME--

--TOO *MATERNAL.* BUT GWEN DOESN'T UNDERSTAND--

-- AUNT MAY'S SO *OLD.* SHE TAKES THINGS TOO *HARD.*

SURE SHE'S GOTTEN ON MY NERVES AT TIMES--

--BUT I STILL *LOVE* HER. NOTHING CHANGES *THAT.*

IF SHE'S--! OH, *NO!*

Dear Peter, I am going away for a wh-- uv it all of d-- o n-- wri--

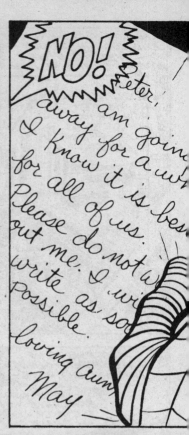

NO!

Peter, I am going away for a wh-- I know it is bes-- for all of us. Please do not w-- out me. I wr-- write as so-- possible.

loving Aun-- May

FOR AN INSTANT HE STANDS *STUNNED*-- HIS MIND AFIRE WITH THOUGHTS OF GUILT-- AND *FEAR*--

WHERE COULD SHE GO--? WHO COULD SHE *STAY* WITH?

SHE CAN'T *HACK* IT OUTSIDE-- SHE'LL BE *LOST*--

-- AND IT'S MY FAULT-- *MY FAULT!*

BUT BEFORE THOSE THOUGHTS CAN GO ANY *FURTHER,* THEY'RE SHATTERED-- BY AN ABRUPT AND UNEXPECTED *INTRUSION!*

OKAY, SPIDER-MAN-- OPEN THIS *DOOR*--

--WE KNOW YOU'RE *IN* THERE, MISTER-- AND THIS TIME-- *YOU DON'T ESCAPE!*

SOMEDAY YOU BOYS IN BLUE WILL *LEARN*--

THERE'S A GREAT BIG *DIFFERENCE* BETWEEN WHAT YOU *SEE*-- AND WHAT YOU *GET!*

6

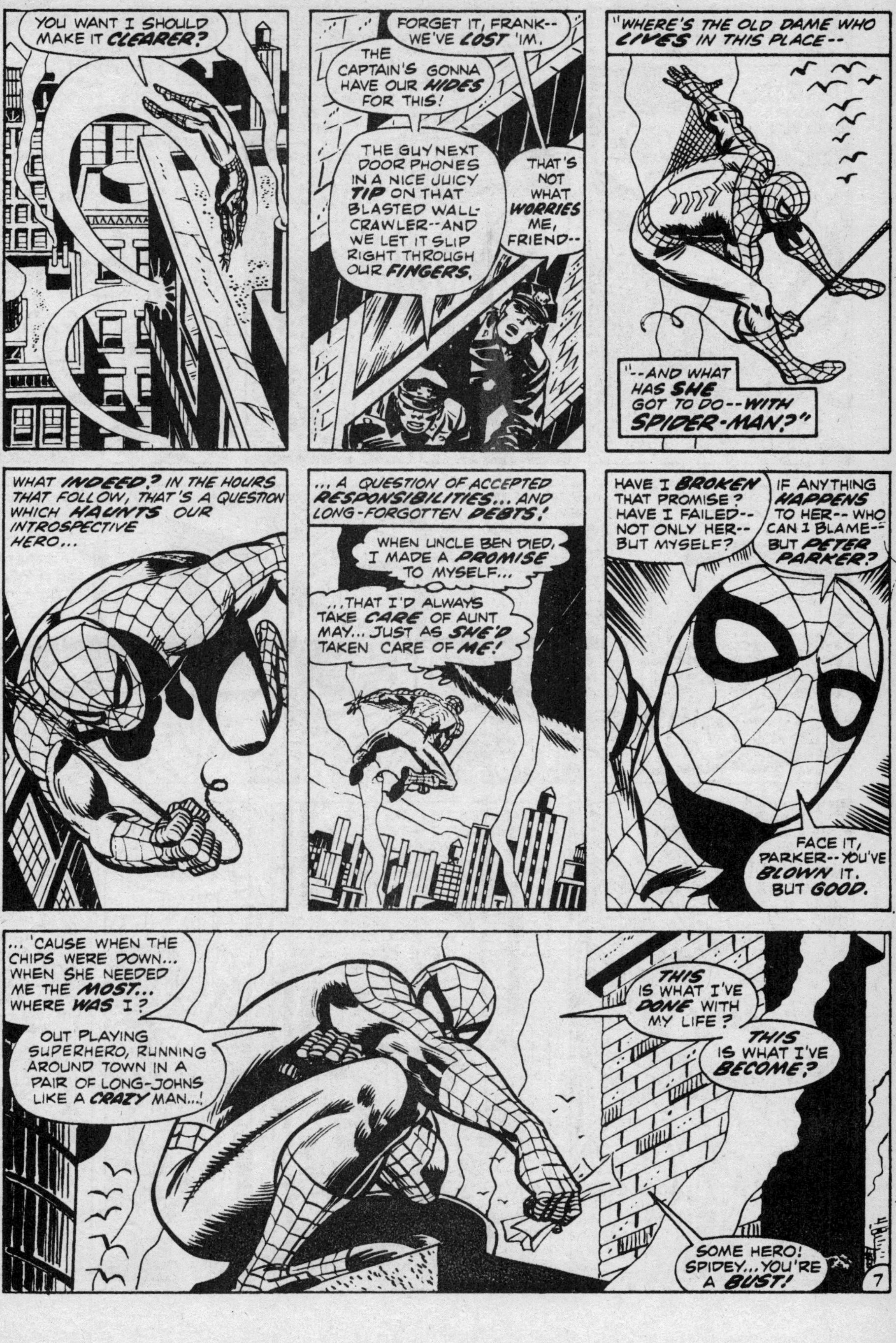
YOU WANT I SHOULD MAKE IT CLEARER?
FORGET IT, FRANK-- WE'VE LOST 'IM.
THE CAPTAIN'S GONNA HAVE OUR HIDES FOR THIS!
THE GUY NEXT DOOR PHONES IN A NICE JUICY TIP ON THAT BLASTED WALL-CRAWLER--AND WE LET IT SLIP RIGHT THROUGH OUR FINGERS.
THAT'S NOT WHAT WORRIES ME, FRIEND--
"WHERE'S THE OLD DAME WHO LIVES IN THIS PLACE--
"--AND WHAT HAS SHE GOT TO DO--WITH SPIDER-MAN?"
WHAT INDEED? IN THE HOURS THAT FOLLOW, THAT'S A QUESTION WHICH HAUNTS OUR INTROSPECTIVE HERO...
...A QUESTION OF ACCEPTED RESPONSIBILITIES... AND LONG-FORGOTTEN DEBTS!
WHEN UNCLE BEN DIED, I MADE A PROMISE TO MYSELF...
...THAT I'D ALWAYS TAKE CARE OF AUNT MAY... JUST AS SHE'D TAKEN CARE OF ME!
HAVE I BROKEN THAT PROMISE? HAVE I FAILED-- NOT ONLY HER-- BUT MYSELF?
IF ANYTHING HAPPENS TO HER-- WHO CAN I BLAME-- BUT PETER PARKER?
FACE IT, PARKER--YOU'VE BLOWN IT. BUT GOOD.
...'CAUSE WHEN THE CHIPS WERE DOWN... WHEN SHE NEEDED ME THE MOST... WHERE WAS I?
OUT PLAYING SUPERHERO, RUNNING AROUND TOWN IN A PAIR OF LONG-JOHNS LIKE A CRAZY MAN...!
THIS IS WHAT I'VE DONE WITH MY LIFE?
THIS IS WHAT I'VE BECOME?
SOME HERO! SPIDEY... YOU'RE A BUST!
7

BUT THEN, AS THE BROODING YOUTH LOOKS UP FROM HIS *DARKER* THOUGHTS...

TALK ABOUT BUSTS... LOOKS LIKE I'VE COME FULL *CIRCLE*.

WELL, WHO KNOWS? MAYBE *JOE ROBERTSON* CAN HELP ME OUT...

YEAH,... HIM AND JOLLY *J.J.J.!*

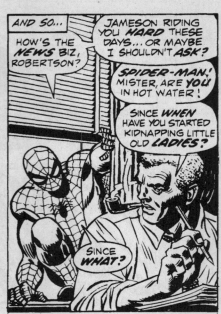

AND SO...

HOW'S THE *NEWS* BIZ, ROBERTSON?

JAMESON RIDING YOU *HARD* THESE DAYS... OR MAYBE I SHOULDN'T *ASK?*

SPIDER-MAN! MISTER, ARE *YOU* IN HOT WATER!

SINCE *WHEN* HAVE YOU STARTED KIDNAPPING LITTLE OLD *LADIES?*

SINCE *WHAT?*

YOU *HEARD* ME, FRIEND. THERE'S A POLICE BULLETIN ON THE WIRES RIGHT *NOW*...

... OR DIDN'T YOU THINK *CITY EDITORS* COULD *READ?*

AND OF ALL PEOPLE MAN-- *MAY PARKER*

WHOA. SLOW *DOWN* A MINUTE.

MAYBE YOU'D BETTER TAKE A GLANCE AT *THIS*, FELLA.

To Peter

THE KIND OF TROUBLE *YOU'RE* IN, MISTER--

--IT BETTER BE *GOOD!*

IT'S GOOD, ALL RIGHT... AND IT'S THE *LAST* FAVOR I DO FOR THAT CRUMB, PETER PARKER.

WILL HE *BUY* IT? WHAT IF HE PUTS TWO AND TWO TOGETHER...

...AND COMES UP WITH YOUR LOGICAL *THREE?*

PARKER, HUH? IF THIS IS ON THE *LEVEL*--

SURE IT IS! PARKER NEEDED THAT *LETTER*-- I GO SNEAK IT OUT FOR HIM -- NOW I'M A BIG BAD *CRIMINAL* TYPE.

--AND SPEAKING OF BIG BAD *TYPES*-- HERE COMES YOUR LOVEABLE *PUBLISHER*.

SEE 'YA *LATER*, BUDDY!

ROBERTSON! WHY AREN'T YOU WORKING ON THAT LATE CITY *EDITION?*

I WANT *FULL COVERAGE* ON THIS SPIDER-MAN STORY--

WE'VE FINALLY GOT THAT WEB-HEADED MENACE RIGHT WHERE WE *WANT* HIM!

8

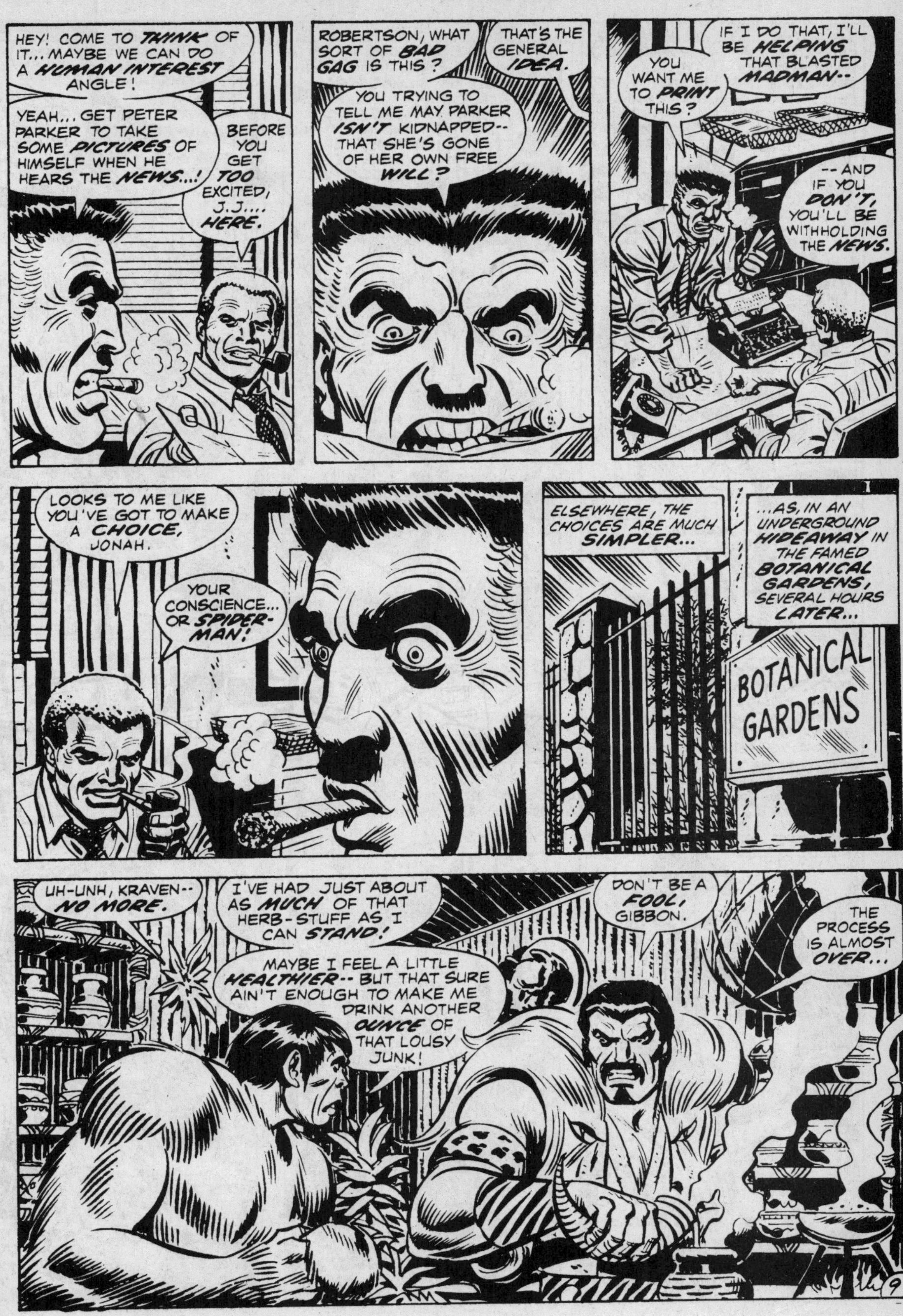

HEY! COME TO THINK OF IT... MAYBE WE CAN DO A HUMAN INTEREST ANGLE!
YEAH... GET PETER PARKER TO TAKE SOME PICTURES OF HIMSELF WHEN HE HEARS THE NEWS...!
BEFORE YOU GET TOO EXCITED, J.J.... HERE.
ROBERTSON, WHAT SORT OF BAD GAG IS THIS?
THAT'S THE GENERAL IDEA.
YOU TRYING TO TELL ME MAY PARKER ISN'T KIDNAPPED-- THAT SHE'S GONE OF HER OWN FREE WILL?
YOU WANT ME TO PRINT THIS?
IF I DO THAT, I'LL BE HELPING THAT BLASTED MADMAN--
--AND IF YOU DON'T, YOU'LL BE WITHHOLDING THE NEWS.
LOOKS TO ME LIKE YOU'VE GOT TO MAKE A CHOICE, JONAH.
YOUR CONSCIENCE... OR SPIDER-MAN!
ELSEWHERE, THE CHOICES ARE MUCH SIMPLER...
...AS, IN AN UNDERGROUND HIDEAWAY IN THE FAMED BOTANICAL GARDENS, SEVERAL HOURS LATER...
BOTANICAL GARDENS
UH-UNH, KRAVEN-- NO MORE.
I'VE HAD JUST ABOUT AS MUCH OF THAT HERB-STUFF AS I CAN STAND!
MAYBE I FEEL A LITTLE HEALTHIER-- BUT THAT SURE AIN'T ENOUGH TO MAKE ME DRINK ANOTHER OUNCE OF THAT LOUSY JUNK!
DON'T BE A FOOL, GIBBON.
THE PROCESS IS ALMOST OVER...
9

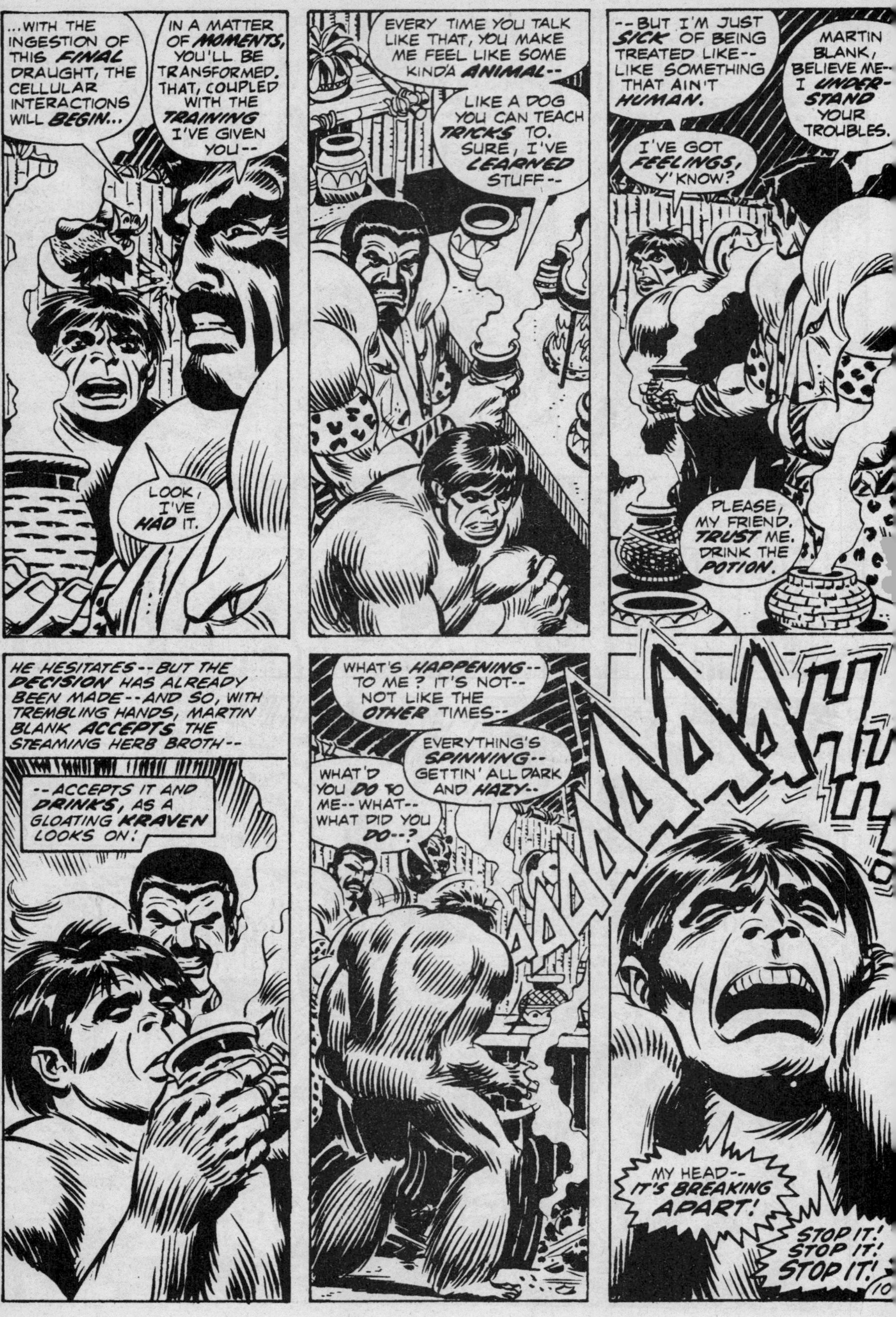
...WITH THE INGESTION OF THIS FINAL DRAUGHT, THE CELLULAR INTERACTIONS WILL BEGIN...
IN A MATTER OF MOMENTS, YOU'LL BE TRANSFORMED. THAT, COUPLED WITH THE TRAINING I'VE GIVEN YOU--
LOOK, I'VE HAD IT.
EVERY TIME YOU TALK LIKE THAT, YOU MAKE ME FEEL LIKE SOME KIND'A ANIMAL--
LIKE A DOG YOU CAN TEACH TRICKS TO. SURE, I'VE LEARNED STUFF--
--BUT I'M JUST SICK OF BEING TREATED LIKE-- LIKE SOMETHING THAT AIN'T HUMAN.
I'VE GOT FEELINGS, Y'KNOW?
MARTIN BLANK, BELIEVE ME-- I UNDERSTAND YOUR TROUBLES.
PLEASE, MY FRIEND. TRUST ME. DRINK THE POTION.
HE HESITATES--BUT THE DECISION HAS ALREADY BEEN MADE--AND SO, WITH TREMBLING HANDS, MARTIN BLANK ACCEPTS THE STEAMING HERB BROTH--
--ACCEPTS IT AND DRINKS, AS A GLOATING KRAVEN LOOKS ON!
WHAT'S HAPPENING-- TO ME? IT'S NOT-- NOT LIKE THE OTHER TIMES--
EVERYTHING'S SPINNING-- GETTIN' ALL DARK AND HAZY--
WHAT'D YOU DO TO ME--WHAT-- WHAT DID YOU DO--?
AAAAAAAAAH
MY HEAD-- IT'S BREAKING APART!
STOP IT! STOP IT! STOP IT!
10

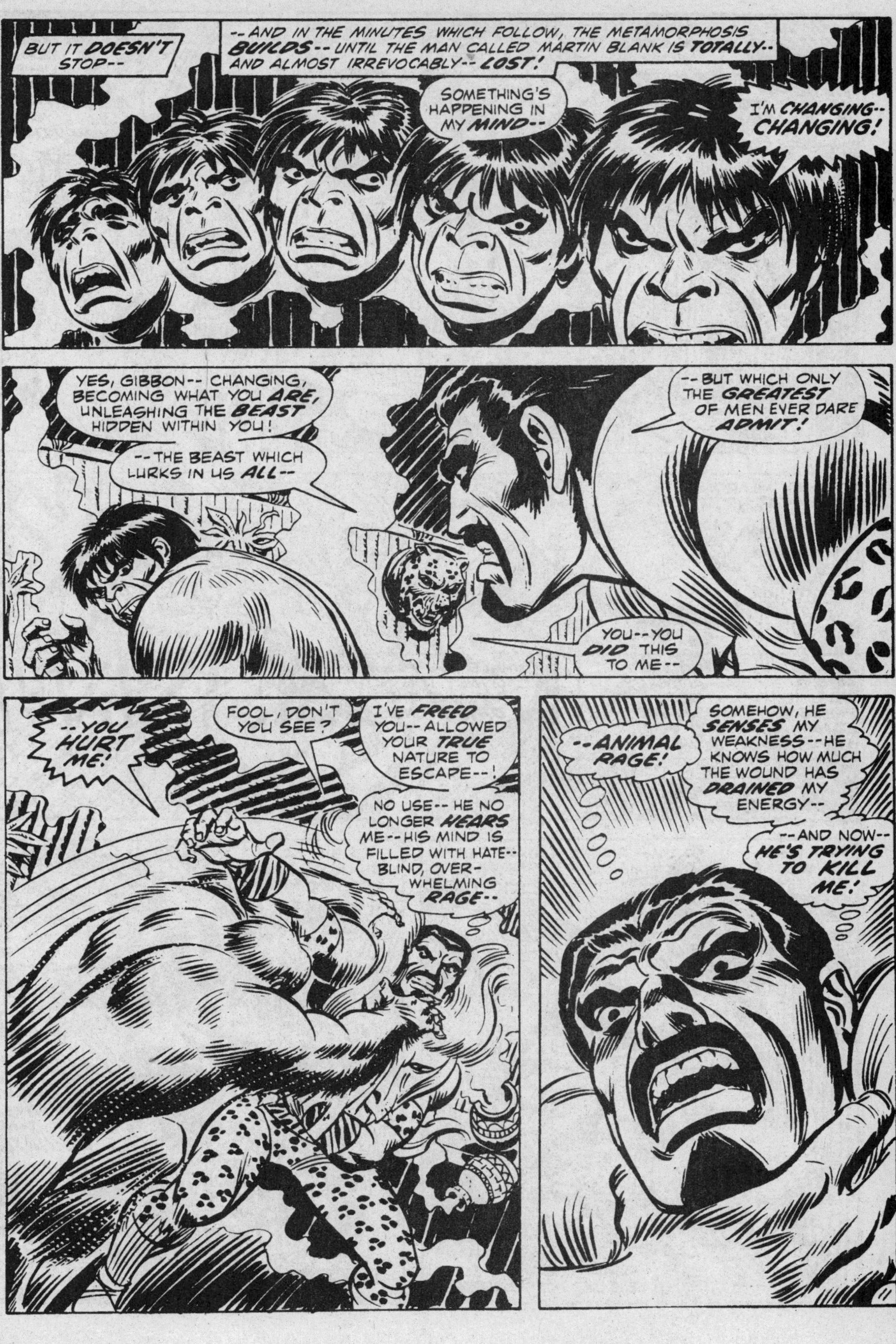
BUT IT DOESN'T STOP--
--AND IN THE MINUTES WHICH FOLLOW, THE METAMORPHOSIS BUILDS-- UNTIL THE MAN CALLED MARTIN BLANK IS TOTALLY-- AND ALMOST IRREVOCABLY-- LOST!
SOMETHING'S HAPPENING IN MY MIND--
I'M CHANGING-- CHANGING!
YES, GIBBON-- CHANGING, BECOMING WHAT YOU ARE, UNLEASHING THE BEAST HIDDEN WITHIN YOU!
--THE BEAST WHICH LURKS IN US ALL--
--BUT WHICH ONLY THE GREATEST OF MEN EVER DARE ADMIT!
YOU--YOU DID THIS TO ME--
--YOU HURT ME!
FOOL, DON'T YOU SEE?
I'VE FREED YOU-- ALLOWED YOUR TRUE NATURE TO ESCAPE--!
NO USE-- HE NO LONGER HEARS ME--HIS MIND IS FILLED WITH HATE-- BLIND, OVER-WHELMING RAGE--
--ANIMAL RAGE!
SOMEHOW, HE SENSES MY WEAKNESS--HE KNOWS HOW MUCH THE WOUND HAS DRAINED MY ENERGY--
--AND NOW-- HE'S TRYING TO KILL ME!
11

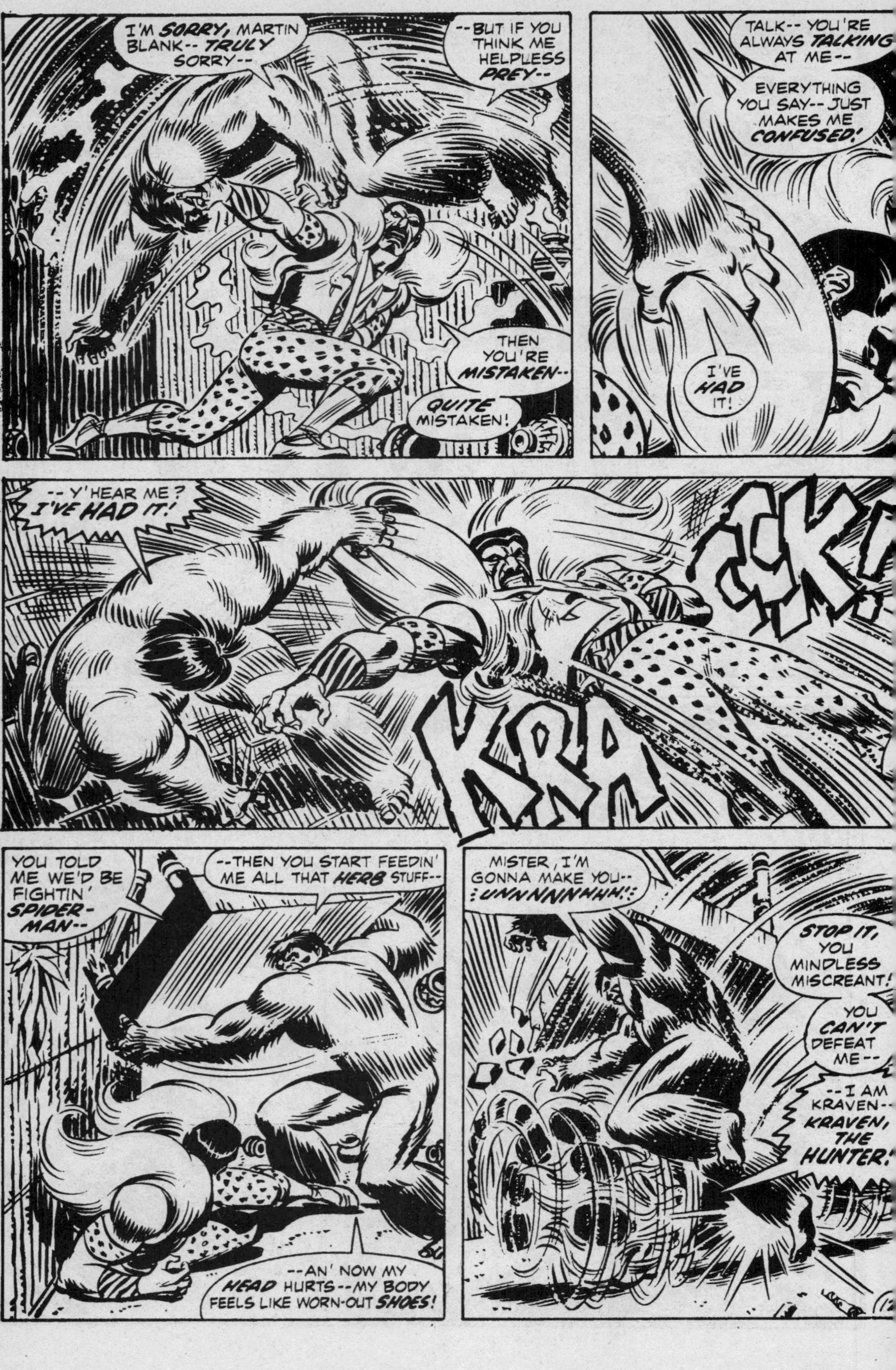
I'M SORRY, MARTIN BLANK-- TRULY SORRY--
--BUT IF YOU THINK ME HELPLESS PREY--
THEN YOU'RE MISTAKEN--
QUITE MISTAKEN!
TALK-- YOU'RE ALWAYS TALKING AT ME--
EVERYTHING YOU SAY-- JUST MAKES ME CONFUSED!
I'VE HAD IT!
-- Y'HEAR ME? I'VE HAD IT!
KRA
YOU TOLD ME WE'D BE FIGHTIN' SPIDER-MAN--
--THEN YOU START FEEDIN' ME ALL THAT HERB STUFF--
--AN' NOW MY HEAD HURTS--MY BODY FEELS LIKE WORN-OUT SHOES!
MISTER, I'M GONNA MAKE YOU-- UNNNNNHHH!
STOP IT, YOU MINDLESS MISCREANT!
YOU CAN'T DEFEAT ME--
--I AM KRAVEN-- KRAVEN, THE HUNTER!

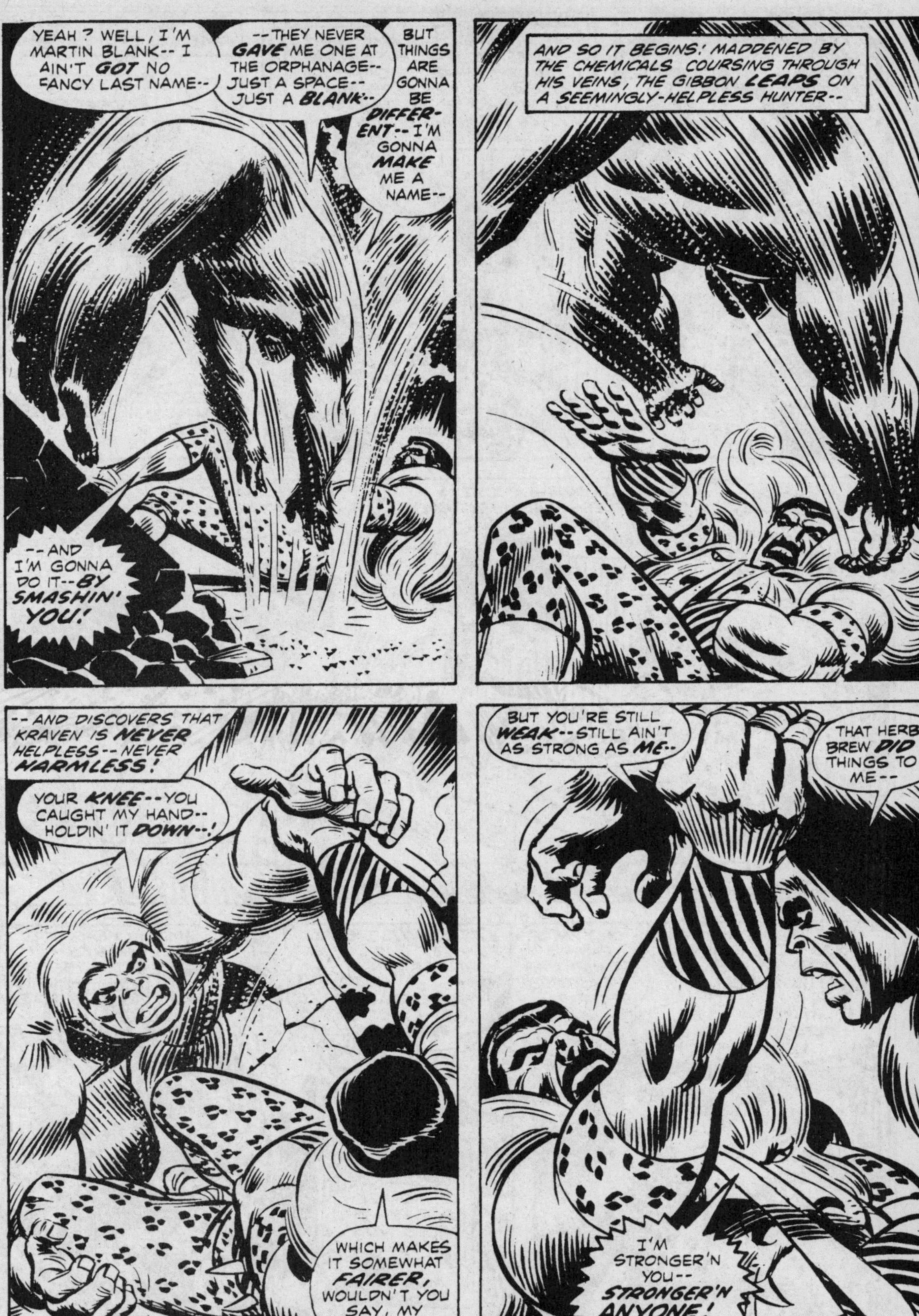
YEAH? WELL, I'M MARTIN BLANK-- I AIN'T GOT NO FANCY LAST NAME--
--THEY NEVER GAVE ME ONE AT THE ORPHANAGE-- JUST A SPACE-- JUST A BLANK--
BUT THINGS ARE GONNA BE DIFFERENT-- I'M GONNA MAKE ME A NAME--
--AND I'M GONNA DO IT--BY SMASHIN' YOU!
AND SO IT BEGINS! MADDENED BY THE CHEMICALS COURSING THROUGH HIS VEINS, THE GIBBON LEAPS ON A SEEMINGLY-HELPLESS HUNTER--
--AND DISCOVERS THAT KRAVEN IS NEVER HELPLESS--NEVER HARMLESS!
YOUR KNEE--YOU CAUGHT MY HAND-- HOLDIN' IT DOWN--!
WHICH MAKES IT SOMEWHAT FAIRER, WOULDN'T YOU SAY, MY FRIEND?
BUT YOU'RE STILL WEAK--STILL AIN'T AS STRONG AS ME--
THAT HERB BREW DID THINGS TO ME--
I'M STRONGER'N YOU-- STRONGER'N ANYONE!
13

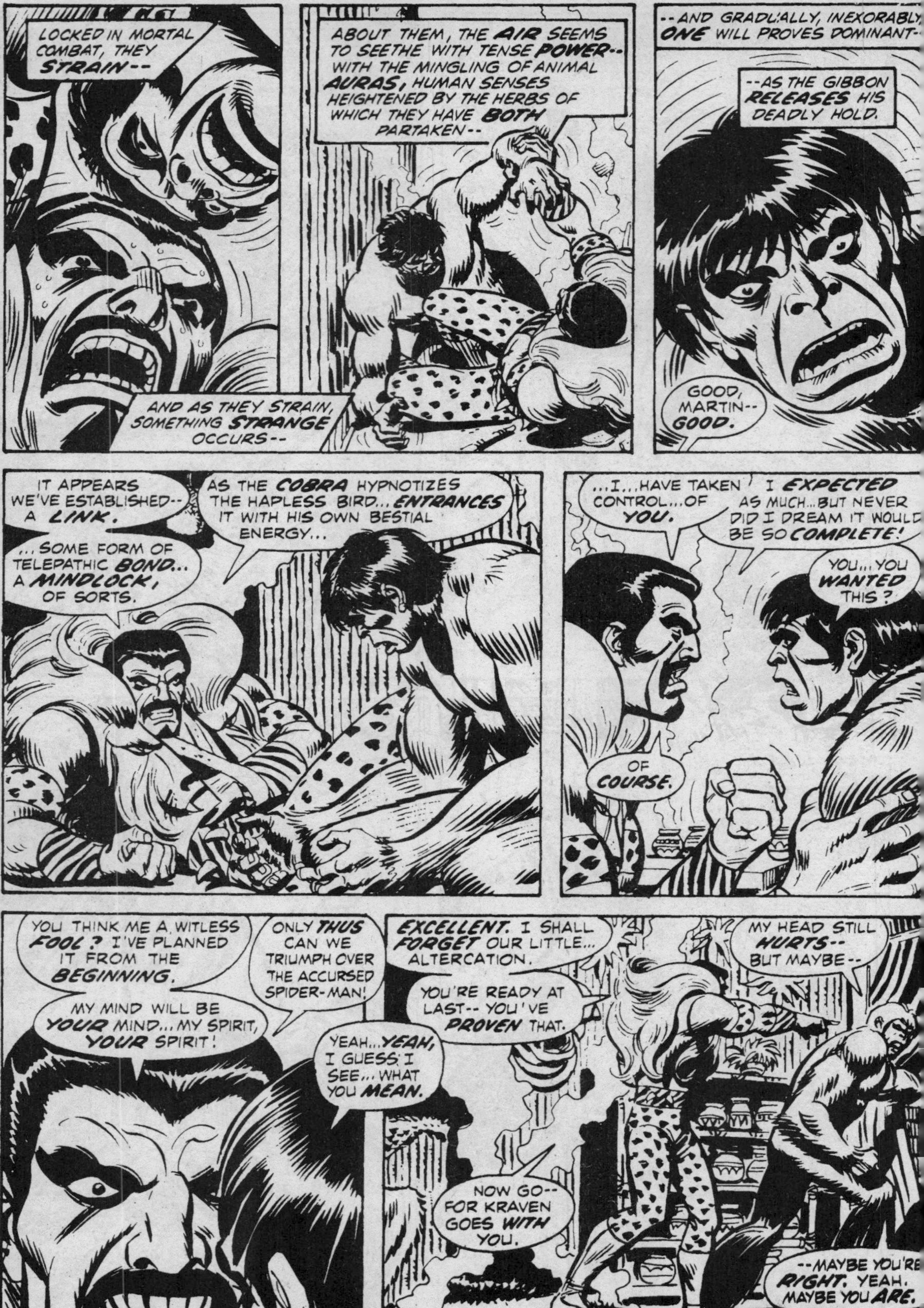
LOCKED IN MORTAL COMBAT, THEY STRAIN--
AND AS THEY STRAIN, SOMETHING STRANGE OCCURS--
ABOUT THEM, THE AIR SEEMS TO SEETHE WITH TENSE POWER-- WITH THE MINGLING OF ANIMAL AURAS, HUMAN SENSES HEIGHTENED BY THE HERBS OF WHICH THEY HAVE BOTH PARTAKEN--
--AND GRADUALLY, INEXORABLY, ONE WILL PROVES DOMINANT--
--AS THE GIBBON RELEASES HIS DEADLY HOLD.
GOOD, MARTIN-- GOOD.
IT APPEARS WE'VE ESTABLISHED-- A LINK.
...SOME FORM OF TELEPATHIC BOND... A MINDLOCK, OF SORTS.
AS THE COBRA HYPNOTIZES THE HAPLESS BIRD... ENTRANCES IT WITH HIS OWN BESTIAL ENERGY...
...I...HAVE TAKEN CONTROL...OF YOU.
I EXPECTED AS MUCH...BUT NEVER DID I DREAM IT WOULD BE SO COMPLETE!
YOU...YOU WANTED THIS?
OF COURSE.
YOU THINK ME A WITLESS FOOL? I'VE PLANNED IT FROM THE BEGINNING.
MY MIND WILL BE YOUR MIND...MY SPIRIT, YOUR SPIRIT!
ONLY THUS CAN WE TRIUMPH OVER THE ACCURSED SPIDER-MAN!
YEAH...YEAH, I GUESS I SEE...WHAT YOU MEAN.
EXCELLENT. I SHALL FORGET OUR LITTLE... ALTERCATION.
YOU'RE READY AT LAST-- YOU'VE PROVEN THAT.
MY HEAD STILL HURTS-- BUT MAYBE--
NOW GO-- FOR KRAVEN GOES WITH YOU.
--MAYBE YOU'RE RIGHT. YEAH. MAYBE YOU ARE.

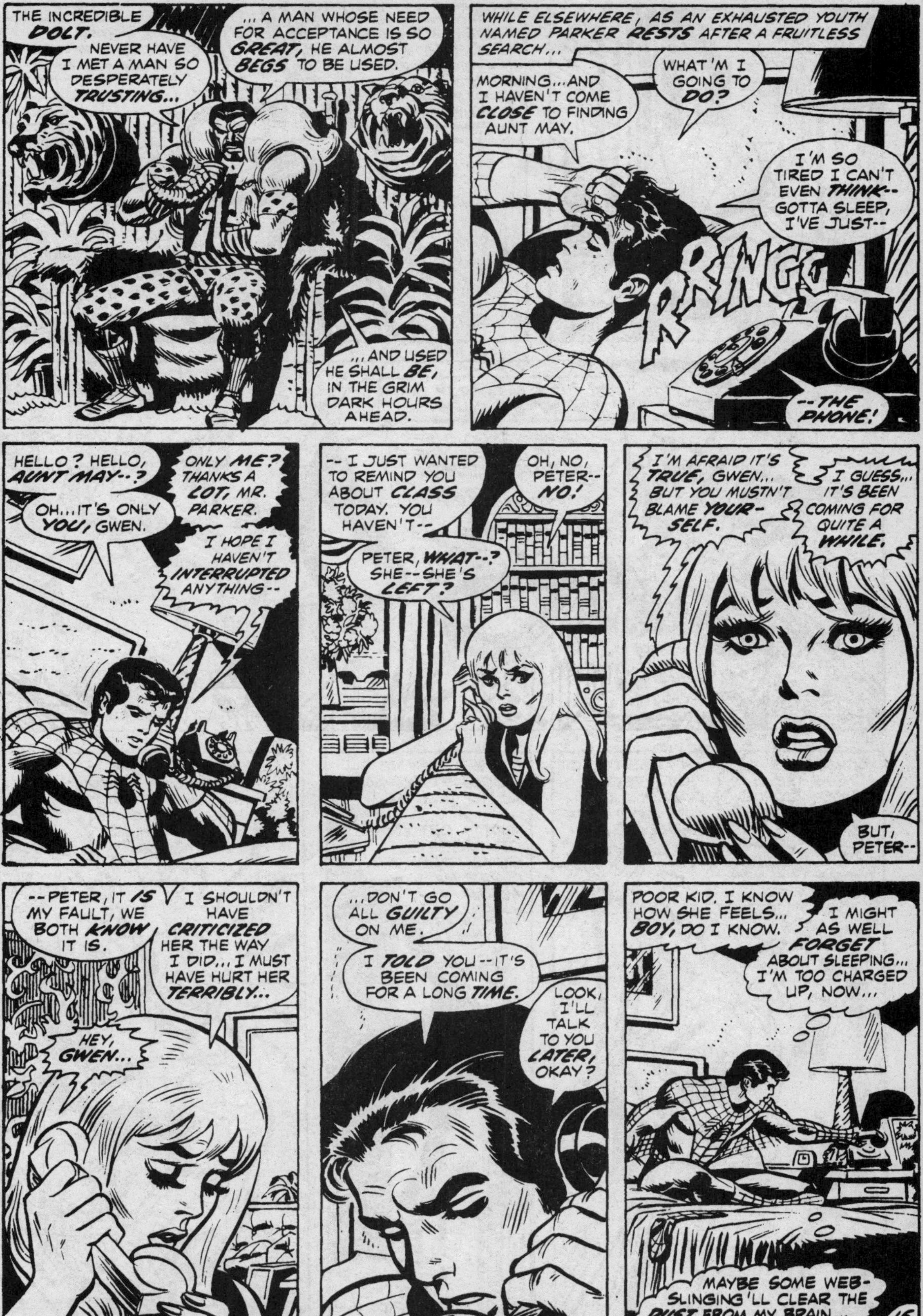
THE INCREDIBLE DOLT.
NEVER HAVE I MET A MAN SO DESPERATELY TRUSTING...
... A MAN WHOSE NEED FOR ACCEPTANCE IS SO GREAT, HE ALMOST BEGS TO BE USED.
...AND USED HE SHALL BE, IN THE GRIM DARK HOURS AHEAD.
WHILE ELSEWHERE, AS AN EXHAUSTED YOUTH NAMED PARKER RESTS AFTER A FRUITLESS SEARCH...
MORNING...AND I HAVEN'T COME CLOSE TO FINDING AUNT MAY.
WHAT'M I GOING TO DO?
I'M SO TIRED I CAN'T EVEN THINK-- GOTTA SLEEP, I'VE JUST--
RRINGG
--THE PHONE!
HELLO? HELLO, AUNT MAY--?
OH...IT'S ONLY YOU, GWEN.
ONLY ME? THANKS A LOT, MR. PARKER.
I HOPE I HAVEN'T INTERRUPTED ANYTHING--
-- I JUST WANTED TO REMIND YOU ABOUT CLASS TODAY. YOU HAVEN'T--
OH, NO, PETER-- NO!
PETER, WHAT--? SHE--SHE'S LEFT?
I'M AFRAID IT'S TRUE, GWEN... BUT YOU MUSTN'T BLAME YOURSELF.
I GUESS... IT'S BEEN COMING FOR QUITE A WHILE.
BUT, PETER--
--PETER, IT IS MY FAULT, WE BOTH KNOW IT IS.
I SHOULDN'T HAVE CRITICIZED HER THE WAY I DID... I MUST HAVE HURT HER TERRIBLY...
HEY, GWEN...
...DON'T GO ALL GUILTY ON ME.
I TOLD YOU --IT'S BEEN COMING FOR A LONG TIME.
LOOK, I'LL TALK TO YOU LATER, OKAY?
POOR KID. I KNOW HOW SHE FEELS... BOY, DO I KNOW.
I MIGHT AS WELL FORGET ABOUT SLEEPING... I'M TOO CHARGED UP, NOW...
MAYBE SOME WEB-SLINGING'LL CLEAR THE DUST FROM MY BRAIN...
15

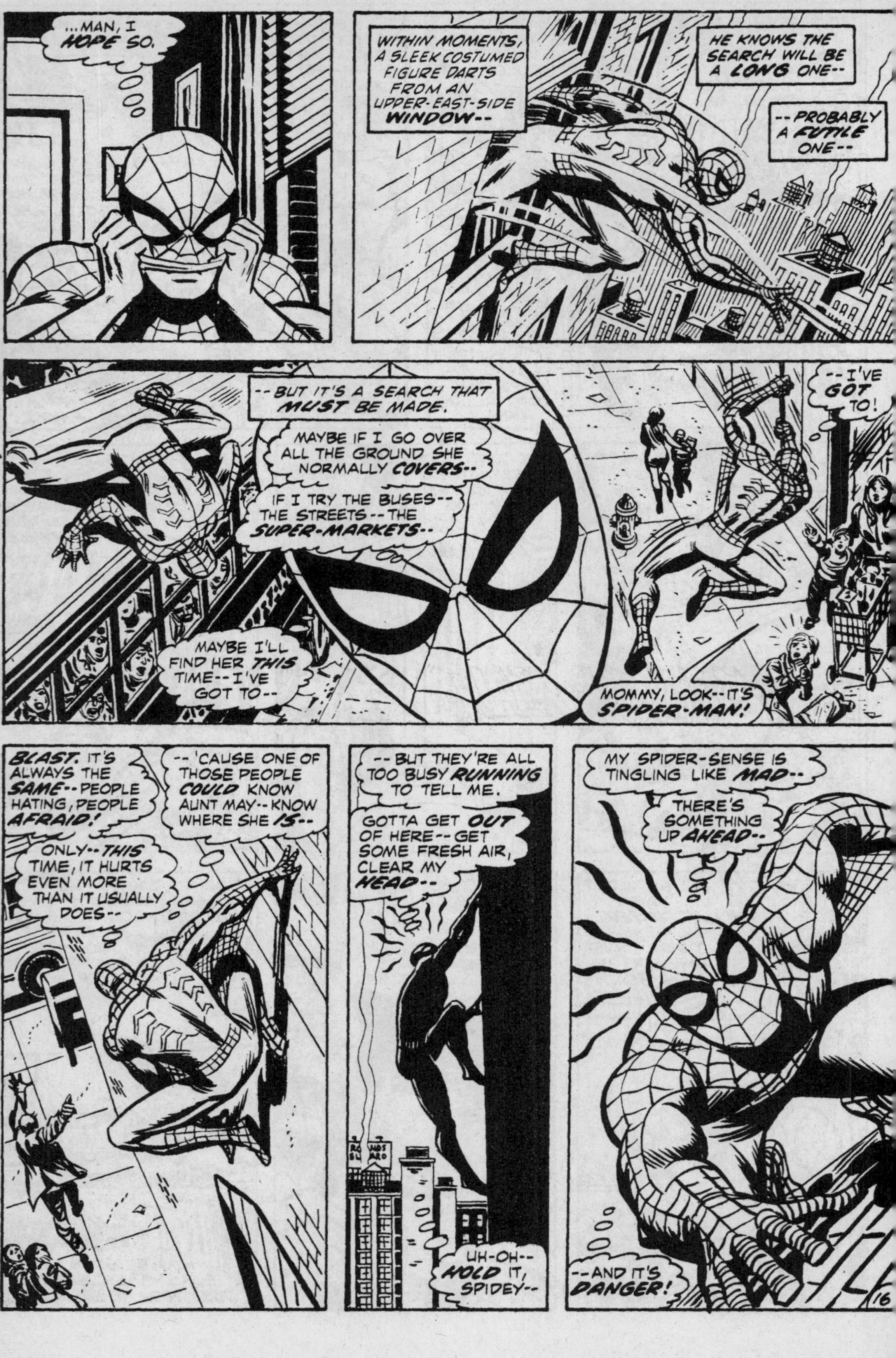
...MAN, I HOPE SO.
WITHIN MOMENTS, A SLEEK COSTUMED FIGURE DARTS FROM AN UPPER-EAST-SIDE WINDOW--
HE KNOWS THE SEARCH WILL BE A LONG ONE--
--PROBABLY A FUTILE ONE--
--BUT IT'S A SEARCH THAT MUST BE MADE.
MAYBE IF I GO OVER ALL THE GROUND SHE NORMALLY COVERS--
IF I TRY THE BUSES-- THE STREETS-- THE SUPER-MARKETS--
MAYBE I'LL FIND HER THIS TIME--I'VE GOT TO--
--I'VE GOT TO!
MOMMY, LOOK--IT'S SPIDER-MAN!
BLAST. IT'S ALWAYS THE SAME--PEOPLE HATING, PEOPLE AFRAID!
--'CAUSE ONE OF THOSE PEOPLE COULD KNOW AUNT MAY--KNOW WHERE SHE IS--
ONLY--THIS TIME, IT HURTS EVEN MORE THAN IT USUALLY DOES--
--BUT THEY'RE ALL TOO BUSY RUNNING TO TELL ME.
GOTTA GET OUT OF HERE--GET SOME FRESH AIR, CLEAR MY HEAD--
UH-OH-- HOLD IT, SPIDEY--
MY SPIDER-SENSE IS TINGLING LIKE MAD--
THERE'S SOMETHING UP AHEAD--
--AND IT'S DANGER!
16

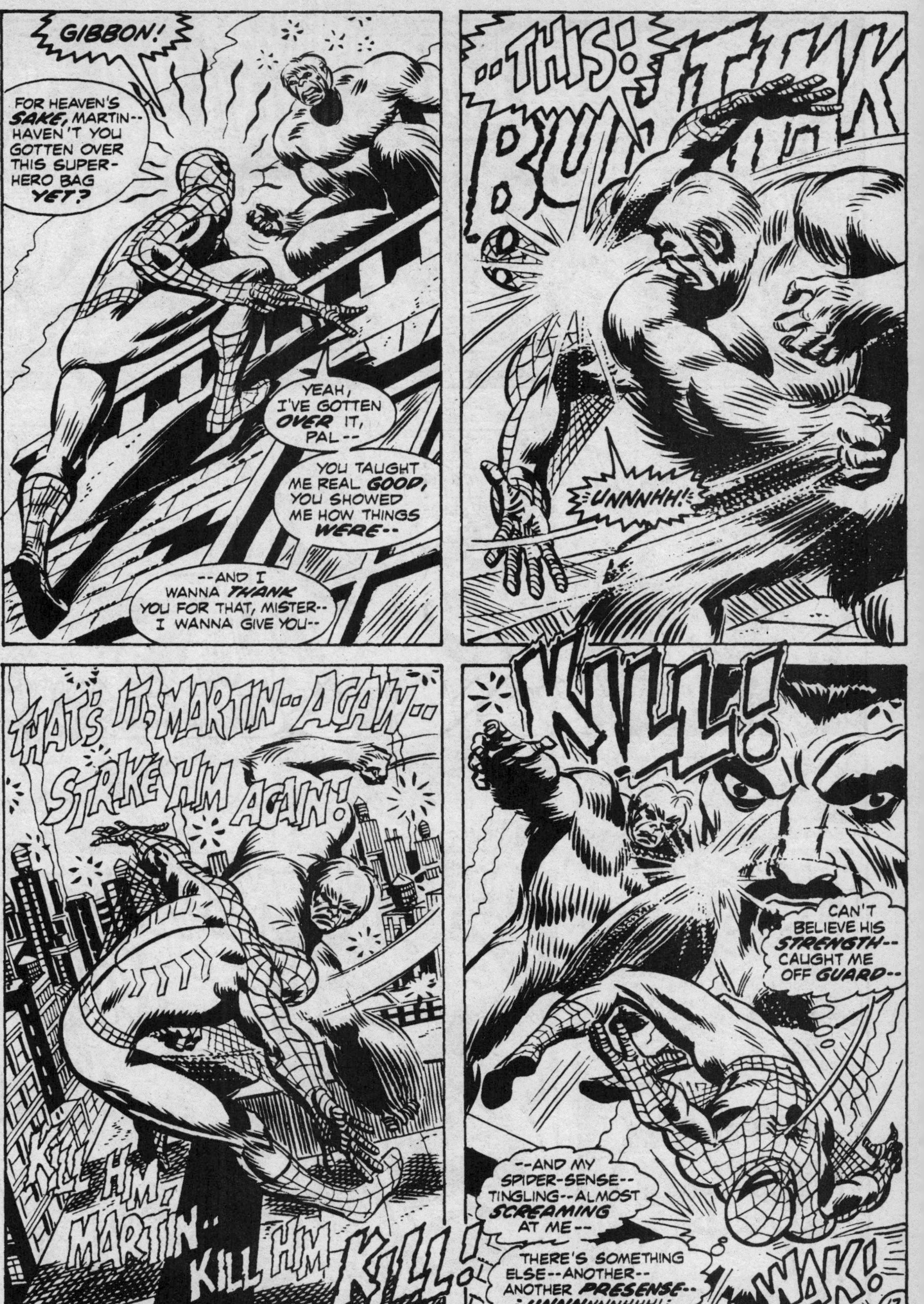
GIBBON!
FOR HEAVEN'S SAKE, MARTIN-- HAVEN'T YOU GOTTEN OVER THIS SUPER-HERO BAG YET?
YEAH, I'VE GOTTEN OVER IT, PAL--
YOU TAUGHT ME REAL GOOD, YOU SHOWED ME HOW THINGS WERE--
--AND I WANNA THANK YOU FOR THAT, MISTER-- I WANNA GIVE YOU--
--THIS!
BUNTHOK
UNNNHH!
THAT'S IT, MARTIN--AGAIN--
STRIKE HIM AGAIN!
KILL HIM, MARTIN-- KILL HIM KILL!
KILL!
CAN'T BELIEVE HIS STRENGTH-- CAUGHT ME OFF GUARD--
--AND MY SPIDER-SENSE-- TINGLING--ALMOST SCREAMING AT ME--
THERE'S SOMETHING ELSE--ANOTHER-- ANOTHER PRESENSE-- UNNNNNNHHH!
WAK!
17

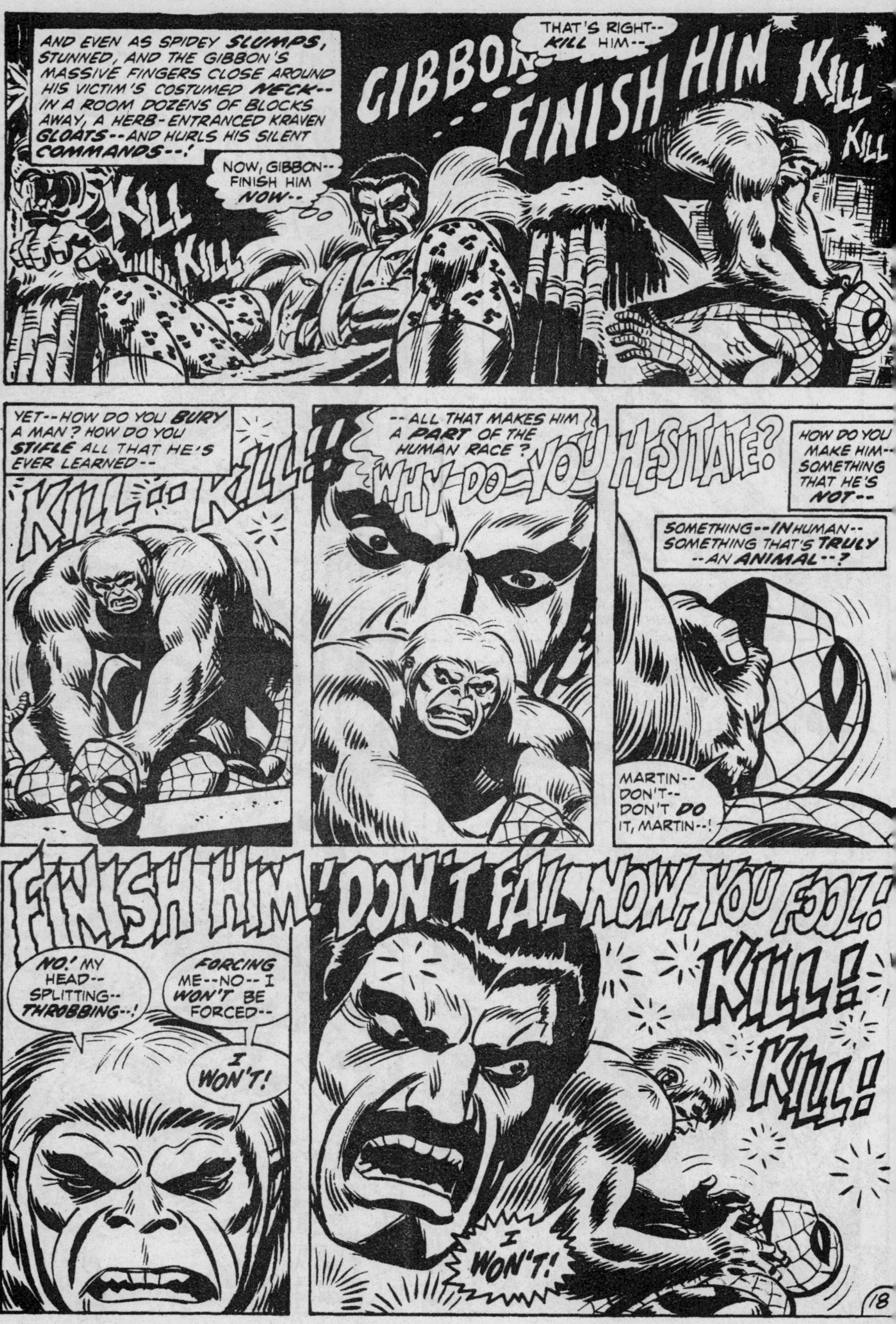
AND EVEN AS SPIDEY SLUMPS, STUNNED, AND THE GIBBON'S MASSIVE FINGERS CLOSE AROUND HIS VICTIM'S COSTUMED NECK-- IN A ROOM DOZENS OF BLOCKS AWAY, A HERB-ENTRANCED KRAVEN GLOATS--AND HURLS HIS SILENT COMMANDS--!
THAT'S RIGHT-- KILL HIM--
GIBBON... FINISH HIM KILL KILL
NOW, GIBBON-- FINISH HIM NOW--
KILL KILL
YET--HOW DO YOU BURY A MAN? HOW DO YOU STIFLE ALL THAT HE'S EVER LEARNED--
KILL--KILL!!
--ALL THAT MAKES HIM A PART OF THE HUMAN RACE?
WHY DO YOU HESITATE?
HOW DO YOU MAKE HIM--SOMETHING THAT HE'S NOT--
SOMETHING--INHUMAN-- SOMETHING THAT'S TRULY --AN ANIMAL--?
MARTIN-- DON'T-- DON'T DO IT, MARTIN--!
FINISH HIM! DON'T FAIL NOW, YOU FOOL!
NO! MY HEAD-- SPLITTING-- THROBBING--!
FORCING ME--NO--I WON'T BE FORCED--
I WON'T!
KILL! KILL!
I WON'T!
18

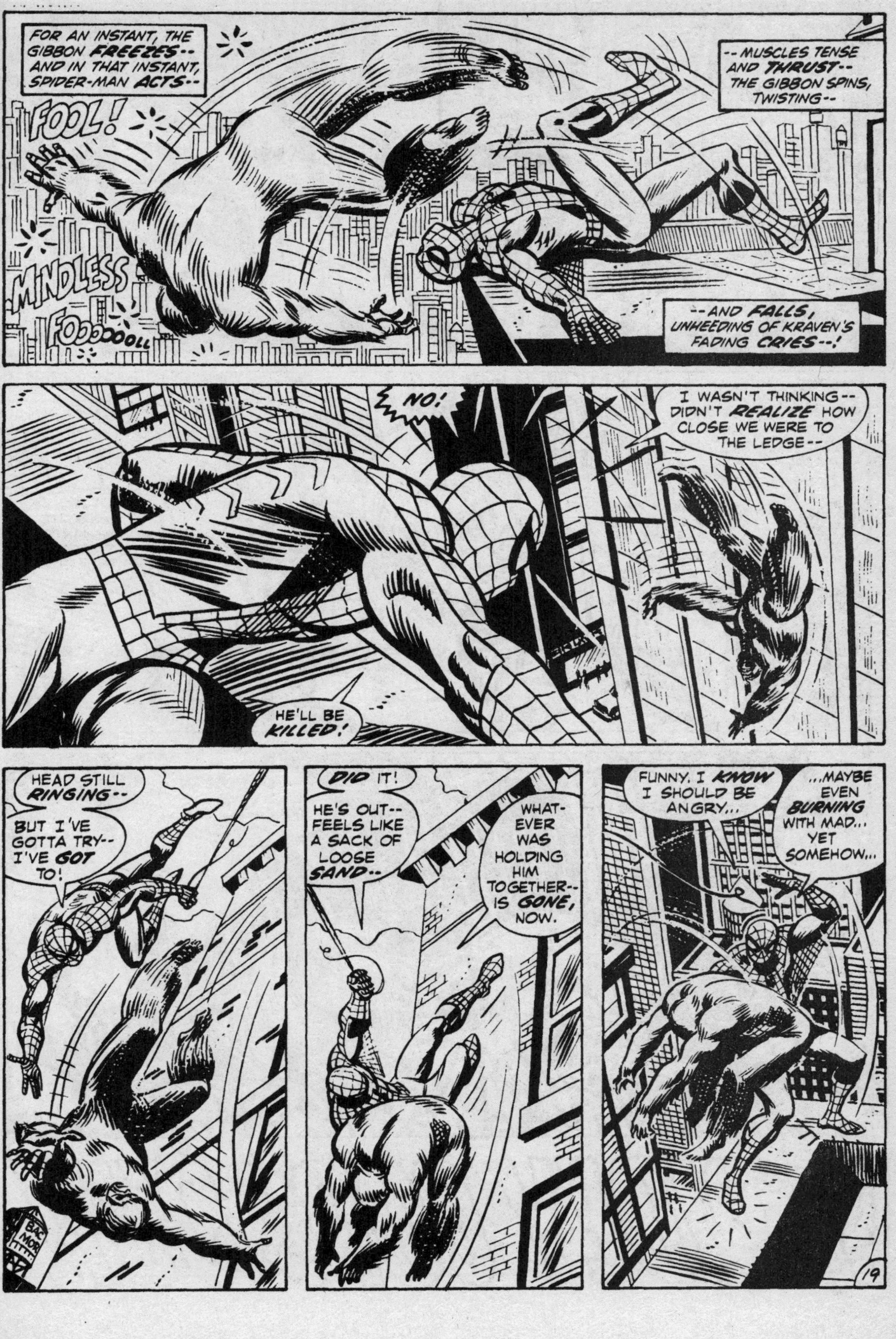
FOR AN INSTANT, THE GIBBON FREEZES-- AND IN THAT INSTANT, SPIDER-MAN ACTS--
FOOL!
MINDLESS
FOOOOOOOLL
--MUSCLES TENSE AND THRUST-- THE GIBBON SPINS, TWISTING--
--AND FALLS, UNHEEDING OF KRAVEN'S FADING CRIES--!
NO!
I WASN'T THINKING-- DIDN'T REALIZE HOW CLOSE WE WERE TO THE LEDGE--
HE'LL BE KILLED!
HEAD STILL RINGING--
BUT I'VE GOTTA TRY-- I'VE GOT TO!
DID IT!
HE'S OUT-- FEELS LIKE A SACK OF LOOSE SAND--
WHATEVER WAS HOLDING HIM TOGETHER-- IS GONE, NOW.
FUNNY. I KNOW I SHOULD BE ANGRY...
...MAYBE EVEN BURNING WITH MAD... YET SOMEHOW...
19

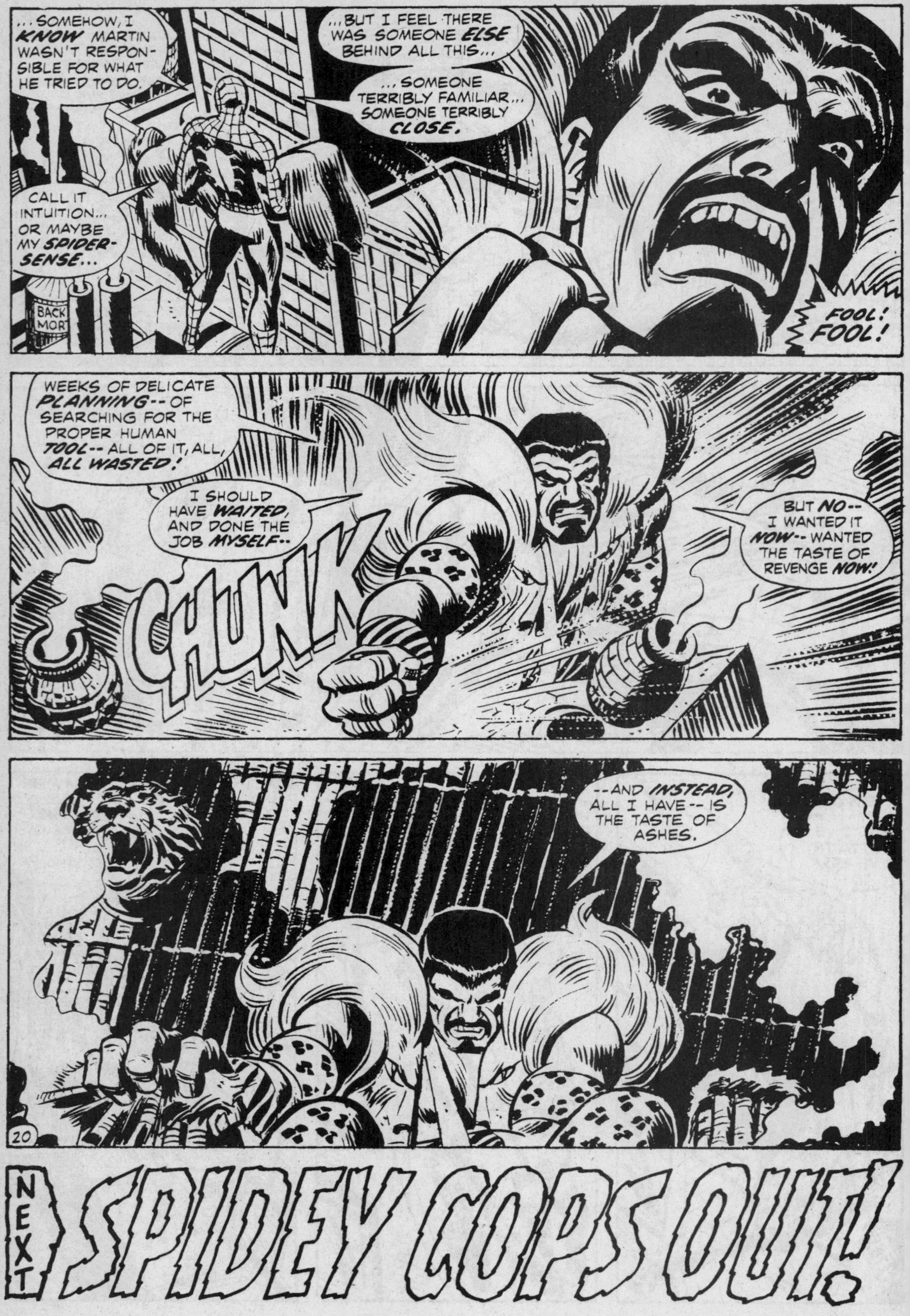

...SOMEHOW, I KNOW MARTIN WASN'T RESPONSIBLE FOR WHAT HE TRIED TO DO.
...BUT I FEEL THERE WAS SOMEONE ELSE BEHIND ALL THIS...
...SOMEONE TERRIBLY FAMILIAR... SOMEONE TERRIBLY CLOSE.
CALL IT INTUITION... OR MAYBE MY SPIDER-SENSE...
BACK MORT
FOOL! FOOL!
WEEKS OF DELICATE PLANNING-- OF SEARCHING FOR THE PROPER HUMAN TOOL-- ALL OF IT, ALL, ALL WASTED!
I SHOULD HAVE WAITED, AND DONE THE JOB MYSELF--
BUT NO-- I WANTED IT NOW-- WANTED THE TASTE OF REVENGE NOW!
CHUNK
--AND INSTEAD, ALL I HAVE-- IS THE TASTE OF ASHES.
20

NEXT SPIDEY COPS OUT!

SPIDER-MAN
MARVEL COMICS GROUP TM
20¢
112 SEPT 02457
the AMAZING SPIDER-MAN ®
APPROVED BY THE COMICS CODE AUTHORITY
TM
GO ON, WORLD!
HURT EACH OTHER--KILL EACH OTHER--DO ANYTHING YOU WANT!
I JUST DON'T CARE ANY MORE!
ROMITA
SPIDEY COPS OUT!

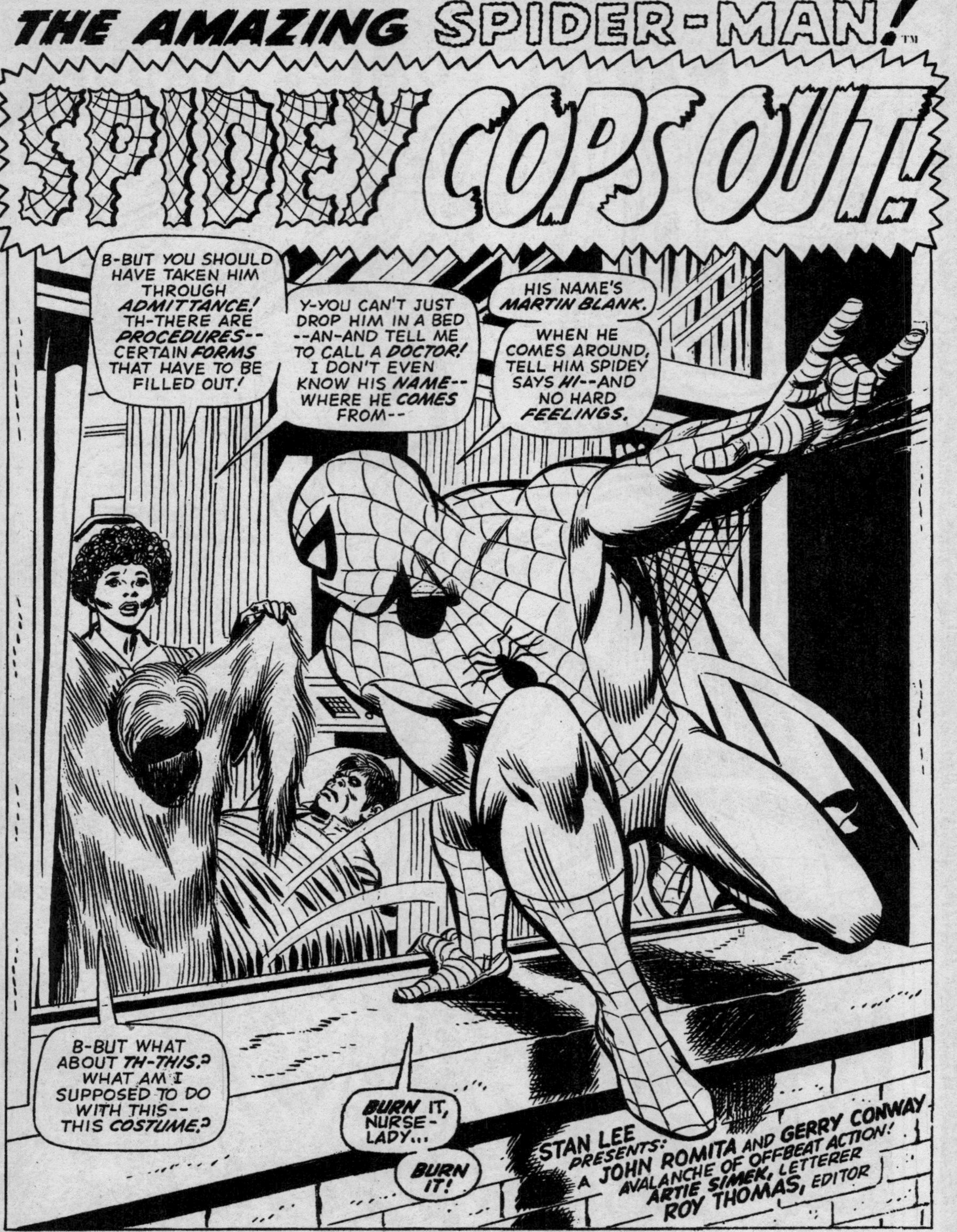

THE AMAZING SPIDER-MAN!™
SPIDEY COPS OUT!
B-BUT YOU SHOULD HAVE TAKEN HIM THROUGH ADMITTANCE! TH-THERE ARE PROCEDURES-- CERTAIN FORMS THAT HAVE TO BE FILLED OUT!
Y-YOU CAN'T JUST DROP HIM IN A BED --AN-AND TELL ME TO CALL A DOCTOR! I DON'T EVEN KNOW HIS NAME-- WHERE HE COMES FROM--
HIS NAME'S MARTIN BLANK.
WHEN HE COMES AROUND, TELL HIM SPIDEY SAYS HI--AND NO HARD FEELINGS.
B-BUT WHAT ABOUT TH-THIS? WHAT AM I SUPPOSED TO DO WITH THIS-- THIS COSTUME?
BURN IT, NURSE-LADY...
BURN IT!
STAN LEE PRESENTS: A JOHN ROMITA AND GERRY CONWAY AVALANCHE OF OFFBEAT ACTION! ARTIE SIMEK, LETTERER ROY THOMAS, EDITOR

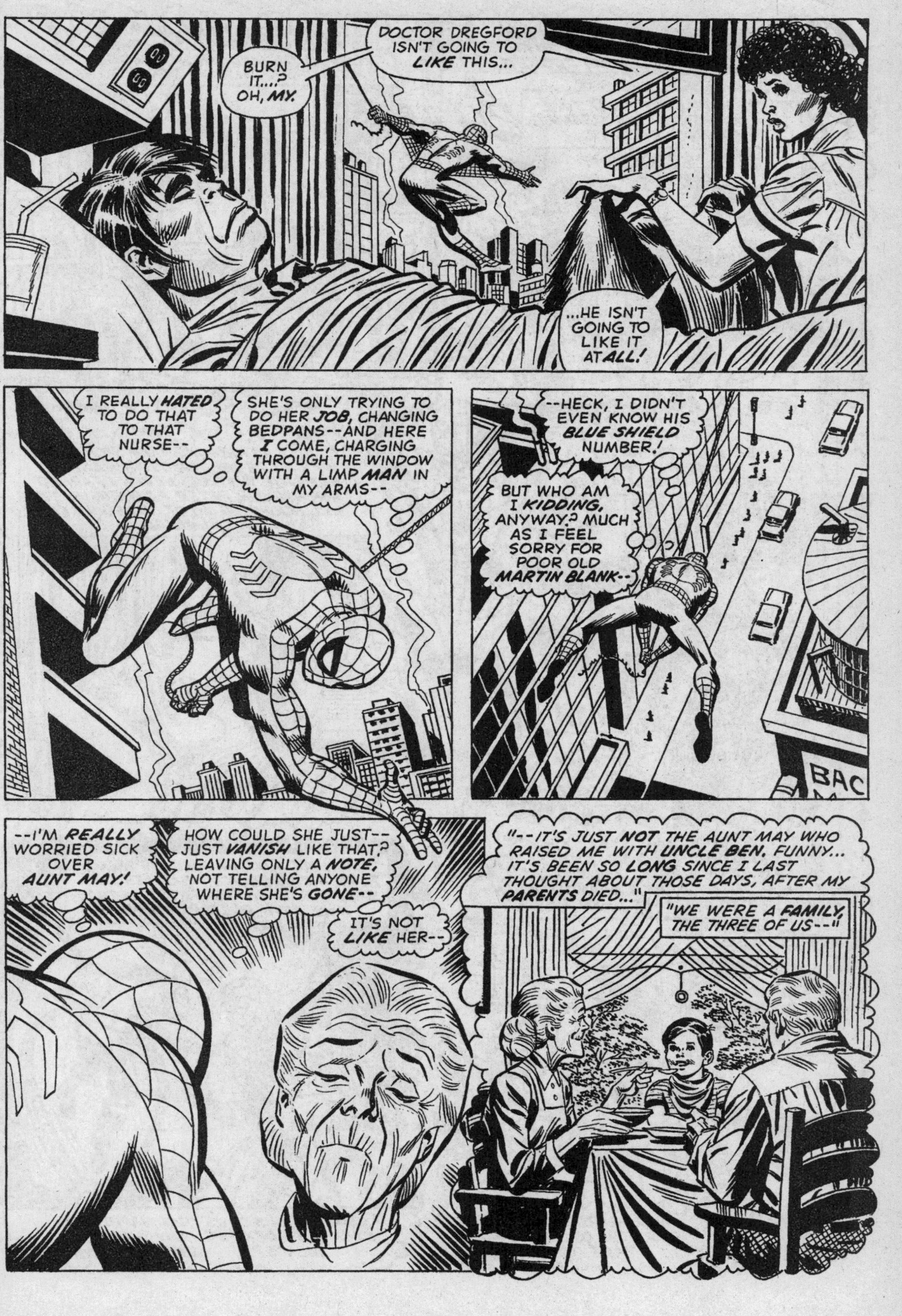
BURN IT...? OH, MY.
DOCTOR DREGFORD ISN'T GOING TO LIKE THIS...
...HE ISN'T GOING TO LIKE IT AT ALL!
I REALLY HATED TO DO THAT TO THAT NURSE--
SHE'S ONLY TRYING TO DO HER JOB, CHANGING BEDPANS--AND HERE I COME, CHARGING THROUGH THE WINDOW WITH A LIMP MAN IN MY ARMS--
--HECK, I DIDN'T EVEN KNOW HIS BLUE SHIELD NUMBER!
BUT WHO AM I KIDDING, ANYWAY? MUCH AS I FEEL SORRY FOR POOR OLD MARTIN BLANK--
BAC
--I'M REALLY WORRIED SICK OVER AUNT MAY!
HOW COULD SHE JUST--JUST VANISH LIKE THAT? LEAVING ONLY A NOTE, NOT TELLING ANYONE WHERE SHE'S GONE--
IT'S NOT LIKE HER--
"--IT'S JUST NOT THE AUNT MAY WHO RAISED ME WITH UNCLE BEN. FUNNY... IT'S BEEN SO LONG SINCE I LAST THOUGHT ABOUT THOSE DAYS, AFTER MY PARENTS DIED..."
"WE WERE A FAMILY, THE THREE OF US--"

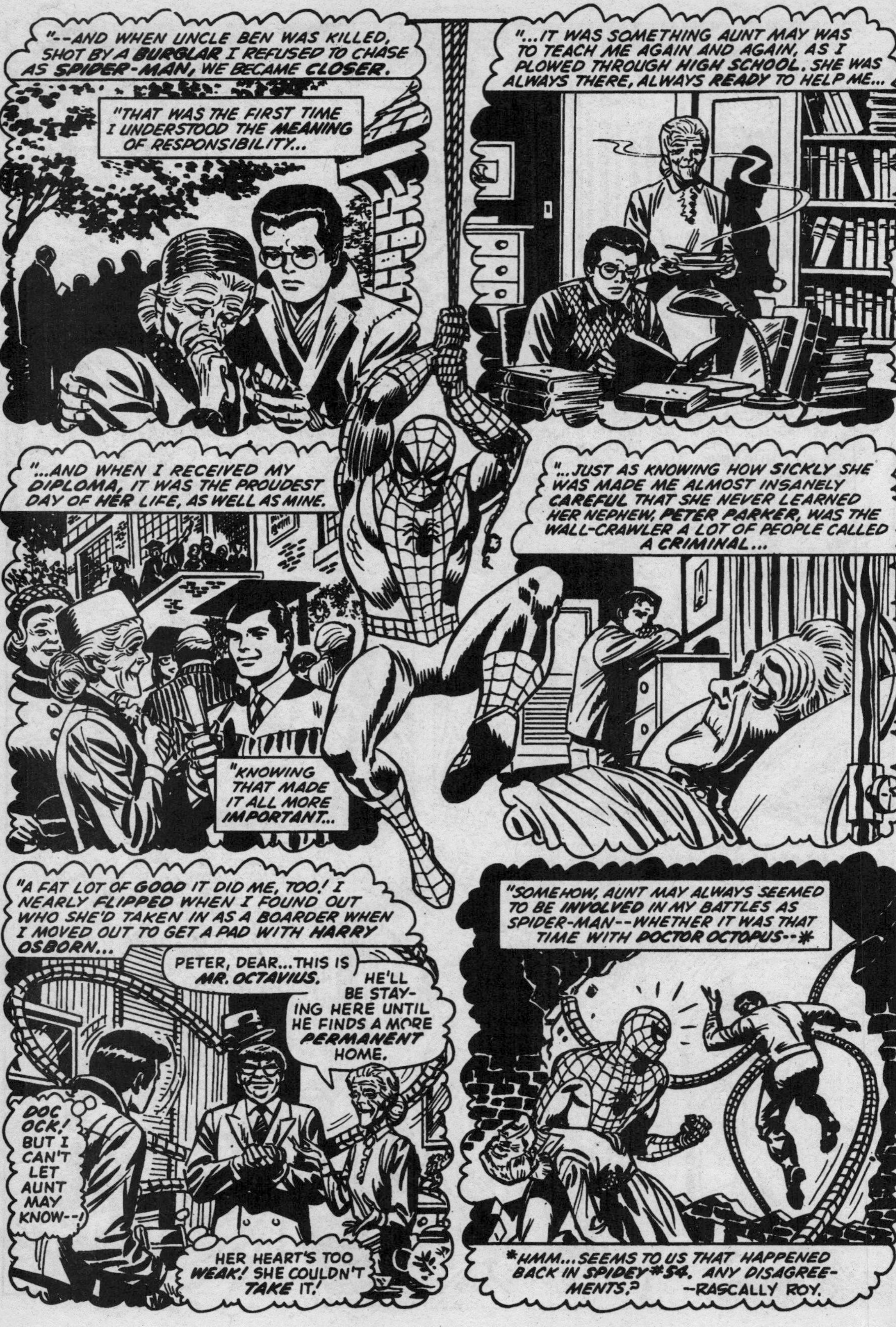
"--AND WHEN UNCLE BEN WAS KILLED, SHOT BY A BURGLAR I REFUSED TO CHASE AS SPIDER-MAN, WE BECAME CLOSER.
"THAT WAS THE FIRST TIME I UNDERSTOOD THE MEANING OF RESPONSIBILITY...
"...IT WAS SOMETHING AUNT MAY WAS TO TEACH ME AGAIN AND AGAIN, AS I PLOWED THROUGH HIGH SCHOOL. SHE WAS ALWAYS THERE, ALWAYS READY TO HELP ME...
"...AND WHEN I RECEIVED MY DIPLOMA, IT WAS THE PROUDEST DAY OF HER LIFE, AS WELL AS MINE.
"KNOWING THAT MADE IT ALL MORE IMPORTANT...
"...JUST AS KNOWING HOW SICKLY SHE WAS MADE ME ALMOST INSANELY CAREFUL THAT SHE NEVER LEARNED HER NEPHEW, PETER PARKER, WAS THE WALL-CRAWLER A LOT OF PEOPLE CALLED A CRIMINAL...
"A FAT LOT OF GOOD IT DID ME, TOO! I NEARLY FLIPPED WHEN I FOUND OUT WHO SHE'D TAKEN IN AS A BOARDER WHEN I MOVED OUT TO GET A PAD WITH HARRY OSBORN...
PETER, DEAR...THIS IS MR. OCTAVIUS.
HE'LL BE STAYING HERE UNTIL HE FINDS A MORE PERMANENT HOME.
DOC OCK! BUT I CAN'T LET AUNT MAY KNOW--!
HER HEART'S TOO WEAK! SHE COULDN'T TAKE IT!
"SOMEHOW, AUNT MAY ALWAYS SEEMED TO BE INVOLVED IN MY BATTLES AS SPIDER-MAN--WHETHER IT WAS THAT TIME WITH DOCTOR OCTOPUS--*
*HMM...SEEMS TO US THAT HAPPENED BACK IN SPIDEY #54. ANY DISAGREEMENTS? --RASCALLY ROY.

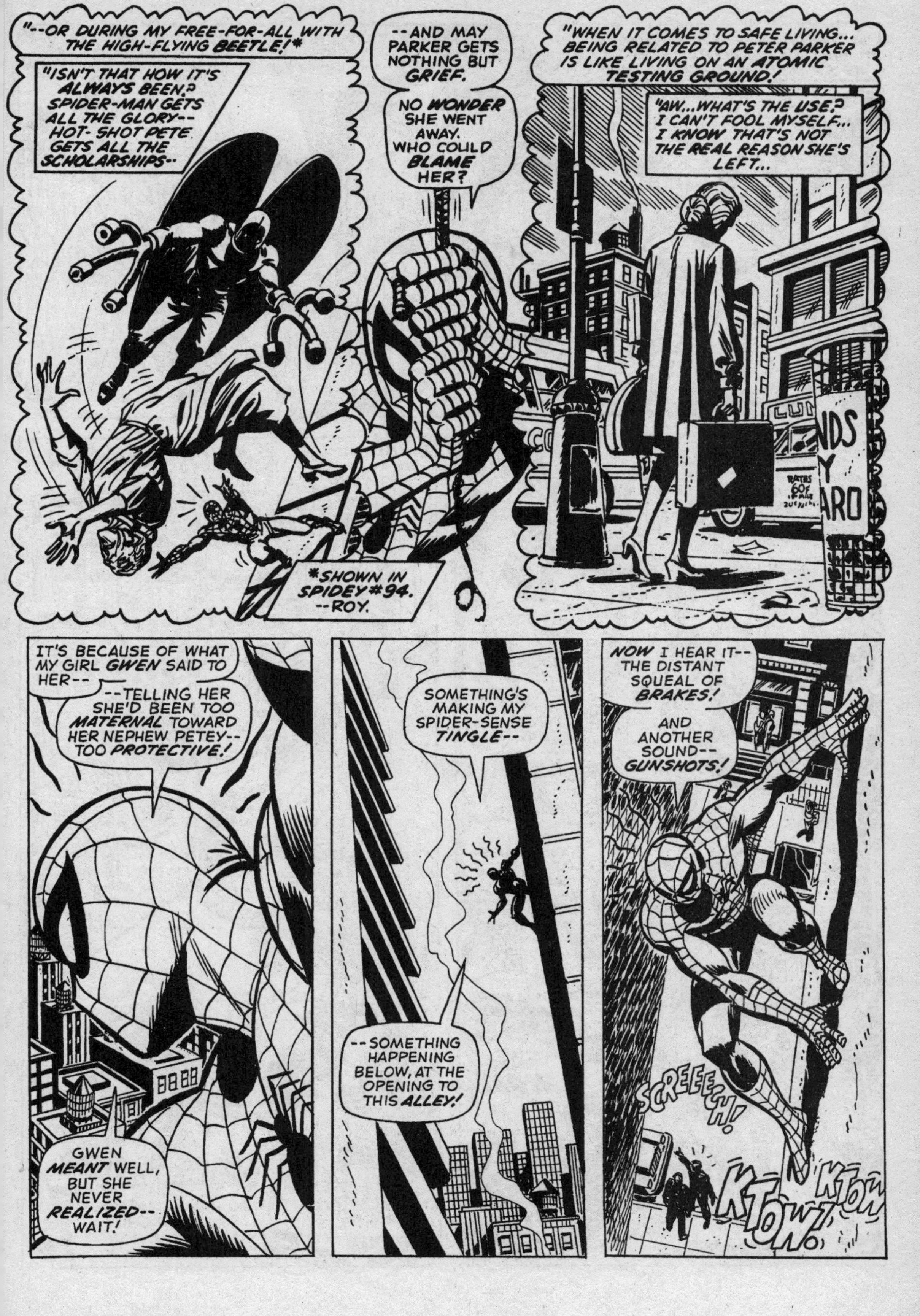
"--OR DURING MY FREE-FOR-ALL WITH THE HIGH-FLYING BEETLE!*
"ISN'T THAT HOW IT'S ALWAYS BEEN? SPIDER-MAN GETS ALL THE GLORY-- HOT-SHOT PETE GETS ALL THE SCHOLARSHIPS--
--AND MAY PARKER GETS NOTHING BUT GRIEF.
NO WONDER SHE WENT AWAY. WHO COULD BLAME HER?
*SHOWN IN SPIDEY #94. --ROY.
"WHEN IT COMES TO SAFE LIVING... BEING RELATED TO PETER PARKER IS LIKE LIVING ON AN ATOMIC TESTING GROUND!
"AW...WHAT'S THE USE? I CAN'T FOOL MYSELF... I KNOW THAT'S NOT THE REAL REASON SHE'S LEFT...
IT'S BECAUSE OF WHAT MY GIRL GWEN SAID TO HER--
--TELLING HER SHE'D BEEN TOO MATERNAL TOWARD HER NEPHEW PETEY-- TOO PROTECTIVE!
GWEN MEANT WELL, BUT SHE NEVER REALIZED-- WAIT!
SOMETHING'S MAKING MY SPIDER-SENSE TINGLE--
--SOMETHING HAPPENING BELOW, AT THE OPENING TO THIS ALLEY!
NOW I HEAR IT-- THE DISTANT SQUEAL OF BRAKES!
AND ANOTHER SOUND-- GUNSHOTS!
SCREEEECH!
KTOWW!
KTOW

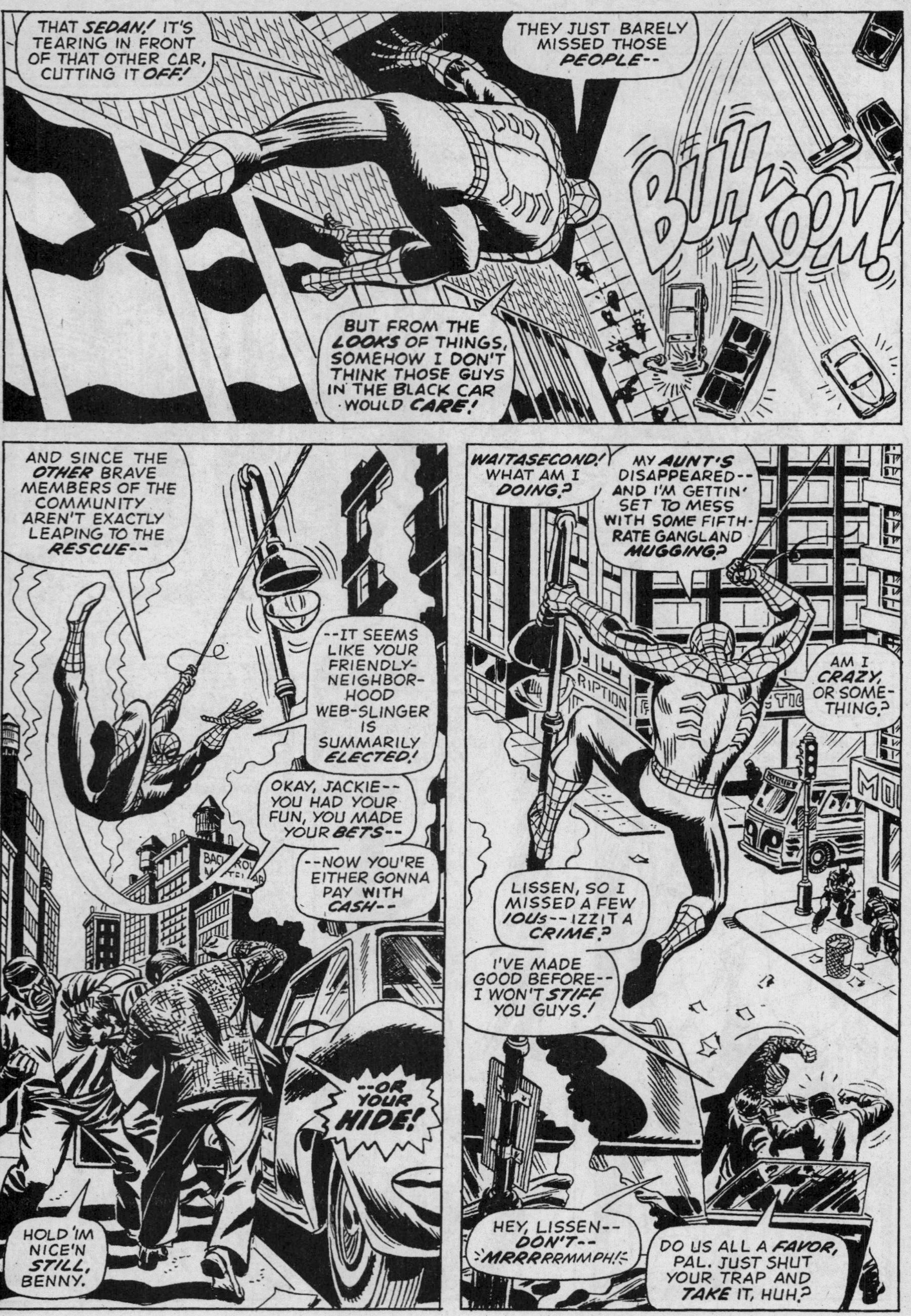
THAT SEDAN! IT'S TEARING IN FRONT OF THAT OTHER CAR, CUTTING IT OFF!
THEY JUST BARELY MISSED THOSE PEOPLE--
BUHKOOM!
BUT FROM THE LOOKS OF THINGS, SOMEHOW I DON'T THINK THOSE GUYS IN THE BLACK CAR WOULD CARE!
AND SINCE THE OTHER BRAVE MEMBERS OF THE COMMUNITY AREN'T EXACTLY LEAPING TO THE RESCUE--
--IT SEEMS LIKE YOUR FRIENDLY-NEIGHBOR-HOOD WEB-SLINGER IS SUMMARILY ELECTED!
OKAY, JACKIE-- YOU HAD YOUR FUN, YOU MADE YOUR BETS--
--NOW YOU'RE EITHER GONNA PAY WITH CASH--
--OR YOUR HIDE!
HOLD 'IM NICE'N STILL, BENNY.
WAITASECOND! WHAT AM I DOING?
MY AUNT'S DISAPPEARED-- AND I'M GETTIN' SET TO MESS WITH SOME FIFTH-RATE GANGLAND MUGGING?
AM I CRAZY, OR SOME-THING?
LISSEN, SO I MISSED A FEW IOUs-- IZZIT A CRIME?
I'VE MADE GOOD BEFORE-- I WON'T STIFF YOU GUYS!
HEY, LISSEN-- DON'T-- MRRRRRMMPH!
DO US ALL A FAVOR, PAL. JUST SHUT YOUR TRAP AND TAKE IT, HUH?

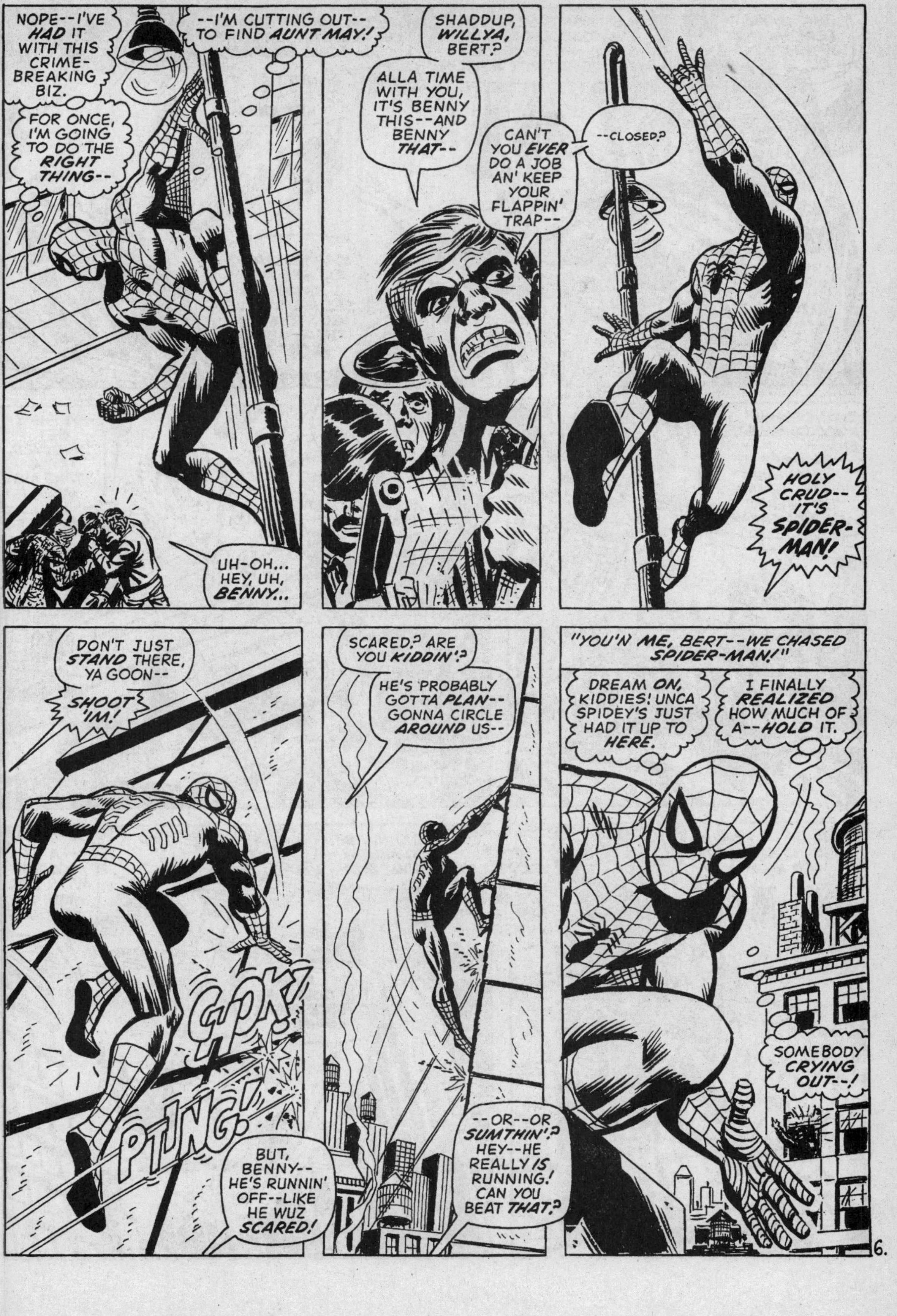
NOPE--I'VE HAD IT WITH THIS CRIME-BREAKING BIZ.
FOR ONCE, I'M GOING TO DO THE RIGHT THING--
--I'M CUTTING OUT-- TO FIND AUNT MAY!
UH-OH... HEY, UH, BENNY...
SHADDUP, WILLYA, BERT?
ALLA TIME WITH YOU, IT'S BENNY THIS--AND BENNY THAT--
CAN'T YOU EVER DO A JOB AN' KEEP YOUR FLAPPIN' TRAP--
--CLOSED?
HOLY CRUD--IT'S SPIDER-MAN!
DON'T JUST STAND THERE, YA GOON--
SHOOT 'IM!
GPOK!
PTING!
BUT, BENNY--HE'S RUNNIN' OFF--LIKE HE WUZ SCARED!
SCARED? ARE YOU KIDDIN'?
HE'S PROBABLY GOTTA PLAN--GONNA CIRCLE AROUND US--
--OR--OR SUMTHIN'? HEY--HE REALLY IS RUNNING! CAN YOU BEAT THAT?
"YOU'N ME, BERT--WE CHASED SPIDER-MAN!"
DREAM ON, KIDDIES! UNCA SPIDEY'S JUST HAD IT UP TO HERE.
I FINALLY REALIZED HOW MUCH OF A--HOLD IT.
SOMEBODY CRYING OUT--!

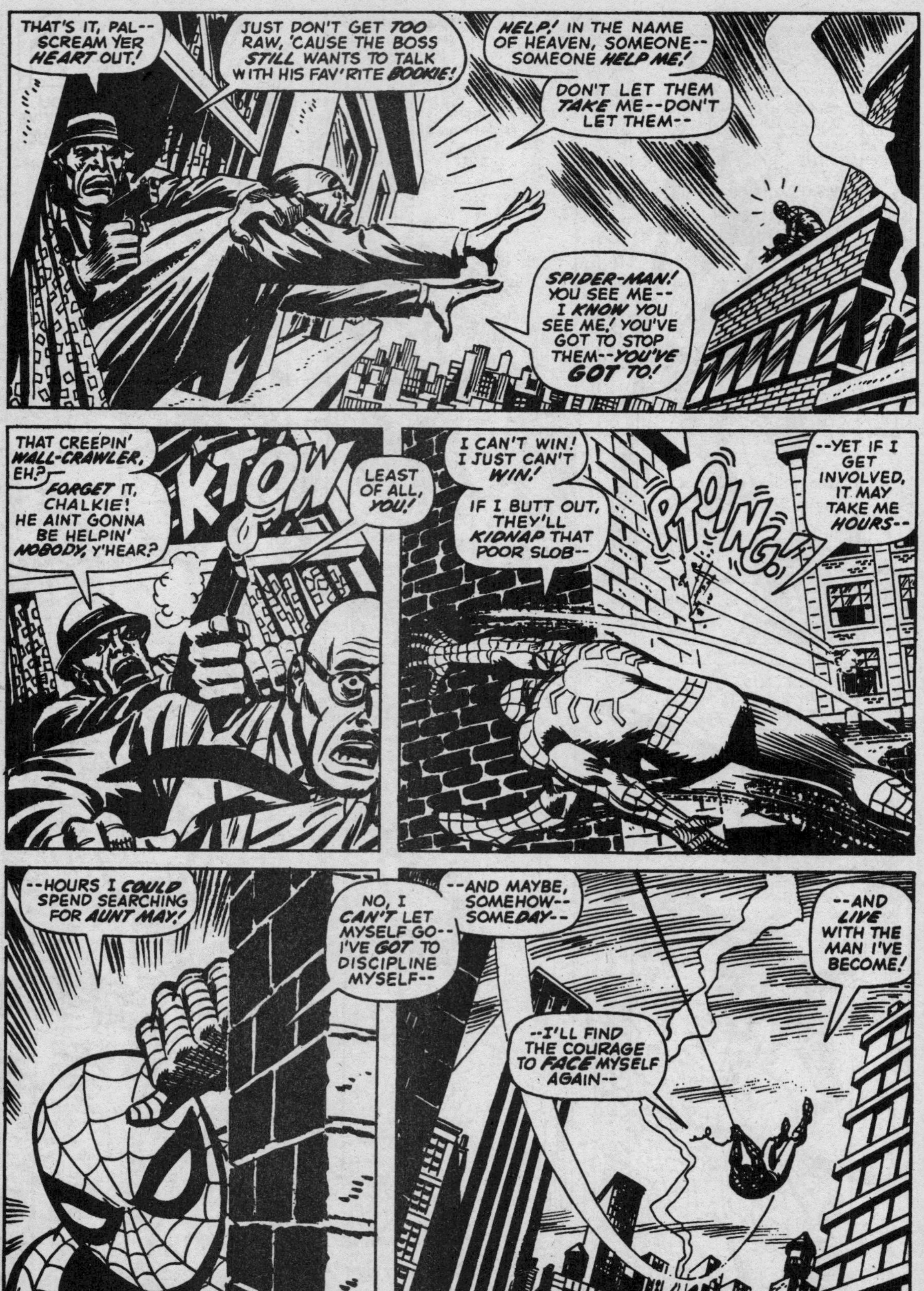
THAT'S IT, PAL-- SCREAM YER HEART OUT!
JUST DON'T GET TOO RAW, 'CAUSE THE BOSS STILL WANTS TO TALK WITH HIS FAV'RITE BOOKIE!
HELP! IN THE NAME OF HEAVEN, SOMEONE-- SOMEONE HELP ME!
DON'T LET THEM TAKE ME--DON'T LET THEM--
SPIDER-MAN! YOU SEE ME-- I KNOW YOU SEE ME! YOU'VE GOT TO STOP THEM--YOU'VE GOT TO!
THAT CREEPIN' WALL-CRAWLER, EH?
FORGET IT, CHALKIE! HE AINT GONNA BE HELPIN' NOBODY, Y'HEAR?
KTOW
LEAST OF ALL, YOU!
I CAN'T WIN! I JUST CAN'T WIN!
IF I BUTT OUT, THEY'LL KIDNAP THAT POOR SLOB--
PTOING!
--YET IF I GET INVOLVED, IT MAY TAKE ME HOURS--
--HOURS I COULD SPEND SEARCHING FOR AUNT MAY!
NO, I CAN'T LET MYSELF GO-- I'VE GOT TO DISCIPLINE MYSELF--
--AND MAYBE, SOMEHOW-- SOMEDAY--
--I'LL FIND THE COURAGE TO FACE MYSELF AGAIN--
--AND LIVE WITH THE MAN I'VE BECOME!

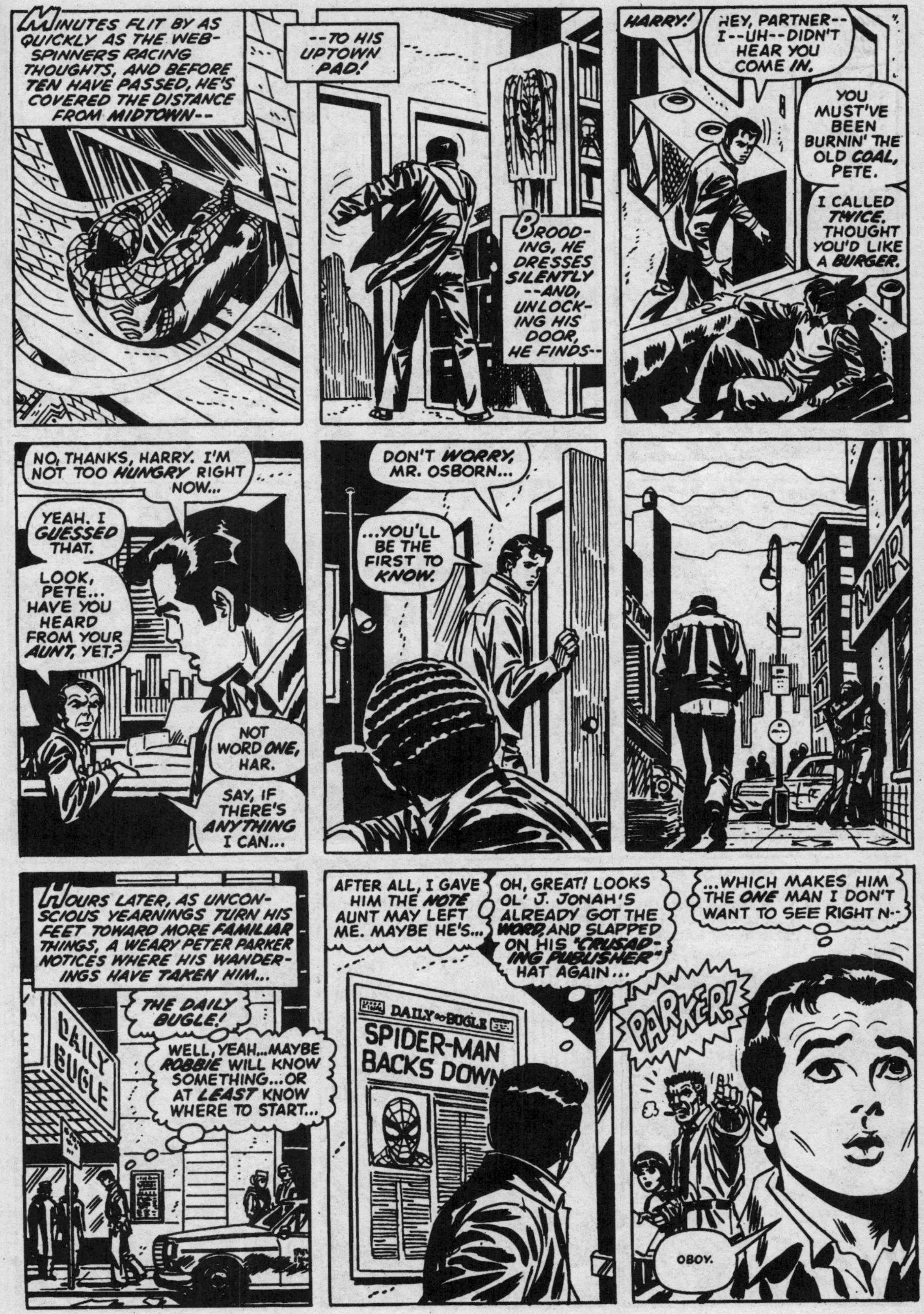
MINUTES FLIT BY AS QUICKLY AS THE WEB-SPINNERS RACING THOUGHTS, AND BEFORE TEN HAVE PASSED, HE'S COVERED THE DISTANCE FROM MIDTOWN--
--TO HIS UPTOWN PAD!
BROODING, HE DRESSES SILENTLY --AND, UNLOCKING HIS DOOR, HE FINDS--
HARRY!
HEY, PARTNER-- I--UH--DIDN'T HEAR YOU COME IN.
YOU MUST'VE BEEN BURNIN' THE OLD COAL, PETE.
I CALLED TWICE. THOUGHT YOU'D LIKE A BURGER.
NO, THANKS, HARRY. I'M NOT TOO HUNGRY RIGHT NOW...
YEAH. I GUESSED THAT.
LOOK, PETE... HAVE YOU HEARD FROM YOUR AUNT, YET?
NOT WORD ONE, HAR.
SAY, IF THERE'S ANYTHING I CAN...
DON'T WORRY, MR. OSBORN...
...YOU'LL BE THE FIRST TO KNOW.
HOURS LATER, AS UNCONSCIOUS YEARNINGS TURN HIS FEET TOWARD MORE FAMILIAR THINGS, A WEARY PETER PARKER NOTICES WHERE HIS WANDERINGS HAVE TAKEN HIM...
THE DAILY BUGLE!
WELL, YEAH...MAYBE ROBBIE WILL KNOW SOMETHING...OR AT LEAST KNOW WHERE TO START...
DAILY BUGLE
AFTER ALL, I GAVE HIM THE NOTE AUNT MAY LEFT ME. MAYBE HE'S...
OH, GREAT! LOOKS OL' J. JONAH'S ALREADY GOT THE WORD, AND SLAPPED ON HIS "CRUSADING PUBLISHER" HAT AGAIN...
DAILY BUGLE
SPIDER-MAN BACKS DOWN
...WHICH MAKES HIM THE ONE MAN I DON'T WANT TO SEE RIGHT N--
PARKER!
OBOY.

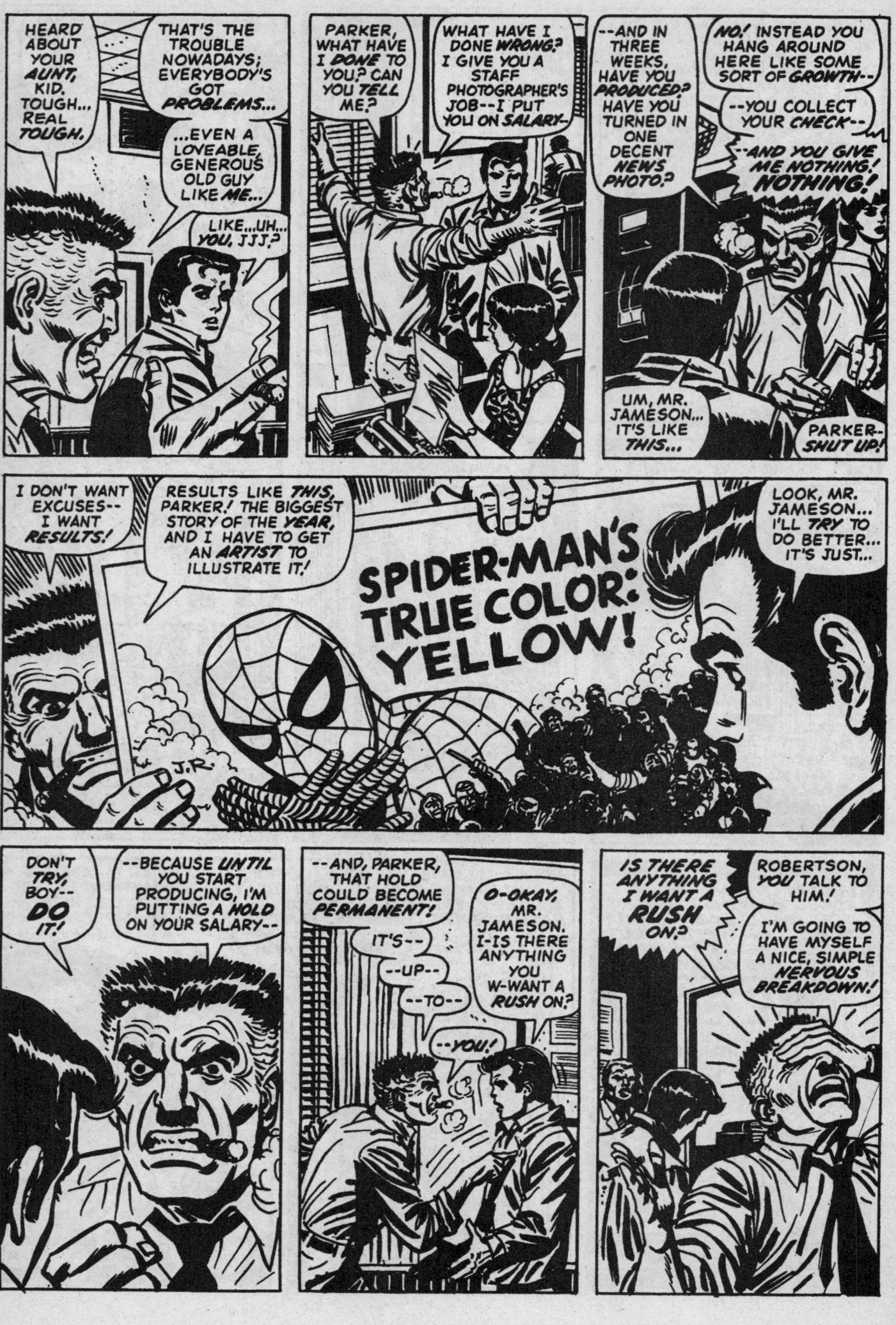
HEARD ABOUT YOUR AUNT, KID. TOUGH... REAL TOUGH.
THAT'S THE TROUBLE NOWADAYS; EVERYBODY'S GOT PROBLEMS...
...EVEN A LOVEABLE, GENEROUS OLD GUY LIKE ME...
LIKE...UH... YOU, JJJ.?
PARKER, WHAT HAVE I DONE TO YOU? CAN YOU TELL ME?
WHAT HAVE I DONE WRONG? I GIVE YOU A STAFF PHOTOGRAPHER'S JOB--I PUT YOU ON SALARY--
--AND IN THREE WEEKS, HAVE YOU PRODUCED? HAVE YOU TURNED IN ONE DECENT NEWS PHOTO?
NO! INSTEAD YOU HANG AROUND HERE LIKE SOME SORT OF GROWTH--
--YOU COLLECT YOUR CHECK--
--AND YOU GIVE ME NOTHING! NOTHING!
UM, MR. JAMESON... IT'S LIKE THIS...
PARKER-- SHUT UP!
I DON'T WANT EXCUSES-- I WANT RESULTS!
RESULTS LIKE THIS, PARKER! THE BIGGEST STORY OF THE YEAR, AND I HAVE TO GET AN ARTIST TO ILLUSTRATE IT!
SPIDER-MAN'S TRUE COLOR: YELLOW!
J.R.
LOOK, MR. JAMESON... I'LL TRY TO DO BETTER... IT'S JUST...
DON'T TRY, BOY-- DO IT!
--BECAUSE UNTIL YOU START PRODUCING, I'M PUTTING A HOLD ON YOUR SALARY--
--AND, PARKER, THAT HOLD COULD BECOME PERMANENT!
IT'S--
--UP--
--TO--
--YOU!
O-OKAY, MR. JAMESON. I-IS THERE ANYTHING YOU W-WANT A RUSH ON?
IS THERE ANYTHING I WANT A RUSH ON?
ROBERTSON, YOU TALK TO HIM!
I'M GOING TO HAVE MYSELF A NICE, SIMPLE NERVOUS BREAKDOWN!

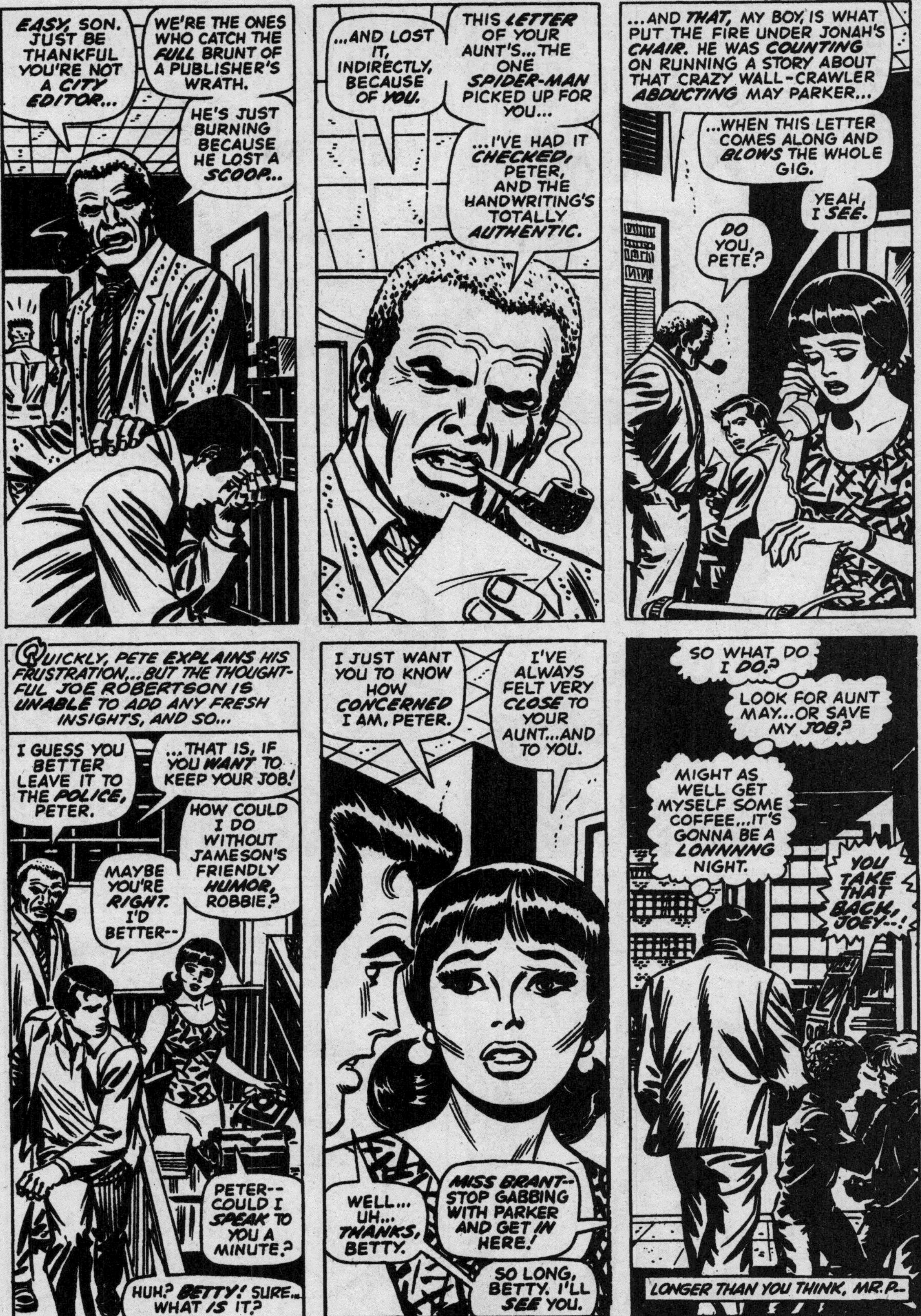

EASY, SON. JUST BE THANKFUL YOU'RE NOT A CITY EDITOR...
WE'RE THE ONES WHO CATCH THE FULL BRUNT OF A PUBLISHER'S WRATH.
HE'S JUST BURNING BECAUSE HE LOST A SCOOP...
...AND LOST IT, INDIRECTLY, BECAUSE OF YOU.
THIS LETTER OF YOUR AUNT'S...THE ONE SPIDER-MAN PICKED UP FOR YOU...
...I'VE HAD IT CHECKED, PETER, AND THE HANDWRITING'S TOTALLY AUTHENTIC.
...AND THAT, MY BOY, IS WHAT PUT THE FIRE UNDER JONAH'S CHAIR. HE WAS COUNTING ON RUNNING A STORY ABOUT THAT CRAZY WALL-CRAWLER ABDUCTING MAY PARKER...
...WHEN THIS LETTER COMES ALONG AND BLOWS THE WHOLE GIG.
YEAH, I SEE.
DO YOU, PETE?
QUICKLY, PETE EXPLAINS HIS FRUSTRATION...BUT THE THOUGHTFUL JOE ROBERTSON IS UNABLE TO ADD ANY FRESH INSIGHTS, AND SO...
I GUESS YOU BETTER LEAVE IT TO THE POLICE, PETER.
...THAT IS, IF YOU WANT TO KEEP YOUR JOB!
HOW COULD I DO WITHOUT JAMESON'S FRIENDLY HUMOR, ROBBIE?
MAYBE YOU'RE RIGHT. I'D BETTER--
PETER--COULD I SPEAK TO YOU A MINUTE?
HUH? BETTY! SURE... WHAT IS IT?
I JUST WANT YOU TO KNOW HOW CONCERNED I AM, PETER.
I'VE ALWAYS FELT VERY CLOSE TO YOUR AUNT...AND TO YOU.
WELL... UH... THANKS, BETTY.
MISS BRANT-- STOP GABBING WITH PARKER AND GET IN HERE!
SO LONG, BETTY. I'LL SEE YOU.
SO WHAT DO I DO?
LOOK FOR AUNT MAY...OR SAVE MY JOB?
MIGHT AS WELL GET MYSELF SOME COFFEE...IT'S GONNA BE A LONNNNG NIGHT.
YOU TAKE THAT BACK, JOEY--!
LONGER THAN YOU THINK, MR. P--

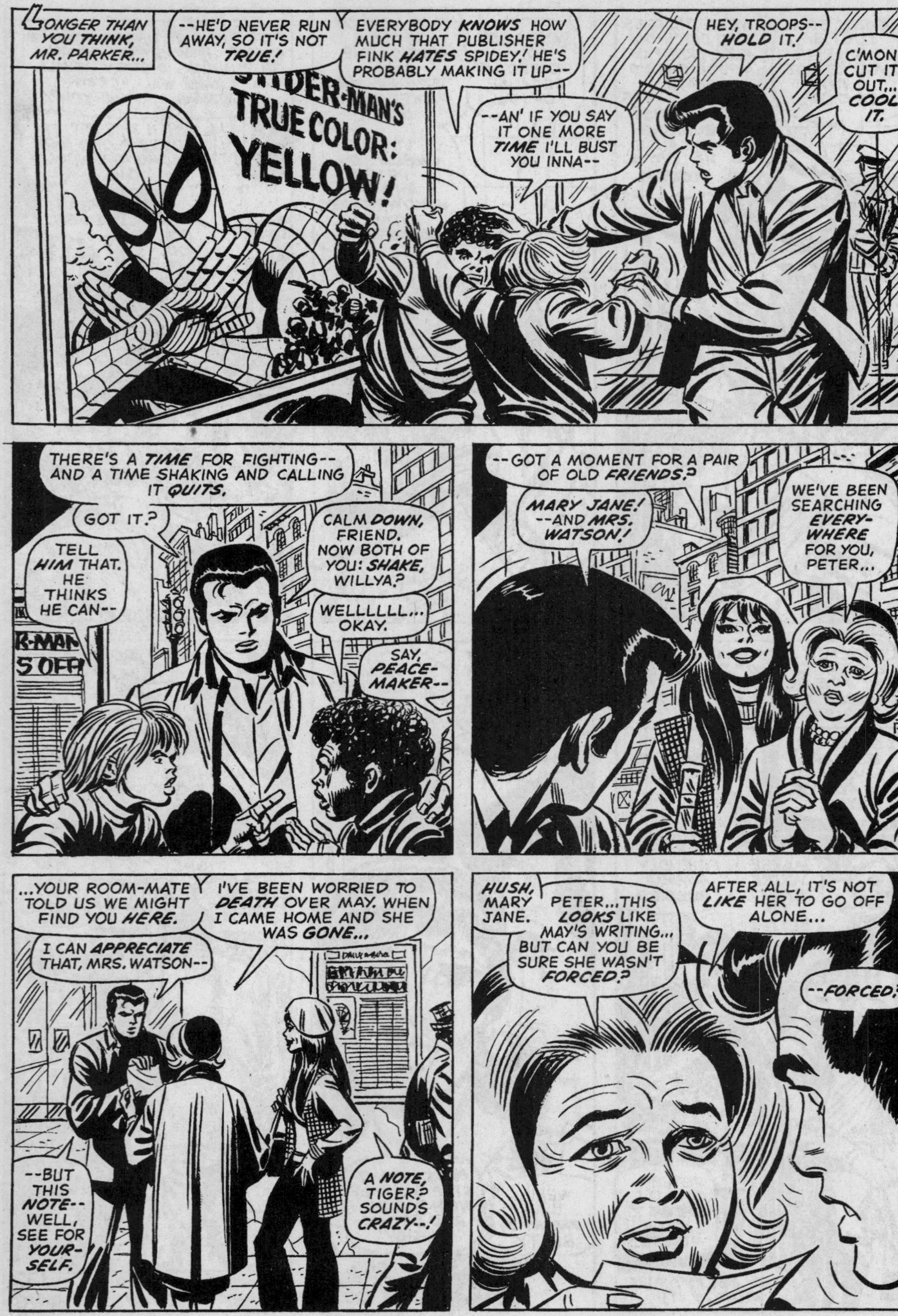
LONGER THAN YOU THINK, MR. PARKER...
--HE'D NEVER RUN AWAY, SO IT'S NOT TRUE!
EVERYBODY KNOWS HOW MUCH THAT PUBLISHER FINK HATES SPIDEY! HE'S PROBABLY MAKING IT UP--
--AN' IF YOU SAY IT ONE MORE TIME I'LL BUST YOU INNA--
HEY, TROOPS-- HOLD IT!
C'MON, CUT IT OUT... COOL IT.
SPIDER-MAN'S TRUE COLOR: YELLOW!
THERE'S A TIME FOR FIGHTING-- AND A TIME SHAKING AND CALLING IT QUITS.
GOT IT?
TELL HIM THAT. HE THINKS HE CAN--
CALM DOWN, FRIEND. NOW BOTH OF YOU: SHAKE, WILLYA?
WELLLLLL... OKAY.
SAY, PEACE-MAKER--
--GOT A MOMENT FOR A PAIR OF OLD FRIENDS?
MARY JANE! --AND MRS. WATSON!
WE'VE BEEN SEARCHING EVERY-WHERE FOR YOU, PETER...
...YOUR ROOM-MATE TOLD US WE MIGHT FIND YOU HERE.
I'VE BEEN WORRIED TO DEATH OVER MAY. WHEN I CAME HOME AND SHE WAS GONE...
I CAN APPRECIATE THAT, MRS. WATSON--
--BUT THIS NOTE-- WELL, SEE FOR YOUR-SELF.
A NOTE, TIGER? SOUNDS CRAZY--!
HUSH, MARY JANE.
PETER...THIS LOOKS LIKE MAY'S WRITING... BUT CAN YOU BE SURE SHE WASN'T FORCED?
AFTER ALL, IT'S NOT LIKE HER TO GO OFF ALONE...
--FORCED?

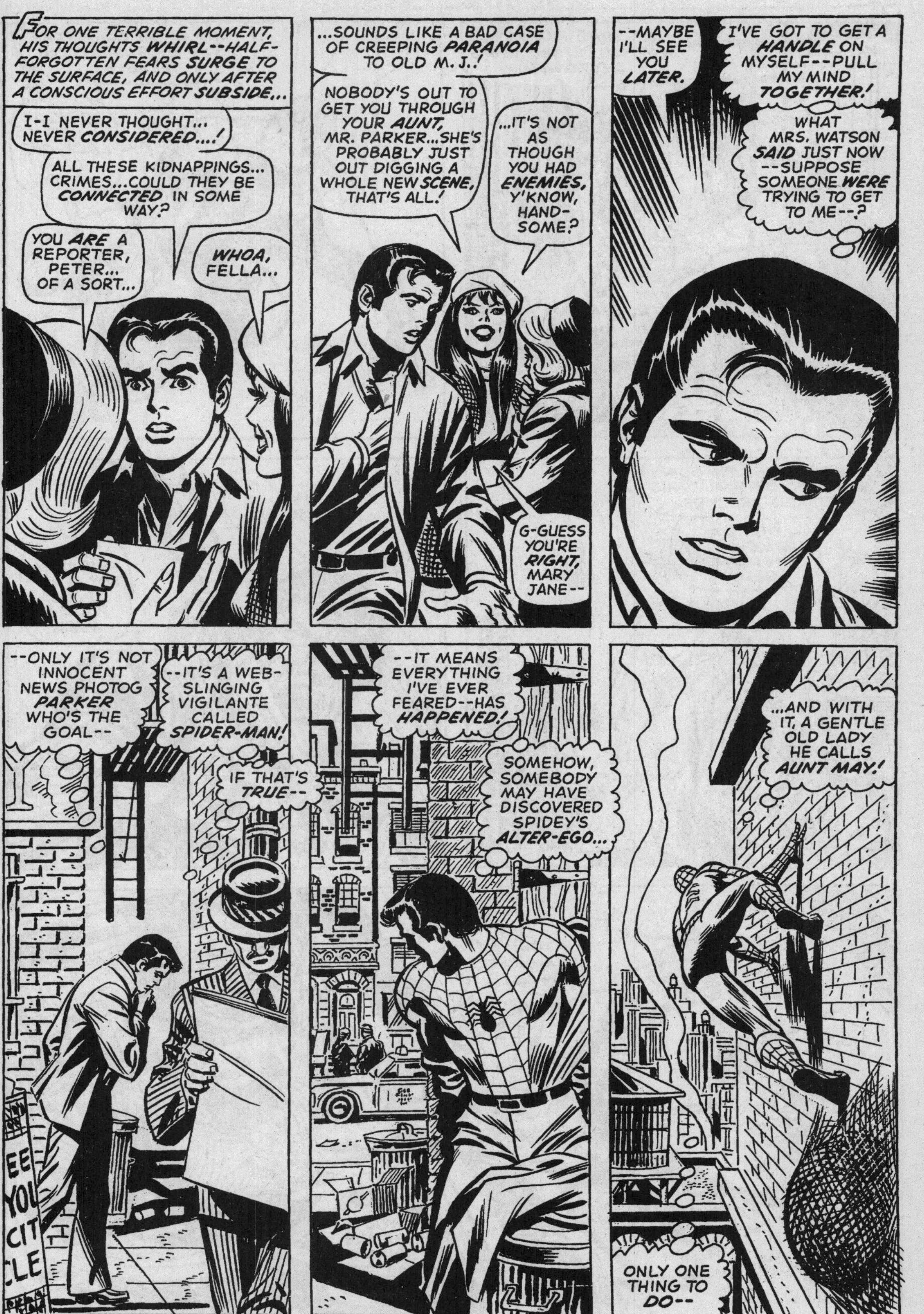
FOR ONE TERRIBLE MOMENT, HIS THOUGHTS WHIRL--HALF-FORGOTTEN FEARS SURGE TO THE SURFACE, AND ONLY AFTER A CONSCIOUS EFFORT SUBSIDE...
I-I NEVER THOUGHT... NEVER CONSIDERED...!
ALL THESE KIDNAPPINGS... CRIMES...COULD THEY BE CONNECTED IN SOME WAY?
YOU ARE A REPORTER, PETER... OF A SORT...
WHOA, FELLA...
...SOUNDS LIKE A BAD CASE OF CREEPING PARANOIA TO OLD M.J..!
NOBODY'S OUT TO GET YOU THROUGH YOUR AUNT, MR. PARKER...SHE'S PROBABLY JUST OUT DIGGING A WHOLE NEW SCENE, THAT'S ALL!
...IT'S NOT AS THOUGH YOU HAD ENEMIES, Y'KNOW, HAND-SOME?
G-GUESS YOU'RE RIGHT, MARY JANE--
--MAYBE I'LL SEE YOU LATER.
I'VE GOT TO GET A HANDLE ON MYSELF--PULL MY MIND TOGETHER!
WHAT MRS. WATSON SAID JUST NOW --SUPPOSE SOMEONE WERE TRYING TO GET TO ME--?
--ONLY IT'S NOT INNOCENT NEWS PHOTOG PARKER WHO'S THE GOAL--
--IT'S A WEB-SLINGING VIGILANTE CALLED SPIDER-MAN!
IF THAT'S TRUE--
--IT MEANS EVERYTHING I'VE EVER FEARED--HAS HAPPENED!
SOMEHOW, SOMEBODY MAY HAVE DISCOVERED SPIDEY'S ALTER-EGO...
...AND WITH IT, A GENTLE OLD LADY HE CALLS AUNT MAY!
ONLY ONE THING TO DO--

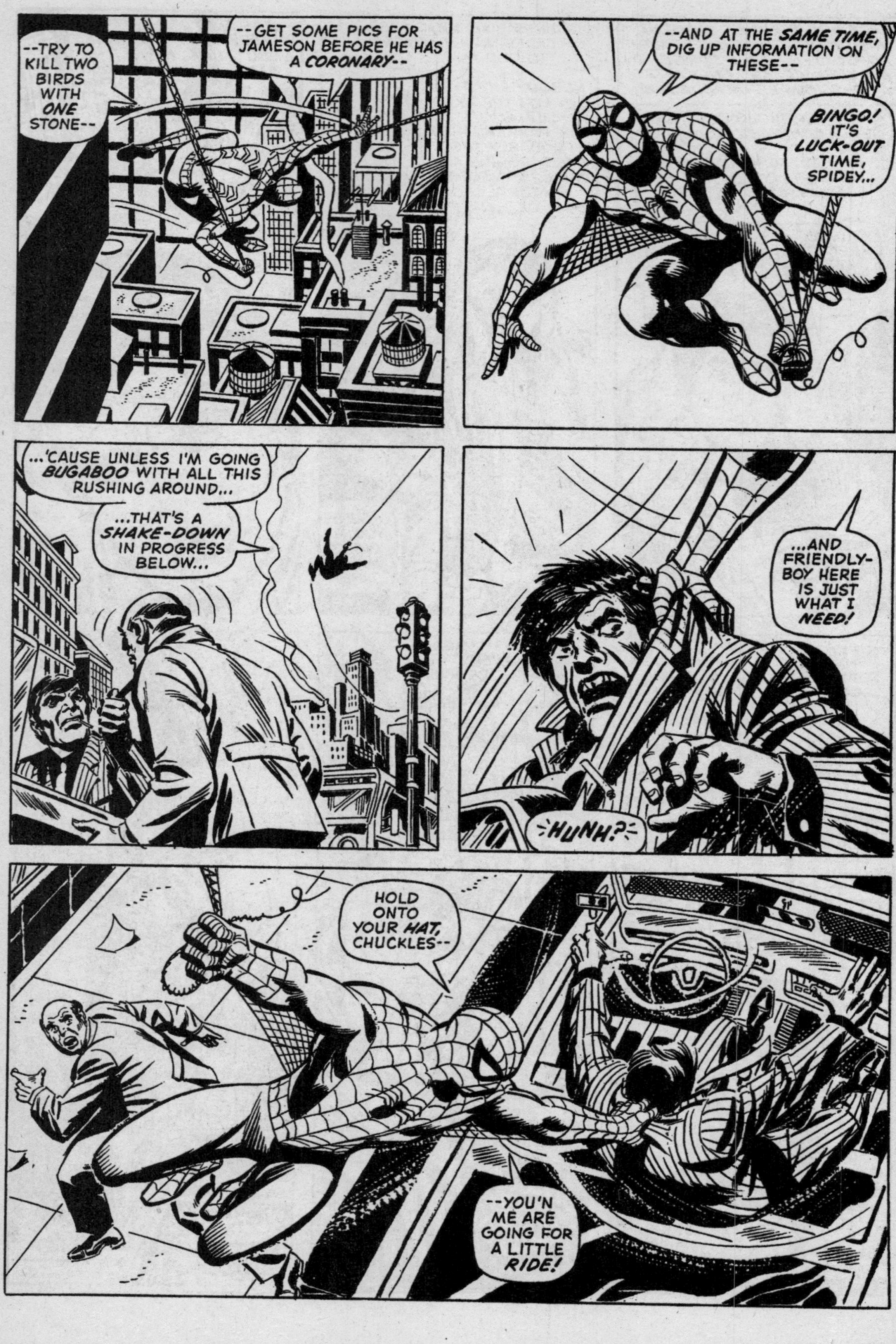
--TRY TO KILL TWO BIRDS WITH ONE STONE--
--GET SOME PICS FOR JAMESON BEFORE HE HAS A CORONARY--
--AND AT THE SAME TIME, DIG UP INFORMATION ON THESE--
BINGO! IT'S LUCK-OUT TIME, SPIDEY...
...'CAUSE UNLESS I'M GOING BUGABOO WITH ALL THIS RUSHING AROUND...
...THAT'S A SHAKE-DOWN IN PROGRESS BELOW...
...AND FRIENDLY-BOY HERE IS JUST WHAT I NEED!
HUNH?
HOLD ONTO YOUR HAT, CHUCKLES--
--YOU'N ME ARE GOING FOR A LITTLE RIDE!

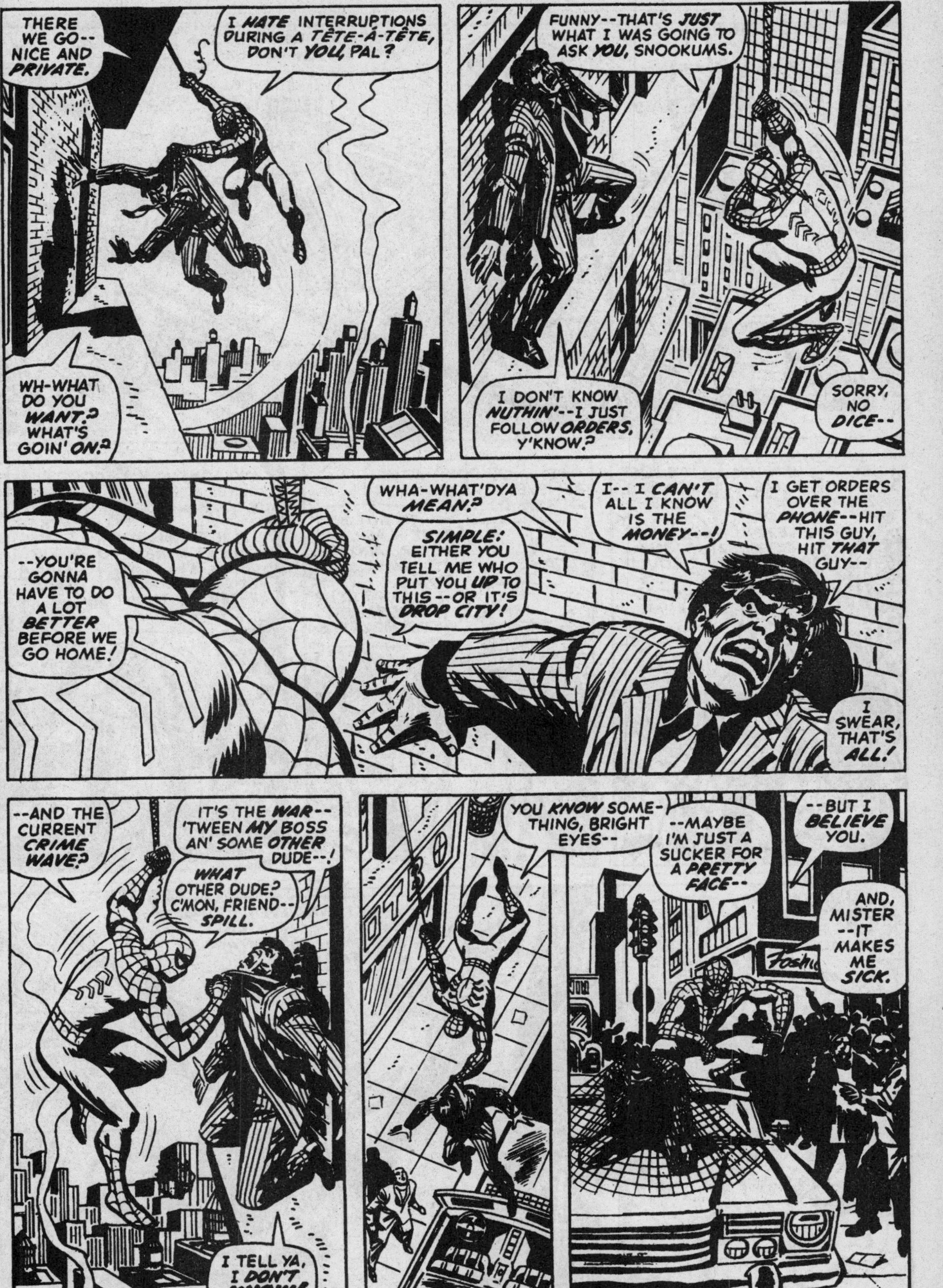
THERE WE GO--NICE AND PRIVATE.
I HATE INTERRUPTIONS DURING A TÊTE-À-TÊTE, DON'T YOU, PAL?
WH-WHAT DO YOU WANT? WHAT'S GOIN' ON?
FUNNY--THAT'S JUST WHAT I WAS GOING TO ASK YOU, SNOOKUMS.
I DON'T KNOW NUTHIN'--I JUST FOLLOW ORDERS, Y'KNOW?
SORRY, NO DICE--
--YOU'RE GONNA HAVE TO DO A LOT BETTER BEFORE WE GO HOME!
WHA-WHAT'DYA MEAN?
SIMPLE: EITHER YOU TELL ME WHO PUT YOU UP TO THIS--OR IT'S DROP CITY!
I--I CAN'T ALL I KNOW IS THE MONEY--!
I GET ORDERS OVER THE PHONE--HIT THIS GUY, HIT THAT GUY--
I SWEAR, THAT'S ALL!
--AND THE CURRENT CRIME WAVE?
IT'S THE WAR--'TWEEN MY BOSS AN' SOME OTHER DUDE--!
WHAT OTHER DUDE? C'MON, FRIEND--SPILL.
I TELL YA, I DON'T KNOW!
YOU KNOW SOME-THING, BRIGHT EYES--
--MAYBE I'M JUST A SUCKER FOR A PRETTY FACE--
--BUT I BELIEVE YOU.
AND, MISTER--IT MAKES ME SICK.

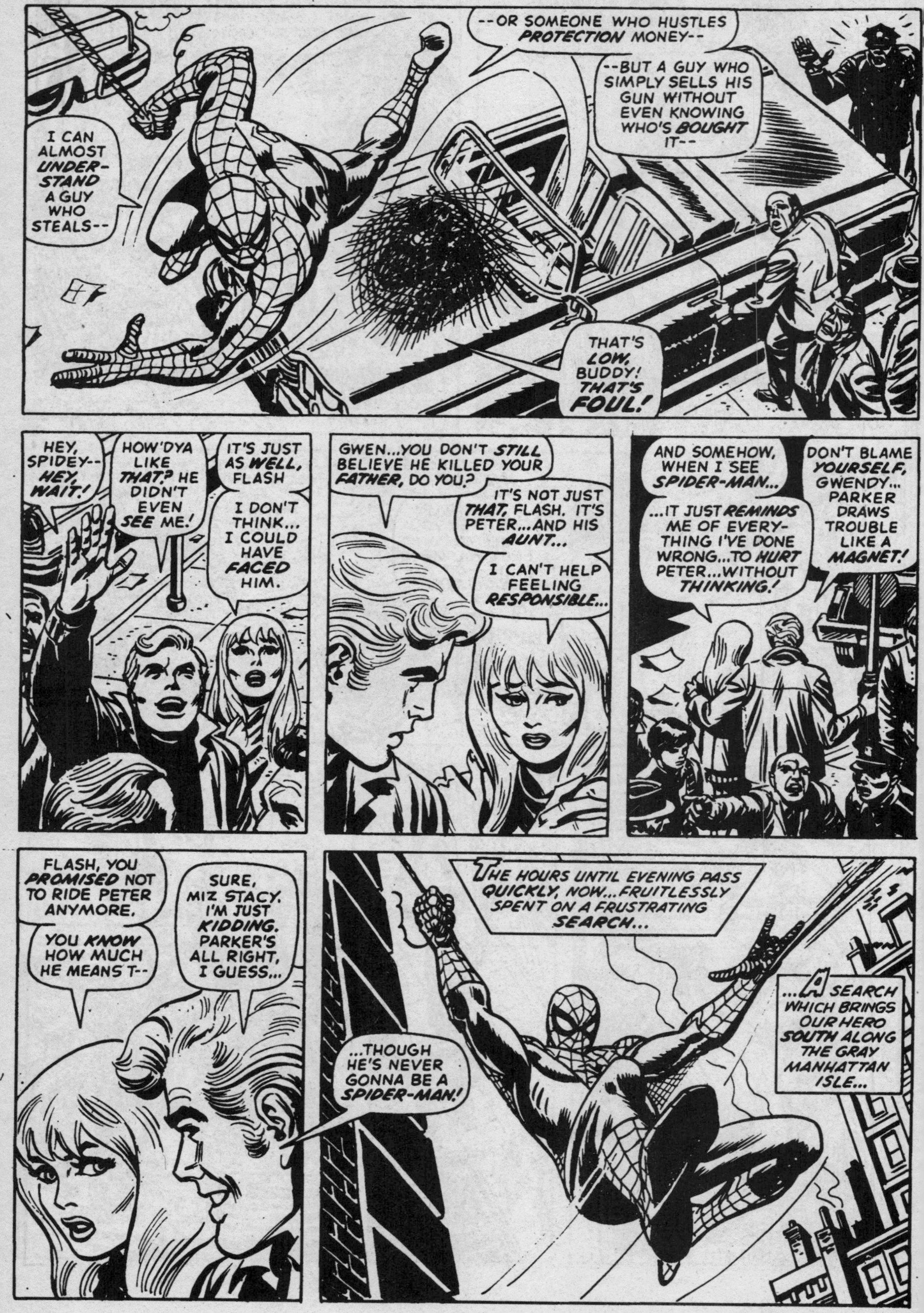
I CAN ALMOST UNDERSTAND A GUY WHO STEALS--
--OR SOMEONE WHO HUSTLES PROTECTION MONEY--
--BUT A GUY WHO SIMPLY SELLS HIS GUN WITHOUT EVEN KNOWING WHO'S BOUGHT IT--
THAT'S LOW, BUDDY! THAT'S FOUL!
HEY, SPIDEY--HEY, WAIT!
HOW'DYA LIKE THAT? HE DIDN'T EVEN SEE ME!
IT'S JUST AS WELL, FLASH
I DON'T THINK... I COULD HAVE FACED HIM.
GWEN...YOU DON'T STILL BELIEVE HE KILLED YOUR FATHER, DO YOU?
IT'S NOT JUST THAT, FLASH. IT'S PETER...AND HIS AUNT...
I CAN'T HELP FEELING RESPONSIBLE...
AND SOMEHOW, WHEN I SEE SPIDER-MAN...
...IT JUST REMINDS ME OF EVERYTHING I'VE DONE WRONG...TO HURT PETER...WITHOUT THINKING!
DON'T BLAME YOURSELF, GWENDY... PARKER DRAWS TROUBLE LIKE A MAGNET!
FLASH, YOU PROMISED NOT TO RIDE PETER ANYMORE.
YOU KNOW HOW MUCH HE MEANS T--
SURE, MIZ STACY. I'M JUST KIDDING. PARKER'S ALL RIGHT, I GUESS...
...THOUGH HE'S NEVER GONNA BE A SPIDER-MAN!
THE HOURS UNTIL EVENING PASS QUICKLY, NOW...FRUITLESSLY SPENT ON A FRUSTRATING SEARCH...
...A SEARCH WHICH BRINGS OUR HERO SOUTH ALONG THE GRAY MANHATTAN ISLE...

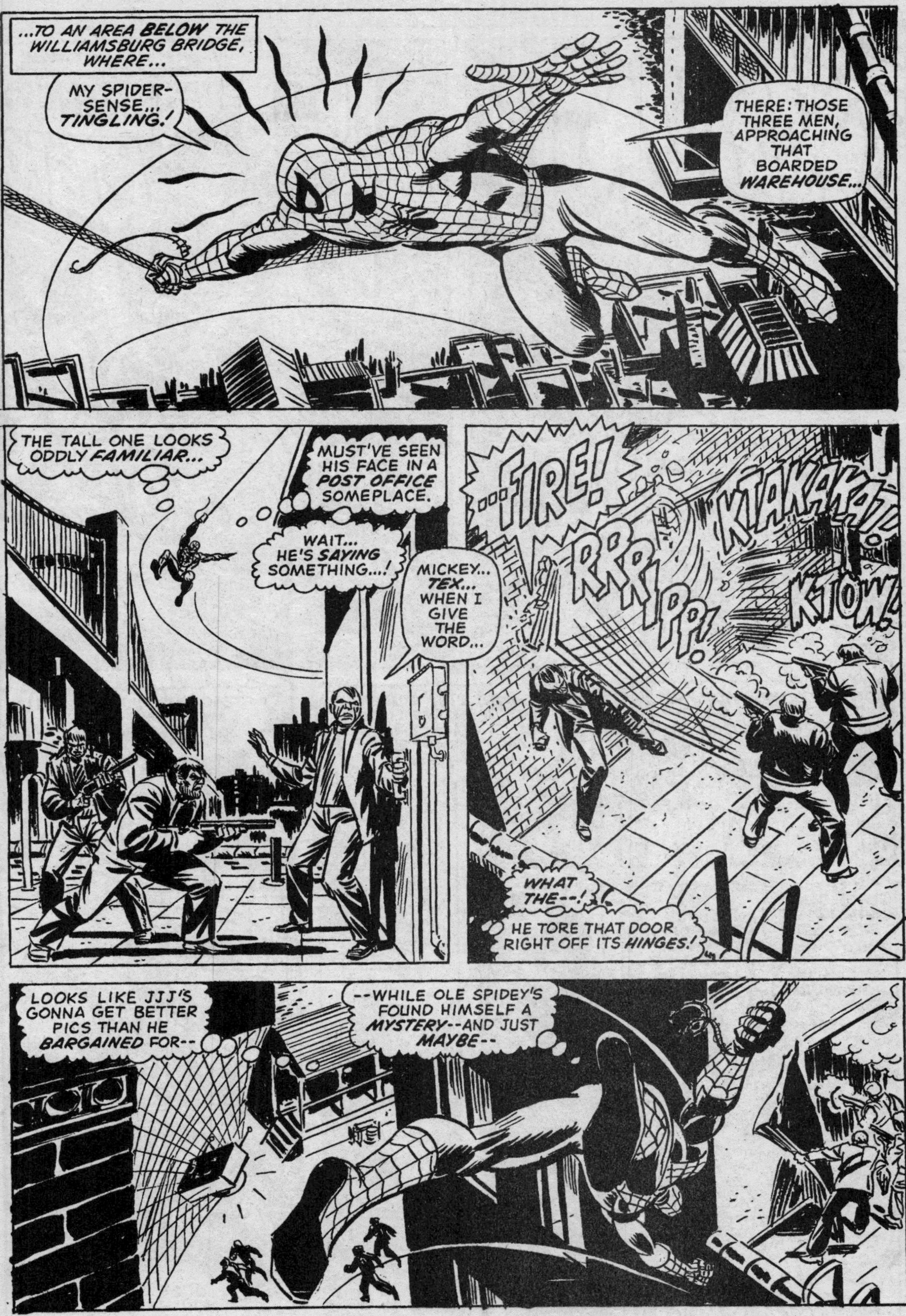
...TO AN AREA BELOW THE WILLIAMSBURG BRIDGE, WHERE...
MY SPIDER-SENSE... TINGLING!
THERE: THOSE THREE MEN, APPROACHING THAT BOARDED WAREHOUSE...
THE TALL ONE LOOKS ODDLY FAMILIAR...
MUST'VE SEEN HIS FACE IN A POST OFFICE SOMEPLACE.
WAIT... HE'S SAYING SOMETHING...!
MICKEY... TEX... WHEN I GIVE THE WORD...
...FIRE!
RRRIPP!
KTAKAKAT!
KTOW!
WHAT THE--!
HE TORE THAT DOOR RIGHT OFF ITS HINGES!
LOOKS LIKE JJJ'S GONNA GET BETTER PICS THAN HE BARGAINED FOR--
--WHILE OLE SPIDEY'S FOUND HIMSELF A MYSTERY--AND JUST MAYBE--

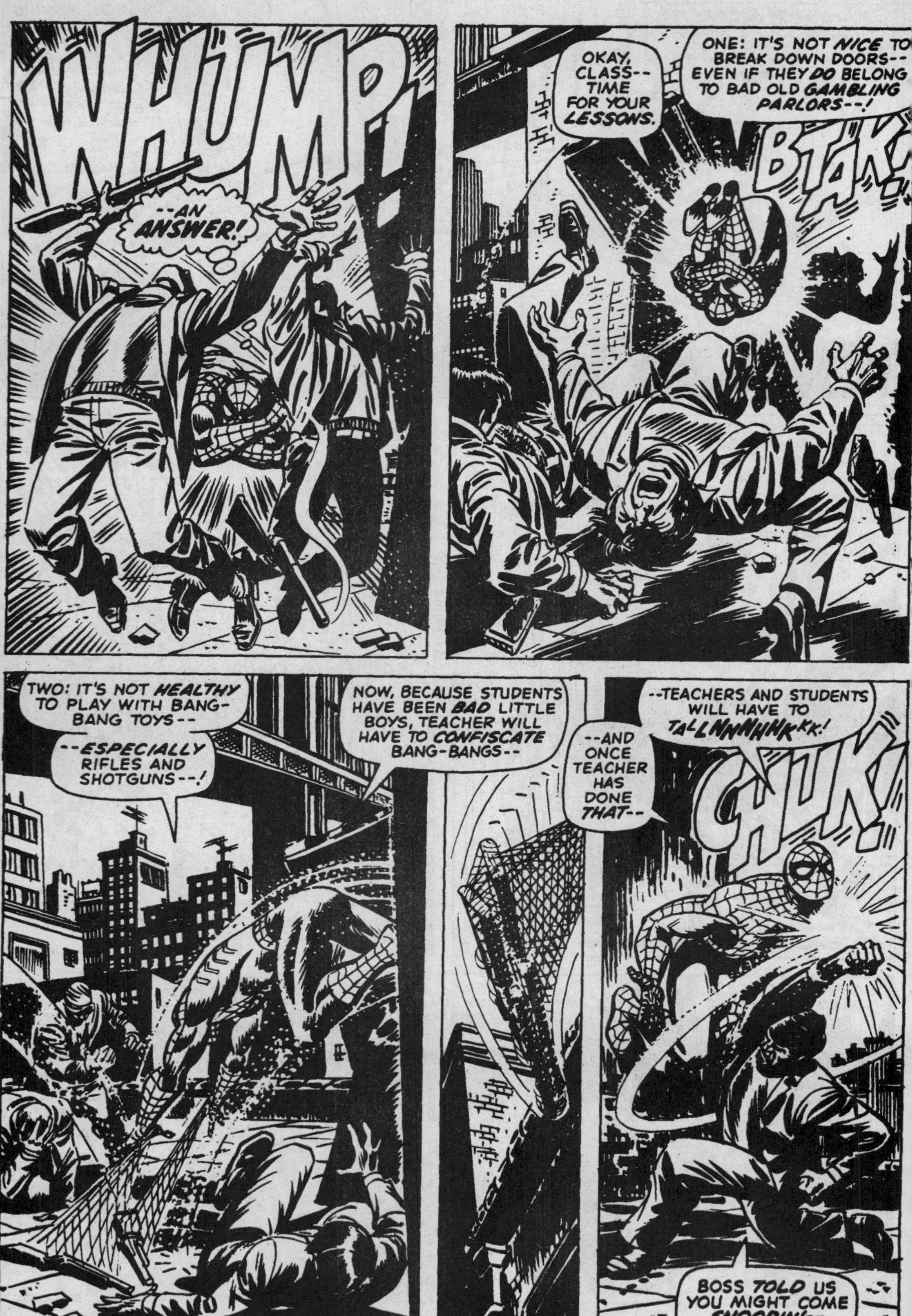
WHUMP!
--AN ANSWER!
OKAY, CLASS--TIME FOR YOUR LESSONS.
ONE: IT'S NOT NICE TO BREAK DOWN DOORS--EVEN IF THEY DO BELONG TO BAD OLD GAMBLING PARLORS--!
BTAK!
TWO: IT'S NOT HEALTHY TO PLAY WITH BANG-BANG TOYS--
--ESPECIALLY RIFLES AND SHOTGUNS--!
NOW, BECAUSE STUDENTS HAVE BEEN BAD LITTLE BOYS, TEACHER WILL HAVE TO CONFISCATE BANG-BANGS--
--AND ONCE TEACHER HAS DONE THAT--
--TEACHERS AND STUDENTS WILL HAVE TO TALLNNNHHKKK!
CHUK!
BOSS TOLD US YOU MIGHT COME SNOOPIN'--

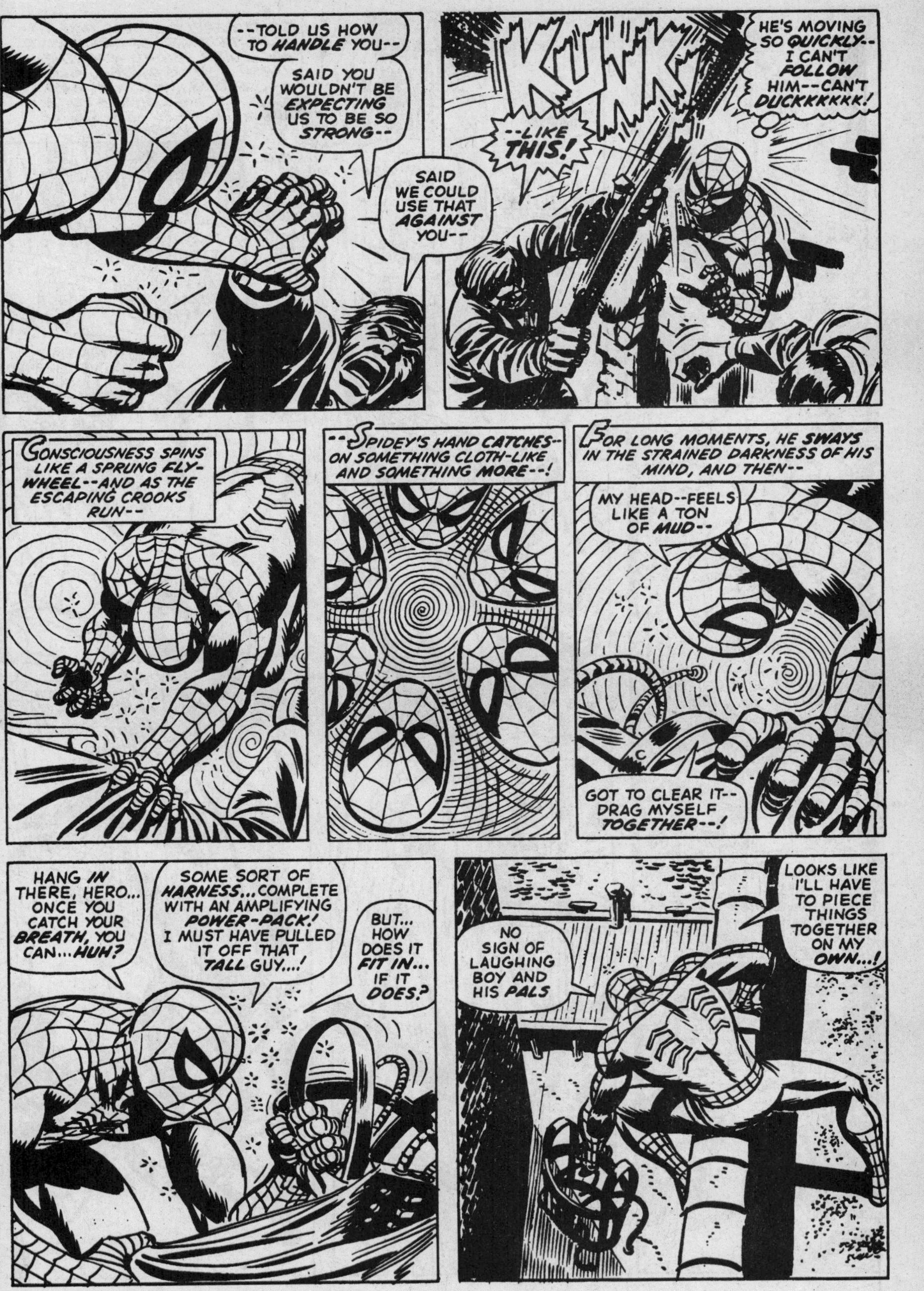
--TOLD US HOW TO HANDLE YOU--
SAID YOU WOULDN'T BE EXPECTING US TO BE SO STRONG--
SAID WE COULD USE THAT AGAINST YOU--
KUNK
--LIKE THIS!
HE'S MOVING SO QUICKLY-- I CAN'T FOLLOW HIM--CAN'T DUCKKKKKK!
CONSCIOUSNESS SPINS LIKE A SPRUNG FLY-WHEEL--AND AS THE ESCAPING CROOKS RUN--
--SPIDEY'S HAND CATCHES--ON SOMETHING CLOTH-LIKE AND SOMETHING MORE--!
FOR LONG MOMENTS, HE SWAYS IN THE STRAINED DARKNESS OF HIS MIND, AND THEN--
MY HEAD--FEELS LIKE A TON OF MUD--
GOT TO CLEAR IT--DRAG MYSELF TOGETHER--!
HANG IN THERE, HERO... ONCE YOU CATCH YOUR BREATH, YOU CAN...HUH?
SOME SORT OF HARNESS...COMPLETE WITH AN AMPLIFYING POWER-PACK! I MUST HAVE PULLED IT OFF THAT TALL GUY....!
BUT... HOW DOES IT FIT IN... IF IT DOES?
NO SIGN OF LAUGHING BOY AND HIS PALS
LOOKS LIKE I'LL HAVE TO PIECE THINGS TOGETHER ON MY OWN...!

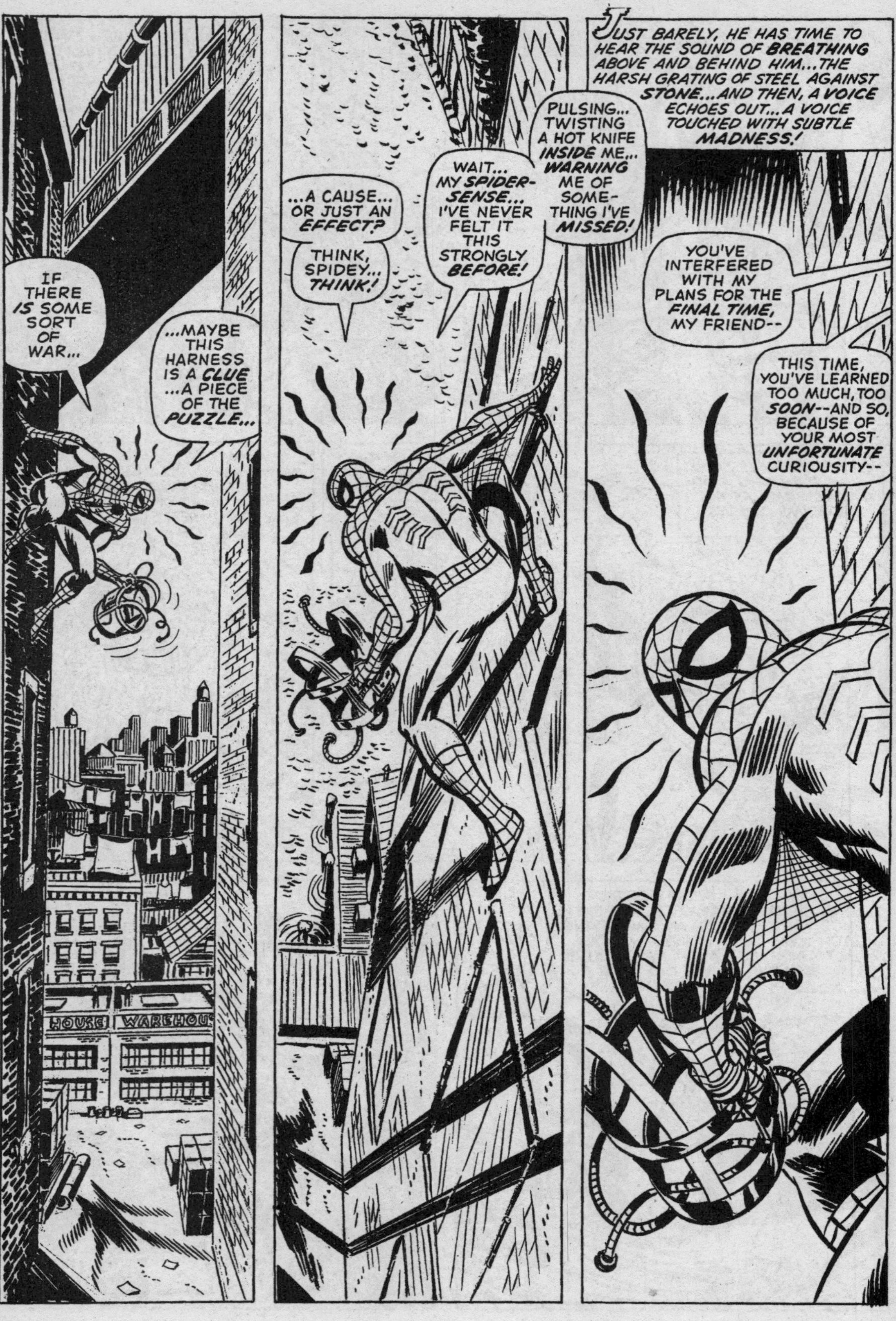
IF THERE IS SOME SORT OF WAR...
...MAYBE THIS HARNESS IS A CLUE ...A PIECE OF THE PUZZLE...
HOUSE
WAREHOU
...A CAUSE... OR JUST AN EFFECT?
THINK, SPIDEY... THINK!
WAIT... MY SPIDER-SENSE... I'VE NEVER FELT IT THIS STRONGLY BEFORE!
PULSING... TWISTING A HOT KNIFE INSIDE ME... WARNING ME OF SOMETHING I'VE MISSED!
JUST BARELY, HE HAS TIME TO HEAR THE SOUND OF BREATHING ABOVE AND BEHIND HIM...THE HARSH GRATING OF STEEL AGAINST STONE...AND THEN, A VOICE ECHOES OUT...A VOICE TOUCHED WITH SUBTLE MADNESS!
YOU'VE INTERFERED WITH MY PLANS FOR THE FINAL TIME, MY FRIEND--
THIS TIME, YOU'VE LEARNED TOO MUCH, TOO SOON--AND SO, BECAUSE OF YOUR MOST UNFORTUNATE CURIOUSITY--

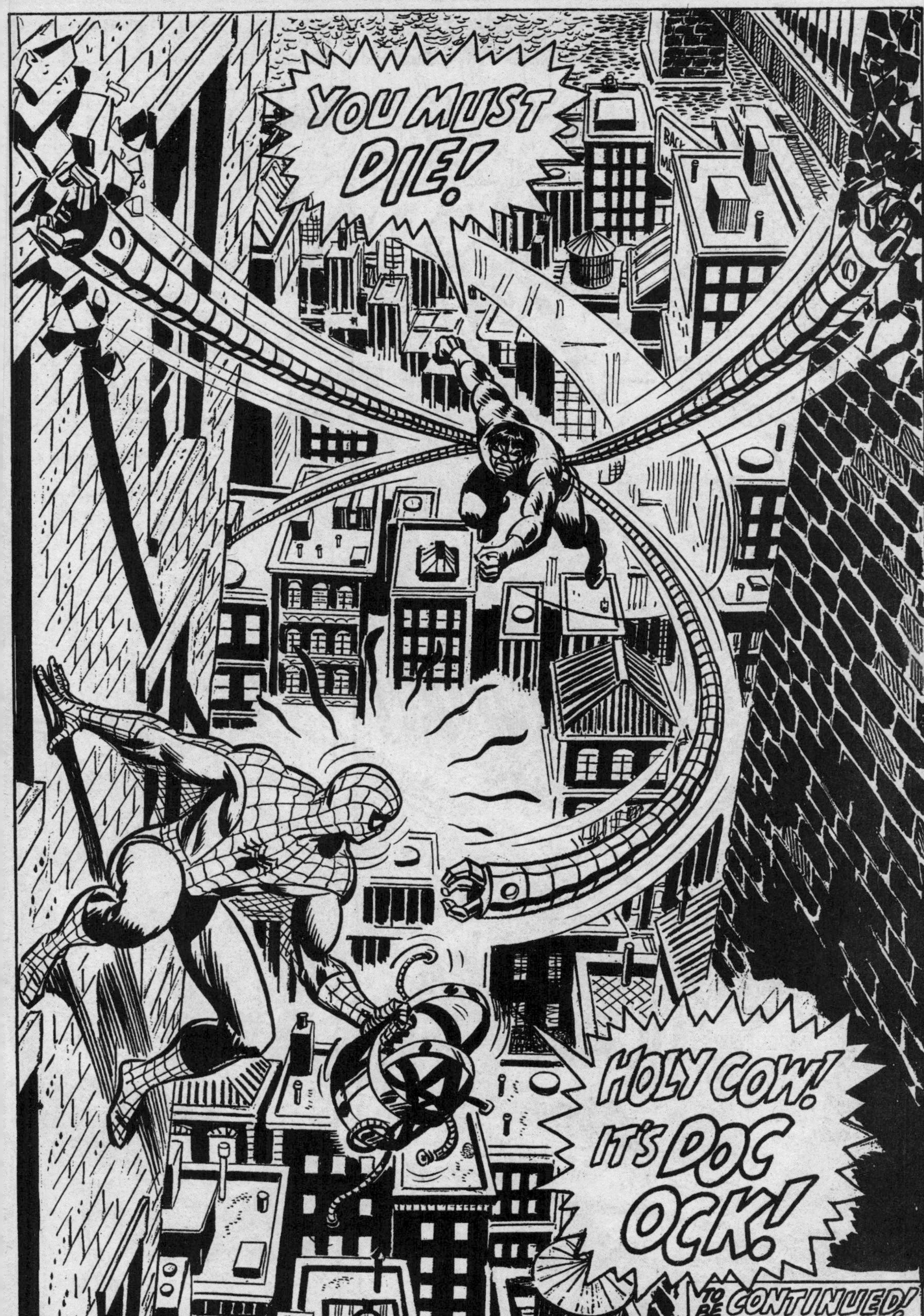
YOU MUST DIE!
HOLY COW! IT'S DOC OCK!
TO BE CONTINUED!

SPIDER-MAN
MARVEL COMICS GROUP
20¢
113
OCT
02457
APPROVED BY THE COMICS CODE AUTHORITY
the AMAZING SPIDER-MAN
HANG ON TO YOUR WEBBING! DOCTOR OCTOPUS IS BACK!
ROMITA
Photo by Peter Parker
EXCLUSIVE TO THE BUGLE! THE MYSTERIOUS MASKED SPIDER-MAN DEFEATED BY THE SUPER-POWERED KILLER KNOWN AS DR. OCTOPUS!

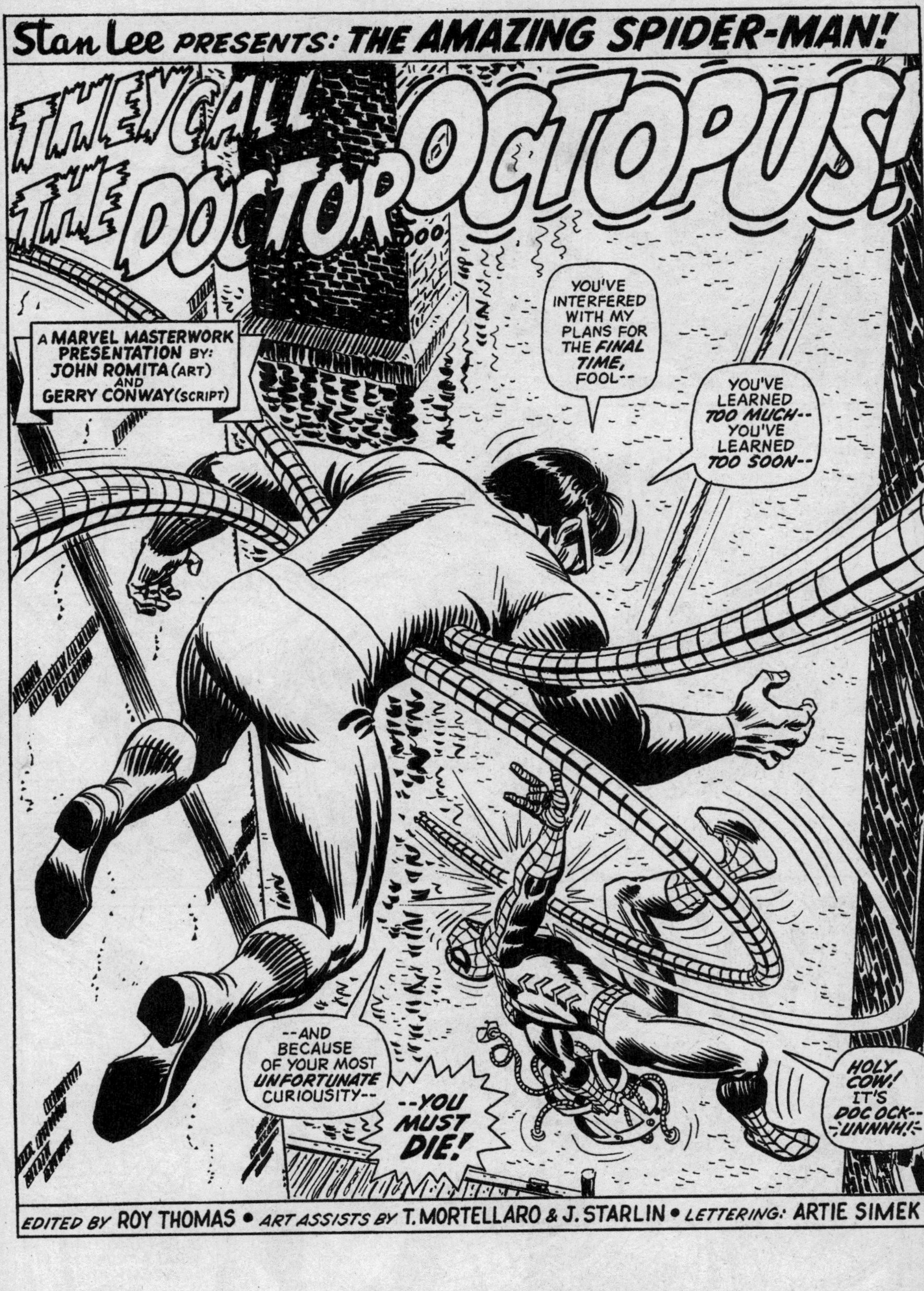
Stan Lee PRESENTS: THE AMAZING SPIDER-MAN!
THEY CALL THE DOCTOR OCTOPUS!
A MARVEL MASTERWORK PRESENTATION BY: JOHN ROMITA (ART) AND GERRY CONWAY (SCRIPT)
YOU'VE INTERFERED WITH MY PLANS FOR THE FINAL TIME, FOOL--
YOU'VE LEARNED TOO MUCH-- YOU'VE LEARNED TOO SOON--
--AND BECAUSE OF YOUR MOST UNFORTUNATE CURIOUSITY--
--YOU MUST DIE!
HOLY COW! IT'S DOC OCK-- UNNNH!
EDITED BY ROY THOMAS • ART ASSISTS BY T. MORTELLARO & J. STARLIN • LETTERING: ARTIE SIMEK

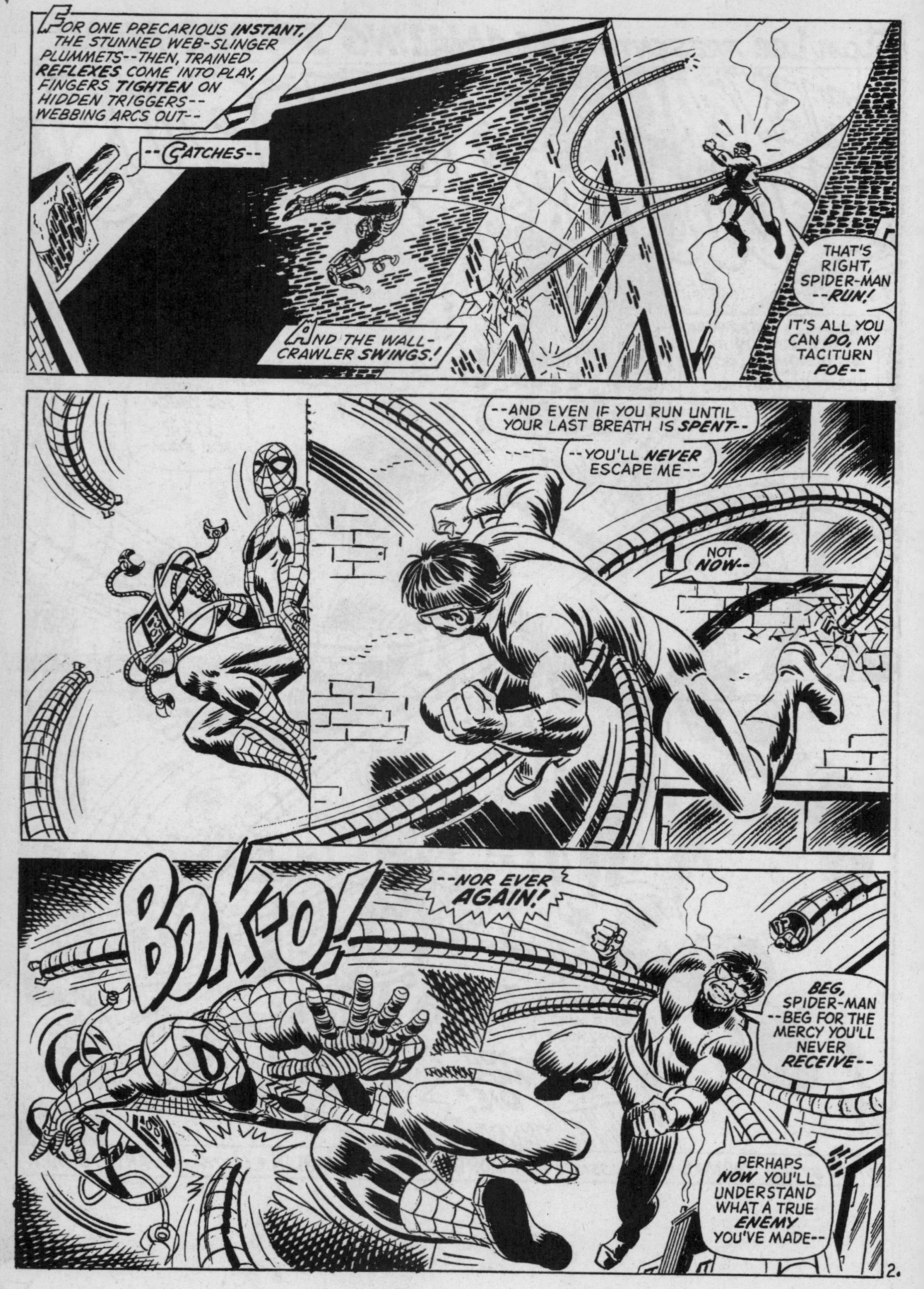
FOR ONE PRECARIOUS INSTANT, THE STUNNED WEB-SLINGER PLUMMETS--THEN, TRAINED REFLEXES COME INTO PLAY, FINGERS TIGHTEN ON HIDDEN TRIGGERS--WEBBING ARCS OUT--
--CATCHES--
AND THE WALL-CRAWLER SWINGS!
THAT'S RIGHT, SPIDER-MAN --RUN!
IT'S ALL YOU CAN DO, MY TACITURN FOE--
--AND EVEN IF YOU RUN UNTIL YOUR LAST BREATH IS SPENT--
--YOU'LL NEVER ESCAPE ME--
NOT NOW--
BOK-O!
--NOR EVER AGAIN!
BEG, SPIDER-MAN --BEG FOR THE MERCY YOU'LL NEVER RECEIVE--
PERHAPS NOW YOU'LL UNDERSTAND WHAT A TRUE ENEMY YOU'VE MADE--
2.

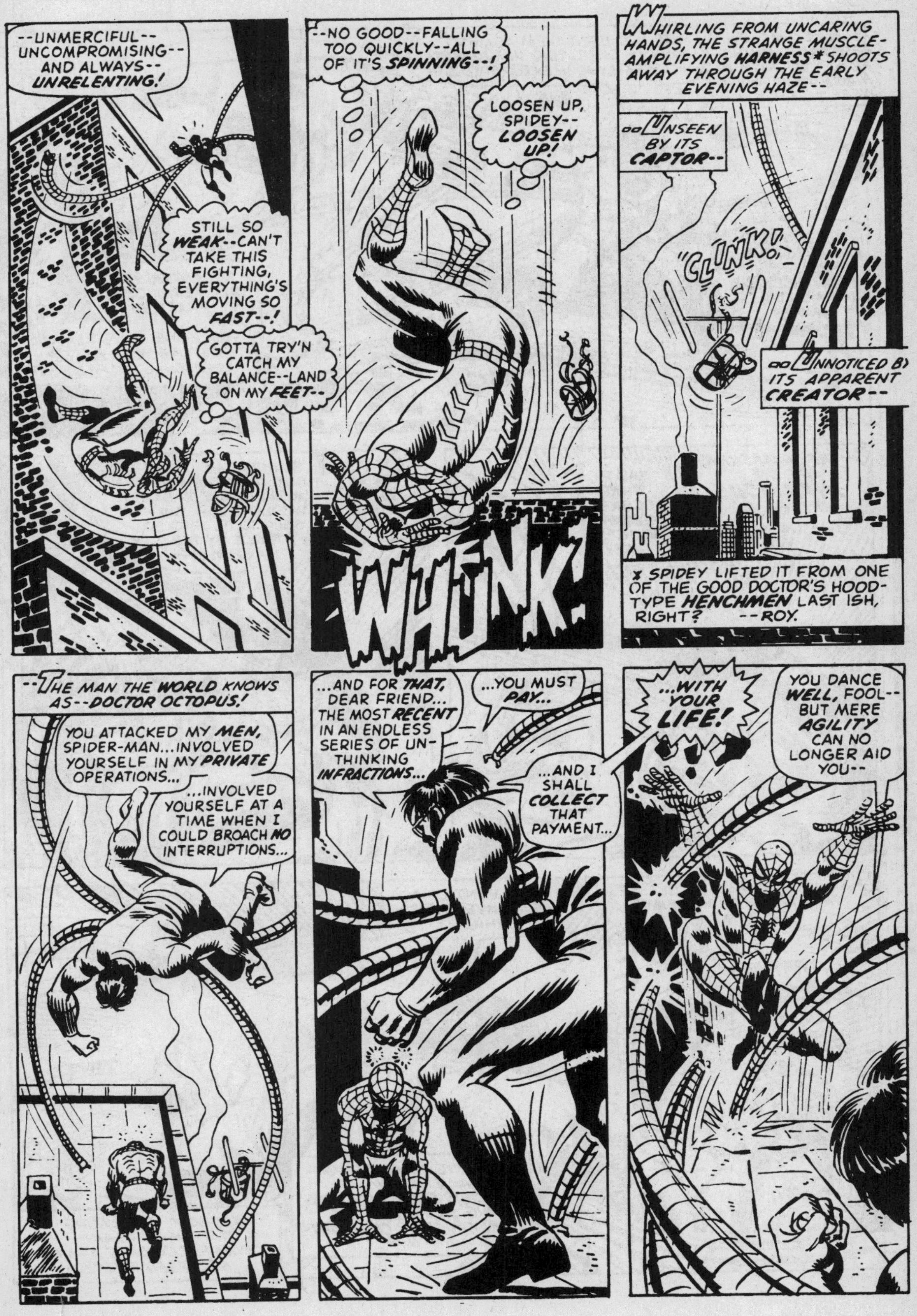
--UNMERCIFUL-- UNCOMPROMISING-- AND ALWAYS-- UNRELENTING!
STILL SO WEAK--CAN'T TAKE THIS FIGHTING, EVERYTHING'S MOVING SO FAST--!
GOTTA TRY'N CATCH MY BALANCE--LAND ON MY FEET--
--NO GOOD--FALLING TOO QUICKLY--ALL OF IT'S SPINNING--!
LOOSEN UP, SPIDEY-- LOOSEN UP!
WHUNK!
WHIRLING FROM UNCARING HANDS, THE STRANGE MUSCLE-AMPLIFYING HARNESS* SHOOTS AWAY THROUGH THE EARLY EVENING HAZE--
--UNSEEN BY ITS CAPTOR--
CLINK!
--UNNOTICED BY ITS APPARENT CREATOR--
* SPIDEY LIFTED IT FROM ONE OF THE GOOD DOCTOR'S HOOD-TYPE HENCHMEN LAST ISH, RIGHT? --ROY.
--THE MAN THE WORLD KNOWS AS--DOCTOR OCTOPUS!
YOU ATTACKED MY MEN, SPIDER-MAN...INVOLVED YOURSELF IN MY PRIVATE OPERATIONS...
...INVOLVED YOURSELF AT A TIME WHEN I COULD BROACH NO INTERRUPTIONS...
...AND FOR THAT, DEAR FRIEND... THE MOST RECENT IN AN ENDLESS SERIES OF UN-THINKING INFRACTIONS...
...YOU MUST PAY...
...AND I SHALL COLLECT THAT PAYMENT...
...WITH YOUR LIFE!
YOU DANCE WELL, FOOL-- BUT MERE AGILITY CAN NO LONGER AID YOU--

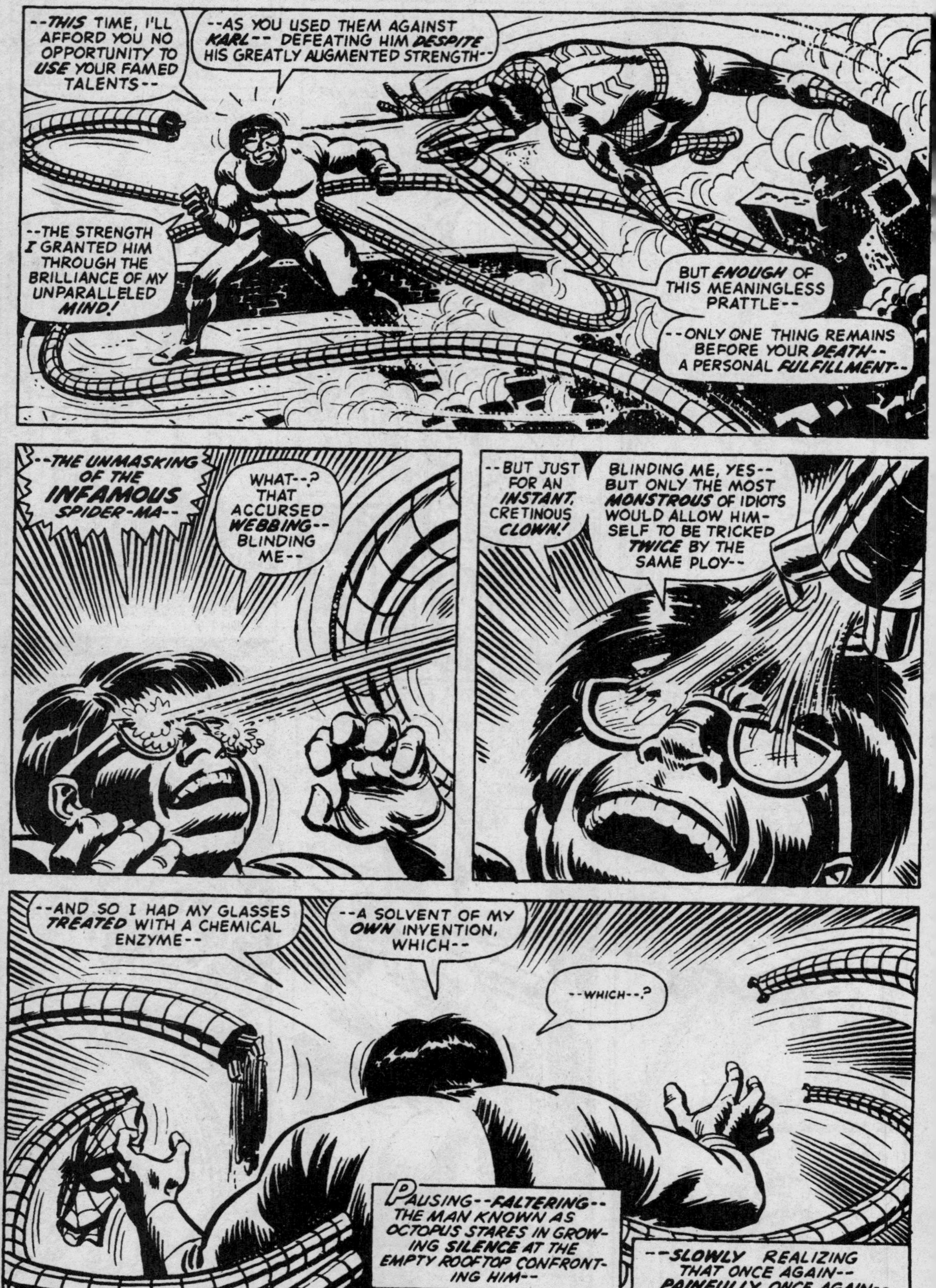

--THIS TIME, I'LL AFFORD YOU NO OPPORTUNITY TO USE YOUR FAMED TALENTS--
--AS YOU USED THEM AGAINST KARL-- DEFEATING HIM DESPITE HIS GREATLY AUGMENTED STRENGTH--
--THE STRENGTH I GRANTED HIM THROUGH THE BRILLIANCE OF MY UNPARALLELED MIND!
BUT ENOUGH OF THIS MEANINGLESS PRATTLE--
--ONLY ONE THING REMAINS BEFORE YOUR DEATH-- A PERSONAL FULFILLMENT--
--THE UNMASKING OF THE INFAMOUS SPIDER-MA--
WHAT--? THAT ACCURSED WEBBING-- BLINDING ME--
--BUT JUST FOR AN INSTANT, CRETINOUS CLOWN!
BLINDING ME, YES-- BUT ONLY THE MOST MONSTROUS OF IDIOTS WOULD ALLOW HIMSELF TO BE TRICKED TWICE BY THE SAME PLOY--
--AND SO I HAD MY GLASSES TREATED WITH A CHEMICAL ENZYME--
--A SOLVENT OF MY OWN INVENTION, WHICH--
--WHICH--?
PAUSING--FALTERING--THE MAN KNOWN AS OCTOPUS STARES IN GROWING SILENCE AT THE EMPTY ROOFTOP CONFRONTING HIM--
--SLOWLY REALIZING THAT ONCE AGAIN-- PAINFULLY, ONCE AGAIN-- HE'S BEEN TRICKED--

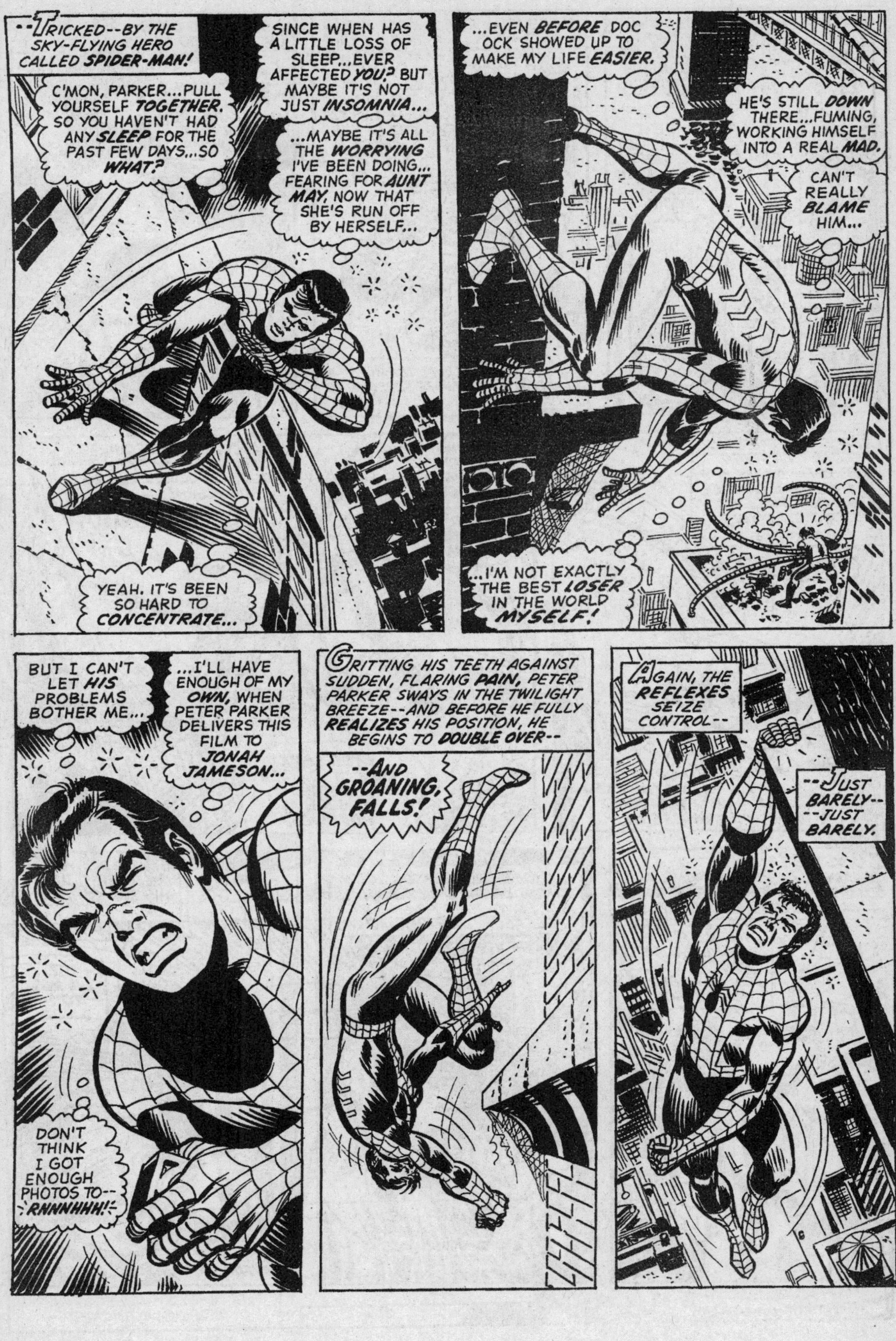
--TRICKED--BY THE SKY-FLYING HERO CALLED SPIDER-MAN!
C'MON, PARKER...PULL YOURSELF TOGETHER. SO YOU HAVEN'T HAD ANY SLEEP FOR THE PAST FEW DAYS...SO WHAT?
SINCE WHEN HAS A LITTLE LOSS OF SLEEP...EVER AFFECTED YOU? BUT MAYBE IT'S NOT JUST INSOMNIA...
...MAYBE IT'S ALL THE WORRYING I'VE BEEN DOING... FEARING FOR AUNT MAY, NOW THAT SHE'S RUN OFF BY HERSELF...
YEAH. IT'S BEEN SO HARD TO CONCENTRATE...
...EVEN BEFORE DOC OCK SHOWED UP TO MAKE MY LIFE EASIER.
HE'S STILL DOWN THERE...FUMING, WORKING HIMSELF INTO A REAL MAD.
CAN'T REALLY BLAME HIM...
...I'M NOT EXACTLY THE BEST LOSER IN THE WORLD MYSELF!
BUT I CAN'T LET HIS PROBLEMS BOTHER ME...
...I'LL HAVE ENOUGH OF MY OWN, WHEN PETER PARKER DELIVERS THIS FILM TO JONAH JAMESON...
DON'T THINK I GOT ENOUGH PHOTOS TO--RNNNHHH!
GRITTING HIS TEETH AGAINST SUDDEN, FLARING PAIN, PETER PARKER SWAYS IN THE TWILIGHT BREEZE--AND BEFORE HE FULLY REALIZES HIS POSITION, HE BEGINS TO DOUBLE OVER--
--AND GROANING, FALLS!
AGAIN, THE REFLEXES SEIZE CONTROL--
--JUST BARELY-- --JUST BARELY.

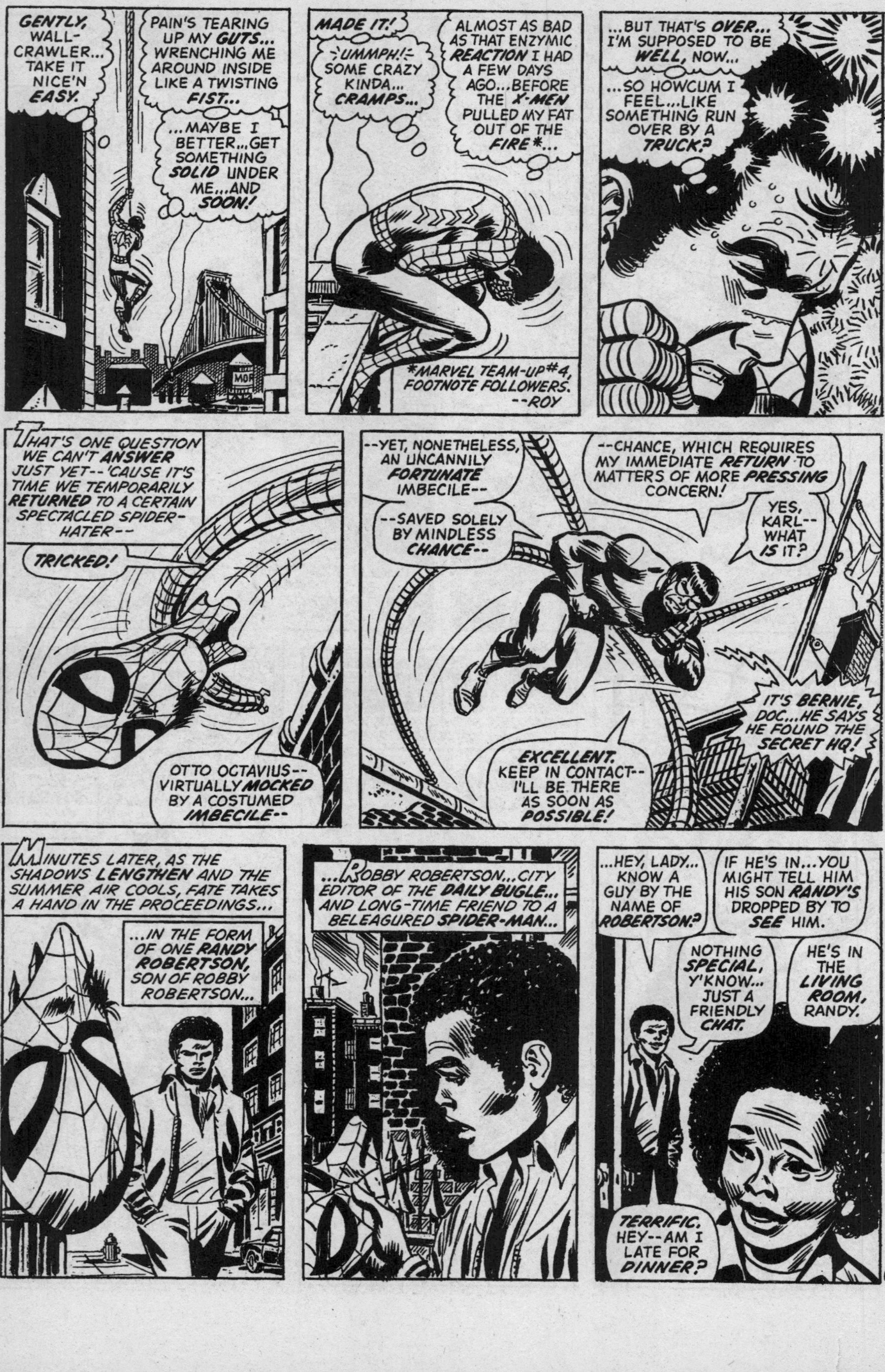
GENTLY, WALL-CRAWLER... TAKE IT NICE'N EASY.
PAIN'S TEARING UP MY GUTS... WRENCHING ME AROUND INSIDE LIKE A TWISTING FIST...
...MAYBE I BETTER...GET SOMETHING SOLID UNDER ME...AND SOON!
MADE IT!
UMMPH! SOME CRAZY KINDA... CRAMPS...
ALMOST AS BAD AS THAT ENZYMIC REACTION I HAD A FEW DAYS AGO...BEFORE THE X-MEN PULLED MY FAT OUT OF THE FIRE*...
*MARVEL TEAM-UP #4, FOOTNOTE FOLLOWERS. --ROY
...BUT THAT'S OVER... I'M SUPPOSED TO BE WELL, NOW...
...SO HOWCUM I FEEL...LIKE SOMETHING RUN OVER BY A TRUCK?
THAT'S ONE QUESTION WE CAN'T ANSWER JUST YET--'CAUSE IT'S TIME WE TEMPORARILY RETURNED TO A CERTAIN SPECTACLED SPIDER-HATER--
TRICKED!
OTTO OCTAVIUS--VIRTUALLY MOCKED BY A COSTUMED IMBECILE--
--YET, NONETHELESS, AN UNCANNILY FORTUNATE IMBECILE--
--SAVED SOLELY BY MINDLESS CHANCE--
--CHANCE, WHICH REQUIRES MY IMMEDIATE RETURN TO MATTERS OF MORE PRESSING CONCERN!
YES, KARL--WHAT IS IT?
IT'S BERNIE, DOC...HE SAYS HE FOUND THE SECRET HQ!
EXCELLENT. KEEP IN CONTACT--I'LL BE THERE AS SOON AS POSSIBLE!
MINUTES LATER, AS THE SHADOWS LENGTHEN AND THE SUMMER AIR COOLS, FATE TAKES A HAND IN THE PROCEEDINGS...
...IN THE FORM OF ONE RANDY ROBERTSON, SON OF ROBBY ROBERTSON...
...ROBBY ROBERTSON...CITY EDITOR OF THE DAILY BUGLE...AND LONG-TIME FRIEND TO A BELEAGURED SPIDER-MAN...
...HEY, LADY... KNOW A GUY BY THE NAME OF ROBERTSON?
IF HE'S IN...YOU MIGHT TELL HIM HIS SON RANDY'S DROPPED BY TO SEE HIM.
NOTHING SPECIAL, Y'KNOW... JUST A FRIENDLY CHAT.
HE'S IN THE LIVING ROOM, RANDY.
TERRIFIC. HEY--AM I LATE FOR DINNER?

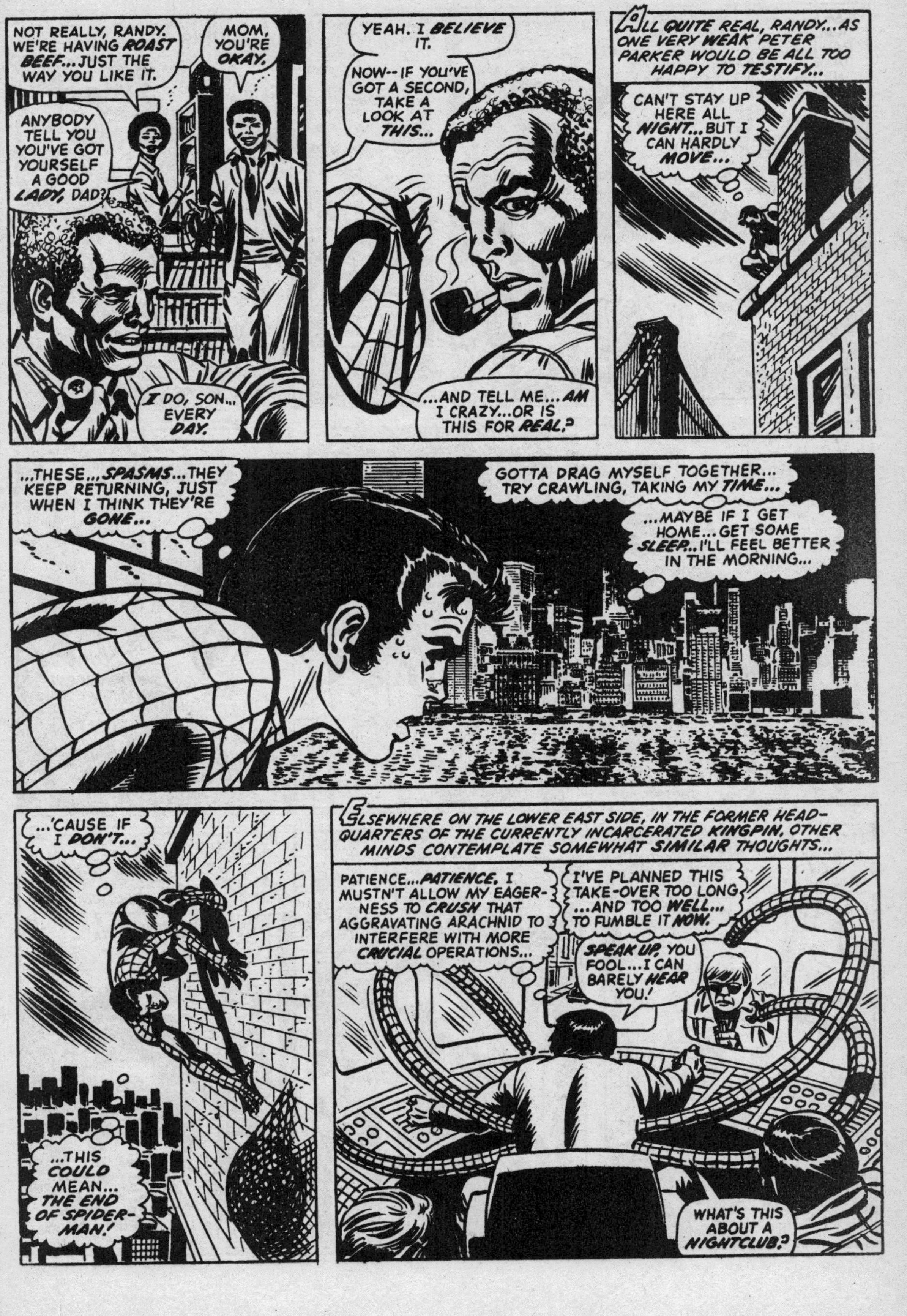
NOT REALLY, RANDY. WE'RE HAVING ROAST BEEF... JUST THE WAY YOU LIKE IT.
MOM, YOU'RE OKAY.
ANYBODY TELL YOU YOU'VE GOT YOURSELF A GOOD LADY, DAD?
I DO, SON... EVERY DAY.
YEAH. I BELIEVE IT.
NOW-- IF YOU'VE GOT A SECOND, TAKE A LOOK AT THIS...
...AND TELL ME... AM I CRAZY...OR IS THIS FOR REAL?
ALL QUITE REAL, RANDY... AS ONE VERY WEAK PETER PARKER WOULD BE ALL TOO HAPPY TO TESTIFY...
CAN'T STAY UP HERE ALL NIGHT... BUT I CAN HARDLY MOVE...
...THESE... SPASMS... THEY KEEP RETURNING, JUST WHEN I THINK THEY'RE GONE...
GOTTA DRAG MYSELF TOGETHER... TRY CRAWLING, TAKING MY TIME...
...MAYBE IF I GET HOME... GET SOME SLEEP... I'LL FEEL BETTER IN THE MORNING...
...'CAUSE IF I DON'T...
...THIS COULD MEAN... THE END OF SPIDER-MAN!
ELSEWHERE ON THE LOWER EAST SIDE, IN THE FORMER HEADQUARTERS OF THE CURRENTLY INCARCERATED KINGPIN, OTHER MINDS CONTEMPLATE SOMEWHAT SIMILAR THOUGHTS...
PATIENCE... PATIENCE. I MUSTN'T ALLOW MY EAGERNESS TO CRUSH THAT AGGRAVATING ARACHNID TO INTERFERE WITH MORE CRUCIAL OPERATIONS...
I'VE PLANNED THIS TAKE-OVER TOO LONG ...AND TOO WELL... TO FUMBLE IT NOW.
SPEAK UP, YOU FOOL... I CAN BARELY HEAR YOU!
WHAT'S THIS ABOUT A NIGHTCLUB?

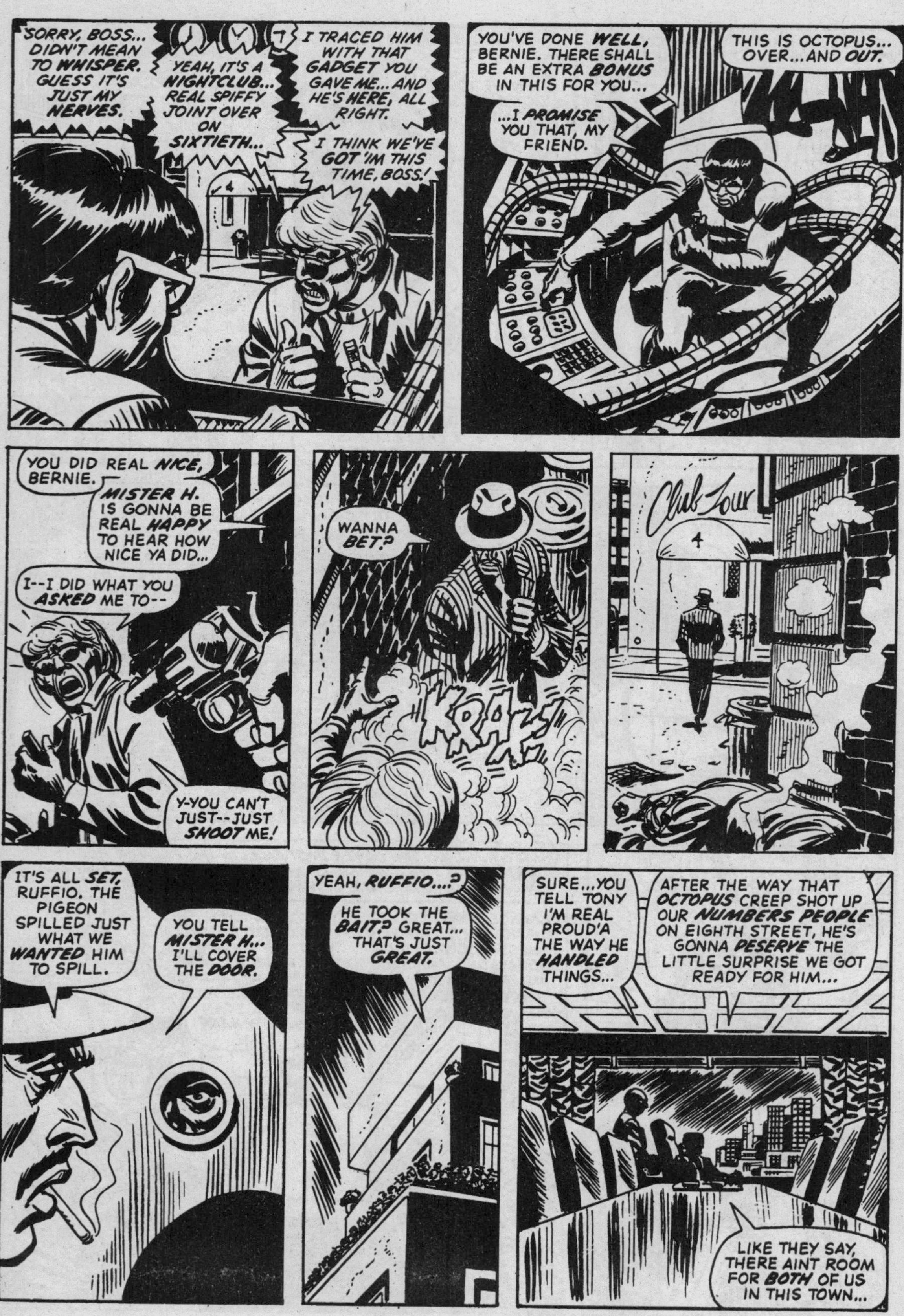
SORRY, BOSS... DIDN'T MEAN TO WHISPER. GUESS IT'S JUST MY NERVES.
YEAH, IT'S A NIGHTCLUB... REAL SPIFFY JOINT OVER ON SIXTIETH...
I TRACED HIM WITH THAT GADGET YOU GAVE ME... AND HE'S HERE, ALL RIGHT.
I THINK WE'VE GOT 'IM THIS TIME, BOSS!
YOU'VE DONE WELL, BERNIE. THERE SHALL BE AN EXTRA BONUS IN THIS FOR YOU...
...I PROMISE YOU THAT, MY FRIEND.
THIS IS OCTOPUS... OVER... AND OUT.
YOU DID REAL NICE, BERNIE.
MISTER H. IS GONNA BE REAL HAPPY TO HEAR HOW NICE YA DID...
I--I DID WHAT YOU ASKED ME TO--
Y-YOU CAN'T JUST--JUST SHOOT ME!
WANNA BET?
KRAK
Club Four
4
IT'S ALL SET, RUFFIO. THE PIGEON SPILLED JUST WHAT WE WANTED HIM TO SPILL.
YOU TELL MISTER H... I'LL COVER THE DOOR.
YEAH, RUFFIO...?
HE TOOK THE BAIT? GREAT... THAT'S JUST GREAT.
SURE... YOU TELL TONY I'M REAL PROUD'A THE WAY HE HANDLED THINGS...
AFTER THE WAY THAT OCTOPUS CREEP SHOT UP OUR NUMBERS PEOPLE ON EIGHTH STREET, HE'S GONNA DESERVE THE LITTLE SURPRISE WE GOT READY FOR HIM...
LIKE THEY SAY, THERE AINT ROOM FOR BOTH OF US IN THIS TOWN...

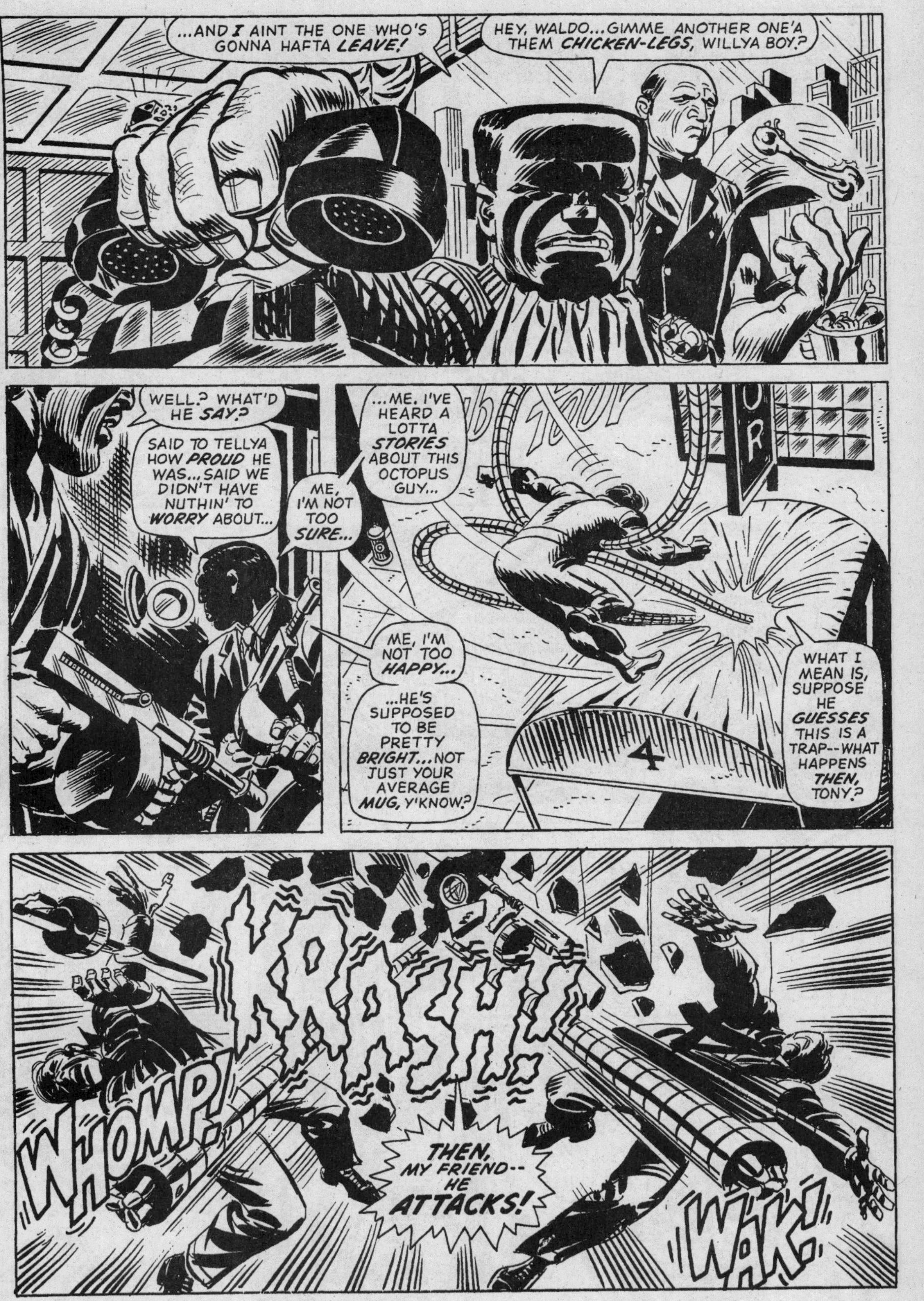

...AND I AINT THE ONE WHO'S GONNA HAFTA LEAVE!
HEY, WALDO...GIMME ANOTHER ONE'A THEM CHICKEN-LEGS, WILLYA BOY?
WELL? WHAT'D HE SAY?
SAID TO TELLYA HOW PROUD HE WAS...SAID WE DIDN'T HAVE NUTHIN' TO WORRY ABOUT...
ME, I'M NOT TOO SURE...
...ME. I'VE HEARD A LOTTA STORIES ABOUT THIS OCTOPUS GUY...
ME, I'M NOT TOO HAPPY...
...HE'S SUPPOSED TO BE PRETTY BRIGHT...NOT JUST YOUR AVERAGE MUG, Y'KNOW?
WHAT I MEAN IS, SUPPOSE HE GUESSES THIS IS A TRAP--WHAT HAPPENS THEN, TONY?
KRASH!
WHOMP!
THEN, MY FRIEND--HE ATTACKS!
WAK!

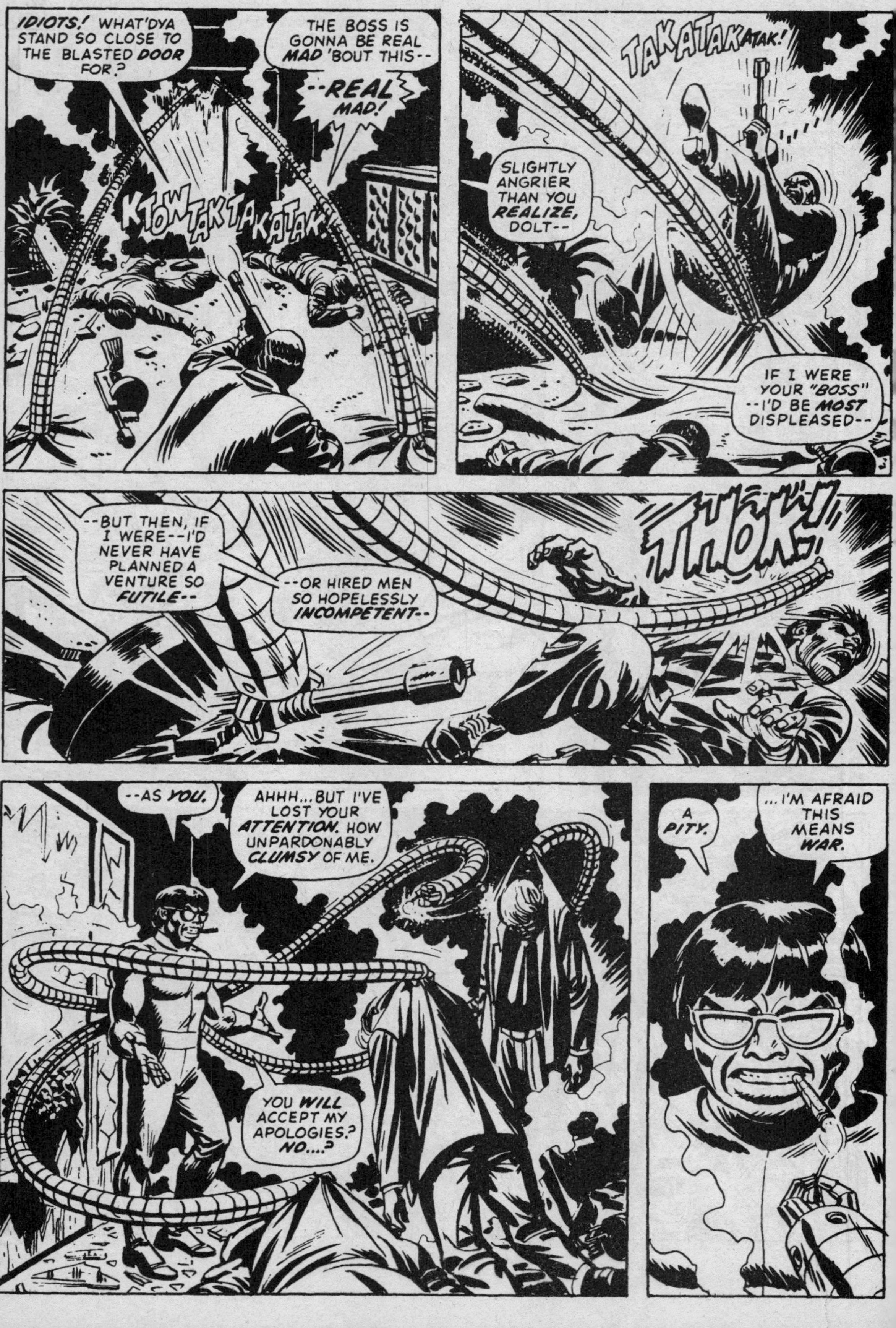

IDIOTS! WHAT'DYA STAND SO CLOSE TO THE BLASTED DOOR FOR?
THE BOSS IS GONNA BE REAL MAD 'BOUT THIS--
--REAL MAD!
KTOWTAKTAKATAK!
TAKATAKATAK!
SLIGHTLY ANGRIER THAN YOU REALIZE, DOLT--
IF I WERE YOUR "BOSS" --I'D BE MOST DISPLEASED--
--BUT THEN, IF I WERE--I'D NEVER HAVE PLANNED A VENTURE SO FUTILE--
--OR HIRED MEN SO HOPELESSLY INCOMPETENT--
THOK!
--AS YOU.
AHHH... BUT I'VE LOST YOUR ATTENTION. HOW UNPARDONABLY CLUMSY OF ME.
YOU WILL ACCEPT MY APOLOGIES? NO...?
A PITY.
...I'M AFRAID THIS MEANS WAR.

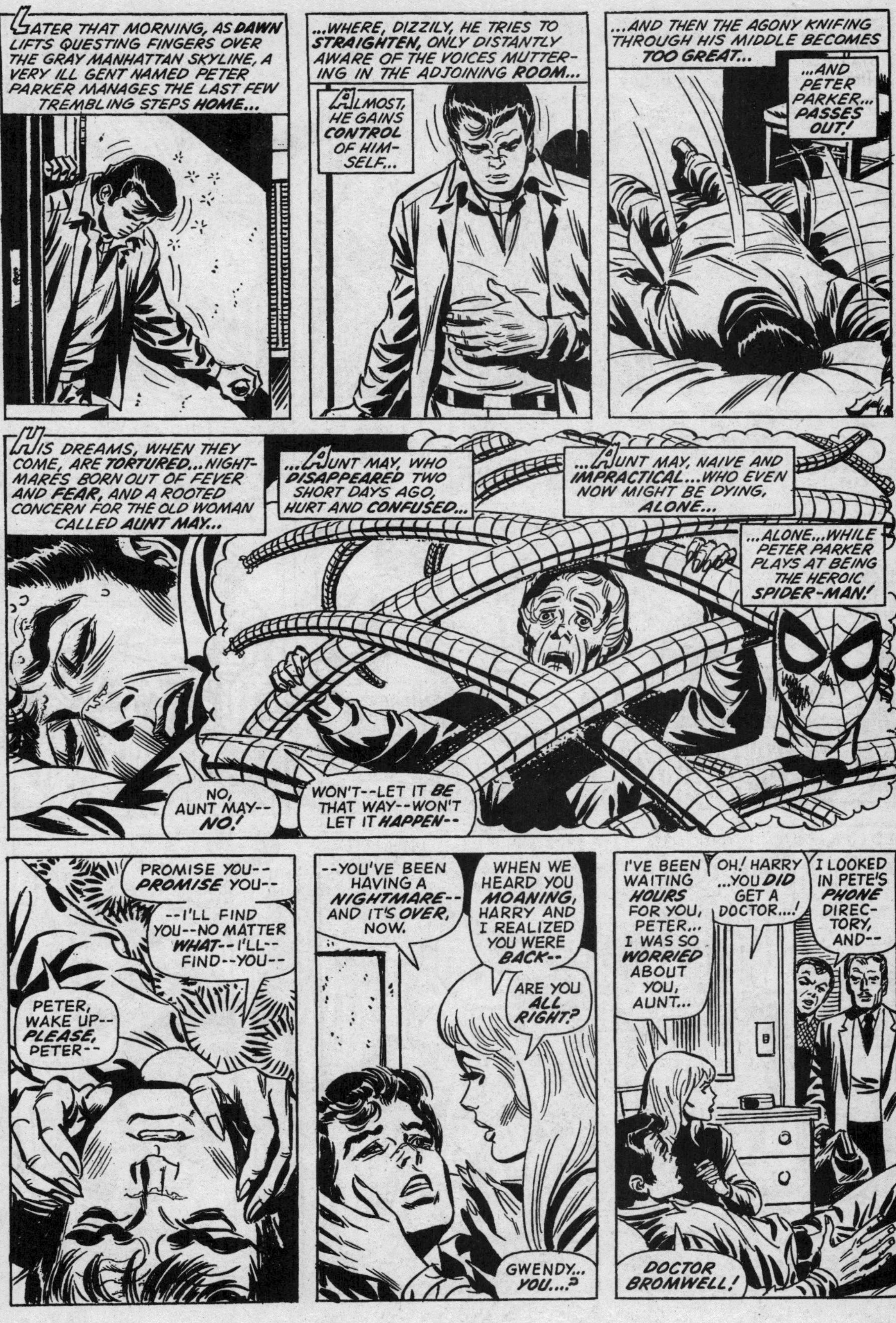
LATER THAT MORNING, AS DAWN LIFTS QUESTING FINGERS OVER THE GRAY MANHATTAN SKYLINE, A VERY ILL GENT NAMED PETER PARKER MANAGES THE LAST FEW TREMBLING STEPS HOME...
...WHERE, DIZZILY, HE TRIES TO STRAIGHTEN, ONLY DISTANTLY AWARE OF THE VOICES MUTTERING IN THE ADJOINING ROOM...
ALMOST, HE GAINS CONTROL OF HIMSELF...
...AND THEN THE AGONY KNIFING THROUGH HIS MIDDLE BECOMES TOO GREAT...
...AND PETER PARKER... PASSES OUT!
HIS DREAMS, WHEN THEY COME, ARE TORTURED...NIGHTMARES BORN OUT OF FEVER AND FEAR, AND A ROOTED CONCERN FOR THE OLD WOMAN CALLED AUNT MAY...
...AUNT MAY, WHO DISAPPEARED TWO SHORT DAYS AGO, HURT AND CONFUSED...
...AUNT MAY, NAIVE AND IMPRACTICAL...WHO EVEN NOW MIGHT BE DYING, ALONE...
...ALONE...WHILE PETER PARKER PLAYS AT BEING THE HEROIC SPIDER-MAN!
NO, AUNT MAY-- NO!
WON'T--LET IT BE THAT WAY--WON'T LET IT HAPPEN--
PROMISE YOU-- PROMISE YOU--
--I'LL FIND YOU--NO MATTER WHAT--I'LL--FIND--YOU--
PETER, WAKE UP-- PLEASE, PETER--
--YOU'VE BEEN HAVING A NIGHTMARE-- AND IT'S OVER, NOW.
WHEN WE HEARD YOU MOANING, HARRY AND I REALIZED YOU WERE BACK--
ARE YOU ALL RIGHT?
GWENDY... YOU....?
I'VE BEEN WAITING HOURS FOR YOU, PETER... I WAS SO WORRIED ABOUT YOU, AUNT...
OH! HARRY ...YOU DID GET A DOCTOR....!
I LOOKED IN PETE'S PHONE DIRECTORY, AND--
DOCTOR BROMWELL!

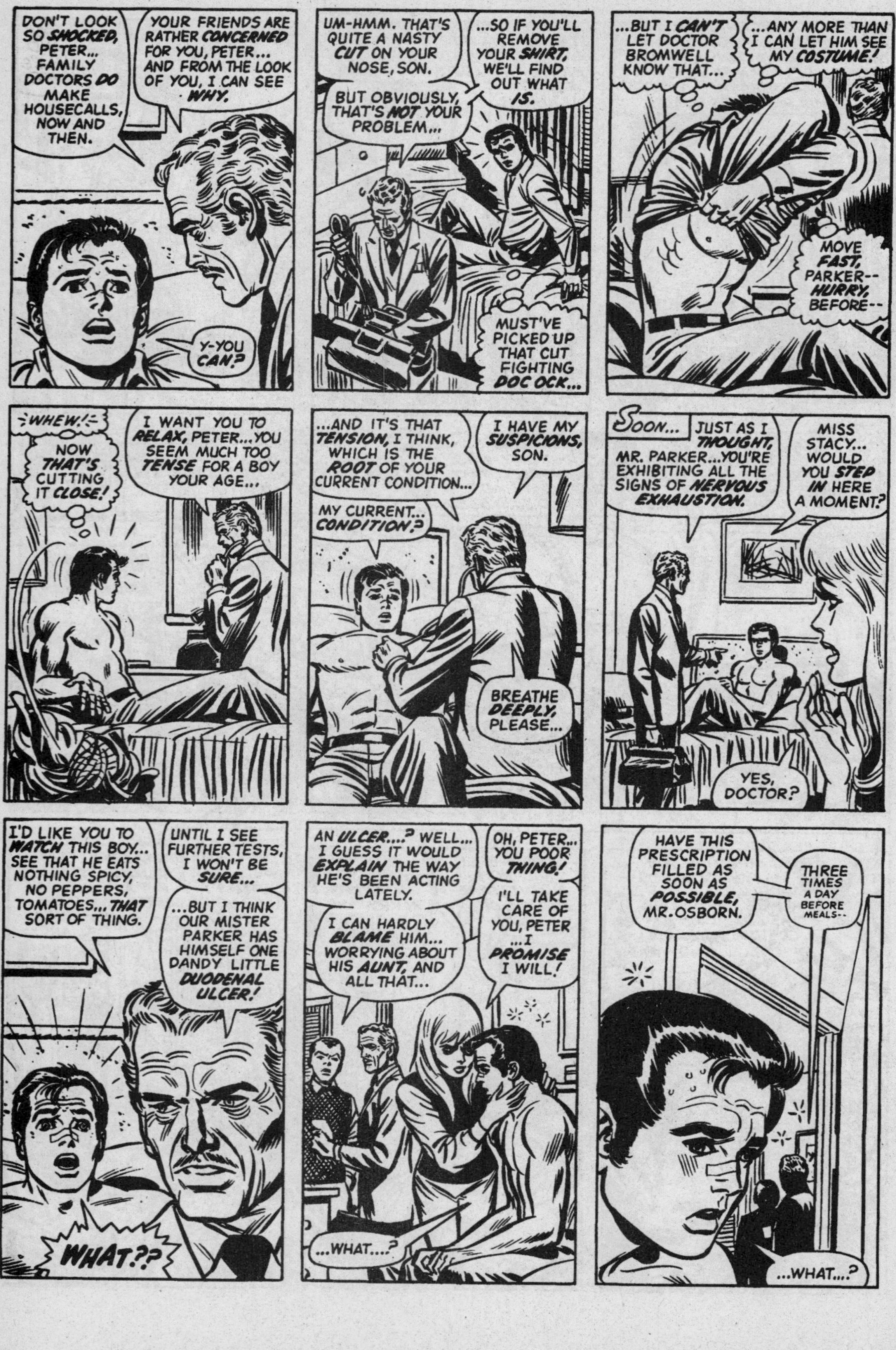
DON'T LOOK SO SHOCKED, PETER... FAMILY DOCTORS DO MAKE HOUSECALLS, NOW AND THEN.
YOUR FRIENDS ARE RATHER CONCERNED FOR YOU, PETER... AND FROM THE LOOK OF YOU, I CAN SEE WHY.
Y-YOU CAN?
UM-HMM. THAT'S QUITE A NASTY CUT ON YOUR NOSE, SON.
...SO IF YOU'LL REMOVE YOUR SHIRT, WE'LL FIND OUT WHAT IS.
BUT OBVIOUSLY, THAT'S NOT YOUR PROBLEM...
MUST'VE PICKED UP THAT CUT FIGHTING DOC OCK...
...BUT I CAN'T LET DOCTOR BROMWELL KNOW THAT...
...ANY MORE THAN I CAN LET HIM SEE MY COSTUME!
MOVE FAST, PARKER-- HURRY, BEFORE--
WHEW!
NOW THAT'S CUTTING IT CLOSE!
I WANT YOU TO RELAX, PETER...YOU SEEM MUCH TOO TENSE FOR A BOY YOUR AGE...
...AND IT'S THAT TENSION, I THINK, WHICH IS THE ROOT OF YOUR CURRENT CONDITION...
I HAVE MY SUSPICIONS, SON.
MY CURRENT... CONDITION?
BREATHE DEEPLY, PLEASE...
SOON...
JUST AS I THOUGHT, MR. PARKER...YOU'RE EXHIBITING ALL THE SIGNS OF NERVOUS EXHAUSTION.
MISS STACY... WOULD YOU STEP IN HERE A MOMENT?
YES, DOCTOR?
I'D LIKE YOU TO WATCH THIS BOY... SEE THAT HE EATS NOTHING SPICY, NO PEPPERS, TOMATOES... THAT SORT OF THING.
UNTIL I SEE FURTHER TESTS, I WON'T BE SURE...
...BUT I THINK OUR MISTER PARKER HAS HIMSELF ONE DANDY LITTLE DUODENAL ULCER!
WHAT??
AN ULCER....? WELL... I GUESS IT WOULD EXPLAIN THE WAY HE'S BEEN ACTING LATELY.
I CAN HARDLY BLAME HIM... WORRYING ABOUT HIS AUNT, AND ALL THAT...
OH, PETER... YOU POOR THING!
I'LL TAKE CARE OF YOU, PETER ...I PROMISE I WILL!
...WHAT....?
HAVE THIS PRESCRIPTION FILLED AS SOON AS POSSIBLE, MR. OSBORN.
THREE TIMES A DAY BEFORE MEALS--
...WHAT....?

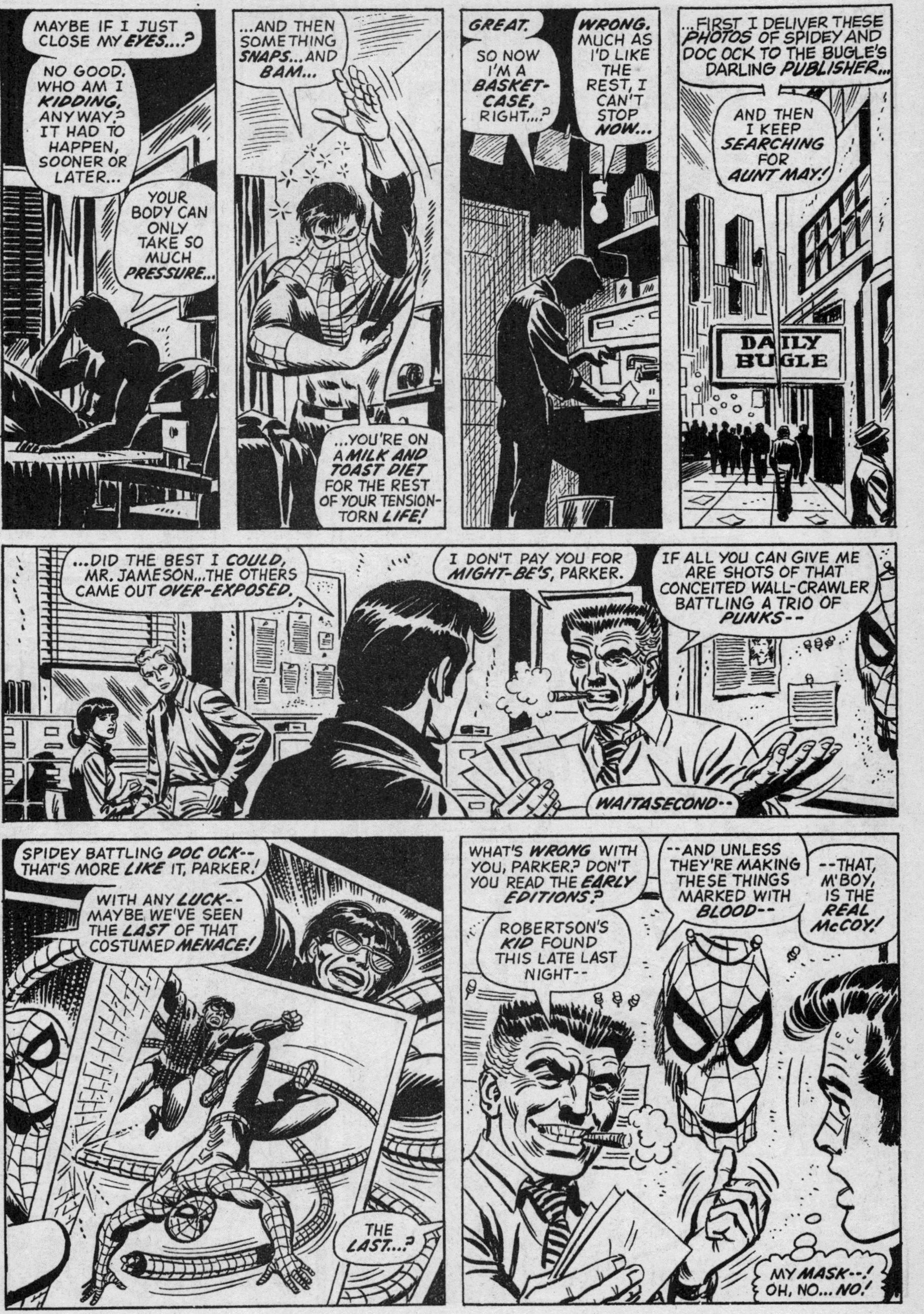
MAYBE IF I JUST CLOSE MY EYES...?
NO GOOD. WHO AM I KIDDING, ANYWAY? IT HAD TO HAPPEN, SOONER OR LATER...
YOUR BODY CAN ONLY TAKE SO MUCH PRESSURE...
...AND THEN SOMETHING SNAPS... AND BAM...
...YOU'RE ON A MILK AND TOAST DIET FOR THE REST OF YOUR TENSION-TORN LIFE!
GREAT.
SO NOW I'M A BASKET-CASE, RIGHT...?
WRONG. MUCH AS I'D LIKE THE REST, I CAN'T STOP NOW...
...FIRST I DELIVER THESE PHOTOS OF SPIDEY AND DOC OCK TO THE BUGLE'S DARLING PUBLISHER...
AND THEN I KEEP SEARCHING FOR AUNT MAY!
DAILY BUGLE
...DID THE BEST I COULD, MR. JAMESON...THE OTHERS CAME OUT OVER-EXPOSED.
I DON'T PAY YOU FOR MIGHT-BE'S, PARKER.
IF ALL YOU CAN GIVE ME ARE SHOTS OF THAT CONCEITED WALL-CRAWLER BATTLING A TRIO OF PUNKS--
WAITASECOND--
SPIDEY BATTLING DOC OCK--THAT'S MORE LIKE IT, PARKER!
WITH ANY LUCK--MAYBE WE'VE SEEN THE LAST OF THAT COSTUMED MENACE!
THE LAST...?
WHAT'S WRONG WITH YOU, PARKER? DON'T YOU READ THE EARLY EDITIONS?
ROBERTSON'S KID FOUND THIS LATE LAST NIGHT--
--AND UNLESS THEY'RE MAKING THESE THINGS MARKED WITH BLOOD--
--THAT, M'BOY, IS THE REAL McCOY!
MY MASK--! OH, NO...NO!

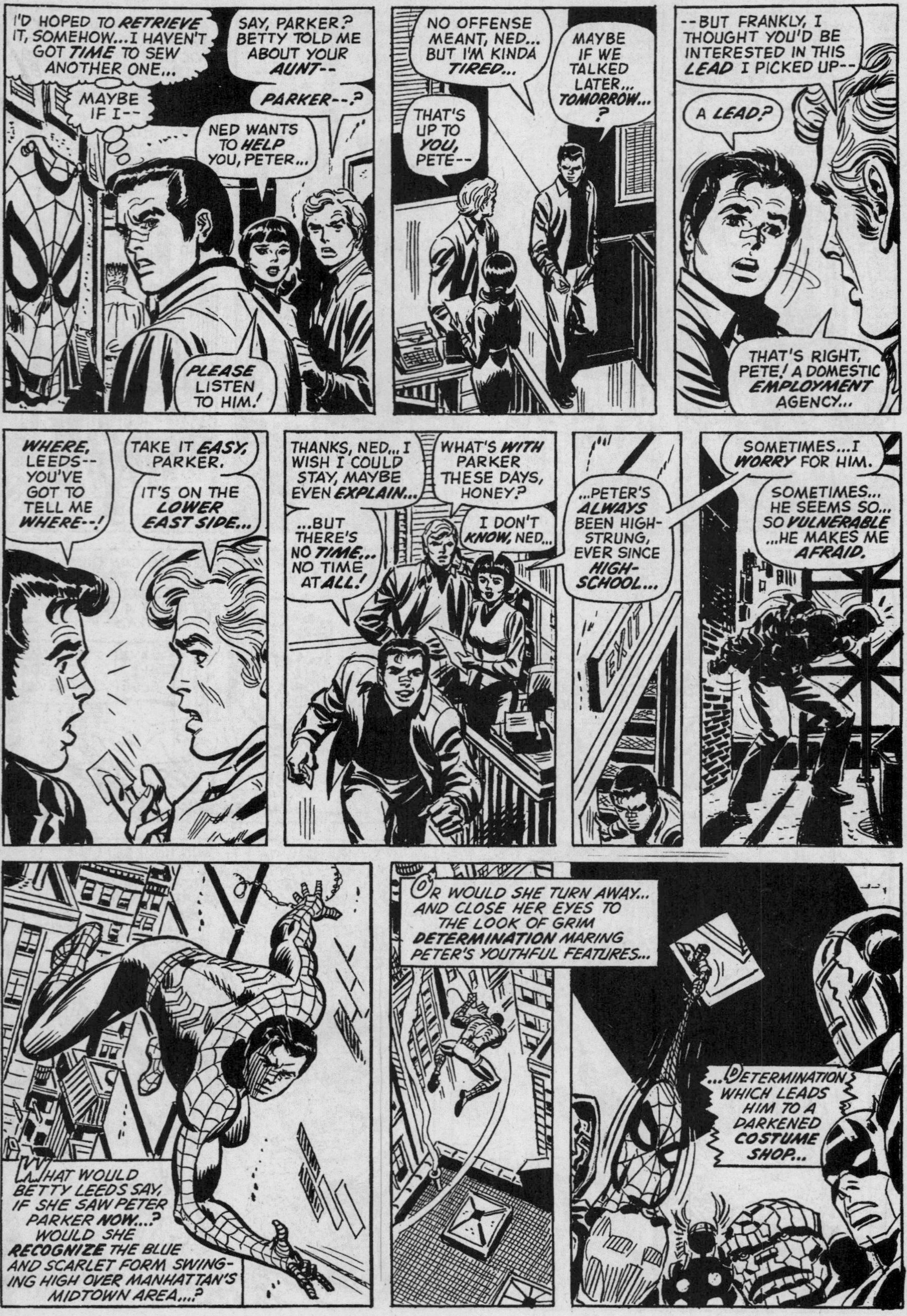
I'D HOPED TO RETRIEVE IT, SOMEHOW... I HAVEN'T GOT TIME TO SEW ANOTHER ONE...
MAYBE IF I--
SAY, PARKER? BETTY TOLD ME ABOUT YOUR AUNT--
PARKER--?
NED WANTS TO HELP YOU, PETER...
PLEASE LISTEN TO HIM!
NO OFFENSE MEANT, NED... BUT I'M KINDA TIRED...
MAYBE IF WE TALKED LATER... TOMORROW...?
THAT'S UP TO YOU, PETE--
--BUT FRANKLY, I THOUGHT YOU'D BE INTERESTED IN THIS LEAD I PICKED UP--
A LEAD?
THAT'S RIGHT, PETE! A DOMESTIC EMPLOYMENT AGENCY...
WHERE, LEEDS-- YOU'VE GOT TO TELL ME WHERE--!
TAKE IT EASY, PARKER.
IT'S ON THE LOWER EAST SIDE...
THANKS, NED... I WISH I COULD STAY, MAYBE EVEN EXPLAIN...
...BUT THERE'S NO TIME... NO TIME AT ALL!
WHAT'S WITH PARKER THESE DAYS, HONEY?
I DON'T KNOW, NED...
...PETER'S ALWAYS BEEN HIGH-STRUNG, EVER SINCE HIGH-SCHOOL...
EXIT
SOMETIMES... I WORRY FOR HIM.
SOMETIMES... HE SEEMS SO... SO VULNERABLE ...HE MAKES ME AFRAID.
WHAT WOULD BETTY LEEDS SAY, IF SHE SAW PETER PARKER NOW...? WOULD SHE RECOGNIZE THE BLUE AND SCARLET FORM SWINGING HIGH OVER MANHATTAN'S MIDTOWN AREA....?
OR WOULD SHE TURN AWAY... AND CLOSE HER EYES TO THE LOOK OF GRIM DETERMINATION MARING PETER'S YOUTHFUL FEATURES...
...DETERMINATION WHICH LEADS HIM TO A DARKENED COSTUME SHOP...

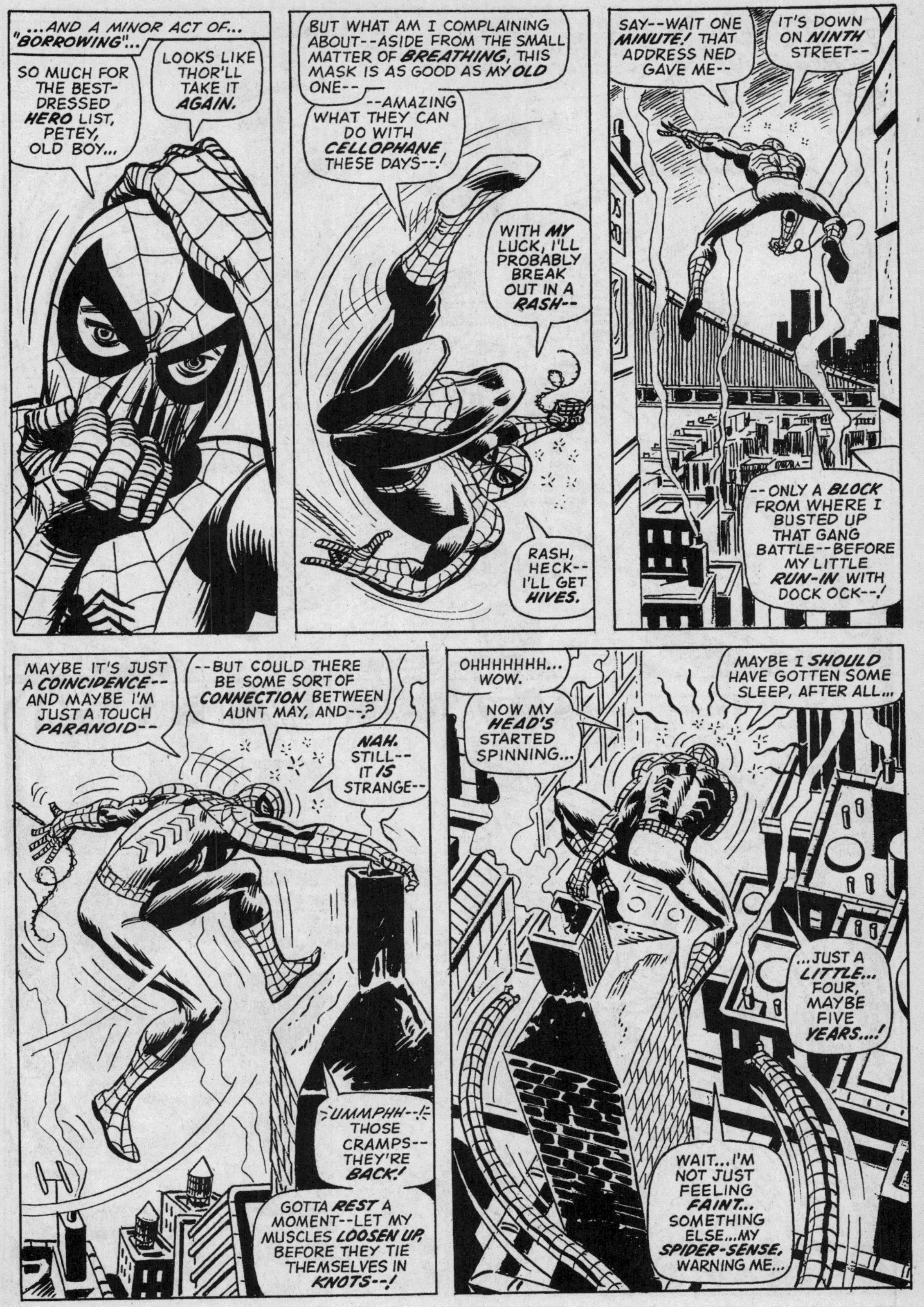
...AND A MINOR ACT OF... "BORROWING"...
SO MUCH FOR THE BEST-DRESSED HERO LIST, PETEY, OLD BOY...
LOOKS LIKE THOR'LL TAKE IT AGAIN.
BUT WHAT AM I COMPLAINING ABOUT--ASIDE FROM THE SMALL MATTER OF BREATHING, THIS MASK IS AS GOOD AS MY OLD ONE--
--AMAZING WHAT THEY CAN DO WITH CELLOPHANE THESE DAYS--!
WITH MY LUCK, I'LL PROBABLY BREAK OUT IN A RASH--
RASH, HECK-- I'LL GET HIVES.
SAY--WAIT ONE MINUTE! THAT ADDRESS NED GAVE ME--
IT'S DOWN ON NINTH STREET--
--ONLY A BLOCK FROM WHERE I BUSTED UP THAT GANG BATTLE--BEFORE MY LITTLE RUN-IN WITH DOCK OCK--!
MAYBE IT'S JUST A COINCIDENCE-- AND MAYBE I'M JUST A TOUCH PARANOID--
--BUT COULD THERE BE SOME SORT OF CONNECTION BETWEEN AUNT MAY, AND--?
NAH. STILL-- IT IS STRANGE--
UMMPHH--! THOSE CRAMPS-- THEY'RE BACK!
GOTTA REST A MOMENT--LET MY MUSCLES LOOSEN UP, BEFORE THEY TIE THEMSELVES IN KNOTS--!
OHHHHHHH... WOW.
NOW MY HEAD'S STARTED SPINNING...
MAYBE I SHOULD HAVE GOTTEN SOME SLEEP, AFTER ALL...
...JUST A LITTLE... FOUR, MAYBE FIVE YEARS...!
WAIT...I'M NOT JUST FEELING FAINT... SOMETHING ELSE...MY SPIDER-SENSE, WARNING ME...

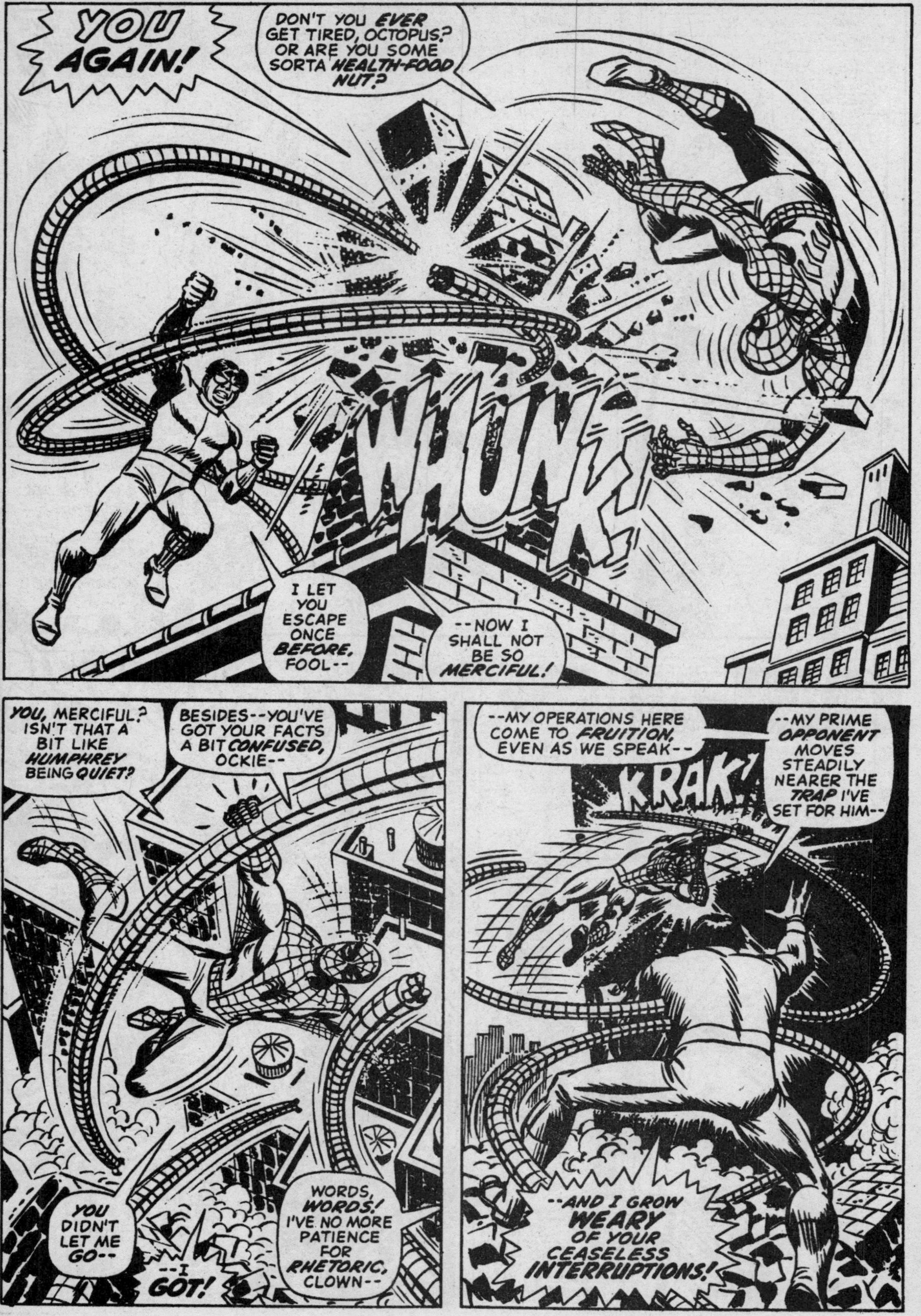
YOU AGAIN!
DON'T YOU EVER GET TIRED, OCTOPUS? OR ARE YOU SOME SORTA HEALTH-FOOD NUT?
WHUNK
I LET YOU ESCAPE ONCE BEFORE, FOOL--
--NOW I SHALL NOT BE SO MERCIFUL!
YOU, MERCIFUL? ISN'T THAT A BIT LIKE HUMPHREY BEING QUIET?
BESIDES--YOU'VE GOT YOUR FACTS A BIT CONFUSED, OCKIE--
YOU DIDN'T LET ME GO--
--I GOT!
WORDS, WORDS! I'VE NO MORE PATIENCE FOR RHETORIC, CLOWN--
--MY OPERATIONS HERE COME TO FRUITION, EVEN AS WE SPEAK--
--MY PRIME OPPONENT MOVES STEADILY NEARER THE TRAP I'VE SET FOR HIM--
KRAK!
--AND I GROW WEARY OF YOUR CEASELESS INTERRUPTIONS!

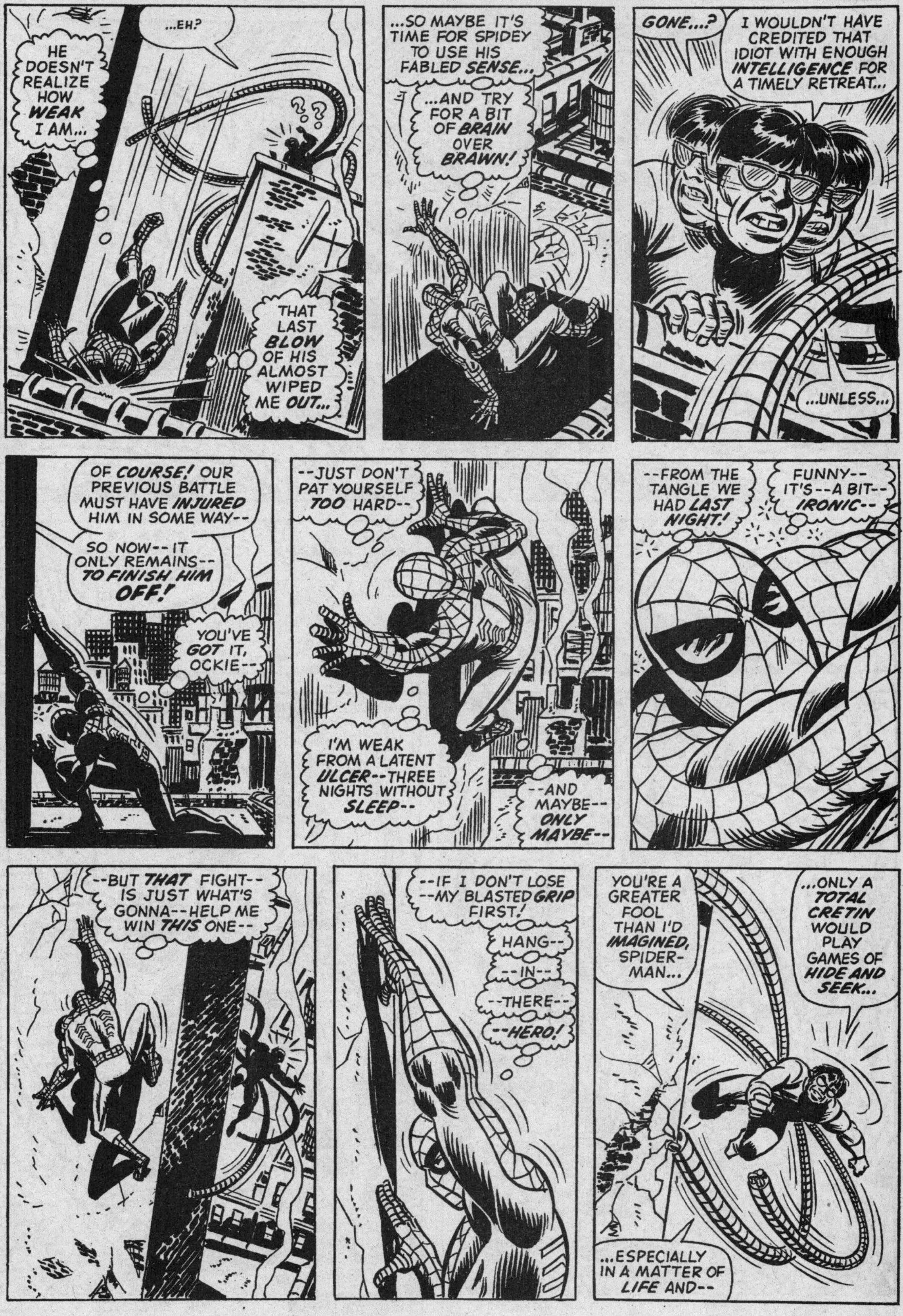

...EH?
HE DOESN'T REALIZE HOW WEAK I AM...
THAT LAST BLOW OF HIS ALMOST WIPED ME OUT...
...SO MAYBE IT'S TIME FOR SPIDEY TO USE HIS FABLED SENSE...
...AND TRY FOR A BIT OF BRAIN OVER BRAWN!
GONE...?
I WOULDN'T HAVE CREDITED THAT IDIOT WITH ENOUGH INTELLIGENCE FOR A TIMELY RETREAT...
...UNLESS...
OF COURSE! OUR PREVIOUS BATTLE MUST HAVE INJURED HIM IN SOME WAY--
SO NOW--IT ONLY REMAINS--TO FINISH HIM OFF!
YOU'VE GOT IT, OCKIE--
--JUST DON'T PAT YOURSELF TOO HARD--
I'M WEAK FROM A LATENT ULCER--THREE NIGHTS WITHOUT SLEEP--
--AND MAYBE--ONLY MAYBE--
--FROM THE TANGLE WE HAD LAST NIGHT!
FUNNY--IT'S--A BIT--IRONIC--
--BUT THAT FIGHT--IS JUST WHAT'S GONNA--HELP ME WIN THIS ONE--
--IF I DON'T LOSE --MY BLASTED GRIP FIRST!
HANG--
--IN--
--THERE--
--HERO!
YOU'RE A GREATER FOOL THAN I'D IMAGINED, SPIDER-MAN...
...ONLY A TOTAL CRETIN WOULD PLAY GAMES OF HIDE AND SEEK...
...ESPECIALLY IN A MATTER OF LIFE AND--

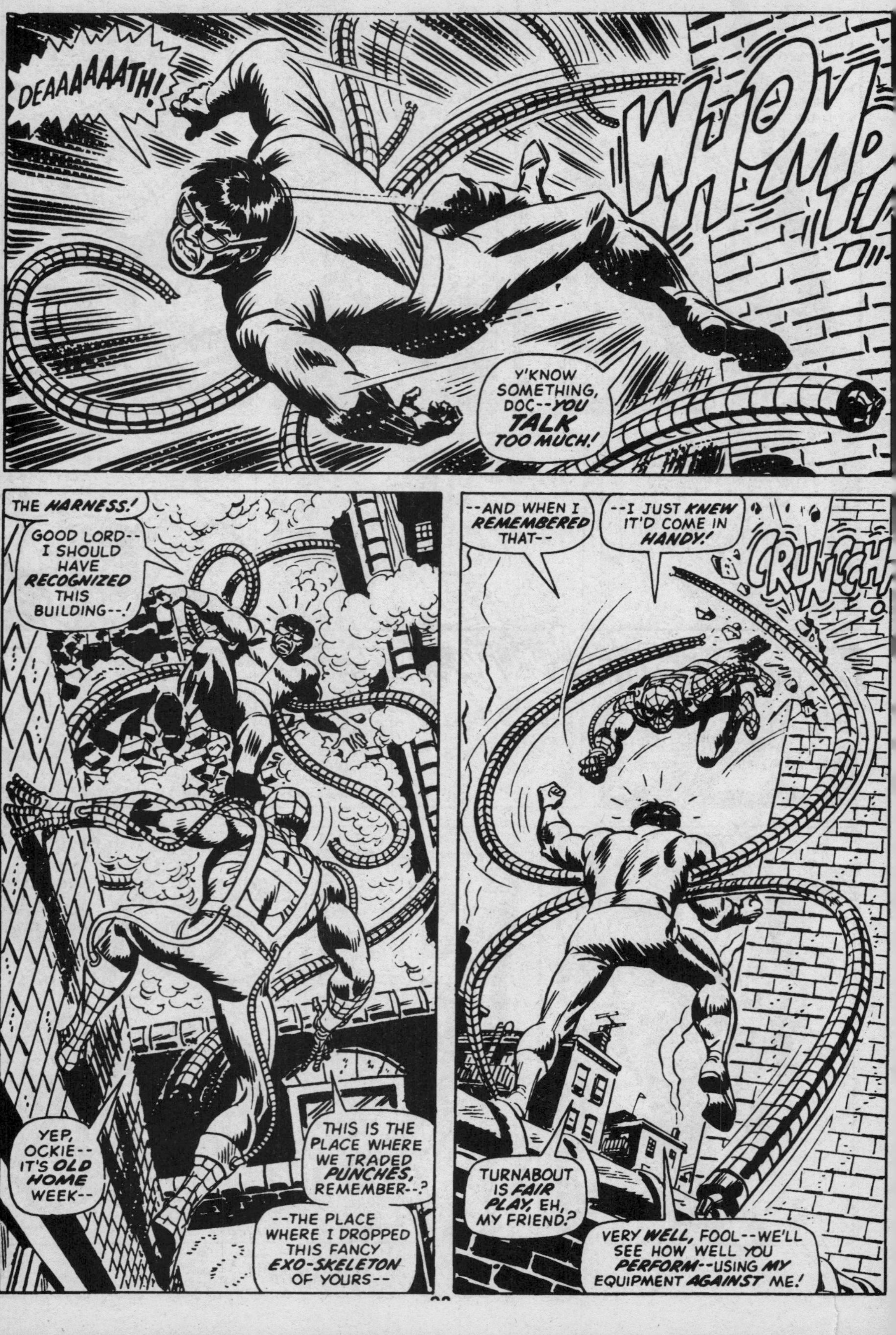
DEAAAAAATH!
Y'KNOW SOMETHING, DOC--YOU TALK TOO MUCH!
THE HARNESS!
GOOD LORD-- I SHOULD HAVE RECOGNIZED THIS BUILDING--!
YEP, OCKIE-- IT'S OLD HOME WEEK--
THIS IS THE PLACE WHERE WE TRADED PUNCHES, REMEMBER--?
--THE PLACE WHERE I DROPPED THIS FANCY EXO-SKELETON OF YOURS--
--AND WHEN I REMEMBERED THAT--
--I JUST KNEW IT'D COME IN HANDY!
CRUNCH
TURNABOUT IS FAIR PLAY, EH, MY FRIEND?
VERY WELL, FOOL--WE'LL SEE HOW WELL YOU PERFORM--USING MY EQUIPMENT AGAINST ME!

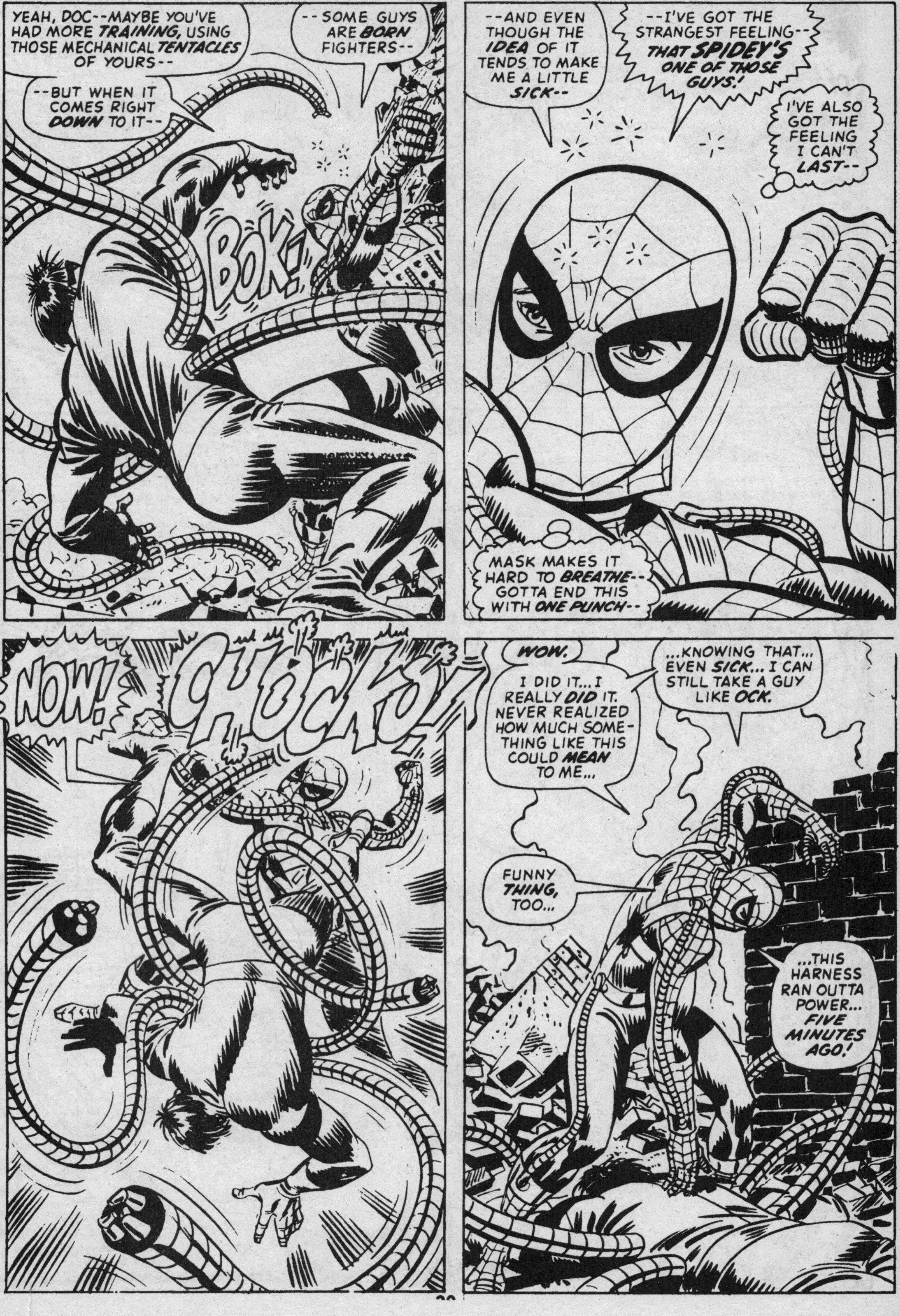
YEAH, DOC--MAYBE YOU'VE HAD MORE TRAINING, USING THOSE MECHANICAL TENTACLES OF YOURS--
--BUT WHEN IT COMES RIGHT DOWN TO IT--
--SOME GUYS ARE BORN FIGHTERS--
BOK!
--AND EVEN THOUGH THE IDEA OF IT TENDS TO MAKE ME A LITTLE SICK--
--I'VE GOT THE STRANGEST FEELING--
THAT SPIDEY'S ONE OF THOSE GUYS!
I'VE ALSO GOT THE FEELING I CAN'T LAST--
MASK MAKES IT HARD TO BREATHE--GOTTA END THIS WITH ONE PUNCH--
NOW!
CHOCK!
WOW.
I DID IT...I REALLY DID IT. NEVER REALIZED HOW MUCH SOMETHING LIKE THIS COULD MEAN TO ME...
...KNOWING THAT... EVEN SICK... I CAN STILL TAKE A GUY LIKE OCK.
FUNNY THING, TOO...
...THIS HARNESS RAN OUTTA POWER... FIVE MINUTES AGO!

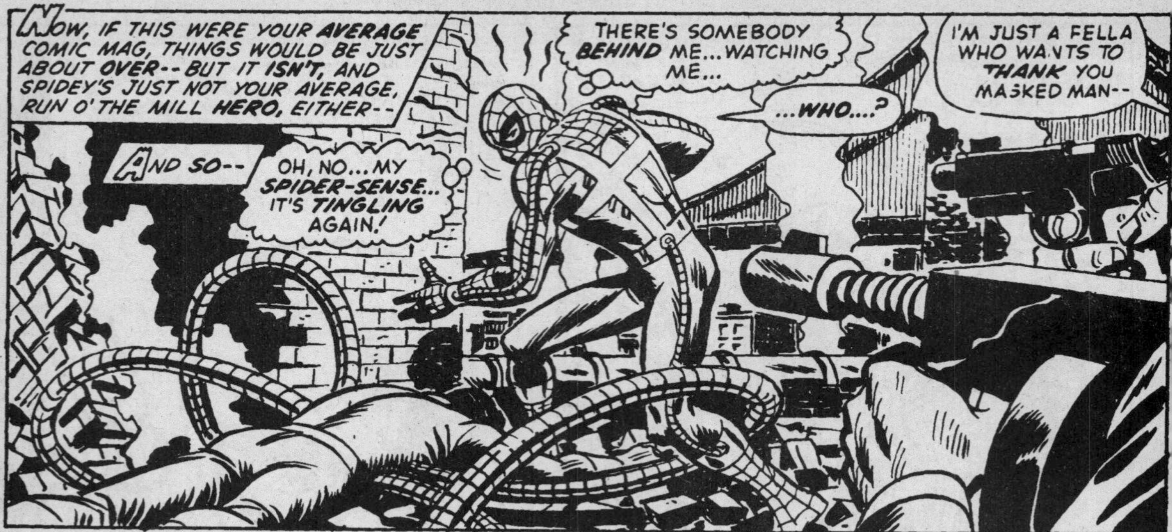
NOW, IF THIS WERE YOUR AVERAGE COMIC MAG, THINGS WOULD BE JUST ABOUT OVER-- BUT IT ISN'T, AND SPIDEY'S JUST NOT YOUR AVERAGE, RUN O' THE MILL HERO, EITHER--
AND SO--
OH, NO... MY SPIDER-SENSE... IT'S TINGLING AGAIN!
THERE'S SOMEBODY BEHIND ME... WATCHING ME...
...WHO...?
I'M JUST A FELLA WHO WANTS TO THANK YOU MASKED MAN--
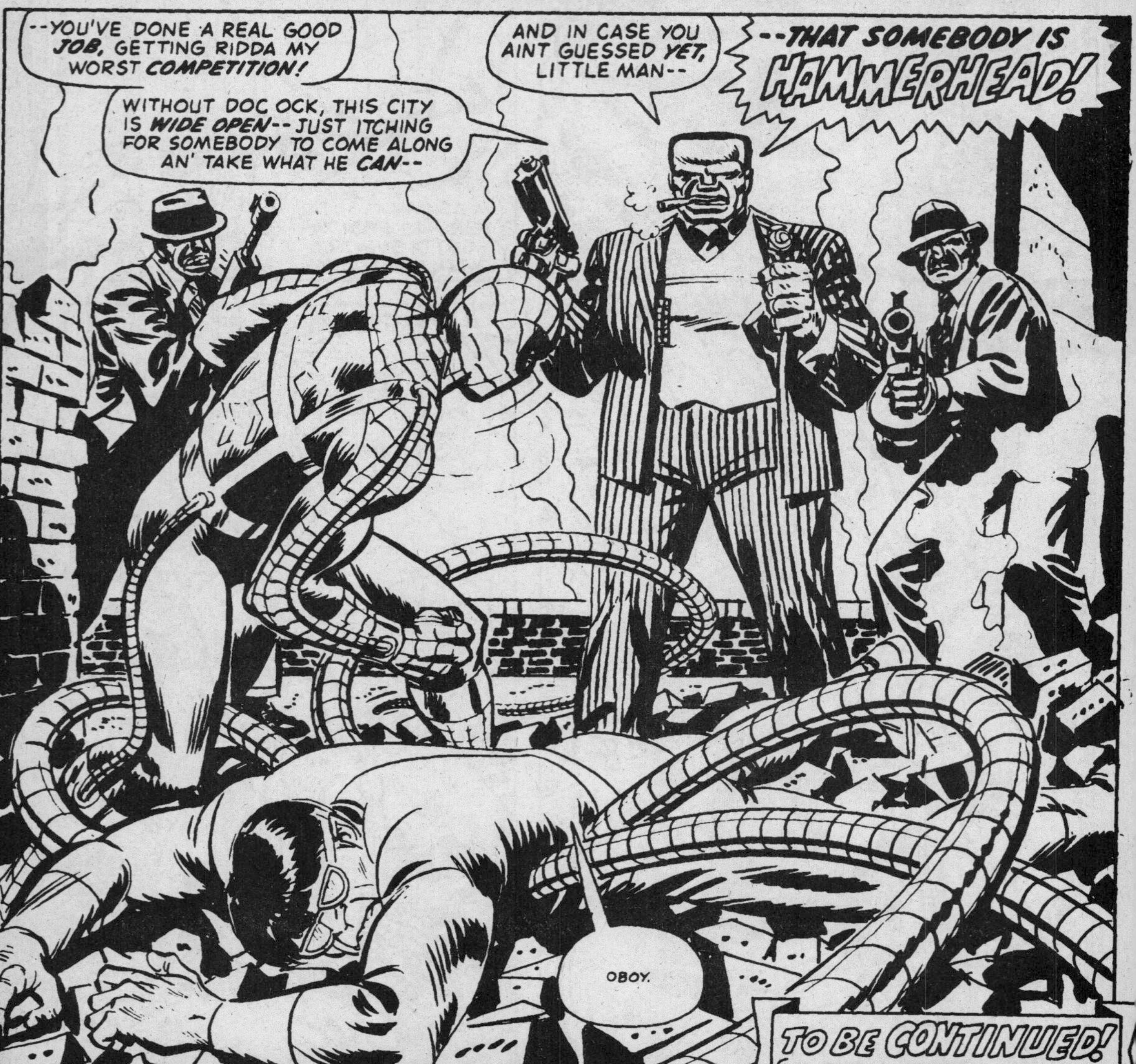
--YOU'VE DONE A REAL GOOD JOB, GETTING RIDDA MY WORST COMPETITION!
WITHOUT DOC OCK, THIS CITY IS WIDE OPEN-- JUST ITCHING FOR SOMEBODY TO COME ALONG AN' TAKE WHAT HE CAN--
AND IN CASE YOU AINT GUESSED YET, LITTLE MAN--
--THAT SOMEBODY IS HAMMERHEAD!
OBOY.
TO BE CONTINUED!
(YOU EXPECTED A HAPPY ENDING, MAYBE.?)

Original art for the front cover to the First Edition of *Essential Spider-Man Vol. 5* By John Romita

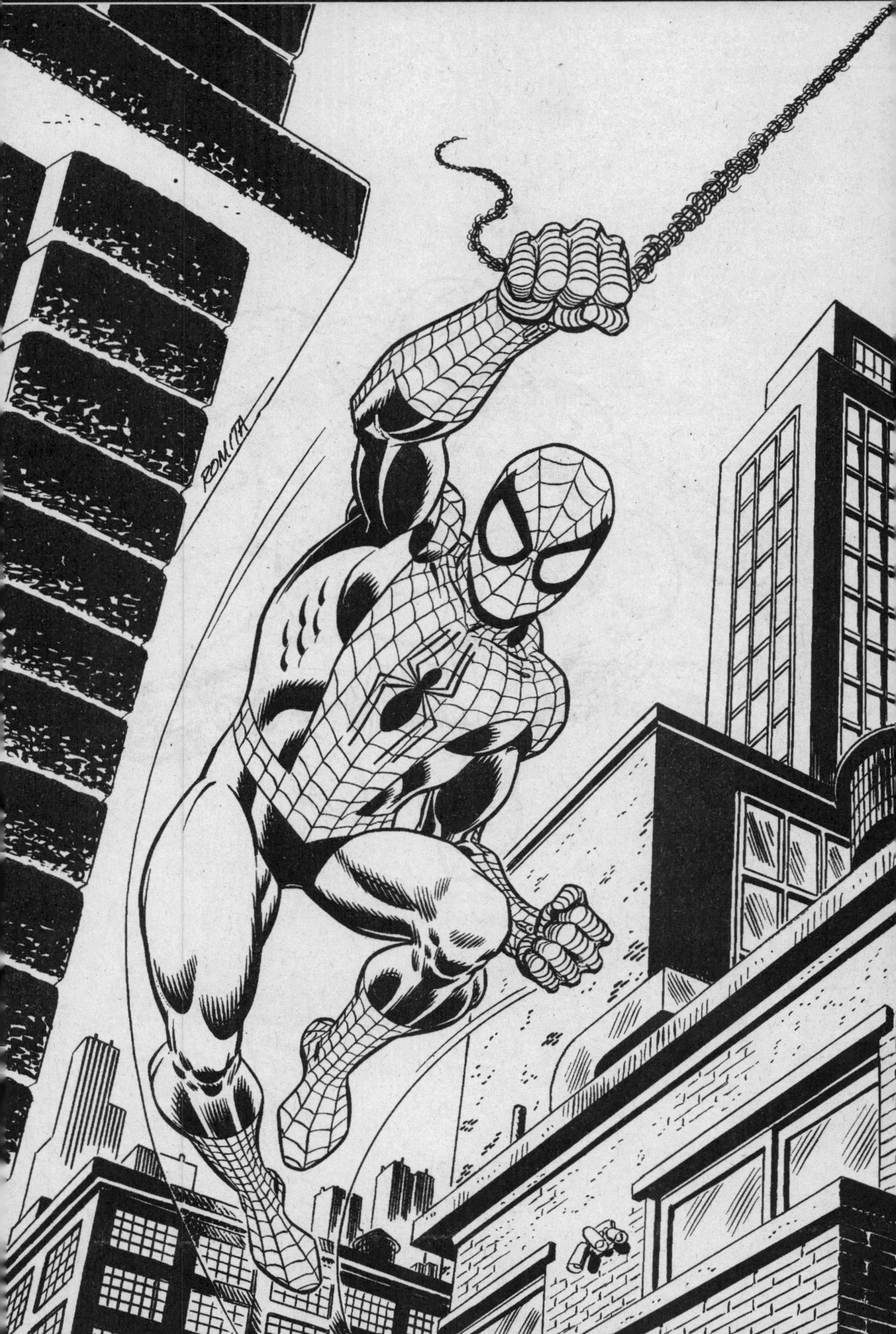
ROMITA

aracter design sheet for the Prowler, then called the Stalker, by John Romit
1969. John's son, John Romita Jr., conceived the character.

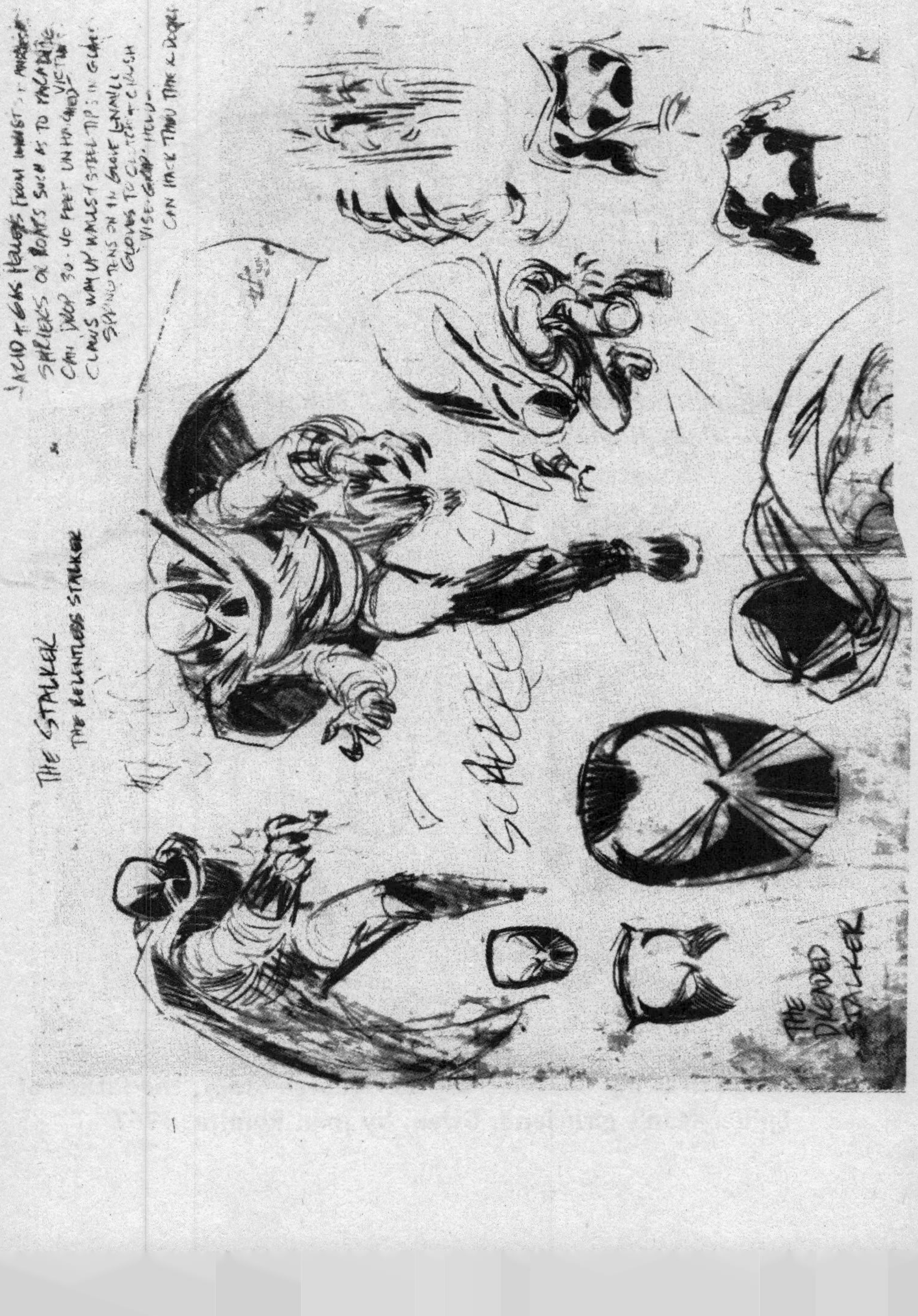
THE STALKER
THE RELENTLESS STALKER

Original character design for Joe "Robbie" Robertson,
The Daily Bugle's city editor, by John Romita, 1967

CAPT.
STACY

WHITE HAIR +
EYEBROWS

HE'S SLIM + TALL -
NOT TOO OLD -

CANE NOT TOO
RAGGED + CROOKED -

Initial design drawing of Police Captain George Stacy, the father of
Spider-Man's girlfriend, Gwen, by John Romita, 1967